Birdsall

P9-AQI-182

EXPERIMENTAL
PSYCHOLOGY

ROBERT S. WOODWORTH

COLUMBIA UNIVERSITY

NEW YORK
HENRY HOLT AND COMPANY

PREFACE

T HE small beginnings of this volume go back to 1910 or earlier, when I worked up the then available literature on practice and memory into a few chapters of readings for a college course in experimental psychology. This material was mimeographed and from year to year chapters were added on imagery, association, reaction time, space perception, judgment and thinking. In 1920 my colleague, Professor Poffenberger, collaborated in pulling together, rounding out and organizing this rather scattered material, and a mimeographed "Textbook of Experimental Psychology" was issued under our joint authorship for the use of our students, graduate and undergraduate. At about that time I determined to go ahead to full publication, but much work remained to be done. Difficult questions of experimental method and of interpretation were attacked from time to time. Meanwhile the experimental literature was increasing by leaps and bounds, so that while I was making progress I was continually falling farther behind. In 1930 I set to work with grim determination. Finally, early in the present year, when the accumulated manuscript had grown to a rather alarming bulk, my long-suffering publishers granted me still a few months time for a final critical revision.

It is interesting, now that the bibliography is fully assembled, to distribute the titles according to their dates of publication. The graph pictures the rapid expansion of laboratory research in psychology. A few scattering titles date from the earlier centuries and from the first half of the nineteenth, and there would have been more references to this early period if the chapters on the senses had been treated historically. But the upswing began about 1850 and still continues. There is no sign of a recession here, but quite the contrary. In my opinion the recent period is outstanding in quality as well as quantity of original research. Yet the older work must not be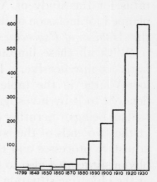
shelved and forgotten. In some cases it was so well done as to remain classic and to provide the stock experiments for generations of students. In other cases, though less fortunate, it made a definite contribution to the development of scientific method in psychology. Some of the pioneers of experimental psychology—Helmholtz, Galton, Binet, to mention only a few—were distinctly great men. However, I have not had it on my conscience to trace the development of each topic. I have not attempted to do over again the work which Boring has so well begun.

iii

Often the beginnings of experimental study have seemed well worthy of a note, and in a few chapters the history is quite important for an understanding of the problems at issue.

As to the scope of the book, a few restrictions should be understood. As explained in the Introduction, the whole field of individual differences and correlations, now so extensively cultivated and so fully presented in recent books, has been left aside. Nor has any attempt been made to include experiments in social psychology (for which reference may be made to the work of Murphy, Murphy and Newcomb, listed in the Bibliography) or to those in child development (see Goodenough and Anderson). I could not keep altogether away from animal experiments in learning and problem solving, but have made no attempt to cover animal psychology in any adequate way. Nor have I dealt with abnormal, educational and applied psychology. Once more, I have kept away from physiology in the main. All of these branches are of great interest to me, personally, but the scope of the book is fully broad enough when confined as it is to the usual content of a course in experimental psychology, in which the students and subjects are young human adults. I should have liked to include chapters on work and motivation, but must content myself with a reference to Robinson's comprehensive chapter on the "Work of the Integrated Organism" in Murchison's *Handbook*, and to such treatments of motivation as are given by Troland, Young and Gordon Allport.

Though this book is closely tied to the laboratory, it does not supply laboratory directions nor go into much detail regarding apparatus and instrumental technique. A supplementary chapter on recording apparatus for the study of Action, written by G. R. Wendt and originally planned for inclusion in this book, will appear on a more adequate scale in the *Archives of Psychology*, 1938, No. 228.

With all these limitations, the book is still rather voluminous and fairly comprehensive. The general field of perception and judgment looms large in the table of contents, as it should from the attention devoted to it by investigators. It is certainly central in the behavior of human beings. Scrutiny of the chapters on learning and problem solving, at the two ends of the book, will reveal close relationship between these adjustive processes and the perception of objective facts. Perception is obviously related also to the study of the senses and the cues they afford of the objective situation. All in all, then, quite a degree of unity can be found in such a book in spite of the diversity of topics and experiments.

Because of these close interrelations between the various topics, the order of chapters cannot escape being somewhat arbitrary. Some preliminary acquaintance with psychology and its terminology is assumed, and the order of chapters can be altered to suit the requirements of the reader or teacher. Cross references and the Index should make it easy to start in almost anywhere.

The treatment is eclectic in the sense that I have felt free to incorporate methods and results from any investigator, without regard to his theoretical leanings. He may have hoped to build up factual support for the tenets of his school, but this hope of his is beside the point when the evidence on a particular problem is under consideration. Care may be needed to disentangle the strands of fact and systematic bias which he has woven into a smooth and attractive fabric, but if the factual strands can be separated they will be perfectly good contributions to the particular problem. A distinction can be made between theories which have the character of systems appertaining to the different schools, and more specific theories of learning or conditioning or visual perception of space. With the latter type of theory the experimenter is directly in touch, and consideration of such theories is quite in line with the purpose of this book. It would be quite inappropriate to make a general experimental psychology the vehicle for expounding a system. It may be true, as has been said, that the present author represents the functional school of psychology, in the broadest sense of the word. Psychology does seem to be a study of the functioning of the organism in its environment. This seems so much a matter of course to me that probably it underlies the discussion of many topics. I would warn the reader especially against a probable theoretical bias in the chapters on Conditioned Response, Maze Learning, Perception of Color, and Problem Solving. Study of these topics has served to clarify my own systematic view, but any explicit presentation of this view must wait for another occasion.

If the question is raised how any one man can expect to cover and pull together all these various topics, each of which demands a specialist to do it justice, the answer is, first, that it cannot be done, and second, that it can be done to a degree by aid of students conducting researches in different lines under the professor's supervision. Over a period of several decades, I have in this way come into direct contact with nearly every major topic included in the book. It would be a pleasure to give credit where credit is due, by mentioning the names of all these virtual collaborators. Failing this, I must at least allow myself the privilege of citing specific assistance received from several colleagues in the final stages of preparation. Professor E. G. Wever honored me by a critical perusal of the chapter on Hearing, and Dr. G. S. Razran by reading the chapter on the Conditioned Response. Mrs. Enrica Tunnell, Psychology Librarian, made herself responsible for the Bibliography and Author Index. Drs. Gladys C. Schwesinger and Mary R. Sheehan have critically read the entire proof.

The admitted youth and immaturity of experimental psychology make it a fascinating field of study and one where the student can rather quickly penetrate the zone of unsettled problems and original investigation. Such an effort as is here made to digest and organize the results already achieved should assist the student in gaining perspective. It pictures for him a live, progressive enterprise, carried on by many enthusiastic workers whose efforts, scattered over a wide field and not coördinated by any higher authority, still reveal an underlying unity of purpose. This body of investigators has a very respectable record of ground already covered, of methods proved and selected, of early false assumptions outgrown, and of positive contributions to knowledge.

Columbia University   R. S. W.
July 22, 1938

CONTENTS

CONTENTS

CONTENTS

CHAPTER I

INTRODUCTION

W HEN experimental psychology first appeared on the horizon, about the year 1860, it was felt to be very much of an experiment itself. Whether it could succeed, outside of a very limited field, was doubtful. The philosophical type of question discussed by most psychologists of the day did not lend itself to laboratory investigation. Questions of detail regarding the senses and sense perception, already examined to some extent by the physicists and physiologists, could be taken over into the psychological laboratory, and other similar questions would doubtless turn up and keep the laboratory going, but the prospective scope of the work appeared quite restricted. Even so, the prospect was attractive to some psychologists, discontented with the endless disputations of the schools and eager to get down to questions which could be settled by an appeal to the facts of observation. Though the answers lacked broad philosophical import, the experimenter felt he was making some progress in the study of mentality and personality. The old philosophical questions tended to fade from his sight and new questions arising in contact with the concrete realities of experience and behavior appeared more and more vital. With all his grubbing for facts there was still plenty of room for discussion—discussion of problems actually in process of solution, of the significance of results obtained, of methods suited for further advance. As in the other sciences, so in psychology progress came largely from close scrutiny of details which were found to embody important principles. Meanwhile many of these apparent details proved to have a practical bearing on the daily life of human beings.

As regards the scope of experimental psychology, a few decades of intensive work by able pioneers showed that it was by no means narrow. Memory, training, conditioning were attacked and the whole field of human and animal learning was found to be accessible by experimental methods. Thinking, invention and problem solution yielded important results. Something could be done with emotion, motivation and even willing. Almost any form of human activity can be surveyed in a preliminary way with good prospects of finding an opportunity for some incisive experiments. Today we are inclined to claim for experimental psychology a scope as wide as that of psychology itself, while admitting that we do not yet know exactly how to subject some of the biggest problems to a rigorous experiment. Until these problems are attacked experimentally, they probably will not be solved.

Two important fields offering serious difficulty to the experimenter are those of child development and the genesis of maladjustments. Workers in both these fields employ tests and other laboratory techniques to good advantage in their efforts to trace the course of normal and abnormal development. But a truly incisive experiment in development would be like those in experimental embryology, where the experimenter takes a hand in the process of development by controlling essential conditions and introducing factors which modify the process. In so doing he is able to discover the factors in development. It is true that every educational procedure is experimental—for it may not work in a given case—and the same is true of every mode of treatment applied to a juvenile delinquent, a neurotic or a psychotic patient. The teacher and the psychotherapist would be psychological experimenters if it were feasible for them to know exactly where they started in handling an individual, exactly what they did and exactly where they came out. Their experiments almost necessarily lack precision and do not yield definite data which can be built into a science. "Almost necessarily," we say; hopeful beginnings in the study of the young child presage a day when there will be true experimentation in this field.

An experimenter is said to *control the conditions* in which an event occurs. He has several advantages over an observer who simply follows the course of events without exercising any control.

1. The experimenter makes the event happen at a certain time and place and so is fully *prepared* to make an accurate observation.

2. Controlled conditions being *known* conditions, the experimenter can set up his experiment a second time and repeat the observation; and, what is very important in view of the social nature of scientific investigation, he can report his conditions so that another experimenter can duplicate them and check the data.

3. The experimenter can systematically *vary* the conditions and note the concomitant variation in the results. If he follows the old standard "rule of one variable" he holds all the conditions constant except for one factor which is his "experimental factor" or his "independent variable." The observed effect is the "dependent variable" which in a psychological experiment is some characteristic of behavior or reported experience. In an experiment on the effect of noise on mental work, noise is the independent variable controlled by the experimenter, and the dependent variable may be speed or accuracy of work or the subject's report of his feelings.

As regards the rule of one variable, it applies only to the independent variable, for there is no objection to observing a variety of effects of the one experimental factor. With careful planning two or three independent variables can sometimes be handled in a single experiment with economy of effort and with some chance of discovering the interaction of the two or more factors (Fisher, 1936).

Whether one or more independent variables are used, it remains essential that all other conditions be constant. Otherwise you cannot connect the effect observed with any definite cause. The psychologist must expect to encounter difficulties in meeting this requirement of scientific work. He has to contend with differences between individuals, inequalities in the materials used (problems to be solved, for example), and changes due to motivation, practice and fatigue. He can often overcome these difficulties by some system of compensating factors. Suppose the efficiency of work under two conditions, noise and quiet, or, in general, A and B, is to be compared. If the subjects work first under condition A and then under condition B, B will probably show better performance because of the practice effect. We may meet this difficulty in several ways: (1) give the subjects abundant preliminary practice; (2) use the double order of conditions, ABBA; (3) use two groups of subjects, one in the order AB and one in the order BA, and combine the results from the two groups. The experiment must be carefully planned in advance, always with an eye to some defensible way of handling the data.

To be distinguished from the experimental method, and standing on a par with it in value, rather than above or below, is the comparative and correlational method. It takes its start from individual differences. By use of suitable tests it measures the individuals in a sample of some population, distributes these measures and finds their average, scatter, etc. Measuring two or more characteristics of the same individuals it computes the correlation of these characteristics and goes on to factor analysis. This method does not introduce an "experimental factor"; it has no "independent variable" but treats all the measured variables alike. It does not directly study cause and effect. The experimentalist's independent variable is antecedent to his dependent variable; one is cause (or part of the cause) and the other effect. The correlationist studies the interrelation of different effects.

The same psychologists, from the early days, have contributed to the two lines of study, and the contact between the two should remain close. The experimentalist needs to use the statistical techniques devised by the correlationist, or some of them, and the correlationist often bases his tests on laboratory experiments. Some psychological problems can be attacked by both methods, but on the whole the immediate problems are somewhat different. Excellent books are available on the methods and results of the comparative method—on tests, individual differences, correlations and factor analysis. There is good reason for not attempting to cover both lines of study in the same book, and good reason for attempting to bring together the methods and results from a variety of fields which have been cultivated by the experimentalist. Controversies between the schools can be (happily) left aside; experiments contributed by all the schools, as well as by the large number of experimental psychologists who are not attached to any school, can be utilized for their intrinsic value. The main question to be answered is: How? What goes on when we learn, remember, observe, read, solve a problem, meet an emergency? Both the survey type of experiment and the crucial test of a hypothesis are deemed worthy of attention in the present exploratory stage of scientific work in psychology.

CHAPTER II

MEMORY

I F WE were required to place first in chapter order that topic which
has most engaged the attention of experimental psychology, we
should be in doubt whether the honor belonged to learning and learned
reactions or to sensation and perception. Counting in the older work
and the work done by physiologists and physicists as well as psychologists,
we should doubtless find more under the latter head. Learning would
be a close second. It runs out into many subtopics: practice and skill,
transfer of training, conditioning, animal learning, educational applications. The part of this broad field first cultivated by experimental
psychologists was the memory of human adults.

When the experimentalist speaks of memory he refers not to a "faculty," but to the act or process of remembering. Common speech
employs the word "remember" in two somewhat different senses. We
speak of remembering a fact or incident and of remembering how to do
an act. You perhaps "remember standing on the bridge at Niagara
Falls and watching the little steamboat on the river below"; and you
"remember how to skate" after a summer's intermission. The expression
"remember how" is inaccurate; for you cannot tell how you skate.
What you can do is to skate. You perform easily an act which it cost
you some trouble to learn.

Both sorts of remembering can be included under the conception
of a learned response. A continuous series of cases extends from the
revival of one's own experiences at one extreme to the automatic performance of a learned movement at the other, and the whole series
belongs together. The difference between the extremes is a matter
deserving of attention, but the likeness is more fundamental. All varieties of learning and remembering belong together in one big chapter of
psychology.

Subdivision of the memory function. When anything is said to be
remembered the implication is that it has been *learned* and that it has
been *retained* during an interval in which it was not actively remembered.
Learning, retaining, remembering are three successive stages in the
whole memory function. Learning goes by various names: experience,
practice, memorizing, conditioning, fixation or the establishment of a

response.   Retention may be incomplete, in which case we speak of a partial forgetting.   Remembering takes many forms which can be fairly well classified under the heads of *recall* (or reproduction) and *recognition*. The performance of a learned motor act belongs under the head of recall or reproduction.   Recognition is seemingly though not really passive; it is in some ways the easiest and simplest form of remembering, and quite possibly the most primitive form.   Learning and remembering are active processes regarding which both objective and introspective data can be secured.   Retention is not directly observable but can be approached by way of recall, recognition or re-learning.   In learning, work is done by the organism; this work leaves after-effects which we may include under the noncommittal term, *trace*.   What is retained is this trace.   The trace is a modification of the organism which is not directly observed but is inferred from the facts of recall and recognition.

EXPERIMENTAL METHODS FOR THE STUDY OF MEMORY

In the early days of experimental psychology, there was little immediate prospect of a successful attack on the "higher mental processes," and effort was concentrated on sensory and motor processes.   It was an important forward step when Ebbinghaus (1885) published his experimental study of memory.   He devised methods for making a quantitative study of learning and retention: the "learning" and "saving" methods, later (1902) also the "prompting" method.   His lead was quickly followed by other inventive psychologists who improved the methods of Ebbinghaus and added new ones.

When we speak of a "method" for studying memory (or for studying esthetics or psychophysics) we refer not to the concrete apparatus and material used, but to the general plan or scheme of an experiment.   A "method" is a procedure which will yield a score.   The score may be the time required to reach a certain standard or criterion of mastery, or the number of trials required to reach the criterion, or the number of errors committed, or the number of items recalled or recognized after a given amount of "study," or some measure of excellence of performance. The subject's task may consist in learning the "lesson" up to a certain criterion of mastery, in learning as much as he can in one trial, etc. Experimenters have exercised their ingenuity in devising such methods as well as in selecting materials and building apparatus suited to the several procedures.   Methods of similar character have been used in studies of animal maze learning (p. 140).

Because the memory methods represent a definite achievement of experimental psychology, and also because the results of any experiment must be judged and interpreted in the light of the operations by which they are obtained, we begin our study of memory by examining these methods.

MEMORY SPAN FOR DIGITS

972	641	853
1406	2730	4097
39418	85943	21659
067285	706294	302481
3516927	1538796	6479038
58391204	29081357	71520863
764580129	042865129	039418276
2164089573	4790386215	5168047392
45382170369	39428107536	94350182765
870932614280	541962836702	176298305914

Immediate memory span. This simple method, introduced by Jacobs (1887), furnishes an answer to the question, how large a quantity of a given sort of material can be reproduced perfectly after one presentation. In a typical experiment, E has at hand lists of 3–12 digits and instructs O as follows: "I will say some numbers; when I have finished, you are to repeat the numbers in the same order." E starts with a short list and advances to longer ones, going far enough to reach O's limit. O has only one trial with any one list.[1]

The score in this experiment is the length of list which O can recite perfectly after one hearing. The concept of span, derived from the span of the hand, conveys the idea of width of grasp. How much can be spanned or grasped at once? To guard against favorable and unfavorable accidents, it is best to give the subject more than one list of each length and to go somewhat beyond the point at which he first makes an error. Occasionally he succeeds with a longer list where he has failed with a shorter one. If there were no variability of performance, a single list of each length would be enough and the result would show, for example, that O succeeded with all lists up to and including 8 digits and never beyond that point. His span, then, would be 8 digits. Even though the span shows a rather remarkable degree of constancy, there is always some variation and we have to take account of it in our measure. Two inadequate measures are: The longest list which O *always* gets right; and the longest list which he *ever* gets right. A true average span can be obtained by giving, say, 3 lists of each length and allowing a credit of ⅓ for every perfectly recited list. Suppose O gets all the lists correct up to and including 6 digits: we credit him with 6 as a basal value. If above that value he succeeds twice with a 7-digit list, not at all with 8, once with 9, and no further, then his total score is $6 + \frac{3}{3} = 7$.

To bring this computation into line with regular statistical procedure we must add to the score just obtained half the step-interval, here 0.5. The logical justification for this addition can be made clear by considering some instances. Suppose that O reproduced perfectly all the lists up to and including 8 digits, but none greater. Then we know that his span was always great enough to compass 8 digits but never great enough

---

[1] For "E" and "O" and other abbreviations, see the Index.

to compass 9. We therefore credit him with a Mean span of 8.5. Suppose, again, that he succeeded in half of the lists of 9 digits and failed in all the lists of 10 or more. Then his Mean, or at least his Median, is obviously 9 digits, since his span reached that number just half the time; 9 digits fell just at his 50 percent level. On this matter see further the discussion on p. 402.

The reader familiar with the Binet tests will observe that this is the same scoring system as is used there. In treating the methods of psychophysics (p. 402) we shall find that this method of computing the average span is the same as the summation method of computing a threshold by the method of Constant Stimuli. Instead of the summation method the Urban or curve fitting method can be used (Guilford & Dallenbach, 1925).

The method of retained members. In an unstandardized way this method is used in the schoolroom whenever an examination is scored in terms of the number of items correct. As an experimental method it was used by Bolton (1892) and by many successors of whom we list a few contributing to perfect the method: Binet & Henri, 1894; Smith, 1896; Pohlmann, 1906; Lyon, 1916; Raffel, 1934. The quantity of material presented must exceed the memory span; the quantity reproduced is the score. The length of the presented list needs to be standardized for a given experiment.

This method is convenient and can be used with a variety of material. It is easy to score, if we are satisfied with a simple count of the correctly reproduced items. When two Os reproduce correctly the same number of items, but one O gives the correct order and the other not, the first O clearly shows the greater memory of the presented list; but as soon as we try to devise a scoring system which shall allow partial credits, we find any system arbitrary.

The method of retained members has been applied successfully to memory for the substance of prose passages. It is necessary to choose a passage which can be divided into fairly equal units of meaning (Henderson, 1903).

METHOD OF RETAINED MEMBERS

Connected passage of 100 words, divided into "ideas" or meaning units, for scoring.

A bear, / climbing over the fence / into a yard / where bees were kept, / began at once / to smash the hives, / and to rob them / of their honey. / But the bees, / to avenge the injury, / attacked him / in a whole swarm together; / and, though they were too weak / to pierce / his rugged hide, / yet, with their little / stings, / they so tormented / his eyes / and nose, / that, unable to endure / the smarting pain, / he tore the skin / off his ears / with his own claws, / and received ample / punishment / for the injury / he did the bees / in breaking / their waxen cells.

Besides the scoring problem, there is another difficulty in the use of this method. It often fails to give a complete measure of the amount retained. It gives the recalled members, rather than the retained members. O may be convinced that he is retaining items which he cannot at the moment recall, and his conviction is often verified by a later recall of the missing items (p. 66).

The learning method. The name does not fully characterize the method, which might be called the *learning-time* method. It measures the time (or number of trials) required by O to reach a certain standard or criterion of mastery. The criterion may be one perfect recitation of the "lesson," or two perfect recitations. Exactly when the criterion is reached may not be sure if O is allowed to decide when he is ready to recite. An optimistic person may try before he is fully ready, while a cautious person studies longer than necessary and "overlearns" the lesson.

The learning method has the advantage of being applicable to a great variety of material which need not be divisible into separate items. It is scored as a whole.

The prompting and anticipation methods (Ebbinghaus, 1902; Robinson & Brown, 1926). These modifications of the learning method serve two purposes: to overcome the uncertainty as to when O has learned the list, and to trace the progress of learning. After one or a few presentations of the list, O attempts to recite, is quickly prompted whenever he hesitates and corrected whenever he makes an error. The list is gone through in this way time after time until O successfully recites it without prompting.

Several scores are possible. The total time or number of trials to reach the criterion can be used just as in the regular learning method. A more characteristic score is the number of prompts necessary before O reaches the criterion. This score corresponds to one used in maze learning, the number of errors committed before the maze is learned.

This method furnishes a score of errors, prompts or items correctly anticipated for each trial and so makes it possible to construct a learning curve for the list as a whole. It is further possible to trace the progress of learning in each separate item in the list. We can tell on which trial a given item was first anticipated and whether it remained in control after once being mastered.

The saving method. O has learned a certain lesson which may be a list of nonsense syllables, a poem, a maze, a motor skill. After an interval he is unable to reproduce the lesson. He *relearns* it by the same procedure as before and to the same criterion of mastery, and the time (or number of trials) required for the relearning is compared with that required for the original learning. If there is any retention, some saving will be found. The saving is the difference between the original learning time and the relearning time, and the percent of saving is found by dividing this absolute saving by the original learning time. For time we may substitute number of trials or number of errors or prompts, though these different measures of saving will not ordinarily give the same percentage.

In strictness we should compare the relearning time, not with the original learning time but with the time it now takes to learn an equivalent lesson. This refinement is important when the learning and relearning are carried out under different conditions. For example if you wish to discover how well material learned by a subject under the influence of alcohol is retained the next day, it will not do simply to compare the learning and relearning time. Instead O should learn 2 equivalent lessons on the second day, a new one and one originally learned under the alcoholic condition. The question is how much of the work required to learn a new list is saved by virtue of the previous learning.

The saving method can be used for other problems than that of retention. How much of the work otherwise required to learn a certain performance is saved by virtue of the fact that O has previously learned another performance? This is the problem of transfer (p. 180).

The method of paired associates (Calkins, 1894, 1896; Jost, 1897; Müller & Pilzecker, 1900; Thorndike, 1908). Think of learning a Latin-English vocabulary; when you come to recite you are given the Latin words as cues, or the English words, but you are not expected to recite the list right through. There are many practical instances where the task of memory is to connect items in pairs: names and faces, goods and prices, objects and the places where they belong. Two types of experiment come under this general head.

1. Items are studied in pairs so that later when the first item of the pair is presented the other can be given in response. The score is the number of correct responses. The test follows either one or several presentations of the material, but obviously the number of presentations must not be sufficient to give a 100 percent score in the test.

Paired associates and the prompting method can be combined. After one presentation of the list in pairs, the stimulus word of each pair is presented and O is allowed a certain time (2–3 sec.) for response. He is prompted whenever he fails. The trials can be continued till a

PAIRED ASSOCIATES: UNRELATED WORDS TO BE MEMORIZED IN PAIRS

1.	crush	dark	11.	nuisance	true
2.	umbrella	prospect	12.	master	steep
3.	sailor	allow	13.	sulphur	riot
4.	cedar	captain	14.	preach	raisin
5.	mischief	gift	15.	minnow	promise
6.	salute	path	16.	invite	apricot
7.	school	grocery	17.	soldier	stone
8.	bashful	satisfy	18.	cabbage	doll
9.	ride	occasion	19.	escape	overcoat
10.	clean	perverse	20.	irksome	eagle

perfect score is attained, and O's progress can be traced trial by trial for each item and for the whole list.

2. In another form of the method, O studies the entire list as in the Ebbinghaus learning method but he is stopped before learning is complete and tested with separate items to which he responds by giving the items next following in the list.

Recognition method. Here we have two radically different submethods:

A. *Accuracy of recognition of a single stimulus.* The familiar psychophysical experiment in comparing successive weights or sounds is converted into a memory experiment by lengthening the interval between the two stimuli compared. By this means loss can be demonstrated even in the first half minute after presentation (Wolfe, 1886; Lehmann, 1889; Bentley, 1899; Whipple, 1901, 1902).

B. *Number of items recognized.* For example, 20 pictures are shown one at a time, and then shuffled with 20 other pictures and the whole 40 shown one at a time; in this recognition test O responds Yes or No to each picture, meaning by Yes that he recognizes it or judges that it was shown in the first presentation (Binet & Henri, 1894; Smith, 1905; Strong, 1912, 1913; Achilles, 1920).

The scoring of a recognition test offers some statistical problems. Let us call the stimuli first presented the "old" stimuli and the recognition of any such stimulus a correct recognition. And let us call the stimuli mixed with the old stimuli, in the recognition test, "new" stimuli and a recognition of one of them a false recognition. Then a raw score is simply the number of correct recognitions, and dividing this number by the number of old stimuli gives the percent of correct recognitions. This would be a good measure if O never falsely recognized any of the new stimuli, but if he does he must be penalized somehow. One way is to subtract from the percent of correct recognitions the percent of false recognitions. That gives us the formula:

Score = (percent of old stimuli recognized) − (percent of new stimuli falsely recognized).

If, as is customary but not at all necessary, the number of new stimuli equals the number of old stimuli, this formula reduces to the familiar:

$$\frac{\text{Right} - \text{Wrong}}{N},$$

where N = the whole number of stimuli in the recognition test, that is, new + old. "Right" = the number of correct responses to all stimuli, and "Wrong" similarly.

The purpose of using some new stimuli along with the old in the recognition test is to afford a check upon O's responses. If we needed no check we would simply show him the old stimuli, instructing him to say which he recognized. If we introduce new stimuli and he recognizes as large a percent of them as of the old, he gives no evidence of any memory at all, consequently his score should be zero as it is by the above formula.

In the recognition test described, an O who is guessing has an even chance of getting any stimulus right or wrong, no matter how many new stimuli are mingled with the old. To reduce the chances of being right by guessing, a *multiple choice* test is used (Baldwin & Shaw, 1895 a; Zangwill, 1937 a; Hanawalt, 1937). Each "old" stimulus is shown in a group of new stimuli and O's task is to select the old one. If there are 4 new stimuli in the group with a single old stimulus, the chances of being right by guessing are only one in five. The recognition test can be made hard or easy by selecting new stimuli more or less like the old. Recognition is often said to be easier than recall, but its ease or difficulty depends upon the similarity of the new and the old, between which recognition must distinguish.

The reconstruction method (Münsterberg & Bigham, 1894; Gamble, 1909; Smith, 1934). In this interesting method what has to be reproduced is the order or arrangement of the stimuli. The stimuli are first presented in a certain arrangement, then this arrangement is broken up and the stimuli are handed to O with instructions to reconstruct the original order. The arrangement may be a simple serial order of the stimuli or it may be a more complex two-dimensional pattern, or even a three-dimensional one. Verbal material can be used; but the method lends itself to the use of colors, shapes and other concrete material.

The score may be a measure of correspondence between the reconstructed and the original arrangement. In case of simple serial order the Spearman formula for correlation by rank differences is an adequate measure. For two- or three-dimensional patterns, a rough score could be obtained, even though an adequate formula might be difficult of derivation. A totally different method of scoring is possible since evidently the trials can be continued until the subject is able to make a perfect reconstruction, the score being the time or number of trials necessary in order to reach a standard of mastery.

MATERIALS USED IN MEMORY EXPERIMENTS

The recognition and reconstruction methods lend themselves to the use of concrete material. The methods that require O to *reproduce* what he has learned are limited by O's powers of expression. He cannot be expected to reproduce a picture though he may be asked to make simple drawings. Verbal material is especially easy to express.

For scoring purposes it is convenient to have material consisting of equal units, such as words, two-place numbers, or nonsense syllables. Connected passages can be broken up (for scoring purposes only) into phrases or "ideas" which can at least be counted, though they are not strictly equal units. The learning and saving methods do not require any such division into equal parts, when the score is the time or number of trials required to master the whole lesson.

Nonsense syllables. Ebbinghaus (1885) introduced this device not for the purpose of having something difficult to learn but to provide a large quantity of material of fairly uniform difficulty—uniform because entirely lacking in previously established associations *between one item and another*. Unrelated words, substituted for nonsense syllables, give good results, but are not uniformly unrelated; some word sequences suggest a connected meaning and are easily learned, while other sequences are difficult. Nonsense syllables should be more uniform in this respect.

Ebbinghaus, in preparation for his experiments, constructed 2,300 nonsense syllables by a mechanical process. Each syllable consisted of a vowel or diphthong with initial and final consonants. Familiar to Germans were 11 vowels and diphthongs, 19 consonants suitable for beginning a word and 11 suited for an ending, with *ch* and *sch* included as single consonantal sounds. He wrote out all the possible combinations on slips of paper, shuffled them and drew for each list as many as required, till every syllable had been used, when the slips were reshuffled. Some of these syllables were familiar words, but these were not thrown out; all syllables were taken just as they came. Ebbinghaus was his own O, an exceptionally stable and well-trained O; and he learned many lists so as to even out inequalities.

Müller & Schumann (1894) introduced greater precision by removing some of these inequalities. They found that alliteration, assonance, or rhyming of neighboring syllables made a soft spot in a list, and that sometimes two adjacent syllables spelled a familiar word and so were easily learned. They secured 12-syllable lists sufficiently uniform to be called "normal" by mechanically following certain rules:

1. No two syllables in the same list shall have the same initial consonant, or the same final consonant, or the same vowel. (They found it possible to use 12 vowels and diphthongs.)

2. The initial consonant of a syllable shall never be identical with the final consonant of the preceding syllable.

3. The list is to be read by O in trochaic rhythm, two syllables being regarded as a foot with accent on the first syllable of each foot. The first and last consonants in a foot shall not be identical, though the initial and final consonants of a single syllable may be the same.

4. Though a single syllable may be a familiar word, no two or more adjacent syllables shall constitute a familiar word or phrase. They may suggest a word or phrase but shall not correctly spell a word or phrase.

In English-speaking countries, psychologists have usually assumed that the syllables must not be familiar words, and that they must consist of only three letters. These two assumptions, along with the existence of numerous monosyllabic English words, greatly limit the number of available nonsense syllables and make it impossible to follow Müller & Schumann's first rule, since we are limited to six vowels. Nor can we use the simple consonantal sounds which are spelled with two letters, as *ch, sh, th*. Moreover, it has seemed desirable to avoid syllables which, though not correctly spelling familiar words, readily suggest them.

Glaze (1928) attempted to measure the meaningfulness or "association value" of every nonsense syllable consisting of three different letters. Fifteen students were shown one syllable at a time and allowed not over 3 sec. to say whether the syllable conveyed any meaning. Certain syllables, as pil and wom, suggested some meaning to all the 15 Os, certain others to 14, others to 12, and so on down. Of the 2,000 syllables tested, 100 suggested no meaning to any one. Glaze's published syllables enable investigators to construct lists of probably equal suggestive value—though Glaze's sample of the population was rather small and narrow. Glazé himself assumed that the best syllables were those of lowest association value, but when he tried memorizing lists of these best syllables he found the task not only difficult but "extremely trying." The syllables most lacking in suggestiveness are uncouth and almost repulsive in appearance. Some of them are scarcely pronounceable, as kyh, quj, xiw. However, they need not be pronounced if the instructions call for oral or written *spelling* of the syllables. Groups of three consonants can be used.

Hull (1933 a) tried out 320 syllables under conditions of actual learning. O memorized a list and also reported immediately any meaning suggested by each syllable as it came. (Lists of 16 syllables, shown at the rate of 2 sec. per syllable, 3 presentations of each list, 20 lists rotated among the 20 student Os.) The "association value" averaged about half that of the same syllables in Glaze's experiment, as might be expected since Glaze's Os were looking for suggested meanings, while Hull's were learning the sequence of syllables. The correlation between the association values of the same syllables in the two experiments was not high—only .63 when corrected for attenuation—and the correlation between Hull's sub-groups of 10 Os was only .64, indicating a lot of individual variation in the suggestiveness of a nonsense syllable. Nevertheless the obtained association values of various syllables can be used first to build syllable-pairs which shall have equal summed association values, and from these pairs to construct lists each of which shall be fairly uniform throughout its extent. Hull (1935) found that in such lists, consisting of alternate higher-value and lower-value syllables, the high-value ones were learned only a little more quickly than the low-value. In learning a list, the sequences of syllables probably count for more than the suggestiveness of single syllables.

In view of the limitations of three-letter syllables, four-letter syllables have been used by Gamble (1909, 1927) and also (in laboratory classes) by the present author. The initial or final consonant is double, or the vowel sound is expressed by two letters, or a final silent *e* is used to indicate a "long" preceding vowel, as in *tade*. There are plenty of vowel sounds and diphthongs in English speech, and it is possible to construct lists of at least 15 syllables no two containing the same vowel or diphthong and all readily pronounced; for example,

meev	goje
jish	hool
glet	fape
crad	kise
lerm	roif
sark	twic

thog   bune
chuz   nowk
daux   whab

Over 10,000 four-letter syllables, some of them being English words, can be constructed from the following elements:

Initial consonant or double consonant			Vowel or diphthong	Final consonant or double consonant			
b	bl	sm	a	b	lb	rj	ts
c	br	sn	e	c	rb	lk	ct
d	ch	sp	i	d	lc	nk	ft
f	cl	st	o	f	nc	rk	lt
g	cr	sw	u	g	rc	sk	nt
h	dr	th	a—e	j	ld	rn	pt
j	fl	tr	e—e	k	nd	rm	rt
k	fr	tw	i—e	l	rd	lp	st
l	gl	wh	o—e	m	lf	mp	lv
m	gr		u—e	n	mf	rp	mv
n	kl		ee	p	nf	sp	rv
p	kr		oo	r	rf	cs	lx
r	pl		au	s	lg	fs	nx
s	pr		ay	t	rg	ks	rx
t	qu		oi	v	ch	ls	bz
v	sc		ow	x	sh	ms	dz
w	sh			z	th	ns	gz
y	sk				lj	ps	lz
z	sl				nj	rs	rz
							vz

With a single initial consonant, use either a single vowel and a double final consonant, or a two-letter vowel with a single final consonant; with a double initial, both the other elements must be single letters. Such syllables have given satisfaction in laboratory classes, but have not been standardized nor had their association values determined.

Nonsense dissyllables, "paralogs," are not offensive in appearance or difficult to pronounce, and probably can do good service.

PARALOGS

A few of the 43,200 dissyllables prepared by the Division of Anthropology and Psychology, National Research Council (Dunlap, 1933).

babab	gokem	medon	runil
defig	kupod	nigat	tarop
fimur	latuk	polef	zuzuz

Apparatus. Ebbinghaus (1885) simply spread a list of nonsense syllables before him and read them at a rate of $\frac{2}{5}$ sec. per item, keeping time with a metronome or with the ticking of his watch. An early objection to this simple procedure, an objection which has turned out *not* to be

FIG. 1. Memory apparatus. The Lipmann apparatus so modified as to be driven by a constant speed electric motor instead of by clockwork. The works are concealed from O by an aluminum screen; through a window he sees one line of the material at a time. As shown below, the paper strip containing the "lesson" is bound around a drum. When the drum is in place on its shaft, the peg on the small wheel engages the cogs of the drum and gives the drum each time a quick push which brings the next line into view. Reduction gear shown above causes the driving wheel to rotate once in 3 sec., which is the interval between exposures when only one peg is inserted. A more rapid rate can be secured by inserting two or three pegs. The drum in the picture contains a list of paired associates arranged for learning by the prompting method. On seeing the word "umbrella," for example, O tries to give its associate before being prompted by the next following exposure.

very serious, was that the simultaneous presence of several items in the field of view made it possible for associations to be established which otherwise would be impossible, for instance backward associations. Müller & Schumann (1894) avoided this objection and standardized the procedure by pasting the list around a drum which rotated behind a screen and exposed one syllable at a time through a little window in the screen. Some Os found it fatiguing to the eyes to read the moving syllables. The drum should move in quick jumps or steps alternating with stationary moments during which the successive items are exposed. Such intermittent motion was provided by Ranschburg's card-changer (1901); by Wirth's memory apparatus (1903), in which a long band carrying the syllables was driven by clockwork and checked from moment to moment by electromagnets timed by a metronome; and also, very conveniently, by Lipmann's memory apparatus (1904, 1908), in which the drum is driven intermittently by a transmission device, the whole apparatus being self-contained and mechanical. These devices have been improved by more recent makers (Fig. 1).

MEMORIZING

In practically all memory experiments on human subjects O is instructed to learn a given "lesson," as we may call it, and he devotes himself attentively to this task, so that memorizing is a good name for the kind of learning that goes on in the laboratory.

Several challenging facts can be demonstrated with very simple material and procedure, as in a test for digit span. The fact that the span may run up to 6, 8 or 10 digits indicates some process of synthetic apprehension. The fact that the memory span is limited presents something of an enigma; for if you can recite 6 digits immediately after hearing them, why can you not hold these, take on 6 more and recite the whole 12? If you run over a list of 12 a few times, then you can recite it in its entirety. This effect of repetition is a third fact to be explained; a fourth is the forgetting of the list in a few minutes or hours, and a fifth fact is the possibility of relearning the material with less expenditure of time and effort than was required for the original learning. These fundamental facts have been amplified and quantified in various respects.

Dependence of learning time on the quantity of material. The memory span measures the amount of a given material that can be reproduced after a single reading:

2 digits at age of $2\frac{1}{2}$
3 digits at age of 3
4 digits at age of $4\frac{1}{2}$
5 digits at age of 7
6 digits at age of 10 (revised Stanford-Binet scale).

The average for college students without preliminary practice is not over 8. Intensive training of kindergarten children for 78 days increased their average span from 4.4 to 6.4 digits and so brought them up to the 10-year level. After the long vacation in which no further practice occurred, they averaged 4.7, about down to their original level and probably no further above it than could be accounted for by growth (Gates & Taylor, 1925). College students by intensive practice increased their span about 20 percent, the maximum rising from 10 to 14 digits. Though they were not tested later for permanence of this skill, probably some of it remained, since it depended upon a technique of grouping the digits (Martin & Fernberger, 1929). Fig. 2 brings out a fact that should not be forgotten, namely that the individual memory span is not a fixed quantity but varies from trial to trial. When the list is long, O is by no means passive; he watches for number relationships or associations, and his most useful technique is grouping, usually by threes or fours.

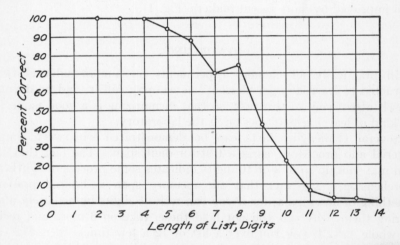

Fig. 2. (After Oberly, 1928.) The variable memory span of an individual. After hearing a list of digits read in a monotonous tone at the rate of one digit per second, O attempted to write it down. In order to score, his reproduction had to be perfect. In the course of five sessions he tried 50 lists of each length. The graph shows that his reproduction was always perfect with the lists of 2–4 digits and that the percent of perfect responses decreased gradually as the list lengthened. The irregularity in the middle of the curve is probably of no significance. The curve might well be smoothed in that region. Where the curve crosses the 50% line we have the indicated Median span, and where it crosses the 25% and 75% lines we have the Quartiles. The Mean computed according to the method of Constant Stimuli (p. 402) is 8.5 digits for this O, and the SD is 2.8 digits. The 100 students tested gave individual Means·ranging from 6 to 12 or 13 digits, and a general average of 9 digits. It made little difference whether the length of list was increased progressively or whether the various lengths were presented in haphazard order.

Lists exceeding the memory span. If O learns a list of 8 digits in one reading (or in 5 sec.) how many readings (or how much time) will it take him to learn a list of 16 digits? This problem cannot be solved by simple proportion, since as a matter of fact when the memory span is exceeded, the time for memorizing takes a sudden jump. If one reading sufficed for 8 numbers, 3 or 4 may be needed to learn 9. A group of 160 unpracticed college students gave an average digit span of 8, but when more than 8 digits were presented in a list the number reproduced fell on the average to 6. Only 5 percent of the Os were able to equal their span when the number presented exceeded the span (Gates, 1916). Digits are rather peculiar materials because there are so few of them and they are so frequently used. When the list consists of disconnected meaningful words, the result is different. Binet & Henri (1894) found with one subject:

5 words presented . . . 5 words reproduced
10 words presented . . . 7 words reproduced
49 words presented . . .17 words reproduced
100 words presented . . .25 words reproduced

The absolute number reproduced increases with the number in the list, but the percent decreases. When a long list of meaningful words was presented, the number reproduced exceeded the subject's memory span. This was an experiment by the method of Retained Members. A similar result is obtained by paired associates and also in recognition experiments, as seen in the adjacent tables.

LEARNING AND RETENTION IN RELATION TO LENGTH OF LESSON
Method of paired associates

	No. word-pairs in list			
	5	10	20	30
Recalled after 1 hearing	3.4	6.0	10.1	10.6
	68%	*60%*	*50%*	*35%*
" " 2 hearings	4.7	8.0	14.2	16.5
	94%	*80%*	*71%*	*55%*
" " 3 "	5.0	9.1	16.9	21.4
	100%	*91%*	*84%*	*71%*
Recalled 2 days later (retention)	0.2	1.6	7.2	10.2
	4%	*16%*	*36%*	*34%*

The table combines the results of two experiments conducted by the author (1915 b) on a group of 25 students. Pairs of unrelated words, similar to those on page 10, were read to the group at the rate of one pair in 6 sec. The instructions were, "Learn the pairs of words so as to respond with the second word of each pair when the first word is given. When I have gone once through the list, I shall begin again at the beginning, and give the first word of the first pair, allowing you 5 sec. for writing the second word of that pair, if you remember it. After the 5 sec. are up I shall tell you this second word so that you may further impress it on your mind. So I shall proceed through the list three times." The procedure thus combined the prompting and paired associates methods.

In the first experiment, E began with a list of 5 pairs and advanced to the longer lists in order; in the second experiment, with different word-pairs, he began with the longest list and proceeded to the shorter ones—so that the practice effect in the two experiments combined should not altogether favor the long lists. For the retention test, the stimulus words (first words) of the four lists were shuffled, and there was no further prompting. A curious fact, confirmed by several repetitions of the experiment on other Os, is that the long lists, though presented no oftener, are much better retained than the short lists. The same time was given to each word-pair in the long and short lists. In learning, this constant time gave larger returns when there were only a few pairs in a list, but for retention the constant time allowance did most for the pairs in the long lists. The harder task stimulated O to find meaningful relations between the words in each pair.

RECOGNITION IN RELATION TO LENGTH OF LESSON

(*From Strong, 1912*)

No. advertisements presented	5	10	25	50	100	150
No. correctly recognized in immediately following test	4.11	8.15	18.23	30.80	56.40	60.60
No. "new" ads. falsely recognized	.04	.10	.30	1.70	4.53	5.68
Net score	4.07	8.05	17.93	29.10	51.87	54.92
Net percent recognized	81	80	72	58	52	37

Each "lesson" consisted of a number of full-page magazine advertisements exposed by E at the rate of one per sec. Immediately after this presentation O was handed a collection of advertisements containing duplicates of those just shown mixed with an equal number of "new" ones, and he sorted out those which he was absolutely sure had just been shown. There were 40 students in each sample, and the table gives the averages. The number recognized increases with the number presented but not so fast. The number of new specimens falsely recognized also increases. The net score here is Right minus Wrong; it increases with the length of lesson, but the percent decreases.

The total time required to learn a list of items must obviously increase with the length of the list, since more time is taken for each single reading. The only question is whether the *time-per-item* (or the number of readings) increases with the length of the list. Does more work have to be done on each item when the number of items is large? Such is the fact, as shown in Figs. 3 and 4. Experiments with nonsense syllables, from Ebbinghaus down, have yielded the same general result—increase in learning time-per-item with increase in the number of items in the list, though there are large differences in the absolute times taken by different Os. Two practiced Os of Henmon (1917) averaged per syllable:

12 sec. when the list contained 10 syllables
20 sec. "   "   "   "   20   "
29 sec. "   "   "   "   30   "

The rate of increase of time-per-item varies in different series, but

Thurstone (1930) shows that many series agree approximately with the statement that the time-per-item increases as the square root of the number of items (beyond the memory span).

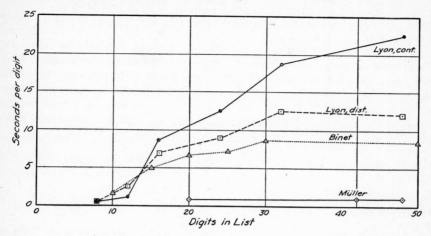

FIG. 3. (Data assembled from several sources.) Increase in time-per-item to memorize digit lists of increasing length. Time-per-item seems the best measure of the increasing difficulty of longer lists. The time-per-list can be found from the graph by multiplying the time-per-item by the number of items.

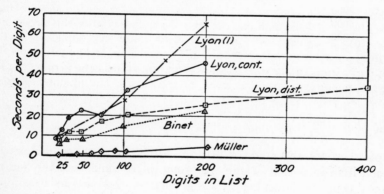

FIG. 4. The same as Fig. 3, on a reduced scale, and covering the whole range of lengths of list. The horizontal scale is more reduced than the vertical with the result that the curves are steeper. This difference of scale needs to be allowed for in comparing the two figures.

The Os in these experiments were probably all unusually expert in memorizing, only such Os having been induced to memorize very long lists. But the general dependence of difficulty on length of list, which shows in these series, would certainly be found with ordinary individuals. The least practiced O in this group is the one labeled "Lyon (1)." She was the most expert among 14 students of about twenty years of age selected by Lyon (1917) as presumably good memorizers, and the only one who stuck it out through the list of 200 digits which took her 1 hour 49 minutes to learn. Lyon himself, who was a practiced memorizer, made about the same record as this student when using the same method of continuous study ("Lyon, cont."). When he used the method of one reading per day ("Lyon, dist.") his time was considerably less and he was able to memorize a list of 400 digits, which may be more than one could master by continuous study because of fatigue, boredom or lapse of effort. The data taken from Binet (1894) and Müller (1911) were obtained from two "lightning calculators," Binet's subject being a professional, and Müller's a mathematician of remarkable facility with numbers and an extraordinary interest from childhood up in numerical relations. In all these experiments the number lists were presented visually, being laid before O, each list as a whole.

If we ask why more time-per-item must be devoted to a longer list, the answer is probably to be sought in some sort of interference between the items or, better, between the processes involved in learning them (p. 231).

With *meaningful material*, as prose or poetry, exceptions are encountered in which a long passage is learned in as few readings as a shorter one; but on the whole it is safe to say that the same rule holds here as in the learning of lists of items. The following data are extracted from Lyon (1917) who memorized prose passages, giving them one reading a day:

No. words in passage	Total time	Time per 100 words
100	9 min.	9 min.
200	24	12
500	65	13
1000	165	16.5
2000	350	17.5
5000	1625	32.5
10000	4200	42
15000	5475	36.5

Relative difficulty of the beginning, middle and end of a list. Not all parts of a list of numbers or nonsense syllables are equally easy to master when the list is being learned as a whole. The middle is learned more slowly than the beginning and end. The prompting or anticipation method is suited to study this matter. Ebbinghaus (1902) learned 48 lists of 10 words and counted up the number of promptings necessary for each item in order. The more promptings, the slower the learning. His total count is shown below.

Position in list	1	2	3	4	5	6	7	8	9	10
No. of promptings	0	3	6	9	23	24	32	25	23	6

The first item required no prompting; it was always recalled without assistance, and the next few items nearly always. The last item also seldom required prompting, but items 5–9 were only slowly mastered. Ebbinghaus explains this result in terms of attention. He says that O's attention if left to itself is at first directed to the beginning and end of the list. This is not an ultimate explanation, for the question immediately occurs, why the attention should be distributed in this way rather than uniformly throughout the list. The answer is, perhaps, that O starts a list in a state of comparative freshness and freedom from load; as he advances he becomes encumbered with the items already taken in. This progressive loading up would by itself produce a steady gradient from the beginning to the end of the list. The reversed gradient at the end results somehow from the free pause allowed at the end of the list. The last items have a chance to strike home or to be reviewed.

A more complete picture of this effect of serial position in the ease of learning an item is provided by Figs. 5 and 6.

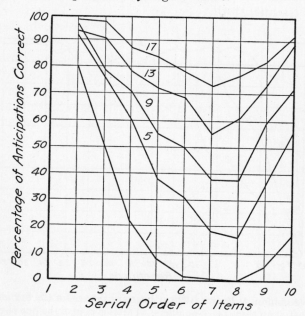

FIG. 5. (Robinson & Brown, 1926.) Effect of serial position in memorizing a list of 10 three-place numbers. There were 8 lists and 11 Os, and each point on the curves gives the percent of successes in the 88 attempts to "anticipate" a number by reciting it before it was shown. The numbers were shown at the rate of one 3-place number every 2 sec. The curve marked "1" shows the result after the first presentation of the list, the curve marked "5" shows the successes after 5 presentations, etc. Each three-place number had to be completely reproduced in order to count as a successful anticipation; no partial credits were allowed. By following the curves upward from "1" to "17" one gets an impression of the gradual mastery of the list from both ends inward. The first item in the list was always given as a cue so that the results furnish no score for this position. Other experiments indicate that it would score nearly 100 percent from the first trial.

THE MEMORIZING PROCESS

The most incisive question to be asked regarding a memory experiment is: How? How is the material memorized? If we could answer this question, we should have both a scientific understanding and the basis for practical rules of efficiency and economy in memorizing.

There are several ways of experimenting on this problem. The most obvious way is that of introspection. O should be able to tell us something of his aim and procedure. We cannot expect introspection to go to the bottom of the dynamic process, yet what it reveals is sometimes important and not open to serious question. For example, the syllables *viz hus* remind O of the word vicious and are quickly learned; but after a few readings, this "association" drops out of mind, the syllable pair having become perfectly familiar on its own account. Such reports are common in memory experiments and there is no reason to doubt their essential truth.

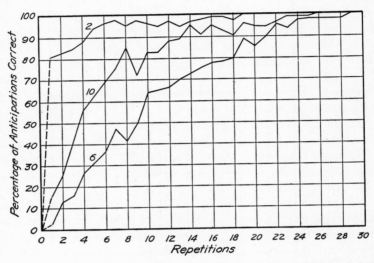

FIG. 6. (Robinson & Brown, 1926.) Learning curves for the beginning, end and middle of a list of 10 three-place numbers. The curves give the percent of successful anticipations at each trial, the results from 8 lists and 11 Os being pooled. The curve marked 6, for example, shows the gradual increase in success in reciting the sixth item which was mastered more slowly than item 10 or item 2.

For an objective attack upon our problem, we may systematically vary the conditions under which learning occurs. For example, E seeks to prevent "associations" by speeding up the presentation to 2–3 syllables per second. O now has not time to work out any relations among the different syllables, except the very obvious ones. Memorizing is somewhat disturbed by the rapid rate. O is under greater strain and requires more readings but not always more total time. The device of speeding up the presentation does not succeed wholly in reducing the learning to the so-called mechanical level (Ogden, 1903; Gamble, 1909, 1916).

E may exert some control over O's condition during the learning by administering a drug such as alcohol or caffeine, or by the instructions. It would be futile to forbid O the use of "associations," but E can exert a certain amount of control by conveying the information that far fetched relationships are usually found to be more hindrance than help.

If we ask in advance of experimentation what O needs to learn in order to recite a list of nonsense syllables, certain requirements seem obvious.

1. The items themselves must be learned; previously unfamiliar syllables must become known.

2. The items must be localized in the list. This requirement could be satisfied either (a) by learning the location of each item or (b) by learning the sequence of items.

Different meanings of "association." This word, much used in memory studies, has at least three meanings. When O says that in learning a list he found an association to help him, he means a meaningful connection between two items or a meaning suggested by a single item. This is not the scientific usage. The scientific meaning of association is broad enough to cover all connections between items or between stimulus and response. There are however two scientific meanings of the term, which should be kept apart:

1. *The factual meaning.* Two objects are said to be associated when one reminds you of the other. No theory is involved. If we find as a matter of fact that item A given as a stimulus evokes the response B, then we can say that A and B are associated, or that an association exists between A and B.

2. *The explanatory concept* of association implies a *direct* connection within the organism, probably within the brain, between the mechanisms concerned with items A and B. The mere fact that A calls up B does not prove that the brain process is a direct shift from the A to the B activity. The transition might take place by way of some integral activity embracing both A and B, and the association theory might therefore need to be replaced or at least drastically revised from its classical form. Some of the experimental results may throw light upon this matter. Meanwhile we shall speak of an association between A and B in the factual and not the explanatory sense.

Associations between the items of a list. When a list has been learned to the point of being recited straight through in correct order, what associations have been formed? Will each item, given alone as a stimulus, call up the following item, or must we give O a running start by allowing him to begin at the beginning of the list? If the latter is the case, we cannot speak of a factual chain of associations linking the items in serial order. When a list has been only partially learned, the items are recalled with omissions and displacements of order. Must we not then speak of associations connecting non-sequential items? From the (explanatory) conception of association by contiguity, we should expect the factual associations to be stronger the greater the contiguity between two items, i.e., the less their distance apart in the presented list. Ebbinghaus (1885) put this matter to a test by an ingenious modification of the saving method. His experiment was divided into two-day units. For each unit he drew from his stock 6 sets of 16 nonsense syllables, and from each set he prepared two lists of the same syllables in different orders. One of these lists, called the original list, was learned on the first day, and the other, a derived or rearranged list, was learned on the second day so as to show how much saving would result from the previous learning of the same syllables in a different order. As regards these different orders, at one extreme we have the case of no difference, the original list being simply relearned; and at the other extreme we have shuffled or scrambled order, a chance rearrangement of syllables from the original list or from several of the original lists which were learned on the same day. In the intermediate cases the second day's lists were derived from the originals by skipping alternate syllables, by skipping twos, threes, etc., or by reversing the order of the original list. Denote by the numbers 1–16 the syllables in their original order; then the arrangement of certain derived lists was as follows:

Skipping ones:	1	3	5	7	9	11	13	15	2	4	6	8	10	12	14	16
Skipping twos:	1	4	7	10	13	16	2	5	8	11	14	3	6	9	12	15
Skipping threes:	1	5	9	13	2	6	10	14	3	7	11	15	4	8	12	16
Reversed	16	15	14	13	12	11	10	9	8	7	6	5	4	3	2	1

On one day, then, Ebbinghaus learned 6 original lists and the next day he learned 6 derived lists. His procedure in memorizing was to have the list spread before him and to read it through and through at the rate of $\frac{2}{5}$ sec. per syllable, grouping three or four syllables into a "foot" and accenting the first syllable in each foot. When he felt able to recite, he looked up from the paper and had a try, but if he was stuck at any point in the list he returned to the paper and read on through the list before trying again; and he was free to interpolate one or more readings before trying again to recite. When he had recited a list once perfectly he took 15 sec. for recording the time, and then started on the next list. To memorize 6 original lists of 16 syllables required about 21 minutes of concentrated effort. The experiment comprised 17 two-day units for each type of derived list, so that each entry in the following table is the average obtained from $17 \times 6 = 102$ lists of 16 syllables, memorized first in the original and next day in the derived order, all the work being done by a single O who was in excellent practice. (For the reversed order, the number of lists was only 60.) The times are given in seconds per unit of 6 lists.

	Time for learning original lists	Time for learning derived lists	Time saved in learning derived lists	P.E. of time saved	Saving in percent
Relearning original lists	1266	844	422	15	33.3
Skipping ones	1275	1138	137	16	10.8
Skipping twos	1260	1171	89	18	7.0
Skipping threes	1260	1186	73	13	5.8
Reversed	1249	1094	155	15	12.4
Scrambled lists	1261	1255	6	13	0.5

As indicated by the values of P.E., there is a statistically reliable saving of time in learning all the derived lists, except the scrambled ones. The time saved in learning a systematically derived list is reliably greater than in learning a scrambled list, and reliably less than in relearning the original list. The differences between the several derived lists, in time saved, are not reliably different, though the indication is that the saving diminishes in proportion as more syllables are skipped. It is certain from the data that reversed lists are learned with less saving than occurs when the original list is relearned.

It may seem incredible that there should have been no saving in learning the scrambled lists. One would expect that mere familiarity with the syllables of the original list would facilitate their learning in any order whatever. So it would, undoubtedly, with an O just making the acquaintance of nonsense syllables. But we must remember that Ebbinghaus had first prepared and written down his 2300 nonsense syllables, and that he had used the same syllables repeatedly in the course of his protracted experiments. To obtain each line in the table, he used $17 \times 6 \times 16 = 1632$ syllables, or over $\frac{2}{3}$ of his entire stock.

These results were taken to mean that there are formed during the original learning of a list of syllables not only the direct serial associations which link each item to its predecessor, but also remote associations linking non-adjacent items, and backward associations; the backward associations being weaker than the forward, and the remote weaker than the direct. By "association" we mean here, in a factual sense, not indeed that A actually recalls C, but that the sequence A-C is more readily learned if the sequence A-B-C has been previously learned. Similarly, with regard to "backward associations," we mean that the sequence B-A is more readily learned if A-B has been previously learned.

Ebbinghaus summarized his results in these words (as translated by Ruger & Bussenius, 1913):

With repetition of the syllable series not only are the individual terms associated with their immediate sequents but connections are also established between each term and several of those which follow it. . . . The strength of these connections decreases with the number of the intervening (syllables). . . . Certain connections of the members are . . . actually formed in a reverse as well as in a forward direction. . . . The strength . . . was however considerably less for the reverse connections than for the forward ones.

In spite of the remarkable excellence of this pioneer study, the conclusions of Ebbinghaus go beyond his evidence. He says that "connections are established between *each term* and several of those which follow it." But his results can be explained just as well by supposing that *some* terms, not all, are thus connected. In the derived list obtained by "skipping ones" there would be some saving if only the following remote associations had been formed in learning the original list: 1–3, 5–7, 9–11, 13–15; the other alternate terms need not be associated at all.

Similarly, there would be some saving in the reversed list provided just a few backward associations had been formed. The method used was global; it measured the saving for the list as a whole and not for the separate parts.

Rhythmical grouping. Ebbinghaus read the lists of syllables rhythmically because, like subsequent investigators, he found it impossible to avoid some grouping and accenting. He did not raise the question whether this grouping played any part in memorizing the list and establishing associations between the items. Once the question is raised, as it was raised by Müller & Schumann (1894), it is clear that imposing a regular rhythmical pattern upon a list of syllables amounts to organizing the list to a certain degree and may well contribute to the learning process. One wonders also whether the items composing a group are not more strongly associated, forward and backward, than equally distant items in different groups, and whether the accented syllables of successive groups are not associated more strongly than unaccented items in adjacent groups. Müller & Schumann proved that, in fact, the grouping is a definite factor in learning a list and in determining what associations are formed. These investigators used 12-syllable lists which were exposed on the surface of a cylinder revolving behind a screen; through a slit in the screen one syllable at a time was visible. The drum revolved once in 10 sec., allowing about ⅚ sec. for each syllable with a slight gap or pause at the end of the list before it began again. The list was learned when O correctly spoke every syllable before it appeared. O was instructed to read the list aloud in trochaic rhythm, accenting the odd-numbered syllables. Most Os went beyond the instructions and read in a more elaborate rhythmical pattern. They made a slight break or caesura after the sixth syllable, thus dividing the list into two parts each of which contained three trochaic feet, with strong accents on syllables nos. 1, 5, 7, 11. A pneumograph record showed that an inspiration was generally taken after the sixth syllable and another at the end of the list. Thus the customary rhythmical pattern was as follows:

$\angle$ _, _ _, $\angle$ _ (breath) $\angle$ _, _ _, $\angle$ _ (breath)

There was a slight accent also on syllables 3 and 9.

This mode of reading suggests, what O's introspection confirmed, that each foot was taken as a unit, and each half of the list as a larger, looser unit. What associations would be expected with this mode of apprehending the list? Three classes of associations could be expected:

1. A close linkage of the two syllables in the same foot.

2. An association between successive feet, each foot being taken as a whole.

3. An association of feet and syllables with their positions in the rhythmical pattern.

To investigate the reality of these associations, Müller & Schumann designed a modification of the Ebbinghaus experiment with derived lists. On the first of two days they memorized several lists, and on the second day they learned lists constructed of pairs of syllables from the original lists. These pairs were sometimes the original trochaic feet, as 1–2, 3–4, and sometimes they consisted of adjacent syllables from different feet, as 2–3, 4–5. The plan of the experiment can be expressed in a formula, the letters A,B,C,D denoting the original lists and the subscripts denoting the place of each syllable in its original list. Thus B_8 denotes the 8th syllable in original list B.

On the first day four original lists were learned:

$$A_1 \, A_2, \, A_3 \, A_4, \, A_5 \, A_6, \, A_7 \, A_8, \, A_9 \, A_{10}, \, A_{11} \, A_{12}$$
$$B_1 \, B_2, \, B_3 \, B_4, \, B_5 \, B_6, \, B_7 \, B_8, \, B_9 \, B_{10}, \, B_{11} \, B_{12}$$
$$C_1 \, C_2, \, C_3 \ldots \ldots \ldots \ldots \ldots \ldots C_{10}, \, C_{11} \, C_{12}$$
$$D_1 \, D_2, \, D_3 \ldots \ldots \ldots \ldots \ldots \ldots D_{10}, \, D_{11} \, D_{12}$$

On the second day the derived lists either preserved the original feet, as:

$$A_5 \, A_6, \, C_9 \, C_{10}, \, D_9 \, D_{10}, \, B_5 \, B_6, \, C_3 \, C_4, \, D_3 \, D_4$$

or else they used adjacent syllables from different feet, as:

$$A_6 \, A_7, \, C_{10} \, C_{11}, \, D_{10} \, D_{11}, \, B_6 \, B_7, \, C_4 \, C_5, \, D_4 \, D_5$$

The results of this experiment on two Os gave averages as follows:

No. readings to learn an original 12-syllable list	20
No. readings to learn a derived list with the original feet preserved	13
No. readings to learn a derived list consisting of adjacent syllables from different feet	20

There was a saving of $(20 - 13) / 20 = 35$ percent when the old feet were preserved, but no saving when there was the same amount of adjacency but no feet preserved. The inference was that the associations carried over from the original to the derived list were associations between the two members of the same foot, and not between adjacent syllables as such. The experiment was varied in several ways and on the whole gave evidence of some association between adjacent members of different feet, but this association was much weaker than between the two members of the same foot.

Association of syllables or feet with their position in the list was brought out by derived lists of these two sorts:

$$A_1 \, A_2, \, B_3 \, B_4, \, A_5 \, A_6, \, B_7 \, B_8, \, A_9 \, A_{10}, \, B_{11} \, B_{12}$$
$$A_3 \, A_4, \, B_1 \, B_2, \, A_7 \, A_8, \, B_5 \, B_6, \, A_{11} \, A_{12}, \, B_9 \, B_{10}$$

The first of these two derived lists preserves the original position of every foot, while alternating feet from the two original lists; the second derived list displaces the feet from their original positions. The number of readings required to learn the original lists averaged 10.9; to learn derived lists of the first sort, 8.6; of the second sort 10.1. We conclude that learning an original list consists partly in locating the syllables in the rhythmical pattern. A derived list which changes the locations of the syllables requires more new learning than one which leaves every item in its original place.

Müller & Pilzecker (1900) pursued the matter further by the method of paired associates. They presented 12-syllable lists of nonsense syllables to be learned; when a list was once recited correctly, they introduced a pause of three minutes, during which O read something easy and amusing, and then they tested him by presenting as stimuli single syllables from the list with instructions to respond in each case by the first syllable that came to mind. The time of each response was measured with a chronoscope and voice key (see pp. 311, 313). When the stimulus was an odd-numbered syllable of the original list the most common response was the following syllable, but when the stimulus was an even-numbered syllable the most common response was the originally preceding syllable. In each case the most common response was the other syllable *from the same foot.* The percents of cases and the average reaction time (RT) are shown below:

When the stimulus was	an odd-no. syllable	an even-no. syllable
the response was the		
following syllable	50% (RT, 3.1 sec)	7% (RT, 7.4 sec)
preceding syllable	4% (RT, 6.5 sec)	38% (RT, 3.4 sec)

Since there are a few responses that go forward or back across the boundaries between feet, the authors believe that Ebbinghaus's serial and backward associations must be genuine, though quite weak. The cohesion of a (barely learned) list of items depends mostly on the grouping and locating of the items.

Further evidence regarding remote and backward associations. The work of Müller and his coworkers rather leaves the impression that backward associations, remote forward and even direct forward or straight serial associations are secondary results of the grouping and locating activity. One must bear in mind, however, that the learning was not carried very far in these experiments—only to the point of one correct recitation, at most. If the lists are read over and over after this point has been reached, the recitation becomes more and more fluent, till finally O rattles off the series automatically. The series has become a motor habit, dependent mostly, one would suppose, on straight serial associations. There is some evidence for this view.

Some results of Ebbinghaus are shown in Fig. 7: increase the number of readings of a list and you increase proportionately the saving in relearning the original list but you increase only slightly the saving in learning a rearranged list. Nagel (1912) went further; he pushed the original learning to the point of great overlearning; after once reciting the list correctly, O read it 20 times more and then recited it 20 times. Next day he learned a rearranged list with a loss of 10 percent instead of a saving. The original order of syllables, greatly overlearned and automatic, actually interfered with the later attempt to learn the same syllables in a different order. In a control experiment the same O learned the original list only to the point of one correct recitation, and the next day learned a rearranged list with a saving of 36 percent. Cason (1926) in a variety of experiments got little evidence of either remote or backward associations except when the material was underlearned in the first place. Both of these authors are very skeptical regarding remote and backward as-

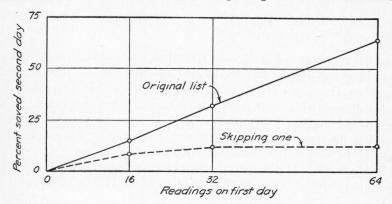

Fig. 7. (Data from Ebbinghaus, 1885.) Saving in relearning original list and in learning derived lists; in the latter alternate syllables are omitted (see p. 26). As the number of readings in the first learning increases the saving in relearning the original list increases markedly, while the saving in learning the derived list shows scarcely any increase. Each data point gives the average of 48 or more lists.

sociations and point out ways in which O, while learning the original list, may incidentally associate non-adjacent syllables; and Nagel is inclined to explain most of the positive results as resulting from associations of the syllables with their positions. Hall (1928) obtained good evidence of remote forward associations (skipping ones), when two precautions were observed: (1) the original lists are not overlearned; (2) the derived lists are learned after a sufficient lapse of time to permit the interferences to die out. When certain syllables have been learned in a sequence and then immediately the same syllables have to be learned in a different order, or with new syllables inserted, the already learned sequence is bound to interfere with the learning of the new one; but such interference (also called associative inhibition) dies out in time (see p. 225).

Displacement of items in reciting a partially learned list. In learning a list to recite straight through, both the items and their locations or order have to be learned. Often an item is known but recited out of its proper position. Preplacement is more common than postplacement—a fact which has aroused some interest, especially because it seems analogous to the premature turning to the right or left which is found in maze learning (p. 138). It is difficult to devise a method for bringing out the significance (if any) of preplacement in reciting a list. If O simply recites what he can, without prompting, his omissions will shorten the list and make it impossible to say what position he has assigned to many items. If he is prompted, the cards are stacked against postplacement, since only by losing track of what has gone before in the same recitation can O postplace an item; he would have to repeat an item already covered in the recitation or prompting. Some postplacements do occur but they are much less frequent than preplacements; the latter become more numerous as more items are learned, and then become less frequent and smaller as more and more items get located and as perfect recitation is approached (Lumley, 1932; Mitchell, 1934). Hull (1935) finds that a dose of caffein somewhat increases the number of preplacements. It makes O disinclined to hold back a syllable for the most likely position—so we might interpret the result. Hull's interpretation may come to the same thing; he speaks in terms of Pavlov's "delay inhibition" which is known to be diminished by caffein in the conditioned reflex experiment (p. 97).

Spatial grouping. A long list exposed as a whole can be read rhythmically, and can also be seen as divided into more or less regular groups. Even when the items are exposed successively, a "visually minded" O may assign each item to its place in an imaginary row or column, perhaps a column of fours. A list presented to the ear may be immediately translated into visual terms and given a spatial arrangement. Each item may be assigned to one of O's fingers or be projected to a definite part of the room. Many spatial schemes have been adopted as helps in memorizing (Müller, 1911, 1913, 1917; Gamble & Wilson, 1916; O'Brien, 1921).

Grouping, whether rhythmical or spatial, provides a blank form into which the items are inserted. The practiced O usually has a regular schema with a place for every item, and his memorizing consists in placing the items in the schema. Remembering the list consists largely in finding the items in their places.

Are grouping and locating of any real service? All this activity of rhythmical or spatial organization might be a natural recourse of one who is confronted by a difficult task, without being of any real service. It might be like scratching one's head in perplexity. The question is whether serial associations do not do the real work. In an experiment of Gamble & Wilson (1916) lists of 18 nonsense syllables were exposed in 3 horizontal rows, each syllable being in its own little square. O's task was to learn the syllables by pairs so that when any odd-numbered syllable was later shown, the following syllable could be given in response. Localizing the syllables was no part of the assigned task but it was made easy by the form of exposure. At each presentation O had barely time to read the list once at the rate of a syllable per second. The list was read rhythmically with strong accents on the odd-numbered syllables. After a few presentations there was an interval of 3 minutes and then came the test in which each odd-numbered syllable was exposed and O attempted to give the paired syllable. The stimulus syllable was sometimes exposed in its original location and sometimes elsewhere, and O was asked to say whether it was in its original position, or what its original position had been. The average score of the 7 Os was 49 percent of right associates, and 76 percent of right localizations. The location of the items had been better learned than the sequences. Locating the items, though not required, was a comparatively easy matter. Did it have any value in learning the pairs? When a syllable was correctly localized its associate was correct in 60 percent of the cases, but when localization was incorrect the associate was right in only 15 percent. This objective evidence strongly suggests that localization was a step in the process of associating the pairs.

Irregular grouping and locating. Cut-and-dried spatial or rhythmical patterns are favored by the practiced memorizer, who follows a regular, predetermined procedure, knowing exactly how to attack each new list. The less experienced O adopts a more fluid method, a method which doubtless corresponds quite well with the way in which meaningful material is memorized. He explores the list, finds easy groups or striking items and uses these as landmarks, attaching other items to them as well as to the beginning and end of the list. O attacks the digit list:

$$4\ 0\ 8\ 2\ 7\ 9\ 6\ 3\ 4\ 8\ 5\ 1\ 0\ 7\ 3\ 2\ 4\ 5\ 5\ 3\ 4\ 7\ 6\ 0$$

He notices the double 5 near the end, that this double 5 is preceded by the small numbers 3 2 4 and followed by the small numbers 3 4 and so he has a group of 7 organized around the double 5; this group of 7 is preceded and followed by the number 7, and the first of these 7's is preceded by 10, while the last is followed by 60. Meanwhile he has probably learned the first few members, so that only a small portion remains to be organized.

Aids in memorizing a nonsense list. The word *aid* is used here as a substitute for the non-technical use of "association." A variety of meanings and relations may be found or read into the list. Müller (1911) made a study of the various kinds of aids employed in memorizing. The chief classes are:

1. *Familiar items or groups.* If a nonsense syllable immediately suggests a word it stands out and is easily located in the list. If a sequence of two nonsense syllables readily combines into a meaningful word, this little sequence is quickly mastered. If a sequence of digits makes a familiar date, like 1492, that part of the list is easy.

2. *Relations and patterns* found in the list give it character and make learning easy. The pattern may be visual or auditory in character. Three adjacent syllables, *zax ron sem*, consisting wholly of short letters may attract attention on that account. Number groups 507, 811 rhyme with each other. Any arithmetical relations are likely to be seized upon by a memorizer who is fond of numbers. Müller's star performer whose span was at least 25 digits had at his finger tips all sorts of numerical relations. He knew all the squares, cubes and prime numbers up to 1,000, and every 3-place number immediately made meaning for him. Take the sequence:

$$357864$$

If we read 256 instead of 357, the whole sequence consists of familiar powers of 2; we learn it so and make the necessary correction.

3. *Suggested meanings, extra ideas.* The memorizer is usually very much on the alert for suggestions which will give a richer meaning to nonsense material. Even when the meaning is far-fetched it may serve a purpose. A nonsense syllable which suggests some word with an interesting meaning stands out and becomes a landmark. More commonly the suggested meaning links two items of the list. The following examples are taken from experiments with paired associates:

Word-pair	*Suggested meaning*
marble-punish	marble-pumice-punish
marble-punish	being punished for playing marbles "for keeps"
disease-argue	disease-ague-argue
simmer-tarry	both slow
simmer-tarry	cemetery
excuse-slave	no excuse for slavery
above-conceal	above-ceiling-conceal

A pair of unrelated words that thus suggests a meaning, however fanciful, is quickly learned and well retained, though occasionally the extra idea alone, without the response word, is recalled. It is important to notice that these extra ideas tend to drop out of mind as the learning advances; they have done their work and are discarded (Reed, 1918; O'Brien, 1921). Short-circuiting occurs, the transition from item to item, instead of taking the circuitous route by way of the extra idea, becomes a direct association. Such short-circuiting is certainly common in ordinary learning. You may learn a telephone number by aid of some little mnemonic device, but if you use this number often, you know it directly. You may learn the meaning of a new word by looking up its derivation, but with repeated use of the word you no longer think of the derivation. What these extra ideas accomplish is to hold certain items together until a direct association has been established between them.

Association by contiguity. There is probably no doubt that two items must be contiguous in experience in order to become associated, but is contiguity sufficient? When we learn from Müller and Schumann that items included in the same group are closely associated whereas those equally contiguous in space or time but included by O in different groups are only weakly associated, we query whether some synthetic act on O's part may not be necessary in order to accomplish the association. An experiment with paired associates strengthens this suspicion. A list of 20 pairs of unrelated words was presented orally to a group of 16 students who were instructed to learn the pairs so as to respond with the second word of each pair when the first was given. The list was read 3 times in the same order and then the subjects were asked to anticipate, if possible, the first word of each pair after giving the response word of the preceding pair. The second members of the pairs were recalled in 74 percent of the cases but the following first members in only 7 percent. Yet the list had been so presented that contiguity in time between two items within the same pairs was scarcely greater than that between two adjacent items of different pairs. The reason why O was able to give the second member of each pair in response to the first, but unable to give the first member of the next pair, was perfectly clear to O himself. He had examined each pair with the object of finding something characteristic about it, whereas he had disregarded the sequence of pairs as being of no concern to him. He had reacted to each pair as a unit but had made no unitary response to adjacent items from different pairs. The results suggest that unitary response rather than stimulus contiguity is the essential factor in establishing an association (Woodworth, 1915 a; Reed, 1918; Thorndike, 1932).

Summary of the memorizing process. "If we look back over this account of the associations formed in memorizing, we cannot fail to be impressed with their great variety—serial associations, remote and backward associations, associations with position, connections of items within a group and of group with group, and extra ideas entering in various ways. We may well be struck also with the importance of perception or apprehension in the learning process—perception of relations, patterns and meanings. To look at a list of numbers or nonsense syllables, you would think that the thing to be done was to forge links between the adjacent terms, but the actual learning proceeds largely in quite another way. It does not start with elements and unite these, but it starts with groups, or even with the whole series, and proceeds largely by analysis and the finding of parts and relations."

The quotation is from the first mimeographed edition of this chapter written in 1913 before the influence of Gestalt psychology began to be felt. The conclusions expressed were based mostly upon the work of G. E. Müller. They have not been overthrown but rather confirmed by more recent studies. The importance of an initial orientation in the material to be learned, of locating and grouping the items, and of finding or inventing meaningful relations has become ever more certain with the progress of investigation.

RECALL

In order of time, recall and recognition come after retention, but there is some sense in studying them first because they are used as indications of retention. We can make our study brief for the reason that less is known about these two processes than about the process of learning. The learning process is perhaps more amenable to experimental control. However, there is a modicum of scattered information on recall. Some relevant findings are given under the head of Retroactive Inhibition (p. 227) and in the chapters on Association and Thinking.

Under the head of recall may be included all cases in which previously learned reactions are made, and there is a great variety of such cases.

1. Recall of lists, items, facts, material of any sort which has previously been learned and is now intentionally remembered.

2. Execution of any learned act.

3. The calling up of sensory images.

4. Reverie or "free association," without any intention of recalling—"one idea calls up another."

5. Controlled association such as occurs in adding, reading or conversation. Here the intention is directed toward some other result than the mere recall. In adding the intention is to find the sum of this column of figures; in reading, to get the meaning of this news item; but the process consists largely in the recall of number combinations and word meanings.

6. Thinking, as in problem solution and the mastery of novel situations. Recall furnishes raw material for thought.

Direct and indirect recall. By "direct" is here meant not necessarily quick, but free from detours and intermediaries. Indirect recall is also called "mediate." Items A and B have been associated, as in a Paired Associates experiment, and A is later given as a stimulus with instructions to respond by saying the paired item and then to report the process intervening between stimulus and response, so far as it can be caught by introspection. Sometimes there is nothing to report, but sometimes there were words, images, thoughts, feelings intervening between stimulus and response; and sometimes these intermediaries obviously led the way to the response. O has learned the word-pair, "above—conceal" by inserting the word, "ceiling" which has a similarity of meaning with one of the given words and a similarity of sound with the other. In the recall test O reaches the response word by way of the inserted word.

Michotte & Portych (1913) used pairs of related words, as "mathematics—algebra," "epic—hero," "lion—king." A list consisted of 12 pairs and was exposed just once for O to learn, each pair being shown for 4.5 sec. In the recall test, which came immediately, after a day, or after a week, the first words of the pairs were the stimuli. With the relatively meager amount of learning, direct recall was infrequent: in the immediate test about ⅕ of the correct recalls were reported as being direct; in the later tests, when memory had become indistinct, the instances of direct recall were still fewer.

Among the various intermediaries reported, two classes are of special interest. There was an obviously useful sort, when a meaningful relation, noticed in learning a pair, came up in recalling the correct response word. The recall here followed the same route as had been used in learning the pair. The route did not always lead to the goal; the intermediary might be too general to yield the exact word required. ("Above" suggests "ceiling," but then what?) When O was stuck another kind of intermediary often appeared: images and ideas were suggested by the stimulus word though not previously used in learning the pair. Here we see O engaged in *searching* for the response word and endeavoring to get some lead from the stimulus word—just as, in trying to recall a name, we look the person over and call up the circumstances in which we met him. Such leads are only moderately hopeful.

Searching for names is a recall process well deserving of study. William James (1890, I, 251) gave a vivid introspective description:

Suppose we try to recall a forgotten name. The state of our consciousness is peculiar. There is a gap therein; but no mere gap. It is a gap that is intensely active. A sort of wraith of the name is in it, beckoning us in a given direction, making us at moments tingle with a sense of our closeness, and then letting us sink back without the longed-for term. If wrong names are proposed to us, this singularly definite gap acts immediately so as to negate them. They do not fit into its mould. And the gap of one word does not feel like the gap of another. . . . The rhythm of a lost word may be there without a sound to clothe it; or the evanescent sense of something which is the initial vowel or consonant may mock us fitfully, without growing more distinct.

The false names that come up during such a search afford some objective clues to the nature of the process of recall. These false names, especially the first one to come up, show similarity of one kind or another to the true name. Wenzl (1932, 1936) has collected cases and finds the similarity to reside sometimes in the initial sound, sometimes in the rhythm of the whole name (number of syllables, accent), and sometimes in the atmosphere of the name, elegant, aristocratic, commonplace, gloomy, foreign. Wenzl suggests a law of recall: the process of recalling a name starts with general characteristics of the name and advances toward the specific. Woodworth (1929, 1934) from his own collection of cases reaches a similar conclusion. A few examples will show various ways in which the name first recalled resembles the name sought.

Name first recalled	*Correct name*
Rogers	Richards
Schniermann	Spranger
Picquard	Lapicque
Casenaugh	Ranelagh
Walliston	Warburton
Stevens	Stowell
Field	Pearl
Ferguson	Gallagher
Hirschberg	Fishberg
Cobb	Todd
Saxegaard	Stangeland
aspasia	azalea
sycamore	sassafras
Philena	Ophelia

You get the right kind of name—right in some respect—before you get the right name. Often, of course, the right name comes directly.

Speed of recall. Recall time, a form of reaction time, is the interval between the recalling stimulus and the motor response (usually verbal). It can be measured in a Paired Associates experiment, roughly by a stopwatch and much more accurately by a chronoscope with a voice key to pick up O's reaction. It is quite variable, the promptest recalls taking about half a second and the slow ones reaching several seconds or an indefinite time. The speed of recall depends greatly on *recency*. In the experiment of Michotte & Portych (1913) the average time for correct responses was as follows:

Immediately after learning	1.5 sec.
One day after learning	2.4 "
One week later	3.0 "

Müller & Pilzecker (1900) used nonsense syllables. One list was read over many times but not tested for 24 hours, while another list, read only a few times, was tested immediately. The older, better learned lesson gave fully as many correct recalls but they were slow in comparison with the responses from the recent lesson. Old-established responses, unless recently reviewed, come slowly; newly formed associations are quick. Reading and conversation depend for their ease on quick-acting temporary associations which are useful in the given context.

The nimbleness of just-formed associations is sometimes an inconvenience. When we have run off the track in trying to remember a name, the wrong name recalled acquires recency value and blocks the correct name. The new association keeps getting in ahead of the slow, old response. The same trouble occurs in athletics or playing a musical instrument; a false move is apt to be immediately repeated and an interval of rest may be necessary before good form can be recovered. The rest interval allows the recency value of the error to die away. The same cause may be responsible for the often noted fact that a problem after being well opened up must be laid aside before a good solution can be reached. In doggedly grinding away at the problem one is likely to get into a rut from which one cannot escape because of its recency. After a rest the problem may reveal a new lead and be readily solved (an instance of "incubation"; see Index).

Condition of readiness. A name is "on the tip of your tongue," yet it does not emerge—it is for the moment below the "threshold of recall." It is partially aroused, sub-excited, as is shown by the peculiar feeling of nearness and by the fact that a little extra push in the right direction will give complete recall. If A and B have been associated, and some time later A is presented without recalling B, it nevertheless makes B easy to recall or relearn. It puts B into a condition of readiness, the reality of which has been shown in a variety of experiments (Ebbinghaus, 1885; Müller & Schumann, 1894; Müller & Pilzecker, 1900; Ohms, 1910; Meyer, 1914). We will cite only the experiment of Ohms. Nonsense words were studied and later tested by Paired Associates. When a word failed of recall it was spoken to O through a poor telephone, or visually exposed for only a small fraction of a second. The auditory or visual presentation was not good enough to enable O to understand nonsense words, but he could often understand one when the stimulus for its recall had just been given. If a name is "on the tip of your tongue" and some one pronounces it indistinctly to you, that extra push may be enough to bring the name up above the threshold of recall. The response is in such a condition of readiness that it can be evoked by an otherwise inadequate stimulus (cf. p. 231).

Memory images. Many individuals possess the power of calling up "before their mind's eye" pictures of scenes, objects or faces which they have seen; they are said to have strong powers of visual imagery. Some, again, have the power of vividly reproducing sounds "before their mind's ear" and are said to be strong in auditory imagery; and similar powers exist in smell, touch, and perhaps other senses. A memory image is typically a lifelike or vivid reproduction of sensory experience.

An "idea" of an object is not necessarily or by definition an image of the object, for it is conceivable that one might think of an object without having a lifelike representation of it. Whether this is ever actually the case must be found out by observation; but at least the lifelikeness of representation which is the peculiar property of the image is not necessarily implied in the words *thought* and *idea*.

The existence of great individual differences in imagery was first announced by Fechner (1860), and later, with fuller evidence, by Galton (1880). Fechner asked his subjects to call up an image of a certain object, and found that while some reported success, others were able, at the best, to get a momentary glimpse, after which the image gave way to a bare thought of the object ("ein blosses Gedankending"). Galton employed the familiar "breakfast table" questionary. He asked his subjects to call up a picture of their breakfast table as they sat down to it in the morning, and to report whether the objects were well-defined, the brightness comparable to that of the actual scene, the colors distinct and natural. From his first subjects, scholars and scientific men, he obtained answers which surprised and somewhat disconcerted him, for many of them reported an absence of images, and were inclined to regard the "mind's eye" as a pure invention of the poets. On distributing his questionary more widely, however, he received many quite different reports. "I can see my breakfast table or any equally familiar thing with my mind's eye quite as well in all particulars as I can do if the reality is before me," was one of the strongest replies. "One or two objects are much more distinct than the others, but the latter come out clearly if attention be paid to them" was the reply of an individual with apparently about average power. Galton arranged his subjects in the order of their power of imagery as indicated by their reports, and was thus able to show where the average (or rather the median) lay.

Galton was followed by other investigators who found some individuals strong in visual imagery, others strong in auditory or in motor imagery; and thus there grew up a theory of imagery types: the visualist, strong in visual imagery but weak or mediocre in other forms; the audile, strong in auditory imagery; the motile and other types.

The motor type is well represented in psychological literature by Stricker (1880, 1882). His word-images, instead of being visual or auditory, were almost entirely kinesthetic—though whether they were true images or sensations from actual articulatory movements was not easy to determine. He believed himself to be typical of all people, and proposed a test to demonstrate the motor nature of verbal images: hold the mouth open and try to think of such words as "bubble," "mutter," "wisp," which cannot be actually spoken without closing the mouth. Some individuals are unable to imagine these words with their mouths open, and this inability indicates that their word-images are motor. Stricker's images of soldiers marching were felt in his own limbs.

The auditory individual can imagine the words "bubble," etc., perfectly well with his mouth in any position; his word-images are distinctly auditory; he is unable to see a printed word without hearing it; marching soldiers are not seen, nor felt in his legs, but heard in the form of foot-falls and a swishing indicative of movement through the air; any attempt to imagine the flight of a bird or of a shooting star results in hearing some sound vaguely symbolic of the movement; auditory imagery of music affords him great pleasure.

Individuals of other types are probably rare. Toulouse (1897) in his psychological examination of Zola found the novelist to belong more or less to the olfactory type, since he thought of persons, streets and houses in terms of odors.

Besides these "pure types," a "mixed type" was found necessary to take care of individuals who reported imagery of several senses and no marked preponderance of any one modality. As investigation progressed, the mixed type was found to be very common and the pure types correspondingly rare. Betts (1909) expanded Galton's questionary so as to give a fair chance for images of every modality. He asked O to call up landscapes, faces; voices, tunes; the feeling of velvet and sand; the taste of sugar, salt; the odor of roses, onions; the kinesthetic impressions of running, kicking; organic sensations like headache and hunger. O graded each image on a scale of 7 degrees from "perfectly clear" to "no image." The surprising result was that those Os who ranked their imagery high or low in one sense tended to do about the same in the other senses also, so that there was a positive correlation between the reported vividness of imagery of the different senses, instead of the negative correlation demanded by the type theory. The average grade assigned to the visual and auditory images was only slightly higher than the average assigned to other modalities. The average fell between "very clear" and "moderately clear" except for olfactory images where it fell a little below "moderately clear."

Experience in giving this questionary to classes of students shows that they tend at first to grade their images very high but that after hearing the distinction between image and idea discussed many of them wish to lower the grades. At first they identify any clear memory of a fact with a vivid image of it but after discussion they see the distinction.

Objective tests of imagery. In view of the necessarily unstandardized nature of an individual's ratings of his imagery it was hoped to develop objective tests. They were based on the assumption that visual work requires visual imagery, auditory work auditory imagery. The only criterion for validating an objective imagery test is the subjective report of a trained observer. Many objective tests were tried out by Angell (1910) and by Fernald (1912) and found to have low validity, though some of them were useful in combination with a subjective report. The causes of their breakdown furnish a valuable psychological study.

1. *Association method.* O is given 5 minutes in which to mention objects having characteristic colors and 5 minutes for objects having characteristic sounds. He is judged a visualist if his list of color-objects is longer and an audile if his sound list is longer. The objection is that a person may recall a violin as being a sounding object without any image of the sound.

2. The style of an author is analysed and the relative frequency of sight words, sound words, etc. is determined. An author who often mentions sounds or sounding objects is diagnosed as an audile. If he abounds in graphic descriptions of scenes he is called a visualist. The objection is the same as in the previous paragraph. Instances are on record in which an author remarkable for his vivid descriptions of scenes reports himself *not* a visualist. There is nothing to prevent the non-visualist from seeing what is worth seeing and remembering it so as later to incorporate it in his writing.

3. *Learning by the eye or the ear.* O learns lists of words or syllables presented to the eye and other lists presented to the ear. If he learns more readily with visual presentation he is called a visualist, if with auditory presentation an audile. The trouble is that the visualist can easily translate heard words into visual terms, and the audile can translate in the opposite direction, so that the modality in which the words are presented is no criterion of the imagery used in learning and recall. The audile need not have a quick ear, he may have become deaf, he may see a syllable better than he can hear it. Adults whether audiles or visualists are found to learn nonsense syllables more readily when they are visually presented.

4. *Method of distraction.* A visual process, the theory runs, will be most readily disturbed by extraneous visual stimuli. While learning lists of words, O is subjected in one case to auditory distraction, in another case to visual, and in a third case is required as a kinesthetic distraction to hold his tongue between his teeth. If his learning is most

hampered by visual distraction, he is judged to be learning visually. As a matter of fact, one who is learning visually may be most disturbed by the motor distraction, simply because of its general distracting effect.

5. *Spelling.* Words are pronounced to O who is instructed to spell them backwards. If he had a photographic image of the word, he could simply read the letters backwards. Fernald (1912) found no subject able to accomplish this feat. Those who had relatively good visual images complained that the letters did not all stay in place. Those who had no visual images were sometimes reduced to the awkward expedient of repeatedly spelling the word through, each time ticking off one letter. With a little practice much more efficient methods are possible. The word is broken up into syllables and each syllable separately reversed. Familiar combinations such as *th*, *sh* and the diphthongs are handled as units. Such devices are found valuable even by those with visual imagery. On the whole, those reporting visual imagery do somewhat better than other subjects in this form of test.

6. *The letter square* (Binet, 1894; Fernald, 1912; Müller, 1917). Nine or 16 or 25 letters, arranged in a square, are presented. In learning,

k	m	t	q		2	6	4	3	0
c	b	r	w		5	9	7	1	8
z	l	d	h		0	8	3	9	5
f	x	g	j		4	1	6	2	7
					9	4	0	5	3

FIG. 8. A letter square and a number square for memorizing. Words or syllables are sometimes given a similar arrangement.

O is to read the letters from left to right, but in the subsequent test he is required to name the letters in vertical columns, or oblique lines. The original assumption was that the visualist, having a picture of the square before him, would easily read off the letters, while the auditory or motor person would be bound fast to the sequence in which he learned the letters and be unable to meet the requirements of the test, except by slow and circuitous devices. This old assumption was found to be erroneous in two respects. (1) Even the most visually inclined Os are unable to maintain a complete visual image from which they can read at will in any direction. Müller, using a square of 25 digits, found that his most competent visual learner recited the digits forward in 8 sec., but required 24 sec. to recite them downward and 59 sec. to recite them in oblique lines. (2) The old assumption, that the auditory-motor learner must have extreme difficulty in reciting in any but the forward direction, failed to take account of the grouping and localizing activities that go on in memorizing a list (p. 32). Both the visual and the auditory-motor learner group and locate the items, and both meet the demands of the letter square test by utilizing the learned groups and locations. They work in much the same way.

7. *Description of a picture.* The well known testimony or *Aussage* test was used by Fernald (1912) with introspective reports of imagery. Verbal imagery as well as visual would be expected since O in examining the picture may name the objects. Both kinds were reported, the visual predominating and appearing here in some Os who reported very little in other tests. Visualization was a distinct help in fullness of description, though the verbalizers were more accurate in the sense of making fewer false statements regarding the picture.

From Galton's results it should be clear that the functional importance of images cannot be estimated entirely from the results obtained with trained psychologists or other mature individuals engaged in scientific work. Davis (1932) repeated some of Fernald's work with undergraduate Os, after some preliminary instruction on the topic of imagery. In a test for memory of tones, 79 percent of the Os reported using auditory imagery and those who so reported were more accurate in most cases than those who reported other images or no images. Similarly in a test for memory of nonsense figures, 71 percent reported visual images and made better scores than those reporting non-visual or no images. In a test for finding rhymes, those who reported using auditory imagery showed the "better ear"; they did not offer "nose," "dose" or "noose" as a rhyme for the stimulus word "lose," nor "most" or "post" as a rhyme for "cost." Bowers (1932) by quite different methods found evidence for the use of concrete, meaningful images in memory for lists of words.

Generalized images. The philosopher Berkeley (1710) in a famous passage denies the possibility of generalized images or, as he calls them, general notions or abstract ideas. He says:

Whether others have this wonderful faculty of abstracting their ideas, they best can tell. For myself, I find I have indeed a faculty of imagining, or representing to myself, the idea of those *particular* things I have perceived, and of variously compounding and dividing them. I can imagine a man with two heads, or the upper parts of a man joined to the body of a horse. I can consider the hand, the eye, the nose, each by itself abstracted or separated from the rest of the body.—But then whatever hand or eye I imagine, it must have some particular shape and colour. Likewise the idea of man that I frame to myself must be either of a white, or a black, or a tawny, a straight, or a crooked, a tall, or a low, or a middle-sized man. I cannot by any effort of thought conceive the *abstract* idea.

According to this famous doctrine of Berkeley, parts of a thing which could be cut off and exist separately can be imagined separately; but qualities which can only exist embodied in a thing cannot be imagined apart from the thing, nor can the thing be imagined without its qualities. Introspective studies have shown, however, that things are sometimes imaged without all their qualities. Koffka (1912) obtained evidence from an experiment in which E called out a word and O waited passively for an image to appear. The images were usually illustrative of the meaning of the stimulus word. In the large collection thus obtained, some images represented objects without a full complement of qualities:

"Image of a coin, but of no special denomination."
"Image of an animal, what kind of animal I do not know, except that it was an animal from which fur can be got."
"Image of the number 1000, but with the number of zeros indefinite."

Similarly in reading, where we might expect a rapid succession of images illustrative of the meaning, such images are meager and fleeting.

How are images distinguished from perceived objects? An image taken for a real object amounts to hallucination. Some of Galton's subjects reported images that were "equal in all respects to a real sensation." How then were they known not to be real sensations? Usually, no doubt, images differ from sensations in possessing less vivacity or vividness. As Hume said (1748):

Everyone will readily allow, that there is a considerable difference between the perceptions of the mind, when a man feels the pain of excessive heat, or the pleasure of moderate warmth; and when he afterwards recalls to his memory this sensation, or anticipates it by his imagination. These faculties may mimic or copy the perceptions of the senses, but they never can entirely reach the force and vivacity of the original sentiment.

The occasional existence of very vivid images and the frequent occurrence of very faint and vague sensations make it difficult to accept this criterion as decisive.

The difference may be one of localization, since a real object is in a fixed place. It is not indeed in a fixed part of the field of view, since O can himself move. But the visual memory image is more mobile. Sometimes it is not definitely localized, sometimes it is localized inside the head, sometimes in the distance where the original object was, sometimes out in front of the subject or on the wall in front. Martin (1911, 1912) found that many persons were able to perform what seems at first an impossible feat. They could look at an object, call up beside it an image of the same object, and compare the image and the object while both were present. Her Os reported that the image was usually less vivid in color, vaguer in outline than the real object, and that it had to be built up with effort whereas the real object was there all at once. Another difference and probably an important one was that the real object revealed more and more detail on continued examination, while continued study of the image revealed nothing more than had been previously noted in the real object.

Can O be fooled into taking an image for a real object or vice versa? Külpe (1902) and Rieffert (1912) seated O in a dark room on the wall of which they threw very faint lights of various colors, shapes and sizes.

Sometimes, after the ready signal, no objective stimulus was given, but O was likely to get an image. He was to decide whether his visual impression was an image or a percept. A strong objectifying tendency was manifested in the frequent mistaking of an image for a percept. Rarely it happened that a real light was taken for an image. O's judgment was determined by his own attitude and direction of attention and by the attending circumstances, rather than by anything in the impression itself.

In a more striking experiment of Scripture (1896) and Perky (1910) O was led to mistake an actual sensation for an image. Perky seated O before a screen in a well lighted room and asked him to project on the screen the visual image of an object such as a banana. As soon as O started to project his imaginary banana on the screen an assistant working in an adjoining room threw a very faint picture of a banana on the screen and very gradually increased its intensity till O reported that he had a good image. Intent on his effort to conjure up a good image O mistook the picture for his own. This result was obtained from 27 college and graduate students, men and women alike, with no exceptions.

The experimental results are in good agreement on the negative conclusion: No absolute difference exists between an image and a percept, and there is no sure criterion by which one can be distinguished from the other. Subjectivity or objectivity is supplied by the context and by O's attitude more than by the character of any single impression. In the kinesthetic modality it is especially difficult to distinguish between sensations and images. Involuntary slight movements are likely at any moment to produce kinesthetic sensations which may be mistaken for images. Speech movements in reading or thinking are likely to be the source of apparent verbal-motor "images." When as in drowsiness or actual sleep we lose our hold on the objective situation, our images immediately take on an hallucinatory character.

Eidetic images. The behavior of some individuals in describing their visual images is very striking. They say they *see* the images, not imagine them, and they behave as if a real object were before them. Yet they are not hallucinated, they know that the object is not really there. Such individuals were first described by Urbantschitsch (1907) who believed it necessary to distinguish between the ordinary memory images, which are imagined, and these percept-like memory images which are "seen." The name *eidetic*, intended from its derivation to convey the idea of an especially vivid image, has been used by Jaensch and his associates, who have found the phenomenon very worthy of psychological attention and who in fact have endeavored to tie it up with personality traits (Jaensch, 1920, 1922, 1927, 1930; Kroh, 1922). The literature of the subject, already very extensive, has been reviewed by Allport (1924) and by Klüver (1926, 1928, 1932).

Few adults report eidetic images but a considerable proportion of children from 6 years up to puberty behave in the way described. A college student described by Purdy (1936) still retained eidetic imagery, not only visual but also of other senses.

A typical procedure in examining a child for eidetic imagery is to allow him 10–60 sec. to look at a picture. He is not to stare but to let his eyes move naturally over the picture, since afterimages are not desired. At the end of the exposure, he looks toward a grey screen and is asked "what he sees there." The spontaneous answer of most persons is that they see nothing on the screen, but the eidetic individual reports that he sees the picture. He behaves as if it were there. His eyes move from one part to the other, he leans forward and looks hard in attempting to discover a detail, his face may express emotions appropriate to the picture. The image may persist for 2–3 minutes and it can be renewed to some extent on another day.

A good eidetic subject, when asked to describe the picture as he sees it on the screen, will often give an astonishing amount of detail. If questioned, he may be able to count the buttons on the coat of a figure, or to work out one by one the letters in a poster printed in a foreign language. Is the eidetic image equivalent almost to a photograph? It is not really much like a photograph. These details are not all present at once. The image develops gradually; when a question is asked regarding a certain object, it may take some time before the object will clear up sufficiently to yield the answer. Small details come out while adjacent parts of the picture remain blank (Klüver, 1930). The number of details reported is by no means the whole number that could be found in an actual picture. And the spontaneous report of the eidetic child when compared with that of other children is actually no more complete or accurate as to details (Meenes & Morton, 1936). Moreover the eidetic image is plastic; many Os can change it voluntarily or it will change in response to suggestion. The objects can be changed in color or size, and can be made to move about in the image. Another important fact is that the eidetic child secures a good image only of a picture that interests him. The eidetic image undoubtedly belongs under the general head of memory images (Allport, 1928).

In studying eidetic imagery we are studying recall, and as in other cases we cannot hope to understand recall without examining the learning process. Exactly what is the eidetic child doing while he is studying the real picture? He seems to be immersed in the visual impression. Probably he takes in the general effect and many details. He sees objects rather than masses of light, shade and color such as a painter would look for. So much we know from the eidetic child's description of his image. But he probably notices much more visual detail than most of us see in a picture. When he has got his image on the screen, we place the picture before ourselves and ask him about the details, and it seems to us that he finds many details in the image which he probably did not see while examining the picture. If so, he is doing something which apparently cannot be done with an ordinary memory image.

Ordinarily we cannot read off even from a vivid memory image any facts regarding the original object which we did not observe in the object itself. Whether the eidetic subject can do so, must be left uncertain for the present.

RECOGNITION

As the topic of recall can be broadened to cover association and imagery, so recognition can be made to include the perception of objects. An object is "recognized" as an individual thing or person; it is "perceived" as an object of a certain class. In both cases use is made of past experience, though there may be no conscious reference to the past.

The recognitive processes differ functionally from those of recall in that recognition starts with the object given whereas recall has to find the object. In recall, A is given as a stimulus and some other object, B, is recalled. In recognition, A is given and the same A is recognized. It would seem that recognition is the simpler process. If so, recognition is not to be explained in terms of recall.

Recall and recognition often go together. A fact is recalled and known to be a fact from one's past. It may be dated and located in one's past, more or less definitely, as when you recall a scene and know when and where you saw it. There is no such definite recognition when you recall a bit of the multiplication table. Unconscious plagiarism affords striking examples of recall without recognition.

Ease or difficulty of recognition. Often a face or a name which cannot be recalled is recognized promptly when presented. In a sense, then, recognition is easier than recall. After a list of words or other items has been presented, a recall test, by the method of Retained Members, gets back a certain number of items. If now all the items are presented, mixed with "new" ones, some of the old items that were not recalled are recognized. An experiment by a similar method was conducted by Achilles (1920) who, however, used different lists of items for the recall and recognition tests and avoided the objection that attempted recall, by placing items in "readiness," would give an undue advantage to the following recognition. A list of 25 items was placed before O and he was allowed 50 sec. in which to study them. He was then asked at once to write down all the items he could recall, or else he was shown a list of 50 items including the 25 "old" ones mixed with 25 new ones and asked to write "Yes" or "No" before each item according as he judged it old or new. There were lists of nonsense syllables, of disconnected words, and of proverbs. The recall and recognition scores, the latter penalized for errors (p. 11), were as follows (averages from 96 Os):

	Syllables	*Words*	*Proverbs*
Recall score	12%	39%	22%
Recognition score	42%	65%	67%

The recognition scores here greatly exceed the recall scores. But the advantage of recognition depends partly on the exact form of the tests. A recognition test may be made very difficult by using new items that closely resemble the old.

So, in an experiment of Lehmann (1888–89) a gray color was produced by mixing white and black in equal proportions on the color wheel (180° of each). After 30 sec. either that same gray or one some degrees whiter was presented to be judged same or different. Results:

	Amount of difference between grays					
	60°	45°	35°	20°	12°	8°
Net recognition score	87%	90%	70%	63%	20%	17%

As the old and the new became very much alike discrimination failed and the recognition score approached zero.

Further light on this matter is obtained from the table and description below.

RECOGNITION ACCORDING TO DEGREE OF SIMILARITY

(*Data from Seward, 1928*)

	Identical	*Similar*	*Slightly Similar*	*Dissimilar*
Positive response				
Frequency	71	54	27	8
Confidence	63	57	43	26
Quickness	51	46	38	38
Negative response				
Frequency	29	46	73	92
Confidence	48	50	60	71
Quickness	37	36	46	56

In G. H. Seward's experiment (1928) from which the above table is taken, 30 fancy papers of varied design and color were shown, with 2 sec. exposure for each and blank intervals of 4 sec. When the series was finished, O occupied himself for 10 minutes with a vocabulary test and was then given the recognition test, which included 10 of the original fancy papers, 10 rather similar papers, 10 slightly similar, and 10 very different designs. As each specimen was shown O judged whether it had been present in the original series and reacted positively or negatively by pressing one of two telegraph keys, so that his reaction time could be taken. He also rated the confidence of each judgment. Each O's confidence ratings and reaction times were transmuted into a relative scale in which 100 represents his maximum quickness or confidence of response. There were 108 Os, students, and each column in the table summarizes 1080 judgments. All the trends are statistically reliable.

Reading down the first column of figures we find that the response to an identical specimen is positive recognition in 71 percent of cases, negative in 29 percent. The positive recognitions have an average confidence of 63 (on the 0 to 100 scale) and an average quickness of 51 (on a similar scale). The negative response, non-recognition of the identical stimulus, is less confident and slower.

As you go from left to right in the table, the positive response becomes less correct and the negative response more correct. Frequency, confidence and quickness follow these changes in correctness, though without wholly keeping pace. If we compare the two sets of perfectly correct responses, positive to identical stimuli and negative to dissimilar stimuli, we see that the latter has the advantage on all counts. The "No" response to a wholly different stimulus, though negative in form, is definite and emphatic in meaning. The impression of newness or not-belonging is fully as distinct as the impression of familiarity.

CHAPTER III

RETENTION

LEARNING modifies the organism in such a way that a performance acquired perhaps with much labor can be easily done when a later occasion arises. We may call this modification of the organism the memory trace without committing ourselves to any theory as to its nature. The trace is invisible by any technique at present developed. What is retained is properly this trace. Retention itself is not directly observed but its effect is seen in the later performance of a learned act. In memory experiments the evidence of retention consists in recall, recognition, or in the fact that apparently forgotten acts are relearned in less time and fewer trials than were necessary for the original learning, or than are now necessary for learning an equivalent but previously unlearned act. Recall, recognition, and relearning are the three experimental tests of retention. None of these is a perfect test. Recall is the least adequate

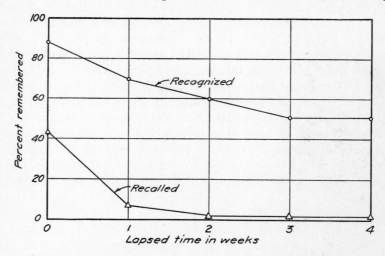

FIG. 9. (Data from Burtt & Dobell, 1925.) Retention tested by both recall and recognition. The material consisted of paired commodity and trade-brand names, 100 such pairs being shown to a class by projection lantern, and sets of 20 from the 100 being used for the tests after different intervals. In the recall tests, the commodity names were the stimuli and the brand names were to be given as far as remembered. Following each recall test came a recognition test in which O selected from 4 brand names the one which he believed had been paired with the commodity. The recognition score is much higher than the recall score. Both curves show the negative acceleration (progressive flattening) characteristic of curves of forgetting.

50

index of retention, for often as we know from common experience an item that cannot be recalled at a given moment is still retained, as is proved by its being recalled later. Recall is a response which depends upon the conditions of the moment as well as upon the trace.

An item which cannot be recalled can often be recognized (Fig. 9). Recognition is better than recall as an index of retention. Relearning also is a better index than recall. A list of nonsense syllables or a poem once learned may be entirely "forgotten" in the sense that none of it can be recalled and still it may be relearned with surprising ease and quickness.

Perseveration and consolidation. Before commencing a study of retention we may consider certain complexities which make its measurement difficult, especially soon after learning. When the overt learning process has come to an end, we are by no means sure that the whole process of forming the trace is finished. The physiological process involved, whatever it may be, quite possibly continues for a time. Indirect evidence of such a process of consolidation is obtained from the fact of retroactive inhibition (p. 227)—intense activity immediately after learning impairs retention as if it prevented the trace from being properly established. A physical or mental shock will sometimes do the same (retrograde amnesia).

After O has memorized a list of nonsense syllables or a stanza of poetry, snatches of the list or poem may come back to him without effort on his part. This "perseveration" often occurs soon after learning, in moments of relaxation. Familiar examples are the running of a tune in the head soon after it has been heard and the spontaneous occurrence of visual images derived from the scenes of the day, as one is dropping off to sleep. Individuals differ greatly in this matter of perseveration. Müller and Pilzecker (1900) found that some Os after learning a list of nonsense syllables were able to lay it aside completely and never think of it again until the retention test a day later. In other subjects bits of the list spontaneously came up from time to time. Some persons on relaxing for a minute spontaneously think of engagements and other items of recent interest which do not occur to other persons unless there is a definite stimulus to recall them. Interesting activities, interrupted before their completion, seem especially likely to recur in this spontaneous way (Zeigarnik, 1927).

Perseveration amounts to an involuntary review and certainly deepens the trace of such material as definitely perseverates. It may indicate, though this is not so certain, that all the material just studied, whether consciously perseverating or not, is undergoing a process of consolidation.

Theories of retention. While most of the experiments on retention do not deal directly with these theories, relevant bits of evidence will crop up from time to time in this chapter and in the chapter on memory for form. What happens to the trace in forgetting? One theory likens forgetting to a process of fading, another to a process of breaking up, a third to a process of becoming more generalized and less distinctive.

When we speak of forgetting as due to the lapse of time, we do not really mean that mere time does anything to the trace. Time is not a force or agency; only the processes that go on in time accomplish results. We are forced to ask what processes occurring in time impair the trace so that it no longer serves for recall or recognition. We think of two general classes of processes going on in the organism, the organic or metabolic processes, and the processes or acts that we call behavior. Perhaps, like the atrophy of a disused muscle, forgetting is due to the metabolic economy of the body; an unused organ or structure may lose out in the competition for nutrition. Or, perhaps, an unused act loses out in competition with other acts and forgetting is a phenomenon of interference (p. 223). Such possibilities are not readily subjected to a crucial test but meanwhile much can be learned regarding the empirical laws of forgetting.

The curve of forgetting. Among the various experiments included by Ebbinghaus in his pioneer work on memory (1885) the one most often cited is his quantitative study of the loss of retention with the lapse of time. Having before him several theories of the cause of forgetting, he thought none of them very good, and believed that the best program for an experimentalist was to leave the theories for the time being and build up a knowledge of the facts which any theory must explain. His specific problem took this form (translation by Ruger & Bussenius, 1913): "If syllable series of a definite kind are learned by heart and then left to themselves, how will the process of forgetting go on when left merely to the influence of time or the daily events of life which fill it?" His procedure was to learn lists of nonsense syllables, lay them aside for a certain interval, relearn them and note the saving in time or number of readings, due to the partial retention of the effects of the first learning. In the course of this investigation he learned over 1200 lists each containing 13 nonsense syllables. A learning session lasted 18–20 min. during which he learned 8 such lists. He took the first list and read it through and through at a steady rate of one syllable every $\frac{2}{5}$ sec. till it could be recited twice without hesitation and with a consciousness of being correct. After a pause of 15 sec. another list was studied and so on till the 8 lists had been learned. The total time to learn these 8 lists was the original learning time for this unit of work. After a certain lapse of time this same set of lists was relearned to the same criterion. Even after a lapse of 31 days the relearning of a set of 8 lists always showed a saving as compared with the original learning. If 1010 sec. were required for the original learning of the 8 lists, and 31 days later 803 sec. were required to relearn them, the saving was 207 sec. = 20.5 percent of the original time.

Learning efficiency may differ at different hours of the day and Ebbinghaus found that it did so in his case. It took him 12 percent longer to memorize a list at 6–8 p.m. than at 10–11 a.m. When therefore he wished to determine the loss of retention for an 8–9 hour interval the original learning came in the favorable time of the day and the relearning in the unfavorable. A deduction of 12 percent of the relearning time was therefore made before computing the saving.

Different lists were learned for each interval. It would not do at all to relearn the same lists after 8 hours, then after 24 hours, and again after 2 days. This procedure gives a practice curve, not a curve of forgetting, for every time the same list is relearned it is more strongly impressed. After several relearnings it can be retained without appreciable loss over a considerable period.

The results of Ebbinghaus are shown in an accompanying table and also in Figs. 10 and 13. There was never any doubt that the work of Ebbinghaus was very thorough and accurate, and the objection that

RETENTION AFTER DIFFERENT INTERVALS

(*Ebbinghaus, 1885*)

Interval	*No. experiments*	*Range of saving percent*	*Mean saving percent*	*PE*$_M$
$\frac{1}{3}$ hour	12	45–64	58.2	1
1 "	16	34–54	44.2	1
8–9 hours	12	28–48	35.8	1
24 "	26	15–46	33.7	1.2
2 days	26	12–46	27.8	1.4
6 "	26	3–40	25.4	1.3
31 "	45	7–44	21.1	0.8

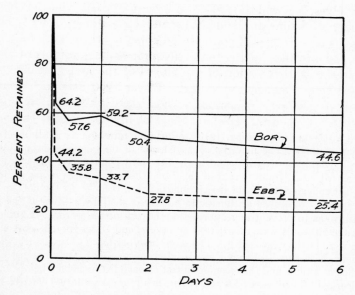

FIG. 10. (Data from Ebbinghaus, 1885 and Boreas, 1930.) Curve of retention of lists of nonsense syllables, as determined by the saving method. The Ebbinghaus curve is from one O about 40 years old, who learned and relearned over 1200 13-syllable lists. The Boreas curve gives the average for 20 students, each learning one 15-syllable list for each interval. Continuation of these curves is included in Fig. 13.

it represented the retention curve of only one individual has now been met by the results of several studies which have all yielded results conforming to the general type of the Ebbinghaus curve. Even the work of Strong (1913) carried out by the recognition method gives essentially the same curve. Its main characteristic is a rapid fall immediately after learning and a gradual flattening out as the interval is prolonged. Forgetting becomes more and more gradual as time advances.

In some of the curves retention is plotted against the logarithm of time. The long and short intervals can thus be got into the same graph without crowding the short ones—that is the practical advantage. Besides, retention declines approximately in proportion to the log of time, and the graph shows to the eye how closely the data conform to this logarithmic law of forgetting. To conform perfectly the data points must lie on a straight line.

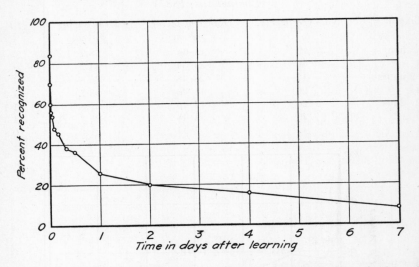

FIG. 11. (Data from Strong, 1913.) Curve of retention as determined by the recognition method. The material consisted of "all the common ordinary words," not over 3 syllables in length, found in the Standard Dictionary. Lists of 20 words were presented visually and were read aloud by O "slowly enough to grasp the meaning, but fast enough not to form associations between them." At the bottom of each list was a short problem in arithmetic to be solved mentally as soon as the list had been read, so as to prevent any immediate rehearsal of the words. In the recognition test the 20 words were mixed with 20 others, and O designated those which he was sure were in the original list. The score here plotted is that of these confident recognitions, with penalty for new words falsely recognized. Only one list of words was studied at a time, and the recognition test on each list was given before any other list was learned. There were 5 Os and 15 lists in all for each interval between learning and test.

If we take the simplest logarithmic equation between retention (R) and time interval (t), namely

$$R = A - B \log t,$$

we have the two constants, A and B, to be determined for each curve. We can determine their values by the method of least squares or, roughly, by the eye, aided by a thread stretched through and between the data points (plotted on a logarithmic abscissa) so as to fit the points as closely as a straight line can be made to do. When t = 1, log t = 0, and the constant A is thus found to have the corresponding value of R. Thus, if time is measured in minutes, A is the

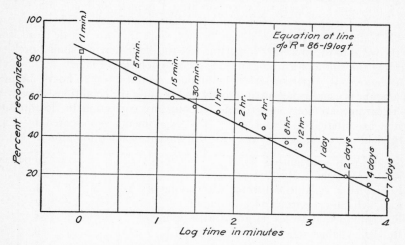

FIG. 12. Same data as Fig. 11, with scores plotted against the logarithm of time. The straight line, drawn in simply by the eye, is a fairly good fit, and the inference is that the retention decreased just about in step with the logarithm of time—or that forgetting (loss of retention) increased as the log of time.

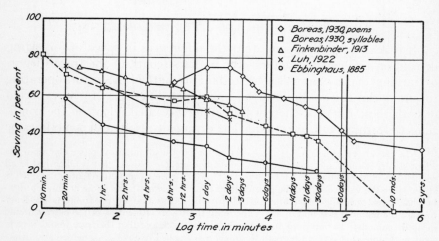

FIG. 13. Several retention curves plotted on a logarithmic abscissa. A straight line would fit any of them fairly well, aside from a dip at 8 hours when no correction has been made for diurnal variation, and aside from the drop at 10 months which suggests an eventual complete loss of barely learned nonsense material. The lessons were syllable lists except for the uppermost curve, which was obtained from 20 students whose high retention of poetry may be due in part to voluntary or involuntary rehearsal during the interval between learning and retention test.

percent of saving at the end of 1 minute; it is the ordinate of the fitted straight line at t = 1. To get the value of B we note the value of R for some other value of t. Thus if t = 10 time units, log t = 1, and B = A − R; i.e. B is the loss in retention from 1 minute to 10 minutes. If we were counting our lapsed time in hours instead of minutes, A would be the retention after 1 hour and B the loss from 1 to 10 hours. The equation says simply that the retention after lapsed time t equals the retention after 1 minute (or hour) minus log t times the loss occurring between 1 and 10 minutes (or hours).[1] These "parameters," A and B, have no special significance, since they are not deduced from any theory as to the process of forgetting (see the discussion of a similar problem regarding the curve of learning, p. 171; see also Johnson, 1932).

A convenient A-parameter is the amount retained for 24 hours, because this amount is usually measured directly and because the conditions of learning and relearning are then comparable without any correction for learning efficiency at different times of day. The experiments represented by Figs. 10–14 yield quite a range of values for the percent of retention after 24 hours:

Strong, words recognized	26	percent
Krueger, words recalled	27	"
Ebbinghaus, syllables relearned with saving of	34	"
Luh, syllables relearned with saving of	52	"
Finkenbinder, syllables relearned with saving of	58	"
Boreas, syllables relearned with saving of	59	"
Boreas, poems relearned with saving of	75	"
Radosavljevich (1907), syllables relearned by adults	74	"
" " " " children	79	"
" poems relearned by adults	80	"
" " " " children	79	"

FACTORS AFFECTING THE SPEED OF FORGETTING

It is reasonable to assume that the differences in speed of forgetting depend on two general factors: the initial strength of the trace (degree of learning, depth of impression), and the strength of the factors operating to annul the trace. Besides the individual differences to be expected in both these respects, there will be differences dependent on the conditions of learning and retention. The divergent results can sometimes be

---

[1] In the above equation, log t is negative for fractional values of t (smaller than the adopted unit of time) and therefore the value of R is greater than A. If t is taken just small enough R will have the value 1 (or 100 percent), which means complete retention; and if t is still smaller the value of R will be greater than 1, which seems at first thought an absurdity, but has a real meaning. Retention of 100 percent means that no relearning is necessary because the material is still at or above the recall threshold. Retention of 150 percent would mean that the material was well above the recall threshold, and that the trace would have to weaken considerably before the recall threshold was reached.

Some of the curves of retention plotted against log t seem to differ significantly from a straight line. Ebbinghaus preferred for his curve, not the linear logarithmic equation given above but one allowing for some curvature in the plot against log t, namely:

$$\text{Percent of retention} = \frac{100\,k}{(\log t)^{\,c} + k}$$

With k = 1.84 and c = 1.25, this equation gave a good fit to his data; but the parameters, once more, have no special rational significance.

attributed to different ways in which the experiments were conducted. Ebbinghaus learned 8 lists at a sitting with only 15-second rests between lists, so affording the least possible chance for perseveration and rehearsal and the maximum opportunity for retroactive inhibition. Radosavljevich on the contrary gave a rest of 3–4 minutes after each list, and it is not surprising that his Os forgot more slowly than Ebbinghaus.

Certain factors in the initial strength of the trace have been worked out experimentally.

1. **Underlearning and overlearning.** A lesson is said to be under-learned when it has not been brought up to the criterion of one perfect recitation, and overlearned when studied after the criterion has been met. The additional study must be carried on with the same close attention as before; mere inattentive reading of the lesson does not

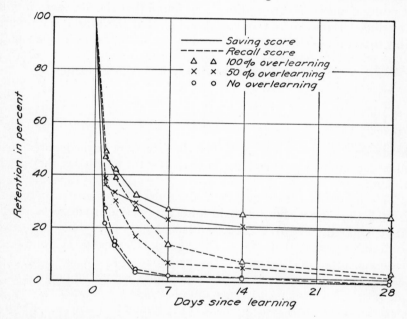

Fig. 14. (Data from Krueger, 1929.) Retention after overlearning. Lists of 12 monosyllabic words, all nouns, were presented on a rotating drum at the rate of 2 sec. per word. After 4–5 presentations, on the average, O anticipated all the words in a list. The number of presentations needed in each case to reach this criterion was noted, and in some cases learning stopped there, but in other cases additional presentations were given till the total number was 50 or 100 percent greater than the number needed to reach the criterion. After an interval of 1 day or more, O relearned the list to the same criterion, and two retention scores were obtained: the regular saving score and the "recall score" which was the number of correct anticipations on the first relearning trial. Separate groups of 20 students relearned after the different intervals. Errors due to inequality of the word-lists were avoided by using the same lists for each interval and by rotating the lists among the members of each group. The averages plotted have high reliability. On the graph the label "100% overlearn-ing" means that the number of additional presentations was equal to the number required to meet the criterion.

count as overlearning. When this requirement is met, an overlearned lesson is better retained than one barely learned, and, in general, retention is roughly proportional to the amount of the original learning (Ebbinghaus, 1885; Krueger, 1929). The result cannot be depended on unless O is well trained (Luh, 1922; Cuff, 1927).

2. **Distributed and repeated learning.** It makes a difference whether the readings given a list or stanza or (probably) any lesson are massed in one continuous series or spaced out and distributed over several sittings. The lesson can usually be learned in fewer spaced than massed readings (p. 211), and retention is definitely better after spaced readings. Such is the general outcome of a variety of experiments, the first being again one of Ebbinghaus (1885), who learned and relearned on successive days lists of nonsense syllables and stanzas of Byron's *Don Juan*—always to the point of one perfect recitation—and found that the necessary number of readings decreased from day to day, i.e., that the lesson was progressively better retained. Some of his results are shown below and in Fig. 15.

No. Readings Required to Learn and Relearn

Day No.	1	2	3	4	5	6
12-syllable list	16.5	11	7.5	5	3	2.5
80-syllable stanza	7.8	3.8	1.8	.5	0	0

The stanzas, though much longer than the lists, were learned more quickly and better retained—so much better that after the fourth day they needed no more study.

This is one of the most practical results of memory experiments: Material that one wishes to retain for a long period needs to be studied and re-studied. The result seems reasonable, but carefully scrutinized it contains a puzzle. On each successive day O learns to the same standard of one correct recitation. At the end of each day, he has reached the same degree of mastery. Why then should not forgetting proceed at the same rate? We are forced to conclude that *the trace becomes stronger and stronger with each relearning.* What is the same at the end of each day's learning is not the trace but the immediate recitability or recallability of the lesson, and recall obviously depends not alone upon the trace but also upon the momentary condition of readiness. Readiness depends very much on *recency* of impression.

The results of this work of Ebbinghaus and of similar experiments of his own were formulated by Jost (1897) in the following law: *If two associations are now of equal strength but of different ages, the older one will lose strength more slowly with the further passage of time.*

What Jost means by strength of associations is the same as availability or reproducibility of a lesson. Since availability is demonstrated by recall at the moment of testing we may speak of it as recall value and reformulate the law as follows: If two associations (or lessons) of different ages have equal recall value at present, the older one has more retention value and will be retained better for the future.   Retention value is the same as strength of the trace.

This law of Jost's can even be deduced from the general shape of a retention curve.   As a lesson becomes old it reaches a flatter part of the curve and its further decline will be slow.   Therefore a young lesson momentarily at the same retention level as an old one is on a steeper part of the curve and doomed to decline more rapidly.

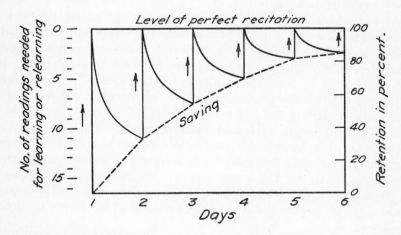

Fɪɢ. 15. (Data from Ebbinghaus, 1885.)   Forgetting is made slower and slower by repeated learning of the same lesson.   The "lesson" in this case was a list of 12 nonsense syllables, or, rather, a set of 9 such lists learned in immediate succession in a sitting of about 15 minutes, and relearned day after day, always to the point of one correct recitation.   The number of trials to learn (relearn) decreased day by day; the saving increased; retention was better and better.   The arrows indicate the daily learning by which mastery was pushed up to the recitation level.   The curves show the probable course of forgetting during each successive period of 24 hours.   The data are the average results from learning and relearning 63 lists.

Jost really announced two laws and the one not yet stated usually goes by the name of Jost's Law: *If two associations are of equal strength and different ages, further study has greater value for the older one.*   This law while consistent with the retention curve could probably not be deduced from it.   He set up this law first as a hypothesis to account for the advantage of spaced over massed learning, after finding that this advantage could not be due to fatigue or loss of attention in the massed learning.   In scouting around for other possible factors, Jost got the idea that an old association might profit more than a new one from repetition or exercise.   To test the hypothesis lists of 12 nonsense syllables were used.   An "old" list was one which had been read 20–30 times on the preceding day and which now gave a recall score of 9 percent (average of 2 Os, tested by paired associates, the odd-numbered syllables being the stimuli).   A "new" list had been read 4–6 times and was tested only a minute afterward, giving a recall score of 40 percent.   So the dice were loaded against the hypothesis, and yet old lessons were more quickly mastered than new ones. For the two Os the averages were:

Old lists, recall score 9%, mastered in 10 readings
New lists, recall score 40%, mastered in 14 readings

Jost's data are rather meager for founding a "law," but more recent experiments could be cited in corroboration, particularly the results of Krueger (1929) shown in Fig. 14.

All these findings on distribution of learning and on the relations of retention, recall and relearning fit together very nicely and undoubtedly embody some fundamental law even though that law has not yet been formulated in any adequate way. There is reason to believe that the law adumbrated by all these results is fundamental in the physiology of learning. Much the same relations can be traced in the response of the muscle to exercise and rest.

3. Effect of length of lesson upon retention. Experimenters are agreed that when longer and shorter lessons are learned to the same criterion of one correct recitation (or of 2 correct recitations) subsequent retention is better for the longer lesson. Ebbinghaus's original result has been practically duplicated by later experimenters. He learned lists of different lengths and relearned them after 24 hours, with a saving as follows:

12 syllables, learned in 17 readings, relearned with saving of 35 percent
24   "   "   " 45   "   "   "   "   " 49   "
36   "   "   " 56   "   "   "   "   " 58   "

At first thought it is surprising that the harder lesson is better retained, but the mystery clears when we notice that the harder lesson required longer study. The stronger retention results from the greater study and is consistent with results previously discussed. To bring a long lesson up to the point of correct recitation more overlearning of parts is necessary. In Paired Associates the present author has found that a longer lesson is better retained even if it is not read any more times (see table, p. 19). A short lesson can be learned without special effort, but when a keen individual is confronted with a long lesson he is stimulated to organize the material and bind the items together by relations and meanings. The strong structure thus developed is more durable than the relatively loose structure which suffices for immediate reproduction of a short list.

4. Retention of different kinds of material. It is not universally true that the lesson which requires more reading is better retained. Meaningful material though quickly learned is better retained than nonsense material. Instances of this are shown in the table on p. 56 and in the Boreas curves in Fig. 13. Motor skill such as in typewriting has been found to be retained with little loss over long periods. We have to remember that such a performance is enormously overlearned in comparison with the syllable lists used in the laboratory.

Vivid impressions are better retained than "run of the mine" impressions. This common observation deserves mention if only to offset our (experimentally justified) emphasis on frequency and recency. In ordinary life it is difficult to make perfectly sure of the effect of vividness, because the vivid impression perseverates and is reviewed and so acquires frequency in addition to its original vividness. But we can fairly attribute some of the good retention of meaningful material to its vividness in comparison with nonsense material. Several experimenters (Calkins, 1894, 1896; Jersild, 1929) have demonstrated that a vivid item in a list is favored in immediate recall, and Van Buskirk (1932) demonstrated the same for later recall and relearning. His Os learned two 9-syllable lists: in the first list all the syllables were in uniform letters, black on white; in the second list one syllable, occupying the least favored position in the list (as indicated by the results with the first list), was in large red letters on a green background. This syllable was quickly learned; it was recalled by a large number of Os in a test one week or two weeks later and, when not at once recalled, was quickly relearned.

5. **The effect of sleep immediately after learning.** A suggestion that forgetting may progress slowly during sleep is contained in many retention curves and was put into words by some of the older investigators. When Jenkins & Dallenbach (1925) took this suggestion seriously enough to subject it to an experimental test they obtained evidence that sleep following at once after learning did favor retention considerably, as judged from a subsequent recall test. Their two student Os memorized lists of 10 nonsense syllables to the point of one correct recitation and were tested later by Retained Members. The intervals between learning and the retention test were spent either in sleep or in daytime activities. The two Os gave similar results which are averaged below.

PERCENT OF SYLLABLES RECALLED

Interval between learning and recall

	1 hour	*2 hours*	*4 hours*	*8 hours*
Interval of waking	46	31	22	9
Interval of sleep	70	54	55	56

The scores were much higher after sleep than after equal intervals of activity, and they were as high after 8 hours as after 2, provided the time was spent in sleep. The authors drew a challenging conclusion: "The results of our Study as a whole indicate that forgetting is not so much a matter of the decay of old impressions and associations as it is a matter of the interference, inhibition, or obliteration of the old by the new."

This pioneer experiment was followed up by van Ormer (1932) who used the saving method and made the necessary corrections for learning efficiency at different hours of the day. Syllable lists were first learned either in the morning or just at bedtime and relearned after intervals of waking or of sleep. The saving was definitely greater after sleep, especially with the 8-hour interval (Fig. 16). This author accordingly agrees with the just-quoted conclusion of Jenkins & Dallenbach, to the effect

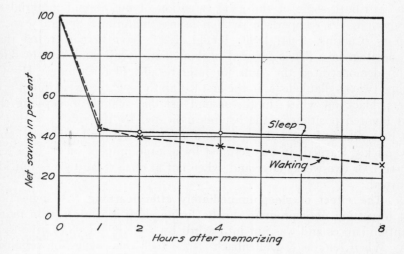

FIG. 16. (After van Ormer, 1932.) Effect of sleep immediately after memorizing. Two adult, well-practiced Os learned lists of 12 nonsense syllables to the point of one correct recitation, 3 lists per sitting, and relearned these lists after 1, 2, 4 or 8 hours spent either in sleep or in the daily activities of a (graduate) student. The lists were learned either at 9:30 a.m., or at 11:30 p.m. It took more readings to memorize a new list at 11:30 p.m. than at 9:30 a.m., 11 and 16 percent more for the two Os. To make the results of the day and night series comparable, these percents were deducted from the 11:30 p.m. scores. Similarly, the memorizing efficiency was determined for each of the relearning hours and corrections have been made reducing all hours to the 9:30 a.m. standard. After all corrections have been made there still remains a difference in favor of sleep, and the difference is statistically reliable in the case of the 8-hour interval. Each data point represents the average of 2 × 8 × 3 = 48 lists learned and relearned.

that forgetting, being slower in sleep, must result not from mere lapse of time or "atrophy through disuse," but from "obliteration of the learned material by the waking activity."

According to this view, daytime activity obliterates traces which have already been established. A possible alternative is that sleep immediately after learning favors the "consolidation" of the trace, while activity at that time interferes with this process. Heine (1914, p. 225) designed her experiment with this second alternative in mind. Lists of syllables were memorized either just at bedtime or 2–3 hours earlier, and relearned at the same hour the next day. The 3 Os who followed this schedule gave the following average percents of saving:

RETENTION AFTER 24 HOURS

	Learned early in the evening	*Learned just before retiring*
Subject L	34%	44%
" C	36	49
" W	35	42
Average	35	45

Other Os, too, learning morning and night, showed better retention of the lists learned just before retiring. We cannot conclude simply that forgetting is slow during sleep, for in this experiment the two conditions were alike in the amounts of sleep and activity intervening between learning and the retention test. It was *sleep just after learning* that was shown to be beneficial.

Suppose you partly learn one lesson in the morning and complete the learning that evening, and another time begin a lesson in the evening and finish next morning—will it make any difference? Spight (1928) found a difference of about 10 percent in favor of the evening-morning arrangement. This was the average result from 51 students who learned lists of 14 word-pairs and were tested by Paired Associates. At the first sitting the list was repeated often enough to give 50 percent of right responses, and in the second sitting, 12 hours later, repetitions were continued till the score was 100 percent. The averages follow.

	Morning-evening	*Evening-morning*
Trials to reach 50%	1.86	1.89
Additional trials to reach 100%	3.66	3:02
Total trials	5.52	4.91

The evening period varied for different Os all the way from 7 to 10 o'clock and we cannot tell from the mere averages whether all of these Os found the evening-morning arrangement better, or only those Os who retired shortly after the learning. The results have a very practical bearing, but from all the evidence yet furnished by the experimenters we cannot decide between three possibilities:

1. Sleep directly after learning favors consolidation of the trace.

2. Sleep directly after learning delays the onset of forgetting which thereafter takes its usual course.

3. Sleep directly after learning eliminates altogether the first rapid drop in the retention curve, so that forgetting thereafter proceeds but slowly and the material is well retained for a very long time.

This last alternative seems too good to be true but deserves a try-out; and the whole problem has many ramifications still awaiting exploration.

"REMINISCENCE"

All the standard retention curves show a rapid drop soon after learning, unless indeed the lesson has been overlearned or reviewed. What

should we think of a curve that *rose* for a few hours or days before starting
to decline?   In terms of pure retention the suggestion is absurd; we cannot
retain more than we already have.   Consolidation might occur, though
it is difficult to believe it continues for more than a day and a night at
most.   Ballard (1913) defined "reminiscence" as a process opposite to
forgetting and believed he had evidence of such a process going on for
several days.   His extensive experiments on London school children
of about 12 years of age, accustomed to memorize poetry as a regular
school exercise, consisted in the partial learning of a poem followed by
immediate reproduction of what they knew, and by retests day after
day.   The scores went up:

> If the immediate score is called 100,
> The score after 1 day averaged 111
> "   "   " 2 days   "   117
> "   "   " 3 "   "   113
> "   "   " 4 "   "   112
> "   "   " 5 "   "   111
> "   "   " 6 "   "   99
> "   "   " 7 "   "   94

This poem was specially interesting to the children; a less interesting
one gave less reminiscence.   Young adults showed only a little, while
6-year-olds showed even more reminiscence than the 12-year-olds.

Is reminiscence due simply to reviewing?   Ballard was not unmindful
of an obvious explanation which would destroy the significance of his
results: the children might have reviewed the poem in the intervals and
they might even have done so together and so supplemented each other's
memories.   He found indeed that many of the children had gone over
the poems in their own minds and that children so reporting showed more
reminiscence than the others; but he did not believe the whole effect to
be so explained.

A check on Ballard's results was made by Williams (1926) who repeated the experiment on over 4,000 school children and college students
in Chicago.   He allowed 5 minutes for partial memorizing of a poem, and
the same time for a list of 30–50 short abstract words.   Sub-groups
were tested at different intervals.   The group averages showed reminiscence only with the younger children and only with the poem, in the latter
case being as follows.

	Immediate recall	*Delayed recall*
Grades 3–4, average age 9.7 years	4.95 items	5.38 items
Grades 6–7, " " 12.7 "	8.68	8.61
Grades 10–11 " " 16.2 "	12.28	11.42
College students	15.37	12.67

Williams doubted whether reminiscence meant anything more significant than voluntary and involuntary rehearsal of the material during the
interval between test and retest.

Meanwhile, Nicolai (1922) without using the name had observed the raw fact of reminiscence with quite a different sort of memory material. Providing himself with a large assortment of toy objects—brush, hammer, apple, bear, etc.—he placed a certain number of them in a box standing on a table and exposed the contents of the box for 10–15 sec. by lifting the lid. In one such experiment on children of 12–13 years, 10 objects were exposed and the successive recall scores averaged as follows:

Test 1, immediately after exposure					5.4 objects
"	2,	after ½ hour			5.1 "
"	3,	"	1	"	6.3 "
"	4,	"	5	"	7.0 "
"	5,	"	24	"	7.8 "
"	6,	"	4 days		7.6 "
"	7,	"	4 weeks		7.4 "

He modified the experiment by using equivalent groups of children and testing each group only twice, immediately after the exposure and at one of the longer intervals. He now got no progressive increase of score as the interval was lengthened, but the retest score was still always higher than the immediate recall. As to rehearsal during the intervals, Nicolai believed that possibility was excluded for the first hour at least since the children were fully occupied in school exercises.

Another experiment which affords data on reminiscence without using the name is that of English, Welborn & Killiam (1934). College students in psychology classes were given psychological selections of several pages to study. Retention was tested not by recall but by a form of recognition, the familiar true-false examination. The true-false items were of two sorts: those repeating almost verbatim certain sentences from the selections read, and those paraphrasing the substance of sentences or paragraphs. One group of 226 students was tested four times on the same material, with average raw scores as follows:

	Interval between learning and test			
	10 min.	*24 hours*	*14 days*	*30 days*
Verbatim items	37.7	37.2	33.7	33.5
Substance items	19.1	21.9	24.8	26.9

While the score in verbatim items shows some falling off, the score in substance items increases progressively; and the same result was obtained in several similar experiments. The increase in substance score was not entirely due to repeated tests, for in one experiment the only retest was given 55 days after learning with these results:

	Test after	*10 min.*	*55 days*
Verbatim items		32.8	25.8
Substance items		13.8	18.6

The authors conclude that memory for substance runs a different course from verbatim memory and must therefore be a different function. But even if the students did not exactly rehearse the substance of the selections they were all the time becoming more familiar with psychology and better able to judge the truth or falsity of a psychological statement.

A definite effort to eliminate this haunting possibility of review during the interval was made by G. O. McGeoch (1935) in her experiments on large groups of school children, who studied poems for 5 minutes with recall tests at once and after 24 hours. After the tests were completed, the children were asked to report whether they had thought of the lines during the interval and were given to understand that such reviewing was quite in order. Of the younger children (Grades 3–4), 84 percent reported more or less reviewing, and of the older group (Grades 9–11) there were 70 percent. So far, it looks bad for reminiscence! But, strangely enough, there was as much evidence for reminiscence in the recall scores of those individual children who denied as of those who reported reviewing. The author concludes that reminiscence is a genuine fact and not merely the result of rehearsal during the interval.

Other possible explanations. If reminiscence is not wholly due to reviews, are we thrown back upon a consolidation process continuing for days and days? Warner Brown (1923) offered another factor for consideration. He pointed out that a recall score is a very imperfect measure of retention—as we have already seen—because items which lie below the recall threshold at one moment may be recalled later when conditions happen to favor them. Consider two successive recall tests on the same material: the items recalled in the first test are thus relearned and made more secure, while other items not recalled in the first test have some chance of emerging in the retest and increasing the total score.

This explanation assumes no strengthening of a trace except by actual recall or relearning. All unused traces are becoming gradually weaker. But recall, depending on cues and other momentary conditions (as well as on the trace), may capture an item on a later test which eluded pursuit on an earlier test. By repeated attempts at recall, one can sometimes get back an entire poem or piece of music which at the first attempt was very fragmentary.

Brown put his hypothesis to the test by two parallel experiments, one with newly learned and the other with old material. In one experiment words were orally presented thus: *"Hat,* he had a *hat* on his head; *hat,"* and so on through a list of 48 unrelated words. The whole list was finally pronounced once more to the class. There was an immediate recall test, with a second test after a half-hour lecture. The average recall scores were:

No. words recalled in first test	25.48
Of these there were recalled in second test	22.44
Additional words recalled in second test	4.33
Total score in second test	26.77

Most of the words recalled in the first test were recalled in the second, too; and a few of those not recalled at first came up the second time. The results conform perfectly to the hypothesis, though they could also be explained in terms of consolidation—especially if the lecture was restful. In the other experiment a large class of University of California students was given 5 minutes in which to write as many as possible of the names of the 48 United States; then came a half-hour lecture and a second attempt to recall the names of all the States. Here are the results:

Av. no. States recalled in first test	36.41
Of these there were recalled in second test	34.37
Additional States recalled in second test	5.29
Total score in second test	39.66

The absolute scores are higher than in the former experiment, but the relations are the same. Here consolidation can have played no part, since the material was very old and any consolidation process long past. Besides Brown's interpretation there is, indeed, one other possibility which will be mentioned in a moment.

The emergence of additional items in a retest was further examined by Raffel (1934), using 100 disconnected words as material. These she presented visually one at a time at the rate of 1½ sec. per word, going through the list 5 times in the same sitting. Her recall tests took somewhat the form of a free association test, the instructions being, "Now I want you to say 150 words, more words than there were on the list. Try to say words from the list, but if you think of a word say it, even if you know it was not on the list. For instance, if you feel yourself on the track of a word but think of others in the meantime, say the others too." Many correct items were obtained of which O was very doubtful. Two groups, each containing 12 educated adults, were treated somewhat differently as can be seen from the table:

	Group C		Group D	
	Words recalled for the first time	*Total score*	*Words recalled for the first time*	*Total score*
On 1st day (immediate test)	43.2	43.2	35.0	35.0
On 2nd day	3.8	34.7	3.5	27.7
On 3rd day	2.8	36.1	No test	
On 4th day	1.8	36.1	No test	
On 5th day	1.1	35.3	1.4	24.9
On 6th day	.5	35.8	1.5	27.2
On 7th day	.4	35.1	.9	26.5

The first thing to notice is the emergence of fresh items day after day even when the total score declines. Retention can scarcely be improving when recall is going down, and therefore the emergence of additional items cannot reasonably be attributed to improved retention. Brown would explain it by chance variations in the cues and other recall conditions, but Raffel gives a different interpretation. If we follow down the Group D column and compare the run of the Total scores with Group C, we see that the omission of the test for two days was followed by a smaller score and the resumption of tests by increased score, just as if an effort to recall today improved the chances of recall tomorrow. In the same way the effort of Brown's Os to remember the States, at the beginning of the hour, seems to have improved recall later in the hour. Do we not often notice that our effort to recall a name, though unsuccessful at the moment, is followed by the emergence of the name a few minutes later? Raffel speaks of a "facilitating effect of recall" which is not limited to the items actually recalled at the time. "Recall probably acts on the learning material as a whole, and not only on the units that are reproduced."

This conception of the matter reminds us of the "condition of readiness" (p. 38). It is quite likely that the effort to recall the names of the States, in Brown's experiment, put some names which were not recalled into a condition of readiness and so improved their chances of being recalled later. When material has been learned as a whole, or when linkages have been established between different parts of the material, the later recall of some parts may well put the rest into a condition of readiness which would amount to a slight review.

All the facts of reminiscence, it would seem, can be explained by the reviewing which sometimes takes place, by the varying chances of recall and conditions of recall, and by the condition of readiness into which previously learned material is put by the effort to recall it. The assumption of a long continued process of consolidation seems unnecessary.

CHAPTER IV

MEMORY FOR FORM

L ISTS of nonsense syllables, numbers or unrelated words, so much used in studies of learning and retention, certainly give an air of artificiality to the laboratory experiments. Are these laboratory performances anything more than stunts or games with no real bearing upon what human beings do in their daily life?

From time to time, such criticism of the usual experiments on memory has been voiced by psychologists, as by Bartlett (1932). He fully recognizes the necessity of simplifying and standardizing the experimental conditions, but he believes that the simplification that occurs in memory experiments is more apparent than real. Nonsense syllables are apt to be given meanings by the learner and disconnected items are grouped and connected in more or less meaningful ways. Controlling the stimulus conditions does not limit O's mode of response. Bartlett undertakes to make the memory experiment more realistic by the use of materials that are intrinsically interesting, materials such as are learned in actual life. He uses pictures, simple and complex figures, stories, anecdotes and discussions. Similar materials have been used by several other experimenters both before and after Bartlett.

In spite of criticism the ordinary memory experiment is justified by its results. The charge of unreality is less serious than it seems. A list of syllables presents a problem to the learner and the way he solves any problem is of psychological interest. Moreover such problems occur all the time in daily life although on a smaller scale than in the laboratory. A name is nonsense until it has been attached to its object. A sequence of numbers in a street address, letters in the designation of a radio station, or syllables in a word is essentially a nonsense list. If raw facts could not be learned, our higher intellectual processes would be everlastingly handicapped. Imagine arithmetical work without the addition and multiplication tables at your finger tips! The laboratory experiment is more intensive than the usual learning process but for that very reason it should throw into relief the essentials of learning. The same general findings are obtained with different classes of material, numbers and words as well as nonsense syllables. The curve of forgetting shows the same general character with various types of material.

The usual memory experiment deals with content rather than form. The distinction between form and content need not, for our purposes, be regarded as anything profound or ultimate. When a letter square is memorized (p. 42) the letters are the content, while the form is the square in which they are arranged. After a single brief inspection O could report, "I know there is a square of 16 letters but what letters are in each part of the square I still have to learn." The square form is learned instantly and remembered long after the letters have been forgotten. A list of 12 nonsense syllables also has form, the form of a row or sequence. O usually gives it more form by rhythmical or spatial grouping (p. 28). If he learns many lists he probably throws them all into the same rhythmical form. This form is a frame or blank schema into which the concrete syllables are fitted. The form being simple and uniform offers no difficulty; the filling or content has to be learned with some expenditure of effort. So we may say that the ordinary learning experiment, while involving form as well as content, is too easy on the side of form to test O's powers of learning and remembering.

MEMORY FOR STORIES

Bartlett's studies can be brought under the head of memory for form. In the case of a story, form is represented by plot and atmosphere. "The house that Jack built" has a definite form which is easily grasped (learned) and often retained even when the content has been lost. In one of Bartlett's stories, two young Indians out on the water are met by a war party in canoes who invite them to participate in a raid. One begs off, the other goes and in the fighting is wounded. Brought back home he lives through the night but dies at sunrise. This rather definite story form was readily grasped and well retained, while details dropped out or were changed. The original story made some mention of ghosts, an incidental item as it seemed to the English students who served as Os in the experiment. Rightly understood, the story centers around the ghosts and has quite a different plot or meaning from the common-sense outline just given. The true plot was not perceived and the ghosts tended to drop out of the story. Reading the story O *reacts* in his own way, forms his own conception. In reproducing the story he omits, modifies or adds details and so improves the consistency of his story. Usually, however, some striking details remain even if they are not well fitted into the general scheme.

In attempting to reproduce a story from memory, one really *constructs* a story, preserving the form as one has grasped it and such details as one has retained, but almost inevitably drawing upon one's general stock of ideas for rounding out a consistent story. After a long interval one may admit that too few fragments remain to justify any attempt to tell the story. Only the general "atmosphere" may remain and the story would have to be constructed out of whole cloth.

In the reproduced or reconstructed story there is much evidence of what may be called rationalization and assimilation, though both of these terms are likely to be misinterpreted. They do not mean here simply that O assimilates the half-forgotten material to his general "apperception mass" of ideas, nor simply that he remolds the story into conformity with his own desires and preferences. Such general assimilation and rationalization do play a part, but there is something more specific. O has "reacted" to the original story in a certain way, has found a certain "form" in the story. It has appeared to him, perhaps, as a bit of primitive folklore. When he tries to recall the story he tends to mold the remembered material into coherence with this "form."

Henderson (1903), using somewhat similar materials in a memory experiment, reaches similar results. He speaks of simplification and generalization by combining similar items (condensation), modification of details to make them more meaningful, omission of incongruous and superfluous details, and domination throughout by the general meaning of the story. Similar changes were noted by Crosland (1921), Hausen (1933), Lewis (1933). When a "crime" is enacted before a class of students, false impressions of what is going on may arise and the facts may be twisted into conformity with this false conception of the whole incident. In an experiment of the present author the students were told that a memory experiment would be performed and saw the professor and an assistant set up a screen on the lecture table and busy themselves with placing objects behind the screen. Then the professor attempted to light the desk lamp but without success till a student from the front row stepped up and screwed in the bulb. As this student resumed his seat the professor gave the screen a push which sent it clattering to the floor; whereupon the professor and his assistant hastily removed the objects that had been concealed by the screen and intimated that the experiment was spoiled. Two days later the students gave testimony regarding the incident and they all agreed that the student from the front row, "butting in," had accidentally knocked down the screen, some of them explaining exactly how he happened to do so. The students grasped this incident in a form that made sense, and adjusted the details to fit the form. The art of a sleight of hand performer or of a writer of detective stories consists largely in suggesting false conceptions of what is going on. (For references on testimony experiments see Whipple, 1915; Lipmann, 1933.)

THE LEARNING OF VISUAL FORMS

Studies of form learning have been made mostly with visual material which is convenient partly because unfamiliar figures can easily be prepared and partly because the reproductions can be drawn with pencil on paper and so made quite objective. Such reproductions are used for tracing the learning process and for following the progress of forgetting. The "reconstruction method" (p. 12) lends itself to the study of memory for form; a figure can be built of pieces of wire which are then scrambled and given to O with instructions to reconstruct the original figure. The recognition method also can be used, and retention can be tested by the method of relearning. It is interesting to notice that psychologists who despise nonsense syllables may make much use of nonsense figures. Both sorts of experiment have opened up important theoretical questions and thrown light on their respective problems.

As a "fundamental experiment" in the learning of form, let the reader examine one of the figures shown here and then close the book and reproduce it with pencil on paper. The differences between the original and the reproduction are due partly to incomplete perception, partly to forgetting during the short interval, and partly to the exigencies of drawing. To trace the process of learning a figure, glance at it repeatedly and draw after each glance. To trace the process of forgetting, delay the reproduction for an hour, a day, a week.

F IG. 17. A few of the many types of figures used in experiments on the learning and retention of visual forms.

Experimental devices for impeding the process of learning a figure. A simple figure is "learned" or mastered so quickly by an adult that E is forced to introduce hampering conditions which slow the process and make it possible to examine the results of incomplete learning.

In what was perhaps the earliest of all these experiments, Philippe (1897) presented figures to the sense of touch (and kinesthesis) instead of visually. A solid object, a button or an iris flower in metal was handed to O who was allowed a short time for examining it with his hands and then indicated its shape by a drawing. After a second similar examination his drawing was much improved.

Other experimenters, while presenting a figure visually, have either used a complex figure or collection of figures, or else have allowed insufficient time for complete learning.

Kuhlmann (1906), one of the earliest workers in this field, allowed 10 min. for learning a collection of 5–9 figures. He depended largely on introspection for his evidence regarding the learning process.

Judd & Cowling (1907) presented a single, moderately complex figure for 10 sec., had it drawn by O, and repeated the exposures until the drawing showed complete mastery of the figure. This method of repeated presentations was followed by Piéron (1920) who allowed 5 sec. per exposure, and by Fehrer (1935) who reduced the exposure time to a fraction of a second.

Gibson (1929) combined two sources of difficulty. He exposed a long series of simple figures, each for 1.5 sec., called for reproduction of all that were remembered, and continued in this way through several sittings till all the figures were correctly reproduced.

The learning curve. As a quantitative study the experiment of Piéron (1920) most definitely answers the standard questions. He presented figures consisting of 10 straight lines of different lengths, crossing at different angles. Such a figure was more difficult to learn than a 10-digit list of numbers; it took as long to learn as a 20-digit list. After each brief exposure the reproduction was scored for accuracy. The learning curve, and also the curve of forgetting, had approximately the same form with this material as with lists of numbers.

Is the learning of a figure a "photographic" process? We speak of "sense impressions" and of "receiving an impression" of an object, and are likely to conceive the receptive process as analogous to photography —as if in looking at an object we took a picture of it. The memory image would be a revival of this picture. Reference back to the topic of imagery (p. 42) will make this conception appear improbable. When first attempting to memorize a figure so as to reproduce it from memory, O may attempt to establish a visual image of it, but he soon finds that he cannot depend on his image for accurate reproductions. He consequently

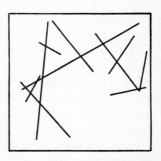

Fig. 18. Type of nonsense figure used by Piéron (1920) in experiments on learning and retention.

resorts to a more active type of memorizing in which he analyzes the presented figure (Piéron, 1920). When well-trained Os attempted to memorize some figures by pure visualization, and other figures by analysis and association, the latter method gave much better reproductions. Another method was to establish a motor image by tracing the seen figure, but it too was inferior to the analytic method (Moore, 1910). Even when O has a vivid image of the figure, he is apt to disregard it in making his drawing and to rely on what he calls his memory or knowledge of the figure itself. He knows more about the figure than is included in his image. He may report only the scrappiest kind of image and still make a good drawing from memory (Martin, 1913; Wulf, 1922).

Exploring the presented figure. One who is to reproduce a figure from memory engages in exploration. He searches for characteristics which define the figure sufficiently for his purpose. There are two main lines of attack which have been noticed by the experimenters. Kuhlmann (1906) speaks of a direct attack in which the figure is critically examined, the lines traced, the details noted and often named. The indirect attack consists in asking "What is it like?" The two modes of attack may be called (1) *figural analysis* and (2) *reification*. The one studies the figure simply as a figure, the other looks for a thing. Bartlett (1932) concludes that the fundamental line of attack is "effort after meaning." A familiar figure is named; an unfamiliar one is described as somewhat like a known object, or else as a pattern constructed according to a certain plan.

Granit (1921), too, distinguished two modes of grasping nonsense figures: schematizing the figure, and "association by similarity." Young children used the latter mode almost exclusively; for them a figure must be a "picture of something" and the only question was, "a picture of what?" They found or fancied some resemblance to a thing. The adults were more geometrical; they noted symmetry, rhythm, the repetition of identical parts.

Schema with correction. A nonsense figure, by definition, does not closely resemble any familiar thing nor does it conform exactly to any simple geometric form. If it is likened to a thing, note must be taken also of the way in which it differs from the thing. If it is seen as a geometric form, due account must be taken also of its idiosyncrasy. In either case the process amounts to schematization plus correction. In the same way, a nonsense syllable is often seen as a familiar word with a difference; and very similar is the reaction of a child who calls a squirrel on first sight a "funny kitty." The new = the old with a correction. Such is apparently the general line of attack in assimilating new experience. This type of learning process has been observed by several experimenters who have worked with nonsense figures. Kuhlmann (1906) reported it; the best schema which his Os could find for a given figure required some correction to enable them to give a satisfactory reproduction. Thus a certain figure was seen as "a square with a nick on the right side." Piéron's Os took some of the long lines (see Fig. 18) as a frame into which the shorter lines were fitted; but sometimes the schema adopted turned out to be too simple to allow for all the details; the schema then had to be modified.

A figure which conforms exactly to a known geometric form or to the outline of a familiar thing is, of course, easy to learn; but so is a figure which fails to conform in an easily definable way, i.e., a figure in which the necessary correction is easy. So we may generalize some findings of Fehrer (1935). She gave her Os repeated brief exposures of figures and determined the number of exposures required for a correct drawing. The difficulty of some figures measured 15 times that of others. Among the easiest were: semicircle, circle, square, diamond, oblong, triangle—regular figures requiring no correction. But it is noteworthy that among the easiest were also: a triangle with a gap at each corner; an oblong with a gap in one of the long sides; a small square placed askew in a larger square. These last are irregular figures which can however be described by a simple schema with a simple correction.

Stages in the learning of a figure. An unfamiliar figure becomes known by a process which takes time. Does it become known first in parts which are then combined to make a whole, or is it first known as a whole in which parts are found later? Does the process advance from chaotic complexity to organized unity; or in the reverse direction, from an undifferentiated totality to an articulated multiplicity? These *a priori* alternatives were set up without due consideration of the reactive character of perception. The unfamiliar figure presents a problem to be solved, and if it is at all difficult we may expect stages of questioning, of trying out and rejecting false leads, and of final satisfaction with some percept. The trial-and-error nature of the process stands out clearly in the pastime of finding the "hidden picture" (see Fig. 19.)

Fig. 19. (Street, 1931.) Type of hidden picture used by Leeper (1935 a). Some of the figures were easy and some quite difficult. Each figure was first exposed for 20–180 sec., according to its difficulty, with instructions to identify it as soon as possible. The series was shown a second time with explanation of each. Some weeks later each figure was exposed for only half a second and was practically always (in 97% of 930 cases) recognized if it had been "correctly" perceived. The typical process of finding the hidden object "was that the figure would change as an entirety from one pattern to another . . . one unification might appear which was not very satisfactory . . . the figure would next transform itself . . . until finally, perhaps, the correct figure was seen. It is interesting that once an organization had been achieved, however, even when it was considered by a subject as being clearly incorrect, it was found hard to exclude that organization and see something else."

Stages in the process of learning a figure have been studied by the method of repeated exposures. Judd & Cowling (1907) presented a fairly difficult figure in 10-sec. exposures, with reproduction after each exposure. Some of the Os proceeded from part to whole and others from whole to part. Some worked methodically from left to right, first making sure of a few segments and in later exposures adding new segments. Others first got the general outline and then concentrated on parts that were still vague.   This latter method seemed at least as efficient as the former.

FIG. 20.   Nonsense figures used by Judd & Cowling (1907).

Fehrer (1935) traced the course of learning from O's reproductions of a figure after successive very brief exposures.   Instead of any stereotyped order of events there was a great variety of actual processes.   The cases were classified as follows:

Increasing complexity	32%
Decreasing complexity	27
Both by turns	25
No change in complexity	16
	100

In the cases of "no change in complexity" the correct number of parts was present even in the first reproduction but some error remained to be corrected.   The most general formula for the course of learning a figure, according to Fehrer, distinguishes three stages:

1.   An initial state of inaccuracy and instability.
2.   A premature, incorrect stabilization.
3.   A gradual or sudden elimination of the stable error.

We might say: a questioning stage, a false answer which tends to persist and is eradicated with difficulty.

If a figure is presented to indirect instead of foveal vision the form is of course less easily and less minutely perceived.   With repeated exposures of this sort, stages can be made out which are very similar to those just mentioned.   After a period of varying reproductions O settles down into a stable drawing for each figure.   The line of development is neither from part to whole nor from whole to part, but "from a labile, plastic, unstable beginning to a condition of stability" (Drury, 1933; see Fig. 21).

Side lights on the stages in reaching a clear percept of a figure are afforded by several interesting experiments in which, instead of repeated brief exposures, the presentation is at first very inadequate and is gradually made better.

A.   The figure is first presented at the extreme periphery of the field of view to an O who has received preliminary training in maintaining fixation while directing his attention to what is shown in indirect vision (Zigler et al.,

1930). As the figure is gradually moved inward, its appearance undergoes changes which can be roughly divided into four stages:

1. "Figureless field—a vague, blurry, hazy or cloudy, shapeless field or spot."
2. "Formless figure—a faint spot or splotch on the background."
3. "Form-like figure"—not enough shape to be definitely named.
4. "Clear figure," when the figure is about 10° from the fixation point.

FIG. 21. (Drury, 1933.) Nonsense line figures used in experiment on indirect vision. One figure at a time was exposed for 1/10 sec. at a point which was either 10° or 22° out from the fixation point. The 12 figures used were shown in chance order and repeated at intervals in several sittings. After each exposure of a figure O attempted to reproduce it in a drawing and to describe it verbally. The figures did not suggest familiar objects and there was no obvious "effort after meaning."

B. The figure is at first very small and is gradually increased in visual size by an optical device (Wohlfahrt, 1932). The stages in perception are about as follows:

1. A roundish spot is seen, sometimes with a slight suggestion of shape, as "comma-like," "cross-like."
2. The slant of the longest dimension is seen, but the figure remains roundish, wavering, almost ameboid.
3. Straight lines and angles appear; the external contour clears up while the interior of the figure is a mass of curves or zigzags.
4. The interior begins to clear up, in the form of blocks or nuclei.
5. Interior lines begin to appear, sometimes to O's astonishment since what has been a puzzle suddenly becomes clear and stable.
6. The figure is distinct throughout and is accepted as satisfactory.

C. Figures cut out of gray paper and pasted on a ground of nearly the same gray are shown first in low illumination which is raised gradually (Hempstead, 1901). At the lowest illumination the figure is not seen at all. "Presently, portions of the figure began to appear. The form might begin as a mere 'suggestion' of something. . . . What portion was seen first seems to have been a matter of accident, except that a long line was apt to be perceived earlier than a shorter one." In attempting to reproduce in drawing what was seen, O is likely to add completeness to the seen shape, "under the guidance of the two principles of symmetry and similarity," the latter principle being that uncertain parts are made to correspond with what is already sure. Hempstead gives some interesting examples of the drawings which do not, however, fall cleanly under his two principles. In all such drawings O is almost forced to go beyond what he has seen (Fig. 22).

RETENTION OF VISUAL FORMS

Reproduction as an index of retention. Memory for figures has been studied by having O draw the figure as well as he can after an interval. Now even with verbal material recall is admittedly not a perfect index of retention, and the same admission must emphatically be made when the recall, or reproduction, is made in a drawing. Evidently O's drawing ability is a limiting factor. Often he cannot get down on paper exactly what he wishes to show. If his memory of a figure is vague he scarcely knows how to represent that vagueness and is almost forced to draw a definite figure which he knows must differ from the original. Kuhlmann (1906) stated the case in emphatic terms: "Recall is very largely not recall at all, and can never be described even half correctly by calling it reproduction. It is rather a construction, not a reconstruction, a construction of a certain result that is accepted in place of the original, and far from a reconstruction of a past perception." In short, memory is only one among several factors in drawing a figure from memory.

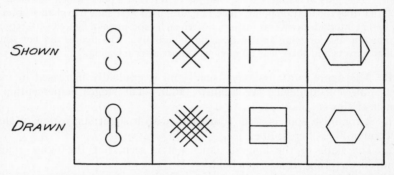

FIG. 22. (Hempstead, 1901.)   Reproduction of imperfectly presented figures.

To bring out the other factors let us first consider the act of copying a figure while it is being presented. The drawing which O makes is determined by three factors:

1. What he is trying to do.
2. What he is able to do—his available responses.
3. The stimulus figure.

What is O trying to do? Simply to copy the seen figure. But how minutely is he supposed to copy it? Shall he reproduce the imperfections of the original, shall he include all the details or only the general shape, shall he copy the exact size or only the shape, shall he bother about the excellence of his own lines and the beauty of his drawing? O's set and purpose will differ according to his understanding of the task. Usually he will strive for general effect and disregard details.

O's ability to reproduce the figure depends on his drawing ability and on his acquaintance with geometrical and decorative forms and with the shapes of various objects. Instead of slavishly following the lines of the given figure he is likely to find resemblances to known figures and to use these resemblances in his drawing.

Now lay aside the original and let O reproduce the figure from memory. The factors of task and ability remain as they were, while in place of the stimulus-figure he has the much less complete memory trace. He is in doubt at certain points and would like to consult the original. He is not sure whether a certain line was exactly vertical or slightly inclined, but he has to draw it one way or the other. It is impossible for him to limit his drawing to that which he remembers, when his memory is vague. His drawing is only partly controlled by the memory trace and corresponds only imperfectly with the trace.

Results obtained by the method of reproduction need therefore to be checked by other methods such as recognition and relearning.

Errors committed in the reproduction of a figure. Many experimenters have obtained drawings of figures from memory, compared the drawings with the originals and found them changed in characteristic ways. We will first notice the classifications made by authors who were not concerned to prove or disprove any special theory of the memory trace. Philippe (1897), the first investigator to use the method, classified the transformations under three main heads:

1. Detail is lost or becomes vague and confused.

2. New detail is substituted.

3. Most frequently, the reproduction becomes generalized and approaches the typical form of some object. "The image appears to evolve toward a pre-existing type which exercises over it a sort of attraction. . . . Useless details drop out and disappear to leave room for what is necessary for the whole. All normal life develops thus."

Kuhlmann (1906) from the introspections of his Os judged that many errors resulted from dependence on verbal description. In the presence of the figure O describes it to himself but on later recalling his description he finds it insufficient. A large share of the errors could be placed under two heads:

1. Object assimilation: O remembered the thing which he found the original to resemble and his drawing deviated from the original in the direction of the associated thing.

2. Regularization of several kinds:

a. "Certain parts of a form approaching in character that of parts of certain familiar geometrical forms tended to be drawn more like the latter."

b. "Lines that were not quite vertical or horizontal tended to be made just vertical or horizontal."

c. "Parts of a form that were not quite perpendicular or parallel to each other tended to be made just perpendicular or parallel."

d. "Parts that were not quite equal in length tended to be made equal."

e. "There was a tendency to arrange parts symmetrically."

Meyer (1913) used the method of Paired Associates. She assigned a name to each of 6 figures, repeated the series several times, and 24 hours later gave the names with instructions to draw the figures. The errors seemed to result from three main causes:

1. "Collective apprehension" of the figure as a whole with neglect of details.

2. Object assimilation.

3. Intraserial assimilation, confusion of two figures in the series.

Bartlett (1932) in a somewhat similar experiment which he called "picture writing," obtained transformations such as have been mentioned and in addition:

1. Exaggeration of unusual characteristics.

2. Increased complexity of certain figures.

3. Right-left reversals, which were very common in asymmetrical figures.

A Gestalt theory of forgetting. New impetus was given to this line of memory study when Wulf (1922), working under Koffka's direction, drew from his results certain challenging conclusions. He called in question a theory of G. E. Müller, according to which forgetting consists mainly in an increasing indefiniteness of the memory trace, so that reproduction after a long interval loses distinctive character—except, indeed, when a particular feature of the original aroused special interest, in which case that feature may be exaggerated in reproduction. Wulf believed his results to prove that the memory trace tended not toward vagueness but toward "better figure." Memory was governed, he believed, by the same laws as those found by Wertheimer to hold for perception. "The most general law which governs all the memory changes is the law of pregnance which says that every gestalt becomes as good as possible. In perception the 'possible' is sharply limited by the existing stimulus complex, but in memory the 'engram' or trace, freed from this limitation, can transform itself in the direction of pregnance. Therefore figures, in memory, tend toward definite outstanding forms." Or, as Koffka restated the theory (1935, p. 496): "If Wulf's conclusion is right the change which any pattern undergoes must be determined by the pattern itself. . . . According to the nature of the pattern lines may gradually become straighter or more curved, longer or shorter. . . . In cases of very irregular patterns the internal forces of organization will . . . be in conflict with the external ones" —i.e., with the stimulus complex—"the perceived forms will be under stress. Therefore, if the trace retains the dynamic pattern of the original excitation, it will be under stress too, and the changes which occur within it will be such as to reduce those stresses."

This theory involves two assertions capable of being put to experimental test. First, a reproduced figure is asserted to be better or more pregnant than the figure as originally seen. Second, the changes are progressive, increasing with the lapse of time since the figure was seen. Goodness or pregnance of figures may prove to be a rather fluid, subjective concept, difficult to define and utilize to everyone's satisfaction, but progressive change ought to be demonstrably the fact or not the fact.

Do figures become "better" in reproduction? Wulf classified the alterations under the three heads: *normalization, emphasis,* and inherent or *autonomous structural change.* A normalized figure is one that deviates from the original in the direction of some familiar object or form, one that shows "object assimilation." An emphasized figure accentuates some part or character of the original. A figure that has undergone autonomous structural change is one which, in Koffka's terms, has yielded to the stresses inherent in its form. Increased symmetry is given as one example of this sort of change. The other two sorts of change, also, are said to conform to the law of the good figure. Memory obviously takes its start not from the objective figure, but from the figure as perceived by O. If he originally saw in it a resemblance to some familiar object or standard form, and in reproduction makes it still more like that model—or if he originally emphasized some feature of it and in reproduction emphasizes that feature still more—in either case the change is in the direction of pregnance. As Werner (1924) said in further developing the Gestalt theory, "The apprehension or definition of a perceived figure is always such as to express as sharply as possible the essence of the structure as the subject gets it." Therefore Wulf regarded all three sorts of memory change as good evidence for the Gestalt law. His proof was complete, except that it depended on very highly *interpreted* data, so that confirmation by other investigators is especially necessary. There have been several repetitions of Wulf's experiment.

What are the concrete alternatives? Before examining the experimental results, we may well ask what results would be predicted by the two opposing theories. According to Müller's theory, which probably would be accepted in the main by most psychologists, the memory trace weakens or disintegrates and loses the distinctive characteristics of the original figure, except that a characteristic which was emphasized in perception will persist longer than other characteristics and so be accentuated in the reproduction. The present author would restate this theory as follows: Any figure that is not extremely simple presents various features, as we may call them, including details and characteristics of the figure as a whole. Some of these features suggest familiar forms or objects. The same objective figure can be seen in a variety of ways according to the features that stand out or are emphasized in perception. What stands out may be either a detail or a character of the whole figure. Both stand out in the common learning process of schema-with-correction. Besides the features specially emphasized, O may be more or less aware of other details and peculiarities of the figure. So much for the learning process. The theory next assumes a true process of forgetting; the trace weakens or dies out; features which were barely noticed die out more rapidly than those that were emphasized. *The trace after a sufficient interval no longer defines any complete figure;* O is thrown back upon his general stock of "available responses."

From this hypothesis we can predict that the attempted reproduction of a figure will practically never contain all the features of the original. With the dropping out of some features others are bound to be exaggerated. Resemblance to a familiar object or standard form will probably be accentuated. We may expect some tendency toward simple and symmetrical figures especially after forgetting has gone pretty far, for why should O introduce fine details and specific characteristics into his drawing when his whole memory has become vague? (If you present O an incomplete figure and ask him to complete it, he produces either a symmetrical figure or the outline of some object—Lund & Anastasi, 1928.) When the memory trace has become too weak to exert much control, the drawing is sure to be simple and may be symmetrical. But the main inference from this theory is that actual forgetting will occur.

According to the Gestalt theory, it would seem, actual forgetting will not occur. The trace instead of weakening is becoming more stable by yielding to its internal stresses. It always defines a complete figure. Disintegration should not occur; a reproduction should always be better integrated than the original, unless the original figure was the ultimate in this respect. Wulf regards object assimilation and accentuation of a feature as conforming to the law of good figure. It is hard to reconcile this view with the strict Gestalt conception represented by the quotation from Koffka. Wulf, and also Werner in the quotation above, seem to be making a concession to the reaction theory of perception. From this modified Gestalt theory we get the same predictions as from the reaction theory, except indeed that there will be no true forgetting, but ever-increasing conformity of the reproduction to some type of figure. According to the strict Gestalt theory of forgetting, the forces at work to modify the trace must be figural, object assimilation can occur only when the object has a good figure, and accentuation, when it occurs, must produce a good figure even if the whole has to be radically transformed. If the original figure was a square with rounded top and the roundness was accentuated in perception, this part might so dominate as to round out the whole figure into a circle, but it could not simply bulge and unbalance the whole figure.

This business of restating an author's theory is hazardous and the distinction between a strict and a loose Gestalt theory of forgetting may be unacceptable to those best qualified to judge. The crucial experiment to decide between the rival theories is more difficult to devise than it seemed at first. The experiments we have to survey are exploratory rather than crucial, but it should be possible to discover whether true forgetting occurs and whether reproductions tend toward good figure in the strict sense.

Are reproduced figures "better" and more "pregnant" than the originals? The changes of various sorts revealed by the experiments already cited were not scrutinized in the light of the Gestalt theory. Recent writers have usually had this theory in mind, though most of them have approached the question with some skepticism. Such was not the attitude of Perkins (1932), a warm adherent of Gestalt psychology, who reported, after obtaining drawings from a large number of students, that "all changes were in the direction of some balanced or symmetrical pattern" and that the changes were progressive until finally, 50 days after the original presentation of the figures, nearly half of the reproductions showed "perfect or semiperfect symmetry." He had a very liberal conception of symmetry, indeed, including under it all kinds of regularization and simplification and even object assimilation. The results of Allport (1930), however, indicate a tendency toward true symmetry in reproduction. Using as subjects 350 school children of 10–13 years, he exposed two figures, one bilaterally symmetrical and the other containing some asymmetry, and found that the asymmetry was lost in a large percent of the delayed reproductions, while the symmetrical figure showed no tendency to become asymmetrical. The tendency toward symmetry was not universal, and the same was true in the results of Fehrer (1935), who compared the drawings of college students, made immediately after presentation, with the originals, in respect to simplicity, accentuation, and symmetry. The percent of cases showing each kind of change was as follows:

Simplified	17.6	Complicated	18.4
Accentuated	18.3	Leveled	21.9
More symmetrical	16.0	Less symmetrical	6.7

There was a balance in favor of increased symmetry, but none in favor of simplification; and the tendencies toward Leveling and Accentuation were nearly equal (as indeed Wulf had found them). The author proposes a "statistical" theory of the errors of reproduction, according to which many types of change are possible, each having only a certain probability.

Another experimenter attempting an objective classification of the changes in immediate reproduction, with college students as Os, was Gibson (1929). He obtained the following frequencies:

Type of change	Gross frequency	Percent frequency	
Intraserial assimilation	108	16	
Object assimilation	95	14	
Completion	48	7	
Disintegration	26	4	
Conformity to verbal analysis	17	2	
Reproduced without definite change	689	57	100
Not reproduced	431		
No. figures exposed	1,120		

Intraserial assimilation was favored by the procedure, which exposed in quick succession a large number of figures, some of which were quite similar. Object assimilation is seen to be a very strong factor. Under "Completion" were included drawings which closed gaps in the presented figure, and under "Disintegration" cases where the gap was widened (emphasized). Completion tends to occur when the figure is apprehended as a single form in spite of the gaps, disintegration when it is seen as consisting of two adjacent figures. Errors due to verbal analysis occur when the names given by O to parts of the presented figure mislead him in reproduction. The fact that a majority of the drawings show no definite change is itself of some theoretical importance, since most of Gibson's figures had gaps or asymmetries or "internal stresses." None of them was a perfectly good figure and according to the strictest Gestalt theory we could predict that all the reproductions would deviate from the originals. What Gibson most emphasizes is the importance of past experience in determining how O shall perceive a figure. "The types of change here observed may all be explained, it is believed, by the supposition that the experience of the individual has brought into existence certain habitual modes of perception, and that these perceptual habits, rather than the laws of configurations, condition the changes observed. . . . In general, the nature of a change found in the reproduction depends upon the manner in which the figure was apprehended."

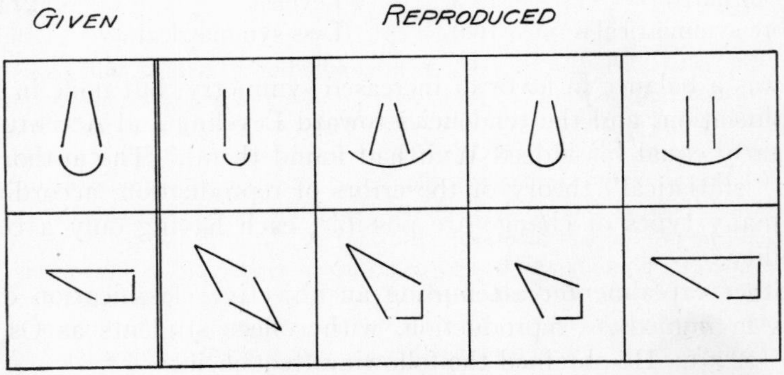

GIVEN   REPRODUCED

FIG. 23. (Gibson, 1929.) Two stimulus figures with immediate reproductions by several Os.

The importance both of past experience and of present "set" is well brought out in an experiment in which E's naming of an ambiguous figure just before the exposure had a tendency to steer O's perception and immediate reproduction in the direction suggested (Carmichael, Hogan & Walter, 1932; see Fig. 24).

Delayed reproduction. The changes so far mentioned occurred in immediate reproduction. On any theory we should expect more pronounced changes after a long interval of forgetting. Warner Brown (1935) and Hanawalt (1937) present data on delayed reproduction uncontaminated—and this is important—by reviews during the interval. Both used Wulf's figures, which are unbalanced and allow plenty of leeway for changes in the direction of good figure. (A few of these stimulus figures are shown in Figs. 25, 26, 28.) They were enlarged so as to be used in group experiments.

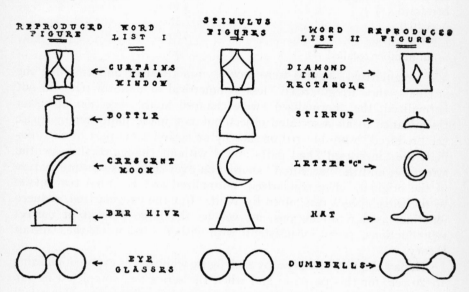

FIG. 24. (Carmichael et al., 1932.) Reproduction of named ambiguous figures. O was informed that he would be shown a series of figures which he was to reproduce, after the series was finished, "as accurately as possible, but in any order." Just before exposing each figure, E said "The next figure resembles . . .," giving one of the alternative labels shown in the chart to the right and left of the stimulus figure. When the series had been run through, O drew all he could remember; and the series was repeated till he produced recognizable drawings of all the 12 figures (of which only 5 are shown here). Some of the 86 college students who served as Os were given one set of names, others the alternative set. While many of the drawings deviated but little from the originals, many showed a definite influence of the suggestion. The examples shown here were chosen as showing pronounced modification.

In the learning period of Warner Brown's experiment (1935), each figure was exposed separately for 5–10 sec., reproduced after a wait of 30 sec., and kept in mind for about 5 min. while O answered questions on the imagery and associations awakened by that figure. Eight figures were thus presented. Unexpectedly, 14–17 days later, the Os were given a recall test. They were provided with blanks containing spaces for 8 drawings and were asked to reproduce the designs. On the average each O produced recognizable drawings of 5.46 of the 8 originals, with 2.16 approximately correct. The author experienced some difficulty in classifying the changes that appeared in the reproductions and admits that some of them could be classified otherwise; but with as great objectivity as possible he obtained the frequencies:

Class of alteration	Gross frequency	Percent frequency
Regularized	421	21
Irregularized	228	11
Normalized	191	10
Reduced	171	9
Increased	140	7
Accented	59	3
Correct	790	39
Total number recalled	2,000	100

The "regularized" figures were more symmetrical or uniform than the originals; the "irregularized" less symmetrical or uniform but still not normalized; the "normalized" were changed in the direction of better resemblance to an associated object but not made more symmetrical; the "reduced" were blurred or sketchy or lacked some part of the original; the "increased" had parts added without change of the essential structure; and the "accented" showed an over-emphasis of some feature of the original. The regularized, normalized and accented correspond to the three classes recognized by Wulf. But the irregularized, reduced and increased reproductions, as well as the large percent of correct reproductions, seem inconsistent with either version of the Gestalt theory.

Hanawalt (1937) had O copy each figure while it was exposed, allowing 15–20 sec. for this purpose; and when the series was completed he ran it through again and secured a second copy of each figure. One result came to light immediately: part of the change usually attributed to the memory trace was present in the direct copies which sometimes evened out irregularities and sometimes accentuated them. See the upper part of Fig. 25.

After copying the presented figures, some groups of Os had nothing further to do with them for several weeks. They were then asked to reproduce them. There were many failures to remember a figure and in the figures reproduced there were various changes, not all of which were in the direction of better or more pregnant figure (Fig. 26). After doing his best to reproduce the figures, O was given a recognition test. Each of the original figures was presented in a collection of similar figures, consisting mostly of drawings which had actually been made by other Os in their efforts to reproduce the original, and O selected that one of the collection which seemed to him most like the original. When the collection contains a drawing much like O's own reproduction, will he select it or will he select the original? If reproduction were a fair index of the state of the memory trace, O would certainly choose a drawing resembling his own. Out of about 300 such choices (when the test came 4 or 8 weeks after the presentation, and when O's drawing differed from the original), we find:

> 38% like O's own drawing
> 44% like the original

14% midway between O's drawing and the original
3% unlike either O's own drawing or the original

On the average, recognition is more correct than recall, as we should expect from other work (pp. 47, 50). Again on the average, we can say that the reproductions exaggerate the change which has occurred in the memory trace. In many cases where the drawing would indicate a distortion of the trace the recognition test shows the trace to be approxi-

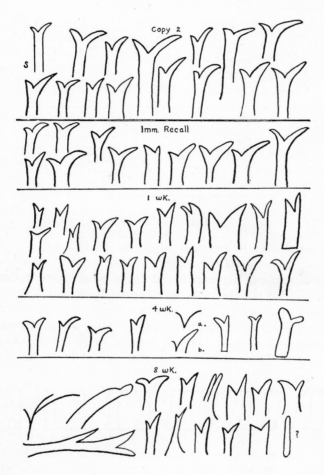

FIG. 25. (Hanawalt, 1937.) Drawings from copy and from memory. The original is marked S. The first collection gives sample drawings by different Os while the original was before them. After copying the figure twice, each O reproduced the figure once only, separate groups attempting reproduction after the different intervals stated: immediately, after 1 week, after 2 weeks, or after 8 weeks. The first 3 Os in the 8-week group reported that the figure reminded them, respectively, of a "figure branched like a tree," of a "tree bud," and of a "tree stem." Another O said it "resembled an M." The reproductions are not selected but include all that were made from memory of this figure.

mately true to the original, though too weak to control the process of reproduction effectively. Zangwill (1937 a) obtained similar results.

To sum up: the kinds of change appearing in drawing a figure from memory are too various to be brought fairly under the concept of better or more pregnant figure, and the changes in the drawings are likely to exaggerate any qualitative changes which may have occurred in the trace.

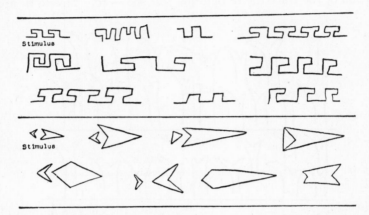

FIG. 26. (Hanawalt, 1937.) Two stimulus figures with attempted reproductions after several weeks by Os who had not reproduced them in the interval. The question is whether the reproductions are consistently in the direction of "good figure."

Are the changes in a remembered figure progressive in time? It is clearly essential to the theory expounded by Wulf and Koffka that the memory trace of a figure shall change progressively in the direction of a good, stable figure, i.e., in the direction of yielding to the internal stresses of its dynamic structure. This implication of the theory is fully admitted, and even insisted on, by these authors. Here, it would seem,

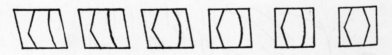

FIG. 27. (Perkins, 1932.) Successive reproductions of a figure by the same individual.

we can escape from the snares of subjective judgment and obtain perfectly irreproachable evidence for or against the theory. One need but note the changes from each reproduction of a given figure to the following and see whether they run in a consistent direction. But even here different examiners will reach different conclusions. For example, the above series of reproductions is offered by Perkins (1932) and by Koffka (1935, 141 ff., 493 ff.) as a good example of progressive change.

Looked at casually this series of reproductions shows a gradual change toward symmetry. Close scrutiny shows some halting and some retrograde changes.

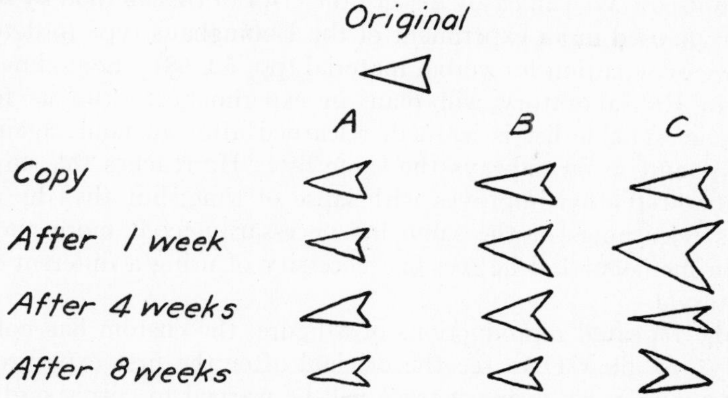

Original

A   B   C

Copy

After 1 week

After 4 weeks

After 8 weeks

FIG. 28. (Hanawalt, 1937.) Repeated reproductions from memory of a given original. Each O copied the original while it was in view and reproduced it 3 times from memory. Individuals A and C show progressive accentuation of the dent, while B oscillates.

Wulf (1922) stated as his main result that the changes in reproducing the same figure are progressive in any individual, though sometimes in the direction of sharpening and sometimes in that of leveling. He gives 20 series of reproductions. In the present writer's opinion, only one of these 20 shows an unequivocal progression; 10 show progression in some respect along with non-progressive change in some other respect, while the remaining 9 are unequivocally non-progressive. Kuhlmann (1906) obtained repeated reproductions after 2–90 days from learning, and concluded: "The errors made in the successive drawings . . . fall into three classes. (a) By far the majority of the errors appeared in the first drawing . . . and remained constant in the later drawings. A smaller number did not remain permanent. (b) Some of these remained the same in character but increased in degree in a constant direction, generally indicating a definite cause of error at work. (c) Others changed in character." Gibson (1929) found that alterations once made usually persisted as long as the figures were reproduced at all; but Object Assimilation and Completion showed some tendency to increase from reproduction to reproduction. Allport (1930) noted a slight tendency for an asymmetrical figure to become progressively more symmetrical.

The net result of the preceding survey is that completion, regularization, symmetry and object assimilation are sometimes progressive. But progressive change is by no means the universal rule. Frequently the reproductions remain stable for months after the original experience, and sometimes we note in the series a wavering back and forth or some other irregular course of change.

A question of method. There is a serious methodological error in many experiments which have attacked the question of progressive change in the memory trace of a figure. The method of *successive reproductions* has been used. We can easily discern the error of this method by imagining it to be used in an experiment of the Ebbinghaus type to determine the curve of retention for verbal material (pp. 52, 58). Sometimes a beginner in the laboratory will plan an experiment to run as follows: A nonsense-syllable list is learned, relearned after an hour, again after 24 hours, and so on—always the same list. He reaches the surprising result that retention improves with lapse of time; but then he notices that his relearnings of the same list necessarily fix it more and more firmly in memory; and he sees the necessity of using a different list for each interval.

In the repeated reproductions of a figure, the custom has not been, of course, to allow O to see the original after the first exposure. For that very reason his memory trace will be warped to correspond to the alterations present in his own reproductions. When the original figure reminds him of a certain object, and that object is remembered during reproduction of the figure, the drawing is apt to deviate from the original in the direction of the object. So much seems certain. Therefore, the memory trace being reset to the figure as reproduced, the next reproduction may very well deviate still more toward the associated object.

Hanawalt (1937) proved the seriousness of this error of method by comparing the results of two procedures, after figures had been learned by copying them, as already described. One procedure was the usual one of having the same Os reproduce the figures at intervals. In the other procedure different groups of Os were used for the different intervals and no O reproduced the figures more than once. As far as concerns the number of figures reproduced, the result was what would be expected from experiments with verbal material: with single reproductions, the number recalled decreased as the interval increased; but with repeated reproductions, there was little decrease.

NUMBER OF FIGURES REMEMBERED, OUT OF 8 SHOWN
(*Hanawalt, 1937*)

	Immediately	After 1 week	After 4 weeks	After 8 weeks
Single reproductions	6.9	5.7	4.8	4.4
Repeated reproductions	6.9	6.6	6.6	6.5

This result is evidence for *true forgetting*. A trace used from time to time is kept alive, but left inactive it dies out. The same effect is seen in the figures which are remembered: reproduced at intervals they suffer less change than when reproduced only after a considerable interval. This is true both of the details and of the general outline or distinctive form of the figures.

We are left in a quandary reminiscent of the indeterminacy principle in physics. We cannot observe the state of a memory trace without letting it act and so strengthening and perhaps distorting it and altering its subsequent history. Successive recognition tests are open to the same objection as successive recalls. The method of equivalent groups of Os, used by Hanawalt, does not permit us to follow the fortunes of the single trace. But we can predict from the Gestalt theory that, with prolongation of the interval, the average reproduction should become progressively better, more pregnant, freer from internal stresses. Fig. 25 contains all the reproductions obtained for one stimulus figure. It is hard to discern any progressive change except that an increasing proportion of the drawings become very poor representations of the original. This sort of progressive change occurred with all the figures. In the case of some figures measurement revealed a small average change in some definite direction, as accentuation of a characteristic.

Results from the method of successive comparison. One form of the recognition method (p. 11) calls for the comparison of two stimuli which are separated by a time interval. Errors in memory for figures can be studied by this method (Irwin & Seidenfeld, 1937). A nonsense figure was exposed for 5 sec. under instructions to observe it carefully with a view to comparing it with a similar figure to be shown later. After several figures had been exposed, there was an interval of 3 min. and then the *same* figures were shown again and O answered such questions as these: "Is the gap in this circle larger or smaller than in the one previously shown?" "Is this dot figure more or less square than the previous one?" About ⅔ of the Os said that the gaps had been smaller in the original circle and triangle than in the (identical) figure shown the second time, and a bare majority said that the dot figure had been squarer the first than the second time. These results are consistent with the Gestalt theory of forgetting; one could say that the memory traces of the original figures had changed in the direction of better figures, though with numerous exceptions. Repeating the recognition test after 10 minutes and again after a week showed no further change in this direction.

Conclusion. Evidence for any progressive change in the direction of better figure is extremely meager, and evidence of real forgetting is abundant. Taken as a whole the evidence speaks for the reactive character of learning and reproduction and against the assumption of any positive formative process in retention itself.

CHAPTER V

THE CONDITIONED RESPONSE

WHILE engaged in his long continued, fundamental and very fruitful experiments on digestion, Pavlov about 1900 (see his book, 1927) became interested in the "psychic secretion" of saliva. It was produced, for example, when food was shown to a hungry dog, before it actually reached his mouth. The salivary response to food in the mouth was a typical reflex, but the response to seen food was probably a learned response. Pavlov called it a conditioned reflex. The visual stimulus, the sight of food, he called a conditioned stimulus for the salivary reflex. He found by experiment that the salivary response could become conditioned to almost any stimulus: the ticking of a metronome, the flashing of an electric light, a thermal or vibratory stimulus to the skin, a sequence of musical notes or a visual pattern. The conditioned "alimentary" or feeding response included, besides the secretory part, the motor reaction of turning toward the source of food and making incipient eating movements. Pavlov directed his attention chiefly to the glandular response, because it could be measured. The duct of one of the salivary glands was brought through the cheek and implanted in the external surface so as to deliver the saliva to the outside, where it could be collected by a suction apparatus and measured in drops or in fractions of a cubic centimeter.

PAVLOV'S RESULTS AND CONCEPTIONS

The fundamental experiment. When the dog has recovered from the operation the experimenter, first making friends with the dog, conducts him to the laboratory and begins a process, which may take four or more half-hour sessions, of adapting the dog to the experimental conditions. The dog stands on a table with slings under his fore and hind legs which prevent him from moving away. The receiving tube is gummed to his cheek over the opening of the duct. The experimenter retires to the adjoining room from which he operates the apparatus for delivering the conditioned stimulus and the food.

In order to condition the salivary secretion to the beating of the metronome, say at 120 ticks per minute, E lets the metronome sound for just a few seconds and then applies the food. After an interval of some minutes, he repeats this combination. The trials are given at somewhat irregular intervals so that the dog may not become conditioned to the interval itself. The time during which the metronome ticks (before food) is gradually increased to 10, 15, 20 or 30 sec. Conditioning is most quickly achieved when the time is short, but some delay in supplying the food is necessary in order to give the conditioned response a chance to show itself. After a few trials, not over 5, one may expect to see a small amount of saliva secreted during the beating of the metronome and before the actual presence of food. This amount increases and after 10 or 15 trials CR is well established for the time being, though it may need some renewal at the next session. An animal which has already acquired the salivary response to the metronome acquires the same response to another stimulus, as a bell, in fewer trials. Individual dogs differ; some of them, in Pavlov's terminology, being more susceptible to excitation and others to inhibition. Both kinds make good subjects when understandingly handled. Success in this experiment requires careful attention to the needs of the dog. He should be taken for a walk before the experiment and be given a drink of water, he should be hungry, wide awake and alert, free from any painful or irritating stimulus and well adapted in advance to the laboratory, the apparatus and the experimenter.

Extinction and restoration. A conditioned response, whether new and just formed in the day's session or old and well established by repeated sessions, is quickly brought into a condition of temporary extinction which might better be called suspension. The conditioned stimulus is applied repeatedly at rather short intervals, 2–5 min., but no longer is it followed by the unconditioned stimulus. The metronome, is made to beat its regular 15 or 30 sec. but no food is presented. On the first of these trials saliva flows abundantly during the beating of the metronome. But the amount secreted becomes less in successive trials till after 6 to 10 unreinforced stimuli no secretion at all is registered. The motor component of CR, the movement of the head toward the food, also drops out. A rest of two hours will restore CR though perhaps not fully; a day's rest will do more toward this spontaneous restoration. Quicker restoration is obtained by reinforcing the metronome, that is, by resuming the metronome-food combination, or even by simply raising the animal's alimentary excitability by a little food given a few minutes before the metronome is tried.

Evidently this so-called extinction is very different from forgetting. CR is not eliminated from the animal's repertory. It is suspended, held in abeyance, one might almost say suppressed—Pavlov says inhibited. That it is not forgotten is clear from the fact that a "natural conditioned reflex," one formed in the usual course of life and doubtless used on many occasions, is easily extinguished in the laboratory. Show the dog some food just out of his reach and you get salivary and motor response. Remove the food without allowing him to eat, and repeat this procedure at short intervals; the salivary flow is progressively decreased to zero, with spontaneous recovery.

MEAT POWDER PRESENTED AT A SHORT DISTANCE BUT NOT GIVEN TO THE ANIMAL

(Pavlov, 1927, p. 58)

Time of presentation	Amount of secretion in drops
11.33 a.m.	20
11.36	12
11.39	6
11.42	2
11.45	0
11.48	0
Rest of two hours	
1.50 p.m.	3

Without regard to the physiological mechanism involved it is clear that *extinction, like positive conditioning, is a process of becoming adjusted to a temporary situation*—in the one case to a situation in which the beating of a metronome is regularly followed by food, and in the other case to a situation in which food shown is regularly taken away. With the passage of time (and of miscellaneous events which happen in time) the adjustment reverts toward the normal and usual. All the facts so far brought forward can be included in this formula.

Pavlov sometimes spoke in similar common-sense terms. He spoke of conditioned stimuli as "signals" of the biologically important facts of the environment. The metronome in the laboratory becomes a signal that food is immediately to be presented. During an extinction experiment, the same stimulus becomes a signal that food is *not* going to be presented. Though the main facts of conditioning can be stated in terms of signals or of adjustments to the environmental situation, there are certain details which cannot be so explained. An intense conditioned stimulus gets a larger salivary response than a weak stimulus of the same modality. Purely as a signal, a loud dinner bell is no better than a soft one, but the intense stimulus produces greater general *excitation* and larger responses. During a prolonged experiment in which no stimuli are given except such as have never had any signal value or such as from extinction have lost their signal value, the dog is apt to become drowsy and slump in his harness, and in this condition of *inhibition*, as Pavlov called it, he responds only weakly even to perfectly good conditioned stimuli which have not been extinguished.

Differentiation. When the salivary response has been conditioned to one stimulus, it can be elicited by similar stimuli ("sensory generalization"). If the stimulus has been a metronome beating at the rate of 120 per minute, the response will be obtained also with a rate of 60 per minute. Differentiation between these two rates can now be established by interspersing them in an experimental session, always reinforcing the 120 rate with food, and never reinforcing the 60 rate. The response to the unreinforced stimulus is gradually extinguished. After differentiation is complete, saliva flows regularly at the 120 rate of the metronome but not at the 60 rate. Stimuli differing as widely as this are readily differentiated. The experimenter proceeds to push the differentiation further; in a long series of trials he gradually increases the slower, negative rate, and may succeed in pushing it up to 100 per minute without breaking down differentiation. This method can be used for measuring the difference limen in animals.

Differentiation of tones according to pitch has apparently been pushed very far in Pavlov's laboratory. Differentiation of sounds according to the direction from which they come has proved, as one might expect of dogs, to be easily established and very precise. Differentiation of tactual stimuli according to their location on the skin is practicable. In one series of experiments (Pavlov, 1927, p. 220) 6 vibratory tactual stimulators were attached to the dog's right fore paw, right shoulder, two places on his right side, right thigh and right hind paw. At first only the shoulder stimulus was used, but when the salivary response had been conditioned to this particular stimulus it was made also when any of the other points were stimulated. Now the thigh was made a negative point, stimulation there not being reinforced while stimulation on the shoulder continued to be reinforced. With differentiation established it was found that strong response was obtained from the fore paw, the shoulder and the front part of the trunk, no response from the hind paw and thigh, and a small positive response from the rear part of the trunk, which being intermediate in position between the positive and negative point was intermediate also in its effect upon the salivary secretion.

Result of Stimulating Points on Skin, After Localized Conditioning

(Pavlov, 1927, p. 221)

Place stimulated	*Amount of secretion in drops*
Front paw	6
Shoulder (positively conditioned)	8
Side near shoulder	7
Side near thigh	3
Thigh (negatively conditioned)	0
Hind paw	0

Another form of the differentiation experiment adds an important new fact. The salivary response is first firmly conditioned to the stimulus A and also to the stimulus B. (There is no special difficulty in attaching this same response to a large number of separate stimuli.) A new stimulus N is now occasionally combined with A and the combination NA is always left without reinforcement. Differentiation is thus established between the positive stimulus A and the negative combined stimulus NA. When this has been accomplished it is found that N has acquired negative value or in Pavlov's terms inhibitory properties, for when N is combined with B it abolishes or diminishes the response to B, i.e., NB gives zero or a small response. Pavlov attached great importance to this result. It shows that extinction not only removes the positive CR but also establishes a negative response. In the same way the negative stimulus in differentiation gives a negative reaction. If the animal were able to verbalize, he might say in response to the positive stimulus, "Food coming," and in response to the negative stimulus, "No food coming." In Pavlov's terms the positive stimulus gives an excitatory effect, the negative stimulus an inhibitory cerebral effect.

Distraction and interference. Whether positive or negative, CR is an unstable reaction, easily disturbed by changes in the environment. Even a well established CR may fail in a lecture room demonstration. The distractions of an ordinary laboratory room—a sudden noise, a change of illumination when a cloud passes over the sun, an odor brought in by the wind, an unwonted movement of E—arouse what Pavlov called the "investigatory reflex." The animal looks, listens, sniffs; he is readjusting himself to a changed situation. His positive and especially his negative conditionings drop out for the moment. To minimize distractions and improve the regularity of the experimental results Pavlov isolated the animal in a sound-proof room and provided noiseless mechanical devices for applying the stimuli. He finally had a special laboratory built for conditioning experiments.

Experimentally, distractions were introduced so as to study their effect. The distracting stimulus was applied just a moment before a stimulus which had become positively or negatively conditioned. An old-established CR was not much disturbed, but any newly and barely established response was likely to be abolished for the moment. A just-established CR was omitted, a just-extinguished CR reappeared, a just-established differentiation was lost. This doing away with a negative CR Pavlov interpreted as the inhibition of an inhibition—a *disinhibition*. The more general term, external inhibition, denoted the interference of one activity with another, as the investigatory response interferes with a CR.

Internal inhibition. This one of Pavlov's physiological concepts is rather difficult to grasp. It implies an inhibition which is internal not simply to the organism but to a particular activity. Unlike external inhibition (interference or distraction), which is a momentary affair, internal inhibition develops progressively. A stimulus repeated without reinforcement, as in the extinction and differentiation experiments, gradually develops inhibitory properties; and even a reinforced stimulus, used many times in succession, loses power, the secretion diminishing from trial to trial. In an experiment lasting for weeks or months, a strong CR may grow weak and disappear; its long-used stimulus acquires inhibitory properties, deadening properties, so that it destroys the power of other conditioned stimuli. When the metronome has become a deadening stimulus, its use must be discontinued and new conditioned stimuli substituted in order to liven up the animal and enable the experimenter to proceed with his research.

The delayed CR. Here we find the best examples of internal inhibition. Pavlov's procedure, we recall, involved applying the conditioned stimulus for 15 or 30 sec. before reinforcement by the food or other unconditioned stimulus. At an early stage in its establishment the CR appears promptly at the beginning of the conditioned stimulus—as soon as the metronome starts to beat. But if the reinforcement is always delayed for 30 sec. the salivary response also is delayed until finally it appears only shortly before the presentation of the food (adjustment to the delay). The total response is now a two-phase affair, negative followed by positive. In some animals the negative phase is clearly revealed in motor behavior; the animal slumps in his harness, closes his eyes and appears almost asleep during the first 15 sec.; then he wakes up, and shows anticipatory movements and salivary secretion during the last part of the delay. A distracting stimulus introduced during the negative phase inhibits that phase and causes the secretion to flow at once. The same distraction introduced during the positive phase of the delay may diminish the amount of secretion.

Effects of a Distracting Stimulus on the Negative and the Positive Phases of a Delayed Conditioned Response

(Pavlov, 1927, p. 96)

In this experiment a vibratory tactual stimulus was regularly continued for 3 minutes before the administration of the unconditioned stimulus. When the delayed response was well established, a distractor was introduced either in the first half of the delay period or in the last half. The distractor was a previously unused whistle of moderate loudness. Results are here selected from two experimental sessions.

Stimulus	*Secretion in successive half minutes*					
	1	2	3	4	5	6
Tactual alone, average	0	0	1	3	9	12 drops
Tactual + whistle sounding during first 3 half minutes	3	2	6	6	8	6 "
Tactual + whistle sounding during last 3 half minutes	0	0	1	3	0	2 "

Trace CR. Let the metronome tick half a minute, then let a silent interval of half a minute follow before the administration of food: with careful management a conditioned response to the metronome can be established with the salivary flow commencing during the silent interval and shortly before the food arrives. This is called a trace conditioned reflex because obviously the original stimulus is not the direct inciter of the response. The trace of the stimulus in the organism releases the response (or in terms of adjustment the organism becomes set for food to be received after a definite silent interval). A similar result is obtained when the trials succeed at perfectly regular time intervals. If food is given without preliminary signal at regular intervals of 10 min., saliva will begin to flow a little before the end of each 10 min. interval. The trace CR like the delayed CR is a two-phase affair, the first, inactive phase according to Pavlov being a phase of internal inhibition. The trace CR is apparently more difficult to establish than the delayed CR.

The delayed and trace CRs, even though always reinforced, are liable to the gradual wearing out which Pavlov called progressive internal inhibition. Suppose the metronome to tick for 30 sec. on every trial before the application of food: the onset of salivation becomes progressively delayed till near the time for food; the negative phase of drowsiness becomes longer, until, in a long experiment, the animal fails to wake up and take food, though he is still hungry and will eat eagerly if taken from the table and given the same food on the floor. Shortening the period of delay to 5 sec. will liven up the animal and restore the CR. There are other practical ways of combatting drowsiness so that the experiment can proceed: give more enticing food or larger portions of food; avoid long delays between trials; remove the animal from the table and give him a recess. Some dogs go into an ecstasy of motor activity when released and then contentedly resume their position in the harness.

Sleep and internal inhibition. The drowsiness which comes over the animal in a prolonged experiment on the delayed CR appears to common sense as the *cause* of the disappearance of the salivary response. We naturally say the animal ceases to respond because he is sleepy. Pavlov asked *why* the animal becomes drowsy. He answered that drowsiness is a condition of internal inhibition which starts with the CR that is wearing out and diffuses over the entire cortex.

One factor should not be overlooked: though the animal is fed on each trial, he is fed *only a small amount*. He cannot pitch in and eat heartily in a dog's way. Each trial culminates not in eating but in prematurely ceasing to eat. The generalized internal inhibition amounts to a "loss of interest" in the situation and a loss of contact with the situation (drowsiness). These non-physiological terms have at least the merit of re-emphasizing the animal's general adjustment which must be an essential factor in the inhibitions as well as in positive conditioning.

Experimental neurosis. If the drowsy dog has "lost interest" in the situation, there is another condition which amounts to complete rejection of the situation. It was found possible to condition the alimentary response even to painful stimuli. A weak electric shock or series of shocks could be used in place of the metronome, with reinforcement by food at the end of so many seconds of shock. When salivation was established as a CR to this electrical stimulus, the shock was gradually increased and still the alimentary response occurred. But when the shock became too strong or was used too frequently, something seemed to snap—salivation ceased, the food was rejected and a violent defense reaction occurred. Weakening the electric stimulus did not now restore the CR. The animal became restless and excited and could not be used in further experiments for a period of months.

A more surprising way of producing experimental neurosis consists in pushing differentiation too far. In one experiment the positive stimulus was a circle of light on a screen before the animal, showing for 30 sec. before food was given. When the CR was well established a negative stimulus was occasionally introduced consisting of an ellipse of light of the same area and brightness as the circle but very long and slender (ratio of axes 2 to 1). Differentiation between the circle and this ellipse was easily established. In the course of weeks of work, the shape of the ellipse was gradually approximated toward the circle without breaking down the differentiation. When the ratio of axes became 9:8, however, not only did the animal fail to discriminate with any regularity but his whole behavior in the experimental room underwent an abrupt change. In place of his previous quiet alertness, he began to squeal and wriggle and bite the apparatus. The next day, on being brought into the experimental room, he started barking and when put on the stand was unable to differentiate even between the narrowest ellipse and the circle. In Pavlov's terms, "The clashing of excitation with inhibition led to a profound disturbance of the usual balance between these two processes." In terms of adjustment, the animal was no longer able to maintain his previously successful adjustment because of the increased difficulty of the task, and his reaction was to reject the whole situation.

Psychological value of Pavlov's work. Pavlov's work on the conditioned reflex, carried on over more than thirty years with the assistance of numerous collaborators, is certainly an important contribution to psychology. The experiments can be called psychological because they were studies of the behavior of the intact animal in well defined environmental conditions. Pavlov himself insisted that they were purely physiological because the methods were objective and because he rejected all such "psychological" concepts as understanding, desire, expectation and disappointment. He endeavored to formulate his results in terms of two opposite factors, excitation and inhibition, which he accepted as physiological fundamentals. Another fundamental concept was obviously necessary, that of some connection established by the conditioning process between the cortical mechanisms excited by the two stimuli, the conditioned and the unconditioned. He said, "Under suitable conditions a new connection must be formed at the very first occurrence of the stimulus excitation and become strengthened by every repetition." It is this last conception which has most awakened the interest of psychologists.

CR is a form of learned reaction—so much cannot be doubted. Psychologists have thought it might be the most rudimentary form, but this can be doubted. Certainly not all the "laws of CR" are laws of learning. The distraction effects—external inhibition and disinhibition

—are more closely related to the psychology of attention. "Experimental neurosis" is related to the psychology of control, conflict, strain and breakdown and may throw light on human neuroses. It would be a mistake to tie up CR exclusively with the psychology of learning.

A prime question for the experimentalist is whether the results so carefully worked out by Pavlov in the limited field of the salivary secretion of dogs can be verified in other laboratories, on other species of animal, and with responses of the striped and smooth muscles as well as of the glands. Experimental work has broadened out in these various directions, with results quite definitely confirming most of Pavlov's findings. Sometimes the distractors do not distract, and sometimes the extinguishing procedure fails to extinguish a CR. Individual differences are much in evidence, as indeed was clearly brought out by Pavlov, and it is not surprising that there should be species differences and age differences. Slight changes in the external conditions sometimes make a large difference in CR.

The main exception to our statement that Pavlov's empirical findings have been widely confirmed has to do with the "irradiation" experiment, elaborated from a differentiation experiment described above on p. 95. The findings so far as there stated have been confirmed on human subjects (Bass & Hull, 1934). Pavlov's irradiation was conceived as a spread of excitation or of inhibition, starting from the brain center directly excited or inhibited, and diffusing gradually over the whole cortex. Physiologically it is a difficult notion to accept. Experimentally, it demands a precision of results almost or quite exceeding the possibilities of so unstable a process as the CR, and Pavlov's own data do not give the notion any real support (Loucks, 1933; 1937). For that reason we have not included it in our list of Pavlov's findings. Those we have included seem to be well confirmed as pure behavioral facts.

Interpretation is a different matter. Here we may expect much disagreement. Pavlov's terminology was intended to suggest physiological interpretations which can be disregarded in psychology. "Internal inhibition" is an example. Pavlov pictured it as a functional anesthesia or sleeplike state which might affect the whole cortex or be confined to one particular center. It was almost sure to have some "spread," and therefore the negative phase of a delayed CR possessed "inhibitory properties" which would show in a lowered response to any conditioned stimulus applied during this phase, a deduction which has received some support from an experiment of Rodnick (1937).

Various interpretations of the phenomena of inhibition are possible. The drowsiness of Pavlov's dogs during the long waits in the experiment may have resulted from their having nothing to do, restrained as they were on the stand. In experiments on monkeys who were free to move about the cage during an interval of waiting, Wendt (1936 b) found them anything but drowsy. They filled in the time with activity of some sort. Wendt takes the view that inhibition of one activity is always incidental to the execution of some other activity—"reciprocal inhibition." In this view Pavlov's internal inhibition is just a special case of his external inhibition. Another view is taken by Wenger (1936, 1937) growing out of his experiments in conditioning newborn human infants. CR went out and came back again without apparent cause except that it was apt to disappear when the child became very quiet and to reappear when he showed some general activity. While admitting inhibition of the "external" type, Wenger believes the "internal" type must also be recognized, but reinterpreted so as to be the result, instead of the cause, of muscular relaxation. He adopts the theory that afferent currents from tense or active muscles are necessary to keep the brain active. Pavlov might conceivably have adopted this retroflex theory of internal inhibition, but it is more likely that he would have come back with a question as to the cause of the muscular relaxation.

TYPES OF CONDITIONING EXPERIMENTS

There are so many streams of post-Pavlovian study of CR that one scarcely knows how to arrange the material. It could be arranged according to the unconditioned reflex on which the conditioning is built— salivary, autonomic, knee jerk, lid reflex, hand withdrawal from shock. Or it could be arranged according to species of animal, with special reference to the question whether human beings can be conditioned. It could be arranged according to the formal procedure of the experiment, for not all conditioning experiments are alike when closely examined. Or we could set up certain important questions to be answered, as: "Is CR in human adults based on a voluntary response?" "On the contrary, is voluntary control based on conditioning?" "Is CR best conceived as an adjustment to the situation?" "Is it a reflex attached to a new stimulus?" "Is backward conditioning possible, or must the conditioned stimulus always precede the unconditioned?" "Does the conditioning experiment furnish a fundamental scheme of the learning process?" Such questions cannot be attacked without some preliminary account of the concrete experiments. The order of treatment adopted here, for want of a better, is to stay in the animal laboratory long enough to identify the different forms of procedure which properly come under the head of conditioning; next to advance to the human laboratory and ask what conditioned responses have been established in human beings; and finally to attack the "important questions" some of which will inevitably be touched upon in describing the various experiments.

Definition of a conditioning experiment. Now that some knowledge of CR has become common property, there is a tendency to broaden and flatten the meaning of the term, so as to speak of "becoming conditioned to the noises of the street" when we mean becoming negatively adapted to them, or to say "becoming conditioned to a friend's peculiarities" when we mean that we have learned how to deal with them. The term conditioning is made to cover all forms of learning. From the psychologist's point of view such broadening makes the premature assumption that all learning can be reduced to conditioning in the strict sense of the term. The experimentalist in particular demands that conditioning should be defined operationally, that is by reference to the procedure of the conditioned response experiment. So we find Hilgard (1936 a) limiting CR data "to laboratory experiments in which there occurs an alteration in response tendencies in respect to a (conditioned) stimulus by virtue of its repeated presentation in a controlled relationship with another (unconditioned) stimulus which with relative regularity evokes a response from the beginning of the experiment."

Nothing is said in the above definition regarding the original response to the conditioned stimulus. This stimulus must be strong or definite enough to arouse attention at least—looking, listening, sniffing and so forth—some form of "investigatory response." But it should not originally arouse the same response as the unconditioned stimulus—or, if it does, the two similar responses to the conditioned and unconditioned stimuli should at first be separate and distinguishable in the record. We are justified in reformulating our definition as follows: *a CR experiment presents repeatedly in a constant time relationship two stimuli which at the outset arouse discrete responses. The question is whether the organism develops a pattern of response to these two stimuli.* Difficult to formulate for animal experiments is the additional underlying assumption that the synthesis is established *involuntarily*.

Even under our strict definition, there are several procedures possible in a conditioning experiment. The conditioned stimulus cannot serve as a "signal" unless it precedes the unconditioned; the experiments where it does not precede will be deferred to the topic of "backward conditioning" later in the chapter. In all other procedures we have a sequence of two sensorimotor units: the conditioned stimulus and its original response, and the unconditioned stimulus and its response. The arrangements may be such that CR (c) produces the unconditioned stimulus, as food; (b) avoids the unconditioned stimulus, as a shock; or (a) does neither, the unconditioned stimulus arriving in due time no matter what response is made to the conditioned stimulus. The behavior pattern developed will differ according to the procedure. We will consider these three procedures in reverse order, beginning with (a) which is obviously the procedure used by Pavlov.

a. CR neither produces nor avoids the unconditioned stimulus. This procedure is well illustrated by an experiment of Liddell and coworkers (1934) which presents several points of interest for later consideration. These experimenters found the sheep to be an excellent subject for conditioning experiments. The animal stands on a table restrained from locomotion by a harness similar to the one used by Pavlov. An electrode is bound to the sheep's fore leg near the shoulder and electric shocks of moderate intensity are applied. A few seconds before each shock, a metronome begins to tick and it keeps on till the shock arrives. The shock when first given arouses violent struggling which may last for half a minute. After a few repetitions of the stimulus-pair the animal begins to struggle at the sound of the metronome. With his violent leg and trunk movements go agitated breathing and heart beat and the psychogalvanic response. As the experiment proceeds this diffuse CR gives way gradually to one that is localized and precise: at the sound of the metronome the sheep raises his head and ears, assumes a crouching position and half flexes the leg that carries the electrode; when the shock comes, the animal flexes the leg completely, replaces it on the ground and relaxes. Though the CR here does not escape the shock, it may have some value to the animal as a preparation for receiving the shock. The leg being already half flexed is jerked less violently by the reflex to the shock.

The description of this experiment would be incomplete without some account of the animal's general adjustment to the laboratory and to the experimenter and his doings.

The sheep or lamb selected for conditioning must at first be caught and forced into the laboratory. It is usually necessary to lift the animal on to the table and tighten the loops under the legs to prevent escape by struggling. It makes every effort to free itself by lunging, crouching, and jumping. Even though a bucket of oats is within reach and another sheep is standing quietly in the corner, it continues attempts to escape. In a very few days, however, it offers less opposition to the restraining routine. It is more easily led to the laboratory, eats from the bucket on the table, and crouches less frequently in the harness. Within a few days or weeks *opposition changes to willingness.* The sheep is more easily caught in the barn, stands quietly while a chain is fastened around its neck, and now it leads the experimenter from the barn to the laboratory, often tugging at its leash. Mounting the inclined platform to the table, it eats from the bucket of oats and allows the loops to be adjusted without struggling. It stands quietly when food is taken away, and even when the loops are removed from the limbs.

By the preliminary training the animal becomes adjusted to the general situation and is brought to the point of foregoing locomotion and miscellaneous activity. In the intervals of a few minutes between trials he stands in a condition of "alert quiet." The value of the conditioning experiment is that it isolates a bit of behavior for study under controlled conditions. A peculiarity of the sheep as a laboratory animal is that it will not stand quietly in harness on the table unless there is another sheep in sight. Consequently a "social sheep" is provided, eating its oats in the corner in sight of the experimental animal.

Different species of animal behave differently in harness. The white rat when strapped to a board and exposed to shocks in one leg, preceded by a warning signal, quickly develops an excited CR with struggling and squealing but makes very slow progress toward the precise, localized type (Kappauf & Schlosberg, 1937). The importance of the general situation is shown by the fact that the same animal, when free to move about a cage or runway, receiving a shock in his feet from a floor grid, preceded by the sound of a buzzer, rather quickly advances from his first excited conditioned response to a precise short run or jump which escapes the shock (Warner, 1932; Hunter, 1935 a, b). This last experiment evidently belongs under our next heading.

b. CR escapes the objectionable unconditioned stimulus. In the procedure adopted by Culler and his associates (1935) for experiments with dogs, the animal is restrained by a harness and frame, with one fore paw resting on a grid from which a shock is received; the animal terminates the shock when he lifts his paw, and escapes the shock altogether

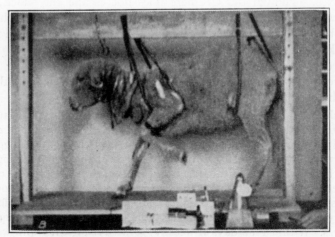

FIG. 29–A. (Liddell, James & Anderson, 1934.) Well developed CR to metronome, the unconditioned stimulus being a brief series of shocks to the foreleg. At the shock, the leg is drawn up still further.

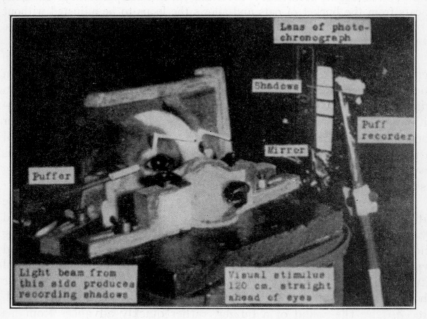

FIG. 29–B. (Hilgard & Marquis, 1935.) The dog's body is in a specially constructed box. Paper eyelashes, glued to the lids, intercept a cross-light and cast shadows on the lens of a Dodge pendulum photochronograph. The unconditioned stimulus is a puff of air against the right eye, recorded by a puff from a side tube against the puff recorder. The conditioned stimulus is a flash of light, part of which is reflected by the mirror to the photographic record.

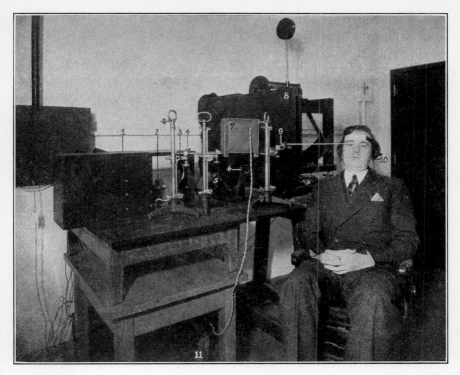

FIG. 29–C. (L. Dick, to appear in *Ar Ps*, 1938.) Attached to the lid by adhesive tape is a lever, its far end carrying a small concave mirror which reflects a beam of light upon a moving strip of sensitive paper. The conditioned and unconditioned stimuli are auditory.

1. Light source for time line.
2. Telechron motor; on the armature is a revolving toothed wheel which interrupts the light from (1) at regular intervals.
3. Plano-convex lens.
4. Mirror which reflects light from (9) to (6).
5. Wash light.
6. Slit of photochronograph, and marker to record presentation of stimuli.
7. Light source for response record.
8. Dodge pendulum photochronograph.
9. Concave mirror, on end of lever, reflecting light from (7) to (4).
10. Earphones for presentation of stimuli.

by lifting his paw at the sound of a tone which starts 2 sec. before the shock. The shock at first brings excited behavior, and after a few tone-shock combinations the excited behavior starts at the tone and before the shock. This excited type of CR gives way in the course of 100 or more repetitions to a perfectly matter-of-fact lifting of the paw at each sounding of the tone, the foot being replaced when the time for the shock has passed. The same procedure was tried on dogs deprived by operation of the entire cerebral cortex (Culler & Mettler, 1934; Girden & Culler, 1937). The decerebrate dog developed the diffuse, excited type of CR almost as quickly as the intact animal, but made no progress in hundreds of trials toward the adaptive response of lifting the paw only. That any conditioning at all is possible in the absence of the cortex is a finding of great interest, and equally important is the inability to acquire the skilled and practical movement.

When the animal escapes the shock by lifting the paw at the sound of the bell, he has no direct evidence that the shock is in the grid nor any precise indication of when the grid is safe again. His replacement of the paw on the grid is apt to be somewhat hesitant. The procedure was improved by introducing a buzzer to serve as an index of the condition of the grid (Finch & Culler, 1935; Culler & others, 1935). The buzzer was wired in parallel with the grid so as to sound while the grid was "hot" and at no other time. The animal after training lifted his foot at the tone and replaced it promptly and firmly when the buzz ended. On replacing his paw, "the dog breathes freely again, and visibly relaxes."

In the procedure without buzzer there is no "reinforcement" except when the animal omits the CR and so gets the shock. The buzzer, when used, serves as a substitute reinforcement and makes the CR much more stable. If the shock is cut out but the buzzer continued, extinction is very slow, but it is rapid with both shock and buzzer eliminated:

Sessions required for extinction with buzzer silent   4
   "   "   "   "   "   "   sounding   15

Buzz has become a sign of hot grid, no-buzz a sign of cold grid. The behavior sequence developed by conditioning is as follows:

Hear tone, lift paw, wait for buzz to cease, replace paw and relax.

Schlosberg (1937) has shown that a stable and successful avoidance response cannot be regarded as a pure example of conditioning. Successful avoidance means absence of reinforcement by the unconditioned stimulus and should therefore lead to extinction.

c. CR produces the unconditioned stimulus. This form of conditioning experiment has been found suitable for work with children by Ivanov-Smolensky (1927; see Razran, 1933 a, p. 48), and for work with rats by Skinner (1932, 1933, 1935). In Skinner's experiment the unconditioned stimulus is a pellet of food delivered by a machine when a bar over the food pan is pressed down. The rat is placed in a cage containing very little except the food pan and the bar. When the rat in exploring the cage places his paws on the bar and presses a little, the food pellet falls with a click into the pan. The machine contains an ample supply of pellets and delivers one every time the bar is depressed, at the same time recording the fact on a kymograph which thus gives a time record of the animal's responses. The stimulus-response unit conditioned in this experiment is not a new unit, like the metronome-saliva connection established in the Pavlov experiment. It is originally present as an exploratory response, and is transformed into a definite food-getting response. It is extinguished by stopping the supply of pellets or by the rat's becoming satiated. It shows spontaneous recovery after extinction.

The Skinner experiment bridges the gap between the more usual experiment in conditioning and the puzzle-box experiment so much used in the study of animal learning. The field of possible trial and error is limited by the bareness of the cage, and the trials are repeated at the animal's option; otherwise it is a typical learning experiment. Yet Skinner and also Hilgard (1937) have shown it to be a genuine conditioning experiment. As in the Pavlov experiment we start with the following sequence of events: conditioned stimulus—investigatory response, followed promptly by food—eating. The difference between the two experiments lies in the investigatory response: Pavlov's dog pricked up his ears, Skinner's rat depressed a lever and so produced an environmental result. If the rat let his pressure become too weak he got no more food; if the dog allowed his ear movements to fade away the food came just the same. Pricking up the ears could undoubtedly be established in the conditioned behavior sequence if the experimenter arbitrarily gave food only when this movement was made. Almost exactly this result was obtained by Grindley (1932) in an experiment on a guinea pig. Food was given when the animal turned his head to the right at the sound of a buzzer. Typical conditioning and extinction results were obtained.

CONDITIONING IN HUMAN CHILDREN

It is of special interest to determine how early in life a conditioned response can be developed. The feeding bottle is used as the unconditioned, a sound or light as the conditioned stimulus. CR is easily established in the second month after birth, and differentiation between two sounds in the third month (Kasatkin & Levikova, 1935 a, b). And this is not the lower limit. D. P. Marquis (1931) tried a similar experiment on neonates in a maternity hospital. Ten infants were never fed during the first ten days from birth except in the laboratory where they received mother's milk by bottle. The baby lay on a cot which registered body movements, and the sucking movements were registered by a tambour system with a receiving bulb under the chin. Feeding time was divided into several short periods before each of which a buzzer sounded. It sounded for 5 sec. and then the bottle was given. After 3–6 days signs of conditioning appeared; crying and general activity ceased at the sound of the buzzer and mouth opening and sucking movements began before the reception of the bottle. Since the cerebral cortex, from its lack of myelinization and of "brain currents," is believed not to be functional in the first ten days after birth, the result is in line with the conditioning found in decerebrate animals, and indicates the possibility of subcortical conditioning.

On older children, Pavlov's main findings have been duplicated in the Russian laboratories of Krasnogorski and others (see Razran, 1933 a). Saliva is collected from the ducts of one or more glands through a cup attached by suction to the inner surface of the cheek or to the floor of the mouth.   The cup and a surrounding groove are hollowed out of a metal disk, the two cavities being provided with separate tubes leading out of the mouth.   The inner cup is fitted over the opening of the duct and held in position by exhausting the air from the outer groove.   Young children are rather easily conditioned, and the more so up to the age of three or four.   Beyond that age conditioning becomes progressively less dependable.

CONDITIONING OF HUMAN ADULTS

The fact just mentioned, that conditioning becomes less dependable as the human child grows up, suggests that an O must perhaps be naive in order to be conditioned.   An adult who does become conditioned in a laboratory experiment is likely to feel that a trick has been played on him and that he has been "fooled."   Quite a variety of reflexes have been used in attempts to condition human adults.

The salivary response.   An early experiment by Lashley (1916), in which he collected the saliva by a device similar to the one just described, gave rather negative results.   A more convenient way of securing the saliva was employed by Razran (1935): a roll of dental cotton is weighed, placed in the mouth for one minute, and weighed again.   The increase in weight measures the saliva collected.   O refrains from swallowing even during the intervals of 1–2 min. when no roll is in the mouth, and thus a series of rolls gives the output in periods of 2–3 min.   With this technique Razran obtained the salivary CR from nearly all of 37 students. But the CR was notably unstable, appearing and disappearing and varying in amount.   It did not increase progressively with the progress of training, nor did the extinction procedure succeed with any regularity. When two or more Os served together, more regular CRs were obtained, as if the Os were less self-conscious.

In this experiment, O's *attitude* made a great difference.   The attitude could be positive or favorable, negative, indifferent, sometimes shifting from positive to negative.   These attitudes explain the frequent failure of adults to be conditioned and the instability of the CR.   The fact seems to be, not that the human adult has lost the power of being conditioned, but that he exercises more control over his responses (Razran, 1936).

Conditioned withdrawal.   As he explains in his book (1933), Bekhterev the "reflexologist," a contemporary and rival of Pavlov in CR work, became dissatisfied with the salivary response and believed that a motor CR would mean more for human behavior.   He found that withdrawal of the hand or foot from an electric shock was a response which could be conditioned in adults.   With regard to the question whether the adult's response was a true reflex, he admitted that suggestion and knowledge of the situation played a part; but he showed that the motor CR, when well established, was not easily checked or inhibited, and that when O tried to mimic his own CR the voluntary imitation was very imperfect. Many variations of the experiment have been conducted in Bekhterev's laboratory (see Razran, 1934).

This conditioned withdrawal experiment was adopted by Watson, the behaviorist (1916). The subject's hand rested on two electrodes, a broad one under the heel of the hand and a small one under the tip of the middle finger where the shock was felt. The conditioned stimulus, a bell, was sounded alone to make sure that it gave no hand withdrawal before conditioning. "We give next the bell and shock simultaneously for about five trials; then again offer the bell. If the reaction does not appear, we give five more stimulations with the bell and current simultaneously,—etc. The CR makes its appearance at first haltingly, i.e., it will appear once and then disappear. Punishment is then again given. It may next appear twice in succession and again disappear. After a time it begins to appear regularly every time the bell is offered."

We notice that though the withdrawal of the hand did not escape the shock then being given (since bell and shock were simultaneous), further shocks were avoided as soon as O took the hint and withdrew his hand at every sound of the bell. O learned what was expected of him, so Watson believed, and yet the response showed the characteristics of an involuntary movement: it came in, not at once, but after 15–30 trials, and at first it was a diffuse bodily response, later becoming restricted to the hand.

Modified forms of the hand withdrawal experiment. An often used procedure was introduced by Hamel (1919): the sound is given 1–2 sec. *before* the shock. If O withdraws his hand promptly at the sound he escapes the shock, otherwise he gets it on every trial. Hamel had no success with this procedure as long as he used a weak shock, but when he made the shock strong enough to be dreaded, he found O reacting quickly to the sound. Quickly, yes—but with a latency of about 190 ms, about the same as the voluntary reaction time to the same stimulus and much too long for a striped-muscle reflex. From this objective evidence, and from the introspection of his Os, Hamel concluded that the so-called conditioned hand withdrawal was essentially voluntary or at least controlled by mental factors. Schilder's results on repeating this experiment (1929) show the importance of attitude. The warning signal was a flash of light and the shock was strong though endurable. The five adult Os were given no instructions but assumed that their task was to keep their hand on the electrode and take the shock. When the hand did withdraw before the shock, they felt silly and ashamed and increased their effort to keep the hand in place. It is not strange that no progressive conditioning was obtained in the long experiment of 15–25 sessions.

Neither the original Bekhterev-Watson experiment nor Hamel's modification is well adapted for inquisitive adults. If given no instructions they usually assume that E wishes them to take the shock and that they are beating his game if they escape the shock by hand withdrawal; whereas E regards the experiment as a success if O does withdraw. Suppose E were frank with O and instructed him as follows: "I will give you strong shocks preceded (or accompanied) by sounds. I wish to discover how soon you will learn to avoid the shock by withdrawing the hand at the sound." The experiment would lose all point.

A possible improvement is to minimize O's conscious participation by giving him some interesting *occupation during the experiment.* In an experiment of Thorndike & Lorge (reported by Thorndike, 1932, pp. 412, 604), O had an interesting book to read. An electric bell sounded frequently, and usually a strong shock in the fingers followed. As soon as O lifted his fingers, the shock ceased, and if he lifted them promptly at the sound of the bell he escaped the shock. The instructions were to place the hand on the electrodes and let it behave normally. From time to time, during a sitting of 1–2 hours, the shock was omitted as a test of conditioning.

From O's point of view, the bell, shock and hand movement were distractions that disturbed his reading. There was no way of avoiding both the shocks and the hand movements, but hand-lifting could be avoided by taking the shocks as they came, or else the shocks could be avoided by lifting the hand at the sound of the bell. Few Os adopted either of these solutions deliberately, but most of them gravitated either toward consistent withdrawal at the sound or toward consistent absence of response to sound and shock alike. How many of them were conditioned, it is hard to say; it depends on the criterion adopted. All but 3 out of 31 made at least a few hand withdrawals in the tests without shock, but only 4 of the 31 reached the rather severe criterion of 9 out of 10 consecutive responses to bell alone. The authors regard the method as not successful in producing regular and automatic CR.

In still another modification of the shock-withdrawal experiment the electrode is attached to the hand so that the *withdrawal movement does not escape the shock.* (This is the Pavlov type of CR experiment, p. 102.) We have already noted the success of this method with sheep, and it is fairly successful with human adults, to judge from an experiment of Hilden (1937). A flash of light was followed by a strong shock. A photographic record was made of the (amplified) action currents of the extensor forearm muscle which produced the withdrawal movement, and of the overt hand movement also. As is well known, action currents will reveal slight muscular contractions which do not move the hand, and they start about 50 ms before an overt movement becomes visible. The Os were informed that the shock could not be escaped, and that the hand would probably jerk upward when the shock was received. They were to replace the hand and wait for the next flash and shock which came

10–40 sec. later. Of 56 college students, 21 (or 37 percent) were conditioned in the course of an hour, meeting the criterion of five successive responses to the light alone. An extinction series followed.

When the flash-shock interval was half a second, the CR preceded the shock. In its development it showed first as a weak action current without overt movement and increased irregularly till overt movement occurred. In extinction the reverse occurred, the overt movement disappearing before the action currents. Such was the typical process though in some cases the CR came in abruptly at full strength. The latencies are interesting for their bearing on the nature of the CR. The averages are shown in the table. For comparison the reaction time of voluntary responses to the light was measured.

LATENCIES OF VOLUNTARY REACTION, OF CONDITIONED RESPONSE, AND
OF THE REFLEX RESPONSE TO SHOCK

(Condensed from Hilden, 1937)

	Action current latency	Hand movement latency
Voluntary reaction	269 ms	318 ms
Conditioned response	280	329
Reflex to shock	63	120

According to the latencies CR is clearly different from the reflex but might be a voluntary reaction to the light. There was other evidence that it was not voluntary and had not developed voluntarily.

a. All the Os reported that it was involuntary.

b. Some reported trying, without success, to inhibit the response to the light alone, when they observed it occurring.

c. Some entered the experiment with full determination not to become conditioned, but were conditioned.

d. CR had no value to O as a means of avoiding the shock (though it may have lessened the unpleasant jerk of the reflex to shock).

e. CR came in gradually, disappeared gradually during extinction.

The conditioned eyelid response. Desirous of escaping from the suspicion that the CR was nothing but a voluntary movement in disguise, Cason (1922 a, b) sought for other reflexes which could be conditioned in human subjects. He tried the reactions of the pupil of the eye to light (see p. 117) and the wink or lid reflex. He succeeded in conditioning the lid reflex and it has proved to be one of the best reflexes for a human conditioning experiment (Switzer, 1930; Shipley, 1934; Hilgard, 1931; Bernstein, 1934; Miller & Cole, 1936; Rodnick, 1937). There are several reliable unconditioned or natural stimuli, besides the shock used by Cason; a blow on the cheek near the eye, a sharp sound, a puff of air against the eye ball. For stimuli to be conditioned a sound can be used, not too intense, a flash of light, not too strong, a tactual stimulus to the wrist. It is desirable to have the movement of the lid recorded, as can be successfully done by a light lever writing on a smoked drum and attached

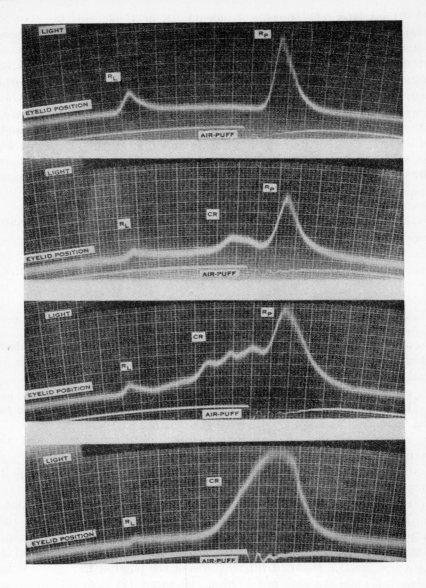

FIG. 30. (From Hilgard, 1936 c) The conditioned eyelid response in a human subject. The conditioned stimulus was a sudden moderate increase in the illumination of a disk toward which O's eyes were directed. This stimulus gave in this O a slight reflex response, marked R_L on the tracings. The unconditioned stimulus was a puff of air against one eye, which gave a strong reflex response, marked R_P. The light preceded the puff by 400 ms. The first record shows the separate responses to the two stimuli, before conditioning, and the other records show different varieties of the behavior pattern developed by conditioning. The bottom record shows what we may probably regard as the most perfect or best adapted pattern, with the CR merging smoothly into the following reflex. Time in 1/20 sec. (strong vertical lines) and 1/100 sec.

to the lid by a silk thread or a hair. Or a receiving tambour may be mounted over the eye and connected with a recording tambour by air transmission. Probably the most adequate recording system is photographic. An artifical eyelash of white paper is stuck to the lid and its movement photographed by a light athwart the eyes. The stimuli and time intervals can be recorded on the same film. The best interval to use between the conditioned and unconditioned stimuli is about 400 ms; the conditioned response then shows as an *anticipatory partial closure* of the lid, with a latency of about 200 ms after the conditioned stimulus. Test trials omitting the unconditioned stimulus—which are a nuisance because they tend toward extinction and slow the process of conditioning —can be dispensed with because of the anticipatory occurrence of CR. See Fig. 29, B and C, pp. 104, 105.

It is not absolutely necessary to obey the usual rule of CR experimenters, to the effect that the stimulus to be conditioned must not give "the" response before conditioning. It is difficult to follow this rule in experimenting on the eyelid which is likely to give a small reflex wink to any sudden stimulus. The short latency of this reflex separates it clearly from the CR, as shown in the record here given.

What is developed by the process of conditioning the wink is a rather definite, though not completely stable or uniform, behavior sequence. To quote Hilgard (1931): "A subject sees a light and the light is followed by a sound to which he automatically winks. After a number of such presentations the subject begins to wink slightly before the reflex to sound, and the reflex wink finds the lid already in motion. . . . The light has come to serve as a signal that the sound and wink are to follow. The tendency to wink to the light becomes more regular until . . . the subject seems to have acquired a set to wink to the light."

The latency of the reflex wink to sound, shock, or a puff of air against the eyeball is notably short, about 40 ms. When a reflex wink is elicited by a weak flash of light its latency is about 110 ms. Contrasted with these quick responses is the CR, which follows the conditioned stimulus with an extremely variable latency, averaging perhaps 200 ms, longer, or certainly no shorter than the voluntary reaction time of a lid response to light, which is 160–180 ms. As far as latencies indicate, the conditioned lid response might be voluntary, but we have the same evidence here as in hand withdrawal that it is involuntary. The subject may be unaware of the conditioned winks or annoyed by them, thinking he is being "fooled." The CR comes in gradually, increasing in frequency and amplitude as the series of trials advance, whereas a voluntary response comes in abruptly and is usually a complete lid closure as contrasted with the partial closure characteristic of CR. Though involuntary, the CR is tied up with conscious processes such as expectancy. O knows what is coming.

The conditioned lid response is more dependable than most others, with human adults. In an hour's session nearly every O gives at least a few anticipatory winks, and in about half of the Os a fairly stable pattern is developed. Retention is good for as long as 20 weeks (Hilgard & Campbell, 1936).

Conditioning is easier when the response is included in some larger, meaningful performance. Miller & Cole (1936) attacked this question directly. To O it was a reaction time experiment. After a ready signal he felt a tug on the wrist, reacted by pressing a key and so gave himself a shock on the cheek which elicited a reflex wink. Conditioning was extremely rapid, with nearly 100 percent of anticipatory lid responses from the 25th trial on to the end of the series of 80 reinforced trials. For the extinction series which then followed, the subjects were divided into two groups: one group continued to close the key on feeling the tug—but the current was off and they received no shock—while the other group were instructed to cease making the hand reaction. When the hand reaction was continued the conditioned lid response continued, too, and was not extinguished for many unreinforced trials, 50 or more on the average. The other group, ceasing the hand reaction, reached extinction of the lid response almost instantly, in 2 trials on the average. The results indicate, as the authors urge, that conditioning is not so much the attaching of a response to a new stimulus as it is the integrating of a particular response into a larger action system. "From the beginning of training, the hand and lid are forced into a temporal pattern of activity. . . . The result of training in this situation is the integration of the two movements. . . . The hand movement provides a reaction system into which the conditioned (lid) response may be integrated as it develops. . . . Such an integration provides the basis for more thorough conditioning than is customarily obtained." Experiments with hand withdrawal (Newhall & Sears, 1933) and even with salivation (Razran, 1936) agree in indicating that human adults are most easily conditioned when the CR is made an integral part of a larger performance.

Conditioning the knee jerk. The very first published experiment on conditioning was apparently one of Twitmyer (1902) who, without using the name, discovered the CR in the course of an investigation of the knee jerk. This reflex is elicited by a blow struck on the patellar tendon just below the knee, the actual stimulus being the sudden stretch of the quadriceps muscle above the knee. Twitmyer's Os while in a semi-reclining position, the lower leg hanging free, were given a single tap of a bell as a ready signal, and ½ sec. later received a blow on the tendon. After three or four sessions, when the bell-blow combination had been given 125 times, the leg of one O gave a quick kick at the sound of the bell, without receiving the blow. Much surprised, E followed up this observation by omitting the blow occasionally and giving the bell alone, and he obtained the same response from each of his six Os after 125–230 repetitions of the combined stimuli. The frequency of this CR increased as the experiment progressed. It was more frequent when O clenched his fist or in other well-known ways facilitated the knee jerk. Though perfectly conscious of these responses to the bell alone, O was unable to inhibit them and insisted that they were involuntary. Twitmyer's interpretation assumed that every incoming sensory impulse diffuses itself over the entire nervous system and that, after many repetitions of bell followed by knee jerk, a "habit of interaction between the two involved centers" is developed. "The connecting pathway of discharge has become well worn so that the sound of the bell alone is an adequate stimulus to the movement."

Later investigators, repeating Twitmyer's experiment with improved technique, agree that the knee jerk can be conditioned—or, at least, that a CR of the quadriceps muscle can be built up on the basis of the knee jerk. Instead of recording the foot movement, they prefer a direct record of the thickening of the quadriceps and find the muscle to show conditioned contractions which are too weak to move the foot. They have thought it best to supply O with reading matter or some other interesting occupation so as to minimize his conscious participation in the leg movements.

Schlosberg (1928) gave a bell tap $\frac{1}{3}$ sec. before the blow on the tendon, while O was reading or otherwise occupied, and obtained some anticipatory quadriceps responses and some responses to the bell alone in test trials. He obtained the CR from 44 of his 49 adult Os, but emphasized its instability. It was least undependable when the knee jerk was facilitated by clenching the fist at the sound of the bell. In motor characteristics it was quite different from the knee jerk itself. The knee jerk has a very short latency (30 ms) and a quick pick-up or recruitment, while the CR showed a long latency (250–500 ms) and a slow pick-up. Graphic records showed a close resemblance between the CR and a voluntary kick, and the testimony of some Os (Schlosberg, 1932) indicated that CR was semi-voluntary in some cases. One said, "I feel as if I could stop the kick, if I wanted to, but I am just letting it go on." The author says, "The conditioned knee-jerk seems to be a bit of behavior more or less broken off from our usually integrated patterns." His physiological interpretation distinguishes between the true knee jerk, which is a quick spinal reflex, and the superimposed cerebral component of the movement seen in reinforcing the knee jerk by clenching the fist. What becomes conditioned is the cerebral component, not the spinal reflex.

A similar conception was suggested by the experiments of Wendt (1930). Instead of using a bell, he struck a blow on each patellar tendon, $\frac{1}{5}$ sec. earlier at the left knee than at the right. The first blow, besides eliciting the reflex of its own leg, was the conditioned stimulus for a kick of the other leg. Some form of CR was obtained from 15 of the 17 adult Os. There were two types of CR, one of medium and one of long latency, both being much slower than the reflex knee jerk, as shown by the averages:

	Latency	Recruitment time
Reflex knee jerk	30–40 ms	40 ms
Medium-latency CR	120–180	60
Long-latency CR	200–300	100

The medium-latency response was bilateral and easily obtained. In one O it even appeared prior to any conditioning, in the preliminary trials when only one tendon was struck. The author considered it a pre-existing brain-stem reflex which was simply sensitized by the repeated bilateral stimulation of the legs.

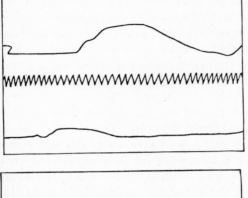

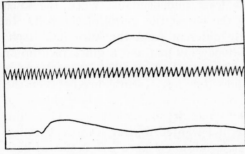

The long-latency response appeared only after many trials and was unstable and easily extinguished. It was always confined to the leg stimulated second; it fused with and reinforced the second knee jerk. It had the earmarks of cortical adaptation to the stimulus pattern—of an involuntary cortical participation in what was going on in the legs.

Conditioned autonomic responses. Special theoretical importance has been attached to the question whether these involuntary responses can be conditioned, because conditioning is conceived as an involuntary process. Though autonomic activity is largely unconscious it is closely related to emotion and effort as best seen in the case of the psychogalvanic response (p. 282). Several autonomic responses have been successfully conditioned.

FIG. 31. (From Wendt, 1930.) Reflex, conditioned, and voluntary "knee jerks." The stimulus in each case was a blow on the left patellar tendon, showing as a slight nick in the tracing, followed by the knee jerk proper of the left quadriceps. In 1, there then follows a voluntary kick of the right leg, and in 2, a conditioned response of the right leg. Time in 1/50 sec. cycles.

1. *Contraction and dilation of the pupil of the eye.* The circular fibers of the iris, which constrict the pupil, are controlled by the cranial autonomic, and the radial, dilator fibers by the sympathetic. The pupil contracts reflexly to increased illumination of the retina and dilates in decreased illumination. The pupil also contracts in looking at a near object and dilates in looking at a far object (so that anyone can contract

or dilate his pupil at will by directing his eyes to objects at different distances). Further, the pupil dilates in excitement and at any sudden stimulus—an index of sympathetic activity, much like the psychogalvanic response.

Cason (1922 a) undertook to condition both the contraction and the dilation of the pupil, basing his attempt on the pupillary reflexes to light and dark. The bell which he used as a conditioned stimulus gave pupil dilation before conditioning. One training series consisted of 400 trials like this: O is in the dark with dilated pupil, a bright light is turned on for a second causing the pupil to contract, and simultaneously the bell rings. At the end of this training series it would be very nice to give the bell without the light and observe whether the pupil contracted—if the pupil could be observed in the dark. The best that could be done in the tests before and after training was to observe the size of the pupil under the influence of light-plus-bell and under the influence of light alone. Before training light-plus-bell gave a larger pupil than light alone, after training light-plus-bell gave a smaller pupil than light alone. There was some conditioning of pupil contraction to the sound of the bell.

To obtain conditioned dilation, the training series consisted of trials which began with the light on and the pupil contracted; the light was turned off and the bell rang while the pupil was dilating. Light-plus-bell gave a larger pupil than light alone, both before and after this training, but the difference was greater after than before, giving evidence of the desired conditioning. Several variations of the experiment gave confirmatory results. The conditioned pupillary responses were slowly established and quickly extinguished.

Conditioned Pupillary Responses

(*Cason, 1922 a*)

Effect of sounding a bell on the pupil diameter, under constant illumination. Comparable results were obtained from four Os whose pupil diameter was 4 mm without the bell. In the training series, bell and dilation were combined for two Os, bell and contraction for the other two.

Bell, before conditioning, made the pupil	.21 mm larger
Bell, after conditioning to dilation, made the pupil	.34 mm larger
Bell, after conditioning to contraction, made the pupil	.26 mm smaller

A word about Cason's apparatus. He measured the horizontal diameter of the pupil by a pupillometer consisting of a small telescope through which E viewed O's eye. The telescope contained two vertical hairs the separation of which was adjusted by E so as just to enclose the pupil.

Hudgins (1933) used similar apparatus with an attachment which recorded on a drum E's adjustment of the vertical hairs. During the tests, before and after training, E kept pace with the pupil changes which were thus (approximately) recorded on the drum. Hudgins wished to discover whether the pupil could be conditioned to verbal commands spoken by E or O, such as "Contract!" and "Relax!" Direct conditioning to such stimuli was not accomplished, but success was achieved by a training process consisting of several stages. In stage 1, the stimulus to be conditioned was a bell which sounded along with the light and while the pupil was contracting. When conditioned response to the bell had been established, (in 200–225 repetitions of bell-plus-light, divided between two sessions), stage 2 followed: the light and bell circuits were closed when O squeezed on a hand dynamometer. E commanded, "contract," O squeezed, the bell rang, the light shone in his eyes and his pupils contracted. After 3–4 seconds, E commanded "relax" and stopped the bell; O relaxed his hand, the light went out and the pupils dilated. After 200 trials of this sort, the bell was omitted and the command "contract" plus hand squeeze gave pupil contraction, while the command "relax" plus hand relaxation gave pupil dilation. In stage 3, O received the verbal commands, repeated them subvocally, and squeezed and relaxed with his hand so turning the light on and off, as before. After 200 trials of this sort the hand movements were omitted, and the pupil obeyed the mere verbal commands, whether spoken by E or (either aloud or subvocally) by O himself. Once established, the CR to verbal command was much less easily extinguished than the CR to the bell. *In this experiment voluntary control of the pupil was built up by a process of conditioning.*

One easy experiment in conditioning the pupil seems not to have been tried, though it would almost surely succeed. Use as the unconditioned response the dilation that occurs at an electric shock, and for the stimulus to be conditioned something very mild, like a picture of a tree or the spoken words, "Very good." Use the mild stimulus as a warning signal, applying it regularly a second or two before the shock.

2. *The conditioned psychogalvanic response (PGR).* The reason for venturing the prediction just made with regard to pupil dilation is the known fact that PGR, a closely related response, is readily conditioned to a warning signal. Darrow (1932, see p. 288) and others have so found. Switzer (1934, 1935 b) and Rodnick (1937) have obtained delayed conditioned PGR, with shock as the unconditioned stimulus and a steady faint light lasting for the 15–20 sec. preceding the shock as the warning signal or conditioned stimulus. Only a few trials are needed to establish the CR. Its latency, measured from the onset of the light, increases from about 5 sec. in the first few trials to about 10 sec. after many repetitions—a result closely paralleling that obtained by Pavlov with the delayed salivary response.

3. *Vasomotor conditioned responses.* If one hand is thrust into cold water the other hand also becomes cold through vasoconstriction, or if the first hand is held in warm water the other becomes warm through vasodilation. These crossed vasomotor reflexes lend themselves to a conditioning experiment. Menzies (1937) measured the temperature of the crossed hand by aid of a thermopile and succeeded in conditioning the vasomotor response to such stimuli as buzz, light, body posture, and

spoken or imagined words. The CR was fairly stable and resistant to extinction.

SIGNIFICANCE OF THE CONDITIONED RESPONSE

From the numerous experiments it is clear that various kinds of responses—of the glands and of striped and unstriped muscles—can be conditioned in men as well as animals. The peculiarities of human conditioning are however important. Man likes to maintain control over his behavior, and his favoring or disfavoring attitude toward a response is a strong factor in determining whether it shall be established. The conditioning process succeeds best in the human subject when it forms a part of some performance in which he is actively engaged. A response at first entirely involuntary, like dilation of the pupil, may be conditioned to verbal commands and so become subject to some measure of voluntary control.

It has seemed to psychologists that CR might afford the key to a theory of learning. The laws of conditioning might be accepted as fundamental and tried out on other forms of learning to see whether they hold good. Analogies can easily be found but the real question is whether from the laws of conditioning we can definitely predict what will happen in maze learning, problem solution, memorizing a list of nonsense syllables or a poem, or in impressing a scene on our memory. Serious attempts to make and test such predictions are under way (Hull, 1934 b). Here we will merely examine two characteristics of CR which seem at first sight quite out of line with other types of learning. These have to do with "extinction" and with the question of "backward conditioning."

The problem of extinction. One of Pavlov's laws is that repeated application of the conditioned stimulus, without the unconditioned, causes a progressive decline to zero of CR. Let us first ask whether this law holds good of human conditioning. It seems to hold good, but with exceptions. The exceptions are numerous if we take the law as demanding a regular, progressive decline. Individuals show much irregularity, but the average for a group does show a gradual decline. Such a result has been obtained with the conditioned wink (Shipley, 1934; Hilgard & Campbell, 1936), with hand withdrawal (Hilden, 1937), and with the PGR (Switzer, 1935 a). The conditioned pupillary response according to Hudgins (1933) was quickly extinguished except when the stimulus was a verbal command. The vasomotor responses established by Menzies (1937) were in general not easily extinguished. The salivary response seldom showed regular extinction in Razran's experiments (1935). Responses indicative of an emotional state of dread seem rather resistant to extinction (Watson & Raynor, 1920; Wever, 1930). Like conditioning itself, extinction depends much upon set and attitude; but on the whole a theory of human learning should reckon with the reality of an extinguishing process.

Carried over to the memorizing of a poem the law of extinction would seem to demand that the poem should never be recited without constant reinforcement from the printed page; the oftener it was recited independently the more it would be extinguished and lost. Memory experiments, on the contrary, show that such recitations make for quick learning and firm retention (p. 208). The apparent contradiction vanishes when two facts are recognized: (1) extinction is not forgetting; (2) recitation is reinforced.

Extinction is not forgetting. The extinguished response is not lost but suspended, as was clear from spontaneous recovery and disinhibition in Pavlov's experiments (pp. 93, 96). It is true that repeated extinctions with never any reinforcement will finally put CR out of commission—apparently by firmly establishing the contrary response.

But may not a once-extinguished response be at least partially forgotten? Is retention of the response just as good after extinction? Hilgard & Campbell (1936) in the experiment already cited (p. 114) first established a conditioned lid response to a light, and at the end of the training extinguished the response in one group of students, leaving it unextinguished in the other group. Tested on the following day the two groups showed no difference. "The permanent effects of extinction, if any, are slight."

Recitation is reinforced. The unconditioned stimulus, or reinforcement, plays a double role in the conditioning experiment. It localizes and also motivates the CR. A shock delivered to the dog's right fore paw localizes the response there, and also makes it worth while to lift the paw from the grid. These two roles, as Culler & Finch showed (1935), are not inseparable. In their experiment already cited the shock was accompanied by a buzz which served as an index that the grid was "hot." The buzz had no localizing effect, but it took the place of the shock as a motivating factor. When the shock was discontinued but the buzzer left in the circuit, extinction was very slow, though it was rapid when buzzer and shock were both removed (p. 106).

In memorizing a poem the printed page is the localizing or directive unconditioned stimulus, but the motivating reinforcement comes from some other source, often social in nature. In laying aside the book for a try at recitation, the learner does not remove the motivating factor. He is eager to see if he can recite. In arithmetic, reinforcement is afforded by checking the answer; in learning a piano piece, by the sound of the piece as played from memory. Human beings show great fertility in finding substitute incentives, and their conditioned responses may thus be made very resistant to extinction.

But human learned responses are often extinguished, without being forgotten. A child has a brother George. He reads a story in which there is much talk of George, and at first thinks of his brother, but this response becomes extinguished as he gets into the story. It is extinguished only within the context of the story and is spontaneously recovered as soon as he shuts the book and gets back into the real environment. To be in possession of a learned response does not mean that you are forced to make it every time its stimulus occurs. You know the color names but are not compelled to say them whenever you see the colors. There must be some incentive. So the facts of extinction do not throw CR out of line with other learning (Peak & Deese, 1937).

The question of backward conditioning. In memory experiments, as in ordinary experience, there is evidence of backward associations (p. 27), but in conditioning experiments it seems illogical to expect a response to become attached to a following stimulus, and the conditioned stimulus is almost always made to precede the response to be conditioned. This apparent discrepancy between conditioning and other learning has been attacked in two ways. Some experimenters have sought to disprove the reality of backward associations, while others have sought to prove the reality of backward conditioning.

Pavlov's experience (1927, p. 27) showed that the conditioned must precede the unconditioned stimulus in order to establish a stable CR. A metronome which began to tick a few seconds *after* food was given acquired inhibitory rather than excitatory properties—it became, in fact, a signal to stop eating, since only a small portion of food was given. In later experiments (Pavlov, p. 393) it was discovered that very early in the training series the metronome following the food did have excitatory properties, which gave way to inhibitory as the sequence impressed itself on the organism.

From Pavlov's findings we should expect some backward conditioning after a very short training series, but none after a long series; and this is about the conclusion to draw from the apparently contradictory results obtained with human adults. Switzer (1930) obtained backward conditioning of the lid reflex in 18 out of 20 students after a training series lasting only 5–15 minutes and comprising 7–60 paired stimuli. A smart tap just below the eye elicited the reflex wink which was immediately followed by the sound of a buzzer. Cason (1935) after a training series lasting 2½–4 hours got no clear instances of backward conditioning. He used no artificial stimulus to elicit the wink, but arranged apparatus so that every natural wink during O's reading immediately produced a click from a telegraph sounder.

Systematic studies of the most favorable interval between the two stimuli were made by Bernstein (1934) for the lid reflex and by Wolfle (1932) for hand withdrawal. An interval of $\frac{3}{10}$ sec., with the conditioned stimulus preceding, was about the most favorable. A few scattering CRs were obtained when the two stimuli were simultaneous or when the conditioned stimulus followed the unconditioned.

A spurious appearance of backward conditioning can arise from a factor pointed out by Grether (1938). A rhesus monkey, loosely restrained in a chair, was given a fear stimulus to which he gave a characteristic response. An electric bell sounded 3 sec. after the fear stimulus. After 10 repetitions of this combination the monkey gave the characteristic fear response to the bell alone. Same result from a second monkey. A good instance of backward conditioning, so it seemed till two control monkeys were given the series of 10 fear stimuli, while in the chair, but without any use of the bell. At the end of this series the control monkeys gave the fear response to the bell or to any sudden noise. All the animals gave the same response when brought back to the room on another day, replaced in the chair and again given the bell as a stimulus, but outside the laboratory the bell aroused no fear response. The fear response had become conditioned to the laboratory situation; it had been sensitized by the series of fear stimuli.

It is too early to state a categorical conclusion on backward conditioning, but the concept is certainly not a safe one to assume in explaining other phenomena of learning.

Is the conditioned response the original reflex attached to a new stimulus? On first hearing of the CR some psychologists, including the present writer, fell into this "substitute stimulus" conception, which was rather convenient for a theory of learning and which fitted some of the facts fairly well. The salivary CR (considered apart from the accompanying motor response) is like the natural salivary reflex, only weaker, and the same is true of the conditioned psychogalvanic response and of the primitive, excited response to a bell or buzz which is immediately followed by a shock. The more exact analysis possible in the case of the wink, knee jerk, and hand withdrawal reveals, not the original reflex simply attached to a substitute stimulus, but a qualitatively different response. The lid reflex and the knee jerk are quick throw movements, and this quick throw is not present in the CR. The primary or lower reflex centers are apparently not involved in the CR, and it is somewhat misleading to speak of the "conditioned knee jerk" or of the "conditioned lid reflex."

The qualitative difference between the original reflex and the fully developed CR is sometimes striking in the animal experiments. The rat which at first gives a jerky hop on receiving a shock from the floor acquires the CR of jumping over a fence into a safe place (Warner, 1932). The sheep, though unable to avoid the shock, comes to assume a definite position of readiness. The dog gives up his first agitated struggling and lifts his paw calmly from the grid at the warning signal. We should not, indeed, make these statements too absolute; some dogs never do give up struggling, and the withdrawal movement, though deliberate in some dogs, retains in others the sharp, brief character of the withdrawal to shock (Kellogg, 1938).

Conditioning develops a behavior sequence. A temporal pattern shows clearly in the tracings of the lid response (p. 112). CR shows as the first phase of a compound act culminating in the reflex. The same would obviously be true of the sheep's CR as described. Even the salivary CR is a preliminary phase in a sequence culminating in taking the food.

When the two stimuli, conditioned and unconditioned, are given simultaneously, no motor pattern is developed, as far as we know, and the conditioning may consist simply in a fusion or confusion of the two stimuli. O becomes conditioned to the stimulus complex as a unit.

The behavior sequence, when it occurs, is an adjustment to the sequence of stimuli received. It is a temporary adjustment to the peculiarities of the environment. It shows the tendency of the organism to participate as a whole in the response elicited by the unconditioned stimulus. It is an index of cortical participation in reflex activity.

Adjustment to the objective situation is shown by certain experiments in the transfer of a CR from one muscle to another. In an experiment by Gibson and coworkers (1932), students were conditioned to withdraw the right hand from an electrode at a buzz which began $\frac{1}{10}$ sec. before the shock. When after 10–52 repetitions they began to show conditioned withdrawal to buzz alone, they were requested to shift their position so as to place the left hand on the electrode. The buzz stimulus was then given alone and 8 out of 13 Os withdrew the left hand from the electrode. This transferred CR was made by different muscles from those supposedly conditioned; but the CR was still a withdrawal from the same object. It should be added that O's attention in this experiment was occupied in reading aloud.

Instead of transferring the CR from one hand to the other Wickens (1938) transferred it from the extensor to the flexor movement of the same finger. In the training series the middle finger of the right hand rested, palm down, on an electrode and withdrew from the strong shock by an upward movement. The conditioned stimulus was a buzz preceding the shock by about half a second. When CR to buzz had been established, E turned O's hand palm up in the same apparatus and gave the buzz. Of 18 students, 10 immediately responded by an upward movement of the finger and all but one of the remainder acquired this movement after a few reinforcements. Considered as an upward withdrawal from the electrode this response was the same as the one originally conditioned, but considered merely as a muscular movement it was antagonistic. It was not a particular movement that had become conditioned but a withdrawal from a particular object.

As an index of adjustment to the temporary environment through participation of the cortex in activities which seem at first sight to be confined to the reflex level, the conditioned response is not as simple an affair as it once seemed. It is perhaps no more simple than other types of learned response, and we cannot regard it as an element out of which behavior is built. It does open a window into the dynamics of behavior and it furnishes a tool for the investigation of the senses in animals, of drug effects, and even of nervous strain and breakdown.

CHAPTER VI

MAZE LEARNING

I F WE are to have any general laws of learning we should evidently base them on a wider survey of learning processes than is afforded by human memorizing of verbal material. A variety of materials should be used and animals and young children as well as adults should be given a chance to show how they learn. The human adult makes free use of language and of intellectual devices which are probably not fundamental in learning. The simpler animal processes, if we can discover them, will provide a frame into which the elaborate human learning can be fitted, as we have already found in the experiments on conditioning.

The maze has been a favorite type of "lesson" first for animal and later for human subjects. It has sometimes been regarded as distinctly a motor problem. Closely considered its distinctive characteristic is spatial rather than motor. With the introduction of "temporal" and "mental" mazes both the motor and the spatial characteristics are minimized and one wonders what is left of the typical maze. The remaining characteristic which differentiates maze learning from the learning of typical verbal material is that in the latter the right responses are given, while in the maze they have to be discovered by the learner. The maze contains blind alleys; it presents a series of "choice points" at which the right alternatives have to be found by exploration.

ANIMAL MAZE LEARNING

We could not do justice to the subject of learning without venturing a little way into the field of animal psychology, where a large share of the experimental work on learning has been done. The technique of the animal laboratory, the differences between different species and even between animals and man, are matters with which we shall not concern ourselves.

The famous "canon" of Lloyd Morgan (1894) warns us not to attribute an animal's performance to the operation of a more intellectual process such as reasoning, if it can be understood in simpler terms. This rule has been heartily adopted in animal psychology and is obviously a good rule in the abstract, but it leaves the question open as to what processes are the simpler. The animal psychologists have usually assumed movement to be simpler than perception. Judging by ourselves we should say that nothing is easier than seeing an object and that no learned reaction is simpler than recognition.

Early animal experiments in maze learning. Shortly before 1900, Thorndike at Harvard and Columbia, and Small at Clark University introduced cats, dogs and rats into the psychological laboratory, and invented two types of experiment which soon became standard in animal psychology and later in human psychology as well. Thorndike did more with the puzzle box or problem box, Small more with the maze. The problem box requires manipulation of some device such as a string or door button, while the maze calls for locomotion. In terms of environmental objects the maze calls for learning a path, the problem box for mastering a tool (in a broad sense). Somewhat arbitrarily, in

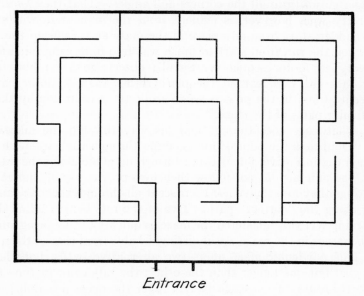

Entrance

FIG. 32. Ground plan of the Hampton Court maze as used by Small and his successors.

the present book the problem box experiment is classed with thinking and the maze is considered here under the topic of learning.

Small's study (1899, 1900) was qualitative rather than quantitative, and for that very reason his careful observations still deserve attention as an introduction to maze learning. He built a small-size reproduction of the famous Hampton Court maze and used it as an instrument of research. It is a complex, unstandardized maze and later students have devised many other forms in the effort to control the variables (Warner & Warden, 1927). Small's maze, measuring 6 × 8 feet over all, was constructed of wire mesh on a sawdust-covered wooden floor. Food was placed in the central room of the maze, and two white rats were placed together at the entrance. Undoubtedly they could smell, if not see, the food. Working independently they explored back and forth throughout the maze, pausing to dig in the sawdust or bite the wires, wandering in the blind alleys and retracing the main path. The first one reached the food in 13 min. The animals remained in the maze all night and on the next day covered the distance from entrance to food box in 3 min. On subsequent trials the time was still shorter and the "errors" (entering a blind alley or retracing in the main path) decreased to 1 or 2 per trial. In an intermediate stage of the learning, the rats would hesitate near the entrance and then "flash" through to the goal. They would enter a previously explored blind alley slowly and run out quickly. When not very hungry, "they 'play by the way,' strolling nonchalantly into the blind alleys, now sniffing listlessly, now with half-eager curiosity in all the corners and angles. That they *know* their way pretty well, however, is evident from the manner in which they take a sudden start from any place in the maze and 'flash' to the end." Even when the run from start to finish was free from errors, it was not a stereotyped motor sequence. Small's observations led him to the theory that the rats learned the place rather than a motor pattern. "The central fact in the process seems to be the recognition by the rats of particular parts of the maze."

By what cues does the rat find his way through the maze? By smell? Doubtless the odor of food coming through the wire-mesh walls furnished the incentive, but it could furnish no guide along the intricate path. The animals did not follow their own previous trails, for in their wanderings they must have left their scent all through the maze and not simply along the "correct" path. Two of the rats became blind during the learning, yet they mastered the maze as quickly as the seeing animals. Their behavior in the maze was indistinguishable from that of the normal rats. This particular maze offers two alternative paths, both leading to the goal but one longer than the other; the rats came in time to use the shorter route almost exclusively. After the maze was well learned, the experimenter opened a short cut which the rats, both blind and seeing, very quickly adopted. Small inferred that neither sight nor smell, but probably touch and kinesthesis, furnished the essential data for the rat's maze running.

The sensory cues in maze learning and maze running. The experiments of Small were repeated, improved in technique and greatly extended by Watson (1907). He confirmed Small's observations on the behavior matrix in which learning occurs. "Anyone familiar with the habits of the rat knows that 'curiosity' is the key note of his existence. A new situation means the releasing of a great amount of motor energy. This takes the form of a minute examination of all the surrounding territory. . . . This type of behavior stands out in bold relief against that of the fully trained animal. In the latter case the food is the emotionally exciting object." At first the rat does not venture far from the entrance; he explores a little distance, runs back and pauses a while at the entrance, then explores a little further; as a result he learns to traverse the maze in both directions. On his first exploration of a blind alley the rat is apt to go to the end of it, on the next trip only part way, and on the third he may merely hesitate at its entrance. In the final stage of mastery, the rat runs without hesitation and covers distance at the rate of two feet a second or more.

Watson sought to discover on which of the senses the rat depended for guidance in learning and running the maze. His method was to exclude one sense at a time and determine (a) whether animals that had already learned the maze could still run it without error, and (b) whether previously untrained animals could learn the maze as quickly as the normal animal.

Visual cues were excluded by darkening the room: animals trained in the light ran the maze correctly in the dark, and previously untrained ones learned as quickly in darkness as in the light. To make perfectly sure, Watson blinded some rats by removing their eyeballs, an operation from which rats recover quickly. Blind rats learned the maze as quickly as normals, and animals blinded after learning the maze showed only a slight loss in efficiency. It appeared that the essential cues were not furnished by the sense of sight.

Other rats were deprived of the sense of smell by an operation which removed the olfactory bulbs, a link in the afferent path from the nose to the brain. These anosmic animals learned the maze as readily as normals, or showed no disturbance in running a previously learned maze.

Two rats were made partially deaf by removing from each ear the tympanic membrane and ossicles and then filling the middle ear with paraffin. They learned the maze as quickly as normals.

The cutaneous senses could not be destroyed by any feasible operation, but the soles of the feet were anesthetized in trained animals without disturbing their running of the maze. Cutting short the vibrissae had the immediate effect of making the animal insecure in his movements, but 48 hours later the running of a familiar maze was perfectly normal; and previously untrained animals, without vibrissae, learned the maze in the usual time. Assuming that any important tactual cues must come from the vibrissae or soles of the feet, Watson believed that he had pretty well excluded this sense, as well as sight, smell and hearing.

By the logic of exclusion, therefore, Watson concluded that the essential cues in maze learning and running were furnished by the muscle sense, by kinesthetic receptors. Other internal senses, such as the organic and that of the semicircular canals, might play some role. The external senses were inessential, though undoubtedly employed in exploring the maze.

This conclusion obviously needed to be checked, if possible, by an experiment in which the kinesthetic sense was excluded. Much later, Lashley found a way of achieving this result in large measure, though not completely (Lashley & Ball, 1929). The afferent path from the muscles of the trunk and legs runs up the dorsal columns of the spinal cord and can be transected after exposing the cord in the neck region. After general recovery from this operation, the rat gives evidence of poor kinesthetic sensitivity by his sprawling gait, by dragging his legs in running or turning a corner, and by stepping on the dorsal surface of the fore paws. Rats that had learned a maze before this operation ran it perfectly or almost perfectly after the operation, so far as "errors" were concerned. Because of their inefficient gait they took more time, but they ran the true course without straying into blind alleys. Rats that underwent the operation before training learned the maze as readily as normal rats (Ingebritsen, 1932). These facts "argue against the primary importance of kinesthesis in maze learning" or in following a previously learned path.

By our previous logic we should now be forced to look to the organic sense or the semicircular canals for the required cues—were there not some weak links in the argument. Kinesthesis has been only partially excluded, and hearing has been only partially excluded. The same is true of touch, and Dennis (1929) found that this sense does play an important role in the maze running of blind rats. He blinded some rats, cut their vibrissae, and set them to learn a simple maze. Careful observation showed that they were touching the walls with the flank and the side of the head, and finding their way by these contacts.

That the albino rat, though his vision is not keen, can readily learn to run a maze by the aid of visual cues alone, when these are provided, is made clear by the work of several experimenters (Vincent, 1915; Walton, 1930; Robinson & Wever, 1930). If a rat has learned a maze by aid of visual cues and is then transferred to another maze of the same pattern but without the visual cues, he has to learn the maze all over again. Snygg (1935) made two duplicate mazes, and painted the one black throughout and the other black in the true path but white in the blind alleys. One group of rats had 45 trials in the all-black maze and was then transferred to the black-white maze; another group just the reverse; with results as follows, in terms of median number of trials to reach a certain criterion of learning:

First group:

| All-black maze learned first | 34 trials |
| Black-white maze learned second | 6 trials |

Second group:

| Black-white maze learned first | 7 trials |
| All-black maze learned second | 45 trials |

Two inferences are justified:

1. The rats utilize good visual cues when they can get them.

2. The rats did not carry over any automatic motor habit but were dependent on cues from the maze.

Open and enclosed mazes. In this study of cues it is important not to limit the experiments to a single type of maze. The original mazes, whether built of wood or of wire mesh, were enclosed alley mazes. They afforded no general view of the maze and so excluded one of the chief advantages of vision. They favored tactual cues from the walls of the narrow alleys. Vincent (1912) and more especially Miles (1930) introduced the open maze, or elevated maze, in which the passages are strips of wood, 1–2 inches wide, supported from beneath at such a height that the rats will not jump down and far enough apart to prevent jumping across from one passage to another. There are no side walls to afford contacts, but vision is unobstructed.

When open and enclosed mazes of the same pattern and size are tried on comparable groups of normal rats, the open maze seems to be slightly easier to learn, though the difference is not large or constant. With blind rats there is a large difference, the open maze being much harder for them. Blind rats are at a decided disadvantage in the open maze (Tsang, 1934, 1936) but not in the enclosed maze (Weaver & Stone, 1928; see their results on p. 139).

MEAN SCORES OF GROUPS OF BLIND AND SEEING RATS
IN ENCLOSED AND OPEN MAZES

(From Tsang, 1934, 1936)

The score here is the total number of blind alleys entered by a rat in his first 150 trials

	Enclosed maze		Open maze	
	M	SD_M	M	SD_M
Normal rats	99	14	75	9
Blind, first group	120	30	281	54
" second "	108	10	244	18

The revised conclusion, so far, is that no one sense furnishes the "essential cues." Either good visual cues or good non-visual cues are utilized, according as one or the other class is more available.

Alternative and multiple cues. Once we admit the possibility of alternative cues we see that Watson's experiment is capable of further development. What will be the effect of depriving the same rats of both sight and smell? According to our original logic, when we have found that neither blind rats nor anosmic rats are at any special disadvantage in learning an enclosed maze, we infer that neither sight nor smell furnishes "the essential cues" and that therefore a blind-anosmic rat should learn the maze about as well as the normal. Lindley (1930) found quite a different result, using an enclosed maze with groups of rats: normal, blind, anosmic, and blind-anosmic. The normal group learned this maze (up to a certain standard or criterion of learning) in a median number of 12 trials, the blind in 14, the anosmic in 27; but for the blind-anosmic group no median could be obtained, since only

27 percent of the group succeeded in learning the maze. For the open maze we have the extensive data of Honzik (1936) who obtained averages from large groups, 42 or more rats in each group, and tried several combinations. The learning curves are fairly represented for comparative purposes by the mean errors at the 12th and 24th trials.

MEAN ERROR PER RAT IN RUNNING THE OPEN MAZE

(From Honzik, 1936)

	after 12 trials	after 24 trials
Normal rats	.1	less than .1
Deaf rats	.2	.1
Anosmic rats	.2	.1
Blind rats	1.5	1.1
Blind-deaf rats	4.2	3.9
Blind-anosmic rats	5.8	5.4
Blind-deaf-anosmic rats	6.2	6.4

As the initial error score on this maze is about 6.5, the blind-deaf-anosmics made practically no progress in 24 trials. The three groups of seeing rats—normal, deaf and anosmic—differ but little and are reliably superior to any of the blind groups. But to be merely blind is much less of a handicap than to be in addition either deaf or anosmic. The blind rat in the open maze can use either noise cues or odor cues, the latter being better according to the figures, and the difference being statistically reliable. But the blind-deaf-anosmic group, dependent on touch and kinesthesis, were apparently not learning the open maze at all, or only very, very slowly. The author comments as follows: "The conclusion that is forced upon us by the results with blind-deaf-anosmic rats is not that kinesthesis has no function in learning but that an act cannot be learned by kinesthesis alone. It is probable that only after learning on the basis of exteroceptive stimuli has begun can kinesthetic impulses begin to take some part in the perfecting of the habit." Other investigators have expressed similar opinions.

Another type of experiment goes back to Carr's important study of 1917, and has more recently been adopted by Honzik (1933, 1936) and by Wolfle (1935). The principle is this: if an animal is using certain cues in finding his way through a maze, his run will be disturbed by altering these cues. For example, if the direction of the light has been an orienting factor, moving the source of light will disturb the well-learned run. If the disturbance lasts only one or two trials, it may be due simply to the distraction of novelty, but if much new learning is necessary, the direction of light was a positive factor in the maze habit. Another form of the experiment consists in continually changing certain stimulus conditions—as the direction of light—during the learning of the maze, and thus retarding the learning if it is really dependent on these conditions. By this method the cues can be more completely analyzed than is possible by blinding, etc. Honzik finds that both intra-maze and extra-maze visual stimuli serve as cues to the seeing rat. Most interesting are the olfactory cues which can be obtained by a rat from a clean open maze built of wooden strips. Both Honzik and Wolfle built such mazes of inter-changeable sections. Normal rats learn the maze almost though not quite as quickly when the units are continually interchanged as when they remain fixed in position; but blind rats make slow progress when the units are con-tinually interchanged. From the way in which the blind rat sniffs at these pieces of wood, it appears that they furnish differential olfactory cues. Many other experiments of this type have been tried.

What is learned in the maze—the motor pattern theory. Distinct from the question of cues is the question, what use is made of the cues. Blind and seeing rats use different cues but acquire essentially the same motor performance. If we ask what is learned, the most obvious answer is, a sequence of movements. "First turn left, 5 leaps forward, turn right, 4 leaps, jog right and left, 4 leaps, turn right, 3 short leaps, U turn to right, 2 leaps, turn left, 2 leaps, jog left, 1 leap, jog right, 2 leaps, turn left, 3 leaps, turn left, 1 leap, jog left, 4 leaps, slow down, jog right, left, right, left, turn right, jog right and left, resume speed, 3 leaps, turn right, 1 leap, U turn to left, 2 leaps, turn left, 3 leaps, U turn to right, 4 leaps, turn right, 4 leaps, jog right and left, 3 leaps, turn right, 5 long leaps, turn right, 3 leaps to finish"—such might be a verbal description of a trained rat's run through the Hampton Court maze. For a short sequence, as 2 straight runs with a turn between, the con-ception would seem possible; but so long a sequence could scarcely be learned without some sort of framework to hold the parts together.

Watson (1914) worked out a direct stimulus-response theory of maze running which called for no framework or pattern. He conceived of the perfected run as a *chain reflex*, in which each movement was a response to the kinesthetic stimuli produced by the preceding movement (or movements?). "Each movement executed would arouse new contact and kinesthetic impulses which in turn would release the succeeding movement (p. 212). . . . When the useless movements are eliminated the correct movements arise serially without any chaining or linking in any material sense" (p. 260). In the light of more recent work Watson's emphasis on "contact and kinesthetic impulses" must be withdrawn, and the chain reflex theory stated in broader terms: each movement brings the animal into another part of the maze from which new extero-ceptive stimuli are received, and the next movement is a response to the new complex of internal and external stimuli.

Positive evidence for the chain reflex theory in its kinesthetic form was claimed from the results of an interesting experiment of Carr & Watson (1908). They constructed a maze in which certain passages could be shortened or lengthened without any change in the required turns. Animals trained in the short form attempted to turn at the old places when the passages had been lengthened, while animals trained in the long form dashed head on against the ends of certain shortened pas-sages. What we can properly infer from these results is that the rats were running rapidly and with little use of certain available visual cues.

A companion experiment of the same authors consisted in placing a trained rat down in the middle of the maze instead of at the entrance. After a few such trials the animals could run from the middle promptly to the food box. In the first two or three trials they were somewhat at a loss till they had explored a little, when they seemed to pick up a cue

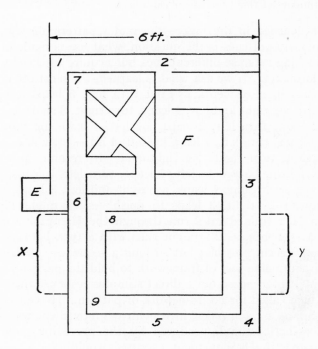

Fig. 33. Maze used in experiments by Carr & Watson, 1908. In the experiment on shortened and lengthened alleys, the section X–Y could be removed or inserted. Rats that had learned the full-length maze often ran into the wall at point 4 when first placed in the shortened maze, and also at point 9, but not (for some unknown reason) at point 7. Rats that had learned the short maze ran into alley 8 on being placed in the lengthened maze. In the test for ability to find the way from the midst of the maze, the rats were set down at points 3, 5 and 6, sometimes headed forward and sometimes backward. The animals often worked their way back toward the entrance and reached 2, 1 or even E before starting their customary rapid run to the food box.

and dart for the goal. As they usually turned at least one corner before picking up the cue, the conclusion was that the cue was a "kinesthetic unit," a certain sequence of movements and resulting kinesthetic stimuli.

The behavior of these animals when first put down in the middle of the maze was interesting in other ways. They very seldom entered any blind alleys; they often picked up the cue while proceeding in the reverse direction; and 85 percent of their explorations were backward toward the entrance from the point where they were inserted into the maze. They showed the same retracing behavior as in the early stages of learning a maze, very often going back nearly to the entrance before starting their dash for the goal. Such behavior seems illogical; if they "know" the way to the entrance, why not turn at once toward the goal? They seemed to go back for a good start, and in every way they showed more acquaintance with the maze than can be included in the concept of a motor sequence.

Against the motor pattern theory. There are still other indications of patterning in the trained animal's run through the maze. He does not advance to a corner and make a square turn, military fashion, as if he only got his cue when he reached the corner; but his curved path shows that he begins to make the turn before reaching the corner. It would probably be impossible to run the maze as rapidly and smoothly as he does without anticipation and overlap (see p. 159). Breaking up the run into a series of leaps and turns is very artificial, anyway. For all that, the pattern must necessarily be stereotyped, if what the animal learns is essentially a sequence of movements. Scattered through the reports of the various investigators are many observations showing variation in the motor performance. When Watson (1907) trimmed a rat's vibrissae and placed him immediately in the maze, the animal bumped into the walls or, as if feeling insecure, hugged the walls and clung to the floor, making slow progress but keeping out of the blind alleys and in some cases completing his run without error. The motor sequence was greatly altered but the "maze habit" was not lost. By aid of a camera lucida, Dennis (1929) traced on paper the course taken by the rat in successive runs, and found it to vary from trial to trial even when the maze had been well learned.

Macfarlane (1930) forced his rats after learning a maze to shift from running to swimming or vice versa. The maze was immersed in water to a depth of 8 inches. In this condition the animals had to explore and traverse the maze by swimming. To enable them to walk, a false floor was inserted in all the passages, one inch below the surface of the water. The appearance of the maze was thus not changed. As shown in the adjoining table there was no increase in errors when the transfer from one form of locomotion to the other occurred early in training, and only a slight increase when it occurred after the maze had been well learned. Yet the leg movements are different and much more numerous in swimming than in wading. When the animals after learning the maze by swimming found solid bottom under their feet for the first time, "they halted, sniffed, stood upright, tested the strength of the wire mesh above them and *then*—traveled down the correct alley. The entire run, for the most part, was made in this hesitant manner." These animals were not carrying over any fixed motor pattern, but they did carry over something which enabled them to follow the learned path.

Errors Following Change in Mode of Locomotion
(*After Macfarlane, 1930*)

Each group of 18–20 white rats was given a certain number of trials with one form of locomotion and then shifted to the other form, by inserting or removing the false floor of the maze. The table shows the average number of errors per individual in the trial just preceding and in that just following the change of conditions.

	Swimming to running		Running to swimming	
	Before	*After*	*Before*	*After*
Shift after 4 trials	7.1	6.3	4.4	3.5
Shift after 12 "	1.3	1.8	1.1	1.4
Shift after 33 "	.2	2.1	.3	1.1

Gross disturbances of gait induced by cerebellar operation do not prevent a rat from traversing without error a maze learned before the operation (Lashley & McCarthy, 1926). Nor does amputating one leg and so compelling the rat to traverse the maze on three legs prevent an errorless performance of a previously learned maze (Dorcus & Gray, 1932). The evidence, all in all, is fully convincing that something different from a motor pattern is learned.

The temporal maze. A human subject in the Hampton Court maze might say to himself after the first trial, "All I have to learn is the correct choice at each junction point. I'll take note of them in proper order." On the second trial he could take mental note of the choices—LRRLLLL (L = left, R = right). Thereafter he need make no errors. That a rat could build up any such key to the maze may well be doubted for two reasons. We can scarcely credit the rat with the right-left distinction, as a purely organismic distinction apart from any environmental differences. And we can doubt that the pure element of order is within his capacity.

An experimental test of this latter question was devised by Hunter (1920). The "temporal maze" is built in the form of a square-cornered figure 8, with certain doors and blocks controlled by the experimenter, who may "force" the subject to make the turns, RLRL, before the exit door to the food is opened. This is the "simple alternation" problem. In "double alternation" the subject must make 2 successive turns to the right, then 2 to the left. All the choices are made at the same point (P in the Figure) whereas in the ordinary maze, the "spatial maze," the choices are made at different places. A spatial maze calling for any sequence of choices, as RLRL or RRLL, is easily learned by the normal rat; and much longer spatially distributed series of choices are easily learned. But the rat has extreme difficulty even with the pure temporal sequence RLRL, and only by a carefully planned course of preliminary training can the rat be led to run RRLL correctly (Hunter, 1929; Hunter & Nagge, 1931). Human adults and older children, put into this maze with no instructions, find the solution in a few trials, using methods which are probably beyond the rat's capacity. They soon see they have a puzzle to solve, and they formulate the solution in words and numbers, "Go twice to the right, twice to the left, and so on" (Gellermann, 1931). As Hunter commented in 1920, "The work on the temporal maze indicates that it is all but impossible to set up a mere temporal sequence of kinesthetic processes (or of movements, he might have added) in the rat. Running the spatial maze therefore must require cues which have space location as well as temporal position. In other words the rat must recognize in terms of space where he is in the maze."

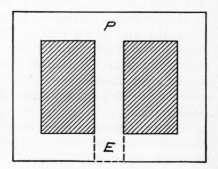

FIG. 34. (After Hunter, 1920.) The temporal maze. By manipulating doors or blocks at and near E, the experimenter compels the subject to take the right and left alleys at the choice-point, P, in a certain time order.

The hypothesis of place learning. Since neither chain reflex nor motor pattern accounts for the rat's behavior in the maze, we ask once more what it is that the animal learns. The most obvious answer, which has been given repeatedly by investigators in describing the rat's concrete behavior, though avoided in their theories, is simply that the rat learns the place. By place we mean a concrete situation containing *objects in spatial relations*. By learning the place we do not imply that the animal acquires a memory image which he can call up in the absence of the place; we need not credit him with any power of ideational recall. We do credit him with the simpler power of recognizing a presented object or situation. We credit him with some power of perception or observation, so that he can discover the character of different objects and parts of the maze. He observes the food-containing character of the food box, the dead-end character of a blind alley, the particular odor of a bit of floor—and the *location* of these parts in relation to each other. The maze, at first a vague total, comes to have parts in definite location and with definite characters.

The main objection likely to be brought against this conception is that it is anthropomorphic—a very serious charge! Let us play safe by setting up this conception not as a conclusion but as a hypothesis for testing. There is no objection to using, in animal psychology, concepts based on human experience provided we treat them definitely as hypotheses and provided also we define them in such a way that they can be subjected to actual test in animal experiments.

For example there is no logical objection to Maier's (1931 b) concept of animal reasoning, defined as a putting together in one act of what has been learned at two different times; or to Krechevsky's (1932) "hypotheses" in rats when hypothesis is defined as something in the animal rather than in the external situation which leads to consistent behavior through a series of trials; or to Hunter's (1913) suggestion of "symbolic processes" in such animals as make a correct delayed reaction after an interval in which they have lost the pointing posture. All of these forms of behavior, however, can be explained by the single hypothesis of place learning. In the reasoning test the animal puts together parts of a maze, or locale, which he has explored at different times. The rat's "hypothesis" is some character of the apparatus which he has discovered and which controls his responses (though because of E's manipulations that character does not hold good all the time). A particular door seen at one moment to have the character of leading to food can by some animals be recognized as having that character, even after some delay. We must not digress to give these experiments any adequate consideration.

The hypothesis of place learning is consistent with all the facts of maze learning so far mentioned, particularly: (1) the animal's exploration of a new maze; (2) his use of alternative cues from different senses; (3) his facility in finding his way from any point of a learned maze to the food box; (4) his quick adoption of short cuts; (5) his relative helplessness in the temporal maze.

Exploration and "latent learning." What does exploring do for the rat? What effect does it leave behind? It changes the animal somehow as is seen from the mere fact that he stops exploring after a while. When replaced in a familiar maze after a day's interval he explores a little before running for the goal (Lashley, 1918), but this re-exploration takes much less time than the original exploration of a strange maze. What is the difference between a rat in a strange maze and the same rat after exploring?

The difference lies partly in emotional adjustment. Placed in a strange enclosure a rat is apt to divide his time between crouching in a corner and trying to escape. After exploration these signs of timidity disappear. Within a familiar enclosure, where he has been fed, he masters a problem box much more quickly than control rats who have not had the opportunity for preliminary adjustment. After learning a problem box the rat learns a maze much more quickly than control animals which have not had similar experience. He seems to acquire a habit of "working" in laboratory apparatus (Warden, 1925; Jackson, 1932).

A more specific acquaintance with the particular maze explored is indicated by experiments on "latent learning"—experiments in which the animal explores the maze without any food being present in the food box. In this first stage of the experiment the animal does not acquire any fixed path from the entrance to the food box, but in the second stage, when food is placed in the food box, he learns the correct path quickly. He learns it in less time and with fewer errors than the control animal which has not explored this particular maze but has spent the same time in a "maze" of similar construction without any blind alleys. The preliminary experience of the experimental and control animals is intended to equate the factor of general emotional adjustment. Varied in several ways (Lashley, 1918; Blodgett, 1929; Tolman & Honzik, 1930; Haney, 1931; Daub, 1933) this experiment gives consistent evidence for what is called "latent learning," i.e., learning that is not revealed by the animal's path through the maze, until food has been found in the food box. Our hypothesis is that latent path learning is actual place learning. There are three processes in learning a maze: (1) getting acquainted with the maze as a place, (2) learning a path within this place, and (3) developing a skilled motor sequence in following this path.

More detailed study of maze learning. Tracing the rat's course through the maze, we ask not only how many errors he makes, but which particular errors are most quickly eliminated and which are most persistent. In terms of place learning we ask what parts, features and characteristics of the maze are most quickly learned. This whole matter is under such active investigation at the present writing that we should be rash if we drew any conclusions. Experiments indicate the reality of the factors listed below.

1. *General orientation in the maze.*

a. If the wire cover of a maze is removed, some rats find their way along the tops of the partitions quite directly to the food box, though necessarily by an entirely new route (Lashley, 1929, p. 137).

b. Blind alleys opening in the direction of the food box resist elimination longer than blind alleys opening away from the food box (Spence & Shipley, 1934).

c. In a maze offering many equally good paths to the food box, rats vary their path while avoiding excess distance (Dashiell, 1930; Gilhousen, 1933; doubted by Buel & Ballachey, 1935).

2. *Learning the location of two goals in the same maze.* Place food at the end of one path and water at the end of another path in the same maze, and place a rat in this maze when he is hungry and when he is thirsty. He learns rather quickly to take the path either to food or to drink, provided the two boxes are in distinct parts of the maze. The problem is made much harder by using a single goal box which must be approached by one route when food is present and by another route when water is present (Hull, 1933; Leeper, 1935).

3. *Orientation toward an intermediate goal or landmark.* The use of intermediate landmarks is so clearly evident in human maze learning (see later) that it is probably present in rats also, when the maze pattern affords good landmarks.

4. *The entrance region as a base of operations.* Early in his explorations

the rat returns often to the entrance; when placed at the entrance of a fairly well learned maze, after a day's interval, he explores a little near the entrance before embarking on his run; and when put down in the middle of the maze he is apt to go back to near the entrance before "getting his cue" for a rapid run to the goal. If he gets his cue by exploring near the entrance, an "error" there does not mean that that part of the maze is unfamiliar but rather that it is familiar.

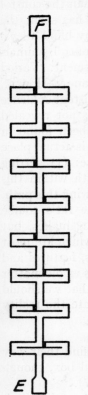

Fig. 35.

(Buel, 1934.) A linear maze set up as a "simple alternation" problem, re-quiring the choices LRLR-LRLR. General orientation is no guide in the choices. The linear maze has somewhat the character of a temporal maze, and is difficult for a rat, though easily mastered by human ver-bal devices.

5. *Goal gradient.* Rats have been found to run the last part of the maze very rapidly. Sometimes they elim-inate the last blind alley early in the learning process. One can easily suppose that the last correct passage quickly acquires the character of leading to food. The goal gradient hypothesis is that, other things being equal, blind alleys will be eliminated in reverse order, beginning with the one closest to the goal (Hull, 1932; 1934 a).

6. *The maze pattern.* As a matter of fact, other things are not equal in most mazes, and the goal gradient seldom appears clearly. One blind alley may be easy and the adjacent one hard. The arrangement of the alleys is an important factor (or includes a number of factors not yet disentangled). When the maze pattern remains the same, the same blind alleys are found to give special difficulty: in an open and enclosed maze (Miles, 1930); with blind and seeing rats (Weaver & Stone, 1928; Lindley, 1930); for rewarded and unrewarded animals, food present or absent (Tolman & Honzik, 1930); for the first trial and later trials, though the correlation is not so close here (Ballachey & Buel, 1934).

7. *Anticipation.* The final correct move is often made prematurely, or "anticipated" in a behavior sense, if the maze affords an opportunity for such anticipation. In a linear maze (Fig. 35), suppose the last unit requires a right turn: this choice is quickly learned but tends to spread back into the adjacent units (Spragg, 1933, 1934; Buel, 1934; Buel & Ballachey, 1934; Snygg, 1936).

8. *Performance preferentials.* This term, suggested by McCulloch (1934), is defined as "a determiner in the organism which leads to one performance in preference to another . . . . . in the achievement of a goal object." Several varieties of performance preferential have been discovered.

a. Position habits such as the preference for the right (or left) alley at a junction, resulting from the individual animal's anatomical structure (Yoshioka, 1928), from previous training, etc.

b. Forward-going tendency (Dashiell & Bayroff, 1931), a tendency to resume the original direction after detouring an obstacle.

c. The wall-following tendency of the rat (Waters, 1937).

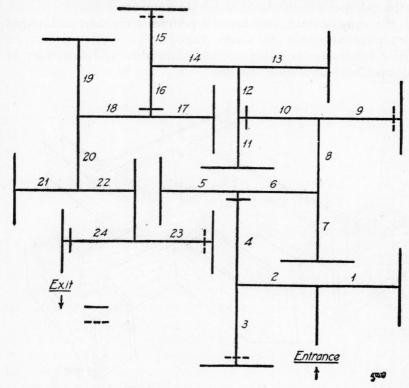

FIG. 36. The short cross lines show the location of doors used to limit back-tracking. When the animal had passed a door it was closed behind him by E. The false doors, indicated by broken cross lines, appeared the same as the true doors but were never closed.

RELATIVE DIFFICULTY OF BLIND ALLEYS
(*Weaver & Stone, 1928*)

The maze is shown in Fig. 36 with alleys designated by numbers. The table gives the mean number of times per 5 trials each blind alley was entered at different stages of practice, by 19 blind rats and by 66 seeing rats (with extra weight on the mean of 12 seeing littermates of the blind animals).

Trials	Group	Numerical designation of blind alley											
		1	3	5	7	9	11	13	15	17	19	21	23
1–5	Blind	2.9	1.7	3.1	2.2	2.4	1.3	1.3	2.6	.7	1.2	3.3	2.5
	Seeing	1.8	2.5	4.0	2.5	3.1	1.1	.9	2.9	.5	1.0	4.8	2.5
6–10	Blind	1.8	1.8	2.8	.6	1.0	.6	.5	.7	.3	.2	1.9	2.1
	Seeing	.7	2.0	3.7	.5	.8	.8	.2	.8	.1	.3	2.5	.9
11–20	Blind	1.1	1.2	2.0	.4	.4	.3	.1	.2	.1	.2	.8	.8
	Seeing	.9	1.2	1.4	.2	.3	.4	.2	.5	.2	.0	.8	.2
21–30	Blind	1.1	.6	.8	.1	.1	.1	.1	.1	.1	.1	.3	.4
	Seeing	.5	.7	.8	.2	.5	.2	.1	.5	.1	.1	.4	.1

d. "Centrifugal swing" (Schneirla, 1929; Ballachey & Krechevsky, 1932). In swinging around a corner a rapidly moving animal may be brought close to the entrance of a particular alley and enter that alley through motor convenience rather than any other reason.

e. Economy of effort, showing as a preference for short rather than longer alternative routes (De Camp, 1920).

These factors are probably not all independent and some may be found superfluous on further analysis.

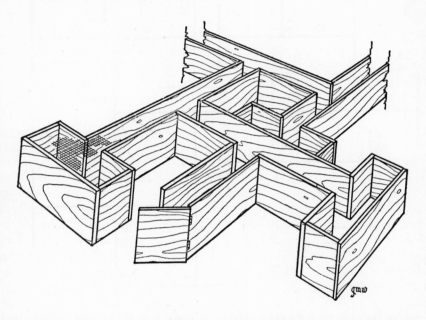

Fig. 37. (Stone & Nyswander, 1927.) Detail of construction of the T-maze, the plan of the whole maze given in Fig. 36. The door here shown is at the entrance; the interior doors are not shown. A little of the wire mesh ceiling is shown at the left of the figure.

Scoring methods for the maze. Scores found useful as measures of animal learning can also be used with human subjects. We will list the most used scores:

1. Number of trials to reach such a criterion as 3 successive perfect runs, or 9 perfect in a sequence of 10 runs. Higher or lower criteria can be adopted to suit the difficulty of the maze and the problem of the investigator.

2. Total number of errors committed before reaching the criterion of mastery.

3. Total time consumed in trials before reaching criterion of mastery.

4. Total time or errors in a specified number of trials counted from the beginning of training.

5. Errors per trial, from which learning curves can be drawn.

6. Time per trial, similarly.

7. The errors can be counted for each blind alley separately.

It is customary to pool the data from a number of individual animals treated in the same manner, and to compare the averages for groups subjected to different conditions. Individual rats are likely to give irregular learning curves and to vary one from another.

HUMAN MAZE LEARNING

One object in borrowing the maze from the animal laboratory is to see how well human subjects perform a task which even rats do very well. Presumably the human being will use intellectual devices which are beyond the rat. Another object is to diversify the material used in the study of human learning.

Reference has already been made (p. 134) to the temporal maze which the human subject masters easily by naming and counting the necessary moves. A full-size spatial maze for the human subject would be an unwieldy piece of laboratory equipment. Usually he is given a miniature maze to trace with the hand. In a few interesting experiments he has had a man-size maze to explore, but never under conditions affording proper scope for man's ability to find his way about. If an open maze were laid out on the floor the human subject looking down on it could trace the paths with his eyes alone, for he is capable of the close visual observation required. In an alley maze the walls would need to be extremely uniform or he would distinguish one part from another by little scratches and smudges. Experimenters have felt that they must not make the problem so easy for the human subject and consequently they have blindfolded him or restricted his vision.

Full-size human mazes. Hicks & Carr (1912) constructed an outdoor maze with alleys 2 ft. wide bounded by wires strung 2½ ft. from the ground. Blindfolded adults and children were run in this maze and compared with rats in mazes of similar pattern. The average number of trials to learn was practically the same for the three groups. The biggest difference was in the first trial in which the rat entered each blind alley on the average seven times, the child four times and the adult only once. The adult was evidently checking off the blind alleys almost as fast as he found them.

We already discern three characteristics of human maze learning: keen vision (when vision is allowed), attentive checking of results, and the use of language.

Perrin (1914) made effective use of an outdoor maze in an amusement park. It was approximately circular (dodecagonal), nearly 50 ft. in diameter, with alleys 2 ft. 4 in. wide, walls of wire mesh 7 ft. high, and a smooth board floor. A platform over part of the top afforded E an opportunity to record O's moves. Blindfolded, O used both hands in feeling his way. Having the services of several very competent psychologists, Perrin asked for retrospective reports as to their method of solution. "The reports show that without exception the net result from the first trial was a knowledge of the general spatial relations. The relation of exit to entrance, the general course of the true path, was acquired by everybody in the first trial." Like the rats, then, the human subjects were learning the *place* and got a general orientation early in the process. They did not develop any accurate conception of this complicated maze, for the maps which they made after each trial were distorted in respect to angles and distances. Even these scientifically-minded individuals were forced from time to time to abandon their preferred method of planful exploration and engage in simple wandering. Emotional excitement sometimes played a useful role by driving the subject out of a complicated blind alley in a wild search for something different.

The trough maze (Warner Brown, 1932) is a feasible piece of indoor apparatus. The passages are boards 1 ft. wide laid on the floor with side walls 3 in. high to guide O's feet. Besides the tactile-kinesthetic cues picked up by the feet there are apt to be auditory stimuli from the street which give the blindfolded O a general orientation in space. Instead of being blindfolded some Os wore about the head and shoulders a cardboard box open at the top and affording a view of the upper part of the room; these Os learned the maze much more quickly than those who were blindfolded. General orientation in the room was thus a great aid in learning the maze. The cues from the feet enabled O to become acquainted rather quickly with the beginning and end of the maze and with some intervening localities which were characteristic enough to stand out as landmarks. An analysis of what O learned in this maze reveals three factors: (1) orientation in space, (2) the location of certain identifiable objects, (3) a sequence of moves or passages.

Hand mazes, usually with blindfold. Corresponding to the open or elevated maze we can construct a path of wire tacked to a wooden base; O's finger is laid directly on the wire and traces the path. In place of the alley maze we have a slot or groove to be traced with a stylus or pencil held in the hand. Here O has no direct contact with the maze, and yet he is aware of the movement of the stylus through the alleys. His tactual sensations are "projected" as they are when, exploring objects with a rod held in the hand, we seem to feel with the end of the rod. In tracing a stylus maze O is definitely aware of alleys, corners, stops. If he had to memorize a mere sequence of tactual impressions, the problem would be very different and probably much more difficult.

In tracing a stylus maze placed on the table before him, O has the advantage of orientation with respect to his body; right and left, forward and back, are definite directions. After a single trial he knows the general course to be followed and the approximate location of the goal, and the maze breaks up into a number of special problems localized in different parts of the general course.

According to Perrin (1914) who tried the same Os in a stylus maze and in his open-air maze, the learning process was essentially the same in both cases. His Os attempted to work the problems out intellectually by planning and reasoning. Some of them tried to build up a visual image of the entire maze, others to reach a verbal description of the pathway, while others sought rather for direct acquaintance with the maze as a place in which to move. None of these methods had any special advantage in the pattern used by Perrin, which was similar to the Hampton Court maze. The essential thing was to discriminate, memorize and combine the parts. "Certain passages early acquired familiar 'tangs,' due to their direction, extent, position, etc. Practically every passage had something analogous to a local sign."

Anticipation, which we have found a behavioral fact in rats running the maze, was a reportable conscious experience in the human subjects. Most of them tried always to foresee the next turn. They also reported what may be called "mental backtracking"; they endeavored to maintain contact with their base of operations at the entrance by keeping in mind the moves made and passages traversed up to any given point. Mental backtracking and anticipation helped in combining the parts and organizing the whole pathway.

When his Os had learned the maze, Perrin tested them, still blind-folded, in a number of ways. He constructed a much smaller maze of the same pattern and found that they traced it with no difficulty and with no errors even on the first trial. He rotated the original maze through 90 or 180 degrees and again obtained very few errors. He asked them to trace backward from goal to entrance, and they did so without trouble. He transferred the pencil to their left hands and obtained some errors due mostly to awkwardness. The readiness with which they readjusted themselves was surprising in view of the changed patterns of tactual-kinesthetic cues. What remained unchanged was the objective situation and their knowledge of that situation. The new cues gave the old meanings. The subjects who had a visual image of the maze could "turn it around" when the maze was reversed, and the new tactual-kinesthetic cues fitted all right into the reversed schema.

Visible mazes for human subjects. The question has been how to arrange matters so that the human subject can use his eyes without finding the problem altogether too easy. Porteus (1924, 1933), in his well-known maze tests for social and practical intelligence, allows no errors to be corrected. As soon as a blind alley is entered by the pencil even a short distance, O is stopped and placed back at the entrance of a duplicate maze. He must look far enough ahead to avoid all errors. Scored in this way, Porteus believes the maze to be a test for "prudence, forethought, mental alertness and power of sustained attention" as against "impulsiveness, irresolution, suggestibility, nervousness and excitability." Leeper & Leeper (1932) presented a very complex visual maze to be traced, the instructions being to keep the pencil on the paper and retrace out of all blinds entered. Credit was allowed for avoiding a blind in proportion to its complexity. The authors compared the success of two groups, one of which had the same maze pattern every time but in varied sizes, while the other group had the same pattern always in the same size. The slight difference found between the learning curves of the two groups justified the conclusion that the pattern is the main thing and the absolute size relatively unimportant—a conclusion agreeing with that obtained by Perrin with the unseen stylus maze. The result is less surprising with a visible maze than with one in which O is dependent upon tactual-kinesthetic cues.

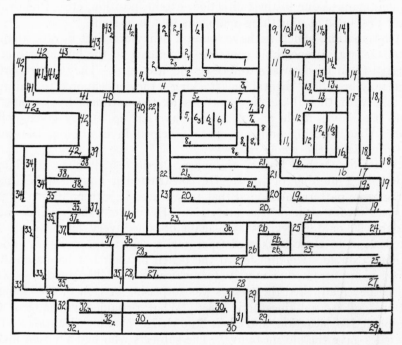

Fig. 38. (From Perkins, 1927.) A maze learned by human subjects. The passages in the original were ¾ in. wide. The lines were drawn on paper and the maze was laid on a glass-topped table and brightly illuminated from below. The subject sat on a high stool, looking through a tube 1 in. in diameter, and moving the tube along the passages in exploring and running the maze. He saw only a small bit of the maze at a time. The experimenter followed the subject's course on a numbered maze (the original had no numbers on it).

Other experimenters have allowed *partial instead of complete vision of the maze*. In one experiment (Perkins, 1927) the maze was drawn in black ink on a large sheet of paper and was placed on a glass-topped table and illuminated from below. Looking through a tube, O saw a short section of a single alley; by moving the tube he explored the maze. In the first trial he got his bearings and learned the general course of the true path. He then analyzed the path into a series of parts, each running in a certain direction. Of the blind alleys, the first two and last two gave little trouble, and the most difficult led in the direction of the next correct turn or else in the general direction of the part of the path where they occurred. We see here two sources of difficulty which have been found also in rats; (1) goal pointing, only in this case the pointing is not toward the ultimate goal but toward some intermediate goal which marks a change in the course; (2) anticipation of a correct turn. Another result was that the human subject seldom entered an alley part way; he either explored it to the end (in the early trials especially), or hesitated at the entrance without entering, or passed by without hesitation.

Perkins intended to allow her subjects about as much use of vision in a finger maze as they would have in a full-size enclosed maze. Much the same result is accomplished by the simple device of Smith (1927), who used a circular maze drawn on paper and covered by a cardboard screen, which was pivoted at the center and had a radial slit. O in-

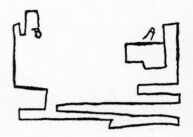

Fig. 39. (From Perkins, 1927.) A subject's drawing of the maze-path after his sixth trial in traversing it. A = starting point, B = goal.

Total count of entrances into each blind alley by 15 human adult subjects:

Serial number of blind alley

2	4	6	8	10	12	14	16	18	20	22	24	26	28	30	32	34	36	38	40	42
22	9	71	55	87	48	47	39	42	95	24	48	57	44	91	59	54	35	82	25	16

serted his pencil in the slit at the entrance point and followed the path along, pushing the slit with his pencil as he went, and thus obtaining a view of a small section at a time. He could also see bits nearer and farther from the center along the same radius and some Os were able to use this surplus view. The blinds near the entrance or near the goal were found to be the easiest.

Vision of the surroundings but not of the maze. The stylus maze can be concealed by covering the maze with a screen. In one experiment (Carr & Osbourn, 1922), the stylus carried a large shield, a circular disk of aluminum attached to the stylus below the handle. O saw his hand but not the maze. A group of adults learned a certain maze in 15 trials under this condition whereas a comparable group, blindfolded, required 22 trials to learn the same maze. With the eyes open, the subject showed more confidence and better spatial orientation.

If O has the opportunity of inspecting the maze before being blindfolded, we should expect him to have a decided advantage. Twitmyer (1930) allowed certain individuals extensive opportunity for visual acquaintance with a stylus maze, since they first acted as experimenters while their laboratory partners, blindfolded, were learning the maze. As experimenters they watched their partners' moves very attentively though with no expectation of serving as subjects. On a later day they were blindfolded themselves and set to learn the same maze. They had an initial advantage of spatial orientation and of good emotional adjustment and maintained their advantage for 10 trials at least as shown in the learning curves of Fig. 40. As the curves also show they

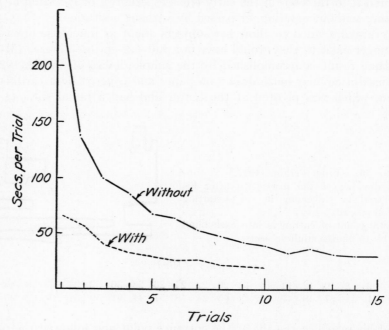

FIG. 40. (After Twitmyer, 1930.) Learning curves for a stylus maze by blindfolded subjects, with and without previous visual acquaintance with the same maze.

did not fully know the maze till they practiced it themselves; they had to learn the "feel" of the maze and of its parts. A maze does not feel the same as it looks.

Two other ways of providing partial visual guidance in learning a stylus maze were devised by Carr (1921). In one way the maze is concealed under a screen but O has before him a plan or map of the maze, which is found to facilitate learning. In the other device the surface of the maze is in full view, but invisible stops are inserted in the bottom of the groove which is expanded to make room for a metal disk pivoted to the end of the stylus. O sees the entrance, the goal, and the general arrangement of the grooves but cannot by vision distinguish the true path from the blind alleys. He learns in quick time because of two great advantages; he sees the choice points, and he can take note visually of the location of the stops, even though he cannot see them. Carr has made a study (1930) of various sorts of teaching and guidance and their value to the maze learner. In school and in life we expect much teaching and coaching, but what kind of assistance to give and at what stage in the learning to give it, are questions not likely to be answered right except by the help of an experimentalist.

An electrical equivalent of Carr's hidden-stop maze has been used by several investigators (Haught, 1921; Barker, 1931). O sees a large square board on which are rows of metal points, one inch apart in both directions. Armed with a metal stylus he starts at an assigned point and proceeds one step at a time toward an assigned goal. The metal points which he touches are the ends of screws or bolts which extend through the board, and are so wired on the reverse side, in series with a buzzer or other indicator, as to inform O when he is on the true path and when he has entered a blind. His task is to find and learn the correct sequence of points to be touched with his stylus. It is an advantage to the learner to have a visible framework on which he can mentally

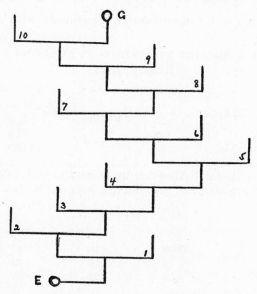

Fig. 41. (Warden, 1924 b.) U-maze pattern used in study of methods of learning.

locate the correct path as he finds it. This form of maze is well suited for standardization and for use in a variety of experiments on learning.

How the maze is learned. The blindfolded O learning a stylus maze is necessarily limited to tactual-kinesthetic cues, but is free to utilize these cues in different ways. Warden (1924 b) made a study of the learning methods used by college students. The U-maze which they learned, though simple to the eye, offers difficulty to the blindfolded subject, and these students required on the average 69 trials to master it.

They were given no suggestions in advance as to efficient ways of learning, but after the learning was completed they were asked to describe their methods. The chief methods reported were: (1) verbal formula, (2) visual image or schema, (3) motor learning. Probably all of the subjects began with motor learning, i.e., with an effort simply to make the right moves in the right places. The majority found their progress too slow and sought for some helpful device. Some attempted to build up a visual image, others used a verbal and numerical description which could be reduced to a mathematical form, as: "Left one; right three; left two; right one; left two; right one." Usually the verbal description was not quite so concise. One student after learning the maze reported as follows: "Well, I made a U-shaped turn at the entrance, then three turns away out to the right, then I found that I had to drop back a couple of places," etc. As shown in the table the verbal schema was the most effective and the motor learning the least. The visual learners fell in between and Warden is inclined to believe that they were using partly verbal and partly motor methods.

Husband (1931 a, b) repeated this experiment with different maze

MODES OF ATTACK ADOPTED BY SUBJECTS IN LEARNING A STYLUS MAZE
(*Warden, 1924*)

Mode of attack	No. Os adopting it	Trials required to learn	
		Mean	Range
Verbal formula	25	32.2	16–62
Visual scheme	18	67.9	41–104
"Motor learning"	17	123.9	72–195

MODES OF ATTACK ADOPTED BY SUBJECTS IN LEARNING A STYLUS MAZE AND THREE FINGER MAZES
(*Husband, 1931 b*)

	Trials to learn			
	Stylus U	Finger U	Finger X	Finger T
Verbal learning	14	10	10	9
Motor learning	52	23	55	9

patterns and with "high-relief finger mazes" (Miles, 1928 a) as well as stylus mazes. (In the stylus maze, keeping the stylus pressed against one edge of the groove, O may pass an alley on the other side without knowing it; in the finger maze, he follows along the wire with his finger and is fully aware of any branch in the path. Accordingly the finger maze is much easier to learn.) Few of Husband's Os reported a clear visual method, though quite a proportion of them could not be classified as verbal or motor. Those who could be so classified showed the same difference as in Warden's experiment. Those who counted the turns learned much more quickly than those who depended upon motor learning. The results are not quite the same with all maze patterns. The adjacent table shows the verbal or counting method to be far superior in the linear maze. Most Os soon found that this maze would be almost insoluble by pure motor learning, there was so little spatial character to differentiate one choice point from another. At the other extreme was the fourth maze, which had good two-dimensional character, and here the counting method was no better than the motor. Probably

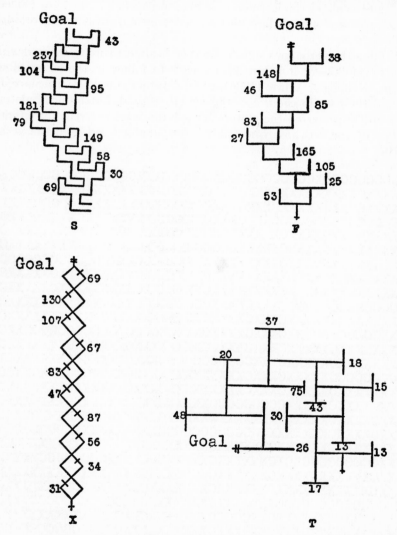

FIG. 42. (From Husband, 1931 a.) A stylus maze and three finger mazes, learned by comparable adult groups of 20 subjects. X is a linear maze, S and F are semi-linear; and these three are alike in the sequence of correct choices. T has a general circular course and is much easier than the others. The numbers give the count of entrances into each blind alley. Study of these numbers indicates the following operative factors: (1) quick learning of the first and last moves; (2) tendency to keep to the general course; (3) tendency to anticipate outstanding moves.

the so-called motor learning is really place learning, in human beings as well as in rats. Pure place learning is closely bound to the actual place and is successful only when the place has plenty of spatial character. T. C. Scott (1930) found a similar though more complex maze pattern that was easily learned by a combination of motor and visual methods. But the linear and semi-linear mazes approach the nature of the temporal maze, and demand the learning of a bare order of right and left choices. Such mazes are sure to be difficult except by aid of counting or some similar scheme.

Though the verbal or counting method is almost sure to succeed when rigorously followed, it is not always easy to follow in the concrete situation. Kellogg & White (1935), using a rather simple stylus maze, instructed their Os in the use of the verbal method, but found that over half of them preferred the motor method and were not reliably inferior, on the average, to those who followed instructions and used the verbal method.

```
ACCCCCCCCCCXCCCCCCCCCCCCCCCCCCCCCXXXCCCCCCCCCCCCCCCCZ
XXXXXCXXXXXXXXXXCXXXCXXXCXCCXCXXXXXXXXXCXXXXXXXX
XXXXXCXXXXXXXXXXCXXXCXXXCXXXXCXXXXXXXXXXCCCCCCXXX
CCCCCCCCCCCCCCCCXXXCXXXCXXXXCXXXXXXXXXXCXXXXXXXC
XXXXXXXXCXXXXCXXXXXXXXXXCXXXXCCCXCCCCCCXXXXXXXC
CXXXXXXXXCXXXXCXXXCCCCCCCCXXXXXCXXXXXXCXXXXXXXXC
CCCXXXXXXCXXXXCXXXXXXXXXXXXXCCCCXXXCCCCCCCCCCCCCC
CXXXXXXXXXXXXXXXXXXXXXXXXXXXXXXXXXXXXXXCXXXXC
CXXXXXXXXXXXXXXXXXXXXCXXXXXXXXXCXXXXXCXXXXC
CCCCCCCCCCCCCCCXXXCXXXXCCCCCCCCCXXXCXXXXXCXXXXC
CXXXXXXXXXXXXXXCXXXXCXXXXCXXXXXXXXXXXXCXXXXXXXXC
CXXXCCCCCCCXXCXXXCXXXXCXXXCCCCCCCCCCCCCCCCCXXC
CXXXXXXXCXXXXXCXXXXCXXXXCXXXXXXXXXCXXXXXXCXXXXXCC
CXXXXXXXCXXXXXCXXXCCCCCCCCCCCXXXCXXXXXXCXXXXXXCX
CCCCCCCCCXXXXXCXXXCXXXXXXXXXXXXXCXXCCCCCXXXCXXCC
CXXXXXXXCXXXXXCXXXCXXXXXXXXXCXXXCXXXXXCXXXCXXXC
CXXCXXXXCXXXXXCCCCCCCCCXXXXXCXXXCXXXXXXCXXXCXXXC
CXXCXXXXCXXXXXXXXXXXXXXXXXXXCXXXCCCCXXXCXXXCXXXC
CXXCXXXXCXXXXXXXXCCCCCCCCCCCCXXXXXCXXXCCCCCCCCC
XXXCXXXXCXXXXXXXCXXXXXXCXXXXXCXXXXXCXXXXXXXXXX
XXXCCCCCCCCCCXCXXXXXXCXXXXXCCCXXXXCCCCCCCCXXXXX
XXXCXXXXXXXXXXCXXXXXXCCCCCXXXCXXXXXXXXCXXXXXXXX
XXXCXXXXXXXXXXCXXXXXXCXXXXXXCXXXXXXXCXXXXXXXXC
CCCCCCCCCCCCCCCXXXXXXCXXXXXXXCXXCCCCCCCCCCXXXC
XXXXXXXCXXXXXXXCXXCCCCCXXXXXXXCXXCXXXXXXXXXXXC
CXXXXXXXCXXXCXXXCXXXXXXCXXXXXXXCXXCCCCCCCCCCCCCC
CXXXXXXXCXXXCXXXCXXXXXXCXXXXXXXCXXXXXXXCXXXXXXXC
CXXXXXXXCXXXCCCCCCCCXXCCCCCXXXCXXXXXXXCXXXXXXXXC
CXXXXXXXXXXXCXXXXXXXXXXCXXXXXXXXCXXXXXXXCXXXCCCCCC
CCCCCCCCCCCCCCCXXCCCCCXXXXXXXCXXXXXXXCXXXXXXXC
CXXXXXXXXXXXXXXXXXCCXXXCXXXXXXXXCXXXXXXXXXXXXXXC
CCCCCCCCCCCCCCCCCCCXXXCXXCCCCCCCCCCCCCCCCCCCCCCC
```

FIG. 43. A letter visual maze (Burtt, 1926, p. 71.)

Order in which the blindfold subject masters the alleys. The "backward elimination of blind alleys," or goal gradient, is scarcely visible in the results from the stylus or finger mazes. Warden (1924 a) found that the beginning and end of the maze were mastered before the middle— the same result as is obtained in memorizing a list of nonsense syllables (p. 22). A subject using the verbal method throughout is almost sure to eliminate errors in the forward direction, since his verbal formula will be constructed from the beginning onward. Other factors are likely to enter. Even in learning a linear maze, which has the minimum of spatial character, there is a tendency to shift prematurely out of a sequence of right or left choices. If the maze has more spatial character, the general course of the true path comes to be a center of reference so that blind alleys leading far from this central line are avoided. To recapitulate, the same factors are important both in learning a partially seen maze and in blindfold learning: the beginning and end stand out and are quickly learned; in the interior of the maze, certain parts stand out or certain moves are prominent, and these moves are likely to be anticipated; the direction of the goal and the general course through the maze are learned early and make some errors easy to eliminate and others difficult.

These principles help to explain the surprising fact (see p. 138) that with the same maze pattern the same blinds are easy or hard whether the pattern is presented as a stylus maze or as a finger maze (Nyswander, 1929); whether it is traced with the right or left hand, and specially if mirror patterns are traced by the two hands (Warden, 1924 a); whether it is learned by the verbal, visual or motor method (Warden, 1924 b). The inequality of the blind alleys is reduced by the verbal method, as one would expect, and still the same alleys remain the most difficult.

Even without any blind alleys a complicated path, containing many right-angle turns, offers considerable difficulty to a blindfolded subject (Sanderson, 1929).

If we examine a single individual's reactions to a single alley, we perhaps expect to find him exploring the alley to its end on the first trial, penetrating it less and less deeply in successive trials, then merely hesitating at the entrance and finally running straight past. Such gradual elimination of the single alley seems *not* to be characteristic of human learning. When partial vision is allowed, as we have already seen (p. 145), an alley is usually traversed to its end if it is entered at all. The blindfolded O in a stylus maze gives a similar result (Kellogg & White, 1935): partway traversal of the blind alleys is less than $\frac{1}{5}$ as frequent as complete traversal. McGeoch & Peters (1933) made a special study of this question in terms of the time consumed in each alley. A stylus maze, of the same pattern as shown in Fig. 41, was cut from bakelite and had a smooth brass contact in the floor of the groove just inside the entrance to each blind alley. When the brass stylus made contact on entering and on leaving an alley, a record was made on a drum along with a time line.

The time spent in a blind alley was typically about 8 sec. on the first trial, fell to 4 sec. after two or three trials, and remained at that level as long as the alley was entered at all. The alleys seemed to be entered or avoided on an all-or-none basis. An alley might be re-entered after it had apparently been eliminated, but each time it was entered the regular 4 sec. was spent in it. The reason may be that an alley is entered not in pure motor automatism but either for exploration or on the assumption that it is part of the true path.

Other uses of the maze in studies of human learning. Apart from the analysis of maze or place learning, the stylus and finger mazes have been found useful in experiments on a variety of problems: on whole and part learning (Pechstein, 1917; Cook et al., 1935; Cook, 1936, 1937); on transfer (T. C. Scott, 1930; Husband, 1931 b); on incentives and law of effect (Tolman et al., 1932; Muenzinger, 1934; Silleck & Lapha, 1937); on retention and the curve of forgetting (Tsai, 1924). With regard to retention, there is an old view to be tested under comparable conditions, the view that skilled motor performances are much better retained than verbal material. An act practiced to the point of skill is greatly "over-learned" (p. 57) in comparison with a poem or list of nonsense syllables learned to the criterion of one perfect recitation. McGeoch & Melton (1929) avoided this source of error by having stylus mazes and nonsense syllable lists learned to the same criterion of one perfect performance. Their mazes and syllable lists were about equally difficult as judged by number of trials to learn. Relearned after an interval of one week, the two sorts of material showed about the same amount of retention. Van Tilborg (1936) used a finger maze and a verbal or "mental" maze (see below), equated in difficulty by a preliminary experiment. Both mazes were then learned to the criterion of two perfect trials in succession, and relearned to the same standard after an interval averaging 51 days. As retention was about equal for the two types of maze, the author concludes "that verbal habits are retained equally as well as are non-verbal ones, and that there is perhaps no difference in the degree of retention of the two kinds of habits when original learning as judged by common criteria has been equal."

AVERAGE LEARNING AND RELEARNING SCORES OF 24 ADULT SUBJECTS
(*Van Tilborg, 1936*)

Trials	*to learn*	*to relearn*	*% saving*
Mental maze	17.7	10.1	43
Finger maze	20.5	12.6	38
Time	*to learn*	*to relearn*	*% saving*
Mental maze	1306 sec.	649 sec.	50
Finger maze	922	432	54
Errors	*to learn*	*to relearn*	*% saving*
Mental maze	70.0	23.8	65
Finger maze	65.6	27.0	58

Mental mazes. When is not-a-maze a maze? A true maze has spatial character; subtracting this what do we have left for a metaphorical maze? We are thinking of a maze to be learned, of course. A maze has a serial character; it presents a series of situations or choice points in a constant order. At each point it presents two or more alternatives. Which is right can only be discovered by exploration. When discovered the right alternative must be remembered. All we can demand of a non-spatial maze is that it present a series of pairs of alternatives, and provide some means by which O can discover which alternatives are right. This task of discovery can be made easy or difficult.

Van Tilborg (1936) made the task of discovery as easy as possible. His mental maze consisted of 20 pairs of nonsense syllables, the first few being:

gik	*yil*
pog	mek
tev	jom
bex	vaf
yun	*zug*

The italicized syllables were "right." The instructions were: "When I pronounce two names (syllables), simply choose one. If your choice is correct I will immediately pronounce two more. If you choose the wrong name, I will repeat the correct one. Repeat this correction after me." The student Os learned this maze in an average of 17.7 trials. If they had been learning a list of 20 nonsense syllables, it would have taken at least twice as many trials. Here they did not have to recall the syllables in order, but simply to recognize them as they were presented.

The idea of a mental maze originated with Peterson (1920), who made the task of exploration very difficult. He apparently desired to place the human subject somewhat in the position of a rat in a strange place. His first procedure allowed retracing or backtracking (see Fig. 44 and legend). If O chose a wrong alternative, he was not told it was wrong but simply given the next pair of alternatives. O was apt to wander back and forth in the early part of the maze, hearing the same letters time after time, before he hit upon the rule, more or less definitely, always to choose the new letters and leave the old ones behind—a rule which is implicit in the concept of a maze but was not obvious to most of the Os. Learning was slow but O came finally to avoid backtracking and later to avoid blind alleys and so follow the "shortest path" from entrance to goal.

In a modified procedure Peterson (1922) inflicted punishment for each error by setting O back to the entrance and offering him once more the first pair of alternatives (N-V in the diagram). Nothing was said of punishment, and some Os seemed quite contented to hear the experimenter pronounce the same letters time after time. The first trial might extend to 15 minutes or more. Eventually even a passive O becomes weary of the continued repetition of the early letters, varies his choices and so gets ahead in the maze. The main result was that in spite of the tremendous frequency piled up for certain wrong choices, these choices were finally eliminated. Learning of the true sequence took place against the principle of frequency rather than in accordance with that principle.

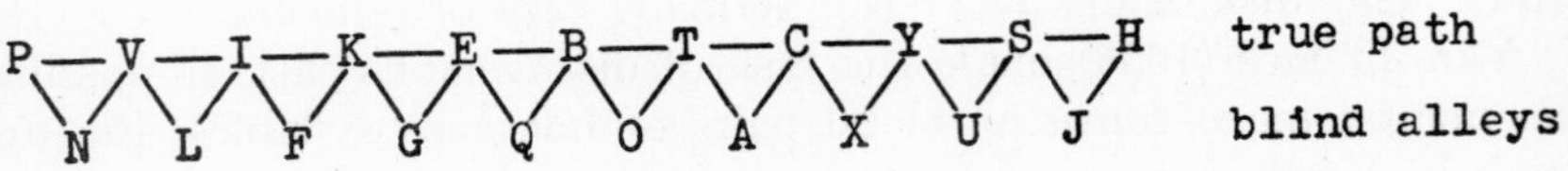

FIG. 44. Operating diagram for Peterson's mental maze.

Experimenter's procedures. Offer choices as follows:

1. *Peterson's revised (1922) procedure.* At each point in the true path, offer the two nearest letters in the general forward direction; thus when the subject has just chosen K, offer him a choice of E and G. Whenever he chooses any letter in the blind alley list set him back to the start by simply offering V and N.

2. *Peterson's first (1920) procedure, with retracing allowed.* (a) From any blind alley offer the two nearest letters in the true path, one ahead and one behind; thus when the subject has just chosen X offer him a choice of C and Y. (b) When the subject has made a forward choice, offer him the two nearest letters in the general forward direction; thus if he has just been at either K or G and has chosen E, offer him B and Q. (c) When the subject has made a backward choice offer him the two nearest letters in the general backward direction; thus if he has just landed on E from either B or Q, offer him K and G.

3. *Without retracing.* (a) As above. (b) When the subject has just chosen any letter in the true path, always offer him the two nearest letters in the forward direction; if he has landed on E from K, G, or Q, in any case offer him B and Q.

The experimenter is not to explain his procedure to the subject, nor to say anything about the "true path," "forward and backward," or "getting set back to the start." The experimenter says nothing but letters (after the original instructions) except that he informs the subject when the goal has been reached and tells him how many errors he has made (or, perhaps better, how many steps he has taken). Count as an error a movement in either direction along any northwest-southeast line in the diagram, as from V to L or from L to V; no other moves can be counted as errors.

Reference to a maze in the instructions is superfluous and confusing to the subject. For minimum guidance it might be better to instruct O as follows: "Every time I name two letters you are to choose one of them; your starting point is the letter P and we will see where we come out; V N." When the subject has reached the last letter H the experimenter says: "That is the goal. You can reach it in fewer steps. Let us begin again, start with P—N V."

Peterson's "rational learning" experiment (1918) can be regarded as a mental maze with exploration made easy if O grasps the import of the instructions. "This is a memory-reason test. The letters, A, B, C, D, E, F, G, H, I, J, are numbered in a random order from 1 to 10. I call out the letters in their order and you are to guess numbers for each letter till you get the correct number, when I say 'Right.' Then I call out the next letter, and so on. This is continued till you get each number right the first guess." The subject is further told to use all the mental powers at his command, so as to minimize the number of errors and the number of trials needed. Considered as a maze, this problem offers ten alternatives at each choice point. The rational way of avoiding excess errors is to eliminate a number from further guessing as soon as its connection with a certain letter is established, since the instructions imply that the same number can be the correct choice only once in the series.

Mental mazes can be varied in many ways and can be embodied in concrete situations. Lumley (1931) used a "typewriter maze": the experimenter prepares a list of letters in random order, and O's task is to discover the first letter by striking key after key until a loud click signals the correct choice; he then advances to the second letter, with no restriction against repeated choice of the same letter. Essentially the same setup was employed by McTeer (1931 a, b) who called it, not a maze, but a "finger-response ten-unit multiple-choice serial-order learning problem." Each of 10 typewriter keys was assigned one of the numbers from 1 to 10, and a chance order of these numbers had to be discovered and learned. Since the same number was not repeated, the problem was one of "rational learning."

CHAPTER VII

PRACTICE AND SKILL

IN WHAT is traditionally known as the practice experiment the same task is performed many times, its success being measured, and the interest lies in the improvement and other changes that occur. If O seeks to better his performance in speed, accuracy, ease, or "form," improvement in the desired respect is practically certain. It is surprising how much improvement will be made under experimental conditions by subjects with long experience in the same task. Four typesetters of 9–26 years experience volunteered for an experiment on the effects of alcohol and were put to work at their regular jobs under the eye of a psychologist who kept the time and measured the output. In the control quarter-hour of each day (unaffected by alcohol) every man improved. Taking the total output of the first quarter-hour as 100, the output on successive days was 100, 103, 110, 117. The surprising thing is not so much that test conditions act as a spur to a greater than usual output, but rather the fact that the improvement is gradual. These experienced Os are *learning* something (Aschaffenburg, 1896).

There is no essential difference between practice and learning except that the practice experiment continues longer. A typical learning experiment comes to an end when O has attained some criterion, such as three successive trials without error. The mere fact that he recites a list of nonsense syllables without error or runs through a maze without entering blind alleys does not mean that he has reached the limit of his ability. What is called "overlearning" in other experiments is essential to a complete practice experiment. As long as improvement continues, so long the learning process is still going on; and when the limit of improvement has been reached, one may "keep in practice"— prevent forgetting—by further repetitions of the performance.

Habituation. Dodge (1923 a, b) habituated a subject to rotation by turning him 6 times in a horizontal plane at the rate of one revolution in 3 sec. The rotation was stopped suddenly and the after-nystagmus of the eyes photographed. So much constituted one trial. There were 19 trials a day for 6 days, the rotation being always in the same direction. The after-nystagmus decreased from trial to trial during the day and also from day to day. We see here a high-level reflex decreasing as the result of continued practice under very constant conditions. In a sense we can speak of improvement since the after-nystagmus was of no benefit to the organism.

156

In another experiment which included 77 practice days distributed over a period of 21 months, Dodge (1927) tried the effect of often-repeated stimulation on the knee jerk and eyelid reflexes. The knee jerk showed little change in amplitude but did increase in latency (become slower). The wink changed little in latency but decreased notably in amplitude. In general, these habituation effects are in the direction of *negative adaptation*.

Muscular tension during the progress of learning. According to common observation the beginner in any difficult task appears tense,

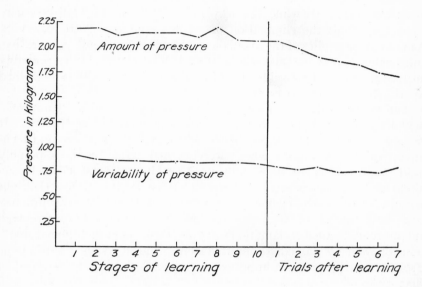

FIG. 45. (GHISELLI, 1936.) Key pressure during the learning and overlearning of a simple task with constant time allowance. The task was a "mental maze" embodied in a keyboard with three keys side by side, one of which must be pressed every three seconds at the flash of a signal lamp. The correct order in which to press the keys (as right, left, center, left, right, center, left) was to be discovered and learned. About ten trials were needed to master a series of seven responses. The trials were continued after perfect responses had been attained, the tempo remaining the same, so there could be no effort for speed. The apparatus registered the pressure exerted by O's hand on the keys. The curves show the average of 22 subjects. The pressure did not fall much during the learning but did so in the "overlearning" trials. The variability of the individual subject from trial to trial decreased with practice.

knitting his brows, clenching his fists, or in other ways exerting superfluous muscular energy. Similar symptoms of diffuse effort are observed in work under conditions of distraction (p. 157). With practice, it is reasonable to expect, the tension would gradually decline. A stylus which recorded the hand pressure in tracing a blindfold maze was used by Stroud (1931 b). As learning progressed, the expected decline in pressure appeared, provided the maze was difficult, but with easy mazes the pressure progressively increased, for when O found the maze easy he exerted himself to learn it quickly and make a good score. Tension depends on O's zeal as well as on the difficulties encountered. Even the expert may develop great muscular tension when he is trying for a record.

QUALITATIVE IMPROVEMENT

Underlying gain in speed and accuracy are changes in the manner in which a task is performed. As executed after practice the performance need not be the same as at the outset. What remains constant is the result accomplished, while the way in which it is accomplished may change. Besides the elimination of surplus muscular effort, we think from our maze studies of the avoidance of blind alleys, literal or figurative. And elimination is not necessarily the whole story; there are probably positive factors in true skill. Improvement of *form* has been examined experimentally in a variety of performances.

The bow and arrow. Lashley (1915) traced the course of improvement in archery, using an outdoor range and full-sized equipment. It was left to the Os to discover for themselves the proper form and technique, except for one O who, receiving instruction, made especially rapid progress. There were many positive bits of technique to be acquired, as in sighting along the arrow and in loosing it with just the right adjustment of muscular tension. In the first hundred trials progress took place by leaps and bounds as old knowledge and habits were revived and put to use. Such exclamations as, "Oh, I've caught on to something!" were followed by immediate improvement. Lashley says, "During the first part of the practice improvement is made largely by a series of what Thorndike has called 'insights,' such as those found so constantly by Ruger in the solution of mechanical puzzles." At a later stage improvement is slow and O is not aware of the causes of his gain which may continue for thousands of shots.

Mechanical puzzles. In Ruger's experiment (1910) O after "solving" a puzzle continued practice and found many trials necessary before first-rate manipulative skill was attained. The process of acquiring skill was about as follows. The manipulation was broken down into a series of steps which were mastered one by one and then combined by aid of anticipation. By looking ahead and preparing for the second step during the motor execution of the first step, the hesitation between the steps was eliminated and the performance became a smooth whole. We get the same picture from Schlieper (1929) who used an especially tricky puzzle containing a series of pitfalls to be avoided by skillful movement. At first O attacked the whole puzzle crudely and discovered the pitfalls by falling into them. He then resolved the task into a series of steps which needed to be mastered before being recombined into a well-structured total performance. The constant urge forward toward the goal was a unifying force.

Telegraphy. A landmark in the early study of practice was the work of Bryan & Harter (1897, 1899) on the acquisition of skill in sending and receiving telegraphic messages. Students of telegraphy were tested weekly and their methods and those of experts were examined. Several stages in learning were distinguished. The beginner first learns the alphabet of dots and dashes. Each letter is a little pattern of finger movements in sending, a little pattern of clicks in receiving. It is something of an achievement to master these motor and auditory *letter habits*. At this stage the learner spells the words in sending or receiving. With further practice he becomes familiar with word patterns and does not spell out the common words. The transition from the letter habit to the *word habit* stage extends over a long period of practice, and before this stage is fully reached a still more synthetic form of reaction begins to appear. "The fair operator is not held so closely to words. He can take in several words at a mouthful, a phrase or even a short sentence." In sending he anticipates, as in other motor performances; but in receiving he learns to beware of anticipation because it may lead him astray. Instead, he learns to "copy behind," letting two or three words come from the sounder before he starts to copy. Keeping a few words behind the sounder allows time for getting the sense of the message.

The gist of this study is contained in the two catch words, *higher units* and *overlap*. Even a letter habit is a higher unit in comparison with a single click or finger movement. The expert telegrapher has at his command a hierarchy of lower and higher units corresponding to letters, words and phrases. These are positive factors in skill. They would obviously be impossible without the two forms of overlap: anticipation in sending, copying behind in receiving.

Typewriting. Quite in line with the study of telegraphy is Book's work (1908) on the acquisition of skill in typewriting. He wired the machine so as to time every movement of the operator, the type itself recording the correctness or incorrectness of the responses. As the subjects in this experiment were psychologists, introspective observations were obtained, not in the regular practice series but in special sessions held every few days at which O tried to observe his method of work.

The stages in learning to typewrite by the "touch method," with the keyboard concealed by a screen, were about the same as in telegraphy. (a) O either memorized the keyboard or had a diagram of it before him. Striking a letter was at first a complicated process. O looked at his copy, picked out the letter to be written, determined the location of this letter from memory or from the diagram, then with his fingers located the correct row and the correct letter and finally struck. (b) After a few hours of practice he knew the keyboard and the position of every letter. At this stage his great concern was to hit each letter by a single stroke, i.e., to have an accurate letter habit. When letter habits were acquired, speed increased and a feeling of mastery supervened. (c) Further practice gave results unexpected by the learner. He found himself anticipating the sequence of finger movements in a short familiar word. Habits were developing for groups of letters such as prefixes, suffixes and short words. The single movements could be trusted at this stage, but care was necessary to keep them in the right order. With practice the order of finger movements for a word became familiar. "A word simply means a group of movements which I attend to as a whole. I seem to get beforehand a sort of 'feel' of the whole group." The adjustment for writing a whole word became more and more accurate, the single letters were no longer thought of, and each word became an automatic motor sequence. (d) Familiar phrases were similarly organized, the thought of the phrase calling out the whole series of connected movements. Yet expert typewriting is not exactly a writing in phrase units. Book had some highly skilled operators write on his wired machine, and their records showed no pauses between phrases. The movements followed one another at a uniform rate even when unfamiliar words or phrases in the copy forced attention to details. The expert "copied behind." The eyes on the copy were well ahead of the hand. "The advantage of thus getting copy several words ahead of the hand is that special attention can be given to difficulties which may arise, for all words and letters are not equally easy even for an expert." (Cf. p. 734)

It is true, then, in typewriting as in telegraphy that the expert performance is far from being the beginner's performance executed more rapidly. Many things that the beginner does, the expert has eliminated, such as spelling out the copy letter by letter. Many things that the expert does are beyond the ken of the beginner, as word habits and overlap. Without attempting a complete summary of the factors in improvement we may emphasize: (1) elimination of surplus movement, (2) precision acquired by attention to detail, (3) working in larger units and (4) increased time span, illustrated by anticipation and copying behind.

Card distributing. A laboratory task patterned after the railway mail clerk's job was devised by Kline (1920). O had before him a distributing case of 9×6 compartments or boxes, of which 2 were blank and the remaining 52 were labeled in irregular order with the identifying symbols found on the corners of playing cards. Each card was to be thrown into the box bearing its own number, but while clubs and hearts were to be thrown into their own boxes, spades were thrown to the diamond boxes and diamonds to the club boxes; for example, the queen of spades must be thrown into the box labeled queen of diamonds. Along with this complication went certain simplifications which O had to discover for himself; thus the deck as handed to him for each trial was always stacked in the same order. The learning process went through several stages:

1. Learning the rules of the game, especially the substitutions which required careful attention at first but soon became automatic.

2. Learning the locations of the boxes. Those around the outside were learned first, those near the center gave the most trouble.

3. Discovering and memorizing the constant order of the cards.

4. Motor patterns. Since each sorting demanded the same sequence of movements, parts of the sequence became familiar, "just like going over an old trail."

5. Integration of these partial motor patterns into one complete pattern. When O, while distributing one little series of cards, was able to look ahead and anticipate the following group, he was in a fair way to pass smoothly from group to group through the whole pack.

Along with this increasing mastery of the space and time arrangement went improved form and coordination. At first the left hand merely held the pack; later it followed around with the right hand and the left thumb pushed the next card forward for the right hand to seize. It must not be supposed that the whole learning process was smoothly progressive; at a certain stage O was inclined to force the issue by main strength and to put in so much muscle as to bring confusion.

Mirror tracing. Much used in practice experiments is a task introduced by Starch (1910 a). O traces the outline of a star or other figure

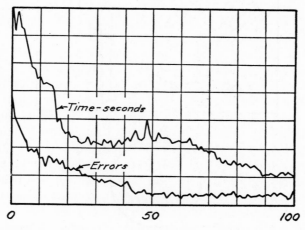

FIG. 46. (Starch, 1910 a.) Learning curve of one subject in mirror-tracing. One trial a day. After the first rapid improvement in both time and errors simultaneously, the periods of rapid improvement in time are periods of little improvement in errors, and vice versa.

which lies on the table before him, screened from direct view but visible in a mirror standing vertically beyond the figure. In this position the mirror reverses the forward and back directions while leaving right and left unchanged. A right-left line requires the usual eye-hand coordination, a front-back line must be reversed, and an oblique line must be reversed as regards its front-back component and left unchanged as regards its right-left component. O scarcely has time to make this analysis and finds that he cannot plan his moves effectively. He has to feel his way by a sort of trial-and-error, though his movements are far from random, as shown by the fact that he can learn a good deal from watching another O, and by the large positive transfer effect from hand to hand—after learning with the right hand O needs little additional practice to succeed with the left hand (Starch; Siipola, 1935; see also p. 186).

To facilitate counting the errors, a double-contour star is often used; it provides a narrow lane through which O moves his pencil, and an error consists in touching either boundary line. The lane can be cut in a brass plate and traced with a metal stylus, so wired that contact with either side closes a circuit and records an error on an electric counter. Because

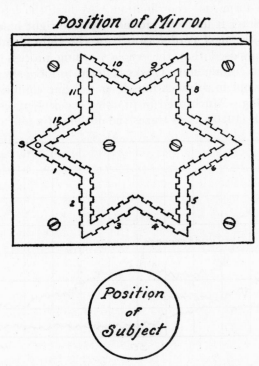

FIG. 47. (Waskom, 1936.) Snoddy's mirror-tracing setup. O starts at the left and proceeds in the anticlockwise direction. The slot is 6 mm wide; the brass stylus has the shape and size of a lead pencil. The brass plate through which the slot is cut is mounted on a smooth sheet of glass lying flat on a table, and is screened from O's direct vision, while visible by reflection from the vertical mirror.

O can slide the stylus along one edge and so get a small error score while still unable to trace properly, Snoddy introduced the niches shown in Fig. 47, and with this and other apparatus has made extensive studies of mirror drawing (1920, 1926, 1935). In the first trial, probably in the very first move, O gets into a niche and finds it surprisingly difficult to get out. The edge seems to hold the stylus by "magnetism" which is really his own push in the wrong direction. Finally he relaxes or makes a reverse movement and is free; and the next niche is less troublesome because he is less stubborn. Competent introspective observers threw some light on the first step in this learning process. They learned to make short movements, keeping very close watch so as to check instantly a movement in the wrong direction while allowing a correct movement to continue. Where the going was difficult, they kept the eyes close in front of the stylus point; in easier places they let the eyes get farther ahead. At first one can move correctly to a point 1–2 mm away, and after practice one succeeds at longer distances, takes longer steps; but with too much effort for speed one falls again into error (Waskom, 1936). In mirror-tracing one learns to follow a new set of visual cues; it is a kind of place learning.

Switchboard learning. So we may label the elaborate experiment of Van der Veldt (1928). O sat at a table on which, slightly tilted toward him, was a board about 3½ ft. long by 1½ ft. wide (110 × 50 cm). Scattered over this board were 12 round openings (diameter 4 cm) which were lighted up one at a time by small electric bulbs underneath. Each opening was assigned a syllable for its "name." O looked directly over the board at an exposure apparatus which showed these names, and as each name was exposed its bulb was lighted. Forbidden to turn his eyes toward the board, O was required to locate the illuminated spot in indirect vision and to touch it with his hand. In one form of the experiment O had to learn several zigzag patterns of movement around the switchboard. The "names" were two-letter syllables combined into six-syllable nonsense words like fo-ru-ke-na-bi-ly. One of these words was exposed, the lamps corresponding to the 6 syllables were lighted in succession, and O was instructed to move his hand from lamp to lamp as they were lighted. After a short interval the next word was similarly presented, and so on through a list of five words. On the first few trials O's impression was one of *chaos;* he saw the complicated word and the rapid series of lamps but could establish no connection. Some of the Os attempted to learn each pattern of lights as a whole, but they made poor progress. For most of them the only escape from chaos was by way of *analysis;* they had to attend to the separate lamps and the separate syllables and connect each lamp with its syllable, paying no attention for the time being to the sequences. Using this analytic method they were able, after 25–50 presentations of the series, to touch each lamp correctly as its syllable was shown. Practice was continued without further lighting of the lamps.

Even before analysis had completed its work, synthesis was treading on its heels—*grouping* occurred, short sequences of syllables and of lamps became familiar. The groups were visual patterns or motor patterns or both at once. Within the limits of each group O moved quickly and easily from lamp to lamp. The groups enlarged and coalesced till O had a complete *schema* for the sequence of lamps demanded by each "word." The schema was visual or spatial in character. The word called up the schema and the schema guided the series of hand movements. The connections between the separate syllables and their respective lamps became superfluous and tended to be forgotten, so that eventually O could not tell the location for any isolated syllable. With further practice the schema itself tended to drop out, because the nonsense word had acquired as its direct meaning the appropriate motor sequence. O simply read the word and promptly executed the sequence of movements. Even in this final, *automatic* stage, the learned act was not a stereotyped series of muscular contractions; for a pattern learned with the right hand could readily be executed with the left hand also; and it could be executed on a miniature scale—just as one can readily write one's characteristic signature in any size of letters.

From this and other studies it appears that the typical process of learning a complex motor act proceeds from whole to part and back to whole again. The whole at first is unorganized and chaotic; parts are discovered, mastered separately, interrelated and combined, and so the whole becomes organized.

QUANTITATIVE CHANGES IN PRACTICE

The learning curve. Repetition of a performance by a well motivated subject gives progressive improvement. If a measure of success on each trial is plotted, the success measure being the ordinate and the amount of practice up to and including the given trial being the abscissa, we have a learning curve, also called a practice curve. The latter name is superfluous. The learning curve rises or falls according to the measure adopted. It falls if the measure is errors per trial as is customary in the maze, or if the measure is time per single performance of a given act; it rises if the measure is amount accomplished per trial or per unit of time. Thorndike (1913) gives a large collection of such curves and discusses many puzzling questions of proper measurement. To obtain a complete learning curve we should start with no previous training and continue until O reaches the limit of his ability. Most actual curves are cut short at both ends since we neither start from absolute zero of practice nor do we carry the subject to his absolute limit.

The slope of the learning curve indicates the rate of improvement. If this rate were constant through the learning, the "curve" would be a straight line. Almost any learning curve shows on the contrary a negative acceleration; it flattens out as practice advances; the rate of improvement decreases.

The practice curve is typically jagged as would be expected from the numerous variables inherent in O's physical and emotional condition. More interest attaches to the general shape of the curves, that is to the course of improvement throughout the learning process. Horizontal parts of the curve, showing no improvement, are particularly intriguing. Of such three sorts are possible: initial level, final level and intermediate level.

1. *Initial level.* For convenience we will speak of the curve as rising rather than falling with practice. An initial level would mean that O's

achievement was zero or near zero for a number of trials at the start. Initial level is quite absent from most learning curves which rise steeply from the base line and show negative acceleration throughout. But this abrupt rise from the base line may be an artifact due to the inadequacies of our experiment. We probably have not caught our subject at the very beginning of his learning of the given performance, and we probably have no complete measure of his achievement during the first few trials. The first trial in a maze, for example, takes a long time during which O learns a good deal about the alleys. If we could trace a learning curve within this first trial we might find an initial phase of positive acceleration, if not an initial level.

In ball tossing practice, an initial level appears at or near the zero score (Swift, 1903; Batson, 1916; Peterson, 1917). The subject has to keep two balls going, by tossing and catching with one hand, and his score is the number of balls caught. This may remain at or near zero for a good number of trials and may rise very slowly at first. In the first few trials the subject is acquiring the rudiments of the game, even though unable to score.

In conditioned reflex experiments, initial level is the rule. It is a zero level before the first sign of conditioned response appears. The conditioned salivary secretion in Pavlov's experiment did not appear on the second trial but only after several trials. Human subjects usually require a considerable number of stimuli before the first conditioned knee jerk or wink appears.

2. *Final level.* Here we may distinguish two kinds, the good enough level and the physiological limit. Unless O is strongly motivated he will never reach his physiological limit but his improvement will taper off to a routine level. All of us are contented with such a level in most performances, as we do not aspire to be experts in every line. The idea of a physiological limit is clear in the case of a strength or speed test, also in acuity of vision and hearing. The receptors, muscles and nerve connections are not capable of indefinite improvement. The reaction time cannot go much below 100 ms just as the 100 yard dash does not improve much below 10 sec. An individual's limit, of course, may be considerably inferior to these group records.

Psychologists have become wary of accepting the terminal level in a practice curve as a true physiological limit. Often it has happened that increased incentive or improved methods or conditions have brought a later rise from what seemed to be the limit.

3. *Intermediate level.* From the time of Bryan & Harter, an intermediate level has been known as a *plateau*. In a learning curve it is a level or nearly level part preceded and followed by steeper parts. What seems to be a final level may turn out to be only a plateau.

The plateau—under what conditions does it occur? The Bryan & Harter curve for sending telegraphic messages shows no intermediate level as that for receiving messages does. This intermediate level was by no means "good enough"; it was below the level at which the learner could be considered for a regular job. He was thoroughly well motivated and trying to improve, though sometimes discouraged when he made no improvement week after week. Bryan & Harter thought that some kind of learning must be going on below the surface. They set up the hypothesis that the plateau was a period during which the lower-order habits were being perfected but were not yet sufficiently automatic to permit the development of the higher habits. As a check on this hypothesis they tested a learner each week in receiving disconnected letters and disconnected words, as well as connected messages; and the results (Fig. 49) proved that even during the plateau progress was being made in receiving letters and words. When these lower skills had reached

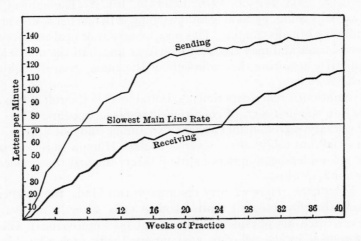

Fig. 48. (From Bryan & Harter, 1897.) Learning curves of one student of telegraphy, tested once a week in sending and receiving connected messages.

a fairly high level the receiving of messages took a sudden jump, and the plateau came to an end.

These authors admitted another possible factor which would explain the absence of a plateau in the curve for sending messages. The sender sets the speed and can slow down when he meets any difficulty, as the receiver cannot do. In receiving the learner must be allowed time to spell out any word that happens to give him trouble. Until his vocabulary of auditory-click words reaches nearly 100 percent of those in common use, his receiving rate will remain low. The same factor accounts for the difficulty in learning to understand a spoken foreign language and for the plateau which Swift (1906) found to occur there.

Two questions regarding the plateau have engaged the attention of later experimenters: (1) whether it is a necessary characteristic of learning curves, and (2) whether the factors suggested by Bryan & Harter are sufficient to explain all cases in which it occurs. The first question is easily answered, for no true plateau, as distinguished from minor oscillations, can be seen in many learning curves. Thurstone (1919) took weekly tests of 60 students of typewriting who practiced 10 hours a week for 28 weeks. Only 2 of the 60 showed definite plateaus. An initial phase of positive acceleration preceded the usual long phase of negative acceleration so that the whole curve had somewhat of an S shape. Similar curves have been obtained in performances as diverse as walking a tight wire (Johnson, 1927) and memorizing a poem (Stroud, 1931 a), improvement being measured in the first case in terms of distance walked before falling, in the second case by number of lines recited.

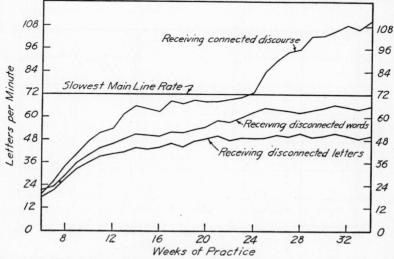

FIG. 49. (From Bryan & Harter, 1899.) Learning curves of another student who had begun the study about 6 weeks before the first of the weekly tests. The three curves show progress in *receiving:* bottom curve, disconnected letters; middle curve, disconnected words; top curve, connected discourse.

With regard to causative factors, the importance of an appropriate learning attitude was emphasized by Book (1908). Some of his Os, after reaching a fair degree of proficiency in typewriting, felt satisfied and let their attention stray from the work. Others became too eager, tried to force their progress and broke down.

Another possible factor is suggested by Batson (1916) and Kao (1937). They reason that a plateau is more likely in complex than in simple performances. In a complex performance O may concentrate on one part for a time and improve there while remaining at a standstill in the other parts and in the total act. If he takes the whole performance as a unit, whether it be simple or complex, his progress should be steady and show no plateau. The extensive experiments of these two investigators favor their hypothesis to a certain extent. They find that a complex performance need not show a plateau if learned as a whole, and that sometimes, if not always, a plateau appears when O concentrates for a time on one part of the performance.

In one of Batson's experiments, a wooden disk, 10 inches in diameter, revolving horizontally, brought into O's view a series of small depressions, each containing a shot to be seized with a small pair of tongs and thrown at a target about 2 ft. away.   The successful act involved accurate aim at the shot, prompt seizing with the tongs, and an accurate throw at the target; and the whole act must be repeated 8 times in about 5 sec., to make a perfect score.   We might expect O to concentrate his efforts successively on the three part acts.   No one proceeded quite so methodically, but one who concentrated on different parts at different times did give a plateau.   Kao obtained similar cases (p. 223).

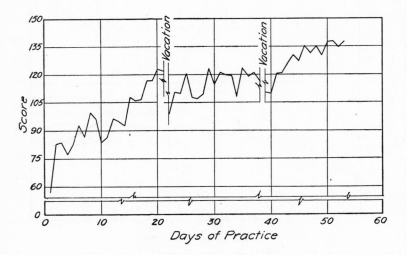

FIG. 50.   (Data from Smith, 1930.)   Learning curve of one subject, practicing the game of ringball with two hands (see Fig. 51).   Each hand had a ball.   The alternate throws of right and left hand were timed by a metronome to occupy about 3 seconds each.   A set consisted of 20 shots with each hand, and a day's practice contained 5 sets.   The practice came three times a week, but was interrupted by two vacations, after each of which there was a low start with prompt recovery.   But after the first vacation the previous rapid progress was not resumed; instead we see a plateau lasting 6 weeks and only left behind after the following vacation.   The cause of the long arrest of improvement, though not perfectly clear, seemed to be a lack of equality and coordination between the different parts of the performance, especially between the two hands.   The right hand needed to hold back, apparently, and let the left hand catch up, before the two could work well as a team.

These results agree very well with those of Smith (1930).   University students practicing acts of skill furnished many instances of intermediate levels, "periods of arrested progress in the acquisition of skill," lasting longer than the usual daily and weekly fluctuations.   Most of these plateaus were explained by nervous or emotional strain, loss of interest, illness, or interruption of the practice; but a certain number seemed to result from factors inherent in the learning process.   When O regarded a task as complex, he was inclined to concentrate for a time on one phase of the process—on accuracy to the neglect of speed, or on the work of one hand in a two-handed performance. Such one-sided concentration of effort, even if advantageous in the long run, kept the score down for the time being.

The inherent causes of arrested progress are summed up by the author in the phrase "difficulties of coordination." Coordination is impeded by: (1) undue attention to one part of the task, (2) oscillation of attention from one part to another, (3) conscious effort to coordinate, (4) carrying over of errors from one part of the performance to another (as in a two-handed performance), and (5) lack of balance between the skill attained in different parts of a complex task. If the task is taken as a unit by the performer, a plateau will probably not appear, though progress is not necessarily rapid.

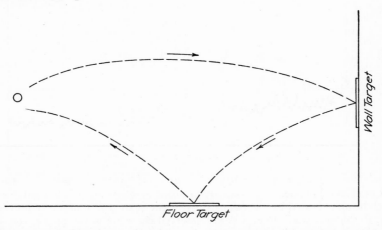

Fig. 51. Diagram of a throw at ringball. The game is to make such a hit on the wall target that the ball in its rebound will hit the floor target and come back to the hand.

Certain simpler causes of a plateau have been pointed out by Hunter (1929) and by Ruger (1910). Hunter's experiment was on maze learning by rats, the maze in question being fairly easy except for a strong tendency to anticipate the final correct move. Only 2 out of 24 animals overcame this difficulty and these 2 did so only after a long plateau in which they regularly made one error per run. Generalizing, we may expect a plateau when some parts of the task are easy and others difficult. Ruger using mechanical puzzles required O to continue practice up to a high degree of skill. There were many cases in which O after running along on an uneven level for many trials changed his method for the better and improved; and in at least 80 percent of these cases O reported that the better method was based on a conscious analysis of the difficulties encountered. Quite generally, we may believe, the rise from a plateau results from a *change of method*, whether consciously adopted or not. On this understanding, the plateau is the final level for one way of performing the act and the rise from the plateau is a second, superimposed learning curve.

Attempts to find a mathematical equation for the learning curve. Disregarding minor oscillations which are accidental so far as concerns the general course of learning, we see enough similarity in learning curves to justify a search for a mathematical formula. The curves differ, to be sure, in initial and final levels of skill and in the amount of practice required by the learner to pass from his initial to his final level. The formula will therefore include "parameters," constant for the single curve but differing from one curve to another.

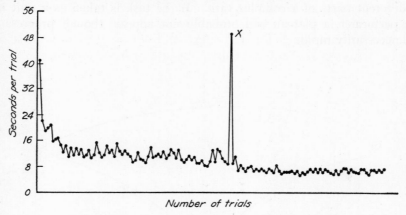

FIG. 52. (Data from Ruger, 1910.) Progress of a subject in learning to manipulate a mechanical puzzle. The trials are arranged in order from left to right, the time of each being indicated by the ordinate. Descent of the curve means improvement. At X, the subject studied out a newly observed character of the puzzle, consuming much time in one trial but permanently improving the level of his performance, and also decreasing its variability.

To free the curve from accidental irregularities we may combine the single trials into blocks, or we may use averages from a group of Os, though in so doing we may wash out general as well as individual characteristics of the curve. For example if every individual had a plateau but at slightly different parts of the curve, the combination would show smooth progress with no trace of a plateau.

If a number of individual curves are fairly similar in shape, they can be combined into a "Vincent curve." Divide each curve into tenths (or some convenient number of equal parts) along the base line, and determine the ordinate at each division. Average the ordinates of all the subjects at the first tenth, at the second tenth, etc., and finally plot the curve of these average ordinates. The work can be done either graphically or arithmetically. There are some sources of error, the chief one being the necessarily arbitrary criterion of completed learning; a change of criterion will change the form of the curve (Vincent, 1912; Kjerstad, 1919; Hunter, 1934; Hilgard & Campbell, 1937).

Empirical and rational equations of the learning curve. The curve shows to the eye the relation between y, the increasing achievement, and x, the amount of practice that has yielded this achievement. Its slope shows the changing rate of progress. An equation between x and y would embody these relations in a statement more compact than ordinary language and more definite than the impression obtained on looking at the curve. If an equation could be found which fitted all learning curves, or a whole class of learning curves, it would be of service in predicting what to expect from any single learning process and would furnish a norm by which to judge the eccentricities of single curves. One who knows his equations can think of several which will give an approximate fit to the typical learning curve. He may proceed "empirically" to find which form of equation gives in general the best fit, and the equation selected will have the values just mentioned.

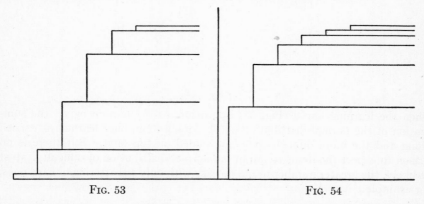

FIG. 53   FIG. 54

FIG. 53. Diagram to show how an S-shaped learning curve could result from a normal distribution of item difficulty.

FIG. 54. How a learning curve with negative acceleration could result from a skew distribution of items.

Not being based on any theory of learning, the empirical equation does not have the value of affording a check on theory. A rational equation is derived from a theory, or hypothesis, and the degree of its fit to the data gives a check on the hypothesis. It is easy to formulate rather vague theories conforming in a general way to the known facts, and one theory may conform about as well as another. If, however, a theory is definite enough to be embodied in an equation, it can be tested quantitatively by its fit with actual data. Each parameter in a rational equation of the learning curve must have a definite psychological meaning, and the changes in the parameter with changes in experimental conditions afford a check on the theory.

One approach to a rational equation regards learning as work applied to a maze or list of nonsense syllables where achievement in each trial is scored in number of items correct. The *rate of effective work* is shown by the increase in score per trial (or unit of time), i.e., by the *slope* of the curve. If the rate of effective work were constant throughout a learning process, the slope would be constant and the learning curve would reduce to a straight ascending line—provided achievement is measured in a constant unit. Theory must take account of the actual curvature of most learning curves. Two ways are open: either the rate of effective work is not constant or the units of achievement, the items learned, are not equal in difficulty.

The items—syllables in a list or alleys in a maze—are not of equal difficulty, when all factors in difficulty are considered, including position and interrelations as well as the characteristics of each single item. Some items demand more work than others, and the learning curve depends on the frequency of items of each degree of difficulty. Suppose the frequencies to be as follows:

Relative amounts of work required	Number of items
1	1
2	5
3	10
4	10
5	5
6	1
	32

Then the learning curve (Fig. 53) approximates the normal ogive, the summation of the normal distribution curve. Each item, once learned, is carried along and the more difficult items are added on top of it. But there is no reason to expect the items to fall into a normal distribution of difficulty. Just as likely, the greater number would be easy with only a scattering of hard ones; for example:

Relative amounts of work required	Number of items
1	15
2	9
3	4
4	2
5	1
6	1
	32

The summation (Fig. 54) has some resemblance to the usual learning curve. A plateau could result from a bimodal distribution of difficulty. A skillful experimenter could prepare lists or mazes which would yield quite a variety of learning curves.

So much for unequal difficulty of items. Regarding the rate of effective work, it probably changes as the learning advances. Work is effective so far as it goes into the learning of items not yet mastered. But the items already learned must be carried along as a *load* requiring the expenditure of energy—as is seen from the fact that they are sometimes lost after being once recited correctly—and this load increases with the progress of the learning and diverts a larger fraction of the energy from the effective work. On this basis the learning curve would show decreasing slope, negative acceleration, from start to finish. But the material already learned may sometimes function as a *carrier* rather than a load, especially when the items are coherent or logically interrelated. On this basis there would be positive acceleration throughout, which of course would not square with the data. To take account of learning curves which start with increasing slope and pass over into decreasing, an equation can be constructed containing two factors, one based on the idea of load and the other on that of carrier.

Quite a different approach is that of Gulliksen (1934) who develops a rational equation for the learning of a *single* item, such as the correct response in a discrimination experiment. He assumes with Thorndike (1932) that O has initial tendencies of certain strengths to make the correct response and the wrong response, and that each success adds a definite increment to the right tendency, while each error subtracts a certain amount from the wrong tendency. From these assumptions an equation is developed which fits some data rather well. Undoubtedly there is a future for this type of analysis, which demands both mathematical knowledge and a sense for psychological realities. References to other important studies of this general kind can be found in Gulliksen's paper.

The effect of practice on variability. To ordinary observation, practice makes an individual more regular. He approaches his task in a more uniform manner and follows a routine. There may be details to which he has given no attention, and in which he continues to vary. His performance has been stripped of many unnecessary movements, and it is a fair question whether what remains is relatively any less variable than the original, untrained performance.

When we go to the quantitative results for an answer, we find ourselves in doubt as to how the variability shall be measured. Notice, for example, the time required by one of Ruger's (1910) subjects for taking apart a mechanical puzzle which called for head work and also for deft finger work. Leaving out the very first trial, which is likely to be very long by accident, we have, for trials 2–11, the time in seconds as follows:

315   344   525   236   154   2388   244   2738   365   409   M = 772,   SD = 904

The times for trials 41–50 are:

18.4   16.8   16.8   19.9   19.6   18.3   16.9   13.3   20.0   13.1   M = 17.3,   SD = 2.4

The first set of times is absolutely much more variable than the second, as shown by the values of SD. But was O's *rate of work* less variable? To find rate of work, we consider output per unit of time, rather than time per unit of output. When O took 315 sec. for the single performance, his output was at the rate of 3600/315 = 11.4 units per hour. Transforming the values in this way we have the following rates of work, in units of output per hour:

In trials 2–11:

11.4   10.5   6.9   15.3   23.4   1.5   14.8   1.3   9.8   8.8   M = 10.4,   SD = 6.2

In trials 41–50:

196 214 214 180 184 197 213 271 180 275   M = 212, SD = 32.8

The variability of output or rate of work has increased as the result of practice. This is what we should expect: a fast worker would probably vary more in units of output per hour than a slow worker whose maximum output was too small to allow of much absolute variation. The relative variability, obtained by dividing each SD by its M, presents a still different picture. We have from the above figures:

SD/M for time per performance, early   1.17; late   .14
SD/M for output per hour,   "   .60; "   .15

By either measure, the relative variability diminishes (in this example) as the result of practice.

The effect of practice on variability differs with the nature of the task. In a ball tossing task (two balls, one hand), we find the number of catches in the ten trials of the first day to be (Batson, 1916):

1   2   2   2   3   3   3   1   2   2   M = 2.1, SD = .7
                                         SD/M = .33

And on the 45th day:

116   88   72   94   80   53   179   222   47   124   M = 108, SD = 53
                                                       SD/M = .49

Here the relative as well as the absolute variability of output increases with practice. It could hardly be otherwise in ball tossing, where a single error ends the trial, and where the player after gaining some skill will occasionally push his score to a very high count. By contrast, in maze running, where the score is errors per trial, there are at the final practice level no errors at all, or almost none, so that the variability comes down to near zero. The subject will still vary in his performance, but the score does not reveal the variation.

If some one asks, "But which is the correct measure of true variability?" we are not sure that the question has any sense. Measures are made for a purpose, for different purposes, and any of the variabilities measured may be useful for some purpose. If you were betting on a horse, the variability of time per unit of his past performances would be the important measure. If you were forecasting the output of a day's work, variability of output per unit of time would be better. Relative variability might seem the best indicator of true, essential variation, were it not for certain pitfalls that beset this measure.

Are individuals made more alike or more unlike by equal training in a performance? That is a question regarding *group* variability, and it is a question of importance in relation to the problem of heredity and environment. For if training makes individuals more alike, the individual differences that appear in advance of special training must be due to differences in previous opportunity; but if training makes individuals more unlike, there must be inherent differences between them. One would expect a straightforward answer from a good practice experiment, except that we do not know what variability to measure. If we take the variability in time per unit of performance, the absolute variability of the group is pretty sure to decrease as the result of practice, but if we use the variability of output per unit of time, we get the opposite result. If we use relative variability, we run afoul of the tricks of this measure, the chief of which is that we often do not know the absolute zero from which to measure the performance (Chapman, 1925). Suppose we were training a group in arithmetic and included in every test of proficiency ten very easy examples which every individual in the group did quickly and correctly. These examples contribute nothing to the group variability which will remain the same even if we give no credit for them. If we do score them we increase every one's score by 10 points, and increase by that amount the denominator in our measure of relative variability, SD/M. We thus artificially lower the relative variability. Padding of a less obvious sort is likely to be present in any performance chosen for a practice experiment. An effect opposite to padding has been more emphasized: the test material may not cover the lower ranges of the ability in question, so that the arbitrary zero of the score may lie well above the absolute zero. Another difficulty lies in the unequal units in which the performance is scored. A gain of one example in the more difficult part of a collection of arithmetic examples is a bigger gain than a gain of one unit in the lower part of the scale. In contrast, a gain of one catch in ball tossing, when the score is already 100 catches, is a smaller gain than the early advance from 1 catch to 2. These difficulties are perhaps avoidable by suitable *scaling* of the test material, as pointed out by Anastasi (1934) who also discusses other sources of error in measuring the effects of practice on variability.

CHAPTER VIII

TRANSFER OF TRAINING

W HETHER skill acquired in practicing one performance spreads to other performances—whether the mastery of one situation is a good preparation for handling another situation—is not only a very practical question but also a rather fundamental problem in psychology. A theory of learning must explain the mechanism of transfer, so far as transfer occurs, and a theory of thinking must interpret the fact, if it is a fact, that original thought on a new problem uses past experience with other problems. Freud's transference which at first seems altogether different from the psychologist's transfer does in fact conceive of an emotional attitude acquired or learned in dealing with certain persons, the parents, and transferred later in life to some other person who stands *in loco parentis.*

Transfer is one form of interaction between learning processes or between learned reactions. Other forms, interference and retroactive inhibition, will be considered in the next chapter. Conceivably the learning of one act might facilitate or hamper the subsequent learning of another act, and might affect favorably or unfavorably the retention of an act already learned or its execution (recall). The many possible varieties of interaction have not all been examined experimentally.

Terminology. *Transfer* means the carrying over of an act or way of acting from one performance to another. *Transfer effect* means the effect of this transferred act upon the execution or learning of the second performance. The distinction becomes clear when we notice that the effect may be positive or negative. A habit of speedy work carried over from a highly skilled to a new performance may impede the learning of the latter. In such cases it has been customary to speak of "negative transfer," but rather illogically, since it is not the transfer which is negative but the effect upon the second performance. Negative transfer would logically mean that an act acquired in the first performance was somehow reversed in being transferred. If the habit of speedy work acquired in learning one performance gave rise to slow, cautious attack upon another performance, that could be called negative transfer. When an act is carried over but impedes the learning of a second act we obviously have positive transfer and a negative transfer effect.

True negative transfer has been demonstrated in certain cases. It is called, in those cases, transfer of fatigue. Bills & McTeer (1932) conducted a fatigue experiment in which the primary task was the writing of the letters a b c, a b c, . . . continuously and as rapidly as possible without errors. In one condition O continued this unchanging task for 16 minutes, in other conditions the task was changed in alternate minutes to writing abd, abd . . . (one letter changed), or to writing ade, ade. . . . (2 letters changed), or to writing def, def. . . . (all letters changed). The output was greatest when all the letters were changed and least when there was no change. The authors conclude: "In transferring from one type of work to another type, there will be a tendency for the level of performance in the second task to be detrimentally affected in proportion to the number of identical elements in the two tasks. In alternately working on two tasks, there will be a tendency for the decrement developing in both tasks to be proportional to the number of elements common to both." We can speak here of negative transfer; the reactions fatigued in the first task are less likely on that account to be made in the second task. We can imagine an act to become distasteful when O is forced to make it repeatedly in a certain situation. On shifting to another situation in which this act though possible is not forced upon the subject, he avoids it. This negative transfer might have either a beneficial or a detrimental effect upon the second performance. So there can be negative transfer with a positive transfer effect.

Another bit of terminology may best be clarified at the outset. The theory about which most of the experiments on transfer revolve, in the hope sometimes of proving and sometimes of disproving it, is called "the theory of identical elements." The word *element* has caused confusion. The element transferred can obviously not be either a single sensory quality or a reflex, since it is a learned response. It does not conform to either of these traditional concepts of a psychological element. It might be an association between stimulus and response (Reed, 1918). Warren's dictionary defines element as "a constituent part of any phenomenon, event, or system; usually, the most simple sort of constituent." In connection with transfer the former, less specific meaning is obviously intended. Bills and McTeer in the article just cited speak of the writing of a letter as an element, though this act is a complex learned performance. The logic of the problem shows that element cannot here be meant in an atomistic sense. What the theory of identical elements demands is that transfer should be of concrete performances, whether simple or complex makes no difference to the theory. Confusion will be avoided by using the word "constituent" or "component" in place of "element" and by speaking of the theory of identical components.

An older theory goes by the name of "formal discipline." It supposes that a faculty or power is developed like a muscle by exercise on one sort of material and is thus prepared for any use. In its educational application the theory holds that memory, trained in learning poetry or vocabularies, will be better able to handle law cases or the details of a business, and that reasoning power, exercised in geometry, is prepared to handle scientific or social problems. If we substitute for "faculty" a more modern-sounding word such as "function" there is nothing repugnant or absurd about this theory, but it obviously is hard to check except by the method of exclusion, i.e., by finding cases in which one function is improved by the exercise of another function, though there is no transfer of concrete acts or ways of acting. General brain development may conceivably be stimulated by any intensive intellectual exercise.

METHODOLOGY OF TRANSFER EXPERIMENTS

Two general methods have been used, the first being more obvious to experimenters in the human laboratory and the second to those in the animal laboratory, though both were first used on human subjects.

The fore- and after-test method. This method was the first in use (Volkmann, 1858) and has been much employed in human experiments. Let two tasks be labeled A and B. The subjects are practiced in task A, and before and after this practice they are tested in task B. The question is whether B shows an improvement (or possibly a deterioration) from fore-test to after-test, and whether this improvement can be attributed to the intervening practice.

There may be improvement not attributable to transfer. Task B has received a certain amount of practice in the fore-test, and we must expect some resulting improvement in the after-test. This practice effect may be very large, since improvement is often quite rapid in the first few trials of a new task. A *control group* is needed, to take the fore-test and after-test like the practice group, but without the intervening practice. The plan of such an experiment will be:

Plan 1

Practice group: Fore-test in B.....Practice in A.....After-test in B.
Control group: Fore-test in B......................After-test in B.

Subtracting the gain of the control group from that of the practice group we obtain the *net gain* attributable to transfer. The control group in transfer experiments was employed in a small way by Thorndike & Woodworth (1901) and became standard practice with the work of Winch (1908), Dearborn (1909) and Sleight (1911).

It is necessary to match the practice and control groups for initial ability in task B, as can be done by making the division into groups on the basis of the fore-test results. We must be justified in assuming equal gains for the two groups, except for the effect of transfer. But we know that Os who make a low initial score are likely to show a large gain. If we should use a control group scoring far above or below the practice group in the fore-test, our computed "net gain" would be too large or too small, respectively.

Instead of matched groups, we can sometimes use matched tasks, equated by previous standardization. We can then dispense with the control group and also with the fore-test, thus:

Plan 2

Practice on A . . . . . After-test on B; A and B being equated tasks.

Here, because of the equality of tasks, the first trial on A is equivalent to a fore-test of B, so far as test scores are concerned. The matched tasks are usually very similar: two mazes, two substitution tests, two card-sorting tasks, etc.

The successive-practice method. The method of fore-test and after-test has the disadvantage of looking for transfer at only one stage in the process of mastering the test performance. This performance, which we call B, has been slightly practiced in the fore-test but is still in an early stage of mastery at the time of the after-test when the transfer from A is examined. There are several objections to limiting the study of transfer to this single stage. There may be some initial awkwardness in shifting from well-practiced A to little-known B, with a resulting negative transfer effect which would pass off on further repetition of B and leave a positive transfer effect. Or, on the contrary, the benefit derived from A may be limited to a few trials of B and give way soon to a zero transfer effect. Once more, if performance A has been brought to a high degree of skill, by the development of "higher units," etc., such skill can perhaps not be used in a relatively raw performance such as B is in the after-test. The rudiments of B must be mastered before the higher skill can be transferred from A. In order to afford a full opportunity for transfer from one performance to another, we therefore expand the after-test into a practice series on B. The fore-test becomes superfluous except as a means of equating groups, and we have the successive-practice method used on human subjects by Bair (1902) and on animals by Webb (1917) and many later experimenters.

The general plan of a successive-practice experiment is to have the same subjects learn first A and then B. If we know that A and B are equally difficult, we need only ask whether B, coming second, is learned more easily than A. To depend on equated tasks would however unduly limit the scope of transfer study. The scope becomes indefinitely wide if we use a matched control group, which simply learns task B, while the transfer group has previous practice with task A. We compare the learning of B after A with the learning of B "from scratch." The tasks A and B can be as dissimilar as we like, provided our groups are equated. Still another plan is to practice one group on A followed by B, and the other group on B followed by A, and pool the groups for first learning and for second learning. Neither tasks nor groups need be strictly equated in this procedure. To the two plans listed under fore- and after-test we add three involving successive practice.

Plan 3

A single group learns A . . . . . learns B;　A and B being equated tasks.

Plan 4

Transfer group learns A . . . . . learns B.
Control group . . . . learns B;　the two groups being equated.

Plan 5

Group I learns A . . . . . . learns B.
Group II learns B . . . . . learns A; the data from A and B being pooled.

The matching of groups sometimes necessitates a fore-test, and sometimes is accomplished in other ways. The method of "co-twin control," used by Gesell & Thompson (1929) and also by McGraw (1935), gives one of a pair of identical twins certain training and then tests both twins or starts both on a second task to be learned.

Measures of the transfer effect. Unless attention is given to the matter in planning the experiment, the results, while clearly demonstrating the presence of a transfer effect, may afford no proper measure of its amount. Consider the results obtainable from Plan 1: the net gain shows the amount of transfer effect in terms of the original unit of measure, as so many seconds or so many errors, but this raw measure does not tell us how complete a transfer effect we have obtained nor enable us to compare the transfer effects obtained in two quite different experiments. We should like to express the transfer effect on a scale of percents, running from 0 to 100. Plan 1, or any of the Plans, furnishes a criterion of zero transfer, but Plan 1 gives no 100 percent mark. It does little good to express the net gain as a percent of the original score in the fore-test; the net gain might run far above 100 percent if expressed in terms of output per unit of time, and could never reach 100 if expressed in time per unit of work. In errors the gain might reach but could not exceed 100 percent, so that here we should be better off though the measure would have no great reliability. What we need is a criterion of a 100 percent transfer effect. Two operational meanings could be attached to this expression.

1. Complete transfer effect is equal to the direct practice effect. We cannot expect a greater gain in any other task than we find in the one directly practiced. When we are using equated tasks, as in Plan 2, complete transfer would mean that the after-test score in B equalled the final practice score in A; and zero transfer would mean that the after-test score in B was equal to the initial practice score in A. So Plan 2 can afford a percent measure of the transfer effect. Plan 3 evidently does the same, and so does Plan 5 when the two tasks are pooled. When we are depending on matched groups, as in Plan 4, we can compare the first trial on task B of the transfer group with the first and last trials of the control group on this same task. If the practice group scores only as much as the first trial of the control, we have zero transfer effect; if it equals the last trial of the control group we have 100 percent transfer. But this measure makes little sense unless we have some way of equating the amount of practice devoted by the practice group to A and by the control group to B.

2. Complete transfer effect, in a successive-practice experiment, is analogous to complete retention in a memory experiment, and is shown by 100 per-

cent saving in learning task B, just as complete retention is shown by 100 percent saving in relearning. The second task is perfect (according to the criterion of learning adopted) on the first trial. Zero transfer effect means here that no saving in the learning of B results from the previous learning of A. If the two tasks are matched, as in Plan 3, zero transfer effect means that as much work must be put on task B as on task A to reach the same criterion of learning. If it takes 20 trials to master A and then takes 12 trials to master B, the saving in trials is $20 - 12 = 8 = 40$ percent of complete transfer effect. (Saving can also be measured in time or in errors.) Saving is computed in the same way in Plan 5. In Plan 4 we compare the learning of B by the transfer and control groups; if the transfer group requires 12 trials to the control group's 20, the transfer effect is, again, $(20 - 12)/20 = 40$ percent. It takes 40 percent less work to learn B because of the carry-over from A.

These different measures of transfer, and some others which make sense (Cook, 1933 a), are not mathematically equivalent; they give different percent values of the transfer effect from the same data. Visual comparison of the successive practice curves affords a good check on the computations. All through we are measuring the transfer effect and not transfer itself. Some of the "identical components" carried over may impede the new learning while other components are assisting it; in which case the amount of transfer would exceed the transfer effect.

CROSS EDUCATION, THE TRANSFER OF SKILL FROM ONE BODILY
MEMBER TO ANOTHER

It is worth noting that the scientific study of transfer began with our old friends, the psychophysicists. E. H. Weber, the author of Weber's law, observed in 1844 that some children trained to write with the right hand were able without further training to produce very good mirror-writing with the left hand. Weber himself possessed a knack which is useful to a biological lecturer in sketching on the blackboard the outline of a bilaterally symmetrical animal—the knack of drawing with both hands simultaneously, the left hand producing a mirror-image of what is drawn by the right hand. A professor of surgery reported to Weber that he found it economical, in teaching certain delicate operations which must be performed sometimes with one hand and sometimes with the other, to train his students only in the use of the left hand, because the right hand without further training would take over the skill acquired. Weber did not publish these observations at the time but later communicated them to Fechner who published them in 1858 along with similar observations of his own.

Transfer of perceptual skill. This paper of Fechner on the bilateral transfer of motor skill was appended to a longer paper by A. W. Volkmann, his brother-in-law, who had collaborated with him in certain psychophysical investigations, including some prolonged experiments on the tactual discrimination of two points from one, i.e., on the two-point threshold (p. 451). Volkmann had noted three rather remarkable phenomena: (1) a very marked increase in sensitivity (decrease of the two-point threshold) in the practiced skin area; (2) an almost equal improvement in the corresponding area of the other hand or arm; and (3) the rapid disappearance of this acquired sensitivity in a few days of disuse. The transfer was not general but was confined to areas adjacent or symmetrical to the area receiving the practice. There was good transfer from the tip to the base of the same finger (volar side) and from one finger to another, but not from finger to forearm. Volkmann inferred from the transfer effects that the change due to practice was in the brain and not in the skin.

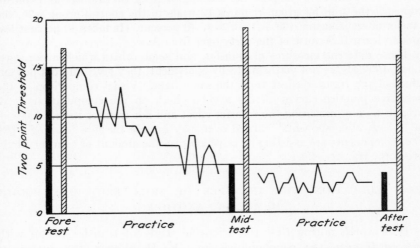

FIG. 55. (Data from Volkmann, 1858.) Practice in the two-point threshold with bilateral transfer. The tip of the left middle finger received the practice, with fore-, mid- and after-tests of the right middle finger (shown by black bars) and of the volar surface of the left forearm (cross-hatched bars). The ordinate shows the percent of errors, which decreased greatly in the practiced finger and in the symmetrical, unpracticed finger, but scarcely at all in the forearm.

Dresslar (1894) obtained the same results from two adult subjects when the practiced area was on the forearm. The two-point threshold went down in four weeks of practice from 27 mm to 3 mm on the directly practiced area. On the bilaterally symmetrical area, the fore-test gave a two-point threshold of 27 mm and the after-test of $3\frac{1}{2}$ mm. Adjacent regions of the forearm were not fore-tested, but afterwards their sensitivity was by no means equal to that of the practiced and symmetrical areas. After practice the points applied to the skin *felt* very different in the practiced area and the adjacent areas. From other work (Messenger, 1903; Boring, 1920) we can be pretty sure that the improvement consisted in becoming acquainted with the feel of two points and of one. At distances so small that the two points are not sensed as two there is still a difference which O can learn to interpret correctly. These slight cues of one and two must differ greatly in differently structured regions of the skin, but may be essentially the same in bilaterally symmetrical areas. With this understanding of the matter there is nothing very mysterious about Volkmann's results, though at first they are surprising.

A similar result in indirect vision was reported by Franz (1933). Various simple figures were presented 8° out from the fixation point, and O practiced recognizing and distinguishing them till he acquired considerable facility. When the practice was confined to one eye, an after-test showed equal facility with the other eye—as indeed would be expected from the fact that corresponding parts of the two retinas are connected with the same part of the visual area of the brain (p. 327). It was also true that the figures could be displaced to somewhat different parts of the field of indirect vision—parts still at the same distance from the fixation point but in other directions—and still show the transfer effect. Somewhat different parts of the area striata, the direct receptive area of the cortex, were here involved in the practice and in the after-test; but presumably the cues for discrimination remained about the same.

Bilateral transfer of motor skill. From many experiments it appears that skill acquired with one hand can often be carried over to the other hand or even to the foot—often but not in every case. Several motor performances were studied by Scripture and his students (1894), es-

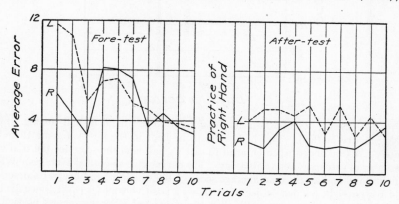

FIG. 56. (After Davis, 1898.) Transfer (?) from right to left hand in lunging at a target with a fencing foil. The lunge was first explained to the Os, who had never fenced; each O was allowed two or three preparatory lunges, and then a record was taken of 10 thrusts at the target with the right hand followed by 10 with the left hand. The Os now practiced for ten days, 10 thrusts a day, *with the right hand only*, before the final test of both hands. The graph shows the average error of four Os in each trial of the fore- and after-tests. If we take the mean of the 10 trials of the fore-test, and of the after-test, we seem to have evidence of transfer. Thus we have:

	Fore-test	After-test	Gain
Right hand	5.3 cm	2.4 cm	2.9 cm
Left hand	6.3	3.9	2.4

But the graph shows rapid improvement of the left hand in the fore-test, and no gain whatever from the end of the fore-test to the beginning of the after-test. All the apparent transfer can therefore be attributed to the practice of the left hand itself.

pecially by Davis (1898). O practiced hand steadiness, gripping a dynamometer, lifting a five pound dumbbell till fatigued, tapping with the foot, or lunging at a target. The practice was confined to one hand or foot, and other members tested before and after the practice showed improvement in most cases. The absence of control groups left the evidence insecure. Fig. 56, from one of these studies, illustrates one of the pitfalls of transfer experiments.

Ball tossing showed transfer from the right hand to the left in 5 of Swift's 6 subjects (1903, see p. 165). In terms of saving, the transfer effect was large, amounting to about ⅔ of the work which would otherwise have been required from the left hand. The most obvious factor in the transfer effect was the carrying over of efficient methods of handling the balls, of throwing them so as to avoid collisions, and of recovering control after a poor throw.

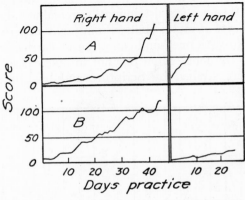

FIG. 57. (Swift, 1903.) Transfer from right to left hand in ball tossing. Successive practice method. Two balls were to be kept in the air by tossing them alternately. A trial ended when O failed to catch a ball, and the score for the trial was the number of catches. Ten trials a day. The curves give smoothed averages. When the right hand had attained an average score of 100, the left hand began its practice. A and B were right-handed subjects. A shows a positive transfer effect, since his left hand improved much more rapidly than the right; but B's curve shows no sign of transfer, perhaps because, though quite skillful, he was not analytical in his work.

Somewhat similar to ball-tossing, though simpler, is the game utilized by Munn (1932) in a transfer experiment with practice and control groups of 50 students each. Both groups took a fore-test of 50 trials with the left hand; the practice group then made 500 trials with the right hand in the course of an hour, the control group resting for this length of time, and finally both groups took the after-test of 50 trials with the left hand. (The experiment was conducted as an individual, not a group experiment.) The groups were not matched for initial ability. From Munn's published data, however, we can select two groups of 25, matched individually for sex and for fore-test scores, with the following result:

Mean fore-test score of each group	47 points
Mean after-test score of practice group	80 "
" " " " control "	55 "

Net transfer gain = 80 − 55 = 25 points, a reliable gain as shown by the original data. The data are more fully utilized in Fig. 58. According to the running comments of the Os, what is transferred here, as in ball tossing, consists largely of technique.

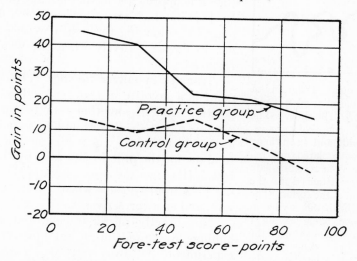

FIG. 58. (Data from Munn, 1932.) Gain and transfer in relation to original score. The Os are grouped according to their fore-test scores, with a class interval of 20 "points," and the average gain for each class is shown by the ordinate. For example, those Os in the control group, who made an initial score of 20 points or less, made an average gain of 14 points; the Os in the practice group whose initial score was 20 or less gained 45 points. The net gain, or transfer effect, is represented by the distance between the two lines; it was greatest for the Os who made low initial scores.

The subjects in Van der Veldt's experiment (1928; see p. 163) after thoroughly learning to touch a series of points with the right hand did so easily and rapidly with the left hand; and they showed no tendency to reverse the movement of the left hand so as to execute a mirror image of the movement learned with the right hand. The *place relations* which had been learned were easily followed with either hand.

Quite similar is an experiment of Cook (1934 a) in which a path was learned without the aid of sight by following a groove with a stylus (Figs. 59, 60). Transfer from each hand to the other, from each foot to the other, and from each hand to each foot, was tested with different groups of Os, and the effect was positive in every group. What was transferred? The *groove* remained the same and in the same position, and skillful *management of the stylus*, so as to avoid binding by excessive pressure, was carried over to some extent from one operating member to another. With a finger maze containing blind alleys, also, the same author (1935) found a strong positive transfer effect from either hand to the other. Since the maze remained unchanged in position, the movements made with the second hand were not symmetrical with those of the first hand and did not call for the corresponding muscular contractions on the other side of the body. It was not a motor pattern, in the strict sense, that was transferred, but an *acquaintance with the maze* as a place. In fact the experiment seems the same in principle as that already described (p. 133) in which rats after learning a flooded maze by swimming through it were found to run it almost perfectly when the water was removed.

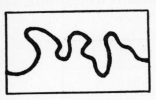

FIG. 59. Diagram of stylus "maze" used by Cook (1934 a). The heavy line shows the course of a groove, ¼ in. wide and 48 in. long. The groove flared out beneath so as to accommodate a washer attached to the lower end of the stylus. The washer held the stylus in the groove, while leaving it free to move along the groove. The stylus rod was attached to a handle or, for use with the foot, to the under side of a sandal. Vision of the maze was excluded by a screen. O was informed that the path extended in general from left to right and that it was winding but had no blind alleys. He was to try for speed.

Transfer in mirror tracing. This experiment is a favorite in transfer studies, and a positive effect, sometimes quite large, is usually reported. Ewert (1926) found some of the older claims excessive because of failure to allow for the practice afforded by the fore-test. His own experiments still showed a net gain from transfer when a control group was used as a corrective.

Not exactly mirror-tracing, but mirror-aiming, was used in a hand-foot transfer experiment by Bray (1928). Instead of tracing a star, O hit at a target with a pencil held in the hand or strapped to the foot. Some of the quantitative results are shown in Fig. 61.

A summary of Bray's findings will throw the facts of bilateral transfer into relief.

1. The transfer was not simply bilateral. There was a positive transfer effect from hand to foot, and from foot to hand.

2. The transfer effect obtained after a small amount of practice was not increased by prolonging the practice.

3. The benefit of the preceding hand practice was shown mostly in the early part of the foot practice. The rudiments, rather than the later acquisitions, are transferred. This conclusion, however, is disputed by Cook (1933 a, b).

4. What, concretely, was transferred? O's retrospective reports, along with E's observations, revealed the following items:

a. Acquaintance with the mirror effect in this particular situation.

b. Some method, differing with the individual, of allowing for the mirror effect in correcting the aim. The very first hit usually fell to one side or the other of the vertical line which served as target. In correcting his aim for the second hit, O inevitably went in the wrong direction because of the mirror effect. The third hit often went still further away. Finally, with much effort, O forced his hand or foot in the opposite direction to that indicated as right by the mirror. In time he worked out some method of correcting his aim without succumbing to the mirror illusion. The commonest method was to disregard vision except for noting an error and to depend on kinesthesis for correcting it. Another method consisted in making a reverse correction; if the mirror shows you too far to the right, go still farther to the right. Still another was to take the frame of the mirror as the guide and to correct by moving toward or away from the frame.

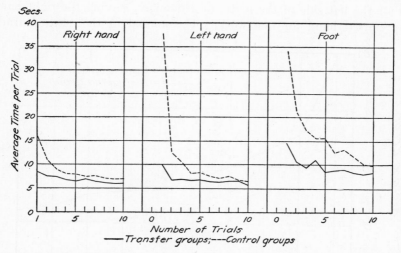

FIG. 60. (Data from Cook, 1934 a.) Transfer in following an unseen groove with a stylus. The course of the groove is shown in Fig. 59. Groups of 30 students had, first, 20 trials with one hand or one foot; and, second, 10 trials with one of the other three members. Dotted lines show first learning (first 10 trials only), solid lines second learning, and the distance between shows amount of transfer effect. Results from both feet were so nearly identical that they have been combined. The figures show clearly (1) that the saving is less for the right hand than for the more awkward members, and (2) that the saving from transfer is small after the first few trials.

c. Avoidance of the impulsive over-correction which was common in the early trials; and learning to let well enough alone and simply repeat a movement which came fairly close to the mark—for a movement can be repeated quite easily while an attempt at correction may suffer from the mirror effect.

d. Escape from the nervousness and self-consciousness which some Os manifested at the beginning. "After a few trials the nervous attitude disappeared and was replaced by an air of confidence. Usually, but not always, the confident attitude was carried over to practice with any other limb." ·

5. Some of this transferable material could be put into O's possession by a course of instruction with demonstrations but without any actual

practice.   As we have noted in another place (p. 161) one can learn some of the technique of mirror-tracing by simply watching another person's efforts.

Neurology of bilateral transfer.   It seems almost certain that the locus of any practice effect is the cerebral hemispheres and that practice leaves behind some change in the neural structure or condition. In case of bilateral transfer, the operating mechanisms have in part a different cerebral localization, since the right side of the body is connected most directly with the left hemisphere, and the left with the right. Lashley (1924) cauterized the right precentral gyre, i.e., the motor area for the left side of the body, in a monkey, leaving the right hand the preferred hand for fine work.   The animal in this state learned

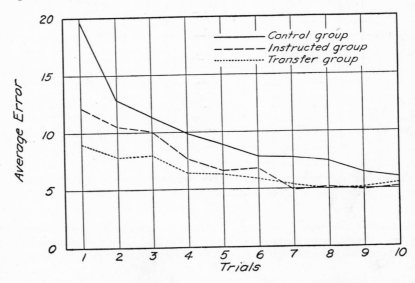

Fig. 61. (From Bray, 1928.)   Transfer from hand to foot in mirror target practice. The target was a vertical line on a frontal-parallel sheet of paper straight in front of O's hand or foot, concealed by a screen from direct vision but visible in a mirror. The mirror was vertical, perpendicular to the plane of the target and somewhat to O's side. It reversed right and left. For the hand practice, the pencil with which the hits were made was held in the right hand; for the foot practice, the pencil was attached to a light block of wood which was strapped to the right foot, and the foot hung free in front of the target, the thigh being supported while O sat in an elevated chair. The hits were required to keep time with a metronome beating 72 times per minute; a forward jab at the target was made at one beat and a backward movement to the starting point at the next beat, and so on till 10 hits were made at the target, the 10 hits constituting one "trial."   O tried to correct his aim between hits and in so doing was at first misled by the mirror reversal. The control group of 24 students did the foot practice without previous hand practice; the transfer group of 37 students had at least 10 "trials" with the hand before starting with the foot; the instructed group of 17 students had no previous practice but were made familiar with the setup and with the mirror effect by visual demonstration and were told an efficient way of correcting their errors and escaping from the mirror effect. The curves indicate that the instruction helped the feet considerably but not as much as actual hand practice.

to open three latch boxes, manipulating the latches with the right hand and using the left arm only as a prop. In a second operation the motor area for the right hand was destroyed, leaving the right hand weak and stiff and the left now the preferred hand. Tested with the same latch boxes the animal in the first few trials tried to use the right hand, as he had learned to do, but shifted to the left hand with very little further practice. Evidently neither motor area could have been the locus of the neural change produced by the practice. From Lashley's description of the animal's behavior, it is clear that acquaintance with the boxes as objects was retained. After the second operation the monkey attacked the latches in the right way but was weak and awkward with his right hand and simply substituted the more convenient member. In the original learning he had probably developed no new motor coordinations but had merely adapted old movements to the characteristics of the latches and boxes which he learned by vision combined with manipulation. The locus of such learning, from all we know of the brain, may extend widely over the cortex, into the premotor, parietal and occipital regions.

Aside from the facility with which a movement is duplicated mirror-wise by the other hand—a facility which points to some mechanism for bilateral innervation of symmetrical muscles—all the instances of transfer which we have seen belong at a relatively high level of cerebral function. On the motor side we find transfer of technique and good management—ways of escaping the mirror illusion and of avoiding collisions in ball tossing—and on the sensory side we find acquaintance with objects such as latches and mazes, and acquaintance with geometrical forms in indirect vision and with the feel of two points applied close together on the skin. Each of these bits of knowledge and skill depends on some high-level cerebral mechanism—to be conceived as wide-spreading rather than confined to a small area of the cortex—and transfer shows that the same mechanism is available to both hands and to the feet as well when they execute the movement. A better statement is that either hand is available for the use of the same cerebral mechanism; for the core of the act corresponds to the cerebral mechanism and not to the muscles or receptors employed.

MEMORY TRAINING

It is rather curious that, while positive results on bilateral transfer have awakened surprise, such results have been expected when the broader question of transfer was broached and the relatively negative results sometimes announced have been received with skepticism. The belief in "formal discipline" seems deeply ingrained. Belief in the efficacy of memory training, certainly a wide-spread belief, was emphatically called in question by William James. In his view retentiveness was a physiological trait which varied with the individual constitution, with age and with the condition of health, but was not susceptible to training. He endeavored to put his hypothesis to test by some experiments (1890, I, p. 666) which were the first experiments on transfer, aside from those on cross education. His subjects first measured their speed of learning the verses of one poet, then trained themselves at length in memorizing those of another poet, and finally came back to the first poet and determined whether they could memorize his poems more quickly than before. The results showed little transfer effect, and such improvement as did appear was attributed to better methods of memorizing rather than to any improvement in retentiveness. James concluded that the power of retention was not affected by training and that "all improvement of memory consists, then, in the improvement of one's habitual methods of recording facts."

Rapid improvement in memorizing a particular kind of material. James did not state how much his Os gained in the practice series itself, but from other experiments in the learning of poems it is certain that great improvement can occur. Ebert & Meumann (1905) conducted a practice experiment in memorizing nonsense syllables and found great improvement, which consisted largely in better technique. The learners tried out various devices to assist in the memorizing, abandoned those which were found useless and kept the good ones. They found rhythmic grouping a help. They learned to avoid farfetched "associations." They discovered, to their own surprise, that they were capable of memorizing lists of nonsense syllables, and gained confidence and interest in the work. They eliminated worry, strain and the useless muscular reactions which occur in performing an unfamiliar and difficult task. They became "adapted" to the experimenter and to the laboratory conditions.

Small evidence of transfer to other kinds of material. In the study just mentioned Ebert & Meumann were interested specially in the question of transfer. Before and after the practice in memorizing nonsense syllables they tested their Os in learning letters, numbers, disconnected words, vocabularies, prose, poetry, and meaningless visual figures. The after-tests usually showed more or less improvement over the fore-tests, from which the authors inferred a positive transfer effect. The lack of a control group in their experiments was a serious methodological defect, as Dearborn (1909) proved by repeating their experiment minus the practice series. Fore-test, after-test and intervening lapse of time were the same as in Ebert & Meumann's experiment, but Dearborn's Os had no memory practice in the interval. "The results indicate that a considerable part of the improvement found must be attributed to direct factors in the test series, and not to any 'spread' of improvement from the practice series."

Reed (1917) repeated Ebert & Meumann's entire experiment on a practice group of 8 students, with a control group of 5 students. The practice, lasting 15 days, half an hour or an hour a day, consisted in memorizing lists of 12 nonsense syllables and resulted in marked improvement in this special task. The time required to learn a list of 12 nonsense syllables was reduced by half. In the after-tests the practice group usually showed some improvement but so did the control group, and none of the net gains and losses shown in the adjacent table are statistically reliable. The two groups were far from matched in some of the fore-tests—a fact which makes comparison difficult. The results do show pretty clearly that the spread of ability from special memory practice is relatively small and undependable, and that more extensive research is necessary to demonstrate its reality or unreality.

TIME REQUIRED TO MEMORIZE (IN MINUTES)
(*Reed, 1917*)

	Fore-test	*After-test*	*Gain*
16 lines of poetry			
Practice group	21.5	19.3	2.2
Control group	18.7	18.8	− .1
Transfer gain			2.3
10 lines of prose			
Practice group	23.4	23.5	− .1
Control group	29.8	27.7	2.1
Transfer gain			−2.2
Latin-English vocabularies, totalling 70 items			
Practice group	42.6	47.6	−5.0
Control group	55.1	54.6	.5
Transfer gain			−5.5
24 nonsense visual diagrams			
Practice group	17.3	9.6	7.7
Control group	12.2	9.9	2.3
Transfer gain			5.4

The experiment of Sleight (1911) can be called fairly adequate and is perhaps all the better for having been done on young subjects (84 school girls, average age 12 years, 8 months). On the basis of fore-test results in ten various memory tasks, four equated groups were formed. Three groups practiced memorizing either poetry, or the substance of prose passages, or tables of measures and similar quantitative facts. The work schedule was : fore-test. . . .3 weeks practice. . . . mid-test. . . .3 weeks practice. . . .after-test. The control group took the fore-, mid- and after-tests but occupied themselves with arithmetic or other school work while the other groups were engaged in memory practice. The test materials were carefully prepared and rotated so as to avoid errors due to unequal tests.

Sleight's results showed no general improvement in memory resulting from the practice. Net gains and losses of the practice groups were equally numerous, and very few of them were statistically significant. The two groups which practiced memorizing poetry and tables of measures showed significant positive transfer effects in the memorizing of nonsense syllable lists, apparently due to the device of using rhythm. In a similar though less extensive experiment on adult subjects, Sleight found one significant transfer effect but a negative one: after practice in learning the substance of prose passages the adult Os showed a net loss in memorizing relatively meaningless material, which they reported to be quite distasteful after the more interesting work of the practice period. Aside from these few instances, the net gains and losses were small and show a chance distribution (Fig. 62).

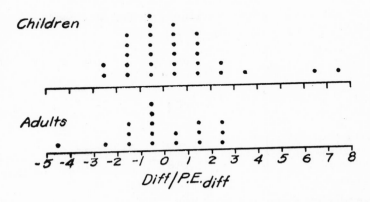

FIG. 62. (Data from Sleight, 1911.) Distribution of net gains and losses in the final tests after memory practice. Children: 3 practice groups and 10 tests, yielding 30 net gains or losses which are here expressed as multiples of their respective PE$_{diff}$. By chance about half of these differences would lie between ±1 PE$_{diff}$. Actually 13 of the 30 differences lie between these limits. The distribution could result from zero transfer effect and chance variation, except for the two large gains which are mentioned in the text. The second distribution is from Sleight's similar experiment on adults and shows one clear negative effect and an apparent surplus of small positive effects.

Memory practice vs. memory training. This distinction is sometimes made: in "practice" O repeats a performance time after time in his own way; in "training" he receives instruction in methods which can be carried over from one performance to another. Memory training ought to show a greater transfer effect than memory practice, provided the instructor knows the best techniques of memorizing. This hypothesis was tried out by Woodrow (1927). He divided a class of students into three groups. The control group did only the fore- and after-tests. The practice group devoted a total of three hours (in 8 periods spread over 4 weeks) to memorizing poetry and nonsense syllables. The training group divided the same total time between instruction and exercises in "proper methods of memorizing," their exercises, like the work of the practice group, being confined to memorizing poetry and nonsense syllables. The fore- and after-tests covered memory span for consonants, memorizing Turkish-English vocabularies and dates of events, verbatim memorizing of poems and prose passages, and learning the substance of information items.

In the after-tests the practice group was only about equal to the control, while the training group definitely surpassed both the other groups in every test. "In short, the experiment shows that in a case where one kind of training—undirected drill—produces amounts of transference which are sometimes positive and sometimes negative, but always small, another kind of training with the same drill material may result in a transference, the effects of which are uniformly large and positive."

What were these "proper methods of memorizing" in which training was given? Woodrow gives the following list.

1. Learning by wholes.
2. Use of active self-testing.
3. Use of grouping and rhythm.
4. Attention to meaning and use of images and symbols to embody meaning.
5. Mental alertness and concentration.
6. Confidence in one's ability to memorize.
7. In certain cases, as in learning nonsense syllables, the use of secondary associations.

Woodrow's experiment did not extend to the point of determining which of these elements of technique were of most value in transfer. They are bits of technique which learners have been found to adopt in memorizing and which seem to account for their great improvement in practice confined to a single type of material, such as nonsense syllable lists, or stanzas of a given author's poem.

When we consider the matter carefully we are struck by the fact that even in continued practice with one type of material, the large improvement which usually occurs can be regarded as a transfer effect. The specific associations established in learning one list of nonsense syllables are different from those required in another list. Yet learning the first list is an assistance in learning the second. There is a positive transfer effect from list to list. What can be transferred? O improves his technique, becomes better adapted to the task and more confident. All the results obtained in these memory studies are consistent with James's original conclusion that improvement in memory consists in better methods of memorizing. It is also likely, though on this point there is little experimental evidence, that the process of *recalling* what has been memorized can be improved by practice. Students seem to develop a technique of marshalling their information to special advantage when it is wanted in examinations—a performance in which they have much practice even if little that can be called "training."

TRANSFER IN OBSERVATION AND JUDGMENT

Early experiments. Thorndike & Woodworth (1901) called in question the whole doctrine of formal discipline and attempted to submit to an experimental test the alternative hypothesis that such a function as observation was really a group of functions varying with the thing observed.   They practiced their subjects in certain tasks and tested them before and afterward in similar tasks.   In one experiment the practice consisted in estimating rectangular areas of 10–100 sq. cm. After each estimate O was informed of the true area, and thus his improvement was assured.   Before and after this training he was tested in estimating the areas of rectangles of different sizes and also of triangles and other shapes.   Similar experiments bore upon the estimation of length of line, and weight of objects.   The general result was that improvement from fore-test to after-test though often present was irregular and undependable and seldom as great as the improvement in the particular function trained.

The same authors made much use of cancellation tests.   The Os practiced cancelling all the words containing both the letters e and s in many pages of a book.   Before and after this practice they were tested in cancelling words containing other letters: i-t, s-t, e-a, e-r.   The speed of cancelling words containing e-s went up during the practice by about 38 percent, while the speed in cancelling the other required words increased from the fore- to the after-test by about 21 percent.   A control group improved 9 percent.   A small positive transfer effect was thus indicated, due, as far as the authors could discover, to carrying over methods, ideas and useful habits from the practice to the after-test. For example, one O had a tendency to overestimate small areas such as were used in the practice series.   Discovering this error he corrected it and carried over the correction to the test series with larger areas, not always to his advantage.   In cancelling, some rules which can be transferred are: not to let the eyes get too close to the page, and not to become interested in the passages through which one is working.   But the high speed developed in cancelling e-s words was due largely to finding out and remembering which common words contain those letters, and this very specific adaptation could not be usefully transferred. There was sometimes a transfer of emotional adjustment.   An O who was timid and over-cautious in the fore-test became adjusted to the experimental situation in the long practice series and attacked the after-test with confidence.

The conclusion drawn by these authors from their experiments aroused considerable dissent at the time: "Improvement in any single mental function need not improve the ability in functions commonly called by the same name.   It may injure it.   Improvement in any single mental function rarely brings about equal improvement in any other function, no matter how similar, for the working of every mental function-group is conditioned by the nature of the data in each particular case. . . . There is no inner necessity for improvement of one function to improve others closely similar to it, due to a subtle transfer of practice effect. Improvement in them seems due to definite factors, the operation of which the training may or may not secure." The authors occasionally spoke of these definite factors as identical elements or common elements. Thorndike later (1903, 1913) gave a more definite statement of this theory: "A change in one function alters any other only in so far as the two functions have as factors identical elements." As examples of such identical elements he cited: specific movements and associations, ideas of aim and method, an attitude of confidence or of care, habituation to distraction or strain.

As between the theories of formal discipline and of identical elements (better, components, see p. 177) psychological discussion has usually favored the latter, since it has seemed certain that there must be something common to two functions if training the one has any effect on the other (H. E. O. James, 1930). Not all psychologists have been pleased with the phrase, "identical elements," and not all have agreed that the transfer effect was typically small in amount. Whipple (1928) points out that experiments on adults, whose general adjustments and work habits are well established, may show little transfer where children would show much more. G. W. Allport (1937) comments on the small scale of transfer experiments in comparison with the training given in school or in life.

Transfer from school subjects. Thorndike (1924), and Brolyer, Thorndike & Woodyard (1927) have examined the transfer values of high school studies. They gave an intelligence test to thousands of high school students before and after a year of study and classified them according to the school subjects studied. They asked whether those who had studied Latin, mathematics, physics and chemistry showed any larger gain in the intelligence test than those who had taken commercial and manual courses. There was a net gain of 7 points on the part of those who had devoted their time to the more intellectual courses. It does not follow that this gain was due to the courses taken, for the home life and other out-of-school experiences of the group taking the classical course may well have been more intellectually stimulating, more informative or more in line with the content of the intelligence tests.

Negative transfer effects. The identical components theory, if formulated so broadly as to satisfy everybody, is merely a frame into which more definite knowledge of transfer can be fitted. In the early discussions it was shown by Judd (1902, 1905, 1908) that negative transfer effects deserved equal attention with positive, in tracing out the dynamic interrelations of different performances. He gave some interesting examples. A subject who knew nothing of the Müller-Lyer illusion (p. 647) and who was not informed of his errors, was given practice in adjusting one of the principal lines to apparent equality with the other, and his adjustments gradually approached objective equality, the illusion being thus overcome. All this time the figure had been presented in one constant position. When now it was reversed right and left, the illusion returned in exaggerated amount and was not overcome by further practice. The practice had involved a specialized position habit which, being transferred, had a negative effect on correctness of response. Another O, however, who knew about the illusion, though fully subject to it and overcoming it only gradually in the first practice series, readjusted himself rather easily to the reversed position. His *cognitive grasp* of the situation enabled him to derive a positive instead of a negative transfer effect from the practice series.

This conclusion of Judd was reinforced by his results in another, often-cited experiment (1908). The task was to throw a dart and hit a target under water. To succeed, a correction must be made for the refraction of light which displaces the visual position of the target, and the correction varies with the depth of the target below the surface of the water. Two groups of 10–12 year old boys served as subjects. One group was carefully instructed in the theory of refraction, while the other group received no such instruction. Both groups practiced first with the target 12 inches under water and both improved at about the same rate, but when the target was later shifted to a position only 4 in. below the surface, the instructed group readjusted their aim rather quickly while the uninstructed had to learn all over again. Judd concludes that transfer may be helpful or detrimental according to O's cognitive grasp of the situation, according to his knowledge and ability to generalize. The same conclusion is reached by Orata (1928) after a comprehensive survey of the accumulated literature on transfer.

The negative transfer effect noted by Judd is of the nature of a correction for a constant error, the correction being carried over to another performance in which it is inappropriate. Negative effects of another sort have been found in cancellation where the task calls for rapid picking out of certain items from a mass of somewhat similar items. After practice in one special task of this sort, O is likely to carry over a set for the old items or a habit of speedy work which leads to error in a new task.

So Kline (1914) found evidence of detrimental transfer from cancellation of the letters *e* and *t* to cancelling a prescribed part of speech in prose texts. The practice with the letters was quite extensive, taking 30–40 minutes a day for 14 days; but the control group showed more improvement in the after-test. The practiced Os reported an interference effect on shifting to the cancellation of parts of speech. One said, "The practice with *e*'s and *t*'s hindered me in dealing with the parts of speech. I think it was because I became accustomed to looking for *e*'s and *t*'s and the tendency was to cross out those letters rather than the parts of speech." This is a good example of positive transfer with negative transfer effect. We see also that this O had a cognitive grasp of the situation and still suffered from transfer.

Similar interferences and also an important speed transfer are seen in the extensive data of Martin (1915) on transfer in cancellation. His subjects were boys 11–13 years of age, 36 in the practice group and 40 in the control group. All the boys were first assembled and given an initial test series, consisting of 2 one-minute trials in several cancellation tasks. The practice group and the control group were nearly equal in this initial test, the practice group being slightly superior. The practice group then worked 40 min. a day for 16 days on a single task, the cancelling of words containing both *a* and *t* in English prose from a book of no special interest to these boys. Improvement was marked. At the beginning of practice the average number of words cancelled was 10.26 per min.; at the end of practice the average had risen to 26.65 words per min. The errors consisted mostly in omitting words that should have been cancelled. Accuracy was therefore measured by dividing the number of words cancelled by the number that should have been cancelled in the reading matter covered by the subject. So measured the accuracy of the practice group in its special task was 79 percent at the start and increased gradually to 96 percent at the finish. When the practice was completed, the boys of both groups were reassembled and put through the same tests as at the outset. The gain from fore-test to after-test of the control group was deducted from that of the practice group, and the remainder was taken as the net gain or transfer effect. The transfer effects thus computed are shown in an adjoining table.

Net Gain in Other Cancellation Tests Resulting From Intensive Practice in Cancelling English Words Containing Both a and t

(*Martin, 1915*)

To be cancelled	*Gain in speed*	*P.E.*	*Gain in accuracy*	*P.E.*
a-t words in Spanish prose	6.44 words	0.38	1%	1.92
a and t in a mixed letter series	4.91 letters	1.25	6%	1.30
A in a mixed letter series	3.99 A's	1.39	− 1%	0.62
B in a mixed letter series	1.13 B's	0.93	− 3%	1.06
Number groups containing both 4 and 7	1.08 groups	0.83	− 7%	1.13
e-s words in Spanish prose	0.02 words	0.36	−16%	2.11
e and s in a mixed letter series	− 3.89 letters	1.78	− 3%	0.75

What these boys learned in their long and intensive practice in cancelling English a-t words included: (1) facility in finding a and t; (2) knowledge of English words containing, or not containing, both of these letters; (3) a habit of rapid work in cancellation. Of these transferable factors, the first would help in the first three tests in the table, and the first and second might interfere with the execution of the last two tests—as the results indicate. The speed habit could be and apparently was carried over into all of the after-tests, with bad results on accuracy. This type of negative transfer effect is probably rather general. When one is adjusted for a rapid tempo one does not readily slow down—say at the entrance to a village after the open road.

One of the early experimenters who was strongly convinced of the reality of transfer was Coover (1916). Positive and negative transfer effects are apt to mask each other in the objective results. Introspection reveals changes of method during practice, tending in general toward simplification; and a brief after-test does not afford sufficient opportunity for utilizing what has been learned. Therefore, he concludes, most transfer experiments do not go to the heart of the problem. Some of his objective results are shown in Fig. 63.

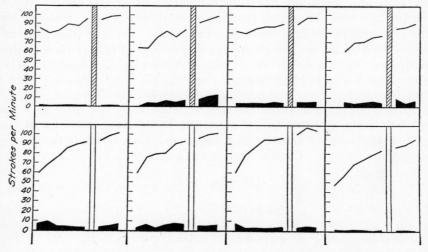

FIG. 63. (Data from Coover, 1916.) Do these results indicate transfer? The curves show the course of practice in a four-choice discrimination experiment. Four keys of a typewriter were used, and the copy appeared one letter at a time as O struck the keys. Each point on the curves shows the speed in a day's work consisting of 100 responses. Each curve shows the performance of a single individual. The four in the upper line interrupted the typewriter practice for 27–41 days at the point indicated by the shaded vertical bar, and engaged in card-sorting practice during the interval. The four Os in the lower line were the control group, their typewriting practice being interrupted for 27–41 days but with no card-sorting or other special practice in the interval. The black areas show the number of errors. The two Os in the upper line who show transfer of speed from card sorting do so at the expense of increased errors. The results have been sometimes cited as evidence for positive transfer effect in rapid discrimination, but the reader must use his own judgment.

TRANSFER IN MAZE LEARNING: HUMAN AND ANIMAL

The method here has usually been that of successive practice. The subject learns one maze and is then given another to learn. If the second maze is learned more rapidly than the first—under proper control— a positive transfer effect is shown. Harmful or interfering transfer can also be shown.

It is rather curious that giving one maze after another is called a transfer experiment, whereas the memorizing of one list of nonsense syllables after another is usually regarded as direct practice. The usage customary in maze studies is logical, since the concrete material learned differs from one maze to the next as also from one nonsense syllable list to the next.

The study of transfer in maze learning began with Webb (1917), who used rats and human subjects. The latter learned stylus mazes of the same pattern as the enclosed mazes learned by the rats. There were several maze patterns, some designed to give a negative transfer effect (an alley which was blind in one maze was a part of the true path in the other, etc.). The expected negative effect was not obtained except in certain parts of a maze; the maze as a whole always showed a positive effect. Transfer was fully as good in the rats as in the human subjects. Hunter (1922) using a different maze pattern confirmed Webb's finding that the transfer effect from one maze to another was usually positive.

The work of Webb was repeated with different mazes in the same laboratory (University of Chicago, under Carr) by Wiltbank (1919). Five mazes were used, each group of rats learning the five in a different order and finally relearning the one with which it had started. The transfer effect was positive throughout. Combining all the groups we have the percents saved in each successive maze as given in the following table.

PERCENT SAVED IN THE LEARNING OF SUCCESSIVE MAZES

(*After Wiltbank, 1919*)

	Maze No. 2	No. 3	No. 4	No. 5	Relearning No. 1
Saving in trials	42	41	54	52	71
" " errors	70	79	82	82	94
" " time	83	87	91	90	92

On the whole the positive transfer effect is cumulative up to and including the fourth maze learned; and the relearning of the original maze shows some retention of the original learning in spite of the other mazes learned in the interim. The justification for this last statement is the sharp increase in the last column in trials and errors saved. The author himself is dubious regarding both of the conclusions we have just drawn, because he finds many exceptions; but on the whole the conclusions seem warranted by the data.

Wiltbank next asked whether there would be any transfer from a *partially* learned maze. He allowed a group of rats only 2 trials in the first maze before running them in the second; another group, 4 trials; etc. The results showed no positive transfer effect until the first maze had been fairly well learned. Thus we find:

Trials in first maze before shifting	2	4	8	16	Complete learning
Percent saved in second maze	−13	−13	−4	+41	+42

Probably there was more confusion between two partially learned mazes than between one already well learned and a new one.

The author further inquired whether a maze already partly learned would benefit from the interpolated complete learning of another maze. He gave groups of rats 0, 2, 4, 8 or 16 trials in a first maze, interpolated complete learning of a second maze, and then resumed learning of the first one. Counting up the entire number of trials, errors, etc., required for the learning of the first maze, he obtained results as follows:

No. trials in first maze before learning second maze	Saving in total		
	Trials	Errors	Time
0	43	61	53
2	45	55	19
4	33	−5	−8
8	22	−33	−32
16	−11	−43	+24

There is little positive transfer effect except to a maze that has been learned only a little or not at all. When a maze has been very largely mastered, the values which might be transferred to it from another maze have already been derived from the learning of the maze itself, and the specific responses brought over from the other maze are likely to be misfits and to cause confusion.

The performance of some individual rats was noteworthy. Out of 7 rats given 2 trials in the first maze before the interpolated learning of the second, 3 on coming back to the first maze made errorless runs from the start, though they had not done so in the original trials in this maze. Similar cases occurred after 4 and 8 original trials in the first maze. These animals had acquired some technique in running the interpolated maze which sufficed for perfect running of the original maze. It was apparently a technique of staying out of blind alleys. All the blind alleys in Wiltbank's mazes were similar in being straight and fairly short. Though the author, following the tradition of his time, did not assume any visual guidance in the rat's maze running, later work (p. 128) makes it safe to assume such guidance. The technique of avoiding blind alleys may have consisted in utilizing the uniform visual appearance of these straight blind alleys as viewed from their entrances. If the rats learned to discriminate visually between blind alleys and alleys with an open turn at the far end, a large share of the positive transfer effect from maze to maze is explained.

Further evidence for a technique of avoiding straight blind alleys was obtained by Dashiell (1920). He discovered another adjustment which can be transferred from one maze to another similarly located, an orientation of the rat in the general direction of the food box. We have already cited the findings of other experimenters to the effect that a rat carries over from maze to maze, and even from a problem box to a maze, a general adaptation to the laboratory, a habit of searching for food in any such apparatus and a habit, one might say, of working for his food in the laboratory situation—all of which give a strong positive transfer effect (p. 136).

TRANSFER IN TERMS OF STIMULUS AND RESPONSE

Since transfer of general adaptation and of familiarity with apparatus and material had already been sufficiently demonstrated, Poffenberger (1915) avoided this type of transfer by using Os who were already familiar with the laboratory and with test materials of the general type to be used in his experiment. Specific stimulus-response units were introduced which if transferred ought to work beneficially or detrimentally. For example the practice group responded 100 times over a period of nine days to a list of 50 adjectives by saying the opposite of each. In the fore- and after-tests this group along with a control group responded to the same list of adjectives by giving an appropriate noun for each. Thus the stimulus word *broad* called in the practice series for the response *narrow*, but in the test series for *street* or *shoe* or some other appropriate noun. Well drilled associations must be laid aside in order to respond correctly in the after-test. The results showed the expected negative transfer effect, since the practice group made no gain from fore- to after-test while the control group gained 20 percent in speed.

The same practice group cancelled the 3's in a sheet of mixed numbers, or, alternately, the 5's, having 50 trials of each kind. In the fore- and after-tests a sheet of six-place numbers was used in which the numbers containing both 3 and 5, or those containing both 4 and 7, were to be cancelled. The practice in finding 3 and 5 separately should help in finding the numbers containing both 3 and 5 but could afford no specific preparation for finding the numbers containing 4 and 7. As a matter of fact the practice group made a net gain in the 3–5 test but none in the 4–7 test. From these and similar experiments Poffenberger concludes that either positive, negative or zero transfer effect can be obtained by so selecting the materials that stimulus-response units established by practice shall be useful, interfering or irrelevant in the later performance. In his words, freely quoted:

1. Where there are no identical bonds between stimulus and response in the two processes, the influence of one test upon another will be neither positive nor negative.

2. Where a given process involves one or more bonds previously formed, there will be a positive transfer effect.

3. Where one test necessitates the breaking of previously formed bonds and the formation of new ones, there will be a negative effect.

Wylie (1919) analyzed the transfer problem as follows: when O passes from one task to another he may find new stimuli calling for old responses or old stimuli calling for new responses. Wylie sets up the hypothesis (practically identical with Poffenberger's conclusion) that *the transfer effect is positive when an old response can be transferred to a new stimulus, but negative when a new response is required to an old stimulus.*

Wylie arranged an experiment to test the first part of this hypothesis on rats. His apparatus (Fig. 64) comprised a food box and an adjacent

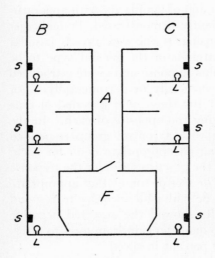

FIG. 64. Diagram of apparatus used by Wylie (1919). F, food box in which the rat gets a preliminary nibble, being then thrust out into the alley, A, from which he finds his way back to the food box by one of the side alleys, B and C. S,S,....small sounders emitting clicks when the rat has entered the "wrong" alley; L,L....small lights for similar use. Grids in the floor of the side alleys deliver shocks for the same purpose.

main alley from which two side alleys led back to the food box. His procedure was first to motivate the rat by giving him a nibble of food in the food box, then to push him out into the main alley and let him find his way back by one of the side alleys. When the rat entered one of the side alleys, E sometimes lighted up that alley as a signal that the door from that alley into the food box was closed and the door from the other side alley open. Sometimes E did not give the signal but left the door open from the alley which the rat had entered. The rat learned in a long series of trials to enter an alley, whisk around quickly if the light came on, otherwise continue. The learned response to the light was, then, to turn and run to the other alley and so to the food box. When this response had been learned with light as the stimulus, E substituted a sound for the light, or with another group a shock for the light. Still other groups first learned to respond to sound or shock and were shifted to another stimulus. The group learning first to respond to a given stimulus served as a control for the groups shifted to that stimulus after learning another stimulus.

Wylie's results showed a positive transfer effect in all groups. Transfer of the response from one stimulus to another was greatly facilitated in certain groups by a transitional series in which both the original stimulus and the new stimulus were given simultaneously. The main conclusion is that a response can be transferred from one stimulus to a substitute stimulus provided the total situation remains otherwise unchanged.

TRIALS REQUIRED TO LEARN WITHDRAWING RESPONSE
(*Wylie, 1919*)

Response to sound signal:

original learning	526 trials
after learning same response to light	152 "
after learning same response to shock	313 "

Response to light signal:

original learning	199 "
after learning same response to sound	150 "
after learning same response to shock	146 "

Response to shock signal:

original learning	191 "
after learning same response to light	158 "
after learning same response to sound	124 "

The hypothesis quoted from Wylie was subjected to a test by Bruce (1933) with human Os who first memorized a list of nonsense syllable pairs, and then learned another list which might (1) consist of entirely different syllables, (2) preserve the original stimulus syllables with new response syllables, or (3) preserve the original response syllables with new stimulus syllables. A sample of the results is given below.

TRANSFER EFFECT IN LEARNING NEW RESPONSES OR NEW STIMULI
(*After Bruce, 1933*)

Sample of original material	Items changed	Sample of changed material	Percent of trials saved
xal-pom	Both syllables	cam-lup	16
lan-qip	Stimulus syllable	fis-qip	37
req-kiv	Response syllable	req-zam	− 9

The 16 percent saved by these previously untrained Os in learning a second list of entirely new syllables is the usual practice effect, which represents, as we have said, a transfer of adaptation and memorizing technique. The second line of the table shows an additional positive transfer effect when the old responses are attached to new stimuli. The third line, which is to be compared with the first, shows a negative transfer effect when a new response has to be attached to an old stimulus.

The differences are not entirely reliable, but are pretty well confirmed by other experiments of the same author.

Studies of transfer as distinguished from transfer effects. In an experiment on transfer proper we seek direct evidence that a response learned in the first situation is actually made in the second situation. There could be several varieties of a transfer experiment so conceived. When O has learned a certain response to a certain stimulus, E could present the same stimulus in a different setting and see whether the response was still evoked. Or, the stimulus could be modified. The original stimulus is for example a visually presented figure which is given a name. When the association is well established, similar figures are substituted to see whether they get the same response. Experiments of this type by Yum (1931), Gulliksen (1932), and McKinney (1933) have shown that the greater the similarity between the old and new stimuli the greater the probability of getting the same response. We will examine Yum's results. He used the method of Paired Associates (p. 10). In one experiment the first number of each pair was a visual figure, fairly simple and symmetrical but not representative of any object. There were 15 figures, each paired with a three-letter name. Having learned these 15 pairs one day, O was tested the following day with a series of stimuli, identical with the original figures or modified by the addition of extra lines, which more or less masked the original figure (p. 638). With 26 students, the percent of recall was 85 when the original figure was presented, and fell off with increasing degrees of

Transfer of Response to Similar Stimuli
(*After Yum, 1931*)

Sample stimulus pair as learned	Change in recall test — Nature of change	Change in recall test — Sample	Percent of recall
Fight—ledger	No change	Fight—	50
Snake—wealth	1st degree	Serpent—	33
House—breeze	2nd degree	Barn—	11
REB–QIM—wolf	No change	REB–QIM—	68
TOQ–BEX—jury	2nd letter of 1st syllable	TIQ–BEX—	60
WUL–GIC—vase	2nd letter of 2nd syllable	WUL–GOC—	54
HUD–LEP—fist	1st letter of 1st syllable	XUD–LEP—	40
VAH–MIZ—nose	1st letter of 2nd syllable	VAH–PIZ—	41
KAJ–ZOY—view	1st & 2nd letters of 1st syllable	NEJ–ZOY—	39
JEC–POR—mask	1st & 2nd letters of 2nd syllable	JEC–NAR—	38

The SD_M of these percents ranges from 0.25 to 0.45. The change of the first letter of either syllable gives reliably less recall than the change of the second letter of either, and the unchanged stimulus gives reliably more recall than any changed stimulus.

masking or dissimilarity in the following series of percents: 66, 49, 45, 36. The same general procedure was used with other stimuli, as shown in the table on p. 204.

Many kindred experiments could be found in which no mention is made of transfer. Klüver (1931, 1933) speaks in terms of "equivalent stimuli." His subjects, monkeys, first learned to respond to a certain stimulus by pulling a box toward their cage by means of an attached string, and were then tested with more or less similar stimuli in order to discover which stimuli were equivalent to the original one, not in the sense of being indistinguishable but in the sense of evoking the same response. In this way, the author urges, the intimate nature of the response is revealed; for the response includes a perceptual as well as a motor component. The non-equivalent stimuli are specially informative in this regard. The monkeys learned to pull in the smaller of two white boxes and continued to pull in the smaller when the absolute sizes were changed. But they did not carry over this response when boxes of equal size were marked with larger and smaller white squares. The response was therefore a response to a size relation between objects (boxes), not between visual figures.

TRANSFER OF PRINCIPLES

We have already noticed the transfer obtained by Woodrow from memory training in which the subjects were taught efficient memorizing technique, and Judd's evidence for transfer of principles. Other experiments in different fields have given similar results.

Bagley (1905) reported a classroom experiment by Squires in which the arithmetic teacher made a point for some weeks of insisting very strongly upon neatness in the arithmetic papers. Meanwhile the other teachers made no such requirement. The result was that the children produced much neater papers in arithmetic than previously but without any noticeable effect on their language and spelling papers. Ruediger (1908) repeated this experiment with an important difference. In each of three schools where the experiment was tried, the teacher who insisted upon neatness also emphasized the value of neatness in general and held it up as an ideal in dress, business and in the home, without however making any reference to other school subjects. The children in this experiment did improve in the neatness of their papers in other subjects.

Particularly convincing is the experiment of Cox (1933) on the transfer of manual skill after "training" in contrast to mere "practice." The manual operations studied were those involved in assembling and stripping an electric lamp holder. One part of the lamp holder, the "container," was used in the practice and in the training, and other parts of the total operation were used in the fore- and after-tests. The practice group alternately assembled and stripped 40 containers a day for 11 days, trying for speed. The training group devoted the same total time to the work, but most of the time was given to instruction in the principles of manual skill illustrated by exercises based on the container operation, with a few daily speed tests in assembling and stripping the container. These two groups and a control group took the same fore- and after-tests. The practice group showed no reliable evidence of transfer, but the training group showed a large net gain. One is curious to know what principles of manual skill were taught with such success. The teaching dealt with five main points: (1) orderly arrangement of parts on the work bench, (2) what to observe visually while engaged in the manual operation, (3) what to observe through the fingers, (4) how to apply effort and attention most economically throughout the operation, and (5) how to combine effort and observation under conditions of actual work. Each matter of importance was embodied in an exercise based upon the container operation. After the particular point of each exercise had been explained it was performed several times as an exercise in observation rather than speed. The results indicated that such training led to manual proficiency far exceeding that obtained by uninstructed practice.

GAIN IN TIME FROM FORE-TEST TO AFTER-TEST

(After Cox, 1933)

Operation	Control group	Practice group	Training group
Assembling screw and block	17 sec.	23 sec.	37 sec.
Stripping " " "	9	9	34
Assembling porcelain units	75	50	163
Inserting wedges	9	7	21
Wiring the lamp holder	43	74	162

The practice group makes sometimes more, sometimes less gain than the control, but in no case is the difference reliable, while the gain of the trained group is reliably greater in almost every instance.

Difficulty of transfer. Of many ramifications of the concept of transfer, one of the most interesting is its use as a criterion of insight (Ruger, Köhler, see p. 757). If O has seen the principle of one problem he may apply it in a similar problem. The more definitely the principle is isolated, even to the extent of formulating it in words, the more chance of transfer. The transfer of principles, of skill, or of any achievement does not occur as a matter of course in a novel situation. Transfer is uncertain in two ways: (1) the new situation may not look like the old and may not put O on the track of the previously acquired principle or habit; (2) and even when the old habit or knowledge is revived, it may not be perfectly suited to the new situation and may do more harm than good. In short, transfer may not occur or if it occurs it may produce a negative transfer effect. The best training does not obviate the need of readjustments and of fresh practice in the new performance.

We think of principles as "abstract." But if they are embodied in words they are concrete bits of behavior and their transfer from one situation to another creates no difficulty for the theory of identical components. Any idea that can be recalled, or any attitude that can be reinstated, is concrete enough to qualify. Perhaps anything that can be learned can be transferred. But does not everything that can be learned have the concrete character of an act or way of acting?

CHAPTER IX

ECONOMY AND INTERFERENCE IN LEARNING AND REMEMBERING

A STUDY of the conditions favorable and unfavorable to learning, retention and remembering is obviously of practical importance not only for those who are teaching children but for adults who hope still to learn any appreciable amount. This line of investigation is of theoretical value also for the light it can presumably throw upon the processes involved. A large number of factors and variables offer themselves for examination. Most of the studies which have been made can be classed under two heads: economy in learning, and interference exerted by some activity upon learning and remembering. Quite a number of relevant points could be gleaned from the topics already covered and there are other experiments specifically directed toward these two general problems.

From work already cited the importance of good memorizing technique stands out clearly. We have noticed the value to the learner of rhythmical and other grouping, of locating, and of meaningful aids or "associations." These last are of service in proportion to the readiness with which they suggest themselves and the amount of meaningfulness or connectedness which they introduce into otherwise disconnected material. A farfetched association may do more harm than good. Practiced memorizers as compared with beginners in these experiments rely less on extraneous associations and more on relations and patterns inherent in the material.

RECITATION AS AN AID TO LEARNING

In memorizing any sort of material which one can reproduce—a list of words or syllables, a connected passage, a poem, a vocabulary, a piano piece, a visual figure—O can proceed by reading, listening or looking, or he may have a try at reproducing, when the material is partly learned. Ebbinghaus and most of his successors have followed this method of partial recitation, "consulting the book" whenever stuck. Witasek (1907) found with adults that the recitation method was definitely superior in number of repetitions to learn, though not necessarily in total time of learning because of the time consumed in hunting for an item before giving up and being prompted. It was best to begin recitations early, long before the complete list could be recited.

This and several other early experiments on the subject were fully analyzed and summarized by Gates (1917). Practically all the experiments favor recitation. Gates attempted to discover how early the recitation should begin. In his experiment, the method of Retained Members was used. A constant time was allowed for studying the material, but the time was differently divided between reading and recitation. Immediately after the learning and again some hours later, a recall test was given. School children from the third to the eighth grade were tested and also college and graduate students. In all cases the best recall scores were obtained when a considerable proportion of the time had been devoted to recitation. The optimum division of time as between reading and recitation appeared for the adults to be about as follows:

20 nonsense syllables—begin reciting after 2 min. (4–6 readings)

26 lines of poetry—begin reciting after 3–5 min. (3–6 readings)

Similar results from children are shown below.

THE VALUE OF RECITATION IN MEMORIZING
(*Gates, 1917*)

Material studied	16 nonsense syllables		5 short biographies, totaling about 170 words	
	Percent remembered		*Percent remembered*	
	immedi- ately	*after 4 hours*	*immedi- ately*	*after 4 hours*
All time devoted to reading.................	35	15	35	16
⅕ of time devoted to recitation..........	50	26	37	19
⅖ of time devoted to recitation..........	54	28	41	25
⅗ of time devoted to recitation..........	57	37	42	26
⅘ of time devoted to recitation..........	74	48	42	26

The time devoted to study was in all cases 9 minutes, and this time was divided between reading and recitation in different proportions as stated in the first column at the left. Reading down the next column, we find that when nonsense syllables were studied and the test was conducted immediately after the close of the study period, 35 percent were remembered when all the study time had been devoted to reading, 50 percent when the last ⅕ of the study time had been devoted to recitation, and so on. The next column shows the percents remembered four hours after the study period. Each subject in these experiments had before him a sheet of paper containing the lesson to be studied, and simply read till he got the signal to recite, when he started reciting to himself, consulting the paper as often as necessary, and proceeded thus till the end of the study period. The subjects in these particular experiments were eighth grade children; younger children, from the third grade up, and college students, gave the same result.

Three facts stand out in this table: (1) The best results were obtained when a large proportion of the time was devoted to recitation. (2) The advantage was still present in the test conducted several hours after the learning, showing that recitation is as important for retention as for efficient learning. (3) The advantage of recitation was greater in the nonsense material than the connected material; this result has been obtained by other experimenters.

One reason, if not the only reason, for the relatively small advantage of recitation in learning connected material is that in re-reading such material time after time, one inevitably anticipates what is coming and therefore is reciting while reading.

The advantage of recitation is probably even greater than is shown by the figures. When material has been only partly learned and cannot be completely recited, the time allowed for recitation is partly devoted to reading. When most of the time is assigned to reading, part of it really goes into recitation because of the tendency, already noted as specially strong in the case of meaningful material, to anticipate what is already known. The figures then show the advantage of recitation with some reading over reading with some recitation. Some Os are almost incapable of learning nonsense material if they resolutely abstain from all recitation.

Advantages of recitation. Recitation furnishes an immediate goal to work for and is more stimulating than continued reading of the lesson. It is somewhat like running a race against a competitor as contrasted with jogging along the track all alone. Then, too, recitation forces the learner to utilize what he has already learned, to depend upon himself instead of on the book. He discovers what he already knows and what he has still to master.

From supplementary experiments with trained Os and from their introspections, Gates analyzed the advantage in recitation in more detail. A number of specific points are worth noting. In the first place there are very few individual exceptions to the rule that recitation is an advantage. A few have been reported by other experimenters but Gates found none among 50 students. When the Os, either children or adults, were asked after the experiment to indicate their preference, nearly all of them preferred to have recitation introduced early in the learning. Recitation was an advantage because it led to speaking the syllables, subvocally at least, and thus getting a more adequate idea of them than was possible by mere visual imprinting. Rhythmical grouping of the items was favored by recitation and so also was the localization of items in the list. Gates says: "In reading, the syllables are handled more as isolated terms; the learner tries to imprint each by itself. In recitation more of an attempt is made to make the material over into some sort of pattern, a more or less highly organized structure." In recitation O applies his effort effectively, by skimming over what is already known and concentrating on parts that are still giving trouble.

Repeated reading of the same material may degenerate into an inattentive droning, and though the Os in this experiment did not allow themselves to lapse in this way, they did make reports like the following: "Reading most fatiguing—monotonous—took all my energy to keep up interest."

Recitation, attempted too early, wastes time and may establish errors. The stages in an efficient learning process are about as follows:

1. *Exploration.* This can be subdivided: (a) an initial survey of the whole lesson in the first 1–2 readings; (b) more detailed exploration through which O becomes familiar with the material. Up to this point reading is probably better than recitation.

2. *Organization by trial and error.* Organization requires active response and will not ordinarily come from simply looking at the material; the pattern found is really a response pattern. O must have the courage to take a chance and put what he already knows to the test of recitation.

3. *Mechanization.* If recitation is repeated often enough the aids utilized in learning become short-circuited (p. 34).

In learning the *substance* of meaningful passages, recitation would presumably take the form of outlining. The first outline even if broad and sketchy provides a schema into which the details can be fitted in later recitations. The advantage of such a procedure, though probable, is not yet experimentally proved. In memorizing a piano piece, preliminary analysis of its structure has been shown to be a definite aid (Rubin-Rabson, 1937).

MASSED VS. SPACED LEARNING

Agreement between experimenters regarding the factor next to be considered is only less complete than in respect to recitation. They have almost uniformly found an economy of learning time when that time is distributed over several sittings (spaced or distributed learning) in comparison with the results obtained when the same total learning time is concentrated into one continuous sitting (massed learning).

Results with various materials. Ebbinghaus and later Jost (p. 58) obtained this result in learning lists of nonsense syllables, and later experimenters have found the same. It takes fewer readings to reach the criterion of one perfect recitation of the list when the readings are distributed over several days than when they occur in immediate succession; and the recall score by Paired Associates is also better. The same result was obtained with lists of digits by Lyon (1917, see p. 21).

In verbatim memorizing of prose and poetry, Lyon obtained rather ambiguous results, but in memory for the substance of a prose passage of 1550 words, according to the results of English, Welborn & Killian (1934; see p. 65), who tested memory by a true-false examination, the material was about 7 percent better known after 4 readings one day apart than after the same number of readings in immediate succession. An interval of 3 hours between readings was as good as one of a day, while an interval of 3 days was no better than none at all.

Book (1908) and Pyle (1914) obtained evidence of better progress in learning to typewrite when the practice was distributed than when there was considerable massing; and Lashley (1915) found the same, quite definitely, for the acquisition of skill in archery. In learning to follow the outline of a star seen in a mirror ("mirror tracing," see p. 161) 20 trials yield much slower progress when massed than when a recess of 1 minute is inserted after each trial, and an interval of 24 hours between trials gives still more rapid progress (Snoddy, 1926). Verifying this result, Lorge (1930) finds it to hold also for mirror reading, for practice in memorizing, and to some extent for the substitution test. This author calls attention to an obvious reason why the superiority of spaced practice, or indeed of any procedure, cannot be maintained indefinitely: whatever procedure is used, O finally approaches a physiological limit or the limit of measurable success, at which all procedures must come together.

It is important for the theory of this phenomenon to add that the advantage of spaced learning is fully as clear in animal as in human learning. The dancing mouse (Yerkes, 1907) learns a black-white discrimination habit in fewer trials given 2–5 per day than given 10 or more a day. The white rat (Ulrich, 1915) learns a puzzle box or a maze better with spaced than with massed trials. These early findings have been confirmed by many later experimenters.

In adapting a rat to laboratory conditions, apparatus and handling, the animal psychologist is accustomed to distribute this preliminary training over several days. Presumably, better adaptation is thus secured than by compressing the process into a single sitting.

In athletics, too, distribution of training is the custom. Would it be worth while to try the experiment of massing a week's exercise in a single afternoon? We can scarcely doubt that more strength is gained from distributed exercise.

Variations of the experiment. The advantage of spaced learning or training seems to be very general. In the hope of finding clues to an understanding of the phenomenon psychologists look for exceptions, for conditions in which the rule breaks down. Complete solution of the problem would require the trying out of many variables: the length of the sitting or *block* of consecutive trials, the length of the *interval* between blocks, the *difficulty* of the task, the *stage* of learning at which the massing or spacing is introduced, and others. Most tangibly put, the problem is to determine the *optimum* block of trials and interval between blocks for tasks of each difficulty and for each stage of learning. As the optimum is simply one point on a *curve* of relationship, what we eventually wish to determine is the whole curve. This is a large order, especially as the several variables are probably interdependent.

Block and interval. These two variables are almost certainly inter-related, though in many experiments one has been held constant while the other was varied. In Jost's experiment (1897), the interval was always one day, and the block contained 2, 6 or 8 consecutive readings of a list of nonsense syllables. After a total of 24 readings a recall test yielded a much higher score for the smaller blocks.

Piéron (1913) held the block constant at 1 reading and varied the interval. His results with one well-practiced O came out as follows:

Interval between readings	30 sec.	5 min.	10 min.
No. readings to learn	11	6	5

Lengthening the interval beyond 10 min., up to as long as 2 days, made no further change.

In some other experiments both block and interval have been varied. Perkins (1914) used blocks of 1, 2, 4 and 8 readings of lists of 14 nonsense syllables, and with every size of block she used intervals of 1, 2, 3 and 4 days. In every case a total of 16 readings was given to each list, and memory was tested 2 weeks after the last reading. The results from 4 Os showed that the size of block was a very important factor, the length of interval much less important.

Size of block	1	2	4	8	readings
Percent correct	75	58	31	13	

Interval	1	2	3	4	days
Percent correct:	39	50	47	43	

There is some indication, not very reliable, that a two-day interval is best. There is clear evidence of an inverse relation between size of block and amount learned in 16 readings of syllable lists by these adult Os.

An animal experiment of Warden (1923) reached somewhat more definite results as to interval. Groups of 10–15 white rats learned a rather difficult maze; the blocks were of 1, 3 and 5 trials; the intervals were 6 hours, 12 hours, 1 day, 3 days. There were thus 12 different conditions, with a separate group of rats learning under each condition. The results can be stated in terms of average number of trials required to reach the criterion (9 out of 10 errorless trials).

TRIALS REQUIRED TO LEARN A MAZE

(*Warden, 1923*)

Size of block Interval	1 trial	3 trials	5 trials	Mean
6 hours	45	62	74	60
12 hours	37	55	64	52
1 day	46	65	86	66
3 days	72	91	86	83
Mean	50	68	77	65

From the agreement between the rows, and between the columns, the indications are strong that the one-trial block is the best, and that the 12-hour interval is better than any other tried. Incomplete results with a 5-day interval showed still slower learning than at 3 days. The interrelation of the two variables seems from the figures to be about as follows: as you increase the size of the block, a long interval becomes somewhat less unfavorable.

Stages of learning. Two stages were distinguished by Lashley (1918): the stage of exploration and adjustment, during which the right response is found, and the stage of fixation of the right response. In the exploratory stage, he suggested, massed practice is a disadvantage because it tends to stereotypy of performance at a time when varied reaction is a necessary means of discovering the right response. He supported this view by showing (1917) that rats learning a maze repeated the same error oftener in successive massed trials than in trials separated by a day's interval. McGinnis (1929) found the same to hold good for maze learning by preschool children. Of two groups of students learning a stylus maze (Carr, 1919), the group having 1 trial per day made more rapid improvement in the first 10 trials than the group having 10 trials at one sitting; the conditions were then shifted and the two groups soon came to an equality. These results indicate the advantage of spaced trials in the first stage of learning.

Recognizing the same two stages of learning, Cook (1934 b) made just the opposite prediction as to the best location for spaced trials. During the exploratory stage, when O has made a significant discovery, right then is the time to fix it by immediate repetition; delay may allow it to be forgotten. Permanent fixation, however, according to all indications, is best promoted by well-spaced repetitions. Human Os learning rather simple puzzles furnished Cook with some evidence in favor of his analysis.

Both Lashley and Cook may be right in principle. Even in the first stage of learning we must distinguish between the discovery of the right response, probably favored by spacing, and the first step toward fixing this response, favored by immediate repetition. Continuous repetition, in everyday experience, often gets us into a rut from which we escape by delaying further practice till another day. We are also familiar with the strong inclination to repeat at once any surprisingly successful act. Spaced learning, but with freedom allowed to capitalize promptly any desirable variation, may be the most practical rule.

Difficulty of task. Arguing once more from the same premises, Cook (1937 b) predicted that easy tasks would be best attacked in massed trials, difficult tasks in spaced trials. He tested this deduction on groups of students learning high relief finger mazes of different length and number of blinds, and found in fact that with increasing length of the maze the advantage shifted from massed to distributed learning. It was also true that massed trials gave an advantage at the beginning of practice and gradually lost this advantage to the spaced trials. Also, for some unknown reason, massed trials favored accuracy, spaced trials speed of performance.

The fact that massing is more suited to easy than to difficult tasks could probably be predicted from somewhat different premises, and at any rate has been found in other experiments. Lyon (1917, see also p. 21) needed less time to memorize a list of only 12 digits in continuous readings than when he read it once a day. With longer lists the advantage was on the side of distributed readings, and when the list was extremely long (100–200 digits) the advantage of distributed readings was great. A simple maze is likely to be learned in fewer massed than spaced trials, by either rats or human Os (Pechstein, 1921). In a difficult maze, as in the experiment already cited of Warden, the advantage goes to spaced trials. It should be possible, accordingly, to find a maze of intermediate difficulty which should be equally easy to learn by either massed or spaced trials. This deduction was tested by S. A. Cook (1928) using a maze which the rats needed about 15 massed trials to master, as compared with the 6 massed trials needed in Pechstein's simple mazes and the 60 or more required in Warden's maze. It made practically no difference in Cook's medium-difficulty maze, whether trials were given 1, 2 or 20 a day. Even here, indeed, there was some advantage on the side of massing in the early trials, and some for one-per-day after about 15 trials. One might expect, then, that the best of all procedures would start the practice with a large block of trials and progressively diminish the block. This procedure was tried by Cook and did show a slight though unreliable advantage over other arrangements.

Possible factors of advantage in massed and spaced learning. The advantage of spaced trials is so general, even though not universal, that we should look for general causative factors. Rehearsal of the performance in the rest intervals, almost necessarily an ideational rehearsal, may occur sometimes in human subjects, but can scarcely be predicated of the rat. Fatigue, boredom and wandering of attention can scarcely be present in a block of only two trials and cannot therefore explain the advantage of single spaced trials nor the advantage of allowing an interval, in some cases, of at least 6–12 hours.

The tendency to get into a rut and make persistent errors, in an uninterrupted series of trials, and to vary the performance after a longer interval, has been mentioned and is undoubtedly important in some cases. The recency value of an unsuccessful act may lead to its repetition in an immediately following trial, and the loss of this recency value overnight will give some alternative act a chance. Forgetting in this sense gives an advantage to spaced trials. Forgetting of a just discovered successful act works the other way. And there is another tendency that works against the immediate repetition of an act, even a successful one. A rat that has taken either of two equally short paths to the foodbox, if immediately replaced at the entrance, is almost sure to take the other path on the second trial (Wingfield & Dennis, 1934; Dennis, 1935). Presumably, a rat just emerging from a blind alley does not often turn and instantly explore it a second time. When a rat, after a day's interval, is placed at the entrance of a familiar maze, he is apt to explore a bit near the entrance and enter the first blind alley (p. 136). Human adults show a little of this same orienting tendency (T. W. Cook, 1937 b). These little behavior traits give some advantage to massed trials.

When all these factors are allowed their due weight, there is still the probability of a "physiological" factor. The muscle profits from an alternation of exercise and rest and cannot be forced into rapid increase of strength by massing the exercise. The size and internal structure of the muscle fibers improve after exercise, and this nutritive after-effect takes some hours to reach completion. The same after-effect, occurring in the nervous system, may "consolidate" the memory trace of an activity (p. 51), and this consolidation may well be one of the factors in giving advantage to spaced learning.

WHOLE OR PART LEARNING

Should a memory lesson of any considerable length be studied as a whole or divided into parts and each part be memorized separately? The alternatives have sometimes been called "global" and "piecemeal" learning. School practice leans toward the maxim, "One thing at a time and that done well," while the custom of some actors and musicians inclines toward the global method. The question was put to an experimental test by Lottie Steffens (1900). She observed the spontaneous procedure of a number of educated adults and found that all of them used mixed methods but always with much separate reading of parts, when a nine-line stanza was to be memorized. They were skeptical of the efficiency and even of the possibility of a strictly global method. She then conducted some lengthy experiments with 5 adults and 2 children, in which some stanzas and lists of nonsense syllables were learned piecemeal, and others by reading through and through. The global method took less time. This was true of every O and of both syllable lists and stanzas of poetry. The advantage of the global method ranged from 2 to 26 percent in different experiments and averaged about 12 percent. The advantage did not always appear at first; some practice with the unaccustomed global method was usually necessary before O could work it successfully. The whole or global method keeps each item in its proper place and relations and for that reason, apparently, was better.

Whole and part learning of verbal serial material. Similar results have been obtained by several later investigators.

Larguier des Bancels (1902) found that poems learned globally were better retained over a period of some days than others learned part by part. This was true at least of adults.

Pentschew (1903) also devoted special attention to retention which he found generally better after the global learning. With regard to economy in the original learning his results, properly evaluated, do not show any decisive advantage for either method. His adult Os, or some of them, found the global method very strenuous, when it required them to learn 16–40 lines of poetry without any division into parts, and they almost inevitably read more slowly in the global learning. As Pentschew sums up his findings, global learning was decidedly better in terms of the number of readings required to learn a poem or list of syllables, though in respect to learning time the part method was often superior. If some readings were slower than others, the reading ceased to be a proper unit of measure; and Pentschew committed the further error of counting the reading of a part the same as a reading of the whole. For example, O learned the first half of an 18-syllable list in 7 readings, the second half in 9 readings, and then needed 6 readings of the entire list before it could be recited. Pentschew counted 22 readings and compared this number with the 18 readings required to learn another list globally. Instead of 22 he should have counted $(7 + 9)/2 + 6 = 14$ readings for the part method. Counting as he did, he obtained a large but spurious advantage for the global method. His results really show no distinct advantage for either method.

Pyle & Snyder (1911), with one well-trained O, found a definite advantage in the global method of memorizing poetry, even up to a selection as long as 240 lines, the learning being distributed over several days.

Lakenan (1913) practiced learning poetry by the two methods. At first the part method gave her better results but after considerable practice the advantage shifted to the whole method.

Meyer (1925) found that 48 out of 53 adults and older children did better by the global method. Their learning time averaged about 15 percent less by the global method, and the advantage held good with syllables, poetry and prose (to be memorized verbatim). Because recitation is known to assist learning, the instructions in this experiment called for reciting soon and as much as possible. There was more reciting, as would be expected, in the piecemeal learning, and yet the whole learning came off better, so far as concerned learning time. Retention tests showed no consistent advantage for either method.

So far, the results favored the whole method for the complete memorization of lists, poems or prose selections. Some later writers have obtained apparently discordant results which, however, need to be scrutinized rather carefully.

Thus Pechstein had inexperienced Os learn lists of 32 nonsense syllables, each O learning just one list either as a whole or in 4 parts. Six Os learned by one method, and six by the other. The average time for the whole learners was 1772 sec., for the part learners 1654 sec.; but whether this is anything more than a chance difference we cannot tell as no variabilities are given. Pechstein used three other methods, which can be schematized by letting the four parts be denoted by the numbers 1, 2, 3, 4. The learning proceeded as follows:

In the whole method: 1–4
In the pure part method: 1, 2, 3, 4, 1–4
In the progressive part method: 1, 2, 1–2, 3, 1–3, 4, 1–4
In the direct repetitive method: 1, 1–2, 1–3, 1–4
In the reversed repetitive method: 4, 3–4, 2–4, 1–4

The progressive part method came out the best in Pechstein's small sample.

In a laboratory exercise Reed (1924) had 113 students learn selections of poetry consisting of 4 stanzas, each student learning 3 such selections, one globally, one stanza by stanza, and one by the progressive part method. His results:

Method of study	Whole	Part	Progressive Part
Av. time in minutes	5.95	5.45	5.21
No. students doing best by each method	26	31	56

Presumably, some practice is necessary before one can get full value from the whole method, especially as the part or mixed method is habitual in school memorizing.

An experiment on school children by Winch (1924) was carefully controlled, in that the groups learning poetry by the whole and part methods were equated for memorizing ability on the basis of preliminary tests. The children were accustomed to memorizing poems. The results came out in favor of the part method, though not strongly.

No appreciable difference between the whole, part and progressive part methods of memorizing 12 lines of poetry was found by G. O. McGeoch (1931) in groups of average and very bright children.

These results are not so discordant as might seem, once we allow that some practice in the whole method is necessary before it can be properly handled. It appears likely that a learner can build up a technique for global learning that will give better results than can be achieved by piecemeal methods. The progressive and other mixed methods consist largely of whole learning, and even the "pure part" method culminates in enough readings of the whole list or passage to make possible its recitation as a whole. After each part has been learned separately, several readings of the whole may be necessary to unite the parts.

When the learning is to culminate in recitation of an entire list or passage, the whole method is the one that drives straight at the goal. It begins at once to locate each item in its proper position and to establish all the necessary connections. The part method may facilitate close attention to important details. What it does, more certainly, is to provide intermediate goals (successful recitation of parts) which stimulate and encourage the learner. The whole method is frightening to the beginner, and if he is a fidgety person who cannot bide his time while exploring and organizing the material, he probably cannot master the method.

Whole and part learning of mazes. A maze, like a poem, has eventually to be gone through as a whole, and we might expect the advantage to remain with the whole method. Pechstein (1917, 1921) obtained results indicating that a difficult maze was best learned piecemeal by either rats or human Os. The most efficient method, he believed, was to divide the maze into parts small enough so that each could easily be learned in a few massed trials, and to unite the parts also in massed trials. A truly difficult stylus maze was used by Barton (1921). It contained 31 blind alleys and was learned:

in 83 minutes by whole learners (mean of 12 students);
in 80 minutes by the "direct repetitive" method (11 students);
in 61 minutes by pure part learning (9 students).

One great advantage of the part method, in Pechstein's judgment, is the opportunity it affords for transfer. The maze-running ability acquired in learning the first part can be carried over to the second part. This advantage, obviously, would be confined to beginners in maze running. Hanawalt (1931, 1934) used for her subjects rats and students already experienced in maze running, and found a distinct advantage for the whole method over the part and mixed methods. After the parts had been separately learned much learning was still necessary, just as in lists of nonsense syllables, before the whole was mastered. With the human Os, learning a large maze visible only a bit at a time (see p. 144), 37 percent of the total time was used in learning the four separate parts and 63 percent in putting them together into a complete run. The Os were not told they were getting the whole maze of which they had learned the parts, and as a rule there was no recognition of the parts. Yet the learning of the parts was of some value in the subsequent learning of the whole.

Mazes of different types and lengths were used with human subjects by Cook (1936, 1937). In the gross no decisive advantage appears for either the part or the whole method. Much depends on the size of the maze and of the parts into which it is divided. For a given O at a given stage of practice there is an optimal size of unit in which to learn a maze. This unit would of course be larger than his memory span; it must give him something to work out by repeated trials. If the part is smaller than his most economical unit, the whole method may be better, and if the whole is larger than his best learning unit, the part method may be better. With practice the size of the best learning unit increases, and it is apt to be larger with quick than with slow learners. Practice also increases O's efficiency in putting the learned parts together and to that extent favors the part method. Some Os who do not readily adjust themselves to a new problem find the part method objectionable because it demands a greater number of such adjustments, one for each part and one for the whole maze. The most important consideration, in Cook's judgment, concerns the size of the optimal learning unit. The maze presents a problem demanding intelligent perception of patterns and relations and prompt repetition in order to fix what has been learned. Too large a unit weakens O's grasp on the relations and prevents prompt repetition of what has been learned. It spaces the repetitions too widely, just as may be done by distributing the trials in time (p. 214). One comment may be offered: whatever the size of O's best learning unit, there are certain important guiding facts which can only be learned by traversing the whole maze. These are the general direction of the goal and the general course of the right path. Such general orientation may best be acquired early, so as to provide a frame or schema into which the parts can be fitted. One or two initial trials of the whole maze may be desirable even if the details are to be learned part by part. The same reasoning would apply to the learning of a poem or prose passage, of a visual form, or of anything possessing important whole properties.

Whole and part learning of paired associates. The advantages claimed for the whole method have been based on the assumption that a whole list, passage, or maze is eventually to be mastered. Many kinds of lesson do not require any such building of a unified pattern. In Paired Associates, only the items composing each pair have to be connected. A vocabulary need not be learned as an ordered list. It can be studied "as a whole" in the sense that it is read through and through from beginning to end, with attention always directed to the individual word pairs; or it can be studied piecemeal, one small group of words being read through and through before passing to another group.

Warner Brown (1924) presented an artificial vocabulary, English paired with nonsense words, as a whole, or by parts each consisting of a single pair—which is certainly reaching the limit in the piecemeal direction. By the part method each pair was presented or read 12 times before passing to the next pair. By the whole method the list of 12 pairs was read through 12 times. The recall score was higher by the whole method. This finding was fully confirmed by Davis & Meenes (1932) and by G. O. McGeoch (1931) with somewhat different material.

A more practical sort of vocabulary experiment was that of Seibert (1932), who used English-French pairs, to be learned so as to give the French in response to the English word. It was more practical because the "parts" were not limited to a single pair. (It seems scarcely possible to read a single pair 10 times on end with full attention.) A vocabulary contained 12 word-pairs and was read 6 times, either as a whole or by parts. The learning was done at the beginning of a class period; the first test came at the end of the period, 50 minutes after learning, and there were later tests for retention. The average scores of 44 students, in percent of the perfect score, were as follows:

PERCENT RECALLED AFTER LEARNING VOCABULARIES BY DIFFERENT METHODS

(Seibert, 1932)

Size of study unit	1 pair	4 pairs	6 pairs	12 pairs (whole lesson)
Percent remembered				
after 50 minutes	35	39	44	49
after 2 days	31	33	34	47

The differences between the extreme values are statistically reliable, the smaller differences only probable. With further retests on the same material the differences became smaller as would be expected since each retest constituted a review of whatever was then remembered.

Card sorting provides another example of paired associates. Each kind of card is thrown into a particular box and has to be associated with the location of that box. Cards bearing the numbers from 1 to 10 (9 omitted because likely to be confused with 6) were sorted into a case of 3 × 3 compartments or boxes labeled in irregular order (Crafts, 1929). In learning by the pure part method, O first practiced row by row; he sorted two packs containing only the numbers in the first row, then two packs containing only the numbers in the second row, and then two packs containing only the numbers in the third row. After these six trials he commenced sorting packs containing all the numbers. By the whole method, O began and continued with packs containing all the numbers. Six trials by the whole method put O farther ahead in the total task than six trials by the part method (average from groups of 16 students, equated on the basis of a preliminary card sorting test). But the Os who had begun with parts caught up in a few trials and spent less total time in the learning because the sorting of 3 numbers went much more quickly than the sorting of 9. The results were more unequivocally in favor of the whole method when the sorting task was made more difficult by requiring each number to be thrown into a box bearing a specified other number.

The substitution test is logically similar to the card sorting and vocabulary tasks and belongs under the general head of Paired Associates. In a letter-number substitution experiment (Crafts, 1930) O uses a key of 12 letters, each letter being paired with a number which is to be substituted for it on a sheet of letters. In learning by the whole method, O uses the complete key from the start; in the pure part method he practices first with only 4 letters, then with 4 others, and then with the remaining 4; and finally attacks the entire task. Here the advantage of the whole method is reduced but not entirely eliminated.

In these later experiments the effort has been to get away from the wholeness—the more or less integrated pattern of response—which is built up in learning a poem, a prose passage, a list of nonsense syllables, a maze; and so to test the view that the whole method owes its advantage to keeping the pattern intact throughout the learning process. Crafts had expected to see the whole method lose its advantage in card sorting, and when it still showed an advantage he concluded that the spatial relations of the sorting case became systematized in whole learning. In the substitution test, where the opportunity for systematic wholeness of response was small, the advantage of the whole method was also small. Therefore the whole method does apparently owe some of its advantage (when it has any) to the opportunity it affords for developing a complete pattern of response. Another factor which could operate in the absence of system has been pointed out by Davis & Meenes (1932): the part method masses the repetitions of the same response, while the whole method spaces them somewhat, so that the advantage of spaced learning would go to the whole method.

Part and whole learning of simultaneous coordinations. Quite as interesting as the sequences of response which are developed in learning a list or a maze are such simultaneous combinations as are executed by use of both hands. Should the hands be practiced separately before the whole act is attempted? A few experiments have been directed to this and similar problems and the results, as usual, sometimes favor the part and sometimes the whole method of learning.

A two-handed "finger exercise" was the task assigned by Koch (1923) to her student Os. Numbering the fingers, from the thumb out, 1, 2, 3, 4, 5, she required the hands to execute the following simultaneous movements, at a rapid rate prescribed by a metronome:

Left hand: 3 2 1 5 4 2 1 4 5
Right hand: 2 4 3 2 1 5 4 5 2

That is, the third finger of the left hand and the second finger of the right were to move simultaneously. The movements were recorded by two typewriters, each hand operating a prescribed 5 keys of one typewriter. One group of 45 Os learned this performance with both hands simultaneously. It was at first a very confusing task, at the high speed demanded. Another group first learned the right and left hand sequences separately and then put them together. Each hand was practiced until 6 perfect runs were made, and the combined hands were then practiced to the same criterion, which was reached on the average in 51 min. from the beginning of the work. The whole learners required an average of 67 min. to reach the same criterion. Thus the experiment spoke definitely for the part method.

Piano practice offers a good opportunity for work on this problem, since the parts to be played by the right and left hands can be practiced separately, or both can be played together from the start. In the latter procedure the tempo would have to be very slow at the start in order to avoid mistakes and hesitations. R. W. Brown (1933), an experienced pianist, practiced three pieces by the "hands-together" method and three equally difficult pieces by the "hands-separate" method. In the latter, however, in order to keep track of progress, one performance with the hands together followed each pair of practices with the separate hands. The two parts were "put together" progressively as they were mastered. The tempo was controlled by a metronome set at a low speed at the beginning of practice and increased in speed as the learning progressed. The ultimate goal was the playing of the piece at the standard tempo for that piece. In all three pairs of equated pieces the goal was reached in less time by the hands-together method, about 25 percent less on the average. The hands-separate method was not specially inferior in the early stage of practice, but in proportion as the separate parts became speedy, the difficulty of combining them increased. The hands-together method afforded more musical pleasure to the learner.

A two-handed task quite different from piano playing was tried by Beeby (1930). Each hand held a stylus with which it moved along a metal strip 1 cm wide, endeavoring to avoid breaking the contact between stylus and strip, the eyes being kept closed. Each metal strip had the form of a square on the table, with sides of about 14 cm. Both hands moved around the squares in anticlockwise direction. One group of adult Os practiced from the start with both hands together, another group first learned right and left hands separately and then advanced to the two-handed performance. This latter group carried over some skill from hands-separate to hands-together and had an initial advantage in attacking the total problem. But this initial advantage was soon lost. At the end of 40 trials in the two-handed performance the group which had first practiced the separate hands was inferior to the group which had had only the two-handed practice. The time devoted to the separate hands was entirely wasted. The whole method was superior for this particular performance at least.

Somewhat the same result can be gleaned from the graphs in Kao's paper (1937, see above p. 167). Here only one hand was used but it had three requirements to meet. It had to thrust forward in a certain direction, at a certain instant of time, and with a precisely graded force, in order to accomplish a certain result. Aiming, timing and the control of force were first practiced separately by one group of students, while another group attacked the whole problem at once. The group with separate practice carried over some of their acquired skill into the total performance and maintained their initial advantage for many trials, but did not save enough time in learning the whole performance to compensate for the time devoted to the part practice. The time spent in part practice, while not wholly wasted, could better have been devoted to whole practice.

The net result of all the studies of part and whole learning seems to be something like this: the parts are easier to learn than the whole and the learner is often happier and better adjusted to the problem when beginning with the parts. He carries over some of the skill and knowledge gained in learning the parts into the subsequent learning of the whole performance. But he finds that putting together the parts is a serious problem requiring much further work. In the end he may have saved time and energy by commencing with the parts—or he may not—much depending on the size and difficulty of the total task and on the learner's poise and technique. If he can adjust himself to the whole method and handle it properly, he can learn quite complex performances effectively by the whole method. In a practical situation it is probably best to start with the whole method while feeling free to concentrate at any time on a part where something special is to be learned.

INTERFERENCE

Interference is nearly equivalent to the negative transfer effect (p. 176). If practicing one act makes another act easier to perform, we speak of transfer; if practicing one act makes another more difficult to perform we speak of interference. A distinction is made between two kinds of interference. If practicing one act makes the *learning* of another more difficult, this effect is called *associative interference;* if practicing a new act hampers the *execution* of an already learned act the effect is called *reproductive interference*. In one case it is the learning process that is disturbed, in the other case the remembering of what has been learned (in the broadest sense of remembering).

Sometimes we hear a tune which reminds us of a long known piece of music and we try to remember the old piece but cannot get the just heard piece out of our heads so as to give the old one a chance. The same sort of thing happens in trying to recall a name. In such cases of reproductive interference the recency of one act gives it a temporary advantage over another well known act.

A little information on reproductive interference can be gleaned from our previous discussions of recall and transfer (pp. 38, 202).

Most of the definite experiments are more concerned with associative interference.

In terms of stimulus and response a schema of the two kinds of interference can be constructed by letting S = a stimulus and A and B two different responses. Then we have:

1. *Associative interference.* Learn S—A, then learn S—B. Is the learning of S—B impeded by the previous learning of S—A?

2. *Reproductive interference.* First learn S—A, then S—B, finally return to S—A and see whether it can still be executed without difficulty, whether it needs to be relearned and whether it is even more difficult to relearn than it was originally to learn.

Can two inconsistent habits be retained? A preliminary answer to this type of question was afforded by an early experiment of Münsterberg (1892). He asked whether the formation of a new habit contrary to an old one actually eliminated the former from the individual. He took a habit of his own as the basis for informal experimentation. Long accustomed to carry his watch in his vest pocket, he began on a certain day to carry it in his trousers pocket, and recorded the false movements made till the new habit was well established. He then returned the watch to his vest pocket and found less time needed to regain the old habit than had been needed to learn the new one. When the vest pocket habit was again established, he changed the watch once more to the trousers; and alternated in this way several times. He reports that the number of false movements, and the period of confusion in shifting, decreased with each change. The coexistence of the two contrary habits within the nervous organism was demonstrated. While one habit was in active use, the other, though suppressed, was not eliminated or forgotten. Bair's typewriter experiment confirms this conclusion (1902).

Interference in card sorting. A very convenient task for studying interference is that of sorting cards (p. 220). Bergström (1892, 1893) used a pack of 80 cards, 8 of a kind, to be sorted into 10 piles, the location of each pile being designated by a sample card. Two altogether different arrangements of the piles were prescribed, and the pack was sorted alternately according to the two arrangements. When the interval between sortings was only 3 sec., interference was marked, but as the interval increased the effect rapidly decreased, and in 24 hours had entirely vanished.

The experiment was repeated in improved form and with more subjects by Culler (1912). The cards were sorted into pigeonholes labeled with sample cards; and two sets of pigeonholes, A and B, demanded different arrangements of the cards. One squad sorted alternately in the two arrangements, another squad sorted four times by the same arrangement before changing, and a control squad sorted throughout by the same arrangement. Between trials a rest of 30 sec. was taken. The results are presented in the adjoining tables, in which each vertical column gives the average time for the series of trials on the same day.

Several important conclusions are clearly indicated:

1. There is a genuine interference between the two performances. Compare the control group with the two interference groups in respect to the run of the day's work. (Reading down any column we see the run of a day's work.) The control group, except on the last day when it has apparently reached its limit, shows improvement throughout each day's work. Its first sorting is usually the slowest for the day. In the interference groups the first sorting each day is usually the quickest; as soon as the contrary performance is introduced the work becomes slower.

2. In spite of interference, there is improvement with practice, most clearly seen by following along the horizontal lines. Each day's work is better in every part, with a few minor exceptions, than the corresponding part of the preceding day's work.

3. Interference depends greatly on recency. At the beginning of each day's work the effect of previous practice is strongly in evidence, and the first trial shows little interference holding over from the day before. During each day's work the interference effect is so strong as to mask the further improvement that is being made, under the surface, and that will be revealed by the work of the following day.

4. Though the strong effect of interference is temporary, there is some sign of a small permanent effect. The squads subjected to interference made less improvement from day to day than the control squad. The control squad had the same amount of daily practice with arrangement A as the other squads who worked also with arrangement B. This work with B, even in the long run, hindered their progress in arrangement A.

Card Sorting Practice Without Interference: Control Group

(Culler, 1912)

The numbers give the average time per trial for a squad of 8 persons

			Days of practice			
	1	*2*	*3*	*4*	*5*	*6*
Arrangement of sorting case						
A	119	79	72	68	70	59
	100	78	70	69	65	59
	93	78	65	65	63	60
	93	76	69	67	63	60
	86	77	70	64	62	57
	85	74	68	66	62	59
	83	75	67	66	62	57
	79	77	67	65	61	57

Sorting Cards Alternately In Two Arrangements

(Culler, 1912)

Each number gives the average time per trial for a squad of 6 persons

	Days of practice					
	1	2	3	4	5	6
Arrangement of sorting case						
A	113	88	73	70	69	71
B	118	97	87	83	82	75
A	108	92	84	76	78	72
B	115	91	86	78	79	76
A	103	90	86	77	75	72
B	104	89	86	82	79	75
A	100	85	84	82	75	72
B	104	87	84	78	76	72
A	99	89	83	75	77	72
B	99	86	86	76	76	73
A	98	86	85	77	75	70
B	96	84	86	76	77	72
A	95	82	82	77	75	73
B	95	84	83	78	77	74
A	90	86	80	77	76	72
B	100	88	83	77	74	71

Sorting Cards In Two Arrangements

(Culler, 1912)

Each number gives the average time per trial for a squad of 14 persons

	Days of practice					
	1	2	3	4	5	6
Arrangement of sorting case						
A	116	91	81	75	74	69
	101	80	74	68	68	64
	96	79	73	66	65	64
	91	76	71	65	64	63
B	125	105	93	87	84	81
	104	87	80	76	73	72
	94	82	73	73	73	67
	89	78	72	70	68	65
A	112	100	91	89	84	83
	96	85	81	78	74	71
	90	82	77	74	71	67
	85	77	71	72	70	66
B	110	96	83	85	82	80
	95	81	77	77	72	71
	87	79	75	73	70	67
	86	78	73	70	67	66

RETROACTIVE INHIBITION

Suppose a memory lesson to be tested half an hour after learning, the interval being sometimes left idle and sometimes occupied by learning another similar lesson: retention is found to be better after the idle interval. In one of Müller & Pilzecker's experiments (1900), the recall score after an idle interval was 56 percent as against 26 percent when the interval was filled with strenuous mental activity. The impairment of recall by mental activity interpolated between learning and recall was given the name "retroactive inhibition," a name fairly descriptive of the facts though open to some logical objection. Genuine retroaction in time, changing already completed responses, is of course inconceivable. It must be the *after-effects* of the learning that are disturbed by later activity. The disturbance is revealed by the still later attempt to remember the lesson, but to suppose that the interpolated activity has no effect until this later time is just as illogical as to suppose it to work backward. Obviously the interpolated activity must have an effect at the time when it occurs.

Two opposed theories of retroactive inhibition have been offered, the anti-consolidation theory of Müller & Pilzecker (1900) and the transfer or interference theory of DeCamp (1915) and Webb (1917). Having discovered *perseveration* (p. 51), Müller & Pilzecker utilized this concept in their anti-consolidation theory. The associative responses which are so intensely active during learning do not lapse instantly into quiet but perseverate for a short time at least, and during this after-activity continue to strengthen and consolidate the traces. Rest immediately after learning favors perseveration and allows for full consolidation of the traces, while strenuous mental work just at this time cuts short the after-learning and leaves the traces weak.

The transfer theory of retroactive inhibition supposes, in a word, that the original and interpolated activities do not remain separate in memory. There are several possibilities. The traces of the original lesson and of similar interpolated material may simply become mixed up, so that on trying to remember the lesson you get items belonging to the other material; or the traces formed in the original learning are actually used and so modified in the subsequent learning of similar material. If an integrated response pattern is first learned—like the running of a certain maze or the complete recitation of a list of nonsense syllables—subsequent dealing with another list or maze may disrupt the original pattern, by using some of its parts in new combinations.

There are many variables to be worked out experimentally: kind of interpolated activity, amount and strenuousness of that activity, its exact temporal location within the learning-recall interval, length of the interval, degree of the original learning, ability and training of the learner. See review of the literature by Britt (1935). Most theoretical interest has attached to variations in the kind of interpolated activity and in its exact location within the interval.

Nature of the inhibiting activity.   According to the anti-consolidation theory, the amount of retroactive inhibition should depend less on the kind of interpolated activity than on its strenuousness.   The strenuousness or energy variable has not been worked out systematically.   Easy reading gives less retroactive inhibition than solving difficult problems, though both are very different in kind from the original lesson.   For a completely inactive condition, sleep would be ideal, but since it cannot be brought on instantly after the learning, the best approximation in German laboratories seems to have been the reading of *Fliegende Blätter*, and in American laboratories the reading of *College Humor*.   Such mild activities favor the retention of what has just previously been memorized.

It has become perfectly clear from many experiments that retroactive inhibition is especially strong when the interpolated activity is very *similar* to the original learning.   If the original lesson is a list of four-place numbers, the maximum inhibition is obtained by learning other four-place numbers.   If the original lesson is an arrangement of 5 chessmen on the board, the maximum inhibition is produced by learning another such arrangement (Robinson, 1920; Skaggs, 1925).   The amount of inhibition increases with the degree of similarity, as illustrated by results in the following table.

INCREASE OF RETROACTIVE INHIBITION WITH INCREASED SIMILARITY OF THE ORIGINAL AND INTERPOLATED TASKS

(*McGeoch & McDonald, 1931*)

The original activity consisted in memorizing a list of adjectives.   The interpolated activity consisted sometimes in learning another list of adjectives, synonyms of those in the first list; sometimes in learning a list of antonyms of the original adjectives; sometimes in learning a list of adjectives unrelated in meaning to the original ones; sometimes in learning a list of nonsense syllables; and sometimes in learning a list of 3-place numbers.   These various interpolated tasks were used with different groups of Os, all of whom at the end of the 10-minute interval attempted to recall the original list and also relearned it.   Greater retroactive inhibition is indicated by lower percent recalled, and by more readings to relearn.

Interpolated activity	Percent recalled	Readings to relearn
Rest	45	5.17
Learning numbers	37	5.08
Learning syllables	26	7.17
Learning unrelated adjectives	22	6.67
Learning antonyms of original	18	7.00
Learning synonyms of original	12	9.08

The similarity of the two activities may lie in the *material* used or in the *operation* performed.   With learning pairs of consonants for the original activity, cancelling consonants is similar in material, while learning number pairs is a similar operation.   Either kind of similarity will give retroactive inhibition, and the greatest effect is obtained by combining both kinds in the interpolated activity (Gibson & Gibson, 1934).

These results favor the transfer or interference theory as against the anti-consolidation theory. The same is true of Nagge's results (1935) obtained by making the interpolated activity different from the original learning, not in material nor in what we would ordinarily call operation (since both the original and the interpolated activities consisted in learning lists of nonsense syllables) but in the conditions under which the two activities were carried on. An obvious way of changing conditions was to take O into a different room for the interpolated activity, bringing him back to the first room for the retention test. The two rooms differed greatly in size, contents and lighting. This purely environmental difference did not have any effect on the amount of retroactive inhibition. But when (without changing rooms) the original list was presented to the eye and the interpolated list to the ear—or the reverse—retroactive inhibition was diminished. The "operation" may have been somewhat different, since a list may be attacked in different ways according to the mode of presentation.

The well-known dissociation between the waking state and the hypnotic trance—shown in many cases by posthypnotic amnesia (Hull, 1933)—suggests that retroactive inhibition should be small if the original learning and the interpolated activity occur in different states. This prediction was verified in another of Nagge's experiments. After learning one list of nonsense syllables, O was hypnotized and learned a second list; on being reawakened he was tested for retention of the first list, and retroactive inhibition was found to be slight though still present. The experiment and results are more fully presented in the following table.

RETROACTIVE INHIBITION IN RELATION TO WAKING AND
TRANCE STATES

(*Nagge, 1935*)

Condition of original learning (and of retention test)	Interpolated condition	Saving score in percent
1. Waking	Waking activity	38
2. Trance	Trance activity	48
3. Waking	Waking rest	49
4. Waking	Trance activity	50
5. Waking	Trance rest	63
6. Trance	Waking activity	64
7. Trance	Trance rest	64
8. Trance	Waking rest	78

The trance state was one of deep hypnosis. The original material was a list of 12 nonsense syllables, and the interpolated activity consisted in learning another such list. The interpolated activity began 10 minutes after, and the retention test 55 minutes after, the end of the original learning. The scores given are the averages for 10 male subjects. The P.E. of the average runs from 1.7 to 3.8, but the P.E. of the differences depends also on the correlations between the several conditions. The differences of 12 or over are all fairly reliable. The most important comparisons for our purpose are those between Conditions 1 and 4, and between 2 and 6. Also, the difference between Conditions 4 and 5 (which is about 3 times its P.E.) indicates *some* retroactive inhibition between activities carried on in the two states; and the same indication appears on comparing Conditions 6 and 8.

Temporal position of the disturbing extra activity. Must the interpolated activity follow the original learning *immediately* in order to produce any retroactive inhibition? One might think so from the anti-consolidation theory; and Müller & Pilzecker (1900) supported this theory by finding a pause of 6 minutes, after learning and before starting the interpolated work, to diminish the inhibition considerably. A similar result was obtained by Skaggs (1925) while according to Robinson (1920) it makes no difference whether a 5-minute work period comes at the beginning, middle or end of a 20-minute interval between learning and recall. McGeoch (1933) found fully as much inhibition when the work came just before recall as when it came directly after learning; and this statement held good whether the total interval was as short as 20 minutes or as long as 6 days. Whitely (1927) even found that the extra activity, instead of being interpolated, could *directly precede the original learning*, and still lower the retention score 1–2 days later. Here we have to speak not of retroactive, but of *proactive inhibition*, since an earlier activity impairs the traces of a later activity. Further evidence of proactive inhibition was found by von Restorff (1933).

Whitely's experiments are interesting in another way. For memory material he used lists of words and phrases, each list being drawn from a certain field, as English literature, mathematics, or athletics; and the extra activity consisted in answering questions in the same field or in quite a different field. We might expect the related material here to be of positive benefit to recall; but no, retroactive inhibition was greater with related than unrelated material.

With proactive inhibition admitted, the results in this paragraph do not rule out the anti-consolidation theory. They are quite in accord with the supposed importance of perseveration. Let there be two activities, A directly followed by B. Perseveration of A brings it into conflict with B, to the detriment of both. B exerts retroactive inhibition on A, and A exerts proactive inhibition on B. An extra activity coming just before or after the learning may prevent the proper formation of traces; coming just before the recall test it may, by perseverating, disturb the process of recall. Nothing in all these results contradicts the transfer theory, however, except perhaps the fact that strenuous though unrelated activity exerts some retroactive inhibition.

Internal retroactive inhibition. Grant retroactive and proactive inhibition between two temporally adjacent lessons, and you can hardly deny its presence within a single lesson composed of a number of items. Work on the later items weakens the hold already gained on the earlier items; and the longer the list, the greater the amount of this mutual inhibition. Were there no such inhibitory factor at work, O could grasp the amount of one memory span, grasp another equal amount, and then recite the whole double span. Mutual inhibition is partly, though not wholly, accountable for the difficulty of memorizing a long lesson (cf p. 19).

Working with Köhler, von Restorff (1933) showed that retroactive inhibition was akin to the heaping-up or *cumulation effect* that occurs when many items of the same kind are learned together. She presented a list containing two kinds of items, many of one kind and only one of the other, such as:

List 1	List 2
lat	74
92	rin
dop	38
zum	53
tef	26
dap	81
lus	45
fed	67
mol	92
sig	19

Each list was presented only once, at the rate of 1.5 sec. per item, and O busied himself in memorizing a prose passage for 10 min., after which he wrote all of the list he could remember. Of the cumulated items (syllables in some lists and numbers in others) the average score of 15 Os was 22 percent; while of the isolated items the average score was 70 percent. Other experiments agreed in showing much better retention of relatively isolated than of cumulated items (Köhler & von Restorff, 1935).

In another experiment of this series (Ortner, 1937) the traces of recently learned items were found to be a help in reading the same items when almost illegible because of poor light and focus. Items which had recently been clearly seen were read, in poor exposure, more easily and correctly than perfectly new items (see p. 38). With this fact established, Ortner proceeded to look for the cumulation effect. A list containing 8 nonsense words and 2 numbers, or 8 numbers and 2 nonsense words, was first exposed. When it had been clearly presented 3 times, O occupied himself in reading for half an hour, and was then given a poor exposure of the same items, with instructions to read them as well as possible and to say which ones he recognized.   The average percents for 8 Os were as follows:

	Correctly read	Recognized
Cumulated items	36	49
Isolated items	81	91

The traces of the isolated items functioned better than those of the cumulated items.   Thus the detrimental effect of cumulation was again demonstrated.   Another interesting fact: more items were recognized than were read correctly.   Items incorrectly read were sometimes recognized, indicating that a trace not definite enough to yield a perfect reproduction may still make recognition possible.   Recognition can get along with less complete or distinct traces than are required for accurate reproduction.

The theory of Köhler and his associates likens the field of memory traces to the visual field, and likens the cluster of traces formed in learning a list to any small region in the visual field.   If this small region contains a mass of similar figures, the general character of the region is clearly seen but the individual figures are scarcely distinguished; any divergent figure within this mass is apt to stand out distinctly.   So in the trace field; when any part of it consists of similar items, their individuality is lost.   One remembers the general character of the cumulated items but not the specific character of each single item.   This theory of retroactive inhibition can be classed with the transfer theories.   It is expounded fully and with more experimental evidence by Koffka (1935, pp. 481–493).

Is recognition affected by retroactive inhibition?   The careful experiments of Heine (1914) led to a negative conclusion on this question. Lists of nonsense syllables were presented, and the interval between the presentation and the recognition test was either left idle or filled with strenuous mental activity such as studying several pictures with a view to passing an examination on them.   The results showed no retroactive inhibition in 9 educated adults.   Heine's inference was that recognition must have some other basis than the associations which are responsible for recall.

Retroactive inhibition is not easily demonstrated in recognition —to that extent later experiments confirm this early work—but indirect evidence is fairly convincing.   How else shall we explain the relatively poor recognition of items from a long list (p. 20)?   The same fact in recall memory is explained by appealing to retroactive inhibition as a causative factor.

Direct evidence on the question is obtained by introducing conditions which make recognition more than commonly difficult (p. 48).   When the "new" items included in a recognition test are very similar to the "old" items, O finds it difficult to distinguish the old from the new, his recognition score is low and retroactive inhibition can be demonstrated (Lund, 1926).   In one experiment (Gibson, 1934) the original lesson consisted of 10 nonsense words, and the recognition test included words altered from the originals by the change of one or two letters, as, for example:

Original	Altered forms	
MAREN	MARER	MARUR
SETIR	SATIR	BATIR

There were fewer correct and more incorrect recognitions when the interval of 5 minutes was occupied with memorizing nonsense words of the same general form (though not specifically resembling the originals) than when it was occupied with looking at pictures. In another experiment (McKinney, 1935) recognition of nonsense syllables was definitely impaired by the use of many quite similar syllables in the interpolated activity and in the recognition test.

A simple geometrical figure can be half concealed by incorporation into a more complicated figure (p. 640); this way of making recognition difficult was employed by Zangwill (1938). The interval between the original presentation of the simple figures and the later attempt to identify them in the complex figures was occupied either with an informal lecture (rest condition) or in the memorizing of still other figures. There was some retroactive inhibition. An interesting result, quite in line with that obtained with verbal material by Ortner (p. 232), was that O's attempt to reproduce a figure, after recognizing it, sometimes showed a right-left or up-down reversal or some other inaccuracy—indicating once more that a trace may be good enough for correct recognition and still lack the precision needed for correct reproduction. Ordinary experience would certainly bear out this conclusion.

We are logically forced to conclude that retroactive inhibition affects recognition, though probably to a smaller degree than it affects recall, because of the superior efficiency of recognition. In terms of consolidation, we can suppose that less firmly established traces suffice for recognition than for recall. In terms of the transfer theories, the traces can become indistinct through interaction between them, and still suffice for recognition.

CHAPTER X

FEELING

CERTAIN distinctions though not very important in the laboratory may well be made at the outset of this study.

1. **Feelings and emotions.** The traditional distinction makes feeling an elementary process, emotion a complex of feeling and sensation. It is doubtful, however, whether the distinction between elementary and complex can be carried through in the laboratory, and consequently there is no good reason for keeping the two topics apart.

2. **Emotion and state of the organism.** Anyone will unhesitatingly classify as emotions: anger, fear, disgust, joy and sorrow; and as states of the organism: hunger, thirst, nausea, fatigue, drowsiness, intoxication. Now that physiology has revealed a peculiar organic state in fear and anger, why do we continue to call them emotions and deny that name to fatigue or drowsiness? It is hard to find a valid distinction, unless it be that the typical emotion is aroused by external stimuli and is directed toward the environment, whereas a state of the organism, such as hunger or fatigue, originates in intraorganic processes and has no direct relation to the environment.

3. **Emotion and desire.** In the concrete, desire and emotion go together. Psychological theory separates them, but whether they can be separated in the laboratory—or in the clinic—is very doubtful.

4. **Feeling and valuation.** When we make a spontaneous judgment of value such as "That is beautiful" or "ugly" we have a feeling of pleasure or displeasure. For that reason the study of esthetics is often included under the general head of the psychology of feeling. If one has to make many esthetic judgments the feeling may diminish and leave only an intellectual perception of the qualities of beauty and ugliness. It is more in line with the realities of laboratory practice to separate esthetics from feeling and group it with studies of judgment.

Methods of impression and expression. In ordinary life we get some knowledge regarding a person's emotion either from his testimony or from his facial expressions and movements. In the laboratory method of impression, a stimulus is applied to O, who is instructed to report the impression it makes upon him. He may be asked for a complete introspective report or simply to pass judgment on the stimulus.

The assumption or hope behind the method of expression was that O would necessarily express his feeling if not in his face then in his breathing, heart action or some physiological process. Symptoms were sought for each type of feeling, by correlating the subjective report with the objective expression. So far definite, dependable symptoms of feelings have not been discovered. From the original point of view the method of expression has broken down. The recording of various physiological processes in emotion continues to be of interest.

In the following pages we will first examine some of the attempts by the method of impression to obtain descriptions of feelings and emotions, and go on in the following chapters to the results obtained by the method of expression.

INTROSPECTIVE STUDIES

Just what can be hoped for from introspective studies of feeling and emotion? We might get some light on the question whether pleasantness and unpleasantness exhaust the list of feelings. We might discover whether feeling is after all a kind of sensation. The question of "mixed feelings" (simultaneous presence of pleasantness and unpleasantness) could be examined. An attempt might be made to differentiate introspectively between the emotions.

The observer in an introspective experiment on feeling needs to adopt a special attitude toward the situation that is presented to him. Rather than perceiving the situation and dealing actively with it he must immerse himself in it and live it, at the same time trying to observe the emotional experience that comes over him.

The number of elementary feelings. Traditionally the number is two, pleasantness and unpleasantness. Wundt (1896, 98ff) made a decided break with tradition when, in developing a comprehensive theory of feeling, he postulated three dimensions: pleasantness-unpleasantness, excitement-quiet, and tension or expectancy with its opposite, relief or relaxation. The total feeling at any moment though a unitary state could be located somewhere along each of these dimensions. It might be mildly pleasant, very excited and quite relaxed, or show other combinations, just as a point on the earth can be identified by its latitude, longitude and altitude.

Here it would seem was a problem for introspective study, though Wundt himself appealed more to the method of expression, seeking without much success to discover circulatory and respiratory variables corresponding to the three dimensions. Titchener, though a pupil of Wundt, was extremely skeptical of the new theory, regarding which he raised two questions: (1) Were these three dimensions really independent? (2) Were not excitement, tension and so on complexes of sensations rather than elementary feelings? In putting these questions to the test of experiment Titchener (1902) presented tones of different pitch, various colors, or a metronome beating at different rates. Two tones having been sounded, O reported which was more pleasant, or in another series which was more exciting. With the metronome beats, O reported in one series which rate was more pleasant and in another which aroused more tension.   The subjects readily used any of Wundt's categories, but were not always in agreement as to their meaning.   The opposite of excitement, which Wundt had called "depression," was especially confusing.   When depression was taken to mean sadness the results made it equivalent to unpleasantness, but if depression was taken to mean quietness, it was nearly equivalent to pleasantness.   The high tones were more unpleasant than the low ones and they were also more depressing but less quieting.   Certain medium rates of the metronome, about 60–70 per minute, were least unpleasant and at the same time least tense.   (This terminological difficulty could have been avoided. Wundt's scheme evidently requires that the three dimensions shall be conceived as independent of each other.   Consequently they must be named and defined so as to prevent the confusion of one dimension with another.   To avoid the connotations of common speech we might substitute for excitement-depression the terms stimulating-unstimulating, or we might invent new terms.)   As the result of his experiments, Titchener made two points against the tridimensional theory: (1) the dimensions were not independent (as naively understood), pleasantness and unpleasantness being the only true and independent feelings; (2) Wundt's other dimensions though perfectly sound categories for the description of complex states were not true elements of feeling but complexes of kinesthetic and organic sensations.

The introspections obtained in this early experiment did not observe the distinction of "process" and "meaning" which later became so important in the Titchener school.   In a somewhat similar experiment with Os well versed in this type of introspection, Yokoyama (1921) found that colors were compared in respect to pleasantness without any genuine feeling on O's part.   The judgments of value had become mechanized through practice.   Slight organic sensations were detected but they faded out in a prolonged experiment, leaving very little "process" to be observed.   Other experimenters also (Johnston, 1906) obtained reports of bodily sensations in experiments on the pleasantness and unpleasantness of colors, tones, etc., provided the instructions required O to look for such sensations.   Chest expansion, abdominal contraction, jaws set, cringing, slight nausea, pleasant thrills in chest and abdomen, unpleasant chills and stiffening are some examples.   Lindworsky (1928) obtained similar reports of organic and kinesthetic sensations when O was given verbal stimuli intended to call up past experiences or imaginary situations that would arouse pleasure, fear, vexation or sorrow. He concludes that there are no "higher feelings"—nothing elementary or specific deserving this name—but that the state of feeling in a life situation consists of bodily sensations arising from the fundamental biological responses of approach and withdrawal.   From Wohlgemuth's (1919) elaborate and fully reported experiment on highly competent introspective observers, the conclusion drawn was that the only true feelings were pleasantness and unpleasantness which were *not* sensations or sensory complexes. It was true however that pleasantness and unpleasantness were often localized at the point of stimulation; this was so of touch and taste, but not so often of sight and hearing. The pleasantness of a taste seems to be in the mouth, while that of a beautiful color lies not in the eyes, nor always in the object, but rather diffusely in O himself.

In the course of time, Titchener inclined to the view that pleasantness and unpleasantness might after all be sensory in character, and it was in his laboratory that Nafe (1924) obtained expert introspections indicating that these feelings were identical with certain tactual qualities. To make introspection easier Nafe avoided strong stimuli, and presented mild stimuli of all modalities with instructions to attend to the affective side of the experience, and to make an effort "to get affection palpable under observation"; also to look for concomitant organic sensations "with a view to determining whether affection is simply a meaning laid over the organics." As an example of the introspections thus secured, here is a report of the experience produced by sweet chocolate: "The characterization, pleasant, applies to the experienced complex, the predominant components of which were the quality of sweet and a brightness or lightness reminiscent of bright pressure. The brightness or lightness character was not so much a part of the experience as an aspect of it. It covered the whole experience." Some of the adjectives used by the Os in their effort to convey the quality of pleasantness were: bright, sparkling, shimmering, mild, misty, vaporous, airy, fluffy, smooth, soft, oily. Some of those used for unpleasantness were: dull, drab, rigid, stiff, gloomy, heavy, dense, thick, cold, hard, rough, grating, somber. After prolonged experience Nafe's subjects agreed with his view that *pleasantness is identical with bright pressure* or contact and *unpleasantness with dull pressure*. Organic sensations were found whenever O looked for them, but they appeared not to constitute the feeling.

"Bright pressure" here is a technical term designating the sensation from light contact, especially moving contact or contact with a number of points. Bright pressure is not far removed from tickle. Pleasantness and unpleasantness according to this finding are identical in quality with the sensations obtained by light touch on the skin and by pressure through the skin upon the subcutaneous tissues. Query: are these affective sensations localized? Nafe's observers were not inclined to give any definite localization, but Hoisington (1928) reported from the same laboratory that the same observers, on becoming more expert in losing sight of the external object and immersing themselves in the feeling experience, were aware of a vague localization which on "waking up" proved to be in the abdominal region for the dull pressure of unpleasantness, and in the upper part of the body for the bright pressure of pleasantness.

To meet the objection that the whole procedure is very esoteric,

Hunt (1931) conducted a check experiment on relatively untrained observers. With colors as stimuli he instructed O on one day to rate each color as pleasant, unpleasant or indifferent and on another day to describe the experience under the categories of bright pressure, dull pressure or neither. His definitions of bright and dull pressure deserve to be quoted: Bright pressure "resembles . . . a touch quality lying between bright pressure and tickle. It is a diffuse bodily feeling with expansive qualities. In addition to its decided brightness it may be described as buoyant, lively, elusive and welling. It is like expansiveness of the body." Dull pressure is like tactual dull pressure "or between dull pressure and strain. It is not extended, and has qualities of constriction. It is dull, inert, heavy, sinking, leaden, condensed and like bodily contraction." Each color was rated many times by each O both on the pleasantness-unpleasantness scale and on the brightness-dullness scale. Hunt worked out the correlation between the scores of the several colors in the two scales and found it high for every one of his Os. This was the result at Harvard; but at Bryn Mawr, where the experiment was repeated by Converse (1932), the correlations were too low and scattered to support the theory. She believes the positive correlations, when obtained, may be the result of pure suggestion, since " 'bright' suggests joyous, happy, pleasant states, while 'dull' suggests dead, unpleasant states." In short, bright and dull pressure will have to receive more matter-of-fact names before such experiments can be properly conducted.

One wonders whether Nafe's original experiment would give the same result in other laboratories. Nafe had worked at Cornell. Young (1927) at Illinois obtained from a few of his subjects reports much like Nafe's, indicating that pleasantness was at least *like* bright pressure; most of his Os, however, gave no such reports but inclined to characterize pleasantness and unpleasantness as bodily attitudes of acceptance or avoidance, or as appertaining to the pleasant or unpleasant object. It seemed that there was a lot of vague, elusive experience to report and that each O picked out what he was looking for.

If we turn to the extensive studies of Phelan (1925) made at Louvain with very competent observers who were well aware of the need for distinguishing between feelings and mere judgments of value, we find nothing definitely opposed to Nafe's findings, but we do find emphasis on the immense qualitative variety of feelings. The reports do not lend themselves to arrangement along the single scale of pleasantness-unpleasantness. We find another distinction, that between objective and subjective feelings. In an objective feeling the pleasantness or unpleasantness is an aspect of the sensation or inherent in the object; for example: "The color was disagreeable in itself objectively"; "The stimulus had an objectively disagreeable character which I could translate into the words, 'That's a dirty noise.'" Subjective feelings, on the contrary, were feelings of one's personal condition; for example: "I express my state better by saying 'That is disagreeable for me to see' than by saying 'That color is disagreeable.' " Subjective feelings were most numerous when the stimulus was a picture or object, recalling a memory, and least numerous with olfactory and gustatory stimuli. It appeared that pleasantness and unpleasantness by themselves are neither subjective nor objective. Never occurring pure, they are always attached either to an object or to the subject. In one case the object is pleasant, in another case the person himself is in a pleasant state. Both subjective and objective feelings are accordingly meaningful; and the question is whether Nafe's observers really succeeded in sinking themselves so completely into the feeling itself as to shake off these meanings, or whether bright pressure and dull pressure were not special names for subjective feeling.

The word "bright" applied to cutaneous sensation is obviously figurative. Common usage, as reflected in the dictionary, gives no warrant for the combination, "bright pressure," which nevertheless is readily understood. Wherein lies the similarity between a light which is literally bright and a pressure which is figuratively so? The similarity may lie simply in the affective tone of the two sensations. If the subject in one of these experiments, responding to a visual stimulus and avoiding objective reference, describes his subjective feeling as "reminiscent of bright pressure," the "pressure" may be body sensation and the "bright" may be merely an index of positive affective response.

Mixed feelings. Psychologists have long disagreed as to the possibility of experiencing pleasantness and unpleasantness at the same time. They have agreed that such parallel or simultaneous feelings are unusual. The question is analogous to one in attention: Can we attend to two things at once? The observer is likely to stumble into two pitfalls in either of these problems. In the case of attention a distinction must be made between divided attention and attention to a compound object or group of objects. The other pitfall consists in failing to distinguish between absolutely simultaneous attention to two objects and rapid alternation of attention between them. In the same way the observer in attempting to decide whether mixed feeling exists must distinguish between the presence of an ambivalent object and the combination of pleasant and unpleasant feeling, and he also must distinguish rapid alternation of the feelings from true simultaneity. Only introspection (if any method) can answer such questions.

One method of approaching the question of mixed feelings is to present a pleasant stimulus to one sense and an unpleasant stimulus simultaneously to another sense. Johnston (1906) used this method, presenting colors, tones and tactual surfaces in different trials. His Os sometimes reported that both pleasantness and unpleasantness were present at the same time, but more commonly there was a summation or a fusion.

The same method was employed by Alechsieff (1907). Solution of quinine was placed in the mouth while a bottle of rose oil was held to the nose. ˙The report of one trial runs as follows:

At first O is aware only of a lukewarm liquid in his mouth, but soon he gets a strong bitter sensation which evokes a strong feeling of unpleasantness. He tries to set aside the bitter sensation and when that fails swallows the liquid, so intensifying the bitter and the unpleasantness. At this moment he becomes aware of the rose oil perfume. For an instant he forgets the unpleasantness, the odor calms him and gives him a strong feeling of pleasantness. But soon it seems to him as if the rose oil had been taken away, because he again gets the quinine taste and the unpleasant feeling. Pleasantness and unpleasantness alternate in this way till the end of the trial, always coming in succession and never simultaneously. When the pleasant feeling is dominant in O's consciousness, the unpleasant feeling is wholly absent, and vice versa.

All of Alechsieff's cases were of this type. There were no reports of true mixed feelings.

Instead of presenting two stimuli simultaneously to different senses Kellogg (1915) exposed a pleasant and an unpleasant picture alternately, by means of a Dodge tachistoscope, at the rate of 10 alternations per minute. His instructions were: Give yourself up to the experience in a normal way and report on feelings and anything else of interest. He obtained reports of mixed feelings in a minority of cases but admitted that the experiences were "decidedly complex and somewhat difficult to introspect." When a surgical picture alternated with a comic picture, the disgust at the surgical picture persisted during the exposures of the comic one and yet the comic feeling was aroused.

Using a similar technique Wohlgemuth (1919) also obtained occasional reports of the coexistence of pleasant and unpleasant feeling, and of the coexistence of two pleasant feelings attached to different objects.

On the other side of the question, Young (1918) reported results obtained with several methods and from well trained Os. One method consisted in establishing a mood and attempting to superimpose on the mood the opposite feeling. For example, while O was very hungry, he received as stimulus the odor of food. Young obtained reports of simultaneous pleasantness and unpleasantness, but on critically examining such reports he found them vitiated by what he called the "meaning error." O was simultaneously aware of two objects or facts, one pleasant and the other unpleasant, and improperly reported the two feelings to be simultaneous. Young decided that there was no real evidence for mixed feelings.

Phelan (1925), in an interesting experiment, paired a pleasant taste with an electric shock, and presented the pair many times, trying to make the taste disagreeable by association with the shock. Such conditioning was not obtained; the taste remained as pleasant as before. The taste and the shock were experienced as distinct events, but in a few instances both feeling tones, one pleasant and the other unpleasant, seemed to be present simultaneously.

After careful scrutiny of the evidence we have cited and of that from still other experiments, Beebe-Center (1932) formulates his conclusions thus: "There are no mixed feelings in the sense of coexistence of pleasant or unpleasant elements or groups of elements with hedonic tone as an attribute." Still, "it is possible under particularly favorable conditions, for a pleasant object and an unpleasant one to be experienced simultaneously." The results are quite analogous with those on the division of attention (p. 711).

A general conclusion, not exactly forced by the evidence from introspective studies of feeling, but at least rendered attractive, is that the feelings are reactive attitudes of the organism. Pleasantness and unpleasantness correspond to the attitudes of acceptance and rejection, excitement and depression to the momentary level of muscular activity or readiness for activity, tension and relaxation to the degree of muscular tension. The various emotions may correspond to more specific attitudes.

CHAPTER XI

EXPRESSION OF THE EMOTIONS

THE PSYCHOLOGIST has several good reasons for devoting some attention to the face and its expressions, as well as to the voice, gestures and other expressive movements and postures. He wishes to describe emotional behavior. If he has the behavioristic point of view, he regards emotion as motor and glandular activity; and though the visceral component of emotional behavior may be more important, the external components are more easily observed. If there are several distinct emotions, there should be as many behavior patterns distinguishable in the face, voice and gestures.

The approach from the James-Lange theory is not very different. The behaviorist regards the emotion as a motor pattern, while the James-Lange theory says it consists of the sensations produced by the motor pattern. Where the behaviorist would examine the motor pattern only, the James-Lange adherent would examine the motor pattern in connection with an introspective report of sensations and feelings.

Questions of heredity and environment present themselves. Is the motor pattern built up in experience or is it unlearned and hereditary? Related questions are whether the visible or audible behavior pattern is readily understood by other persons, whether it excites the same emotion in the beholder (sympathetic induction of emotion), and whether such sympathetic response, if genuine, is itself learned or instinctive.

Apart from these difficult genetic and developmental problems, social psychology is directly concerned with the individual's ability to read the emotional state of another from the face, voice and other expressive movements. Facial expression serves as a sign language, a medium of communication—but how good a medium?

With such questions in the background, one approaches the study of facial expression hopeful of significant results and ready to lend an ear even to the preliminary results so far obtained.

Antecedents. The psychologist was preceded in this line of study by the anatomist, the painter and the actor. A great anatomist, Sir Charles Bell (1806, 1844), well known for his discovery of the distinct sensory and motor roots of the spinal nerves, pointed out the value of anatomy for the painter and the special importance of knowing the facial muscles which produce the different expressions. As to the question whether these facial movements are primarily expressive or practical, he believed the latter alternative to be the better general theory. When

242

an angry dog bares his teeth, it is a practical movement. Physiologically the facial movements, like those of speech, are connected with the general function of respiration. Yet Bell believed that certain muscles peculiar to man (better, to the primates), such as the corrugators that "knit" the brows or the triangularis that depresses the corner of the mouth, have no other function than that of expressing the finer shades of emotion.

The greatest of the early students of emotional expression was Charles Darwin, who followed up his *Origin of Species* and *Descent of Man* by a work which was a contribution to psychology as much as to the theory of evolution, his *Expression of the Emotions in Man and Animals* (1872). Disagreeing with Bell, Darwin held that every facial movement was primarily "serviceable," and that its expressive function was derived from the practical function according to one or another of his three principles of emotional expression.

1. The principle of "serviceable associated habits." Many expressive movements are remnants or vestiges of practical movements. Originally directed to the securing of practical results, these movements became automatic habits and might even be inherited. But they were modified in two respects. On the side of the stimulus, they became associated with situations which were merely analogous with the original exciting causes; and on the side of the response they were weakened and toned down till only vestiges of the original practical movements remained.

2. The principle of "antithesis." Opposite impulses tend to opposed movements. If one emotion gives a certain movement, the opposite emotion will give the opposed movement even though the latter never had any practical value.

3. The principle of the "direct action of the excited nervous system on the body"—of the overflow of nervous activity into all available motor channels. Muscular trembling is an example.

Most characteristically Darwinian is the first principle. The expression of grief in the adult is toned down from the frank crying of the infant. The vocal part of crying is a practical call for help, and the facial part was originally an adjunct to the vocal. The wide open mouth involved the muscles which depress the corners of the mouth, and this little movement remains as a sign of grief after vocal crying has been eliminated. Similarly, firm closing of the mouth, originally adjunct to the practical movement of straining, remains as a symptom of mental effort and determination. Raising the upper lip and showing the canine teeth in anger may be a remnant of practical teeth-baring in simian combat.

Darwin's principle of antithesis can be used to explain laughter which is the opposite of sobbing in that sobbing involves spasmodically interrupted inspiration, laughter expiration.

Piderit (1859), a German anatomist who lived for many years in Chile, wrote on facial expression both before and after Darwin. Like

Bell, he hoped to make anatomy useful to the painter and sculptor. In many paintings he found a lack of harmonious facial expression, which stimulated him to analyze the total expression of the face into elementary expressions of the several features, in the belief that combining such elements would insure a harmonious total.

In Piderit's theory, expressive movements are not mere remnants of practical movements. They have a present utility which can be discovered without going back into individual and racial history. The facial muscles, he believed, are adjuncts of the sense organs, serving to assist or impede the reception of stimuli. Just as opening or closing the eyes facilitates or impedes the reception of visual stimuli, so certain positions of the nose facilitate smelling while other positions keep out unpleasant odors. A sweet substance is savored by pressing tongue and lips against the front teeth, a bitter taste minimized by lowering the tongue away from the roof of the mouth.

In developing his theory Piderit suggested that an object thought of should give the same facial response as when present to the senses. With an unpleasant thought, the mouth behaves as if avoiding a bitter taste, the eye region as if avoiding an unpleasant sight, the nose as if

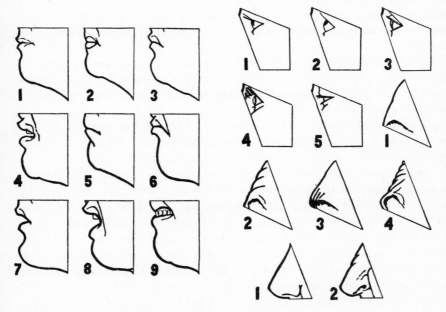

Fig. 65. (Boring & Titchener, 1923.)   Piderit features.

Mouths: 1, normal; 2, sweet; 3, bitter; 4, very unpleasant; 5, stubborn; 6, stubborn and unpleasant; 7, attentive; 8, unpleasant and attentive; 9, snarl or sneer.

Eyes: 1, normal; 2, exalted; 3, attentive; 4, very attentive; 5, inattentive, withdrawn.

Brows: 1, normal; 2, attentive; 3, unpleasant or thoughtful state; 4, unpleasant attention.

Noses: 1, normal; 2, unpleasant attention.

avoiding a foul odor. A pleasant thought gives open eyes, a "sweet" mouth, and a sweet nose if the individual's nose is sufficiently mobile. In general, movements such as impede the reception of stimuli express unpleasant emotion. Receptive movements may express attention as well as pleasure. Wide-open eyes express attention, suddenly raised brows surprise, extremely raised brows amazement, half shut eyes indifference. Similarly, Piderit recognized the open mouth of listening or other attention, the stubborn mouth (agreement with Darwin here), and the appraising or sampling mouth, with lips protruding. Many combinations of these elements are possible.

Piderit illustrated his analyses by drawings. Simple line drawings they were, profile and front views, stripped of all accessories that could suggest emotion. Such bare outlines afford the fairest test of the reality of the proposed elementary expressions.

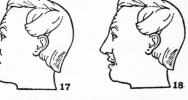

Fig. 66. (Boring & Titchener, 1923.) Compounds of Piderit features: 17, bewildered; 18, amazed.

Judgments of facial expression. The experimental psychologist took his cue from Darwin and Piderit. Darwin himself introduced one of the typical experiments. Obtaining some photographs intended to represent several emotions he showed them "without a word of explanation," and asked for a judgment of the emotions expressed. Among his 20 judges there was general agreement regarding some of the photographs but little agreement on others. Where the judges disagreed, Darwin concluded that the picture did not truly express the emotion, though he himself, on first examining it and being told what emotion it represented, had been fully satisfied. The experiment convinced him that suggestion was a factor in reading facial expression.

On the basis of Piderit's drawings, Boring & Titchener (1923) prepared interchangeable features which could be inserted in a profile drawing of a human face. With an assortment of brows, eyes, noses and mouths, they built up 360 compounds and found, strangely enough, that almost every compound was accepted by some O as a genuine expression, even when the parts were contradictory. When O had entered into the spirit of the game, he saw the Piderit elements in the separate features and intelligible expressions in the built-up faces.

The question remained whether these compounded expressions would convey the same meanings to observers who received no guidance or suggestion from the experimenter. This question was put to the test in an experiment of Buzby (1924) and of Fernberger (1928). Some of the Piderit faces were shown to students who were supplied with a list of emotion names from which to select the most appropriate name for each facial expression. The results, as presented in the next table show that the Os did not agree closely with each other or with the theoretical meanings of the expressions. If we accept the faces as correct, and regard the experiment as a test of ability to read facial expression, we conclude that these students did poorly. If we assume that in such a matter the pooled judgment of a large number of unprejudiced observers is correct, we must conclude that the faces were not very expressive of the supposed emotions. The expressions were however very unequal in success. The "dismayed" face seldom gave the impression of dismay, more often suggesting simple attention. The "bewildered" face usually conveyed the impression of something akin to bewilderment, if we count the 26 percent of "amazed" and the 14 percent of "quizzical." We have to reckon with some vagueness in the use of these emotion words.

How the Piderit Faces Appeared to 1382 Students

(Buzby, 1924 and Fernberger, 1928)

The list of names at the left of the table was provided and each subject selected what seemed to him the best-fitting name for each of the five faces. The table gives the percent selecting each name, an "e" denoting less than ½ of 1%.

	Intended expressions of the faces shown				
	Dismayed	Horrified	Disdainful	Disgusted	Bewildered
Terms used					
Pleased	e	1	e	0	e
Displeased	3	1	4	2	e
Stubborn	2	e	9	1	e
Attentive	45	0	1	0	11
Quizzical	18	e	1	0	14
Inattentive	1	e	5	0	3
Dismayed	5	3	2	e	6
Reverential	5	0	3	e	5
Affable	2	e	e	0	2
Bewildered	8	2	1	e	32
Amazed	2	7	e	0	26
Horrified	e	57	0	e	e
Raging	e	11	e	e	0
Disapproving	4	2	14	7	1
Disdainful	2	2	34	9	e
Angry	e	2	1	e	0
Contemptuous	1	3	19	33	0
Disgusted	1	10	6	48	0
	99	101	100	100	100

Where the facial expression is susceptible of different interpretations, there is room for suggestion. Fernberger (1928) tried the effect of suggesting a "false" interpretation. To several groups, totaling 658 students, he showed these same five faces, assigning to each a "false" designation and asking the subjects to judge whether the given face expressed the designated emotion well, fairly well, poorly or not at all. His results are seen in the following table.

EFFECT OF SUGGESTION ON THE INTERPRETATION OF FACIAL EXPRESSION
(Fernberger, 1928)

Expression intended *Response suggested*	*Dismayed* *quizzical*	*Horrified* *attentive*	*Disdainful* *displeased*	*Disgusted* *contemp-* *tuous*	*Bewildered* *reverential*
Percent selecting this response without suggestion	18	0	4	33	5
Percent accepting the suggestion *	74	10	77	95	70

*The "percent accepting the suggestion" judged the face as expressing the suggested emotion well or fairly well.

The suggestion worked except when conflicting strongly with the intended expression. Probably suggestion affects our ordinary reading of a person's emotion from his face, only that the suggestion is conveyed by the situation in which the person is placed and by his total response. "Reading the emotion from the face" amounts in large part to reading the emotion into the face. As Fernberger puts it, the results "indicate that little can be determined of an emotional state in another individual from the perception of an abstracted facial expression completely divorced from a general, total stimulus-situation. If a stimulus-situation is indicated, the emotional state is judged in accordance with that situation rather than in accordance with the facial expression."

Judgments of posed facial expression. The Piderit profiles are not merely "divorced from the total situation"; they are outline drawings, and photographs of actual faces might be more accurately judged. Photographs would escape from the criticism of Arnheim (1928) who prepared silhouettes with some parts identical and found that the part was changed in its appearance by being brought into different combinations. He inferred, going to be sure beyond his evidence, that Piderit's analytical way of studying facial expression was entirely beside the mark.

As a service to artists, Rudolph (1903), a painter with some anatomical knowledge, made a study of facial expression, and published some hundreds of photographs of a male actor in various poses, the photographs being retouched and somewhat idealized by the author. Rudolph's own theory was that all facial expressions were based on a few primitive types, which fundamentally were movements of approach and withdrawal. His actor subject possessed a very mobile and expressive face and the collection of photographs is a storehouse from which psychologists have drawn. Collections of female poses have been provided by Feleky (1914, 1924) and by Ruckmick (1921, 1928).

The experimental procedure is to take facial poses intended by the actor to express certain emotions and to try them out on unprejudiced observers. Sometimes O is provided with a list of emotion words, sometimes he is free to use his own words.

Langfeld (1918) used 105 of the Rudolph poses, and instructed his 11 Os to give a name descriptive of each pose. His most successful O gave 58 percent of "correct" names (agreeing closely with the actor's intention), and the least successful 17 percent. These low percents have led subsequent writers to say that facial expression is not read with much success; but the mere percent correct is a very inadequate measure, as we shall see.

Langfeld also tried suggestion, by presenting each picture a second time with a name purporting to be correct (but actually incorrect in half the cases), and asking whether this name was acceptable. Incorrect names were often accepted even though O had previously given a correct interpretation of the same poses. One O accepted as many as 47 percent of these false suggestions, another as few as 16 percent. On the whole suggestion had considerable effect—a result quite in line with that obtained with the Piderit faces.

Another important result is improvement through instruction and training (F. H. Allport, 1924). A class of 12 college women were shown by lantern 14 of the best Rudolph poses, and made an average score of 49 percent correct. E then gave a brief but comprehensive lecture on facial expression, covering the anatomy of the facial muscles and the contribution of each part of the face to each major type of emotion: Pain-Grief, Amazement-Fear, Anger, Disgust, Pleasure, Attitudinal, (including doubt, determination, etc.). After this instruction the same pictures were presented again, and the average score rose to 55 percent.

Repeating this experiment, Guilford (1929) used 96 Rudolph poses, divided into four approximately equivalent sets. The average scores made by the 15 Os were:

Set 1, before instruction 27%
Set 2, after study of the facial muscles 27%
Set 3, after re-showing of Set 2 with correct names given, and after study
     of Allport's six groups and his analysis of expression 32%
Set 4, with special directions to analyze 39%
Set 1, repeated at end 41%

The implications of this improvement through training in the judgment of facial expression are rather uncertain. Allport infers that the ability to interpret facial expression is acquired by learning, not inborn, and that the differing ability of different individuals results from their differing attention to this matter. The fact that the individuals who score high in the initial test improve little, in comparison with those whose initial score is low, may be explained, Guilford suggests, by supposing that training in analysis does not help those who take the face as a whole in reading its expression, which very likely is the best way to read faces.

As to the method by which one attempts to diagnose the emotion expressed in the face, introspections were obtained by Langfeld and other experimenters. So far as the observer can tell, there are two main methods: imitate the pose and notice "how it feels"—the method of empathy; or, imagine a situation in which the pose would be appropriate. Neither is a sure method.

How accurately can facial poses be interpreted? The low percents of "correct" judgments obtained in several experiments have seemed to justify the conclusion that reading facial expression is mostly a myth, and that we depend in real life on the situation in which a person is placed and on what he says and does, rather than on his face, to reveal his emotion. The results do *not* justify such a conclusion, because there has been no *measure* of the degree of error. The judgments have simply been classified, with more or less leniency, as right or wrong. We need to scrutinize the judgments, asking *how far wrong* they are. We need a scale, rough though it may be, for measuring the error.

A B

Fig. 67. (Feleky, 1924.) Two poses, A intended for surprise and B for hate, on which the judgments of 100 observers came out as shown below:

A		B		B—Continued	
surprise	52	ugliness	13	sneering and contempt	1
wonder	12	disgust	11	bore	1
astonishment	10	hate	8	dread-anger-defiance	1
amazement	9	disdain	8	bitterness and hardness	1
admiration	3	scorn	7	fury	1
awe	2	aversion	5	sullen anger	1
dismay	2	repugnance	5	sulkiness	1
pretended astonishment	1	defiance	5	pouting	1
playful interest	1	irritation	2	childlike pettishness	1
earnestness	1	bitterness	2	disagreeable	1
enthusiasm	1	hardness	2	suspicion	1
rapture	1	contempt	2	self-assertion	1
hope	1	sneering	2	self-sufficiency	1
romantic love	1	loathing and dislike	2	displeasure	1
friendliness	1	dislike	2	perturbance	1
altruistic pride	1	loathing	1	weeping	1
repugnance	1	antipathy	1	mental pain	1
		disgusted dread	1	pain	1
		disregard	1	timidity	1
				sorrowful pity	1

Fortunately for our purpose, Feleky (1924) reports in full the judgments of 100 observers on 86 poses, photographs of an actress posing for various emotions. O was furnished a list of emotion names but was free to use any word or words that seemed most appropriate. The responses to two poses are appended to Fig. 67 and certainly give a first impression of wide scatter and much disagreement. Of all the poses, that for surprise gave the greatest concentration of responses and yet only 52 percent used the word "surprise." Examining the list more closely we find much use of approximate synonyms. Adding the votes for "wonder," "astonishment" and "amazement" to those for "surprise," we have 83 percent of the Os in approximate agreement on this pose. Similarly, most of the responses to the other pose in Fig. 67 refer to emotions that are not far apart. The first impression of wide scatter gives way to an impression of concentration within a small part of the whole range of emotions.

We should notice what names are *not* used to characterize a given pose. Few would regard pose B in Fig. 67 as expressive of love, happiness or mirth, and in fact none of Feleky's Os did so; nor did any of them take pose A to express contempt. The complete absence of overlap between the two lists of responses shows that we have two "populations," statistically, and not two samples of random guessing.

It is a likely hypothesis, therefore, that good correlation exists between the poser's intention and the observer's judgment. This hypothesis will be confirmed if we can find an order of the emotions such as to show a good correspondence between pose and judgment—provided also the order is reasonable on other grounds. If we can arrange the emotions in a single series, with similar emotions adjoining, we can obtain a rough measure of the error of each judgment. Probably the whole variety of emotions cannot be arranged in a linear series, but 10 important ones are so arranged in the following table. The order is adjusted to the votes of Feleky's 100 Os, so as to make the frequencies run a

DISTRIBUTION OF JUDGMENTS FOR A ROUGH SCALE OF POSES

(Data from Feleky, 1924)

19 poses, two for each of the named emotions except Determination, with judgment of each pose by 100 observers. The entries give frequencies in percent; the "scattering" judgments could not be located on the scale.

| | Poses | | | | | | | | | |
Judgments	Love	Happiness	Mirth	Surprise	Fear	Anger	Suffering	Determination	Disgust	Contempt
Love	10	2		1			1			
Happiness	68	63	51	4		1	1			
Mirth	9	27	49					3		
Surprise	1	1		77	5	7	1			
Fear				6	66	28	17	4	1	
Anger				1	19	31	1	30	22	2
Suffering				1	6	14	70	3	2	1
Determination		1			1	7		52		2
Disgust				1	1	2	1	63	7
Contempt					2			3	12	86
Scattering	12	6	0	10	2	9	7	4	0	2
	100	100	100	100	100	100	100	100	100	100

regular course in both vertical and horizontal lines, with more overlap between adjacent than non-adjacent columns and rows. In other words the order is adjusted to give the maximum correlation between pose and judgment, and so to test the hypothesis that a good correlation exists.

The table undoubtedly shows agreement between the judges rather than unlimited scatter. It shows a positive correlation between pose and judgment. However, the attempt to obtain a linear scale has not been wholly successful. "Suffering" and "determination" cannot be perfectly fitted into the series. According to the frequencies, suffering belongs next to fear, and determination next to anger; but fear and anger, still according to the frequencies, must not be separated. If suffering were located on a branch line from fear, and determination on a branch line from anger, the main line would be quite regular.

The first three emotions in the series, love, happiness and mirth, overlap greatly with each other but scarcely at all with any of the others. If these three are combined, and if suffering is combined with fear, and determination with anger, we have a scale of 6 steps which is very satisfactory as far as the frequencies go. The judgment is seldom displaced more than one step in this coarse scale, and if the steps are assumed to be equal, the correlation of pose and judgment is +.92. Other data, from Ruckmick (1921) and from Gates (1923), obtained with other sets of poses, fit neatly into the same scale.

CONDENSED SCALE OF FACIAL EXPRESSION
(Data from Feleky, 1924)

	Poses					
Judgments	Love Happiness Mirth	Surprise	Fear Suffering	Anger Determination	Disgust	Contempt
Love Happiness Mirth	93	5	1	2		
Surprise	1	77	3	4		
Fear Suffering		7	79	24	3	1
Anger Determination		1	10	60	22	4
Disgust			2	1	63	7
Contempt				3	12	86
Scattering	6	10	5	6	0	2
	100	100	100	100	100	100

Other evidence that a posed emotion can be fairly well recognized from a still photograph of the actor's face is given by Kanner (1931). Some of the Feleky poses were shown to groups of students, totaling 409 individuals. They were not furnished any list of emotion names but were instructed (1) to give the "best term" for each pose, (2) to state the situation to which the actor was probably reacting, and (3) to guess what the actor would say along with his facial expression. With all these responses taken into account, each O was rated on a 10-point scale, and a score of 7 points or more was counted as a success. Nearly all the Os did much better than chance, and nearly every pose gave better than a chance percent of successful responses. The poses were quite unequal in this respect, Surprise being recognized by 77 percent of the Os, Fear by 70 percent, Horror by 62 percent, Shame by 53 percent, Rage by 50 percent, Suspicion by 27 percent, Pity by 19 percent.

Children's judgments of posed facial expressions. Six pictures from Ruckmick's collection were tried on children of 3–14 years by Gates (1923). There was a gradual increase with age in the percent of approximately correct judgments. With a liberal allowance for childish vocabularies, the pose for laughter gave 70 percent correct judgments even at ages 3–4, and an increase to 100 percent at age 10. Surprise and contempt, on the contrary, got practically zero scores at ages 3–5. The level of 50 percent correct was attained at different ages for the different facial expressions:

> Pose for laughter . . . . below 3 years
>   "   "   pain . . . . at 5–6 years
>   "   "   anger . . . . at 7 years
>   "   "   fear-horror . . . . at 9–10 years
>   "   "   surprise . . . . at 11 years
>   "   "   contempt . . . . above 14 years

Children and adults differ in the relative difficulty of the several expressions. Contempt, the hardest for the children, is among the easiest for adults, and there are other discrepancies. Laughter is however about the easiest for both children and adults. Anger usually gives low scores and wide scatter of the judgments. Surprise is easily understood in the Feleky and Ruckmick poses, but not in the Rudolph poses. There are probably cultural differences in the conventional expression of anger; and individual actors have their specialties, some registering one emotion more successfully and some another.

Spontaneous facial expression. Granted that actors express in their faces a variety of emotions to a recognizable degree, it does not follow that the faces of everyday folk are spontaneously expressive. There is probably a strong element of convention in stage expressions, as there is a strong element of control and suppression in the facial behavior of the ordinary adult. It would be worth while to photograph the spontaneous expressions of children and adults, while undergoing emotion, and to check such photographs as the poses have been checked, by submitting them to the judgment of unprejudiced observers. The difficulty is to secure the photographs under known conditions of emotion.

Sherman (1927) took motion pictures of infants a few days old, in situations presumed to produce different emotions:

> Rage   (restraint of the infant's head)
> Fear   (sudden loss of support)
> Pain   (needle prick)
> Hunger   (feeding overdue)

Students and other observers attempting to judge these pictures were unable to distinguish the several conditions, even though they had a picture of the whole baby and a motion picture at that. Apparently, at this tender age, there is practically only one expression for all these unpleasant situations.

Schultze (1906, 1909) had better luck with older children. He placed before them pictures intended to arouse different emotions, photographed the children while they were examining the pictures, and presented the photographs to judges who endeavored to identify the picture at which the children must have been looking. The judges had some success, and the reproduced photographs certainly show characteristic differences of facial expression.

Dunlap (1927) obtained unposed facial expressions by applying to adults in the laboratory stimuli calculated to arouse laughter, startle, pain, disgust, strain, relaxation. His special interest was in the relative expressiveness of the eyes and the mouth. He took two photographs of the same person, expressing very different emotions, cut the photographs in half horizontally, and combined the upper half of one with the lower half of the other. The result was, in general, that the synthetic expression was dominated by the mouth. A face with sober eyes and laughing mouth appeared unquestionably to be laughing. The laughing mouth dominated the face, and the same was true to a considerable degree of the disgusted, startled, pained or strained mouth. Dunlap's photographs certainly indicate that unposed facial expressions differ with the subject's emotional state.

Objective analysis of spontaneous facial expressions. An especially thoroughgoing attempt to bring genuine emotions into the laboratory was made by Landis (1924). In a three-hour session he introduced 16 situations intended to produce varied emotions and to build up finally a strongly excited and irritated state. He obtained the irritation but did not secure any specially agreeable states. His Os took the whole affair rather seriously and were probably set for endurance rather than enjoyment. They were for the most part psychologists going through unpleasant experiences in the presence of another psychologist and for his benefit. For that reason, perhaps, the facial expression did not differ markedly from one situation to another. Considerable muscular tension showed in the lines of the face and increased with the progress of the trying experience. The eyes were partly closed much of the time, and the upper lip was raised or drawn to the side. A smile was present even in situations which must have been disagreeable.

Landis made an analytical, objective study of the photographs taken during the several situations, so as to determine which muscles were active in each expression. He looked for patterns of muscular action characterizing particular emotions. The ideal positive result would be to find a certain pattern present in all the faces photographed in one situation and never present in any radically different situation. The ideal negative result would be to find all the situations, all the reported emotions, alike in their pattern of muscular contraction. The actual result lay between these ideal extremes and, in Landis's judgment, much more to the negative side. He reached the conclusion, "So far as this experiment goes, I have found no expression other than a smile, which was present in enough photographs to be considered as typical of any situation." There were expressions, or facial postures, characteristic of individuals, but not characteristic of emotions. It must be admitted, however, that the range of emotions actually aroused was rather narrow, that the Os were probably not expressing their emotions freely, and that the analytical data are difficult to handle by any recognized statistical procedure. A poker-faced individual can undergo a variety of experiences without revealing his emotions, and still the naive face may be very expressive.

Vocal expression of emotion. Almost certainly the voice does express emotion, though that statement is based more on common experience than on experimental evidence. When Sherman (1927, 1928) finds an observer unable to tell from the sound of the voice alone whether a baby is crying from hunger, from colic, or from restraint, the differences in question are slighter than those between the sound of a baby's crying and the sound of his cooing or laughing. Certainly we can tell by the sound whether a person is laughing or not, and there are various other tones and intonations which we believe we can recognize—until some experimenter proves the contrary—the determined tone, the sarcastic tone, the coaxing tone, and others.

The sound of the voice may differ in loudness, in pitch, in timbre, and in inflection, the last amounting to a slide in pitch. It is safe to say that "raising the voice"—which means raising its pitch or increasing its loudness, or both—occurs naturally in excited states. Apparently the baby doesn't have to learn to cry more loudly as he becomes more "worked up."

That change in the timbre of the voice may go with changing emotional state is suggested by the "sweet voice" and the "harsh voice" which we believe we can distinguish and interpret. But there is a minimum of scientific evidence on this point.

Inflection was studied by Merry (1922) from transcribed phonograph records. He used records of actors and orators delivering impassioned speeches, and found an extraordinary mobility of the pitch of the voice. Far from using a monotone, these artists in vocal expression move rapidly up and down a large share of their whole voice range. E. H. Sothern, in Shylock's speech, showed a total range of over two octaves, while single inflections or glides of his voice extended a full octave and more. How much of this modulation of the voice is the spontaneous expression of emotion, and how much is histrionic convention, we do not know.

The voice is commonly said to "tremble" with excitement. A trembling would have to be either a rapid waxing and waning of loudness, or a rapid rising and falling of pitch. Both of these kinds of trembling occur not only in emotion but at all times. The pitch always wavers slightly. Even the best singers seldom maintain a constant pitch for more than half a second (Schoen, 1922).

As singing, like other forms of musical performance, attempts to give expression to emotion, the singing voice has been examined to see how the emotion is actually expressed. Quite a series of studies on the singing voice came from Seashore's laboratory at the State University of Iowa. Attention was directed especially to that peculiar ringing heard in the voices of professional singers and known as the *vibrato*. It is a sort of tremulo effect, though it should not be called tremulo, because the tremulo is regarded as objectionable, whereas the vibrato is used by the best singers. The difference between the two is only a difference in degree, a vibrato being smoother and better controlled.

The vibrato consists in a periodic rise and fall in the pitch of the sung tone, or in a periodic waxing and waning in its loudness, or in both. An artificial vibrato can be produced by machinery which does either of these things to an otherwise uniform tone. Such "synthetic" vibratos were studied by Tiffin (1931), who produced the tone by a rapid series of flashes of light falling upon a photoelectric cell which operated a loud speaker by aid of an amplifier. He obtained a pitch vibrato by periodically hastening and slowing the series of flashes, and a loudness vibrato by periodically varying the amount of light in the flashes. Thus he produced 5-8 pulsations per second in the tone, and this pulsating tone was heard as a vibrato. It apparently made no difference whether it was the vibration rate or the intensity of the tone that was made to vary; an observer could not readily distinguish these two kinds of pulsations. The tone did not seem to oscillate in pitch even when such was the objective fact; it seemed to maintain a steady pitch but to pulsate in some undefined way. A periodic variation even as small as 1-2 cycles per second, in a tone of 420 cycles, could be heard as a pulsation by the average person.

The pitch variations produced by singers are much larger than this. According to measurements by Metfessel (1928) of phonograph records of eleven great singers, the rate of the pulsations averages 7 per second. The accomplished singer, while ostensibly sustaining a tone of constant pitch, actually lets his voice range above and below that pitch, about a quarter of a tone in each direction, covering a width of half a tone in all, and does this so rapidly and evenly that the effect on the hearer is of a pulsating or ringing tone.

Both the rate and the width of the vibrato vary from singer to singer and from moment to moment. The rate varies from 5 to 10 pulsations per second in superior singers, but does not often pass the limits of 6 and 8 per second. The width varies from 0.1 to 1.35 full tones, but does not often pass the limits of .25 and .85 full tones.

According to Kwalwasser (1926), the vibrato appears in the singing of many children, but seldom in adults, without voice training. Singers with some training tend to have a vibrato with a width of a quarter of a tone, half as great as that of the stars. Untrained voices do not maintain their pitch any more closely than trained, but waver irregularly and so do not give the vibrating effect. Trained singers were unable to sing without vibrato; they did not succeed even in decreasing it to any considerable degree. When asked to exaggerate it, however, they about doubled their usual vibrato width.

The process of learning to execute the vibrato was revealed by the experiments of Wagner (1930). He found that some young boys could acquire it after preliminary training in voice production and singing. They started with rhythmical panting, and, under the guidance of a skilled vocal teacher, after a few lessons produced a pulsating tone. Adults whose vibrato, after some training, was slow, could be taught to increase its rate by keeping time with a metronome, three or four pulsations to the beat.

With all these facts before us regarding the vibrato, shall we regard it as expressive of emotion, or not? Schoen's original interest in 1922 was based upon the supposed relation between this "trembling of the voice" and the muscular trembling which is often observed in strong excitement. But it appears that the vibrato is very much a matter of technique, and that it is used practically all the time by professional singers, without much regard to the particular emotion appropriate to a given song. Probably the emotion actually felt by the singer along with his vibrato is one of mastery rather than one of being "shaken."

CHAPTER XII

BODILY CHANGES IN EMOTION

THE OLD commonly accepted "seat of the emotions" was somewhere inside the trunk rather than in the head or limbs. The heaving chest and throbbing heart of the angry man, and the digestive upset that sometimes ensues, are certainly evidence that something out of the ordinary is occurring in the interior of the body. The normal routine of organic processes is disturbed because of something abnormal in the individual's relations with the environment. Evidently the nerves and nerve centers are concerned, and the modern physiologist would locate the "seat" of the emotional disturbance somewhere in the brain rather than in the visceral organs that show the disturbance. Rather than attempt to summarize the important discoveries of physiology regarding the role of different parts of the brain, of the glands and other internal organs, in emotional behavior, we may better refer to the physiologists themselves (Cannon, 1929; Bard, 1934; Dunbar, 1935), and limit our account to the lines of experiment in which psychologists have been active. That means that we shall consider respiratory and circulatory changes which can be observed in the normal human subject, and also certain important electrical phenomena which will be treated in the following chapter.

RESPIRATION IN EMOTION

Besides the movements of breathing, with which we shall concern ourselves in the following pages, the general function of respiration includes the gaseous exchange between the air and the blood in the lungs, and between the blood and the tissues. This chemical side of respiration is beginning to attract the attention of psychologists, as in studies of the metabolic rate during mental work (Harmon, 1933) and in studies of psychological processes, including emotion, at high altitudes (McFarland, 1932, 1937). Emotional excitement involves muscular activity and so increases the consumption of oxygen. Low oxygen tension in the air sometimes induces euphoria and sometimes irritability. Experimental study of emotion in relation to chemical respiration is rather lacking as yet, but there have been a number of experiments on breathing movements during emotional states.

The respiratory movements serve two primary functions. One, obviously the more important, is the ventilation of the lungs, making possible the gaseous exchange between the air and the blood. The other is that of a bellows supplying the air to operate the vocal cords. Emotion may disturb either of these primary functions. There may be an involuntary raising of the voice, or a catch in the voice; and there may be an alteration of the regular breathing movements.

Neuromuscular mechanism of respiration. The regular operation of the respiratory mechanism affords a necessary base line from which to measure the disturbances in emotion. Anyone desirous of making a thorough study of these disturbances must of course acquaint himself with the physiology of the breathing movements. Only a sketchy outline will be attempted here.

The muscles which enlarge the cavity of the chest in inspiration are principally the diaphragm and the intercostals. In quiet expiration little muscular contraction occurs, since the elasticity of the lungs and the return of the chest by gravity to its resting position suffice to expel a quantity of air. In more active expiration the muscles of the abdominal wall play the principal part, and in rapid, forcible breathing many muscles contribute either to inspiration or to expiration.

The smooth muscles surrounding the bronchial tubes control the bore of the tubes and so the resistance offered to the passage of the air. They receive bronchoconstrictor fibers from the cranial autonomic and bronchodilator fibers from the sympathetic, so that the tubes are wide open in the "emergency reaction" of the body. Probably this part of the autonomic system like other parts to be mentioned later plays a role in emotional conditions.

The main respiratory apparatus belongs to the skeletal system and not to the autonomic. The diaphragm, intercostal and abdominal muscles are striped muscles, controlled directly by the central nervous system. The phrenic nerve issuing from the cervical cord supplies the diaphragm and is the principal motor nerve of breathing. The chief sensory nerve is the vagus which supplies the lungs with sensory fibers. These are stimulated by the stretching of the lung tissue in inspiration and, acting on the respiratory center in the medulla or bulb, inhibit that center and check inspiration. The stimulus to inspiration seems to arise within the center by the local effect of venous blood. Excess of carbon dioxide in the blood stimulates the center to strong activity; a few deep, rapid, voluntary inspirations reduce the carbon dioxide content of the blood, lower the activity of the respiratory center and cause a temporary cessation of breathing.

This mechanism though relatively self-contained is responsive to stimulation of almost any sensory nerve. Cold suddenly applied to the skin will cause a reflex catch of the breath, as will also the unexpected inhalation of a sharp vapor such as ammonia or chlorine. Irritation of the nose or throat interrupts the regular breathing rhythm and gives a sneeze or cough. In swallowing the respiratory movements are inhibited. The influence of the cortex upon the bulbar center is seen in voluntary control of breathing, in the peculiar breathing of speech or singing, and in the momentary arrest of breathing which is apt to occur in attending to a faint sound or to a sudden interesting thought. In short we have here a reflex-automatic mechanism serving a metabolic function but very responsive to all that is going on in the behavior of the organism. Our problem is to examine the responses of this mechanism in emotion. Any effect will probably show a recovery phase. Since the metabolic needs continue, any momentary disturbance will have a compensatory after-effect. Any stimulus which causes a momentary arrest of breathing will probably be followed by a compensatory increase of breathing, and any stimulus which causes rapid breathing in excess of the metabolic needs will probably be followed by a compensatory reduction of breathing.

Pneumographs. From a movement with so much muscular power behind it a graphic record is easily obtained. The mere rate of breathing is easily recorded. If one wishes to analyze the breathing movement so as to discover for example whether the expiration is the usual quiet passive affair or an active muscular contraction, more elaborate recording instruments are necessary. The total respiratory activity could best be attacked by some record of the amount of inspired and expired air. A few typical pneumographic devices will be mentioned.

1. *Chest girth recorder*. An elastic belt strapped around the chest changes in length with the respiratory movements. The belt consists of a rubber tube distended by a weak spiral spring inside; the tube is closed at both ends and connects by an air-tight joint with a smaller rubber tube which leads to a recording tambour. We have here a closed body of air the volume of which is increased during inspiration and decreased during expiration. With these changes in volume go reverse changes in the internal pressure of the body of air, which are recorded by the tambour lever. In the usual upright position of the tambour, inspiration draws the lever down, expiration forces it up, but the tambour can be inverted so as to give a rise for inspiration and a fall for expiration —a picture that is more readily understood.

2. *Breath current recorder*. O wearing a gas mask inhales fresh air through one tube and exhales through another tube into a gas bag. Each tube has a one-way valve. On the out-going tube between the mouth and the valve a side tube is inserted leading to a recording tambour. The pressure inside the tambour will be positive during expiration and negative during inspiration. The device can be made sensitive enough to record the slight pressure thrusts that occur in speech and even in silent speech (Rounds & Poffenberger, 1931).

3. *The body plethysmograph* (Golla & Antonovitch, 1929). O is seated inside a box; the double lid folds down over his shoulders, leaving his head protruding through a neck hole. The joints of the box are air tight and the neck is sealed by an inflated rubber collar. With careful adjustment the subject can be made comfortable. The air inside the box connects by tubing with a tambour or gas tank recorder. The advantages claimed for this type of pneumograph are that the subject

can be kept unaware of the record being made of his breathing, and that the recorded changes in body volume give a fairly accurate measure of the amount of inhaled and exhaled air.

Measurements of the breathing records. Horizontal distances in the record denote time; vertical distances indicate, directly, pressure changes within the recording tambour. More or less indirectly they indicate changes in amplitude of breathing, i.e., in the volume of inspired and expired air, and changes in the position of the chest or abdomen produced by the activity of the respiratory muscles. Very careful calibration would be required before the breathing record could be made to yield any absolute measures of muscular contraction or air volume; but *changes* in amplitude can be read from the curve within the compass of a single continuous record. For example, a series of shallow breaths followed by a deep breath can be detected with certainty.

The time characteristics of the breathing curve are read off and measured with relatively high accuracy. The points at which inspiration and expiration start can usually be located, and from them we determine the duration of the respiratory cycle and of its two phases, inspiration and expiration. A pause at the end of inspiration or expiration cannot be sharply delimited and is best counted as part of the preceding phase.

Changes in rate and amplitude of breathing. Muscular exercise, as everyone knows, hastens and deepens the breathing. It is interesting to note (Cannon, 1932) that respiration and circulation increase with the beginning of the muscular activity and do not delay till oxygen dearth and excess of carbon dioxide have actually developed. There is a physiological anticipation of the needs of the muscles. Might not imagined or suggested muscular activity have the same effect and give increased respiration? The author once observed an individual who could speed up his pulse by simply imagining himself to be running a race. Respiratory movements can be speeded up voluntarily, but the question is whether they increase involuntarily in excited "states of mind." Rehwoldt (1911) had his Os engender an emotion by recalling or imagining some emotional experience, such as a scene from a drama, and he found that respiration was increased when O reported excitement. There is agreement among experimenters that the breathing tends in excitement to be both fast and deep. This is the clearest known correlation between respiration and emotion. Pleasantness and unpleasantness show either increased or decreased breathing, usually increased, apparently because both pleasant and unpleasant stimuli are apt to be stimulating.

Another clear correlation is that between momentary attention and partial or complete inhibition of breathing. Sudden stimuli will make the subject "catch his breath." If he is listening to a faint sound, arrested breathing eliminates disturbing respiratory sounds; if he is trying to read letters at a great distance, his fixation is steadier if the breathing movement is suspended (probably a marksman holds his breath while pulling the trigger); and the kinesthetic sensations from the chest may be a distraction which one avoids at a moment of intense mental application (Suter, 1912). In continued mental work, no matter how attentive, this inhibition of breathing naturally does not continue, but the breathing tends to be shallow and quickened. Skaggs (1930) compared the breathing in quiet relaxation and in several kinds of activity, and noted the following effects, along with much variation:

1. In mental multiplication, compared with the resting condition, breathing was usually quick and shallow.

2. In anxious expectancy, the rate tended to increase and the depth to remain normal.

3. After a shock or surprise, too, the rate was high and the depth about normal, and the breathing was irregular.

The results are explicable by supposing that: (1) in mental work, unaccompanied by increased muscular activity, maximum efficiency is sought by keeping the breathing as quiet as possible while maintaining the normal supply of oxygen; (2) in excitement there is an actual increase in muscular activity calling for increased respiration, or at least a physiological readiness for muscular activity.

As to irregular breathing, varying in depth or rate or both, we know one definite cause for it, namely the use of the breath for speech. Fossler (1930) finds the rate much more irregular in speech than in the resting condition. Expiration is much prolonged and varies greatly in duration from one cycle to another; inspiration is shortened and varies considerably. The reason is obvious—one wishes to talk continuously but one must stop to take breath. The vocal cords are operated by the expired air which is paid out economically and replenished by rapid inspirations whenever time can be spared from the talking.

An interesting experiment was that of Blatz (1925) who smuggled a genuine fear into the laboratory. A trick chair tilted the unsuspecting, blindfolded subject suddenly backward into a nearly horizontal position, while a pneumograph registered his breathing and an electrocardiograph the rate and force of his heart beat. There were 21 Os. The heart showed definite symptoms. The pulse shot up from 84 to 104 beats, on the average, receded promptly to 87 only to rise again to 97 after which it gradually slowed down but remained irregular. The force of the heart beat was increased and remained high during the after-period of six minutes while O rested in a reclining position.

O returned on another day for a repetition of the experiment. Expecting the chair to fall he showed in advance a strong rapid pulse. When the fall actually came, the cardiac changes were the same as on the first occasion—the same in kind though less in degree. The subjects did not make overt movements of saving themselves as they had on the first occasion, and they reported no fear the second time. The author draws the conclusion that a genuine emotion of fear requires the overt escape reaction as well as the internal organic changes.

As to the respiratory effects, the rate went down from 14 cycles a minute before the original fall to 11 cycles immediately after; it returned toward normal at first quickly and then gradually. It did not, as usual, run parallel to the rate of the heart beat. The first effect of falling was to *lengthen the inspiration.* If the fall of the chair occurred during an inspiration, that inspiration was prolonged, and when it occurred during expiration the expiratory movement stopped abruptly and gave way to inspiration. This "catch in the breath" seems like an exaggerated form of the familiar arrest of breathing which occurs at any sudden shift of attention.

Relative duration of inspiration and expiration. This last effect and the previously mentioned long expiration during speech both suggest that some scientific use might be made of the time ratio of inspiration and expiration. This suggestion was first made by Störring (1906) and has proved to be quite fruitful. Störring introduced the *Inspiration-Expiration Ratio,* I/E, in which I = the duration of inspiration, and E = that of expiration. Some authors have omitted the pauses from the measure of I or E, others (as recommended above) have included them, counting I as extending to the beginning of the expiratory movement, and E as extending thence to the beginning of the next inspiration. It makes quite a difference which measure is used.

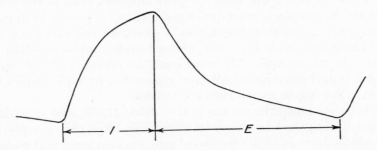

Fig. 68. Diagram of a single cycle in the breathing curve. I = inspiration, E = expiration.

Statistically, the I/E ratio is not a very good measure. It is all right for single cases but not good for averaging, when the single ratios differ considerably; though the geometrical mean, or more simply the median, can be used without distortion of the results. A simpler and more intelligible measure is the I-fraction, here recommended. *The I-fraction is obtained by dividing the duration of inspiration by the duration of the whole cycle.* It shows what proportion of the time is occupied by inspiration. Since all the air used is drawn in during inspiration, and since inspiration is ordinarily the active muscular phase of the cycle, the I-fraction shows how much of the time is consumed in the necessary labor of supplying air. The use of the air for metabolic purposes is of course continuous; the use for voice production is usually confined to expiration. The I-fraction during speech shows how much of the time is consumed in the necessary task of taking in the air for voice production. According to the records of 13 Os, obtained by Fossler (1930), the I-fraction in speech averages .163, individual averages ranging from .090 to .258. That is, we have to sacrifice on the average about ⅙ of our speaking time for supplying the necessary air. In ordinary quiet breathing the I-fraction averages about .40–.45, somewhat less than half.

Provided I and E are so measured as to comprise the whole cycle, there is a simple arithmetical relation between the I-fraction and the I/E ratio. Either of these measures being given the other can be computed. If

$$f = \text{the I-fraction; and}$$
$$r = \text{the I/E ratio; then}$$

$$r = \frac{f}{1-f} \text{ and } f = \frac{r}{1+r}$$

For example, I takes 1 second and the whole cycle 3 seconds; the I-fraction = ⅓ = .33, and the I/E ratio = ½ = .50.

Some corresponding values of the two measures can be found in the following reduction table.

I/E ratio	I-fraction	I/E ratio	I-fraction
.10	.09	1.10	.52
.20	.17	1.20	.55
.30	.23	1.30	.57
.40	.29	1.40	.58
.50	.33	1.50	.60
.60	.37	1.60	.62
.70	.41	1.70	.63
.80	.44	1.80	.64
.90	.47	1.90	.66
1.00	.50	2.00	.67

When one of these measures increases, so does the other, but the changes in I/E are larger—exaggerated, we might say. The absolute limits of the I-fraction are 0 and 1.00, while I/E has no upper limit. There is of course an E-fraction = 1.00 − the I-fraction.

Some early results with the I/E ratio were:

1. It is low in attentive mental work, such as mental multiplication, and the greater the reported feeling of tense attention the lower the ratio (Suter, 1912). The I-fraction averaged .30 for brief periods of attentive mental work.

2. It tends to be low when O reports a feeling of tension (Drożyński, 1911).

3. It is high in excitement, the I-fraction being then over .60 (Rehwoldt, 1911).

4. It is very high in posed wonder, i.e., when O imagines a wonderful

or surprising situation and expresses his feeling by face and gesture (Feleky, 1916); the I-fraction averaged .71 for six Os, ranging from .62 to .78. O tends to hold his breath in inspiration. This is the same result as obtained by Blatz (1925) after the backward drop of the chair; the I-fraction in his Os ranged from .50 to .80 just after the fall.

5. It is very low during laughter (Feleky, 1916), the I-fraction ranging from .18 to .28 with a general average of .23. This figure is near that quoted above for speech, and the cause of the small I-fraction is the same: the breath is drawn in rapidly in both laughter and speech and paid out bit by bit in the vocal function.

To recapitulate in tabular form, the I-fraction averages:

in speech	.16
in laughter	.23
in attentive mental work	.30
in the resting condition	.43
in excitement	.60+
in posed wonder	.71
in sudden fright	.75

In singing, which requires more "wind" than speech does and allows only scraps of time for replenishing the bellows, the I-fraction goes down to very small values.

The most dramatic experiment in which the I/E ratio has played a part is that of Benussi (1914 a). How the author hit upon this idea he does not explain, but he conceived that the I/E ratio would furnish an objective index of *lying*. He arranged an experiment as follows. The subject is placed in the situation of a witness in court. He is handed a card containing letters, numbers or both, arranged in a regular way, and he is to give either true or false testimony regarding the contents of that card, according to a secret sign placed upon it. Oral questions are put to him by the examining "lawyer" as to whether the card contains letters or numbers, how many, in what arrangement; and finally he must read the letters in order; but if his task is to lie he must answer every question falsely, trying however to appear truthful to a "jury" sitting there before him. The jury tries to judge from the witness's general behavior whether he is lying or telling the truth, while the experimenter judges entirely by the pneumograph record.

The jurymen in Benussi's experiment did no better than chance, but Benussi from the breathing records made nearly 100 percent of correct judgments in over a hundred trials. He used entirely the I/E ratio (the I-fraction would of course have served him just as well). He compared the ratio before and after each answer, measuring 3–5 cycles immediately before O's response and 3–5 cycles immediately after it. In a sample of 10 double experiments, half with lying and half with truth-telling, the median I-fraction is as follows:

	Before O's answer	*After O's answer*
Truth told	.39	.32
Lies told	.40	.50

The difference between the breathing of the truthful and lying witness might be attributed to the harder intellectual task of the liar who must make his false statements con-

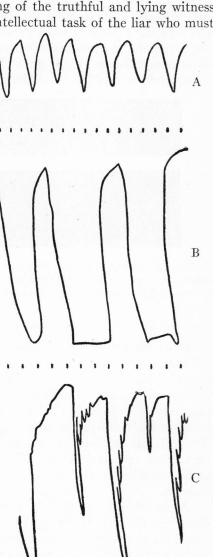

sistent to escape detection by the jury. To check on this possibility, Benussi tried a modified experiment in which it was understood in advance between the witness and the jury whether the report on a given card was to be true or false. The intellectual task remained as before but the emotional situation was flattened out. The result was that the I/E ratio behaved the same in this pretended lying as in truth-telling. Benussi concluded that the breathing in genuine lying was dominated by the emotional situation. Since the I-fraction is essentially the same before either true or false statements, what we have to explain is the difference *after* the testimony. The increased I-fraction after lying can be explained as the result of (suppressed) excitement. The decreased I-fraction after a true statement might mean that O immediately became attentively expectant of the next question.

Benussi found that voluntary control of breathing did not eliminate the index of lying, and he hoped the test would prove practical. Those who have repeated the experiment (Burtt, 1921; Landis & Gullette, 1925) have not obtained very satisfactory results; the blood pressure test for lying is perhaps better (p. 273). It is possible that the exact conditions of Benussi's experiment have not been dupli-

FIG. 69. (Feleky, 1916.) Breathing curves during posed emotions. A, normal; B, pose for "wonder"; C, laughter. The curves read from left to right. Inspiration carries the curve down, expiration up. Time in seconds.

cated. It would make a difference how rapidly the questions were fired at O and how promptly he was forced to reply.

Somewhat akin to this experiment is one on distraction (p. 706). The I-fraction decreases under distraction for a very simple reason: O uses speech in overcoming the distraction and consequently prolongs the expiratory phase. Even in whispering, though no blast of expired air is required to produce vibration of the vocal cords, the I-fraction diminishes. Ponzo (1915) finds the I-fraction small in silent reading, though not so small as in reading aloud.

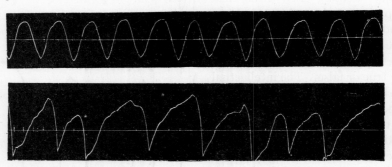

Fig. 70. (Morgan, 1916). Pneumograph record of a subject working at a code substitution test. The upper line shows the breathing during quiet, the lower line the breathing during noise. The downward thrust of the tracing records inspiration in this case.

CIRCULATORY CHANGES IN EMOTION

When the circulation of blood is affected by emotion it is because an emotional episode breaking in on the regular work of the heart makes special demands which are met by some change in the circulation. The circulatory change—blushing, paling, high blood pressure—is not primarily an "expression" of the emotion. Darwin's view of emotional expression as consisting of originally practical responses is quite pertinent here. Emotional demands cut across the routine metabolic function of circulation and respiration. Without even a sketch of the physiology of the circulation we will note certain variables which are related to emotion.

Apart from the quality or composition of the blood, the variable of direct metabolic importance is the *flow*, the quantity of blood passing through an organ in a unit of time. Instead of attempting to measure the flow, we take such measurements as the rate and force of the heart beat, the arterial blood pressure, and the volume of some part of the body, as the arm or hand. The flow depends on the driving force (the blood pressure in the arteries) and on the resistance encountered in the small arteries and capillaries. Smooth muscle in the walls of the small arteries responds to the vasoconstrictor and vasodilator nerves; constriction increases the resistance and retards the flow, dilation increases the rate of flow, provided the arterial pressure is maintained.

The *arterial blood pressure* depends on two factors: (1) the output of blood from the heart and (2) the total resistance encountered. Increased output or increased resistance raises the blood pressure. With each contraction or systole the ventricle forces a quantity of blood into the elastic large arteries, while, at the other end of the arterial system, blood is steadily being forced through the capillaries by the pressure in the arteries. The systolic pressure is the maximum reached during a given heart cycle and the diastolic the minimum. Within a given cycle the systolic pressure may be 120 mm of mercury and the diastolic 80; the difference, here of 40 mm, is called the pulse pressure.

The *output of the heart* depends upon the intake of blood from the large veins. The intake varies with two conditions of special interest. (1) Active exercise dilating the small arteries in the muscles increases the flow from the arteries into the veins and through the veins back to the heart; the whole circulation is speeded up. (2) In quiet conditions the large veins, especially those in the abdominal area, relax and hold a large quantity of blood which flows only slowly back to the heart. When the large veins constrict they force blood rapidly into the heart and the heart increases its output, quickly raising the blood pressure in the arteries. This is the most important circulatory change directly related to the emotions. Any startling stimulus or sudden exertion of muscular force causes vasoconstriction in the abdomen, forcing blood rapidly to the heart, raising its output and the blood pressure and causing a quick rise in the volume of the hand or any other distensible organ. This distension may be quickly counteracted by local constriction in that organ.

The heart is an automatic organ; it continues to beat even when removed from the body if provided with proper blood. The rate and force of the heart beat are regulated by two sets of nerves. The *sympathetic accelerates* the heart; the vagus contains fibers of the *cranial autonomic* system which *inhibit* or retard the heart. The heart rate is also influenced by hormones, especially adrenin which accelerates it.

The cardiac and vasomotor centers in the medulla are responsive to stimuli from almost any source. Momentary stimuli (such as sudden change to lighter or darker illumination) accelerate the heart momentarily. Inhibitory reflexes arise from the depressor nerve which is a small sensory branch of the vagus distributed to the aorta. High blood pressure in the aorta stimulates the depressor nerve and reflexly diminishes the heart beat and vasoconstriction, so lowering the pressure. A similar reflex regulatory mechanism has its sensory endings in the carotid sinus at the junction of the external and internal carotid arteries, the chief arteries of the brain and head. Excessive pressure in this region acts reflexly to reduce the heart beat and vasoconstriction and so lowers the general blood pressure.

Instruments for recording circulatory changes in man. Such instruments have been devised in various forms. The force of the heart beat, which can be felt between the ribs, is picked up mechanically by a receiving tambour and conducted by air transmission to a recording tambour. The electrocardiograph amplifies the changes of potential which occur with each heart beat and makes them audible, visible or recordable on moving photographic film.

A plethysmograph or volume recorder is made to fit the finger or arm. The member is sealed airtight but not under pressure in a glass tube and communicates its changes of volume to the air in the tube which is connected by rubber pipe with a recording tambour.

A sphygmograph or pulse recorder is affected by the changes in pressure in the artery as the pulse wave passes the point of application.

The sphygmometer or sphygmomanometer gives a measure of the blood pressure. A rubber belt or cuff encircling the upper arm is inflated to a pressure measured by a manometer inserted in the system. When the inflation pressure exceeds the systolic blood pressure the blood cannot get through the arm past the cuff but as soon as the pressure in the cuff sinks below systolic pressure the pulse waves will pass and can be felt or heard below the cuff.

The cardiotachometer (Boas & Goldschmidt, 1932) gives a continuous record of the *rate* of the heart beat. Two small electrodes are placed on the chest, one over the base of the heart and the other near the apex; from these the main peak of the electrocardiogram is led through amplification to a relay which operates an electromagnetic counter and a graphic registering device. The flexible leads can be as long as 100 ft., permitting O to work or play freely while his heart rate is being recorded. The instrument gives an accurate measure even at high rates which can scarcely be counted by feeling the pulse.

The circulation in sleep. Though it would be extravagant to speak of sleep as an emotion, it can be thought of as furnishing a base line for the study of emotion, and the changes in going to sleep and awaking are instructive for comparison with emotional changes. Boas & Goldschmidt (1932) obtained continuous heart rate records from over 100 adults in various activities. A "basal heart rate" was obtained in the same conditions in which the basal metabolic rate is measured, that is in the post-absorptive resting state while O is lying awake in the morning long after the last meal and before engaging in the activities of the day. This basal heart rate averaged 61 for the male subjects and 70 for the female. In ordinary indoor occupations the average male rate was 78 and the female 84, with wide individual variations. In sleeping the male average was 59 and the female 65, not much less than the basal waking rate. In some Os the heart rate went down to 40 during sleep, in some it rose to 170 or higher during muscular exercise. Noises during sleep, especially during the light sleep just before awaking, caused a momentary quickening of the heart. The pulse also rose when O turned in bed. In awakening there is sometimes a quick rise of heart rate, sometimes a gradual rise which begins before awaking and continues afterward. The heart rate curve for a full night's sleep varies with the individual, in some showing an early drop to a low level which is maintained until awaking, in others showing a progressive decline until awaking, in still others showing more oscillation with a gradual rise for the last hour before awaking. As judged from the heart rate there are different ways of sleeping and different ways of waking up.

Landis (1925) took the blood pressure of male students, in going to sleep, during sleep and in awaking. In ordinary going to sleep the systolic pressure fell from 108 to 94 mm of mercury in two or three minutes; this typical result was obtained even when the subject was reclining instead of lying flat in bed. Normal quiet awaking showed a gradual rise of the blood pressure, as from 94 to 108 mm in two minutes. When O was awakened by an alarm clock the rise was more rapid, for example from 92 while asleep to 114 within 50 sec. This sudden rise was followed by a decline back to 104 in another 20 sec. The picture varied, however; sometimes the rise was more gradual even on being wakened by an alarm clock.

An experiment by Shepard (1906, 1914) was quite comprehensive since in addition to heart rate, breathing rate and hand volume he was able to record the *changes in brain volume* in two young men whose skulls had been trephined because of head injury. A portion of the skull had been removed and the scalp sewed together over the hole. The brain could be felt to pulsate as in a baby's fontanelle. A piece of cork, attached to the rubber diaphragm of a receiving tambour, was bound firmly over the opening in the skull, the tambour being connected by air transmission with a piston recorder. After some preliminary sittings the subjects became well adjusted to this instrumentation and took the experiments as a routine matter; they sometimes slept all night in the laboratory while their brain volume, arm volume and breathing were being recorded.

Shepard's setup was very complete and accurate and he obtained many records with consistent results. So, though his results differ from those obtained in earlier less complete experiments, they are probably correct. In agreement with other experimenters he found the general blood pressure low and the hand volume large during sleep. These findings indicate general vasodilation during sleep. The arterial pressure being low and the small arteries generally dilated, the brain circulation would necessarily be diminished, unless the brain vessels were dilated like those elsewhere.

Because the skull is rigid and its liquid and semiliquid contents incompressible, it is often assumed that the brain volume (inside an intact skull) must be constant, and that the brain vessels are incapable of active constriction and dilation. However, the several openings by which nerves and blood vessels enter and leave the skull afford some leeway for expansion and contraction of the contents of the skull. In the brain as elsewhere the walls of the arteries contain elastic and muscular tissue and nerve endings, so that there is good reason to believe that these arteries can change their bore.

At any rate Shepard's results show a definite *increase* of brain volume in going to sleep and a definite decrease on awaking. The brain volume always rose as sleep came on and remained fairly high throughout sleep. Stimuli not strong enough to waken the subject caused a fall of volume, sometimes preceded by a slight rise. Waking always brought a fall in brain volume.

These changes obviously cannot be explained by the changes in general blood pressure. They are the opposite of what could be explained by this cause, for in going to sleep increasing brain volume goes with falling blood pressure, and in waking the blood pressure rises while the brain volume sinks. The changes can be accounted for perfectly by assuming vasodilation in the brain (as elsewhere) in going to sleep, and vasoconstriction in waking up. It would not follow, however, that the *flow* through the brain was increased in sleep, for the speed of the whole circulation is low during sleep because of the small output of the heart.

Startle, surprise and sudden shifts of attention. Here we will take note first of Shepard's results on his trephined subjects during the waking state. Stimuli then gave an increase in brain volume, not a decrease as was the case during sleep. A sudden loud noise gave a compound response: first a rise, than a small fall and finally a further rise of volume. The same startling stimulus gave a rise of hand volume followed by a fall. The net result was rise in brain volume, fall in hand volume.

These seemingly complex results are not inexplicable. We have a right to assume a constriction of the large abdominal veins in response to a startling stimulus, with consequent increase of blood poured into the heart and increased output into the arteries. The first effect in both hand and brain is an increase of volume. Vasoconstriction in the hand soon reduces the volume there, while brain vasoconstriction, we may assume, is comparatively ineffective so that the net result is increased brain volume. The whole thing is a consistent sympathetic reaction. But how then shall we explain the *fall* in brain volume on disturbance during sleep? We need only assume, further, that the brain vessels are so much relaxed during sleep that their constriction in response to a startling stimulus amounts to a big change, sufficient to counteract the increased heart output.

With startling stimuli, a loud whistle or a pistol shot, the heart rate takes a sudden jump and quickly returns toward normal. Blood pressure takes a similar course. Blatz (1925) in the falling chair experiment (p. 261) found that this fear-provoking stimulus gave a prompt acceleration of the heart, with an average rise of 20 beats per minute followed by quick recovery and a subsequent secondary rise which was smaller but more prolonged.

Expectancy. Returning for a second day of the experiment, Blatz's Os showed a high pulse rate in *anticipation* of the fall of the chair. A. E.

Nissen (1928) obtained blood pressure readings from two patients in the dentist's chair. The pressure rose sharply when the dentist came into the room; in fact, the rise at this time was more regular than when he began his operations. Even the expectation of a neutral stimulus, announced a few moments in advance, tends to raise the pulse rate, increase the volume of the brain and decrease the volume of the hand (Shepard, 1906).

Mental activity. Muscular activity increases the heart rate and the flow of blood for excellent physiological reasons. Mental activity is likely to involve some muscular activity and for that reason to increase the circulation. Mental arithmetic, involving very little muscular activity, produces no noticeable increase, and in fact the heart rate may sink during the prolonged muscular inactivity of this particular experiment. In other kinds of mental work some increase in the pulse rate is found, especially if the conditions involve competition or working against time.

Excitement. From much experimental evidence it is perfectly clear that excitement speeds up the circulation. Tigerstedt (1926) measured the blood pressure of 13 students before and after an important six-hour examination, and found it very high, 165 mm on the average, beforehand; 152 mm, still high, afterward. In another experiment he had a student step forward and face the class, who passed remarks while this student's blood pressure was being taken. The average from 10 students was 166 mm. These same students then reported individually to the professor for several successive days and gave average blood pressure, day by day, of 152, 140, 139, 130, 129 mm, the last reading being down near the norm for young adults. Tigerstedt concluded that the high pressure in the earlier days of this series was a hangover from the exciting conditions under which the measurement had first been made, a sort of conditioned response.

Other tests of circulation and respiration before examinations are summarized by Brown & Van Gelder (1938). These authors themselves measured a large number of students. One group of 17 college seniors, before and after the sessions of a two-day final comprehensive examination in psychology, were above their normal state by the following amounts:

	First day		Second day	
	Before	*After*	*Before*	*After*
Systolic B.P.	15 mm	2 mm	4 mm	0
Pulse rate	23 beats	5 beats	16 beats	4 beats
Breathing rate	3 cycles	−1 cycle	1 cycle	0

As remarked by Luria (1932) individuals differ in their anticipatory reaction to an examination, some being relatively immune to this influence.

Landis & Gullette (1925) piled one emotional situation on another through a long sitting. Though they did not obtain differential reactions to the different situations, the general reaction was high blood pressure during the whole sitting.   In the effort to produce severe emotional upset, Landis (1926) induced three psychologists to undergo a two-day fast and a sleepless night, after which they were given the strongest electrical stimulation that they could stand for as long as they would endure it.   There were many symptoms—inhibition of stomach contraction and of rectal contraction, gasping, nausea and gagging, marked sweating, incoordination of behavior—and along with these signs of excitement went a marked rise in the blood pressure.

That stimulation of the circulation is not confined to unpleasant excitement is shown by a record of Boas & Goldschmidt (1932) in which they demonstrated the wide range of application of their cardio-

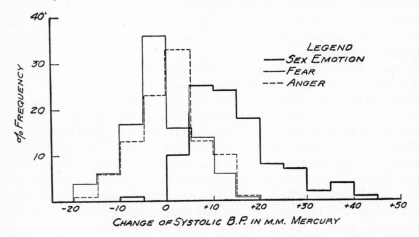

FIG. 71. (Data from J. C. Scott, 1930.)   Rise of systolic blood pressure during a motion picture episode which aroused a sex emotion reported as at least "moderate" by 88 of 100 subjects tested.   The episodes intended to arouse fear and anger were less successful according to the introspective reports.   The graph shows the distribution of responses.

tachograph by obtaining a complete record of heart rate during sex behavior of a married couple, and found sharp peaks (143–146 beats per minute) during orgasm.   A milder degree of pleasurable excitement was shown by a man listening to a phonograph record of a song which was connected in his mind with a woman of whom he was very fond. On hearing this song his pulse rate increased from 64 to 121.

The problem of introducing any strong pleasurable emotion into the laboratory has been a difficult one for the psychologist.   O needs to become so well adapted to the recording instrument that he forgets all about the record being taken.   This seems to be fairly well accomplished by the cardiotachograph.   The subject needs also to lose himself in the situation, forgetting that it is an experiment.   This need is met by the motion picture.

J. C. Scott (1930) showed a forty-minute motion picture to 100 medical school sophomores, taken one at a time into the laboratory. The film contained a love scene, an episode likely to arouse anger in which the hero was badly treated, and a third episode intended to arouse fear, in which the city was destroyed by earthquake and the hero was in danger. These episodes were separated by about ten minutes of relatively neutral film. O sat alone in a room watching the show, his blood pressure being recorded by means of the Tycos recording sphygmometer which although not giving a continuous record enables the experimenter to obtain the pressure at intervals without being in the immediate presence of the subject. At the close of the picture O gave a retrospective estimate of the degree of his emotion in viewing the different episodes. From these reports the sex emotion was most successfully aroused, and it showed a definite rise of blood pressure in nearly every one of the subjects. It must be remembered that moderate changes in blood pressure amounting to a rise or fall of 10 mm occur without obvious cause, either emotional or physiological. The subjects in this experiment had been adapted to the laboratory situation by previously coming several times and having their blood pressure taken.

A neat physiological demonstration of abdominal vasoconstriction in fright and excitement is provided by an experiment on a dog (Barcroft & Florey, 1929; Drury, Florey & Florey, 1929). By a preliminary operation a bit of the lining of the dog's intestine was grafted into the skin while still retaining its own proper nerves and blood vessels. Thus a sample of the intestinal mucous membrane was exposed to view. Whenever this dog was frightened, as by the approach of a strange person, the membrane blanched, showing vasoconstriction. The latency of this reaction was 4–5 sec., much longer than that of the external signs of fright, a fact which may be, as the authors suggest, a telling point against the James-Lange theory of emotion. Again, the dog was held by one of his friends while another called him from a distance; and the patch of mucous membrane blanched, while the external behavior indicated excitement, not fear or anger.

Blood pressure in deception. Soon after Benussi had introduced his respiration test of lying, Marston (1917) performed a similar experiment with blood pressure as the indicator. Ten students served as subjects, testifying before a "jury." O's friend was supposed to be accused of a crime and O tried to save his friend by establishing an alibi. O could choose whether to follow a ready-made "true" alibi or to invent a "false" one. He was examined before the jury who rendered a verdict according to their impressions of O's truth or falsity. At intervals before and during the examination O's blood pressure was measured by the experimenter who rendered a verdict based entirely on rise of blood pressure and was correct in 103 out of 107 judgments. The true witnesses showed only a small rise, not over 5 mm, while the liars gave a gradual increase amounting to 16 mm on the average. These American students like the Europeans in Benussi's experiment proved themselves fairly competent liars so that the jury had only a 50–50 chance of reaching a correct verdict. The students preferred lying (under the experimental conditions) to the rather humdrum task of telling the truth. Their reported emotions included interest in deceiving the jury, a feeling of adventure, fear, and occasionally anger on being cornered by the "attorney."

Marston attributed the blood pressure rise to this emotional state of the lying witness rather than to the intellectual activity involved. In control experiments with intense mental work—arithmetic, studying a lesson, inventing a story—his Os showed no large rises but usually a decline in blood pressure. In a later experiment (1923) he studied the blood pressure changes in a variety of situations, more or less exciting, and got considerable rises in most of them as shown in the accompanying table.

MAXIMUM RISE OF BLOOD PRESSURE DURING A SITTING OF 10–40 MINUTES

(Marston, 1923)

	Average for 10 Men	10 Women
Resting with eyes covered	11 mm	19 mm
Reading story	9	15
Reading difficult psychological book	8	14
Reading newspaper	5	19
Conversing with one of opposite sex, met for the first time	14	28
Narrating story read 2 weeks previously	7	15
Narrating exciting personal experience	9	20
Narrating own actions for last 24 hours	6	24
Cross-examination on story read	7	13
Cross-examination on exciting experience	7	16
Cross-examination on own actions for last half day	12	28

Results equally favorable for the blood pressure test of deception, at least under laboratory conditions, were obtained by Chappell (1929) in a true-or-false-alibi experiment similar to Marston's but without any jury. Chappell's truth tellers showed an average rise of 5 mm with very few going above 12 mm increase, while his liars averaged 19 mm with very few less than 12 mm. The use of 12 mm as a critical value separated the sheep from the goats in 87 percent of the individual cases.

In control experiments Chappell found: (1) a blood pressure rise in an intelligence test which worried the subjects; (2) no rise in mental arithmetic free from all worry; and (3) no rise in making false statements where there was no test situation involved. Chappell concludes that the blood pressure rise, where it occurs, is due to excitement rather than to lying. The test can therefore be used successfully "when the deception situation gives rise to excitement and when other causes of excitement are eliminated."

Larson (1923, 1932) has made practical use of a combination of respiration and circulation records during the examination of suspects by the police. He lays more stress on the circulation but uses the respiratory symptoms to help out. He inflates an arm cuff to a pressure intermediate between systolic and diastolic and connects the cuff to a recording tambour. He does not pretend to secure thus an absolute measure of the blood pressure (see Chappell, 1931, for critique of this procedure), but his record shows rises and falls in blood pressure, hastening and slowing of the heart, irregular fluctuations, and combinations of circulatory and respiratory symptoms which he uses judiciously and not according to any rigid formula. Confronted with these objective evidences of emotional disturbance at critical points in the examination, many suspects have broken down and confessed. Larson does not believe that the results of the deception test should be introduced as evidence in court. Rather, it is a tool for the detective force, and much of its value comes from the elimination of innocent suspects. Though both guilty and innocent suspects may be under high tension at the beginning of the test, the innocent one calms down as he finds it easy to answer the questions truthfully while the guilty one finds himself in difficulty. Sometimes the test gives a false lead with very nervous suspects or in the case of one who is guilty enough but not guilty of the particular crime under investigation.

CHAPTER XIII

THE "PSYCHOGALVANIC REFLEX" OR "GALVANIC
SKIN RESPONSE"

A MONG the electrical phenomena of life which have attracted the
attention of physiologists, there is one of special psychological
interest because of its apparent connection with emotion. Perhaps
we should speak of two phenomena and call them by the names of their
respective discoverers, Féré (1888) and Tarchanoff (1890).

It was known that when an electric current was passed through the
human body, the electrical "resistance" of the body was high and subject
to large variations. Féré passed a weak current through electrodes
on the forearm, having a galvanometer in the circuit, and applied to O
such stimuli as a tuning fork, an odor, a colored glass held before the
eyes. The galvanometer responded by a quick deflection, indicative
of increased flow of current due to decreased bodily resistance. Féré
obtained deflections also on the occurrence of a "sthenic" emotion;
and suggested that these observations might open up an interesting
field for psychological experiments.

Féré's attention was first attracted to these electrical phenomena
by the case of a woman with abnormally dry skin who was troubled
with sparks from the skin and hair, especially in cold, dry weather.
In collaboration with the celebrated physicist d'Arsonval, he measured
the static charge on this woman's skin and found it to run up to several
hundred volts after friction between the skin and the clothes. But
on applying stimuli—a blue glass before the eyes or a whiff of ether—
this charge largely disappeared. Féré was inclined to attribute these
changes to the generation of electricity in the subject's body. But
d'Arsonval (1888) showed that it was absolutely impossible for any such
voltages to be generated in the human body. He pointed to external
friction as the source of the charge on the dry skin, and to "cutaneous
secretion modified by the sensory stimuli" as the cause of the sudden
loss of charge. This incident is interesting because it shows the phenomenon in a form which has not been followed up, and also because
d'Arsonval at the very beginning put his finger on the sweat glands as the
probable locus of the response.

Tarchanoff (1890) approached the matter from a different angle.
He found that any two parts of the skin, connected through a galvanometer, would usually show a difference in potential. A weak

current would be found passing through the galvanometer in a certain direction. This endosomatic current could be neutralized by a weak external current passed in the opposite direction and the galvanometer needle thus brought to zero. After this had occurred a stimulus to O often gave a deflection of the galvanometer needle, with a latency of 1–3 seconds. Tarchanoff obtained this response not only with sensory stimuli but also on inducing shifts of mental activity.

Féré, then, passed an external current through O and found O's resistance to decrease in response to certain stimuli. Tarchanoff used no external current (or just enough to compensate for the slight potential difference between two points on the skin), and the changes which he observed on stimulation must have been action currents generated in O, probably in O's skin. The two phenomena are elicited by the same stimuli, and, as we shall see later, they are undoubtedly both manifestations of the activity of the sweat glands. Though they differ physically they are both indicators of the same physiological activity.

The name "psychogalvanic reflex" was introduced by Veraguth (1906, 1909), who made a comprehensive study of the Féré effect. The name has the merits of a good sign post, and is better in that respect than "galvanic skin response," which is preferred by recent workers in the field because they are surer of the skin than of the psyche as the source of the phenomenon. In the present chapter we will call it PGR, and if any reader objects to the psychic implications of the "P," he can read "perspiratory."

Rudiments of the necessary technique. Dealing as he does here with electrical phenomena, the experimenter needs some knowledge of electricity to keep out of pitfalls that would vitiate his results. Any adequate description and explanation of the apparatus required would take us too far afield. Some of the most helpful references, as to circuits and electrodes, are the following: Prideaux (1921), Richter (1927, 1929 a), Jeffress (1928), Darrow (1930), Davis (1930), Davis & Porter (1931), Seward & Seward (1934), Forbes & Landis (1935), Forbes (1936).

When no external current is used, we have to do with minute changes in skin potential and must employ delicate recorders or amplifiers. Non-polarizable electrodes are applied to two portions of the skin, as the palm and the forearm. Since the potential changes in the skin under the two electrodes are often out of step with each other, it is well to shortcircuit the skin under *one* electrode by one or two punctures with a needle, so establishing electrical connection between the external part of the circuit and the well-conducting body fluids. Or, the indifferent electrode can be applied to the mucous membrane inside the mouth, where there are no sweat glands. This setup will also give a measure of the skin resistance to a weak impressed current.

When an external current is used, the Wheatstone bridge is useful. The requirements of quantitative work include a measurement of the resistance level from which any PGR starts as well as a measurement of the PGR itself. The PGR shows itself in the galvanometer as an increase of current due to decreased resistance of the skin, and is best measured as a decrease in skin resistance. It is necessary or at least desirable to maintain the current flowing through the skin at a constant intensity, because the resistance of the skin (due to polarization by the impressed current, p. 280) varies with the current, and also because the galvanometer deflections must be evaluated in accordance with the current. These requirements are met by a particular arrangement of the Wheatstone bridge, such that three arms contain known constant

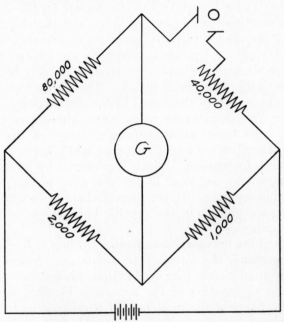

FIG. 72. A Wheatstone bridge for measuring resistance levels and magnitude of PGR. No current will flow through the galvanometer G when the potential is equal at the opposite corners of the square connected through the galvanometer. The remaining two corners, being in direct connection with the poles of the battery, have a certain difference in potential. As you follow along either of the two circuits between these poles, the potential difference decreases in proportion to the resistance traversed. With the resistances indicated (the 40,000 ohms being the resistance of O plus that of the adjustable coil), the potential is equal at the two ends of the bridge. Let O's resistance decrease: the balance is disturbed and current flows through the galvanometer, causing the needle to swing. E may now increase the resistance in series with O, noting the amount added, till the needle comes back to zero. By introducing known resistances in place of O the amplitude of the galvanometer deflections can be calibrated and so the temporary drops in O's resistance which constitute the PGR can be measured.

Most circuits in actual use complicate the simple diagram shown here to provide a galvanometer shunt, known resistances to be substituted for O, amplification for the current changes, etc.

The galvanometer deflections can be read, traced by hand on a kymograph as they occur (they are slow enough to allow of such tracing) or photographed.

resistances, while the fourth arm includes a large, adjustable resistance in series with O. When the level of O's resistance changes (as it always does, usually declining in the course of an experimental sitting), the resistance in series with O is adjusted to compensate for the changes in O's resistance, and thus the total resistance in O's circuit is kept constant. The resistance in the circuit remaining constant, and also the impressed voltage, the current through O is kept constant, and measurement in absolute units is possible.

Non-polarizable electrodes are indicated for quantitative work. A metallic electrode in contact with the skin behaves like a small battery and generates unmeasured current and polarization. Perhaps no sequence of contacts between the skin and the external metallic conductor is perfectly free from polarization. One electrode which gives good results consists of a zinc plate (having a good dry junction with the external copper wire), covered with a pad of gauze, chamois or kaolin filled with zinc sulphate solution.

PHYSIOLOGY OF PGR

Evidently the proper approach to an understanding of PGR is from below up. First we should know its physics, then its local physiology and its neurophysiology, and finally we should look into its psychology.

Physics of the response. Physically the Féré and Tarchanoff effects are quite different though both are indicated by deflections of the galvanometer. The Tarchanoff effect requires a very sensitive galvanometer since the potentials that come to light in this procedure are very small, of the order of 5–10 millivolts. The magnitude of the Féré effect may be a thousand times this depending on the voltage of the impressed current. The Tarchanoff effect appears as a swing in either direction, indicating a current flowing sometimes in one direction and sometimes in the other. These little currents must be generated in the body, and the Tarchanoff effect thus shows that the total response of the organism to certain situations involves the generation of such currents (Wells & A. Forbes, 1911).

The Tarchanoff effect is likely to be weak and irregular unless special care is taken in locating the two electrodes. If one of them, the "indifferent electrode," is placed in the mouth where there are no sweat glands, or on a portion of the arm which has been punctured and so short-circuited, then there is no interference between the electrical waves generated in two portions of skin and consequently the wave picture is much clearer, though it often shows a double wave, one relatively quick and the other slow in starting and long drawn out (Richter, 1927; Jeffress, 1928; T. W. Forbes & Bolles, 1936). What is revealed by Tarchanoff's procedure consists undoubtedly of action currents originating in the skin under the "active electrode."

The Féré effect consists in an increased flow of the impressed current through the body, due to a diminution of the effective resistance of the body. This bodily resistance is peculiar and not like the passive resistance of an ordinary poor conductor. When suitable methods are used to measure its development in time, it is found to be very small at the first instant after the current is turned on but to increase to a maximum in less than a millisecond, after which it tends to decrease slowly. (Strohl, 1921; Hozawa, 1928; Gildemeister, 1928; James & Thouless, 1926). Something happens in the body very quickly to impede the flow of the impressed current. Another peculiarity is that the resistance decreases when the impressed voltage is increased; a passive conductor does not behave in this way. The Féré effect is a relatively quick and brief decrease in this enigmatical resistance.

The peculiar resistance is satisfactorily explained as the result of *polarization*. When an electric current is passed through a mass of living cells it has to penetrate cell walls which are semipermeable membranes, not open to the passage of all ions. The ions which carry the current bank up against the cell walls; so that each such wall constitutes a polarization cell with polarity opposite to that of the impressed current. At the cell wall an electromotive force (E. M. F.) arises counter to that of the impressed current, though weaker. The impressed voltage is partly neutralized by this counter E. M. F. and so the current is diminished. The greater the impressed voltage the greater the polarization, but the latter does not fully keep pace with the former, so that a high tension current is less impeded than one of low tension, with the result stated above, that the apparent resistance decreases as the voltage of the impressed current increases.

With this understanding of body resistance we can see that the Féré effect consists in a partial and temporary *depolarization* of the cell walls (or some of them) through which the current is passing. As far as the galvanometer is concerned, the effect amounts to a temporary decrease in the body resistance of the subject. The electrical phenomena, on careful analysis, prove to be fully in accord with the polarization-depolarization conception of the matter (Gildemeister, 1928; Thouless, 1929; Davis, 1930).

Local physiology of the galvanic response. That the skin under the electrodes is the locus of both the Féré and the Tarchanoff effects is clear from experiments in which the skin under one or both electrodes has been punctured. When direct connection is thus made with the internal body fluids under one electrode, the body resistance is cut in half, and if the skin is punctured under both electrodes the resistance drops nearly to zero (Richter, 1926). The blood and lymph channels inside the body afford good conduction, and nowhere but in the skin itself could the high apparent resistances, 50,000 to 100,000 ohms and up, possibly occur. As to the Tarchanoff effect, the fact that the electric waves generated under two electrodes on unpunctured skin show interference which disappears when puncture is made under one electrode indicates that these waves also originate in the skin.

If there is no puncture the current probably traverses all the cells of the skin under the electrodes and polarizes the epithelial cells as well as the sweat gland cells; but the quick depolarization which occurs in response to a pistol shot or to a bit of surprisingly good news must be located in skin cells that are responsive to nerve impulses, and one thinks then of the sweat glands or perhaps of the smooth muscle in the cutaneous blood vessels. The Tarchanoff action currents also must originate in a burst of activity in some such cells.

The depolarization which gives the Féré effect is just what is known to occur at the walls of active cells. In cell activity the walls become more permeable and let some of the banked-up ions pass, diminishing the counter E. M. F. which has been impeding the flow of current.

After long discussion of the varied evidence physiologists have come to agree with the original suggestion of d'Arsonval (1888) and of Tarchanoff (1890) that the galvanic skin phenomena, both action currents and depolarization, are due to activity of the cells of the sweat glands. Some of the evidence follows:

1. Atropin, which is known to inhibit the sweat glands, abolishes or reduces the galvanic skin phenomena (Wells & Forbes, 1911; Gildemeister, 1928; Mall, 1936 b), and the effects of other drugs also conform to their known effects on these glands. Hyperthyroidism lowers the resistance (Vigouroux, 1879) and exaggerates the Féré effect (Prideaux, 1921).

2. Darrow (1929 c, 1932) obtained through a microscope a motion picture of a small bit of skin surrounded by one of the electrodes, and his film shows quite convincingly the emergence of droplets from the sweat pores during PGR. These droplets are not visible to the naked eye, and they disappear quickly.

Up to this point we have carefully distinguished between the two effects, Féré and Tarchanoff; but if we are right in accepting both of them as indices of sweat gland activity there is no reason for continuing to keep them separate, and we may use our symbol PGR for both. Jeffress (1928) took simultaneous photographic records of the Féré effect from one hand of the subject and of the Tarchanoff effect from the other hand and found them to vary together as far as magnitude was concerned, the correlation between them in this respect being $r = +.96$. He also found the average latency of the two effects to be the same. The reflex is rather slow, its latency ranging from 1 to 3 seconds. The two phases of the Tarchanoff wave may however represent somewhat different mechanisms, the second phase only being dependent on the sweat glands (Forbes and Bolles, 1936). There are also differences in the responses obtained from the palms and from the back of the hands which may indicate two different mechanisms at work (Richter, 1929 a). There may be quite a complex of phenomena here awaiting analysis. But for most known psychological purposes the two effects can be treated as equivalent.

Neurophysiology of the PGR. These little bursts of glandular activity begin to look interesting when we remember that the sweat glands are innervated by the sympathetic division of the autonomic nervous system. We recall the other effects of sympathetic activity—acceleration of the heart, constriction of blood vessels, rise of blood pressure, inhibition of digestion, contraction of the sphincters of the bladder and anus, dilation of the bronchi, liberation of adrenin from the adrenal glands, of sugar from the liver and of red blood corpuscles from the spleen, erection of the cat's fur and of the porcupine's quills, gooseflesh and dilation of the pupil—the complex "emergency reaction" (Cannon, 1915). We remember also that the sympathetic is supposed to act diffusely so that all these effects occur together, though there can be degrees of this mass activity. So we get the suggestion that *PGR is an index of this whole sympathetic activity*, and probably so delicate an index that it is obtainable even when the sympathetic is only very slightly aroused, i.e., when the emergency is itself very slight and far removed from the primitive situations in which the emergency reaction is of practical utility to the organism.

The particular role of perspiration in this emergency reaction complex is not wholly clear. One prime function of sweat is by evaporation to cool the skin and so to eliminate heat from the body, and that function is obviously important when the emergency calls for violent muscular activity. But the abundant sweat glands of the palms and soles seem poorly located for serving the function of heat elimination, because the soles are apt to be in contact with the ground and the palms in contact with some object or in a cupped, half-closed position, so that the sweat is prevented from evaporating or is wiped off before it can evaporate. Darrow (1936) has pointed to another use which is actually made of sweat upon the hands and feet. A certain amount of moisture on the palms enables the hands to get a firmer grip as is seen "in the behavior of the workman who spits upon his hands to obtain a better grip, as also in the action of a clerk who more hygienically moistens his fingers with a sponge." A firm hold on the ground or on a stick or limb of a tree is of obvious importance in primitive emergencies. The dry palm which is said to be characteristic of sleep signalizes the antithesis of an emergency adjustment. Imperceptible moisture such as is furnished the palms and soles by slight activity of the sweat glands would evidently be an asset in the prehistoric (and prehuman) struggle for existence. From this point of view the PGR is not simply an index of general sympathetic activity but a manifestation of a glandular response which is of direct service in emergencies.

We should look for a moment at the physiological evidence that PGR is actually dependent upon innervation by the sympathetic division. It is possible to cut the sympathetic chain at such a point that all sympathetic fibers to an arm or leg are severed. PGR is abolished and the level of skin resistance is raised in the limb affected by this operation.

The sympathetic therefore exerts a "tonic" influence on the sweat glands of the palm, keeping them in a state of continued moderate activity, and it can also arouse them to momentary spurts of greater activity (Richter, 1929 b). Whether there is any parasympathetic innervation of the sweat glands (from the cranial and sacral autonomic), as is the case with most of the organs having a sympathetic nerve supply—the parasympathetic being always antagonistic to the sympathetic in its effect on any organ—cannot be made out from present evidence though there are some indications of such a double nerve supply.

In the human the sympathetic chain is sometimes interrupted by the growth of a tumor. In one such case (Richter, 1927) a tumor in the neck blocked the sympathetic innervation of one arm and of one half of the head and upper chest. The pupil on the affected side was constricted (unbalanced action of the pupilloconstrictor fibers of the cranial autonomic), the skin on the affected side was noticeably warm (unbalanced action of the vasodilator fibers of the cranial autonomic), and there was no sweating in the affected area even in a hot air bath, though there was abundant sweating in the same area after hypodermic injection of pilocarpine which presumably stimulates the sweat glands directly. Skin resistance was high in the affected area (except after pilocarpine) and PGR could not be obtained by a pistol shot, automobile horn or pinprick, though these stimuli gave the usual response on the normal side. The evidence from animals and humans alike is clear that PGR is mediated by the sympathetic.

There seems to be a center for the sympathetic in the region of the interbrain, though different attempts to locate it have not given precisely the same results. Wang & Richter (1928) stimulated that portion of the hypothalamus known as the tuber cinereum and believed to be a "vegetative center," and obtained widespread sympathetic effects, including dilation of the pupil, rise of general blood pressure and PGR in the cat's foot pads. This last response was also obtained on stimulation of the motor area of the cortex (Wang & Lu, 1930). PGR is thus seen to belong both to the thalamic and to the cortical action system.

Can PGR be accepted as an index of general sympathetic activity? Mention was made above of the common view that the sympathetic acts as a unit, or diffusely by a sort of mass action. Uhlenbruck (1934) obtained simultaneous records of PGR and of vasoconstriction (plethysmograph) from different fingers of the same hand, in response to painful stimuli, and found the two responses to occur together and with the same latency. He proposed therefore to substitute the broader term "autonomic reflex" for the more limited PGR. Gildemeister (1928) who had previously observed dilation of the pupil occurring along with PGR, thought well of this suggestion. ("Autonomic reflex" is however too broad; "sympathetic reflex" would be better.) Schoonhoven (1925), obtaining simultaneous records of PGR, blood pressure and pupil diameter, reports that the blood pressure changes do not always run parallel to the changes in the pupil; and Darrow (1929 a) repeating Uhlenbruck's experiment with the extra refinement of obtaining PGR from the same fingers as were enclosed in the plethysmograph, and also recording changes in the general arterial blood pressure, found that the three sympathetic effects to be expected from strong sensory stimulation —local vasoconstriction, rise of blood pressure, and the PGR—were not always coincident and synchronous. (It must be remarked however that records of blood pressure and finger volume do not show the exact instant at which the smooth muscles of the vessel walls contract in response to stimulation by the sympathetic nerve fibers; PGR is probably much more precise as an indicator of the moment of sympathetic activity.) One is left with the impression that the sympathetic does not always act as a unit and that PGR is not an infallible index of any activity going on in the sympathetic division. Yet it is probably a pretty fair index.

PSYCHOLOGY OF PGR

Now that we have found PGR to be an index of activity in the sympathetic division of the autonomic, we ask what psychological use can be made of such an index. The answer, in general terms, is that it will show the participation of the sympathetic in emotion, mental work, overt behavior. Is the sympathetic active in all emotional states or only in certain emotions? Is its activity confined to emotional states? Does PGR give an objective index of emotion, as psychologists believed at first? In the laboratory we have two interrelated questions to attack. In terms of stimulus we ask what types of situation elicit this response. In terms of response we ask in what types of action PGR is involved. The experimenter deals directly with situations which he can control, but he can also record other elements of response besides PGR, and when he comes to interpret his results he is concerned with the total response. Sympathetic activity doubtless occurs as part of a larger action pattern, and the ultimate question is whether we can characterize and delimit this larger pattern.

Our perspective in approaching these psychological problems will be clearer if we first examine the slow changes in skin resistance that are found when an external current is used (the Féré procedure). PGR appears as a relatively quick lowering of resistance with partial or complete recovery in a few seconds, up to 15 or more. These momentary changes can best be understood in relation to the slower changes which occupy some minutes. The slower changes are changes of state, while PGR is an act, or part of an act.

Slow changes in skin resistance. Besides its psychological interest, the level of skin resistance must be considered in evaluating the magnitude of PGR, which tends to be greater the higher the resistance from which it starts. Skin resistance is very low during profuse sweating, when polarization in the sweat gland cells is at a minimum. In most cases the resistance is lower in the palm than in the back of the hands, because sweat glands are more abundant in the palm (Syz & Kinder, 1928). The psychological interest begins to emerge when we examine the course of the skin resistance during an experimental session. When O has been harnessed into the recording apparatus and readings are started, his palmar resistance is usually found to be rather low, and it sinks slowly while he is waiting to see what E will do to him; if E gives him electric shocks or loud noises, PGR is elicited and the resistance level is lowered; when a rest period is announced the resistance tends upward only to go down again when announcement is made that the experiment will soon be resumed. See an especially full record by Darrow & Heath

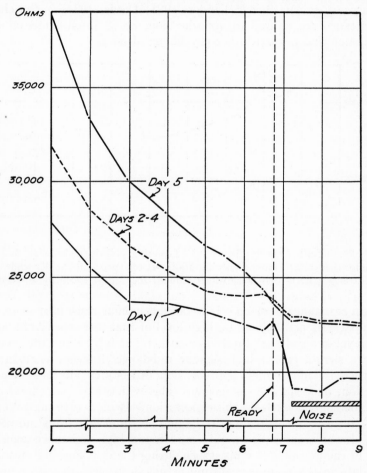

Fig. 73. (Data from Davis, 1934.) Change of resistance during an experimental session lasting 9 minutes. After 6¾ minutes of quiet, a ready signal was given and 15 sec. later came a loud, rough noise which continued to the end of the record. There were 8 adult Os, and 5 sessions on successive days. The curves for days 2–4, being much alike, are averaged in this graph. The increase of resistance, day by day, shows habituation to the experiment.

(1932, p. 62), and see also the resistance changes plotted in Figs. 73 and 74. If the experiment is repeated day after day, O's skin resistance is progressively greater at the start of each session and, while declining in the course of each session, it tends to remain higher than on the first day. As O becomes accustomed to the situation his sympathetic is less involved. The resistance is low during active mental work, and still lower during work under conditions of distraction (Davis, 1934).

The decline in skin resistance during a sitting cannot be attributed to any local effect of the current passed through the skin, for the decline occurs even in experiments in which the current is passed only for brief periods at the beginning and end of the session when the galvanometric readings are taken (Syz & Kinder, 1928; Davis, 1934). The changes in resistance are related to apprehension, relief, intense mental work, habituation and perhaps other psychological factors.

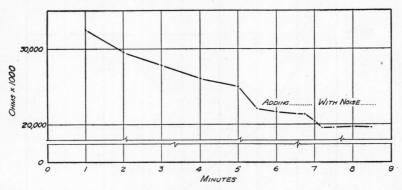

FIG. 74. (Data from Davis, 1934.) Lowering of skin resistance: first while waiting for the work to start, then while adding at top speed, and finally while adding with distraction by a loud noise which reduced the adding speed by 10 percent.

Skin resistance in sleep. If we accept palmar resistance as an index of sympathetic activity, and a high level of that resistance as indicating a low level of steady or "tonic" sympathetic activity—and the reverse—then we should expect high palmar resistance in sleep, since in quiet sleep there is a minimum of apprehension, expectancy, alertness, readiness for action, or feeling of emergency. The evidence of experiment shows fairly good agreement with this expectation. Waller (1919) and Wechsler (1925) measured the palmar resistance at intervals from morning to night, during waking hours only, and found high resistance soon after rising in the morning, low resistance during the day, and high resistance again late in the evening. During actual sleep, according to numerous observations (Farmer & Chambers, 1925; Richter, 1926; Freeman & Darrow, 1935), palmar resistance is high with a rapid fall on waking. Landis & Forbes (1933) were able to confirm this result only on the palm and not always there; and Jones (1930 a) on examining sole-leg resistance in eight infants under one year of age—infants from whom he obtained good PGR—could find no change in sleep. Confining our conclusions to the palm and to adults, we have fairly harmonious testimony to high resistance during sleep with a fall on waking. The results of Waller and Wechsler can mean that some subjects, at least, are relatively inert on first awakening and that their resistance does not immediately drop to the level found in the middle of the day, while toward the end of the day these subjects become relatively inert again.

Davis & Kantor (1935) experimented with hypnotized subjects. O was put under light hypnosis and it was suggested to him either that he would now sleep deeply or that he was unable to move his arms and legs. The latter suggestion tends to produce a more alert type of hypnosis than the former. Suggestion of deep sleep tended to raise the resistance while suggestion of the more alert condition tended to lower it. The authors conclude that "the lethargic condition of hypnosis resembles sleep in the behavior of skin resistance; the active hypnotic condition resembles the waking state."

PGR obtained by sensory stimuli. When difficulty is encountered in obtaining this response the reason is usually to be sought in inadequate electrical apparatus. With a good setup the response is practically certain on the application of a strong electric shock or a pistol shot. Other dependable stimuli are: pinching or pricking the skin, striking the face, unexpectedly touching the skin, tickling. Odors and flashes of light have been used with success. Stimuli of any modality, it appears, can elicit PGR, and they need not be very intense, though the more intense stimuli are more certain to give the response. It would be going much too far to assert that *every* stimulus that reaches the organism gives this response. Stimuli arrive every instant, but "spontaneous" responses, occurring in the absence of any stimulus applied by the experimenter, appear only sporadically during a sitting.

Not all stimuli are equally effective (Fig. 75). Effectiveness is gauged by the percent of trials in which a given stimulus gives the response, or (if the apparatus is adequate) by the amplitude of the galvanometric deflections. Another measure which one would expect to find correlated with amplitude is the quickness of the response; but Davis (1930) finds the latency of PGR about the same for strong and weak stimuli, though the amplitude is greater with strong stimuli. The latent period was longer for visual than for auditory stimuli, being 1.7 sec. for a sound and 2.1 sec. for a light—a result which recalls the longer reaction time to light than to sound (p. 324) and also the everyday fact that sounds, more than flashes of light, are apt to be startling.

PGR is readily obtained from the cat, the electrodes being applied to the pads of the feet; also from young dogs and from several other animals. Pinching or pricking the skin is an effective stimulus when a cat is awake. Even under anesthesia (Wang, Pan & Lu, 1929) a dependable PGR is found in the cat's forefoot when electrical stimulation is applied directly to a large sensory nerve from the hind limb.

Conditioned stimuli for PGR. Many experimenters have observed that the sensory stimulus need not actually be applied in order to give PGR. *Warning* that a shock is soon to be applied gives a fall of resistance, either abrupt or gradual, and the threat of repeating a shock, pinch or loud noise will sometimes give a larger response than the actual application of the stimulus. From these facts one would expect PGR to be readily conditioned and experiment shows that such is the case. A few repetitions of an innocuous click along with a strong shock established a conditioned PGR to the click, and extinction was

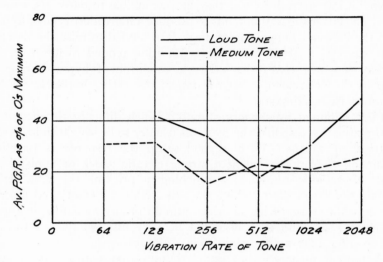

Fig. 75. (Data from Misbach, 1932.) Average PGR to tones of different pitch but of equal subjective loudness. Loudness equality was first worked out on one group of subjects, and the equated tones were given as stimuli to a second group. The tones were given in chance order, and each tone was turned on gradually so as to avoid startle. Both frequency and magnitude of PGR were greater for high and low tones than for those of middle pitch. The data points in this graph were obtained by multiplying frequency by average magnitude of responses obtained, each O's magnitude of response being first expressed as a percent of his maximum actual response. Smoothing would evidently give a relatively flat curve for the tones of medium intensity and a steeper dip toward the center for the loud tones. (The tone of 64 cycles could not be amplified sufficiently to bring it up to the upper loudness level.)

obtained by a few quick repetitions of the click alone (Darrow & Heath, 1932, p. 62). Similar results were obtained with a faint light as the conditioned stimulus (Switzer, 1933). In fact PGR is one of the most readily conditioned responses in human adults. In infants, 3–9 months old, unconditioned PGR was obtained with weak shocks, loud sound, removal of the bottle during nursing, or sudden loss of support; but visual stimuli were ineffective until after conditioning. A few combinations of a faint glow of light with a weak shock established conditioned PGR to the glow, and once established this conditioned response persisted for 7 weeks without further reinforcement (Jones, 1928, 1930 a, b).

PGR in response to meaningful situations. Less manageable than the simple sensory stimuli but quite as effective at times are phonograph records of stirring music, or of any music interesting to O, and motion pictures. Individual differences are revealed by use of films of travel and adventure. A mechanically minded man gives PGR at sight of machines in action, a child at sight of animals playing, an adolescent girl at fine clothes or in later adolescence at the picture of a handsome man, a youth at the picture of a pretty girl, and all adolescents respond to beautiful scenery. If O can be induced to talk freely of his personal troubles PGR often appears during the recital (Mall, 1936 b).

PGR in the free association test. Most sensory stimuli so far considered appear to work by virtue of suddenness, intensity or in some such primitive way. Words as stimuli must work through the meanings called up, since the response is not made indifferently to all words. Peterson & Jung (1907) conceived that PGR might make a good "complex indicator" (p. 364), along with slow verbal reaction; and their results satisfied them that such was the case. Whately Smith (1922) spoke 100 stimulus words as stimuli for free verbal response and concluded that PGR was a very good indicator of emotion. The ten words in his list which gave the largest average PGR from 50 educated subjects, and the ten which gave the smallest average, are as follows, with numbers indicating the relative magnitudes of the galvanometer deflections:

1.	Kiss	73	91.	Carrot	18
2.	Love	59	92.	Bury (berry)	18
3.	Marry	58	93.	Hunger	18
4.	Divorce	51	94.	White	18
5.	Name	49	95.	Glass	18
6.	Woman	40	96.	Give	17
7.	Wound	38	97.	Flower	16
8.	Dance	37	98.	Pond	15
9.	Afraid	37	99.	Pencil	15
10.	Proud	37	100.	Swim	14

Jones & Wechsler (1928) tried most of the above words on 35 students and obtained very nearly the same order of the stimulus words as regards the magnitude of the response.

Correlation of PGR with reported emotion. So far we have been studying PGR from the stimulus side; now we turn to the question, what the total activity may be of which PGR is a part. Is the total activity an emotion, necessarily? If so, the amplitude of PGR should correspond with the intensity of the emotion. Wells & Forbes (1911) gave words as stimuli and required O to estimate the intensity of the emotional response to each word, using a scale of four degrees, A, B, C, F, with A indicating the greatest intensity. The average magnitude of PGR was greatest for the A cases, next for the B cases, and so on, but with many exceptions. The magnitude of PGR could not serve as an index of the reportable emotionality of the single experience. Essentially the same result was obtained by Wechsler (1925) and by Syz (1926 b). The latter investigator used as stimuli words and phrases suggesting various life situations. The subjects, medical students, listened to the stimuli without making any verbal response at the time, but later, after the list of stimuli had been gone through twice, it was laid before them and they were asked to indicate which stimuli had aroused emotions. The table below gives a few of the stimuli, with the percent of Os who gave PGR to each stimulus and the percent who reported an emotion.

Stimulus word	Percent of Os giving a PGR on 1st hearing	on 2nd hearing	Percent reporting emotion
O's first name	84	68	36
O's last name	74	40	28
Kiss	72	40	34
Misspent youth	48	20	4
Unpaid bills	36	24	2
Cheating	28	22	10
Mother	26	12	30
Stupid	18	24	0

The decreased percent of galvanic responses on second hearing exemplifies the adaptation effect which will be noticed later. The discrepancies between the first and third columns are specially emphasized by the author. PGR occurred a vast number of times without any remembered and reported emotion, and on the other side a good many emotions were reported where there had been no PGR. No one hesitates to admit experiencing emotion on hearing the word "Mother," as one may on hearing "Unpaid bills". The conclusion drawn by Syz from these discrepancies is the opposite of what might perhaps be expected. Instead of condemning PGR as invalid because of its frequent conflict with verbal report he accepts PGR as the better index of emotion and condemns the verbal report as unreliable.

Dysinger (1931) obtained immediate instead of delayed reports from his Os. In the course of three sittings he presented 150 stimulus words intended to run the gamut from very pleasant ("darling," "vacation") through indifferent ("basket," "make") to very unpleasant ("suicide," "vomit"). After each stimulus word O reported its pleasant or unpleasant effect on him, using a five-point scale. Meanwhile a galvanometer was registering PGR. Pooling the results from the 13 Os (so far as comparable) we find PGR to be smallest, on the average, when the stimulus word was "indifferent," as seen from the mean PGR readings:

Effect of stimulus:	very pleasant	129
	pleasant	98
	indifferent	79
	unpleasant	101
	very unpleasant	147

(The SD_M for these values is about 6; the unit is arbitrary.) The increased PGR with either pleasantness or unpleasantness, shown here, is particularly interesting.

What kind of emotion is reported with PGR? In the experiments of Bayley (1928) and Patterson (1930), the reports indicated kind as well as intensity of emotion. Bayley's stimuli, intended mostly to arouse fear, included loud noises (whistle, pistol), holding a lighted match till it burned the fingers, electric shock received on making error in arithmetic example, preparation for taking drop of blood from finger, reading of gruesome story, oral quiz on laboratory apparatus, subsequent assurance that the quiz was not serious, piece of chocolate candy, statement that the experiment was "all over." Patterson sought to awaken surprise rather than fear by giving O a jar to hold which contained mercury, by showing O his own face in a mirror when he was expecting to see a skull, by reading a ghost story to O and inserting a sentence from a mathematical book, by dropping a pile of scrap tin in the midst of soft music. When the cases were sorted according to reported *intensity* of the emotion aroused, there was a fair positive correlation, ranging from .53 to .88, between this intensity and the magnitude of PGR (Patterson). When the cases were sorted according to *kind* of emotion, the two studies agree in showing the largest average PGR for startle, medium for apprehensive expectancy, small for relief and for indifference. One O who was informed during the experiment of his election to an honor society reported "joy" and gave an extremely large PGR.

Another experiment combining PGR with immediate verbal report is that of Abel (1930) in which O was given a variety of problems to solve and was asked to report the "attitude" or "state of his functioning organism." The reports were sorted into two main classes: reports of "predicament" or sense of encountering difficulty; and reports of "ease" or smooth progress toward the solution of the problem. The frequency of PGR was determined for these two classes and was found to be:

> 76 percent for "predicament"
> 16   "   "   "ease"

The author's conclusion is that PGR is an index not so much of feeling or emotion as of an attitude of the organism directed toward *overcoming difficulty*. This organic attitude is often experienced as a "predicament."

As pointed out by Landis & Hunt (1935) PGR occurs in such a variety of mental states that a fallacious case can be made out for its connection with any one state by employing only stimuli suited to produce that state. These authors consequently presented varied stimuli intended to arouse fear, amusement, sex emotion, pleasantness and unpleasantness, and other states. O was required after each response "to give a verbal description of what happened in your consciousness during the period of stimulation." When the galvanic responses were sorted according to the mental state reported by the Os, the average PGR in ohms (account being taken of both frequency and magnitude of PGR) came out as follows:

Subjective state reported	Mean PGR
Tension	1248 ohms
Startle, surprise, fear	846
Confusion	740
Amusement	514
Expectancy	401
Inhibition, uncertainty	319
Unpleasantness	260
Effort	169
Pleasantness	105

The authors conclude that PGR, while not attached specifically to any one conscious state, is "more nearly related to startle or to tension than to anything else."

PGR during mental work. PGR is not limited to states which we ordinarily regard as emotional. The slow decline of skin resistance, as well as the brief deflections which we call PGR, occurs in adding, learning nonsense syllables or solving problems. Prideaux (1920) points out that PGR during mental work need not result from the mere intellectual labor, since as he says, "Very often a strong affect is produced by the surprise at the question or by the embarrassment and possible annoyance that the solution of the problem may be incorrect." Wechsler (1925) makes a similar comment: O "feels he is being tested, that by the correctness of his answer he will make a favorable or unfavorable impression." He gave problems of the type, $7 + 3 + 6 \times 5 - 6 \ldots$, and found PGR largest at the start and finish, i.e., at the moments when the problem was attacked and when the answer was stated, rather than during the arithmetical work.

A special study of PGR in mental arithmetic was made by Sears (1933) with 24 college women as subjects. He gave: (1) easy examples to be done without any time limit or demand for speed; (2) easy examples to be done rapidly; (3) more difficult examples. When a whole list of 20 examples was easy and done at leisure, PGR showed a gradual decline. When the first 10 examples were easy and the second 10 difficult, there was an abrupt increase of PGR at the onset of the difficult examples. When all the examples were easy and the first 10 done at leisure and the last 10 with a time limit, there was a sudden increase of PGR with the beginning of effort for speed. In short there was a gradual decrease of PGR with continuance of the same kind of work, but an abrupt increase in PGR on shifting to more speedy or difficult work, and also an abrupt decrease on shifting from more rapid or difficult to more comfortable work.

In the work of Bartlett (1927) we find illustrations of the minute analysis necessary in order to identify the precise stimulus that gives PGR during continued mental activity. In one experiment O counted "one, two, three . . ." as rapidly as possible, either silently or aloud. Counting aloud gave much larger deflections. But as merely talking aloud gave no deflections it was not the speech movement that aroused PGR. Careful observation showed that in counting aloud O stumbled in his speech, and Bartlett attributes the deflections to this stumbling, accompanied as it probably was by an "awareness of possible failure."

PGR in combination with bodily movements. One very sure way to obtain the galvanometric deflection from a subject is to ask him to draw a deep breath or to cough. PGR does not occur with ordinary quiet breathing, but does occur regularly with deep breathing. Besides the cough, other respiratory movements in which it occurs includes the sneeze, sigh, laugh, clearing the throat, and the yawn. Claparède (1924) shows that yawning is associated with stretching. Though the experiment may not have been tried, there is no doubt that PGR would accompany the stretching movement. Yawning and stretching, Claparède urges, are preparatory movements with a wakening effect. Straining is another movement accompanied by PGR. It occurs in other vigorous muscular movements (Starch, 1910 b), as well as in quick or accurate movements such as those of aiming or the reaction time experiment. One may generalize from these observations that PGR accompanies energetic or attentive muscular movement and also preparation for such movement.

Negative adaptation of PGR. We have already spoken of a habituation effect showing as a rise of the skin resistance level from day to day in a continued experiment (p. 285). This rising level of resistance means a decline in the activity level of the sweat glands and of the sympathetic division of the autonomic. What we are here calling negative adaptation of PGR is the same fact, probably: with repetition of the stimulus or of the total situation the response decreases in magnitude and disappears. Farmer & Chambers (1925) found that Os who were used day after day in an intensive experiment came finally to give no PGR even to strong stimuli; but a restful week-end in the country restored them to condition and PGR reappeared. Davis (1930), measuring the magnitude of PGR quite accurately, found a decrease on repetition of the stimulus (the flash of a neon light) at one-minute intervals. The average reaction for 15 Os was as follows:

First flash	1099	ohms decrease of resistance			
Second flash	268	"	"	"	"
Third flash	190	"	"	"	"

Seward & Seward (1934) using 12 adults as Os, applied in each daily session a series of five strong electric shocks at one-minute intervals, and recorded skin resistance and PGR, respiratory changes, and general bodily movement. They wished to discover how much adaptation and habituation occurred within the daily session and from day to day. Each day O gave a subjective rating of the intensity and unpleasantness of the shock, and adaptation appeared in these ratings, since the shocks became less unpleasant and seemed less intense as the long experiment advanced, anxiety and apprehension decreased and the shocks were taken less as disturbances and more as localized, objective stimuli. This adaptation appeared also in the records of bodily movement, respiration and PGR. Taking the record for the first day as 100, we have for sample days throughout the experiment:

Day No.	1	8	15	22	29
Body movement	100	91	47	19	11
Respiration	100	84	66	26	14
PGR	100	82	81	81	75

We see that PGR decreased in amplitude from week to week, but much less than the muscular response to the shock. Within the single sitting, also, there was progressive adaptation as seen in the following average relative values.

Shock No.	1	2	3	4	5
Body movement	100	64	55	50	50
Respiration	100	77	70	64	60
PGR	100	78	71	69	69

Here again there is less adaptation in PGR than in the muscular responses to the shock.

In the association test also, PGR decreases on repetition of the same list of words (p. 290), and it tends to decrease even within the word list, especially for the more neutral words, those later in the list giving smaller deflections than similar words early in the list (Jones & Wechsler, 1928). This negative adaptation cannot be a fatigue of the sweat glands, for a shift to a radically different stimulus will restore PGR to full force (Sears, 1933). The receptors may of course become negatively adapted to a continued stimulus (p. 467) but the adaptation of PGR is probably central rather than peripheral.

Psychological significance of PGR. From the time of Féré and Tarchanoff it has been clear that PGR is often associated with emotion. Psychologists hoped it might serve as a convenient index of emotion. Peterson & Jung (1907) believed it to be an index, not entirely of conscious emotion but often of an unconscious complex, the stirring of which by a stimulus word would elicit the physiological expression of emotion. Aveling (1926) held, on the basis of his results, that PGR was a better index of conation, including effort and striving, than it was of feeling and emotion. Landis (1930) reviewing these and other suggestions came to the conclusion that PGR was a phenomenon of great generality, not associated specifically with any mental state, and consequently of little value as an index of any psychological process. In further work Landis

& Hunt (1930) reached a somewhat less skeptical conclusion. It seemed possible to them "to set up tension not as an exclusive correlate but as that conscious experience best correlating with the galvanic skin response." They recognized that PGR is primarily an index of sympathetic activity, and showed that from this point of view "the outstanding fact is the general participation of the sympathetic system in the behavioral picture," particularly in emotional behavior and more particularly in startled or tense behavior. It is "a fairly adequate indicator of 'change of direction of mental activity' but in no sense is it an adequate or direct measure of these changes."

We should include in our theory the relatively slow changes in resistance level which are perhaps easier to interpret than the quick changes which constitute PGR. Low palm resistance indicates a relatively high level of sympathetic activity. Using this index we saw that the level of sympathetic activity rose while O was waiting for something to happen; that it rose higher when something began to happen, as a series of strong stimuli or the performance of a mental task; and that it rose still higher when the difficulty of the task increased. On the other hand, sympathetic activity declined when O was resting quietly in the assurance that all was over. There was pretty good evidence of high palmar resistance, i.e., a low level of sympathetic activity, during sleep and inertness. We wish, if possible, to derive from these facts a general statement of the behavior situation in which the level of sympathetic activity is high or low. A generalization suggested for the reader's consideration is the following: sympathetic activity is high during actual muscular activity and during the condition of readiness for such activity; and it is high also during strenuous "mental" activity or readiness for such activity; but sympathetic activity is low in inactivity, rest and unreadiness for action. As Thouless (1925) has put it: "The condition of low resistance is apparently a condition of preparedness to react to a stimulus."

In attempting to fit PGR into this theoretical framework, we should remember the PGR elicited in an anesthetised cat (p. 287). In this case and others which the physiologists have unearthed, PGR is part of a subcortical, reflex sympathetic activity. When we get PGR as a conditioned response or as a response to a ready signal, to a verbal stimulus, or to any situation which acts by its meaning rather than by its mere sensory magnitude, we have evidently to do with sympathetic activity aroused by the cortex, and it is this type in which we are especially interested. What type of cortically controlled behavior is accompanied by PGR?

The experimenters agree that startle is especially associated with strong PGR, and that apprehensive expectancy is also a common condition under which considerable magnitudes of PGR are found. The situation giving rise to startle and apprehension can well be called an emergency (Sears, 1933). The response can be characterised as a shift from unpreparedness toward preparedness (Bartlett, 1927), or as a mobilization for action (Darrow, 1936). Primitive emergencies demand mobilization of muscular energies. In the subtler emergencies of mental work or of civilized social contacts the organism may derive no advantage from this primitive mobilization, but it continues to mobilize whenever any quick readjustment is necessary. PGR in mental work is like the muscular straining that accompanies mental effort; both are carried over from the more primitive to the more subtle situations.

So far our interpretation conforms very nicely to the view of Cannon (1915) as to the emergency function of the sympathetic. The emergencies of the laboratory are rather slight but then the sympathetic reaction indicated by PGR may also be relatively a small affair. Can we make this conception square with the fact occasionally noted, of moderate or even strong PGR in response to a joyful situation? We have been accustomed to think of sympathetic activity as going with fear and anger, with situations of danger and frustration. If we think back to primitive conditions of life, however, we easily see that there are at least three types of emergencies, calling for quick, energetic muscular activity.

1. Danger, calling for escape or avoidance.
2. Frustration, calling for fighting and attack.
3. The presence of prey, calling for quick seizure.

In primitive conditions the prey will escape unless it is seized promptly, or some rival may capture it. From the way in which the young child grabs at a beautiful new toy or other specially desirable object, one can readily imagine, though the experiment seems not to have been tried, that PGR would occur in this situation.

We have been speaking throughout in behavior terms. If we wish to catch the moment of experience at which PGR is initiated (some second or two before it appears) we need very sharp introspection. It will not be enough to report the experience of some seconds as pleasant or unpleasant, joyful, excited and so on. We must attempt to note an exact second of experience. Those who have most seriously attempted such introspective studies (Bartlett, 1927; Abel, 1930; Patterson, 1930) characterise this moment of experience as showing a sense of check or predicament, the shock of encountering something for which one is not prepared, a brief maladjustment, usually with quick recovery.

In the association test when a stimulus word touches upon a complex and gives PGR, we need not suppose that some unconscious emotion is what gives PGR; it is probably the conscious sense of touching on a dangerous topic.

PGR is not subject to voluntary control. Gregor (1927) reports an experiment in which O attempted to suppress PGR or tried to exaggerate it, but without success in either case. There is some evidence of an inverse correlation between the amount of PGR and the amount of overt emotional reaction. Jones (1930), working with young children, found that a very weak electric current applied to the skin produced an inhibition of arm and leg movement, but frequently gave a marked PGR. Somewhat stronger stimuli produced crying or thrashing around, with small or no PGR. Landis (1932 b), recording PGR from older children who were engaged in a difficult motor task (pursuitmeter), obtained few PGR from those of his subjects who' cried or showed fear or anger overtly. With adult subjects Prideaux (1921) got little PGR when a stimulus was so exciting as to arouse much muscular movement, but when movement was suppressed there was apt to be a large galvanic response. Seward & Seward (1934) however, found no clean-cut inverse correlation between the two measures of response to an electric shock. Here as at many other points in this field there is abundant room for further investigation.

CHAPTER XIV

REACTION TIME

T HE FREQUENT reference in psychology to the time or speed of a performance is not due to over-emphasis on the value of rapid work. Time as a dimension of every mental or behavioral process lends itself to measurement, and can be used as an indicator of the complexity of the performance or of the subject's readiness to perform. A technical difficulty at once suggests itself. "The speed of thought," we say; but as soon as we set about measuring the time occupied by a thought we find that the beginning and end of any measurable time must be external events. We may be able in the future to use "brain waves" as indicators of the beginning and end of a mental process, and even now muscle currents enable us to penetrate the organism a little way with our timing apparatus; but in general it has seemed necessary to let the timed process start with a sensory stimulus and terminate in a muscular response.

A typical experiment. O is seated at a table on which is a telegraph key. At the fore-signal "Ready" he closes the key with his finger and is prepared to raise the finger instantly on receiving a certain stimulus. Apparatus is present for recording the time between the application of the stimulus and the opening of the telegraph key by O's reaction. This time usually lies between 100 and 200 ms (where 1 ms = 1 millisecond = 1/1000 sec.; also written 1σ and read "one sigma"). The task here is about the simplest possible. It can be complicated in various ways.

Under the head of method in reaction time ("RT") work we shall need to say something of timing apparatus, but first we will consider the general logic of the experiment or, in other words, the nature of the tasks that can fruitfully be assigned and the kinds of problems that can be attacked in an experiment of this character.

THE REACTION TIME METHOD IN THE LIGHT OF ITS HISTORY

The RT experiment has a long and interesting history. A cynic might say that its interest was altogether historical, but we shall see that it is still a live experiment for which new uses are constantly being found. The history makes an instructive study in psychological method. Faulty procedures have been tried and found unworkable, problems hopefully attacked have been found insoluble by use of the reaction time, and the reasons for these failures, as well as for the successes, are really quite important contributions to the science of psychology.

Reaction time as a means of measuring the speed of nerve conduction.
The RT experiment was invented about 1850 by no less a person than
Helmholtz, one of the discoverers of the law of conservation of energy,
the inventor of the ophthalmoscope, and best known to psychologists
for his great works on the senses of sight and hearing. As a young
physiologist Helmholtz undertook to find out whether electrical methods
of measuring very short time intervals would not prove adequate to
measure the speed of nerve conduction, which the authorities of the
day, including his own master, Johannes Müller, believed much too
rapid to be measured. Helmholtz worked first on a motor nerve of the
frog. He stimulated the nerve as far as possible from its muscle and
again as close to the muscle as possible and determined in each case the
latency of the muscular response, i.e., the time interval between the
stimulus and the beginning of the muscular contraction. This interval
was a little greater when the nerve was stimulated at a distance from the
muscle, and the time difference corresponded to a speed of transmission
along the nerve of about 26 meters per sec., on the average of several
experiments.

Desirous of obtaining the figure for human nerves, Helmholtz re-
sorted to the following device: "A slight electric shock is given to a man
at a certain portion of the skin, and he is directed, the moment he feels
the shock, to make a certain motion as quickly as he possibly can, with
the hands or with the teeth." Keeping the reacting movement constant
he applied the stimulus to different parts of the skin, expecting to find
the RT longer, the further from the brain the point of stimulation
and the longer, therefore, the length of sensory nerve traversed. On
the whole his expectation was realized and he was able to compute an
average speed of about 60 meters per sec. for human nerves. But the
results were so variable that he had little confidence in this figure and
later abandoned it. (It was not so far from the now accepted value of
66–69 meters per sec., Münnich, 1915.)

Helmholtz's report of his work on nerve transmission (1850, 1852),
though sometimes cited as the original reference on reaction time, deals
wholly with the experiments on frog nerves. Apparently the only report
he made of his RT study was a paragraph or two in a popular lecture
published as a pamphlet (1850 a) and soon translated into English
(1853). He refers to it in a later study (1867) of human nerve transmission by a different method. Even though rather meagerly published,
Helmholtz's RT experiment was soon widely known and quickly followed
up by other investigators.

Helmholtz's conclusion that the RT method is unreliable as a
means of determining the speed of nerve conduction was confirmed by
later experiments, as by Cattell & Dolley (1895 c). They eliminated
some of the variability by using very well trained Os, and still they
found that the RT might be longer when the stimulus was applied at
the elbow than when applied at the wrist—the shorter nerve path giving

the longer RT. There were two causes for this anomaly. One part of the skin was more sensitive than another, and where the stimulus was more strongly felt it gave the quicker reaction. And even when the sensory effect of two stimuli was equalized, the RT was shorter where the afferent and efferent nerves were (presumably) more closely connected in the nerve centers, as from skin to muscles of the same limb.

The failure of the RT experiment to furnish a measure of nerve conduction is instructive because it shows that the bulk of the time required for even so simple a response is consumed in the nerve centers and that this central process must be complex and variable. It is no mere redirection of a nerve impulse from the sensory to the motor nerve.

The astronomer's contribution—the personal equation. This story has been well told by Sanford (1888–89) and in some of its later developments by Bowie (1913). Astronomers in seeking to build ever greater precision into their instruments were warned by certain curious incidents that the limiting factor was the uncertainty of the human observer. One standard observation in which great precision is desirable is that of timing the transit of a star across the meridian of a given observatory. The telescope is pointed straight north or south (at the necessary elevation); the star enters the field and passes over a grid of vertical hair lines, the middle line being the exact meridian. At what exact time does the star pass this middle line?

An old standard procedure is the "eye and ear method." The observer first reads the time to the second from his clock and counts additional seconds by listening to the strokes of the pendulum. He notes the exact position of the star at the stroke just before and at the stroke just after it crosses the meridian. From these two positions he computes the time of transit to the tenth of a second.

The first indication of unreliability in this method came in 1795 when Maskelyne, head of the Greenwich observatory, discharged an otherwise capable assistant because of a habit of recording all transits about half a second too late. The only way the chief had of estimating the error of his assistant was by comparison with his own observations which he naturally assumed to be correct. A note of these facts in the Greenwich observatory report caught the attention of the German astronomer, Bessel, some decades later, and led him to test astronomers against each other, with the result that no two agreed precisely on the time of a given transit. Usually the difference between two skilled observers was well under a second. It seemed at first to be a constant difference between any two specified individuals, so that their observations could be harmonized by use of a constant correction or "personal equation," such as Jones − Smith = 0.35 sec. Further investigation showed that it was by no means constant. It varied with the magnitude of the star and with its rate of movement across the telescope field, and its constancy as between two observers was only temporary.

The personal equation stated the difference between two observers, not the absolute error of either one. By use of apparatus for presenting an artificial star and recording objectively the true time of its transit, the error of the single observation was later measured and found to be sometimes positive and sometimes negative. Some observers tended to get the moment of transit too late, others too soon. This was the germ of Wundt's "complication experiment" (1862, 1894); its resemblance to the RT experiment is not very close.

In the hope of making their transit data more precise the astronomers developed the "chronographic method." The strokes of the pendulum are automatically recorded on a moving drum and the observer signals the passage of the star across the meridian by pressing a telegraph key and so leaving a record on the drum. Since the observer sees the star approaching the line he can anticipate, and the beginner tries to make his signal synchronize with the transit; but he is instructed to "wait until the instant when the star is apparently bisected by the line and then press the key as soon as possible thereafter," since the latter procedure is found more regular. In tests with artificial stars, the transit is sometimes signalled as much as 70 ms too early, and sometimes as much as 250 ms too late. Evidently the observer who signals the transit before it occurs, or even who signals it exactly when it occurs, is not reacting to the transit as a stimulus; his RT could not be zero or a negative quantity. Mitchel (1858), a pioneer American astronomer (also a general in the Civil War), constructed apparatus for producing artificial transits which could also deliver *momentary* stimuli, visual or auditory, and thus obtained true RTs ranging from 137 to 223 ms. The chronometric method of signaling a transit, as well as the eye and ear method, has been developed into a psychological experiment with interesting results[1] (Alechsieff, 1900; Günther, 1911; Hammer, 1914).

The astronomers have found a still better method: the telescope is provided with a movable vertical hair line which the observer brings into coincidence with the star and keeps on the star while it passes across the field. The time when this moving hair line crosses the meridian is automatically recorded. Since the star moves steadily, the observer can keep the hair line on it with very little error. The method resembles the "pursuitmeter" experiment in which however the "star" or target is given an irregular motion (Miles, 1921).

A very definite contribution to the study of reaction time was made by a Swiss astronomer, Hirsch (1861–1864), in collaboration with his engineering colleague, Hipp. The latter had just invented the famous Hipp chronoscope, for many years the standard apparatus for measuring RT. With this instrument Hirsch measured what he called the "physio-

---

[1] By use of suitable catch tests (stopping or extinguishing the "star" before it reaches the line), O can be trained either to react or to synchronize with fair consistency (SD of single trials, 30 to 45 ms). When O is synchronizing he will certainly be "caught" if the star goes out much less than 200 ms before it is due to cross the line. He cannot halt in less than that time which is about the same as the RT of a positive movement to a visual stimulus.

logical time" of sight, hearing and touch and obtained values which have remained fairly standard averages:

RT to visual stimulus	200 ms
RT to auditory stimulus	150 ms
RT to electric shock on hand	140 ms

Why should the visual reaction take longer than the others? Presumably because of some difference in the senses. The RT experiment provided a means of investigating the latency of the different receptors and has been used extensively for this purpose. Some of the results will be discussed later.

Timing mental processes. Credit for extending the scope of the RT experiment to the study of mental or central processes belongs to Donders (1868), a Dutch physiologist well known for his contributions to the physiology of the eye. It seemed to him that each mental act such as sensation, discrimination, volition and choice probably occupied a certain time, like the time of the heart beat or of a muscle twitch. How could the "physiological time" of these central processes be determined? Perhaps by starting with the simple reaction of Helmholtz and Hirsch and advancing progressively to more complex reactions. Complicate the simple reaction by the "insertion" of additional processes. "If I found out how much the physiological time was thus lengthened, the duration of the inserted act, I judge, would thus become known."

An experiment involving discrimination and choice was conducted by applying an electric stimulus to either foot and demanding a reaction by the hand on the same side as the stimulus. Each hand had its own reaction key, and O was ready to react with either hand, but the stimulus had to be identified before the correct hand could be selected. The simple reaction Donders called the *a-reaction*, and this reaction requiring discrimination and choice he called the *b-reaction*. The b-reaction in the experiment described took 66 ms longer than the a-reaction, and Donders concluded that the 66 ms were consumed in the "inserted" processes of discrimination and choice. He next sought to separate these two processes and believed he could eliminate "choice" by giving two or more stimuli to be distinguished while having only one motor response. This type he called the *c-reaction*. Of the two or more stimuli, given in random order, O is to respond only to one, and always with the same movement. It is like the simple reaction except that O has to disregard certain stimuli which may be much like the prescribed positive stimulus. He must discriminate between the stimuli but does not go through the process of selecting the right movement. So Donders reasoned.

In an experiment to try out the method, Donders used speech sounds as stimuli. E pronounced one of the five syllables, "Ka, Ke, Ki, Ko, Ku," under the following conditions:

a-reaction: the stimulus was always "Ki," and the response also was always to be "Ki."

b-reaction: the stimulus was any one of the five syllables, and O was to respond with the same syllable.

c-reaction: the stimulus was, again, any one of the five syllables, but O was to respond only to "Ki," using this syllable as his response.

The speech vibrations were recorded on a moving drum. The average RTs were as follows:

$$a = 197 \text{ ms}$$
$$b = 285 \text{ ms}$$
$$c = 243 \text{ ms}$$

By subtraction, then,

$c - a = 46$ ms, the time occupied by sensory discrimination.

$b - c = 42$ ms, the time occupied by choice or motor selection.

Apart from the reliability of these values which is probably low because of the variability to be expected in the speed of mental processes, the validity of the whole procedure rests on two assumptions:

1. The c-reaction includes no act of choice or motor selection.

2. In a complex reaction, certain additional acts are *inserted* into the simple reaction and their time can be found by *subtraction* of the simple RT from a complex RT, or of a less complex from a more complex RT.

The later history of the method is concerned to quite an extent with the validity of these two assumptions of Donders.

Early work in Wundt's laboratory—the d-reaction. The physiologists and astronomers who did the first RT work were precursors of experimental psychology. Wundt, starting as a physiologist, came as early as 1860 to conceive of the possibility of a physiological psychology, as he called it. It could start with work already accomplished by the physiologists on the senses, muscular movement and the nervous system, and develop their methods for use with mental processes. Introspection would remain essential in psychology, but must be supplemented by experiment in order to unravel the complex phenomena revealed by introspection. One of the most promising leads was by way of time measurement. At first (1862, 1863) Wundt pinned his hopes to the already mentioned complication experiment which he adapted from the personal equation of the astronomers; but a little later (1874) he concluded that the work of Donders afforded the better lead.

It seemed to Wundt, however, that Donders had erred in assuming no motor or choice element in the c-reaction. While in the b-reaction the choice is between one movement and another, in the c-reaction there is a choice between movement and no movement. Wundt devised a d-reaction, intended to differ from the simple reaction by the insertion of discrimination only. It could be called a cognitive reaction. There were two or more stimuli, and only one motor response which was to be made in every case but not until the stimulus had been identified. As soon as O knew which stimulus he had received he was to signal the fact by closing (or opening) the telegraph key. Wundt's conception was that in the simple reaction O signaled as soon as he became aware of a stimulus, while in the d-reaction he signaled when he recognized or identified the stimulus. Just so, the astronomical observer was supposed to *signal* when he saw the star right on the meridian line. It seems a straightforward and obvious conception but contains a serious flaw, as we shall see.

In 1879 Wundt opened at Leipzig the first active psychological laboratory and in his program of research the timing of mental processes had a prominent place (1880, 1883). The plan was to use the simple reaction as a base line and to complicate the process a step at a time, so obtaining the time occupied by various mental processes.

Even the simple reaction, as Wundt conceived it, included a sequence of three processes: (1) entrance of the sensory impression into the field of consciousness, (2) entrance into the focus of attention, and (3) the voluntary release of the signaling movement. He saw no possible way of timing these three processes separately.

The next step above the simple reaction was the d-reaction; and the difference d − a would give the time occupied in discrimination or cognition. The Donders b-reaction included discrimination and choice, and b − d would give choice time. Association time could be found by requiring O to signal "at the moment when an idea reproduced by association made its appearance in consciousness." Subtracting from the associative RT that of the d-reaction would give the time occupied by the process of association.

The prospect opening before the new laboratory was very hopeful, but everything depended on the d-reaction. The first two studies in the series were encouraging. Friedrich (1883) found cognition time to increase with the complexity of the stimulus, and Trautscholdt (1883) found association times running about 700–900 ms. But the next investigator, Tischer (1883), began to find difficulties. Cognition time (d − a) was sometimes suspiciously short, almost zero. Two well trained Os found themselves unable to make the d-reaction anything different from the simple reaction. Kraepelin (1883, 1892), later famous as a psychiatrist, was one of the early workers in Wundt's laboratory, and used the RT technique in a study of drug effects. The simple reaction and the b-reaction gave him trustworthy results, but the d-reaction could not be kept distinct from the simple reaction, especially under the influence of alcohol or some other drug. Cattell (1886, 1887, 1888) gave up trying to use the d-reaction because he either slid into the simple reaction or else hung back excessively. Berger (1886) put his finger on the source of trouble. The motor response, in the d-reaction, is not dependent on the identification of the stimulus, for the response is the same for all stimuli. In the b-reaction each stimulus calls for a different motor response; and in the c-reaction one stimulus calls for a movement and the others for no movement; in both these forms the reaction will often be false unless held back until the stimulus is identified. There is no such check on the d-reaction. As Berger said, "Certainty that discrimination has actually taken place at the time when the re-action movement is released is possible only if the movement depends on the discrimination." For there is nothing to prevent two cerebral processes from occurring simultaneously. Two responses, one perceptual and one motor, may take their start simultaneously from the same stimulus. If the motor response is not made to depend on the perception, it can start at once, as in the simple reaction. The brain is not a one-track road.

Berger's critique, along with the difficulties encountered by the other investigators, pretty well disposed of the d-reaction, though Wundt himself was not wholly convinced. They disposed of the "signaling" conception of the RT experiment. Of course one can signal the time of an occurrence, if allowed some latitude. The school child can raise his hand "as soon as" he sees the answer to a question. But can he signal the instant of the occurrence with a precision of $\frac{1}{10}$ of a second, as is expected in RT work? The subject in a RT experiment does not first see and then signal but performs a much more closely integrated act.[1]

The simple reaction conceived as a "prepared reflex." We have passed over the work of Exner (1873, 1874), a Vienna physiologist who was the first to use the term, "reaction time," and who from his intro-spections was led to a very different view of the reaction process from that of Wundt and others. He says, "Every one who performs this experiment (i.e., serves as subject) for the first time is struck by the little control he has of his movements when the task is to execute them as quickly as possible. . . . While one is awaiting the stimulus with tense attention one feels an indescribable something going on in his sensorium (brain), which prepares for the quickest possible reaction. . . . If the sensorium is in this state, the reaction is involuntary, i.e., no new will impulse is needed after the entrance of the stimulus in order that the reaction shall follow." The only voluntary act is the preparation. The preparation amounts to a set of the nervous system, a "Bahnung" or facilitation of a particular sensorimotor response. In the simple reaction the way is prepared in advance so that the process runs straight through to its predetermined goal.

[1] The d-reaction comes to life at intervals. It was scotched again by Fernberger (1934) in connection with an experiment in lifted weights. For measuring the time required to reach a judgment, O was asked to squeeze a bulb simultaneously with his verbal report, the hand movement being the same whether the judgment was "heavier," "lighter" or "equal." Since the hand movement did not depend on the judgment, there was nothing to insure cognitive as against simple reactions; and it was found that the Os "were anticipating the judgment by pressing the bulb too soon and before the judgment had been completely formulated." Ac-cordingly the hand squeeze was eliminated and a voice key used to register O's verbal responses —and the RT went up abruptly from 260 to 460 ms.

Cattell in Wundt's laboratory reached the same conclusion. He could detect very little perception or will during the simple reaction, which he regarded as a prepared reflex. This view, with Berger's rejection of the d-reaction, threatened to undermine Wundt's whole program of research on the time of mental processes. But almost immediately there emerged from the Leipzig laboratory a discovery which seemed to put new life into the undertaking.

Sensorial and muscular reactions. Ludwig Lange (1888) conceived that the simple reaction would be a different process, "sensorial" or "muscular," according as expectant attention was directed toward the stimulus to be received or toward the movement to be made. His instructions for the muscular reaction were, "not to think at all of the coming sense impression, but to prepare as vividly as possible the innervation of the movement to be made"; and for the sensorial reaction, "to avoid altogether all preparatory innervation of the movement, but to direct the whole preparatory tension towards the expected sense impression, with the intention, however, of letting the motor impulse follow immediately on the apprehension of the stimulus, without any unnecessary delay." The natural attitude lay somewhere between these extremes. By practice some Os could acquire either of the extreme attitudes, but more readily the muscular. In practicing for the sensorial attitude, O passed through a stage of very slow reactions, which were not really "simple" reactions. Success in the sensorial reaction required the simultaneous avoidance of two errors: the error of preparatory muscular tension and the error of lingering over the stimulus, once it had arrived. Premature and false reactions did not occur with the sensorial attitude, but were frequent with the extreme muscular attitude. The muscular attitude was felt as a state of mild muscular tension and the reaction often involved other muscles besides those of the reacting hand. The sensorial attitude was completely free from sensations of muscular tension.

Three Os after training in the two types of reaction gave the following average values for RT to sound:

	Muscular reaction	*Sensorial reaction*
Subject N. L.	125	223
Subject L. L.	123	230
Subject B.	137	224

Thus the sensorial RT was about 100 ms longer than the muscular.

Lange regarded the muscular reaction as a prepared reflex, but the sensorial reaction conformed to Wundt's analysis and included processes of perception and will. Wundt accepted the distinction with great satisfaction because it harmonized the views of experienced workers like Exner and Cattell with his own theory and introspection. Exner and Cattell must react in the muscular way, he himself in the sensorial way. Wundt decided that the sensorial attitude gave a "complete reaction" while the muscular attitude gave an abridged or short-circuited reaction. Only the complete reaction could serve as the base line for timing the additional processes of cognition, choice and association.

Difficulties with the sensorial reaction. The way seemed open for a new attack on the time of mental processes, but now everything depended on the stability of the sensorial reaction. Experience in the Leipzig laboratory soon showed a lack of stability which unfitted this type of reaction for precise measurements. Only a minority of the Os available in the laboratory could follow the instructions and give satisfactory results (Titchener, 1893). Extreme variability of the sensorial RT pointed to an inconstancy of O's attitude (Dwelshauvers, 1891; Alechsieff, 1900). There seemed to be two sensorial attitudes: one in which O was set to react just as soon as he got the stimulus, and one in which he was set to cognize the stimulus before reacting (Martius, 1891). As an experimental series progressed, O tended more and more toward the muscular reaction—a fact which showed the inconsistency of two laboratory requirements: to use the sensorial reaction, and to use only well-practiced Os (Külpe, 1891, 1892). This last investigator also pointed out that *pure* sensorial and muscular reactions were scarcely possible, since, after all, O is ready for both stimulus and response. "The general prescription, to respond to a defined stimulus by a defined movement, accompanies all reactions like a faint ground melody and is intimately bound up with the whole adjustment of the subject." The natural, relatively neutral attitude, conforming best with the requirements of a unified performance, might well be the best for regular results.

From outside the Leipzig laboratory, especially from the newly established American laboratories, came further questionings regarding the two types of reaction. Cattell (1893) who had started laboratories at the University of Pennsylvania and later at Columbia University, tried out the sensorial and muscular reactions on three trained Os, with results as follows when the stimulus was an electric shock:

	Muscular reaction	*Sensorial*
Subject C.	143	143
Subject J.	119	122
Subject D.	281	202

For the two quicker Os the direction of attention made no difference in the RT. Their reactions, whether sensorial or muscular, were apparently automatic and of the "prepared reflex" type. The third O's RT was *lengthened* by attention to the movement—just as, in ordinary life, the smooth, automatic act of going down stairs is disturbed by attention to one's legs. Cattell doubted altogether the general validity of Lange's quantitative results.

Baldwin (1895 b, 1896), who inaugurated the Toronto and Princeton laboratories, also found one of his three Os distinctly quicker in the sensorial reaction, and suggested that the imagery type of the individual made a difference. A visualist or audile would more readily adopt the sensorial attitude, one of motor type the muscular attitude. , He argued that Wundt, in accepting Lange's results as standard, was basing his psychology on only one type of individual. Titchener (1895, 1896), having come to America and set up his laboratory at Cornell, defended the Leipzig school and held to the importance of the sensorial-muscular distinction. From the new laboratory at Chicago, Angell (1896) found one of two Os quicker at first in the sensorial reaction and one in the muscular; but the difference disappeared with practice. Thus:

	Early in practice		Late in practice	
	Sensorial	*Muscular*	*Sensorial*	*Muscular*
Subject A.	195	149	133	127
Subject M.	163	178	132	134

Angell explained individual differences in another way than Baldwin: the individual who profits from attending to the reaction movement is the slow-moving individual, while one who is quick with his hand may better attend to the stimulus; attention tends to go where it is needed.

Later investigators have usually found the muscular response quicker than the sensorial, but the difference has ranged from 10 to 50 ms, in relatively untrained Os, and has not approached the 100 ms which Lange regarded as normal. The best explanation for the retardation of the sensorial reaction is probably very simple: in the sensorial form O is not quite so ready to react. The muscular attitude is a single-minded readiness to react, while attention to the coming stimulus diverts a fraction of the energy, the size of this fraction varying with O's understanding of the instructions (Moore, 1904; Ach, 1905; Bergemann, 1906; Breitwieser, 1911; Williams, 1914).

The importance of catch tests. An important contribution from the Leipzig laboratory to the RT method was the principle formulated by Wirth (see Kästner & Wirth, 1907, 1908; Wirth, 1927): a type of reaction cannot be demarcated by instructions alone, in the absence of objective checks. Such checks are afforded by *Vexirversuche* or "catch tests," which were not unknown to previous workers but had not been systematically employed as a prime requirement of method. In the simple reaction O may be so eager to react quickly that he sometimes overshoots the mark and "reacts" before the stimulus. The presence of these impossible "negative RTs" indicates that some of the shortest positive RTs also are spurious, so that O's average RT is too small by an undefined amount. To train O out of his excessive readiness E occasionally gives the Ready signal but *omits the stimulus*. Only when O can pass the catch tests with practically no false reactions can his RTs be accepted as genuine.

The catch tests must not be numerous; otherwise the simple reaction will be concerted into a c-reaction. O must be reasonably sure of getting the positive stimulus on any given trial; he must be set for the simple reaction. But he must retain enough control over his hand to keep it quiet till the stimulus arrives. By experience with the interspersed catch tests he learns how far he can go in the direction of motor readiness and still avoid false reactions.

In reporting the results of a RT experiment, then, it is important to state the nature of the catch tests used and O's degree of success in passing them.

As applied to the simple reaction, catch tests rule out the extreme muscular form in which premature reactions are common. It rules out the extreme sensorial form as defined by Lange, for O must be trained to react as quickly as he can while still avoiding false reactions. No one has devised a form of catch test distinguishing the sensorial from the natural reaction. The choice (or disjunctive) reactions carry their own checks: in the b-reaction O will sometimes make the wrong response if he is too ready, and in the c-reaction he will sometimes react when the stimulus calls for no reaction. As to the d-reaction, no check can be devised for it, apparently, and for that reason, again, it has no value in accurate work.

Discarding of the subtraction method. It will be recalled that Donders, in his pioneer study of the time of mental processes, assumed that a complex reaction consisted of a simple reaction with certain additional processes *inserted*, and that the time occupied by the additional processes could be obtained by subtracting the simple RT from the complex RT. The earlier studies from Wundt's laboratory employed this subtraction procedure, though the results were sometimes disconcerting. A major contribution from Külpe's laboratory at Würzburg was the discrediting of this procedure and its underlying assumption. The pertinent papers are by Ach (1905) and Watt (1905). Ach studied the simple and disjunctive reactions, Watt the associative reaction. (Watt's work is more fully described on p. 790.) After each reaction, O gave a full introspective report, and one important finding was that O had much more to report regarding the period of getting ready to react than regarding the reaction itself. The reaction usually seemed to O almost automatic, a "prepared reflex," but the preparatory period often revealed effort, determination to react quickly and correctly, and adjustment for the required type of reaction. The preparatory set or adjustment differed according to the task to be performed. In preparing for a simple reaction, motor readiness reached a higher pitch than in preparing for a disjunctive reaction. These results showed the invalidity of the subtraction procedure. The disjunctive reaction is not the simple reaction with discrimination and choice inserted; the two reactions differ from the start.

If the progress of time is represented by a line extending from left to right, with fore-signal, stimulus and response marked on it, we have a diagram of the whole process.

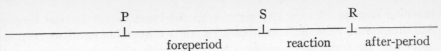

The foreperiod extends from the Ready signal or fore-signal, P, to the stimulus, S; the reaction time from S to the response movement, R; and the after-period extends for a short but indefinite period beyond R. The after-period contains the completion of the motor response, and may include much of the perceptive process which Wundt supposed to come within the reaction time; for, as Berger suggested, clear perception of the stimulus may run concurrently with the motor response. Different types of reaction differ right through from foreperiod to after-period.

If we cannot break up the reaction into successive acts and obtain the time of each act, of what use is the reaction time? It affords a means of studying the *total reaction* as dependent on the stimulus, the task, and the conditions in which the task is performed. Variations in the total RT throw light on the dynamics of the performance. It is with this understanding that the RT method is employed in the more recent work.

REACTION TIME APPARATUS

Without attempting to work out the details of an actual laboratory setup we can at least notice the instrumental problems and get some idea of their solution. The time to be measured extends from the beginning of the stimulus to the beginning of the response. These two instants must be made to register themselves on an instrument or record which shows the elapsed time. For rough timing of a reaction lasting several seconds, a stop watch reading to the fifth of a second may give a fine enough measure and we may depend upon E to register the instants of S and R by his own manipulation of the stop watch. For a RT of less than a second, certainly, a finer measure and some means of automatic registration are necessary.

If we ask how fine a measurement is required our best answer is found in the scatter of the RT. When a sufficient number of RTs have been timed we shall want to assemble them in a distribution table containing 10–20 step intervals. When the RT ranges from 100 to 200 ms, the step interval should not be less than 10 ms and the instrument should accordingly read to 1/100 sec. A practiced O in the simple reaction may show a much smaller scatter and the reading should be correspondingly fine. A unit of 1/500 sec. is probably fine enough for any RT work; some of the best instruments when in good running order measure to the single millisecond.

Graphic and "scopic" registration. The chronographic method registers S and R by marks upon a steadily moving surface—a kymograph drum or photographic film—and the RT is found by measuring the distance between these marks and taking account of the speed of the moving surface. Unless the speed is known to be constant, the time is simultaneously inscribed on the same surface by the vibrations, say, of a 100-cycle tuning fork, and the count of vibrations between the S and R marks gives the RT. The regularity of the tuning fork (at a constant temperature) makes this method a good check on the accuracy of other methods. But the counting of the vibrations is laborious. In the scopic method, S and R are automatically registered upon a dial or other scale by a pointer which moves at a known speed, and the time is read off from the scale. The main problems are to secure uniform speed of

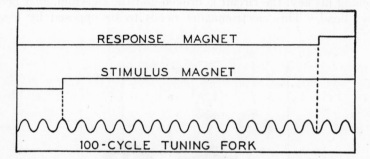

RESPONSE   MAGNET

STIMULUS   MAGNET

100-CYCLE TUNING FORK

FIG. 76. Diagram of a chronographic record of reaction time. Three writing points are synchronized so as to write simultaneously in the same vertical line on a horizontally moving drum. One writing point inscribes the vibrations of a tuning fork and so provides a "time line"; the other two are moved by electromagnets in circuit with E's stimulus key and O's response key. The RT here measures 135 ms. For an actual chronographic record (photographic) see p. 112.

movement, and to impress the instants of S and R upon the mechanism.

The chronoscope. Most of the usable models contain two main parts, a constant-speed motor and a clutch. The motor carries the pointer around the dial at a known rate, while the clutch allows the pointer to move only during the S–R interval.

For a *motor*, the Hipp chronoscope, much used since 1861 for RT work, has a clockwork driven by a weight and governed by a lamella vibrating 1000 times per sec. The lamella is so mounted as to engage the cogs of a certain wheel in the clock; it blocks the motion of this wheel except for part of each vibration and allows the wheel to advance one cog per ms. Thus controlled the clock becomes a constant-speed motor and carries a pointer around the dial at the uniform rate of one scale division per ms.

The advance of electrical engineering has made available the constant-speed electric motor which is sturdy and relatively foolproof and does not require rewinding (Dunlap, 1917, 1918; Renshaw, 1931; King, 1934; Jenkins, 1936).

It is the clutch rather than the motor that creates the great problem in devising a chronoscope. Motors can be obtained with speeds varying only a fraction of one percent, but when the pointer is shifted into and out of gear with the motor a large constant error may occur. The application of the stimulus to O must at the same time automatically throw the pointer into gear and O's reaction must throw it out of gear and bring it to a quick stop.

The clutch is usually operated by electromagnets. The circuit may pass in series through an electromagnet, through E's key which also throws in the stimulus, and through O's response key. At the fore-signal, O closes his key. E then closes his key which gives the stimulus and completes the circuit, activating the electromagnet. When O reacts by opening his key, the circuit is broken and the electromagnet becomes (nearly) dead. This electromagnet needs to be opposed by a spring

Fig. 77. (From C. H. Stoelting Company, Chicago.) Chronoscope and accessories. The experimenter sits on the near side, O on the far side of the table. A, bulb used for certain responses; B, voice keys for experimenter and subject; C, visual stimuli; D, tactual stimulator; E, Dunlap chronoscope; F, sound stimulus; G, tuning fork for regulating chronoscope; H, experimenter's stimulus keys.

or better by another electromagnet, so that when the circuit is broken the movable armature will snap back. The pointer, attached to the movable armature, is thrown into gear with the motor by the first electromagnet and out of gear by the opposed magnet or spring.

A source of error can easily be discerned in this setup. Unless the two pulls on the armature are properly balanced, the shift of the pointer into gear and out of gear will not be equally quick, and the pointer will not remain in gear for precisely the true length of time. Variations in the current and in the residual magnetism of the cores of the electromagnets make readjustments necessary when the magnet is opposed by a spring. It is better to oppose one magnet by another like magnet and to arrange the circuit so that the same current is switched from one magnet to the other by the stimulus and response keys.

Now that the 60-cycle alternating current is supplied with a frequency variation of much less than one percent, it can be used for RT work by aid of a telechron, an impulse counter, or some similar inexpensive instrument. The electromagnetic clutch in these little instruments is very quick (Miles, 1931 a).

The *galvanometer* was used as a chronoscope in Helmholtz's original RT experiment, and it has the advantage of being noiseless and of dispensing with the troublesome clutch. The extent of swing of the needle depends on the quantity of current passing through the coil. With a constant intensity, the quantity of current is proportional to the time and thus the swing of a galvanometer can be calibrated in terms of time (Klopsteg, 1917). A *condenser* can be used in much the same way, the current intensity being constant and the voltage accumulated during a short time interval furnishing a measure of that time (Klingler, 1931). These instruments placed in a Wheatstone bridge make it possible even to measure the "negative RTs" that occur in the transit experiment and whenever O gets ahead of the stimulus (Günther, 1911; Klingler, 1931). Premature reactions can also be timed by arranging the stimulus key so that it starts the chronoscope 200 ms before it delivers the stimulus; all the readings will be 200 ms too long and are rectified by subtracting that amount (Woodrow, 1932).

Regulation of the chronoscope is an essential part of RT work. The forces acting on the clutch are put in proper balance by using the chronoscope to time a physical process such as the fall of a steel ball from rest through a certain distance, and adjusting until true readings are obtained. The chronoscope should be regulated to give a true measure of an interval equal to about the average RT which is to be measured (Schlosberg, 1937 a).

Stimulus and reaction keys. Given adequate time-measuring apparatus, E's next problem is to devise arrangements for making or breaking a circuit simultaneously with the S and with the R. The reagent's key is usually a simple affair, though it may need careful designing to fit some of the more complicated circuits. The old standard is a simple telegraph key, which is held closed by O from the fore-signal to the reception of the stimulus and then released by quickly raising the hand. If the reacting movement is a downward pressure on the key, the indicated time will be longer when the force required to depress the key against its spring is greater. This element of variability is eliminated by using the upward movement for the reaction. The circuit can be arranged so that the upward movement either breaks or makes the current through the chronoscope magnet.

For disjunctive and especially for associative reactions a speech key is very desirable, and the problem here is by no means simple. Lip keys, jaw keys, chin keys and voice keys have all been used, but the difficulty with all of them is that the articulatory movements and sound vibrations differ from one spoken word to another, and the time lost in the activation of the key varies accordingly. Probably the voice key, well managed, gives the best service—unless it be a microphone or an oscillograph with photographic registration (Dunlap, 1921).

Stimulus keys or stimulators must be adapted to the sense stimulated and should not give any stimulus besides the one intended. If a visual stimulator makes a noise, the response, in case of a simple reaction, will probably be made to the noise rather than to the light, since response to sound is quicker than to light. Expecting O to disregard the noise and react only to the light is about the same as expecting him to make a consistent d-reaction. A neon lamp lights up and also goes out with no significant latency of its own and so affords a good stimulus for the simple reaction to light. For the ear, the "sound hammer" or a telegraph sounder furnishes a convenient noise though not usually of known intensity. To obtain a tonal stimulus free from initial noise is not so easy. Jenkins (1926) used a thermionic receiver inserted into the external auditory meatus and operated by an alternating current. Modern developments in telephone and radio engineering provide facilities for this sort of psychological work.

A tactual stimulus key delivers a quick pressure on the skin at the same instant that it makes or breaks a circuit. For better control of the intensity, a small weight carried by a lever is made to fall through a known arc before striking the skin (Cattell & Dolley, 1895). Stimuli for the senses of taste, smell, pain and temperature ought to be free from incidental stimulation of the sense of touch—an almost impossible requirement.

FACTORS IN THE SIMPLE REACTION TIME

Instead of attempting to dissect out of the well integrated simple reaction the times consumed in successive mental processes, we will study the effect of different conditions in the hope of finding factors which increase or decrease the reaction time. The procedure is that of holding all conditions constant except one which is varied systematically.

1. **The factor of readiness.** It is almost a matter of course that the reaction will be the quicker the greater O's readiness to react at the moment when the stimulus is applied. How shall the readiness factor be controlled and varied? If there were no fore-signal of any kind, O might be taken by surprise and fail altogether to make the prescribed response. Presumably readiness will depend on the *length of the fore-period*. A foreperiod of 2 seconds, varied slightly from trial to trial to prevent O from attempting to synchronize his finger movement with the stimulus, has been regarded as about the optimum for quick reaction. Experiments in which the foreperiod has been systematically varied have given results favoring something like this same interval.

Breitwieser (1911) found individual differences in two respects: in promptness of adjustment, and in the persistence of adjustment. Some Os got fully ready in a foreperiod of only 1 sec., while others, more numerous, required 2–3 sec. to give the minimum RT. Some Os sustained their readiness for as long as 10 sec., while in others it showed a decline if the foreperiod exceeded 4 sec.

Telford (1931) tried out a half-second foreperiod. The auditory stimuli came in a continued series at intervals of ½, 1, 2 and 4 seconds, the intervals being mixed in chance order and no other ready signal used except the preceding stimulus. On making each reaction O knew that another stimulus would arrive shortly. The average result for 29 untrained Os was as follows:

Interval between stimuli (= foreperiod)	½	1	2	4	sec.
Mean RT	335	241	245	276	ms
SD	64	43	51	56	ms

In spite of the wide variation shown by SD, the RT at 1 or 2 sec. was reliably shorter than at either ½ sec. or 4 sec. The one-second interval was as good as any.

Woodrow (1916) extended the foreperiod to 20–24 sec., using auditory stimuli on three well-trained Os. It made a difference whether the foreperiod remained the same for a series of trials or whether it varied irregularly and without warning. When it remained the same for a series of trials, so that O could adjust himself to its length, the optimal length was 2–4 sec. When it varied irregularly, there was no clear optimum and the reaction was slow throughout—about as slow as at the longest foreperiods in the regular procedure. Maximum readiness in these

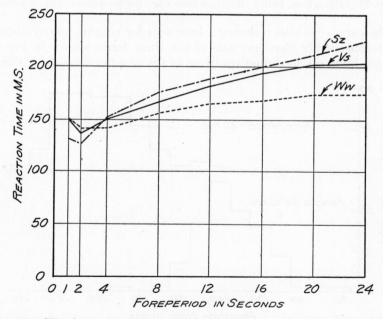

Fig. 78. (Woodrow, 1916.) Reaction time according to length of the foreperiod, when this period is the same for a series of trials. The curve for each O is given separately.

Os was not attained in much less than 2 sec., and was not maintained for much more than 4 sec.

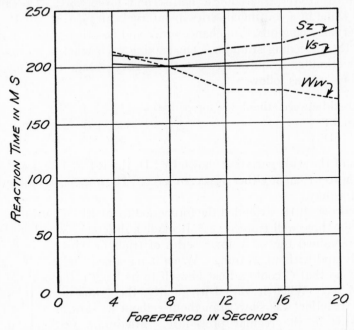

FIG. 79.   (Woodrow, 1916.)   Reaction time when the foreperiod varies irregularly.

The *curve of readiness* during a long wait for an anticipated stimulus might conceivably have any one of the three forms shown in Fig. 81. O might build up maximum readiness in the first few seconds and main-

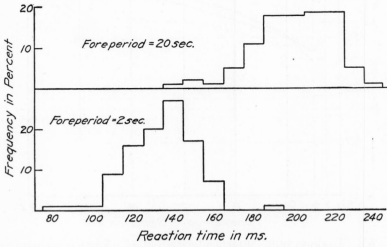

FIG. 80.   (Woodrow, 1916.)   Distributions of RT after short and long foreperiods, from Subject Vs.

tain it as well as he could. More probably, after becoming accustomed to the length of the foreperiod, he would delay getting ready till the stimulus was about due. (Compare the "delayed conditioned response," p. 97.) Since he could not tell exactly when it was coming, he probably

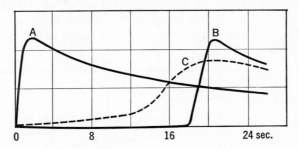

Fig. 81. Possible curves of readiness in a long foreperiod. The fore-signal comes at 0. If curve A is correct, readiness is immediately pushed to a maximum. If B is correct, readiness is pushed to a maximum at the moment when the stimulus is expected. If C is correct, there is no sharp peak of readiness in a long foreperiod.

would not push his readiness to the maximum at any moment. This reasoning favors curve C, and certain incidental results of Woodrow favor it also. There are no very short RTs after a long foreperiod, as there would be if readiness were pushed to a peak. Another fact speaks against curve A. When foreperiods of various lengths were mixed, a short one following a long one often caught O napping and gave a very long RT. It seems that O adjusts his readiness curve to the length of foreperiod he has just experienced.

2. **The factor of magnitude of stimulus.** The stimulus can be varied in intensity, extent or duration. From the time of the early experimenters it has been clear that the RT is long when the stimulus is very weak,

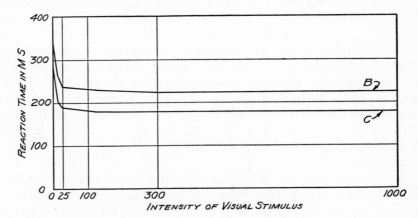

Fig. 82. (Berger, 1886.) The simple RT becomes shorter with increasing intensity of a visual stimulus. The stimulus is measured in relative values. B and C are the two subjects.

and several experiments have traced the relationship up through a considerable range of intensities. The early results of Berger (1886) show the RT decreasing rapidly from weak to medium intensities of the stimulus. The curve approaches a level, suggesting that very intense stimuli would not give a much shorter RT. Wundt (1911) believed, on the basis of his early experiments, that the RT increased again at high intensities, because, as he explained, one could never be fully ready

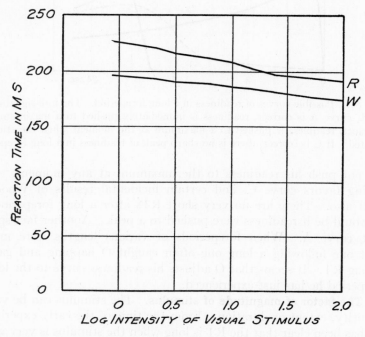

FIG. 83. (Froeberg, 1907.) Reaction time plotted against the logarithm of intensity. Visual stimulus. R and W are the two subjects.

for a very intense stimulus, but this statement has never been adequately tested. Froeberg's results (1907), not differing essentially from Berger's, show an approximately linear relationship between the RT and the logarithm of the stimulus intensity—the RT decreases by equal steps as the intensity increases by equal ratios. Such a statement, in connection with Weber's law, would make RT depend on the "subjective" or physiological intensity of excitation as against the physical intensity of the external stimulus.

However, Piéron (1919, 1932 a), working with auditory stimuli, obtained values of RT which show far from a linear relationship with the logarithm of stimulus intensity. The RT does not decrease as fast or as far as would be demanded by a logarithmic formula. The RT reaches what is practically a minimum at intensities which are quite moderate—a conclusion consistent with all the results at hand. A stimulus of medium intensity gives about as quick a reaction as can be obtained.

The RT has somewhat the same relation to the *extent* of a visual stimulus as to its intensity: within narrow limits, at least, corresponding to foveal vision, increasing the area of the stimulus decreases the simple RT (Froeberg, 1907). A larger area affords a chance for spatial summation of stimuli (p. 563).

As to *duration* of the stimulus, one would think at first that it could make no difference in the RT; for if O reacts to the beginning of the

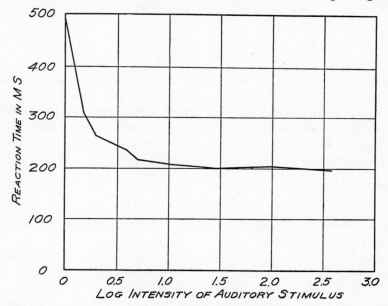

FIG. 84. (Piéron, 1919.) Reaction time plotted against the logarithm of stimulus intensity. Auditory stimulus, its lowest intensity being approximately the stimulus threshold. Piéron works out an equation for this and other curves of the relation of RT to stimulus intensity. He supposes the RT to be composed of two parts, not successive in time. There is an irreducible basal RT required for nerve conduction, receptor and effector latencies, and central processes which take a certain minimum time; and there is a reducible margin which is reduced to zero by sufficiently increasing the stimulus intensity. Let k = the irreducible minimum, which = RT at high intensities. Let i = intensity measured as a multiple of the stimulus threshold, at which $i = 1$. If the reducible margin were exactly in inverse proportion to i, we could write it as a/i, and the equation for RT would be,

$$RT = a/i + k$$

Piéron finds that usually the term a/i needs to be modified in order to give a good fit. He finds it necessary to introduce a third parameter, such as b in the formula,

$$RT = a/(i + b) + k$$

To fit the data in this figure the parameters take the values: $a = 87.9$, $b = -0.70$, $k = 197$; so that

$$RT = 87.9/(i - 0.70) + 197,$$

where the irreducible minimum RT (under the conditions of this experiment) is 197 ms, the value at stimulus threshold is 490 ms, and the reducible margin at the stimulus threshold is $490 - 197 = 293$ ms.

stimulus, the thing is done and further continuance of the stimulus could have no effect on the RT.   And yet we know that the apparent intensity of a light increases with its duration up to a maximum time of about 50 ms (temporal summation, p. 564).   So it is a fair question whether the RT does not decrease within the same limits.   Froeberg (1907) found a slight quickening of the reaction as the visual stimulus increased in duration from 3 ms to about 50 ms.   His averages from two Os, each of whom made 400 reactions at each point, are given below.

Duration of stimulus in ms

	3	6	12	24	48
RT of Subject R	201	199	196	193	191
" " " W	181	179	177	175	173

Though the differences are very small, their P.E. is not over 0.7 ms for Subject R, and not over 0.6 ms for Subject W, so that all but the adjacent values are reliably different.   Wells (1913) extended the stimulus series to longer durations, and obtained the following average values for the simple RT to visual stimuli (from 6 Os and a total of 6,000 reactions at each point):

Duration of stimulus	10–12	25–31	64–66	144–150	1000 ms
Av. reaction time	180	175	177	178	185

There is certainly no indication of any quicker reaction at stimulus durations exceeding 50 ms.

Within narrow limits, then, increasing the intensity, extent or duration of a stimulus hastens the reaction.   And another similar factor, in the visual field, is the *contrast* between the stimulus and its background. Rudeanu (1933) used as stimulus the starting of the chronoscope pointer; as soon as O saw the pointer start to move, he reacted and so stopped the pointer.   The pointer was black, and the dial face against which it was seen was either white or black.   As we might expect (though why?) the RT was shorter when the background was white.   The average RT for each of four Os was as follows:

	Black pointer seen against	
	white ground	black ground
Subject V	186 ms	297 ms
" F	190	275
" R	175	218
" J	179	205

3. **Summation and facilitation.**   A combination of simultaneous stimuli may give a quicker response than any one of these stimuli alone. The effect of increasing the area or duration of a visual stimulus can be taken as an example, and even the effect of increased intensity may belong here, since a more intense stimulus probably arouses a larger

number of receptors. An interesting instance of summation is given by Poffenberger (1912): the RT is shorter in binocular than monocular stimulation by the same light. Each of three Os gave this result by a reliable margin:

	Monocular	*Binocular*
Subject T	201	185 ms
Subject P	175	160
Subject A	191	178

The effect on RT is rather surprising in view of the fact that the apparent brightness of the light, the sensory effect, is scarcely different with monocular and binocular stimulation. A similar effect in hearing was noted by Bliss (1893) when a sound was admitted to both ears or confined to one: RT to monotic stimulation, 147 ms; to diotic, 133 ms.

If two stimuli, a light and a sound, are applied simultaneously, it is futile to tell O which one to regard as the stimulus; such instructions cannot be consistently followed, as our discussion of method has indicated. The RT is less than to light alone but not less than to sound alone (Dunlap & Wells, 1910). In Todd's experiment (1912) three stimuli were applied singly and in combination, with results from three Os as shown below.

Stimulus	*Reaction Time of Subjects*			
	M	P	T	Av
Light	168	176	186	176
Electric	141	135	152	143
Sound	135	132	160	142
Light and electric	139	137	151	142
Light and sound	133	135	159	142
Sound and electric	125	122	145	131
Light, sound and electric	120	124	138	127

Light does not hasten the response to sound or to electric shock, but sound and shock give a quicker reaction when combined than when given singly.

In a somewhat different experiment by Jenkins (1926) the assigned stimulus was light (a bright spot in a dark room), which came on and went out at intervals of about 4 sec. O reacted to each onset and to each cessation of the light. Part of the time a tone was sounding, and the auditory condition accompanying the visual stimulus was any one of these four, irregularly interspersed: continued sound, cessation of sound, continued silence, onset of sound. Continued silence is of course the ordinary condition in an experiment with visual stimuli, and the question was whether the other three auditory conditions would affect the RT. All three proved to have a facilitating effect. The five Os gave a total of 2,000 reactions for each entry in the table at the top of the next page.

Stimulus

Condition	Onset of light	Cessation of light
Continued quiet	230	200
Continued sound	214	190
Cessation of sound	191	173
Onset of sound	171	158

The differences shown in this table of averages appear consistently in the records of the individual subjects. It is fairly certain that the reaction to light is facilitated by the simultaneous onset or cessation of sound.

An extra stimulus, however, does not always have a facilitating effect. Todd (1912) found an inhibitory effect when an electric shock *preceded* by a fraction of a second the light to which O was reacting. On the average of two Os, he obtained the following reaction times:

To light with no extra stimulus	181 ms
To light preceded by shock at interval of 360 ms	200
" " " " " " " " 180	220
" " " " " " " " 90	175
" " " " " " " " 45	170
To light and simultaneous shock	139

A shock coming 180–360 ms before the visual stimulus delays the reaction, while one coming very shortly before the stimulus facilitates the reaction. The relationship looks much the same as that found in the reinforcement of the knee jerk. The strength of the knee jerk is increased by simultaneously clenching the fist or by clenching it just before the blow on the patellar tendon; but if the clenching precedes the blow by 0.5–1.0 sec., the knee jerk is weakened rather than strengthened (Bowditch & Warren, 1890).

Facilitation by incentives. The facilitating factors just considered may be called "peripheral" since they act directly on the sense organs. We have previously noted two classes of "central" facilitating factors, both concerned with the preparation to react. "Sensorial" preparation was less effective, less facilitating, than "muscular" preparation. And a short and uniform foreperiod gave greater readiness than a long or irregular foreperiod. Another central facilitating factor can be classed under the head of incentives. In the experiment of Johanson (1922) one incentive consisted simply in informing O just before each reaction what his time had been in the preceding reaction. A still more effective incentive consisted in passing an electric circuit through O's reaction key in such a way that he automatically got a shock in his finger whenever his RT exceeded a certain time (adjusted to O's speed). The three conditions—no incentive, knowledge of results, and shock—were rotated so as to give no one any advantage of position. The results are shown in the form of distribution curves.

It is surprising that well practiced Os, "doing their best" all the time, yet increase their speed by 15 percent under the spur of special incentives. The result is, however, quite in line with the other facts of summation and facilitation. The simple RT is not a fixed quantity, but is affected by many influences—though it apparently has a physiological limit in the neighborhood of 100 ms.

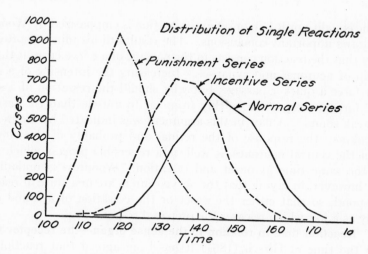

Fig. 85. (Johanson, 1922.) Change in the distribution of reaction time under the influence of incentives. Auditory stimulus. In the "incentive series" O was informed of his last RT; in the "punishment series" he received a shock in the finger when the reaction was at all slow. Each curve shows the distribution of 3,600 single reactions obtained from three Os whose times were nearly the same.

4. **Reaction to the cessation of a sound or light.** Is it possible to react to cessation as easily as to onset? From ordinary experience no special difficulty would be expected, but if a stimulus is conceived as energy applied to a sense organ, how can the cessation of energy be a stimulus? The termination of a stimulus might terminate a response, but here we are thinking of something different, a positive reaction set off by the mere ceasing of a sound or light.

Experiment has shown no great difference in the RT to onset and cessation. The results cited from Jenkins show even quicker reaction to the cessation than to the onset of light. This was true of each of five Os and also of two Os in the experiment of Holmes (1923). The reason, as suggested by these two authors, may lie in better visual fixation of a light that is there than of the faint fixation point present before the light is presented. Wells (1913) found only 3 of his 6 Os giving quicker reactions to cessation than to onset of light, and the 2 Os in Salow's experiment (1913) reacted more quickly to the onset of light. Woodrow (1915) used both light and sound, and his 5 Os quite consistently gave the *same* RT to onset and cessation, as illustrated by the averages from one O:

	Onset	*Cessation*
Sound, medium intensity	119	121 ms
" weak "	184	183
" liminal "	779	745
Light, strong "	162	167
" Weak "	205	203

The equality of RT to onset and cessation is emphasized by Woodrow, who draws important conclusions. The results to his mind disprove the theory that the reaction consists in the passage of a nerve current through a chain of neurones and synapses. Increasing the intensity of a sound might force a quicker passage, but why should the cessation of a strong sound force its way more quickly from ear to muscle than the cessation of a weak sound? A flaw in this argument was indicated by Holmes and by Jenkins: the response of the retina, and probably of the inner ear and of the central neurones as well, is a reversible process which might take the same time at onset and cessation. Woodrow is undoubtedly right, however, in saying that the nerve centers are in a state of readiness to respond, so that either the onset or the cessation of a sound comes simply as a jolt which releases the prepared response.

5. **Reaction time in relation to the sense organ—the receptor factor.** From the time of Hirsch (1861) it has been agreed that reaction to a visual stimulus is somewhat slower than to an auditory or tactual. Typical values are:

Reaction time to light		180 ms
" " " sound		140
" " " touch		140

Sometimes the RT to an electric shock applied to the hand or face is 10–20 ms shorter than that to sound, but this result is not universal. In a large sample of individuals some are found who react as quickly to light as to sound (Wells et al., 1921).

The rather surprising slowness of reaction to light raises the question whether the comparison rests on a fair basis. In view of the dependence of RT on the intensity of the stimulus, fairness demands that the stimuli applied to the different senses be equated in intensity—not however in physical energy but in effective intensity, measured in relation to the sensitivity of the receptors. Three ways of meeting this demand suggest themselves:

a. Work at the stimulus threshold. The just perceptible intensity of light and sound are equal in relation to the sensitivity of the two senses. Using this approach Wundt (1874) found a RT of about 330 ms to liminal light, sound and touch. According to this finding the RT does not depend on the sense stimulated but upon the effective intensity of the stimulus. But the values obtained are of doubtful validity because at the threshold O is often uncertain whether a stimulus has been received, and if catch tests are given he will react to some of the zero stimuli.

b. Measure the stimulus in "sensation units," i.e., in multiples of the stimulus threshold—in decibels in the case of sound (p. 437). Apparently this promising approach has not been tried.

c. Increase the intensity until the minimum RT for each sense is reached. From the fact that the minimum RT is reached at quite moderate intensities, such as are customary in RT work, we reach the tentative conclusion that the usual values, 180 ms for sight and 140 ms for hearing and touch, are fair to these three senses.

Sight, hearing and touch (proper) stand in a class by themselves as regards RT, because pure stimuli can be applied to them. It is almost impossible to apply timed stimuli to the warmth, cold, pain, smell and taste receptors without also exciting the receptors for touch. And the touch receptors get their mechanical stimuli before the thermal or chemical stimuli can penetrate to the appropriate receptors. O gets a touch sensation a fraction of a second before the temperature, taste or smell sensation to which he is supposed to react. If he adopts the "muscular" or the "natural" attitude, he gives simple reactions to touch; but if he is cautioned not to react till he senses the warmth, cold, taste or smell, he is placed in the difficult situation of an O trying to make consistent d-reactions.

Attempts were made by very competent experimenters to measure the RT to *taste* stimuli (von Vintschgau & Hönigschmied, 1875, 1876, 1877; Kiesow, 1903). The stimulus solution was applied to the tip of the tongue by aid of a little brush mounted on a suitable circuit key. The stimuli were:

for Bitter, quinine bisulphate, saturated solution;

for Salt, sodium chloride, saturated;

for Sweet, cane sugar, nearly saturated;

for Sour, phosphoric or citric acid, diluted to avoid injury to the tongue.

The mouth was rinsed with lukewarm water after each stimulus. O was instructed to react as soon as he detected the least trace of a taste sensation. The average values for the simple reaction are given below for three Os.

Stimulus	Salt	Sugar	Acid	Quinine	Touch on tongue
V. & H.'s subject H	160	164	168	220	151
V. & H.'s subject D	597	752		993	125
Kiesow's subject	308	446	536	1082	

The first O differs altogether from the other two and was probably reacting to touch most of the time. The other two Os were undoubtedly reacting to taste but not with a typical simple reaction. Their slow reaction to the bitter stimulus was to be expected with the stimulus applied to the tip of the tongue which is relatively insensitive to bitter.

For *olfactory* stimulation Moldenhauer (1883) constructed a stimulator which blew a puff of odorous air into the nose and at the same instant started the chronoscope pointer. The noise of the blast of air and the sensation of touch and cool from the nostrils distracted the Os at first and produced false reactions, but after some practice the Os became "fully certain that they were reacting only to the odor." As a check, the simple RTs to the noise of the blast and to the cutaneous sensation were determined, with results as follows from the three Os:

Reaction to the	sound	touch	odor
Subject 1	138	—	263
" 2	164	187	210
" 3	185	214	390

The figures indicate a slower reaction to odor than to sound or touch, but doubt remains whether the reactions to odor were genuine simple reactions, since they were not released till O was sure that he was getting something besides sound and touch.

Reaction to a *painful stimulus*, instead of being very quick as one might expect, is slow, and the pain sensation itself has a long latency. Except by good management, an experiment on RT to pain will suffer from the defects which seem unavoidable in taste and smell. Luckily, superficial pain without any touch sensation can sometimes be obtained by applying to the skin a sharp point with very weak pressure. Eichler (1930) used for this purpose the technique of von Frey: a slender bristle, tipped with a thorn from a thistle plant, is so mounted that the chronoscope pointer starts at the moment when the thorn is lowered upon the skin. The weak pressure usually gives a double sensation, touch followed by pain, but in some trials only pain is felt. O makes a simple reaction to every stimulus, and reports afterward whether the sensation was touch followed by pain, or pain only; E then sorts the RTs into these two classes. Four Os consistently gave much longer RTs when pain only was felt:

	Touch and pain	Pain only
Subject A	340 ms	870 ms
Subject B	240	992
Subject C	255	740
Subject D	238	930

The slow reactions to touch are accounted for by the extreme weakness of the stimulus. But the stimuli that happened to give only pain were no weaker and yet gave much slower reactions.

Why should the reaction to pain be so very slow, why should the reaction to light be slower than to sound, and in general why should the RT differ according to the sense stimulated? The difference might lie in the sense organs or in the nerve centers. Receptor cells may differ in latency, and another peripheral variable is the time taken by a stimulus to reach the receptors. When acid is applied to the skin it takes 3–10 sec. to reach the receptors so as to give a pain sensation (Lebermann, 1922). Warmth applied to the surface must penetrate the skin a certain small distance before reaching the warmth receptors (p. 463). The transmission of mechanical pressure to the touch receptors, or of pressure oscillations through the ear to the auditory receptors, is in comparison practically instantaneous. Light of course reaches the retina with no loss of time, but the rods and cones are probably not excited by light and the mediating photochemical process may take a little time. Or, it may be, the central process in a visual reaction is more elaborate than in the simplest reaction to sound or touch—more elaborate or less directly connected with the muscles.

The left cerebral hemisphere is connected with the right hand and with the right half of the field of view (through the left half of each retina). Consequently the neural connections are more direct from a stimulus in the right half of the field of view to a reaction of the right hand, than if the reacting hand is on the other side from the stimulus. From these neural connections one would expect a quicker response of the hand on the side of the visual stimulus (when the latter lies to the right or left of the fixation point). Poffenberger (1912) finds a small but reliable difference in the expected direction (about 6 ms in each of two well-trained Os). This finding illustrates what is meant by speaking of more or less direct central connections between stimulus and response.

The RT to light differs with the

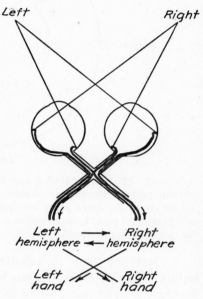

Fig. 86. Hand reaction to stimulus presented in indirect vision. The eyes are supposed to be looking straight forward. If a stimulus appears on the left side, the neural connections are to the right hemisphere; and if the right hand is to respond, use must apparently be made of the commissural connection between the hemispheres, so that the response mechanism involves an additional step.

part of the retina which receives the light. The further out from the fovea the stimulus is applied, the longer the RT. It is quicker when the spot of light strikes the upper than the lower half of the retina, and quicker when the nasal than when the temporal half is stimulated. Quickness of reaction runs parallel with acuity of vision (tested by perception of letters and others figures). Acuity decreases from the fovea out, as the RT increases. Acuity at the same distance from the fovea is somewhat better on the (more important) nasal half and on the (more important) upper half of each retina; and where the acuity is better the RT is shorter.

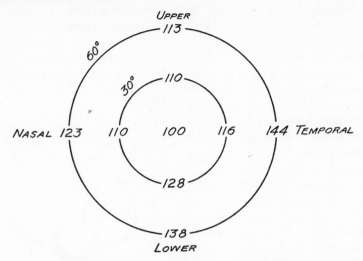

FIG. 87. (Data from Hall & von Kries, 1879.) Reaction time to stimulation at different parts of the retina. Stimuli were applied at the fovea and at points 30° and 60° from the fovea along the horizontal and vertical meridians. The RT at each peripheral point is expressed as a percent of that at the fovea, the percents for the two Os being averaged.

6. **Reaction time in relation to the response movement—motor factors.** The RT gives only one fact regarding the concrete performance. A complete description would include the characteristics of the reacting movement and the behavior during the foreperiod and during the after-

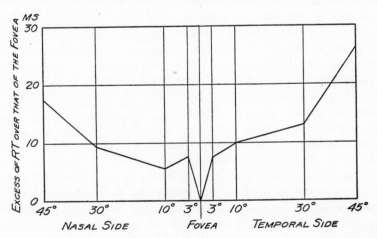

FIG. 88. (Data from Poffenberger, 1912.) Reaction time to stimuli applied along the horizontal meridian of the retina. The level of the base line represents the RT to foveal stimulation, and the ordinate shows the excess RT at each peripheral point. Two Os, each eye stimulated separately, gave a total of 400 RTs for each point.

period, the latter including Ponzo's "recovery response" by which the finger is replaced in position on the key (Hirsch, 1936, 1937). These motor phenomena can be used to indicate something of the state of the organism before, during and after the reaction, and some of them may affect the RT itself. A few interesting facts have been gleaned from the literature.

As between the two hands, it makes little difference which is used; the RT is the same within about 5 ms. Some Os show about that difference in favor of the preferred hand, others in favor of the non-preferred. As between the two feet, also, the difference is very small, but the hand is 16–60 ms quicker than the foot (Slattery, 1893; Cattell & Dolley, 1895; Kiesow, 1903). The difference between the several fingers is small (Gatewood, 1920). The voice reaction is slower than that of the hand (Wells, 1924), because of the inadequacy of voice keys or because of the complex movement of voice production. Reymert (1923) found the lips as quick as the hand, while a backward head movement was slower than the foot.

A complex movement, even though well prepared, gives a relatively long RT. A movement aimed at a particular point is slower in starting than a free movement. The RT for stopping a movement or changing its direction is longer than that for starting the same movement (F. N. Freeman, 1907; Isserlin, 1914).

The role of *muscular tension* is a matter of interest. The large extensor thigh muscle, the quadriceps, is likely, especially in unpracticed Os, to show considerable involuntary tension during the foreperiod, with relaxation after the reaction (G. L. Freeman, 1931). The preliminary tension in the hand and arm that are to react depend very much on the key that is used. If strong pressure is needed to hold the key closed during the foreperiod, such pressure is exerted; but if the hand and forearm are supported and make a free movement for the reaction, their muscles may show no preliminary tension whatever. Needle electrodes inserted directly into these muscles may lead off no action currents during the foreperiod (Hathaway, 1935).

When muscular tension is voluntarily induced by the instructions, or enforced by the apparatus, the RT is shortened, especially if this foreperiod tension is in the direction of the reaction movement, so as to give the movement a "flying start" (Scripture & Burnham, 1896; Angell, 1911; G. L. Freeman, 1933).

Graphic records of the finger pressure on a spring key (Smith, 1903; Judd, 1905; Williams, 1914; Rolder, 1922) reveal quite a variety of behavior during the foreperiod. The finger may remain motionless, oscillate, gradually increase its downward pressure, or gradually decrease the pressure. Though there is no close relation of the RT to these foreperiod patterns, it is true that some of the quickest Os let the pressure decrease toward the end of the foreperiod, as if anticipating the reaction; while some of the slower Os who testify to a "sensorial" attitude let the pressure gradually increase. When the stimulus comes, the first response is sometimes an increase of the downward pressure. This movement is antagonistic to the required release of the key and necessarily lengthens the chronoscope record of the RT, even when the graphic record shows the first, antagonistic response to have been as quick as a "muscular" reaction. The time consumed by this first phase is 30–40 ms (Smith, 1903; Williams, 1914). Williams gives an attractive explanation: when attention is on the coming reactive movement, that movement is allowed to get a slight start during the foreperiod; but when attention is directed to the coming stimulus, the hand involuntarily increases the downward pressure during the foreperiod; in either case the first effect of the stimulus is to release more energy into the momentarily dominant muscle group. This explanation does not cover the whole range and variety of foreperiod behavior.

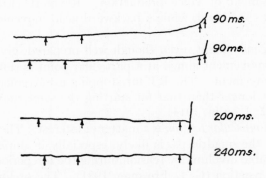

FIG. 89. (Williams, 1914.) Graphic records of finger pressure in foreperiod and reaction. Each tracing begins after O has depressed the spring key into position. The first two little arrows show the beginning and end of a ready signal (buzzer), the third arrow marks the instant of the stimulus (sound hammer), and the fourth shows when the key opened and halted the chronoscope pointer (often perceptibly later than the very beginning of the reaction). The first two tracings are from an O who gave quick reactions of "muscular" type, the last two from an O who gave slow reactions of "sensorial" type. The first O tended to raise his finger gradually toward the close of the foreperiod as if partially releasing the reaction, while the second O had somewhat the contrary tendency. In reacting the second O very often began with an "antagonistic" movement, the first almost never. Out of 260–280 recorded reactions, these two Os gave the following percent frequencies:

	Quick O	Slow O
Finger rises toward end of foreperiod	56	14
Finger presses " " " "	3	27
Finger steady " " " "	32	41
Antagonistic, biphasic reaction	3	71
Sharp upward monophasic reaction	90	24

Full tracings of the reaction movement under quite a variety of mechanical conditions have yielded miscellaneous and sometimes conflicting results. It seems to be established that the reaction movement need not have great force in order to give a short RT, and that there is practically zero correlation between the RT and the force of the movement. A slowly beginning movement may become forcible through a delayed impulse sent in to the muscles in the effort to "catch up"; and a false reaction is apt to be very weak as if partly checked (Delabarre et al., 1897; Moore, 1904; Kornilov, 1922; Hanes, 1929; Mayerhofer & Pauli, 1934).

Action currents led off by electrodes applied to the skin over the reacting muscle give a RT 30–40 ms shorter than is shown by the finger on its key (Vörckel, 1922), and a similar difference is found between the action current latency and the latency of mechanically registered muscle thickening in the patellar and Achilles tendon reflexes (Nystrom, 1933). When a simple reaction is executed by a movement of the whole forearm from the elbow, the interval between the start of the action currents and the start of the mechanically recorded arm movement runs up to 60–120 ms (Hathaway, 1935). Quite a slice of the ordinary RT is thus consumed in setting in motion the finger or arm and the reaction key. These electrical techniques should eventually make it possible to measure the time consumed in the sense organs, motor organs and peripheral nerves and so show how much must be assigned to the nerve centers. The central lost time of the flexion reflex runs as low as 4 ms (Creed et al., 1932); that for the simple reaction is probably as much as 70 ms.

THE DISJUNCTIVE REACTION

Leaving behind now the simple reaction with its single stimulus and single response, we encounter two main classes of complex reactions, the disjunctive and the associative. The associative reaction will be considered in the next chapter. The disjunctive reaction is an either-or affair. There are two or more alternative responses, and each must be made to a prescribed stimulus. "Reaction with discrimination and choice" is another name for the same thing. Included under the head of disjunctive reactions are the Donders b-reaction and c-reaction.

An example of the b-reaction: react to red with the right hand, to blue with the left.

An example of the c-reaction: react to red, but do not react to any other color.

The disjunctive RT is longer than the simple RT, from 20 to 200 ms longer, and the b-reaction runs a little slower than the c-reaction. In the b-reaction, two motor responses are held in readiness, but neither of them must be allowed to reach "hair-trigger" readiness; otherwise many false reactions will occur. In the c-reaction, too, motor readiness must be held down, because the stimulus that calls for a reaction occurs in only about half the trials. The attitude is apt to be "sensorial" rather than "muscular."

Practice effect. Slow at first, the disjunctive reaction becomes decidedly quicker with practice, as shown in an accompanying table and in Fig. 90. The simple reaction also improves with practice, and keeps ahead of the disjunctive, though by a narrowing margin. There is no evidence that the disjunctive would ever catch up.

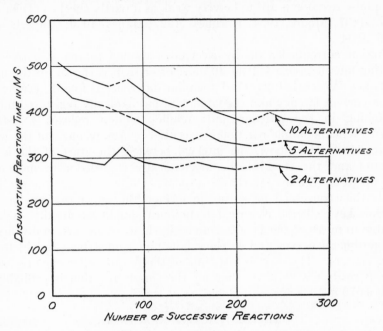

Fig. 90. (Data from Merkel, 1885.) Practice curves in disjunctive reactions. The stimuli (visual) were the Arabic numerals 1 to 5, assigned to the fingers of the right hand in due order, and the Roman numerals I to V similarly assigned to the left hand. In any given experiment, two, three or any number up to the whole ten of these stimuli were used. The curves show the results from one O who practiced for four days and made about 300 reactions with 2 stimuli and fingers, with 5, and with 10. The dotted segments are the breaks between each day and the next.

Practice in Simple and Disjunctive Reactions
(von Kries & Auerbach, 1877)

Parallel training was given two Os in the simple and the c-reaction to electric shocks. For the simple reaction the shock was applied to the left hand and the response was made with the right hand. For the c-reaction the shock was applied to either of two parts of the left hand and the right hand responded to only one of these two locations of the stimulus. The table shows the average RT for the two Os combined, on the first and seventh days of practice.

	Initial RT	*Final RT*	*Final/Initial*
Simple reaction (a)	145 ms	130 ms	90%
c-reaction	248	152	61
c — a	103	22	

The disjunctive RT increases with the number of alternatives. It is harder to keep a large team of stimulus-response units in readiness, without allowing any one to get out of hand. The chief evidence for this statement is the experiment of Merkel, described in the legend of Fig. 90, which gave the following results:

Number of alternatives	Reaction time
1 (simple reaction)	187
2	316
3	364
4	434
5	487
6	532
7	570
8	603
9	619
10	622

The table gives the averages for nine Os, omitting the tenth because, as pointed out by Wirth (1927), this O's exceptionally short times are invalidated by false reactions.

The more similar the alternative stimuli, the longer the disjunctive RT. Naturally, it takes more time to distinguish two stimuli that are almost alike than two which differ greatly. Yet one would hesitate to predict that more time would be required to discriminate between red and yellow than between red and green. One would rather expect the difference to be perceived instantly in either case. The question was tried out by Henmon (1906). O had two reaction keys, one for each hand; he saw two colors side by side, and reacted with the hand on the same side as a specified color. When red and green were being used, O reacted always to the red, with the right hand when red was on the right, with the left hand when it was on the left. The table on page 334 gives the results obtained with one O, who served in all varieties of the experiment.

FIG. 91. (Henmon, 1906.) Two lines were presented side by side, and O reacted with the hand on the side of the longer line. His average RT is given at the left.

These differences, even the smallest, are well above the difference threshold, and few if any errors would be made in distinguishing them, given a second or two in which to make the comparison. Even among these supraliminal differences, the larger ones take less time to see and use in governing the response. Besides Henmon's evidence for this statement, we have similar findings from von Kries & Auerbach (1877)

Stimuli to be distinguished	*Average reaction time*	*P. E. of average*
White and black	197 ms	1.1 ms
Red and green	203	1.2
Red and yellow	217	0.7
Red and orange	246	0.7
Red and (orange + 25% red)	252	0.8
Red and (orange + 50% red)	260	0.8
Red and (orange + 75% red)	271	0.8
Lines 10 and 13 mm long	296	0.9
" 10 " 12.5 "	298	0.8
" 10 " 12 "	305	0.8
" 10 " 11.5 "	313	0.9
" 10 " 11 "	324	1.0
" 10 " 10.5 "	345	1.0
Tones differing by 16 cycles	290	1.3
" " " 12 "	299	1.3
" " " 8 "	311	1.3
" " " 4 "	334	1.4

on the time required to discriminate directions of sound, and from Lemmon (1927) on discrimination of number of exposed lights, Fig. 92.

VARIATIONS AND USES OF REACTION TIME

A well developed experiment like that on RT ought to prove a serviceable tool in scientific investigations and in tests for practical aptitudes. It can serve as a tool if it has significant relationships with other traits and performances. To follow the work on individual differences and correlations would take us outside our defined field of study and we must content ourselves with a few brief citations and references.

That unpracticed individuals differ in RT is sufficiently brought out by the distribution curve in Fig. 93, p. 336. With practice some improve more than others and their positions in the distribution change considerably but even at or near their respective physiological limits they differ in RT (Blank, 1934).

Variation of the RT from one trial to another. A relatively untrained O gives quite a *skew* distribution of the single RT values, as shown in Fig. 94. With training the scatter is much reduced, but the skewness persists in some cases (Cattell & Dolley, 1895) though not always (Friedrich, 1928). The skewness admits of an easy interpretation: the quickest reaction depends on perfect adjustment in every respect, and the factors that make for imperfect adjustment can delay the reaction greatly and give a few very long RTs.

Many distribution curves of the single reactions of an individual appear *multimodal* and suggest that the "population" of RTs is heterogeneous. The simple reaction may not always be the same thing. This possibility, not yet fully tested by experiment and statistical analysis, has been emphasized by Johnson (1923): "There are a limited number of reactive mechanisms, having different latent times; those having the shorter times are the harder to excite and hence are less frequently excited under unfavorable conditions . . . the effect of training in reaction time work consists largely in increased frequency of use of the more quickly acting mechanisms."

Organic factors. Body temperature, for example, might probably affect the RT, though not in an easily predictable way. According to van Biervliet (1894) the day-to-day variations in pulse rate are accompanied by variations in RT, though this effect was not found in all the students tested. One of them, fairly typical, gave the following results:

Pulse rate	Reaction time
70–80 per min.	130 ms
80–90	126
90–100	121
100–110	117

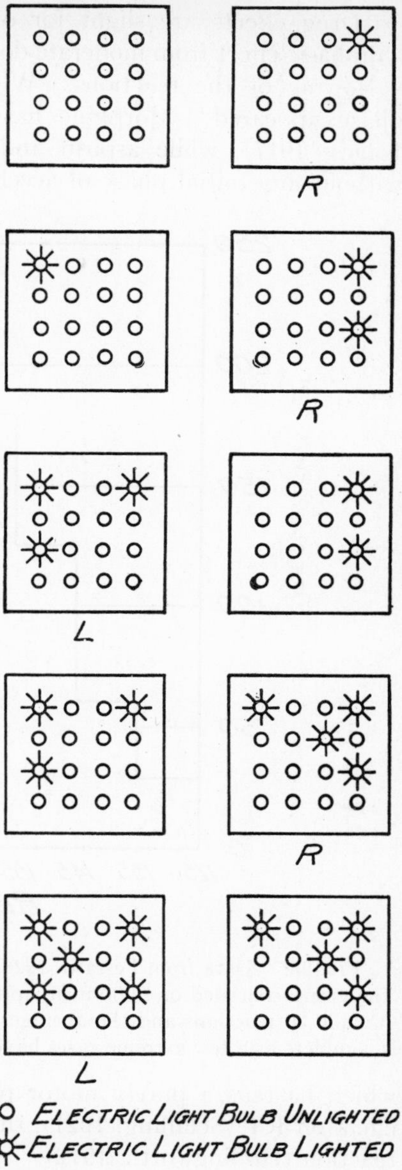

FIG. 92. (Lemmon, 1927.) Sample stimuli given in pairs, O to react with the hand on the side of the larger number of lights burning. Two square frames stood side by side, each containing 16 bulbs. After a Ready signal, 1–5 of the bulbs in one frame were lighted, and one fewer in the other frame. O had thus to discriminate 1 from 0, 2 from 1, 3 from 2, etc. The simple RT to light was also measured, and 40 reactions of each sort were taken from each of 113 college students, with the following average results, which recall Weber's law:

Stimuli to be discriminated	Average reaction time	S.D. of distribution	Percent of false reactions
Simple reaction	199 ms	25 ms	
1 and 0 lights	290	30	3
2 and 1 "	475	62	2
3 and 2 "	566	101	5
4 and 3 "	656	150	7
5 and 4 "	741	212	15

Drug effects are slight for ordinary doses. Kraepelin (1883) got a diphasic effect from moderate doses of alcohol, a quickening followed by a slowing of the reactions. With larger doses, only the retardation phase appeared. Morphine has a similar diphasic effect (Macht & Isaacs, 1917), while aspirin and other antipyretics show retardation without any initial phase of acceleration (Macht et al., 1918). Caffein,

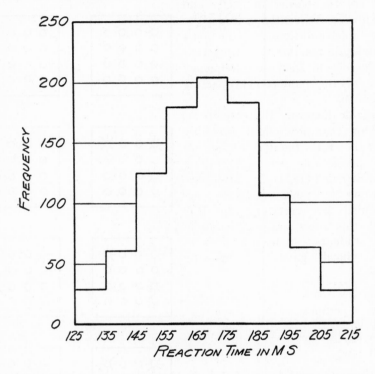

FIG. 93. (Data from Fessard, 1926.) Group distribution of simple RT to sound. The group consisted of 1,000 men, applicants for jobs as machinists in Paris. Each O made 30 reactions and the averages are plotted. Neither tail of the distribution is complete as a few extreme cases have been omitted.

which hastens a purely motor performance such as tapping, has little effect on RT (Schilling, 1921), though large doses hasten the disjunctive reaction (Hollingworth, 1912).

The behavior of manic-depressive patients would lead one to expect a very long RT in the depressed condition and a short RT in the excited condition, but tests give about the same RT in both conditions; the reaction is rather slow in both (Wells & Kelley, 1922).

The *age* of the individual can be counted as an organic factor. The young child, in spite of his short nerve paths and general liveliness, does not give a short RT, but quite the reverse. The RT decreases year by year to about the age of 20, and remains near the minimum for most of the life span, increasing somewhat in old age. Even in old age some individuals give a short RT (Miles, 1933). The long RT of the young child may reveal a lack of perfect "set." See Fig. 95.

Correlations of the reaction time. In spite of the large variation from trial to trial, the average of 40–100 simple RTs affords a rather

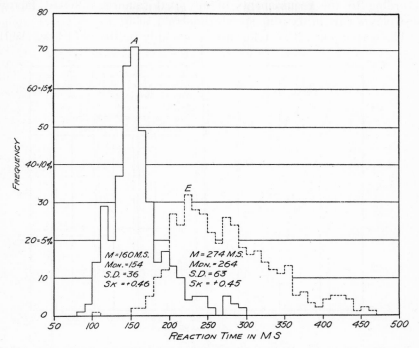

Fig. 94. (Data from Jenkins, 1926.) Distribution of single RTs. Each of two Os made 400 simple reactions to the cessation of a light (p. 321), A having had some previous training in RT experiments, E having had none. Both distributions are skew with the long tail extending to the right. M = arithmetical mean, Mdn = median, S.D. = standard deviation, Sk (a measure of skewness) = $3(M - Mdn)/S.D.$

precise measure of the untrained individual's initial standing in a group, the reliability coefficient being about .90 (Sisk, 1926; Lemmon, 1927).

As between the simple RT to light, sound and touch, the inter-correlations are fairly high, .70 to .85 (Sisk, 1926; Lanier, 1934).

Changing the reaction movement lowers the correlation; when the stimulus was always a sound but the response was made with finger, thumb, elbow, foot, head, lips or jaw, the intercorrelations ranged from .40 to .80 (Reymert, 1923).

As between the simple and the disjunctive RT, the correlation is still lower, .30 to .50 (Lemmon, 1927; Lanier, 1934). Disjunctive reactions have shown a high correlation with each other but no great variety of such reactions has been tried on the same individuals.

Between the simple RT and the latency of the eyelid reflex to a sudden noise, Lanier gets a correlation of zero.

As between the RT and such serial performances as tapping, color naming, cancellation, only low correlations have been found, .15 to .30 or a little higher.

The correlations lead to the conclusion that speed of action depends on no one factor such as speed of nerve conduction or synapse latency. According to the requirements of any performance, different factors must play a part in securing speed (Seashore, 1930).

The correlation with intelligence is probably positive but low. With

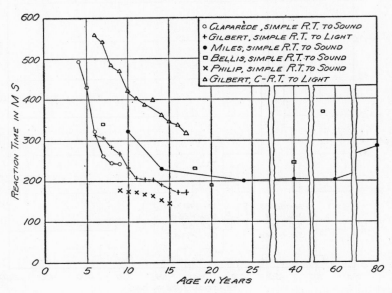

FIG. 95. (Data from Bellis, 1932–33; Claparède, 1925; Gilbert, 1894; Miles, 1931 b, 1933; Philip, 1934.) Reaction time in relation to age. Samples of the various age groups were tested.

college students, it ranges from 0 to +.35, when intelligence is measured by a paper and pencil test including many items. In such serial performances much time is lost on certain items, and the total time or score does not reveal O's true speed in an intellectual act. When single acts are timed, the correlation with RT has come out as high as .60–.75 (Peak & Boring, 1926; McFarland, 1930).

Reaction time outside the laboratory. Though serial action is more common in everyday life, simple and disjunctive reactions occur when one is set to respond in a certain way to one or more known stimuli. Instances are easily found in athletics, as the runner starting at the pistol shot or the football team charging at the motion of the ball. Miles (1931 c) devised a chronograph of rugged construction, which recorded the RTs of seven men at once. The men assumed the stance for charging and at an auditory stimulus lunged forward against rods placed a few inches in front. Thus measured, the simple RT was quite long, averaging 389 ms, and it was a bit longer in the heaviest men. It was 40 ms less for the best football players, and it differed somewhat according to the player's position in the team, being

360 ms, on the average, for 18 backs;
385 ms, " " " , for 40 line men;
444 ms, " " " , for 5 centers.

The words "on the average" need emphasis, for there was much variation within each group and the correlation of RT and playing skill was quite low.

The automobile driver cannot hope to equal the short RT of the laboratory, because his preparation is not so good; he does not get a Ready signal two seconds before the emergency. He has to shift his own internal transmission when the stimulus arrives. A second or two must be allowed him for shifting his set and adjusting himself to the new situation which has arisen. If he is really startled, several seconds may be needed. In the laboratory, an unexpected pistol shot or magnesium flash will produce a momentary inability to continue a rapid performance (Lubrich, 1932). On the road, however, the driver shows less fright than perseveration; he persists for a second or two—sometimes too long—in what he is already doing.

In another laboratory experiment (Westerlund & Tuttle, 1931), O has before him a row of three bulbs, which when lighted are red, yellow and blue; thus,

Y   R   B

To the yellow O responds with the left hand, to the blue with the right hand, to the red with the foot. The yellow and blue stimuli come in a rapid random series, and the red is interpolated at long intervals. In one condition O has also to do some adding while engaged in the RT work. The adding slowed the hand reactions but quickened the interspersed foot reactions. Thus, on the average:

	Hand reaction to *blue and yellow*	*Occasional foot* *reaction to red*
Without adding	490	1040
With adding	640	910

Without the adding O became so much absorbed in the hand reactions that he often failed to shift promptly to the foot reaction; with the adding his attention was less concentrated and the shift was easier. On the road, the driver needs to keep his field of attention broad, and not let it become concentrated on one possibility, since what happens may be something else. Ordinary conversation is probably an advantage—contrary to the old ideas—in the way just indicated as well as in keeping the driver awake in a long, monotonous turn at the wheel.

CHAPTER XV

ASSOCIATION

T HE STUDY of association antedates by many centuries the beginnings of experimental psychology. Aristotle spoke of association by contiguity, by similarity and by contrast, and these "laws of association" were prominent in the psychology of the eighteenth and nineteenth centuries. The subsidiary laws of recency, frequency and vividness were formulated about the beginning of the nineteenth century (Brown, 1820).

The main aim of the associationist school of psychology was to reduce all the laws of association to a single one, association by contiguity in experience, and to show that all mental operations could be explained as processes of association. One difficulty in the way of this last reduction was pointed out at the very outset by Hobbes (1651):

The train of thoughts, or mental discourse, is of two sorts. The first is unguided, without design, and inconstant; wherein there is no passionate thought to govern and direct those that follow . . . in which case the thoughts are said to wander, as in a dream. . . . The second is more constant, as being regulated by some desire and design.

The distinction drawn by Hobbes has been adopted by the experimentalists, who speak of "free" and "controlled association." In free association the laws of association are supposed to have full sway, while in controlled association an additional factor plays a part. "Unrestricted" and "restricted" association would be somewhat more objective terms. E may instruct O to respond to each stimulus word by saying its opposite, so imposing a restriction on the responses. Since O readily follows such instructions he clearly is exerting some control over his associative processes.

The free association experiment was first tried by Galton (1879-80) with himself as subject. He prepared 75 stimulus words (mostly nouns), wrote each on a separate slip of paper and laid them away for several days. He then took one slip at a time and laid it "under a book, but not wholly covered by it, so that when I leant forward I could see one of the words, being previously quite ignorant of what the word would be." He started a stop watch at the instant when the word caught his eye and stopped it when the word had suggested two different ideas. He immediately reviewed these two ideas and sought in memory for their origins and the connection of each with the stimulus word. He went through his list of stimulus words four times at intervals of about a month, and on assembling his data found that he had revived 505 ideas in a total of 660 sec., or at the rate of one recall per 1.3 sec. These 505 recalled ideas were however not all different, since 57 had come up twice, 36 three times, and 29 four times in the four presentations of the stimulus words. Those which recurred several times dated largely from his boyhood and youth, while those that came up only once were apt to date from adult life and sometimes from quite recent events. He was able to classify the revived "ideas" as follows:

Visual and other images of past scenes or events................ 32.5%
"Histrionic representations," acting out an event or an attitude
such as that of "abasement"................................... 22.5
Purely verbal: names, phrases, quotations.................... 45.

Galton found this experiment laborious but illuminating. "It would be very instructive to print the actual records at length, made by many experimenters . . . but it would be too absurd to print one's own singly. They lay bare the foundations of a man's thoughts with a curious distinctness, and exhibit his mental anatomy with more vividness and truth than he would probably care to publish to the world."

Galton's lead was promptly followed in Wundt's new laboratory, first by Trautscholdt (1883) who introduced the technical improvement of having an experimenter to announce the stimulus word and take the time, and then by Cattell (1886, 1887) who used the lip key and voice key, alternatively, so as to obtain a chronoscope reading of the associative reaction time. To make the timing wholly automatic, E uses a voice key in speaking the stimulus word, and O a similar key in speaking the response word; or the stimulus word is exposed visually. Cattell & Bryant (1889) modified the experiment by using a *list* of stimulus words, exposed visually, with time for the whole list taken by a stop watch. They also introduced the method of *continued* association: E gives a stimulus word and allows O a certain time for saying as many separate words as suggest themselves. The stop watch is used for rough timing of single reactions, E starting the watch as he speaks the stimulus word and stopping it when O starts to respond; or, perhaps better, E keeps the watch running, gives the stimulus word as the pointer passes a definite mark and notes the reading when O starts to respond (Murphy, 1917; Cason & Cason, 1925). Trautscholdt and Cattell extended the experiment to various forms of controlled association.

The association experiment has been used largely as a test for individual differences which lie outside the scope of this book; but there are some valuable results relating to the process of recall.

The association and memory experiments compared. From the association experiment just described, we can see that it is a form of reaction time experiment. A stimulus word (or object) is presented, and

O's response is timed and recorded.   Evidently the response is furnished from previous learning; it is a recalled response.   The association experiment *starts* with recall and differs thus from the memory experiment which starts with the original learning process.   The associations considered in a memory experiment are formed specially for the purposes of the experiment, and to make this possible either nonsense or at least unfamiliar material is used.   The association experiment, on the contrary, makes use of associations which have been formed in the ordinary course of life.   The association experiment is less complete than the memory experiment and does not control the formation of the associations nor the frequency, recency, etc. of their use.   Certainly the memory experiment (which was invented almost simultaneously with the association experiment) is the better of the two; but there is room also for the association experiment because it deals with the ordinary materials of thought and reveals something of the process of handling such materials.

Varieties of associative response.   Under this head can be included any previously learned response: reading a word, naming an object, giving the sum of two numbers, etc.   Most used in the laboratory are the "other-word" responses, the stimulus being a word and the response restricted to the extent that it must be some other word.   In controlled association the response must stand to the stimulus word in some prescribed relation, while in free association there is no such restriction, but O is instructed to speak or write the first other word called up by the stimulus word.   He is usually required to respond with a *single* word, not with a phrase or sentence.

How free is "free association"?   Other-word responses are evidently somewhat restricted and artificial.   In ordinary life we do not often respond to an isolated word by simply saying another word.   Many persons unfamiliar with the psychologist and his peculiar ways cannot believe that he wants nothing more definite.   They suspect him of seeking to discover how well they understand the stimulus words and set themselves, more or less intentionally, to give "sensible" answers.

Koffka (1912) attempted to secure genuinely free associations by instructing O to maintain a passive attitude, to let the stimulus word call up an image, and then to make a simple hand reaction.   Even here O commonly made the task more specific.   One O involuntarily set himself to give word reactions as quickly as possible, another to realize completely the meaning of the stimulus word, a third to call up an image of some individual thing or person of the kind mentioned in the stimulus word, and a fourth to pass from the object designated by the stimulus word to some other related object.   Apparently it is almost impossible to secure perfectly free association in an experimental setting.   Even in day dreaming there is usually some degree of control, shown by the dream's following along a certain line for some time before shifting to another.

The overt response is even less free than the first inner association, for O often rejects the first response that suggests itself because it seems foolish, embarrassing or in some way unsuitable. Wells (1911 a) concluded that the free association test still deserved its name in that good performance depended on freedom from hampering sets and obstructions.

Data yielded by the association experiment. Besides the associative reaction time, we obtain the verbal response which can be examined from several points of view. In controlled association the response can be scored as right or wrong, and in free association its character can be noted. All in all there are five types of data obtained in free association experiments.

1. The frequency or commonness of the response.
2. The logical or other relation of the response to the stimulus word.
3. The associative reaction time.
4. Signs of embarrassment or of suppression, indicative of an emotional "complex" or of "guilty knowledge."
5. The introspective (retrospective) report of O, which may reveal the origin of the association or the process of reaching the response.

We will devote the rest of this chapter to the first four types of data in their order, utilizing the introspective data from time to time to throw light on the questions discussed.

I. RELATIVE FREQUENCY OF DIFFERENT RESPONSES TO THE SAME STIMULUS WORD

As soon as the free association experiment was tried extensively (Cattell & Bryant, 1889) it became clear that any familiar stimulus word evoked the same response from many Os, and that the relative frequency of different responses to the same word was a matter of interest. Tried on a sample of a given population, the experiment becomes one in social custom and individual conformity. Thumb & Marbe (1901) used as stimulus words: nouns of family relationship, as *father, cousin;* adjectives having easy opposites; pronouns; verbs; adverbs of place and of time; and the number words 1–10. These were all arranged in mixed order, and presented orally for oral reaction. When eight Os had been examined, it was found that nearly every stimulus word had its favorite response. To *Vater* the response was *Mutter* from 5 of the 8 Os; to *gestern* (yesterday) the most frequent was *heute* (today). To each of the first nine numbers the common response was the next larger number; to the adjectives used the most common response was the adjective of opposite meaning. By using the same list of words in a class experiment E could make a hit by predicting (after the response words had been written but before they were reported) the most common response to each stimulus word (Saling, 1908). For such prediction to succeed the procedure had to be always the same and the groups tested fair samples of the same population. Esper (1918) repeated Thumb and Marbe's experiment in America with substantially the same results. Schmidt (1902) in Germany interspersed with other words different forms of the verb (as *to rain, I stand, he ate, broken*) and found that the verbs usually called up verbs, either another form of the same verb or another verb in the same form.

The Kent-Rosanoff frequency tables. In the hope of providing a basis for the use of free association in discovering individual peculiarities, especially of an abnormal sort, Kent & Rosanoff (1910) selected a list of 100 familiar English nouns and adjectives, though a few could be taken as verbs, and gave them orally to each of 1,000 normal subjects, mostly adult men and women of varying education and occupation. The subject was seated with his back to the experimenter and requested to respond to each stimulus word by one word only, "the first word that occurs to you other than the stimulus word." If O responded with a phrase or by repeating the stimulus word or some grammatical variant of it, that stimulus word was given again at the end of the list. Assembling the results from the thousand Os, the authors prepared a table of all the responses to each stimulus word, with the frequency of each response. The responses to one stimulus word are shown on the page opposite.

There is a similar table for each stimulus word. Three ways have been used for obtaining the individual's score.

1. Simply count the number of "individual reactions," defined as reactions having a frequency of zero in the tables. Some variants of form or meaning should be counted as equivalent to those actually found in the table, and rules are provided for scoring these doubtful cases. Normal persons with only common-school education have given an average of 5.2 individual reactions for the list of 100 stimulus words, while college-educated subjects, perhaps because of their larger vocabulary, have averaged somewhat more, 9.3 individual reactions. But some dementia precox patients, whose responses appear incoherent and unrelated to the respective stimulus words, give 25–50 percent of individual reactions.

2. Count the number of high frequency responses given by the individual. This is nearly the reverse of the preceding.

3. The most comprehensive measure would seem to be the median frequency value of the individual's responses. This measure shows with how large a fraction of the population the individual's free associations tend to agree on the whole. If this median value is high, the individual runs to common responses, if low, he runs to unusual responses (which may be extra high grade, eccentric, or incoherent).

Other association frequency tables. There are good reasons for repeating the Kent-Rosanoff experiment with the same stimulus words, but with other groups or "populations." The individual can be fairly compared only with his own population—a college freshman with a frequency table derived from college freshmen (Foster, 1929, p. 321). Besides, the comparison of different populations is interesting, as we shall see.

Woodrow & Lowell (1916) prepared frequency tables of the responses of 1,000 Minneapolis school children, aged 9–12, to 100 stimulus words, 90 of which were taken from the Kent-Rosanoff list. The children

Stimulus word: NEEDLE

Frequency in 1,000 subjects	*Response word*
160	thread
158	pin(s)
152	sharp
135	sew(s)
107	sewing
53	steel
40	point
26	instrument
17	eye
15	thimble
12	useful
11	prick(s)
9	pointed
7	cotton
6	work
5	implement
5	tool
4	cloth
4	darning
4	knitting
4	sharpness
3	article
3	fine
3	metal
2 each	books, button (s), clothes, coat, dressmaker, hurt, hypodermic, industry, pricking, small, sting, thick, thin,
1 each	blood, broken, camel, crocheting, cut, diligence, embroidery, handy, help, hole, home, housewife, labor, long, magnetic, material, mending, nail, ornament, patching, pincushion, shiny, slippers, stitching, surgeon, tailor, use, using, weapon, wire, woman
1,000	

were tested in groups and wrote their responses to the oral stimuli. O'Connor (1928) used the Kent-Rosanoff stimulus words and obtained oral responses from 1,000 adult men, mostly in industry. This sample differed from that of Kent and Rosanoff in containing no children, no women, and few, if any, representatives of the agricultural and personal service occupations. That gives us three large samples to compare: children, men and women representing the general adult population, and men in industry. The men in industry differ from the men and women in the same direction as the latter differ from the children, as can be seen from the *most frequent* response of each group to some of the stimulus words, as given on p. 346.

The shifts are striking and curious. Very few children give the opposite of *dark* or *soft*, while more than half of the "men in industry" do so. (Why the men in industry should show the adult type of response more decisively than the men and women can only be guessed in the absence of definite information on the make-up of the two samples.) A similar shift appears in the *coordinate* responses: table—chair, man—woman, and mountain—hill. The children tend to "stay by" the thing mentioned;

Stimulus	Response	1,000 Children	1,000 Men and women	1,000 Men in industry
TABLE	eat	358	63	40
	chair	24	274	333
DARK	night	421	221	162
	light	38	427	626
MAN	work	168	17	8
	woman	8	394	561
DEEP	hole	257	32	20
	shallow	6	180	296
SOFT	pillow	138	53	42
	hard	27	365	548
MOUNTAIN	high	390	246	171
	hill	91	184	364

they tell something about that thing, complete or enlarge upon the idea conveyed by the stimulus word; whereas the adults jump to a related, parallel idea. This difference is typical, though naturally not holding of every individual or of every response of any individual.

To show that the shift to opposites is characteristic of the adults, we examine the 20 adjectives contained in the whole list which have familiar opposites, and we find the average frequency of response by naming an opposite to be:

For the children	43
For the men and women	298
For the men in industry	473

To show the shift to coordinates, we may examine first the responses to the six color names included in the list: black, white, red, yellow, green, blue.

Response	1,000 Children	1,000 Men and women	1,000 Men in industry
some colored object	530	348	243
the word "color"	232	218	208
another color	33	291	414

Such a response as "red—blue" was very uncommon in the children, but common in the adults. The following table contains other examples of the shift to coordinates.

Stimulus-response		*1,000 Children*	*1,000 Men and women*	*1,000 Men in industry*
HAND	foot	0	239	321
BOY	girl	33	319	509
SOLDIER	sailor	0	58	102
DOCTOR	lawyer	1	36	161
LION	tiger	13	102	237
SHEEP	lamb	108	187	241
SALT	pepper	29	142	213
CHEESE	butter	49	136	194
WINDOW	door	2	57	107
STREET	road	60	91	124
CITY	town	110	258	452
MOON	sun	14	120	194

The great frequency of coordinate and contrast responses in adults is not to be interpreted as indicative of a strong tendency to think in these terms. The experiment as usually carried out is distinctly an experiment with words. When, instead of color names, actual bits of color were shown to college students (Dorcus, 1932) with instructions to write the first word thought of other than the name of the color itself, the response words were mostly names of colored objects, and very few coordinate colors were named. We are not to suppose that seeing a color commonly leads the adult to think of another color, but only that one color *name* tends to suggest another color name when the task is to give word responses. More in general, the frequency of opposites and coordinates in the responses of adults need not mean that "association by contrast" or by coordination is specially characteristic of adult thinking; for, again, the experiment is bound up with the use of words.

The parts of speech in stimulus and response. Many authors have studied the question whether the part of speech used in the response conforms to that of the stimulus word. Thumb and Marbe found it so, but their stimulus material was rather peculiar in including many pronouns, adverbs, number words, etc. Other experimenters (Bourdon, 1895; Crane, 1915; Jung, 1919; Menzerath, 1908; Wreschner, 1907–9) have obtained rather varying frequencies, but the general run of samples is about as follows:

	Percent frequency of response by		
	Noun	*Adjective*	*Verb*
To noun stimulus	70	20	8
To adjective stimulus	45	50	3
To verb stimulus	50	5	35

Adverbs also occur among the responses, and some pronouns and inter-jections. Much depends on the particular nouns, adjectives or verbs used as stimulus words, and upon the particular "set" which the subjects adopt. In general, two tendencies can be seen in the above table: a tendency to respond by a noun, and a tendency to make the response correspond grammatically with the stimulus word.[1]

II. CLASSIFICATION OF RESPONSES IN FREE ASSOCIATION

One curious fact that is readily noted in examining the responses made by different subjects to the same stimulus word is the variety of rela-tionships between stimulus and response. We have spoken of the contrast, coordinate and "completion" relationships, and others can be found. We should be able to learn something regarding individual and cultural habits and preferences of thought by noting the relations of response to stimulus words. Otis (1915) observed the following kinds of response in children:

I. O simply repeats the stimulus word, a common response in normal children 4–5 years old.

II. O gives a word unrelated to the stimulus word, a common response in five-year-olds. The stimulus word acts simply as a trigger releasing a word which the child has got by looking at objects in the room; as

> lamp—coat
> dream—collar
> bread—hat

III. Clang associations, the stimulus word evoking a word of similar sound, without regard to meaning; as

> table—able
> dark—hark
> music—use it

This type of response is not peculiar to any particular age, but occurs sporadically.

IV. Sentence responses, common at ages 4–7. For example:

> table—I eat off a table
> dark—It's dark at night
> soft—Snow is soft

V. Normal one-word responses, common in children from age 6 up.

The "defining" response. The more-than-one-word response, ob-tained from young children in spite of instructions, has usually the charac-ter of a rough definition, as if O were aiming to make clear to himself the meaning of the stimulus word or to demonstrate to E that he knew it.

---

[1] It has also been found (McClatchy, 1922) that when some of the stimulus words are local in their reference (as names of local buildings, clubs, etc.) the responses are likely to have a similar local reference.

Such defining responses are frequent in the responses of adults of low intelligence (Wehrlin, in Jung, 1919). Some examples:

> Angry—when you're angry
> Mountain—the big mountain
> Father—when you have a son of your own
> Table—made of wood
> Flower—in the garden
> Bird—flies
> Frog—is an insect
> Eel—fish

The last two instances are *supraordinates*, a class of response which is not peculiar to Os of low intelligence. In normal adults, the supraordinate response is even the most frequent to certain stimulus words:

> Citizen—man   Frequency 275 per 1,000
> Cabbage—vegetable   "   386 "   "
> Eagle—bird   "   593 "   "
> Bible—book   "   371 "   "

Under the head of definitions can be brought the *synonyms*, which are frequent responses to certain stimulus words:

> Blossom—flower   Frequency 509 per 1,000
> Swift—fast   "   318 "   "

The response in these cases is a *more familiar* equivalent of the stimulus word. Synonyms are frequently given as responses to relatively unfamiliar stimulus words (Murphy, 1917). Defining responses of one sort or another are frequent even with well-educated Os when the stimulus words are taken from a learned or scientific vocabulary (Rosanoff, 1918). For example:

> Ameba—animal   Frequency 108 out of 1,000
>   —protozoa   "   92 "   "   "
>   —biology   "   83 "   "   "
> Cerebellum—brain   "   671 "   "   "
> Odyssey—Homer   "   455 "   "   "
>   —Greek   "   119 "   "   "

But we also find a considerable frequency of coordinates:

> Ameba—paramecium Frequency 32 out of 1,000
> Cerebellum—cerebrum   "   127 "   "   "
> Odyssey—Iliad   "   197 "   "   "

Those Os who were specially familiar with the natural sciences were more likely than others to give coordinates in response to stimulus words taken from the sciences. It will be admitted that the coordinates just listed reveal more acquaintance with their respective stimulus words than can be inferred from the defining responses. You would hardly expect a biologist to give the response, *ameba—animal*. He would be more specific. Probably the first inner response to a stimulus word is to know its meaning. If the word is very familiar, O is free to shift quickly to some related object or fact; but if the word is relatively unfamiliar, its meaning or its sphere of meaning becomes explicit and so yields the response word.

Evaluating responses. Occasionally a subject is encountered who gives very few of the matter-of-fact responses illustrated, but seems impelled to tell in every case whether he (or she) likes the thing mentioned. Such persons show to an extreme degree a type of response which occurs sporadically in many subjects. Of 1,000 men and women, in response to the word *mutton*, 10 said *delicious, nice, disagreeable, dislike, hate,* or *horrid*. Some stimulus words bring more of these responses, the word *woman* giving no less than 33 different value words, such as *angel, artificial, beautiful, cross, good, graceful, inexplicable, kind, liar, perfection, pleasure, pretty, sweet, weak.*

Classification for clinical use of the free association test. Formerly more than at present it was hoped that an individual's favored type of response would reveal his mentality and personality. Many classes were at first distinguished, but with continued clinical experience the tendency has been to combine them into larger classes, since there seemed to be no special significance attaching to most of the minor classes. Wells (1911 c) for a time used the following rather elaborate classification, adapted from Jung (1919):

Class	*Example*
1. Failure to respond	
2. Egocentric	Success—I must
3. Egocentric predicate	Lonesome—never
4. Evaluation	Rose—beautiful
5. Matter-of-fact predicate	Spinach—green
6. Subject-verb	Dog—bite
7. Object-verb	Deer—shoot
8. Cause-effect	Joke—laughter
9. Coordination	Cow—horse
10. Subordination	Fruit—apple
11. Supraordination	Table—furniture
12. Contrast	Black—white
13. Coexistence	Sunday—church
14. Identity	Blossom—flower
15. Phrase completing	Forward—march
16. Word completing or compounding	Black—board
17. Assonance	Pack—tack
18. Syntactic change	Deep—depth

These classes were regarded as falling within three larger groups: the emotional, including classes 1–4; the matter-of-fact, classes 5–14; and the purely verbal or linguistic, classes 15–18. Failure of response is included in the emotional group on the ground that a strong emotion aroused by the stimulus word may distract O and inhibit reaction; but other interferences may give the same result. With failures are classed the naming of present objects unrelated to the stimulus word. Interjections also are classed with the emotional responses. Wells (1927) found that clinical purposes were better served by combining the classes into five, which he names:

I. Egocentric or subjective
II. Supraordinate
III. Contrast
IV. Miscellaneous
V. Speech habit

Here the Supraordinate and Contrast classes are left untouched, the Speech Habit includes classes 15–18 in the more detailed classification, the Egocentric class is expanded to include classes 1–7, and all the others are thrown into the Miscellaneous group which usually includes about 45 percent of all responses. The Supraordinate class, though usually small, is retained as an index of the "defining" tendency which largely disappears after adaptation to the experiment, provided the stimulus words are familiar. The Contrast class is retained as an index of O's readiness to adopt the quick and efficient type of reaction.

The Egocentric or Subjective class serves as an index of O's tendency to make an emotional or at least personal reaction to the stimulus words, and is made to include even the matter-of-fact predicates because of the difficulty of drawing a clear line, in practice, between them and the valuation responses. There is a strong negative correlation between the number of an individual's Egocentric and Contrast responses.

Uncertainties of classification. Almost every investigator who has attempted to classify the responses in free association has commented on the arbitrary decision required in many cases, and when two investigators have worked together with the same system of classification they have found it impossible to agree in the placement of certain responses. Some investigators have pointed out that each O should cooperate in the classification of his own responses or at least give introspections to guide in the classification; but such introspections are often unreliable even if feasible. Some of the difficulties can be seen in the following frequent associations:

Man—animal: supraordinate or coordinate?
Man—male: supraordinate noun or predicate adjective?
Hand—foot: coordinate, contrast, or similarity?
Red—color: supraordinate or adjective-noun?
Salt—sweet: coordinate or contrast?

In such cases as *Man—animal* or *Salt—sweet* we are of course concerned not with the best scientific relationship but with the way O sees the matter. Does he, or did he at the moment, think of man as a kind of animal or as distinguished from animals? Did he think of salt and sweet as coordinate primary tastes or as contrasting tastes?

The uncertainties are increased, especially with English words, by the identity in form of many nouns, adjectives and verbs, as can be gathered from the following frequent associations:

> Needle—thread
> Lamp—light
> White—light
> Hammer—nail
> Whisky—drink

One distinction which cannot be made with any assurance is that between speech habit and the meaningful categories. *Black—board* can reasonably be classed as word completion, especially with school children; but some psychologists would regard *Command—obey* as mere phrase completion, while others would take it at its face value as a contrast response.

A proposed classification. For experimental if not for clinical use, the facts cited and others to be now stated indicate the following as a sound psychological classification of most of the responses in free association:

1. Definitions, including synonyms and supraordinates
2. Completion or predication, broadly conceived
3. Coordinates, including contrasts
4. Valuations and personal associations

Class 1 might be called the "arriving" response, Class 2 the "staying by" response, and Class 3 the "jumping away" response; these three being matter-of-fact in distinction from the more emotional or personal responses of Class 4. Class 1 is to be expected when the stimulus word is relatively unfamiliar, so that the first explicit response is that of arriving at its meaning. Class 2 corresponds to a combination tentatively suggested by Murphy (1923) as involving "carrying out an idea" rather than "addition of a new idea." As the present author conceives it, it would include many responses classed under "coexistence" as well as the "matter-of-fact predicates."

Responses of Class 3 "jump away" from the meaning of the stimulus word to something which, while different, is coordinate. They might be called "and/or associations," as one of these conjunctions can readily be supposed inserted between stimulus and response words. Stimulus and response belong under some supraordinate concept which however is so familiar it need not become explicit. Examples are: *lion—tiger, hand—foot, man—woman, man—boy, table—chair, physics—chemistry, red—blue,* as well as any pair of opposites. Opposites are really coordinates; *up* and *down* have something in common which neither shares with *east* or *soft* or *bitter*.

These theoretical considerations are not the main reason for combining contrast and coordinate responses. The two sorts behave alike. An individual who gives few opposites in a free association test is likely to give few coordinates. The correlation between the number of opposites and the number of coordinates given has been found to range from +.42 to +.90 in various samples (Conrad, 1931; Crosland,[1] 1929; Kelley, 1913; Murphy, 1921; O'Connor, 1934).

If stimulus words like *man* or *hand* are included in an opposites test, a coordinate response is given with little hesitation.

Contrasts and coordinates are alike in being more frequent with adults than with children (p. 346). Murphy (1917) tried the free association experiment on university students and professors, devoted to literary or to scientific studies, and found contrasts and coordinates to be much more frequent with the scientists while "contiguity associations," corresponding to our Class 2, Completion and Predication, were much more common with the literary group. It would be hazardous to conclude that literary people, more than scientific, preserve the childlike spirit and are more prone to "completion" and "dwelling on" an idea than to "jumping away" to a related idea, yet something of the kind may be true.[2]

There does seem to be some psychological basis for the fourfold classification suggested; but it is doubtful whether any such scheme can win general acceptance at the present time.

Superficiality (or economy) of responses. Cutting across the classifications so far considered is a scale of meaningfulness *vs.* superficiality. The steps in the scale are somewhat as follows:

1. Most meaningful: the stimulus word calls up a particular experience.
2. The stimulus word calls up a particular object, though not a particular experience of it.
3. The stimulus word calls up a meaningful associate without any help from speech habit or purely verbal association.
4. The stimulus word calls up a familiar verbal associate, as in phrase completion or word compounding.
5. Mere clang association: the most superficial response.

Ziehen (1898, 1900) by retesting the same boys at intervals from ages 9 to 14, found that the type of response tended to become more superficial with increasing age. Recall of particular experiences decreased from 24 percent of all responses to 11 percent, and responses involving the recall of particular objects (including steps 1 and 2) decreased from 82 percent to 14 percent.

Jung (1919) finds that some educated adults tend to superficial re-

[1] The correlation in Crosland's sample of 47 college students was computed by the present author and found to be +.72.

[2] Freyd (1924) found contrast responses more frequent with life insurance salesmen than with students of the mechanical arts.

sponses, especially of step 4. They conceive the experiment "entirely as a verbal one; they endeavor by maintaining a ready speech-excitation to affix the first word that comes up, without entering more closely into the meaning of the stimulus word." Less educated Os are more inclined to say something meaningful about the object named in the stimulus word, regarding it as a question or challenge to show their knowledge. He also found that the distraction of making pencil marks in time with a metronome, at 60 strokes per minute, tended to make the responses more superficial.

The responses become more superficial also in fatigue (Aschaffenburg, 1897), under the influence of alcohol (Kraepelin, 1892; Smith, 1922), and with practice in the free association experiment (Wells, 1911 a; Wreschner, 1907–9). Psychotics respond surprisingly like normals, so far as the classification of their responses is concerned (Murphy, 1921, 1923) except indeed that egocentric or subjective responses are relatively few in the excited phase of manic-depressive insanity, and relatively frequent in the depressed stage (Wells, 1927). The psychotics show no "regression to the infantile" condition in their word responses, but conform more to adult frequencies than to those obtained from the 1,000 children (Murphy, 1923).

III. ASSOCIATIVE REACTION TIMES

Reaction times are divided into simple, disjunctive and associative, of which the first two were considered in the preceding chapter. The disjunctive is longer than the simple; the associative is longer still.

Since associative reactions are usually spoken and recorded by use of lip or voice keys, we need the simple vocal RT as a base line. Cattell (1886) gives averages obtained from two well-trained Os reacting to visual stimuli:

For the simple RT to light,
    with hand reaction   148 ms
    with speech reaction   175

For the disjunctive RT to 2 colors
    with hand reaction   317
    with speech reaction   376

For the disjunctive RT to 10 colors
    with speech reaction   547

The last reaction was more properly associative than disjunctive, since O depended on his previous associations between the colors and their names. The comparatively long average RT to the 10 colors is due largely to the incomplete familiarity of some of the color names. It took 650 ms to name orange, 577 ms to name brown or violet, and only 483 ms for blue and green. No doubt all these names seemed "perfectly familiar," but the RT showed a difference.

Associative reactions will be arranged in a scale of "directness," which proves to be also a scale of quickness.

1. **Reading reactions.** These are perfectly direct, or seem so to the experienced reader. When his eyes light on a printed word he seems actually to *see* the word, instead of seeing a complex little figure symbolizing the word and strongly associated with it. In an experiment O is shown words, letters or numerals and responds by reading them aloud. Cattell obtained the following average RTs from his two trained Os:

Reading	single letters	409 ms
"	short words	388
"	long words	431
"	one-place numbers	360
"	two-place numbers	396
"	three-place numbers	443

The RT, though always measured from the visual exposure of the stimulus to the *beginning* of the vocal response, was longer for the longer words and numbers because, probably, more time was needed to perceive them. But we notice that a short word was read as quickly as a single letter—an important result in the psychology of reading (see p. 715).

2. **Naming objects.** Here O is shown colors or pictures of familiar objects and responds by saying their names. It takes longer to name an object than to read its name (Cattell, 1886; Woodworth & Wells, 1911). In an experiment of Lund (1927) a color-naming test sheet was used, containing little squares of five colors—red, yellow, green, blue, black— 20 squares of each color in random order. The time for the whole series of 100 reactions was taken with a stop watch. There was a similar blank of five forms—circle, square, cross, star, triangle—and other blanks containing the printed *names* of the colors and forms arranged in the same order. Besides going straight through the series in the usual way, O was tested in *finding* all the reds, then all the yellows, etc. Of these various tasks, reading the names was the easiest but finding the names was the hardest, as seen from the average time per item obtained from 28 college students:

Reading a name	360 ms
Naming a color	560
Naming a form	800
Finding a color	560
Finding a form	730
Finding a word (name)	1000

Why should it take longer to name colors than to read the names of the same colors? The colors are easier to see than the names, as the above experiment shows; and the motor process of naming is the same in both cases. The difference must lie in the intervening central processes. The association between a seen word and the saying of the word must be closer than between a seen color and saying the color name. The difference may be due to practice: every time we notice a printed word we read it, silently at least; but we often see a color without naming it. As a result, not only is the association between printed and spoken word more practiced, but also it has no strong competitors. About the only response to a seen word is to read it, whereas there are many possible responses to a seen color, form or object.

One who serves as subject in experiments in color naming and in reading the color names believes that the association is more *direct* in reading the names. A word is its own name, and as soon as you recognize the word you have its name ready to speak. But when you have an object to name you have first to recognize it and then to recall its name. There must be an additional associative step in naming an object.

When a small group of dots is exposed (as in the "span of apprehension" experiment, p. 690) and O responds as quickly as possible by saying the number, we have a kind of naming reaction. The RT is about the same as for naming a color or object, provided the number of dots is quite small; it increases with the number of dots, even within the limits of the span of apprehension (Warren, 1897). Von Szeliski (1924) exposed cards containing 1–10 dots with instructions to call out the number as soon as possible into a voice key. Here is a sample of his results:

Number of dots exposed	Average reaction time for calling out the number
1	424 ms
2	437
3	484
4	553
5	636
6	827
7	1189
8	1060
9	1451
10	1124

The course of these figures shows some irregularities, which disappear when the results from several Os are pooled. The time certainly increases with the number of dots to be counted, but even with small numbers it is longer than the time for reading short words or one-place numbers.

3. **Other-word associations, restricted and partially restricted.** Less direct than either reading or naming is the typical association test in which O responds to a stimulus word by saying another word. The response may be either free or restricted, as we have seen. It may be wholly restricted, so that only one particular word is correct; or partially restricted, more than one response being correct though only those which meet certain requirements. In addition or multiplication the response is completely restricted, in an opposites test almost completely, in a

verb-object test much less so. Compare the species-genus or supraordinate test, illustrated by

horse—animal
copper—metal

with the genus-species or subordinate test, illustrated by

animal—horse
metal—copper

The latter is less restricted, since several animals or metals are well known to the subject and any one of them can be named. The average RT has come out as follows (Woodworth & Wells, 1911):

Species—genus	1540 ms, P.E. 70 ms
Genus—species	1840 ms, P.E. 70 ms

(The difference of 300 ms is reliable, given the correlation of + .70 between the two tests.) The closer restriction in the species-genus test seems to facilitate the response. Cattell (1887) gives other instances. In the following table [1] of his results, completely restricted responses are marked with an R:

R	Addition of two one-place numbers	690 ms
R	Multiplication of two one-place numbers	870
	Country—city (as England—London)	780
R	City—country	810
R	Month—season (as July—summer)	770
	Season—month	910
R	Month—following month (as May—June)	780
R	Month preceding month (as April—May)	1210
R	Famous man—occupation (as Raphael—painter)	820
R	Author—language (as Homer—Greek)	790
	Language—author	1000
	Author—book (as Homer—Iliad)	1330
	Whole—part (as house—door)	920
	Noun—adjective (as rock—hard)	790
	Verb—object (as aim—gun)	920
	Verb—subject (as swim—fish)	1050
	Genus—species	1040

These other-word reactions are distinctly slower than Cattell's reading and naming reactions; and the partially restricted responses tend to be slower than the wholly restricted. (The Country-city associations could almost be regarded as wholly restricted since, with the countries named, there was usually some one city standing out as the only likely

---

[1] Cattell's published tables give "recall times," times required for calling up the required word. They were computed by subtracting from the total associative RT the naming RT for words, which averaged 409 ms for the two Os. I have added this 409 ms to the published figures in order to make all our RT data directly comparable.

response.) Of course not all restricted responses are quick and easy: multiplication is slower than addition, and the preceding month is harder to get than the following month. These differences may be due to previous drill. In general, there is little justification for assigning any definite RT for any particular class of associative responses, because different examples of the same class will vary enormously. The stimuli used in the experiments were selected to be familiar and easy. That on the whole the restricted responses were quicker than the partially restricted appears in the adjacent distribution of Cattell's averages.

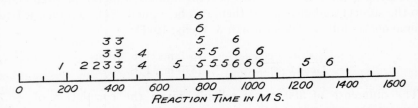

Fig. 96. Distribution of RT averages for the several classes of reactions, from Cattell's data:

1 = simple speech reaction to light
2 = disjunctive reactions
3 = reading reactions
4 = naming reactions
5 = other-word reactions, restricted
6 = other-word reactions, partially restricted

Free association time. Many experimenters have taken the time for free other-word responses, using either the stop watch or the chronoscope, and have (usually, not always) obtained skew distributions, with occasional responses delayed for 3–10 seconds. The median has usually been over one second but under two. Here are some of the averages from fair numbers of individuals:

Aschaffenburg (1895): 1150 ms
Jung (1919): 1800 ms; men, 1600; women, 2000 ms
Wreschner (1907): 1600 ms
Cason & Cason (1925): 1520 ms with the distribution of individual averages showing an S.D. = 400 ms
Murphy (1917): 1276 ms, going down to 1033 ms on repetition of the stimulus list

Menzerath (1908) and also Wells (1911 a) repeated the test on a series of days, and found the average to go down from 1750 to 1200–1300 ms. This result is rather remarkable, since new stimulus words were used on each succeeding day. The practice effect did not consist in strengthening particular stimulus-response connections. With practice the very long RTs became few, though the minimum remained at about 1200 ms throughout, as Wells found. The gain in average speed was probably due to better adaptation to the experiment, greater freedom from inner obstruction, and the adoption of more facile and "superficial" types of response. On repeating the original list of stimulus words at the close of the long experiment, Wells noted such changes in response as the following:

Stimulus word	Response before practice	Time	Response after practice	Time
bank	building	2.6 sec.	England	1.8 sec.
axle	hub	2.2	grease	1.2
spread	distance	3.4	bed	1.4
sister	Anna	5.0	brother	1.4
suffer	weak	2.2	pain	0.8

The later responses given in this list are "superficial" in being phrase completions, word compoundings or familiar pairs. Such responses are facilitated by speech habit. With practice O tends to be satisfied with such responses and so to cut down his average time, though he continues to give some responses of a less purely verbal sort.

All the above RT averages are from adults. Children are slower in free association, one investigator (Anderson, 1917) giving the following results:

Age	No. subjects	Average of indiv. Medians	Fastest indiv. Mdn	Slowest indiv. Mdn
8 years	15	2600 ms	1600 ms	5000 ms
10	26	2300	1400	5000
12	22	1700	1000	3000
14	18	1570	1000	3000
Adult	10	1500	1000	2200

The free association time differs somewhat with the part of speech of the stimulus word, as indicated in the accompanying summary table, which may also serve to show the usual run of these RTs.

FREE ASSOCIATION TIME ACCORDING TO PART OF SPEECH OF THE STIMULUS WORD

Stimulus word	1	2	3	4	5	6
Noun, abstract	979	1480	1950	1310	1852	
Noun, concrete	779	1330	1670	1175	1426	1640
Adjective		1450	1700	1140	1353	1550
Verb	910	1440	1900	1237	1526	1675

Sources: 1, Cattell and Bryant (1889), mouth key, single reactions, av. for 2 Os
2, The same, lists of 10 stimulus words, timed for list, av. per word for 2 Os
3, Jung (1919), single reactions timed with stop watch, av. for 26 adult Os
4, Wreschner (1907), voice key, single reactions, av. for 17 educated adults, each responding to 150–200 stimuli from each part of speech

5, Crane (1915), single reactions, lip key, av. for 30 college students,
responding to 10–50 stimuli of each class

6, Menzerath (1908), voice key, av. for 8 educated adults, about 50
stimulus words of each class

The free association time differs somewhat with the type of response—egocentric, predicate, contrast—but the main fact is that the more verbal responses are quicker than the more meaningful and personal.

Relation of free association time to the frequency of the response.   At first thought there should be no relation of any significance between the individual's RT in giving a certain response and the number of other people who give the same response; but Thumb & Marbe (1901) found as a matter of fact that the more frequent responses were quicker.   They spoke of this relation as a "law" and it has been called Marbe's law.   It has been confirmed by several other investigators, whose data are embodied in an adjacent figure.   Cason & Cason (1925) have checked the result by correlating the RT of the response with the frequency value of that response as given by Kent and Rosanoff.   The correlation was

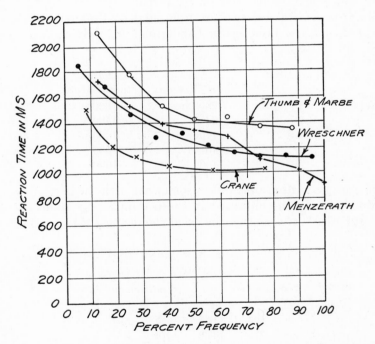

Fig. 97.   Relation of reaction time in free association to the frequency of the response in four samples of the population.   Data from: Thumb & Marbe (1901) with 8 O's and 140 stimulus words; Wreschner (1907) with 20 O's and 750 stimulus words; Crane (1915) with 30 O's and 145 stimulus words; Menzerath (1908) with 8 O's and 215 stimulus words.   Altogether over 20,000 reactions are summarized in this figure.   Menzerath secured 100 percent frequencies by use of especially familiar speech combinations as "einmal—zweimal," "rechts—links," "Tick—tack," "Bim—bam," and for this reason his RT curve does not flatten out at the highest frequencies.

worked out for the 100 responses of each individual separately, and was found negative in each of the 28 individuals examined, ranging from −.11 to −.59 with a general average of about −.33. The negative sign means that the greater the frequency value of a response, the shorter was its RT.

Another necessary check on "Marbe's law" is presented in Fig. 98, which dispels any suspicion that the effect might be due merely to the

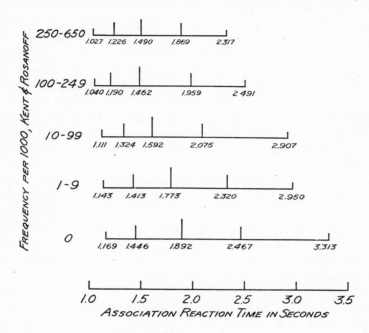

Fig. 98. The distribution of associative reaction times, for responses of low, medium and high frequency value. (Data from Crosland, 1929, computations by present author.) The responses of 47 Os to fifty of the Kent-Rosanoff stimulus words were divided into five groups according to frequency value. Responses not occurring in the Kent-Rosanoff tables, having thus a frequency value of zero, formed the first group; next came the responses given by 1–9 of the 1,000 persons tested by Kent and Rosanoff; and so on. A distribution was made of the RTs of the responses falling in each of the five frequency groups; and the figure shows the median, quartiles, and 10- and 90-percentile marks for each such group. The ends of each horizontal line lie at the 10- and 90-percentiles, the median is indicated by a large mark and the quartiles by the two smaller marks. The trend of the median is to shorter and shorter RT with the greater frequencies; and the same trend is seen in each quartile, etc.; so that the result is general and not due merely to exceptionally slow, unusual responses.

occurrence of extra slow reactions. Occasionally a delayed and unusual response can result from the tapping of some exciting personal experience; but that is not the whole story.

Why should the frequent responses be quick? Claparède (1903) suggested that quickness was the cause and frequency the effect. If O has a quick response available, that response would usually get the start of a slower response. But can we assume without further explanation that the same response will be quick for all Os, or for a large enough share of the population to give the group results just cited?

Cason & Cason (1925) take somewhat the same ground as Claparède: "If the subject's reaction is delayed, responses which are more and more foreign to the original stimulus word are formed, and his response has less probability of being a common one." Slowness is the cause, infrequency the effect. This view is certainly based on genuine observations, but may not do justice to the generality of the result shown in Fig. 98. Crane (1915) urges, on the other side, that frequency is cause and quickness effect, because group frequency would mean frequent individual experience. This explanation must hold especially well of the more verbal associations such as familiar opposites and phrase completions.

Is the reaction quicker in free or controlled association? An a priori argument could be put up for either alternative. The "first word suggested," in free association, ought to be quicker than a response subject to restrictions. Such was Wreschner's conclusion from his data (1907), but he used many difficult stimulus words in his tests of controlled association. You can delay the restricted response to any length by giving a difficult task (as the opposite of *rash* or *lonely*). But the set for opposites certainly facilitates the correct as against the incorrect responses, and it might operate to hasten an easy response. The question was reopened by May (1917). He says, "It is a general observation of psychologists that free associations take longer than controlled. . . . In order to test this matter I took several hundred free-association reactions and found the median reaction time was about 1.046 seconds against the median time of 1.102 seconds of the controlled reactions taken under similar conditions." There was practically no difference. But we have as yet no answer to the crucial question, whether the *same response to the same stimulus* is quicker in free or controlled association. Take the stimulus word *dark* which usually evokes its opposite in a free association test; will it give this response more quickly when O is set for opposites?

Factors in the associative reaction time. The question, how all the time is consumed, has some point when we compare the associative RT of 1000–2000 ms with the simple RT of only 100–200 ms. The associative reaction is both slow and exceedingly variable.

Directness is a factor. When introspections are taken in a free association experiment (Cattell, 1889; Aschaffenburg, 1895; Ziehen, 1898; Cordes, 1901; Mayer, 1901; Menzerath, 1908) O sometimes reports that the response word was reached by an indirect process, since he first thought of some object, situation, or "sphere of thought," out of which the response word emerged. Large differences in the single RTs are thus accounted for; and we have seen reasons for believing that the reading reaction is essentially more direct than the naming reaction, while any other-word reaction is still more indirect. Another fact accounted for by "directness" is the quick reaction that occurs when stimulus and response words are linked by speech habit.

Interference is an important factor. Sometimes O reports that two or more responses struggled for utterance, one getting in the other's way. It is probable that such interferences often impede the naming reactions and contribute to their slowness as compared with plain reading. It is also probable that restricted association eliminates interferences which impede the free or the partially restricted response. In wholly restricted association the set facilitates one particular response, but where more latitude is allowed two or more responses may compete.

Sometimes interference occurs in the form of distraction; the stimulus word may remind O of some interesting experience on which he dwells for a moment to the neglect of his task of responding. Sometimes a pleasant or unpleasant emotion delays the response. Sometimes O reports a short period of blankness in which nothing seems to occur and no progress is made toward a response; these blank periods probably indicate some kind of interference. Quick free association depends on freedom from such interferences and on a set for the more superficial or at least impersonal responses.

IV. DETECTIVE AND DIAGNOSTIC APPLICATIONS OF THE FREE AS-SOCIATION EXPERIMENT

The free association test has been used as a means of identifying a criminal from among other suspects, and as a means of discovering the emotional complex supposed to underlie a neurosis. No attempt will be made here to impart the special skill required for success in these efforts, but some facts of psychological interest may be gleaned from a brief account.

Detecting guilty knowledge. A theft has been committed. Stimulus words are selected which should remind the offender of the scene and circumstances of the crime. If 20 significant words can be found, they are mingled with 80 harmless words and the list of 100 stimulus words is presented orally, O being instructed to respond to each with the first other word suggested. The list is run off rapidly so that any emotional disturbance aroused by one word may carry over and affect the following responses. The response words and their RTs are recorded, O is carefully watched for signs of emotion, and sometimes a psychogalvanic or blood pressure record is taken (pp. 273, 276). The theory is that the significant words should elicit responses directly revealing guilty knowledge or, if such responses are suppressed, should give long RT and signs of emotion.

Introduced by Wertheimer (1905) this detective experiment has been tried many times in the laboratory with made-up "crimes," and sometimes in the examination of suspects in an actual case. Some psychologists found it untrustworthy (Crane, 1915), while others got excellent results (Crosland, 1929).

Need of "control" subjects in detecting a culprit. The association test is apparently undependable when applied to a single person in the attempt to answer the question of his guilt; but it is more reliable when a number of persons are tested to discover which one of them is guilty. The need for comparison between the results of a number of subjects can be seen in the case of one of the main indicators—excessive RT to the significant stimulus words. A bit from the middle of a list used in a case of dormitory theft (Crosland, 1929), with the responses and RTs of the person who later confessed, follows:

Stimulus word	Response	RT
bread	butter	2.6
flag	American	2.1
hip pocket	pants	5.2
light	dark	2.3
German	English	2.1
milk	butter	2.1
cottage	cheese	2.1
laugh	cry	3.0
cat	dog	1.8
desk drawer	desk	4.5
ocean	rain	2.3

This subject's RT to the two significant words is suspiciously long. But we have to expect that the response to such rather special stimuli will be longer than to the general run of ordinary words. We find that the average RT of seven other Os who were put through this same list was 2.5 sec. for *hip pocket* and 1.7 sec. for *desk drawer*, longer in the first case but not in the second than their average RT for the non-significant stimuli. The guilty person's average RT to the 20 significant words in the entire list was nearly double his average RT to the non-significant words; whereas the other seven Os showed comparatively little difference in RT to the significant and the non-significant. Other indicators besides the RT were taken into account, and combined into a single statistical measure of probability of guilt. Properly used the method is laborious; at best it cannot detect every guilty person; and occasionally it may pick the wrong culprit, one, for example, who somehow knows the circumstances of the crime though not himself guilty. But it has succeeded in a good number of cases in leading to confession.

Detecting complexes. This use of the free association test was introduced by Jung & Riklin (1904; see Jung, 1919). A "complex" here is a system of desires, emotions and memories, containing an element of strain, failure, dissatisfaction or sense of guilt. It is often a love affair, sometimes a business difficulty or a family trouble. Complexes are said to be "repressed" and "unconscious" when not readily called to mind; other complexes are perfectly conscious and yet O is reticent regarding them, and may not recognize their connection with any neurotic trouble.

The psychotherapist in his search for the troublemaker sometimes derives useful clues from the association test.

The discovery of a complex is a kindred problem to the detection of a criminal. There is, however, one important difference. The detective knows the crime but not the culprit; the psychotherapist knows the culprit but not the "crime." The psychotherapist does not know in advance what stimulus words will suit the individual case, but he can set traps for the complexes commonly encountered in clinical practice, arising from the sex life and its frustrations, from discontent with one's personal appearance or abilities, from disappointed ambition, from economic stress. Stimulus words calculated to tap such complexes are therefore included in the list, along with a padding of presumably neutral words. O takes a relaxed sitting or reclining position in a quiet (sometimes a partially darkened) room, and the examiner instructs him, as in other uses of free association, to respond to each stimulus word by saying the first other word suggested. As soon as the list of 100 stimulus words has been completed, it is gone through again with instructions to try and recall the response made to each stimulus word on the first round.

The evidence that a complex has been touched by any particular stimulus word is furnished by peculiarities in the response, called "complex indicators" (Jung, 1919), such as the following:

Long RT or complete failure to react.

Repetition of the stimulus word before reacting or as the sole reaction.

Misunderstanding of the stimulus word.

Response having no obvious relation to the stimulus word, far-fetched, extremely personal, or merely a clang-association.

Signs of excitement or embarrassment, laughing or smiling, stammering, interjections, whispered or shouted response.

Failures to recall the original response to a word when that word is given in the reproduction test. If the stirring of a complex has disturbed the easy flow of association on the first trial, the response may be difficult to recall.

The psychogalvanic reaction may be taken along with the association test, and is likely to show large deflections when an emotion is stirred (p. 289).

Experimental checking of validity of the indicators. There are two ways of obtaining some estimate of the trustworthiness of a complex indicator. Follow up the indicated complex and see if it is genuine in the individual subject. Or, check one indicator against another. The first method corresponds to a test for "validity," the second for "reliability."

The follow-up is constantly used by the psychotherapist. He finally reaches the complex, but often by so tortuous a route that one is not clear at the end whether the complex finally brought to light created the disturbance which served as a complex indicator. An immediate follow-up with cooperative, normal subjects makes a better check on the validity of the complex indicator; where this has been tried (Dooley, 1916) the results have shown that complexes, not perhaps unconscious ones, were actually tapped by certain stimulus words in the experiment, and that delayed reaction, failure to react or failure to recall a response—as well as direct emotional expressions—were the result of stirring up a complex. But not always. No one of the indicators is absolutely dependable.

Long RT is sometimes the effect of temporary interferences or distractions which have nothing to do with any complex (Grossart, 1921; Wells, 1911 a, 1927).

Failure to reproduce some of the original response words is certainly to be expected; a perfect recall score would be almost a miracle of memory.

Signs of embarrassment or excitement sometimes are due to tapping some *recent* experience. Amusement may be aroused by the examiner himself or by the whole procedure, especially in the early part of the list before the subject has settled down to the task (Hubbard, 1924).

Checking one indicator against another was a means adopted by Jung (1919, p. 396) to convince those who doubted in particular that failure to recall a response word was any sign of a complex. He showed that failure to recall went along with other indicators to quite an extent.

This method of attack was further developed by Hull & Lugoff (1921). They used Jung's list of 100 stimulus words on 50 men and 50 women believed to be a fair sample of the normal middle-class population. Taking each single reaction of any subject as a unit, they noted whether it showed one or more complex indicators. They then asked whether the coincidence of one indicator with another, or with all the others taken together, was greater than could be expected by chance; and if so, how much greater, the answer to this question being a "coefficient of association." By this statistical procedure they reached positive results on the whole, as indicated by the following coefficients of association between each indicator and the rest taken together:

Repetition of the stimulus word   + .59
Misunderstanding of the stimulus word + .47
Long RT   + .41
Defective reproduction of response word + .26

Each of these four indicators seems to have a certain reliability as revealing the same kind of disturbance as the others—call it a complex or by some broader term. The first two, which seem the better, are however infrequent. "Repeated use of the same response word," previously regarded as a good indicator, was frequent enough but showed no agreement at all with the others. Regarded as reliability coefficients, the figures just given inspire no great confidence in the test, to be sure; and further studies (Hubbard, 1924) show that irrelevant factors come into play. The mere position of a stimulus word in the series of 100 is a factor; for when the words were arranged in different orders for different Os, on the whole the long RTs came toward the middle of the list, while the failures to reproduce and the "laughing and smiling" came disproportionately from the early part of the list, and thus meant more when they occurred late in the list. The grammatical form of the stimulus word also made a difference, since the nouns gave fewer complex indicators than the adjectives and these than the verbs. The subject may be surprised when a new kind of stimulus word appears, as "to sin" or "to part" or "caring for" after a string of single word stimuli; and may give complex indicators because of mere surprise.

The most complex-arousing words differ somewhat from one investigation to another (Conklin, 1927; Hull & Lugoff, 1921; Wells, 1927), but on the whole they tend to suggest these sides of life:

> Love and marriage
> Friendship
> Quarrels and anger, injustice
> Ridicule, contempt, pity
> Danger
> Expense, money
> Death

CHAPTER XVI

EXPERIMENTAL ESTHETICS

Such a title as the above might refer to the experimenting that artists carry on when they try out their inventions on themselves, their artistic colleagues and their public. In the psychological laboratory experimental esthetics means a study of response to the beautiful, the sublime and tragic, the comic, the pathetic. Such a study ties closely with a chapter on feeling and emotion. The beautiful must be pleasing, the sublime uplifting, the tragic stirring, the comic amusing, the pathetic moving. Man is the measure of all things esthetic and the measure depends upon his feeling rather than purely upon his intellectual perceptions.

Laboratory study of esthetics makes use mostly of the "method of impression" (p. 234), in which O reports the impression or effect produced upon him by a presented object. He must answer such questions as: "Is this object pleasing or displeasing? Which of these two colors is the more attractive? How would you rate this joke on a scale of funniness?" Ostensibly O is reporting his feelings. But in a prolonged experiment his attitude becomes that of a critic who must evaluate the merits of the objects presented, and his responses become cool and matter-of-fact, with very little feeling, as has been found in careful introspective studies by Ledowski (1908) and Yokoyama (1921). If the instructions were, "Report how much feeling is aroused in you by this object and whether it is pleasant or unpleasant," we might secure from well trained Os reports of actual feeling, but usually the instructions are understood to mean, "Is this object pleasing or displeasing?", and O makes a report about the object rather than about his own subjective state. The objective attitude is more easily adopted and more consistently maintained. The consequence is that the results of experimental esthetics belong under the head of judgment rather than feeling.

Judgment defined. Such a term must be defined first as a *function*, as a relation between situation and result achieved. When this function has been identified, we can attempt an introspective description of the process of judging. We can present suitable situations and get O to make the judgment response and to report his experience. So we might conceivably reach a definition of judgment in terms of content. An attempt of this sort was made by Marbe (1901). Functionally he defined judgment as any reaction that can be characterized as true or false. He found no specific content characteristic of the judgment, no particular sensation or image or feeling or attitude occurring regularly in all judgments. Apparently judgment cannot be defined in terms of content but only as a function.

Marbe's functional definition, however, in terms of true and false, is not entirely satisfactory. It does not cover the esthetic judgment. In matters of taste there is no objective fact regarding which either true or false statements can be made. As a more inclusive definition of judgment the following is suggested: *A judgment is an answer to a question.* The question may be asked by someone else or by oneself. It need not be formulated in words. But in the absence of questioning, an impression or a response would not be a judgment. According to this definition, some percepts are judgments and some are not. If you look out of your window and see a cloud in the sky, this observation by itself is scarcely a judgment, but if the sight of the cloud suggests, however inarticulately, the query whether it is clouding over, and if further looking gives you an answer to this query, then you definitely have made a judgment.

Whether or not this question-answer definition of judgment will prove to be universally satisfactory, it certainly applies well enough to the experimental work, both on esthetic judgments and on the "psychophysical" judgments of magnitude, intensity and quality. In all such experiments the instructions include a question which O is to answer. The instructions specify some *dimension,* as extent, time, intensity, quality, goodness or beauty. Within this dimension certain steps or *categories* are specified, in terms of which O is to report his answer to the question. Two categories may be used, "good, bad"; or three as "heavy, medium, light"; or four as "very pleasing, slightly pleasing, slightly unpleasing, very unpleasing"; or a larger number.

If a judgment is functionally an answer to a question, the process of judgment must include a rising gradient of certainty. The process starts with uncertainty and reaches sufficient certainty to justify at least a tentative answer. In many cases the gradient does not reach the level of full certainty and the judgment is qualified as doubtful. The upward slope of certainty may be gradual or abrupt, and the judgment slow or quick in its development.

Beginnings of experimental esthetics. It is somewhat surprising to learn that Fechner, the father of psychophysics, deserves the same title in the field of experimental esthetics (1871, 1876). Fechner was a man of wide interests, including literature and the arts. It seemed to him the time was ripe for an empirical science of esthetics, not to supplant but to supplement the more philosophical treatises which approached the subject as he said "from above." He thought it should also be approached "from below," by gathering facts and working inductively toward principles. Working from above down, one started with general principles, on which there was no way of securing agreement, and attempted to deduce the rules of art, but could never reach certainty or clarity. Starting from below, one might be limited for a long time to relatively unimportant findings, but they would at least be clear and, if confirmed by other experimenters, would command universal acceptance.

In investigating esthetic problems from below, one would obviously begin with individual likes and dislikes, choices and preferences. By pooling results from many individuals one could through statistical procedure arrive at group standards. When individual idiosyncrasies were ironed out by averaging, one could even obtain esthetic norms with some claim to validity, at least for a given social group.

Besides this psychological approach Fechner used another empirical method which may be called ethnological. In seeking the most esthetic shape of a rectangle, he not only ascertained the preference of many individuals but also measured many specimens of picture frames, visiting cards and book covers, where the proportions are not rigidly determined by practical requirements and some leeway is left for taste. It should not be assumed in advance that the forms or colors current among a group are necessarily preferred by the majority of individuals. The group standards might be affected by economic and other social factors cutting across the psychological factor of individual likes and dislikes. At any rate it appeared to Fechner that the psychological approach through the laboratory was worth trying.

The utility of an experimental esthetics may or may not reach as far as the artist's studio. At least the decorator and the industrial artist will be grateful if the psychologist shows how the greatest number of people can be pleased. If the right shape and color of a container will cater to pleasure as well as use, why not try out the possibilities on a fair sample of the prospective public and be guided by the general preference? Quite apart from such practical applications, experiments on esthetic judgments have a legitimate place in pure psychology. The main purpose is to study esthetic interests, their sources, development and mode of operation, and in general to chart the individual's course in his quest of the beautiful.

METHODS OF EXPERIMENTAL ESTHETICS

Since in both cases we are concerned with the judgments of an observer upon objects presented to him, our methods in esthetics and in psychophysics are naturally somewhat alike. In psychophysics we ask such questions as "Which of these two weights is the heavier?", and in esthetics such questions as "Which of these figures is the more pleasing?" Or, in psychophysics, we give O a fixed and an adjustable weight, asking him to adjust the second till it seems equal to the first when lifted with the hand. Similarly in esthetics we give O a rectangle of fixed width but adjustable length and ask him to adjust it to the most pleasing proportion. In both fields we have two main methods: securing judgments on ready-made objects, and adjusting an object to meet certain specifications.

In psychophysics E knows the weights or other objects which O is trying to judge, and E can therefore measure O's errors. In esthetics there is no error to measure, because there is no objective standard against which an error could be measured. For that reason the methods of esthetics are somewhat simpler than those of psychophysics.

The adjustment or production method. For example, O is asked to draw a rectangle which shall have for him the most pleasing proportion of length and breadth. To obviate difficulties in drawing, E provides an adjustable rectangle by laying a long strip of white paper on a sheet of black paper and furnishing a second black sheet with which O covers so much of the white strip as will leave the visible remainder a white rectangle of the preferred shape. More adequate apparatus, free from extra lines, can be set up in a dark room by illuminating a sheet of milk glass from behind and covering it with black paper except for a rectangular strip the length of which can be adjusted by a movable sheet of black. Confining our experiment for the time to the single O, we obtain from him enough settings to yield a distribution, from which we can see where the settings centered and how much they scattered, and from which we can compute the Mean and SD, etc. A small scatter indicates definite preference; a wide scatter means that O can be pleased by quite a range of rectangles. Settings from many Os show by their distribution whether agreement is close in the population sampled and what shape or shapes of rectangles are most popular.

The second main method, in which ready-made figures or other objects are judged, has several varieties. The objects are shown singly, by pairs, or all together, and O's task is either to compare them or to judge each one separately. We will consider the methods of choice, of ranking, of rating, and of comparison by pairs.

The method of choice. Fechner prepared 10 rectangles of cardboard, ranging from a perfect square to an oblong only $\frac{2}{5}$ as wide as long. Spreading them in irregular order on a table, he asked O to select the most pleasing and also to indicate the least pleasing. O was instructed to consider the bare shapes without regard to any use or association. After several hundred individuals had made their choices he counted the votes for each rectangle. (If an O could not decide between two rectangles, half a vote was assigned to each of them.) The distribution of choices was rather scattered but did show a definite mode, with some indication of a secondary mode. Rectangles receiving many positive votes received few negative ones.

This method, on its face, is a census and gives merely the frequencies of different choices in the population sampled. Fechner believed that it gave more than that. Assuming that some one shape is inherently most pleasing, he argued that irrelevant factors would deflect some choices to this or that side but still leave the ideal shape as the center and mode of the distribution. He concluded that the modal choice was an index of the most pleasing shape, and that the falling off in votes on each side of the mode was a fair index of the relative pleasingness of the different shapes. It is probably a rough index rather than a fair one.

The ranking method, or order of merit method. Had Fechner asked his subjects after making their first choice to indicate the next best and the next, and so on down the list, he would have obtained more complete information on relative pleasingness. Later experimenters, especially Cattell (1902, 1903, 1906), introduced this expanded method. Usually the whole lot of objects is presented together, and O is given latitude as to exactly how he shall proceed, so long as he comes through with a complete rank order. Some experimenters have asked O first to sort the objects roughly into grades, and then to rank the items in each grade and revise the whole order.

A single ranking of a collection of objects shows their relative pleasingness or value to one individual at one particular time. We can go much further by having him rank them on a second occasion, and by having several individuals rank the same objects. Two rankings by the same O indicate how stable his preferences are with respect to those objects. When several judges have ranked the same objects we compute the mean rank assigned to each object. The pooled ranks are free from the idiosyncrasy of the individual judge and furnish a social and quasi-objective appraisal of the objects. We can see how well the judges agree on the whole and regarding which objects they are in good or poor agreement, and we can discover which judges are most representative of the social judgment expressed by the pooled ranks.

The ranking method will be illustrated by a sample of Cattell's data on scientific merit (1906). He asked 10 representative astronomers, serving as judges, to rank a whole list of astronomers. The judges worked, not like an ordinary jury, but each one independently and privately. Our table takes account only of the 10 astronomers who came out at the head of the list. Adding the rank numbers vertically and dividing by the number of judges we obtain the Mean Rank for each person judged. We notice that a certain one of the astronomers was ranked first by every judge; his scientific merits were evidently quite outstanding. (In a similar ranking of the psychologists of that day, William James received unanimous first choice.) Agreement was not so good regarding the second man on the list who was once given ninth place. Where the Mean Rank is almost the same for two persons, VIII and IX for example, the difference is probably not reliable.

Before noticing the formulas beneath the table, consider what information can be obtained regarding the "items" (here the persons judged), and regarding the judges. The SD of the ranks assigned to the same item shows how variable an impression is produced by that item and can furnish a measure of the reliability of its Mean Rank. Comparing the ranks assigned to the several items by one judge with the respective Mean Ranks we can see how nearly the judge agreed with the pooled judgment of the whole group of judges.

Ranking of 10 Leading Astronomers by 10 Judges
(*After Cattell, 1906*)

Person judged

Judge	I	II	III	IV	V	VI	VII	VIII	IX	X
A	1	2	4	3	9	6	5	8	7	10
B	1	4	2	5	6	7	3	10	8	9
C	1	3	4	5	2	8	9	6	10	7
D	1	3	4	5	2	6	10	8	7	9
E	1	9	2	5	6	3	4	8	10	7
F	1	4	9	2	5	6	7	3	10	8
G	1	3	5	10	2	6	9	7	8	4
H	1	3	5	7	6	4	8	10	2	9
J	1	2	8	4	9	6	3	7	5	10
K	1	2	4	5	9	8	6	3	7	10

Sum	10	35	47	51	56	60	64	70	74	83
MR = Mean Rank	1.0	3.5	4.7	5.1	5.6	6.0	6.4	7.0	7.4	8.3 Av MR = 5.5
MR^2	1.00	12.25								Av MR^2 = 34.23

n = no. items = 10; m = no. judges = 10

(1) Av MR $= \dfrac{n+1}{2}$, always; here $= \dfrac{10+1}{2} = 5.5$

(2) SD$_{MR}$ = SD of the Mean Ranks

$= \sqrt{\text{Av } MR^2 - (\text{Av } MR)^2} = \sqrt{34.23 - 5.5^2} = \sqrt{3.98} = 2.00$

(3) SD$_n$ = SD of the first n whole numbers
(or of any n consecutive whole numbers)

$= \sqrt{\dfrac{n^2-1}{12}} \qquad = \sqrt{\dfrac{99}{12}} = \sqrt{8.25} = 2.87$

(4) t $= \dfrac{SD_{MR}}{SD_n} \qquad = \dfrac{2.00}{2.87} = .70$

(5) Av r = Av correlation of all the rank orders

$= \dfrac{mt^2-1}{m-1} \qquad = \dfrac{4.90-1}{10-1} = +.43$

As to the psychological significance of such a table of results, we cannot do better than quote the original statement of Cattell (1903, 1906):

It should be distinctly noted that these figures give only what they profess to give, namely, the resultant opinion of ten competent judges. They show the reputation of the men among experts, but not necessarily their ability or performance. Constant errors, such as may arise from a man's being better or less known than he deserves, are not eliminated. There is, however, no other criterion of a man's work than the estimation in which it is held by those most competent to judge.

Though scientific merit is scarcely an esthetic dimension, it belongs under the broader head of human values, and Cattell's remarks would hold good, in their general import, of judgments of beauty or goodness.

Measures of agreement between the rankings. The amount of agreement between any two judges is measured by the correlation coefficient, either the product-moment formula or the rank-difference formula, the two being mathematically equivalent when the data consist simply of ranks. Any judge's ranks can be correlated with the Mean Ranks by the product-moment formula. But it would be very desirable to have a measure of the general agreement among all the judges or rankings. Such a measure would serve as an index of the reliability of the Mean Ranks as a whole, and would also enable us to compare different groups of judges; for example, it would answer the question whether men or women were more uniform in their color preferences.

There are two good measures of general agreement among the rankings, shown beneath the preceding table by the formulas for t and for Av r.

Consider first the Mean Ranks. If all the judges were in perfect agreement, one item would always be ranked 1 and would have a Mean Rank of 1; another item would have a Mean Rank of 2; and so on. The Mean Ranks would be the numbers 1, 2, 3 . . . . n; and the SD of the Mean Ranks would be that of the first n whole numbers. Any disagreement between the judges causes the Mean Ranks to fall together and have a smaller SD. The ratio t, between the actual and the maximum possible SD of the Mean Ranks, thus gives a measure of the agreement among all the rankings. When t = 1, the agreement is perfect; when t = 0, the agreement is the least possible, less than chance.

The correlation coefficient is a more familiar measure. The average correlation could be found by first finding the correlation between the judges, two by two, and then averaging, but the computation would be laborious with any large number of judges. Fortunately Av r can be computed directly from t, by Formula (**5**), which deserves a little discussion. If t = 1, the equation gives Av r = 1, perfect agreement. If t = 0, Av r is negative, indicating opposition rather than chance relationship. For chance, put Av r = 0, and the equation gives

$$t^2 = \frac{1}{m}$$

If m, the number of rankings, is 10, we have $t = \sqrt{.10} = .316$. As m increases, the chance value of t approaches zero.

With regard to the *proof* of the formulas:
(1) Av MR is the average of all the ranks given by all the judges and therefore = the Mean of the first n whole numbers.
(2) SD is found with zero as the "Guessed Average" or Assumed Mean, the actual average being the correction.

(3) See Yule, 1929, p. 143.

(4) The equation defines t.

(5) This equation can be derived from one given by Woodworth (1912, p. 108) or from one given by Kelley (1923, pp. 213, 217).

One more formula may be added for the purpose of estimating the reliability of Av r.

The regular measure for the SD of an r, namely,

$$SD_r = \frac{1 - r^2}{\sqrt{n}}$$

gives the SD of the single r and is thus the predicted SD of a distribution of r's of which the r obtained is a sample. What we have obtained is a Mean of such a distribution. The distribution contains $m(m - 1)/2$ values of r, but only m independent measures, corresponding to the number of judges or rankings. Therefore in passing from the SD of the distribution to the SD of the Mean, we divide by the square root of m. We have thus

$$SD \text{ of } Av\ r = \frac{1 - (Av\ r)^2}{\sqrt{mn}} \qquad (6)$$

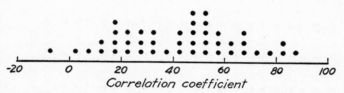

Fig. 99. Distribution of correlations between the rankings of astronomers by individual judges. As a check on formulas (5) and (6), the 45 separate correlations were computed and M, SD and SD_M were computed for this distribution, with results as follows:

	From the formulas	*From the distribution*
Av r	.4252	.4252
SD_{dist}	.2591	.2268
SD_M	.0819	.0717

Agreement is exact in respect to Av r (as it must be since the two computations are mathematically equivalent), but only approximate as regards SD; the SD of r, as computed from r itself, being only a probability value.

The utility of the formulas is better illustrated by the adjacent large table of data from Strong (1911). 20 advertisements were ranked by each of 100 men, and also by 95 women. The body of the table shows the frequencies with which the men ranked each item first, second, etc. The frequencies in each column are used to compute the Mean Rank, and SD_{MR}, t and Av r are computed from the Mean Ranks, as before. The women's Mean Ranks and derived values are given at the bottom of the table, and the net result is that agreement among the women was closer than among the men, though it was still far from close.

The rating method. This resembles the method of single stimuli in psychophysics (p. 425). The objects to be judged are presented one at

RANKS ASSIGNED TO 20 ADVERTISEMENTS BY 100 MEN

Advertisement no.

Position	1	2	3	4	5	6	7	8	9	10	11	12	13	14	15	16	17	18	19	20
1	14	7	6	10	10	6	5	3	1	12	5	1	7	0	1	7	5	0	0	0
2	20	13	7	6	1	4	3	8	1	7	3	3	6	0	5	5	6	2	0	0
3	11	7	7	4	15	6	6	2	4	7	9	4	3	1	2	6	4	3	0	0
4	11	11	8	7	5	5	5	6	4	6	9	6	3	0	2	3	3	2	3	0
5	5	8	11	5	10	4	7	8	7	7	2	5	10	3	1	4	3	4	0	0
6	9	7	11	1	10	1	8	3	7	6	5	3	6	3	3	5	7	7	0	1
7	10	9	6	12	3	2	4	10	9	4	2	6	3	3	3	3	7	3	1	2
8	3	8	6	4	8	5	7	5	10	3	8	5	8	5	4	1	2	3	1	1
9	2	12	7	3	3	5	4	4	4	5	4	8	6	7	5	7	3	5	4	3
10	4	3	3	8	5	4	9	6	6	6	6	6	7	2	2	3	8	7	2	4
11	3	0	2	6	8	3	5	3	5	3	3	14	3	7	10	4	6	7	2	0
12	3	0	5	3	5	8	5	5	9	7	7	2	7	8	9	5	6	9	4	5
13	1	3	3	2	3	7	9	2	6	8	6	11	5	6	6	9	5	4	4	1
14	0	0	4	7	4	10	3	3	5	3	4	5	5	6	7	8	3	2	9	4
15	0	3	4	8	2	5	3	3	6	3	3	3	4	7	13	8	8	4	9	7
16	2	2	4	1	2	6	3	8	2	5	3	3	4	14	12	2	0	6	11	7
17	1	1	4	6	4	4	3	7	5	0	9	7	5	6	7	5	6	3	13	8
18	0	4	1	3	1	5	7	5	5	5	3	2	6	13	3	8	3	10	9	12
19	1	0	1	3	0	3	2	8	3	2	6	2	1	9	5	3	11	3	12	14
20	0	1	0	1	1	7	2	1	1	2	3	2	1	3	0	7	2	12	16	38
MR	5.12	6.89	7.83	9.11	7.60	11.03	9.64	10.28	10.32	8.66	10.13	10.47	9.43	13.96	12.19	10.98	10.72	12.58	15.71	17.35

SD_{MR} = 2.817,   t = .489,   Av r = .231,   SD of Av r = .021

Mean Ranks for 95 women

	1	2	3	4	5	6	7	8	9	10	11	12	13	14	15	16	17	18	19	20
MR	4.62	4.92	6.37	7.48	8.60	11.57	9.54	9.46	9.74	8.56	10.65	9.00	10.21	13.77	12.10	13.00	13.78	14.01	15.01	17.68

SD_{MR} = 3.326,   t = .577,   Av r = .326,   SD of Av r = .020

a time and the subject expresses a judgment on each. He locates each object along some absolute scale, and no comparison of one object with another is called for. This absolute scale may have two steps, as "good" and "bad"; it may have three, as "good," "bad" and "indifferent." The first use of this method apparently was by Major (1895) who used a scale of seven steps:

1. very pleasant
2. moderately pleasant
3. just pleasant
4. without affective tone
5. just unpleasant
6. moderately unpleasant
7. very unpleasant

The rating method is used extensively for obtaining estimates of the personality traits of individuals; for this use reference is made to books by Symonds (1931), Garrett and Schneck (1933), and Guilford (1936). Sometimes the ratings are made in letter grades, sometimes on a percent basis, 100 denoting the maximum degree of a trait and zero the complete absence of the trait. Where the dimension in question extends from positive to negative, as in the case of pleasantness and unpleasantness, it is desirable to designate one step of the scale as denoting the indifferent level, which is in a sense an absolute zero.

At first thought this method appears to ask too much of the judge. Having only one item present at a time, he can make no direct comparisons, and is dependent on memory for his subjective scale. As a matter of experience, however, the method is rather easy and comfortable for the judge, and gives reasonably consistent results. Its administrative advantages are obvious, especially when any large number of items has to be judged, for then the ranking method becomes very unwieldy. Think of ranking 100 objects in order! Still more unwieldy is the method of comparison pair-by-pair which we shall consider in a moment.

It is not easy to standardize the individual's subjective rating scale, or to insure uniformity in the scales and rating procedures of different judges. E can help by training the judges in advance of the experiment proper. Otherwise each judge calibrates his own subjective scale as best he can and the scales differ in two respects: (1) One scale may be displaced bodily as regards the other; thus one judge systematically gives lower ratings. (2) One judge's scale may be excessively coarse, so that he gives most of the items nearly the same ratings; his distribution is narrow. These two difficulties can be overcome by transmuting the raw ratings into a SD scale. The average rating and the SD of the ratings are found for each judge and his ratings are then converted into SD units measured up and down from his own average. Suppose two judges rate the same 100 objects on a seven-point scale with frequencies as follows:

| | First judge | | Second judge | |
Scale units	f	SD units	f	SD units
1	2	− 2.85	5	− 2.10
2	8	− 1.70	5	− 1.45
3	40	− .55	20	− .81
4	40	+ .60	35	− .16
5	10	+ 1.75	10	+ .48
6	0		15	+ 1.13
7	0		10	+ 1.77

$$N = 100 \qquad\qquad N = 100$$
$$M = 3.48 \qquad\qquad M = 4.25$$
$$SD = .87 \qquad\qquad SD = 1.55$$

If a certain object X was rated 5 by the first judge and 7 by the second, their agreement was almost perfect, according to the SD ratings. If another object Y was rated 4 by both judges, its mean SD rating would be $(+ .60 − .16)/2 = + .22$. The transmutation need not ordinarily be carried to two places of decimals. The SD scale has the disadvantage of losing the "absolute zero" out of scales that extend from good to bad through an indifference point.

Comparison by pairs. The objects are presented two at a time and O expresses his preference between each two. He reports which of the two is more pleasing or which he places higher in whatever dimension is being considered. This procedure was introduced by Cohn (1894) who used it in the study of color preferences, and called it the method of "paarweise Vergleichung," a phrase which has often been translated "paired comparisons," though it properly should be "pair-by-pair comparisons," since it is the items, not the comparisons, which are paired. The purpose of the method is to simplify O's task by demanding only a single comparison at any moment; and because of this simplicity the method has often been regarded as the standard method of experimental esthetics. When each item is paired with every other, the total number of pairs is $n(n − 1)/2$. With 5 items to be compared, the number of comparisons is 10; with 10 items, 45; with 20 items, 190; with 30 items, 435; and the number of pairs becomes impossibly great with any large number of items. The subject's esthetic sense becomes exhausted. The relative preference for the items is determined just as well by the shorter and more agreeable ranking method (Barrett, 1914), and probably also by the rating method. The method of pair comparisons does afford a means of analyzing minutely the subject's process of judgment and its fluctuations and inconsistency.

In conducting a Pair Comparison experiment, it is well to prepare a list of the pairs in shuffled order and to check O's preference in each pair as presented. Since time and space errors are possible (see p. 438), i.e., since O may have a tendency to prefer the second member of a pair when one follows the other in presentation, or to prefer the upper one, or the right-hand one, etc., when the pair is presented simultaneously, the experimenter in preparing his list of pairs should, roughly at least, equate the items in time or space position. The experiment is sometimes doubled, by presenting each pair twice, once in each time or space order; but this doubling lengthens what may already be a rather wearisome procedure.

The judgments obtained from a single experiment on one O can be charted in a triangular form which shows the choice between each two items, as in the following table. The preference score for each item is the count of its entries in the whole table. Blue-Green was preferred 3 times, Green 3 times, Red 2 times, Yellow 2 times, Brown 0 times, Pink 5 times. Pink was most preferred.

SAMPLE PAIR COMPARISON DATA TABLE, WITH COMPUTATION

Six colors were compared pair by pair, the one preferred being designated by its initial, etc., at the proper intersection.

	Blue-Green	Green	Red	Yellow	Brown	Pink	
Green	BG						
Red	BG	G					
Yellow	Y	G	R				
Brown	BG	G	R	Y			
Pink	Pk	Pk	Pk	Pk	Pk		
P = Preference score	3	3	2	2	0	5	Av P = 2.5
P^2	9	9	4	4	0	25	Av P^2 = 8.5

p = Relative preference score

$= \dfrac{P}{n-1}$	.60	.60	.40	.40	0	1.00	Av p = .50
p^2	.36	.36	.16	.14	0	1.00	Av p^2 = .34

n = no. items = 6

n − 1 = no. comparisons of each item with all the others

(7) $\text{Av } P = \dfrac{n-1}{2}$ 　　　　(7a) $\text{Av } p = \dfrac{1}{2}$

(8) $SD_P = \sqrt{\text{Av } P^2 - (\text{Av } P)^2}$ 　　(8a) $SD_p = \sqrt{\text{Av } p^2 - (\text{Av } p)^2}$

$\qquad = \sqrt{8.5 - 2.5^2}$ 　　　　　　$\qquad = \sqrt{.34 - .50^2}$

$\qquad = 1.5$ 　　　　　　　　　　$\qquad = .30$

(9) $SD_n = \sqrt{\dfrac{n^2-1}{12}}$ 　　　(9a) $SD_{pn} = \sqrt{\dfrac{n+1}{12(n-1)}}$

$\qquad = 1.71$ 　　　　　　　　　$\qquad = .34$

(10) $t = \dfrac{SD_P}{SD_n}$ 　　　　(10a) $t = \dfrac{SD_p}{SD_{pn}}$

$\qquad = \dfrac{1.50}{1.71}$ 　　　　　　　$\qquad = \dfrac{.30}{.34}$

$\qquad = .88$ 　　　　　　　　　$\qquad = .88$

Proof of the formulas

(7) Each item is compared with the (n − 1) other items and, on the average, each item gets half the preferences.

(8) Same as for equation **(2)**, p. 374.

(9) Same as **(3)**, p. 375. If all the preferences were perfectly consistent, in perfect agreement, some one item would be preferred to all the others, the next-preferred item to all the others except the first, and so on down to the least-preferred item which would get a zero score. With n items, perfectly consistent scores would be:

$$n-1, n-2, n-3 \ldots 2, 1, 0.$$

The SD of these preference scores is the SD of n consecutive whole numbers.

(10) The ratio t has the same meaning here as in formula **(4)**, p. 374. It measures the consistency of the whole table of preferences. An Av r cannot be computed here because we have no m, no number of judges or rankings. Since Av r in the ranking method is always less than t^2, we are likely to get a fairer impression of the amount of consistency in Pair Comparisons by considering t^2 rather than t. For maximum consistency of the choices, t = 1; for maximum inconsistency, t = 0; for chance, by aid of the SD of a binomial

distribution, we get $t = \sqrt{\dfrac{3}{n+1}}.$

We should also provide some measure of scatter which here means the same as inconsistency of preference. The table shows a little contradiction between the preferences involving Yellow. Such irregularities are usually present in the data from Pair Comparisons, due to fatigue, contrast and similar factors. The formulas below the table afford a measure of the consistency of judgment in this form of experiment.

We may apply this measure of consistency to the very interesting data of Folgmann (1933) on the preferences of musicians for the work of great composers. In preparation for the experiment, E selected 19 representative composers, including most of the recognized leaders, and paired the name of each with the name of every other one. The instructions required the subjects "to underline the name of the one composer of each pair whose *music you prefer* in general, *not* taking the personality or greatness of the composer into consideration. . . . To make this experiment valid, it is absolutely necessary not to omit any pair, even if it is difficult to make a choice." The subjects were members of the Philadelphia, Boston, Minneapolis and New York Philharmonic Orchestras, 308 individuals in all. Beethoven was directly compared with Wagner by each of the 308 musicians, and 197 = 64% of them gave the preference to Beethoven. Beethoven was preferred to each of the other composers by a larger or smaller margin, and on the average his p score was 87.2 percent, or .872. The p score for each composer is given in the following list:

Beethoven	.872
Brahms	.798
Wagner	.774
Mozart	.772
Bach	.748
Schubert	.650
Haydn	.591
Debussy	.565
Schumann	.527
Mendelssohn	.479
Tschaikovsky	.422
Berlioz	.399
C. Franck	.370
Chopin	.357
Verdi	.325
Stravinsky	.305
Grieg	.291
MacDowell	.129
V. Herbert	.128

From these p values we obtain $t^2 = .5216$, which would indicate, so far as results from the two types of experiment are properly comparable, that the agreement among the musicians was just about as great as among the astronomers who gave $t^2 = .4824$. The agreement is very far from complete in either case.

RESULTS OF EXPERIMENTAL ESTHETICS

Without attempting to cover the field of esthetics, in many parts of which beginnings of an experimental attack could be found, we will at least take note of some of the results obtained in studying color and visible form.

Color preferences. From the readiness with which many persons express their preference for certain colors and their dislike for other colors, we should expect that an experiment would yield quite definite results for the individual, along perhaps with marked individual differences. At the World's Fair in St. Louis, 1904, the present author in collaboration with F. G. Bruner studied color preferences by the method of choice. A large assortment of little skeins of colored worsted (those used in the Holmgren test for color blindness) was placed in a loose pile on the table and O indicated the color that pleased him most and the one that pleased him least. Though some Os had difficulty in selecting a color without regard to any special use, nearly all seemed to go by the immediate impression. Of several hundred Os the largest number chose pink and the next largest a pale blue. When all the preferred colors were arranged according to their position in the spectrum, the reds (including pink) predominated. The least pleasing colors were usually dark, dull shades. A few bright colors, mostly orange and reddish purple, were designated as the least pleasant (or most unpleasant), these same colors being sometimes chosen as the most agreeable.   The greens were seldom assigned either first or last place.

An earlier experiment of the same kind was made by Jastrow (1897) at the Chicago World's Fair of 1893. He used colored papers and obtained a result differing from that just cited in that the most frequently preferred color was blue in case of men, red in case of women.   Other samples of color preferences, from children or adults, have been taken by Winch (1909), Washburn (1911 a), Katz & Breed (1922), Garth (1924) and Michaels (1924), with results which, as assembled by Chandler (1934), leave a rather confused impression.   On the whole, red and blue are more often preferred than yellow and green.   Several factors other than wave length (hue) affect the esthetic impression.   Brightness and saturation must obviously be factors, and so are area (Washburn, 1911 b) and the background (von Allesch, 1925).   The surface texture is important; colored papers are not so pleasant as the same colors in silk or worsted.

Dissatisfied with the rather crude experiments of his predecessors and with their discrepant results, von Allesch (1925) hoped to secure more uniformity by carefully controlling the conditions.   He used a color wheel and measured the proportions of each mixture.   The color was seen through a window in a gray screen and appeared not as the surface color of an object but as free, expanse color (p. 539).   He used many Os and repeated the experiment often with each O.   Even under these conditions one O differed from another and the same O varied from time to time.   The instructions were then modified so as to obtain a free report on the esthetic impression produced by each stimulus color. Still the results varied.   The same color gave quite different esthetic impressions in different trials.   It was even described differently, saturated at one time, pale or dark at another time.   The same color was described as yellowish red, straight red, and even bluish red, in different trials.   O's standard of hue and saturation varied according to the colors which had just been exposed.   In spite of all this variation, the esthetic impression of a given color was not wholly chaotic, for bright colors were never called gloomy; saturated red, orange and yellow were never felt to be "cold" nor greyish blue to be "warm."   Many colors, however, were regarded as lively and cheerful at one time and again as quiet and sad.

In one of these experiments O was asked to try to get a certain prescribed effect from the color stimulus.   When the prescribed effect was "cheerfulness," the task was easy with red, orange and saturated blue, but difficult with dark blue and impossible with a blue that approached black.   Von Allesch's conclusion from his extensive research is formulated in these words: "No color is beautiful, none ugly, but any color can be either at a given moment or in a given place."   Chandler's rather more adequate statement is that "no color is invariably and unconditionally pleasant or unpleasant, exciting or soothing, dignified or tawdry."

In support of this conclusion, we may recall the dark, dull colors which are indicated by many individuals as unpleasant. Much use is made of these shades in wearing apparel and in buildings, exterior and interior. Is it possible that we voluntarily surround ourselves with distasteful colors when we are perfectly free, as a social group, to use the bright pinks and blues which are preferred in a collection of colored worsteds? Even dull shades must be passably agreeable. Another strange fact is that some Os will designate a bright orange or greenish yellow as very unpleasing—yet no one exclaims against the orange of the sunset or the greenish yellow of early spring foliage.

Color combinations. There are supposed to be rather definite rules governing the esthetic effect of color combinations. Here again, nature

PERCENT OF EXPOSURES WHEN EACH COLOR PAIR WAS
ACCEPTED AS PLEASANT

(von Allesch, 1925)

	R		O		Y		YG		G		GB		B		V	
R		35	60	62	40	27	32	40	52	40	57	50	40	57	47	50
	35		45	42	45	35	60	57	47	45	37	55	30	42	35	40
O	60	45		42	35	30	50	47	60	45	35	52	37	55	85	57
	62	42	42		60	47	55	42	65	55	50	57	50	37	55	40
Y	40	45	35	60		37	42	45	60	35	60	47	45	40	47	37
	27	35	30	47	37		55	57	40	55	42	47	60	50	42	45
YG	32	60	50	55	42	55		40	47	40	47	52	55	60	45	47
	40	57	47	42	45	57	40		55	40	42	85	50	52	60	45
G	52	47	60	65	60	40	47	55		62	40	55	62	55	35	47
	40	45	45	55	35	55	40	40	62		60	30	45	57	40	55
GB	57	37	35	50	60	42	47	42	40	60		47	55	62	40	40
	50	55	52	57	47	47	52	85	55	30	47		50	40	42	40
B	40	30	37	50	45	60	55	50	62	45	55	50		32	40	45
	57	42	55	37	40	50	60	52	55	57	62	40	32		47	60
V	47	35	85	55	47	42	45	60	35	40	40	42	40	47		37
	50	40	57	40	37	45	47	45	47	55	40	40	45	60	37	

Mean
percent
for each
color   46   43   49   51   45   45   48   50   52   47   48   50   46   50   46   46
Mean for all pairs = 47.6% accepted as pleasant
Distance apart of colors in color circle

1	2	3	4	5	6	7	8	*steps*
47	45	47	51	46	49	48	47	percent accepted

R = red; O = orange; Y = yellow; YG = a color midway between yellow and green; G = green; GB = a color midway between green and blue; B = blue; V = violet. There were 16 single colors in all, including intermediates between those labeled in the margins of the table. Between V and R occurs purple, which occupies the last line and the last column in the body of the table. All possible pairs of these 16 colors were presented, one pair at a time, by use of a color wheel, and each pair was either accepted as pleasant or rejected as unpleasant. The series was gone through twice with each of 10 Os; the number accepted is here reduced to percent. For convenience, the table is duplicated above and below the diagonal. Reading along the first line, or down the first column, we find that the pair consisting of red and a reddish orange was accepted as pleasant in 35 percent of the trials; the pair consisting of R and O in 60 percent; the pair consisting of R and a yellowish orange in 62 percent; and so on. Adding the numbers in a column and dividing by 15 we obtain the average percent of cases in which pairs containing a given color were accepted. These percents occupy a line below the body of the table and do not differ much nor reliably. To find whether the amount of dissimilarity of the colors composing a pair was a factor in its acceptability, we add up diagonally (remembering that the color series is circular, so that the 50 at the bottom of the first column should be included in the diagonal of pairs of adjacent colors, and similarly that the little diagonal, 47, 40, close to the lower left-hand corner, should be added to the diagonal showing pairs of colors two steps apart, etc). So we obtain the percents accepted for adjacent colors, etc., as given in the last line of the table. These percents also differ little and not reliably; so that the conclusion from this experiment is that the dissimilarity of the colors forming a pair had little general effect on the acceptability of the pair. A few of the single pairs differ from the general mean more than would be expected by chance.

breaks the rules. Blue sky seen through green trees, mingled green and yellow in spring, mingled red and yellow in autumn, do not offend our tastes. In the laboratory a pair of colors is presented side by side and rated on a scale of pleasantness and unpleasantness. Colors of many hues, saturations and degrees of brightness are paired. From the results it is difficult to deduce any rules, except the rule that any color pair is sometimes pleasant and sometimes unpleasant. When colors are reported as not going well together, it is not because they clash so much as because they lead in different directions so that O cannot do anything unified with the pair (von Allesch, 1925). The correlation between the pleasantness of the pair and that of its constituent colors is positive but far from close. Quite often a pair of separately pleasant colors is unpleasant, and even a pair of disliked colors may be pleasant (Washburn, 1921).

The rather indefinite results obtained with color pairs are illustrated in the table on p. 383.

Esthetics of simple forms—the rectangle. Apparently the idea of an experimental esthetics was first suggested to Fechner in connection with the much debated question of the most pleasing proportion. An old theory held that simple ratios of width to length, such as 1:2, 2:3, 3:4, would necessarily appeal to the beholder. That beauty was inherent in simple ratios was an idea that had come down from the Pythagoreans. An example was seen in the vibration rates of harmonious tones, though Helmholtz (1862) had made it clear that the harmony came from the absence of beats rather than from the simple ratios in themselves.

Fechner wished to discover whether rectangles of which the two dimensions stood in a simple ratio made any special appeal "to the eye." He also had in mind the vaunted claims of the "golden section," the mathematical name for which is "extreme and mean ratio": the whole is to the larger part as the larger is to the smaller;

$$1 : x = x : 1 - x,$$

from which $x = .618^+$. In a rectangle, to have the golden section, we make the width .618 of the length. This ratio lies between the simple ratios, ⅗ and ⅝, and is not itself a simple ratio. Certain theorists held that the golden section best presented "unity in diversity" and therefore gave the ideal proportion.

To test these theories, Fechner placed rectangles of different proportions before O and asked him to indicate the most and the least pleasing. A mere rectangle, we might suppose, could have no esthetic effect one way or the other. Fechner's first result, an important psychological result, was that nearly everyone was able to select a most pleasing rectangle, though often after hesitation and sometimes with an inability to decide between two or more, usually rather similar rectangles. This experiment was repeated by Lalo (1908) and the results of both experimenters are in the adjoining table, with the distributions of the votes

PREFERENCES FOR RECTANGLES: PERCENT OF ADULTS CHOOSING EACH SHAPE IN SAMPLES EXAMINED BY FECHNER IN GERMANY, 1876, AND BY LALO IN FRANCE, 1908

Ratio of width to length	Best rectangle		Worst rectangle	
	Fechner	*Lalo*	*Fechner*	*Lalo*
1.00	3.0%	11.7	27.8	22.5
.83	.2	1.0	19.7	16.6
.80	2.0	1.3	9.4	9.1
.75	2.5	9.5	2.5	9.1
.69	7.7	5.6	1.2	2.5
.67	20.6	11.0	.4	.6
.62	35.0	30.3	0	0
.57	20.0	6.3	.8	.6
.50	7.5	8.0	2.5	12.5
.40	1.5	15.3	35.7	26.6
	100.0	100.0	100.0	100.1

for best and for worst rectangle. Several results stand out in the table. Looking first at Fechner's results we see a rather definite mode at the ratio .62, which is the golden section. From this high point the percent falls off in each direction, yet not suddenly. There is rather a broad mode reaching in Fechner's data from .57 to .67. We can say that a rectangle whose width was about 6/10 of its length had the advantage. The narrowest rectangles were scarcely chosen at all. The square (ratio $= 1.00$) was chosen by a large enough number to suggest a second mode.

In Lalo's data this second mode shows up more distinctly. A good number of his subjects chose the square as the most agreeable rectangle. Equally striking is a third mode at the other extreme, the slenderest rectangle being chosen by 15 percent of the subjects. Lalo's main mode still remains in the same region as Fechner's. And there were almost no votes against the golden section and adjacent rectangles as being the worst of the lot.

These results rather deflated the claims of the golden section. Although it was the modal choice, individuals were found to differ widely and there was no sharp falling off from the high point at .62 as there would be if a particular mathematical ratio were a governing factor. In music a slightly mistuned interval is not almost as pleasant as the true interval but quite unpleasant. In music the exact ratio counts heavily, but nothing so precise holds good in the esthetics of the rectangle.

Witmer (1894) obtained similar results with a mode extending from .57 to .65. Individual choices were found to differ definitely from the general mean. Witmer asked his Os to rate the degree of pleasure as the differently shaped rectangles were passed before them. Their reports

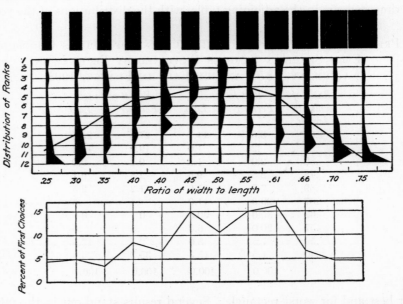

FIG. 100. (Data from Thorndike, 1917 b.) Each of 200 Os ranked the rectangles shown at the top, which were presented all at once but with better spacing than here shown. O ranked them in order of preference, and the distribution of ranks assigned to each rectangle is shown just below it. The line cutting across these distribution curves gives the median rank for each rectangle. The preference curve is not quite the same as judged by the median rank and by the percent of first choices, though the discrepancy is not great. Two of the rectangles were duplicates but did not get precisely the same ranks.

showed that the pleasure fell off gradually on each side of the most preferred figure. Slight deviations from the square (which also was pleasing) were found to be unpleasant because they looked like mis-shapen squares; but if a rectangle of ratio .65 was most pleasing, slight deviations from this proportion were only slightly less pleasant. "Unity in diversity," Witmer held, was the key to any liking for a rectangle. The square has superlative unity but lacks diversity. A very slender rectangle presents a maximum of diversity but is not easily grasped as a unity. A medium rectangle, corresponding approximately to the golden section, offers sufficient diversity to be interesting but not enough to prevent a firm grasp of the whole shape. It is the visible shape, not the mathematical analysis, that gives esthetic pleasure.

Rectangles have been tried by several experimenters with results similar in general to those of Fechner, though American students lean to the slenderer rectangles. Several of the experimental methods have been employed. Thorndike (1917 b) used the method of rank order. He presented a chart of 12 rectangles and asked O to designate his first choice, second choice and so on down to the worst. His results, shown in Fig. 100, further deflate the claims of any particular ratio, since every rectangle was ranked in every position. The median rank shows no real peak but an approximate level from .40 to .60.

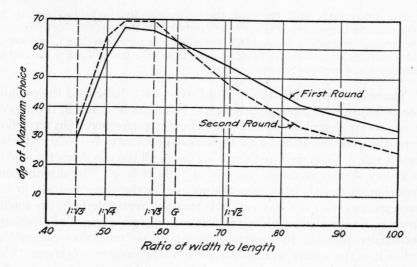

Fig. 101. (Data from Weber, 1931.) Preference for rectangles as affected by practice. The rectangles were projected on a screen, long side vertical. Two were shown at a time and a preference registered by each of 68 women college students, every rectangle being compared with every other twice in the course of each round. The ratios of width to length included the golden section, G, the simplest root ratios, and intervening ratios. The results brought out by the graph are (1) that there are no peaks indicative of any special advantage possessed by the root ratios or by the golden section, and (2) that on the second round there is a definite shift of preferences toward the slenderer rectangles.

Weber (1931) used the method of pair comparisons and obtained the results shown in Fig. 101. Like Thorndike's curve of median rank this curve of Weber's shows no sharp peak. No precise ratio shows any great advantage over the neighboring ratios. Weber was especially interested in testing the claims of the "root ratios" (Hambidge, 1920). According to this theory the rectangle would have the most pleasing shape when the width was to the length as 1 to the square root of 2, or 1 to the square root of 3, etc. There is nothing in Weber's results to indicate that any precise shape is outstandingly pleasing. He repeated the experiment after an interval of two weeks and found a definite shift of preference toward the slenderer rectangles. He believes that the slenderer rectangles present more difficult problems of unified apprehension and that after practice with rectangles these more difficult problems are solved with some zest, while the square or less slender rectangles become stale and trite.

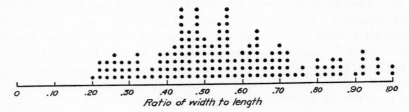

FIG. 102. (Data from Haines & Davies, 1904.) Rectangles produced by 23 students under instructions to adjust length and width to the most pleasing proportion. The rectangle was solid white on black, presented on a vertical surface 1.3 m from O, and was 10 cm long, the width being adjusted to suit O's taste. Each O had four or more trials; and each dot records one trial.

Haines & Davies (1904) and also Davis (1933) have used the production or adjustment method, in which O is free, as he is not in the experiments so far described, to indicate his exact preference. On repetition some Os were consistent with their first preference, but others varied considerably. The preferred shape scattered all the way from the square to a very slender rectangle, only ⅕ as wide as long. The distributions appear multimodal, but the peaks are not in the same position in the two experiments. We may conclude that any rectangle from the square down to a very slender oblong is pleasing to some persons and perhaps potentially pleasing to everyone, and that no particular proportion, unless it is the square, stands out above its immediate neighbors. This conclusion implies that ratios as such have nothing directly to do with the esthetic effect. What the subject sees is not a ratio but a shape. In most cases he is unaware of any specific ratio. If he thinks of the rectangle as a visiting card or as having a particular use, his choice will be governed by that idea, but apart from use it would seem that any rectangle is potentially pleasing, the same as any color.

Other figures besides the rectangle have been used in preference experiments from time to time. Fechner himself used several. His unpublished results on the ellipse were brought to light by Witmer (1894), and show the following distribution of first choices:

Minor axis as fraction of major	Percent of first choice
1.00 (circle)	1.2
.83	.6
.80	8.3
.75	14.7
.67	42.4
.62	16.7
.57	13.1
.50	1.6
.40	0
	98.6

The preference ran to somewhat larger ratios for the ellipse than for the rectangle, and this result was confirmed by Witmer's own experiments, which gave:

	Range of individual means	Group mean
Rectangle	.57 to .65	.61
Ellipse	.61 to .70	.65

Ellipses are preferred a little fatter than rectangles, perhaps because of the tapering of the ellipse toward each end. Preferences for the circle as against the ellipse were very few—which seems strange in view of the very frequent use of the circle in objects which make some claim to elegance. Probably the ellipse appears more recherché.

With isosceles triangles, standing on their bases, it makes a difference what range of proportions is presented for choice. Presenting a chart of triangles which were all taller than they were wide, Thorndike (1917 b) found the preferences to center around 1.60 (ratio of altitude to base), while Witmer (1894), using a chart of triangles lower than wide, found the choices centering around .41. Probably in each case we have a "series effect" or "central tendency," a tendency to choose toward the middle of the presented series rather than at either end (see p. 445). Witmer found this tendency to be present in an experiment with rectangles. He had at hand a whole series differing by small steps of slenderness. When he presented together a short series of adjacent shapes, the Os chose the middle of this short series. Thus:

when the series was nos. 7, 8, 9, 10, 11, the choice was 9
" " " " " 8, 9, 10, 11, 12, " " " 10
" " " " " 9, 10, 11, 12, 13, " " " 11
" " " " " 10, 11, 12, 13, 14, " " " 11
" " " " " 11, 12, 13, 14, 15, " " " 11

The series effect is seen to break down if pushed too far. It holds only within a range where the objects are all nearly equal in attractiveness.

About the simplest form that can have proportion is a straight line divided into two parts. Angier (1903) used a luminous horizontal line (opal glass illuminated from behind), divided by a narrow steel strip the position of which was adjustable by the subject, who was instructed *not* to divide the line in the middle (usually the first preference) but at some other point which gave a pleasing effect. Each O varied in his setting from trial to trial, and the mean settings for the nine Os ranged from .55 to .69 with a group mean of .62; the longer segment was .62 of the whole line. Though the group average coincided with the golden section, Angier urges that the exact average has little significance and that the wide range of pleasing proportions is the important result.

Balance. Angier's Os, college students, found the unequal division of the horizontal line more interesting and stimulating than the perfect symmetry of equal division. They reported that they could somehow place an emphasis on the shorter segment and so restore the balance.

Pierce (1894, 1896) presented a visual field divided by a vertical line, on one side of which was a narrow stripe and on the other side a similar but shorter stripe. The subjects adjusted the distance of the shorter stripe until they were pleased with the appearance of the whole field. They located the short stripe farther from the central line than the long stripe. They thus achieved a balance between the two sides of the field much as a small weight on the long arm of a balance will balance a large weight on a short arm. Puffer (1903) used a similar setup except that she employed a rectangular frame and no central line. She found that when one of two figures was weighted in any way, as by its size or its inherent interest, the field could be balanced by placing the less weighted object farther from the center. Legowski (1908) obtained similar results though with wide individual variation. The "balance," according to introspection, consisted in an equality of areas or angles. O's main requirement was that the field must show *some* sort of regularity.

Expressiveness of lines. The wide range of judgment noted in all the preceding experiments was possible because all the figures were well drawn and symmetrical. It is easy to obtain marked distaste for figures violating this principle. When asked to draw a beautiful line, Lundholm's (1921) subjects tried to make one that was smooth, curved, symmetrical, continuous, with rhythm, or repetition, and expressive of a single idea. For an ugly line they drew an unorganized mass without continuity, with mixed angles and curves, intersections and unrelated spaces. Lundholm also asked his subjects to draw lines expressive of sadness, calmness, laziness, gentleness and seriousness. To express these qualities they drew wide sweeping curves, with no straight line combinations and few sharp curves. On the contrary when they wished to express merriment, playfulness, agitation or fury, they drew sharp waves or zigzags. These various lines seemed primarily to express motor activity, as indicated by the subjects' introspections:

"Small waves make the movement of a line go more quickly. The calm line has slow, long curves."

"Angularity of a line expresses violence of movement. . . . A long curve always expresses slowness."

"Angular motion represents hard and painful feeling. Angles even tend to express strength, vivacity—sharp angles distress, broader angles, power, determination, calmness. Curves express grace and are usually pleasant. Short curves, grace and liveliness, long curves, beauty, indolence, calmness. Curves in general express the weaker and less forcible emotion."

Individual differences were not prominent in Lundholm's results. Yet though the results and the introspections seem reasonable, other investigators have found some individual variations in repeating the experiment (Poffenberger & Barrows, 1924; Chandler, 1934).

Sources of the pleasure in simple forms. Is the pleasure derived from simple forms a direct esthetic effect of the forms themselves, or is it the result of association and empathy? A rectangle or ellipse may suggest some pleasant or unpleasant object, or some use, and be judged accordingly. Such associations, frequently reported in the experiments, lend warmth to the figures and heighten the esthetic effect. But they are not always present (Legowski, 1908). Empathy is sometimes reported as a determining factor in the preference for symmetry and balance, but scarcely in the choice of the most pleasing rectangle or ellipse. As far as introspection can tell, the pleasing impression of a figure may be perfectly direct and consist in the often suggested unity-in-diversity.

Experimenters who have cultivated a field long and intensively deserve a hearing even when their conclusions go somewhat beyond their data. Witmer (1894) concludes that while a square or circle pleases by its internal symmetry and equality, an oblong may show a still more pleasing unity of diverse parts. A well proportioned rectangle must not be so slender as to fall apart nor so fat as to look like a square gone wrong. It should be a happy mean, a good, typical rectangle. Pierce (1896) says somewhat the same in different words: "The esthetic consciousness is the feeling resulting from a realization by the object of a tendency suggested by it. Any form that . . . suggests a general tendency which is satisfied by the elements it contains, apperceived as a whole, may be beautiful. . . . It seemingly makes no difference what the general tendency is as long as the object carries out this tendency."

Weber (1931) considers that any figure sets a problem; it demands to be seen as a unit. Too easy a problem kills interest, too great difficulty spoils the esthetic effect.

Lalo (1908) holds that when the observer succeeds in laying aside all associations and all reference to the arts his judgments cease to be truly esthetic. The golden section has been used freely by the artists of certain times and places, and avoided at other times and places. The same is true of other shapes, of colors and of musical chords. Beauty is not a purely individual matter, but an affair of the artistic standards of the time and place. It differs from one school to another, and fashions in beauty come and go.

CHAPTER XVII

THE PSYCHOPHYSICAL METHODS

Logically, "psychophysics" means a science of the interrelations of the psychical and the physical—the mind-body problem. Fechner (1860), who introduced the word psychophysics, meant it to cover all kinds of psychophysical relations, so far as they could be studied scientifically. He found something to say of sleep and waking, after-images and memory, and brain physiology. But the most promising line of attack led by way of stimulus, sensation and judgments of weight, brightness, loudness and other magnitudes.

In order to investigate such questions Fechner had first to devise and revise suitable methods of experimentation and of mathematical treatment of results. A large portion of his book on *Psychophysics* was devoted to the mapping out of these "psychophysical methods," as they are still called, though they have found varied uses outside of the special field for which Fechner designed them.

Fechner was one of the immediate precursors of experimental psychology. He approached the subject from the side of physics, also with a strong philosophical interest which might be classed as mystical or pantheistic. He believed that the material world had an all-pervasive psychical aspect, or "daylight side," into which man has some glimpse through his own conscious experience; and he dared to hope that laws of interrelationship between the physical and the psychical could be discovered, just as in his time the mechanical equivalent of heat and other laws of the transformation and conservation of physical energy had been found.

Fechner found Weber's law in existence, though not yet named. He named it, conducted numerous experiments to test its validity, and transformed it into an equation which seemed to him to reveal a sensation equivalent for physical energy.

Fechner's story has been well told by Boring (1929), and the prolonged and many-voiced debate that he stirred up, as to the possibility and nature of a measurement of sensation, has been thoroughly covered by Titchener (1905) and by Foucault (1901).

Fechner's psychophysical interpretation of his results has found no acceptance among psychologists, but his methods are still called psychophysical. Many have used them and many have contributed to their further development and improvement.

Measurement of sensation. Much of the debate over psychophysics has been concerned with the question whether sensation is in any proper sense measurable. Fechner himself said that only the crudest form of measure was afforded by direct observation of sensation and that the only effective measure must be indirect, that is, in terms of the stimulus. But if it were entirely impossible to gauge the intensity of the sensation directly there would be no validity in any indirect measure that might be applied. Let us note certain obvious possibilities.

1. *Classification.* Given a collection of colored papers it is perfectly possible to classify them, by putting those that look alike together and separating those that are different. The classification can be more or less fine or minute. Here is no measurement as yet. But if we have a physical measure of the objects which are classified together we can at least determine how broad the classes are and so take a step toward measurement of the sensory impression.

2. *Serial arrangement or order.* In many cases we perceive not only difference of kind but also difference of degree, and can arrange objects or classes in a regular order, because the same sort of difference occurs repeatedly and cumulatively. The ability to perceive gradations and to arrange objects in an ordered series is a fundamental and significant fact in psychology. Lines can be arranged in order of length, time intervals in the order of their duration, boxes in the order of their weight, sounds in the order of loudness, tones in a pitch series, and colors in a circular chromatic series. Odors can be arranged in an order of agreeableness. Historical personages can be arranged, roughly at least, in the order of their eminence.

In all these cases the important point is that the series is arranged simply on the basis of *direct impression*. The subject needs no knowledge of the physics of light; if a full assortment of colors is placed before him he can build up a color circle by starting with any color and placing next it the color which most resembles it, and next to that the one which most resembles it, and so on.

An ordered series looks like measurement, for we can number the items in order. The ordinal numbers so obtained do however lack something of true measurement, and must if possible be turned into cardinal numbers by the introduction of a unit of distance.

3. *The scale or graduated series.* Often the observer goes beyond mere serial arrangement and notices that the steps in his series are unequal. When he has arranged the available bits of color into a color circle, he may find gaps in the series, where the adjacent colors are rather dissimilar. Now if he can detect unequal steps, he can also certify certain steps as being equal for him, *equal-appearing intervals*. If a whole series is divisible into equal steps, the step is obviously a unit of distance along the series. By counting the steps between items in the series we are able to state, for example, that two particular items are twice as far apart as two others. We are using cardinal numbers, we are measuring

distances along a scale. The scale is subjective, and the units only sub-jectively equal; but the point is that this type of subjective measurement is genuine and that without some such start we should probably never conceive of measurement. A well developed and much used subjective scale is seen in music; the violinist tunes his four strings to equal intervals by ear, and not by counting the vibrations.

Absolute and conventional zeros. In the physical scale of temperature, neither the Fahrenheit nor the Centigrade zero is anywhere near absolute zero. They are purely conventional points from which degrees are counted up and down, so that each temperature may have a definite and permanent number. Using the Fahrenheit scale we note a tempera-ture of 70° today as against 60° yesterday, a rise of 10°, but we cannot say that it was 6/7 as warm yesterday as today, because these degree numbers do not tell the complete measure of temperature for either day. Without an absolute zero we can measure distances or differences but not single magnitudes and their ratios. Presumably silence and darkness would be appropriate absolute zeros from which to measure loudness of sound and brilliance of light; and the task of building up a series of equal-appearing intervals from these zeros may not be impossible.

The threshold or limen. It is a fundamental fact of psychology, and of physiology as well, that, *at any one moment*, a stimulus must reach a certain strength in order to be perceived or to elicit a response, and also that the difference between two stimuli must reach a certain amount in order to be perceived or to make any difference in the response. To arouse any response a stimulus must be above the momentary *stimulus threshold*, and to make any difference in the response a stimulus difference must exceed the momentary *difference threshold*. As a symbol for difference threshold (limen) we use the letters DL.

An example of the stimulus threshold is afforded by the watch test for hearing. If a watch is first held close to the ear and then carried slowly away, at a certain distance it ceases to be heard. The difference threshold is illustrated by many everyday facts. When a bright light is already burning the addition of a single candle does not make the room perceptibly brighter. The stars are invisible by day because they add only slight increments to the brightness of the sky. To hear a pin drop you must have quiet; otherwise the slight increment of sound will be below the DL for intensity of sound.

As its name implies, the threshold is a *transition point*. The stimulus threshold is the transition point between stimuli too weak to elicit a response and stimuli strong enough to elicit that response. The difference threshold is the transition point between differences too small and those large enough to be perceived.

Variability of responsiveness. Equally fundamental with the fact of the threshold is the fact of its variation. It varies not only with the individual, but from moment to moment. It varies with fatigue, practice and other determinate conditions, and it varies continually from unknown causes. In attempting to measure any threshold we encounter this variation and are forced to recognize that our measure will be only an average. Our measure of DL will be the mean of a number of momentary DLs. To complete our task we must obtain a measure of the scatter of these DLs, probably their Standard Deviation, SD.

The stimulus threshold is evidently a measure of sensitivity—an inverse measure, since the lower the threshold the greater or keener the sensitivity. The DL affords a similar measure of differential sensitivity. Not quite so obviously, the SD also is an inverse measure of these sensitivities. The less the momentary thresholds vary, the better is the perception. In a discrimination test, the SD as well as the DL can be used as the measure of achievement. The SD, as we shall see, is the more dependable measure.

The task of psychophysics calls for measurement of thresholds and variabilities and for reduction of the data to comprehensive statements such as Weber's law. The preliminary task of devising adequate methods has proved so fascinating as to absorb a surprisingly large fraction of the energies of the psychophysicists from Fechner (1860) down to the present.

As in experimental esthetics, so here, O's task may consist in adjusting a stimulus till it meets his requirements, or in giving his judgment on a presented stimulus (or pair of stimuli). The latter general method is used in a variety of ways, and it will be convenient to deal with four main *psychophysical methods:*

1. The adjustment method.
2. The method of serial exploration.
3. The frequency method.
4. The reaction time method.

These methods will now be described, especially as regards the arithmetic of handling the data.

THE ADJUSTMENT METHOD

This method, or group of methods, can also be called the *equation method*, and the most common form of it is also called the *method of average error*. A constant standard stimulus, S, is presented, and a variable stimulus which O adjusts to apparent equality with the standard. He makes enough trials to give an average and SD of his settings. The average shows his "constant error," and the SD gives a measure of sensitivity.

When the standard and the adjustable stimulus are presented under different conditions, we speak of the *method of equivalents*. For example, O adjusts a vertical line to apparent equality with a horizontal standard, and thus measures are obtained of the amount and variability of the horizontal-vertical illusion. This type of problem can be handled also by the frequency method.

METHOD OF AVERAGE ERROR: TREATMENT OF DATA
(*For list of symbols, see Index.*)

O repeatedly adjusts a Variable stimulus to subjective equality with a constant Standard. In computing the results it has been customary to determine:

AE, the Crude Average Error, which is 1/Nth of the sum of the single errors with their signs disregarded;

CE, the Constant Error, which is 1/Nth of the algebraic Sum of the single errors;

VE, the Variable Error, which is the Average Deviation of the settings or reproductions.

It is preferable to follow modern statistical practice, and substitute SD for AD as the measure of variability; and likewise to substitute SE for AE. Then the following equation holds good of the three "errors,"

$$SE^2 = SD^2 + CE^2 \tag{11}$$

It is also important to notice that

$$CE = M - S, \tag{12}$$

where M is the average of the settings or reproductions. CE is positive when this average exceeds the Standard, negative when it falls short of the Standard.

In computation it is convenient to collect the settings in step intervals and to proceed by the "Short Method" (Garrett, 1937) using S as the AM. The deviation of any setting from S we call e, the single error, and the "correction" by which we obtain the true from the Assumed Mean is CE. In the example below, the step interval = 1, and the step numbered 7, for example, extends from 6.5 to 7.5.

Steps	Tally sheet	f	e	fe	fe²
10	.	1	+4	+ 4	16
9	..	2	+3	+ 6	18
8	..	2	+2	+ 4	8
7	....	4	+1	+ 4	4
S = 6	....	7	0		
5	....	12	−1	−12	12
4	....	10	−2	−20	40
3	....	7	−3	−21	63
2	....	4	−4	−16	64
1	.	1	−5	− 5	25
		N = 50		+18	250 = Sum fe²
				−74	
			Sum fe =	−56	

$$CE = \frac{\text{Sum } fe}{N} = \frac{-56}{50} = -1.12$$

$$SE^2 = \frac{\text{Sum } fe^2}{N} = \frac{250}{50} = 5.00; \ SE = 2.236$$

$$SD^2 = \frac{\text{Sum } fe^2}{N} - CE^2 = 5.00 - 1.2544 = 3.7456; \ SD = 1.935$$

$$M = S + CE = 6.00 - 1.12 = 4.88$$

THE METHOD OF SERIAL EXPLORATION

The name above attempts to characterize the experimental procedure and the way of handling the results. More used is the name, *method of limits*, and still commoner is *method of just noticeable difference*, which we shall also employ. Serial exploration is the most direct method of locating a threshold. Suppose you wished to determine the least audible sound. Providing yourself with a physically measurable source of sound you would start with an intensity well below the stimulus threshold and increase the intensity by small steps till O reported hearing the sound;

FIG. 103. Geometrical representation of the relation of crude error to constant error and variability, when SD and SE are used. In comparing the results of different authors it must be remembered that SE is larger than the usual "Average Error," just as SD is larger than the Average Deviation.

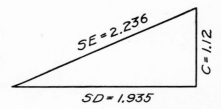

or else you would start with an easily audible sound and go down till O ceased to hear it. You would probably make two tests, one with an ascending and one with a descending series. In the ascending series the transition point lies between the last inaudible and the first audible intensity; in the descending series, between the last audible and the first inaudible intensity; and the Mean of these two transition points would give a measure of the momentary stimulus threshold.

Two difficulties are often encountered in this experiment:

1. Suggestion may arise from O's knowing when the stimulus is being increased; he may imagine he hears the sound before he really does. He may yield to other similar suggestions if the procedure is "with knowledge." Several devices are available for making the procedure "without knowledge." Repeat a stimulus occasionally before the regular series is continued. Interpolate catch stimuli such as blanks or definitely supraliminal intensities. Start the ascending series at different intensities, vary the length of step. Continue the ascending series well above the threshold and reverse the direction without warning.

2. Reversals of judgment within a single series are a natural result of O's variability. In an ascending series O reports hearing the sound at one point, and as the series is continued he reports not hearing it at a greater intensity. Two transition points would be indicated for this single series. *The convention is to count only the first change of response within each series.*

When the direct method is applied to the measurement of least noticeable *differences*, two stimuli are presented for comparison: the Standard is kept constant throughout the experiment; the Variable, in a descending series, is decidedly stronger than the Standard and diminishes by steps until the judgment changes to "equal" and then to

METHOD OF LEAST NOTICEABLE STIMULUS OR DIFFERENCE: TREATMENT OF DATA

1. Applied to the determination of a Stimulus Threshold.

(Data from Titchener, 1905, II, p. 6)

Lower limit of audible pitch

Stimulus in cycles/sec.	Alternate	descending	and	ascending	series					
	↓	↑	↓	↑	↓	↑	↓	↑	↓	↑
24	+									
23	+									
22	+		+							
21	+		+							
20	+		+						+	
19	+		+				+		+	
18	+		+		+		+		+	
17	+		+		+		+		+	
16	+	+	+		+		+			
15	+	−	+	+	+	+	+		+	+
14	−		−	?	−		?	+	?	−
13	−				−		−			−
12	−				−		−			−
11					−		−			−
10	−						−			
9		−								
8					−		−			
7							−			

T = 14.5　15.5　14.5　14.5　14.5　14.5　14.5　13.5　14.5　14.5

M = 14.5;　SD = .45

If the series are combined in pairs, and the average T for each pair taken as the single determination we have:

Av T =　　15.0　　　　14.5　　　　14.5　　　　14.0　　　　14.5

　　M = 14.5;　SD = .32

2. Applied to the determination of a Difference Threshold.

In a descending series, locate the *first* transition from plus to not-plus, and the first from not-minus to minus; and similarly in an ascending series locate the first transition from minus to not-minus, and the first from not-plus to plus. (Note the different scoring of the last two columns, in spite of identical entries, one however being scored downward and the other upward.)

Responses in alternate descending and ascending series

Values of s	↓	↑	↓	↑	↓	↑	↓	↑	
8	+	+		+	+	+			
7	+	+	+	+	+	+	+	+	
6	+	+	+	=	=	?	+	+	
S = 5	=	?	−	+	+	+	?	?	
4	=	−	−	−	−	=	+	+	
3	−	−		−	−	−	=	=	
2	−	−			−	−	−		
1	−						−	−	
T(+) =	5.5	5.5	5.5	4.5	6.5	4.5	5.5	3.5	M = 5.125
T(−) =	3.5	4.5	5.5	4.5	4.5	3.5	2.5	2.5	M = 3.875

Limen

Interval =	2.0	1.0	0	0	2.0	1.0	3.0	1.0	M = 1.25
Av T(+&−)		4.75		5.0		4.75		3.5	M = 4.5

PSE = point of subjective equality = Mean av T = 4.5; SD_{dist} = .59

CE = PSE − S = 4.5 − 5.0 = −.5

"Interval of Uncertainty" = Mean Limen Interval = 1.25; SD_{dist} = .97

DL = ½ Interval of Uncertainty = .625; SD_{dist} = .48

(The Limen Interval for each series = T(+) − T(−). The Av T(+&−) is computed for each *pair* of descending and ascending series and gives the point of subjective equality for that double series.)

"weaker." An ascending series starts with decidedly weaker and proceeds to equal and stronger. There are four transition points: plus-equal and equal-minus in the descending series; minus-equal and equal-plus in ascending. Two of these may coincide in a single series, as when O shifts abruptly from plus to minus.

This direct method is sometimes said to be suited only for rough preliminary measurements; but by repeating the series a sufficient number of times one can determine the average transition point with any desired accuracy. It is the only method that gives a genuine DL. When, as occasionally happens, an individual gives no responses except + and −, his data provide no way of measuring DL but the average transition point and SD are still obtainable.

A modification of the direct method, intended to give greater reliability to the single series, is the *method of serial groups*. In place of a single stimulus at each value of V, the stimulus is repeated a certain number of times, and a certain proportion of *plus* or *minus* responses is required in order to count that step as plus or minus. Stratton (1902 a), who invented the method, required 9 out of 10 *pluses* to count the step as positive; while Thorne (1934) required only 2 out of 3, seeking thus to obtain a threshold that should be fairly accurate for the moment when it was obtained, and so to trace the changes in the threshold which occur from moment to moment.

FREQUENCY METHOD A: CONSTANT STIMULI WITH ONLY TWO RESPONSE CATEGORIES

In many parts of psychology a measurement problem is encountered which is not handled by the usual methods of statistics, because the separate responses are not measurable. They can be classified as right or wrong, or under some set of categories, and the *stimuli* can be measured or scaled. The memory span (p. 7) and the span of apprehension (p. 686) are examples, and another is found in the Binet tests. Each response in the Binet tests is scored simply as passed or failed, but measurement is possible because the test items have been scaled. Some items have been found to be at the level of the average six-year-old child, others at the seven-year level. The items are arranged in an age scale. If a child passes a six-year item, the indication so far is that his mental age is at least 6 years; if he fails a ten-year item the indication is that his mental age is below 10. But how shall we put together his complete tally of items passed and failed so as to determine his mean mental age? Binet (1908) worked out a method suited to his scale, and this method is fundamentally the same as the psychophysical *method of constant stimuli* which we owe to Fechner (1860), Müller (1879), Spearman (1908) and Urban (1909).

Instead of measuring the single responses, we classify them and determine the frequency in each class at each step of the stimulus scale.

Dividing the absolute frequencies by the number of times the particular stimulus was presented we obtain the *relative frequency* of different classes of response to that stimulus. Relative frequency is expressed as a decimal fraction; a relative frequency of .38 means that a certain response was given in 38% of the trials. If there are only two categories, so that every response falls under one or the other, we designate the two relative frequencies by the letters p and q, where

$$p + q = 1.00, \tag{13}$$

and if there are three categories, such as "greater," "smaller" and "equal," we will denote their relative frequencies by a, b and m, where

$$a + b + m = 1.00 \tag{14}$$

The transition zone. The measurement problem presented by a table of relative frequencies can be brought out by comparing the broad jump and the high jump in athletics. Each *broad jump* is directly measured on the ground, and if we wished to go beyond athletic practice and obtain a complete statement of O's performance we should simply record all the single jumps and obtain the M and SD. The single *high jump* is not measured; we only know whether it cleared the bar at the height used in that trial. In the chart below, the bar is set at the heights indicated and each success is marked +. We count the successes and

s in inches		p	f
A = 50		0	
			2
49	++	.10	
			0
48	++	.10	
			1
47	+++	.15	
			2
46	++++	.25	
			3
45	+++++++	.40	
			4
44	+++++++++++	.60	
			4
43	+++++++++++++++++	.80	
			2
42	+++++++++++++++++++	.90	
			1
41	++++++++++++++++++++	.95	
			1
B = 40	+++++++++++++++++++++	1.00	
			$\overline{20}$ = N

obtain the value of p for each height within the transition zone, the zone in which both categories occur. The transition zone is bounded below by a Basal Value, B, at and below which every trial is a success (or assumed to be such), and it is bounded above by an Apical Value, A, at and above which every trial is a failure. At B, and for every value of the stimulus below B, $p = 1.00$ and $q = 0$; at and above A, $p = 0$ and $q = 1.00$. Such are the data, and the problem is to find M and SD of the transition zone, i.e. the M and SD of the distribution of transition points.

There are several ways of computing the required M and SD:

1. Arithmetical treatment of data (Spearman).
2. Graphic treatment of data.
3. Linear interpolation.
4. Fitting a normal ogive to the data.
5. Fitting a normal ogive to weighted data (Müller-Urban).

1. **The Spearman arithmetical method of computation** is the same in principle as Binet's method of computing Mental Age. It can be illustrated by our chart of hypothetical high jump data. Let O have 20 trials at each height from 40 inches, which he clears every time, up through 50 inches which he fails every time. Thus B = 40 inches, A = 50 inches. His score at each intervening height is shown in the chart, and the p column furnishes the data for computation.

The arithmetical method of computation has two equivalent forms, the Summation Method and the Distribution Method.

a. **The Summation Method of computation.** Give full credit for the basal height and partial credit for each step within the transition zone, in proportion to the relative frequency of successes at that step. O's Mean is at least 40 inches; if he had cleared 41 inches every time, we should add an inch, and his clearing it .95 of the time is the same for averaging purposes as clearing .95 inch every time; therefore we add .95 inch to the basal value of 40 inches. He clears the next higher step .90 of the time, thus adding .90 inch to his score; and so on. In short, take the sum of the p values within the transition zone, multiply by i, the step interval, which here = 1 inch, and add to the basal score. *Add in also ½ the step interval.* For suppose that O had cleared 40 inches every time, and 41 inches never, we should then know that his transition point varied between the limits of 40 and 41 inches and that the most probable value to assign for the Mean transition point was the midpoint of the step interval, 40.5 inches.

As a check, we can also compute M by starting from above and using the values of q (which always = 1 − p). Add up the values of q lying within the transition zone, multiply by i and subtract from A, subtracting also i/2 for the same reason that we added it to B in the other computation. The alternative formulas are:

$$M = B + i/2 + i \text{ Sum } p \tag{15}$$
$$M = A - i/2 - i \text{ Sum } q \tag{16}$$

The equally important formula for computing SD is appended without proof, in alternative forms:

$$SD = i \sqrt{2 \text{ Sum } p' - \text{Sum } p \,(1 + \text{Sum } p)} \qquad (17)$$

$$SD = i \sqrt{2 \text{ Sum } q' - \text{Sum } q \,(1 + \text{Sum } q)} \qquad (18)$$

Here p' is the sum of the p values up to and including a given value of p. We start from the small end of the p values and cumulate them. Similarly the q' values are obtained by cumulating the q values from the small end. The high jump data are treated in this manner in the following example.

s	p	p'	q	q'
50	0		(1.00)	
49	.10	.10	.90	4.75
48	.10	.20	.90	3.85
47	.15	.35	.85	2.95
46	.25	.60	.75	2.10
45	.40	1.00	.60	1.35
44	.60	1.60	.40	.75
43	.80	2.40	.20	.35
42	.90	3.30	.10	.15
41	.95	4.25	.05	.05
40	(1.00)		0	
	4.25	13.80	4.75	16.30
	= Sum p	= Sum p'	= Sum q	= Sum q'

B = 40 inches; A = 50 inches; i = 1 inch

(15) M = B + i/2 + i Sum p;   also M = A − i/2 − i Sum q   (16)

= 40 + .5 + 4.25   = 50 − .5 − 4.75

= 44.75 inches   = 44.75 inches

(17) $SD = i \sqrt{2 \text{ Sum } p' - \text{Sum } p \,(1 + \text{Sum } p)}$

$= i \sqrt{2 \times 13.80 - 4.25 \times 5.25}$

$= i \sqrt{27.60 - 22.3125}$

$= i \sqrt{5.2875}$

= 2.30 inches

also

(18) $SD = i \sqrt{2 \text{ Sum } q' - \text{Sum } q \,(1 + \text{Sum } q)}$

$= i \sqrt{2 \times 16.30 - 4.75 \times 5.75}$

$= i \sqrt{32.60 - 27.3125}$

$= i \sqrt{5.2875}$

= 2.30 inches

b. **The Distribution Method of computation** obtains an ordinary distribution of the transition point by subtracting adjacent frequencies. In the chart on p. 401, the transition point lay above 40 in 20 trials but above 41 in only 19; therefore it lay between 40 and 41 in 1 trial. It lay between 41 and 42 in 1 trial, between 42 and 43 in 2 trials; and so on as given in the column headed f. We can compute M and SD from these f values, in the ordinary way:

Interval		f	d	fd	fd^2
49–50		2	+5	+10	50
48–49		0	+4	0	0
47–48		1	+3	+ 3	9
46–47		2	+2	+ 4	8
45–46		3	+1	+ 3	3
44–45,	AM = 44.5	4	0		
43–44		4	−1	− 4	4
42–43		2	−2	− 4	8
41–42		1	−3	− 3	9
40–41		1	−4	− 4	16

$$N = \text{Sum } f = 20 \qquad +20 \qquad 107 = \text{Sum } fd^2$$
$$i = 1 \text{ inch} \qquad -15$$
$$\text{Sum } fd = + 5$$

$$M = AM + c$$
$$= 44.5 + .25$$
$$= 44.75 \text{ inches}$$
$$c = \text{Sum } fd/N$$
$$= +5/20$$
$$= + .25$$
$$SD = i \sqrt{\text{Sum } fd^2/N - c^2}$$
$$= i \sqrt{107/20 - .0625}$$
$$= i \sqrt{5.2875}$$
$$= 2.30 \text{ inches}$$

The Summation Method demands less computation; the Distribution Method has the advantage of being familiar. Also it can be used in the rare instances where the experimental series of stimuli does not proceed by equal steps. But in using the Distribution Method one must be prepared for *negative frequencies*, which occur whenever the p values show an "inversion of the first order," becoming greater when they should become smaller. As the different values of p are obtained from different samples, such inversions will occasionally occur. But they need cause no trouble in the computation if the negative sign is carefully observed, as illustrated in the example on p. 405 (data from Bressler, 1933). Weights were lifted, a standard of 100 grams followed by a weight of 112, 108 . . . 80 grams, which was judged +, − or = as compared with the Standard. In the table, s = the value in grams of the variable weight, and p = the relative frequency of minus judgments.

The Summation Method gives the same results much more conveniently.

The cut tail error. The arithmetical method in either of its forms is based on the assumption of a "complete series." When, as often, the series of stimuli used in the experiment does not extend far enough to give p = 1.00 at one end and p = 0 at the other end (or nearly those values), the value of M computed from the short series is displaced,

Constant Stimuli data computed by the Distribution Method

s	p	f	d	fd	fd^2
112	0				
		.10	+4	+ .40	+1.60
108	.10				
		.02	+3	+ .06	+ .18
104	.12				
		−.02	+2	− .04	− .08
100	.10				
		.48	+1	+ .48	+ .48
96	.58				
		.20, AM = 94			
92	.78				
		.18	−1	− .18	+ .18
88	.96				
		−.03	−2	+ .06	− .12
84	.93				
		.07	−3	− .21	+ .63
80	1.00				

$$N = \text{Sum } f = \overline{1.00}$$
$$i = 4 \text{ grams}$$

+1.00	+3.07
− .43	− .20

$$\text{Sum } fd = + .57 \qquad +2.87 = \text{Sum } fd^2$$
$$ci = + .57\, i$$
$$= +2.28 \text{ grams}$$

$$M = AM + ci$$
$$= 94 + 2.28$$
$$= 96.28 \text{ grams}$$
$$SD = i\sqrt{\text{Sum } fd^2/N - c^2} \qquad = i\sqrt{2.87 - .57^2}$$
$$= 1.60\, i$$
$$= 6.40 \text{ grams}$$

though often very little, while the obtained value of SD is sure to be smaller than its true value and often considerably smaller. Partial correction of this error is afforded by a simple modification of the arithmetical method, the **double step** device. If the experiment has employed 7 values of the variable stimulus, use in computing only the 1st, 3rd, 5th and 7th of these stimuli, with their respective values of p, just as if the experimenter had doubled his step interval and used only these four stimuli. The points where p is assumed to reach 0 and 1.00 are thus pushed farther out and the assumption is less in error. The error of cut tails and the correction obtained by "double step" will be illustrated in an example from Bressler, which will also be used later for other methods. The original series of stimuli is here complete and furnishes correct values of M and SD, with which the values obtained from the cut series can be compared. See p. 406.

2. **Graphic treatment of data.** The values of s are laid off on the base line and at each point is erected an ordinate proportional to the corresponding value of p. A smooth curve can be drawn to fit the data

M and SD for judgments "heavier" computed by Summation

s	Complete series		Shortened series		Double step	
	q	q'	q	q'	q	q'
(124)					(1.00 assumed)	
120	(1.00)		(1.00)		.99	2.71
116	.99	4.90	.99	4.83		
112	.97	3.91	.97	3.84	.92	1.72
108	.92	2.94	.92	2.97		
104	.77	2.02	.77	1.95	.62	.80
100	.62	1.25	.62	1.18		
96	.38	.63	.38	.56	.18	.18
92	.18	.25	.18	.18		
88	.04	.07	(0 assumed)		(0 assumed)	
84	.03	.03				
80	0					
Sums	4.90	16.00	4.83	15.41	2.71	5.41

Value of A   120 grams   120 grams   124 grams

Value of i   4 grams   4 grams   8 grams

Compute M

$120 - 2 - 4.90 \times 4$ $120 - 2 - 4.83 \times 4$ $124 - 4 - 2.71 \times 8$

$= 98.40$ grams $= 98.68$ grams $= 98.32$ grams

Compute SD²

2×16.00 2×15.41 2×5.41

$- 4.90 \times 5.90$ $- 4.83 \times 5.83$ $- 2.71 \times 3.71$

$= 3.0900$ $= 2.6611$ $= .7659$

SD $=$

1.758×4 1.631×4 $.875 \times 8$

$= 7.03$ grams $= 6.52$ grams $= 7.00$ grams

points as closely as possible. It is safe to assume that the true curve is like an ogive in merging at one end with the base line and at the other with the horizontal line, p = 1.00, and also in having somewhere near the middle an inflection point. One may assume, further, that the true curve has no inversions of the first order—no places where an ascending curve takes a dip, etc.; and that it has no inversions of the second order— no irregular changes in slope. The slope should become gradually steeper from either end to the inflection point, and the curve should be nearly a straight line for some distance where it is steepest. The smooth curve drawn in "by the eye" should meet these specifications and at the same time pass as impartially as possible over and between the data points, steering a middle course.

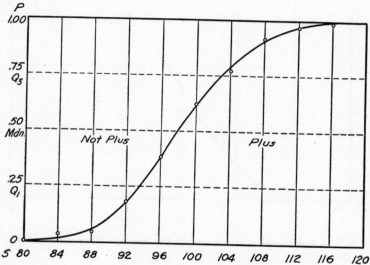

Fig. 104. Freehand ogive drawn to fit the data points of the Complete series on p. 406. For similar freehand curve fitting see pp. 687, 690.

The graph affords a view of the transition zone as a whole, and serves as a check against gross errors of computation. The Median and Quartiles can be approximately located by noting where the curve crosses the horizontals for p = .25, .50 and .75. Sometimes a cut tail can be rather safely reconstructed by continuing the smooth curve beyond the last data points.

3. **Linear interpolation.** This procedure gives us not M and SD, but the Median, Quartiles and Q. We proceed in the regular way for computing Mdn and the Quartiles, except that the "counting up frequencies from one end" is already done for us in our values of p. In the present example we have:

$$\text{Mdn} = 96 + 4 \times (.50 - .38)/(.62 - .38) = 98.00$$
$$Q_1 = 92 + 4 \times (.25 - .18)/(.38 - .18) = 93.40$$
$$Q_3 = 100 + 4 \times (.75 - .62)/(.77 - .62) = 103.47$$
$$Q = (103.47 - 93.40)/2 = 5.03 \text{ grams}$$

Because of some skewness usually to be found in the data we cannot expect the Mdn to coincide with the M, nor Q to be exactly .6745 SD. If we are willing to assume that the skewness is an accident of sampling, we can compute a smoothed value for Mdn = M by taking (Mdn + Q_1 + Q_3)/3, which gives us here an estimate of M = 98.29, rather close to the "correct" value obtained from the complete series by summation (Brown & Thomson, 1921, p. 60). The value for SD obtained by multiplying Q by the theoretical ratio, 1.4826, is 7.46, rather greater than the correct value of 7.03.

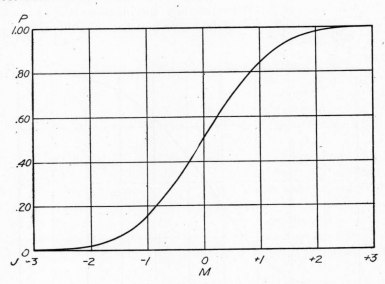

FIG. 105. A normal ogive, incorporating the corresponding values of p and j as given in Table I, p. 415.

4. **Fitting a normal ogive to the data.** Here we assume that the data would fall into a normal ogive, except for sampling errors, and we make use of a table of the normal probability curve which has been worked out by aid of the calculus. (Fortunately, if we are willing to take the table on faith, we need not know anything more of the calculus.) In the normal ogive, to each value of p (or q) corresponds a value we will call j, which is the number of SD units that the point lies above or below M. For example, when p = .84, the point lies 1 SD above M, and when p = .16, the point lies 1 SD below M. By "the point" we really mean the abscissa of the data point, i.e., the value of s, along the base line, which has yielded a given value of p. We thus have, for each value of s used in the experiment,

$$s = M + j \times SD \qquad (19)$$

i.e., any value of s can be expressed as lying j SD units above or below M, j being taken as + on one side of M and as − on the other side.

The experiment gives us a value of p for each s, and a table of the normal ogive (as Table I) gives the value of j corresponding to the obtained p. We can thus substitute in Equation (**19**) the corresponding values of s and j, as is done below for the "Shortened series" of our example (p. 406).

s	p	j	equation
116	.99	2.3263	116 = M + 2.3263 SD
112	.97	1.8808	112 = M + 1.8808 SD
108	.92	1.4051	108 = M + 1.4051 SD
104	.77	.7388	104 = M + .7388 SD
100	.62	.3055	100 = M + .3055 SD
96	.38	− .3055	96 = M − .3055 SD
92	.18	− .9154	92 = M − .9154 SD

Taking any two of these equations and solving them simultaneously would give values of M and SD; but the different pairs of equations would give different values because of sampling errors, as we assume, i.e., because the values obtained for p are not exactly correct.

This difficulty is met, in Fechner's *Method of Right and Wrong Cases*, by concentrating all the laboratory work upon just two values of s and so determining two p values with great accuracy. The experiment starts with several values of s and after preliminary trials is narrowed down to two values which promise to yield p values above and below .50. Linear interpolation between these two values will then give an accurate Median (Linder, 1933), though it will give no measure of variability. Assuming a normal ogive, as Fechner did, we can obtain both M and SD. From the above data, extracting the equations for s = 100 and s = 96, we have:

$$100 = M + .3055 \text{ SD}$$
$$96 = M − .3055 \text{ SD}$$

from which we find M = 98.00 grams, SD = 6.55 grams. These values are in fair agreement with those obtained from the complete series by the following method.

Müller's *Method of Constant Stimuli*, usually employed, utilizes the data from any number of values of s, and may obtain the most probable values of M and SD by the principle of Least Squares, the same principle by which the product-moment coefficient of correlation was derived. What we want here is in fact a formula for the *regression of j on s.* We want a formula that shall give us the most probable value of j for each value of s, with all the obtained values of p taken into account. On our assumption of a normal ogive, s and j are two measures of the same quantity, expressed in different units. If the data should conform precisely with the assumption, the correlation between s and j would be +1.00; the actual correlation between s and j shows how closely the data do conform with the assumption.

Our problem could be solved for each set of data by finding the correlation of s and j and the regression equation of j on s. This has been done once for all in letter symbols, and the following formulas give the best fitting or most probable values of SD and M. Some central value of s is taken as the Assumed Mean.

Formulas for fitting a normal ogive to the obtained values of p, by use of Table I, i.e., *without* use of the Müller-Urban weights:

$$SD = \left(\frac{n \text{ Sum } s^2 - (\text{Sum } s)^2}{n \text{ Sum } sj - \text{Sum } s \times \text{Sum } j}\right) i \qquad (20)$$

$$M = \left(\frac{\text{Sum } s \times \text{Sum } sj - \text{Sum } s^2 \times \text{Sum } j}{n \text{ Sum } sj - \text{Sum } s \times \text{Sum } j}\right) i + AM \qquad (21)$$

In these formulas,

n = the number of values of s considered;

s = any value of the variable stimulus, expressed in terms of the step interval as unit, and counted up and down, + and −, from a central value of s, which is the AM;

Sum s = the algebraic sum of the s values;

Sum s^2 = the sum of the squared values of s;

(Sum s)^2 = the square of Sum s;

j = the value, taken from Table I, corresponding to a given p, j being + on one side of p = .50 and − on the other side;

Sum j = the algebraic sum of the j values;

Sum sj = the algebraic sum of the products sj, each s being multiplied by its corresponding j, their signs being respected. For convenience, Table I gives values of sj.

Simplified formulas for the case where n is an odd number, so that Sum s = 0, the middle value of s being taken as AM:

$$SD = \left(\frac{\text{Sum } s^2}{\text{Sum } sj}\right) i \qquad (22)$$

$$M = \left(- \frac{\text{Sum } s^2 \times \text{Sum } j}{n \text{ Sum } sj}\right) i + AM \qquad (23)$$

(The simpler formulas can be used even when n is an even number, as 6, by taking the midpoint of the s series as AM and halving i, thus having for s values: +1, +3, +5, −1, −3, −5.)

The use of both simpler and full formulas will be illustrated by use of the data on p. 406, Shortened series. As n here = 7, the simpler formula is first used. Then to make n an even number the uppermost value of the variable is omitted and the results computed by the full formula.

Computation of M and SD by use of Table I, when n is odd

s in grams	s in steps	p	j	sj
116	+ 3	.99	+ 2.3263	+ 6.9790
112	+ 2	.97	+ 1.8808	+ 3.7616
108	+ 1	.92	+ 1.4051	+ 1.4051
AM = 104	0	.77	+ .7388	0
100	− 1	.62	+ .3055	− .3055
96	− 2	.38	− .3055	+ .6110
92	− 3	.18	− .9154	+ 2.7461

$$i = 4 \text{ grams} \qquad \text{Sum } s = 0$$
$$n = 7 \qquad \text{Sum } s^2 = 28$$

+ 6.6565	+ 15.5028
− 1.2209	− .3055
+ 5.4356	+ 15.1973
= Sum j	= Sum sj

(22) SD: $\dfrac{\text{Sum } s^2}{\text{Sum } sj} = \dfrac{28}{15.1973} = 1.842$
$$\times \quad \underline{4 \ (= i)}$$
$$\text{SD} = 7.37 \text{ grams}$$

(23) M: $-\dfrac{\text{Sum } s^2 \times \text{Sum } j}{n \text{ Sum } sj} = -\dfrac{28 \times 5.4356}{7 \times 15.1973} = -1.431$
$$\times \quad \underline{4 \ (= i)}$$
$$- 5.724$$
$$+ \underline{104} \quad (= \text{AM})$$
$$\text{M} = 98.28 \text{ grams}$$

The same, when n is even

s in grams	s in steps	p	j	sj
112	+ 2	.97	+ 1.8808	+ 3.7616
108	+ 1	.92	+ 1.4051	+ 1.4051
AM = 104	0	.77	+ .7388	0
100	− 1	.62	+ .3055	− .3055
96	− 2	.38	− .3055	+ .6110
92	− 3	.18	− .9154	+ 2.7461

$$n = 6 \qquad \text{Sum } s = -3$$
$$i = 4 \qquad (\text{Sum } s)^2 = 9$$
$$\text{Sum } s^2 = 19$$

+ 4.3302	+ 8.5238
− 1.2209	− .3055
+ 3.1093	+ 8.2183
= Sum j	= Sum sj

Compute Denominator:

$$6 \times 8.2183 - (-3) \times 3.1093 = + 58.6377$$

(20) Numerator of SD:

$$6 \times 19 - 9 = + 105; \qquad \text{SD} = \dfrac{+ 105}{+ 58.6377} i = 1.791 \ i$$
$$\underline{4 \ (= i)}$$
$$\text{SD} = 7.16 \text{ grams}$$

(21) Numerator of M:

$$(-3) \times (+ 8.2183) - 19 \times (3.1093) = - 83.7316$$

$$\text{M:} \quad \frac{- 83.7316}{+58.6377} = - 1.428$$

$$\underline{\qquad \qquad 4 \,(= i)}$$

$$- 5.712$$

$$+ \quad \underline{104} \quad (= AM)$$

$$\text{M} = \quad 98.29 \text{ grams}$$

5. **Fitting a normal ogive, using the Müller-Urban weights.** The several equations (as on p. 409) with which we are dealing may not deserve equal weights. The weights should be unequal if the values of p are not equally reliable. If more trials have been given at one value of s than at another, the equations ought strictly to be weighted in proportion to the number of trials. Again, with the same number of trials, p is more reliable the closer it is to 0 or to 1.00 (and the farther from .50). Also, the data points to which we are fitting an ogive are (s,p) values, not (s,j); and Müller introduced a set of weights intended to insure the best fit to the p values. Urban combined Müller's weights with the factor representing the reliability of p, and provided a convenient table for using these weights. Table II is Urban's table with one modification: it conforms to present statistical practice (rather than to Fechner) in using the SD as a unit instead of the "modulus," which = SD $\sqrt{2}$. The formulas for use with the Table are also modified to give SD instead of the traditional "Precision," designated by the letter h, where

$$h = \frac{1}{SD\sqrt{2}} = \frac{.707107}{SD} \qquad\qquad (24)$$

From this it also follows that

$$SD = \frac{.707107}{h},$$

so that it is easy to compute either SD or h, given the other.

Let the weight assigned to any pair of values, s and j, be denoted by w. Then the weighted formula is derived from the unweighted formula given above by simply

a. writing Sum w in place of n, and
b. inserting w after each "Sum" sign, i.e. writing
    Sum ws for Sum s,   Sum ws² for Sum s²
    Sum wj for Sum j
    Sum wsj for Sum sj

Thus we obtain from equations **(20)** and **(21)**:

$$SD = \left(\frac{\text{Sum w} \times \text{Sum ws}^2 - (\text{Sum ws})^2}{\text{Sum w} \times \text{Sum wsj} - \text{Sum ws} \times \text{Sum wj}} \right) i \qquad (25)$$

$$M = \left(\frac{\text{Sum ws} \times \text{Sum wsj} - \text{Sum ws}^2 \times \text{Sum wj}}{\text{Sum w} \times \text{Sum wsj} - \text{Sum ws} \times \text{Sum wj}}\right)i + AM \quad (26)$$

In computation, care has to be taken with the signs: w is always +; the sign of wj (as of j) is + when p is less than .50 and − when p is greater than .50 (or the reverse, as convenient); the sign of ws is + or − according to the sign of s; the sign of wsj is + or − according as the signs of s and j are the same or opposite, and ws² is necessarily +.

Computation with Müller-Urban weights (using Table II, p. 416)

s in grams	s in steps	p	w	wj	ws	ws²	wsj
116	+ 3	.99	.1127	.2622	.3381	1.0142	.7865
112	+ 2	.97	.2499	.4700	.4998	.9996	.9400
108	+ 1	.92	.4718	.6629	.4718	.4718	.6629
AM = 104	0	.77	.8179	.6043	0	0	0
100	− 1	.62	.9666	.2953	− .9666	.9666	− .2953
96	− 2	.38	.9666	− .2953	− 1.9332	3.8663	.5906
92	− 3	.18	.7327	− .6707	− 2.1980	6.5940	2.0120
i = 4			4.3182	1.3287	− 3.7881	13.9125	4.6967
			= Sum w	= Sum wj	= Sum ws	= Sum ws²	= Sum wsj

Compute Denominator:

Sum w	4.3182	
×	×	
Sum wsj	4.6967	20.2813
−		
Sum ws	− 3.7881	−
×	×	
Sum wj	1.3287	− 5.0332
		25.3145

(25) Compute Numerator of SD:

Sum w	4.3182	
×	×	
Sum ws²	13.9125	60.0770
−	−	
(Sum ws)²	(3.7881)²	14.3497
		45.7273

$$SD = \frac{45.7273}{25.3145}i$$
$$= 1.806\ i$$
$$= 7.22\ \text{grams}$$

(26) Compute Numerator of M:

Sum ws	− 3.7881	
×	×	
Sum wsj	4.6967	− 17.7916
−	−	
Sum ws²	13.9125	−
×	×	
Sum wj	1.3287	18.4855
		− 36.2771

$$M = \frac{-36.2771}{25.3145}i + AM$$
$$= -1.433\ i + AM$$
$$= 98.27\ \text{grams}$$

The results of the various forms of computation upon these same data are assembled below from pp. 406, 408, 411 and 413.

	M	SD
Complete series, Spearman	98.40	7.03
Shortened series:		
Double step	98.32	7.00
Linear interpolation	98.29	7.46
Normal ogive, unweighted	98.28	7.37
The same with Müller-Urban	98.27	7.22

The reliability of the M and SD can be roughly estimated by using the ordinary formulas (which are probably not exactly applicable), viz.,

$$SD_M = \frac{SD}{\sqrt{N}} \text{ and } SD_{SD} = \frac{SD}{\sqrt{2N}} \quad \text{(here N = no. trials per single value of s)}$$

In the present example, since N was 500, we obtain an SD of the M of .31, and an SD of the SD of .22. To judge from this example, any of the methods are adequate for finding M, but there is some doubt regarding the SD. Using the Spearman value of SD from the complete series as a criterion, we find sometimes one and sometimes another of the methods of computation to give the best approximation from a cut series. Other examples of comparative results from the several modes of computation are found on p. 691. In practice Summation gives essentially the same values of M as the more laborious methods. The latter tend to give a somewhat larger SD even when the Summation value can be regarded as correct because of the absence of cut tails.

Note on the Tables. Table I gives the SD value corresponding to each value of p in a normal ogive. It was constructed by the author by taking 6-place values of j from the tables of Pearson and of Kelley, multiplying by the values of s, and finally rounding to 4 places of decimals.

Table II is derived from the table of Urban (1912) and more directly from a corrected table obtained from the Cornell University laboratory. The values for w were checked and an error at p = .97 was corrected. With this exception the values of w, ws, and ws^2 are taken from the Urban table. The values of j were taken to 6 decimal places from the tables of Pearson and Kelley, multiplied by the Urban weights and rounded to 4 decimal places. The table has been rearranged somewhat and is carried out only to s = 4, because in practice 4 steps above and 4 below an Assumed Mean fully cover the experimental series.

When the number of trials is not such as to give exact values of p in 2-place decimals, use can be made of the Kelley-Wood table (Kelley, 1923, p. 373 ff). This table gives our j under the heading x; and our w = the product of z/q and z/p, multiplied by the constant factor 1.5708. The values of wj, ws, etc., would then be found by multiplication. This same table can be used to supplement our Table I.

TABLE I. *SD value* $(= j)$ *corresponding to p in Normal Ogive*

p	j	2j	3j	4j	5j
.01 or .99	2.3263	4.6527	6.9790	9.3054	11.6317
.02 " .98	2.0537	4.1075	6.1612	8.2150	10.2687
.03 " .97	1.8808	3.7616	5.6424	7.5232	9.4040
.04 " .96	1.7507	3.5014	5.2521	7.0027	8.7534
.05 " .95	1.6449	3.2897	4.9346	6.5794	8.2243
.06 " .94	1.5548	3.1095	4.6643	6.2189	7.7739
.07 " .93	1.4758	2.9516	4.4274	5.9032	7.3790
.08 " .92	1.4051	2.8101	4.2152	5.6203	7.0254
.09 " .91	1.3408	2.6815	4.0223	5.3630	6.7038
.10 " .90	1.2816	2.5631	3.8447	5.1262	6.4078
.11 " .89	1.2265	2.4531	3.6796	4.9061	6.1326
.12 " .88	1.1750	2.3500	3.5250	4.6999	5.8749
.13 " .87	1.1264	2.2528	3.3792	4.5056	5.6320
.14 " .86	1.0803	2.1606	3.2410	4.3213	5.4016
.15 " .85	1.0364	2.0729	3.1093	4.1457	5.1822
.16 " .84	.9945	1.9889	2.9834	3.9778	4.9723
.17 " .83	.9542	1.9083	2.8625	3.8167	4.7708
.18 " .82	.9154	1.8307	2.7461	3.6615	4.5768
.19 " .81	.8779	1.7558	2.6337	3.5116	4.3895
.20 " .80	.8416	1.6832	2.5249	3.3665	4.2081
.21 " .79	.8064	1.6128	2.4193	3.2257	4.0321
.22 " .78	.7722	1.5444	2.3166	3.0888	3.8610
.23 " .77	.7388	1.4777	2.2165	2.9554	3.6942
.24 " .76	.7063	1.4126	2.1189	2.8252	3.5315
.25 " .75	.6745	1.3490	2.0235	2.6980	3.3725
.26 " .74	.6433	1.2867	1.9300	2.5734	3.2167
.27 " .73	.6128	1.2256	1.8384	2.4513	3.0641
.28 " .72	.5828	1.1657	1.7485	2.3314	2.9142
.29 " .71	.5534	1.1068	1.6602	2.2135	2.7669
.30 " .70	.5244	1.0488	1.5732	2.0976	2.6220
.31 " .69	.4959	.9917	1.4876	1.9834	2.4793
.32 " .68	.4677	.9354	1.4031	1.8708	2.3385
.33 " .67	.4399	.8798	1.3197	1.7597	2.1996
.34 " .66	.4125	.8249	1.2374	1.6499	2.0623
.35 " .65	.3853	.7706	1.1560	1.5413	1.9266
.36 " .64	.3585	.7169	1.0754	1.4338	1.7923
.37 " .63	.3319	.6637	.9956	1.3274	1.6593
.38 " .62	.3055	.6110	.9164	1.2219	1.5274
.39 " .61	.2793	.5586	.8380	1.1173	1.3966
.40 " .60	.2533	.5067	.7600	1.0134	1.2667
.41 " .59	.2275	.4551	.6826	.9102	1.1377
.42 " .58	.2019	.4038	.6057	.8076	1.0095
.43 " .57	.1764	.3527	.5291	.7055	.8819
.44 " .56	.1510	.3019	.4529	.6039	.7548
.45 " .55	.1257	.2513	.3770	.5026	.6283
.46 " .54	.1004	.2009	.3013	.4017	.5022
.47 " .53	.0753	.1505	.2258	.3011	.3764
.48 " .52	.0502	.1003	.1505	.2006	.2508
.49 " .51	.0251	.0501	.0752	.1003	.1253
.50	0	0	0	0	0

Table II.   *Müller-Urban Weights and Products*

p	s = 1 w	s = 1 wj	s = 2 ws	s = 2 ws²	s = 2 wsj	s = 3 ws	s = 3 ws²	s = 3 wsj	s = 4 ws	s = 4 ws²	s = 4 wsj
.01	.1127	.2622	.2254	.4508	.5243	.3381	1.0142	.7865	.4508	1.8030	1.0486
.02	.1881	.3864	.3762	.7525	.7727	.5644	1.6931	1.1591	.7525	3.0099	1.5454
.03	.2499	.4700	.4998	.9996	.9400	.7497	2.2491	1.4100	.9996	3.9984	1.8800
.04	.3036	.5316	.6073	1.2146	1.0632	.9109	2.7328	1.5947	1.2146	4.8582	2.1263
.05	.3519	.5788	.7038	1.4076	1.1576	1.0557	3.1671	1.7365	1.4076	5.6304	2.3153
.06	.3954	.6147	.7907	1.5814	1.2294	1.1861	3.5582	1.8441	1.5814	6.3258	2.4587
.07	.4351	.6421	.8702	1.7403	1.2842	1.3052	3.9157	1.9263	1.7403	6.9613	2.5683
.08	.4718	.6629	.9435	1.8871	1.3257	1.4153	4.4259	1.9886	1.8871	7.5483	2.6515
.09	.5059	.6783	1.0118	2.0236	1.3566	1.5177	4.5531	2.0349	2.0236	8.0944	2.7132
.10	.5376	.6889	1.0751	2.1502	1.3778	1.6127	4.8380	2.0667	2.1502	8.6008	2.7556
.11	.5673	.6958	1.1346	2.2692	1.3916	1.7019	5.1056	2.0874	2.2692	9.0766	2.7832
.12	.5953	.6995	1.1907	2.3813	1.3990	1.7860	5.3580	2.0985	2.3813	9.5253	2.7980
.13	.6215	.7001	1.2430	2.4860	1.4001	1.8645	5.5935	2.1002	2.4860	9.9440	2.8002
.14	.6463	.6982	1.2927	2.5853	1.3965	1.9390	5.8170	2.0947	2.5853	10.3413	2.7930
.15	.6697	.6941	1.3394	2.6788	1.3882	2.0091	6.0273	2.0823	2.6788	10.7152	2.7764
.16	.6921	.6882	1.3842	2.7683	1.3765	2.0762	6.2287	2.0647	2.7683	11.0733	2.7530
.17	.7129	.6802	1.4257	2.8515	1.3604	2.1386	6.4158	2.0406	2.8515	11.4059	2.7208
.18	.7327	.6707	1.4653	2.9307	1.3413	2.1980	6.5940	2.0120	2.9307	11.7227	2.6826
.19	.7515	.6598	1.5031	3.0061	1.3195	2.2546	6.7638	1.9793	3.0061	12.0245	2.6391
.20	.7695	.6476	1.5390	3.0780	1.2953	2.3085	6.9255	1.9429	3.0780	12.3120	2.5905
.21	.7865	.6342	1.5729	3.1459	1.2685	2.3594	7.0782	1.9027	3.1459	12.5835	2.5369
.22	.8025	.6197	1.6051	3.2102	1.2394	2.4076	7.2229	1.8591	3.2102	12.8406	2.4789
.23	.8179	.6043	1.6357	3.2714	1.2085	2.4536	7.3607	1.8128	3.2714	13.0858	2.4171
.24	.8323	.5879	1.6646	3.3293	1.1757	2.4970	7.4909	1.7636	3.3293	13.3171	2.3515
.25	.8460	.5706	1.6921	3.3842	1.1413	2.5381	7.6144	1.7119	3.3842	13.5366	2.2826

TABLE II, *continued*

p	p	s = 1 w	wj	s = 2 ws	ws²	wsj	s = 3 ws	ws²	wsj	s = 4 ws	ws²	wsj
.26	.74	.8590	.5526	1.7180	3.4360	1.1053	2.5770	7.7310	1.6579	3.4360	13.7440	2.2105
.27	.73	.8713	.5339	1.7426	3.4852	1.0679	2.6139	7.8417	1.6018	3.4852	13.9408	2.1358
.28	.72	.8830	.5146	1.7659	3.5318	1.0293	2.6489	7.9466	1.5439	3.5318	14.1274	2.0585
.29	.71	.8939	.4947	1.7878	3.5755	.9893	2.6816	8.0449	1.4840	3.5755	14.3021	1.9786
.30	.70	.9043	.4742	1.8085	3.6170	.9484	2.7128	8.1383	1.4226	3.6170	14.4682	1.8968
.31	.69	.9140	.4532	1.8280	3.6561	.9064	2.7421	8.2262	1.3597	3.6561	14.6243	1.8129
.32	.68	.9232	.4318	1.8464	3.6929	.8636	2.7697	8.3090	1.2954	3.6929	14.7715	1.7272
.33	.67	.9317	.4099	1.8634	3.7268	.8197	2.7951	8.3853	1.2296	3.7268	14.9072	1.6395
.34	.66	.9398	.3876	1.8797	3.7594	.7753	2.8196	8.4586	1.1630	3.7594	15.0376	1.5506
.35	.65	.9473	.3650	1.8945	3.7890	.7300	2.8418	8.5253	1.0950	3.7890	15.1562	1.4600
.36	.64	.9542	.3420	1.9084	3.8168	.6841	2.8626	8.5878	1.0261	3.8168	15.2672	1.3682
.37	.63	.9607	.3188	1.9214	3.8429	.6376	2.8822	8.6465	.9565	3.8429	15.3715	1.2753
.38	.62	.9666	.2953	1.9332	3.8663	.5906	2.8997	8.6992	.8858	3.8663	15.4653	1.1811
.39	.61	.9720	.2715	1.9440	3.8881	.5430	2.9161	8.7482	.8145	3.8881	15.5523	1.0860
.40	.60	.9768	.2475	1.9537	3.9074	.4950	2.9306	8.7916	.7425	3.9074	15.6296	.9899
.41	.59	.9814	.2233	1.9627	3.9254	.4466	2.9441	8.8322	.6699	3.9254	15.7018	.8932
.42	.58	.9853	.1989	1.9706	3.9413	.3978	2.9560	8.8679	.5968	3.9413	15.7651	.7957
.43	.57	.9888	.1744	1.9776	3.9551	.3488	2.9663	8.8990	.5232	3.9551	15.8205	.6976
.44	.56	.9918	.1497	1.9836	3.9671	.2995	2.9753	8.9260	.4492	3.9671	15.8685	.5989
.45	.55	.9943	.1249	1.9886	3.9772	.2499	2.9829	8.9487	.3748	3.9772	15.9088	.4998
.46	.54	.9964	.1001	1.9928	3.9855	.2001	2.9891	8.9674	.3002	3.9855	15.9421	.4003
.47	.53	.9980	.0751	1.9959	3.9918	.1502	2.9938	8.9816	.2253	3.9918	15.9672	.3005
.48	.52	.9991	.0501	1.9982	3.9963	.1002	2.9972	8.9917	.1503	3.9963	15.9853	.2004
.49	.51	.9998	.0251	1.9996	3.9991	.0501	2.9993	8.9980	.0752	3.9991	15.9965	.1003
.50		1.0000	0	2.0000	4.0000	0	3.0000	9.0000	0	4.0000	16.0000	0

When values of M and SD have been computed to give the best fit to the data, one naturally wishes to see the fit. The original data points are plotted as previously described (p. 405), and now M is located on the base line and SD units are laid off to right and left of M. Since the normal value of p,

for M is 0,
for M − 1 SD is .16,
for M + 1 SD is .84,

we thus secure three points on the normal ogive. To obtain more points, lay off the base line in units of 1/4 SD, measuring always from M, and

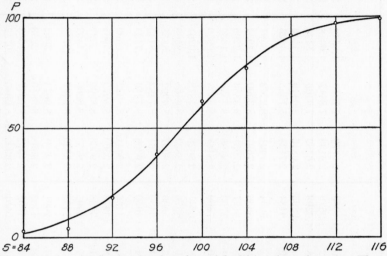

Fig. 106. A normal ogive fitted to the weight-lifting data of p. 406. The values of M and SD used are those found with the use of Müller-Urban weights, but the curve derived from the unweighted formula is scarcely distinguishable from this.

VALUES OF p FOR CERTAIN VALUES OF J

j	p
−2.25	.012
−2.0	.023
−1.75	.04
−1.5	.07
−1.25	.11
−1.0	.16
− .75	.23
− .5	.31
− .25	.40
0	.50
+ .25	.60
+ .5	.69
+ .75	.77
+1.0	.84
+1.25	.89
+1.5	.93
+1.75	.96
+2.0	.977
+2.25	.988

plot the corresponding normal values of p as shown in the accompanying small table which gives p for known values of j instead of (as previously) j for known values of p.

FREQUENCY METHOD B: CONSTANT STIMULI WITH THREE CATEGORIES OF RESPONSE

In a typical experiment by the method of Constant Stimuli, O lifts two weights in succession and compares the second with the first which is the Standard. He would be inclined to judge Heavier, Lighter, or Equal, thus using three response categories; though he may be instructed

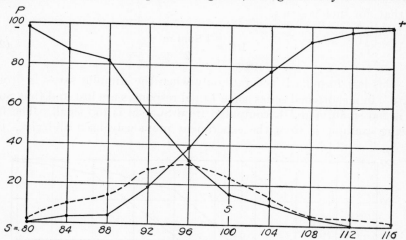

FIG. 107. Data from a 3-category weight-lifting experiment. The Standard was 100 grams and the compared weight ranged from 80 to 116 grams. The ordinate shows the percent of responses falling into each category at each value of s. The sum of these percents is necessarily 100 at each value of s. The ogive ascending toward the right shows the percents of Heavier judgments, which are used in computing M and SD for the transition from Heavier to Not-heavier. The ogive ascending to the left, similarly, shows the transition from Lighter to Not-lighter.

to use only two, Heavier and Lighter. Interesting methodological questions arise in connection with the use of three categories, but the computation is straightforward enough and will be considered first.

With the three categories allowed, there are two mean transition points to be computed: from Heavier to Not-heavier, and from Lighter to Not-lighter. The middle class is combined with the lower one in computing the transition out of the upper class, and it is combined with the upper one in computing the transition out of the lower class.

A graph may be of service in clarifying this situation. See Figs. 107 and 108.

Computation of 3-category data is the same as for two categories, except that (1) it has to be done twice because of the two transitions, (2) a measure must be found for the Point of Subjective Equality, and (3) a measure can be obtained for DL.

DL = 1/2 of the Interval of Uncertainty, which is $M_a - M_b$;

$$DL = \frac{M_a - M_b}{2}, \qquad (27)$$

where M_a and M_b are the mean transition points from A to not-A and from B to not-B, found by any of the methods already listed. It is also true, in case of a *complete series*, as can be easily proved from Equation (**14**), p. 401, that

$$M_a - M_b = i \text{ Sum } m,$$

so that, for such a series,

$$DL = \frac{i \text{ Sum } m}{2} \qquad (28)$$

This last formula is accurate only when the stimulus series is "complete"; in a shortened series some Equal responses are lost and thus Sum m is too small, and DL computed from Sum m is too small. The following example is from the experiment previously used and gives the

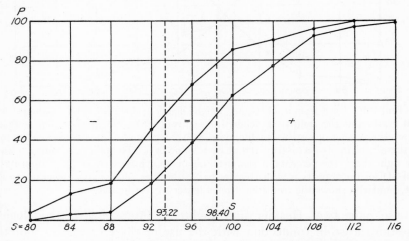

FIG. 108. Another graph of the same data. The lower ogive shows the percents of Heavier judgments, and the upper one shows the percents of (Heavier + Equal) judgments. These two ogives divide the total area between the horizontals into three parts: an area for the Heavier judgments at the right, one for Lighter judgments at the left, and an intervening sloping band for the Equal judgments. In computing the two Mean transition points we answer the question, "Where would the transition points lie if their variability disappeared while the area occupied by each of the three classes of judgment remained unchanged?" The answer is shown by the dotted vertical lines erected at the two Mean transition points. The rectangular area to the right of the right-hand dotted line = the area to the right of the Heavier ogive, and is the area of Heavier judgments when their variability is cancelled. Similarly for the Lighter judgments. The vertical band between the two verticals is equal in area to the sloping band of the Equals. If variability were eliminated the Equals would occupy this band, which is the "interval of uncertainty."

relative frequencies of each of the three categories. Any method of computation can be used; here the Summation Method is followed.

s	a	m	b
120	1.00	0	0
116	.99	.01	0
112	.97	.03	0
108	.92	.04	.04
104	.77	.13	.10
100	.62	.23	.15
96	.38	.30	.32
92	.18	.27	.55
88	.04	.14	.82
84	.03	.10	.87
80	0	.02	.98

$$\text{Sum } a = \overline{4.90} \quad \text{Sum } m = \overline{1.27} \quad \text{Sum } b = \overline{3.83}$$

$A = 120; \quad B = 76$, assumed; $\quad i = 4$ grams; $\quad S = 100$

(16) $M_a = A - i/2 - i \text{ Sum } a = 120 - 2 - 4 \times 4.90 = 98.40$ grams

(15) $M_b = B + i/2 + i \text{ Sum } b = 76 + 2 + 4 \times 3.83 = 93.32$ grams

(27) $DL = \dfrac{M_a - M_b}{2} = 2.54$ grams

(28) Also, $DL = \dfrac{i \text{ Sum } m}{2} = \dfrac{4 \times 1.27}{2} = 2.54$ grams

(17) $SD_a = i \sqrt{2 \text{ Sum } a' - \text{Sum } a \, (1 + \text{Sum } a)} = 7.03$ grams

(17) $SD_b = i \sqrt{2 \text{ Sum } b' - \text{Sum } b \, (1 + \text{Sum } b)} = 7.27$ grams

Av SD $= (7.03 + 7.27)/2 = 7.15$ grams

PSE = Point of Subjective Equality (or Subjective Midpoint), computed thus:

PSE $= \dfrac{M_a + M_b}{2} = 95.86$; this is the midpoint between the **(29)** upper and lower mean transition points.

CE = PSE − S $= 95.86 - 100 = -4.14$ **(30)**

With two categories, as there is no middle class, Sum m = 0, and DL comes out zero. That is, a two-category experiment does not yield any measure of DL.

While there is no mathematical objection to the use of three categories, some unexpected psychological difficulties have come to light in the laboratory. The main question is whether O can use the middle category in any precise, standardized way.

Shall a middle category be allowed? A brief history of the debate on this question is given by Fernberger (1930). The obvious answer is that Equal judgments must certainly be allowed; when two weights seem equally heavy to O he must so report, not misrepresent his impression by guessing Heavier or Lighter. But the difficulty is that O's impression of equality is seldom distinct in these experiments with small stimulus differences. Imagine an experiment in sorting oranges into three bins, according as they are equal to a given standard orange, or larger or smaller. If the oranges come only in three corresponding sizes, the sorter has no doubts and all the middle-sized oranges look practically alike. But if they come in all sizes he has trouble in drawing a line between adjacent classes. Must an orange be *exactly* equal to the Standard in order to go in the middle bin? He notices smaller differences and loses his first impression of equality. No two oranges look precisely alike. He would probably offer no objection if his task were changed so that he sorted into *two* bins according as the oranges were larger or smaller than the Standard. It is fully as easy to divide a continuum into plus and minus as to divide it into plus, equal and minus. And it is just as rational to divide a continuum into two parts as into three.

From O's point of view, it has been proved, either a two-category or a three-category task is perfectly feasible. He responds well to either set of instructions. Many Os prefer the two-category plan (Kellogg, 1930) as being simpler and less confusing. Less frequent is the O (Culler, 1926) who absolutely needs the middle bin to accommodate cases where judgment must be suspended and who feels that the lack of the middle class makes for snap judgments. Culler found in his case a smaller scatter (greater "precision") with three categories, but the data of Kellogg and of Fernberger (1931) do not wholly support this finding. On the whole the SD averages about the same whether two or three categories are used. In short there is no real basis, from the laboratory point of view, for deciding in favor of one method rather than the other.

The relative merit of SD and DL as measures of discrimination. Although the two-category and the three-category procedures are about equally good in the laboratory, the two-category procedure gives no DL. The interval of uncertainty drops out unless there are equal judgments; it is really a measure of the frequency of equal judgments. In experiments conducted on the three-category plan it has sometimes happened that O actually used only two categories, giving zero frequency for the equals. His interval of uncertainty reduced to zero, his DL likewise, and he was on the face of the returns credited with an infinite power of discrimination $\left(\dfrac{1}{\text{DL}}\right)$. The real fact was simply that he preferred to use two categories instead of three. Other Os without going so far as to omit all equal judgments use this category sparingly, and so obtain a small DL. We must remember that O has to find his own criteria of equality and difference. Different Os adopt different criteria and the same O may change his criteria. With a change in criteria goes a change in the number of equals and so a change in the interval of uncertainty and in the DL.

Fernberger (1931 a) has shown that the criteria can be controlled to some extent by instructions. The experiment was one in weight lifting with a standard of 100 grams and the instructions took three diverse forms.

1. Normal instructions such as are commonly given:
Heavier means that the second weight is heavier than the first.
Equal means that the second weight is equal to the first.
Lighter means that the second weight is lighter than the first.
2. Instructions intended to minimize the number of equal judgments:
Lighter means that the second weight is lighter than the first.
Heavier means that the second weight is heavier than the first.
Do not know means that in spite of an effort to find a difference O is unable to tell which weight is heavier.
3. Instructions intended to increase the number of equal judgments:
Heavier means that the second weight of any pair is certainly heavier than the first.
Lighter means that the second weight of any pair is certainly lighter than the first.
Equal means that the second weight seems equal or uncertain.

The table shows the average results from 4 Os:

Tendency of the Instructions

	Minimize equals	Neutral	Maximize equals
Interval of Uncertainty	2.12	4.34	9.80
DL	1.06	2.17	4.90
SD	6.67	6.20	7.29
PSE	94.73	95.46	95.34
CE	−5.27	−4.54	−4.66

Three important results appear in the table:
1. DL was strongly influenced by the instructions which worked as expected to decrease and increase the frequency of Equal judgments. The Os were however affected in different degrees and not brought to a common standard. Fernberger concludes that the difference between individuals in the use of the middle category is partly temperamental, though partly controllable by instructions.
2. SD and CE were not much affected by the instructions; they were fairly stable, and apparently are not strongly influenced by instructional, attitudinal and temperamental factors.
3. DL is not closely related to SD and CE. It therefore measures something different from accuracy of judgment. It measures directly O's inclination to use the middle category, and indirectly the complex of factors responsible for this inclination. It does not measure O's differential sensitivity, his keenness of discrimination.
In making this radical statement, that DL does not measure what its name implies, we are referring only to the DL obtained by the method

of Constant Stimuli. The DL is much more directly obtained by the method of Just Noticeable Difference, and when so obtained has often been used to test Weber's law and found to give the same general result as the SD from other experiments (Holway & Pratt, 1936). As obtained by Constant Stimuli the DL and SD give only low correlations, sometimes positive and sometimes negative (Kellogg, 1930; Bressler, 1933).

The DL obtained by Constant Stimuli is of no use for finding individual differences in keenness of discrimination, because it depends on O's attitude toward the middle category and on his criteria of equality. But perhaps it can be used in comparing the effect on discrimination of different experimental conditions? It can be so used only if O's attitude is not influenced by these conditions. Scattered through the literature are weird results obtained by use of the DL, results which show that the attitudinal factor changes with the conditions.

Oberlin (1936) compared the discrimination of weights lifted by a movement from the wrist, from the elbow, or from the shoulder, the Standard being 100 grams. One of his Os gave the following measures:

	DL	*SD*
Lifting from wrist	.72 grams	9.86 grams
" " elbow	.03 "	6.95 "
" " shoulder	.00 "	6.81 "

According to the DL this O's differential sensitivity was 24 times as good when lifting from the elbow as when lifting from the wrist, and when lifting from the shoulder it was *infinitely* good. He could, according to the DL, detect any difference, no matter how small, when lifting from the shoulder. All the data really mean is that this O did not use the Equal category in this condition. He used this category very sparingly throughout and for some reason avoided it altogether when lifting from the shoulder. The SD affords a truer comparison, and shows the differential sensitivity to have been about 1.5 times as good when lifting from elbow or shoulder as when lifting from wrist.

Köhler (1923) and Lauenstein (1933) presented sound intensities for comparison and noticed that when the time interval between two sounds was lengthened much beyond 2 sec. the frequency of "equals" greatly diminished. Lengthening the interval thus diminished DL and ostensibly improved the discrimination—an absurd conclusion which these authors, of course, did not draw.

A similar result was obtained by Lorenz (1912) in an experiment on discrimination of length. Four pairs of vertical lines were exposed for an instant, with attention directed to one designated pair, and O judged which line of this pair was longer—a fairly easy task. At other times O reported on 2 pairs, on 3, or on all 4—the task becoming subjectively more difficult as the number of required comparisons increased. But for some reason the Os tended to avoid "equals" when attempting to judge 3–4 pairs, and so often gave a smaller DL for 3–4 than for 1–2 pairs. SD increased regularly with the difficulty of the task.

The conclusion is forced upon us that the DL obtained by the method of Constant Stimuli is not a valid measure of differential sensitivity, though it may be of value as a measure of attitude. The SD is a true measure of differential sensitivity, as can be seen clearly in the two-category experiment. A difference correctly judged 75 percent of the time evidently affords a measure of keenness of discrimination—the smaller this difference, the keener the discrimination. But a difference perceived 75 percent of the time is precisely Q, a measure of scatter; and a difference perceived about 84 percent of the time is that other measure of scatter, the SD.

What bearing has this conclusion on our previous question, whether to allow a middle category? Two inferences follow: (1) the middle category does no good, and (2) it does no harm. As to the first statement: if DL is unimportant, the three-category method furnishes nothing that is not furnished by two categories. The second statement requires more elucidation. Going back to the table of Fernberger's results (p. 423) we see that the frequency of Equals makes no sure difference in SD and CE. Kellogg (1930), in comparable data from the same Os in two- and three-category experiments, finds that SD differs very little. This is a very heartening result, for it means that O's attitude toward the middle category is not a disturbing factor if the appropriate measures are used, namely M and SD. The criteria of equality and the attitude toward the middle category are easily changed, but the variability of the receptive apparatus is deep-seated; and it is that variability which we need to measure in studying accuracy of observation, along with the constant errors. We reach a conclusion which will very likely be satisfactory to everybody: in the method of Constant Stimuli, whether or not equal judgments are allowed and whether or not any importance is attached to the DL, at least the value of SD should be reported. Those who believe that the SD is the proper measure can then use it.

FREQUENCY METHOD C: THE METHOD OF SINGLE STIMULI

Instead of presenting paired stimuli, one of which, the Variable, is always to be compared with the other, the Standard (as in the method of Constant Stimuli), the method of Single Stimuli dispenses with the Standard and presents only one stimulus in each trial. This stimulus is to be rated, assigned a value on some scale. The scale may have two steps or categories, as Large and Small; or three steps, Large, Medium and Small; or more than three steps, such as a series of physical units, grams, inches, seconds. Essentially the same procedure is used in esthetics under the name of the Rating Method (p. 375), and also in experiments on the span of apprehension (p. 684).

Wever & Zener (1928) thought this method worth trying in psychophysics, and they found it perfectly feasible in the weight-lifting experiment—a finding confirmed by Fernberger (1931 b). Pfaffmann (1935) found it especially convenient in experiments on discrimination of tastes, because the mouth must be rinsed after each stimulus. Eliminating the Standard cuts down the number of stimuli to one half, while furnishing the same number of judgments.

But, one may ask, what is the basis of judgment, if no Standard is provided? The basis lies in O's quickly acquired familiarity with the series of stimuli used in the experiment. The range of weights, let us say, is 85–115 grams. In relation to this series, 85 grams is light, 115 heavy, 100 medium. The judgment is relative to the stimulus series, but it is "absolute" in form, and the method is sometimes called that of absolute judgment.

The data can be handled by the same methods as in Constant Stimuli. When the scale has two steps or categories, we find M and SD of the transition zone between them. When there are three categories, there are two Ms and two SDs to be found, and also a measurement corresponding to the Interval of Uncertainty, the net width of the middle class, and further something corresponding to the Point of Subjective Equality, which we may call the Subjective Midpoint and denote by the symbol, PSE, computing it by Equation (**29**), p. 421.

When the stimuli are estimated in physical units, M and SD can be found for each stimulus according to the method of Average Error (Bressler, 1933; Long, 1937).

Comparable results from the same Os by Constant Stimuli and Single Stimuli show one striking difference in results: the middle category is much more used by O in Single Stimuli; he is much readier to classify a weight as Medium than to judge it equal to a Standard. He takes a different attitude toward the middle category and uses different criteria. But his discrimination, measured by SD, is just about as good by one method as by the other (Wever & Zener, 1928; Fernberger, 1931 b; Pfaffmann, 1935). When a rather fine scale of physical units is prescribed, as by Bressler (1933), the discrimination is considerably better by Single Stimuli, though the work is more strenuous.

THE REACTION TIME METHOD IN PSYCHOPHYSICS

This method deserves mention though it has been little used. Henmon (1906) found it a practicable method. He used the disjunctive reaction (p. 333), exposing for example two horizontal lines side by side with instructions to react with the hand on the same side as the longer line. The larger the difference, the shorter was the reaction time. The differences used in this experiment must be supraliminal, because O must not make any appreciable number of errors; if he does his reaction time cannot be accepted (p. 308).

Reaction time can be combined with the methods of Constant Stimuli and Single Stimuli. Kellogg (1931) in an experiment on discrimination of brightness exposed a circular field, either half of which could be brighter than the other. O had before him three keys and pressed the middle one if both halves appeared equally bright, otherwise the key on the same side as the brighter semicircle. Without O's knowledge his reaction was timed. In a two-category experiment the middle key was eliminated and O was required to react right or left. The reaction was definitely quicker in the two-category experiment. When three categories were used, the reaction was slower for Equal than for the two outer categories. This last result was confirmed by Fernberger and his coworkers (1934) in an experiment with lifted weights, O speaking his judgments into a voice key. The relatively slow "equal" response agrees with the testimony of many Os to the effect that the impression of equality is seldom strong and clear.

Comparability of the several psychophysical methods. The different methods can all be employed on the same problems, as in testing Weber's Law, but the specific measures are not comparable because O's task is not the same. The SD of Average Error and the SD of Constant Stimuli are both good measures but they do not measure the same thing, and that obtained by Average Error is much the smaller (Kellogg, 1929 a, b). The DL of Just Noticeable Difference is a direct measure since O is looking for the transition point and is aware of the transition when it occurs, while the DL of Constant Stimuli emerges only at the computer's desk. The DL of Constant Stimuli seems to be of little value, while that of Just Noticeable Difference has furnished some of the best data on Weber's Law, the rest coming mostly from Average Error.

CHAPTER XVIII

RESULTS IN PSYCHOPHYSICS: JUDGMENTS OF MAGNITUDE

IN PSYCHOPHYSICAL experiments, the subject's task is to observe and report the apparent magnitudes of physical stimuli, to answer questions regarding weight, length, brightness, loudness, and the like. While the psychophysical methods are used in a variety of experiments, on problems belonging under many topics, the specific psychophysical problems are connected with the stimulus threshold and the difference threshold.

The stimulus threshold. The least quantity of physical energy which excites any given receptive system and produces a reportable sensation is a very small quantity indeed. The least audible sound is produced by oscillatory changes in air pressure against the tympanic membrane amounting to about .001 dyne per square cm, when the vibration frequency of the tone is 2048 cycles. This oscillation is only a billionth part of the ordinary atmospheric pressure. The threshold varies greatly with the individual, as we know, and it is relatively large for low and for very high tones.

With a dark-adapted eye, and a point source of light, the minimum luminous energy visually perceptible is about 17×10^{-10} ergs per sec. (Reeves, 1918 b), not much greater than the auditory stimulus threshold which, measured in ergs, comes to about 4×10^{-10} ergs per sec. Very good physical technique is required to measure these thresholds, but several competent investigators have obtained values of the same general order of magnitude.

The difference threshold looms larger in psychological discussions. We find three main problems to consider: (1) the perceptibility of a difference as related to the magnitude of the difference itself; (2) the perceptibility of a difference as related to the total magnitude of the stimulus; and (3) the curious constant errors, especially the "time error," which are found in judgments of magnitude.

LARGER DIFFERENCES MORE READILY PERCEIVED

No one could question the statement that very large differences are noticed more easily than very small differences. A question arises, however, regarding differences lying within the transition zone, the region of the threshold. If the difference threshold were a constant, as sometimes supposed, any difference smaller than the threshold would be imperceptible and any larger difference simply perceptible, and there would be no degrees of perceptibility. That there are degrees of perceptibility within the transition zone is amply demonstrated by frequency data and by reaction time data, already mentioned. The ogive plot of Constant Stimuli data shows an increase in the frequency of correct judgments as the difference increases. The demonstration is most convincing when very fine gradations of difference are given a thorough trial, as in a weight-lifting experiment of Warner Brown the results of which are shown in Fig. 109. With a few exceptions such as would be

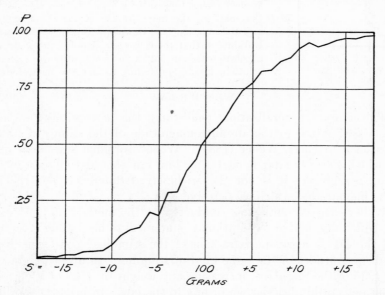

FIG. 109. (Data from Warner Brown, 1910.) Relative frequency of the response Heavier in a two-category weight-lifting experiment. The Standard was 100 grams and the Variable ranged from −18 to +18 grams by steps of 1 gram (with two additional steps of ½ gram adjacent to the Standard). Method of Constant Stimuli, 700 trials at each value of s.

expected from the sampling error, every small increase in the difference gave an increase in the percent of correct judgments. The same investigator, working on the stimulus threshold for taste, found that every little increase in the concentration of a salt solution increased the number of positive judgments (Fig. 110).

Incredible as it may seem that every stimulus, no matter how weak, will sometimes elicit a response, or that every difference, no matter how small, will sometimes be perceived, a broad view of the situation shows that such results are to be expected. The response is determined by a multitude of internal factors as well as by the stimulus. Even a zero stimulus sometimes gives a positive response, when the readiness for that response is very great. A zero green, that is to say a neutral gray, will give the positive response, "green," when the retina has just been exposed to the complementary color (the negative after-image effect). A minus difference in weights is sometimes perceived as a plus difference. With such a receptive system any slight increase in the strength of the stimulus factor will increase the chances of a positive response.

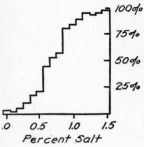

Percent Salt

FIG. 110. (Brown, 1914.) An experiment on the stimulus threshold for taste. Solutions of salt were applied ranging in strength from 0 to 1.5% by steps of 0.1%. The O whose results are plotted made 80 trials with each concentration, judging whether the solution applied to her tongue tasted salt or not. The stronger the solution, the more frequently taste was reported, and this relation held down practically to zero concentrations, so that there was no stimulus threshold in an absolute sense but only a mean transition point between solutions giving and failing to give the taste sensation.

WEBER'S LAW

This famous generalization, concerning the perceptibility of a difference in relation to the absolute magnitude of the stimuli compared, dates back to E. H. Weber (1834). Weber's original statement of the law which Fechner later named after him ran about as follows: in comparing magnitudes it is not the arithmetical difference, but the ratio of the magnitudes, which we perceive.

Weber's experiments were conducted by the method of Just Noticeable Difference, and an "operational" statement of his finding is therefore that the DL is a constant fraction of the stimulus—constant, that is, for all magnitudes of the same kind of stimulus. In lifted weights, DL was 1/30 of the Standard; increasing any weight by 1/30 of itself makes it just perceptibly heavier, according to the law. In brightness of light, under favorable conditions, DL is about 1/100 of the stimulus brightness; adding 1/100 to the brightness of one half of a circular field makes that half just perceptibly brighter than the other. The fraction differs with different senses and different magnitudes to be perceived.

Tested by the method of Average Error, Weber's law does not apply at all to the Constant Error but holds fairly well of the Variable Error, or of the SD. The SD is a fairly constant fraction of the stimulus which is being reproduced.

For testing Weber's law by the method of Constant Stimuli, with either two or three categories, the measure to use is the SD, or some other measure of variability such as h or Q (p. 425).

Broadening the statement of Weber's law. So far, we can say that DL is a constant fraction of the stimulus, or that SD is such a fraction, or that Q is such a fraction. The DL is a difference which is perceived half the time, Q a difference perceived 75 percent of the time, SD a difference perceived 84 percent of the time. Probably it would be safe to generalize to the extent of saying that a difference perceived any specified percent of the time is a constant fraction of the stimulus.

Warrant for such a statement of the law is to be found in experiments which keep the fraction constant and determine whether this constant fraction remains equally perceptible when the absolute magnitude of the stimulus is changed.

In an experiment with lifted weights, many fractional differences were tried, the Standards being 50 and 100 grams. With any given fraction the percent of right judgments (out of 500 trials) was nearly the same for both Standards, though somewhat smaller with the smaller Standard in accordance with the usual deviation from Weber's law. The results are shown in a table.

PERCENT OF RIGHT JUDGMENTS IN LIFTED WEIGHTS
(Brown, 1910)

Fractional difference		.005	.01	.02	.03	.04	.05	.06	.07	.08	
Standard	50 g.	51	54	59	63	71	70	77	84	87	
Standard	100 g.	52	57	60	67	73	76	82	81	85	
Fractional difference		.09	.10	.11	.12	.13	.14	.15	.16	.17	.18
Standard	50 g.	84	89	92	92	93	95	96	98	97	98
Standard	100 g.	88	91	94	92	94	95	97	96	98	98

The table reads, for example, that when one weight was .02 = 1/50 heavier than the other, the difference was correctly perceived in 59 or 60 percent of the trials. If we keep the weights in the same ratio we obtain approximately the same percent of right judgments even when the absolute weights are doubled.

Stimulus ratios too large to give any appreciable number of false judgments can be tried out by the reaction time method, as was done by Henmon (1906) in the case of lengths of seen lines. With a stimulus ratio of 5:6 he obtained discrimination reaction times as follows, each figure being the average of 640 reactions from two Os combined:

Lines in mm	5–6	10–12	15–18	20–24
Discr. RT in ms	326	318	316	313

As usual, a slight increase in perceptibility goes with increase in the stimulus magnitude, for a constant stimulus ratio.

A similar experiment in cutaneous pressure was made by Chiba (1923). The pressure exerted on the skin of the finger by a "pressure balance" was suddenly increased or decreased by $\frac{1}{5}$ of its amount, and O reacted by speaking against a voice key. The difference was perceived correctly in 96 percent of the trials. The average reaction times for a group of four Os were:

	Increase of $\frac{1}{5}$	Decrease of $\frac{1}{5}$
Standard of 25 grams	682 ms	955 ms
" " 50 "	610	734
" " 100 "	587	788
" " 200 "	576	750

The RT is longer (the perceptibility of the difference less) at the Standard of 25 grams, but above that the law is approximately confirmed.

Still larger stimulus ratios can be tried out by the method of "equal appearing intervals," a method which might have been listed among the main psychophysical methods but was omitted because it introduces no new type of computation but utilizes the technique of either the serial, the equation or the frequency method. Two standard stimuli widely different in intensity are presented and O adjusts a variable stimulus to the subjective halfway point between the two intensities. Or a series of stimuli differing by a constant ratio is presented and O reports whether the steps are subjectively equal. The results of this method are not very precise and differ in different fields, but in respect to visual brightness at least they are in good agreement with Weber's law (Ebbinghaus, 1911, p. 600).

A difference perceived in a certain percent of the trials can be called a *perception unit;* a difference perceived in a certain time can also be called a perception unit. Weber's law, in general terms, says that each perception unit is a constant fraction of the stimulus magnitude (constant for a given kind of stimulus and a given task of perception). It also includes the converse statement that any given stimulus fraction or ratio defines a constant perception unit; for example, a difference of $\frac{1}{10}$ in weight will be perceived in a certain fraction of the trials, and a difference of $\frac{1}{5}$ in the length of two lines will be perceived in a certain time.

If DL is a constant fraction of the stimulus, we can write:

$$\frac{DL}{s} = a \text{ Constant};$$

and if SD is a constant fraction of the stimulus, we can write:

$$\frac{SD}{s} = a \text{ Constant}.$$

If we use the symbol, Δs, read "Delta s" or "Increment of s," to stand for any one of these perception units, we can state the law in a general form,

$$\frac{\Delta s}{s} = W \tag{31}$$

where W is called the Weber Fraction. Weber's law asserts this fraction to be constant in spite of variations in s.

Breakdown of Weber's law at the extremes of the stimulus range. Weber's law should be tested over the whole range from the stimulus threshold to intensities as high as can be safely used. Fairly adequate tests have been made in several sense fields. A clear picture of the results is obtained by plotting the obtained values of the Weber Fraction as ordinates against an abscissa representing stimulus intensity. If the fraction is actually constant the graph is a horizontal straight line. Results from the different sense fields agree in giving a line which is approximately horizontal over a middle range of intensities, rising however at the low end and sometimes showing a tendency to rise at very high intensities (Figs. 111, 112, 113).

The first impression created by these curves is that Weber's law has broken down—but how seriously? The middle range, in which the line is approximately horizontal, looks rather short in the graphs when they are drawn, as usual, on a base line divided in equal ratios. If the curve for brightness discrimination (Fig. 112) were drawn on a base line divided in equal arithmetical increments, and on the scale used in the left-hand part where the curve descends rapidly, the level part would reach over a mile to the right.

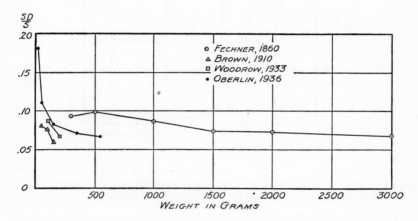

FIG. 111. (Data from several authors.) Weber's law in lifted weights. The weights were lifted successively with one hand. Method of Constant Stimuli. Number of Os: Fechner, 1; Brown, 1; Woodrow, 5; Oberlin, 5. The results, given by the several authors in terms of h, Q or complete distributions, are here reduced to terms of SD, and are seen to be in good agreement as to the absolute values of SD, and especially as to the course of the Weber fraction with change of S.

The flat part really covers 99.99 percent of the whole range of intensities. To be sure the line is not absolutely straight even within this zone but its curvature would be imperceptible if it were drawn on an arithmetical scale. Some one may argue that the equal ratio scale is the only sensible one to use on the base line, because the difference between 1,000 and 1,001 ml is of much less significance than that between 1 and 2 ml. This argument assumes Weber's law as a basis for arguing against it.

However, the actual divergence from Weber's law is not unimportant; it occurs in the region of weak stimuli and indicates special conditions and handicaps of discrimination in that region. Fechner who was quite cognizant of the breakdown of Weber's law at low intensities had an explanation. In weight-lifting the weight of the arm itself has to be considered, in visual discrimination the idioretinal light due to endogenous stimulation needs to be added to the external light in estimating the total stimulus. Always, there is some addition to the external stimulus, and the addition may count heavily when the external stimulus is very weak.

In view of the practical importance of the middle range of intensities, and of the practical importance of perceiving relative rather than absolute differences, it seems fair to say that discrimination is *best* where the

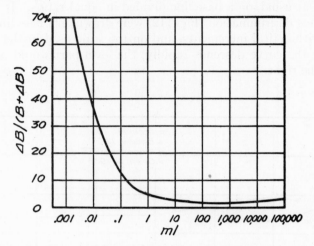

FIG. 112. (Data from König & Brodhun, 1888, recomputed in millilamberts by Nutting, 1908.) Weber's law in brightness. Discrimination of upper and lower halves of a small round field, tested by Just Noticeable Difference. Data from one O.

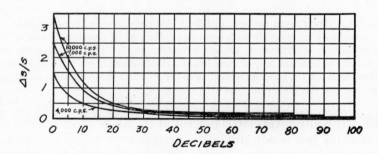

FIG. 113. (Adapted from Riesz, 1928.) Test of Weber's law in discrimination of intensity of sound. The sound was a pure tone produced in a special telephone receiver by the alternating current from an oscillator. Combined with this current was a second weaker current differing in vibration frequency by 3 cycles/sec. and producing beats or fluctuations of intensity in the main tone, the amount of fluctuation being controlled by varying the intensity of the second current. The question for O was whether the tone was heard to beat. Δs was determined at various vibration rates of the main tone, and over the whole range of intensities from near the stimulus threshold to near the pain threshold. The Weber fraction was found to be lowest (the discrimination best) when the tone had a high pitch, about 2,500 cycles, three octaves and more above middle C of the musical scale. In this region the ear is most sensitive to very faint sounds, i.e., the stimulus threshold is lowest. Fig. 114 shows that discrimination of pitch also is best in the region of high tones. Average of 12 Os. "c.p.s." = cycles per second.

Weber fraction is smallest, and accordingly that it is practically optimum through a wide middle range and suffers from hampering conditions at very low and perhaps also at very high intensities.

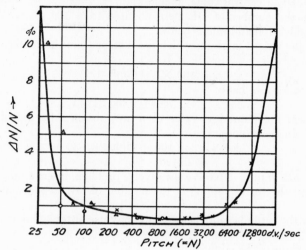

FIG. 114.   (Data from Stücker, 1907; Vance, 1914; Knudsen, 1923.)   Pitch discrimination in relation to vibration rate.   The data give DL obtained by different experimental methods.   Here the curve certainly rises at both ends of the scale.   Pitch discrimination is theoretically not subject to Weber's law, because the perceived difference is physically one of vibration rate and not of intensity or magnitude.   The statement was formerly made that the DL for pitch was a constant absolute quantity, as 2 cycles for a given O.   But when plotted over the whole range of audible vibration rates the curve is similar to that for light and sound intensities, except in showing a marked rise at the upper extreme.   The relative DL is smallest in the two octaves from 800 to 3200 cycles, which are rather high from a musician's standpoint but not very close to the upper limit of audible tone (about 20,000 cycles).

Fechner's summation formula.   Fechner's restatement of Weber's law aroused much controversy but properly considered is only a convenient mathematical device for computing the consequences of Weber's law.

Assume Weber's law to hold for lifted weights, and let the Weber fraction, $W = DL/s = 1/30$. Then $W + 1 = 31/30$ is the constant ratio by which any weight must be multiplied in order to give a just noticeably heavier weight—30/31 in order to give a just noticeably lighter weight.   Start with any convenient weight, as 100 grams, and multiply it by 31/30, obtaining 103.33 grams, which $= 100 + 1$ DL.   To get a weight just noticeably heavier than this, multiply 103.33 grams by 31/30, giving 106.78 grams, which thus $= 100 + 2$ DL.   Proceeding in this way we obtain the following series, which can be extended as far as the Weber constant holds good:

$100 - 4$ DL = 87.71 grams	$100 + 1$ DL = 103.33 grams
$100 - 3$ DL = 90.63 "	$100 + 2$ DL = 106.78 "
$100 - 2$ DL = 93.65 "	$100 + 3$ DL = 110.30 "
$100 - 1$ DL = 96.77 "	$100 + 4$ DL = 114.01 "
100 ± 0 DL = 100 "	etc.

If we wished to find what weight would lie 50 DL above 100 grams, instead of laboriously computing all the intervening steps, we could reach our answer directly by logarithms. First construct a formula for any number of DL steps above or below our central value, as follows:

Let n = the number of DL steps counted from 100 grams as center, n being plus above 100 and minus below.

Let s = the weight in grams which lies n steps from the center.

Then

$$s = 100 \times (31/30)^n$$

Passing to logs we have:

$$\log s = \log 100 + n \log 31/30$$

Now insert the numerical value of n and obtain s by aid of a table of logarithms. In the supposed case,

$$\log s = \log 100 + 50 \log 31/30$$
$$= 2.7120$$

whence s = 515 grams. To solve the reverse problem, insert a numerical value for s and find the corresponding n, the number of DL steps from 100 to that value of s.

To make the formula more general, we may use letter symbols throughout, letting

s = any value of the stimulus;

s_0 = that particular value of the stimulus which is selected as the center or arbitrary zero, analogous to the zero of the thermometer;

r = the constant stimulus ratio by which each value of s must be multiplied in order to give the value lying one perception step higher up the scale (r = W + 1). The perception step is defined in terms of the subject's responses and may be the DL, the SD or some other.

n = the number of perception steps from s_0 to s.

Then

$$s = s_0 \, r^n \tag{32}$$
$$\log s = \log s_0 + n \log r$$

$$n = \frac{1}{\log r} (\log s - \log s_0) \tag{33}$$

To adapt this general formula for use in any particular sense field, we need a well defined perception unit and the numerical value of r which corresponds to this unit. We must select an arbitrary value of the stimulus, s_0, analogous to the zero of the thermometer, above and below which we count our perception units. That is all we need, and the logarithmic formula is merely a convenience, involving no assumptions beyond Weber's law.

For example, to find the location in the musical scale of any assigned vibration frequency, we can take middle C of 260 cycles as our zero and the octave (r = 2) as our perception unit. Equation (33) then reduces to this: n = 3.322 (log s − 2.415). If s = 10,000 cycles, the equation gives us n = 5.265; i.e., the tone of 10,000 cycles is 5.265 octaves above middle C.

Having derived the logarithmic formula, Fechner reduced it to a more elegant and compact (but less usable) form by taking s_0 as his stimulus unit, and by writing C for the constant $1/\log r$. Since log 1 = 0, the equation became

$$n = C \log s$$

In place of n, Fechner used a symbol which he called "sensation," and thus Weber's law took the form,

$$\text{Sensation} = \text{C log Stimulus,} \tag{34}$$

and was read, "The sensation is proportional to the logarithm of the stimulus," sometimes called Fechner's law. Wholly irrelevant controversy arose on the question whether sensation was capable of measurement. As far as the formula is concerned, "sensation" means nothing more than n, a number of perception units which are equal in the sense of equal perceptibility. They are sometimes called "sensation units," but "perception unit" is a truer expression.

Practical use has been made of Fechner's formula. It was desired to have a measure of sound in "sensation units." Weber's law was known to hold good, approximately, for middle intensities of sound and was assumed as the basis of measurement. A stimulus ratio of 10:1 was chosen as the fundamental unit and was named the "bel" (after Alexander Graham Bell). The tenth part of this ratio, i.e., $^{10}\sqrt{10} = 1.259$, was called the decibel and is the unit most often used. The decibel, then, is the stimulus ratio of 1.259 (in power units); and it is also the perception step corresponding to this stimulus ratio and assumed to be constant, in accordance with Fechner's law. This perception step is not far from the DL for intensity of sound, but it is not defined as the DL but as the step corresponding to the stated stimulus ratio. For an arbitrary zero it is customary in this system to use the stimulus threshold. To say that the noise on a certain street corner is 50 decibels above the average stimulus threshold means that it represents noise-producing power delivered at that point equal to 50 decibels = 5 bels = 10^5 = 100,000 times the minimum audible. To say that one voice is 20 decibels louder than another means that the louder one delivers $10^2 = 100$ times the power of the other. No doubt the assumption of Fechner's law leads to slight errors in the count of "sensation units," especially down near the stimulus threshold, but on the whole the system does good service in the hands of the telephone engineers and acoustic experts; and it is interesting to see this dry-as-dust old formula actually put to work in modern developments (Fletcher, 1929).

Interpretations of Weber's law. Here we will do little more than mention the outstanding suggestions that have been offered. Fechner regarded the law as psychophysical in the literal sense of the word. He based his interpretation on his logarithmic formula, (**34**); and regarded this as teaching that the sensation increased more slowly than the stimulus. The sensation plods along step by step while the stimulus leaps ahead by ratios. There seemed to be a lag in the sensation as compared with the stimulus—of the psychical as against the physical in the process of transformation of energy from the physical to the psychical spheres. If we disregard Fechner's concept of the psychical sphere we can locate the lag according to his theory in the sensory areas of the cortex.

Wundt's interpretation, which he called psychological, was a corollary of his doctrine of relativity (1894). Since no stimulus is apprehended as an isolated item but every one in relation to others, it follows that relative rather than absolute differences should be perceived. The lag is thus located in the cortex but not confined to the sensory areas. It is incidental to the total cortical activity of perceiving and judging.

Psychologists in general have been inclined to agree with the physiologists that the lag is not entirely cortical; it may occur largely in the receptors. Hecht (1924, 1934) has shown in the case of brightness discrimination two peripheral factors which singly or conjointly could give an explanation of the Weber's law curves. One factor, photochemical in nature, is seen in the concentration equation for the speed of a chemical reaction. To produce a constant increment in the amount of the photochemical product which is the immediate stimulus of the retinal receptors, the increment of light intensity must have a constant ratio to the initial intensity. The other factor is the presumably varied stimulus threshold of the single receptors. If the distribution of these thresholds has a certain form, the number of fresh receptors thrown into action by an increase in the stimulus intensity could be a constant number for a constant ratio of stimulus increase.

CONSTANT ERRORS AND THE PROCESS OF JUDGMENT

Psychophysical experiments always encounter constant errors which are just a nuisance as far as the test of Weber's law is concerned but which afford clues to the process of judgment and for that reason may prove the most important outcome of the experiments, psychologically. Fechner found space and time errors present in the weight lifting experiment. If one of the two weights lay to the right of the other, some difference in the lifting movement made the two feel unequal. If one was lifted after the other, the second was apt to seem heavier.

For some purposes the experimenter's only concern with such constant errors is to avoid them in advance or to eliminate them by suitable statistics. The space error in lifted weights is avoided by Urban's device (1908) of a rotating table, turned by the experimenter so as to bring each weight in turn directly under O's hand. Both time and space errors are avoided in experiments on light and sound by introducing a momentary variation in the intensity of the stimulus. The subject, for example, sees an illuminated field which sometimes receives a small additional illumination lasting $\frac{1}{5}$ sec., and his task is to observe whether the light wavers or remains steady (Macdonald & Allen, 1930; see also the legend of Fig. 113). The device of parallel series serves for eliminating and measuring a constant error. Let the first-lifted weight be on the right in one series and on the left in a parallel series; compute M for each series, and their average gives an M from which the space error is eliminated, while half of their difference gives a measure of that error.

Among space errors can be counted many of the "geometrical illusions" (p. 643), of which the vertical-horizontal illusion is a simple example. The amount of such an illusion can be measured by any of the psychophysical methods, and these peculiar constant errors have thrown some light on the process of form perception. Apart from these illusions the most intriguing of the constant errors is the *time error*, which is usually negative. This error promises to throw light on the process of "successive comparison."

The sign of the time error. Both in Average Error and in Constant Stimuli the CE is found by subtracting the Standard from the Point of Subjective Equality; CE = PSE − S. The error is positive when PSE is greater than S, negative when PSE is less than S. This is logical but some of its implications may cause confusion. Suppose, in a single trial, the Variable is the same as the Standard but is judged greater: evidently a smaller Variable would give the impression of equality; the Point of Subjective Equality at that moment lies below the objective value of the Standard, and the time error is negative. The sign of the time error will be clear if we think of this error as affecting, not the second stimulus on which the judgment is passed, but the first stimulus which is somehow carried in memory during the interval.

A rough measure of the time error is obtained from the frequencies of plus and minus judgments, when S and V are objectively equal. A balance of plus judgments means a negative time error. Subtract the percent of plus judgments *from* the percent of minus judgments, and the difference, denoted by the symbol D%, shows the sign and something of the size of the time error.

Examples of the time error. In weight lifting from Fechner down, though not universally, a negative time error has been found. The second of two equal weights feels heavier than the first, or gives a larger percent of plus judgments. PSE lies below the standard S.

In sound intensities the same negative time error has been found. The second of two equally intense sounds, separated by a short interval of time, sounds louder than the first.

When a tone of a medium pitch is sounded and sounded again after a silent interval of a few seconds, it is likely to appear higher the second time than the first, showing again a negative time error. The result varies with the pitch, with the time interval and with the range of tones in the series (Wolfe, 1886; Wada, 1932).

When a bright spot on the wall of a dark room is exposed for one second and then again after a dark interval of one second, it is likely to appear *less bright* the second time than the first—an instance of a *positive* time error. This effect soon passes away with the prolongation of the interval (Fullerton & Cattell, 1892; Lauenstein, 1933) and can be explained in terms of retinal adaptation. The first stimulus, received by a dark retina, induces a change in the direction of brightness adaptation, a change which does not entirely pass away in a brief interval of darkness, so that the second stimulus is received by a less sensitive retina. The second impression is weaker than the first though the external stimuli are equal. Anyone thinking that this well-known fact of sensory adaptation furnishes a key to the whole problem of the time error is reminded (a) that the time error is usually negative and not easily explained by adaptation, and (b) that he is tacitly assuming in the observer the ability to compare the two successive impressions, an ability which still remains to be explained.

The puzzle of successive comparison.   The first stimulus has come and gone; the second now arrives and is compared with the first.   How can the two stimuli be laid side by side, even figuratively, when one of them is a thing of the past?   The older theory was that an *image* of the first stimulus was laid beside the new stimulus.   The negative time error— the lowered PSE—was due to the fading of the image.

Though logical enough, this theory did not stand the test of careful introspection.   Schumann (1898, 1902) after long experience with lifted weights testified that he seldom had a kinesthetic image of the first weight at the moment of lifting and judging the second.   The first weight had dropped out of consciousness and was usually not recalled. The judgment was a direct response to the second weight without any conscious reference to the first weight.   Martin & Müller (1899) found *absolute impressions* playing a large role in the judgment of weight. When O had become acquainted with the range of weights used in an experiment, any one of those weights was apt to give him the impression of being light or heavy in an absolute sense.   To be sure, light and heavy are relative, but the relation need not be present in mind.   A "heavy" baby is heavy in comparison with the general run of babies, but those other babies are not thought of while you are lifting the particular baby. Similarly in the experimental situation O builds up a *subjective scale* of weights, a scale of which he is not directly aware but by implicit reference to which he judges the particular weight.   Experiments by the method of Single Stimuli (p. 425) have shown that O readily uses the absolute categories.   He soon becomes adjusted to the range of stimuli used in an experiment.

Further evidence against the image theory of successive comparison was obtained by Whipple (1901, 1902), by Fernberger (1919) and others. (See a review by Needham, 1934 a.)

Trace theory and set theory.   In place of the fading image the concept of a *fading trace* is used to explain the negative time error.   The trace is a physiological after-effect of the first stimulus.   It is "silent," giving by itself no sensation or image, but it affords a level of residual excitation which is displaced by the second stimulus with a resulting "absolute impression."

An alternative conception, not necessarily antagonistic to the trace theory, is that of *set*.   The clearest example is afforded by the Müller-Schumann theory of the perception of lifted weights (1889).   In lifting the first weight O adjusts the force of his lifting movement to the weight encountered.   The second weight he lifts with a force about equal to that found necessary for the first.   He carries over a motor adjustment ("Einstellung") from the first lift to the second.   If the second weight is lighter it comes up quickly and easily but if it is heavier than that for which O is adjusted it comes up slowly. The impression received from the second weight depends upon the adjustment with which it is lifted. The adjustment depends not only upon the first weight in a pair but also upon the whole series of weights to which O has become accustomed in the experiment. It can depend upon many other factors, such as muscular fatigue, warming-up or the visual appearance of the weight. A weight which looks heavier than it is will be lifted with greater force than necessary and accordingly feel light. So the size-weight illusion is explained.

In other fields than lifted weights, the set becomes somewhat less tangible, but the main idea remains that an adjustment for the Standard stimulus is carried over to the moment when the Variable stimulus is received, and that the Variable appears strong or weak according as it is stronger or weaker than the stimulus for which O is adjusted.

The trace as conceived here must decrease or fade out with time; it tends toward zero though perhaps slowly. It is renewed or increased by a repetition of the same stimulus or of any weaker or stronger stimulus of the same kind. The set is not subject to so simple a law. It does not necessarily tend toward zero. As an active adjustment it is subject to "conditioning" and is reinstated after an interval of disuse when O sits down again at the familiar laboratory table to repeat the experiment. Its level can be raised by O whenever he suspects that it has fallen too low. It is subject to fatigue and warming-up, practice and forgetting, and to the stimulating and depressing influences of external and physiological conditions.

In order not to speak continually in terms of one of these theories we need some noncommittal term to designate whatever it may be that does duty for the first stimulus in successive comparison. We will speak of the *effective value* of the Standard at the moment of passing judgment. In case of a negative time error, the effective value of the Standard has declined during the interval. We can use our symbol PSE to denote the *effective value of the Standard* as well as Point of Subjective Equality, because the latter is our index of the former. PSE shows how much S is worth at the moment of judging. If S is 100 but PSE after an interval is 96, the effective value of S has declined from 100 to 96 during the interval.

The time error changes with increasing interval. The interval in question, the S–V interval, is the time elapsing between the first and the second of two successive stimuli. Köhler (1923) devoted particular attention to this matter in order to reach a decision between two theories of the time error. (1) If the time error is due to fatigue or some other direct after-effect of the first stimulus, the time error will disappear when the interval is prolonged. (2) If the time error is due to a fading trace, it will become more and more negative with prolongation of the interval. Köhler found in fact that the time error was zero or positive for 2–3 sec. and then became progressively more negative, and these results were confirmed, in general, by Wada (1932) and Needham (1935 a), though they found a later turn in the positive direction when the interval was considerably prolonged. All of these experiments were done with auditory stimuli. The upswing of PSE directly after the first stimulus is a slight effect but well enough established to demand some attention; it may be due to fatigue, adaptation or refractory period.

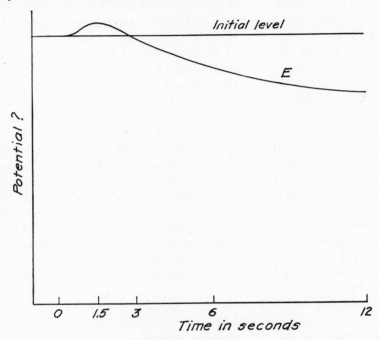

FIG. 115. (After Köhler, 1923.) The fading trace. E here means PSE, which starts from a level corresponding to the first stimulus, rises for a short time above that level and then decreases gradually up to 12 seconds. The ordinate is labeled "Potential?" in allusion to Köhler's conception of the electrical nature of the trace.

The effect of practice on the time error. The practice here is not directed specially against the time error but simply toward doing as well as possible (without knowledge of results). Köhler found, with repetition of the experiment, that the time error diminished and lost its simple curve of increasing negativity. Needham (1934) found that the curve almost reversed itself after several days of practice; it was negative with short intervals and became positive with the longer intervals; and the absolute amount of the error decreased. This practice effect makes the fading trace theory seem ultra-simple, for how can practice cause a trace to increase instead of decrease with the lapse of time during the interval? (Fig. 116.)

Effect of interpolated stimuli on the time error. A novelty in weight lifting was introduced by Guilford & Park (1931) for the purpose of testing Köhler's trace hypothesis. A stimulus interpolated between S and V should displace the level of the trace, i.e., of PSE: if strong, it should raise the level and made V appear unduly weak; if weak, it should depress the level and make V appear unduly strong. In their experiment the weights to be compared were in the region of 200 grams, the S–V interval was 7 sec., and in the middle of this interval an extra weight

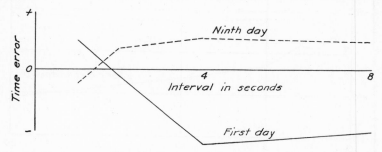

Fig. 116. (Data from Needham, 1934 b.) The time error curve as changed by continued repetition of the experiment. Average curves for 6 Os. On the first day the error was positive at the one-second interval and negative for the longer intervals between Standard and Variable; but after eight days of practice the curve reversed itself and the time error was also diminished in absolute amount.

of 100, 200 or 400 grams was lifted. The Point of Subjective Equality was displaced in the predicted direction. The average for three Os came out as follows:

	Interpolated weight		
	100	*200*	*400 grams*
PSE	188.2	192.5	199.2
Time error (PSE − S)	− 11.8	− 7.5	− 0.8

The heavier the interpolated weight, the higher the level of PSE at the end of the interval. But the effect was very slight. The 400 gram weight raised PSE not to 400 or anywhere near it, but only by 6 or 7 grams, and the 100 gram weight lowered PSE by only 4 or 5 grams. The Os in this experiment reported that they tried to *disregard* the interpolated weight and attend only to S and V, and the objective results showed them succeeding to an extent which is scarcely consistent with a pure trace hypothesis.

Lauenstein (1933) obtained a similar result with tones as stimuli, and formulated the effect of the interpolated stimulus in terms of "assimilation." The trace of the Standard was assimilated with the trace of the interpolated stimulus and so was raised or depressed. He urged that the customary interval of silence between S and V was not vacant but filled with a "zero stimulus" toward which the trace of S was attracted, lowering PSE and producing the usual negative time error. He did not actually try the effect of the zero stimulus; but Pratt (1933 a) did so in an experiment in which the sounds to be compared were separated by an interval of four sec., within which not indeed a continuous background stimulus but a loud or a soft momentary sound or no sound at all was introduced. All the sounds were produced by the falling of a

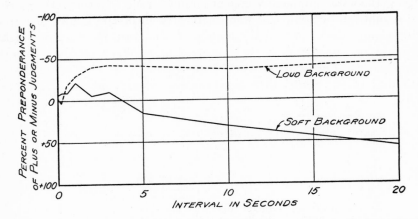

Fig. 117.   (After Lauenstein, 1933.)   Assimilation of PSE to its background. The Standard tone was immediately followed by a background tone which filled the interval of 0–20 sec. before the Variable was given. This background tone was either much louder or much softer than the two tones, S and V, which were being compared. S and V were objectively equal, but the loud background pulled PSE gradually upward and so gave an increasing preponderance of minus judgments for V; and the soft background the opposite.

sound pendulum, from graduated heights. The intensity of the standard was 45° (height of fall). PSE came out as follows:

With loud interpolated sound	48.19°
With soft interpolated sound	42.19°
With silent interval	44.14°

We see *PSE was lowered more by a soft sound than by the silent interval.* The differences though small were reliable on the average of 3 Os.

Why should zero interpolated stimulus have less effect than a weak stimulus? The result is inexplicable by assimilation and shows that Lauenstein's theory does not explain the ordinary time error with a vacant interval. A zero stimulus is successfully "disregarded" by O whereas the interpolated sounds or weights form a part of the stimulus pattern which controls the judgment. Pratt concludes that, at any rate, the idea of fading trace cannot be discarded in spite of the reality of the assimilation effect.

Needham (1935 c) discovered another fact inconsistent with a pure assimilation hypothesis. His observers were comparing the intensity of clicks in one experiment and of brief tones in another. In each case he interpolated into the middle of the S–V interval a brief sound of the same character as was being judged, but much louder or weaker. The rest of the interval was silent. As in the experiments already cited the strong interpolated stimulus raised the level of PSE, the weak interpolated stimulus lowered it. The new fact is that this effect dies out during a vacant interval; the more the interval is prolonged the less remains of the effect of the interpolated stimulus. The positive time error induced by a loud interpolated stimulus dies out as the interval increases from 2 to 4 and 8 sec. This dying out can be explained by the fading trace assumption. But the negative time error induced by a weak interpolated stimulus also dies out—an effect not explained by either assimilation or fading trace. Some other factor must be sought.

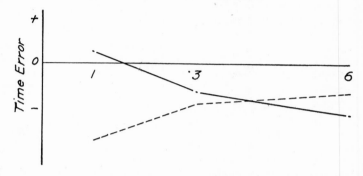

FIG. 118. (From Needham, 1935 c.) Dying away of effects of brief interpolated stimulus. S, V and the interpolated stimulus were each a tone lasting ½ sec. The time error curve after a loud interpolated tone is shown by the solid line; after a weak interpolated tone by the dotted line. Results from two Os combined.

An apparent contradiction between this figure and Fig. 117 is easily explained. Lauenstein's interpolated stimulus continued throughout the interval and had a cumulative effect, whereas the effect of Needham's brief interpolated stimulus died away during the ensuing silence.

Central tendency or series effect. The additional factor required for a full analysis of the time error may be connected with the "indifference point," a phenomenon observed for many years in judgments of magnitude. When Vierordt (1868) attempted to reproduce the duration of an interval, he made short intervals too long, long intervals too short, and intervals of 3 sec. about right. The indifference point, 3 sec. in his own case, differed with the individual and with the conditions of the experiment. Later experimenters located it at various points and regarded it as an index of the natural speed or rhythm of the individual. For recent work on this matter see Stott (1935). The results taken as a whole were confusing because the indifference point varied so widely; but the confusion was cleared up by Hollingworth's discovery (1909, 1910) of the "central tendency" of judgment. The same law was rediscovered by Ipsen (1926) who called it the "series factor." The law is that *the indifference point* has no fixed location but *lies near the middle of the range of stimuli* employed in any experiment. Extend the stimulus range upward and you raise the indifference point. *Below the indifference point the time error is positive; above, negative.* Ipsen showed that the same results were obtained without actually changing the limits of the stimulus range, by simply presenting the low, or high, values of the stimulus disproportionately often. The series effect is a tendency toward the mean of the stimuli used rather than toward the midpoint; i.e., PSE gravitates toward the mean of the stimuli used.

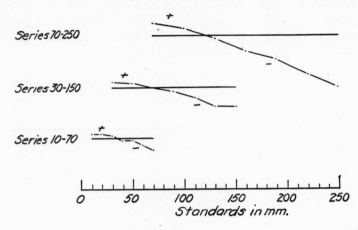

FIG. 119. (Data from Hollingworth, 1909.) Central tendency and the shifting indifference point. An experiment by the method of Average Error, in which O attempted to reproduce the extent of a hand movement, his eyes being closed throughout. The Standard to be reproduced was supplied by a groove through which O moved his pencil. The guiding groove was then removed and O tried to reproduce the length of the Standard by a pencil line drawn on paper. On one day the series of Standards extended from 10 to 70 mm, on another day from 30 to 150, on another from 70 to 250. (Standards presented in shuffled order, 25 trials with each Standard by each of 3 Os, during each day's work.)

The ordinate shows the positive or negative time error for each Standard in each series. The data points give PSE for each Standard. The indifference point of each series lies where the oblique line crosses its base line. The indifference point lies near the middle of each series, but somewhat below it—an evidence for fading trace. For Standards below the indifference point of each series, the time error is positive, etc. Notice the changes in the time error of the Standard of 70 mm with change in the range of the series.

These results, obtained by Hollingworth with hand movements and with judgments of seen areas, and by Ipsen with extent of seen lines, have been closely paralleled in lifted weights by Woodrow (1933) and in sound intensities by Lauenstein (1933) and by Needham (1935 b). The results have been obtained by Constant Stimuli as well as by Average Error.

Central tendency and time error shown also by the method of Single Stimuli. Here no Standard is given, and each stimulus is rated in terms of an absolute scale. Central tendency can still be present because O becomes accustomed to the range and mean of the stimuli employed in an experiment. In a very early use of the method of Single Stimuli, Leuba (1892) presented an assortment of artificial stars which O sorted into five classes or "magnitudes." The results revealed the law of central tendency, which Leuba called a law of sense memory and formulated thus: "There seems to be a natural tendency in us to shift the sensations held in memory toward the middle of the scale of intensities, i.e., toward the united residual of all the past sensations of the same kind."

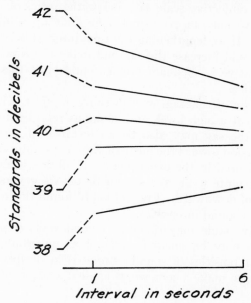

Fig. 120. (Data from Needham, 1935 b.) PSE returning toward the series mean. The Standards were tones of a constant pitch but of 5 intensities, each Standard being used in a shuffled fifth of the trials. A Standard was sounded, followed by a silent interval of either 1 sec. or 6 sec. and then by the Variable, which O compared with the Standard in respect to intensity. The data enable us to compute the approximate PSE for each Standard after each time interval. When the Standard was 42 db, PSE was 41.5 db after 1 sec. and declined to about 40.5 at the end of 6 sec. The weakest Standard of 38 db, on the contrary, shows PSE = 38.5 after 1 sec. and about 39 db after 6 sec.

The curves are convincing evidence of a positive time error affecting the weaker Standards in the series and a negative time error affecting the stronger Standards; and they show a reversion toward the series mean during the interval of 6 sec. Each of the curves is a rudimentary curve of forgetting. We can think of O as adjusted to the general level of tonal intensity used in the experiment, 40 db, and of his adjustment being displaced by each standard and gradually reverting toward the general level.

In developing this method, Wever & Zener (1928) found the negative time error present, in case of lifted weights, a result confirmed by Fernberger (1931) and observed also in sound intensities by Pratt (1933 b) and Needham (1935 a), though not in taste intensities by Pfaffmann (1935). A negative time error here means that PSE, the subjective midpoint, lies below the objective midpoint of the range of stimuli used. Weights of 84, 88, 92, 96, 100, 104, 108 grams are classified as Heavy, Medium or Light; and the result is that more are called Heavy than

Light, and that PSE = 94.5 grams instead of 96 which is the objective midpoint of the series used.

The time error in this situation is quite understandable. Let there be a set or trace corresponding to the general average of the stimuli already received, and let this set or trace have a sinking or sagging tendency. The subjective scale sags below the series of stimuli. Each fresh stimulus, we may suppose, jacks the scale up a bit, but the sag quickly returns. If so, lengthening the time interval between successive single stimuli should increase the sag and make the time error progressively more negative. Needham (1935 a) finds just this effect in case of sound intensities.

As to the cause of this sag, we can think of effort being required to maintain the set at a high level, and of sag as representing a relaxation of effort. But the sag may also be an instance of central tendency. It may be a reversion toward the mean of *ordinary* stimuli as distinguished from the stimuli used in the experiment. If all the stimuli used in the experiment were quite weak, the sag, or better the reversion, should be upward instead of downward. Pratt (1933 b) found this to be the fact in an experiment on sound intensities.

The subjective scale may differ in several ways from an objective scale. Its steps may be unequal, as well as uncertain and unstable. By having the intensities of sound estimated in decibels, Long (1937) found it possible to make a somewhat detailed analysis of the subjective scale.

Similar results in esthetics. Comparisons in experimental esthetics are often by methods similar to constant stimuli and single stimuli, and results are obtained similar to those we have been considering.

1. *Time error.* Danzfuss (1923) presented two chords with an interval of 2 sec. between them, asking his subjects to judge the second as more or less *agreeable* than the first. He found in most Os a tendency for the second chord to be preferred. This is a result parallel to that in weight lifting, where the second weight tends to be judged heavier than the first; it is therefore a negative time error. Beebe-Center (1932) has verified this result with tones and odors, and with intervals of 20 as well as 2 sec., but with a 1.5 sec. interval he finds a positive time error. The pleasurable effect of a brief tone or odor reaches its maximum shortly after the stimulus has ceased—or so it would seem from these results.

2. *Central tendency.* If a set of colored papers is laid before O with instructions to select the most pleasant and the most unpleasant, he has little trouble in following these instructions, though it must be admitted that the "unpleasantness" of any clean piece of paper, of whatever color, is only relative. When the categories of response are designated by the numbers 1 to 5, or 1 to 7, he finds little difficulty in adjusting his judgments to such a scale, whether the stimuli are all pleasant or some pleasant and some unpleasant.

3. *Effect of interpolated stimuli.* Results similar to those obtained in psychophysical experiments go in esthetics under the name of the "law of affective contrast." In an experiment by Bacon, Rood & Washburn (1914) many colored papers were laid before O who selected 6 as extremely agreeable and 6 as extremely disagreeable. From the remaining colors the experimenter selected 18 and exposed them singly for O to rate on a scale of 7 points. Between each 2 of these medium colors was interpolated a very agreeable color (as selected previously by O), and, in a second round, a very disagreeable color. The medium colors received lower ratings when interspersed with the most liked colors than when interspersed with the most disliked. The law of affective contrast, formulated from these results, is that the pleasure of an agreeable experience is heightened by an immediately preceding disagreeable experience, etc. Harris (1929) shows that the effect is not induced entirely by the immediately preceding pleasant or unpleasant color; it is rather a mass effect from the whole series of interpolated pleasant or unpleasant colors. Beebe-Center (1929, 1932) finds the mass effect to hold over from one sitting to another two days later. His experiment had five stages. (1) From a set of 21 odors, O selected the 10 most and the 10 least pleasant. (2) For 5 sittings distributed over a period of two weeks, O was occupied with the 10 least pleasant odors, making comparisons between them as to pleasantness. (3) After a two-day interval the whole set of 21 stimuli was presented for judgment and ratings were obtained on a three-step scale—pleasant, indifferent, unpleasant. (4) For two weeks O was occupied with the most agreeable stimuli. (5) Two days later the whole collection of 21 odors was again rated. The 21 odors received higher ratings after two weeks of occupation with the unpleasant stimuli than after similar occupation with the pleasant stimuli—a mass contrast effect.

"Contrast" here has however no explanatory value since the stimuli which induced the contrast were not in direct contact with those which suffered contrast. What carries the effect over the two-day interval? If we continue to use our noncommital symbol PSE which stands for either trace or set, we can say that occupation with the unpleasant stimuli lowered the level of PSE, occupation with the pleasant stimuli raised it, and the level so reached persisted to some extent over a two-day interval. The result is in conformity with the hypothesis that PSE is not determined simply by the stimuli in the immediate situation but in part by past experience in the laboratory or elsewhere.

4. *Disregarding an irrelevant stimulus.* Harris (see Beebe-Center, 1932) interpolated agreeable or disagreeable *odors* between *colors* which were being rated, and found scarcely any contrast effect. The hedonic tone of the odors had little dependable influence upon the PSE for colors.

CHAPTER XIX

THE SKIN SENSES

SENSATION and sense perception offer a field for scientific exploration which is much vaster than it first appears. The structure and operation of the sense organs and their nerve centers and the contribution they make to experience and behavior have been explored by numberless physiologists and psychologists, and the amount of detailed information obtained is so enormous that our account must be extremely selective.

Sensation and perception. If we should attempt to begin this study with an adequate definition of these terms, we should find ourselves in the midst of a debate that has gone on for many generations of psychologists and philosophers. Where to draw the line between sensation and perception is the particular difficulty. So much as this is clear: *Sensation* points to the sense organs with their nerves and nerve centers as the object of study; *perception* points to the objects of the world which we know through the senses. In the laboratory the distinction between an experiment on sensation and one on perception is reasonably clear. In a sensation experiment we apply stimuli that are quite restricted and typically simple, the attempt being to discover what impression or reaction results from these simple stimuli and their variation. In a perception experiment we present objects or objective facts and attempt to discover how well they are observed. In both cases O is keenly attentive to what is presented and in both cases he gives a verbal report. In a sensation experiment we are interested in the correlation of his report with the stimulus, in a perception experiment we are interested in the correlation of his report with a certain objective fact.

To illustrate: In lifting a loaded pill box in a psychophysical experiment, O perceives the weight of the box. This box is not the stimulus, nor even is the weight of the box the stimulus; the stimulus is the pull of the weight upon the hand, the bending of the joints, the pressure on the skin. O can be trained to attend to these sensations or in other words to attend to the exact stimulus (Friedländer, 1920). Without special training O takes his customary object-directed attitude and judges the weight of the box. He is thus committing what is usually called the stimulus error. A better name originally suggested by Titchener (1909, p. 267) is *object error*. The error consists in attending to the object when one should be attending to the stimulus. It is an error, however, only in an experiment on sensation and not in the psychophysical experiment which belongs properly under perception of magnitude.

Another example, this one from the cutaneous field, is furnished by the *two-point threshold*. With a pair of "touch compasses" two points at graduated distances are simultaneously applied to the skin; sometimes as a check only one point is applied. In a perception experiment, O's task is to distinguish between two points and one. In an experiment on sensation, his attention is directed to the exact impression derived from each application of the stimulus, and he reports whether the impression is compact, elongated, dumbbell-shaped, or clearly double (Boring, 1921). O would be committing the object error in this last experiment if he attempted to decide whether two points or one were being applied. But are not the two points and the one point the stimuli? No, for a stimulus must be defined in relation to the receptors—light is not a stimulus except as it strikes the retina. The tactual stimulus consists in deformation of the skin and stretch applied to the receptors. In describing the sensation O gets as close as possible to the stimulus.

The two-point threshold is smallest on the tip of the tongue (1 mm) and largest in some parts of the back, thigh and upper arm where it is given as 68 mm. It shows a large practice effect (p. 181).

A long known fact which may appear strange is that the two-point threshold exceeds the error of localization in the same region. On the volar surface of the forearm, near the wrist, where the two-point threshold is about 14 mm, the error of localization is about 4 mm. In determining the localization error, E touches a point on O's skin and O, blindfolded, tries to find the point with a stylus. Or, to make conditions more like those in the determination of the two-point threshold, E touches two points successively and O judges "Same place" or "Different place." By this method the localization error measures about $\frac{1}{4}$ of the two-point threshold. Zigler (1935) who obtained this result explains it as follows: when a blunt point is applied to the skin, stimulation is not limited to a point, since the surrounding skin is somewhat stretched. The receptors must be stimulated in decreasing amount from the directly touched point as a center. Localization is probably determined by the center of strongest stimulation, while the whole stretched area is effective in giving a broad impression and obscuring the presence of two points. (See also Boring, 1930. For other methods of studying localization and for results on constant errors of localization, see Cole, 1929; Hulin, 1935; Grannis & Walker, 1936. For values of the two-point threshold see Ladd & Woodworth, 1911; von Skramlik, 1937).

Cutaneous sensation and perception. We have distinguished two types of report which may be demanded: the report of stimulus (or of sensation) and the report of objects (or meanings). The "phenomenal" report is intended to be a third type, a freer type, in which O simply relates his experience on receiving a stimulus. On account of the dominant object-directed attitude of the naive observer, the phenomena reported are mostly properties of objects. Furnished the materials for obtaining a variety of cutaneous experiences, O reports that he feels metal, wood, velvet, paper; or he reports characteristics of objects: rough and smooth, hard and soft, moist and dry, warm and cold, large and small, vibrating, tickling, prickling. These characteristics he usually refers to external objects, though sometimes to the skin which is warm or cold, tickles, itches, etc.

In a study of pure sensation, all objects and meanings are laid aside, and the attempt is made to get as simple sensory impressions as possible and at the same time to exhaust the variety of such impressions, to note their similarities and differences, and arrange them in some sort of system. Titchener's efforts in this direction culminated in his touch pyramid, which he regarded as tentative and as obviously incomplete since warmth and cold were not included.

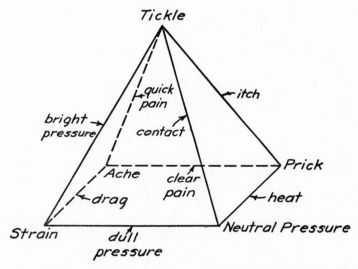

Fig. 121. (Titchener 1920.) The touch pyramid. Salient qualities of sensation are placed at the angles, intermediate qualities along the sides.

Like the perceptual qualities of hardness, smoothness and the rest, these sensory qualities raise the problem of cues. What is the stimulus giving the impression of roughness? Probably a pattern of stimulation. The stimulus for warmth or cold may also be a pattern (Nafe, 1934) but may be a simple and distinct process in the skin. We will leave this question for a moment, and go further into the problem of cutaneous perceptions.

Perception of rough and smooth. In an extensive series of experiments Katz (1925) tested the fineness of this kind of perception and obtained evidence regarding the available cues. From a large assortment of papers he selected a scale of 14, extending from glazed paper at one end, through writing paper, drawing paper, blotting paper and wrapping paper to a very rough cloth paper. Over two sheets of paper to be compared, was laid a sheet of cardboard having windows 4 × 6 inches through which the papers were felt with the fingers, the eyes being closed. With very few errors, O distinguished all the papers with respect to roughness and smoothness. Asked to describe the papers, he characterised most of them with fair success.

O's spontaneous procedure in examining the papers was to move the finger balls from side to side along the surface. When he was required to eliminate this movement and to place his fingers on the paper and take them off immediately, he was unable to perceive roughness and smoothness, though this type of exploration revealed hardness and softness. It appeared that friction between the skin and the paper somehow furnished the cues of rough and smooth. In order to determine whether active movement was necessary, the papers were mounted on a turntable and moved under O's motionless fingers, with the result that he was still able to distinguish the papers though perhaps not quite so well as with active finger movement. Explored with a wooden rod held like a pen the papers were distinguished fairly well. A thin coating of collodion on the fingers hampered the perception very little, but a coating of liquid glue made all the papers feel equally smooth.

Is the up-and-down bouncing movement impressed on the finger by the unevenness of the rough surface sufficient in extent to constitute a stimulus? Katz found that a lightly etched piece of glass felt rough though the up-and-down of the surface amounted to only .001 mm, too little to constitute a mere spatial stimulus, but enough, by friction, to produce irregular vibrations in the skin. These vibrations are even audible and make it necessary to plug the ears with cotton in order to limit perception to tactual cues.

Perception of vibration by the skin. For a handy demonstration of cutaneous vibratory sensation, simply hum a note while partially closing the nostrils. Damp a tuning fork or piano string with the finger and you feel the vibration. Set a tuning fork in vibration and apply its shank or foot to the skin and the vibration will be felt for a longer time. A special "vibration sense" need not be assumed, since the cutaneous receptors for pressure (or "touch proper") are apparently the only ones stimulated (v. Frey, 1915; v. Skramlik, 1937). For testing the cutaneous perception of vibration, the most adequate apparatus uses vibrators driven by radio oscillators, with control of both frequency and amplitude of vibration and with liberal possibilities of amplification (Knudsen, 1928; Roberts, 1932; Geldard & Gilmer, 1934; Hugony, 1935). Several problems in perception can be attacked.

1. *The range of perceptible frequencies, and the intensity threshold at each frequency.* At low frequencies, such as 10 per sec., pulsation is sensed rather than vibration; and there is probably no exact point of transition to the vibratory sensation. Of more interest is the question of an upper limit, but the results indicate no upper limit, provided the amplitude of the high frequencies is sufficiently great. O lays his finger gently on the vibrator and reports when it is activated. By varying

the amplitude, using the psychophysical method of serial exploration (p. 397) E determines the stimulus threshold for each frequency. In the region of 200–300 cycles per sec. amplitudes as small as .001 mm can be sensed as vibration, this being the region of greatest sensitivity. Positive reports have been obtained with frequencies as high as 8,000 cycles per sec., when the amplitude was sufficient (Knudsen, 1928; Goodfellow, 1933; Setzepfand, 1935).

We are not to infer that these high frequencies are transmitted by the cutaneous nerves to the brain. Refractory period would prevent the single nerve fiber from transmitting more than about 500 impulses per sec., probably. When the finger is laid on a vibrator, many receptors and many nerve fibers are thrown into action, but the vibrating stimulus synchronizes the nerve impulses in large measure and thus, we may suppose, yields the characteristic sensation. Experiments on the frog, in which animal about 300 impulses per sec. is the limit for a single nerve fiber, show one impulse for each vibration impressed on the skin, up to about that limit, and a dropping out of some impulses when the frequency exceeds what the nerve fiber can carry (Adrian et al., 1931; Cattell & Hoagland, 1931).

2. *Perceptible frequency differences.* Can the skin duplicate in any degree the ability of the ear to distinguish small differences in frequency (p. 436)? There is a qualitative difference in the sensation obtained from low and from high frequencies applied to the skin, and smaller differences, as between 200 and 225 cycles per sec., can be correctly judged after some practice. After intensive training with these particular frequencies, 400 and 420 cycles can be distinguished, but the interrelations of frequency, amplitude and energy leave it possible that something besides frequency furnishes the differential cues (Knudsen, 1928; Roberts, 1932).

3. *"Hearing" speech through the skin.* Amplified speech vibrations can be felt by the fingers, and different words and phrases differ enough to be distinguished after specific practice. Though the intensity pattern, rather than the frequency pattern, probably furnishes the cues, these tactual vibrations are of some value to the deaf in lip reading and in learning to manage their own voices (Gault, 1927, 1936).

THE FOUR CUTANEOUS SENSES

The traditional "sense of touch" has been broken up by experiment into at least five senses. The first to be split off, early in the nineteenth century, was the muscle sense, kinesthesis. Then, toward the close of that century, the cutaneous sense was broken up into four: the warmth sense, the cold sense, the pain sense, and the pressure sense or sense of touch proper. These four are distinguished because they give radically different sensations, in response to radically different adequate stimuli, applied to different points or "spots" on the skin.

Sensory spots of the skin. The discovery of these spots affords a striking instance of independent investigators reaching the same result almost simultaneously. Three physiologists, Blix the Swede, Goldscheider the German and Donaldson the American conducted the experiment at practically the same time and published their results in that order, within the few years from 1883 to 1885. The full demonstration of the pain points was not achieved till the work of von Frey (1894), another German physiologist.

Von Frey's experiment aimed to make sure whether the pain sense was separate from the pressure sense. He knew of course that strong pressure was likely to give pain while light pressure gave only a sensation of contact. It was therefore probable, if there were two separate senses, that the pressure sense had the lower threshold. Accordingly he needed a graduated series of very weak stimuli. He found that straight hairs, human and other, could be used for his purpose. He used hairs an inch long or more, fastened sideways at the end of light wooden handles. He pressed the free end of the hair vertically against the skin so as barely to bend the hair. It exerted upon the skin a definite pressure which was measured by substituting a delicate weighing balance for the skin. A fine hair, pressed down on one pan of the balance, can barely raise a weight of one milligram placed in the other pan; a stiff hair can raise 100 times as much. A graduated series of hairs being prepared, the threshold of any spot of the skin was determined by ascertaining the weakest hair that gave rise to a sensation. The diameter of each hair was measured by aid of a microscope, and the pressure exerted per square millimeter was computed. Expressed in this last measure, the threshold was as follows on different surfaces (one subject):

STIMULUS THRESHOLD FOR PRESSURE

Tip of tongue	2 grams per square mm
Tip of finger	3
Back of finger	5
Front of forearm	8
Back of hand	12
Calf of leg	16
Abdomen	26
Back of forearm	33
Loin	48
Thick parts of sole	250

The threshold depended partly on the thickness of the skin and partly on the amount of nerve supply. Hairy portions of the skin are shaved before the sensitiveness of the skin itself is measured, because a hair acts as a lever conveying stimulation to the nerve ends about its base, and any pressure sufficient to bend a short hair will ordinarily give a sensation.

Von Frey selected for more minute exploration a small area, one centimeter square, on the skin of the leg. The area having been shaved, he explored it first with very weak hairs and found a few points giving a sensation of contact. Using slightly stiffer hairs he found about 15 points that responded, each one having a threshold of 33 grams per square mm, or less. Gradual increase of the stimulus above this value yielded scarcely any further sensitive points till he reached 200 grams per square mm, above which pressure numerous points gave a pricking and painful sensation. There were thus two sets of spots, one with low threshold giving sensations of contact or pressure, and the other with high threshold giving sensations of pain. The distribution of the two sets was different, as the pressure spots were clustered near the roots of the hairs, while the pain spots were scattered over the whole surface. The pressure spots lie mostly on the "windward" side of the hair, i.e., close over the hair follicle. A few others are found, not close to any hair, even on hairy surfaces; and on the hairless surfaces there are of course many pressure spots (von Frey, 1894, p. 288).

Using a very sharp needle, von Frey pressed it into pain spots and pressure spots, getting sharp pain from the former, and usually only a pressure sensation from the latter. In spots that gave both pain and pressure to the needle stimulation, both pressure receptors and pain receptors might be present.

On the front of the eyeball (cornea and conjunctiva) the sensitive spots were numerous, and their threshold low, but the sensation was always painful, diffuse and outlasting the stimulus. It appeared that these surfaces were provided with a pain sense but not with a pressure sense.

Von Frey (1894) concludes as follows:

1. Punctate stimulation of the skin with graduated mechanical stimuli affords a demonstration of two stimulus thresholds, a lower one for pressure sensation, a higher one for pain sensation. Pressure and pain points are separate in location, the former lying near the hair roots.

2. There are skin areas of some size which feel pressure but not pain and others which feel pain only. . . .

I infer from these facts that pain sensation is mediated by special arrangements, that is by pain points and pain nerves.

The pain threshold was found to differ greatly in different regions, but the differences were not parallel to those of the pressure sense. Some of the thresholds for pain were as follows:

STIMULUS THRESHOLD FOR PAIN

Cornea	.2 gr/mm^2
Conjunctiva	2
Abdomen	15
Front of forearm	20
Back of forearm	30
Calf of leg	30
Back of hand	100
Sole	200
Finger tip	300

For locating temperature spots, the skin is explored with dull-pointed instruments that are a few degrees warmer or colder than the skin. A brass rod, with a conical end and rounded point, is convenient to manipulate but not easy to maintain at a constant temperature. A hollow metal cone can be filled with water kept at a nearly constant temperature by a supply tube leading from a reservoir controlled by a thermostat, with a vent tube to provide for circulation. Very convenient is electrical heating of the brass rod by a loop of resistance wire introduced into a hole drilled along the axis of the rod near its stimulating end, the temperature being regulated by a rheostat.

Explored with a cool stimulus, the skin yields cool or cold sensations at some spots, and not at others. Explored with a warm stimulus, it yields warm sensations at certain spots and not at others. Usually more cold than warmth spots are found.

In general, the pain spots are the most numerous, next the touch or pressure spots, then the cold spots, and finally the warmth spots. The skin has been widely explored by Strughold and others and the results assembled by von Skramlik (1937) from whom a few counts are cited.

SPOTS PER SQUARE CENTIMETER

	Pain	Touch	Cold	Warmth
Forehead	184	50	8	.6
Tip of nose	44	100	13	1.0
Chest	196	29	9	.3
Volar side of forearm	203	15	6	.4
Back of hand	188	14	7	.5
Ball of thumb	60	120		

These results suggest the hypothesis that each sensory spot contains a receptor sensitive to a particular stimulus. One would expect to find warmth receptors in the warmth spots, cold receptors in the cold spots, pressure receptors in the touch spots, and pain receptors in the pain spots. Three questions are raised which can be submitted to experiment: (1) Are the spots stable in their sensitivity, so that the same spot always gives the same sensation? (2) Does the microscope reveal a characteristic end organ in each kind of spot? (3) Does each spot yield its characteristic sensation not only when excited by its "adequate" or normal stimulus, but also on the application of electric or other "general" stimuli? Affirmative answers to these three questions would demonstrate the punctate distribution of the skin senses.

Stability (or instability) of the sensory spots. The original investigators certainly leave the impression that they found stable spots which yielded the same sensation on retest. But when a student in the laboratory has mapped out a small area on the back of the hand, recording on his map each cold spot, for example, and re-examines the same area on another day, he finds rather poor agreement. With the same stimulus he gets about the same number of cold spots, but not exactly in the same locations. Even experienced psychologists find only moderate correspondence in remapping.

Another disturbing fact is that intensifying the stimulus increases the number of spots. Stimuli just slightly warmer or colder than the skin yield a few warmth or cold spots, while stimuli several degrees warmer or colder yield a much larger, though still a limited number (Heiser, 1932). The hypothesis of fixed spots can take care of this fact by assuming some receptors to be more sensitive than others, and

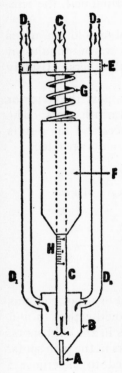

FIG. 122. (Dallenbach, 1927.) Improved thermal stimulator. Either cold water (8–9° C.) or warm water (42–44° C.) was forced into the chamber B through the tube C and out by D_1 and D_2. The projecting copper stimulus point, A, 1 mm in diameter, can be seen by the experimenter as he applies it to the skin, and is kept at a constant temperature by the water in B. The experimenter holds the handle F, supporting the weight of the apparatus through the spring G, and lowering it upon the skin till the handle reaches a certain mark on the scale H. Thus the pressure of A upon the skin is controlled.

by appealing to the undoubted fact that the physical effect of a strong stimulus spreads over an appreciable area of the skin. Increasing the pressure increases the area of skin subjected to stretch, raising the temperature of a stimulus increases the warmed area; and thus a strong stimulus will reach receptors situated some distance from the point of application to the skin.

Still we must admit that these two facts—the apparent instability of the spots and their increasing number with increasing stimulus— are more in line with the alternative hypothesis which discards the idea of an essentially punctate distribution of the skin senses and assumes only that the sensitivity of the skin varies from spot to spot, and in each spot from time to time. This alternative is at least worth keeping in mind.

The instability observed might be due to experimental errors. Dallenbach (1927) found many sources of error, some of which were very hard to avoid. Error arises from inexact mapping of the results. An exact record is necessary because two spots only a millimeter apart may give different sensations. The grid stamped on the skin for purposes of identification, though in indelible ink, rubs off in a few days unless protected by a ring of felt. Where the skin is loose the map is sure to be inexact. The pressure of the temperature stimulator must be kept constant, and the duration of stimulation as well; and the skin itself should be at the same temperature during test and retest. A rise of one degree in its temperature makes the skin less sensitive to warm stimuli, and a fall of one degree makes it less sensitive to cool stimuli. With so many causes of error and variation, perfect agreement of two maps cannot be expected. By using an improved stimulator which permitted precise control of the temperature and location of the stimulus, by securing the services of very competent Os, and by observing all possible precautions, Dallenbach obtained a degree of correspondence which can be seen in Fig. 123.

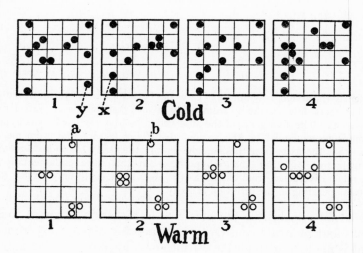

FIG. 123. (Dallenbach, 1927.) Four maps of cold spots and four of warmth spots, obtained on four days within about a week from the same area, 1 cm square, on the upper arm of an individual. The black dots are the cold spots, the little rings the warmth spots.

The number of spots, i.e., the number of square millimeters responding by warmth or cold sensation, was, for the successive mappings, 12, 11, 11 and 14 for cold, average 12; and for warmth, 6, 8, 8 and 8, average 7.5. That is, 12 percent of the cold stimuli, applied a millimeter apart, gave cold sensations; and 7.5 percent of the warm stimuli gave warmth sensations.

If we tally the positive responses on each millimeter unit, we find from the cold maps that 4 spots gave cold every time, 4 gave cold 3 times out of 4, 6 gave cold twice, 8 gave cold once, and the remaining 78 gave no cold responses at all. We can compare these actual frequencies with the theoretical frequencies to be expected on each of two hypotheses: (1) Fixed and separate receptors each accessible to stimulation at one particular spot, so that every spot must give either 4 positive responses or else 4 negatives. (2) For a given intensity of stimulus a fixed percentage of the spots will give positive responses, but it is all a matter of chance *what* spots will give the positive response in any day's trial. If the probability of getting the positive response from any spot on one trial is .12 (or say 1/8), then the chance of getting this response in two successive trials is the square of 1/8 or 1/64; the chance of getting it four times in the four trials is the fourth power of 1/8, or 1/4096. From this as a starting point we can compute the probable percent of single positives, double positives, triple positives, quadruple positives and no positives. We thus derive theoretical frequencies to compare with the observed frequencies, and find the following:

For cold

No. of positive responses from each spot	No. of such spots, as observed	No. of such spots, by chance	No. of such spots, if fixed
4	4	0	12
3	4	1	0
2	6	6	0
1	8	33	0
0	78	60	88
	100	100	100

For warmth

4	3	0	7.5
3	2	1	0
2	2	3	0
1	8	23	0
0	85	73	92.5
	100	100	100

Evidently the actual distribution of cases lies between the two theoretical distributions. The facts differ markedly from either chance distribution or perfect fixity of sensitive spots. The divergence of the observed facts from the fixed spots hypothesis can perhaps be explained by the various disturbing factors that were mentioned above; so that the fixity hypothesis might be fundamentally sound but obscured by disturbing factors. The pure chance hypothesis can scarcely be fundamentally sound, since so much divergence from chance as the facts show could only be due to some real factors operating in the direction of fixity.

While not conclusive, the evidence is rather in favor of localized receptors and punctate sensitivity. In another type of experiment no attempt is made to map all the warmth or cold spots in an area, but the specially sensitive spots are marked for later stimulation and prove to be very dependable. Pendleton (1928, p. 369) after locating 36 cold spots with great care found that only 2 of them ever failed to give the cold sensation.

Search for the receptors of the cutaneous senses. Any theory of cutaneous sensation is incomplete until it can point out the anatomical structures which serve as pressure receptors, pain receptors, warmth receptors and cold receptors. It is incomplete until it can also show exactly how these structures are affected by their respective stimuli. Two methods have been employed in seeking for the receptors. The less direct method is to *compare the distribution* of the four senses over the skin with the distribution of different types of nerve ending. The more direct method is to *excise the spots* and see what nerve endings are present.

Indirect method. Histological examination of the skin reveals several types of nerve endings:

a. Free-branching nerve ends, the most common type of sensory nerve ending, present practically everywhere in the skin.

b. Hair receptors. The root of each hair is embedded in the mass of free nerve endings, and is sometimes said to be specially encircled by some of these endings. At any rate, there is no difficulty in understanding how the hairs can serve as touch receptors, by transmitting pressure to the nerve endings around their roots. The great sensitiveness of the hairs can be understood from the leverage with which they act on these nerve endings.

c. Meissner's corpuscles, found on the hairless portions of the skin. They are usually supposed to serve the pressure sense, and are even called "touch corpuscles."

d. Krause's end-bulbs, spherical in shape, each bulb (like the Meissner corpuscle) containing the ending of a sensory nerve fiber enclosed in a little capsule of epithelial cells.

e. Other end-bulbs of cylindrical and other shapes.

f. Pacinian corpuscles, large and with well developed capsule, found in the subcutaneous tissue (and elsewhere) rather than in the skin itself.

As to distribution, the free nerve endings are everywhere, the hair receptors over the whole hairy surface, the Meissner corpuscles over the hairless areas. The end-bulbs are apparently rather limited in distribution, as they are not easy to find, microscopically, and have seldom been reported in histological studies of the skin.

All regions of the external skin are provided with all four senses. But this is not true of the mucous membrane of the mouth and throat, nor of the front of the eyeball, nor of some portions of the external genital organs. These regions have been explored in the hope of obtaining light on the temperature and pain receptors.

Von Frey (1895) found that the center of the cornea gave a sensation which, even when too faint to be painful, had the characteristics of pain as against touch, namely long latency and slow waxing and waning. The nerve endings there are exclusively of the free-branching variety. In that area, then, the *free nerve ends were obviously pain receptors*. The additional fact of universal distribution over the external skin both of free nerve endings and of the pain sense confirmed the correlation. But the free nerve ends may take care of other senses *besides* pain.

The outer margin of the cornea gives, in addition to pain, sensations of cold though not of warmth; and here Krause's end bulbs are common. From this von Frey concluded that these *spherical end bulbs were probably the cold receptors*, though he left the question open whether such end bulbs are abundant enough in the external skin to take care of its cold sense.

Von Frey's experiments on the eyeball were repeated and improved by Strug-hold (1926). As a stimulator, he used a camel's-hair brush lightly covered with cotton wool, dipped into warm physiological salt solution, shaken out and then applied to the cornea or conjunctiva. He tested the outer skin of the eyelid, the conjunctiva just to the side of the cornea, the conjunctiva just below the cornea, usually covered by the lower lid, and the lower margin of the cornea, obtaining results which are tabulated below:

TEMPERATURE OF STIMULUS

Area tested	28–30°	31°	32–38°	39–46°	47–51°	52–55°	56–68°
Skin of lid	cold	none	warm	warm	hot	burning-hot	burning
Conjunctiva, side	cold	none	none	none	cold	burning-cold	burning
Conjunctiva, below	none	none	none	none	none	burning	burning
Cornea, margin	cold	none	none	burning	unendurably-burning		

The skin of the lid here gives what may be called the normal or regular run of temperature sensations, with a physiological zero at 31° C. The side of the conjunctiva gives no temperature sensation between 31° C. and 46° C., the interpretation being that it has no warmth sense, though it gives "paradoxical cold" (see below) in response to rather hot stimuli. The "burning cold" is interpreted as a combination of this paradoxical cold with the pain aroused by high temperatures.

The second area tested in the conjunctiva had no cold sense, or warmth sense either, and its only response to temperature was the burning sensation which occurred when the temperature was high enough to arouse the pain receptors.

The corneal margin shows the cold sense, no warmth sense, and a low threshold for the pain sense.

The inner corner of the eye, the caruncula lacrimalis, does give warmth and possesses also the pressure or touch sense absent from the conjunctiva and cornea. The touch and warmth sensations we get from the eye come from this inner corner and the outer skin and edge of the lids.

To summarize: the pain sense is present all over the cornea and conjunctiva, and is the only sense present in the middle of the cornea. The margin of the cornea and most of the conjunctiva have also the cold sense, but not the warmth nor the pressure sense.

The glans penis and clitoris have been tested by von Frey (1895) and by Hauer (1926), because of the presence in those areas of spherical end bulbs and of "genital corpuscles" which may be simply a large variety of the same. The pain sense is present, the pressure sense is said to be absent, the warmth sense present but not well developed, and the cold sense present and well developed. Thus the tie-up of the cold sense with the end bulbs is strengthened.

In the mouth, a small area of the mucous membrane on the inside of the cheek opposite the second molar tooth has the distinction of lacking the sense of pain (Kiesow, 1894). The pain sense is the only one present in certain parts of the throat (tonsils and rear wall). Cold is more widely present in this region than warmth and pressure sensitivity. Inside the nose, all the cutaneous senses extend into the nostrils about 1 cm, and pain about 1 cm further (Schriever & Strughold, 1926). No close correlations with different forms of nerve endings have been made out for the mouth, throat or nose.

2. *Direct method: examination of the skin or mucous membrane beneath the sensitive spots.* The conjunctiva of the eye is highly sensitive to cold, and it has numerous Krause end bulbs; moreover the distribution of the cold spots and of the end bulbs is similar as far as general topography is concerned: where the cold spots are numerous the end bulbs are also numerous. But such correlations are indirect evidence. Strughold & Karbe (1925) made a direct attack on the problem by intravital staining with methylene blue, a dye which stains nerve tissue. The procedure was to drop a little methylene blue solution into the eye, and observe the conjunctiva through a microscope until nerve fibers and receptors could be seen. A wait of 2–3 hours was necessary for the stain to take, and by the time the end bulbs became visible the dye had deprived the eye of both the cold sense and the pain sense, for the time being. Accordingly a map of the observed end bulbs was carefully made and the cold stimuli applied to their locations on the following day when the dye had disappeared and the sensitivity had returned. Every spot in which an end bulb had been located gave the cold sensation. This result seems to clinch the question for the eye: its spherical end bulbs are cold receptors.

The matter cannot however be regarded as settled for the external skin. In the first place, there is no sure histological evidence of end bulbs in the skin. In the second place, several investigators, from Donaldson (1885) to Pendleton (1928) have applied the direct method, by locating cold spots, cutting them out, staining the excised bit of skin, and examining the nerve endings. All these investigators have been on the watch for end bulbs but have not seen any.

Depth of the warmth and cold receptors in the skin. If the receptors could be located as to depth, they would probably be easier to find and identify. It has long been believed that the *warmth receptors lie deeper than the cold receptors.* There are several bits of evidence in favor of this view, and no contrary evidence.

First, the reaction time to warmth is longer than to cold—warmth about .18 sec., cold about .15 sec. Probably it takes longer for warmth applied to the surface of the skin to reach the warmth receptors—longer than it takes cold to penetrate to the cold receptors.

Second, the warmth spots are less sharp and punctate than the cold spots. Since the heat conduction must spread, a deep-lying receptor could be stimulated from a wider area of the surface than a receptor lying near the surface.

Third, when the skin is cocainized by the electrosmotic method—the solution of cocaine being applied to the surface and carried in by electricity—it is known that only the superficial layers of the skin are reached by the anesthetic in the first few minutes, and deeper and deeper layers as the anesthetization continues. Schriever (1926) finds that three minutes of electrosmotic cocainization impairs the cold sense considerably, while leaving the warmth sense unaffected. After eight minutes both are gone.

Fourth, data have been secured regarding the conduction of heat into and out of the skin, and regarding the concomitant temperature sensations (Bazett,

McGlone & Brocklehurst, 1930). The temperatures at the surface and at
various depths in the skin were measured by thermocouples connected with
galvanometers, the deflections of the galvanometric needle being recorded on
moving photographic paper. A cold or a warmth spot was first located on the
back of the forearm. A sharp needle was then passed nearly horizontally
through the skin under the cold or warmth spot, at a depth of about one millimeter. The needle being removed, a loop of slender wire was passed through
the hole, and a thermojunction brought exactly below the spot; an X-ray photograph was taken to assist in this adjustment. Another thermocouple was placed
on the surface of the skin directly over the spot. When ready, a warm or cold
stimulus was applied to the spot in question, O reacting as soon as he felt warmth
or cold; the record on photographic paper showed the time of application of the
warm or cold stimulus, the time of O's reaction, and the temperature changes
at the surface and at a certain depth in the skin.

One result of some importance was that a stimulus lasting a few seconds
did not bring even the surface of the skin up to the applied higher temperature
or down to the applied lower temperature. The change of temperature
1 mm deep was much less than at the surface. The following typical result
illustrates these facts:

				Resulting maximum or minimum temperature	
Initial temp.		*Applied temp.*			
at surface	*1 mm deep*	*acting for 6 sec.*		*at surface*	*1 mm deep*
30.6°C.	31.0°	16.8°		25.7°	29.0°
31.2°	31.2°	41.0°		36.0°	33.5°

A temperature 14° below the skin temperature, applied for 6 sec., lowered
the surface temperature only 5°, and lowered the layer 1 mm deep only 2°;
and similarly a temperature 10° above skin temperature raised the surface
5° and the deeper level 2°. These were the effects of a fairly broad stimulus
(11 mm diam.); a punctate stimulus produced still smaller changes, especially
at a depth of a millimeter.

The rate of conduction of heat through the outer layers of the skin was
measured by noting in the records the instant when the galvanometer connected with the deep thermocouple first showed any rise or fall of temperature.
It took about a second or a little more for the heat to reach the depth of 1 mm.
The conduction of heat inward was at a rate of a little less than 1 mm per
second, while the conduction outward (i.e., the penetration of cold) was somewhat slower.

The temperature at a depth of 1 mm starts to rise about one second after
the application of a warm stimulus. It continues to rise during the application
of a brief stimulus and even for a few seconds after the withdrawal of the
external stimulus (Fig. 124).

O signaled the sensation of warmth or cold with a variable reaction time,
a second or more. A constant allowance of .15 sec. was made for the true
reaction time, the remainder was taken as the time required for heat or cold
applied to the surface to reach the receptors, and their depth was computed
from the speed of conduction. Though the several experiments gave somewhat different results, the most probable depth indicated for the cold receptors
was only .15 mm, ± .1 mm, and that for the warmth receptors .6 mm ± .2

mm. These depths would locate the cold receptor in the papillae or in the Malpighian layer, and the warmth receptors in the dermis.

The authors find that the vascular condition of the skin has much to do with the rate of penetration of heat or cold, and suggest that constriction of the capillaries may be an important factor in the stimulation of the cold receptors.

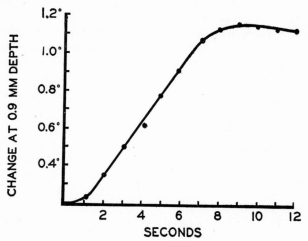

FIG. 124. (Data from Bazett, McClone & Brocklehurst, 1930.) Change of temperature at a depth of 0.9 mm from the surface of the skin, when a temperature 7.5° above that of the skin surface was applied for 5.4 sec. The inner temperature was scarcely affected at all for the first second; it then rose steadily at a rate of 0.18° per sec. for 7 sec. before tapering off and starting to fall. A warmth spot was present in the warmed area, and a sensation of warmth was signaled with a latency of 1.17 sec.

3. **Non-adequate stimulation of the sensitive spots of the skin.** The "adequate" stimulus of any receptor is that agent to which the receptor is specially sensitive. Light is the adequate stimulus for the retina. The adequate stimulus for the pressure sense is a bending or stretching of the skin, for the temperature senses, roughly, warmth and cold, while for the pain sense it is strong pressure, penetration of the skin, strong heat, biting chemicals, etc. The pain stimulus seems to be anything that injures the skin or comes to the point of injuring it. The pain sense, in other words, has a high threshold and is not specially adapted to any particular kind of external stimulus.

In accordance with the principle that was first named "specific energies of sensory nerves," though the specificity is now known to inhere not in the nerves proper but rather in their cerebral connections, we must get a sensation of cold whenever a cold receptor is aroused by any stimulus whatever; and the same with the other receptors.

Von Frey (1894) found that interrupted electric currents gave a piercing sensation at the pain spots and a whirring or hammering sensation at the pressure spots. The pressure spots registered the vibratory character of the stimulus up to as many as 100 pulses per second, and this was true whether the pulses were electrical or mechanical, the latter sort being given by a vibrating tuning fork. The pain spots, on the contrary, gave a continuous sensation even when the pulses were as slow as 5 per second.

Kiesow (1895) applied mechanical and electrical stimuli to temperature spots. He first located and marked for identification the most sensitive warmth and cold spots he could find. A blunt-pointed stick of soft wood, applied to a sensitive cold spot gave a brief cold sensation; applied to a warmth spot it gave a longer-lasting warmth sensation. These results could not be got every time, but at best in about 50 percent of the trials. With electric stimuli his percentage of successes was nearer 75.

But the most significant result obtained from non-adequate stimulation is the *paradoxical cold*. This discovery again goes back to von Frey (1895) who first observed the fact on the conjunctiva, and later on the external skin. Having located and marked a number of cold spots, he went over them with a hot stimulus, and some of them responded by a sensation of cold. Rather a high temperature was needed to arouse the cold spots, 45° C. in most areas, whereas 33° C. is usually high enough to give the sensation of warmth.

Paradoxical cold cannot be obtained by applying a *broad* hot stimulus, because, obviously, the warmth receptors thus stimulated mask the cold. Thunberg (1901) found, however, that paradoxical cold could be got by areal stimulation of well *warmed* skin. He applied a temperature of 45° C. for two minutes to the front of the forearm, and immediately followed with a stimulus at 48° C., which gave a pure cold sensation at first, with some warmth creeping in later. This apparently strange result is explained by the adaptation of the warmth receptors to the 45° C. and their consequent weak response to the 48° C. The feeble response of the warmth receptors permitted the cold receptors in the area to deliver their sensation unmasked.

Paradoxical warmth has been reported a number of times, but is very difficult to obtain.

Paradoxical cold is our evidence for asserting that a moderately hot stimulus applied to an area arouses both the warmth and the cold receptors in that area. It was suggested by Alrutz (1908) that this simultaneous arousal of warmth and cold receptors gave the sensation of *heat*. A still higher temperature would also arouse the pain receptors. Alrutz (1908) gives the following scale of sensations above the physiological zero:

At physiological zero	no temperature sensation
At warmth threshold	barely warm
A little higher	definitely warm
At paradoxical cold threshold	heat resembling warmth
A little higher	heat resembling cold
At pain threshold	burning heat
A little higher	pure pain

The threshold temperatures for heat and burning heat differ somewhat with different individuals, as well, probably, as with the temperature of the environment. Lowenstein & Dallenbach (1930) determined these thresholds in 100 individuals, at a room temperature of 20–25° C., and found the heat threshold to range from 40–46°, with an average at 42–43°, and the burning heat threshold to range from 43–51°, with an average at 46–47°.

The most convincing demonstration that the sensation of heat arises from the simultaneous stimulation of (neighboring) warmth and cold receptors is the *synthetic heat* experiment, in which no genuine heat is applied, but warmth spots are subjected to moderate warmth, and cold spots to cold. Several experimenters have succeeded with this experiment. An effective procedure is the application to the front of the forearm of a "temperature grill" built of small copper tubing. The tubes are parallel, a few millimeters apart, and alternate tubes are warmed and cooled by warm and cold water circulating through them. O is kept in ignorance of the nature of the stimulation. (Burnett & Dallenbach, 1927).

The first sensation is usually cold, followed by heat which often disappears after a few seconds and gives way to cold again. Warmth also is often experienced at some time during the 10–15 sec. of application of the stimulus.

Synthetic *burning* heat has been obtained by the simultaneous application of cold, warmth (not heat) and weak electric shocks (Ferrall & Dallenbach, 1930).

ADAPTATION OF THE SKIN SENSES

All these senses show the phenomenon of "negative adaptation": under continuous, unchanging application of a stimulus they cease after a time to give their characteristic sensations. From ordinary experience we might imagine the *pain sense* to be non-adaptable, but under ordinary conditions the stimulus is more or less intermittent and the sense is afforded intervals for recovery. A sharp needle applied to the forearm with the small pressure of 2.5–25 grams gives cutaneous pain without complication from deep pressure; and the pain fades out in a time which varies in general between 10 and 100 sec. The process of fading may be complicated by momentary recurrence of a pain which has once vanished. A typical case gives the following sequence of reports: "(1) sharp intense pain, (2) sharp pain, (3) pain, (4) dull pain, (5) weak pain, (6) pressure, (7) weak pressure, (8) tickle, (9) nothing." On removal of the stimulus, after-sensations of itching, pricking, heat, etc., are often quite strong (Wells & Hoisington, 1931; Burns & Dallenbach, 1933). When several needles are simultaneously applied to an area 15 mm in diameter on the forearm, adaptation may require as long as 5 minutes but it is eventually complete in practically all cases (Stone & Dallenbach, 1936).

The *pressure sense* ("touch proper") is extremely subject to adaptation. Pull on a glove and then hold the hand perfectly still. The strong initial sensation of pressure fades rapidly till the glove is scarcely felt unless the stimulus becomes intermittent because of pulsating arteries.

Experimentally, the adaptation to steady pressure follows a course which is indicated, for the first few seconds, in Fig. 125. A simpler

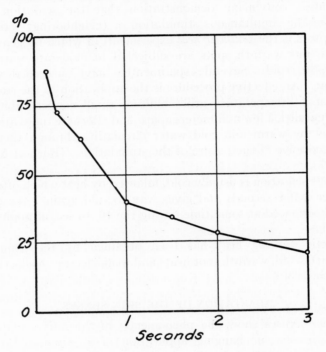

Fig. 125. (After von Frey & Goldman, 1915.) Rapid fading of pressure sensation during steady stimulation. Two neighboring areas on the forearm were stimulated, one with a steady pressure lasting 4 sec., the other with a momentary pressure thrown in at some time during the application of the steady pressure to the other area. In a series of trials the momentary pressure was adjusted till judged equal in intensity to the steady pressure at the same moment. The momentary stimulus provided a yardstick to measure the declining sensation of the steady stimulus. The ordinate shows the momentary pressure judged equal to the steady pressure, in percent of the initial matching value. After 3 sec. application the steady pressure has declined to about 20 percent of its initial matching value.

experiment answers the question, how long a steady pressure can be felt at all. A weight is gently lowered upon the skin and allowed to rest there till O signals that it is no longer felt. A paper disk is first laid on the area to be stimulated so as to avoid temperature sensations. Adaptation time was found to be quite variable, differing apparently with the individual, with the weight applied and with the region of skin stimulated. The averages from 8 Os are shown in the table.

ADAPTATION TIME FOR STEADY PRESSURE
(*Zigler, 1932*)

Applied weight (milligrams)	Back of hand	Forearm	Forehead	Cheek
50	2.42 sec.	2.31 sec.	5.07 sec.	5.71 sec.
100	3.82	3.28	6.22	6.37
500	6.01	4.86	9.96	11.63
1000	6.71	5.60	10.43	13.51
2000	9.52	7.76	16.03	19.36

Though the adaptation time of 2 sec. to the lightest pressures seems very short, there is reason to believe that the receptors, or some of them, adapt almost instantly to a perfectly steady stimulus. They may respond only to *changes* of pressure, to changes in the stretch reaching the fine endings of the sensory nerve fibers. The longer adaptation times may represent gradual mechanical adjustments of the skin to continued pressure, mechanical changes which bring in fresh receptors or cause the stimulation of some receptors to be intermittent (Adrian, 1932; Cattell & Hoagland, 1931).

Temperature sense adaptation. Ordinarily, in a comfortable room, there is little sensation of either warmth or cold from any portion of the skin, though different portions are at different temperatures. This fact indicates some adaptation of the temperature senses. Exposed parts of the skin usually have a surface temperature of 30–32° C., which is 86–90° F., several degrees below the internal body temperature. These exposed parts are adapted to their own temperature, which is the "physiological zero" of the subjective temperature scale.

The physiological zero is not fixed; it varies from one part of the skin to another, and in the same part from time to time according to the surface temperature. If 32° C. is the surface temperature of the hand, water at that temperature will feel neither warm nor cool to the hand. Transfer the hand to water at 35° and you find it definitely warm at first but after a few minutes of steady immersion it becomes neutral. If the hand is then transferred back to water at 32°, the latter feels cool instead of neutral. The physiological zero has been raised, and it can similarly be lowered by holding the hand in water a few degrees below the usual surface temperature of the hand.

The same temperature may seem simultaneously warm to one hand and cold to the other, as in the classical adaptation experiment of Weber (1846). Three bowls of water are provided, at 20°, 30°, and 40° C. Hold one hand in the warm water and the other in the cold water for a minute or two, and then transfer both to the medium water.

Weber's experiments led him to a theory of the adequate stimuli for the temperature sense. The warmth sensation he held to result from a rise in temperature of the skin, the cold sensation from a fall of temperature. With a stationary temperature of the receptors, there would be no sensation, no matter what the temperature.

An opposed theory was formulated by Hering (1877). He held that when the skin was adapted to any temperature, a higher temperature constituted a warmth stimulus, and a lower temperature a cold sense stimulus.

A large share of the numerous experiments devoted to the temperature sense had these two theories in view, but no generally accepted decision has been reached—except, perhaps, that neither theory comes very close to the real physical character of the stimulus as it reaches the receptors. We may as well accept that decision and utilize the experimental data for the light they throw on important questions of fact, such as: (1) What are the limits of temperature within which the warmth and cold senses are capable of adaptation? (2) How rapidly do they become adapted? (3) Do the two temperature senses keep pace with each other in becoming adapted to a given temperature? Does the physiological zero move in adaptation? (4) Is the physiological zero really a zone of some width, and does the width change with the adaptation temperature? (5) Is the whole scale of temperature sensations moved bodily up or down in adaptation to a high or low temperature?

Limits of adaptation. The facts are complex. If the hand is held in water that is only a few degrees above or below the usual skin temperature, the sensations of warmth or cold diminish and cease in a few minutes. If the hand is held in water much above 45° C. (113° F.) the burning heat soon becomes unendurable, and apparently the pain sense does not become adapted to this high temperature until the surface of the skin is cooked. If the hand is held in water as low as 10° C. (50° F.) the sensation of cold persists for a long time and perhaps never does disappear. These facts by themselves indicate that there are limits to the possible range of adaptation, though the exact limits may be difficult to establish.

An introspective account of the process of becoming adapted to a cold stimulus (about 20° C.) is given by Abbott (1914):

> There was scarcely any noticeable change in the sensation for a longer or shorter time, depending on the individual, and then the temperature sensation faded with remarkable quickness. . . . But this first disappearance was not permanent. The sensation returned and there was likely to be a fluctuation . . . for some little time before adaptation was complete and permanent. Each time the sensation returned it was a little fainter and lasted a shorter time.

All of Abbott's subjects reported complete disappearance of the temperature sensation, after a longer or shorter exposure to any temperature within the range of 17.5 to 40° C.

Somewhat similar results were obtained by Gertz (1921), who found that adaptation proceeded intermittently, when the hand was held in cold water, the cold sensation disappearing, reappearing with less intensity and finally disappearing altogether. Adaptation to warm water proceeded more smoothly. But when the cold water was below 18° C., there was, according to Gertz, never a complete loss of cold sensation. A deep sensation of cold, compounded with deep pressure— in short, a numb feeling—persisted even when the skin itself had ceased to deliver the sensation of cold. It was not altogether easy to decide whether the cold came from the skin or from deeper in the hand, and for this reason it was difficult to locate the exact lower limit of cutaneous adaptation. Gertz was inclined to place the lower limit at about 16° C., certainly not lower than 12° C. He placed the upper limit at 41–42° C. We shall have occasion shortly to return to his findings.

Rate of adaptation. The further an applied temperature is from normal skin temperature, the longer time is needed for the skin to become adapted to it. Holm (1903) and Gertz (1921) applied a "temperator" (an instrument for warming or cooling a skin area) and kept the temperature constant till the skin ceased to feel it as warm or cold. The following table shows the time required for the sensation to disappear.

Applied temperature	Duration of warmth or cold sensation	
	(Holm)	*(Gertz)*
45°C	152 sec.	
40°	126	162 sec.
30°	31	
25°	47	52
20°	72	102
15°	112	126
10°	165	
5°	210	

The main result here is the progressive increase of adaptation time as the applied temperature lies further away from the initial surface temperature of the skin (here 31–32°). Holm's results seem peculiar, or exceptional, in that he reports complete adaptation to temperatures as high as 45° C. and as low as 5° C. But his main result, just noted, is probably correct even if adaptation was not really complete.

In another interesting experiment, Gertz managed to change the applied temperature so slowly that no warmth or cold was ever felt. The temperator was at neutral temperature at the start of the experiment and was kept neutral throughout. This result was accomplished when a change of 10°, up or down, occupied 35–45 minutes in the making. A change of 0.2° C. per minute was about the threshold.

We are not to infer from the results so far cited that adaptation proceeds at a uniform rate from the time the hand is plunged into warm or cold water up to the time when that water ceases to feel warm or cold. The adaptation curve is not a straight line. To determine the nature of the curve a different sort of experiment is necessary, such as is described under Fig. 126.

Simultaneous adaptation of the warmth and cold senses—shifting of the physiological zero. Recognizing two temperature senses we must inquire whether adaptation to cold means only an adaptation of the cold sense, or whether the warmth sense also becomes adapted to the low temperature. Adaptation of the cold sense to cold means that the threshold for cold has been pushed down the scale. Adaptation of the warmth sense to cold would mean that the threshold for warmth also has been pushed down the scale. Thus if 20° C. is the adaptation temperature, and if it no longer feels cold (or cool), then the cold sense is adapted

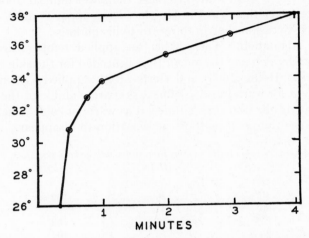

Fig. 126. (Data from Hahn, 1930.) The progress of temperature adaptation. Both hands were first adapted to 38° C. by being held for 5 minutes in water at that temperature. Then the left hand was transferred to water at 26° to become adapted to that new temperature, while the right hand remained in the 38° water. After half a minute, a series of tests showed that the 26° felt just as cold to the partially adapted left hand as a test bowl at 31° felt to the other hand which had preserved its 38° adaptation. The abscissa denotes time from the beginning of immersion in the 26° water; the ordinate shows the temperature of the test bowl which seems the same to the right hand as 26° seems to the partially adapted left hand. At the end of 4 minutes, 26° feels to the left hand the same as 38° seems to the right; both feel neutral and adaptation is complete. The upward trend of the curve shows the approximation toward complete adaptation. The curve resembles a learning curve (p. 164). A curve of similar shape was obtained by Hahn for the process of adaptation between any initial and any final temperature, except that adaptation to extreme temperatures never reached completion.

to 20° C. If a temperature of 21° or 22° now feels warm, then the warmth sense also is adapted to 20°. One sense might conceivably become adapted alone. In that case, adaptation to 20° C. would mean that temperatures between 20° and 32° were neither cold nor warm to the skin; the neutral zone would be expanded to cover all the temperatures down to the adaptation temperature.

The fact of the matter is that, in cold adaptation, temperatures above the adaptation temperature feel warm, and in warm adaptation temperatures below the adaptation temperature feel cool. Thunberg (1901) reports that when the skin has been exposed for some time to 11°

C., a temperature of 12° C. gives a distinctly warm sensation; and that when it has been adapted to 39°, temperatures a little below that give a cold sensation.

A more complete experiment was carried out by Gertz (1921). He dipped the fingers of one hand, as far as the first joint, into a large jar of water kept at a definite temperature, and held them there 15–30 minutes (or so much thereof as was necessary to insure practically complete adaptation). When the fingers were thus adapted, he transferred

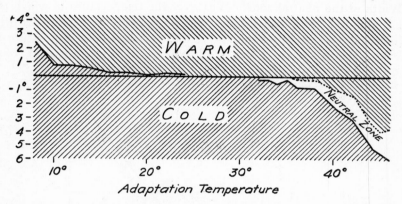

Adaptation Temperature

FIG. 127. (Data from Gertz, 1921.) The warmth-cold transition as affected by adaptation. The fingers were "adapted" to the temperatures indicated along the base. Stimuli above or below the adaptation temperature were then applied. Distances above and below the horizontal line show the difference between the adaptation temperature and the stimulus temperature. The oblique solid line connects the transition points between cold and not-cold (average of 2 Os), and the dotted line connects the transition points between warm and neutral. The figure reads, for example, that when the fingers were adapted to 10°, temperatures up to 10 + 1 = 11° were felt as cold, above that as warm, with no appreciable neutral zone; when the fingers were adapted to 40°, the neutral zone extended from 38° to 39°, temperatures above 39° feeling warm and those below 38° feeling cold (cool).

Gertz's data do not cover the region, 28 − 32°, but various other experiments indicate for this region complete adaptation and a very narrow neutral zone.

them for a few seconds to another jar of water at a little higher or lower temperature, and noted whether this last temperature felt warm, cold or neutral. After this test, the fingers were returned for 2–3 minutes to the adaptation jar and then tested again. The adaptation jar was held at a constant temperature during a series of tests, while the test jar was varied from test to test.

Gertz found only incomplete adaptation to extreme temperatures, either high or low. The best attainable adaptation to 10° C. did not prevent 10.5° C. from feeling cold, and the test temperature had to be raised to 12° C. before warmth began to appear. Similarly, after adaptation to 40° C., 39.5° still felt warm, 38.5° neutral, and not till the test temperature was lowered to 38° did the sensation of cold begin to appear. As he puts it, application of 10° C. adapts the skin not to 10° but to 11°;

and we might say that application of 40° C. adapts the warmth sense to 39°, and the cold sense to 38°. Application of 45° C. adapts the warmth sense to 41° and the cold sense to about 39°. The adaptation of the cold sense to high temperatures is thus less complete than that of the warmth sense, which is itself not fully complete under the conditions of this experiment. One difficulty at either high or low temperatures is that the temperature sensation proper is masked by pain. Gertz's results are more fully shown in the diagram on p. 473.

Width of the neutral zone. Whatever the temperature to which the skin is adapted, the physiological zero can scarcely be a point with no extent whatever. It must require a finite increase of temperature to give the warmth sensation, and a finite decrease to give the cold (cool)

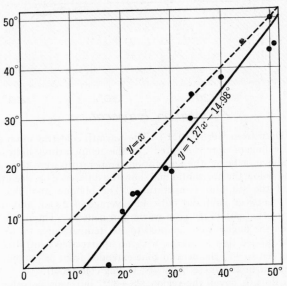

FIG. 128. (Data from Hummel, 1926.) Equivalent stimulus temperatures for differently adapted hands. The Y hand was adapted to 15° C., the X hand to 30° C. The adaptation was scarcely complete since the hand (forefinger) was immersed only one minute before each test. The forefingers were taken from the adaptation jars, rapidly dried on a towel and at once placed in two test jars, and O judged which of the test jars was warmer. In a series of such tests an equation was worked out between the two hands, differently adapted as they were. Each round dot in the graph records one such equation, the ordinate showing the temperature applied to the cold-adapted hand, the abscissa the subjectively equivalent temperature applied to the normal hand. The broken line, y = x, shows where the data points would have fallen if both hands had got the same sensation from the same test stimuli. The full line is the regression line of y on x, the best-fitting straight line to the data. The slope of this line shows that, on the average, a difference of 1.27° in the temperatures applied to the cold hand counted for only as much as a difference of 1.00° applied to the normal hand. Adaptation seems then to have done two things: shifted the physiological zero down a certain number of degrees, and diminished the sensitivity of the cold-adapted hand. Several other experiments have reached results consistent with this conclusion, though the evidence is still far from adequate.

sensation. The sum of these two finite quantities would be the width of the neutral zone. From Gertz's results it appears that the width of the neutral zone is about 0.3° at an adaptation temperature of 35° C., increasing to 1.0° at 40° C., and to 2.0° at 46° C.

If however, the experiment is conducted as a regular experiment in psychophysics, with O keyed up to judge whether the test water is not a shade warmer or cooler than the adaptation water, and if the data are treated by the method of Constant Stimuli (see p. 402) so as to give thresholds of 50 percent correct judgments, then the width of the neutral zone comes out considerably smaller.

In one such experiment, by Culler (1926), the fingers of both hands were used alike. They were first adapted to a given temperature by immersion in a jar of water at that temperature for 3–5 minutes. They were then transferred in succession to two test jars, remaining in each for 2 sec., and then were replaced in the adaptation jar for 12 sec. before making a similar test. O's task was to say which of the two test jars was warmer. One of them was always at the adaptation temperature, and the other a fraction of a degree higher or lower (or sometimes the same). The computation gave the warmth and cold thresholds above and below the given adaptation temperature.

A sample of the results for a single adaptation temperature is the following:

Adaptation temperature = 24.00°C. Each comparison temperature was compared with this.

Comparison temps.	*24.20°C.*	*24.15°C.*	*24.10°C.*	*24.05°C.*	*24.00°C.*	*23.95°C.*	*23.90°C.*	*23.85°C.*
Percent of judgments								
warmer	100	75	58	31	18	10	00	00
equal	00	19	32	35	37	28	15	8
colder	00	6	10	34	45	62	85	92

Computation of these data, by the Summation Method gives—

warmth threshold at	24.079,	SD = .079
cold threshold	23.992,	SD = .094
difference	0.087 degrees	

If we are willing to take as our measure of the neutral zone the difference between the 50-percent thresholds for warmth and cold, we have the very small figure of .087°, less than 1/10 of a degree Centigrade. If we prefer not to admit so many errors (and not to pin our faith on the Equal judgments, see p. 425), we can widen the neutral zone by adding 1 SD to the warmth threshold and subtracting 1 SD from the cold threshold, so obtaining a width of .260° C. for the neutral zone at this adaptation temperature. Culler's results at several adaptation temperatures are as follows:

Adaptation temperature	*Width of neutral zone*	*Median SD*
44 C.	.166	.241
40	.156	.163
36	.117	.096
32	.079	.076
28	.071	.077
24	.081	.099
20	.112	.131
16	.143	.128

Whatever measure we use, we get a result agreeing with Gertz in one important respect: the nearer the adaptation temperature lies to the normal skin temperature of about 30° C., the narrower is the neutral zone, the keener the perception of warmth and cold.

Distortion of the sensation scale in adaptation to high or low temperatures. So far, we have seen that the physiological zero moves up or down in adaptation, and also that the neutral zone widens when the adaptation temperature lies far from the normal temperature of the skin. This last fact leads us to expect some loss of sensitivity to differences of temperature. Will a temperature 5° above (or below) the physiological zero always feel equally warm (or cold), no matter how much the physiological zero has been displaced by adaptation? Very elaborate experiments would be required to answer this question, but the data at hand (see Fig. 128) indicate a loss of sensitivity such that, for example, 8° of warmth (or cold) to the adapted hand feels only as warm (or cold) as 5° to the normal hand.

CHAPTER XX

SMELL AND TASTE

I F TOUCH, kinesthesis, and hearing are called mechanical senses because they respond to mechanical movement or tension, and if the temperature senses are obviously thermal, taste and smell are chemical senses. Sight also may be chemical, i.e., photochemical, since a chemical reaction probably intervenes between the incidence of light and the excitation of the receptors. The pain sense is nonspecific and responds to chemical stimuli among others, as to a drop of acid on the skin. The pain sense is present in the mucous membrane lining the mouth and nose and is responsible for "sharp" tastes and smells. Smell, taste and the pain sense act together in response to certain stimuli and constitute in combination the chemical sense of this region.

SMELL

The olfactory receptors are situated in a little alcove in the upper part of the nose. Each nostril leads upward and back into a rather wide but shallow chamber of irregular shape which opens at the rear into the pharynx. The nasal septum separates the right half of the interior nose from the left. The olfactory alcove lies out of the direct path of the inspired or expired air, but odorous gases penetrate to the receptors by diffusion and also by eddies in the air current. The latter are produced especially by sniffing, which thus has somewhat the same relation to smelling as turning the eyes has to seeing, or as pricking up the ears has to an animal's hearing.

The olfactory receptors are cells embedded in the mucous membrane, with slender branches extending out to the surface and with an axon passing through the cribriform bone into the olfactory bulb of the forebrain. The neural connections from the olfactory bulb lead to the archipallium.

The non-olfactory portions of the nasal cavity are supplied by the fifth cranial (trigeminal) nerve and possess the four cutaneous senses. The upper part of the pharynx, into which the rear passage from the nose enters, contains taste buds and adds a taste quality to some of the odors.

Points in experimental technique. Although it is not always necessary, it is desirable for some purposes to work with pure substances of known chemical composition. Hundreds of such substances, mostly compounds of carbon, are odorous. Even a slight admixture of unknown ingredients

477

may deceive the experimenter, because of the high sensitivity of the olfactory sense. Even when obtained pure, many organic compounds are likely to undergo chemical change on prolonged standing.

Another difficulty: the diffusion of odorous substances through the experimental room may give a mixed stimulus even when a pure substance is held to the nose. Odorous substances also have an unfortunate way of adhering to rubber and even to glass, so that the odor "clings." It can be removed by scouring with chalk, spraying with hydrogen peroxide, or by applying ultraviolet light. Bottles prepared for an experiment are best left stoppered but on an open table with plenty of space about them, so as to prevent the gas of one bottle from adhering to the outside of other bottles and giving mixed stimuli.

For qualitative experiments, small, wide-mouthed bottles are suitable, with enough vapor space left to afford a good whiff. The bottles are of course kept stoppered except for the brief times when they are held under the nose.

For quantitative experiments, especially on the stimulus threshold, a known quantity of the odorous substance is placed in a liter bottle and allowed to evaporate completely. The stimulus is known in milligrams (or thousandths of a milligram) of substance per liter of air, the air being inhaled directly from the bottle.

Stimulus threshold. Expressed in thousandths of a milligram per liter of air the threshold concentration varies greatly with the odorous substance, being about 200 for ethyl alcohol and as low as 0.001 for musk, vanillin or skatol. The actual quantity that acts as the stimulus must be very much smaller than this, since only a small fraction of the liter of air need be inspired and only a small portion of the inspired air reaches the olfactory receptors.

Zwaardemaker's olfactometer. As a test for individual sensitivity, the last-mentioned procedure is cumbersome, and Zwaardemaker (1888, 1925) devised a method which is semi-quantitative. The odorous gas is inhaled through a glass tube of 5 mm bore, one end of which is placed loosely within the forward part of the nostril (since it is known that only air entering this part gets to the olfactory receptors and can be smelt). The glass tube curves first downwards and then outwards from the nostril and passes through a screen. The far end of the tube is graduated in linear units and is inserted into a larger tube or cylinder which contains the odorous substance. This stimulus cylinder is just large enough in bore to slide over the smaller tube and it consists of an odorous solid (such as cedar wood) or of porous baked clay saturated with an odorous liquid. In either case it is protected on the outside by a glass tube—being, in short, a glass tube lined with the odorous substance. Now when the inner tube which leads to the nose is pushed entirely through the odor cylinder and out the far end, inhaling through the inner tube will bring in no odorous gas; but when the far end of the inner tube lies within the odor cylinder, the incoming air picks up odorous substance.

If the end of the inner tube is only 1 cm inside the far end of the odor cylinder, only a small amount of the odorous substance will be picked up; but if the exposure distance is doubled, the amount of odorous substance is increased and (perhaps) doubled. The stimulus threshold is measured by the distance through which the inspired air is exposed to the odorous substance. A norm can be determined for a given instrument and odor tube, and individuals can be compared with the norm.

A double olfactometer, with separate though identical odor tubes for the two nostrils, has been used for measuring the difference threshold for smell and testing Weber's law. According to Gamble (1898) and Hermanides (1909), Weber's law holds and the difference threshold amounts to 30–45 percent for most odorous substances, not differing greatly from one substance to another.

Stimulation applied to a single nostril is called *monorhinic;* applied to both nostrils alike, *dirhinic.* When one odor is applied to one nostril and a different odor to the other, the stimulation is called *dichorhinic.*

Monorhinic stimulation shows that many individuals have keener smell on one side than on the other; and it even happens that the same substance will give a qualitatively different odor on the two sides. Dirhinic stimulation gives much stronger and clearer odor impressions than monorhinic. It is sometimes true that the same substance has a different odor quality in strong and in weak concentration. Thus indol when strong has a fecal odor but when diluted a pleasant flowery odor (Henning, 1924, p. 181). The reaction time to odor stimuli is rather long, varying from 200–300 ms for camphor and peppermint up to as long as a second for beeswax. (Cf. p. 326.)

Individuals differ considerably in their sensitivity to odors in general or to particular odors. Some individuals are permanently anosmic. Temporary anosmia results from nasal catarrh, or from the application of cocaine. Filling the nose with water, which is then allowed to run out, leaves smell temporarily abolished though the other nasal senses soon recover. Holding the nose or blocking the rear passage from the nose to the throat eliminates smell stimulation. Hyperosmia can be produced by blowing strychnine into the nose. Parosmia (distorted olfaction) may occur instead of complete anosmia in colds. All of these conditions should, it would seem, have a value akin to that of color blindness in discovering the primary sensory responses, but thus far they have yielded little definite information.

The same is true of olfactory fatigue or adaptation. Weak odors steadily applied cease to be smelt in a few minutes, and accordingly the procedure in an experiment with such stimuli has to be slow and deliberate. Tobacco smoking produces a temporary partial anosmia and must be avoided for a few hours before an experiment. Strong odors, though they doubtless give partial adaptation, can be smelt for long periods—some odors longer than others. Henning reports no loss of sensation in long experiments with camphor, phenol, garlic, or carnation.

Odor mixture. If we speak of odor mixture, in analogy with the familiar "color mixing" experiment, we must recognize the inaccuracy of both expressions. What we mix are the stimuli, not the color or odor sensations. The stimuli are applied simultaneously in order to discover what sensory response is aroused by the combination. The response varies all the way from dual sensations to complete blending. The results obtained by combining olfactory stimuli are as follows:

1. The commonest result is a blend or fusion of the odors of the two stimuli. The blend is a unitary impression, though resembling the odors of the components. Thus violet combined with H_2S may give a blend resembling both components. The more the components resemble each other in odor, the more likely they are to blend and the more difficult it is to attend separately to one or the other component (Henning, 1924).

2. When the component stimuli are such as give very dissimilar odors, the usual result is a successive smelling of the two odors (Henning), though fusion is not impossible.

3. With dichorhinic stimulation, this successive smelling of the two odors has some analogy with rivalry, though it is not so clean-cut as binocular rivalry and according to von Skramlik (1925), is nothing more than ordinary shifting of attention and should not be labeled rivalry.

4. The two odors may be smelt simultaneously and yet separately. They may appear as a pattern, analogous to a chord of musical tones, or they may be smelt as two distinct and unrelated odors. This high degree of separateness can only be obtained with dichorhinic stimulation, according to Henning, while von Skramlik finds that the same result can be obtained with monorhinic or dirhinic stimulation. He asserts indeed that all the impressions obtained with one form of stimulation can be obtained with the others as well.

5. One odor may mask the other altogether, as happens especially when one odor is much the stronger.

6. Neutralization or "compensation." In this case the combination of stimuli gives no odor whatever. There is a violent controversy over this asserted neutralization. Zwaardemaker (1895, 1925) finds that by carefully selecting the stimuli and carefully graduating their strength he can obtain complete neutralization. Titchener (1916) confirms Zwaardemaker's finding, while admitting that complete absence of odor lasts only for an instant at a time. Henning (1924) denies the phenomenon altogether and reports that he has never been able to obtain it under any conditions; but he does not make it clear that he has put the matter to a thorough and patient test. If certain odor stimuli were related in the same way as complementary color stimuli, this relationship would be very important in olfactory theory, but thus far we have little light or leading from this source.

The results of odor mixture are thus seen to have some analogy with those of color mixture, but not complete analogy. When the odors blend we have the same effect as with colors, but when they maintain a degree of separateness the effect is more like that obtained with combinations of tones.

CLASSIFICATION AND SYSTEMATIZATION OF SMELL QUALITIES

Ordinary experience leaves us with an unorganized manifold of odors and with no start toward a scientific system. In taste we have the common names, sweet, sour, bitter and salt, which are found to be adequate for scientific classification. In color we have a similar set of common names and we find it easy also to arrange the hues in a circular series. In hearing, the names high and low picture the one-dimensional character of the pitch series. But in smell common experience and language give us no clews toward a system. We speak of agreeable and disagreeable odors, but the agreeable have various odor qualities, and the disagreeable likewise. We speak of "sweet" smells, and "sweet" here does not mean simply agreeable, since the odor of camphor is certainly not "sweet" though it is agreeable; but whether olfactory sweetness is simply gustatory or points to some true olfactory quality is not clear. We speak of "sharp" or "pungent" odors, but here we are confusing the olfactory with the other nasal senses. We also speak of "spicy" and of "putrid" odors and here we are approaching a classification of true smell qualities.

The poverty of our odor vocabulary is keenly felt on consulting the dictionary to discover what may be the odor of some chemical substance such as thiophene or geraniol or citral or ethyl acetate. If there were some system or scheme by reference to which the chemist or the botanist could designate the quality of an odor, it would be a great aid in communication, if nothing more.

The first scientist to make a serious effort at filling this need was the Swedish botanist Linnaeus (1756). He distinguished seven classes of odors, namely:

> Aromatic — as carnation
> Fragrant — as lily
> Ambrosial — as musk
> Alliacious — as garlic
> Hircine — as valerian
> Repulsive — as certain bugs
> Nauseous — as carrion

The Linnaean classification did service for over a century. Zwaardemaker (1895, 1925) sought to perfect it by subdividing some of the classes and by adding two new classes, the etherial and the empyreumatic, so as to do justice to the modern products of organic chemistry. Zwaardemaker's full classification (1925) is as follows:

1. Etherial; examples: acetone, chloroform, ethyl acetate, butyrate and valerianate, ethyl ether.

2. Aromatic; sub-classes:

   a. camphorous: camphor, eucalyptol, pinene (turpentine)
   b. spicy: eugenol (cloves)
   c. anisic: anisol, thymol, menthol
   d. citric: citral, geraniol
   e. amygdalate (almondy): benzaldehyde, nitrobenzene

(Other substances mentioned as "aromatic," without designation of sub-class: laurel, resins, volatile acids, lemon, rose, geranium, myrtle, cinnamon, lavender, mint, majoram.)

   3. Balsamic; sub-classes:

   a. flower perfumes: jasmine, orange blossom
   b. lily: ionone, irone (violet root)
   c. vanilla

(Other substances mentioned as "balsamic" without designation of sub-class: lily, jasmine, crocus, orange blossom, lilac, violet, mignonette, heliotrope, lily of the valley, tonka bean, cumarin.)

   4. Amber-musk
   5. Alliaceous; sub-classes:

   a. garlic: acetylene, H_2S, ethyl sulphide, mercaptan
   b. cacodyl: trimethylamine
   c. halogen: Br, I

   (This class is said to contain the compounds of S, P and As, as well as allyl. Onion is typical.)

   6. Empyreumatic: roasted coffee, toasted bread, tobacco smoke, tar, benzol, phenol, xylol, toluol, cresol, guiacol, naphthalin, anilin.

   7. Hircine: caproic acid, other fatty acids, cheese, sweat, bilberry, cat's urine; perhaps also vaginal and sperm odor, chestnut and barberry.

   8. Repulsive (suffocating): flowers of the solanaceae and of coriander, some orchids, some bugs; narcotic odors. (Pyridine is transitional between this class and the empyreumatic.)

   9. Nauseous: rotten meat, indol, scatol, carrion flower.

   These nine classes can be combined into two large groups:

     The nutritive   (classes 1–4)
     The decomposed (classes 5–9)

Henning (1915, 1916, 1924) has attempted a radical revision of this classification. He regards Zwaardemaker's classes 4, 5, 7 and 8 as undeserving of the rank of main classes, while he divides class 2, the aromatic, into spicy and resinous. Henning recognizes six classes:

              Fragrant
              Etherial or fruity
              Resinous
              Spicy
              Putrid
              Burned, empyreumatic

Henning claims for his classification (1) that it is more than a mere classification, being in fact a system, and (2) that it is based on a more comprehensive experimental study of odor qualities than had been attempted by any of his predecessors. He claims to have made the first really psychological investigation of the odor manifold.

Henning's experiment on resemblance and classification of odors. In the belief that a purely psychological experiment would reveal some order in the manifold of odor sensations, Henning set his Os the task not of identifying and naming the odors, but of describing the sensations and noting resemblances and differences between them.

He obtained as stimuli no less than 415 odorous substances, some of which were definite chemical substances, and others natural products. These substances were placed in smelling bottles which were kept ⅓ full so as to furnish an ample quantity of saturated vapor for sniffing into the nose from the broad mouth of the bottle.

The procedure had to be slow, 10–20 stimuli being applied in the course of a day's sitting (probably an hour). The procedure was "without knowledge" and O's eyes were closed. He was instructed "to apprehend and describe the odor exactly and reach a definite judgment without hurrying." He usually took 4–5 seconds for reaching his judgment.

There were two ways in which an odor presented itself to O, as a "Gegebenheitsgeruch" and as a "Gegenstandsgeruch." The first, or "datum odor" is the bare sensory quality, not referred to any objective source but localized in the nose. The second, or "object odor" is almost sure to occur when the source of the odor is seen; it is localized in the odorous object and experienced as a characteristic of the object. The difference is analogous to that between "expanse color" and "surface color" (p. 539) but is more pronounced. The "datum odor" is more suited for the qualitative description that Henning desired to obtain.

Henning tried out a considerable number of individuals and selected those who showed the best power of describing and identifying odors. His main reliance was on six principal Os whose results were apparently in fairly close agreement.

At first the judgments were rather wild or vague, but with experience in the "procedure without knowledge" O soon became able to express a judgment in one of the following forms: (1) correct identification of the odor, (2) correct statement that the stimulus resembled a specified odor, (3) correct assignment of the stimulus to a group of similar odors, as majoram was judged to be a cooking spice, (4) incorrect identification of the odor, as vanilla was said to be heliotrope. These false identifications were utilized as indications of similarities.

Odor series. Though the course of the whole series of experiments is not clearly set forth, what seems to have happened is that the Os agreed in classing certain odors together as similar, certain others as belonging in a different class, and so on; and that they adopted certain outstanding (salient) odors as points of reference and described other odors as more or less like the salient odors, and sometimes as resembling two salient odors and lying between them.   The salient odors corresponded in part with Zwaardemaker's classes, but Henning reduced the number of classes to six.   How far he was *forced* by his data into this selection of six salient odors, and how far his selection represents a *hypothesis* which he tried out and found to work fairly well, is not clear from the published reports.   It is clear that at a late stage of the experiment the Os were given collections of odors with instructions to arrange them in order of similarity, that the Os found it possible to arrange certain odors in a serial order and that all or at least several Os agreed in these arrangements.

Thus a set of spicy odors was arranged in the following order:

> fennel
> sassafras
> majoram
> nutmeg
> anise
> pepper
> ginger
> cinnamon
> cassia
> cloves
> caraway

And another series, beginning with caraway, but running on further, contained:

> bay
> hops
> thyme
> arnica
> lavender
> vanilla
> vanillin

Starting thence, a third series ran:

> heliotrope
> geranium oil
> jasmine
> oil of roses
> orange blossoms
> orange leaves
> orange oil

From that point, a further series ran:

> lemon oil
> strawberry oil

pineapple oil
acetic ether
ethyl ether
acetone

And thence, again:

turpentine
pine
Canada balsam
spruce
mastic
frankincense
cedar wood
eucalyptus
myrrh
juniper

Now this last odor is verging upon fennel, with which we started, so that the whole series thus far could be arranged in a circle. It could be arranged in a form of a triangle, square or other polygon, provided certain odors were sufficiently salient to deserve a position at the corners.

An odor square. Evidently the corners cannot be selected without other grounds than the serial order of the odors. From the serial order alone we have no reason for selecting any special odors as any more outstanding than the rest. If it were true that certain odors possessed a unitary quality whereas others appeared to be composite, we could select the unitary odors as the corners and designate them as the elementary odors and the rest as compounds. But Henning rejects this notion altogether. Admitting that an O untrained in attention to odor quality regards certain odors as unitary and the rest as mixed, Henning rejects this distinction as due merely to the familiarity of certain odors and odor names. He insists that even when an odor shows "double resemblance," i.e., when it seems to belong between two others, it is perfectly unitary as a sensory quality—just as orange color, though obviously resembling both red and yellow and standing between them, is regarded by many psychologists as perfectly unitary in itself. Henning further adduces a fact, which he says he has demonstrated, that the *mixture of two odors does not give the intervening odors.* The mixture gives an odor in which both components can be smelt and which appears as a blend, but it gives no odor which can be matched with the intervening odors of the series. A mixture of cinnamon and vanilla cannot be adjusted to duplicate the odor of caraway; therefore caraway, though intermediate between cinnamon and vanilla, is just as unitary as they are.

What ground, then, has Henning for designating certain odors as salient? It appears that his Os, in running through the series, had the impression at certain points that something radically new was coming in while something old was dropping out. It was like turning a corner and heading for a new landmark. The situation was the same as in running through the spectrum. From red to yellow the orange hues continually lose reddishness and take on more yellow, but as you pass yellow you lose the last trace of red and see a trace of something new, green. In passing green you lose the yellow tinge and begin to see a resemblance to blue, and in passing blue you begin to see a resemblance to red. Accordingly the color circle is often transformed into a square, and by the same logic Henning transforms the odor series (as so far described) into a square. The corners of this square he designates as Fragrant, Etherial, Resinous and Spicy.

It does not appear from the record that Henning's Os were very definite as to the exact corners. They found it easier to arrange a series passing through any corner than to select any one odor as the most typical representative of the fragrant, etherial, resinous or spicy class.

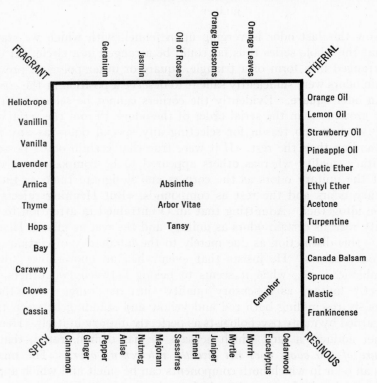

FIG. 129. The FERS odor square, a part of Henning's smell prism.

An odor prism. This square, however, does not include all the odors. There is a distinct class of foul or *putrid* odors typified by H_2S. Between this extra corner and each corner of the square there are intermediate odors: onion toward spicy, tomato toward fragrant, durian fruit toward etherial, fish scales toward resinous. And still another salient odor is exemplified by tar and named *burned* by Henning (empyreumatic by

Zwaardemaker). Odors intermediate between burned and any other
odor can be obtained, according to Henning, by the simple process of
scorching the substance giving that other odor. With these additions
Henning believes he has accounted for all the salient or fundamental
odors. Any unitary odor, he believes, can be located, according to its
resemblances, between two, three or at most four of the salient six.

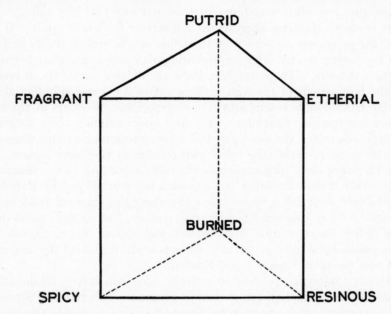

FIG. 130. (Henning, 1915–16, 1924.) The smell prism. The English names,
suggested by Macdonald (1922), have the advantage of providing six different initial
letters to serve as convenient symbols of the salient odors.

As the most appropriate diagram of the whole system of smell qualities, Henning chose the triangular prism, with a salient odor at each
corner. He defines the smell prism in the following terms (1924, p. 370):

The model in its definitive form is the surface of a regular prism, the six
corners designating the turning points in the direction of resemblance.

Any definite point on an edge or surface of the prism cannot, however, be
duplicated by mixture of the stimuli between which the point lies (as is the case
with the color octahedron), for such mixture of stimuli never gives a simple
odor but always (as in the tonal series) a sensation which is a mixture of the
components used.

All odors on the edges and surface of the prism are *simple*. The odors lying
along any edge resemble only the odors located at the two corners bounding
that edge, and are more like the corner to which they lie nearer. In the case of
the simple odors of any surface we notice not merely two resemblances, but—
more or less clearly—more numerous resemblances, resemblances indeed to all
the corners of their surface in proportion to their neighborhood to those corners.

Repetition (analogous to the octave), neutralization (as in the middle of the color octahedron) and contrast are not present in the smell system, but on the contrary every single simple odor maintains its own sharply circumscribed individuality in spite of its numerous resemblances. These resemblances are, as in the color octahedron, only aspects of the simple quality.

Discussion of the smell prism. Only the *surface* of the prism constitutes the diagram. The interior is thought of as hollow and not representing any odor sensations, at least not any that are unitary. It might be used, Henning suggests, as a reservoir for *mixed* odors. If we study the prism we see that a straight line can be drawn on its surface from any corner to any other, representing odor series extending between any two salients. These straight lines are of two sorts, the 9 edges, and the 6 diagonals of the square faces. Now any odor standing along an edge has "double resemblance," i.e., resembles the odors at the two corners terminating this edge. But any odor standing on a diagonal not only resembles the odors at the corners terminating this diagonal but also must resemble the other two corners of the same square. It must therefore have quadruple resemblance, according to the diagram; but whether it does in reality is a question not worked out by Henning. For example, he gives a series extending along the diagonal from Spicy to Putrid, and containing, in order: dill, parsley, leek, celery, asafoetida, garlic, onion, horse radish, mustard oil, and rotten cheese. According to the prism, these odors, especially those near the middle of the diagonal, must also resemble Fragrant and Burned.

Another inference is that no unitary odor can have certain triple resemblances. No odor can resemble Fragrant, Etherial and Burned, for to represent such an odor we should have to go inside the prism, which is forbidden. There are six such impossible cases of triple resemblance according to the diagram, but whether they are impossible in fact was not determined. In the same way, while any odor standing inside a square face has quadruple resemblance, no odor standing inside either of the triangular faces can have anything but triple resemblance.

These restrictions were apparently not intended by Henning, and are merely incidental consequences of the geometrical representation.

Checks on the validity of the smell prism. In spite of the meager evidence presented by Henning, his prism aroused great interest among psychologists, because it reduced to some order the jumbled manifold of smell sensations and because it embodied definite hypotheses that could be checked by experiment.

Dimmick (1927) selected 14 odor stimuli which should lie along the periphery of the FERS face. His 30 subjects attempted to arrange them in serial order. Each O made two arrangements of the same stimuli at a week's interval. The two orders given by the same O often differed, and different Os differed considerably in their arrangements.

Macdonald (1922) and Findley (1924) went to work in a systematic way to test out the resemblances of various odors to the six salient odors of the smell prism. The stimuli used for the salients were as follows:

	Macdonald	*Findley*
Fragrant	Oil of jasmine	Oil of jasmine
Etherial	Citral	Oil of lemon
Resinous	Eucalyptol	Turpentine
Spicy	Anethol	Cinnamon
Putrid	Thiophenol	Hydrogen sulphide
Burned	Pyridine	Oil of tar

Besides these standards there was an assortment of other odor stimuli, each of which was compared with the standards. One standard was first presented (held under O's nose in a wide-mouthed bottle), then the odor to be judged (the comparison odor), and finally a second standard; and O decided whether the comparison odor was more like the first or the second standard. The judgment was supposed to be based wholly on the odor quality, without regard to intensity or to accompanying nasal sensations of cold or pricking. Each comparison odor was thus compared with every possible pair of standards, two or three times in the course of the experiment.

The most striking result of this type of experiment, apart from the great variability of the judgments, was that nearly every comparison odor was at one time or another said to resemble every one of the standards. So pinene, a chemical unit present in turpentine and oil of juniper, obviously a good representative of the Resinous class, was sometimes said to be more like the F, E, S, P and B standards.

Peppermint, compared 20 times with R and P, was said to be more like R 17 times and more like P 3 times; when compared with S and P, it seemed more like S 19 times, and once equally like the two. This consistent set of judgments showed, without doubt, that peppermint is much more Spicy than Putrid! The other comparisons of peppermint indicated that it was as close to any one corner of the FERS square as to any other of this square. Its indicated position on the prism surface would then lie near the center of the FERS square; but if we allow just a little weight to the judgments which placed it nearer to P or B, we should have to assign it a position a little behind the FERS face, bringing it inside the prism, which is supposed to be empty, except for mixed odors. By the same criterion, every odor tested belonged inside the prism, so that the whole theory of the prism seemed to break down.

Henning's reply to this criticism (1924, p. 424) was that the prism showed the relations of odor *sensations*, not of odor stimuli, and that the same stimulus gives different sensations at different times. This rejoinder does not meet a difficulty pointed out by Macdonald (1922), who conducted a second experiment, using only the four standards located at the corners of the FERS square, and asking O to assign a place in this square, or along its sides, to each of 11 stimuli which belonged in this general region and had no marked resemblance to P or B. O found this task quite difficult, though possible with some stimuli. The main difficulty was that a given odor usually seemed to belong inside the square and yet did not resemble all the corners of the square. For example, nutmeg and geraniol seemed intermediate between E and S, requiring a place along the diagonal ES, and yet they did not resemble R nor always F; whereas the middle of the diagonal ES is also the middle of the diagonal FR and an odor intermediate between E and S must at the same time be intermediate between F and R, according to the logic of the prism. Similarly, menthol seemed intermediate between F and R, but did not resemble E and S. There were other odors that resembled F, E and S, and so belonged inside the square, and yet did not resemble R. The mere geometry of the prism unfits it for expressing some of the factual resemblances.

Another difficulty is that F, E and S resemble one another much more than they do R so that the face FERS is not properly a square but a kite-shaped figure. Also it appears that P and B resemble each other closely. Thus the regular prism is far from an adequate representation of the actual relations between odor sensations.

Herrmann (1926), on asking his Os to describe a large number of odors by reference to Henning's six salient odors, encountered vigorous objection. The Os found it unnatural to describe the odors in this particular way, and they did not accept Henning's six as any more outstanding than several other odors—mint and camphor, for example. Herrmann concluded that true corners did not exist and suspected that everyday associations were responsible for the supposed outstanding character of Henning's six fundamentals.

Hazzard (1930) found well-practiced Os able to locate many odors on the smell prism, while certain odors (cinnamon oil, tar, apiol) had no place. One O insisted on dividing the E or fruity odors into two classes: the "clear fruity," resembling F; and the "mellow fruity," resembling P. Hazzard's Os also gave a free description of the odor experience, couched largely in terms of "texture, volume, brightness, extent and temporal course." They could locate the odors along no fewer than ten scales or dimensions: loose—tight, light—heavy, smooth—rough, soft—hard, thin—thick, sharp—dull, bright—dull, lively—inert, surfacy—deep, small—large. Spicy odors were sharp, bright and lively, while Putrid odors were dull and inert; Fragrant odors were soft, loose and light in texture, while Burned odors were the reverse. These "textures" suggest possible cutaneous components in the total nasal sensation.

Sensations accompanying smell. The interior of the nose, as has been said, is provided with the cutaneous senses of touch, pain, warmth and cold, and the throat which receives the inspired air from the nose is provided with taste buds. With these facts in view it is not surprising that inhaled substances may "smell" sweet, sour, pricky or sharp, warm or cold.

The sharp, pungent or biting "smell" of ammonia surely arises from stimulation of the pain receptors in the nose, and the cool or fresh "smell" of menthol from the cold receptors. The sweet "smell" of chloroform doubtless arises from the taste receptors in the throat and probably the sour "smell" of vinegar comes from the same source.

Henning found that untrained Os did not distinguish odor proper from the other sensations obtained in smelling. He mentions in this connection the pricky sensation of oil of mustard, the sweet of jasmine, the cold of garlic, the warm of heliotrope, and the soft, heavy, or sticky pressure sensations of certain perfumes. Training in odor analysis makes it possible to isolate the odor quality partially but not wholly.

These smell-accompanying sensations have been studied with special care by von Skramlik (1925). Out of a collection of 200 odorous chemical substances, tried out on several Os, all but 50–60 gave recognizable sensations besides odor. Over 50 of them were sharp or pricky, about 30 were cold, about 30 sweet, a few were warm and a few were sour.

Von Skramlik's chief question was whether pure odors could be localized as coming from the right or the left nostril in monorhinic stimulation. His procedure was to hold two bottles simultaneously under the two nostrils, one bottle containing an odorous substance and the other distilled water. Keeping his eyes closed, O refrained from breathing while the bottles were being placed in position, and then drew a long breath which he expired through the mouth. He reported in which nostril the odor was localized. The result of the experiment was very curious. Some stimuli could be localized easily, while others could not be localized at all. Those that could be localized were such as give other sensations besides smell, and those that could not be localized were pure odors. (There were some minor exceptions and doubtful cases, in which it was impossible to be sure whether or not the odor was entirely "pure.") It appeared that the olfactory centers made no distinction between right and left, whereas the taste and trigeminal apparatus made that distinction.

Among the "pure" smells were representatives of five of Henning's six classes; thus:

Fragrant: geraniol (roses), terpineol (lily of the valley);
Etherial: limonene (lemon);
Resinous: pinene (turpentine), cadinene (juniper);
Spicy: eugenol (cloves), anethol (anise);
Putrid: indol and skatol (fecal odors).

As examples of the several classes of "impure" smells the following may be cited:

Smell plus sweet: chloroform, bromoform, iodoform, ethyl chloride, nitrobenzol.

Smell plus sour: acetic, propionic, butyric and valerianic acids.

Smell plus cold: camphor, menthol, phenol, eucalyptol, safrol (sassafras).

Smell plus warm: ethyl alcohol, propyl alcohol, amyl alcohol.

Smell plus pain (prick): chlorine, bromine, iodine, ammonia, SO_2, xylol, toluol, formic and acetic acids, acetone, pyridine, nicotine, thiophene.

The presence of these smell-accompanying sensations makes it imperative that *the classification of odor qualities should be revised or at least re-examined experimentally with the object of factoring out the non-olfactory components.* It may be that certain classes would coalesce if the non-olfactory components were eliminated. It might even be that the whole FERS face would coalesce into a single class, if pungency (pain sense), freshness (cold sense) and sweetness (taste) could be factored out. The outcome might be a simplification of the system of odor qualities, or it might be the recognition of fundamental odors which fail to be "outstanding" when blended with non-olfactory components (Komuro, 1922; Ohma, 1922).

THE STIMULUS OF SMELL

On the assumption that smell, like taste, is a "chemical sense," one is at first inclined to relegate the question of the olfactory stimulus to the chemist, handing over to him our psychological information on the system of smell sensations and asking him to indicate the chemical processes that could serve as stimuli for the several odor qualities. The chemist, however, might prefer to turn over his knowledge to the psychologist. The physiologist also would have to be considered and might well be the central figure in an inter-science committee on the question of the smell stimulus, on the question, that is, how different chemical substances, by exciting different receptor processes, give rise to the different odor sensations.

The distinction between stimulus and object is important here. We have been speaking as if vanilla and turpentine and lemon oil and tar were stimuli; which is like naming Turkey red and Paris green and Prussian blue as typical visual stimuli. The visual stimulus is light, not a pigment. The fact that pigments of quite different chemical composition can be used for securing red light is a puzzle for physics and chemistry, not for psychology. But in the case of smell the exact nature of the stimulus is obscure, and instead of naming the stimulus we are forced for the present to speak of the odorous substance which is the source of the stimulus.

The odorous substance affects the receptors by the passage of molecules into the air and the passage of the air into the nose. It dissolves in the air and assumes the gaseous form, and this gas or air-solution reaches the olfactory mucous membrane and delivers the stimulus. If a substance is entirely non-volatile, or if it cannot diffuse into the air under the existing conditions of temperature, it is necessarily inodorous. But it does not follow that all gases, vapors and volatile substances are odorous; oxygen, nitrogen, hydrogen and carbon monoxide are familiar examples to the contrary.

A first step toward a knowledge of the smell stimulus is afforded by the work of the chemists in isolating the essential ingredients of odorous substances and determining their composition and molecular structure. Instead of speaking of vanilla as an odorous substance, we can speak of vanillin, $C_8H_8O_3$, the chemical compound occurring in vanilla and chiefly responsible for its odor; instead of speaking of violets, we can speak of ionone, $C_{13}H_{20}O$; instead of speaking of roses, we can speak of their chief odorous constituent, geraniol, $C_{10}H_{18}O$; and instead of speaking of onions, we can speak of $C_6H_{12}S_2$. These chemical substances can be extracted from their respective flowers, fruits, etc., or in many cases can be prepared chemically from quite other sources such as coal tar. Perfumes, in this era of chemistry, are usually compounded from the known chemical ingredients with the addition of a little of the genuine extract to afford a whiff of some slight additional ingredients which have not yet been identified.

Von Skramlik (1925) gives the chemical formulas for about 200 odorous substances.

Of all the chemical *elements*, about 90 in number, only about 16 seem to play any role in the production of odors (Haycraft, 1888). These 16, according to their chemical families, are:

a. hydrogen
b. carbon, silicon
c. nitrogen, phosphorus, arsenic, antimony, bismuth
d. oxygen, sulphur, selenium, tellurium
e. the halogens: fluorine, chlorine, bromine, iodine

Only the halogens, apparently, are odorous as elements. The great majority of odorous substances are compounds of carbon, "organic" compounds, containing also hydrogen, oxygen, nitrogen—one or more of these three.

Within each of the families, similar compounds have similar odors. In the halogen family, for example, the elements themselves have somewhat similar odors; and their homologous compounds, chloroform ($CHCl_3$), bromoform ($CHBr_3$) and iodoform (CHI_3), also have similar odors. From chlorine through bromine to iodine the atomic weight and other atomic properties change progressively; and to this chemical series corresponds an odor series. The odor of bromine is "heavier" than that of chlorine, and the odor of iodine is heavier still. Similarly the odor of bromoform is intermediate between those of chloroform and iodoform.

There are many series of homologous organic compounds which show a gradation in odor quality and also in odorous power, the latter being measured inversely by the value of the stimulus threshold. The "lower" members of a series, with small or light molecules, have little odor, the intermediate members have more odor, while the still higher members are non-volatile and have no odor. One such series consists of the fatty acids.

Changes in Intensity and Quality of Odor in the Fatty Acid Series

Serial No.	Name of acid	Formula	Threshold in .001 mg per liter	Quality of odor
1	formic	CH_2O_2	25.	pungent
2	acetic	$C_2H_4O_2$	5.	sour
3	propionic	$C_3H_6O_2$	.05	sour
4	butyric	$C_4H_8O_2$	.001	rancid
5	valeric	$C_5H_{10}O_2$	.01	rancid
6	caproic	$C_6H_{12}O_2$	.04	rancid—aromatic

The threshold values are from Passy (1893), the odor qualities are those reported by Zwaardemaker (1922).

The threshold is lowered steadily with the increase in the size of the molecule up to and including butyric acid, beyond which point it remains fairly steady up to about No. 14 of the series, myristic acid, $C_{14}H_{28}O_2$, which is odorless, as are the still higher acids.[1]

So far we have found some regularity; but there are many perplexing facts. Though similar chemical substances give similar odors, the converse is not true, for quite dissimilar chemical substances may also give similar odors. There is no one element that we can hold responsible for all odors of a given class; nor is there any one sort of chemical compound, nor any one atom-group, that we can hold responsible. It appears that we must take account of the molecular structure, as Passy (1892) urged on the ground of the different odors or different odorous power found in isomers (such as butyl alcohol and isobutyl alcohol), the molecules of which contain the same atoms but differently arranged.

Henning (1924) holds that the odor of a substance depends on three factors: (1) the core of the molecule, such as the benzol ring, (2) the atom-groups attached to this core, and (3) the mode or place of attachment. He believes he can make out a fair case for the following relationships between molecular structure and type of odor:

Fragrant: two atom groups attached to adjacent members of an open chain

or benzol ring (an ortho-substitution in the latter case:

Spicy: benzol ring with para-substitution:

Resinous: benzol ring with cross link (or open chain with extra side-link):

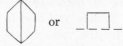

[1] The formulas are more adequately written by separating out the carboxyl group, —COOH, characteristic of the fatty acids, and writing formic acid as HCOOH, acetic acid as CH_3COOH, propionic acid as CH_3CH_2COOH, butyric acid as $CH_3CH_2CH_2COOH$, and so on, thus indicating the open chain character of these molecules.

Etherial: Forked atom group attached to ring or to open chain:

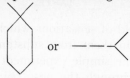 or

Burned: Heterocyclic ring including an N member:

Putrid: Here other elements usually are present, S, Se, Te, As, Sb, Bi, P; but instead of any of these N plays the decisive role in the fecal odors, indol and skatol.

Henning admits that these rules have exceptions and are only first approximations. Zwaardemaker (1922) regards them as interesting though speculative. Macdonald (1922) gives a clear statement of Henning's chemical theory and points out certain difficulties.

Even if these or similar rules were established, we still should not know the stimulus, but should want to know how these atom groups and molecular structures act upon the olfactory receptors. They probably act by vibrations of some kind (Haycraft, 1888; Zwaardemaker, 1922), vibrations of the atoms or atom groups, or vibrations of the electrons. An electronic oscillation would betray itself, in spectroscopic examination, by an absorption band of the odorous gas; and Heyninx (1919), after assembling the known facts on absorption bands of odorous substances, was well pleased with the result as evidence for the vibration theory of the smell stimulus.

The vibrations in question are in the ultraviolet region, with wave lengths of 360 mμ down to 200; and within this region he maps out a complete odor spectrum, with bromine near one end, wave length = 330; and with the following classes in order:

putrid, e.g., CS_2 at 320;
rancid, e.g., butyric acid at 280;
burned, e.g., phenol at 270, xylol at 265, naphthalin at 260;
spicy, e.g., caraway at 255, cinnamon at 240;
fragrant and etherial and resinous, scarcely separated, e.g., geraniol at 220, acetone at 210, camphor at 210.

When the odorous gas is drawn into the nose and comes in contact with the olfactory receptors, then, according to this theory, the electronic vibrations characteristic of the substance excite the receptors and excite them differently according to the vibration rate. It would be premature to take this theory as anything better than a suggestive hypothesis. Like all the other rules that have been suggested it appears to have many exceptions.

TASTE

The complex manifold of sensations which we ordinarily think of as tastes, because we obtain them from substances taken into the mouth, is much simplified by the simple experiment of holding the nose while tasting. Air currents through the nose being thus prevented, the olfactory component of the "tastes" is excluded and substances with very different flavor are found to have the same mouth taste. The mouth itself is supplied with the four cutaneous senses, as well as with kinesthesis from tongue, jaw, lip and cheek muscles; and the temperature, consistency and sometimes the prickiness of the tasted substances are components from which taste proper is not easily abstracted. When all accompanying sensations are excluded or disregarded, the clearly marked tastes of sweet, bitter, sour and salt remain.

These tastes certainly result from stimulation of specialized sense cells in the papillae of the tongue—in the circumvallate and fungiform, not in the filiform, papillae. Taste buds and some gustatory sensitivity are found also in other parts of the mucous membrane lining the mouth and throat. Some papillae respond only to sweet, and some perhaps only to sour or only to bitter; many yield only 2–3 of the four tastes, while many yield all four. Different parts of the tongue are differentially sensitive. Sensitivity to bitter is low at the tip, increases backward along the edges and is highest at the back in the region of the circumvallate papillae. Sensitivity to sweet is just the reverse, while sensitivity to sour is low at both tip and back and highest about the middle of the edges, and salt is best sensed in the forward part of the tongue. The upper surface of the tongue, toward the front and away from the edges, yields no taste sensation (Fig. 131).

These facts certainly suggest four distinct receptive processes, four gustatory elements in the physiological sense. Henning (1921, 1927), however, takes the same view here as in case of smell. He rejects the usual statement that there are only four unitary tastes, all others being compounds. The standard four he regards as salient, as distinctive reference points, but intervening between any two of them he finds a series of tastes which, purely as sensations, are as unitary as the salients. For example, magnesium chloride gives a bitter-salt taste which is not the same as the patently mixed taste of a mixture of quinine and common salt. This mixture betrays its components, while the taste of magnesium chloride cannot be broken up by attention into clear sweet and clear bitter. It is a unitary intermediate, as orange color is unitary while resembling both red and yellow. In the same way, the alkaline taste is a unitary intermediate between sweet and bitter, and the metallic taste, though unitary, resembles sweet, bitter and salt. Bicarbonate of soda gives a unitary taste intermediate between salt and sour. The whole system of tastes Henning proposes to represent by a tetrahedron with the four salients at the corners.

The gustatory *stimulus*, as it reaches the taste buds, is necessarily a chemical substance in aqueous solution. The stimulus for sour is undoubtedly the acid ion, the hydrogen ion; and the stimulus for salt is the anion, such as the Cl in $NaCl$, or the SO_4 in K_2SO_4. Sweet and bitter substances are alike in being only slightly soluble in water and the facts suggest that they act on the lipoid constituents of the taste cells. Instead of saying "act on," it is better to think of a reaction between the sapid substance and a receptive substance in the cell. There may be four receptive substances corresponding to the four main tastes (Crozier, 1934).

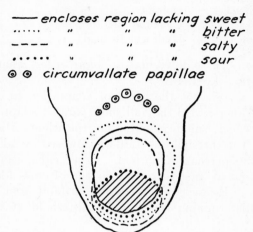

Some light on the nature of the bitter stimulus may come eventually from following up the fact that individuals differ widely in the stimulus threshold for certain bitter substances. A solution which is bitter to most Os is sweet to a few, or even sour or salty. Special interest has been awakened by the wide variation in the stimulus threshold

FIG. 131. (After Henning, 1927.) Diagram of upper surface of the tongue, with lines enclosing the regions *not* yielding the four tastes.

for the bitter substance, phenyl-thio-carbamide, some individuals requiring a concentration thousands of times greater than others to get the taste (Blakeslee & Salmon, 1935; Rikimaru, 1934, 1937).

Taste adaptation. Following up the common experience that a sweet drink tastes less sweet after several swallows, Mayer (1927) conducted an adaptation experiment on three well trained Os. At least an hour after eating the mouth was carefully rinsed and 10 cc of a solution of cane sugar (the adapting solution) was held in the mouth for 2 minutes. One minute was then allowed for rinsing the mouth, and test solutions were applied to determine the stimulus threshold for sugar. The threshold was raised to 10 times the normal; i.e., 10 times the normal concentration of sugar was necessary to give any sweet taste. The experiment was varied in several ways.

When time was the variable, adaptation increased up to 1–2 minutes of exposure to the adapting solution, in which time the maximum effect was reached.

When concentration of the adapting solution was the variable, adaptation increased with the concentration.

When other adapting solutions were tried, adaptation was greatest to sweet, next to bitter (quinine solution), and comparatively slight to salt (NaCl) and to acid (HCl). Typical results from one O, after 2 minutes exposure to each adapting solution, were as follows:

Adapting solution	Ratio of adapted threshold to normal threshold
Cane sugar	11.4
Quinine	3.6
Common salt	1.6
Hydrochloric acid	1.2

These differences are more or less what one would expect from everyday experience.

What is the effect of adaptation to one taste on sensitivity to the others? Do they all show parallel adaptation, or can there be a reverse effect, enhancement? On the whole, Mayer found some enhancement. The threshold for salt was lowered by adaptation to sweet; it was about 30 percent of normal. Other enhancement effects were rather slight, but at least there was no sign of cross adaptation.

Recovery from adaptation (and from enhancement) was followed by determining the stimulus threshold at intervals after the end of the

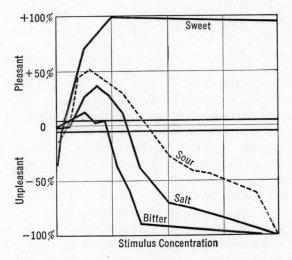

FIG. 132. (Data of R. Engel, 1928.) Preponderance of "pleasant" or "unpleasant" judgments in relation to the concentration of a sapid solution. The ordinate gives percent "pleasant" minus percent "unpleasant." The abscissa is proportional to the concentration, the full length of the base line standing for 40% cane sugar, for 1.12% tartaric acid, for 10% salt, and for .004% quinine sulphate (all by weight). The two parallel lines just above and below the zero level signal the fact that there is typically a neutral zone between pleasant and unpleasant.

Bitter, as shown by its curve, gave at best only a slight preponderance of "pleasant" over "unpleasant" judgments. Sweet always gave a preponderance of "pleasant" except at very low concentration. Sour and salt are intermediate. The curve for sour has been slightly smoothed.

adaptation period. Recovery was gradual and became complete after 10–15 minutes.

Feeling tone of tastes. Why tastes and odors, which are so definitely pleasant or unpleasant, should be regarded as standing low in the esthetic scale, is a question discussed by Hollingworth & Poffenberger (1917).

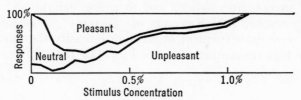

Fig. 133. (After R. Engel, 1928.) The shift from pleasant to unpleasant with increasing intensity of the stimulus. The stimulus was an acid applied to the tongue, in various concentrations as represented by the abscissa. The ordinate of the lower oblique line gives the percent of responses "unpleasant" for each concentration. The ordinate of the upper oblique line gives the percentage of responses ("unpleasant" + "neutral"), i.e., all except the "pleasant" responses. Therefore the space above the upper oblique line represents the "pleasant" responses, that between the two obliques represents the "neutral" responses, and that below the lower line represents the "unpleasant" responses. The figure gives the pooled results from 7 subjects.

They find it necessary to lay weight on the relatively non-social and non-perceptive nature of the senses of taste and smell. Taste affords a good example of the dependence of pleasantness and unpleasantness upon the intensity of the stimulus. In an experiment of R. Engel (1928) a solution was introduced into the mouth and judged pleasant, unpleasant, or neutral. A two-minute pause followed for removing the taste by chewing a little white bread and rinsing the mouth. In this

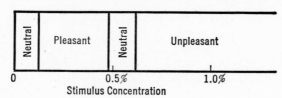

Fig. 134. Average zones and transition points computed from the previous figure. If we imagine the stimulus to be gradually increased in intensity (concentration) from zero upwards, the typical run of responses is: indifferent, pleasant, indifferent, unpleasant. The transition points vary, but their average location can be computed from the data by the same devices as are used in the method of Constant Stimuli, with two special assumptions to fit the present case: (1) the few "unpleasant" responses at and near zero concentration mean "insipid" and can be counted as "neutral"; and (2) the "neutrals" belong in two zones, one below pleasant and the other above, and can be sorted into these two zones, roughly, by assuming that every "unpleasant" (except those close to zero which are counted as neutral) has been preceded by a pleasant-neutral sequence. We thus reach the conclusion that the sour taste produced by about 0.5% tartaric acid is typically neutral; below that pleasant (except for the neutral very faint tastes); and above that unpleasant—with much variation, however, as indicated by the preceding figure.

way graduated solutions of common salt, of quinine, of tartaric acid, and of cane sugar were judged. Adaptation and satiation were avoided, since adaptation makes a bitter solution less unpleasant after a few repetitions, while satiation with a strong sweet solution makes it less pleasant. Apparently no concentration of a sugar solution can be made unpleasant except after satiety and to a few individuals. The other tastes never reached a high percent of "pleasant" judgments, but such judgments were more frequent at medium intensity than at either very low or very high concentrations. See Figs. 132–134.

CHAPTER XXI

HEARING

THE SENSE of hearing like that of sight is the concern of several sciences. The physicist is concerned with the production of sound, with its transmission through the air and other media, with reflection, diffraction and resonance. Heard sounds interest him because their peculiarities—loudness, pitch, timbre, and spatial characters—point to some corresponding peculiarities in the wave motion which is physical sound. The anatomist and physiologist are confronted by the complicated structure of the ear and seek to discover its mode of operation, taking account both of its structure and of its performance as revealed by the phenomena of hearing. The otologist encounters abnormalities of the ear and disturbances and defects of hearing which he desires to correct. The acoustical engineer is concerned with the design of musical instruments, telephones, radios and instruments for assisting the deaf. He needs to apply both the physics and the psychology of sound and has made important contributions to these scientific branches.

In this attack from many angles upon the problems of hearing, what is the particular sector of the psychologist? The varieties of auditory experience seem logically to be his concern, and also the role of hearing in the behavior of men and animals. Experiments in sensation and perception (as previously distinguished, p. 450) belong quite properly, though not exclusively by any means, in the psychological laboratory. The work of the various specialties overlaps to such an extent that we must feel free to utilize contributions from all sources.

Problems in auditory sensation and perception. Heard sounds differ from each other along certain dimensions such as loudness and pitch. Such dimensions need to be discovered and defined and connected with variations in the acoustic stimulus. The enterprise may well begin with sounds that are as simple as possible, and advance to complex sounds, harmony and discord, and the masking of one sound by another. Monaural and binaural hearing need to be compared. As to auditory perception, there is an unlimited field for the study of recognition of speech and of the noises by which objects are distinguished; but the main topic in auditory perception thus far subjected to experimental study is the fascinating problem of space perception.

VARIETIES AND DIMENSIONS OF AUDITORY SENSATION

The psychological distinction between *tones* and *noises* does not correspond exactly with the practical distinction. In a noise abatement campaign, "noise" is undesirable sound, unwanted sound. The sound of an automobile horn in the city street is classified as a noise even though it is a smooth musical tone. In psychology any sound having a well-marked pitch is classified as a tone. It is "higher" or "lower" than another tone. Noises are not wholly devoid of pitch; a rumble is lower or deeper than a rattle; but their pitch is much less definite than that of a smooth tone. Noises may be sudden like a crack or continued like a hiss; they may be rustling, roaring, crunching, grating; and their various qualities are of much practical importance as cues of objective facts. Tones as well as noises differ in quality. The violin tone has a different *timbre* from that of the flute or horn or trumpet. The quality or character of a sound, added to the dimensions of loudness and pitch, completes our first rough list of the varieties of auditory sensation.

Sound waves. Sound reaches the drum of the ear in the form of air vibrations or waves. A simple sound wave, produced by gently striking a tuning fork, is a pendular motion. The particles of air move back and forth like the bob of a pendulum, except that they move in a straight line instead of a curve. The vibration is longitudinal, but can be represented to the eye by a transverse vibration or sine wave. Sound waves travel through the air at a speed of about 1130 feet per sec., one wave following another at a certain frequency. For example a tuning fork with pitch of middle c sends out 260 vibrations per sec. The frequency of these waves we call 260 cycles per sec.; their wave length, the distance from crest to crest, is $1130/260 = 4.34$ ft. Wave length is inversely proportional to frequency. The amplitude of the pendular motion necessarily diminishes as the waves spread radially in the air, but their speed of transmission and their frequency and wave length remain the same. A simple wave has only two independent dimensions, amplitude and frequency.

Correlations of the physical and psychological dimensions of sound. Pitch and loudness are dimensions of sound as heard, not of the physical wave motion. Physically, a sound wave has frequency but not pitch; it has amplitude, energy, intensity, but not loudness. We shall use the word "intensity" to refer only to the physical dimension, and save "loudness" for the psychological. A psychological dimension depends on the characteristics of the organism, and cannot be entirely defined in terms of the stimulus.

Two rough correlations are familiar. As a tone dies away, its frequency does not change but its amplitude diminishes, and with the diminished amplitude goes a decrease of loudness. A small tuning fork vibrates faster than a large one, and its tone is higher. Pitch is correlated with frequency, loudness with intensity. But this is not the whole story.

Pitch, though depending mostly on frequency, depends in a minor degree upon intensity. Increase the intensity of a tone and you *lower* the pitch, unless the tone be of high frequency; above 2500 cycles the effect is the opposite but slight (Zurmühl, 1930; Stevens, 1934 a; Fletcher, 1934. See also Fig. 139, p. 509).

Loudness is much less exclusively dependent on intensity than pitch on frequency. The first thing to notice is that intensity or energy itself is not wholly dependent on amplitude of vibration. For if amplitude

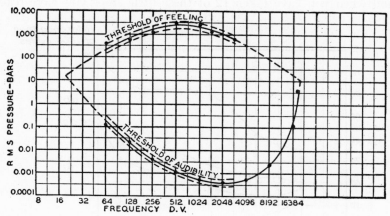

Fig. 135. (From Fletcher, 1929; courtesy of D. Van Nostrand Company, Inc.) Threshold sensitivity of the ear at different frequencies. The ordinate scale here, in root-mean-square pressure, is proportional to the square root of energy per second. The upper curve shows the sound intensities required to arouse a pressure sensation in the ear, a warning that the limit of safe intensities is nearly reached, and at the same time a rough indication of the intensity which gives the maximum loudness for any frequency. The lower curve shows the much smaller intensities required to arouse a sensation of tone at its minimum loudness for any frequency. The parallel dotted lines show the limits between which half of the single observations on normal ears may be expected to fall. (D. V. = double vibrations = cycles.)

remains constant while frequency increases, the more numerous blows upon the tympanic membrane deliver more energy per second. Energy per second equals the square of amplitude × the square of frequency. We have also to take account of the peculiar sensitivity of the ear. It responds only within a certain frequency range, between the limits of about 20 and 20,000 cycles per sec., and it is most sensitive in the middle portion of this range, from about 1000 to 5000 cycles. Less physical intensity is needed to give a just audible tone at these medium frequencies than at low or high frequencies. A little above the threshold nearly the same relation holds: the tone must be physically stronger at low or high than at these medium frequencies in order to seem equally loud (or soft). The relation changes as the intensity is increased; a medium degree of loudness is produced by almost equal intensities throughout the low and middle range of frequencies; while very great loudness is given by smaller intensity at low than at middle or high frequencies. So the whole relation is quite complicated. (Fletcher, 1929; Fletcher & Munson, 1933; Churcher, 1935; Baier, 1936; Stevens, 1936). See Figs. 135, 136.

Scaling the psychological dimensions of pitch and loudness. To scale a dimension is to mark it off in sensibly equal steps. Pitch was scaled by musicians long before the physics of sound was understood. The basic pitch step is the octave; a sub-unit is the equal-tempered semitone which is 1/12 of the octave. Ascend the piano by semitones from middle c, and when you have taken 12 of these little steps you have reached

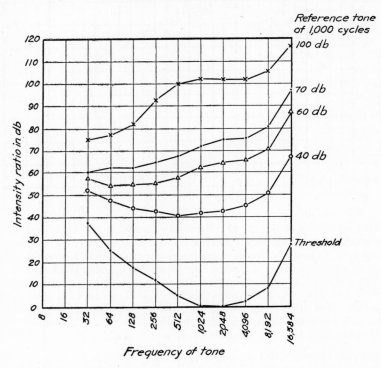

FIG. 136. (Fletcher & Munson, 1933.) Equal loudness contours over the frequency range. Each of the contour lines passes through intensities which, at the different frequencies indicated, give the same loudness effect.

the next c, one octave above your starting point. Within the middle range of musical tones, all semitones are sensibly equal and one jump of an octave seems as great as another. The pitch step of an octave corresponds to a frequency ratio of 2:1. Double the frequency and you raise the pitch by one octave; halve the frequency and you lower the pitch by one octave. The frequency ratio for the equal-tempered semitone is $2^{1/12}:1 = 1.0595:1$. To complete the tie-up of pitch and frequency we need to know the absolute frequency for some particular pitch. If the convention is adopted that middle c shall be 260 cycles per second (or that the a above middle c shall be 436 cycles), the scaling process is complete.

It is true that the octave, as physically defined by the ratio 2:1, shrinks in psychological size at both the upper and the lower extremes of the musical scale, and that the semitone shrinks with it—as can readily be observed by striking in succession two adjacent notes on the piano at either end of the keyboard and noticing how small the difference is to the ear compared with the difference between two adjacent notes anywhere in the middle of the keyboard. This difference is important for music in one way—no one would think of presenting a melody in these very high or very low notes—but it does not make desirable a reform which would be suggested by the psychological scale considered alone, i.e., a wider spacing out of the frequencies at the top and bottom of the scale so as to make the semitones sound as large as in the middle of the scale. The top and bottom notes are used mostly in harmony, and as soon as two or more notes sound at once, the physics of sound waves asserts itself. The frequency ratios have to be kept constant throughout the scale or the harmony is lost.

The loudness dimension also can be scaled. Music has long used a loudness scale with degrees designated by the familiar marks of expression: *ppp*, *pp*, *p*, *mp*, *mf*, *f*, *ff*, *fff*, in order from softest to loudest. The steps between these degrees are not necessarily equal. The modern need for noise abatement creates an engineering demand for a well developed loudness scale. What needs to be abated is not the physical intensity of sound per se, but its loudness; and loudness must be measured somehow by the effects of sound on the organism. The most direct effect is simply the subject's judgment and report of loudness. The problem is to divide the loudness dimension into equal steps, tying the scale to the physical dimensions of intensity and frequency.

What step can be used? Probably one of those worked out in psychophysics: the DL, the SD, or the supraliminal "equal appearing difference." The DL has been tried but has not given a consistent picture. The SD has not been tried, but the equal-appearing difference seems to fill the bill pretty well. O hears alternate tones of the same frequency and adjusts the intensity of one to appear just half as loud as the other. "Just half as loud," we say; but the task is not one which O feels able to execute with great precision. The agreement between Os is however sufficient to warrant using the data and working with averages. By halving and doubling up and down the scale, equal loudness steps are marked off in terms of intensity at one particular frequency, and similar scales at other frequencies can be interrelated and consistency checked by cross comparisons.

Binaural hearing provides somewhat more precise determinations of equal loudness steps, if we can assume that a tone applied to one ear is subjectively half as loud as when led to both ears. O makes a loudness equation between two tones, heard alternately, one by both ears and the other by only one. The equation gives two physical intensities one of which will be twice as loud as the other when both are heard in the same way, either monaurally or binaurally.

Timbre. Having found the physical correlates of pitch and loudness we still have to account for the different qualities of different instruments. How can the sound waves differ? Two simple sine waves are altogether alike if they are alike in both frequency and intensity. But the waves emitted by instruments, and by practically all sources of sound, are compounded of simple waves of differing frequencies, called *partials*, or *fundamental and overtones*. The upper partials are harmonic with the fundamental, in case of musical tones, and the frequencies of harmonic partials are in the ratio of the numbers 1, 2, 3, 4, 5 and so on. A note of 100 cycles sung by a bass voice or played on any instrument consists in the air of a complex wave containing the frequencies 100, 200, 300, 400, 500 and many more. It seemed possible to Helmholtz (1862) that these partials varied in relative intensity from one instrument to another, and produced the varying timbre. He put his hypothesis to the test by using resonators, which were hollow spheres of different sizes, tuned to different frequencies. Each resonator had a wide mouth to admit air vibrations and a small orifice to be inserted into the observer's ear. A resonator "sings" when the frequency to which it is tuned is present in the compound wave reaching it from any source. By this means Helmholtz found some partials strong in the tone of one instrument, other partials strong in another instrument. After practice he was able to hear the overtones without the aid of resonators.

Modern methods provide visual confirmation of these findings. Miller (1922) directed the sound waves by a funnel or horn onto a thin glass diaphragm to which was attached a tiny mirror. A beam of light reflected from the mirror upon a moving film gave a photographic record of the sound waves. It was necessary to correct the wave curves for distortion introduced by the diaphragm and the horn, and to subject the curves to a Fourier analysis by means of a mechanical harmonic analyzer. Fourier's principle is that any wave motion can be imitated to any desired approximation by a sum of simple sine waves in the harmonic ratios 1, 2, 3, 4, . . . of frequency. The harmonic analyzer determines the amplitude of each partial necessary to effect the best approximation to the original wave. If the original wave is really constituted of harmonic partials the analyzer discovers these partials. If the total wave is composed of inharmonic components, the harmonic analyzer shows the frequency bands within which the partials are strong, without identifying them absolutely. The strength of the overtones is sometimes surprisingly great. In the case of the clarinet, partials 7, 8, 9, 10 together deliver 59 percent of the total energy of the wave. In some of the bass notes of the human voice the fundamental gives only 4 percent of the total energy. In the low notes of a piano as many as 42 partials have been identified; the middle notes give 10 or more, while the high notes give very few. The low, middle and high registers of the same instrument may differ considerably in wave composition and in timbre. Fletcher (1929, 1934) obtained similar results by use of an electric harmonic analyzer applied to the currents in a telephone activated by sound.

Timbre depends primarily on the "overtone structure," the intensity pattern of the partials. It depends also on absolute intensity, for if a violin tone is sufficiently amplified its timbre changes, though amplification leaves the relative strength of the partials unchanged. Frequency, too, has an effect upon timbre. By slowing down or speeding up a phonograph turntable, we do not change the relative physical strength of the partials, but we may produce a noticeable change in the quality of the tone (Fletcher, 1934).

Other possible dimensions of tonal sensations. Besides loudness, pitch and, of course, duration, there are other ways in which tones differ. Several psychological dimensions have been suggested: volume, density, brightness, and vocality or vowel quality. The question is whether all these dimensions are to be taken with equal seriousness or whether some of them are merely fanciful ways of describing tonal sensation. Volume was accepted by Stumpf (1883, 1890), who was a recognized leader

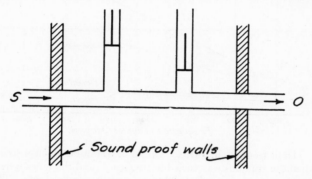

FIG. 137. Diagram of an interference tube assembly. The tone to be purified is led through a long tube, into the side of which are inserted tubes of the same bore. The lengths of the side tubes are regulated by adjustable pistons. To eliminate a certain partial, make the length of a side tube ¼ the wave length of that partial. A wave of this length entering the side tube, and reflected from the piston, gets back to the main tube ¼ + ¼ = ½ wave length out of step with the wave proceeding along the main tube. The wave returning from the side tube, being always in opposite phase, neutralizes the corresponding wave in the main tube. By setting side tubes at different lengths, different partials are neutralized. A strong partial will not be completely annulled by a single interference tube but will be by two or more of the same length, inserted at intervals along the main tube. Though the interference is most perfect when the side tube has exactly ¼ the wave length of a given partial, some interference occurs when the tuning is not exact. A number of side tubes of slightly different length will filter out all possible partials within a given frequency band.

among the early psychological students of tone and music. James (1890, 2, p. 134) insisted that a primitive spatial character inhered in almost all sensations: "In the sensations of hearing, touch, sight and pain, we are accustomed to distinguish from among the other elements the element of voluminousness." Low tones seem more voluminous than high, loud tones more voluminous than weak.

It is also possible, as pointed out by several of the older authors, to describe high tones as brighter and low tones as duller than medium tones. Are these two dimensions, volume and brightness, simply different ways of expressing the same facts?

Vocality or vowel quality, used broadly to include also the sound of such continuing consonants as m, n, r, and s, is certainly a characteristic of speech sounds, but as these are complex, vowel quality might be regarded as a kind of timbre. Köhler (1909, 1910, 1913, 1915) believed that he could demonstrate vowel quality in simple tones.

Rich (1916, 1919) attempted an objective examination of the problem whether these suggested dimensions or attributes were genuine. If

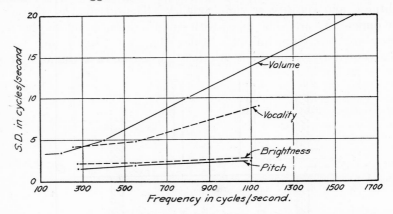

FIG. 138. (Data from Rich, 1919.) Values of SD obtained in discrimination of pure tones, when the stimulus was varied in frequency, and the tones were compared, in different series, as to their pitch, brightness, vocality and volume. The question is whether the run of the SD values in the different series is sufficiently different to justify admitting separate dimensions of tonal sensation. The data on volume are too scanty to give a reliable curve.

For plotting these curves we have used Rich's data on "precision" or "h," transmuted into SD values (p. 412). Rich's DL values show about the same relations.

they were mere metaphors, he reasoned, the judgments comparing tones in brightness or volume would not show sufficient consistency to yield a measure of DL, the difference threshold. Or these supposed dimensions might simply be other names for pitch, in which case the DL for brightness or volume would be the same as for pitch. Rich used Stern tone variators as sources of sound, but purified the tones through a system of interference tubes, which cut out the overtones and left only the fundamental of each composite tone to reach the ear. He presented two tones of different frequency and asked O to decide which appeared the more voluminous. After some preliminary training O was able to make such judgments with confidence. Of the three Os, one required very little training and the third considerable.

Rich's data are summarized in Figure 138. The difference shown between brightness and pitch is too small to justify separating them as two dimensions. Introspectively the subjects were much inclined to identify the two. Bright meant to them high, sharp pointed; dull meant flat, blunt, dark (compare sharp and flat in music). Brightness seemed to be merely a less technical word for pitch and Rich suggested that this dimension might well be called pitch-brightness.

Because the DL and SD values for volume are so much greater than for pitch and brightness, it was logical to accept volume as a separate dimension. Introspectively, judgments of volume were easy and direct. Volume decreased rather slowly as frequency rose.

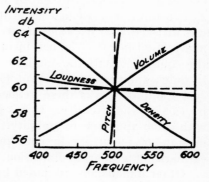

Fig. 139. (Stevens, 1934 b.)   Volume, loudness, density, and pitch equations between tones of differing frequency, the frequency difference being compensated by a difference in stimulus intensity. The rectangular framework represents the physical dimensions, intensity and frequency, while the curves are lines of equal volume, density, etc. The volume line reads that, on the average of several Os, the following stimuli gave equally voluminous tones:

> 400 cycles at 56 db
> 450   "   " 58 "
> 500   "   " 60 "
> 550   "   " 62 ", nearly
> 600   "   " 63.5 db, approx.

The other lines are read in a similar way; thus a tone of about 508 cycles at 64 db was regarded as having the same pitch as the standard tone of 500 cycles at 60 db.

Volume as related to intensity of stimulus. A loud sound seems more voluminous than a weak sound. This relation was approached quantitatively by Halverson (1924) and Dimmick (1933). The output of an audio-oscillator was fed into a telephone or loud speaker and maintained at a constant frequency of 256 cycles in Dimmick's experiment and of 1000 in Halverson's. The amplitude of the wave was varied so that tones of differing physical intensity were presented for comparison by the method of Constant Stimuli. The tones were compared in loudness at one time and at another time in volume, and the DL in volume judgment was 2 to 4 times as great as in loudness judgment.

Volume, therefore, seemed to be a true dimension of tonal sensation, varying both with frequency and with intensity of the stimulus but different from either pitch or loudness. Some later experimenters (Gundlach & Bentley, 1930; Zoll, 1934) on repeating Rich's experiment have obtained less satisfying results; the DL and SD of the volume judgment have not differed much from those for pitch, while some Os have been unable to give consistent judgments of volume.

Volume dependent on the combination of frequency and intensity. Since greater volume goes with greater intensity and with lower frequency, we should be able, by increasing the intensity of a high note, to make it equal in volume to a lower note. This hypothesis was put to the test by Stevens (1934 a) using the equation method. The output of a loud speaker driven by an oscillator was varied in frequency so that two pure tones of different pitch were presented in rapid alternation, 40 single stimuli per minute. Stimuli 1, 3, 5 . . . were tones of 900 cycles per sec. whereas stimuli 2, 4, 6 . . . were a little higher, 950 cycles per sec. O held in his hands a rheostat by which he adjusted the intensity of tones 2, 4, 6 until they seemed equal in volume to tones 1, 3, 5. When he was satisfied with his adjustment, a reading was taken showing by how many db of intensity he had increased the higher tone in order to reach this equation. With the standard remaining at 900 cycles, the comparison stimulus was presented at 925, 950, 1000 and also at 875, 850 and 800 cycles and at each of these frequencies a volume equation was obtained by varying the intensity. It was possible for O to make these equations with some approach to stability. He could attest equality of volume, in spite of inequality in both pitch and loudness. Volume had the earmarks of a separate dimension.

Other dimensions examined by the equation method. This method can be conveniently used for testing the claims of any proposed dimension of tonal volume which varies both with the frequency and with the intensity of the stimulus. Let the standard have a fixed frequency and intensity, and let the comparison tone, alternating with the standard, be set at different frequencies by E and adjusted in intensity by O so as to match the standard in a certain dimension. Tone "density" was tested in this way (Stevens, 1934 c). A very high tone was unhesitatingly pronounced more dense than a low tone, a loud tone more dense than a soft one, and O was easily trained to compare tones in these terms. When the standard was 500 cycles and 60 db, a tone of 600 cycles was weakened to about 56 db in order to seem equally dense. Other similar equations are incorporated in the "density" line in Fig. 139.

Brightness increases with the frequency and with the intensity of the stimulus. Therefore it cannot be identified, as Rich identified it, with pitch alone. Brightness equations obtained in the manner just described were identical with the density equations, and the Os found it impossible to maintain a distinction between the two dimensions, which are apparently the same (Boring & Stevens, 1936).

The experimental evidence supports the claims of four psychological dimensions of simple tones:

1. Loudness, increasing with the intensity of the stimulus and also varying in a complex manner with frequency.

2. Pitch, rising with frequency, and affected in a minor degree by intensity.

3. Volume, increasing with intensity and decreasing with frequency.

4. Brightness or density, increasing both with frequency and with intensity.

If the objection is raised that with only two independent dimensions of the physical stimulus, there should be only two in the tonal sensation, the reply has been made by Köhler (1915 b) and by Boring (1935). Since the heard tone depends on the characteristics of the receptor system as well as on the stimulus, the dimensions of the sensation need not, and do not, correspond one to one with the dimensions of the stimulus. Additional dimensions can arise from peculiarities of the sense organ. The sense cells of the organ of Corti stand in a column of fours and fives on the flexible floor of a long corridor. Sound waves cause this floor to vibrate and thus excite the sense cells. The length of the vibrating portion of the floor may vary, the location of the maximum vibration, the number of cells excited, and the frequency per second of their responses. So there are enough variables to account for four dimensions of sensation. We find a similar state of affairs in color sensation. Homogeneous light is fully defined in terms of its two dimensions of intensity and frequency, but the resulting sensation has the three dimensions of hue, brilliance, and saturation (p. 540).

Vowel quality or vocality. To the human ear (listener, we should say) the differences between speech sounds are certainly more striking than the differences in volume and brightness with which we have been laboring. The vowels and semivowels differ among themselves about as much as the different odors or tastes. How can we rest content with the elimination of vocality from the list of dimensions of tonal sensation? The only excuse for this elimination is that vowel quality, like timbre, is usually believed to be a characteristic not of pure or single tones but of tonal complexes. Have pure tones any vowel quality? One can scarcely answer this question outside of the laboratory, because pure tones do not exist in nature, in the street or in the music room. Before examining the evidence for and against vowel quality in pure tones we will briefly consider the analyses that have been made of vowel sounds as ordinarily spoken or sung.

Though we are concerned with speech sounds as heard and not with the motor process of producing them, we may remind ourselves that the tone of the voice is produced by the vocal cords, while the speech characteristics are introduced by the mouth and nose cavities, as is shown by the presence of vowel and consonantal sounds in whispering, when the vocal cords are inactive. In whispering a vowel, the mouth cavity is shaped for *oh*, *ah*, *eh*, etc., and the air blown out through the mouth starts a feeble vibration of the frequency for which the cavity is tuned. In the *ah* position the mouth cavity is tuned for a frequency of about 1000 cycles, differing somewhat with the size of the individual's mouth and with the exact position he gives it in whispering *ah*. In the *oh* position it is tuned for a lower frequency, somewhere near 500 cycles, and in the *u* (or *oo*) position it is tuned for still lower frequencies, somewhere near

300 cycles. These characteristic vowel tones, as produced in whispering, are called "formants."

It was Hermann's idea (1890) that these same formants were present in speaking aloud. He supposed that the mouth cavity was set into resonance by the voice tone—which, so far, is certainly the fact—and he assumed that the cavity must resound with its own proper frequency. It would accordingly give out the formant of 1000 cycles for *ah* and the formant of 500 cycles for *oh*, no matter what the frequency of the voice tone. There are two objections to this simple theory of vowel sounds. One objection is psychological. Since the formant has a constant pitch for a given vowel, while the voice tone varies in pitch, the formant would often be inharmonic with the voice tone and the two would produce a discord. If the mouth is set for a formant of 1000 cycles, while the voice is sounding a note of 255 cycles, the fourth partial of the voice tone is 4 × 255 = 1020 cycles which would clash with the formant and give rough beats. But if you lowered your voice tone to 250 cycles, the fourth partial would coincide with the formant, the beats would disappear and the whole effect would be smooth. No such beating and smoothing out are observable in the speaking or singing voice.

The other objection is physical. When a resonator is affected by vibrations quite near its own proper frequency it does not resound with its own proper tone but is forced into sympathetic vibration with the impressed tone. In singing or speaking aloud, as distinguished from whispering, the mouth cavity cannot give out its own proper tone but must reinforce any partials in the voice tone which happen to fall near that proper tone. With the mouth set for 1000 cycles and a voice fundamental of 255 cycles, the mouth cavity would reinforce the fourth partial of 1020 and would not give out the clashing tone of 1000.

For these reasons the original Helmholtz theory (1862), though slightly more difficult to grasp than that of Hermann, is now preferred. The mouth in any vowel position reinforces certain partials of the voice tone. Those partials are reinforced which happen to have a frequency near to the proper frequency of the mouth cavity. Any partials lying near 1000 cycles will be reinforced by the mouth in the *ah* position; those near 500 cycles are reinforced when the mouth shifts to the *oh* position. Let a man sing *ah* on the note of 150 cycles: the sixth partial of 900 and the seventh of 1050 are reinforced and give the *ah* quality to the heard tone.

This theory of vowel quality is tested by recording speech sounds and subjecting the records to the harmonic analyzer (Miller, 1922; Fletcher, 1929; Steinberg, 1934). The experimenters have obtained somewhat variant frequencies as characteristic of the vowels, as might be expected from variations in pronunciation. (To secure that particular sound of *a* which is regarded as central in the vowel system, one is instructed to pronounce it as in father, but the *a* in father is sometimes pronounced like the short *o* in pop, or like the *aw* in paw, or even like the flat *a* in dad.) For every difference in pronunciation there is a change in the mouth cavity and in the reinforced frequency band. In spite of these differences the experiments agree in placing the vowel *u* as in true at the lowest frequency, the vowel *o* as in go next, the vowel *a* as in father in the middle, the vowel *e* as in ten higher, and the vowel *i* as in machine highest. Agreement is closest on the vowel *o*, which has a characteristic frequency of 450 to 500 cycles. Some other values in which there is agreement are given in an adjoining table. Often a second frequency band is found in addition to the one listed here.

APPROXIMATE FREQUENCY CHARACTERISTICS FOR A FEW VOCAL SOUNDS

u	(as in true)	about	325 cycles/sec
oo	(as in book)	"	420
o	(as in roll)	"	450
aw	(as in jaw)	"	730
a	(as in father)	"	950
a	(as in bat)	"	1800
e	(as in ten)	"	1900
i	(as in tin)	"	2200
i	(as in machine)	"	2500–3000
m, n, ng		"	250
s		"	5000–9000

Do pure tones have vowel quality? If the vowel *o* as in go always shows a strong frequency band in the region of 450–500 cycles, it is a natural supposition that the converse of this proposition will hold true and that a physically pure tone of 450–500 cycles will give the *o* quality. Köhler (1909) set up this hypothesis, at first very doubtfully. But he found in preliminary experiments with tuning forks that his Os after a little practice detected vowel quality in these relatively pure tones, and that they agreed fairly well on the particular vowel heard at each vibration frequency. Thus they usually reported *oh* for a fork of 550 cycles and *ah* for a fork of 1100.

But tuning forks are not wholly free from overtones. To obtain pure tones, Köhler passed the waves from a tone variator through an assembly of interference tubes (Fig. 137). Knowing from preliminary experiments that the *ah* quality came at about 525 cycles, he started 20 cycles above this frequency and decreased the frequency step by step till O reported that the point of clearest *ah* quality had been reached. This point was approached in both ascending and descending series (p. 399) till a satisfactory average was obtained. How closely the four Os agreed in their mean frequency choices for several vowels is shown below:

Vowel quality	*Subjects:* *1*	*2*	*3*	*4*
u	266	262	261	264
o	528	515	522	521
a	1055	1047	1053	1057
e	2112	2095	2086	2095

The typical values for the vowel and semivowel sounds which Köhler finally adopted are as follows:

Vowel quality	Typical central frequency
m	132
u (as in true)	263
o (as in roll)	525
a (as in father)	1053
e (as in ten)	2100
i (as in machine)	4200
s	8400

These results of Köhler are in rather good agreement with those for spoken vowels (p. 513). The order is the same and the absolute frequencies differ no more than can be attributed to differing pronunciation of the North German and North American Os. The frequency characterizing a spoken vowel gives approximately that same vowel quality when presented as a pure tone. *According to Köhler's findings simple tones do have vowel quality, and vocality should be added to the list of tonal dimensions.* It was true, however, that the vowels heard in pure tones were rather thin as compared with spoken vowels. Full vowel quality may be possessed only by complex tones.

Repetition of Köhler's experiment on vocality. Rich's study already described (page 508) included an experiment similar to the last one described from Köhler, except that the psychophysical method of Constant Stimuli was used. With a frequency of 550 cycles, taken as the Standard, were compared pure tones of 530, 540, 550, 560 and 570 cycles. The subject judged whether the comparison stimulus was more like *u* than the Standard or more like *ah*. Rich used three Standards, 250, 550, and 1140 cycles, corresponding rather nearly to Köhler's central frequencies for the vowels *u*, *o* and *a*. After some training Rich's subjects gave fairly stable results, shown in Fig. 138. The quantitative results did not justify separating vocality from volume; both might be the same dimension. Rich was inclined to reject vocality because the effect of suggestion was difficult to avoid. *The status of vocality remains unsettled.* It may be a dimension of simple tones or only of complex speech sounds.

BEATS AND SUBJECTIVE TONES

The phenomena which we next consider are subjective in the sense of being generated within the organism, not in the sense of being imaginary. They are probably generated in the ear. Difference tones are the best example, but before considering them we should note the phenomena of beats, which to be sure are not strictly subjective since they correspond to periodic interferences in the physical waves which enter the ear.

Beats. Let there be two separate sources giving out simple tones; and let one remain at 256 cycles while the other is raised gradually in frequency (Krueger, 1900). When one source is giving out 256 vibrations per sec. and the other 257, the listener hears only a single tone but this wavers in loudness. It waxes as the two sources come into like phase and wanes as they come into opposite phases with each other. The listener hears one waxing-waning unit per second. When the higher source is raised to 258 cycles, there are two of these units per second, and their number is always equal to the difference in the vibration frequency of the two sources. Up to about 8 per sec. they can be counted by an attentive listener. As the number increases the gentle waxing and waning give way to a beating which is not only heard but also felt in the region of the ear drum. The beats become rattling and unpleasant as the upper source is raised to 284 cycles per sec.; there are then $284 - 256 = 28$ beats per sec., far too many to be counted. Beyond this point the beats become less prominent but the whole tone is rough. The roughness flattens out as the difference in vibration rate becomes still greater— except that beating difference tones come in and are absent only when the two primary tones stand in a simple ratio to each other, as at 320–256, the major third. Beating difference tones will be considered shortly.

The intertone. When the two beating primary tones differ in vibration rate by only a few cycles per second, only a single tone is heard, intermediate in pitch between the two primaries. As the difference increases, say at 256–272, this intertone becomes fainter and fainter and the primaries become separately audible.

Difference tones. The physical cause of difference tones is the same as that of beats, though the mechanism of their production in the ear may be different. Two tones, sounding at once, produce audible beats when their difference in vibration rate does not exceed 40 or 50, but from about the difference of 40 cycles up a low hum is heard which can be identified as a tone having a pitch corresponding to the difference of the two primaries. With the primaries at 256 and 300, this "first difference tone" can be matched in pitch with a separate tone of $300 - 256 = 44$ cycles.

If we let l = the frequency of the lower primary tone; h = the frequency of the upper primary tone; $D_1, D_2, \ldots$ = the frequencies of the first, second, . . . difference tones; we have

$$D_1 = h - l$$
$$D_2 = 2l - h$$
$$D_3 = 3l - 2h$$
$$D_4 = 4l - 3h$$

$\left.\right\}$ Reverse signs when difference is negative

Difference tones are most audible: (1) when they are not too low, and therefore when the primaries are fairly high, as from 500 to 2000 cycles; (2) when the primaries are of good intensity; (3) when the primaries are of equal intensity. The last two conditions are best met by oscillator tones. Fletcher

(1929) reports an experiment in which ten separate sources gave frequencies of 100, 200 . . . 1000 cycles. The waves, combined in a telephone receiver, gave a full, rich tone with a pitch of 100. Physical elimination of the 100-cycle component made no appreciable difference in the tone. The ear, we might say, regenerated the fundamental of 100 cycles as a difference tone which was very strong because generated by every two successive frequencies in the whole complex. The lowest four components, 100, 200, 300 and 400 could all be omitted from the physical stimulus and still be regenerated by the ear in the form of difference tones.

A difference tone can be reinforced or annulled by introducing an extra physical tone of the same pitch, and adjusting the *phase* of this extra tone. At a certain phase position of the extra tone the reinforced difference tone reaches its maximum loudness, while at another phase position, half a wave length from the first, the difference tone is obliterated or reaches minimum loudness. By this interference method the phase of the difference tone and its intensity can be determined. Having these determinate physical characteristics, the difference tone is undoubtedly a physical vibration generated in the ear (Lewis & Larsen, 1937).

Beating difference tones. Let two sources emit the frequencies 400 and 600; they are tuned to a "perfect fifth" with each other. The first difference tone has a frequency of $600 - 400 = 200$, one octave below the lower of the two primaries. The second difference tone is $2 \times 400 - 600 = 200$, the same as the first. Now mistune the fifth, raising it to 601 cycles: the first difference tone is $601 - 400 = 201$, and the second difference tone is $2 \times 400 - 601 = 199$. The two difference tones are now 2 cycles out of step with each other and give two beats per second. In general, when two primaries are tuned to a perfect musical interval, as an octave, a fifth, a fourth, a major third, etc., the difference tones coincide, drop out, or are harmonic with each other and with the primaries; but if the primaries are not tuned to any perfect interval (simple ratio of frequencies) the difference tones beat with each other and make the tonal complex inharmonious.

Subjective overtones. Suppose a simple sine wave is applied to the ear, will it remain simple after passing through the middle and inner ear, or will the resonance and other physical properties of the ear add overtones? A delicate test for subjective harmonics makes use of an "exploring tone" of adjustable frequency, thrown in while a steady tone is sounding. Both are pure tones, simple sine waves. Let the question be whether a pure tone of 400 cycles generates a subjective overtone of 800. If present this overtone must beat with the exploring tone in the neighborhood of 800 but the beats will disappear when the exploring tone is tuned exactly to 800. The results of this experiment were definitely positive. When the primary tone was 400 cycles, subjective overtones were located at 800, 1200, 1600 and 2000 cycles (Fletcher, 1929).

However, this experiment alone does not prove the existence of subjective overtones, since the results can be explained in terms of difference tones. When the primary is 400 cycles and the exploring tone 798 cycles, the first difference tone will be 398, the third difference tone 396, and the two will beat. If we assume several orders of difference tones, we can explain the observed beats without assuming subjective overtones. But we can just as well follow Helmholtz (1862) and assume subjective overtones, and then reduce all difference tones to the first order. The second difference tone, $2l - h$, is evidently the first difference tone between h and $2l$, the latter being the first overtone of l. All the difference tones are of the first order and generated as beats are generated, if only there are real subjective overtones. To make sure of them we must appeal to close observation by the hearing subject, or we must find a way of observing the vibrations in the inner ear.

The latter possibility has been developed in recent years (p. 534) and the "cochlear effect" obtained from an electrode on the round window

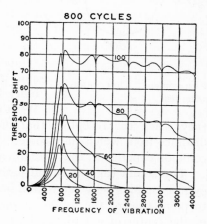

Fig. 140. (Fletcher, 1929; courtesy of D. Van Nostrand Company, Inc.) The masking effect. The masking tone here is a pure tone of 800 cycles; the masked tone has in any single test a constant frequency and is raised in intensity till it can just be detected by the listener. The curves show the stimulus threshold for masked tones of various frequencies when subjected to the masking effect of the 800-cycle tone. Each curve shows the results obtained with a given intensity of the masking tone.

affords good evidence of overtones generated in the ear when a pure tone is used as the stimulus (Stevens & Newman, 1936 b; Wever & Bray, 1938).

Masking of tones. It is familiar knowledge that one sound may be difficult to hear in the presence of another sound. The older scientific results indicated that a low tone could mask or conceal a higher tone but that the reverse was not possible. Recent results (Fletcher, 1929) however show masking in both directions, up and down, the maximum effect being exerted upon tones just above or just below the masking tone in frequency. The stimulus threshold for the masked tone is raised by the presence of the masking tone and the rise in threshold furnishes a measure of masking. A tone of 800 cycles masks a tone of 400 only slightly. The amount of masking increases as the masked tone rises from 400 to 800 where the maximum effect is produced. Above that frequency the amount of masking decreases but not so rapidly as it does below.

In the immediate neighborhood of the masking tone, beats are heard between the two tones and these beats betray the presence of the masked tone and lower its stimulus threshold. This accounts for the little sharp dip at the frequency of the masking tone and its overtone.

LOCALIZATION OF SOUND

The everyday reply to the question, "What do you hear?" would be something like this: "I hear the bell ringing—the children playing—the rain falling." We hear a thing doing something. Things and happenings are recognized by the sounds they make. Along with the identification of the sound-producing object goes localization. The source of a sound is localized instantly and rather accurately, at least in familiar surroundings where we know the probable sources of various classes of sounds and are adjusted to the floor, walls and other reflecting surfaces and sound screens.

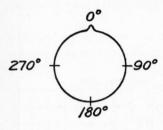

FIG. 141. Sound cage experiment. Description in the text.

When we consider the anatomy of the ear, we wonder how such a mechanism can possibly furnish any cues of distance and direction. The sound waves pass through the narrow external auditory meatus, the tympanic membrane, the chain of ossicles and the oval window before reaching the inner ear where the receptors are located. What can there be left in the sound waves as they reach the receptors that differs according to the direction and distance from which they come? One would almost declare, in spite of common experience, that sounds cannot possibly be localized.

The sound cage or sound perimeter. O is blindfolded or closes his eyes, a sound is delivered to him from a certain direction, and he attempts to point toward the source of sound. In Fig. 141, O's head is placed in the center of a horizontal circle of wire, graduated in degrees with zero at the front and 180° at the rear, 90° being opposite the right ear and 270° opposite the left. O learns to use this scale of degrees or he can face north and use the points of the compass. Vertical circles or arches attached to this horizontal circle make it possible to test localization in all directions. In rough work E walks softly around O, speaking or using a telegraph snapper at various points. Better, a telephone receiver is arranged to emit clicks or tones from any part of the cage. Padding the walls of the room with felt minimizes reflection which would furnish secondary cues. An open field makes a good laboratory for this experiment.

The experiment may follow the method of Average Error. O indicates the apparent direction of each stimulus, and the distribution of his errors is obtained. The method of Constant Stimuli can be used; two clicks are sounded in quick succession and O judges which is farther to the right, etc.

Results with the sound cage. This simple experiment gives certain very definite results (Matsumoto, 1897; Seashore, 1899; Pierce, 1901; Starch, 1908). Right and left are sharply distinguished in localization and practically never confused. The median plane is not confused with right or left, except for small errors. O can also judge with some accuracy how far the source of sound diverges from the median plane. Directions can be best discriminated adjacent to the median plane, front and rear, and least finely opposite the ears.

LEAST PERCEPTIBLE MOVEMENT OF A BUZZING SOUND IN THE HORIZONTAL PLANE, STARTING FROM VARIOUS POSITIONS
(Pierce, 1901)

Starting point	Least perceptible movement
0° (Front)	2.5°
45° Right or left	2.6°
90° " " "	8.7°
135° " " "	6.1°
180° (Rear)	3.3°

The right-left distinction is sharper for high tones and for noises and speech sounds than for medium tones, as is seen in the following data from Starch (1908), which show the least noticeable difference in direction from the standard directions: front, 45° right and 90° right (average of 4 Os).

	0° (Front)	45° Right	90° Right
Tone of 730 cycles	10.3°	28.5°	38.6°
Galton whistle, 10,000 cycles and up	3.8	8.9	35.9
Wooden hammer on wood	2.1	4.1	19.1
Puff of air	2.0	5.5	17.5
Voice saying "now"	1.5	2.3	8.5

Right-left discrimination is good, but up-down and front-back discriminations are poor. Sounds coming from above the level of the ears are not infrequently heard as coming from below and vice versa. Sounds from in front are often heard as if coming from behind. One is tempted to conclude that when secondary cues from familiar surroundings are excluded the only real spatial distinction made by the ears is that between right and left (including amount of rightness and leftness).

This conclusion would however be too negative. Though the up-down and front-back localizations are poor they are definitely better than chance.

For example, let O be seated upon a high stool and let a wire circle extend above and below in the *median plane* of the head with its center at the level of the ears and a radius of two feet. In one such experiment the subjects got 33 percent right where 25 percent would be chance. In a somewhat similar experiment the score was 33 percent correct as against 19 percent chance.

A cue of front and back may be furnished by the *pinna* or external ear which from its position must screen sounds coming from the rear more than those from the front. Only high frequencies would suffer any appreciable diminution from this cause. Pure tones of low and medium pitch cannot be distinguished as coming from in front or behind; but very high tones, and noises such as a click or a hiss which consist mostly of high-frequency vibrations, are fairly well localized in the front-back dimension (Stevens & Newman, 1936 a).

Localization with one ear. The excellence of right-left localization suggests that the possession of two ears is an important factor. Plugging one ear by inserting the finger firmly in the external auditory meatus does in fact impair localization very considerably. Individuals completely deaf in one ear give a history of poor localization immediately after their loss, followed by some improvement. When tested in a sound cage such Os are found superior in localization to normals with ears tem-

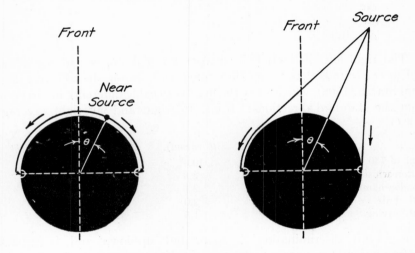

Fig. 142. Binaural distance difference in case of a source of sound close to the head, and in case of a sound a short distance from the head.

porarily plugged, but quite inferior to normals with binaural hearing. They are liable to left-right confusion which practically never occurs in binaural hearing (Starch, 1908; Angell & Fite, 1901).

Judgment of distance of source of sound. When blindfolded Os hear the same sound from different points in the horizontal circle, it seems nearest and loudest if directly in line with the ear. Intensity is apparently the factor determining the judgment of distance (Starch, 1905). Besides the intensity cue of distance, there is some evidence for a pitch cue and a quality cue: high tones and rich tones (abounding in overtones) are judged to come from near at hand.

Possible auditory cues of distance and direction. The sound cage experiment has given us facts to be explained: good right-left localization of sound, relatively poor front-back localization, little distinction between up and down. Explanation must consist in identifying the stimulus cues of distance and direction, and discovering the process of utilizing these cues. At present more is known regarding the cues than regarding the perceptual process.

From the facts already cited it is clear that the main cues of direction are connected with the possession of two ears. The ears must differ in some way. In many individuals they differ in sensitivity and even in the pitch heard from a given vibration frequency, but there is no evidence that these irregular differences are of much importance in localization. The main difference between the ears is that *they are not in the same place.* There is a binaural parallax analogous to binocular parallax though not playing exactly the same role. What difference in stimulation can result from the mere spatial separation of the two entrances for sound? Geometry and physics show that there are several differences, and it then becomes the task of the experimenter to ascertain which of these differences serve as cues.

The geometry of the matter is fairly simple. When the source of sound lies in the median plane of the head, extended into space, the path from the source to one ear is the same in length and curvature as that to the other ear, and the stimuli reaching the two ears are therefore identical (aside from echoes, etc.). But from any source lying outside the median plane the paths to the two ears differ in length and curvature, and the stimuli reaching the two ears necessarily differ. From the path difference there result a binaural time difference, phase difference, intensity difference and quality difference (or wave composition difference). Figs. 142, 143.

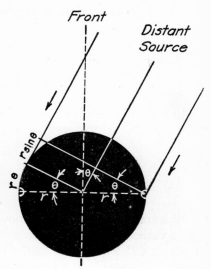

Fig. 143. Binaural distance difference in case of a source distant enough so that the waves to the two ears move in almost parallel lines. The construction lines show the geometry of the formula,

$$D_s = r(\theta + \sin \theta)$$

Let the source be close to one ear: the sound waves travel about 11 inches (27.5 cm) around the head to reach the other ear. This is obviously the maximum distance difference, for if the source is not close to the head, the waves will travel in straight lines tangent to the surface of the head and then around the head for the remaining distance. If the source lies in the aural axis straight out from one ear, at a distance of a meter or more, the distance difference is about 22–23 cm, and this is the maximum for a distant source. Except for sources lying close to the head, the distance difference is practically independent of the absolute distance of the source and depends almost wholly on its direction.

The distance difference for any direction of sound can be ascertained by use of a tape measure, or computed approximately from a formula derived on the assumptions that the head is a perfect sphere and that the source lies in the horizontal plane through the ears. The radius of our spherical head will be on the average about 8.75 cm. The direction of the source is defined by its angle from straight in front, and this "direction angle" is designated by the letter θ. If we denote the binaural distance difference by the symbol D_s, the following formulas enable us to compute the distance difference for any direction:

(1) for a source close to the head,

$$D_s = 8.75 \times 2\theta$$

(2) for a distant source,

$$D_s = 8.75\,(\theta + \sin\,\theta)$$

In this computation, the angle θ must be expressed in radians:

$$180° = \pi \text{ radians} = 3.1416$$

$$90° = \frac{\pi}{2} \text{ radians} = 1.5708$$

$$30° = \frac{\pi}{6} \text{ radians} = .5236$$

Binaural time difference. Sound travels through the air at a speed which varies slightly with the temperature, but is 1,130 feet per second at about 68° Fahrenheit (20° Centigrade). This is the same as 344 meters per second, or 34.4 centimeters per millisecond. For each cm of distance difference between the ears there is a time difference of $1/34.4$ = .029 ms. By the use of this equivalent, we can reduce the distance difference, D_s, to a time difference, D_t, expressed in milliseconds. Substituting in the previous formulas we have:

(1) for a source close to the head,

$$D_t = .254 \times 2\,\theta$$

(2) for a distant source,

$$D_t = .254\,(\theta + \sin\,\theta)$$

These formulas give the maximum and minimum values of the time difference for any direction, as tabulated on p. 523.

There is no time difference between up and down nor between front and back but there is this definite difference between right and left. The question is whether so small a time difference can count in the localization of sound. Near the median plane where discrimination of 3° in difference of direction is possible (p. 519) we should have to suppose that a difference of .03 ms at the ears is a sufficient cue of direction.

BINAURAL TIME DIFFERENCE ACCORDING TO DIRECTION (AND DISTANCE) OF SOURCE OF SOUND

Direction angle	Time difference in milliseconds	
	Source close to head	Source distant
0°	0	0
1°	.009	.009
2°	.018	.018
3°	.027	.027
4°	.036	.036
5°	.044	.044
10°	.089	.088
15°	.133	.132
20°	.178	.176
25°	.222	.218
30°	.266	.260
35°	.311	.301
40°	.355	.341
45°	.400	.379
50°	.444	.416
55°	.488	.452
60°	.533	.486
65°	.577	.518
70°	.622	.549
75°	.666	.578
80°	.710	.605
85°	.755	.630
90°	.799	.653

When the source lies behind the aural axis, reckon its direction angle from the rear; so for $\theta = 100°$, use $180° - 100° = 80°$. See also Fig. 144.

Binaural phase difference. At first thought the time difference cue is lacking in case of a continuous smooth tone which, aside from its beginning and end, acts on both ears simultaneously. Each *wave* from the source will however reach the nearer ear first, and the time difference which we have computed holds good for the arrival of every successive wave. Suppose a distant source to be at an angle of 45° on the right; then according to our table each wave reaches the right ear .379 ms before it reaches the left. Throughout the continuance of the tone there is this constant time difference between corresponding phases at the two ears.

This same fact can be stated as a phase difference. At any given instant the wave entering the two ears is in different phases. The phase difference is measured not in units of time but in fractions of a wave length (or cycle). In a given case, the phase at one ear may be ¼ of a cycle different from that at the other ear. Just when the crest of the wave is reaching the nearer ear, the middle of the rising phase is reaching the other, and when the first ear is in the trough the second is in the falling phase. The phases are always changing at each ear, but the amount of difference, considered purely as a fraction of the cycle, remains constant during the continuation of a tone, provided the tone remains at a constant pitch and the source remains at the same place with respect to the head.

Phase difference, just by itself and without regard to the time difference involved, would make a poor cue of direction, since it depends not only on direction but even more on the wave length (or frequency) of the tone. A phase difference of 1/20 of a cycle would indicate the following directions:

Frequency	Direction angle
62.5	90°
125	45°
250	22.5°
500	11.25°
1000	5.6°
2000	2.8°
4000	1.4°
8000	.7°
16,000	.35°

Similarly for any other specified phase difference. As a cue of direction, phase difference would always have to be corrected for the pitch of the

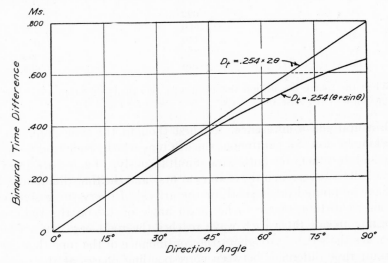

Fig. 144. Binaural time difference as dependent on the direction (and distance) of the source. The oblique straight line shows the maximum time difference for each direction—the source being close to the head—while the curved line shows the minimum, with distant source. If we read this graph along vertical lines, it shows the physics of time difference; for example when the source lies at an angle of 60°, the time difference may be anything between .48 and .53 ms, according to the distance of the source. If we read along horizontal lines we see in what direction a sound will be localized if O follows time difference strictly; thus when the time difference is .500 ms, the direction angle is anything between 57° and 62°, according to the impression of distance which O receives. Experimental results compared with this graph (or with the table above) will show how closely O follows the time difference in his localization of sounds (see p. 531).

tone, and the system of cues would become incredibly complex. Besides, it is difficult to conceive how the auditory mechanism could possibly respond to a phase difference as such. In spite of these improbabilities, it is a matter of history that phase difference was seriously put forward as the main cue in sound localization, the more obvious time difference being overlooked or regarded as too small to have any effect on perception.

Binaural intensity ratio. It may seem that we have been hunting for out-of-the-way cues when a very good one lay right at hand. Must not the stimulus be more intense at the nearer ear, and must not the sound waves lose energy in bending around the head? When we look into the physics of sound transmission through the air, we find that the mere difference in distance of the ears from the source has only a small effect on the intensities, except when the source is close at hand. As to bending around the head, long waves do this with little loss; but the shorter the waves (the higher the frequency) the deeper the "sound shadow" cast by the head, and the more the stimuli delivered to the two ears differ in intensity. With a source 15° out of the median plane, the intensity ratio is as follows, according to threshold determinations by Sivian & White (1933):

for a tone of   300 cycles, intensity ratio <   1 db (1.26)
"   "   "   "   1100   "   "   =   4 db (2.51)
"   "   "   "   4200   "   "   =   5 db (3.16)
"   "   "   " 10,000   "   "   =   6 db (3.98)
"   "   "   " 15,000   "   "   = 10 db (10 to 1)

These ratios are well above the difference threshold at the high frequencies, but are very small for 300 cycles (and under). The intensity ratio is a promising cue at high frequencies only.

Binaural timbre difference. Since the sound shadow of the head affects high frequencies mostly, the upper partials of a complex tone are weak at the far ear, which will hear a comparatively dull (or mellow tone. The pinna acts similarly to weaken the upper partials of a tone coming from the rear.

Experimental testing of various binaural cues. In ordinary hearing the several binaural differences operate together. A sound from the right reaches the right ear with greater intensity, reaches it quicker, and is a richer sound, less robbed of its upper partials than on reaching the left ear. With all cues working together we cannot tell which one is effective in localizing the sound. The experimentalist seeks to control these various factors separately so as to present a time difference with equal intensities at the two ears, or an intensity difference with no time difference.

It should be noted that the experimenter thus produces a *conflict of cues*. If he applies equal intensity to the two ears along with a time difference, the intensity cue indicates a source in the median plane while the time difference locates it on the side of the earlier reception of the sound. Which of the conflicting cues will the listener follow in his localization?

Nomenclature. The word *monaural* is sanctioned by long usage and is perfectly clear in meaning. *Uniaural* is an equivalent term preferred by those who hate to see a Greek prefix combined with a Latin root. *Binaural* is pure Latin. If we stick to the Greek we have *monotic* and *diotic* and we can add *dichotic* (from the Greek root for ear with the prefix *dicho* or *dich* meaning apart, asunder, separately). This word *dichotic* conveys in a nutshell the nature of a whole class of experiments intended to sort out the different cues of direction. The ears are stimulated separately through tubes or telephones. We will use *monotic* to indicate the stimulation of one ear alone, *diotic* for stimulation of both ears in the normal way through the air, and *dichotic* for separate stimulation of the two ears by controlled paths. The dichotic stimuli may at times be identical, while diotic stimuli are nonidentical except when the source (in the open air) lies in the median plane.

We note here that the word *sound* is used with four different meanings: (1) sound is a sensation having the characteristics of pitch, loudness, timbre, vowel quality, volume, brightness, density; (2) sound is a physical wave motion having the characteristics of frequency, amplitude and composition; (3) a "distant sound" refers to the source; (4) in the dichotic experiment the listener hears a "phantom sound" or "sound image." If, for example, the binaural time difference is changed continuously the sound seems to move about in space, but the listener is well aware that there is no object moving around in space. The sound image has somewhat the same reality to him that the image in a mirror has to the adult who is used to mirrors.

Apparatus for dichotic stimulation. This takes two general forms, telephone and speaking tube. Time difference, phase difference, intensity difference and composition difference can be manipulated separately in the leads to the two ears.

An early form of the tube apparatus was that of Bowlker (1908). Having been present in a boat collision off the coast of Maine, Bowlker was curious to know how the direction of a fog horn could possibly be perceived. Suspecting that binaural time difference or phase difference was a factor, he made some experiments in an open field, holding to his ears tubes of sheet aluminum, two inches in diameter and adjustable in length by telescoping. The sound was produced by an organ pipe at a distance of 30 feet. O, facing directly toward the source, got a binaural time difference dependent upon the difference in length of the ear tubes.

The tube apparatus used in dichotic experiments usually resembles a binaural stethoscope. Tubes inserted in the ears, or held very close to them, unite into a single tube which is brought close to the source of sound; or the two ear tubes may be brought together at the source of sound. A time or phase difference is got by introducing into one of the tubes a telescoping part by which the path to one ear is made longer than that to the other. With well-made tubes the intensities at the two ears are the same, but an intensity difference can be introduced by pinching one of the tubes. Several variations of the stethoscope type of binaural apparatus have been used (Wilson & Myers, 1908; Stewart & Hovda, 1918; Halverson, 1927; Shaxby & Gage, 1932). Account should be taken of the fact that the velocity of sound in a narrow tube is somewhat less than in open air.

Another setup uses ear phones, each receiver having its own circuit with amplifiers or attenuators to control intensity and with adjustable condensers to control time and phase. The source for both ears is an oscillator by which the frequency is controlled. The frequency is always the same for both ears. The composition of the sound wave, its overtone structure, can be controlled to some extent by sound filters and other means, though a perfectly pure tone is scarcely obtained from telephone membranes. Clicks at any desired time difference can be produced in the ear phones by an adjustable contact apparatus which interrupts the circuits through the two receivers. (Some descriptions of apparatus: Klemm, 1920; Stewart, 1920; Wittmann, 1925; Banister, 1926 a, b; Shaxby & Gage, 1932; James & Massey, 1932.)

Fusion and separation of dichotically presented tones. Simultaneous tones led to the two ears are heard as a single tone, if they are identical in frequency and composition, i.e., in pitch and timbre. Two pure tones must differ by as much as 6–16 cycles in order to be held apart and assigned each to the stimulated ear. Two complex tones of different timbre are easily held apart; for example, the tone of a blown bottle led to one ear and that of a reed led to the other, simultaneously, are correctly localized on the two sides. More than two simultaneous tones, if very different in pitch, can be correctly assigned to their respective ears by well trained Os. In ordinary life we constantly receive sounds from both sides, with little resulting confusion (Baley, 1914–15 a).

Time difference and intensity difference examined by use of brief sounds. The sound cage experiment proved that a sudden sound or *click* is well localized in the open air. In a dichotic experiment, each ear is provided with a receiver in which a click is produced by breaking the circuit. The intensity of the click is varied by resistances in the circuit. The time difference is controlled by a contact apparatus consisting of a wheel or a pendulum, which operates two keys at any required interval. The telephone receivers must be carefully selected in order to secure clicks of the same quality which will fuse when simultaneously presented to the two ears. When Klemm (1919, 1920) began experimenting with dichotic clicks, he assumed naturally enough that a time difference of a few ms would be as small as could be utilized in perception, but he found that while absolutely simultaneous clicks were localized in the median plane, a time difference as small as 1 ms gave a definite localization to one side; a single (fused) click was heard to come from a certain angle at one side of the median plane. With an improved contact apparatus

Klemm delivered clicks at still smaller intervals, and was surprised to find that a binaural time difference of only a few *hundredths* of a ms was sufficient to give a definite lateral localization of the click. He suspected some experimental error, but the apparatus proved to be physically accurate and the psychological data while showing individual differences were reasonably consistent.

The dichotic click experiment has been performed with some modification of apparatus by several experimenters who have found the minimal effective binaural time difference to vary with individuals between .03 and .3 ms. If in a series of trials the time difference is increased from zero by small steps, O's report passes through the following stages: with a time difference of less than .03 ms, O reports a single sound located in the median plane; as the time difference increases, he reports that the sound is deviating from the median plane by a larger and larger amount; at about .65 ms the location is close to the ear where it stays as the time difference further increases up to 2.5 or more ms, when the single click breaks up into two, one heard on each side (von Hornbostel & Wertheimer, 1920; Wittmann, 1925; Banister, 1926 b; Trimble, 1928).

While Os agree in locating the single click heard with zero time difference somewhere in the median plane, they differ as to the exact place. Some locate it outside the head but often it seems to come from the middle of the head. (The experience of hearing a sound inside the head can be obtained by humming while holding both ears closed.)

Von Hornbostel & Wertheimer (1920) came out definitely in favor of binaural time difference as the essential cue in localization. They believed the intensity difference to be unimportant. When they kept the time difference constant in a series of experiments but varied the intensity difference, localization conformed to the time difference. To be more concrete, let us assume that they give the first click to the right ear and maintain a constant difference of 1/10 of a ms. At first the intensity difference is zero, and the localization is on the right in accordance with the time difference. They progressively *weaken* the stimulus at the right ear, but still the sound is localized on that side until the click at the right ear has become very weak, when the sound image suddenly jumps into the other ear. This experiment shows that a small time difference can prevail over a large opposing intensity difference, but before discarding the intensity cue altogether we should try the reverse experiment.

Klemm (1920) started an experiment with a time difference of zero and an intensity difference (or ratio) of 3 to 1. The sound image was localized on the side of the greater intensity. A time difference was now introduced such that the ear which received the lower intensity received it first. The time difference necessary to compensate for the intensity difference was about .6 ms. A time difference larger than this prevailed over the intensity difference and the sound was heard on the side of the weaker intensity.

Wittmann (1925) also found that when the time difference was zero the click was localized on the side of the greater intensity, and that when the intensity difference was zero the click was localized on the side of the first stimulus. He found that a time difference could be balanced against an intensity difference and vice versa. He reached the conclusion that both time difference and intensity difference are factors in the localization of dichotic sounds.

A given time difference has the same effect in the dichotic experiment as it does in the open air. This is the most important finding from the dichotic click experiment. In the sound cage (which is essentially open air) O can just about distinguish a median position of the source of sound from a position 3° to the right or left. Our table on page 523 shows that the corresponding time difference is .027 ms, and the dichotic experiment shows that this time difference is about the least which will give a localization out of the median plane. A binaural difference of .65 ms in the open air means that the source is directly opposite one ear, and this is where the dichotically presented click is localized when the time difference is this amount. Further quantitative evidence will be reported in connection with dichotically presented tones.

Localization of continuous tones—the "centering" experiment. Once the apparatus is at hand for delivering a tone separately to the two ears, and for controlling frequency, intensity and phase, interesting qualitative results are readily obtained. If the phase difference is zero, so that each wave reaches the two ears simultaneously, the tone seems to come from the side which is receiving the greater intensity. If the intensity difference is zero, the tone is localized toward the side of the ear which receives each successive wave earlier. For quantitative results, O is instructed not simply to say "right" or "left" but to estimate the angle from which the sound seems to come. Or—and this is a more accurate method—the observer has the control of intensity or of phase, which he adjusts until the sound seems to come from the median plane (usually from in front). He *centers the sound.* Centering is used in "sound locators," which assist binaural hearing in determining the direction of an airplane or submarine (House, 1935). We cite first an experiment by the centering method.

Shaxby & Gage (1932) used oscillator tones and had in the circuit a "phase balance" by means of which the phase at one ear could be advanced or retarded. An intensity difference of 2–18 db was introduced which threw the sound image off center, and O by adjusting the phase brought the sound back to center. The larger the intensity difference the greater must be the compensating phase difference (time difference). The result of prime importance was that the time difference required to compensate for a given intensity difference was practically the same at the three frequencies tried, 500, 800 and 1200 cycles per second; whereas the necessary phase difference varied with the frequency of the tone.

For example, to balance an intensity difference of 6 db, the following adjustments were necessary, expressed in phase and time differences:

	Frequency 500	800	1200
Phase difference as fraction of complete cycle	.005	.009	.012
Time difference in ms	.010	.011	.010

And to balance an intensity difference of 14 db, the following were found necessary:

	Frequency 500	800	1200
Phase difference	.011	.019	.025
Time difference	.023	.024	.021

In general, and in spite of some inevitable variability in the settings, the following equation fits the data:

$$1 \text{ db} = .0017 \text{ ms,}$$

i.e., it takes .0017 ms of time difference to offset each decibel of intensity difference, within the rather narrow frequency range employed. That range was however sufficient to provide an answer to the question at issue, by showing that *what counts as a localization factor is not phase difference as such but binaural time difference.*

Estimating the direction of a dichotic tone. Instead of centering the sound, O here has the more difficult task of estimating the direction angle. In one procedure the phase difference is changed gradually and O observes the apparent movement of the sound image or phantom. The phenomena are very striking (Bowlker, 1908; Wilson & Myers, 1908; Hartley, 1919; Halverson, 1922 a, 1922 b). Let a pure tone of 300 cycles be presented by tubes or telephones, with intensity equal and phase the same at both ears: the sound is heard from the median plane, usually straight in front. Now introduce a phase difference, letting the right ear receive the successive waves a little before the left: the sound image moves to the right, and with increasing phase difference it moves around to the right ear. When the phase difference becomes ½ cycle two sounds may be heard, one at each ear; and as soon as the phase difference exceeds ½ cycle the image is on the left and moves toward the front, coming back to the median plane when the phase difference reaches a complete cycle. (In a continuous series of waves, a phase difference of one cycle is obviously equivalent to zero phase difference. Binaural phase difference cannot exceed ½ cycle. When it is precisely that, neither ear is ahead. Imagine two runners on a circular track—when they are just half a lap apart it is impossible to tell from the look of things which one is ahead.)

With change of phase, then, the sound image moves almost in a circle, but not around the head. It moves from in front to one ear, jumps across to the other ear and thence moves forward.

Such are the phenomena when the tone has a frequency of about 300 cycles. Our description would be incomplete and misleading if we left the matter there.

At frequencies much below 300 the sound image reaches the "nearer" ear long before the phase difference reaches ½ cycle and hovers there till that difference is reached; then it shifts to the other ear and proceeds forward. If, on the contrary, the frequency is much above 300 cycles, the image never reaches the ear, but shifts from right to left when its direction angle is only 60°, 30°, 10° or even less, depending on the frequency; the higher the frequency the less

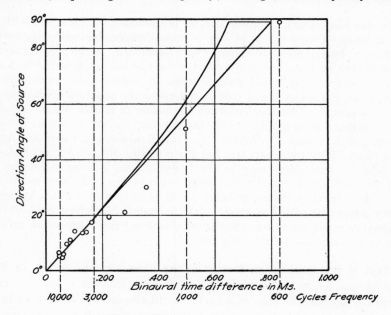

FIG. 145. Results of Halverson (1927) plotted so as to show their agreement with the hypothesis that phase difference operates merely as time difference. The oblique straight line and curve are taken from Fig. 144, with abscissa and ordinate interchanged, so that, read in the usual way, the figure answers the question: Given a certain time difference, X, from what direction, Y, *should* the sound seem to come? The data points show the direction from which a tone *did* seem to come when the phase difference was at or near its maximum, i.e., half a cycle. If phase difference were the controlling factor, the tone would have the same apparent direction angle without regard to frequency, since the phase difference was constant. All the data points would lie in a horizontal line. But the time difference produced by a phase difference of one-half cycle increases as the frequency decreases, so that a subjective localization strictly conforming to the time difference would give data points lying in the oblique strip. It is true that the larger time differences, from .200 ms up, give a smaller direction angle than expected. This underestimation of the larger side-angles is interesting, but does not obscure the main fact, that the location of tones closely follows the time difference.

movement toward the ear before crossing over. These results, quite confusing in terms of phase difference, become clear when stated in terms of time difference. Half a cycle occupies less and less time as the frequency increases. It is the time difference that determines the apparent direction angle of a dichotic sound.

Careful study of O's estimates of direction angle shows them to conform very well with what is demanded for the time difference cue (von Hornbostel

& Wertheimer, 1920; Stewart, 1922; Wittmann, 1925). O's estimates become rather vague when the sound image deviates far from the median plane. In Halverson's experiment (Fig. 145) the tone was led to the ear by tubes. A T-piece received the sound at the source and one of the branches contained a telescoping section by which a phase difference was produced. O's task was to estimate the direction angle at which the sound image shifted from right to left.

Double localization. Another curious phenomenon which agrees with the time difference theory is that of double sound images obtained under certain conditions. One condition has already been mentioned. When phase priority is about to shift from one ear to the other, the sound is often heard at both ears simultaneously. This is not strange when we consider that both ears are actually being stimulated and that at this particular juncture neither ear has a time advantage. Another condition conducive to double images is strong conflict between the intensity cue and the time cue, the time difference favoring one ear and the intensity difference the other (Banister, 1923; 1926 a). Again, if the phase difference equals zero but the intensity difference strongly favors the right ear, two sounds may be heard, one straight in front and one at the right ear (Halverson, 1922 b); the image heard in front conforms to the zero time difference while the image heard at the right conforms to the strong intensity advantage of the right ear. The stimulation received is in fact approximately what would come in the open air from two sources, one straight in front and one opposite the right ear.

Test of the localization factors in the open air. From the dichotic experiments we have learned that both time difference and intensity difference are used as cues of direction. In the case of sudden or intermittent noises, either time or intensity would furnish a good basis for localization. In the case of complex tones, the timbre difference due to the screening out of the higher components by the sound shadow of the head would furnish a good basis, which however has not been much tested experimentally. In the case of pure tones we have to make a distinction between low and high. Low tones bend around the head so that the intensity difference at the ears is slight. At frequencies above 3000 the intensity difference becomes large and probably effective. The time difference provides a thoroughly adequate basis for localization of tones up to about 600, above which it shrinks because of the decreasing wave length. According to Stewart (1922) phase (time) difference becomes almost entirely ineffective at an average of 1260 cycles, varying with individuals.

These laboratory findings led Stevens & Newman (1934, 1936 a) to suspect that the localization of pure tones in the open air would be good at low frequencies, poor at medium, and possibly good again at very high frequencies where the intensity factor would operate powerfully. To test this expectation, they seated the subject on a high stool on top of a building where there was no reflection from side walls. They fastened a loud speaker on the end of a 12-ft. arm which could be moved noiselessly to any angle around the blindfolded subject. They produced tones in the loud speaker by an oscillator adjustable to any frequency from 60 to 10,000 cycles. The tones were not absolutely pure, but they were strained through filters and came out with only weak overtones. The tones were sounded from the front, rear and intermediate positions. O's task was to designate the position of the tone after each stimulus.

The results came out according to prediction. The average error of direction was small at the low frequencies, increased to a maximum at

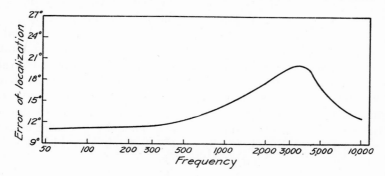

Fig. 146. (Stevens & Newman, 1936 a.) Open-air localization of (nearly) pure tones. The abscissa gives a logarithmic scale of frequencies, and the ordinate shows the average error in degrees of the judgments of direction by two Os.

3000 cycles and diminished until at 10,000 cycles localization was as accurate as at 1000. As far as pure tones are concerned, the open air and the dichotic experiments agree in pointing to time difference as the potent factor in localization of low tones and to intensity difference as the important factor at high frequencies.

A bit of theory. We are not to suppose that the subject *notices* time or intensity differences and *infers* from them the location of sound. The small fractions of a ms which are found to be effective direction cues are imperceptible as time intervals. In order to approach any theory of sound localization, we must think in physiological terms. We can imagine a neural mechanism controlling the movements which turn the head and eyes toward the source of sound. It must be a unitary mechanism capable of turning the head in either direction and responsive to nerve currents from both ears. When the currents arrive from one ear only, the neural mechanism turns the head toward that side. When the currents arrive from both ears, but more from one ear, that side has the advantage. When the current from one ear arrives at the central mechanism ahead of the other and gets in its work first, it has the advantage. Refractory period comes into play and the prior ear maintains the advantage, throughout the duration of a tone.

The supposed mechanism, however, does not operate purely on an all-or-none or a right-left basis. It must be capable of turning the head more or less according to the amount of the time or intensity difference. And it must be such that other factors besides the auditory stimuli can play on it. It must be adjustable to the surroundings, since under ordinary conditions one's knowledge of the situation plays a role in the localization of sounds.

ELECTRICAL INDICATORS OF AUDITORY FUNCTION

The various phenomena of hearing offer a fascinating puzzle for the physiologist as well as for the psychologist. The older physiologists such as Helmholtz had little direct indication of the operation of the cochlea and were forced to base their theories on the anatomy of that organ along with the correlation between the physical stimulus and the psychological response. The action currents of the cochlea and auditory nerve, when made observable by amplification, provide direct indicators of the physiological processes in hearing, as was first demonstrated by Wever & Bray (1930 a, 1930 b). Under anesthesia they exposed a cat's auditory nerve between its exit from the internal ear and its entrance into the medulla. Around the nerve they hooked a fine wire as active electrode while the broad, "indifferent" electrode was placed on the head at some distance from the ear. The electric potentials picked up by these electrodes were led through a shielded cable into a sound proof room, amplified and conducted to a telephone receiver. The experimenter's ear applied to the telephone made a very delicate detector of action currents or other electrical potentials present in the nerve. An oscillograph or other recording instrument can be substituted for the telephone. These experimenters were indeed surprised by the result obtained. When any tone was applied in the normal way to the ear of the animal, the experimenter in the sound proof room, listening at the telephone, heard that same tone. Not only low tones were thus reproduced, but also tones with a frequency of 5000 cycles or more. Words spoken into the cat's ear could be distinctly understood and the quality of the speaker's voice recognized by the experimenter at the telephone. This experiment did two things: as a method it opened the door to a new type of study of the auditory receptors and nerve connections, while the results showed that the frequencies of the sound stimulus were faithfully conveyed into the brain by the auditory nerve.

Cochlear currents. This challenging experiment was immediately subjected to close scrutiny by Adrian (1931), Kreezer (1931), Davis (1933) and others, for there was a good chance of error creeping in with the high amplification employed. It was soon conceded that the Wever and Bray effect was no artifact. These first investigators, however, had observed that the effect could be obtained not only from the auditory nerve but also from any tissue in the immediate neighborhood of the cochlea. Later it was found that the round window between the inner and middle ears was a very favorable place for obtaining the effect. So the currents picked up from the auditory nerve need not be action currents of the nerve itself, but may originate in the cochlea. Each sound wave as it passes through the basilar membrane and the organ of Corti presumably stretches the hair cells and generates an electrical wave which spreads throughout the adjacent tissues. This "cochlear effect" ceases with the death of the animal, though not immediately; it depends upon the hair cells being in fair condition. It is an index of the initial response of the cochlea to the incoming sound wave.

Auditory nerve action currents. To avoid the spread of the cochlear effect to the auditory nerve, Saul & Davis (1932) used comparatively weak auditory stimuli to the ear and so minimized the cochlear effect. They led off from the auditory nerve through very high amplification and found true action currents present. While the latency of the cochlear effect is only about .1 ms, much shorter than the latency of any known vital response, the time elapsing from the arrival of a sound wave at the inner ear to the appearance of the action current in the nerve, is nearer to 1 ms. Action currents, of longer latency, can be picked up even inside the medulla, provided the receiving electrode is placed squarely on the auditory pathway which passes up to the midbrain and interbrain.

Much theoretical interest attaches to the question, how rapid a series of action currents can be transmitted along the auditory nerve? If the auditory mechanism operates on the principle of transmitting faithfully to the center each wave received by the ear, it must transmit up to 20,000 vibrations per sec. and have a recovery period of only 1/20,000 of a sec., quite beyond all analogy with other mammalian nerves.

With his technique for isolating auditory action currents, H. Davis (1934) found the frequency of these currents to keep step with the impressed sound up to at least 700 vibrations. Beyond that the gross frequency did indeed follow sound to 3000 vibrations, but when the intensity of the action currents was observed by aid of an oscillograph, the record showed a sudden drop in intensity at about 800 cycles of the stimulus, a further drop at about 1600, and a final cessation of the synchronous action currents at 3000 or somewhat less. To get the full significance of these findings, we need to dip for a moment into the general theories of hearing.

Auditory theories: the resonance, frequency, and volley theories. Helmholtz suggested that different portions of the basilar membrane were tuned to different frequencies. At the base of the cochlea where the membrane is narrowest, it presumably resounds to the high frequencies; at the apex where it is widest and also most loaded, it would resound to the low frequencies. According to this theory, the impulses sent up from the cochlea along the auditory nerve might or might not preserve the frequency of the sound waves, but in any case the pitch of the heard sound would depend simply on the part of the organ of Corti aroused through resonance.

The frequency theory supposes the basilar membrane to vibrate as a whole and to give rise to nerve impulses which preserve the frequency of the stimulus, so that the auditory brain center receives nerve currents faithfully reproducing the frequency of the external sound. The analysis of a chord or clang into its partial notes, an analysis which Helmholtz attributed to the resonance mechanism of the cochlea, is by the frequency theory relegated entirely to the brain.

An improbable assumption apparently demanded by the frequency theory was that the auditory nerve could transmit impulses up to 20,000 per sec. (the upper limit of hearing). To escape this difficulty it was suggested (Troland, 1929; Fletcher, 1929; Wever & Bray, 1930 c) that the single nerve fiber need not respond to every successive wave of the stimulus. Each fiber may respond only to every second, third or fourth wave. The fibers may fire, not all at once, in a "company volley," but by squads, each wave of the stimulus causing one squad to fire its volley. The auditory nerve as a whole will carry within it a volley for each wave and will transmit the stimulus frequency faithfully to the brain center. According to the results cited from Davis, the whole company of active fibers fires together up to a frequency of about 800 per second; beyond that the company is divided into two squads, firing alternately; at a frequency of 1600 or thereabouts three squads are formed; while above 3000 the squads break up and the firing becomes indiscriminate. The formation of squads is supposed to result automatically from the differing sensitivities and recovery periods of the individual receptors and nerve fibers.

The volley theory has a strong case, but it should be noted that there is no real incompatibility between these two conceptions: (a) that by aid of squad formation the auditory nerve conveys to the brain center the stimulus frequencies, up to 3000; and (b) that different regions of the organ of Corti respond to different frequencies of the stimulus. The whole "company" of receptors aroused by a given tone may be confined to a limited portion of the basilar membrane, the particular portion depending on the frequency of the sound vibration.

In commenting further upon these theories, let us ask ourselves what correlates we can find in the auditory mechanism for loudness, pitch, volume and localization. Consider the totality of nerve impulses reaching the brain center, and ask in what ways this totality can vary. With what variables can we work in constructing a theory? Four variables are admissible: the number of volleys per second, the whole number of fiber impulses per second, the part of the receptor assemblage that is most excited through resonance, and the extent of the excited portion.

As a correlate for loudness of sensation, one thinks first of still another variable, the intensity of the single nerve impulses; but this variable is ruled out by the all-or-none law. Loudness must depend on the total number of fiber impulses reaching the brain center per second from both auditory nerves.

As a correlate for pitch, we might look with favor on the number of volleys per second, since this number corresponds directly with the wave frequency up to nearly 3000 cycles. However, pitch discrimination runs much higher, and we are forced back to the resonance theory. We suppose that the part of the basilar membrane thrown into vibration by the stimulus depends on vibration frequency, and that the pitch of the heard tone depends on the part of the receptor assemblage thus activated. A tone is high because it is mediated by certain particular receptors and their connecting nerve fibers, low because mediated by certain other receptors and fibers.

The activated portion of the receptor assemblage will not only have a certain mean location on the basilar membrane, analogous to the mean of a distribution, but it will have a larger or smaller spread along the membrane. The spread is probably greater for intense than for weak stimuli, and greater for low than for high frequencies. Thus spread makes an adequate correlate for auditory volume.

So far, our theory makes no use of "volleys by squads" nor of the remarkable ability of the single auditory nerve fibers to transmit up to

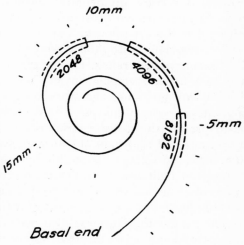

FIG. 147. (Crowe, Guild & Polvogt, 1934.) Diagram of the 2½ turns of the cochlea, showing the approximate location of the receptors concerned in hearing certain high tones. If the basal end of the organ of Corti is atrophied for a distance of 10 mm, the octaves above 2048 cycles are not heard at all. When 4096 cycles can be heard the atrophy does not extend so far from the basal end.

800 impulses per sec. Now unless the impulses coming into the brain center from the two auditory nerves preserved the frequency of the stimulus, they could not preserve the binaural time difference of the waves in a continuous tone, and this essential cue of direction would be lost. The volleys fail above 3000 cycles, and the time difference cue also fails. The volleys may have nothing to do with pitch sensation, but they are necessary for the localization of tones.

Localized injury to the cochlea. If different regions of the basilar membrane are tuned to different vibration frequencies—or if the overlying receptors are responsive to different frequencies—an injury limited to a small part of the organ of Corti should make the subject deaf to tones of a certain frequency band, or at least raise his threshold for that band. Human cases are fairly common with loss of hearing for the high tones. Audiometer tests correlated with post-mortem examination "prove very definitely that the receptors for high tones are located in the basal turn of the cochlea" (Crowe, Guild & Polvogt, 1934).

In animals prolonged exposure to a tone of great intensity at a constant frequency does as a matter of fact impair hearing. On the resonance theory, one would expect to find a localized lesion with impaired hearing in a particular frequency range. For example, exposure to a very loud tone of 1000 vibrations would be expected to produce a lesion in the apical part of the organ of Corti and to impair hearing in the neighborhood of 1000 cycles. Results indicate however that the injury is more wide spread.

Instead of relying upon an intense tone to produce localized injury, it is possible to bore through the bone with a fine dental drill and destroy a portion of the organ of Corti. The exact location must be established by post-mortem examination. Up to the present the evidence obtained by this method supports the resonance theory. Work has not gone far enough to warrant any definite conclusion, since the results by different experimenters are not wholly in agreement. We will content ourselves with references to some of the recent investigations: Finch & Culler (1934), Rawdon Smith (1934), Davis et al. (1935), Wever et al. (1935).

Tensor tympani reflex. Inside the middle ear there is a small muscle attached to the tympanic membrane and called the tensor tympani. Alternative functions suggested for the tensor tympani muscle are: to tune the ear for a specific pitch by adjusting the tension of the membrane; or to protect the delicate structures of the inner ear by damping the membrane and the chain of ossicles. Köhler (1909) with the assistance of an otologist attached a small bit of mirror to his tympanic membrane. A beam of light was thrown into the meatus, the mirror reflected the beam back to a camera and the movements of the membrane were photographed. In response to sounds of different intensity, the membrane took up different positions, evidently caused by differing contraction of the tensor tympani. The response was bilateral, obtainable by isolated stimulation of the opposite ear. Since the reflex varied with the intensity of the stimulus but not with its frequency, Köhler concluded that the reflex had a protective function and not one of accommodation for pitch.

This conclusion has been confirmed by a very different type of experiment. The cochlear electrical effect, used as an indicator of inner ear activity, was measured both before and after anesthetizing the tensor tympani muscle in a guinea pig's ear. Under this anesthesia the cochlear response to low tones was increased, sometimes to the point of shaking bits of the organ of Corti loose from the basilar membrane. The effect of the tensor tympani, therefore, is to weaken intense tones of low frequency and protect the delicate structures of the inner ear. Aside from protection, it weakens the low component of a complex tone as against the high components which are so important in timbre, speech sounds, noises, and their localization (Stevens et al., 1935).

CHAPTER XXII

THE SENSE OF SIGHT

T HE psychology of vision is so vast and diversified a field that five chapters must be devoted to it, and some important topics will even then receive scant attention. We encounter here again the distinction between the sensation experiment and the perception experiment. The present chapter, dealing with the relations of visual experience and the stimulus of light, comes under the head of sensation. Eye movements then claim a chapter, after which the theme shifts to the perception of objective facts revealed by light.

Visual "phenomena." The first step in the whole inquiry might well be the same as in our chapter on the skin senses—to secure the free, unhampered report of the psychologically naive observer on the question, what he sees in the presence of typical fields of view. He would undoubtedly mention things and happenings. If we directed his attention to the visual appearance of things he would speak of colors and of light and shade. If we got him to go further and describe the colors, not in terms of any conventional color system, but simply in their *ways of appearing*, we should probably come out with a list of *phenomenal varieties of color* essentially similar to the list obtained by Katz (1911, 1930):

1. Expanse color, free color, film color (Katz's *Flächenfarbe*, literally two-dimensional color).
2. Surface color (*Oberflächenfarbe*).
3. Bulky or three-dimensional color (*Raumfarbe*).
4. Transparent color.
5. Lustrous color.
6. Luminous color.

The first three varieties, distinguished according to the spatial appearance of color, make an exhaustive list by themselves. A transparent color is also an expanse color (when obtained by holding a smoked or colored glass at arm's length and looking through it at some object), or a surface color (obtained in the same way but with smudges on the glass or other indications of a definite surface through which one is looking), or, finally, a bulky color (obtained by looking at objects through a fog or through a liquid that is not perfectly clear). Bulky color is necessarily transparent.

A lustrous color is seen on looking at silk or polished metal; one sees the proper surface color and also reflected light which appears free and not bound to the surface.

Luminous color may present either a surface or a bulky appearance and is seen on looking into a flame (bulky) or at a translucent surface lighted from behind.

Surface color is distinctly the color of some object. It appears to lie in the surface of an object. It may be flat or curved and extend in any direction, according to the shape and position of the object. It often shows grain or "microstructure," a more or less mottled appearance.

Free or expanse color lacks these object-bound characters. It appears less objective or thingy. Esthetically it is "soft" in comparison with the hardness of a surface color. Its spatial character is rather indefinite except for the inevitable spread-out-ness of all visual appearances, but it usually seems to extend at right angles to O's line of sight. The readiest way of experiencing expanse color is to close the eyes and observe the gray field of idioretinal light or the brighter field obtained by turning the face toward a source of light. A dense fog through which no objects are seen gives the effect of expanse color, as does the clear sky seen by looking upward in an open field. Small bits of expanse color can be seen by looking through a tube at any perfectly uniform surface, free from grain. The tube need not be held close to the eye. Roll a paper tube small enough so that only one uniform color is visible through the tube. The surface character disappears and a mere color expanse is seen blocking the far end of the tube. The tube shows an expanse of color isolated from its objective surroundings and therefore lacking the surface or bulky character of the color of a visible object. (A hole in a card will do as well as the tube. This little instrument, very useful in experiments on object color, is called the hole screen or reduction screen, p. 607.)

Dimensions of visual sensation. Expanse color, free from suggestion of objects, is the best phenomenal variety to use in a study of sensation. Surface colors can sometimes be used, if all the surfaces are similar in texture and stand in the same illumination, so that the object character is a constant which O can easily disregard in comparing the colors. Place before O a large assortment of colored papers, or silks, or worsteds, and ask him to reduce this manifold to order, without any reference to the physics of light. He probably starts by grouping the colors into classes—reds, pinks, browns, yellows, greens, blues. Taking any one class he can arrange its colors into a series running from light to dark. There is certainly a light-dark dimension of visual sensation. We may name it the *brilliance* dimension.

In a sufficiently large assortment of colors, O will be able to segregate a bunch of greens, for example, all approximately alike in brilliance and yet differing in some other respect since some are vivid while others are dull or pale. A series of greens can be arranged according to the vividness or fullness of their green. A pale green or a dull green has very little green in it, being mostly white or gray. We find here a dimension of *saturation*, extending from the full, vivid color to the pale or dull, almost colorless specimen which borders on white or neutral gray.

We now ask O to pick from each class of colors a good representative of strong saturation, and to arrange this collection of saturated colors in some order. With a little patience he will obtain a circular series, extending, say, from red through orange, yellow, green, blue and purple back to red. This is a strictly qualitative series, whereas brilliance and

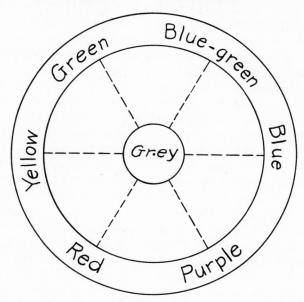

Fig. 148. Outline of the color circle. Complementaries are placed at opposite ends of diameters.

saturation are matters of degree. This important qualitative dimension of the color manifold—a dimension seen in the spectrum or rainbow as well as in our color circle—we call the dimension of *hue*.

The next question is whether the three dimensions of hue, brilliance and saturation are enough to make possible a systematic arrangement of the whole color manifold. Segregate all the colors of the same brilliance, arrange the most saturated hues of this brilliance in a color circle, and ask whether all the paler or duller colors can be matched in hue, each with some one saturated color. This is found to be possible. A pink has the same hue as some particular saturated red, a brown the same hue as some orange or yellow. All the colors of the same hue and brilliance can be arranged in a series extending from the saturated color of this hue to neutral or hueless gray of the same brilliance. Placing the neutral gray at the center of the color circle, and the saturated colors around the circumference, we arrange the saturation series for any hue along a radius. All the colors of any one degree of brilliance have definite places in a filled-in color circle, the center of which is a neutral gray.

The color solid. Having obtained a filled-in color circle for each degree of brilliance, we imagine these circles piled in order from low brilliance to high—from dark to light. We thus obtain a cylinder which may well be made to taper toward the top and toward the bottom, giving a double cone or spindle. The tapering does justice to the fact that full saturation is possible only with colors of medium brilliance.

Though the color spindle provides a place for every color sensation it does not include all the facts capable of being represented in a diagram. Certain hues—like certain tastes and odors—stand out as distinctive, while others appear intermediate between these salient hues. Purple is a reddish blue, and orange a reddish yellow, but can red be seen as a purplish orange—or yellow as a greenish orange? Are not red and yellow more unitary than purple and orange? The average person, asked to state which colors are unitary, names red, yellow and blue—these three; and some Os add a fourth, green. Psychologists are accustomed to accept the four as salient hues and to transform the color circle into a square, with these four at the corners. The color spindle becomes a double pyramid, with maximum brilliance at the upper apex, maximum darkness at the lower apex, and the square of medium brilliance and maximum saturation in the middle.

The axis of the double pyramid is sometimes, misleadingly, said to represent the white-gray-black series. But a perfectly white surface gives all degrees of brilliance according to the illumination; and a dark gray surface, almost black, can be made to give a sensation of high brilliance by using strong illumination. Black, white and gray are properly object colors, not degrees of brilliance (p. 598). Brilliance extends from light to dark, not from white to black; and the axis of the pyramid is the locus of hueless, achromatic visual sensations.

Stimulus correlates of the three dimensions of color sensation. A homogeneous ray of light (all of one wave length, one frequency) can vary in amplitude, intensity, energy per second. These three amount to a single physical dimension when the wave length is constant. Two homogeneous rays can differ in wave length or frequency, a second dimension (and energy per second depends on frequency as well as on amplitude, as in the case of sound waves, p. 503). Most lights, whether straight from their sources or reflected from objects, are not homogeneous but are mixtures of different wave lengths; and the amount of mixture can be regarded as a third dimension of physical light, with white light having maximum mixture and any homogeneous ray having zero mixture.

With three dimensions of color sensation and three dimensions of the physical stimulus, we might hope to find a one-to-one correspondence, though our experience with auditory sensations raises some doubts. As a matter of fact, *brilliance* depends quite definitely on the intensity of the light, when the wave length of homogeneous light, or the composition of a mixed light, remains constant. But brilliance depends just as definitely on wave length. Wave lengths lying outside the range of the visible spectrum (which extends from 760 millimicrons, mμ, at the red end to about 400 mμ at the violet end) arouse no visual sensation whatever; and within the visible spectrum the medium wave lengths, in the general region of the yellow, are much more brilliant for the same quantity of energy than the rays near either end of the spectrum (Fig. 150). Brilliance depends also on adaptation, summation, contrast and other conditions of the receptive apparatus.

Newton's experiment with the prism is fundamental in tracing the dependence of *hue*. He broke up white light into the spectrum, dispersing the rays according to wave length. Advancing through the spectrum we see practically pure red from 760 to 660 mμ, and then get a trace of orange. Wave length 610 is a good orange, 580 a good yellow, 530 a green, 480 a blue, 430 a violet. Minutely examined the spectrum shows many intermediate hues.

If we should take these results to mean that hue is uniquely dependent on wave length, we should be making things far too simple. Hue depends also on the intensity of the stimulus. At very low intensities the spectrum is colorless, there is no differential response to wave length, because only the rods are responding (p. 545). At high intensities red and yellowish green become more yellowish, while greenish blue and violet become more bluish (Purdy, 1931; Troland, 1930, 1934). A certain bluish green and its complementary purple do not change except to lose saturation with increasing intensity of the stimulus. Substantially the same effect is produced by moving the stimulus from the fovea toward the periphery of the retina. Red and yellowish green verge into yellow, greenish blue and violet into blue, and the particular bluish green and purple simply fade out, as do also blue and yellow in the extreme periphery (Baird, 1905). At medium intensities, red and green lose their hue at a smaller distance from the fovea than yellow and blue; but at high intensities red, yellow and blue are sensed even out to the limits of vision (Ferree and Rand, 1919).

Saturation depends very much on mixture of wave lengths. If we start with a homogeneous light and add more and more white we continually diminish the saturation. Wave length also is a factor, since some homogeneous lights, especially red, are more saturated than others, as green. The green of the spectrum, though homogeneous physically, appears somewhat pale and whitish.

Measurement of light. As distinguished from radiation, visible light has to be defined and measured in relation to the sensitivity of the eye. Yet we need to measure light, for psychological purposes, in as nearly pure physical terms as possible, because we need a measure of the stimulus that shall be independent of the organism's response. The measurement depends directly or indirectly on the eye.

In speaking of the dimensions of sensation we have used the word *brilliance* instead of *brightness*, so as to reserve the latter for a physical measure, in accordance with the practice of specialists in light. In looking steadily at a bright surface the eye becomes adapted to its brightness and the brilliance of the sensation decreases, though the physical brightness of the surface remains unchanged.

Let a standard candle be burning at the center of a globe: the total *flux* of light from the candle falls on the inner surface of the globe, no matter what its radius, and is the same at all distances from the source. As the radius increases, the light falling on a unit area, i.e., the *density* of illumination, decreases and is inversely proportional to the square of the distance from the source. If the receiving surface is one meter distant from the candle, the illumination of the surface is said to have a density of a one meter candle. A *meter candle, the unit of illumination*, is the density of illumination received by a surface one meter distant from a one candlepower source. A *lumen, the unit of luminous flux*, is the total light received by one square meter of surface at one meter distance from the one candlepower source.

Let the globe transmit all of the light it receives, diffusing it perfectly into the surrounding space: we wish to measure the brightness of the surface of

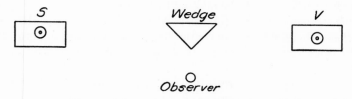

Fig. 149. Diagram of wedge photometer. The wedge consists of two mat paper surfaces making an angle of 90° with each other, each being inclined 45° to its respective source of light. The observer sees a square which is brighter on one half or the other till the two are adjusted to equal brilliance. One source, S, is at a fixed distance; the other, V, is adjusted in distance till the whole field appears uniform. The physical brightness is computed by the law of inverse squares.

the globe as seen from outside. Under the assumptions made, a square meter of the surface of the globe receiving one lumen of flux from the source transmits one lumen; its brightness is one lumen per square meter. One lumen per square meter is rather low brightness; ten times this is a useful *unit of brightness*, the *millilambert*, which is then the brightness of a surface which gives out ten lumens per square meter of surface; in other words, it is the brightness of a perfectly transmitting and diffusing surface placed 1 meter from a 10 candle power source; or, again, it is the brightness of a perfectly diffusing surface illuminated with a density of 10 meter candles. The same definition and unit apply to a perfectly reflecting mat surface. Brightness in its technical use does not apply to a point source of light but only to a *surface* which diffuses so much light per square meter of its area.

Photometry. The photometer is an instrument arranged to enable O to make an accurate equation of apparent brightness between two adjacent surfaces. An easily understood form, though not the most accurate, is the wedge photometer, illustrated in Fig. 149. It is used either for physical measurement, as of the candle power of a lamp, or in a psychological experiment. In the physical measurement the observer makes an equation between a known and an unknown surface and his equation is accepted as an approximate statement of a physical fact. In the psychological experiment E knows the physical fact, the true equation, in advance and O's setting affords a measure of his own accuracy.

ROD AND CONE VISION

The brilliance, hue and saturation of a color sensation depend not only on the stimulus but also, to a marked degree, upon the receiving apparatus and on its condition. The receptor apparatus is "duplex" according to a theory which is now so well established as to count almost as a statement of fact (von Kries, 1929). It is an anatomical fact that the retina contains two types of receptor cells, the rods and the cones, and all the evidence goes to show that they differ in functional characteristics. The rods become adapted to very faint light, far surpassing the cones in this respect. But the rods are exclusively a light-dark sense; they do not respond to differences of wave length by sensations of different hues. And the rods do not contribute much to the accurate perception of form. Some of the evidence for these statements will be presented.

Anatomical differences between the rods and the cones. Though these two types of receptors are very similar, they do show significant differences.

1. The rods are smaller and appear less highly developed than the cones.

2. There are no rods but only closely packed cones in the fovea. The rod-free area is usually not over 2° in horizontal diameter, and a little less vertically. A one-cent coin, held at arm's length, just about fills this area. Rods begin to appear outside the fovea and become more numerous toward the periphery, in proportion to the cones, though there are a few cones even in the extreme periphery.

3. With respect to nerve supply, the cones are the better off. Several adjacent rods feed into one ganglion cell and so into a single optic nerve fiber. Each cone, at least in the fovea, has its own separate path back to the interbrain.

4. "Visual purple" is present in the rods but not in the cones. This substance is rapidly bleached on exposure to bright light and gradually restored in dim light or darkness. It must have something to do with dark adaptation—a suspicion which is fortified by the fact that the responsiveness of the dark-adapted eye to different wave lengths of light corresponds closely with the degree of absorption of the several wave lengths by visual purple (Hecht, 1934).

5. Nocturnal animals possess mostly rods and few cones. This was the fact which first (Schultze, 1866) suggested the idea that the rods were receptors for dim light.

Pathological evidence for the duplex theory. The condition of "night blindness" found in patients who cannot become adequately dark-adapted, and in whom there is some degeneration of the pigment layer at the back of the retina from which the visual purple is derived, is explained as a deficiency of rod vision (Parinaud, 1881). There is also a condition of "day blindness" in which vision is painful and inefficient in strong light and the individual is totally color blind—just as if the cones were undeveloped and unfunctional. His fovea then should be completely blind—a prediction which has been verified in a majority of the cases examined. These individuals must direct their eyes a little to the side in order to see an object, and they commonly show some nystagmus or unsteadiness of fixation (Ladd-Franklin, 1929).

Experimental evidence for the duplex theory. If it is the rods that respond to very faint light, such light should not elicit any response from the fovea which would therefore be night-blind in all persons.

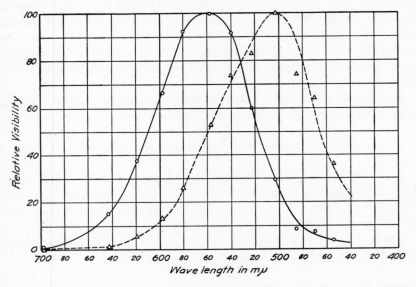

FIG. 150. (Data from Sloan, 1928.) Relative visibility of different wave lengths of light, when of medium intensity (2–10 meter candles, shown by the solid line) and when of low intensity (.001 meter candles, shown by the broken line). This pronounced shift of the visibility curve was not obtained except when the weak light fell outside the fovea of a dark-adapted eye. In the fovea the shift was very slight and uncertain. The data are from one eye of a highly trained O; other published data give nearly the same curves.

In order to test this prediction, the eye is dark-adapted and a faint light thrown upon the fovea alone. Very exact fixation is required; otherwise the light will fall outside the fovea and reach some rods. Instead of a single fixation point, a ring of weakly luminous points is provided. If the ring has a diameter of 3° and is fixated as a whole, the center of the ring will correspond to the fovea. The test light is located in the center of the ring. By such experiments the foveal threshold, during dark-adaptation, is found to be very much higher than that of the parafoveal region (von Kries, 1897). You can see a faint star better by looking a little to one side.

A very weak spectrum has no visible color but only a gradation of brilliance. Its maximum brilliance lies at a wave length of 510 mμ instead of at 560 as is the case in a bright spectrum. The brilliance curve of the spectrum is the same for the normal dark-adapted eye, with dim illumination, as it is for the totally color-blind eye under any illumination. (See Fig. 150; also Geldard, 1933.) In both cases the red end is invisible, the visible spectrum is shortened at that end. The rod apparatus is evidently tuned to a shorter wave length than the cones.

A related fact has long been known under the name of the Purkinje phenomenon. If a red paper and a green or blue paper are matched for brilliance under good illumination and are then taken into much dimmer light, the green or blue appears the brighter. In good light the cones, in dim light the rods, contribute most of the sensation. Consequently the reds are relatively bright in strong light and the greens and blues in dim light. The greens and blues in dim light are not only relatively bright but also whitish because of the colorless contribution of the rods. The Purkinje phenomenon is said to fail when the stimulus is confined strictly to the rod-free region, and also in cases of night-blindness (von Kries & Nagel, 1900; Kohlrausch, 1931).

LIGHT AND DARK ADAPTATION

The visual apparatus adjusts itself in compensatory fashion to the intensity of light to which it is exposed. The pupillary response to light and dark compensates in some measure for changes in illumination, and the sensitivity of the retina also adjusts itself. Some data on the pupil are given below and in Fig. 151.

PUPIL DIAMETER AND AREA AFTER PROLONGED EXPOSURE TO FIELD OF GIVEN BRIGHTNESS

(Average of 7 Os, from Reeves, 1918 a)

Brightness of exposure field	Diameter of pupil	Area of pupil
ml	mm	mm^2
0	8.1	52
.00015	7.8	48
.01	7.2	40
1.0	5.3	22
10	4.0	13
55	3.1	8
100	2.8	6
2000	1.9	3

For any given intensity the amount of light admitted to the retina is proportional to the area of the pupil. Changes in the pupil, as shown by the table, can compensate for a 17-fold increase in the external light. The external light, at different times of the day and night, varies in the ratio of millions to one, so that the pupillary adjustment is relatively a slight affair. Adaptation of the retina goes much further in the way of compensation. Everyone is familiar with the effects of retinal adaptation: after "getting used" to either a dim or a bright illumination, one sees objects much more distinctly than at first. That the retina rather than the cortex becomes light-adapted and dark-adapted is indicated by the bleaching of the visual purple in the light and its reappearance in prolonged exposure to the dark. Another relevant fact is that one eye can be light-adapted and the other simultaneously dark-adapted.

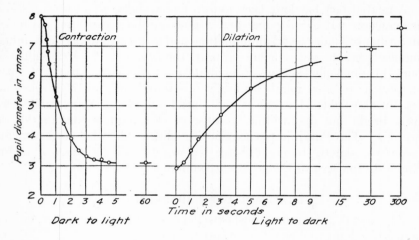

Fig. 151. (Data from Reeves, 1918 a.) Pupillary contraction and dilation. Average results from 6 Os. The contraction curve was obtained by first keeping O in the dark long enough to obtain practically complete dilation and then exposing the eye to a brightness of 100 ml, and photographing it at short intervals during this exposure. The dilation curve had to be built up from several experiments in each of which, starting from practically complete adjustment of the pupil to the bright light of 100 ml, O was kept in the dark for a certain number of seconds and his eye then photographed by aid of a flash of light. The pupillary response to light is a much quicker process than that to darkness.

The progress of adaptation to light or dark is traced by determining the stimulus threshold, the lowest intensity of light which can be perceived at a given time. The rod-free fovea requires separate study, since the rods go much further than the cones in adaptation to dim light. In an experiment of Piper (1903) the test field was a 4–inch square of milk glass, illuminated from behind and placed one foot from O's eyes. The apparatus was set up in a dark room, but O was first sent out of doors for a quarter of an hour in order that the experiment might start with light-adapted eyes. When O returned a first determination of his threshold was made, the illumination of the milk glass being altered till O just barely saw it. O then remained in the dark room and his threshold was measured at intervals till it reached a fairly stable level, as it usually did in 40–60 minutes. At this level it was only 1/3500 of the threshold first determined after entering the dark; and this first threshold was certainly too low, because dark adaptation had advanced to some extent during the minute or two consumed in measuring the threshold. A quicker method of determining the threshold (Blanchard, cited by Kohlrausch, 1931) is to have O look at a large field of known brightness for a certain time, for adaptation, and then to darken the field completely except for a small central portion—the question being whether O can see this central portion. By varying its brightness the stimulus threshold is determined. This method gave results indicating fully a million times the sensitivity in extreme dark as in extreme light adaptation. Since the test field in the experiments so far described was large enough to extend beyond the rod-free region, the results apply to the rods rather than the cones.

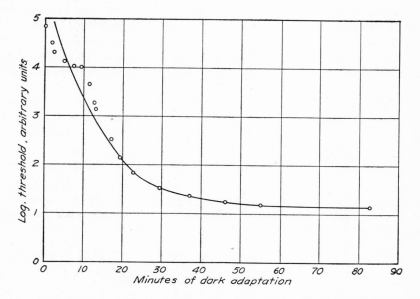

Fig. 152. (Data from Piper, 1903.) The course of dark adaptation of the rods in one O. Because of the slow method of determining the threshold, the first point on the curve does not fairly represent the very beginning of the process when the eyes were strongly light-adapted. The curve should start much higher. The curve sketched in to fit the data points shows that adaptation first proceeds rapidly and then more slowly. Closely examined, the data points show a flattening out at 10 minutes, followed by another rapid drop. Presumably cone adaptation was complete in 10 minutes and the rest is rod adaptation.

Hecht (1934) has fitted a rational curve to similar data and has thus obtained evidence for a photochemical theory of the process of adaptation.

Adaptation of the cones is studied by confining the test field to the fovea. Hecht (1921) used for a test field a small red cross illuminated from the rear. It subtended a visual angle of 2.5°, which is not quite small enough to restrict the field to the rod-free region, but the additional precaution of using red light (a Wratten filter transmitted only the red end of the spectrum) was doubtless effective since the rods are insensitive

to that light. An initial state of light adaptation was secured by directing
the eyes for 5 minutes upon a bright surface. This surface was then
darkened and O had simply to raise his head and look into the apparatus
for the red cross, and to signal when it became visible. A very quick
first determination was thus secured; O remained in the dark and was
retested at intervals. The results indicated a rapid but limited dark
adaptation of the cones. It was nearly complete in 3 minutes, but the
sensitivity was only 100–200 times that in light adaptation. Cook
(1934 c) found about the same amount of change which was almost
complete in 8 minutes though it continued for 10 minutes longer.

Instead of determining the stimulus threshold, Wright (1934) obtained
a brilliance equation between two monocular fields lying side by side
in the combined binocular field of view. One eye was kept in a state of
dark adaptation while the other was exposed to a bright surface. A
match was then made between two test fields, one exposed to each eye.
The light-adapted eye required a much brighter test field than the dark-
adapted eye in order to obtain a brilliance equation. But as the light-
adapted eye recovered from its light adaptation (or became dark-adapted)
by being kept in the dark, less objective difference was needed in order
to obtain the equation. The course of dark adaptation was so nearly
linear for the first few minutes that the initial sensitivity could be estimated by extrapolation. This initial sensitivity was thus determined
after different durations of exposure to light, and by this means Wright
obtained indirectly what is very difficult to obtain directly, a curve
of *light adaptation*. The progress of foveal light adaptation, according
to this evidence, is extremely rapid and is nearly complete at the end of
one minute's exposure to the light.

COLOR MIXING

The dependence of hue on wave length, as already stated, is very
definite. Aside from certain effects of intensity and of peripheral vision,
each wave length gives a specific hue. But the converse of this proposition is not true. Each hue is not bound to a specific wave length. The
same yellow hue which we get from a homogeneous ray of wave length
580 mμ can be obtained from a mixture of 570 and 590, and from an
indefinite number of mixtures centering about 580. Any hue can be
obtained from suitably balanced mixtures of wave lengths, and in fact
most of the colors we see are produced by mixed lights, since homogeneous
rays seldom reach the eye.

The sensation obtained from a mixed light is apt to be less saturated
than that from a homogeneous light, but as far as hue is concerned the
effect is unitary in both cases. The effect is altogether different from that
obtained in the auditory sphere by mixing two wave lengths (or frequencies). Sound *do* and *mi* at once and you do not hear *re;* but superpose
red and yellow and you get, not a red-yellow chord, but an intervening
hue, orange. Color mixture is not a mixture of sensations, but a mixture

of stimuli which gives a unitary sensation. Yellow, though surely a unitary hue, can be obtained by mixing red and green lights, and white can be obtained by mixing yellow and blue.

Mixing pigments. The painter will rebel against the last statement, as he knows from abundant experience that mixing yellow and blue pigments gives green and not white. Yet it is easy to demonstrate that yellow and blue lights thrown together on a screen or directly into the eye, in proper proportions, produce a colorless white and that in other proportions they give either yellow or blue and never green. There is an important physical difference between mixing lights and mixing pigments. Mixing lights is addition, mixing pigments is a double subtraction. The color of a pigment is the light remaining after the pigment has absorbed certain wave lengths. A yellow pigment absorbs certain rays, a blue pigment certain other rays, and the mixture of the two pigments absorbs both sets of rays. Let us take two color filters, one letting the yellow rays pass through, the other the blue rays. If these filters were strictly monochromatic, the yellow one would absorb all the rays except yellow, and the blue one all except blue, and no light whatever could pass through both. If the filters, like most pigments, were not monochromatic, their combination might well transmit a mixture of rays which would be so balanced as to give the sensation of green.

Ways of mixing color stimuli. Mixing pigments will not serve when we wish to *add* one light to another of different wave length. We may extract two rays from the spectrum and superpose them on a dead white screen or throw them directly upon the same part of the retina. We must be able to regulate the intensity of the two rays, as by use of gray filters or by interposing an episcotister in the path of a ray.

A good set of color filters of known transmission can be substituted for the parts of the spectrum without loss of precision in most experiments and with great increase of convenience for the experimenter.

The color wheel by which interlaced paper disks of different colors are rotated above the fusion frequency (p. 565) is an apparatus not to be despised, in spite of the fact that the light reflected from each disk is by no means homogeneous. Ordinarily we do not know the physical variables of our color papers very well and consequently cannot state results in terms of the physical quantities. For qualitative work the difficulty with the color wheel is the low saturation of the papers and the very low saturation of some of the mixtures. Brick red and grass green should give yellow; they do give a brown in which the hue by careful attention is seen to be yellow.

In qualitative work, the goal of a color mixing experiment is simply noting, naming and describing the color produced by the mixture. In quantitative work we must obtain a *color equation*. The sensory effect of the mixture is matched with that of a Standard which may be a homogeneous light or some defined mixture. Though the interest usually lies in hue, the brilliance and saturation must also be matched, for it is almost impossible to certify to an exact equation of hue unless these other characteristics are also equated. The equation should state that the mixture was indistinguishable from the Standard. To secure a perfect match between yellow and a red-green mixture, we must be prepared to reduce the intensity of the yellow and also to lower its saturation by the admixture of white.

Results in color mixing. By mixing red and yellow in different proportions we obtain all the orange hues intermediate between our red and yellow. By mixing red and grass green we get all the hues of orange, yellow and yellowish green. It might seem that we had found

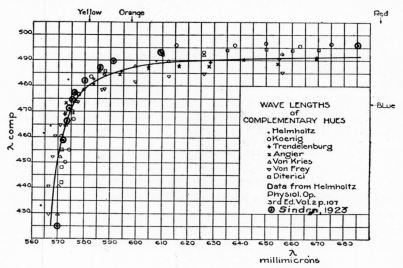

FIG. 153. (Priest, 1920, with added data from Sinden, 1923.) Wave lengths of complementary colors. On the abscissa is given the longer, on the ordinate the shorter, of two complementary wave lengths. Thus for a red of 655 mμ the complementary as determined by different observers ranges from 485 to 493; and for a greenish blue of 495 it has ranged from 585 over to 655, i.e. from yellow to red. The most probable paired values as computed by Priest fall on the curve, but the later measurements by Sinden call for lifting the upper arm of the curve somewhat. λ = wave length.

a rule, to the effect that mixing any two colors of the spectrum gave the intermediate colors. But when we push the matter a little further by mixing red and a bluish green, we get no intermediate hues. If red predominates in this particular mixture we get only unsaturated shades of red; if the bluish green predominates we get unsaturated shades of that same green; and if the red and the bluish green are rightly balanced we get white or gray. Red and this particular bluish green are said to be complementary. If we advance still further and mix red and blue, in different proportions, we obtain all the hues of purple and violet. In the spectrum, these hues are not intermediate between red and blue, but in the color circle they are intermediate "around the back way."

Experimenting with other pairs of colors we obtain similar results. When two colors differ comparatively little in wave length, their mixture gives the intermediate hues; when they differ just enough they are complementary; and when they differ by more than this amount they give the purples.

A systematic search for complementaries shows that individuals differ somewhat (Fig. 153). Some of the values are given below:

PAIRS OF COMPLEMENTARY COLORS

(Wave lengths)

Red	660 mμ	and	Blue-green	497 mμ
Orange	610	and	Green-blue	492
Yellow	585	and	Blue	485
Yellow-green	570	and	Violet	430

We notice that the strict greens, lying between yellow-green at 570 and blue-green at 497, have no complementary wave length. To obtain a colorless mixture with green we have to use *two* other wave lengths, one long and one short. Green is complementary to purple which is a mixture of red and blue.

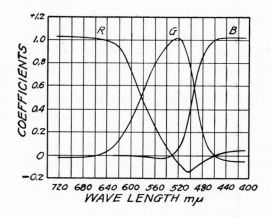

FIG. 154. (From Troland, 1930, p. 160; data from Wright.) Proportions of red (650), green (530) and blue (460) required to match each hue of the spectrum. Average results from 10 subjects. The ordinate scale of "coefficients" was obtained by determining the amounts of the three components necessary to give white and regarding these amounts as the units for the three respective components. The figure reads that if the three components mixed in the proportion, R: G: B = 1: 1: 1, give white, then, for example, the wave length of 600 is matched by mixing the same three components in the proportion, 0.74: 0.28: 0, approximately. When one of the component lines goes below zero, the meaning is that the spectral color in question was more saturated than the mixture and had to be whitened by adding to it a little of the complementary color. Thus the hue of wave length 500 was matched by a mixture of B and G, but some R had to be added to the spectral color to reduce its saturation.

The chromatic power of blue is large in comparison with its low brightness, and if these curves were transformed to read in brightness units the blue curve would shrink almost out of sight.

Obtaining all the hues by mixture of three wave lengths. It is of importance for the theory of the color sense, and for the practice of color printing and color photography, to know how few colors will by various mixtures yield all the hues of the color circle and also white, gray or hueless sensation. From experiments with two colors, already described, we infer that two colors are not enough. We must use at least three, and no two of them can be complementary. For if we selected a pair of complementaries, as yellow and blue, what color should we take for the third? If we took red, mixing it with yellow would give orange, and mixing it with blue would give purple and violet, but we could not get green; and if we chose green instead of red, we could get only the yellow-green-blue series, and not red, purple or violet. Two complementaries and one other component will give us only half of the color circle. But if we choose red, blue, and a yellowish or straight green of wave length between 497 and 570, we can obtain all the hues from mixture of these three. The wave lengths need not be exactly specified; some latitude is permitted. Each component is complementary to a mixture of the other two, and therefore some mixture of all three will give white.

The color mixture triangle. Having properly chosen three component wave lengths, we combine them in various proportions to match all the hues in the color circle. Each match shows the proportions of red and green required to match some orange or yellow hue, or the proportions of green and blue required to match a blue-green, or the proportions of red and blue required to match a purple or violet. We also determine the proportions of red, green and blue required to match white. If we had no white and no differences of saturation on our hands we could represent all our results by a triangle with the three components at the corners and the various hues located along the sides at distances indicating the mixtures found necessary. (The distance of yellow from the red and green corners would be inversely proportional to the amounts of red and green required to match the yellow.) To take account of saturations also we locate white inside the triangle, as in the color circle. Much more color knowledge can be incorporated in the triangle, as illustrated in Fig. 155, and as explained by Troland (1930).

Color blindness. In total color blindness, which apparently is pure rod vision, all wave lengths and all mixtures differ only in brilliance and there are no differences of hue. In order to match all parts of the spectrum, only *one* component is necessary and this one may have any wave length within O's visible spectrum. Totally color-blind individuals are very rare. Relatively common in males is red-green blindness, betrayed by confusion of green with brown, and of pink with pale blue. In the color mixing experiment the red-green blind O needs only *two components*, one from the red half of the spectrum and one from the blue half. With these two, mixed in different proportions, he can match every hue and saturation. In color mixing, the red-green blind eye is dichromatic, as the normal eye is trichromatic.

The Young-Helmholtz theory of color vision, i.e., of cone vision, starts from the fact that three components are sufficient to yield all the colors including white. It assumes separate receptors for three primary color responses, red, green, and blue or violet. It supposes dichromatic vision to lack one of these three primary responses, usually the red or

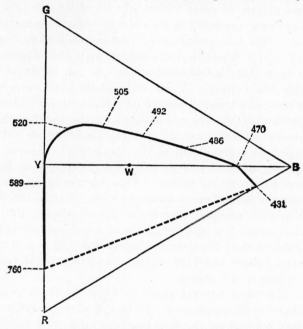

FIG. 155. (After König & Dieterici, 1892.) The color mixture triangle modified to show the mixtures of an ideally saturated green and blue and of a slightly purplish red. The colors of the spectrum are arranged in order on the heavy solid line, and the purples along the heavy dotted line. Inside the heavy line are located colors less saturated, and outside are colors more saturated than those of the spectrum. A line drawn from any point on the spectrum to the point W (white) contains tints all of which have the same hue. Continuing this same line through W we have the tints of the complementary color.

Every point in the triangle stands for a color of a certain hue and saturation, brilliance being disregarded. The straight line connecting any two points contains all the colors obtained by mixing those two particular colors in all proportions. Take two points on the spectrum line, as the sodium yellow, 589, and blue-green, 492; draw a straight line between them, take the middle point of this line, representing equal amounts of the two mixed colors, and draw a line from W through this point to the spectrum line to discover the hue of the mixture.

the green. Red-green blindness should therefore have two forms, red-blindness and green-blindness. This expectation is realized in color mixing experiments, especially in matching spectral yellow with a red-green mixture, since some color-blind individuals, called *protanopes*, require an undue amount of red—i.e., are relatively insensitive to the red rays—while others, the *deuteranopes*, are relatively insensitive to green. The brilliance curve of the spectrum (Fig. 150) is about the same for normals and deuteranopes, while for the protanopes the red is less bright than normal. Some individuals possessing trichromatic vision agree with the protanopes in finding the red end of the spectrum lacking in brilliance, and there are all gradations between normal and protanope in this respect (Tufts, 1907; Kohlrausch, 1931). Probably the protanope combines two defects of color vision, one consisting in low sensitivity to red and the other consisting in the reduction of trichromatic to dichromatic vision. This interpretation of protanopia makes it possible to do justice to a fact which is inconsistent with the Young-Helmholtz theory—the fact that dichromatic vision, so far as direct testimony goes, is yellow-blue vision. A few individuals have been tested who proved to be red-green blind in one eye only and able, therefore, to make a direct comparison of the color sensations of the dichromatic and the trichromatic eye. In dichromatic vision, according to their reports, the red-orange-yellow-green half of the spectrum is reduced neither to shades of red nor to shades of green—as the Young-Helmholtz theory demands—but to shades of yellow. This description of dichromatism is confirmed by the normal eye in indirect vision. A red or green stimulus, on being displaced gradually from the fovea toward the periphery, loses its red or green hue and merges into a dull yellow before finally becoming colorless near the extreme periphery. At a certain distance from the fovea yellow and blue retain their hues, while both red and grass green appear a dull yellow.

Fig. 155 illustrates several possible ways in which normal vision could be reduced to dichromatism. If the eye were green-blind, it would give sensations lying along the R-B line only; if it were red-blind, along the G-B line only; and if it were blue-blind, along the R-G line only. The color equations obtained from protanopes and deuteranopes correspond to those required by the diagram for red-blindness and green-blindness respectively. Anything corresponding to blue-blindness is excessively rare. Thus the triangle affords a picture of the Young-Helmholtz theory of color vision. But another form of dichromatism conforms better with the facts of peripheral color vision and with the testimony of individuals color-blind in one eye only. According to this evidence, the reduced color series extends not from red to blue, nor from green to blue, but from yellow to blue. The Ladd-Franklin theory does justice to these facts by regarding dichromatism as always yellow-blue vision and as due not to the absence of either the red or the green receptor mechanism but to the coalescence of these two systems into a yellow-receiving system (or to the non-differentiation of the red and green out of the more primitive yellow). On this theory the triangle is reduced to the line Y-B in dichromatic vision.

VISUAL AFTERIMAGES

The total response of the visual apparatus to a light of any considerable intensity lasts for some time after the cessation of the stimulus.

After-lag is illustrated by the circle of light seen when a burning coal or bulb is rapidly swung in a circle. The color wheel and the episcotister make use of this lag for obtaining a steady sensation from an intermittent stimulus. This after-lag lasts less than half a second from the cessation of the stimulus. Then there is a blank interval after which a visual effect again appears, the afterimage. Many students require some practice before seeing the afterimage, because it is one of those subjective phenomena which our whole practical life leads us to disregard. It is subjective in the sense of originating in the organism and representing no external fact, but it is definitely sensory and not imaginary. It indicates some peculiarity of the retinal or cortical response. Electric potentials led off from the retina, in an animal experiment, show an after-effect which is undoubtedly correlated with the afterimage.

A few definitions may be of use. The *stimulus field* or *exposure field* consists of the light thrown upon the retina and also of the intervening dark spaces. We cannot leave out of account the surroundings (or "surround") of any particular stimulus which we apply. The *after-field* or *post-exposure* field consists of the stimuli applied to the retina after the primary stimulation but during the observation of an afterimage. This after-field may be bright, dark or colored, and the afterimage depends on the after-field as well as on the exposure field. A convenient homogeneous after-field is afforded by the diffuse light penetrating the closed eyelids and varying with the external illumination.

Afterimage must be distinguished from *after-effect*. The image may disappear and reappear, while obviously some after-effect has persisted. The image may change from positive to negative, but the retinal after-effect need not have changed, for the change may lie in the after-field. We cannot very well speak of an invisible afterimage though we can speak of an invisible after-effect. A *positive* afterimage corresponds to the original impression, light for light, dark for dark. In a *negative* afterimage the light-dark relations are reversed. With regard to color, an afterimage is positive when its colors are respectively those of the original impression, and negative when the afterimage colors are complementary respectively to those of the original impression. Not all chromatic afterimages are either positive or negative; the colors seen are often neither the originals nor their complementaries.

The after-lag is positive; the afterimage may be either positive or negative or both by turns.

Whether the afterimage shall be positive or negative depends primarily upon two variables, the strength of the after-effect and the brightness of the after-field. On a dark after-field the image is likely to be positive, on a bright field negative. What counts here is not the average brightness of the whole field of view but the particular part of the field upon which the afterimage is projected. Thus the afterimage of a lamp filament, projected on a black and white field, is negative on the bright part and positive on the dark part simultaneously.

The strength of the after-effect, though not directly observable, can be inferred from the afterimage phenomena. It depends on two variables, the strength of the original stimulus and the time since the stimulus ceased to act. The after-effect dies away gradually as the retina recovers from the stimulus. The strength of the original stimulus depends on its intensity, duration and area. These statements are justified and amplified by many experiments of which we cite only a few.

Franz (1899) presented a black field (dark room, O dark adapted) containing a small square of light (ground glass illuminated from behind). This square could be varied in area, in intensity of light, or in duration of exposure. The simplest task assigned to O was that of reporting whether he got any afterimage from a given stimulus. The frequency of the reported afterimages increased with the increase of each of the three stimulus variables. The largest square used had a side of 8 mm (in angular magnitude, 1° 32' as seen from O's position a foot distant from the screen). With this area, 1 sec. exposure, and an intensity described as 2/25th candle power, an afterimage was reported practically 100 percent of the time. When the duration of exposure was reduced to 1 ms, or the side of the square to ¼ mm, or the intensity to 1/800 candle power, an afterimage was reported only 15 percent of the time.

To secure a kymograph record which would show the *duration* of the afterimage, Franz instructed O to hold a telegraph key closed while the image was visible, releasing it whenever the image disappeared. On the average of three Os the afterimage lasted 50 sec. when the dimensions of the stimulus were 1 sq. cm, 5 sec., 0.1 candle power. Decreasing any of these stimulus dimensions shortened the duration of the afterimage; increasing any of them gave a longer duration. Provided brilliance were equated, the wave length of the stimulus seemed to have no effect on the duration of the afterimage. In peripheral vision the duration was shorter. An interesting point is that afterimage duration was greatest in the morning when the eyes were fresh, and least when the eyes were fatigued. Early morning, in fact, is a very favorable time for observing afterimages.

A much wider range of intensity and duration was tried out by Berry & Imus (1935). The duration of the afterimage continued to increase up to quite high intensities of the stimulus, and up to durations of the stimulus as long as 60 sec.

Positive and negative afterimages. To the older investigators, as Fechner (1840) and Helmholtz (1866), it seemed perfectly clear that there must be two opposite after-effects of stimulation. Helmholtz said that "continued excitation and diminished excitability are no hypothesis but an immediate expression of the facts"—the positive afterimage showing continued excitation; the negative, diminished excitability. Yet Ebbecke's (1929) experiments show both to be indicators of the same after-effect. For a stimulus he used the light of a bulb with a long straight filament, of 32 candlepower, viewed from different distances. As after-fields he used a series of gray papers or, in many cases, the very convenient and uniform fields afforded by the closed eyes, covered by the hand or exposed to outside light. The afterimage was changed from positive to negative and back by changing the after-field; on a bright field it was negative, on a dark field positive, and on a medium field of just the right brightness it vanished. It was blotted out by a very bright after-field.

Whether positive or negative, the afterimage fades out when projected on a field of constant brightness. Fixate for half a minute a bright spot on a dark ground; then look at a dark field where you see a positive afterimage; when it has faded out, look at a bright field and you find a negative image which fades out in its turn. This alternation can be repeated many times if the original stimulus was strong or long fixated.

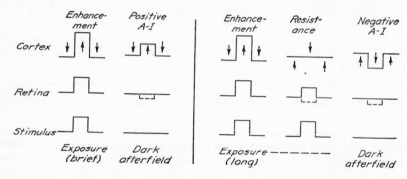

Fig. 156. (Modified from Ebbecke, 1929.) A theory of positive and negative afterimages seen on a dark after-field. Up means brighter, down darker. The stimulus field is a bright spot with dark surround. The retina is assumed to undergo adaptation (indicated by dotted lines) but no after-excitation. The full lines opposite "Retina" indicate the pattern of stimulation sent up by the retina to the cortex. The cortex is assumed to take an active part in the proceedings, a) by enhancing or reinforcing a fresh pattern, and b) by resisting and neutralizing a persisting pattern of stimulation received from the retina. After a brief exposure the cortex is caught in the phase of enhancement and so gives a purely cortical positive afterimage. During a longer exposure the cortex switches into the phase of resistance and so gives a negative afterimage.

Though the image can be revived many times, it becomes continually weaker and more evanescent. Evidently the after-effect is gradually dying out; and evidently both positive and negative afterimages are indicators of the same after-effect.

In another experiment Ebbecke (1929) used instead of the glowing filament a much less intense stimulus, a strip of white paper on a black ground under ordinary illumination, fixated for 60 sec. Now he got a negative afterimage even on a dark after-field, instead of the positive image on dark after-field of which we have hitherto spoken. The reason for this difference is that with a stimulus field of moderate intensity fixated for a long time, local adaptation washes out the stimulus pattern and causes it to disappear even during the continuance of the stimulus, as was vividly described by McDougall (1901). When this adaptation (retinal or cortical) has gone far enough the first afterimage is negative on any after-field.

Ebbecke accounts for all these results by a theory which assumes in the retina not two opposed after-effects, but one effect only; this he regards as after-excitation. The adaptation which wipes out a stimulus pattern he displaces to the cortex or at least to some part of the brain. This denial of retinal adaptation seems unreasonable in view of the difference between rod and cone adaptation already discussed; and there is a difficulty in the way of assuming enough retinal after-excitation

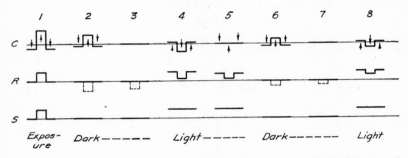

Fig. 157. Positive and negative afterimages according to the brightness of the after-field. The single brief exposure is of a bright spot with dark surround. The first afterimage is positive, exactly as in the first part of Fig. 156; no stimulus pattern is going up from the retina and the afterimage thus depends wholly on the cortical tensions. These tensions are represented as having died out in stage 3, but there is still some retinal adaptation remaining, so that when a bright after-field is used (stage 4) the retina responds unequally and sends up a stimulation pattern, giving a negative afterimage of retinal origin, though enhanced by the cortex. As the retinal pattern remains unchanged, the cortex in stage 5 develops resistances which yield a positive afterimage in stage 6 when the retinal pattern of stimulation ceases. Stages 7 and 8 repeat stages 3 and 4 on a reduced scale because of the progressive recovery of the retina from adaptation.

to account for the afterimages. Prolonging the stimulus up to 60 sec. or more increases the duration of the after-effect, while the "maximum time" (p. 565), beyond which prolonging a stimulus does not increase the level of excitation and the brilliance of the primary sensation, is only a fraction of a second. The excitation effect cannot accumulate beyond this short maximum time, and there should be no more retinal after-excitation after an exposure of 60 sec. than after a very brief exposure.

For these reasons we take the liberty of modifying Ebbecke's theory by assuming the single retinal after-effect to be one of adaptation instead of excitation and by transposing to the cortex the necessary after-excitation to account for the positive after-image. A sketch of this modification of Ebbecke's theory is presented in Figs. 156, 157. The modified theory is based on the following assumed processes:

1. Retinal adaptation. This has to be considered in relation to the stimulus *pattern*, since it is light-adaptation where the stimulus was bright and dark-adaptation where the stimulus was dark. The retina has thus become more or less adapted to the stimulus pattern and sends in to the cortex, when itself stimulated by a uniform after-field, a negative of the original pattern. When the after-field is dark there is no retinal excitation and no pattern of stimulation is sent in to the cortex.

2. A two-phase active cortical response to a pattern of stimulation sent in by the retina. The first phase is one of reinforcement or enhancement of a fresh pattern. If the pattern received from the retina remains unchanged the cortical response is assumed to switch over to a phase of opposition or resistance by which the pattern is cortically annulled.

3. Positive and negative afterimages of cortical origin, occurring when the stimulation pattern is suddenly removed by a uniform after-field. The cortical afterimage will be positive or negative according as the cortex is caught in the phase of enhancement or of resistance.

The supposed cortical processes find some support in other phenomena: enhancement in the contrast effect, resistance in negative adaptation to a distracting stimulus, and the cortical afterimage in the "memory afterimages" of other senses as well as vision.

RELATIVE FREQUENCY OF THE DIFFERENT COLORS IN THE AFTERIMAGE OF A BRIGHT WHITE LIGHT
(*Berry, 1927*)

Out of a total of 2287 colors reported by 12 Os in a series of experiments, the percent of times each hue was reported was as follows:

Red	11%
Orange	10
Yellow	11
Yellow-green	2
Green	9
Green-blue	9
Blue	13
Violet	5
Purple	18
Gray	11

Flight of colors in the afterimage of a bright light. Reasoning from the complementary afterimage obtained after a colored stimulus, we might expect a colorless afterimage to follow a colorless stimulus. As a matter of fact the afterimage of a bright white light shows a sequence of many colors. At one time or another, by one observer or another, all the hues of the color circle have been reported, and the exact sequence reported offers an almost ludicrous variety. Recent investigators, using a considerable number of Os, agree in finding yellow to be the predominant color in the early part of the sequence, with red commonly following, then blue or purple and finally, in many cases, dark green. Rapid immediately after the cessation of the stimulus, the sequence slows down progressively and the colors become darker and less saturated, fading finally into dull gray or black. At any moment the afterimage is likely to show a core of one color surrounded by a ring of another color and perhaps by a halo of yet another. The surrounding color gradually encroaches on the core and supplants it, only to be supplanted itself by another fringe creeping in from the margin. These phenomena certainly indicate something, obscure as yet, regarding the process of excitation and recovery of the visual apparatus (Berry, 1922, 1927; Shuey, 1924, 1926; Bayer, 1933).

Afterimage of a brief flash of light. Measured by the reaction time method, the latency of the afterimage is typically 2–3 sec. It is *longer* for intense than for weak stimuli (Franz, 1899; Creed & Granit, 1928; Feinbloom, 1938), perhaps because the primary excitation process has a greater after-lag. This latent period of 2 sec. is not empty. If O is in a dark room and at least partially dark-adapted, and attempts to observe the sensations produced by a single flash of light, he can report, besides the primary flash, a second flash and a third weak positive effect followed by a negative afterimage (Judd, 1927). All this happens in a couple of seconds. The early phases of this pulsating after-response can be disentangled by *moving a light across the field of view*, the eyes remaining motionless, as in the interesting experiments of Bidwell (1899) and McDougall (1904). The moving stimulus may consist of a bright sector on an otherwise black color wheel, rotated once a second, while the eye remains fixed. Since different parts of the retina are successively stimulated, the phases of the after-response are spread out in the path of the moving stimulus. Working by this method Fröhlich (1921, 1922) and others have identified the following phases in the immediate after-effect of the flash stimulus:

1. The primary sensation
2. A short dark interval
3. A positive afterimage of the same hue as the original
4. A short dark interval
5. A positive afterimage, but complementary in hue to the primary sensation
6. A long dark interval
7. A relatively long but weak positive afterimage
8. A blank interval
9. A negative afterimage, which may last many seconds

The first after-flash of the same color as the original is called the Hering afterimage, the second, weaker one which is sometimes gray, sometimes violet, sometimes complementary to the stimulus color is called the Purkinje afterimage. With a stationary light these two after-flashes cannot usually be separately perceived.

SPATIAL AND TEMPORAL SUMMATION

If we think of the eye, or of the whole visual apparatus, as a light-registering instrument, high efficiency of this instrument will demand good resolving power in both space and time. Poor resolving power in space would mean that sharp lines in the field of view were blurred in vision; acuity would be poor. Acuity is impaired by poor focus of the refracting system of the eye; and even if the optical image of the retina is in perfect definition, acuity would be poor unless the sensitive cells of the retina and their neural connections maintained a high degree of separateness. If the light falling on one cone excited all the neighboring cones over a wide area, vision could apparently not be distinct. Poor resolving power in time would mean a fusion of successive impressions, with inability to distinguish intermittent from steady light.

The fact of retinal lag indicates that resolving power in time cannot be very great. In space, apart from optical defects, acuity seems remarkably good, especially under good illumination and with sharp, strong contrasts between adjacent parts of the field (see data on acuity in Southall, 1937; Luckiesh & Moss, 1937). Experiments on spatial and temporal summation of stimuli reveal some of the limitations of vision in respect to these types of efficiency. From another point of view, spatial summation is interesting as evidence of some amount of interaction between adjacent receptive-neural units.

Spatial summation. If a surface is of uniform objective brightness, a small bit of it appears less bright than a larger bit. Increasing the visible area of the surface from a mere point to the small size of half a degree of visual angle increases the apparent brightness, but further increase has little effect. The brightness threshold, then, is lowered by increasing the area exposed. Evidently more light enters the eye from a broader than from a narrower surface of the same brightness. Perfect summation would require the same quantity of light to be barely perceptible whether it came from a broader or narrower area; area and brightness would be interchangeable factors in perceptibility. Denote brightness by the letter I and area by A, and let K be a constant; then perfect spatial summation would be expressed by the statement: for constant perceptibility,

$$I \times A = K$$

an equation which is sometimes called Ricco's law, and the validity of which is disputed.

An experiment of Piéron (1929) was designed to measure the degree of spatial summation within the confines of the fovea. To confine a stimulus to the fovea is not easy because of wavering fixation, especially in dim light. To overcome this difficulty Piéron used instead of a single fixation point a little square consisting of four red points. To maintain fixation in the blank center of this square was comparatively easy.

Within the square he presented from time to time a circular spot of faint light; and for each size of the circular stimulus spot he determined the brightness threshold. It decreased as the diameter of the stimulus circle increased, up to over 1° which is about the diameter of the fovea. But the summation was not perfect, for the I value did not go down as fast as the A value went up. If we write, instead of Ricco's law, the more general expression,

$$I \times A^m = K$$

we have in the exponent, m, a measure or indicator of the degree of summation. If $m = 0$, the area makes no difference, there is zero summation. If $m = 1$, summation is perfect, as already said. Piéron's data gave $m = 0.3$ which would indicate quite imperfect summation, in the fovea. Other experiments showed a higher degree of summation outside the fovea, and the value of m increased toward the periphery of the retina. Also, the further from the fovea the stimulated area, the broader it can be and still show some summation.

These functional results probably depend on the anatomical fact that in the peripheral zone of the retina several receptor cells connect with a single ganglion cell and optic nerve fiber. The further from the fovea, the more convergence of neural impulses from the receptors.

Summation occurs between *separated* spots, so that the threshold is lower when two spots receive the same intensity simultaneously than when only one of the spots gets the stimulus. The spots cannot be far apart, however—not more than 10′ apart in the fovea, and not more than 2° at some distance from the fovea. Here again we see more summation in the periphery than in the fovea (Beitel, 1934).

Spatial summation must impair acuity unless it is offset by the reverse type of interaction. Graham & Granit (1931) were able to detect an inhibitory or subtractive influence exerted by the brighter of two neighboring spots upon the dimmer one. While the dim spot increased the apparent brightness of the adjacent bright spot, the latter seemed to diminish the apparent brightness of the former. For fuller discussion of this interesting type of interaction see Graham (1934).

Temporal summation. If we ask the apparently sensible question, how long a light must act on the retina in order to be perceived, no direct answer can be given. It depends on the intensity of the light. An electric spark acts only a small fraction of a millisecond and is readily perceived; a very dim light needs an appreciable fraction of a second. If we turn the question around and ask how weak a light can be seen, the answer depends on how long the light acts on the retina. The quantity of light striking a retinal area depends on both the intensity and the duration of the stimulus. If $t =$ the duration, this quantity $= I \times t$, and within certain time limits it is true that, for a given degree of perceptibility, especially for threshold value,

$$I \times t = K$$

There must obviously be a time limit; brilliance cannot go on indefinitely increasing with prolongation of the stimulus. If it did, the weakest stimulus (given steady fixation of the eyes) would in time become visible. If we think of temporal summation as due to the accumulation of the photochemical effect of stimulation, as water accumulates behind a dam, we have to add the concept of leakage which after a certain time balances the inflow and prevents further accumulation (Hecht, 1934).

The *maximum time* during which the sensory effect of a light accumulates is dependent on the intensity of light, being as long as 200 ms (a fifth of a second) for a very dim light and as short as 50 ms for a bright light. It is only below these small values that the product, $I \times t$, determines the brilliance, or that time has any appreciable effect on brilliance.

Intermittent light. Flicker and fusion. If the eye were a perfect light-registering instrument it would give an intermittent sensation whenever the stimulus was intermittent. There would be no "retinal lag." The retinal response would start up instantly with full force at the beginning of each flash of light and stop instantly with the end of each flash. This is too much to expect of any instrument consisting of biological structures, and as a matter of fact we find a lag both at the beginning and at the end of the stimulus. This lag is more an advantage than a disadvantage in perceiving *objects* under intermittent illumination. A modern electric bulb driven by alternating current would show all objects as flickering if the eye had perfect resolving power in time.

A regularly intermittent light can be regarded as consisting of cycles, each cycle composed of a dark phase and a light phase. Frequency is measured in cycles per second. At low frequency O perceives a series of flashes of light; as the frequency is gradually increased the impression changes successively to coarse flicker, fine flicker, and perfectly steady light. The frequency at which all flicker disappears is called the *fusion frequency*. The higher the fusion frequency, the more efficient is the operation of the light-registering mechanism, the better its resolving power in time.

Fusion frequency depends on several stimulus variables: on the intensity of the positive phase and the difference between the two phases; on the time proportion of the two phases; on the area of the flickering field; on the part of the retina stimulated.

Let the negative phase have zero intensity, then fusion frequency increases with the intensity of the positive phase. The increase follows a logarithmic curve expressed by the equation:

$$n = a \log I + b$$

in which n is the fusion frequency in cycles per second, I is the intensity of the positive phase, and a and b are parameters which remain constant under constant conditions of the experiment, though varying slightly from time to time and from O to O. This equation is called the Ferry-

Porter law. It is the same in form as the Weber-Fechner law (p. 436), and the correspondence indicates that fusion frequency can be used as a measure of brilliance or apparent intensity.

Fusion frequency is as low as 5 cycles per sec. at very low intensities, and as high as 50 or 55 cycles per sec. at high intensities. In motion picture projection the retina receives intermittent stimulation since a dark phase intervenes between each two successive frames. Freedom from flicker is secured at a rate of 15–20 cycles (frames) per sec., except when the picture chances to be very bright. According to the equation, n is a linear function of log I, and the plot of fusion frequency against log I should therefore be a straight line. This law breaks down not only at very high intensities, when the receptors are overloaded, but also at low intensities when the rods are doing most of the work—or rather at those fairly low intensities at which the contribution to brilliance is shifting from the rods to the cones. If the rods are excluded, either by using red light to which they are insensitive, or by confining the stimulus to the fovea, the Ferry-Porter law holds very well over the whole range up to the overloading point (Hecht, 1934, p. 741).

Fusion frequency increases with the *area* of the flickering field as well as with its intensity (Granit & Harper, 1930) and the same logarithmic relation holds good:

$$n = c \log A + d$$

where A = area, and c and d are parameters. The fact that a larger area gives higher fusion frequency is further proof of spatial summation and shows that spatial summation assists the resolving power in time.

Fusion frequency differs in different parts of the retina. It is usually said to be higher in peripheral than in central vision. Bring a color wheel just to fusion frequency in direct vision and then turn the eyes somewhat to the side: you find the flicker to reappear in indirect vision. In this experiment quite a broad area of the retina is exposed to the intermittent stimulus. When the stimulus is restricted to a very small area, the opposite result is obtained (Granit & Harper, 1930): fusion frequency is highest in the fovea. The cones, accordingly, have a higher fusion frequency than the rods, and the usual result first cited is due to greater spatial summation in the periphery.

Spatial summation can be well demonstrated by the flicker method (Granit, 1930). Four small spots are made to flash synchronously, and the fusion frequency is determined when all four are used and when only one flashes. The fusion frequency is higher for the four than for the single spot. The difference is greatest when the four spots are close together and when the periphery of the retina is stimulated. If we query how spatial summation can raise the fusion frequency, the answer is that it has the effect of intensifying the positive phase of the intermittent stimulus.

The relative duration of the light and dark phases of the cycle has an effect on fusion frequency, though the relation is rather complex. The longer the light phase the higher its effective intensity rises through temporal summation; but the longer the dark phase, the more complete the recovery and the more nearly zero is the dark phase (Cobb, 1934).

When the two phases of the intermittent light differ not in intensity but in wave length, flicker is much less in evidence. Rotate a color wheel with red and green sectors of about the same brightness, and you get some flicker at low speeds, but any flicker remaining at higher frequencies is due wholly to brightness difference. This principle is used in flicker photometry: you alternate a colored and a white light and adjust the intensity of the white to give minimum flicker; the two will then have equal effective intensity. The equations so obtained do not agree perfectly with those given by direct impression of the relative brightness of two colors (Tufts, 1907).

Once the fusion frequency is reached, further increase of frequency— for example, further increase in the speed of a rotating color wheel— produces no change in sensation. The sensation is the same as would be produced by the same flux of light spread uniformly throughout the cycle—the well-established Talbot-Plateau law. For example, let a color wheel contain ¼ white and ¾ black, and suppose for the moment that the black has zero brightness. Suppose also that the white, under the given illumination, has a brightness of 100 millilamberts. Then the effective brightness of the fused surface is ¼ of 100 = 25 ml. If the "black" sector really reflects enough light to have a brightness of 4 ml, it will contribute during rotation ¾ of 4 ml = 3 ml to the effective brightness of the mixture, which will therefore be 25 + 3 = 28 ml. This principle is constantly assumed and utilized in color mixing.

CONTRAST

We have already noticed one kind of interaction between different parts of the visual field, a very limited spatial summation between neighboring regions. Much more striking is the interaction known as contrast, including brightness contrast and color contrast. Three little squares cut from the same sheet of gray paper and laid on gray, black and white backgrounds no longer look the same. The one on the white background appears darker and the one on the black background brighter than the one on the gray. If these squares are laid on backgrounds of different hues, they no longer appear neutral gray, but more or less tinged with the complementary colors. The gray need not be surrounded by the color or the black or white, it may simply be adjacent.

Stimulation confined to one part of the field of view, which we will call the stimulus region or the inducing region, affects the adjacent region, which we call the test region, inducing in it an opposite type of sensation. The interaction is mutual.

Contrast between adjacent regions is called simultaneous contrast to distinguish it from the successive contrast resulting from retinal adaptation and appearing in the negative afterimage. To obtain pure simultaneous contrast, one must guard against successive contrast by making sure that the test region has not been exposed to the inducing color.

Ways of obtaining strong contrast effect. In the simple experiment with the gray paper on black, white or colored paper, the contrast effect is likely to be slight. If the whole field is covered with *white tissue paper* or gauze, contrast is more striking. Holding the gray with its background *a few inches from the eye*, too near for good focus, and so washing out the contours and texture and depriving the field of object character, favors the contrast effect.

The *color wheel* is a convenient method. The test region here consists of a gray ring surrounded by the inducing color.

With the color wheel a *measure* of the contrast effect can be obtained. Enough of the inducing color is mixed with the gray to neutralize the induced complementary tinge. Since O's standard of neutral gray is unstable, he needs to refer to a neutral gray placed at some distance from the contrast inducing area.

Contrast shadows can be very vivid. The shadow receives diffuse daylight while the surrounding field receives colored light from a special source.

Sometimes a contrast color is so vivid that O scarcely believes it to be subjective, but he can convince himself by looking at the test region through a tube which conceals the inducing region.

Color contrast is best seen when the two regions are of about equal brightness. It can be obtained when the inducing region is of low saturation, but increases with the saturation of that region.

Though contrast colors appear most simply when the test region is gray, they appear also when it is colored. The contrast effect in this case can be understood as follows (Kirschmann, 1927). If the test field were a perfectly saturated color it could undergo no change, but usually it is equivalent to a mixture of some saturated color with white. The white component by contrast is tinged with the complementary of the inducing color and this complementary is mixed with the objective color of the test region. Place red and yellow in juxtaposition: by contrast with the red, some bluish green is mixed with the yellow, and by contrast with the yellow some blue is mixed with the red. Thus any two adjacent colors are modified, each toward the complementary of the other.

Marginal contrast. When the test region is broad, the contrast effect appears most strongly at the margin next to the inducing region. But the effect is not limited entirely to the margin. The test region can even be separated from the inducing region, though the contrast effect diminishes as the distance between the two regions increases.

The contrast effect increases with the amount of objective difference between the inducing and the test regions. According to the experiments of Ebbinghaus (1911, 233–245) and others, the darkening effect upon a gray induced by a surrounding bright field is directly proportional to the brightness difference between the two regions. This law is subject to exceptions at extreme values, but it holds approximately for color contrast as well as brightness contrast. With regard to area (Kirschmann, 1927) the contrast effect is greater the smaller the test region and the larger the inducing region.

Theory of contrast. Is contrast a retinal process or is it cortical and bound up with psychological processes? As usual on theoretical problems,

FIG. 158. (After Sherrington, 1897.) Disk for demonstrating the influence of contrast upon flicker. The ring contains the same proportions of black and white as the rest of the disk, but they are enhanced by contrast which is effective not only in the immediate impression received but also in raising the rate at which the disk must be rotated in order to extinguish flicker. Flicker persists at a higher rate in the ring than in the rest of the disk.

opposite sides of this question were taken by those masters, Helmholtz (1866, 537–566) and Hering (1874, 1876). Hering stood for a strictly physiological explanation in terms of interaction between different parts of the retina; the external stimulus evoked a certain chemical reaction in one region and induced the opposite reaction in the adjacent region. One difficulty was to explain the increased brightness of a gray field surrounded by black. How can black, the absence of a stimulus, have any effect on the adjacent region? The explanation is that white when present over a considerable area darkens itself by *internal contrast*. Each part of any uniform bright area induces the dark reaction in neighboring parts of the same area and a large white area is thus darkened more than a small area surrounded by black. Of many bits of evidence advanced in favor of the peripheral theory, perhaps the strongest is that of Sherrington (1897) who showed that the fusion frequency of a black and white disk could be raised by the contrast effect (Fig. 158). It is scarcely possible that a flicker could be prevented by the psychological factors brought forward by Helmholtz.

Helmholtz's theory is sometimes said to attribute the contrast effect to an error of judgment, but this account of the theory is scarcely adequate. According to his view, the main factor in brightness and color contrast is the same as in many other cases of contrasted objects. A medium-sized man appears tall when standing with short men, short when standing with tall men. A loud note breaking into a soft passage seems remarkably loud, a medium speed following full speed of the automobile seems very slow. The principle, according to Helmholtz, is that clearly perceived differences are enhanced or exaggerated. Another factor in visual contrast comes into operation when the field of view is predominantly of one color: the average color of the field, Helmholtz said, is accepted for the time being as the norm and identified with white. In many cases the predominant color of the field gives the impression of illumination rather than of object color. In yellow illumination a pale yellow appears white or neutral, and a neutral gray stimulus therefore appears tinged with the complementary color. Gelb (1932) presents good evidence that contrast depends on the apparent illumination of the field rather than on adjoining object colors. Quite similar to Helmholtz's emphasis on the average color of the field is Koffka's (1932, 1935) conception of a general level of the field color which serves as a neutral framework in which particular bits of the field have apparent color according to their divergence from this level. These recent writers, however, avoid Helmholtz's intellectualistic phraseology and his reference to "illusions of judgment."

Psychological factors in contrast. Certain psychological factors operate in the direction of *annulling* or correcting the contrast effects which would otherwise tinge and falsify the apparent color of many objects. When a piece of gray paper is laid on a sheet of colored paper, what demands explanation in view of other instances of contrast is its relative absence here. The explanation is, or may be, that the objective character of the field stands out so clearly that the gray is seen in its true color. When the objective character of the field is partially obscured by a superimposed sheet of tissue paper or by holding the field close to the eye, contrast is unescapable. A contemplative rather than an object-directed attitude is favorable for getting contrast colors and can be acquired by practice (Riedel, 1937).

One instance in which the customary object-directed attitude annuls color contrast was used by Wundt in his lectures (Sander, 1928; Riedel, 1937), though perhaps interpreted somewhat differently. Two bits of the same gray paper are laid respectively on white and black grounds, and the one on black appears the lighter. Now lay a narrow strip of the same gray paper so as to form a bridge between the two bits of gray, and the contrast mostly disappears. If this whole field is held close to the eye, contrast reappears very strongly. Conditions which favor clear perception of the objective situation tend to annul contrast.

Contrast plays a useful role in increasing the distinctness of vision by correcting the effect of irradiation, the latter being due to imperfect focus, etc. The biological importance of contrast has been especially emphasized by Hering and his followers (Tschermak, 1929). If perceptual factors annul the contrast effect, is the advantage for distinct vision thereby lost? Not necessarily. The advantage of binocular vision is not lost because the two views are so fused that we are aware of only one. The contrast effect may be lost in the sense that it does not disturb object perception, but it may remain in the distinctness of different parts of the field of view.

Contrast is really an enhanced difference between different parts of the field. When one part is seen as figure and another as ground, it is the figure which seems to carry the enhanced effect. Examine a field in two shades of gray, such a field as can show figure-ground reversal (p. 629). For example let there be alternate stripes of the lighter and the darker gray. The contrast effect consists in an enhanced difference between the light and the dark, but the effect is seen on the figure rather than on the ground. If the dark stripes are seen as figure their darkness is enhanced, if the white stripes are seen as figure their whiteness is enhanced (Wolff, 1934; Riedel, 1937).

The retina and the lower levels of the receptive process probably can make no distinction between ground and surround. In perception there is a distinction. A gray patch surrounded half by black and half by white may seem to stand on the black or on the white. To many eyes it appears whiter when seeming to stand on the black and darker when on the white (Benary, 1924).

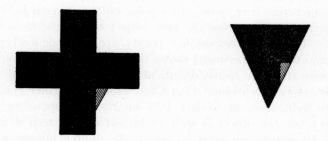

Fig. 159. (Benary, 1924.) Contrast dependent on the background rather than the surround.

Somewhat related to the contrast effect is the effect of bright or of dark surroundings upon the visibility of objects in the central field of vision. Visibility can be tested by an acuity test or by determining the threshold for difference of brightness within the central field. Common experience teaches that glare from bright surroundings interferes with vision. Experiment shows very little of this effect unless the bright surroundings are as close as 5–8 degrees to the central field. If bright light shines into the eye within a few degrees of the objects being examined, visibility is very definitely decreased. We might expect that dark surroundings would be an especially favorable condition, but the best evidence is that the surround should be about of equal brightness with the test field in order to obtain the maximum efficiency of vision (Cobb, 1916; Johnson, 1924).

BINOCULAR VISION

The fact that human beings have two eyes, directed forward and with overlapping fields of view, is of special importance in perceiving the three-dimensional characteristics of things in the world and will loom large in our later chapter on visual space. Apart from space perception, the interrelations of the two eyes raise a number of dynamic problems indicated by the phrases, binocular rivalry, fusion, summation.

Binocular vision is not merely the normal condition, it is practically unescapable. Closing one eye does not put that eye out of commission; it simply gives it a dark field to combine or compete with the bright field of the open eye. We can secure monocular (uniocular, if you prefer) vision of an object, monocular reception of a particular stimulus, but we cannot secure completely monocular vision. If you close the right eye, your field of view includes the objects visible to the left eye, around to the nose, and beyond that, on the right, a dark field around to the normal limit of the right eye's field.

Corresponding points of the two retinas. With both eyes open and directed upon the same small object, that object is seen single in spite of the two optical images, one on each fovea. The foveas are said to be corresponding points (better, spots) because of this single vision. Any point on one retina corresponds to a point on the other if light striking the two seems to come from the same object or at least from the same direction. Though corresponding points are thus defined primarily in functional terms, experiment shows them to correspond geometrically as well since they are nearly identical in their distance and direction from their respective foveas. (See Carr, 1935, for further elucidation.) When the light from an object falls on non-corresponding parts of the two retinas, the object is seen double, or can be seen double after practice. Ordinarily we scarcely notice the double images which are constantly present in the binocular field.

When, as often happens, the light from an object is screened from one eye by some intervening object, we do not ordinarily notice any difference between the monocular and binocular views, nor can we tell which eye is seeing the object; but perhaps we could tell with practice. In an experiment by Thelin & Altman (1929) a small circle of light, 11 ft. distant from O in a dark room, was screened by shutters from either eye. O judged which eye was stimulated and was informed of his errors. In the course of 400 trials, nearly every O showed improvement, except indeed for those accustomed to monocular work with the microscope, who were practically perfect from the start of the experiment.

In a type of experiment which might be called *dichopic* (by analogy with the dichotic and dichorhinic experiments in hearing and smell) discrepant stimulation is applied to corresponding parts of the two retinas. What response will the brain make to such a conflict of cues? It might disregard one retina and respond only to the other, or it might respond to the combination in several ways: by fusion of the monocular fields, by seeing one through the other, or, where possible, by getting a depth effect.

To effect dichopic stimulation, the simplest procedure is simply to close one eye; the result for most of the time is complete unawareness of the dark monocular field. A small mirror held close to one eye at a suitable angle gives a reflected field overlying the directly seen field of the other eye. The stereoscope (p. 655) is a very convenient means of presenting radically different colors or figures to corresponding areas of the two eyes.

Binocular rivalry. Radically different colors or figures presented simultaneously to corresponding areas of the two eyes are not usually combined. At first only one is seen, the other being entirely invisible, but sooner or later a shift occurs, what was invisible coming into view and what was visible disappearing. The reverse shift follows and the alternation becomes more rapid as the double exposure continues.

Using a prism stereoscope, Breese (1899, 1909) presented a red square to one eye and a green square to the corresponding area of the other eye. To increase the discrepancy he ruled parallel oblique lines on each square but in different directions on the two squares. By use of electric keys and markers, O recorded on a kymograph the time during which each field was seen.

Since the two fields were seen alternately, we can speak of a whole cycle as consisting of two phases, a right eye phase and a left eye phase, or a red and a green phase. The kymograph record provided an answer to two main questions, concerning the duration of the cycle and concerning the relative duration of the two phases; i.e., concerning the *rate* of rivalry and concerning conditions of *prevalence* or advantage.

Rate of alternation. When parallel changes were made in the two monocular fields, the following factors were found to change the rate:

1. Light intensity. With low illumination the cycle duration averaged 8.5 sec.; with increased illumination this decreased to as little as 2.5 sec. The intense field gave the rapid alternation.

2. Area of field. The larger the field the more rapid the alternation.

3. Distinctness of lines. When the stereoscope slide was moved out of focus, blurring the lines, the alternation was slower.

4. Central vision gave more rapid alternation than peripheral vision. Increasing the distance from the fovea increased the cycle duration, which averaged:

In central vision	4.9 sec.
3.6° to right or left	9.1 sec.
3.6° up or down	11.1 sec.
7.2° to right or left	10.8 sec.
7.2° up or down	11.8 sec.

Evidently conditions which make for efficient vision favor rapid alternation (p. 327).

Prevalence. In this part of Breese's experiment the two eyes were treated differently in some respect, and the question was, which eye would see its field a larger fraction of the time—which phase of the cycle would be longer. The following factors were effective.

1. Light intensity. The brighter field was visible 60 percent of the time when the intensity ratio was 4 to 1. When the intensity difference is very great—as when both eyes are closed, one being also covered by the hand while a bright light is brought close to the other— the dark field is invisible most of the time.

2. Presence of figures. A field containing lines prevails over a plain field as much as 70 percent of the time. A single letter written on one field remains visible almost the whole time, even while the rest of its field is invisible, and around the letter a halo of its background is usually seen.

3. Movement. When both fields contain figures and the figure on one is made to move, it remains in sight more than half the time.

4. Attention. As between two absolutely plain fields, voluntary effort has no effect, but if there is any perceptible figure, smudge or texture in either field, that field can be held more than half the time by exploring the figuration. When both fields offer a multitude of details, attention to either one will hold it for most of the time.

As to the cause of rivalry, one ready suggestion would attribute it to eye movements—though we should then have to ask what causes the eye movements. Peckham (1936) could find no better than chance coincidence in the time of eye movements and that of rivalry changes as signaled by O. Any adequate explanation would have to cover three points: (a) why response is made to only one at a time of the retinal fields, (b) why the stronger, clearer or more interesting field has the advantage, and (c) why the advantage shifts. Fatigue of the momentarily active response mechanism seems a likely explanation of the third point. The first point is quite in line with the selective response to conflicting stimuli, as observed in reflex action (Sherrington, 1906). As to the second point, evidently selection depends not only on stimulus characteristics but also on the available responses.

Binocular fusion. Rivalry amounts to a cortical response to one or the other of the retinal fields, and to only one at a time. Binocular fusion consists in making a single cortical response to the combination of the two retinal fields. Under what conditions does fusion occur? We have no adequate answer. It occurs, or so we believe, when the two retinal fields are almost alike in color, brightness and pattern. Even here rivalry can be observed under experimental conditions (stereoscope) and may be more common than we suppose. When the fields differ very much, rivalry is the rule and fusion the exception.

The question of *binocular color mixture* is still unsettled in spite of a century of sporadic investigation. If a red glass is held before one eye and a green glass before the other—or if by aid of a stereoscope or just by suitable convergence of the eyes red and green are presented in corresponding areas of the two fields—the usual result is rivalry; but some Os get fusion which in this case gives a yellow mixture of the red and the green. Many competent observers have found it impossible to obtain this fusion, while others have secured it without difficulty.

In a stereoscope experiment of Johannsen (1930) approximately monochromatic colors were presented by use of Wratten filters. With four Os there was never any fusion of the following pairs, one color to each eye: yellow and blue, red and blue, red and blue-green; while fusion occurred practically always with yellow and yellow-green, with blue and blue-green, and with yellow-green and blue-green, i.e., with colors lying close together in the spectrum. Fusion was favored by equal intensities of the two colors, and also by low intensity.

Hecht, however (1928), had good success in obtaining binocular mixture of quite diverse colors of high intensity, by use of the following setup. O faces a square of white cardboard, 1 meter in front of him, from which projects a 250-watt bulb. The bulb strongly illuminates the cardboard and almost forces O's eyes to converge on the glowing filament. He looks at the lamp through a black-inside box which carries a red Wratten filter before one eye, and a green one before the other eye. He thus gets a red square before one eye, a green one before the other eye, the two squares partially overlapping in the binocular field. Fusion instantly occurs in the overlapping part, in most Os, who report seeing red and green at the sides and yellow in the middle. If the filters are yellow and blue, they report white in the middle.

In this experiment the mixture occurs not in the retina but either in the interbrain or in the cortex. Just for convenience, let us say the cortex. The cortex, then, can respond with a sensation of yellow to red and green stimulation coming in separately from the retinas; and it can respond by a sensation of white to yellow and blue from the retinas. If the cortex can do this in binocular stimulation, it can doubtless do the same when the red and green come in from different sets of receptors located close together in the same retina. Therefore, Hecht concludes, yellow and white may be purely cortical responses, and their unitary character offers no obstacle to accepting the Young-Helmholtz three-component theory of the retinal response.

Though the argument is rather convincing, it leaves one or two questions unsettled. It does not account for the fact that dichromatic vision, in the red-green blind individual and in the intermediate zone of the normal retina, is yellow-blue vision. And it leaves us wondering why the cortex does not respond to a mixture of red and green by seeing reddish green—as it responds to a mixture of red and blue by seeing reddish blue. Why should the red and green disappear and give way to the apparently unitary yellow? The Hering and Ladd-Franklin theories offer a conceptual scheme for handling these difficulties, but demand retinal color mixture.

CHAPTER XXIII

EYE MOVEMENTS

B ESIDES the movement of the eyeball as a whole, the topic of eye movements properly includes two sorts of movements that occur inside the eyeball. The ciliary muscle changes the convexity of the lens in accommodation for near and far; and the smooth muscle of the iris narrows and widens the pupil. The iris, controlled by the autonomic nerves, has been studied somewhat in relation to emotion, and the pupillary reflexes have been employed in experiments on conditioning. The movements of accommodation would probably be found of much interest in psychology, but thus far psychologists have concerned themselves principally with the movements of the whole eyeball, and it is to this part of the subject that this chapter will be devoted.

The eyeballs are rotated in their sockets by their "extrinsic" muscles, six in number for each eye. The four rectus muscles exert a straight up, down, right or left pull. The *internal rectus* turns the front of the eye to the nasal side, the *external rectus* to the temporal side, the *superior rectus* upward, the *inferior rectus* downward. The *superior* and *inferior oblique* muscles pull in an oblique direction but probably act always in conjunction with the rectus muscles.

These muscles receive their motor nerve supply from the third, fourth and sixth cranial nerves; the center for these (the lower motor center for the eyes) lies in the midbrain and bulb—more precisely, close to the aqueduct in the midbrain and in the floor of the fourth ventricle in the bulb. All parts of this motor eye center are interconnected by nerve fibers and operate together. Coordination is seen in the movements of each single eye, the several muscles working smoothly together. When the external rectus contracts and pulls the eye outward, the internal rectus relaxes a corresponding amount. Coordination of the two eyes is surprisingly close. When one eye looks to the right, so does the other; the external rectus of the right eye and the internal rectus of the left contract simultaneously. This *conjugate* movement occurs even when only one of the eyes has received the visual stimulus.

Whether binocular coordination is native or acquired is perhaps an open question. Statements can be found in the literature of child study to the effect that the newborn baby is likely to move one eye alone, or to move one upward and the other simultaneously downward. The present author takes leave to doubt the accuracy or at least the generality of such statements, since his own observation of the eyes of newborn children has never revealed any such incoordination.

The conjugate movement brings an object of attention from the periphery to the center of the visual field, the center of clear vision. It brings the optical image of the object to the fovea and surrounding macula or yellow spot. The eyes show another type of coordination in the movement of *convergence*. If an object approaches the eyes, the eyes must converge in order to keep its image on both foveas. Instead of the internal rectus of one eye working together with the external rectus of the other, as in conjugate movements, in convergence the two internal recti act together, and in returning from convergence to the parallel position both external recti act together. With convergence are associated the movements of accommodation and of the iris which focus the lens and adjust the pupil for the distance of the object.

METHODS OF OBSERVING AND RECORDING EYE MOVEMENTS

The facts so far mentioned have long been in the possession of physiologists, but the finer details—some being of great importance in understanding such psychological processes as reading or the perception of objects—awaited the development of accurate methods of observation. For technical analysis see Wendt & Dodge (1938) or Wendt (1938).

1. **Direct observation.** The most important single fact, it is true, was discovered by Javal (1878) without any more special technique than simply watching the eye of a school child who was reading. His very eminent predecessors had assumed the truth of the common belief in "sweeping the eyes over a scene or along a line of print." He found, not a steady sweep, but a series of little jumps with intervening fixation pauses. The eye moved, as he said, "par saccades," from which expression comes the name *saccadic* now applied to this class of quick eye movements. More regarding them is given below.

Good use can be made of a mirror placed to afford E a view of O's eyes. If O is reading, the mirror can be laid on the table beside the book, and both E and O can rest their heads on both hands, so as to minimize head movements. O faces the light and E, sitting opposite, has a good view of O's eyes in the mirror (Erdmann & Dodge, 1898).

For a quick test of eye movements in reading Miles (1928 b) uses a "peephole method." A page of reading matter, with a small hole cut in its center, is held up for O to read and his eyes are watched through the hole, E being sufficiently concealed to avoid distracting the reader.

These direct methods reveal the general character of eye movements, but they do not catch all the very small, quick saccadic movements (Robinson & Murphy, 1932). Nor do they furnish any measures of the speed and extent of the movements, or of the duration and location of the fixations. Some way of recording the movements is desirable.

2. **Mechanical registration.** The first successful recording method, though soon superseded, deserves mention. It was an adaptation of

the standard laboratory method of recording muscular movements on a smoked drum. While the drum is rotating steadily and carrying the smoked surface from right to left, a writing lever connected with the muscle moves up and down and inscribes a curve on the smoked surface. The problem of connecting the eyeball and the writing lever was solved by Delabarre (1898) and Huey (1908). A ring of plaster of Paris, polished smooth, was applied to the cornea in such a way as not to obstruct O's vision. Adhering to the moist surface of the cornea, which was cocainized to avoid pain and winking, the ring was connected by a light rod to the writing lever. The apparatus caused no serious inconvenience to O, and gave fairly good registration, so that the results

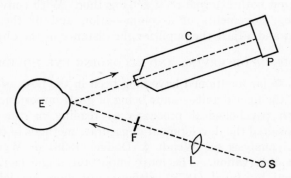

Fig. 160. Scheme of the nucleus of the Dodge setup. E is the eye, much exaggerated in size in respect to the rest of the diagram. Light from the source S, as shown by the dotted lines, is reflected from the cornea into the camera. In the path of the beam are interposed L, a lens which makes the rays of light parallel, and F, a filter of blue glass which moderates the light shining into the eye without greatly reducing its effect on the photographic plate. C is the bellows of the camera, and P is a special plate holder or film holder, arranged to move the plate or film steadily in a vertical direction while the reflected beam is writing its horizontal movements upon the photosensitive surface.

obtained in several experiments have been mostly confirmed by use of more adequate methods.

3. **Photographic registration of corneal reflection.** With photography there will be no load on the eye and no slip or lag in the connections. A beam of light, thrown from the side and reflected from the cornea, can be made to record the eye movement on a steadily moving photographic plate or film. A little further explanation is necessary.

Everyone is familiar with the "bright spot" on the eye, which is any bright light reflected from the surface of the cornea. It moves with the eyes. Why it should move is clear from the shape of the eyeball. If the eyeball were a simple sphere turning about its center, there would evidently be no such motion of the spot. The cornea, however, projects forward from the general spherical surface of the eyeball and is, indeed, a portion of a smaller sphere with an imaginary center in front of the center of the whole eyeball. The result is that, as the eyeball turns, the cornea changes its angle to the incident beam of light and consequently reflects the beam in a different direction. So the reflected beam moves with the eye and can be used to register the eye movement on the steadily moving film. With careful arrangements this method is delicate and accurate. Invented by Dodge (see Dodge & Cline, 1901), this method has been adapted to various experiments and is by all odds the most widely employed.

Dodge's apparatus was arranged to register the horizontal movements of the eyes upon a sensitive plate or film which moved steadily in a vertical direction. Two difficulties had to be overcome: either head movements or irregular motion of the recording apparatus would confuse the record of eye movements. Arrangements were contrived to insure steady motion of the plate. Film has largely supplanted plates, because of the longer consecutive records that it allows. The head can be held fairly steady by a combination of supports for the upper teeth, the bridge of the nose, and the mastoid process behind one ear—with O's attentive cooperation. Some head movement is bound to remain, and it is best to register it along with the eye movement, by reflection from a bright bead fastened to a spectacle frame worn by O. The recorded head movements can be allowed for, when interpreting the eye movement record. The time must be registered, and this is done very conveniently in photographic registration by interrupting the light by a tuning fork or reed vibrating at a known rate (pp. 104, 112).

In order to locate the fixations of the eye on the object which O is examining during the exposure, the record is calibrated while it is being made. O holds his eyes fixed for a moment on certain assigned points in the object—say at each end of a line of print—and thus leaves reference points in the photographic record. The record is later projected upon the actual page and trued by these reference points.

Records of considerable value can be obtained even without a moving film. A time exposure with a stationary film shielded from all light except the beam reflected from the cornea shows the movements and fixations of the eye for a brief period and has the advantage of recording not simply the horizontal movements of reading but the movements in all directions that occur as the eye surveys an object or scene (Stratton, 1902 b, 1906; see p. 585).

3. **The motion picture method.** At first thought the motion picture camera affords an easy and complete solution of the problem of registering eye movements. Movements in all directions can be recorded, timed and measured. But there are difficulties to overcome. How are you going to use the record? Merely running the film through a projector and viewing the picture does not put you far ahead. It gives you no better view than you could get from direct observation of the eyes themselves, except that the film can be run through repeatedly for completing and verifying your observations. Judd (1905) overcame this and other

difficulties. Each frame is projected separately on a sheet of drawing paper and the position of the eye in each successive frame is marked on the paper. A line connecting these points maps the path taken by the eye. Time is known from the rate at which the camera was operated, and if this rate is not dependably uniform, an electric circuit connected with the camera movement can be made to write a special time record on a smoked drum.

We have slurred over a serious difficulty in assuming that the position of the eye in each frame can be marked on the drawing paper. The eye itself, with its smooth surface, round iris and variable pupil, offers no definite point to be marked and followed. Judd found that a small flake of China white, thinly coated with paraffin to make it smooth and durable, could be placed on the cornea over the iris without causing any discomfort. It could be so placed as to remain in position even during winking. It photographed well and showed distinctly in every frame which caught the eye in fixation. When a frame caught the eye in motion, the flake of China white left a faint streak and so recorded the fact of eye movement. It was this white spot that was mapped on the drawing paper and yielded information regarding eye movements and fixations.

A fundamental difficulty is that the motion picture camera yields not a continuous record but a series of exposures separated by blank periods during which the film is advanced. Eye movement of the saccadic type is also intermittent and many of its small movements are so quick and brief (occupying about $\frac{1}{50}$ sec.) that they can occur wholly within the blanks of the photographic record. Judd partially overcame this difficulty by using two cameras, so geared together that the exposures of one coincided with the blank intervals of the other. The rate of the camera can be increased but then strong light must be thrown upon the eye. In spite of all these difficulties some good results have been obtained from moving picture records of the eyes.

4. **The afterimage method.** This oldest of aids in the observation of eye movements did good service for Helmholtz (1856–66) and other physiologists. A strong, sharp afterimage obtained by steady fixation of a small bright light remains fixed with respect to the retina and moves with the eyes. Where it rests, there the eyes are fixated, and when it moves along a page it reveals the shifting of fixation. If it wavers or slides, fixation is unsteady. If O repeatedly fixates the same object, looking aside between times, the afterimage will show whether the eye always comes back precisely to the same point or allows itself some latitude of fixation. The advantages of this method are its convenience and its freedom from instrumental errors. Its obvious limitation is that it demands O's careful attention and does not leave him free to read or observe normally.

Another similar method (Lamansky, 1869) utilizes the brief positive after-sensation following momentary stimulation. When the field of view is dark except for one bright light, every eye movement leaves a visible streak which is a trace of the path of the movement. If the light is intermittent, consisting of 120 flashes per sec., the streak shows this intermittence in the form of a dotted line, and each dot represents $\frac{1}{120}$ sec. Fairly accurate measurements of the speed of some eye movements were obtained by this method before photographic registration was developed.

TYPES OF EYE MOVEMENT

Using his method of photographing eye movements on a moving plate, Dodge (1903) found that several distinct types appeared in the records. Besides convergence, there were two main forms of conjugate movement: the rapid saccadic jump of the eyes to a new fixation point,

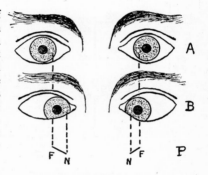

FIG. 161. (Judd, 1907.) Method of studying convergence by use of the motion picture camera. The upper pair of eyes is in the parallel position as if looking at a distant object. The lower pair is strongly converged upon a near object lying below the level of the eyes. (The lid movement which accompanies downward eye movement is not represented in this diagram.) On each iris can be seen a spot of China white, and the dotted lines indicate the method of using these spots for plotting the eye movement.

and the relatively slow pursuit of a moving object. Then there were eye movements compensating for head movements—two types of such. And we might add fixation which, if not a movement, is the most important type of ocular behavior, since it is fixation that gives a view of the object. The function of the saccadic movement is to carry the eye from one fixation to another; the function of the pursuit movement is to maintain fixation on a moving object; and the function of the compensatory movements is to maintain fixation in spite of head and body movements. The types of eye behavior can be set out in the following schema:

1. Fixation on a stationary object.
2. Saccadic movement from one fixation to another.
3. Pursuit movement, maintaining fixation on a moving object.
4. Convergence and relative divergence, securing binocular fixation on shifting between a near and a far object.
5. Compensation for active head movement—a head-eye coordination.
6. Compensation for passive movements—an ear-eye reflex.

All these types of eye movement serve the requirements of clear vision. There are also some self-servicing movements of the eyeball, such as the upward turn during sleep and the slighter upward movement that occurs in the act of winking (Miles, 1931 c).

Fixation not absolute and precise. The eye does not need to operate with mathematical precision, for its "center of clear vision" is not a mathematical point. In returning to the same point on an object it does not come back to precisely the same position. This lack of precision

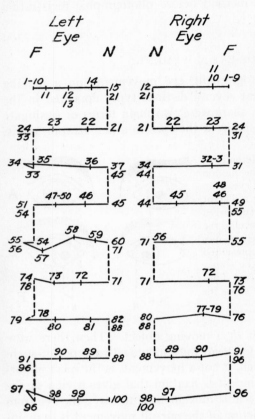

FIG. 162. (Judd, 1907.) Movements of convergence and relative divergence. O's eyes were photographed during repeated shifting to and fro between a near and a far fixation point, situated directly in front of the nose at distances of 30 and 55 cm. The figure shows the plot obtained from the photographs. The vertical dotted lines indicate the fixation pauses, those under F representing the fixations on the far point and those under N the fixations on the near point. The solid lines, horizontal or nearly so, represent the path of each eye in passing between the near and far fixation points. Both eyes were photographed simultaneously, at the rate of slightly over 10 exposures per second. The numbers written on the record are the successive exposures, and can be taken as time units of approximately $\frac{1}{10}$ of a second (more exactly, of 94 ms). The position of each number shows where the spot of China white was found during the successive exposures.

The record starts with the eyes fixating the far point. The left eye remains on this point for the first 10 exposures, moves toward the near point, being caught en route in exposures 12, 13 and 14, and reaches its near fixation by the 15th exposure. It occupied nearly ½ sec. in this movement of convergence, which was interrupted by a definite pause at the point marked 12 and 13.

The right eye began its first movement of convergence before the left, since exposure 10 caught it on the way, and it reached the goal first (exposure 12 as against 15). Both eyes remained fixated on the near point till exposure 21, when they simultaneously moved to the far point, keeping in perfect step during this movement of (relative) divergence, which occupied about 300 ms. In the next movement of convergence, the right eye again took the lead, advancing at first only a short distance (exposures 32–3), then executing a rapid movement to the destination. The left eye made a short conjugate movement along with the right eye (33–34), corrected this and swung into convergence, reaching the near point by exposure 37, nearly 300 ms behind the right eye. Similar behavior occurs further down the record; in fact, with this particular individual, every time the eyes converge, the left eye makes a false start to the left in sympathy with the right eye. Individuals differ in this respect, from habit or because of dominance of one eye or because of lack of perfect balance between the muscles of the two eyeballs.

is easily verified by the afterimage method. The setting sun makes a good object to fixate: look at it, away from it, at it again, for a few times, and then notice the afterimages of the sun. If you find a cluster of suns you know that the eye was in slightly different positions during the several fixations. Using the motion picture camera, McAllister (1905) abundantly verified the result stated. He also found that the eyes did not remain absolutely motionless even during a single fixation lasting for a second. Dodge (1907) was in general agreement.

Convergence and relative divergence. By relative divergence is meant the return of the eyes to or toward the parallel position. In distant vision the ocular axes are parallel, in near vision more or less convergent. When a change of fixation occurs from a near to a far object or the reverse, the task imposed on the eyes is more difficult than in the simple conjugate movement, as is clear from the photographic records.

Movements of convergence were photographed by Judd (1907) with the motion picture camera. A little sample of his results is shown. There was good evidence that such movements are labored. They take much more time than the simple conjugate movements and are often interrupted by pauses. The two eyes do not always keep step; one may pause while the other is moving; one may reach its destination and remain there while the other is still feeling around. When the eyes shift their gaze from a far to a near object, the first attempt is likely to leave them imperfectly converged and the object is "seen double." This double vision is corrected by readjusting the direction of one or both eyes.

One cause of the difficulty appears in records. In passing from a far to a near point the eyes need to turn in opposite directions but they often show first a short movement in the same direction. This easier conjugate movement gets the start of the other and proceeds a short distance before being corrected.

One practical inference is that reading matter should be so held as to minimize the necessity of changes in convergence as the eyes proceed along a line of print. All parts of the *same line* of print should be nearly at the same distance from the eye, so that no change in convergence will be required in reading the line. If a change in convergence is necessary in passing down the page, that is unimportant because the progress of the eyes down a page is slow. Ease of eye movements demands that the page, even though tilted back so as to have the best illumination, should not be tilted to the right or left.

The comparative slowness of movements of convergence and divergence can be observed by a subjective method also, akin to the afterimage method already mentioned. Choose a near and a far object, each of which is distinct and contrasts sharply with a plain background, the near object within a foot or two of the eyes and almost in a direct line with the far object, so that a shift from one object to another requires merely change of convergence. While you look with both eyes at the far object, the near object is seen double; the same happens to the far object when the near object is fixated. As you shift your gaze from one to the other, the double images merge into one, and the merging may take an appreciable time. The merging is the visual result of the comparatively slow sliding into position of the eyes.

The saccadic movement. This is the simple looking movement, a conjugate movement without complication by change of convergence. It is the reaction of the eyes to a stimulus received in indirect vision, and brings the object into the central area of clear vision. It is the movement used in reading and in surveying any stationary object or scene. There are several remarkable facts about this saccadic movement.

It is the most frequent sort of eye movement.

It is only very imperfectly felt by the subject. The sensations of movement from the eye muscles and from the eye socket are slight, especially for short movements, and give no reliable indication when the eye is moving and when it is still. O cannot count his own saccadic eye movements, and in fact, as was said before, he usually has an entirely false impression of the behavior of his eyes in reading or in surveying a scene. He imagines himself to be sweeping his eyes by a continuous gradual movement along the line or about the room, whereas all the objective methods show that he is really moving his eyes by jumps separated by fixation pauses.

It is a coordinated movement of the two eyes. Even if one eye is screened from the page or scene, it still keeps step with the other.

Its starts quickly, and stops quickly, like an automobile, and makes its journey with little loss of time. A movement over a space of five letters of ordinary print, at a reading distance of a foot, takes 15–20 ms, or about $\frac{1}{60}$ sec. The following table from Dodge & Cline (1901) gives the duration of longer movements, their extent being measured by the angle through which the eye swings.[1] The table quotes the average from three subjects.

DURATION OF SACCADIC EYE MOVEMENTS
(*Dodge & Cline, 1901*)

Extent of movement	Duration of movement
5°	29 ms
10°	39
15°	48
20°	55
30°	80
40°	100

The longer movements take longer times, though they are more rapid. Individuals differ somewhat; a distance which one covers in 50 ms may take another, 60 ms. For the same individual and the same

---

[1] For movements of twenty degrees or less, along a page held a foot from the eyes, each degree means approximately $\frac{1}{5}$ of an inch, so that 5° = 1 inch, 10° = 2 inches, 15° = 3 inches, and 20° = 4 inches (more precisely, 4.23 inches).

extent of movement, the time is nearly but not perfectly constant.

The speed of the saccadic movements is not subject to voluntary control; you cannot hasten or slacken them at will. You can make them at will by voluntarily looking from one point to another, and you can even make them at will while the eyes are closed.

The speed of the saccadic movement changes somewhat with O's

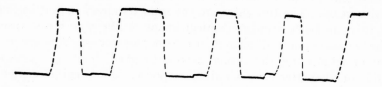

FIG. 163. (Dodge & Benedict, 1915.) Long saccadic movements. The eye shifted back and forth between fixation points 40 degrees apart. The light beam was interrupted 100 times per sec., and the duration of the movements can be found by counting the dashes. The heavy lines are fixations, during which the separate flashes of the light are too close together on the record to be distinguished. Minute saccadic movements can be seen in many of the fixation periods, and the largest of these little jumps, from the record, covered about 4 degrees and took from 10 to 20 ms. As the original eye movements were horizontal, the figure is best seen from the side. For photographic records of eye movements in reading, see p. 722.

organic condition, being slower in drowsiness or under alcohol (Dodge & Benedict, 1915; Miles, 1924, 1929; Miles & Laslett, 1931).

We might expect the reaction time of the saccadic movement to be very short, but it is in fact about the same as that of a hand response to a visual stimulus (p. 324). The saccadic response to a stimulus appearing in indirect vision was found to be 195 ms on the average with a range of individual averages from 125 to 235 ms (Diefendorf & Dodge, 1908).

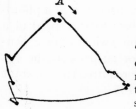

FIG. 164. (Stratton, 1902 b, 1906.) Eye movement in "sweeping the eyes" around a circle. The lines are saccadic movements and the dots fixations. This and similar records by Stratton showed the impossibility of explaining the esthetic pleasure in a seen curve by the supposed smooth sweep of the eyes along the curve.

The pursuit movement. In looking at a moving object the eyes follow it or, better, keep pace with it. They stay right on the object, though with some tendency to fall behind and catch up again. The catching up consists of a saccadic movement. When a moving object in indirect vision catches the eye, a saccadic movement brings the object into central vision and a pursuit movement keeps it there. The speed of a pursuit movement is governed by the speed of the moving object, though there are limits to the eye's ability to keep pace with very slow or very rapid movement. The pursuit movement cannot be executed at will, in the absence of a moving stimulus.

The utility of this type of movement can be seen from a little experiment. Provide two sheets of paper with writing on each, and let one of them be as transparent as possible. Lay the transparent sheet over the other and move it back and forth at moderate speed. When you fixate a word on the moving sheet the words on the stationary sheet are blurred, and vice versa. The two cases are the same as far as the retina is concerned; for in both cases the optical image of one object is stationary on the retina, while the image of the other moves on the retina. An image moving along the retina gives a blurred or streaky sensation because of the after-lag of retinal response. *For distinct vision, the image of the object must be stationary on the retina.* If the external object is stationary, the retina must be stationary; and if the external object is in motion, the retina must keep pace with it. The pursuit movement amounts to a moving fixation.

When a large moving object presents interesting details, the eyes make saccadic movements from one part to another as they do with a stationary object; they fixate one part after another, but each fixation consists in a pursuit movement. Move a printed page from side to side while reading: you can still read without much trouble, advancing from word to word by saccadic movements and fixating by use of the pursuit movement.

Pursuit movements occur not only in watching a moving object while you are stationary yourself, but also in watching stationary objects while you are in motion. As far as the eyes are concerned the two cases are the same. Looking sideways out of a moving vehicle, your eyes fixate, i.e., pursue, one object for a while and then jump to another. The alternation of quick saccadic and relatively slow pursuit movements in such a case is well worth watching in a fellow-passenger.

The characteristics of the pursuit movement are best seen in a photographic record. The eyes quickly adjust themselves to the speed of a uniformly moving object and even to the rhythmic swinging of a pendulum. If the moving object goes out of sight for an instant, the eye immediately falls behind. The pursuit movement requires the constant presence of a moving visual stimulus. See Fig. 165.

COMPENSATORY EYE MOVEMENTS

The two types of movement still to be considered compensate for head movements by reverse movements of the eyeballs in their sockets. If the head movement is to the left and upward, the compensatory rotation of the eyeballs is to the right and downward. The compensatory movements are like the pursuit movement in respect to speed. The pursuit movement could be said to compensate for the movement of an external object, and the compensatory movements could be said to pursue an object whose image tends to move on the retina because of head movement. In spite of this similarity, the pursuit movement and the two types of compensatory movement have important differences in latency and in the stimulus to which they respond.

Head-eye coordination. There are really two very different coordinations of the head and the eyes. When fixation is shifting from one object to another, as in *looking to the side*, head and eyes turn in the same direction, and the distance between the old and the new fixation point may be covered partly by the head movement and partly by the eyes. When the angular distance is small, as in reading, the head may remain motionless, at least in adults, and leave the eyes to cover the

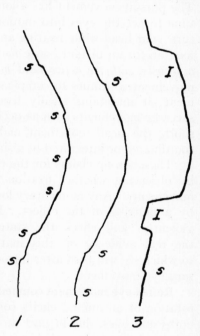

FIG. 165. (After Dodge, 1907.) Tracing of photographic record of pursuit movements. The stimulus was a pendulum, followed for several swings. The pendulum was swinging to the right in each of the three records here reproduced. The lines are to be read upward. (1) Starting from a stationary fixation, the eye jumps into a moving fixation which is corrected by several small saccadic movements, s, s, s. (2) After several swings the pursuit movement has become smooth and accurate, with only a few slight saccadic corrections. (3) Disturbance results when the pendulum is hidden for a part of each swing, as at I. With the visual stimulus gone, the eye falls behind and makes a large saccadic movement on the reappearance of the pendulum.

whole distance; but when an object is far around to the side, most of the angle is covered by the head.

Maintaining fixation during active head movements is quite a different coordination. The eyes move opposite to the head and maintain the original fixation in spite of the head movement. Thus it is possible and even perfectly easy to continue looking at the same object while moving the head. This is the easiest eye movement to observe: watch your own eyes in a mirror while turning the head from side to side. You would almost suppose the eyes to be merely standing still by inertia, but this cannot be the case. The eyes are not loose in their sockets, not as loose probably as the tongue is in the open mouth; and the tongue does not behave in this compensatory fashion when the head is turned from side to side. (The pursuit movement also can be observed in the mirror: hold the head still and turn the mirror. You thus change the direction in which the eyes must look in order to keep themselves in view; the eyes follow themselves readily if the motion of the mirror is not too fast. The saccadic movement cannot be observed in the mirror, because you cannot keep your eyes directed toward your eyes while shifting them from one object to another.)

This compensatory movement is so much like the pursuit movement that one is tempted to regard them as identical. They look alike in the mirror and they accomplish the same result of maintaining fixation when it would otherwise be lost because of the motion of the object along the retina. Why are they not the same? There is one remarkable difference. The pursuit movement has a long latency, about 200 ms. It takes that time to get the eyes into motion toward a moving object. But if you turn your head while fixating an object of interest, you do not lose your fixation for an instant, since *the compensatory eye movement starts simultaneously with the active head movement.* Moreover, the backward eye movement continues to compensate for the progress of the head movement; it maintains steady fixation on the object without any little saccadic movements such as occur during most pursuit movements. In short, the head movement and the compensatory eye movement are coordinated or integrated in a single reaction unit.

These strong claims for the compensatory movement can be checked by observing whether fixation is well maintained during active head movements. Any momentary loss of accurate fixation would be betrayed by a blurring of the object. Read while moving the head—not too violently—and check the statement that no blurring occurs.[1] But the real evidence on this matter comes from photographic records, to which we will turn after introducing the remaining type of compensatory eye movement.

Reflex eye movement compensatory to passive head rotation. Passive rotation of an animal elicits compensatory movements of head, trunk, limbs and eyes, due in part at least to stimulation of the semicircular canals. In the human subject it is the eyes that make the most noticeable of these compensatory movements. He is placed on a turn table or in a rotating chair. When the rotation is such as to turn his face to the right, his eyes slide off to the left. With continued rotation the backward drift of the eyes is interrupted from time to time by a saccadic movement in the same direction as the rotation. After prolonged rotation, when O becomes dizzy, his eyes cease their movements and stare straight ahead. When the rotation ceases (or slackens), the eye movements reappear with reversed phases, the slower movement being now in the direction of the recent rotation and the saccadic movement in the opposite direction. The name *nystagmus* is applied to this peculiar oscillatory eye movement, which also occurs in certain diseases affecting the semicircular

---

[1] As a companion experiment (Dodge, 1907), attach a printed card to a light rod held firmly in the mouth, and move the head from side to side. Here the compensatory movement defeats its own purpose and disturbs fixation, resulting in much blurring.

canals.   Occurring during rotation it is rotation nystagmus; occurring as the after-effect of rotation, it is post-rotation nystagmus.

The evidence for regarding nystagmus and certain other compensatory movements as responses to stimulation of the semicircular canals makes a long and fascinating story, starting with the Mach-Breuer-Brown theory of 1874–75, advancing by way of extirpation and stimulation experiments on animals and by observation of human pathology, and reaching a definitive answer, it seems, in the observations and photographs of Steinhausen (1931–33) who, by injecting a small quantity of black dye into a canal of the pike, made the end organ visible and saw it bending during rotary acceleration and deceleration, quite in accordance with the theory.   To clinch the matter, Mowrer (1935) led off action currents from the vestibular nerve of the terrapin and found them to occur during the starting and stopping of rotation.   Slight inertia currents are set up in the fluid filling the canals, the receptors are subjected to bending and thus stimulated.   Reflex responses to this stimulation play a role in maintaining orientation and steadiness of movement (Dusser de Barenne, 1934).

But are we sure that rotation nystagmus is the result of stimulation of the canals?   When O's eyes are open and directed to some interesting object, rotation provides an adequate *visual* stimulus for a pursuit movement opposite in direction to the rotation; and when the eyes have thus turned as far as is comfortable they will jump to a new object and follow that, just as they do in looking from a moving vehicle.   Thus we have the same nystagmus, apparently, without participation of the canals.   To be sure, post-rotation nystagmus is not thus explained; and a decisive fact is that both rotation and post-rotation nystagmus occur when the eyes are shut.   The latency of the compensatory response to passive rotation averages about 50 ms, varying from 40 to 80 ms in different individuals, while the pursuit movement has a latency of about 200 ms.   There are many other evidences of the genuineness of reflex compensatory movement initiated by stimulation of the inner ear (Wendt, 1936 b).

If we inquire into the utility of this ear-eye reflex, we have to notice that the body and with it the head are subjected to many impressed movements, some of them rotary, and that all such movements disturb eye fixation.   The pursuit and saccadic movements do indeed correct for such disturbance and return the eye to the object of interest, but the much shorter latency of the ear-eye reflex makes a much quicker correction and may thus be of service.   In prolonged rotation there is no adequate compensation, and fixation cannot be maintained.   The environment begins to swim and is soon reduced to a mere streak.   Post-rotation nystagmus is no help to vision but quite the contrary.   It seems to be a necessary mechanical after-effect of prolonged stimulation of the canals.

Photographic registration of compensatory eye movements.   In order to obtain accurate records of the eye movements during active head movement and passive rotation, Dodge sought to develop the photographic method which had proved useful in studying the saccadic and pursuit movements. Long and patient experimentation was finally crowned with success. The main technical problems and their solution may be briefly outlined.

1. The eyes must be photographed while O is being rotated. The solution was to mount the camera on the turntable so that it kept pace with O.

2. The eye movements must be photographed while the eyes are closed, in order to secure a record of a pure ear-eye reflex. If you hold your finger on the closed eyelid and move the eyes from side to side, you can feel the cornea moving under the lid. Substitute for the finger a little block resting lightly on the lid and so pivoted as to turn freely to right and left: the cornea will tilt the block to one side and the other. Cement a bit of mirror to the block, and throw a beam of light upon the mirror: the reflected beam will move with the eye and can be made to write the movement on a moving film.

The eyelid mirror possesses an incidental advantage which simplifies some other problems. A bit of concave mirror can be used which will focus the reflected beam directly on the photographic film without the intervention of the cumbersome camera bellows and lens. The film holder simply has a horizontal slit, past which the film is moved in a vertical direction, while the focused light from the eyelid mirror moves horizontally along the slit.

3. The eye movement record must be uncomplicated by head movements and yet the head must be free to move in the horizontal plane. Its movement was limited to that plane by a swivel head rest placed against the top of the head. The source of light and the film holder were mounted directly over O's head in the axis of the head movements, and O's teeth held a light but rigid frame carrying mirrors which reflected the light from the source to the eyelid mirror and the return beam back to the film holder. O's head is the hub of a wheel and the frame held in his teeth is a spoke at the end of which is a mirror reflecting the light along the line of the spoke. As the head moves, so moves the spoke and the course of the beam along the line of the spoke remains the same. But the eye, turning as it does about a different axis from the head, displaces the beam so that its movement is recorded. Meanwhile the movement of the head is also recorded on the same film by a separate optical system. Both eyes are closed for recording the ear-eye reflex, one eye only for recording the head-eye coordination. There is still more to the whole setup: means for smoothly rotating the turntable, and means for rotating the visible environment around the subject (Dodge, 1921 a, 1923 a, b, c; Wendt & Dodge, 1938).

Of the results of this experiment, mention has already been made of the short latency of the ear-eye reflex and of the fact that this reflex compensates accurately only for small amounts of passive head rotation.

The perfect coordination of active head movement and its compensatory eye movement (the head-eye coordination) was demonstrated by the record—provided at least one eye was open. With both eyes closed this coordination broke down. It is in fact, as already suggested, essentially a maintaining of visual fixation as an integral part of active head movement.

By rotating the visible environment in the same direction as the turntable on which O was seated, but more rapidly, a conflict was created between the ear-eye reflex and the pursuit movement induced by the visible motion; and the working out of this conflict was a fascinating illustration of the interaction of cortical and subcortical mechanisms. The ear-eye reflex is doubtless subcortical, while the pursuit movement depends on the cortex, as do also the head-eye coordination, the saccadic movement and the movements of convergence.

VISION DURING EYE MOVEMENTS

The question whether we see during eye movement may appear a foolish one. Certainly in the pursuit movement we clearly see the moving object which is being fixated. We could not see it clearly unless the eye moved with it. This applies also to the compensatory back movement of the eye during active head movement. During passive rotation we see by virtue of the compensatory eye movements. Do we see during saccadic movements?

The question breaks up into two: Whether we derive from the stimulation received by the retina during a saccadic movement any data that are used in perception, and whether any sensation at all results from the stimulation received by the retina during saccadic movement. The sensation might be disturbing rather than helpful. We have touched already on this matter, in saying that distinct vision of an object is only possible if the optical image of the object is stationary upon the retina— that the retina must be stationary if the object is so and must keep pace when the object moves, in order to avoid the blurring that occurs when the optical image moves along the retina. When the image moves along the retina, the same bit of the retina is exposed to constantly changing stimulation, which, because of the lag of the retinal response, produces blurring. That is the fundamental fact in this whole matter of vision during eye movement.

As the saccadic movements are rapid, the blurring would necessarily be extreme, and there would be no chance for any effective perception. But as these movements are very brief, the disturbance of clear vision would pass unnoticed under ordinary conditions.

A few simple experiments will show that (1) we can see what the retina has to show during saccadic movements, but (2) usually there is very little to see.

Ordinary fields of view present a multiplicity of lighter and darker patches. What the retina has to show during saccadic movements over such a field is of course not the motion of clearly outlined objects, but quick flashes and streaks. These are hard to observe because the contrasts between different parts of the blurred field are slight. When you notice them, you go against a habit of disregarding worthless subjective appearances such as afterimages, or the momentary darkening of the whole field of view that occurs with every wink. If you observe this last disturbance of vision, and note how slight it is, and then consider that the disturbance due to a saccadic movement must be still slighter and briefer, you come to understand what an unobtrusive and evanescent appearance you are trying to catch.

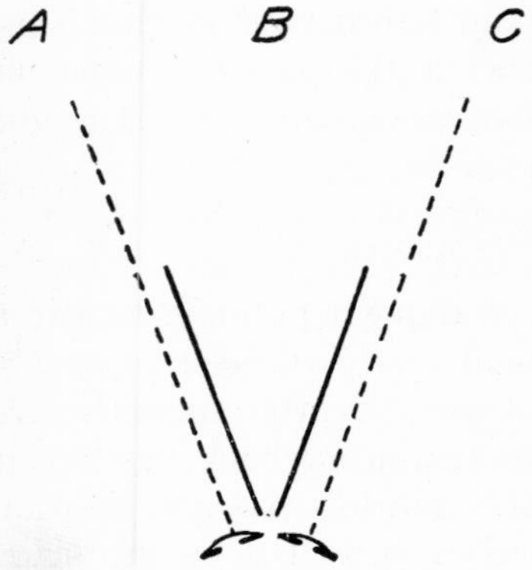

A   *B*   *C*

The task of observing what happens visually during saccadic movement is made easier with a dark background and only a few bright spots in sight. If you look hither and yon across this sort of a field, the streaks of the bright spots are easily observed.

After some practice in observing these streaks of bright light against a dark ground, it is possible to catch the fainter blurs resulting from saccadic movement over an ordinary field of view. One gets an effect something like that due to winking, but reduced almost to the vanishing point, which is all that one could expect from a consideration of the stimulation received by the retina under the conditions.

FIG. 166. Arrangement of screens for concealing B during fixation of either A or C, but permitting exposure of B during eye movement from A to C.

If we could move the field of view past the stationary eye at a speed corresponding to a saccadic movement, we should get the same retinal stimulation. The objective movement must be rapid and brief in order to duplicate the retinal stimulation received during a saccadic movement —40 degrees of movement in a tenth of a second. Some approximation can be got with a mirror. Hold it so you see over your right shoulder but not your face, and shift with as quick a movement as possible to the corresponding position on the left; notice how much you see of your face during the shift. If your face is a high light against a dark ground, you see a streak, but if it is about as bright as its background, it probably makes no impression during the shift. Thus one realizes how little there is to see during saccadic eye movement.

About the best type of experiment under this topic is that of presenting to the eyes during a saccadic movement something that cannot possibly be seen except during the movement. Otherwise it is difficult to be sure that involuntary fixations have not beaten the game. Having another person watch your eyes is a desirable precaution. One way of exposing an object only during eye movement is illustrated in the diagram. Two thin screens are brought up so close to the eye that what lies between the two cannot be seen with the pupil directed toward either A or C; but it is exposed to the eye in the intermediate position, through the slit between two screens. The screen assembly may be made of a piece of stiff paper, by folding it and cutting off a portion of the folded edge so as to leave a slit a millimeter wide. Hold the slit up close to the eyes, touching the lashes, and adjust its position so that you can see B when looking through the slit, but not when you look at either A or C. Then look with a single movement from A to C or from C to A, and notice how much you see of B. If you seem to see B clearly during the course of the movement, have your assistant watch your eyes to detect any involuntary fixation of B. Now vary the field B. In one case have a bright spot there, such as the electric light; and in another case have an object that does not contrast strongly with its background. Place reading matter there, or a large letter. Results comparable to those obtained by shifting a mirror past the stationary eyes justify the conclusion that, *given the same retinal stimulation, it makes no difference whether it is the eyes or the external field that moves.*

If we are correct in this conclusion, there should be clear vision during saccadic movement if only it could be arranged to have an object keep pace with the eyes. The object would have to move too fast for the pursuit movement, and the eyes would have to catch it on the wing, in the course of a shift of fixation. This can be arranged. Riding in a train, if you look down at the adjoining track flying to the rear and shift the eyes from a position forward to one behind, you will sometimes catch a momentary flash with clear vision of the track as if it were motionless. The angular speeds of your eyes and of the track have coincided for an instant; at that instant the retina received a motionless image of a bit of the track. You can sometimes get the same result from a wheel spinning fast enough to make the spokes a blur to the motionless eye: fixate a point to the right of the wheel and then one to the left, shifting the eyes directly from one of these points to the other. If the angular speeds coincide you catch a clear glimpse of a part of the wheel. In the laboratory a similar setup can be arranged with a color wheel. Sectors of different colors can be seen distinctly for an instant over a part of the rotating wheel, by making a saccadic movement across the wheel from one side to the other. The faster the wheel is spinning, the faster must the eye jump; and the only way to have it jump faster is to give it a longer jump to make.

The facts regarding vision during eye movement are thus perfectly straightforward and in accord with the fundamental facts of retinal response to stimulation. Clear vision of an object is obtained only from a motionless image on the retina. The pursuit movement and the compensatory movements provide such images under certain common conditions. The saccadic movement does not provide motionless images under any ordinary conditions; it gives blurs and streaks which, besides being very brief because of the quickness of the saccadic movement, are also very faint with ordinary fields of view. Consequently the blurs and streaks due to saccadic movements are ordinarily not disturbing; since they are of no practical interest they are habitually disregarded and overlooked.

In case this discussion of vision during eye movements should appear unduly labored in view of the simplicity of the facts, a bit of history may be appended. Shortly after 1900, when knowledge of saccadic movements was new and a sudden revision of the older assumption of effective vision during all eye movements became necessary, much mystery attached to the apparent absence of vision during saccadic movements. The ingenious hypothesis of central anesthesia was suggested, the idea being that the nerve impulses corresponding to retinal stimulation during a saccadic movement were shunted aside in the visual cortex and prevented from disturbing the clear perception of the valuable data received during fixation. This hypothesis was energetically discussed at the time, experiments such as described above were made, and the whole matter appeared to be settled. Recently, however, younger psychologists who did not listen in on that old-time discussion have begun once more to feel the mystery which was then cleared away. For the older discussions see Holt (1903); Dodge (1905); Woodworth (1906 b).

CHAPTER XXIV

PERCEPTION OF COLOR

IT IS well-nigh impossible for a normal man, in his senses, to see the picture presented to him by his eyes. He sees what is before his eyes, a field of objects, but he does not see the juxtaposed color patches which constitute his retinal image. He sees objects at certain distances, standing at certain angles, having certain forms, sizes and colors. He sees the objective field as illuminated brightly or dimly, with high lights and deep shadows and all grades of illumination.

A painter, if he wishes to be realistic, must learn to see the picture rather than the field of objects, for he must reproduce the actual picture on his canvas. His success in enabling the beholder to see objects in perspective, and in their proper sizes, shapes and colors, proves that the retinal image affords good cues of these various objective facts. But it required much study and experimentation on the part of the early realistic painters to master these cues. They cannot ordinarily be discovered by introspection. One does not first notice the cue and then get the indicated fact, for it seems to be a general psychological principle that a cue, so far as it is used, is absorbed into the suggested meaning and is no longer observable for itself.

The existence of intriguing psychological problems of perception becomes evident when we consider that the retinal image continually changes without much changing the appearance of objects. The apparent size of a person does not change as he moves away from you. A ring, turned at various angles to the line of sight, and therefore projected as a varying ellipse on the retina, continues to appear circular. Part of a wall, standing in shadow, is seen as the same in color as the well-lighted portion. Still more radical are the changes in the retinal image that occur when we move about a room and examine its contents from various angles. In spite of the visual flux the objects seem to remain in the same places. In short, what we perceive is the objective situation.

A striking instance of the objectivity of perception can be drawn from the auditory field. As we found (p. 519), the auditory space sense is mostly limited to the right-left distinction, dependent on the cues of binaural time difference and intensity difference. Yet a continued sound, as a street noise, observed while we ourselves are turning around, seems to remain in the same place in spite of the varying cues.

Problems in color perception. It is a fact of common observation that coal looks black even in sunlight and that chalk looks white even in shadow. Yet the light reaching the eye from well-lighted coal is very much stronger than that from shaded chalk. The retinal image of the coal is much brighter than that of the chalk, under the conditions, and the stimulus received from the coal is much more intense. O's impression conforms to the object rather than to the stimulus, and he is apt to see no problem here, for if coal is really black why should it not be seen as black in a good light? Not a bad answer, perhaps, but one involving some tacit assumptions that the psychologist would like to make explicit.

Interest in the problem dates from those early giants of physiological optics, Helmholtz and Hering. Helmholtz said (1866, p. 408):

Colors are mainly important for us as properties of objects and as means of identifying objects. In visual observation we constantly aim to reach a judgment on the object colors and to eliminate differences of illumination. So, we clearly distinguish between a white sheet of paper in weak illumination and a gray sheet in strong illumination. We have abundant opportunity to examine the same object colors in full sunlight, in the blue light from the clear sky, the weak white light of the clouded sky, and the reddish yellow light of the sinking sun or of candlelight—not to mention the colored reflections from surrounding objects. Seeing the same objects under these different illuminations, we learn to get a correct idea of the object colors in spite of difference of illumination. We learn to judge how such an object would look in white light, and since our interest lies entirely in the constant object color, we become unconscious of the sensations on which our judgment rests.

Intellectual judgment based on unconscious sensations seemed to Hering (1874, 1876, 1879) an over-schematic and essentially untrue account of the process of color perception. He called attention to the peripheral factors that compensate for changes of illumination. The contraction of the pupil in strong light and its dilation in dim light compensate in some degree for changes in the total illumination of the field. A much more powerful, though slowly acting factor is retinal adaptation to light, dark and color. Brightness and color contrast, believed by Hering to be retinal and not psychological processes, accentuate object colors by brightening the brightest objects in sight, darkening the darkest, and so on. Though these peripheral factors work in the direction of correcting for illumination, Hering admitted that they were not sufficient, and accordingly he introduced a cerebral factor, dependent on attention and past experience. The sensory effect of a stimulus depends on the state of the "sensorium," the structure of which is modified by voluntary and involuntary exercise in perceiving things according to our interests. With a modified sensorium we get a different sensation from the same stimulus, and the color impression which we receive from an object is therefore an actual sensation and not a judgment or unconscious inference. Later (1907, reprinted 1920) Hering elaborated this conception of "memory color":

The color in which we have oftenest seen an external thing impresses itself indelibly on our memory and becomes a fixed characteristic of the memory image. What the layman calls the real color of a thing is a color which has become firmly attached to the thing in his memory; I might call it the memory color of the thing. All the things which are known to us from past experience, or which we believe to be known to us in respect to color, are seen through the spectacles of the memory colors.

Agreeing with Helmholtz to this extent, at least, that the function of vision is to supply information regarding objects rather than regarding light, Hering urged that the "approximate color constancy of seen objects" was one of the most remarkable and important facts in the realm of physiological optics.

Regarding the problem as equally appropriate for psychology, Katz (1911) developed it extensively in connection with his study of phenomenal varieties of color (p. 539, above). He was able to show that "color constancy," or the perception of object color, was not accounted for either by memory color or by Hering's peripheral factors. At first inclined rather toward the Helmholtz theory, he spoke of "allowance for the illumination" and of the central or cerebral "transformation" of color from its stimulus value to its object value. Largely influenced by the important critique of Gelb (1929), Katz in his second edition (1930) withdrew the concept of transformation and rejected Helmholtz's notion of a two-stage process, sensation followed by judgment. Katz still stresses the importance of some sort of "allowance for the illumination" and believes that the general illumination is brought home to O by the total impressiveness (about equivalent to brilliance) of the field of view.

Many psychologists have taken an interest in the problem, and the abridged catchword, "color constancy," has become familiar, along with the parallel phrases, "size constancy," "shape constancy," and others. As a comprehensive term, Thouless (1931) suggested "phenomenal regression to the real object," which might better read "toward the real object." The regression, or approximation, is *from* the stimulus color, size or shape (such as the painter would reproduce) *toward* the object color, size or shape, but the actual impression, i.e., the apparent or phenomenal color, size or shape is usually intermediate between these two "poles" (Brunswik, 1929, 1933, 1934; reviewed by Ansbacher, 1937).

Before introducing the experiments on perception of object color, we may well ask what are the objective facts which the observer is trying to perceive and, since illumination is evidently an important factor, whether it is fair to credit the observer with any ability to perceive or somehow register the illumination so as to allow for it in perceiving the color of the illuminated object.

What are object colors? Object color is a certain physical property of objects, the property of absorbing some of the incident light and reflecting the remainder (or transmitting the remainder in the case of transparent objects). A perfectly black object is one that absorbs all the light that strikes it and reflects none; an ideally white object absorbs none and reflects all; while a gray absorbs and reflects certain proportions of the incident light. The *albedo*, or reflecting power of a substance, is measured by the ratio of the reflected to the incident light. A certain mixture of white lead and lamp black reflects 25 percent of the light; its albedo measure is 25 percent. It reflects more light, absolutely, when it receives more; but it always reflects 25 percent of what it receives. If it is moved from a weaker to a stronger illumination, or the reverse, the observer still sees it as the same gray (approximately), thus in effect perceiving its reflecting power or albedo. We have been perceiving albedo all our lives without knowing it.

An object color of the chromatic series—red, orange, yellow, green, blue, purple—results, according to physics, from *selective* absorption of the different wave lengths of light. A red substance is one which absorbs the short waves and reflects the long; green absorbs predominantly the longest and the shortest visible rays and reflects those of medium length; purple does just the reverse of this last. Aside from monochromatic illumination, which is seldom encountered even approximately, a red substance reflects a redder mixture than it receives; it reddens the light; the stimulus light received from it is redder than the illumination under which it stands. Similarly a blue substance reflects a bluer mixture than it receives from the source of light.

Object color, then, is physically a relation between the illumination received by an object and the light reflected by the object. Of course we do not think of it in such abstract terms. Defined in a rough, common-sense way, it is the power of an object to alter the light, by weakening or reddening it, etc., or by reflecting it unchanged. To perceive object color is to see how the object modifies the light.

White is no specific degree of brightness; it is bright or dim according to the illumination. But under a given illumination nothing can be brighter than white, since it reflects all the light received. If a surface emits more light than it receives, it is luminous and so appears. Black, also has a unique position among object colors. Absolute black would reflect no light under any illumination, but absolutely black surfaces do not exist. An acceptable black may be only the darkest gray present under a given illumination; but it must be the darkest.

In the relatively simple case of the white-gray-black series of colors, if we let M = illumination, A = albedo, and S = the reflected light which enters the eye (the stimulus brightness), we have as the measure of albedo:

$$A = S/M$$

As data for perceiving albedo, the observer therefore needs S, which he certainly gets, and some indication of M, sufficiently good to account for the degree of accuracy which he shows in perceiving A. Reserving till later the question, how he utilizes the data and solves the equation, let us look first into the possibility of obtaining good cues of illumination.

Registering the illumination. We say "registering" so as not to imply in all cases an explicit perception of the illumination. In many cases we certainly do perceive illumination. We notice the change when the light is turned on or off, when the sun goes behind a cloud, when we pass from a dark to a light room. Looking out of the window in the morning for a weather observation, we know instantly from the light on the ground, trees or buildings whether the sun is shining and about how brightly it is shining. Even with closed eyes we notice changes in the light falling on the lids.

Since the eye in early stages of its evolution has no lens or cornea and cannot furnish a picture of objects, it is easy to believe with Bühler (1922) that response to general illumination is more primitive than perception of object color, and that the initial response to each new field of view may be a registering of the general illumination.

Hering (1907, 1920) raised a logical difficulty: we must know the object color in order to utilize the reflected light as an index of illumination, while we must know the illumination in order to use the reflected light as an index of object color. We seem to be involved in a circle. The answer is:

1. In any normal field of view, more than one object is simultaneously visible, and the illumination falling on a particular object can be gathered from the stimuli received from the surrounding objects (Kardos, 1929).

2. The field of indirect vision yields little in the way of object color but affords a total impression of the illumination.

But it is not enough to register the general illumination, since different parts of the visible environment are often differently lighted. Can we perceive regions of different illuminations? Nothing is more certain. High lights and deep shadows are seen as definitely as are object colors. The flecks of sunlight under the trees, the shadow of a house or of a person—examples could be multiplied indefinitely. A shadow is often seen as filling space; a dark corner seems filled with shadow, even when there is no object there to reveal the darkness by its dim reflection. What can we mean by dark empty space, or by dark air? Unless some object is present to reflect what little light penetrates the corner, the dark space is completely invisible, and yet we seem to see it. We evidently take dark space to be an objective fact, just as we take the color of an object to be really present in the dark. Our objective tendency extends to illumination conditions as well as to object colors. We are on the watch for both and are not easily deceived.

A shadow is betrayed by the penumbra or half shadow along its edges, and the same is true of an area of extra illumination. We do not always notice the penumbra as such, but we utilize it in perceiving the shadow (Wundt, 1911). A famous experiment of Hering (1907) demonstrates the importance of the penumbra in the perception of a shadow.

It is the "ringed shadow experiment." Place some small object so as to cast a shadow on a sheet of white paper; the shaded part is seen as white paper lying in shadow. Now outline the shadow with a heavy black line so as to conceal the penumbra: the appearance of a shadow is gone, and the shaded portion appears like gray paper. The reverse experiment can be made by screening the light from the paper except for one spot of light coming through a hole in the screen. Outline that spot in black and it appears like a whiter paper or even a luminous surface. It is important to notice in these experiments that when the indicators of illumination are destroyed, the perception of object color is lost.

What is objectively a shadow can be perceived in three ways, according to conditions; we have mentioned two ways, perception of a shadow and perception of a dark object color. The third is the perception of the *shape* of an object or, more generally, the perception of spatial relations and especially of the third dimension. Suppose the sun is low and shining on the west side of a house leaving the north side in shadow. If you observe these two sides of the house separately, you definitely perceive the shadow on one side and the sunlight on the other; but if you regard the house as a whole the difference of illumination is seen as a difference in direction of the walls, as a manifestation of the shape of the house. When a white towel is hanging from a nail or a crumpled white handkerchief lying on the table, some parts catching the light more strongly than others, the whole appears white, and the numerous shadows, though not noticed separately, serve as indications of the folds and creases and in general of the shape into which the cloth has fallen. The roughness of a wall or the coarse texture of a fabric (its microstructure) is revealed to the eye by numerous little shadows not separately observed but seen as unevenness of surface. A rounded surface shades off from high light to deep shadow, but the gradation is not easily seen in a purely optical way; a novice attempting to reproduce the object in water color or charcoal scarcely knows how to start, though he sees the shape of the object clearly enough, depending for this perception on that very shading which he has such difficulty in analyzing and reproducing. Many other instances could be given in which shadows are not seen as shadows but are utilized in perceiving spatial relations.

Conversely, if the spatial relations are clear from other cues, they will provide cues of illumination. If the three-dimensional form of a box is clearly revealed, its darker side is seen as shaded rather than painted black.

Summing up the non-experimental evidence on registering illumination, we conclude that the general level of illumination is perceived to quite an extent and that differences of illumination within a given presented field of objects are often very clear. Penumbra and the perceived spatial relations of the visible reflecting surfaces afford good cues of the distribution of light and shade.

The observer's intention in everyday situations is that of identifying the color of an object as white, black, gray, blue, etc. Sometimes he wishes to rate it on a white-gray-black scale, or even to match a color now seen in artificial light with a color previously seen in daylight. In other cases he compares two object colors presented simultaneously—a simple matter when the objects get the same light so that only the S values need to be compared. When the objects stand in different illuminations, comparison is often helped by the presence of an objectively uniform background. A wall, a floor, a lawn is visibly of the same material throughout. When different parts of the same wall stand in different illuminations, these differences of illumination are easily discounted because of the spatial and material continuity of the wall. Objects attached to different parts of the wall are seen in relation to the wall. If the albedo of an object is higher than that of the wall, that object will always be brighter than the adjacent wall. Two objects of the same albedo, attached to different parts of the wall, will have the same brightness ratio to the wall in spite of differing illumination. According to Weber's law, equal brightness ratios should be perceived as equal and the two objects in question should appear equally bright in relation to the wall. As the wall is visibly the same throughout, the two objects should therefore appear equal in albedo. Even when the visible field contains nothing so continuous as a wall, the average albedo of different parts of the field may seem to O about the same and so provide him with a base line for rough comparison of object colors in differently lighted parts of the field.

OBJECT-COLOR PERCEPTION UNDER NORMAL ILLUMINATION CONDITIONS

As an introductory experiment we cite the study of Burzlaff (1931). A series of 48 gray papers was prepared, ranging by approximately equal steps from the best white to the best black obtainable. There were two pieces of each gray, 6 cm. square, and one set of the 48 grays was mounted in regular order upon a large medium-gray cardboard, 60 × 80 cm, while the other set was mounted in irregular order on a similar cardboard. The irregular set was placed near a window where it was illuminated by diffuse daylight, and the regular set was placed back in the room, so far from the window that the illumination was only 1/20 that of the irregular set.

O stood near the window, with his back to it, and saw both charts against the same background, the dark rear wall of the room. A certain piece of gray paper on the near chart being designated as the Standard, E with a pointer indicated the grays on the far chart in regular order, asking O to compare each of them with the Standard and tell whether it was the same, lighter or darker. This procedure was gone through six times with several Standards and the points of subjective equality were computed according to the method of Constant Stimuli (p. 421).

The result, in a word, was that O equated approximately the same grays, the one on the near, well lighted chart and the other on the dimly lighted chart. He matched a given gray on one chart with almost the same gray on the other, in spite of the difference of illumination.

Burzlaff's main interest was in testing young children to find whether their perception of object color was as good as that of an adult. The table gives the results for each age group and for five standard grays. Each shade of gray is designated by its approximate albedo, i.e., by the percent of white it contained, this percent being determined by matching the gray with a white-black mixture on the color wheel (gray and color wheel being under the same illumination for this calibration).

DIMLY LIGHTED GRAY SELECTED AS MATCH FOR EACH
WELL-LIGHTED GRAY

(Burzlaff, 1931)

Subjects	Well lighted grays				
	75	51	25	11	6
5 adults	81	53	25	12	6
4 seven-year-olds	80	53	24	12	6
5 six-year-olds	78	55	25	12	6
6 five-year-olds	79	54	25	11	6
5 four-year-olds	77	54	24	11	6

The table reads that adults matched a light gray (75% white) seen in good light by a somewhat lighter gray (81% white) seen under relatively weak illumination; and so on.

There is little sign of any age difference in these results. The four-year-olds match the grays as well as the older children or adults. Until one thinks over the situation, one sees nothing remarkable in such results and is inclined to ask why any person, child or adult, should not see the same gray paper as the same, in good light or dim. Considering that the light reflected from any particular gray into the eye was only 1/20 as much in the dim as in the bright illumination, one begins to see a problem. The stimulus is diminished to 1/20, yet the object color seems the same, or nearly the same. The diminution of the stimulus has *some* effect, for the errors are all in one direction (in the averages): it takes a somewhat lighter shade in the dim light to match a given shade in a bright light. The actual match is a *compromise* between an object-match and a stimulus-match, but is much closer, in this experiment, to the object-match.

Matching color wheel grays in different illuminations. The same author performed another experiment in which conditions were not so favorable for perception of object color. Two color wheels, one placed near the window and the other back in the room where the illumination was only 1/20 as bright, were seen against the same dark background. A certain black-white mixture was rotated on one color wheel, and a similar mixture on the other wheel was adjusted until the two appeared equal to an observer standing near the window. Some of the results are presented in Fig. 167, together with comparable results from the previous experiment in which gray papers on charts were matched.

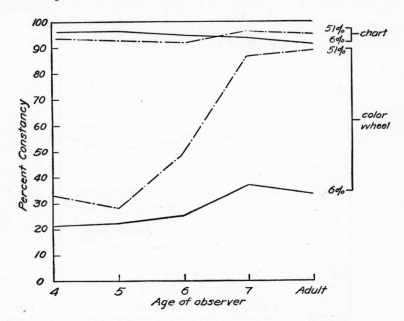

FIG. 167. (Data from Burzlaff, 1931.) Object color perception as dependent on age. Matches were made, by observers of different ages, between a well-lighted and a dimly lighted gray. Had the matches been according to stimulus brightness they would all have fallen on the lower horizontal line, and had they been in strict accordance with object whiteness (albedo) they would all have fallen on the upper horizontal line. They actually fell between these extremes, on the intervening lines. In the experiment with charts they approximated closely to albedo matches, and changed little with age; but in the color wheel experiment they were rather near to stimulus matches at ages 4 and 5 and approached object color matches with increasing age, this being truer of the light gray (51% white) than of the dark gray (6% white).

The diagram brings out three important results:

1. The actual match always (except for scattering individual exceptions) lies between what is demanded by the object color and what is demanded by the stimulus received from the object. It is a compromise between these two ideal values.

2. The actual match approaches much more closely to object color in the experiment with charts of gray papers than in the color wheel experiment.

3. The experiment with charts of grays shows no change with age,

but the color wheel experiment shows a development with age toward accurate perception of object color.

Why was it more difficult to perceive the object color of a rotating color wheel mixture than that of a plain gray paper on a chart containing various shades of gray? The rotation of a color wheel washes out the grain of the paper and so increases the difficulty of separating the surface color and the illumination. Burzlaff lays less stress on this factor than on the simultaneous presence of many grays on the charts. He believes

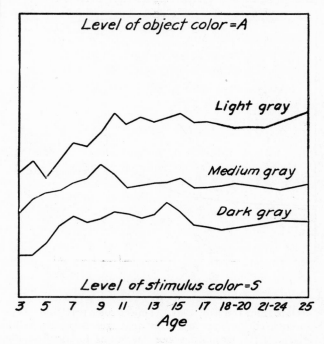

FIG. 168. (Data from Brunswik, 1929.) Age curves in matching grays under different illuminations. Gray of a given albedo was five times as bright under one illumination as under the other.

that "articulation" of the diversified field is important. Other authors have said "organization" of the field. But these words offer no suggestion as to why the effect should be in the direction of seeing the object color rather than the stimulus color. It is more to the point to notice that each chart provided a whole scale of grays mounted on the medium-gray cardboard. The brightness ratio of a given gray to the gray of the cardboard was the same under higher or lower illumination.

Age curves similar to those of Burzlaff with the color wheels were obtained by Brunswik (1929) with squares of gray paper. He however exposed only two squares at a time, at different distances from the source of light. Up to 9–11 years of age, there was increasing approximation toward the object-color level (Fig. 168).

Measurement ratios. Brunswik (1929) introduced a convenient means of expressing the degree of approximation to objective perception. Judgments in these experiments usually lie between two extremes, one conforming to the stimulus and the other conforming to the object. If O matched strictly according to stimulus intensity, he would be showing zero tendency toward "color constancy." If, at the other extreme, he matched exactly in accordance with albedo or object color, he would show 100 percent "color constancy." His actual judgment can be assigned a percent value according to its position in this continuum.

If A = a numerical value for the object,
S = a numerical value for the stimulus, and
R = a numerical value for the response or actual match, then the

Brunswik ratio = (R − S)/(A − S)

as illustrated by the diagram,

S	R	A

For example, a gray mixture on a color wheel consists of 30 percent white and 70 percent black. Its A value is 30. This wheel is placed in low illumination and matched by an observer with a gray mixture on another color wheel standing in illumination that is 10 times as high. A strict stimulus match would be 1/10 of 30 = 3, which is the S value (if we assume for simplicity that the black is absolute black). The actual match by the observer is 15; he is satisfied when the better illuminated mixture consists of 15 percent white and 85 percent black. The Brunswik ratio in this case is

$$(15 - 3)/(30 - 3) = 12/27 = .44$$

Partly because apparent brightness under uniform illumination is rather proportional to the *logarithm* of the physical brightness, and partly for other reasons, a modified ratio proposed by Thouless (1931) is often preferred. The logs of A, S and R are used. So we have the

Thouless ratio = (log R − log S)/(log A − log S)

Color constancy in animals. Since quite young children show about as much tendency as adults to perceive albedo as against stimulus brightness, it is interesting to inquire whether animals also show this tendency. Locke (1935) tested 4 rhesus monkeys and 5 human adults with the same setup and essentially the same conditions and found decidedly more approximation to the object color in monkeys. His subjects gave Brunswik ratios as follows:

Human adults: .10, .13, .13, .19, .23
Monkeys: .47, .53, .59, .65

Moreover the same conditions raised or lowered the ratio with the human Os and with the monkeys.

Köhler (1917 a, b) tried the following experiment on young hens (7–8 months old). He trained them to pick grain only from the darker of two sheets of paper, which were under the same moderate illumination, and then he placed the darker paper in direct sunlight, leaving the lighter paper in weaker illumination. The hens still went to the dark gray paper for their grain, though now it was reflecting much more light than the whiter paper. The brightness ratio of grain to background remained as before.

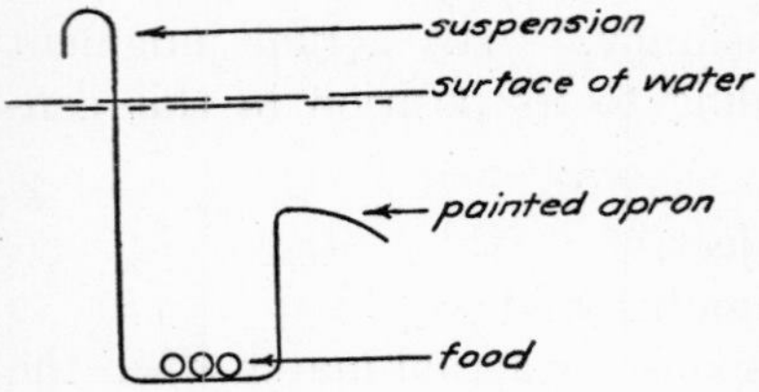

FIG. 169.   (Burkamp, 1923.) Food trough for experiment on aquarium fish.

Katz & Révész (1921) stained some grains of rice a strong yellow color, leaving other rice grains unstained, and trained hens to pick only the white grains. They then threw a strong yellow light upon a white ground containing white grains, and these the hens picked without hesitation, though they were actually reflecting strong yellow light—but not yellower than the ground.

Burkamp (1923) went still further down the vertebrate scale and tested aquarium fishes (Cyprinides). He had two problems in mind: to test the color sense, and to discover whether the fish responded to the stimulus color or to the object color. The procedure, in outline, was to train the fish to seek their food in troughs of a certain color, and then to apply tests showing (1) whether the fish were able to pick out this color from an assemblage of grays and other colors, and (2) whether they could do so even when the illumination was so changed as to alter the stimulus values.

The troughs were made of sheet zinc and were shaped somewhat as shown in Fig. 169. They were suspended near the top of the water so that E could easily see when a fish entered a trough. The "aprons" were painted various colors and shades of gray.

In the training series, which required 9–15 days, two feedings per day, the food was placed in two troughs of a given color hanging among 22 troughs of other colors. When the fish had learned to go to the troughs of the given color, they were tested with a fresh set of 24 troughs, one being the precise color for which the fish had been trained, and others of the same hue but lighter or darker in shade, of other hues, and of various grays. The result, as regards the color sense, was definitely positive, except for confusions between red and yellow.

When the illumination was altered by moving the aquarium closer to the north window, by drawing the shutters, or by passing the light through colored filters, there was very little change in the learned responses. Increasing the light did not make the fish go to the darker shades, decreasing it did not send them to the lighter shades, nor did colored illumination send them to the grays or to non-training colors. Most remarkable was the slight effect of very dim illumination; the fish picked out the object color in very dim light better than the human observer could do. Their "color constancy"—i.e., response to object color—was better than human. Burkamp points out that correction for illumination is even more important for a fish than for a land-living animal, since the fish is subjected to large changes in illumination every time he moves from one depth to another in the water.

Though these results from children and animals indicate that no exalted intellectual process is necessary in correcting for illumination so as to see object colors, it would be going much too far to infer that no learning is involved. The opportunities for learning are certainly abundant from the time the young creature begins to use his eyes. As the mother moves about in sight of the baby, her face, her clothes, pass moment by moment from one illumination to another. If we assume merely that the object during these gradual and partial changes continues to appear to the baby as the same object, he is being conditioned to make all the necessary corrections.

Various normal modifications of the illumination. In everyday life there are several different ways in which the illumination of an object differs from one time to another and from one part of the field to another. Katz and others have tested human adults under these various conditions.

1. *The reduction screen or hole screen.* As already explained (p. 540) the hole screen allows the light reflected from a surface to reach the eye but conceals the surroundings and in particular the illumination conditions. The resulting appearance is one of free or expanse color, not surface color. If therefore the light from two surfaces is received through a hole screen—and if no microstructure or other little cues of illumination are visible (Sheehan, 1938)—the observer can only compare the two spots of light according to their stimulus values. The two spots seem equally bright when the stimuli are equally intense. Thus the hole screen affords a convenient means of matching two *stimuli* or determining their relative brightness and hue. When the screen is removed and the objects are viewed in the objective situation, O usually compares the object colors rather than the stimuli.

It should be noted, however, that O in most of the experiments has not been instructed to compare the object colors. He has been instructed to tell how the two surfaces appear to him, whether one looks brighter than the other, whether they seem to have the same or different colors. The point of view has been "phenomenological." O is supposed to maintain the naive attitude of everyday observation, which undoubtedly is the attitude of looking for object colors. Yet the instructions are somewhat ambiguous and some Os adopt a more "critical" attitude, like that of a painter who tries to recapture the stimulus colors on his canvas. In most of the experiments O has not aimed definitely to capture either the stimulus colors or the object colors; and his observations have in most cases been a compromise between these two.

2. *Illumination perspective* is the term used for the gradation of illumination that depends on the distance of a surface from the source of light. Burzlaff's experiment employed this means of varying the

illumination. With a point source, the illumination of a surface would be inversely proportional to the square of its distance from the source; but in practice the hole screen or an illuminometer is used to establish a physical equation between the stimuli.

3. *The angle of incidence* of the light upon the surface is an important factor. The more obliquely the light strikes the surface, the larger the area over which a given flux of light is distributed and the less dense the illumination. The arrangement of apparatus for one of Katz's experiments is shown in Fig. 170.

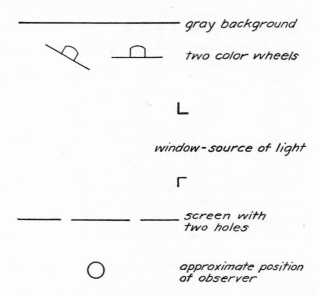

FIG. 170. Setup for varying angle of incidence.

The left-hand color wheel, being further from the window and also receiving the light more obliquely, was so much less brightly illuminated than the right-hand wheel that, when viewed through the hole screen, an all-white disk on the left-hand wheel was matched with 13% white and 87% black on the right-hand wheel. But with the screen removed and direct view of the whole objective situation, the all-white disk at the left was matched with 45% white and 55% black at the right. The Brunswik ratio figures out at .36, the Thouless ratio at .61.

4. *Shadow.* One object plainly stands in the light, the other in shadow, and O makes an equation between them. Katz (1930) describes the setup shown in Fig. 171. In the shadow was a 100 percent white color wheel, to be matched with an adjustable wheel on the bright side of the partition. A match through the reduction screen furnished the S values; and the A value was obviously 100. A match strictly according to albedo would require 100 percent white in the well-lighted color wheel. The actual matches given by two Os were as follows:

	First O	*Second O*
Reduction screen match	1.2% white	2.3% white
Open view match	32.2	27.1
Brunswik ratio	.31	.26
Thouless ratio	.74	.65

The observers found it easy to reach a satisfactory equation when looking through the hole screen, but difficult in open view. They were apt to shift toward the stimulus equation in long-continued inspection

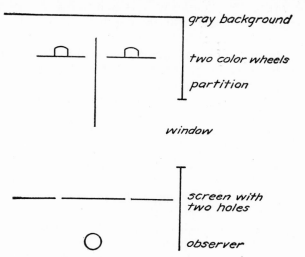

FIG. 171. (After Katz, 1930.) Arrangement of room for shadow experiment.

of the field; the above equations were obtained with a view of only 3 sec. at a time. This difficulty and instability of equating shaded and unshaded grays is a matter of importance to which we shall return.

Instead of a shadow, a spot of additional illumination may be used. For example (Katona, 1929) two gray squares are attached to the wall of the room, both being illuminated by a ceiling lamp and one of them standing in a bright circle of light projected on the wall by a lantern. The brightly illuminated gray is taken as the Standard and other grays are tried outside the bright circle till one is found that appears the same as the brightly illuminated gray. Equations made with and without the use of the hole screen differ as they do in the shadow experiment; the observer makes some allowance for the extra illumination, but not enough.

5. *Looking through colored glass, smoked glass, or an episcotister.* If O is wearing gray glasses, which absorb 9/10 of the light, allowing only 1/10 to reach his eyes, the stimulus he receives from any single surface is the same as if the illumination itself had been reduced to 1/10 by the interposition of a sheet of the same glass between the source of light and the object. If he is wearing yellow glasses, he receives the same

stimulus as if the illumination had been made yellow by a filter of the same glass around the light bulb. If he holds a sheet of gray glass at some distance from his eyes so as to see only a part of the field through the glass, he gets the same stimuli as if this part of the field were under reduced illumination. Thus the sheets of glass can be used in much the same way as a shadow or a colored spot of light, in experiments on the perception of object color, and equations can be obtained between one surface seen through the glass and another viewed directly.

The episcotister (or "darkener") is a rotating disk with a sector or sectors cut out to allow light to pass for a certain fraction of the time. If the cut-out sector is 180°, the light passes through in flashes which aggregate one half of the whole time, and if the speed of rotation is high enough to avoid flicker, the Talbot-Plateau law holds good (p. 567), and the stimulus is the same as if the illumination were reduced to one half. This statement assumes however that the episcotister disk is perfectly black or so screened as to reflect no light into the eye. In some experiments the episcotister surface is colored and gives the effect of colored light falling on the part of the field seen through the episcotister. A white disk with 270° cut out, rotating before a plain dark background, appears perfectly opaque; the darker the disk and the brighter the background, the more the impression of a transparent medium is produced; but the background must show some figure or diversity in order to create this impression (Tudor-Hart, 1928).

In an experiment of Katz (1930, p. 153) O looked alternately through two small windows in a screen. Just beyond one window was an episco-tister, through which he saw a disk of white paper, standing 1.4 m away, its surroundings also being visible. Through the other window a color wheel was seen at the same distance, with no episcotister intervening. Black and white sectors were adjusted on this color wheel until a match was obtained with the white disk seen through the episcotister. The opening of the latter was changed from experiment to experiment, so as to reduce the "illumination" of the white disk to $\frac{1}{4}$, 1/12, 1/36 and 1/120 of that received by the color wheel, and equations were obtained as follows:

Fraction of illumination received through episcotister	.250	.083	.028	.008
Fraction of white in matched color wheel mixture	.330	.280	.240	.230
Brunswik ratio	.107	.215	.219	.224
Thouless ratio	.200	.489	.602	.700

The matches in the second line of the table would have tallied with the numbers in the first line, if O had matched according to the stimuli received, and would all have been 1.000 if he had matched white with white. He actually compromised, as shown by the ratios.

The usual instructions in these experiments, calling for a report of the "appearance" or "phenomenal impression" of the surfaces, leave it uncertain exactly what O is trying to accomplish. In an experiment of Marzynski (1921) the instructions specified that two pieces of white or gray paper should be matched according to object color. One piece was seen directly and the other through an episcotister which cut down the light to 1/90. Of the two Os, one matched the object colors quite closely, and the other showed the usual compromise. Their introspections give some indication of ways of correcting for the illumination. They first tried the method of observing the background and surroundings

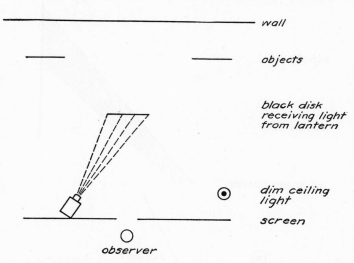

Fig. 172. Gelb's concealed illumination experiment. The lantern at the left is invisible to the observer, and its light is confined to the black disk. The wall and all objects in the room receive the rather dim light from the ceiling lamp. See p. 612.

carefully so as to estimate the depth of the episcotister shadow; but they soon found this deliberate procedure confusing and useless and fell into what they called an "instinctive" procedure. They "looked through" the shadow, as through a veil, and tried to see the object behind and how white it was. This procedure evidently focused attention on the object rather than the illumination.

DECEPTIVE CUES OF ILLUMINATION

If perception of object color, so far as it succeeds, depends on some process of correction for the illumination, it should be possible to mislead O by introducing deceptive cues, and experiments of this sort should bring into relief the cues on which O depends. Hering's ringed shadow experiment (p. 600), in which the penumbra of a shadow or of a spot of extra illumination is concealed by a black ring, subtracts an important cue; the appearance of a shadow vanishes and with it the object color of the shaded spot of white paper. This experiment contains the germ of two strikingly deceptive setups designed by Gelb and by Kardos.

Concealed illumination.   Gelb (1929) presented a wall and several objects standing in the rather dim light of a ceiling lamp, while in the foreground was a disk of black paper, receiving the bright light of a concealed lantern, which fell only on the disk.   No penumbra was visible on the disk or the background (Fig. 172).   O reported a *white* disk standing in the general illumination—white in dim light instead of black in bright light.   But the instant a small bit of white paper was

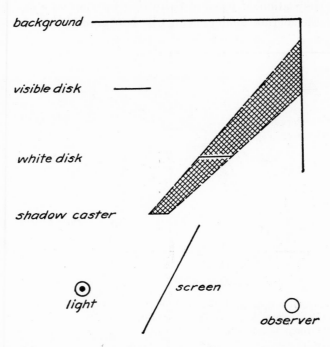

Fig. 173.   The Kardos concealed shadow experiment.   The only visible object shaded by the shadow-caster is the white disk which stands entirely in full shadow. O sees this disk as black or dark gray.   Screening the shadow-caster is unnecessary, for even if O sees it he gets no suggestion that it is shading the white disk.   See p. 613.

held just in front of the disk, in the bright light, the disk was seen to be black.   When the white paper was removed the disk snapped back into its former appearance.   We might have expected O, once made aware of the extra illumination on the disk, to maintain this awareness after the white paper was removed.   So he did no doubt, intellectually, but he needed a concrete visible indicator of extra illumination in order to *see* the illumination, or in order to see an object as receiving the illumination.

How could the bit of white paper make the extra illumination visible? There are two possible ways.   It might have cast a visible shadow on the disk behind it.   Or, if E took care to eliminate that cue, O still got brighter light from the white paper than could possibly have been reflected by any surface from the dim general illumination.   The black could not appear white with the much brighter bit of paper so obviously in the same spot of light. This spot thus revealed itself as under special illumination. What would have been the effect of substituting a plain white disk for the black one, and having only the white in the spot-light? The white disk would send to the eye more light than could be accounted for by the visible illumination. It could only appear *luminous;* and this prediction was verified by Henneman (1935, p. 30).

Concealed shadow. Parallel to this experiment of Gelb is one of Kardos (1934): a good light floods a field of objects, except for one disk of white paper which stands in the shadow of a concealed shadow-

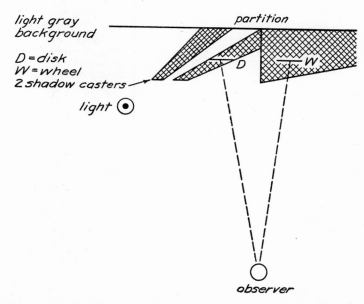

Fig. 174. (After MacLeod, 1932.) Shadow suggestion experiment, described in text below.

caster. The size and position of the shadow-caster are so regulated that the shadow covers the whole disk and nothing more. There is no penumbra or other indicator of shadow on the disk (Fig. 173). O reports a *black* disk standing in the good light. Move the shadow-caster a little to the side so that the edge of the shadow is visible on the disk, and the disk is at once seen to be white—white in shadow instead of black in good light. Return the shadow-caster to its original position, and the appearance of the disk reverts to black-in-good-light.

Suggested shadow. MacLeod (1932) found still another way of deceiving O regarding the illumination of an object. Shadows in the background conveyed a suggestion, more or less potent, that the object was shaded. The object was a disk of light gray albedo (disk D in Fig. 174). It stood always in a concealed shadow and appeared black when the background was free from shadows. But when a visible shadow was introduced into the background, the disk appeared lighter gray and somewhat shaded. The larger the visible shadow on the background, the stronger was this suggestion and the lighter the disk appeared. The suggestion was further strengthened by giving the background shadow a three-dimensional appearance; a shaded corner was introduced by running a small partition forward from the background, just to the left of the disk (not shown in Fig. 174). O saw the disk in front of the shaded corner and got a strong suggestion of shadow on the disk which therefore appeared a lighter gray. These qualitative impressions of O

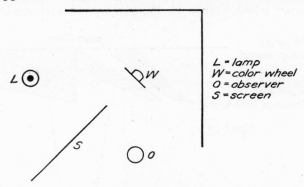

FIG. 175. (After Cramer, 1923.) Colored corner experiment. The walls were papered in some color; the light was white. The color wheel contained a disk of the same paper as that on the walls, along with a disk of white, and the mixture was adjusted till it appeared white. Only a little white was required; the color was attributed partly to the illumination.

were confirmed by color matches between the disk D and a black-white mixture on the color wheel W.

Colored background. Cramer (1923) created a false impression of colored illumination by papering a corner of the room in a uniform color and illuminating it with white light from a concealed source (Fig. 175). The whole corner seemed to be receiving colored light, not quite so saturated as the actual color on the walls. The stimuli in this experiment were ambiguous: they could result from strongly colored walls under white light, or from white walls under strongly colored light. The phenomenal impression lay between these extremes—another instance of compromise perception.

DIVERSITY OF FIELD

Some psychologists are doubtful about "correction for illumination" and incline to explain the results by reference to complexity and "articulation" of the field (p. 604). As already remarked there is no obvious reason why field complexity should make for "color constancy" rather than for any other "organization of the field." But there is one way in which diversity within a field of homogeneous illumination favors recognition of the object colors present in that field. A light gray paper

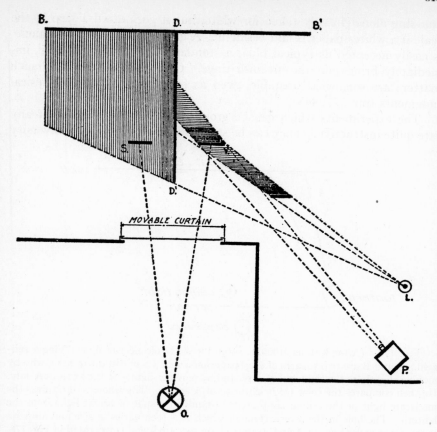

FIG. 176. (Henneman, 1935.) Basic setup for study of field diversity. When the curtain was opened, O saw a limited field divided by the partition DD' into a shaded half on the left, containing a rotating white disk S with white background, and on the right a space with black background, illuminated by the light L and containing a rotating disk V of gray albedo screened from the light L but receiving the spotlight from the concealed lantern P. This was adjusted in intensity by an iris diaphragm till O was satisfied with the match between S and V. The brightness of the two backgrounds, BD and DB' was physically the same as determined by an illuminometer. The shaded half of the field was diversified by the introduction of disks, with results as follows expressed in Thouless ratios:

Homogeneous field around disk S	.290
1 small gray disk near S	.418
1 small black disk near S	.442
3 small black disks near S	.502

The white disk S, then, looked whiter when accompanied by a gray disk and still whiter when accompanied by a black disk. This "contrast" effect can be understood as the result of placing S at the top of a more or less extended scale of brightnesses in its own sub-field (p. 598). Presumably, if a disk brighter than S could have been introduced into the shaded field, S would then have appeared darker and the match would have given a lower ratio.

standing alone is easily taken for white, but it goes down a step in the scale if a whiter paper is laid beside it. A greenish blue, standing alone, is easily accepted as typical blue; a standard blue placed beside it immediately brings out the greenish tinge. Our "mental scales" in such matters are somewhat unstable, even as in esthetic or psychophysical judgments (pp. 377, 448).

The experiments which can be grouped under this head are at any rate quite instructive. They can be subdivided according as the diversity

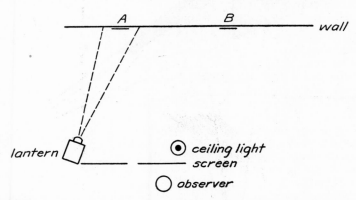

FIG. 177. (After Katona, 1929.) Setup for study of effect of diversifying a sub-field. A and B are two squares of gray paper on a wall 1.8 m distant from O, who by moving slightly to the right sees B only, and by moving slightly to the left sees A only. He then compares the color (or brightness) of A and B. The whole wall receives the moderate light of the ceiling lamp, and A stands in a spot of bright light from the lantern. The hole in the screen through which A is seen varies in size and allows a narrower or wider view of A and its immediate surroundings, as indicated in Fig. 178.

is spatially two-dimensional or three-dimensional. The diversity, it should be understood, lies within a field, or sub-field, subjected to uniform illumination.

Two-dimensional diversity. Unusually complete control of all field conditions was achieved in the experiment of Henneman (1935, see Fig. 176). A white disk standing in shadow was matched with a disk standing (apparently) in good light, adjustable in physical brightness. When the shaded area showed no diversity whatever, being viewed through a reduction screen, there was almost no approach to perception of albedo. As the shaded area was diversified by the introduction of disks of gray or black, the apparent whiteness of the test disk increased.

Diversity can be diminished by restricting the visible extent of a sub-field. When the view is limited to one single uniform surface, we have the familiar reduction screen experiment, with zero diversity in the sub-field, no illumination cues, and almost no approach to perception of albedo. When a somewhat wider view shows more diversity (and also provides some cues of illumination) there is some approach to perception of albedo, and this approach becomes closer as the view is widened. An experiment of this type by Katona (1929) is illustrated in Figs. 177 and 178.

Another diversification tried by Katona consisted in a little picture placed beside the gray square on the wall, 6 feet distant from O and standing in a spotlight. The gray albedo was better seen when the picture was present. How the picture helped was not perfectly clear, but one possibility (not stressed by Katona) is that O derived a cue of illumination from the distinctness of the small picture—for the better the light the better the acuity of vision.

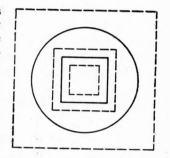

Fig. 178. Extent of visible field in Katona's experiment. The heavy square represents the gray square A of the preceding Figure, and the circle represents the spot of bright light. The 3 broken lines show the alternative views afforded by the peekholes. The smallest hole amounts to a reduction screen, as it allows a view of only a part of the gray square. The medium hole reveals the entire gray square surrounded by a frame of brightly illuminated wall. The largest hole shows the entire bright spot with its penumbra and some of the surrounding wall. In terms of diversity, the small hole shows none, the medium hole some and the large hole much. Viewed through the small hole, A was matched with B in accordance with stimulus brightness, very nearly; through the large hole, nearly in accordance with object color; through the medium hole, in between. The greater the diversity, the closer the approximation to perception of object color. The result can be stated equally well in terms of cues of illumination. When looking through the small hole, O receives no cues of the bright light falling on the gray square, except such as may be afforded by its microstructure. Through the medium hole he sees the brightly lighted wall around the gray square, and through the large hole he sees the whole bright spot with its penumbra.

Cramer (1923), in one of her many experiments, projected pictures upon a yellow screen in a dark room. A white house, well focused, appeared in three dimensions and in its object color; it looked like a white house standing in yellow light. When poorly focused, it lost its object color along with its three-dimensional appearance and became a mere assemblage of stimulus colors. A blue square projected on a yellow screen appeared gray, as it should according to the color mixture; but the picture of a child wearing a blue dress showed very clearly a blue dress in yellow illumination. In the case of the blue square, there was no diversity within the illuminated area, as there was in the two pictures. The importance of good focus, however, shows that something beside mere diversity was operating; indicators of the shape, size and other spatial qualities of the object are strong supports for the perception of object color.

Another experiment of the same author: between the prisms and the slide of a stereoscope was placed a sheet of blue glass. When the slide presented a snow-covered landscape, the observer saw the snow as white in blue illumination, and the white of the snow came out best when there were definite, outstanding objects in the foreground of the picture. Lowering the illumination deprived the picture of depth and made the snow itself appear blue.

Three-dimensional diversity. An experiment of Katz (1930, p. 354) shows the importance of cues of the third dimension in perceiving the true colors of objects. A white disk was set up behind an episcotister and viewed from different distances. From a distance of 7 meters or more, the disk was not seen to be behind the episcotister but appeared to be a dark gray circle lying about in the plane of the episcotister. As O came nearer, the disk appeared to become brighter and to move to its objective position behind the episcotister. To obtain a measure of this change, the white disk was matched with a color wheel mixture viewed directly. In terms of the Brunswik ratio, the approximation to correct perception of the white albedo was, for each distance:

At 7 m distance	.03
" 6 " "	.04
" 5 " "	.04
" 4 " "	.05
" 3 " "	.07
" 2 " "	.11
" 1.5 " "	.14
" 1 " "	.16
" 0.5 " "	.19

These values were all obtained with the disk 20 cm behind the episcotister. When the disk was moved to a distance of 1.5 m behind the episcotister, O remaining at 0.5 m in front of the episcotister, the Brunswik ratio went up to .22. Thus conditions which made it easier to separate the disk from the episcotister, spatially, made it easier also to keep their colors separate.

Another way of assisting O to separate a color seen through an episcotister from that of the episcotister itself was found by G. M. Heider (1932). As shown in Fig. 179, she used a blue episcotister, in front of a black background containing some yellow circles. Part of the background, the outfield, was visible over the top of the episcotister, but was concealed at times in order to discover what difference the outfield made in the appearance of the infield. The infield was a segment of a circle; when seen alone, it appeared dark blue in color from the mixture of the black ground with the blue of the episcotister, and the spots of the infield appeared neutral gray from the mixture of the blue of the episcotister with the yellow circles on the background. The outfield was readily seen to lie in a plane behind the episcotister; the infield when seen alone did not break up into the two planes which were objectively present. But when the outfield also was exposed, the continuity of the background asserted itself and the spots seen through the episcotister appeared to be located on or near the background. With this change in the apparent location of the spots came a change in their apparent color; they became yellowish, like yellow spots seen through a blue veil.

In this experiment, *continuity* was the important factor in keeping the planes of episcotister and background separate, and in keeping their colors separate. The visibly continuous background pulled the spots back into its plane, while the continuous surface of the episcotister carried its blue color through the spots. The two continuities combined made the gray stimulus spots appear as yellow showing through blue.

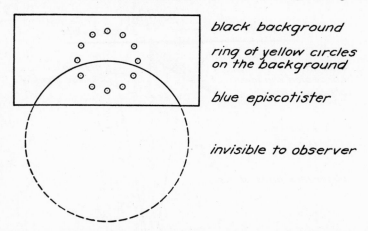

FIG. 179. (G. M. Heider, 1932.) Continuity a factor in separating planes and their colors. A screen concealed everything except the rectangular area, part of which, the outfield, is visible over the top of the episcotister, and is sometimes screened off leaving only the infield visible.

Three-dimensional diversity in a sub-field is important because it furnishes cues of the third dimension and so reveals the objective spatial relations. Conditions of illumination—distance from the source of light, angle of incidence, cast shadows—are bound up with these spatial relations. Therefore three-dimensional diversity functions as a cue of illumination.

Contrast. Two-dimensional diversity within a sub-field operates somewhat differently, as already suggested. It shifts or stabilizes O's scale of object colors. This effect can scarcely be separated altogether from "contrast" in a broad sense. Contrast would seem to be the only one of Hering's factors which plays much role in the experimental studies. Memory color is ruled out by using grays and color-wheel mixtures which have no constant object color. Pupillary diameter and retinal adaptation can hardly be quick and selective enough to count in comparing different parts of the field of view. With regard to contrast, if it is peripheral or at least sub-perceptual in origin, the fact that it is only slightly in evidence when surface color is clearly perceived (p. 568) means that in some instances object color is perceived *in opposition to contrast*. Contrast would then amount to an illumination for which correction is made.

In Gelb's concealed illumination experiment, a separately illuminated black disk appears white, but as soon as a bit of white paper is held in the spot light, the disk is seen as black. Though the bit of bright field would produce some contrast, it seems hardly possible that it should change white to black, except by serving as an index of illumination. MacLeod (1932) obtained similar evidence from a modification of the concealed shadow experiment, as explained under Fig. 180.

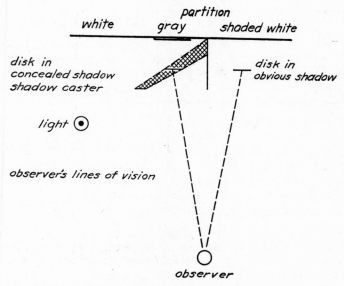

FIG. 180. (MacLeod, 1932.) Color constancy in the absence of direct contrast. The two disks were both white and both shaded, but the one on the right stood in visible shadow and the one on the left in concealed shadow. The immediate background of each disk was the same in physical brightness, one being gray paper, the other white in shadow. Yet the disk on the right was seen as white in shadow, the one on the left as black in good light. Non-adjacent parts of the left-hand field were white, to be sure, but the contrast effect is supposed to be slight between non-adjacent areas.

Attitude in color constancy experiments. In addition to cues of illumination and diversity of field there must be factors in the observer himself which determine the way he sees and matches colors in these experiments. Otherwise the large individual differences would be inexplicable. Under the same field conditions one O will give a Thouless ratio as low as .10, another as high as .80 or even higher; the one matches approximately according to stimulus brightness, the other approximately by albedo. In everyday life we are certainly concerned to see the colors of objects, while the painter aims to do justice to the stimuli that actually reach the eye. In the laboratory most Os show what amounts to a compromise between these two ideal attitudes, but a sample of Os is .

likely to give a bimodal distribution, as if each O was primarily object-directed or else stimulus-directed. Henneman (1935) queried whether these attitudes could be changed by a short course of instruction. Individuals who spontaneously gave a low ratio were instructed in "allowing for illumination" so as to get the albedo of a shaded disk; and individuals whose original ratio was high were made acquainted with the painter's attitude. Most of the individuals were able, after instruction, to shift their attitude to a certain extent. The average Thouless ratios were as follows for the two groups:

Original ratio	.221	.721
Ratio after instruction	.575	.474

Whiteness is not the same as brightness. A white object in shadow may appear white but still it does not look the same as when standing in strong light. The difference is described by Katz (1930) as one of *Eindringlichkeit*, which may be translated, forcefulness or insistence. The shaded white has little insistence. Insistence corresponds to the intensity of the stimulus. In its insistence the impression corresponds to the stimulus while in object color it corresponds to the albedo of the object. It seldom corresponds with either one completely; usually it is a compromise between the two. So far as it corresponds to the stimulus, no special explanation is demanded. So far as it corresponds to the object it must depend on some form of correction for illumination. The immediacy of the impression of object color warns us against assuming the correction to be a secondary process, interpolated between sensation and perception. But if the perceptual apparatus is set or adjusted for an illumination, a stimulus received from that area of illumination will be corrected as it is being received. It is not first received and then corrected but the correction is imposed in the process of perceptual reception. The perceptual apparatus, so conceived, is analogous to a camera with iris diaphragm automatically controlled by a light meter— except that the control can differentiate between parts of the field standing under different illuminations. Recalling our equation:

$$A = S/M$$

we see that if the receiving apparatus is adjusted for M, the S, as received, is reduced to S/M and therefore to A. Perception is direct, immediate.

But perception is seldom complete or exclusive. The perceptual response is not the only response to the stimulus. Katz (1930) finds that the size of the pupil corresponds to the stimulus and not to the phenomenal whiteness of a fixated surface. The afterimage, fusion frequency, the impression received from indirect vision, the difference threshold correspond with stimulus brightness and not with the perceived object color. "Insistence" shows that stimulus intensity has an effect even when corrected for illumination. The total impression seems to combine what have traditionally been called sensation and perception.

Other instances of perceptual constancy. The facts in regard. to perception of object size and shape are parallel to the facts of color constancy. In ordinary life these and other characteristics of objects seem to be perceived very correctly in spite of variations in the stimuli received. Under laboratory conditions the objective facts are seldom perfectly perceived, the necessary corrections for distance, angle, etc., are seldom fully adequate, and compromise responses are the rule, though individuals differ greatly in these laboratory tests (Thouless, 1931–32); some even show "over-constancy," over-correction for the disturbing stimulus variable (Brunswik, 1933, 1934; Sheehan, 1938).

CHAPTER XXV

THE PERCEPTION OF FORM

THE FACT that a common German word for form or shape is *Gestalt* reminds us that this topic comes into close relation with a "systematic" question, a question relating to the theory of the Gestalt school of psychology. It cannot be our purpose here to take issue either for or against this school. We can utilize the numerous contributions made by members of the Gestalt school to the problem of form perception without involving ourselves in any such controversial question. The general problem of form perception was not first seen by the Gestalt school. The fact that wholes or complexes present characteristics which are not readily explained by the parts into which the whole can be analysed has long been obvious to psychologists. John Stuart Mill attempted to meet the problem by his theory of mental chemistry and Wundt by his theory of creative synthesis. Special importance in the history of the problem attaches to the work of Ehrenfels (1890) on *Gestaltqualität* or form quality. A good example is afforded by a musical tune. The tune transposed into another key is made up of different notes, but is still the same tune and easily recognized. The form quality of the tune does not reside in the constituent notes but in their pattern and mutual relations. In the same way the perception of a circular form is obviously not dependent upon the stimulation of any particular retinal receptors, since the circle may differ in size and in retinal position and still be seen as of the same form.

We shall not attempt either to trace the history from Ehrenfels down or to assign carefully to each author his share in the progress achieved. We may note the names of some of the chief contributors: Schumann (1900) discovered several principles of unit formation in the visual field; Benussi (1904) demonstrated important central factors in the perception of form, especially the opposite attitudes of totalizing and analyzing perception; Bühler (1913) demonstrated quantitatively the genuineness and accuracy of form perception; Rubin (1915, 1921) showed the fundamental importance of "figure and ground"; and Wertheimer (1923) worked out the main principles according to which forms are segregated out of the manifold patches and contours of the visual field.

Theories of form perception. Nor shall we attempt any elaborate discussion of general theories of form perception, but shall stick closely to the experimental literature and the hypotheses which have been put to the test of experiment. A brief statement of certain general theories may serve as a background. The following concepts have been employed in the different theories: (1) mosaic reception of stimuli, (2) association, (3) set or *Einstellung*, (4) objective meaning. We have also the concepts of cerebral receptive centers, perceptive centers and association centers. Of theories we may distinguish the following:

1. *The empiristic theory* aims to get along with a minimum number of concepts; it uses only the concept of a pure mosaic of elementary sensations and the concept of associations established in experience. To the associations are assigned the functions (a) of combining the elements into forms and (b) of giving objective meaning to these forms.

2. *The nativistic theory* regards the fundamental spatial and temporal organization of sensory material as a native characteristic of the individual.

3. *The relation theory* of Spearman (1923, 1925) and others considers that the perception of "eduction" of relations is the essential process in the building up of a perception of a total form.

4. *The Gestalt theory* regards relations as a secondary product of analysis of the total form which itself is primary and primitive, inherent in the process of sensory reception, and not dependent fundamentally on learning or experience. This theory minimizes the associative factor and regards the receptive process as being formative or configurational. It denies the existence of any mosaic stage in the process. In place of the mosaic it uses the concept of a dynamic field, all parts of which are interacting from the moment of peripheral stimulation. The forming process is coincident with the receptive process. Central factors such as set or association are not necessary for the formative process. Yet this theory recognizes the reality of set as a central factor modifying the receptive field in the direction of favoring certain formations as against others.

5. *A modification of the Gestalt theory to conform to the facts of brain injuries* (form blindness, etc.) admits that the first receptive centers of the visual cortex have little configurational character and that the formative process occurs mostly in other portions of the visual cortex. Yet this function is not due to association and meaning, but is a primitive physiological process so closely bound up with the receptive process that introspectively no distinction can be made between sensation and perception.

6. A theory held by the present writer regards *perception as a kind of response*, and places much emphasis on the central factors of set and meaning. In ordinary life we see not forms but things, and our effort in sense perception is to know the objective situation. The set for perceiving objective facts dominates the receptive process as a whole. Any momentary assemblage of stimuli is received into a brain already adjusted to the situation as already perceived, and thus the immediately past experience is a very important factor which is embodied in the adjustment or set for the situation. The importance of more remote

past experience is seen from the obvious fact that the objective meaning of sensory impressions is retained from one experience to another. This theory is not tied up with any particular theory of association.

PERCEPTUAL UNITS

If an assemblage of dots is presented they are not perceived each singly nor as a chaotic total mass, but in groups. The grouping is perceptual rather than objective, since it can change in spite of the same objective constellation of stimuli. Yet it does depend upon the objective constellation, since certain groupings are easier with certain constellations, and other groupings with other constellations. Wertheimer (1923) used the criterion of ease in his comprehensive study of the principles governing unit formation in the visual field. He found the following factors especially important:

1. *Nearness or proximity in the field of view.* Dots relatively close together are readily seen as a group.

2. *Sameness or similarity.* Dots of the same color are readily seen as a group in distinction from dots of another color, which may form another group. The likeness may be one of shape instead of color.

3. *"Common fate."* Dots which move simultaneously in the same direction are readily seen as a group. They possess a sort of similarity in their sameness of motion.

4. *Good continuation* or *good figure.* The group follows a uniform direction in some respect. The closed line has the advantage over an open one. Another important case is symmetry or balance of the total figure.

5. *Conformity with the individual's momentary set or Einstellung.* Wertheimer distinguished subjective and objective *Einstellung.* Subjectively the observer can set himself for a certain grouping and so resist the factors of proximity and similarity. By objective *Einstellung,* Wertheimer means essentially the same thing as perseveration. Let dots be arranged in a straight line with alternately smaller and wider spaces between them—O pairs them according to proximity. Let the spaces be gradually equalized—O adheres to the original grouping.

6. *Past experience or custom,* illustrated by a series of words printed without spaces, which can nevertheless be separated and read. Wertheimer urges that this factor must not be too readily invoked. To prove the reality of the experience factor in any concrete case, one must show that the more direct perceptual factors do not account for the grouping obtained.

The first three of these factors refer to objective characteristics of the field of dots. The last two factors are subjective or organismic in that they depend upon conditions within the observer. The fourth factor, good continuation or good figure, occupies a middle ground, since some conditions of "goodness," as closure and symmetry, are described in objective terms, while others depend on the observer and on what he finds easy or pleasing.

Wertheimer found by detailed introspective reports that O saw the groups as parts of a larger whole. With extremely brief presentation the groups were seen as mere blotches or patches of dark color separated

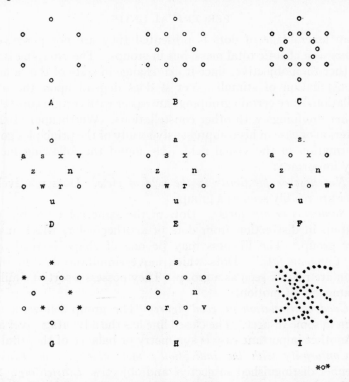

FIG. 181. Dot figures illustrating the factors of nearness, sameness, continuation and good figure. The hexagon so clearly visible in A is somewhat obscured in B by the additional dots, but reappears in C as a leftover group when the addition of still more dots in close proximity to each other brings out the interior hexagon. In D, E and F the sameness of certain items favors grouping them, and the leftovers readily fall into a complementary group, when they make a regular figure, or when, as in G, they are similar; whereas in H, where the leftover items are dissimilar and irregularly arranged, they do not get together readily. I shows the factor of homogeneous continuation, in that the dots are readily seen as lying along straight lines or fairly definite curves.

by brighter streaks. With more deliberate examination these patches broke up into grouped dots.

It is difficult by any form of experiment to obtain exact information on what O really sees. Verbal description is inadequate, and if O is asked to draw, he cannot reproduce all he sees (Rupp, 1923). However clear the total figure may appear, it requires some analysis, some noting of relations, before it can be copied (p. 73).

Attempts to unify the principles of grouping. Musatti (1931) combined these principles into one comprehensive law of homogeneity.

Homogeneity with respect to place is proximity; with respect to quality, similarity; with respect to movement or change, common fate; with respect to direction, good continuation. As to the factors of set and past experience, we may think of homogeneity between what is presented now and what has been prepared for in the immediate or more remote past.

If we think of perception as a reactive process, all the principles have to do with ease of response, and the question becomes, why it is specially easy to make a unitary response to dots which lie near together or are

Fig. 182. (Schumann, 1904.) A dot figure readily shows a variety of grouping.

similar or homogeneous in some respect. From the response conception we can deduce one or two further factors. The reaction must not only be easy but it must be satisfactory or do its job; accordingly a grouping which leaves out some of the dots will be at a disadvantage as compared with a grouping which includes them all—a factor of *inclusiveness*.

We can also deduce that where the factors favoring two or more groupings are about equally balanced the perception will be unstable and tend to *shift* from one response to another, as, indeed, we know to be the fact (p. 697).

Figures seen in three dimensions. Ambiguous figures, easily seen in more than one way, can be constructed of lines instead of dots. Many line drawings readily suggest three dimensions and are called figures of ambiguous or reversible perspective. The Necker cube and the

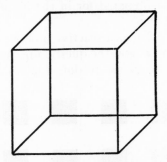

FIG. 183.   The Necker cube.

Schröder staircase are the best known. Geometrically, a line drawing can be the projection upon a plane of any one of many different three-dimensional objects; but only rather simple or familiar three-dimensional objects are actually seen in the drawings. It is also true, geometrically, that the same three-dimensional object, seen from different angles, presents many different plane projections. As shown by Kopfermann (1930) some of these projections are readily seen in three dimensions, others much more readily in two dimensions. It depends according to this author on how "good" the figure is in two dimensions. If it is compact and symmetrical there is little urge toward the three-dimensional appearance. Fig. 185 shows several projections of a cube; those that are unsymmetrical are seen as cubes; the regular hexagon most readily appears as a two-dimensional figure, but with steady examination the three-dimensional appearance comes out. Similarly with the tetrahedron;

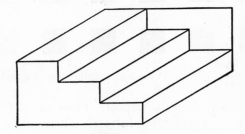

FIG. 184.   The Schröder staircase.

some of its projections, unsymmetrical as plane figures, are seen in three dimensions, whereas others are regular as plane figures and scarcely suggest a three-dimensional appearance.

However we must grant a proneness to see in three dimensions even against the dictates of good figure. The perfectly regular star in Fig.

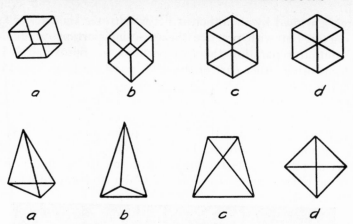

Fig. 185. (Kopfermann, 1930.) Plane projections of cube and tetrahedron.

186 will nevertheless give way if steadily viewed to a three-dimensional appearance which is less symmetrical but more exciting.

FIGURE AND GROUND

The psychological importance of this distinction was first brought out clearly by Rubin (1915, 1921), though of course figure and ground are familiar concepts in the graphic arts. In our everyday looking at the field of view we distinguish the thing from its background, but here we are helped by the perception of the third dimension. It is somewhat more surprising to notice that even a plain drawing on a sheet of paper readily breaks up into a figure and the ground. It does not necessarily so break up; looking at a map in the usual way we do not see one colored patch as the figure and the rest as merely ground. But staring at it tends to make the field separate along some contour into figure and ground. Rubin found it possible with a little practice to bring out any

Fig. 186. This figure though perfectly regular as a flat figure is readily seen in three dimensions.

well-marked part of a field as the figure, leaving the rest as the ground. If the total field consists of a black portion and a white portion meeting in a contour, either the black or the white portion can be seen as figure, the other remaining as ground. If either the black or the white portion is entirely enclosed by the other, it is easier to see the enclosed portion as the figure, but with practice the enclosing portion can be so seen. If the contour separating the two portions is approximately vertical without enclosing either part of the field, reversing figure and ground is easy for the observer. When the shift or reversal occurs the change of appearance is surprising because the shape of the two parts of the field is very different—which is rather curious since these shapes depend on the common contour separating the two parts (Figs. 187, 188).

The phenomenal differences between figure and ground are classified by Rubin as follows: (1) the figure has form, the ground is relatively formless, or if the ground has form it is due to some other figuration

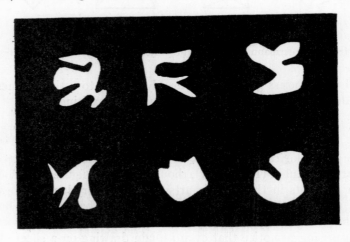

FIG. 187. (Rubin, 1921.) Type of field presented with instructions calling sometimes for taking the enclosed portion as figure, and sometimes for taking the enclosing portion as figure. Reversal is easier if half of the field is covered by a white sheet. In Rubin's experiments the white was replaced by green.

upon it and not to the contour separating it from the figure; (2) the ground seems to extend continuously behind the figure and not to be interrupted by the figure; (3) thus the figure has some of the character of a *thing*, whereas the ground appears like unformed *material;* (4) the figure tends to appear in front, the ground behind; (5) the figure is more impressive, better remembered and more apt to suggest meaning.

We might suspect that the distinction of figure and ground was simply the old distinction between the field of attention and the field of inattention. This criticism would imply that it is impossible to attend to the ground. Granted that the figure is more apt to attract attention, it is possible to attend to the ground as ground. If we define attention in terms of clearness, we cannot say that the ground is simply less clear than the figure, for ground often has the positive property of seeming to extend behind the figure.

Rubin's experiments led to two important discoveries which may be called (1) the figural after-effect and (2) the non-recognition of the field when reversal of figure and ground has occurred.

Figural after-effect. Rubin prepared a large number of nonsense figures by cutting irregular portions out of cards and placing the cards before a lantern with green glass interposed so that on the screen there appeared an irregular green area surrounded by what was sensibly black. With a four-second exposure for each single figure, he presented a series of 9 figures, four times over, with instructions to see the enclosed green area as the figure, the black as ground. This was followed by a series of 9 similar figures with instructions to see the enclosing black area as the figure. The experimenter now shuffled these 18 figures with 9 new ones and presented them in mixed order, after an interval of 30–45 minutes, with instructions to remain passive as regards which part should be seen as figure, but to report in each case whether the figure was the enclosed or the enclosing portion and whether the field was recognized as one previously shown.

The results revealed a moderate tendency to see the same figure on the second exposure as in the original experience. As the subject had divided the field the first time into figure and ground, so he was likely to do the second time, even when remaining passive; 64 percent of the figures were seen in the same way as before, $33\frac{1}{2}$ percent were seen with reversed figure and ground, and $2\frac{1}{2}$ percent were seen in both ways. This carry-over of the same figure-ground organization

FIG. 188. (Rubin, 1921.) Figure and ground. Here the two fields have about an equal chance of being the figure, though the white field, being the same in color as the page, is more likely to be seen as ground.

of a given field from one exposure to another is called by Rubin the figural after-effect.

Non-recognition of reversed fields. Rubin's experiment on recognition of fields with reversed figure and ground was conducted in the same general manner as just described. First O examined 9 fields under instructions to see the enclosed figure, and 9 under instructions to see the enclosing figure. Then these 18 were shuffled with 9 new fields of similar general character and presented in a recognition test with instructions to *look for the enclosed figure*, to report whether they found it and whether they recognized it. In a parallel experiment the learning task was as before but the recognition test called for noting the *enclosing* figure.

The question was whether the fields seen the second time with reversed figure and ground would be recognized. The answer in general was negative. Combining the results from the two experiments, with two Os and a total of 324 fields used, we obtain the following percents recognized:

Figure and ground remaining the same	49
Figure and ground reversed	9
New fields (false recognitions)	6

The percent of reversed fields recognized is little larger than what would occur by chance, as indicated by the false recognitions of new figures.

This experiment proves that a field is not recognized if its division into figure and ground is reversed. What is recognized, then, is not the stimulus aggregate but the perceptual response which we call a figure. Nevertheless the figural after-effect proves that there is some learning at the level of this first perceptual response. There seem to be two

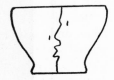

Fig. 189. Reversible contour.

stages in the process of recognition: (1) starting with the stimulus aggregate and ending with the perceived form; (2) starting with the perceived form and ending with recognition. Another stage in the total reaction is present, at times, when the form is seen as a familiar object. Reference may be made to pp. 48, 87 for other experiments on recognition of figures, and to p. 79 for the more difficult task of reproducing figures from memory.

Development of a figure-ground experience. Rubin's study of figure and ground was made with exposures of several seconds. It seemed possible to Wever (1927) that the figure-ground experience, instead of being absolutely primitive and simple, was composed of different features and capable of growing in time. He therefore repeated Rubin's experiment with tachistoscopic exposures from under 10 ms up. The post-exposure field was such as to blot out the afterimage, and the duration of the exposure was used as a measure of the amount of effective stimulation. Wever found, in fact, that with very brief exposures there was no differentiation between figure and ground, but a bare homogeneous appearance, though the figure exposed was black on white. In a somewhat longer exposure O began to see some difference between different parts of the field. There might be a smudge or blotch. This O did not yet call a figure, but if the smudge took on a vague shape, he was willing to call it figure on ground, in the lowest degree of differentiation. With slightly longer times of exposure the contour began to appear, vaguely and incompletely, and somewhat longer exposures gave the complete contour and good brightness difference between the enclosed and the enclosing fields, and the figure was well defined. The depth differentiation, that is, the standing out of the figure in front of the ground, appeared either early or late in the process and varied greatly in definiteness. Under the particular conditions of this experiment minimum figure-ground differentiation appeared with an exposure time of about 10 ms, minimum contour at about 11 ms, good contour at about 14. With still longer exposures the different features of the figure-ground experience improved but not in equal measure, and there was no length of exposure which gave the experience in ideal perfection. When the exposure lasted several seconds the figure took on the appearance of some object, as a bird or a helmet, and this appearance was apt to be stable, in contrast with the fluctuation of mere figure and ground. On the whole the figure-ground experience was decidedly complex.

With a similar tachistoscopic setup and bright post-exposure field to extinguish the positive afterimage and limit the effective time of presentation to that of the actual exposure, Ehrenstein (1930) attacked somewhat different problems of figure and ground. By determining the minimum exposure time necessary for perception of the figure under different conditions he found that the greater the illumination, and the greater the brightness difference between the two parts of the field, the shorter was the exposure time necessary for giving the figure-ground differentiation. He also reports that the better the form (with regard to symmetry, etc.) and the more meaningful the figure (in reference to object significance), the less the necessary exposure time. He denies that the figure necessarily appears to be nearer the observer than the ground and holds that the emphasis upon this characteristic of figure results from the exclusive use of plane patterns. In looking at objects in space with the eye fixed on an object at a certain distance, both the nearer and the farther objects fall into the ground. In looking through a wire screen at a distant object the screen is ground and still appears nearer than the figure. In the division of a total field into figure and ground, the large, broad expanses are likely to go to the ground and the sharply projecting points to the figure. What lies in indirect vision has usually, not always, the appearance of ground. Figure can be seen in indirect vision, as explained on p. 76.

Figure and ground not always seen. That the figure-ground differentiation is not absolutely essential in vision is shown by experiments with a total homogeneous visual field. It is difficult to secure such a field with the eyes open, but Engel (1930), by a combination of screens reaching to the limits of the field of view, with provision for uniform illumination, was able to secure such a field. Metzger (1930) also experi-

mented with it and found that no figure-ground differentiation occurred.
If the illumination was high, the texture of the screen was apt to show and
the screen was seen as an objective surface and localized at its true distance. With low illumination, however, the object character of the
field was lost and a cloudy expanse color effect was obtained (p. 540).
Jablonski (1930) found that the negative afterimage of the homogeneous
total field was rather difficult to obtain, requiring longer than usual
exposure.

A homogeneous total field for demonstration purposes can be obtained
by simply closing the lids, allowing time for residual afterimages to
fade out, and directing the face toward any source of illumination.
Absence of the figure-ground differentiation is clearly demonstrated.

Another evidence that the figure-ground differentiation is not absolutely fundamental in all perception is found in experiments with
dim illumination (Pikler, 1928; Galli, 1934). Let the figure be a square
of gray paper and the background a figured surface like tapestry or
fancy wall paper. Let the illumination, at first good, be gradually
reduced. The following changes in the appearance occur: (1) with
good illumination O sees the figure and the interruption introduced
by it in the background; (2) with lower illumination the figure loses its
sharpness of outline and only its central part remains definitely perceived;
(3) with still lower illumination the ground overcomes the figure and
annuls it, though at certain moments the figure is visible as through a
veil; (4) finally with very low illumination only the ground with no trace
of the figure is seen.

A result in line with the last is that of Helson & Fehrer (1932) to the
effect that a dimly lighted surface is seen as light before its form is
recognizable. The experiment was one in measuring the stimulus
threshold for light. The light was seen through a milk glass screen,
illuminated from behind, in front of which was placed a figure, either
a circle, a triangle, a V-shaped figure, or a square. These were cut
from black cardboard. O being first dark-adapted was seated 275 cm
from the instrument so that the figures fell entirely within foveal vision.
The main result was that light was perceived at a very much lower
illumination than even vaguely perceived form which in turn was perceived at a lower illumination than definite shape.

Non-visual figure and ground. Both figure and ground are characteristically visual phenomena; yet analogies are not wanting in the other
modalities. Vernon (1934–1935) shows how the figure-ground conception
can be applied in hearing. There is a background of relatively uniform
sound; standing out from this ground is some shrill or otherwise sharply
delimited sound analogous to a figure. In music we should think of
the melody as the figure and of the chords and other accompaniment as
the ground. Vernon analyzes the characteristics of figure in music as
follows: figure is apt to be higher in pitch and louder than the ground,
to have a different timbre, to be played by a different instrument. The

figure moves differently from the ground, it has more movement and different rhythm, its crescendos and diminuendos are different from those of the ground. To make the musical figure distinct it is started either before or after the ground; the accompaniment may begin first and when the hearer is used to that, the melody appears, or the melody may be announced first in isolation and later interwoven with the accompaniment and still be recognizable. The figure often contains notes discordant with the accompaniment which are not experienced as discordant but as belonging to the figure.

In the field of bodily movement one can easily think of phasic movement as figure and of posture as ground.

CONTOUR

It needs no argument to prove that figure cannot be perceived apart from contour. If the contour is vague and broad as when one part of the field shades off gradually into another, the shape of either part is indefinite. For these reasons Rubin (1915, 1921) called contour formative of shape, "shape producing." When, as is so commonly the case, the field is divided by the contour into figure and ground, the contour shapes the figure only, the ground remaining shapeless. The tendency of contour is to exert its effect upon the enclosed figure, that is, upon what may be called the concave side of the contour. It exerts its forming influence inward rather than outward.

But though contour gives shape to a figure we cannot say that the shape *is* the contour or that O experiences the contour directly. Some analysis is necessary before he sees the contour. Even in copying a figure with a pencil attention is directed rather to the shape of the figure to be copied than to the exact run of the contour. Rubin reports an interesting demonstration of this fact. Draw on a sheet of paper a wavy line, then draw another line below it so as to mark off a stripe or ribbon of uniform width. When the upper and lower contours of the stripe are examined carefully they are found to be very different. They have to be different in the case of curved contours in order to make the stripe seem equally broad. It is clear that O in outlining the stripe attends to its width rather than to the exact run of the contour.

Shape not identical with contour. When two parts of the field are separated by a contour the two parts may appear very different in shape, though they have the same contour. A more objective demonstration of the same relationship is seen in the non-recognition of a field when figure and ground have been reversed. This result, already cited from Rubin, is confirmed by a similar experiment of Galli & Hochheimer (1934). A rectangular piece of black cardboard was cut in two along a curved but somewhat irregular line, and the two parts were mounted on white cards so that the same contour was presented twice, once with the black at the left and again with the black at the right. These black-white fields were presented tachistoscopically with the curved contour approximately vertical.   After each brief exposure O reproduced the contour as well as possible with pencil.   That the contour looked different according as it ran with the right or left side figure was clear from his different drawings and also from the fact that he very seldom recognized the same contour in the two types of presentation.   It appears that direction, as Mach (1914) pointed out, is an important factor in apparent form, since the same contour will seem different according as it is attached to the right or the left side, above or below.

When you attend to the shape of the figure you are apt to look rather fixedly at some part, but when you are directing your attention to the contour you take it as a path to be followed.   You *follow the contour*

+   1   —   +   2   —   +   3   --

FIG. 190.   (Galli & Hochheimer, 1934.)   Two forms with same contour.

in more or less detail, but exactly what this "following" is cannot easily be determined.   O reports that he feels his eyes moving around the contour (Rubin) but his eyes do not move with regularity around the contour as we know from the photography of eye movements (p. 585).   Rubin found it possible to follow a contour while maintaining the eyes in a fixed position, or even to follow the contour of an afterimage.

What produces contour?   Mach pointed out as long ago as 1865 (see Mach, 1914, p. 217) that contour is not simply a change of color or brightness at some portion of the field of view, for a steady brightness gradient gives no contour at any point.   Contour is a sudden change; mathematically it is a change of change, that is to say, it is the second differential of brightness and not the first $\left(\dfrac{d^2i}{ds^2} \text{ not } \dfrac{di}{ds}\right)$.   A part of the field is prominent in proportion as its brightness differs from the mean brightness of the immediately surrounding field.   A contour is a relatively *abrupt change of gradient* in either brightness or color.   It belongs in the same class of phenomena as marginal contrast.   Contrast enhances contour, and makes the outlines of objects more distinct than they are in the retinal image itself.

Not only peripheral factors like contrast but also central factors enhance and complete contour.   This is brought out especially well by figures (such as Fig. 191) in which a contour is subjectively completed across an objectively homogeneous portion of the field.   The extended contour is often called a "tied image"; at least it is a central addition to the retinal image. In dot figures, contours change with the grouping of the dots—a proof of central origin. Also the contours change with the meaning conveyed by the figure (Zigler, 1920).

Recent studies hold out the promise of a still more penetrating analysis of contour and its formation. Werner (1935) exposed two figures successively (Fig. 192) to the same retinal area, a black square, and a white square of the same size surrounded by a black frame. If the black square was followed, after a vacant (gray) interval of 150 ms, by the framed white square, curiously enough the black square was not seen at all. When the sequence was reversed, both squares were seen. Same results when black and white were interchanged in each figure. The framed square obliterated the plain square, which did not have time to establish itself before

Fig. 191. (Schumann, 1904.) Subjective contour. Note the appearance of a vertical white stripe bounded by straight lines at the right and left where it is separated from the semicircular figures.

being wiped out by the opposed gradient of the framed square; but when the framed square came first its double contour was too strong to be obliterated. By use of this obliteration method Werner found the corners especially strong. It would appear also from his results that parallel contours of opposed gradient reinforce each other in proportion to their nearness.

Fry & Bartley (1935) used the threshold method in studying contours. They determined the minimum difference of illumination or brightness necessary to make a visible contour under different field conditions. They obtained results consistent with the hypothesis that a contour exerts an inhibitory influence upon a neighboring parallel contour and a reinforcing influence upon one which it approaches at right angles. It would seem, however, that it should make some difference whether the gradients of the two parallel contours are in the same or opposite directions. At the present writing this subject of contour formation seems to be in its beginnings.

MASKING OF FIGURES

Though puzzle pictures may seem below the dignity of scientific investigation, they are no more unpromising than dot figures and nonsense figures. By what means can a picture be concealed? Still better, by what means can a simple figure be concealed? We find ourselves facing a fundamental problem in the perception of form. If we knew the factors in form perception, we could so control them as to conceal one form in another.

Since shape depends so largely upon contour one way of concealing a figure is to remove portions of the contour. The observer is forced to reconstruct the figure by supplying the missing contour, as is possible within limits. To reconstruct most of the contour, to go as far as Michelangelo who saw the statue in a block of marble, is to go beyond mere perception.

FIG. 192. (Werner, 1935.) Experiment on the development of contour. The square *a* is of the same size as the interior white space in the frame *b*. Expose them in cyclical sequence to the same part of the retina, with blank (uniform gray) time intervals, longer after *b* than after *a*, so that a cycle runs:

a	20 ms
blank	150 ms
b	20 ms
blank	300 ms

Then *b* only is seen, or at the most the only trace of *a* is a graying of the interior square field. But if *a* and *b* change places, so that *b* comes first, *b* is not obliterated by *a*, but both are seen. The prevalence of *b* over *a* can be observed also in binocular combination of the two figures (as by crossing the eyes, p. 657).

Foley (1935) demonstrated the difficulty of supplying missing contour by requiring O to find small figures within a total figure. He first tested the hypothesis that a part is more easily isolated from a meaningless than from a *meaningful* figure. The results seemed to confirm this hypothesis until the greater *compactness* of the meaningful total figures was pointed out. A second experiment compared three conditions: (A) meaningful whole; (B) equally compact meaningless whole; (C) less compact, broken-up pattern of the same masses. The results showed no difference between the meaningful and equally compact meaningless totals, but a considerable advantage for the broken-up figure, the parts of which were more easily isolated. Then it was noticed that the less compact figure presented the *contour* of the parts more completely. When the three sorts of total figure were equalized in this respect by drawing fine lines across them without destroying their total shapes, the total shape was found to be of no consequence. Since O was all intent on finding parts, the shape of the whole made no difference to him while visible contour of the parts made a great difference (Fig. 193).

In this last experiment, O devoted considerable time to each total figure. In very brief exposures, the regularity or irregularity of the total figure is a factor of some importance; a part is found more quickly in an irregular figure. An irregular total figure gives a first impression of an uninteresting mass and leaves attention free to search for the designated part, while a pleasing total figure delays the search for the part (Seifert, 1917).

Gottschaldt (1926, 1929), guided in part by Wertheimer's laws of good figure, became very skillful in concealing figures. His purpose was

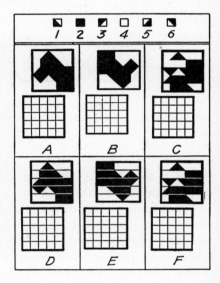

Fig. 193. (Foley, 1935.) Portions of a substitution test. The blank squares are to be filled in with numbers identifying the corresponding parts of the "pictures," according to the key at the top. Picture A suggests an object; B, though equally compact, does not suggest an object; C was made by transposing some of the horizontal rows of A; D, E and F are the same as A, B and C, except that fine horizontal lines equate the three in respect to the visible contour of the separate squares. The whole test contained many sets of figures made up in the same way. The small figures were equally difficult to find in A and B, and easier in C; but the addition of the fine horizontal lines made D, E and F all equally easy.

somewhat different. He wished to check the common belief that a familiar figure is easily seen and that past experience is an important factor in form perception. He believed his results to prove the contrary, but this conclusion is disputed (Moore, 1930; Braly, 1933). He did not show whether a familiar figure was as easily concealed as an unfamiliar one. But he succeeded in concealing familiar figures, and also good figures, by devices which we will consider presently (Fig. 194).

Galli & Zama (1931) conducted a similar experiment to study the masking of figures. Their object was to hamper the process of seeing a figure and in that way to bring the process out into the open. They drew on paper a geometrical figure, as a square or circle, and on the same paper superimposed another figure masking the first to a greater or less degree. The combined figure was presented to O without time limit, and he was instructed to find the masked figure which was present and to describe his experience. The introspections indicated a process somewhat as follows: certain lines not fitting well into the total figure suggest some familiar figure which is taken as a blank schema with missing parts to be found. These parts are found and the masked figure is then seen more or less clearly (Fig. 195).

The main instruction we can derive from both of these experiments is as to ways and means of concealing a figure. In concocting a concealed figure pattern, we can start with a given total figure, note how it naturally breaks up into parts, and extract from it a part which cuts across the natural subdivision or differs in direction from the whole figure. If the whole figure is symmetrical and upright we extract from it lines which will give an unsymmetrical slanting figure.

If a given figure is to be concealed, the rules of the game call for complete presentation of the concealed figure. At least, all its lines must

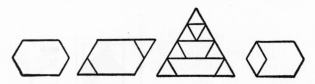

Fig. 194. (Gottschaldt, 1926, 1929.) A figure hidden in more complex figures. The hidden figure (hexagon) is both familiar and "good."

be there so that it can be traced out completely in the lines of the inclusive figure. A large share of the concealed figure can still be *omitted* from the total figure. We can actually *omit much of the contour* of a figure while playing the game and presenting all the lines.

A freely projecting corner is a strong part of the contour of a figure; remove this part by prolonging the lines beyond the corner so that it no longer projects. A free-ending line, if present in the part figure, is a prominent part of the contour; remove it by connecting another line to that free end. A flat end is an important part of a contour; remove it by placing other lines out beyond it. Embed part of the contour in a series of parallel or radiating lines, and so make it impossible to pick out this part of the contour except in direct vision (whereas the figure has to be seen partly in indirect vision). Apart from contour, interior clear space is a prominent character of some figures; remove this character by drawing lines across this space. If the original figure gives an impression of three dimensions, remove this impression by added lines which give the total a two-dimensional appearance; or vice versa.

So there are many characters of a figure which can be subtracted by the addition of new parts. The observer's job in finding the thus-concealed figure is to prune away the additions and so recreate for himself what the "artist" has destroyed. The artist can conceal from the observer even the best and most symmetrical figure—which certainly does not disprove the advantage of such figures in ordinary perception. Similarly the ability of the artist to conceal even the most familiar figures does not disprove the importance of experience in ordinary perception.

The *tactile-motor perception of concealed figures* was studied by Yamane (1935). The figures were made of points stamped in paper (like Braille letters) and arranged in a circle, square, triangle and hexagon. These were concealed somewhat after the method of Gottschaldt. Blind subjects and blindfolded seeing subjects were used. The concealed figures could be found by the hand, but much more time was required than in visual presentation and many more errors were made. A complex figure which can be grasped visually in a few seconds may take a blind person as long as 10 minutes. The factor of good continuation is not

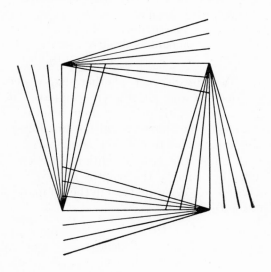

Fig. 195. (Galli & Zama, 1931.) Concealed square. The task is to *see* the square.

specially important in tactile-motor examination. Collective apprehension of the whole figure is difficult while the separate apprehension of small portions is relatively easy. The span of simultaneous apprehension is broad in vision and narrow in tactile-motor examination of figures. That this difference of span is important was proved by artificially limiting the span of visual apprehension: the presented figure was seen through a hole, one cm in diameter, which O could move around so as to see the figure part by part. The results were similar to those obtained with tactile-motor examination.

PROPORTION AS A CHARACTERISTIC OF SHAPE

Our everyday use of such words as *square, oblong, slender* is pretty good evidence that some characteristic of a shape is easily perceived, a characteristic which on analysis comes down to a ratio between length and breadth. Bühler (1913) asked whether proportion is directly perceived, and sought an answer from psychophysical determinations. For a rough preliminary experiment he drew on paper two series of rectangles, one series with a base of 20 mm and an altitude ranging from 7.5 to 12.5 mm, the other series twice as large. When a pair of rectangles, one of the larger size and one of the smaller, was presented for O to judge, he had little difficulty in deciding which was more slender.

For more exact work, rectangles were outlined in fine lines scratched through black shellac on glass, and were exposed by projection in a dark room. Standard rectangle, 340 × 255 mm. Comparison rectangles, base of 600 mm and heights ranging from 535 to 650 mm by steps of 5 mm. The Variable was exposed after the Standard, farther to the right and a little below. Exposure times: ¾ sec. for Standard, interval of 2 sec., ¾ sec. for the Variable. Complete stimulus series, results computed by summation (p. 402). O judged the Variable in relation to the Standard as slenderer, stouter (plumper), or of the same shape.

The main point was to discover whether shapes were as accurately perceived as lengths. If rectangles were compared in shape by an indirect process involving estimation of four lengths, the length and width of each rectangle, the shapes could not possibly be as accurately judged as the single lines, because of the combination of errors. In a parallel experiment under the same conditions in every respect, except that not rectangles but merely the lengths of two vertical lines were compared, two Os were less accurate than in the comparison of rectangles. Their results are shown below:

	DL		SD	
Subject	Lines	Rectangles	Lines	Rectangles
Kü	.012	.009	.031	.021
Ak	.018	.013	.038	.032

These decimal fractions give the DL and the SD divided by the Standard. The relative DL is smaller for the rectangles than for the vertical lines, and the relative SD is also smaller.[1] The advantage of the rectangles over the separate lines is not great, and perhaps the safest conclusion would be simply that proportion is perceived *at least as well* as length.

The introspective reports indicated that two rectangles differing considerably in shape were compared so directly that no process was observable. When they were nearly of the same shape, care was necessary and O was aware of examining the separate dimensions, but without any attempt to compute their ratio, as this procedure when attempted was found to be useless. Bühler tried a number of variations of the experiment. Horizontal lines of different length were exposed one after the other at intervals of 2 sec. The first was divided by a short vertical line into parts having the ratio of 3 to 4. The second was divided in some ratio not far from that, and O judged whether the two lines

[1] The present author has computed the SD from Bühler's tables (1913, pp. 142, 149), as a check on the conclusions drawn from the DL which here as always are somewhat at the mercy of O's attitude towards "equal" judgments (p. 422).

were divided in the same proportion. This proved to be a difficult task at first but after some practice the judgment was about as accurate as with the rectangles.

Lenk (1926) and Schneider (1928) working in the Leipzig laboratory used Wirth's apparatus for quickly altering either or both dimensions of a rectangle and projecting it upon a screen tachistoscopically. The brief exposures were separated by an interval of 1.10 sec. Lenk presented a rectangle followed by a vertical line and instructed O to compare this line with the height of the rectangle. Similarly the rectangle was followed by a horizontal line and O was to compare this line with the width of the rectangle. The height of the rectangle was underestimated in relation to the vertical line exposed immediately after, and this was more the case for broad than for very narrow rectangles. To a smaller extent the width of the rectangle was underestimated with respect to a horizontal line immediately following. Thus we can say that increasing the width of a rectangle makes it seem lower, and increasing the height makes it seem a bit narrower. The horizontal dimension was more resistant to this kind of suggestion than the vertical.

Schneider's Os compared two rectangles, shown successively, and found better discrimination when the rectangles were bisected by a horizontal line, by a vertical line, by both of these lines, or by both diagonals. The advantage conferred by these crosslines seemed to lie in the richer shape given to the whole figure.

THE GEOMETRICAL ILLUSIONS

Errors in apparent length, area, direction or curvature occur in the perception of patterns of lines. Such illusions are normal in the sense that they are the regular result of attempting certain comparisons. A few of them, like the vertical-horizontal illusion, may be due to the structure of the eye or to the position of the lines in the field of view. But the majority depend on the *pattern* of lines. In a general way they are errors in the perception of parts of a figure incidental to the perceived form of the whole figure.

These illusions are often divided into: (1) contrast illusions, (2) confluxion or assimilation illusions. If a short person standing between two tall persons looks shorter than he objectively is, that is a contrast illusion, but if he should look taller than he actually is that would be an instance of confluxion or assimilation.

Like other errors these illusions are to the psychologists more than mere curiosities, for they afford clues to the process of perception. They have long attracted the interest of psychologists and many figures have been devised which give illusory effects. Instead of attempting a full account we will first state the principal theories that have been suggested to explain them, then give a selection of illusory figures on which the reader can try out these theories, and finally report a few experiments of a more analytical character.[1]

[1] A more complete account of such illusions can be found in Sanford (1898), Ladd & Woodworth (1911) or Ebbinghaus (1911).

The principal theories deserving consideration are as follows:

1. *The eye movement theory*, in its simplest form, assumes that the impression of length is obtained by moving the eye along a line from one end to the other. If vertical movements of the eye are more strenuous

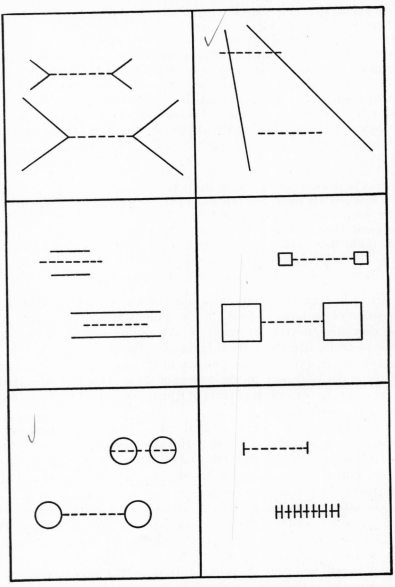

FIG. 196. Several illusion figures. Compare the dotted lines. A crucial test of any theory is the ability it confers not so much to explain facts already known as to predict the results that will occur under certain untried conditions. It would be interesting to see whether the reader can by examination of these illusion-producing figures predict what illusion will occur in each case.

than horizontal, a given vertical distance calls for more effort than the same horizontal distance and therefore seems longer. Again, if the outward lines in one part of the Müller-Lyer figure catch the eye and cause the eye movement to exceed the length of the included line, whereas in the other part of the figure the inward pointing lines cause the eye to move a smaller distance, the first line will seem longer than the second. A less direct form of the eye movement theory admits that actual eye movements do not occur in all cases, but assumes that a tendency to such movement is sufficient to give the impression of length.

2. *The perspective theory*, starting from the undoubted fact that a line drawing readily suggests objects in three dimensions, infers that the apparent length of the lines is affected by the perspective read into the figure. For example, a short vertical line in a drawing may represent a relatively long horizontal line extending away from the observer. The horizontal-vertical illusion can be explained by supposing the vertical to represent such a foreshortened horizontal line. In the Müller-Lyer figure the obliques readily suggest perspective and if this suggestion is followed one of the horizontal lines appears farther away and therefore objectively longer than the other.

3. *The empathy theory* of Theodor Lipps is the same theory by which this author sought to explain the esthetic effects of architecture. He held that even in looking at relatively simple figures the observer's emotional and reactive nature is stimulated. A vertical line, resisting gravity, suggests effort and thus appears longer than an equal horizontal. One part of the Müller-Lyer figure suggests expansion and the other limitation and thus the first line appears the longer.

4. *The confusion theory*. To judge the lines and angles of a figure requires analysis which is difficult because the observer is engrossed in the appearance of the figure as a whole. One of the Müller-Lyer segments taken as a whole is really longer than the other. If O cannot rid himself of this total impression and narrow his attention down to a particular line, he carries over the total impression to the lines which he imagines himself to be judging.

5. *The pregnance or good-figure theory*. The metaphorical use of "pregnance" here is somewhat novel in English, though not far from that used in the expression a "pregnant sentence," meaning a sentence containing a wealth of meaning. Among the German psychologists a "pregnant" figure is one which expresses some characteristic fully. "Goodness" of figure means in part the same thing. When the observer sees a figure as having some characteristic, his tendency is to see this characteristic as fully expressed as the conditions allow, according to the theory. A near-circle is seen as a true circle or as a better circle than it is. If one of the Müller-Lyer figures is seen as consisting of two things standing apart, the apartness will be exaggerated by the observer. If the other figure is seen as a single compact object the compactness will be exaggerated (p. 84).

Some of the more incisive experiments which have been done with geometrical illusions are the following.

1. **Measurement of the illusion under varying conditions.** The method used may be either that of adjustment (p. 395) or of Constant Stimuli. By the former method O is given an adjustable figure and is asked, for example in the case of the Müller-Lyer figure, to make one of the horizontal lines apparently equal to the other. The error is measured and the test is repeated a number of times sufficient to permit computation of the constant error and variability. This method was used by Heymans (1895, 1897) by Thiéry (1895) by Judd and his co-workers (1899, 1902, 1905) and by many subsequent writers. By the method of Constant Stimuli one of the two Müller-Lyer figures is kept

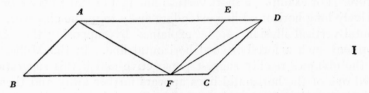

I

FIG. 197. (Sander, 1926.) The Sander parallelogram.

of constant length and used as a Standard, while the other figure is the Variable, presented in a "full series" of differing lengths; O judges on each presentation whether the Variable is equal to the Standard, longer or shorter. This method was used by Ipsen (1926) in an elaborate study of the Sander parallelogram illusion.

The advantages of a quantitative study of these illusions are: (1) that it brings out slighter illusions than can be demonstrated without measurement, (2) that it gives definite facts to be explained by any theory, and (3) that it can be extended to other parts of the figure besides the part which is most obviously subject to illusion.

Some of the results of quantitative study may be briefly cited.

Heymans (1895) made a thorough study of the Müller-Lyer figure and its variants. He found the average strength of the illusion to be 25 percent under optimum conditions: i.e., when the obliques were 1/4 as long as the horizontal segments and made only a small angle with the horizontal. The amount of the illusion was proportional to the cosine of the angle between the obliques and the horizontal, being zero when this angle was 90° and increasing to its maximum when the angle was almost zero.

Judd (1899) found that the illusory effects were not confined by any means to the main lines of the Müller-Lyer figure. All parts within and adjacent to the figure were affected; all the space relations in the immediate neighborhood were distorted by the arrangement of the figure.

Ipsen (1926 a) on measuring the illusion in the Sander figure found it to exceed even that in the Müller-Lyer, which is the typical strong illusion. The greatest error affects the diagonals of the two parallelograms into which the whole parallelogram is divided; but the base lines of the smaller parallelograms are also affected, and so are the areas and angles (Fig. 197).

2. **The practice experiment in illusions.** Heymans (1896) and others had noticed that continued experience with one certain figure diminished the amount of the illusion. Judd (1902, 1905) made a systematic study of this practice effect. O was not informed of his error, but simply examined the figure time after time, each time setting the apparatus

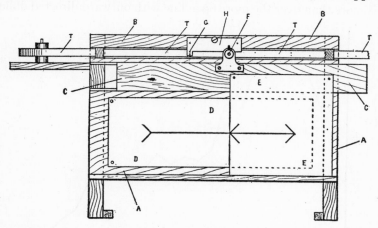

Fig. 198. (Judd, 1905.) Apparatus for measuring and recording the amount of the Müller-Lyer illusion. AABB is a fixed wooden frame, to which is attached the card DD containing one part of the Müller-Lyer figure. CC is a sliding board, adjustable by the subject, and to it is attached a card containing the remainder of the figure. O adjusts the sliding part till the two main lines appear equal. He then records his setting by pressure on the rod F, which makes a pinhole in the ticker tape TT and at the same time makes a double pinhole (like this :) in the tape under G. As G is attached to the fixed frame, whereas F is attached to the sliding board, the distance along the tape between the double and the single pinholes indicates the setting and so the amount of the illusion.

to a subjective equation. The illusion gradually diminished to near zero, and this was true of all three of the illusions tried, the Müller-Lyer, Poggendorff, and Zöllner. This practice effect held good, however, only for the original position of the figure. If it were reversed right and left, the illusion returned in full strength, and in some Os was exaggerated, but in others was overcome by a relatively small amount of further practice. The illusion was revived even in the original figure by standing off and looking at it casually as a whole (p. 195). One might suppose that practice would develop the ability to isolate the main lines and disregard the rest of the figure, but such was not the testimony of these Os, to whom it rather seemed that with practice they became better able to take the figure as a whole and still see it in its true proportions (Fig. 199).

3. **Recording eye movements during examination of illusory figures.**
These experiments were undertaken as a check on the eye movement
theory. Judd (1905) used a motion picture camera to photograph the
eye movements during the examination of several illusory figures both
before and after practice. From the eye movement theory in its simple
form one would expect that a line that was underestimated would be
examined with a short easy movement. But the photographs gave no
support to this hypothesis. The eyes made more fixations on the underestimated line with the inward directed obliques; they seemed to labor
over it more than over the more open line with outward directed obliques.

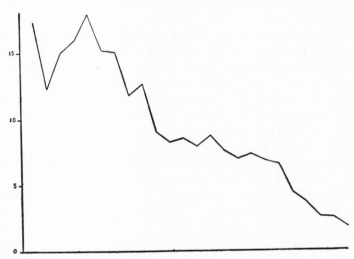

FIG. 199. (Judd 1905.) Decrease of the Müller-Lyer illusion through mere
practice. The subject used the apparatus shown in Fig. 198, making in all 600
settings, 25 per day. At the outset the line included between the outward obliques
was made on the average 17% shorter than the line included between the inward
obliques; at the end of practice this error had decreased to about 2%.

No clean cut explanation of the illusion could be deduced from the eye
movements. Yet the eye movements were not unrelated to the figure
nor to the illusion. Where the figure appears crowded the fixations of
the eye were more frequent, where the figure is more open they were
fewer. The guess might be hazarded that the eye movements were
dependent upon the appearance of the figure rather than the appearance
on the eye movements.

This guess is confirmed by the eye movements during the examination
of a reversible figure (p. 628). It had often been held that the fixation
point determined the appearance, since it is possible to reverse the
figure (though not instantly) by shifting the fixation point. The point
fixated tends to appear near the observer. Zimmer (1913) had his
subjects examine the cube figure while the experimenter watched O's

eyes through a laboratory telescope. Whenever O experienced an involuntary inversion of the cube he pressed a telegraph key, and whenever E observed a movement of O's eyes he pressed another key. The kymographic record showed that the eye movements occurred about a second *after* the inversion rather than before. The relation of cause and effect is probably that O fixates the part of the figure which seems nearest to him, rather than that any part seems nearest which he happens to fixate.

Sisson (1935), on photographing the eye movements during examination of the reversible staircase figure, obtained a somewhat less regular result: 33% of the eye movements were followed by recorded inversions and 46% of the inversions were followed by eye movements. These are the average percents when a rather generous time allowance is made. But if we assume that a change of fixation point must *instantly* cause a reversal of the appearance, "there remain only 5.7% of the total 332 movements that are followed by reversals within a time interval which might indicate causal relationship." Sisson like Zimmer concludes that in all probability the shifting appearance is due to central factors and that the eye movements depend upon the shifting appearance rather than vice versa.

4. **Experimentally controlled attitudes of observation.** In order to bring out central factors in the illusions, Benussi (1904) instructed O in one case to observe with a whole-perceiving attitude, in another case with a part-isolating attitude. The Müller-Lyer illusion was greater in the whole-perceiving attitude than in the part-isolating. Objective conditions increased or diminished the illusion, according as they made the isolation of the required lines easy or difficult.

A sample of the results is shown in the accompanying table. Con-

ATTITUDE AND OBJECTIVE CONDITIONS FAVORING TOTAL AND
PART-ISOLATING PERCEPTION

(Benussi, 1904)

Main lines of Müller-Lyer	white	white	dark gray
Oblique lines	white	dark gray	white
Background	black	black	black
Average illusion under			
whole-perceiving attitude	4.95	2.20	7.66
part-isolating attitude	1.02	− .50	3.20

Each figure in the table is the average of 20–30 measurements, all on a single O; confirmed by results from other Os.

spicuousness of the main lines breaks up the total form and weakens the illusion. But the totalizing attitude, after being practiced, overcame even unfavorable objective conditions.

Benussi later (1912) combined this attitude experiment with a stroboscopic presentation of the Müller-Lyer figure. A series of figures was shown in rapid succession so that the figure appeared to be in motion, as can be understood from the diagram in Fig. 200, and the apparent motion threw the Müller-Lyer illusion in and out again. Müller-Lyer in this simplified form is a shift of the point of intersection toward the inner side of the angle. If O attends strictly to the lines and regards the crossing point only as a pivot, the position of this crossing point does not move, but if attention is directed to the changing shape of the total figure, then the midpoint seems to glide along the vertical line, upward when the side lines move up and downward when they move down.

It is safe to conclude with Benussi (1914 b) and with most of the recent investigators that the typical geometrical illusions are incidental

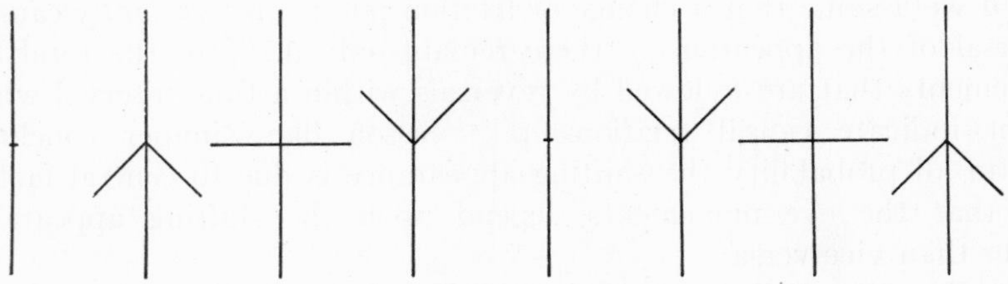

FIG. 200. (Benussi, 1912.) Successive positions of the Müller-Lyer element, shown in rapid succession, and giving an appearance of up and down movement of the point of intersection along with the apparent movement of the side lines.

to the perception of form. They are errors in the apparent size and direction of parts of a figure resulting from the total impression of the figure. We are not to suppose that these illusions occur only in the special figures of the laboratory; they occur in innumerable patterns and designs.

To speak of these illusions as incidental to the total impression obtained from a pattern is to give only a vague, general explanation. Somewhat more definite is the statement of Koffka (1931). For him the guiding principle is always the law of pregnance: "The specific character of the whole enforces itself as strongly as possible. If that character is integral, simplicity is exaggerated; if divided, the division is emphasized." In a similar vein Sander (1928) speaks of an "eidotropic tendency," by which an imperfect form is seen better than it is, an atypical form more typical than it is. The figure gravitates in perception toward its type or eidos. When the given figure suggests a familiar object, perception gravitates toward the typical form of that object, and when the figure suggests some geometrical form perception gravitates toward the true circle, square or other suggested form. Any such gravitation is certain to distort the actual sizes and angles of parts of the figure. But even these formulations would scarcely enable one to predict all the illusory effects, and especially not the quantitative results cited.

CHAPTER XXVI

VISUAL SPACE

T HE EYES serve remarkably well in the perception of spatial relations—
the size and shape of objects and their distance and direction from
the observer. Of the many fascinating problems which arise here for
the psychologist, the one most studied experimentally has to do with the
third dimension of visual space. How can the distance of objects and
their depth or relief possibly be seen? We should like to discover the
cues or sense data utilized in visual space perception and if possible to
unravel the process of utilizing these data. In the present chapter the
main findings on depth perception will be considered in approximately
their historical sequence, so as to get close to the original experimenters.

Perspective and related cues of distance. The first experimenters
on visual space perception were probably the Renaissance painters,
and of these the most experimental and also the most articulate was
Leonardo da Vinci (1452–1519). Leonardo sought for principles by
which realistic reproductions of an object or scene could be achieved.
The picture must duplicate as closely as possible what is presented
to the eyes in looking at an object or scene—that was his fundamental
principle. Objects must be shown in a picture not as they are known
to be, but as they are presented to the eye at a given moment. The
picture must be painted from a single viewpoint.

The third dimension, that is depth or distance, constituted a serious
problem for Leonardo. Painters were having difficulty in securing good
depth effects. The depth or relief of a single object, and the depth of a
whole scene—the distance of the various objects from each other and
from the observer—both gave difficulty. Leonardo found that depth
was revealed largely by light and shadow. He distinguished *attached
shadow* from the more obvious *cast shadow*. The shadow of one object
is cast on another object, as a man's shadow is cast on the ground. The
shadow of an object appears attached to that same object; the shading
of a face, due to the way the light strikes certain parts more than others,
appears to be on the face. Attached shadows show the relief or three-
dimensional shape of a single object, while cast shadows reveal spatial
relationships between objects (p. 600).

The relative distance of objects in the field of view is revealed mostly,
Leonardo found, by *perspective*, of which he distinguished three kinds:
(1) *linear* perspective, the diminution of angular size with increased

distance; (2) *detail* perspective, the loss in the distance of the finer lines, angles, shape and shading of an object; (3) *aerial* perspective, the partial loss of object color from the effect of the air, fog or smoke through which the distant object is seen.

The air tints distant objects in proportion to their distance from the eye. . . . If you wish to try out this perspective of variation and loss of color, go into the country, select objects situated at distances of 100, 200 yards, etc.—objects such as trees, houses, men—and as respects the nearest tree, place a sheet of glass firmly in front of you, keep the eye fixed in location, and trace the outlines of the tree on the glass. Now move the glass to the side just enough to allow the tree to be seen beside its tracing, and color your drawing to duplicate the color and relief of the object, so that when examined with one eye the drawing and the tree shall both seem painted and at the same distance. Follow the same procedure in painting the second and third trees situated at the greater distances. Preserve these paintings on glass as aids and teachers in your work.

This quotation could be embodied in a laboratory manual as a demonstration of different types of perspective. Another experiment is reported in the next quotation.

Suppose several buildings are visible over a wall which conceals their bases, and suppose they all extend to the same apparent height above the wall. You wish to make one appear in your painting more distant than another. Conceive the air to be rather hazy, since in such air you know that distant objects like the mountains, seen through a great mass of air, appear almost blue. . . . Therefore paint the first building beyond the aforesaid wall in its own proper color and make the more distant building less sharply outlined and bluer, and a building that is twice as far away, make it twice as blue, and one that you wish to appear five times as far away, make it five times as blue. This rule will make it possible to tell from the picture which building is farther away and which is taller.

Leonardo found some cues of distance which could not be employed in painting. One such may be called *movement perspective*. The farther away a horse, the more slowly will his galloping carry him across the field of view. More important is Leonardo's discovery of the depth effect due to what has since been named *binocular parallax*.

It is impossible that a painting, though reproducing its object with absolute perfection of line, light, shade and color, can appear with the same relief as the natural object—unless indeed that natural object be seen at a distance and with only one eye. The proof is as follows: Let the eyes a and b regard the object e, with convergence of the central lines of sight, ae and be meeting at point e; the lateral lines of vision will pass beside the object and see space behind it. Eye a sees the whole space fd, eye b the whole space gc. Together the eyes see the whole space fc behind the object. For this cause the object is transparent, according to the definition of a transparent object—behind which nothing is hidden—but this cannot happen to one who looks with only one eye (unless the object is smaller than the pupil of the eye). Thus we have an answer to our question. For in painting, a near object preempts the whole space lying behind it, and there is no way of making any part of this space visible.

This seeing behind a small near object is perhaps the most vivid of all cues of distance. The others mentioned by Leonardo are often called "monocular cues" because they are fully available to vision with a single eye. There are one or two other cues in this class which Leonardo seems not to have specifically mentioned, probably because they are so obvious. The sequence of objects, as of houses along a street, and the partial covering of an object by one that is nearer belong in the class with perspective and shadows.

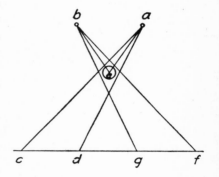

FIG. 201. (Leonardo da Vinci.) Seeing around behind a near object in binocular vision.

Non-visual cues of distance. All of Leonardo's cues are strictly visual. The first suggestion of non-visual cues came from George Berkeley in his "Essay towards a new theory of vision" (1709), published when the author was twenty-four years old. This work of an acute thinker is somewhat annoying to an experimentalist because reliance is placed entirely on common observation and introspection even when the chances for an experiment are excellent. Berkeley's general theory is that the sense of sight gives only light and color, and that the spatial appearance of seen objects is not strictly visual but derived by association from touch and bodily movement. He begins with the perception of distance. "It is, I think, agreed by all that distance of itself, and immediately, cannot be seen. For, distance being a line directed endwise to the eye, it projects only one point in the fund of the eye, which point remains invariably the same, whether the distance be longer or shorter." With respect to remote objects, he continues, the signs of distance are obviously and admittedly experiential, consisting of perspective and the other cues used by painters. But the distance of a near object might conceivably be known from the angle between the axes of the two eyes when converged upon the object. By certain physicists of the day the observer was supposed to compute the distance by a sort of intuitive geometry, and without the teaching of experience. Against this view Berkeley argues that this angle, not being itself perceived, cannot be used in perceiving distance.

I appeal to any one's experience, whether, upon sight of an object, he computes its distance by the bigness of the angle made by the meeting of the two optic axes? . . . Every one is himself the best judge of what he perceives, and what not. In vain shall any man tell me, that I perceive certain lines and angles which introduce into my mind the various ideas of distance, so long as I myself am conscious of no such thing.

In place of these geometrical cues Berkeley wished to substitute: (1) the sensation from the eyes when they are converged, this sensation being more intense the nearer the object; (2) the blurred appearance of an object which is very close to the eyes; (3) the sensation of straining the eyes to see this very near object. These sensations, Berkeley argues, while not inherently sensations of distance, become associated in experience with the distance of objects, otherwise ascertained, and so come to suggest distance.

Of the sensations regarded by Berkeley as cues of distance, the blur of a very near object is visual, but the sensations of convergence and accommodation are tactile-kinesthetic. These latter sensations have played a great role in later discussions of depth perception. The whole subject has been the theme of active discussion and experimentation, especially about the middle of the nineteenth century when the main discoveries were made. We can touch only some of the high spots.

BINOCULAR DISPARITY AND THE STEREOSCOPE

Charles Wheatstone, a physicist, published in 1838 some epoch-making contributions to the science of binocular vision. In him we find a thorough experimentalist at work. Referring back to Leonardo da Vinci's proof that we see behind a small near object in binocular vision, Wheatstone goes on to show that Leonardo had only partly covered the ground. Not only do the two eyes see around and behind the object; they obtain different views of the object itself. This can be proved geometrically, and it can be demonstrated experimentally by examining a small solid object first with one eye and then with the other eye alone. The binocular disparity thus revealed, though ordinarily unnoticed, must contribute to the visible solidity and relief of the object. Binocular disparity is present when the object is three-dimensional or extends into the third dimension, not when a small flat surface lies straight before the eyes and at right angles to the line of sight. Wheatstone continues:

It being thus established that the mind perceives an object of three dimensions by means of the two dissimilar pictures projected by it on the two retinae, the following question occurs: What would be the visual effect of simultaneously presenting to each eye, instead of the object itself, its projection on a plane surface as it appears to that eye? To pursue this inquiry it is necessary that means should be contrived to make the two pictures, which must necessarily occupy different places, fall on similar parts of both retinae.

The simplest way of accomplishing this result is to place two drawings side by side and to look at one with the right eye and the other with the left eye. This is a difficult performance, though it can be learned.

It requires a temporary "dissociation" of the normally combined acts of convergence and accommodation. The difficulty can be lessened by the use of tubes as illustrated in Fig. 202, but to remove it completely Wheatstone designed an instrument which he called the *stereoscope*. It was a mirror stereoscope. Close in front of the right eye was placed a vertical mirror, at an angle of 45° with the frontal plane, so enabling the right eye to see an object located off to the right. Similarly a mirror close before the left eye reflected light from an object placed off to the left. The objects thus presented separately to the eyes were line drawings on cards. Their optical distance from the eyes, by way of the mirrors, required a certain degree of accommodation, and the corresponding degree of convergence was secured by adjusting the lateral position of the cards in the field of view, i.e., by sliding the cards forward or backward in frames parallel to O's median plane (Fig. 203).

Wheatstone tried out his stereoscope with carefully drawn outlines of simple geometrical objects and of complex objects (this was before the invention of photography in 1839) and obtained vivid depth effects. He drew the conclusion that the disparate views obtained by the two eyes from the same (near) object were the prime factor in the perception of depth. His evidences for this conclusion were: (1) the strong depth effect obtained when disparate views are combined by use of the stereoscope; (2) the absence of the depth effect when the views are identical instead of being disparate; (3) the

Fig. 202. Wheatstone, 1838.) Tube apparatus for enabling the eyes to fixate two objects simultaneously. The convergence of the tubes is adjustable.

reversal of the depth effect when the drawings are interchanged, so that the right eye sees what the left eye would normally see and vice versa, a pseudoscopic effect, as he called it. From later experiments we can add: (4) the exaggeration of the depth effect when the views are taken from farther apart than the distance between the two eyes.

An obvious objection is considered by Wheatstone. A one-eyed person, or any person with one eye closed, sees objects in relief very much the same as in binocular vision even though without the full vividness of the depth effect. Wheatstone replies that there are indeed other signs of depth—perspective, etc.—available in monocular vision, and he adds a new and very powerful one which might be called *head movement parallax*. By moving the head from side to side one obtains disparate views in succession instead of simultaneously as in binocular vision. By moving the head a considerable distance sideways we increase the disparity above anything furnished by binocular parallax. In the same way we accentuate Leonardo's seeing-behind effect. Also, distant objects move with the head, or we may say forward, and near objects backward in the field of view. This motion of objects within the field of view is specially striking when the observer is moving rapidly as in a railroad train and looking out to the side. How much actual use is made of this movement parallax in everyday space perception has not been worked out experimentally.

The pseudoscope. Reversal of far and near can be obtained with the stereoscope in three ways: (1) by transposing right and left pictures; (2) by reflecting the pictures, so reversing right and left within each picture separately; (3) by inverting the pictures.

In a later paper (1852) Wheatstone describes a pseudoscope (Fig.

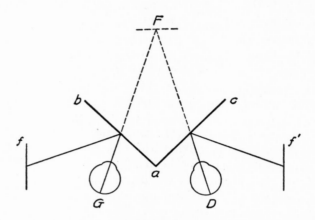

Fig. 203. Diagram of a mirror stereoscope. G and D are the eyes, converged for the distance of the imaginary object F, and receiving foveal stimulation from the objects f and f', by way of the mirrors ba and ca. The position of f and f' can be adjusted to make superposition easy. In a later model Wheatstone mounted f and f' on radii which were turned about a center near the midpoint between the eyes, so that the adjustment of f and f' made no change necessary in accommodation.

204) which makes it possible in viewing a real object to obtain a reflected image in each eye. It shows the object in reversed relief, though many familiar objects are not easily seen reversed. At the first view of an object through the pseudoscope its reversed appearance does not immediately occur.

The natural appearance of the object continues to obtrude itself, when suddenly, and at other times gradually, the converse occupies its place. The reason of this is, that the relief and distance of objects is not suggested to the mind solely by the binocular pictures and the convergence of the optic axes, but also by other signs, which are perceived by means of each eye singly; among which the most effective are the distributions of light and shade and the perspective. . . . One idea being therefore suggested to the mind by one set of signs, and another totally incompatible idea by another set, according as the mental attention is directed . . . the normal form or its converse is perceived. . . . Some very paradoxical results are obtained when objects in motion are viewed through the pseudoscope. When an object approaches, the magnitude of its picture on the retinae increases as in ordinary vision, but the inclination of the optic axes, instead of increasing, becomes less, as I have already explained. Now an enlargement of the picture on the retina invariably suggests approach, and a less convergence of the optic axes indicates that the object is at a greater distance; and we have thus two contradictory suggestions.

Uses of the stereoscope. More familiar than the mirror stereoscope is the prism stereoscope invented independently by Wheatstone and by his contemporary David Brewster; it is the popular form used for obtaining vivid depth effects from double photographs. Prisms are placed before the eyes to bend the rays so that the eyes can converge and accommodate for the distance of the pictures though the latter are placed straight in front of their respective eyes. Convex lenses combined with the prisms magnify the pictures, enable them to be placed nearer to the eyes and do some of the work of accommodation for the eyes (Fig. 205).

Besides its entertainment value and its value in the study of space perception the stereoscope has found a number of technical uses. It can be used to detect counterfeit paper money. A genuine bill and a suspected counterfeit are exposed each to one eye, and the combined view gives no depth effect if the two are identical but shows an apparently rumpled appearance if one differs from the other in slight details. Binocular field glasses by a system of lenses and mirrors widen the interocular distance and so increase binocular disparity and increase the relief of distant objects. Depth can not only be seen; it can even be measured by aid of binocular parallax and disparity.[1]

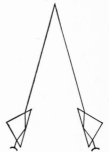

FIG. 204. (Wheatstone, 1852.) Plan of Wheatstone's reflection pseudoscope. Each of the two prisms acts, both to bend the rays and to reflect them by internal total reflection. The result is that each eye's view is reversed right or left.

Some practical points regarding the stereoscope. For viewing stereoscope pictures found in a book, a good aid is a sawed-off prism stereoscope, made from an ordinary commercial stereoscope by removing the slide holder and the rod or strip which carries this holder. Bring the prisms within a few inches of the pictures. The observer may find some difficulty if his interocular distance does not match the distance between the paired pictures.

Many Os are able to combine the pictures by "crossing the eyes," and this method has the advantage that it can be used with drawings of any size and separation. Hold a pencil between the paired views, fixate the pencil and bring it toward you. While maintaining fixation on the pencil point, observe the coming together of the paired pictures. When they have come together, you may be able to remove the pencil and still hold the combined view of the pictures. Since in the combined view the right eye furnishes the picture on the left, and vice versa, the depth effect is reversed from that to be obtained with the stereoscope.

[1] See article on "Binocular instruments" in Encyclopedia Britannica 14th ed.

This device therefore is not satisfactory for viewing photographs of landscapes, but it will serve for examining the drawings employed for the study of space perception.

A good rule in viewing these drawings is to play a waiting game, simply keeping the lines clear and watching for effects that may appear. For easy combination the lines to be combined should be alike in width and color.

The fact that the depth effect does not always appear when the drawings are combined is itself of some importance. It shows that the depth effect is not *forced* by binocular disparity. Whether an individual shall get the effect depends on his readiness as well as on the stimulus. With the simple drawings used for psychological purposes the observer often fails for a time to see any depth. He sees it more readily if he is prepared by knowing what particular effect to look for. Dahlmann (1934) finds that even among figures properly drawn to give a binocular depth effect, some give the effect readily while others appear flat. If the flat figure is symmetrical and "good," the three-dimensional appearance is less likely to develop. Binocular disparity is a stimulus, but the depth effect is a *response*, and it is not the only response which the organism has at its disposal. It seems usually to be the most satisfying response. It leads the observer to exclaim "Oh!" and "Ah!"

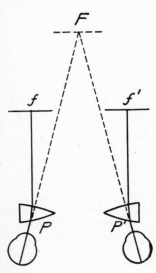

FIG. 205. (Bourdon, 1902.) Plan of a prism stereoscope. The stereoscope slide is composed of the two views, f and f', the rays from which are bent by the prisms P and P' so as to reach the eyes as if from the point F upon which the eyes are converged.

Rule for predicting the stereoscopic effect. For psychological purposes the important thing is not simply to get the depth effect but to note the conditions which give each particular effect. The effects can be predicted from the make-up of the monocular fields by applying a principle which has been variously stated but most simply by Wheatstone: consider the monocular fields (drawings) to be views of a single solid object as seen by the separate eyes; then the depth effect of the combined binocular view corresponds to that object.

Some examples of this rule: (1) Hold a ruler directly in front of you with its back parallel to your forehead. Each eye sees a vertical stripe or rectangle and the two stripes are of the same width. Now if two equal stripes, or pairs of vertical lines, are presented in the stereoscope, one stripe to each eye, the effect is that of a flat surface parallel to your forehead, as the ruler was. (2) Keeping the ruler vertical turn it so that the right edge is further away than the left; then the ruler as seen by the right eye gives a wider stripe than as seen by the left eye. If two stripes of unequal width are presented to the two eyes, the broader stripe to the right eye, the combined view shows the right hand edge farther away. (3) Hold a pencil before you, pointing toward you; with one eye you see it pointing more to the right, with the other more to the left. Draw corresponding projections on paper and present each to its proper eye, and the combined view shows a line pointing toward you.

The figures can be reduced from lines to points and still give a depth effect, or they can be complicated and show the three-dimensional shapes of pyramids, cones, crystals and even whole landscapes. Wheat-

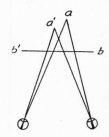

FIG. 206. (Wheatstone, 1838.) Binocular parallax of a two-point figure. When the two points are seen through the plane b′b, which has the place of a stereoscope slide, the separation a′a is necessarily greater for the right eye than for the left, because the right-hand point, a, is further away. If two views showing the points with different separations are presented to the eyes, the combined binocular view gives the depth relation of the two points. See Fig. 207.

stone's rule enables you to prepare drawings which when combined will give the shape of any selected solid.

How the binocular field is made up from the monocular fields. Of many investigators who soon followed Wheatstone's use of the stereoscope in studying space perception, Panum (1858) deserves mention for the important points which his experiments brought to light. He made a comprehensive study of binocular vision as related to monocular. He dealt with the related topics of binocular rivalry, binocular fusion and the depth effect. He noted particularly the following phenomena. (1) *Rivalry of contours;* for example, when one monocular field contains a horizontal line and the other a vertical line, there is rivalry at their point of crossing in the combined field. (2) *Prevalence of contours* over

FIG. 207. (Wheatstone, 1838.) Monocular views corresponding to the situation of Fig. 206. The plane of the paper corresponds to the plane b′b in that figure. If the eyes are crossed the situation is reversed. This figure embodies the essence of all stereoscopic effects.

plain field. In competition with a plain field presented to one eye, a line presented to the other remains in view nearly all the time. In thus prevailing over a plain field a contour carries with it into the binocular field some of its own immediate background. (3) *Binocular mixture of colors,* asserted and denied by previous investigators, but observed by Panum under certain conditions. (4) *Mosaic composition of the binocular field* in so far as the contours in the monocular fields do not overlap. In such cases they simply appear side by side in the combined field— a bird in one field and a cage in the other will be seen binocularly as bird in cage. These four laws, Panum believed, made it possible to predict the composition of the binocular field from two given monocular fields.

Another important preliminary to the study of the depth effect was Panum's observation that when each monocular field contains a strong vertical line so located that the two are not far apart in the binocular field, they have a strong tendency to come together; that is, convergence is adjusted to bring these two lines together. It is almost impossible to

a b   c d

FIG. 208. (Panum, 1858.) Single vision of disparate figures. The disparity consists in the different widths of the two pairs of lines. If convergence is adjusted to combine a and c, it cannot be right for superposing b and d. Yet by looking steadily at the binocular combination, ab and cd are superposed, with a depth effect.

hold them side by side in the binocular field. Suppose each monocular field to be plain with the exception of one vertical line—there is no perceptual or esthetic advantage in combining the two lines. A pair of parallel lines makes fully as good a figure as a single line. Since they are nevertheless combined, we seem to glimpse here a dynamic factor more fundamental in binocular vision than either good figure or

FIG. 209. Two unequal triangles which can be superposed by crossing the eyes or by aid of a stereoscope.

the depth effect. It would have practical value in guiding the infant's binocular vision toward single vision of objects. For example the side of a window would furnish a vertical line in each monocular field, and according to this principle these two lines are combined and the result is single vision of the window.

The nature of binocular disparity. The disparity between the monocular views of a real object in space is a right-left or horizontal disparity—horizontal in the field of view. Drawings prepared for the stereoscope can be made disparate in the vertical direction, the monocular fields

FIG. 210. Two opposite disparities can be overcome simultaneously. This and many similar figures show binocular disparity to be overcome centrally, not peripherally.

containing horizontal lines at different heights. The eyes can overcome slight vertical disparity but the combined view does not yield any depth effect. It is horizontal disparity which, when overcome by adjusting convergence, yields the depth effect.

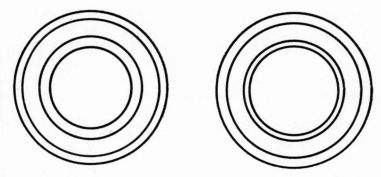

FIG. 211. Panum's circles. Each pair of circles shows opposite disparity at the two ends of the horizontal diameter and the two pairs also show opposite disparity from each other. Watch for the depth effect, which follows exactly from Wheatstone's principle.

But this horizontal disparity is not essentially one of lines or points. The disparity that counts is one of *width;* the width of two stripes (between pairs of vertical lines) is different for the two eyes; or, two points are further apart to one eye than to the other; or, in general, the horizontal width of some part of one monocular figure is greater than the width of the corresponding part of the other monocular figure. *Width disparity, when overcome in binocular vision, gives the depth effect.* Binocular vision is somehow able to superpose widths which are unequal;

it sets aside a fundamental postulate of Euclidean geometry, according to which two triangles, for example, must be equal in order to be super-posed (Fig. 208, 209, 210).

Fig. 212. (Panum, 1858.) Depth effect obtained from a single line in one field combined with one of two lines in the other field—as if the ruler of p. 658 were turned so far that to one eye it showed simply an edge, to the other eye a narrow stripe.

Fusion need not be complete in order to give some depth effect. Slight eye movements are always occurring without necessarily disturb-ing the three-dimensional picture. Typical depth effects can be ob-tained in very brief exposures, too brief to allow a shifting of fixation from one to the other of the lines which fall on non-corresponding parts of the two retinas. Apparent visual movement in the third dimension

Fig. 213. The stereoscopic effect can be predicted from Wheatstone's rule.

occurs when disparate figures are presented in alternation at a suitable rate (about $\frac{1}{5}$ sec. per figure, depending on the amount of disparity). For a modern, experimental analysis of the binocular depth effect, see Werner (1937).

The fusion of disparate figures is not a weakness but an achievement of binocular vision. It is accomplished centrally rather than by any peripheral adjustment, such as accommodation, as proved by the simul-taneous fusion of opposed disparities in Figs. 210 and 211. A complex solid object presents many different disparities for simultaneous fusion.

Double images as cues of distance. Binocular vision not only gives disparate views of the object at which one is looking and on which one is converging, but it also gives double images of other objects in the field of view which lie nearer or farther than the fixated object. The importance of double images in depth perception was brought out by Hering (1861–1864).

If a pencil is held vertically between some object and the eyes, the pencil is seen double while the eyes are fixed on the more distant object, and that object is seen double while the eyes are fixed on the pencil. One of the double images is given by the right eye and the other by the left, but which eye gives which image we cannot tell except by closing

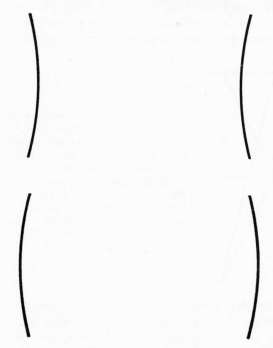

FIG. 214. Combination of differently curved lines.

or covering one eye. By this test or by the geometry of the situation (Fig. 215) it is proved that (1) when the eyes are fixed on the near object the double images of the far object are *uncrossed*, the image on the right side being given by the right eye, etc.; (2) when the eyes fixate the far object the double images of the near object are *crossed*. Therefore crossed double images of an object are a perfect cue that that object lies nearer than the momentary fixation point, while uncrossed double images indicate the reverse. When attention shifts from one object to another at a different distance, the double images which are already present are perfect cues for the readjustment of convergence to the new object. The probability is that these excellent cues of relative distance are actually used.

Because we ordinarily are unaware of most of the double images which are demonstrably present, it might be argued that we cannot use them as cues. But need a cue be noticed to be used? On the contrary, it seems that a sign need not be known except in terms of its meaning. Binaural time difference is an example (p. 533). A cue of distance need not be known to the observer except in terms of distance. Binocular disparity, constantly in use as a cue, is seldom observable for what it is—it is observed only as depth and relief of the object.

Nor does the fact that we cannot usually distinguish between crossed and uncrossed double images, except by the expedient of closing one eye, justify the conclusion that the double images are not used as cues. The falsity of such a conclusion is seen from the following facts. (1) With the stereoscope, interchanging the views presented to the two

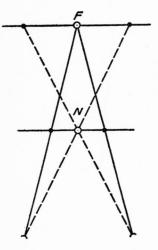

Fig. 215. Crossed and uncrossed double images. If the eyes are converged upon N, F is seen on the right by the right eye and on the left by the left eye. But if the eyes are directed to F, N is on the left to the right eye and on the right to the left eye.

If the right eye is dominant, so that its image is the more *important* of the double images, this important image lies on the right for far objects and on the left for near objects. Thus eye dominance can afford a cue of relative distance.

eyes reverses the depth effect; therefore it does make a difference which eye gets a certain view or image. (2) *Eye dominance.* If a person is asked to bring up the forefinger (of either hand) and point to a distant object, he will be observed to sight with either the right or the left eye, and most Os in repeated trials sight fairly consistently with the same eye. The majority sight with the right eye and are accordingly said to have right eye dominance. (In this test both eyes are kept open.) Consider what happens here. O fixates the distant object and therefore has (crossed) double images of the pointing finger, but he consistently holds the finger in such a position that the right eye's image of the finger shall cover the object, the left eye's image of the finger being disregarded. Therefore it is clear that in practice he distinguishes between the two images.

The fact that we cannot introspectively distinguish between crossed and uncrossed double images, therefore, does not in the least disprove the use of them in distinguishing near from far.

Conflicting visual cues of distance. Under natural conditions the several cues are in agreement, but many laboratory setups are designed to discover their relative strength by pitting one against another. Wheatstone's pseudoscope gave conflicting cues of a real object with resulting oscillation in its appearance. A systematic study of the question was made by Schriever (1925). He used drawings and photographs of solid objects presented by a stereoscope. They gave good depth and reversed depth effects when the only cue present was the binocular disparity. Other cues were then added. *Line perspective* was powerless against disparity; a skeleton cube figure drawn in perspective could be reversed in relief by reversing right and left views. The reversed view showed not a cube, however, but a truncated pyramid with the small end near the observer. Line perspective is in fact an ambiguous cue, taken by itself, since the same drawing can truly represent different solid objects, differently placed (p. 628).

When *shading* was added to perspective and the two together pitted against binocular disparity, the appearance was unstable, though disparity on the whole prevailed. But when *covering* of far by near objects was introduced into the drawings, it proved to be the most powerful cue of all, not to be overcome by contrary disparity. Reversing right and left views in the stereoscope does not enable the observer to see the near object partially covered by the far object, though sometimes an effect of transparency is obtained.

DO CONVERGENCE AND ACCOMMODATION FURNISH CUES OF DISTANCE?

We turn now to Berkeley's theory of tactile-kinesthetic cues from the eyeballs, a theory which has given rise to much experimentation. In view of the excellence of the visual cues already noted, one is inclined to doubt whether non-visual cues are used at all. Yet the eyes in their adjustments to distance almost certainly stimulate tactual and kinesthetic receptors in the eyeball region. The eyes make three adjustments to a near object: accommodation, convergence, and change in the pupil. These three adjustments are coordinated so that as the eyes shift from far to near muscular contraction increases in the ciliary muscle, the internal recti, and the iris. There is thus a possible tactile-kinesthetic cue of distance which would function in this way: O gets a good focus on the object and single vision of it; then the intensity of the tactile-kinesthetic stimulation is somewhat proportional to the nearness of the object.

But is this possible cue actually used in visual depth perception? In order to attack the question experimentally, it is necessary to eliminate the visual cues—if possible—so as to discover what impressions of distance remain. There must be no perspective, aerial perspective, covering, movement parallax or binocular parallax to assist the observer. The difficulty of meeting this requirement will appear as we proceed.

Two sorts of experiment have been tried. The more direct attack is to present a real object in space, and the less direct to present separate pictures to the two eyes by use of a stereoscope. We will consider the direct experiment first. It was introduced by Wundt (1862).

Wundt's thread experiment. O looked through a short flat tube into a room at the far end of which was a smooth illuminated wall; nothing else was visible except a single thread suspended from above and weighted so as to hang vertically through the center of the field of view. Neither the top nor the bottom of the thread was visible but only a middle portion. O's task was to observe the distance of the thread, to turn his eyes aside while E altered that distance, and then to look again and judge whether the thread was nearer or farther than before. There were two conditions, monocular and binocular. Wundt's single

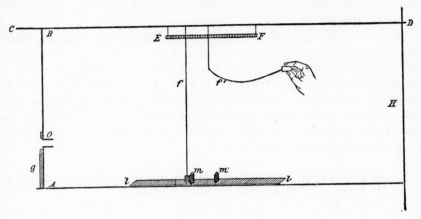

Fig. 216. (Arrer, 1898.) Wundt's hanging thread apparatus, improved form. The view from the side shows the tube *O* (80 mm wide and 40 mm high) through which the observer looks with either one or both eyes toward the gray wall *H* several yards away; the tube, blackened inside, allows him to see only a square portion of the wall, the rest of his field being nearly black. At a variable distance, between the eye and the gray background, a single vertical thread *f* is hanging; it is suspended from the wire *CD*, which extends directly over the observer straight forward to the other end of the room, and lies right over his line of sight. The thread *f* is weighted with a steel bob and kept from swinging by a magnet, *m*. The standard distance is given by the thread *f*, and the comparison distance by *f'*, which is kept out of the field by E while *f* is observed, and then quickly lowered, *f* at the same time being removed from sight: the observer's eyes are closed during this operation. The threads are movable along the wire *CD*, and their separation at any time is measured on the scale *EF*, beneath which is another scale *ll* for setting the magnets under the threads.

The screen *AB*, in front of the observer, carries a chin rest *g*, but the position of the observer's eye is only approximately controlled, and a visual cue of distance is possible if the observer holds his eye not directly beneath the wire but a little to one side. Some observers adopt such devices involuntarily. Arrer's observers made no report of using any such cue.

O, when restricted to the use of one eye, was able after some practice to compare the two distances of the thread with a difference threshold of about 7%. With two eyes he found the task much easier and his difference threshold was reduced to 2%. Wundt concluded that the convergence sensations available in binocular vision yielded a much finer cue than the accommodation sensations alone which were available in monocular vision.

Wundt was assuming (1) that in monocular vision convergence did not occur, at least no accurate convergence, and (2) that the single thread visible before the bright background presented no binocular disparity or other visual cues.

After being widely accepted for thirty years, Wundt's conclusion was called in question by Hillebrand (1894), a pupil of Hering. He challenged both of Wundt's assumptions.

1. It cannot be assumed that convergence is absent from monocular vision, for the two eyes work as a team even when one is closed. This teamwork can readily be observed in conjugate movements by holding the forefinger lightly over the closed lid of one eye while looking around the room with the other; the movement of the projecting cornea can be felt with the finger. The same means can be used with convergence, though it must be understood that the eyeball rotation in convergence is slight in comparison with large conjugate movements. Hold a pencil before the open eye in line with a distant object, and fixate alternately on the pencil and the distant object, and notice whether the cornea of the closed eye can be felt to move. Another check is afforded by first fixating an object with one eye open, and then opening the other eye and noticing whether double images of the object are present for an instant. If so, the closed eye was not accurately directed toward the object, and convergence was imperfect. These check experiments indicate that the closed eye does participate in convergence though not always accurately. Therefore, argued Hillebrand, Wundt's monocular experiment reveals the poverty of the whole tactile-kinesthetic cue, accommodation and convergence together.

2. Wundt's assumption that all visual cues of distance were excluded from his binocular experiment overlooks the double images which were present whenever the eyes were not accurately converged on the thread. Suppose that O's eyes are first directed at the distant wall; they get crossed double images of the thread, an excellent cue of its distance. The superiority of binocular over monocular perception of distance could be explained by the presence of double images in binocular vision.

Hillebrand's straight edge experiment. In Hillebrand's judgment Wundt had failed to make a case for the tactile-kinesthetic cues. Even the (relatively poor) perception of distance shown in Wundt's monocular experiment might be due to visual cues. Any little irregularities in the thread would bulk larger as it came nearer. To obviate this source of error Hillebrand substituted for the thread the vertical edge of a sheet of cardboard, cut very sharp and straight, and forming one side of an upright rectangle, the other three sides being supplied by a screen placed closer to O's eye, and the interior of the rectangle consisting of light from an illuminated background several yards away. O's field of view was dark except for this rectangle of light, three sides of which were too close to be focused on, while the fourth was this vertical straight edge, variable in distance. This straight edge was supposed to lie directly in O's line of sight, and was moved directly toward or from him. Such movement of the straight edge would not change anything in O's field of view

except the mere distance of the edge. Hillebrand used monocular vision
entirely, as he was convinced that any binocular experiment would introduce the visual cue of double images. He employed two conditions, a
"gradual" and an "abrupt" change of distance of the vertical straight
edge. In the gradual procedure, O looked through his tube at the rec-

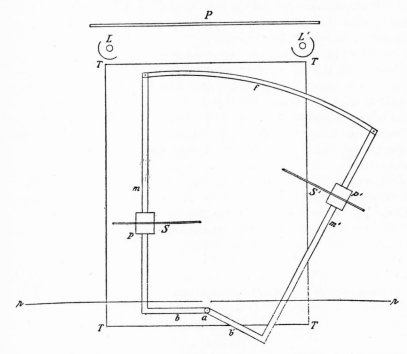

Fig. 217. Hillebrand's apparatus (1894). The figure gives a plan of the apparatus
as seen from above. *T T T T* is a table on which the frame *f m b a b' m'* turns about
the axle *A*. Directly over *a* is the observer's eye looking through a tube which
passes through the screen *r* and affords a view of part of the distant flat surface
P illuminated by the lights *L* and *L'*. O's view of this light surface is however limited,
first by a screen at the end of the short tube through which he looks and second by one
of the more distant screens *S* or *S'*. In the "gradual procedure" *S* is moved along its
rod *m* either to or away from the observer. In the "abrupt procedure" the frame is
swung to the side carrying *S* out of the field and at the same time bringing *S'* in.
What the observer sees at any moment is a rectangle of light, fuzzy on three sides,
where it is bounded by the very near screen, but capable of being sharply focused on
the fourth side where it is bounded by the more distant edge of *S* or *S'*. *S* and *S'*
consist of cardboard beveled to a straight edge. The visible rectangle of light is
not changed in size by changes in the distance of *S* and *S'*.

tangle of light, fixing his attention on the straight edge, which after a time
began to move; and O judged whether the motion was forward or backward. For the abrupt procedure, Hillebrand provided two vertical
straight edges fastened to a frame by which one of them could be moved
out of sight and the other simultaneously brought in at a different distance
from O.

Hillebrand's setup was copied with some improvements by Dixon (1895), Arrer (1898) and Baird (1903). Arrer working in Wundt's laboratory also repeated Wundt's original experiment with the apparatus improved by the addition of a second thread so as to prevent irregularities in the single thread from serving as cues of distance. Arrer found the Wundt thread superior to the Hillebrand straight edge, from O's point of view, because of difficulty in regarding the mere edge of a bright rectangle as an object to be fixated.

As for results, all four of these investigators agreed that monocular perception of a "gradual" approach or recession of the mere edge was almost impossible, though Baird succeeded in obtaining a difference threshold of about 32% of the initial distance. The "abrupt" procedure gave better discrimination, and indeed Arrer with the thread apparatus obtained an average difference threshold of only 2.9%, monocular, as against 2.6%, binocular. With the Hillebrand apparatus, monocular abrupt, Arrer's five Os gave an average difference threshold of 23%, and Baird's four subjects an average of 12%. Baird also used the Hillebrand apparatus with binocular vision and obtained the very low average difference threshold of 1.8%.

The difference threshold for distance follows Weber's law very closely, as is seen in the following table of Baird's averages.

PERCEPTION OF DISTANCE, DIFFERENCE THRESHOLDS $\left(\dfrac{\Delta s}{s}\right)$

WITH THE HILLEBRAND APPARATUS
(Baird, 1903)

Standards in mm	*286*	*333*	*400*	*500*	*667*	*Av. of all*
Monocular, gradual	.340	.367	.340	.297	.265	.322
Monocular, abrupt	.110	.112	.125	.117	.120	.117
Binocular, abrupt	.019	.019	.018	.017	.019	.018

Dixon (1895) gives some interesting introspective notes on the cues in monocular perception with the Hillebrand apparatus. Of three Os two took longer to shift the eye from near to far, and one took longer to shift from far to near; all three were able to use the time needed for getting clear vision as an index of the direction of the change. (Judd by photography—see p. 583—showed in fact that some Os take more time to shift from far to near, and some the reverse.) Dixon also found, on applying atropin to paralyze the muscle of accommodation, that the resulting blur of a near object was used as a cue of nearness. A myopic O, on the contrary, used blur as a sign of farness. Such observations warn us that the visual cues of distance are manifold and apt to be picked up by the observer whenever they are available. It is almost impossible for an experimenter to exclude them all.

Reviewing the results so far, we find agreement on two main points: the especially poor monocular perception of gradual change of distance, and the general superiority of binocular over monocular perception. Binocular superiority seems a definite proof of the use of visual cues, such as double images, in accurate perception of distance. The practical failure of monocular vision to detect gradual movement in the line of sight makes the value of the kinesthetic-tactile cues doubtful. How shall we account for the fair monocular perception of abrupt changes in distance? On this point the experimenters obtained rather discrepant results, and one suspects that visual cues were in some cases present. If the observer's eyes, instead of being centered in the apparatus, were held a little to one side, change of distance would give a lateral displacement of the object in the small visible field—an excellent cue of distance.

Bourdon's bright spot experiment. Wundt's thread has the disadvantage of being a solid object which, though slender, may show some shading and relief and furnish unintended visual cues of distance. Hillebrand's straight edge has the disadvantage of not appearing like an object on which one is inclined to focus. More satisfactory than either of these objects is the circle of light introduced by Bourdon (1902). He constructed a dark lantern out of a black box containing an electric bulb. On the side toward O there was a circular hole covered with paper. Holes of different diameters were used for different distances, or an iris diaphragm was used, its diameter being proportional to the distance, so that the visual angle, or retinal size, of the spot was the same for all distances.

With two lanterns of this sort, placed at the level of O's eyes and side by side in his field of view, one being 20 meters and the other only 1–2 meters from him—all in a long dark corridor affording no view of walls or intervening objects—no O was sure which bright spot was the farther. This was the result with *monocular* vision. If however the head were moved from side to side, the movement parallax immediately revealed the difference in distance. Bourdon concluded that accommodation (plus such convergence as occurs in monocular vision) affords no cue of distance as between objects situated 2 meters or more from the eyes.

Even with both eyes open, and a single bright spot showing, its absolute distance could not be perceived. Placed at 4 meters distance, it appeared to be 3–10 meters away; placed at 22 meters, it appeared 12–25 meters away. In an entirely unfamiliar locality a single bright spot distant 10 meters was sometimes estimated to be as much as 100 or even 500 meters away. It should be remembered that a single flat spot of light offers no binocular disparity nor double images to guide the judgment.

In another experiment Bourdon presented two bright spots successively in binocular vision. One lantern was placed in one long dark corridor, another in a corridor at right angles to the first; the observer standing at the corner turned on his heel to look first at one and then at the other bright spot and endeavored to judge which was farther. The difference threshold for one O was 22%.

Compare with this mediocre discrimination the much smaller threshold obtained from the same O in an experiment which gives full play to binocular disparity, the celebrated *three-needle experiment* of Helmholtz (1856–1866, p. 644). Three needles are mounted vertically in little wooden blocks placed side by side in a plane perpendicular to O's line of sight. Laterally the needles are a few mm apart. The two end needles are fixed in position, and the middle one is moved toward or away from O till he is satisfied that it lies exactly between the other two, in the same plane. He does not see the surface of the table nor the blocks but only the needles. At the distance of 2 meters, Bourdon's subject gave an average difference threshold of only 0.6 mm, or .03% of the distance of 2 meters. This is an incomparably finer distance perception than can be had of a flat object, perpendicular to the line of sight, as in the preceding experiment. It is also much superior to anything that can be done with monocular vision, as can be shown (in the absence of any exact measurements) by the old familiar experiment of taking two pencils, one in each hand, holding one eye closed and attempting to bring the two pencil points close together in front—and then opening the other eye to secure the binocular perception! One is led to conclude that in ordinary life binocular parallax (as also movement parallax) affords cues of distance so greatly superior to anything obtainable from the kinesthetic sensations of convergence and accommodation, that the latter cannot be of much practical use.

But Bourdon's experiments leave the possibility open that accommodation and convergence may furnish effective cues at distances of less than one meter from the eyes. The nearer the object, the more intense the contraction of the ciliary and internal rectus muscles. Later experiments answer this question.

Bourdon's setup was reproduced by Peter (1915). Two lanterns were moved on tracks diverging at an angle of 10° from a point directly below the eye. Each lantern presented a round hole covered with milk glass lighted from behind. The diameter of the holes was proportioned to the distance. O's head was fixed by aid of a biting board. A pendulum tachistoscope allowed 4 sec. total for focusing first on one and then on the other of the two circles of light. Care was taken to remove all reflected light from the outside of the lanterns and to remove any other secondary cues of distance. When one of the bright spots was placed at a constant distance of 130 cm and the other at a variable distance of 30–230 cm, one O gave correct judgments for the distances between 30 and 70 cm; that is he distinguished these short distances from the distance of 130 cm. But beyond 70 cm his discrimination was entirely at sea. The second O was at first helpless at all distances but improved greatly with practice by utilizing the same sort of cues that Dixon noticed, time and difficulty of focusing. He found it more difficult to pass from far to near than from near to far, and adopted the following procedure: to start each observation with accommodation for great distance, and as he increased the accommodation to notice which object became sharp first; that would be the more distant object. When this procedure had become mechanized by practice the depth impression seemed to be immediate and not inferential—a bit of evidence that a "sensory" impression of distance can result from a cue which has been learned.

Since, other things being equal, a larger disk appears nearer, Peter pitted this visual angle cue against the accommodation cue and found that the visual angle always prevailed in monocular vision though not in binocular.

Repetition of the three experiments. Bappert (1923) working with Gelb in the laboratory of Schumann (who had long concerned himself with the problems of space perception) introduced several technical improvements. He modified Wundt's setup by substituting iron rods of different diameters for Wundt's thread. The diameters were proportioned to the distance so that the angular magnitude was always the same. He also repeated Hillebrand's straight edge experiment. Through a little mirror placed before O's unused eye (in monocular vision) E observed the eye movements and noted whether convergence conformed to the actual distance. Hillebrand had assumed that convergence and accommodation followed the distance of the straight edge which he used as an object. But Bappert found in repeating the Hillebrand experiment that the eye movements did not correspond properly with the distance. The lack of correspondence held good both in the gradual movement of the straight edge and in the abrupt changes of its distance. The reason why the eye movements did not correspond to the distance appeared in O's introspections. Due to irradiation and to contrast between the bright surface and the adjoining black, the straight edge appeared about the same at different distances and a clear definition could not be obtained. Therefore Bappert concluded that the Hillebrand experiment was unsuited for answering the question as to the efficacy of convergence and accommodation, because the assumed convergence and accommodation did not occur with any regularity.

He found however that the Wundt thread experiment in the modified form described did actually cause movements of convergence (probably accommodation also) in accordance with the distance of the object. Nevertheless the judgments of distance were very poor. With the nearer rod at a distance of 30 cm, the farther at a distance of 90 cm, though the eye movements corresponded to the objective distance in 93% of the cases, the judgments were correct in only 27%, that is less than chance.

Bappert's most extensive experiment employed the Bourdon light spot. The visible spots were circular holes in screens showing against a moderately illuminated background of ground glass, which was far enough behind the circular holes to render its grain invisible. O was instructed to focus sharply upon the circular edge of the visible spot. There was a 4 sec. exposure of the first spot, a 2 sec. interval and then a 4 sec. exposure of the second spot. By aid of a transparent mirror set at 45°, both spots were presented in the same direction. In this

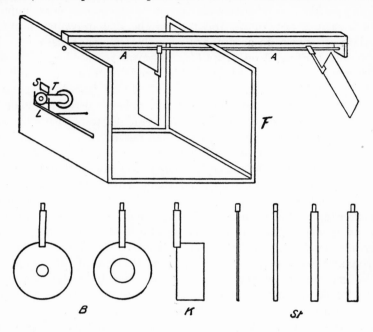

FIG. 218. (Bappert, 1923.) Schumann's apparatus for testing monocular cues of distance. The observer's eye looks through the tube T toward a distant smooth, light background (which is not shown). A little mirror, S, placed before O's other eye enables E to note the actual movements of convergence and relative divergence as one object after another is regarded. A lens-holder, L, enables E to slide any selected lens, convex or concave, before the used eye, to show the effect upon convergence and upon O's report of apparent distance. The screen through which the tube T is inserted cuts out the view of everything except the small cone of space visible through the tube. Into this small space can be brought a rod, a vertical straight edge, or a circular hole in a black disk. Any of these objects can be attached to the shaft A, and brought into or out of the field of view by a quick twist of the shaft. As one object is removed another is substituted at a different distance from O. The back frame F is a support, and does not carry the background which is to be thought of as off to the right beyond the limits of the diagram. The background can be so far away as to show no grain visible to O, and remains at a constant intensity for all distances of the object. When the object is a circular bright spot, O is instructed to see its outline distinctly, and when the straight edge is used, he is to see that distinctly. When the circular spots or the rods are being used, their diameters are chosen to be proportional to the distances at which they are presented; and thus the visual angle is kept constant in spite of change of distance. Care is needed to avoid reflected light from the rods or from the black cardboard in which the round holes or the straight edges are cut. Stops are provided to insure that the twist given to the shaft A shall bring the object to the exact center of the visible field.

experiment, *distances much less than a meter were used and so the gap in Bourdon's work was filled.* The distances to be compared were: (a) 16½ and 25 cm, (b) 25 and 50 cm, (c) 33.3 and 100 cm. The change in accommodation required in each case corresponds to two diopters. In 130 trials with five Os only 19% were correct, 25% reported the opposite change, 51% reported no change of distance, 5% were undecided. Yet in nearly 100% of all these cases the eye movements observed with the mirror were in accordance with the change of distance. These results were confirmed on other Os. Bappert repeated the experiment with a more convenient apparatus designed by Schumann (Fig. 218). With bright spots at a distance of 20 and 100 cm, the diameter proportional to the distance, two subjects in 39 trials got 6 right, 32 contrary, and 1 undecided, though the eye movements were usually correct.

The reader will be struck by the small percent of correct judgments in these experiments. One would expect 50% right by chance, but the percent never reached 50 and on the whole was about 25. The Os must have been following cues which led them wrong. One such cue was indicated by an O who reported "smaller and farther" when the object was nearer (and of the same angular size). The increased accommodation and convergence apparently had the effect of making the object look not nearer, but smaller and therefore farther away.

From all these experiments so far, especially from the work of Bourdon and his successors, we can almost surely conclude that the tactile-kinesthetic sensations of accommodation and convergence contribute very little to the accurate perception of distance. Even at distances as small as 6–12 inches, convergence and accommodation alone seem to have little effect on the perception of depth—except of course as these eye adjustments give rise to changes of blur and double images, that is to visual cues. It might seem appropriate to close the discussion at this point. But we should not neglect the interesting stereoscopic experiments on the effect of convergence, especially as some of the investigators have reached quite different conclusions from that just stated. We must see whether their results can be explained by the factors with which we are already familiar.

STEREOSCOPE EXPERIMENTS ON THE EFFECT OF CONVERGENCE

In what we called the "indirect attack" on the problem, the retinal images are held constant (or approximately so) by placing the object at a fixed distance from the eyes, while convergence is altered by adjustments of the mirror stereoscope. This experiment goes back to Wheatstone (1852).

The prediction. Let us consider in advance what results to expect on the hypothesis that convergence is a controlling factor in apparent distance (in the absence of retinal cues). When the eyes are converged at a certain angle, their lines of sight come together at a certain distance, and an object, seen single, should appear to lie at that distance. The nearer the object, the greater the required convergence; and therefore, conversely, the greater the convergence the nearer the object should appear according to our hypothesis. Accordingly, when the two drawings presented by the stereoscope are combined the object should appear *nearer* as convergence increases. It should also look *smaller;* for the nearer an object that gives a retinal image of a constant size, the smaller that object must be. With greater convergence, then, the stereoscopic object should appear nearer and smaller.

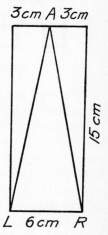

FIG. 219. The angle of convergence as related to the distance of the object. If the eyes L and R are 6 cm apart (on center) and are fixating a point A in the median plane, each line of sight comes in 3 cm, and this amount divided by the forward distance of the object = the tangent of the angle by which each eye is turned inward. Thus,

Distance of object	Tangent of angle	Angle
2 m = 200 cm	3/200 = .015	0° 52′
1 m = 100 cm	3/100 = .030	1° 43′
30 cm	3/30 = .100	5° 43′
15 cm	3/15 = .200	11° 19′

The results. Wheatstone found with increasing convergence a decrease in the apparent size of the object, but the expected decrease in apparent distance was not a regular result with him. Judd (1897) made a similar experiment with a pair of mirrors hinged together and held in front of the eyes so as to give both eyes a view of the same object located behind O's back. By placing the mirrors at a slight angle to each other (convex toward O) Judd increased the convergence necessary for single vision of the object, while the optical distance of the object and consequently the size of the retinal images remained almost unchanged. Judd's finding was that the change of convergence affected both apparent size and distance. His results and Wheatstone's can be compared in tabular form:

	Apparent size		Apparent distance	
	Wheatstone	*Judd*	*Wheatstone*	*Judd*
During the process of increasing convergence	smaller	smaller	unchanged	nearer
At rest after increased convergence	smaller	smaller	nearer	indefinite

The two experimenters are in perfect agreement as to the changes in apparent size: increased convergence (with constant retinal images) makes the object appear smaller. As to the apparent distance, Wheatstone noticed no change during the actual process of changing convergence but did find the object to appear nearer when it was regarded steadily with the increased convergence. Judd, on the other hand, saw the object apparently come nearer during the process of convergence but found that its apparent distance became indefinite during steady fixation with the increased convergence.

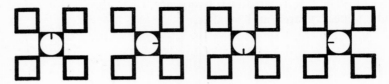

Fig. 220. Repeated figure for convergence experiment.

We need not accuse either author of careless observation since both agree that the apparent distance is fluctuating and unsettled. To quote Wheatstone: "Unless other signs accompany this sensation (that of convergence) the notion of distance we thus derive is uncertain and obscure, whereas the perception of the change of magnitude it occasions is obvious and unmistakable." And Judd says: "Of two objects requiring different degrees of convergence and yielding the same size retinal images the one requiring the greater convergence will seem smaller; it will also appear nearer unless associative factors from past experience come in to disturb the localization."

The postage stamp experiment. The results just cited can be verified with very simple apparatus. Place two identical postage stamps about 3 inches apart on the table, in good alignment. Maintain fixation on a pencil point while you bring it closer and closer to the eyes, starting midway between the stamps. While maintaining this fixation, notice the two stamps coming together; if necessary, true the alignment so that they can be exactly superposed and appear as one. Notice the apparent size and distance of this one. Then relax your convergence and let the two stamps drift apart till you are fixating them normally.

This experiment is essentially the same as the old "wall paper experiment," for which any repeated figure or a typewriter keyboard will serve (Fig. 220). Use the pencil point as before. Adjacent or non-adjacent figures can be superposed by sufficiently increasing convergence. Notice the apparent size and distance of the combined images. With regard to size, all observers will probably agree that the greater the convergence the smaller the combined figures appear. The apparent distance is not so definite; sometimes the combined figure appears nearer, sometimes farther than the objective distance. When the apparent distance is less than the real distance, convergence is apparently the cue; but when the figure appears farther away than it is, the apparent size is the dominant cue.

Improved research stereoscope. In order to reach a valid conclusion on the role of the supposed tactile-kinesthetic cues of distance, all visual cues must be excluded or at least equalized. Carr (1935) invented a new type of mirror stereoscope which permits convergence to be changed with no change in the actual distance of the object and (presumably) with no change of any kind in the retinal images. Each eye looks into a separate tube and the amount of convergence is controlled by the

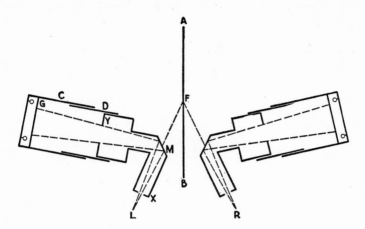

FIG. 221. Carr's mirror stereoscope (Carr 1935, p. 248. Published by Longmans, Green & Co.).

The figure shows a horizontal section of the instrument. The eyes (more precisely, their centers of rotation) are placed at L and R, looking into the tubes. The left eye receives light reflected by the mirror M from the milk glass G which is illuminated from behind. The distance of the surface G can be changed by telescoping the farther section of the tube; G can be brought as close as 25 cm from the eye, or removed as far as 40 cm. But these changes in distance do not affect the size of the retinal image, for that is bounded by a circular hole in the screen Y, placed at a constant distance from the eye. And the changes in distance of G do not affect the brightness of the retinal image, since the area of G exposed increases as the square of its distance, while the light from the unit of area decreases as the square of the distance. If the milk glass were perfectly uniform and free from visible markings and texture, changes in its distance from the eye would make no difference in the retinal image. Close to the eye, at X, is an eye hole which was sometimes only 1/16 in. in diameter, at other times 5/16 in., without noticeable effect on the judgment of distance.

The right eye is treated the same as the left in every respect. Each tube is mounted on a carriage and can be rotated about L and R as centers. With the eyes properly placed and converged, this rotation does not change the retinal images; but by means of the rotation, different degrees of convergence can be enforced on the eyes, in the sense that each eye must look straight into its tube to see its circle of light complete, and to secure single binocular vision of the circle. With any symmetrical position of the tubes, the eyes converge upon a point F somewhere in the straight line BA extending straight forward from the midpoint between O's eyes. F may be called the "virtual fixation point," and its distance the "convergence distance." A metal rod, fixed in the position AB, carries a slider which O grasps (without seeing it) and moves forward or back to indicate the apparent distance of the seen circle of light, much as if O first located the position of a small object with the eyes, and then closed the eyes and brought his finger to the object. It can be done fairly accurately, and thus the hand indicates the apparent distance of an object.

angular position of the two tubes. The distance of the object is controlled by altering the length of the tubes, which are bent (with mirrors at the bends) so that they do not collide when placed in a strongly convergent position (Fig. 221).

Results and critique. Using the Carr stereoscope Swenson (1932) varied actual distance and convergence distance independently, in extensive experiments the main results of which are shown in the table.

APPARENT DISTANCE AS DEPENDENT ON CONVERGENCE
AND ON ACTUAL DISTANCE
(*Swenson, 1932*)

The entries in the body of the table are judged distances as indicated by O's hand. Averages from 5 subjects.

Convergence distance	Actual distance of the milk glass		
	25 cm	30 cm	40 cm
25 cm	24.80	26.51	27.54
30 cm	28.55	29.88	31.74
40 cm	36.95	36.36	39.81

Reading down the columns we see that for any given actual distance of the milk glass, the apparent distance increased with the "convergence distance"; the greater this distance (i.e., the less the convergence) the greater was the apparent distance. Reading the rows horizontally we find the apparent distance dependent in a minor degree also on the actual distance of the milk glass. At any given amount of convergence the apparent distance increased slightly with the actual distance.[1]

The results are interpreted as follows (Carr, 1935). "In these experiments the binocular factor is excluded. The monocular factors that are present remain constant. Only convergence and accommodation are altered. The data constitute a decisive proof of the efficacy of these two factors."

Satisfactory as it would be to accept this conclusion, the setup does not justify it, in the present writer's opinion, because visual cues were not and could not be entirely excluded. Let us consider first the matter of accommodation. Can we assume that it follows the actual distance of the milk glass? We are confronted by a dilemma: (1) if the milk glass is perfectly smooth with no grain or markings, so that it presents exactly the same surface at all distances, then it offers no stimulus whatever to control accommodation; (2) if however the milk glass has enough texture to focus upon, this texture will become visibly coarser the nearer the milk glass is brought to the eyes. The second alternative is more probable in view of the fact that the actual distance of the milk glass

---

[1]The relative rather than the absolute values in this table are significant. In other experiments (Carr, 1935, pp. 261, 265), with convergence and actual distance both set for 25 cm, the apparent distance ranged from 24 to 41 cm, partly in dependence on the size and brightness of the retinal image, but partly in accordance with individual peculiarities. Individuals in general cannot be expected to judge the distance of *F* (see Fig. 221) as accurately as Swenson's subjects did in the experiment quoted.

had some effect on the apparent distance. There was a monocular visual cue of distance.

As to convergence, the question is whether double images were excluded. If O on looking into the apparatus starts from the parallel, relaxed position of the eyes, he gets double images at first, and then by convergence brings the two images together. The initial separation of the double images and their visible movement in coming together afford a visual cue of the amount of convergence required, and a much more definite cue than the kinesthetic sensations of convergence. As we review the experiment it seems absolutely impossible to arrange a setup which will eliminate double images and their movement. The eyes are free to move, no matter how well they are "controlled" by the apparatus. The experimenter can force the eyes to assume a certain position in order to reach single vision, but he cannot prevent them from assuming other positions on the way to single vision.

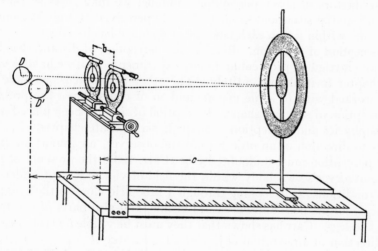

Fɪɢ. 222. (Fischer & Löwenbach, 1935.) Figures to be combined by convergence.

An essentially similar experiment with a different setup was that of Fischer & Löwenbach (1935). O has before him at a distance of 10 inches two black rings, each containing a central black circle which E displaces to produce disparity. O combines the two figures and indicates the apparent distance of the combined image by adjusting a vertical rod which is beyond the actual figures but visible to O. The rod was adjusted to apparent identity of position with the combined image. In fact the adjustment conformed closely to the distance for which the eyes were converged; the convergence distance evidently determined the apparent distance.

These authors, like Carr and Swenson, regard their results as proving the dependence of apparent distance on degree of convergence. Both experiments do prove some connection between convergence and apparent distance, but they do not identify tactile-kinesthetic sensations as the cue. For here again visual cues of convergence were present. The indicator rod would be seen double except when placed at the distance for which the eyes were converged. When both the rod and the ring were seen single, their apparent distance was necessarily the same. No other cue could possibly compete with this perfect visual cue.

Conclusion on cues of distance. The stereoscope experiments have not overthrown the conclusion drawn earlier in the chapter from the more direct type of experiment. All the evidence favors the great predominance of visual cues. They are not only more precise than the tactile-kinesthetic sensations from the eyeball region, but they are tied up directly with the visual field. In ordinary conditions all the cues are integrated, or rather they all work together in giving the perceived spatial field. Except for "close work," the manipulation of small objects right before the eyes, the binocular cues are probably less important than covering, shading and the different kinds of perspective. Without attempting to offer any theory of the dynamic process by which the various factors in space perception combine, we may suppose that the external spatial situation, so far as already perceived at a given moment, is a frame within which each new cue of distance has its effect.

Perception of direction. Because the perception of distance has been the more intriguing problem and more experimented on, we have devoted the chapter to it almost entirely. The other two dimensions have also been worked with to some extent, and so of course have the problems of perception of size and shape. Perception of size has been placed under psychophysics and perception of shape has a separate chapter.

As to direction of an object from the observer, an important factor in its perception must undoubtedly be (Carr, 1935) the presence of parts of the observer's own body within the field of view. Except under artificial conditions, as in looking through a tube held close to the eye, parts of the eyebrow, nose and cheek are visible, and also parts of the trunk, arms and legs. Carr has shown that they must be visible if O is to perceive the direction of an external object at all accurately.

Perception of motion. Brief mention will be made of this important topic, and nothing will be said of the important topic of time perception. Since about 1833, when the stroboscope was invented, it has been known that a series of stationary visual stimuli, not far apart in the visual field, presented in fairly rapid succession with intervening blank intervals, gives the appearance of motion. This psychological principle is utilized in the motion pictures. There is no continuous motion on the screen. The projector presents a series of still views, with blank intervals due to cutting off the light while the film is advanced from each frame to the next. What we see is actually not a moving picture. If a picture should move slowly on the screen, the eyes would follow it and we should simply see the picture move. If its motion exceeded the possible speed of the pursuit movement of the eyes, we should get blurs and streaks and no picture. Terrific blurs and streaks would be seen if the movement of the film took place while the light was on.

Why do we see motion when all there is to see is a series of still views with black intervals? A hasty explanation, sometimes offered by those who should know better, lays everything to the after-lag of retinal sensation (p. 557), the same after-lag which produces the blurs and streaks just mentioned. A moment's thought shows that this after-lag bridges the time gap between the successive views, but not the space gap. It gives temporal continuity to the sensation and prevents flicker (when the views come at short enough intervals to reach or pass the fusion frequency, p. 565). But it does not give the spatial continuity which we see in the picture. If retinal after-lag were all, we should see, not smooth movement but a steplike, jagged series of successive positions.

For analytical work much simpler views than those of the motion pictures are employed. Lines may be ruled on film and exposed with the motion picture projector (Mibai, 1931). A rotating disk, with two windows cut 180° apart and at slightly different distances from the center, will expose alternately two stationary lines placed behind the disk and give the appearance of a back and forth movement (Bishop, 1928). The Dodge tachistoscope (p. 689) is a favorite instrument for such exposures (De Silva, 1926). Exner (1875) used the simplest possible stimulus: two electric sparks exposed to different points of the retina. When the points were close together, the time interval between the sparks could be reduced to 20 ms and still yield a minimal impression of movement. He believed the impression to depend on actual stimulation of the intervening retinal points by "diffusion circles" resulting from imperfect accommodation. He admitted, however, that an impression of movement often occurred when the two stimulated points were much too far apart for this explanation to hold. One of the two points could even be in one retina and the other point in the other retina. Exner therefore appealed to a tendency in the observer to see motion whenever the stimuli received made such an appearance possible. (Apparent motion of a finger can be seen by holding it before the face and opening one eye just as the other is closed; or by placing different figures before the two eyes by aid of a stereoscope and shifting the exposure from eye to eye by alternate winking.)

Wertheimer (1912, 1925) conceived of diffusion circles in the cortex rather than in the retina. The cortical excitation may have some spread and the shift from one stimulus to the next may produce a movement of excitation along the cortex. The impression of movement will thus be fully sensory in character and not inferential or due to associations formed in past experience. For qualitative experiments he found a simple sliding screen effective; a window in the screen exposed, for example, first one and then the other of two vertical lines on a surface close behind the screen. Or, the slide holder of a lantern was adapted to hold a fixed plate and a sliding screen. For quantitative work he used the Schumann rotating tachistoscope (a metal disk with adjustable windows through which stationary figures are exposed).

Wertheimer varied the experiment in many ways, and his results have remained classic, though subjected to minor revisions and to many additions. He worked out the time relations for apparent movement. Let two vertical lines, 1 cm apart at reading distance, be exposed one at a time. If the blank interval between exposures is only 30 ms, the lines seem to stand side by side; if it is 200 ms or more, they are seen successively and with no apparent motion. When the blank interval lies between the limits mentioned, the appearance is often that of a single line moving from one position to the other. The best appearance of movement ("optimal movement") occurs at an interval of about 60 ms. These values are not to be regarded as stable constants; they depend on other variables, such as the spatial distance between the lines, the duration of the first exposure, the brightness of the "blank" interval, and the attitude and expectancy of O.

The appearance of movement, for which there is no obvious physical stimulus, Wertheimer called the Phi phenomenon. His Os sometimes reported an impression of movement when the lines themselves were not seen. There was visual movement without any object seen to move— "pure Phi." Later observers have given somewhat different reports: a "gray flash" (Dimmick, 1920), or a colored flash depending on the hue of the stimulus lines and always carrying the meaning of an object in motion (Higginson, 1926), or simply the invariable presence of an object in motion (Steinig, 1929). Theoretical importance has been attached to these rather elusive varieties of the phenomenon. More tangible is the question whether eye movements can be held responsible for the whole appearance of movement. Wertheimer pretty well ruled out that possibility by showing that two simultaneous movements *in opposite directions* were seen when suitable pairs of lines were presented; and Guilford & Helson (1929) on photographing the eyes found no significant relation between the eye movements and the appearance of movement.

The movement seen has many varieties, partly dependent on the stimulus conditions and partly on O's readiness for getting the various possible appearances. The movement may be a simple sliding as in the case of the two vertical lines. It may be a turning, as when an oblique line is followed by a horizontal line. It may be a motion in the third dimension, as when an inverted V is followed by a V right side up and slightly lower in the field. Steinig (1929) and Fernberger (1934) give many examples of this three-dimensional movement. The same figure sequence is differently seen by different Os and by the same O after different preparations. Wheatstone's rule (p. 658) applies here as well as in the prediction of stereoscopic effects. The stimulus sequence is almost sure to be perceived as an objective movement, a movement of such an object as could give rise to the stimulus sequence. If we start with an objective movement which would produce a certain sequence of stimuli, we can predict that that stimulus sequence will yield the appearance of that objective movement. Since, however, a plurality of objective movements could yield any given stimulus sequence, we always have an ambiguous stimulus and have to expect different appearances, some more frequently realized than others. James's principle (1890) that "perception is of definite and probable things," holds good throughout. General reviews of this subject are given by P. Engel (1928), Mibai (1931) and Koffka (1931).

CHAPTER XXVII

ATTENTION

Fᴜɴᴄᴛɪᴏɴᴀʟʟʏ, attention has a real meaning, as in the expressions, "giving attention" or "catching the attention." Attention is a preparatory stage in perception or exploration. When something catches your attention you proceed to observe it and discover some of its characteristics. In voluntary attention the incentive comes from within rather than without, but still the process goes on to an examination of some object. Though attention to the object continues during the exploration, the peculiar function of attention is best seen in the transition from object to object.

In spite of its functional genuineness, the psychological status of the concept of attention has become more and more dubious. Titchener was successful in inducing many psychologists to drop the functional view of attention and consider only the attributive aspect of clearness. Other psychologists have continued to assign a role to attention in the process of analyzing and synthesizing the content of the visual field, for example, or the content of a list of nonsense syllables which are being memorized. But the Gestalt psychologists, and others, have made it seem that any such explanatory use of the concept of attention amounts to invoking a *deus ex machina* when one ought to look for causes in the dynamic structure of the field itself.

Besides this inclination to place a taboo on the concept of attention, there is an obvious difficulty in segregating certain experiments under this title. Every experiment which gives O a task to perform demands his attention, whether the experiment be one in memory, reaction time, sensation, perception or the solution of a problem. The experiments which usually pass under the name of attention have affinities with other topics. The time-honored experiment on "span of attention" might be labeled "perception of number," and those on fluctuation of attention and on distraction might go under the head of "work and fatigue." Yet these experiments have distinctive characteristics which ought not to be obscured; and for that reason, if for none of greater theoretical weight, it seems desirable to place them together under the old head of attention.

THE SPAN OF APPREHENSION

One of the oldest experiments in psychology, apart from some on the senses, was inspired by the philosophical question whether the mind could apprehend more than one object at a time. The conception of a unitary mind suggested an answer inconsistent with the facts of comparison and discrimination. If the mind is a unit, how can it simultaneously be in two states, perform two acts or be absorbed in two objects? But if it cannot hold two objects together, how can it compare or distinguish them? Such questions called aloud for an experimenter.

Early experiments. In the lectures on "metaphysics" which Sir William Hamilton (1859) gave to his students at the University of Edinburgh from 1836 to 1856, he was accustomed to say:

How many several objects can the mind simultaneously survey, not with vivacity, but without absolute confusion? I find this problem stated and differently answered, by different philosophers, and apparently without a knowledge of each other. By Charles Bonnet the mind is allowed to have a distinct notion of six objects at once; by Abraham Tucker the number is limited to four; while Destutt-Tracy again amplifies it to six. The opinion of the first and last of these philosophers, appears to me correct. You can easily make the experiment for yourselves, but you must beware of grouping the objects into classes. If you throw a handful of marbles on the floor, you will find it difficult to view at once more than six, or seven at most, without confusion; but if you group them into twos, or threes, or fives, you can comprehend as many groups as you can units; because the mind considers these groups only as units.

The experiment as described by Hamilton is crude and primitive in two respects: the conditions were not well controlled, and the data were not reported nor, probably, even recorded. A step in advance was taken in 1871 by W. S. Jevons, usually classed as a logician rather than a psychologist. Referring to Hamilton's statement, he remarks:

This subject seemed to me worthy of more systematic investigation, and it is one of the very few points in psychology which can, as far as we yet see, be submitted to experiment. I have not found it possible to decide conclusively in the manner Hamilton suggests, whether 4 or 5 or 6 is the limit. . . . Probably the limit is not really a definite one, and it is almost sure to vary somewhat in different individuals.

I have investigated the power in my own case in the following manner. A round paper box, $4\frac{1}{2}$ inches in diameter, and with the edges cut down so as to stand only $\frac{1}{4}$ inch high, was placed in the middle of a black tray. A quantity of uniform black beans was then obtained, and a number of them being taken up casually were thrown towards the box so that a wholly uncertain number fell into it. At the very moment when the beans came to rest, their number was estimated without the least hesitation, and then recorded together with the real number obtained by deliberate counting. The whole value of the experiment turns upon the rapidity of the estimation, for if we can really count five or six by a single mental act, we ought to be able to do it unerringly at the first momentary glance.

Excluding a few trials which were consciously bad, and some in which the number of beans was more than 15, I made altogether 1,027 trials, and the following table contains the complete results:—

Estimated Numbers	ACTUAL NUMBERS 3	4	5	6	7	8	9	10	11	12	13	14	15
3	23												
4		65											
5			102	7									
6			4	120	18								
7			1	20	113	30	2						
8					25	76	24	6	1				
9						28	76	37	11	1			
10						1	18	46	19	4			
11							2	16	26	17	7	2	
12								2	12	19	11	3	2
13										3	6	3	1
14										1	1	4	6
15											1	2	2
Totals.....	23	65	107	147	156	135	122	107	69	45	26	14	11
Mean estimate	3.0	4.0	5.1	6.1	7.1	8.0	8.9	9.7	10.5	11.5	12.2	13.1	13.7
SD of estimate	0.0	0.0	0.3	0.4	0.5	0.7	0.7	0.9	1.0	0.9	1.0	1.3	1.0
Percent correct	100	100	95	82	72	56	62	43	38	42	23	29	18

So far as my trials went, there was absolute freedom from error in the numbers 3 and 4, as might have been expected; but I was surprised to find that several times I fell into error as regards 5, which was wrongly guessed in 5 percent of the cases.

But in reality the question is not to be so surely decided by the trial of the first few numbers, as by endeavoring to obtain some general law pervading the whole series of trials.

Jevons proceeds to show how the data can be handled statistically: for each column, i.e., for each number of beans exposed, he computes the average error of estimate and the constant error. He thus uses the method of Average Error (p. 395). Following our own preferences we have added to his table the Mean and SD for each column. With regard to the constant error, we note a slight tendency to overestimate the numbers 5–7 and a stronger tendency to underestimate the numbers above 9. With regard to scatter, the SD increases with the number of beans exposed, somewhat irregularly but without any sure departure from the linear relationship demanded by Weber's law.

Computation of the span. The technique of Jevons was a great advance over Hamilton's: conditions were better controlled, the data were recorded, and an attempt was made to do justice to all the data in reaching a conclusion. Yet neither the experiment nor the statistical treatment was entirely satisfactory. Postponing for a moment the matter of laboratory technique we will consider the question of how to compute a span of apprehension.

How large a number of beans, dots, or other uniform objects can be grasped in one glance—one momentary act of apprehension—so as to be reported correctly? Jevons recognized, and his data show, that the span varies from moment to moment. Whenever a certain number was reported correctly, the span at that moment was *at least as great* as that number. Whenever any error was made, the span at that moment was *smaller* than the number exposed. The problem of measuring a span belongs with other problems of the "high jump" type (p. 401). As pointed out by Fernberger (1921), the data can be adequately handled by the method of Constant Stimuli. For this purpose we extract from the complete table of Jevons only the percent of correct responses for each number of beans exposed, and compute M and SD for the whole stimulus series by any one of the methods used in Constant Stimuli.

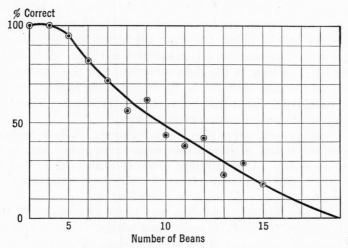

FIG. 223. A graph of Jevons's data on the span of apprehension for number of objects. The ringed points are the actual data, the observed percent of correct judgments for each number of beans exposed. The smooth line is drawn to fit the data as closely as seems possible while maintaining the most general characteristics of an ogive curve. The extension of the curve to the right carries out the general line of the curve and corresponds to the probability that the number of correct responses would not have fallen abruptly to zero if the experiment had been extended to larger numbers of beans. The data here, being rather irregular, leave much leeway to one's judgment as to exactly where the curve had best be drawn. A similar graph with more regular data is shown in Fig. 225.

By following the 50 percent horizontal, one sees it cross the curve at a point corresponding to the number of 9.7 beans, which is thus indicated as the median span. Similarly the quartiles and other percentiles can be located.

Because of irregularities in the data, the different computations give somewhat divergent values, though they agree in locating the Mean span at about 10 beans for Jevons as subject. More regular data from other Os will be presented later.

The tachistoscope. This instrument was the laboratory man's answer to the problem of experimental control. Where Jevons had depended on O to take but a single momentary glance at the beans, suitable apparatus can transfer to E the control of the exposure. The tachistoscope is literally an instrument for giving "briefest views," for giving visual stimuli of very short duration. First devised for the purpose of discovering how brief a stimulus could arouse visual sensation, it was adapted by Cattell (1885–86) for use in span and reading experiments. Here the fundamental requirement is to allow only one glance; the eyes must not have time to change their fixation point during the exposure.

If we placed O in a perfectly dark room, with a card before him containing an assemblage of dots (substituted for beans), and flashed the light on for an instant, we should *not* have a good tachistoscope experiment, because O would not know exactly where to look, would not have his eyes focused for the exact distance of the card, and, being adapted to the dark, would be dazzled by the sudden light. A good setup provides a *pre-exposure field* of about the same brightness as the exposure field itself, so that the eyes are properly adapted in advance. A visible *fixation point* enables O to look in the right direction; and this fixation mark is practically at the same distance as the object to be exposed, so that O's eyes are properly focused and converged in advance. These are the elementary conditions of a good tachistoscope.

Other conditions also are of some importance. A dark *post-exposure field* allows the retinal after-response, or positive afterimage, to supplement the exposure. A very bright post-exposure field washes out the retinal image before it has time to exert its full effect on the brain. Therefore the post-exposure field must be controlled and specified.

When the pre-exposure field gives way to the exposure itself, it should do so without visible motion, or at least without slow motion such as induces a pursuit movement of the eyes and draws them away from their assigned fixation point. Another obviously desirable condition is that the machine should start and stop with little noise.

The *duration of exposure* must ordinarily be long enough to afford a clear view of the field, and short enough to prevent O from getting two views. The upper limit is set by the reaction time of the eyes in shifting from one fixation point to another. This reaction time is fairly long, usually 150–200 ms (p. 585), so that we are safe in using exposures up to 100 ms. Photographs of the eyes during exposures of 100 ms showed in fact no shifts of fixation (Dearborn, 1906). Much shorter exposures afford an adequate view of the field, provided the light is sufficiently strong. With exposures shorter than about 50 ms, the effective stimulation equals the product of time and light intensity (p. 564). A short, bright exposure gives the same sensation as one that is longer and correspondingly less intense. A white card illuminated by a bright electric spark lasting a fraction of a millisecond appears as bright as when illuminated for 50 ms by a weaker light. The exposure can therefore be as short as we wish, with strong illumination; but for experiments on span, reading, etc., there is usually no advantage in striving for a very short exposure (Dodge, 1907).

If the product of intensity and time (up to 50 ms) is kept constant, the exposures appear to O not only equally bright but also equally long. And it makes no difference whether all parts of the field are exposed simultaneously or one part after another, always within a brief time. Hylan (1903) exposed a row of 6 letters successively from left to right or from right to left, and found that O could not detect the difference when the total time was kept down to 24–86 ms, depending on the individual. Interested in this matter of successive exposure of the letters of a word, Kutzner (1916) invented a tachistoscope in which a little window in a horizontally moving screen exposed one letter after another, each letter for 4.5 ms, and all the letters of a long word within a total time of 100 ms. Working with this instrument Stein (1928) found that the word was perceived just the same as when all the letters were exposed simultaneously. He exposed the letters in reverse order and O did not notice that any change had been made. These surprising results could have been predicted from the known facts of retinal lag.

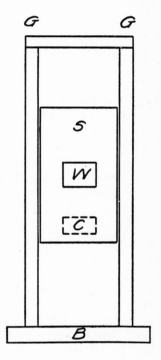

FIG. 224. Diagram of a fall tachistoscope. This old form of tachistoscope may serve for a simple illustration. The screen S, containing a window W, is held at the top by a catch till all is ready, then released and in falling between the grooved guides, exposes through the window the card C, which is held by a frame attached behind to the guides. The screen is brought to a stop by the base B. A stationary screen set up in front of the apparatus has a window at the height of C. Seen through this stationary window, the pre-exposure field is furnished by the lower part of the screen S and the post-exposure field by the upper part of that same screen. The duration of the exposure is governed by the size of the moving window and by the speed of its motion past the card. A fixation point can be mounted on a thread strung across the front of the guides at the level of C. There are many improved forms of tachistoscope. Mention may be made of Dodge's (1907) transparent-mirror tachistoscope, which changes fields noiselessly and without visible motion and has other advantages for accurate work.

The general requirements of a good tachistoscope have been met by a variety of devices. The exposure field is sometimes a small area viewed through a laboratory telescope; sometimes it is large enough to be seen by a class of students. It is illuminated sometimes from the front, by reflected light; sometimes from the rear, by transmitted light. Recently much use has been made of the projection lantern in tachistoscopic work. The change of fields—pre-exposure to exposure to post-exposure—is accomplished in several ways. In the fall tachistoscope, one of the oldest and simplest devices, a screen containing a window first conceals a card behind it, then, in descending, exposes this card through the window and conceals it again. In other instruments the screen is attached to a large pendulum or to the shaft of a motor. With a projection tachistoscope the exposure can be controlled by a photographic shutter. One of the main difficulties in describing a tachistoscopic experiment is to make sure of stating all the conditions which another investigator would need to duplicate in order to repeat the experiment.

Results: the span of apprehension for number of seen objects. With the instrumental and statistical techniques perfected, the century-old question of the span of apprehension has been reopened and sufficient data have been obtained to afford an answer under certain definite

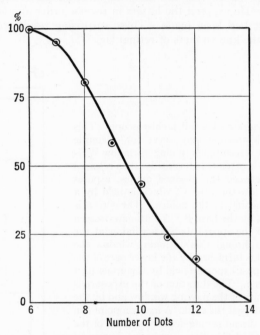

Fig. 225. Percents of correct estimates by the subject labeled F_1 in the adjoining table.

conditions. The conditions need to be specified because the size of the span differs accordingly.

When the requirement is that the *number* of objects shall be correctly apprehended, and when the objects are distinct black dots scattered irregularly over a white card and exposed to clear central vision for a period of from 37 to 100 ms (in the different experiments), the average span for keen adults is about 8. Individuals differ in their average spans, all the way from 6 to 11, and each individual varies from trial to trial about his own average, as indicated by the SD which is large for some individuals and small for others. The table on p. 691 shows the percent of correct estimates for each number of dots exposed.

How the number of objects is apprehended. If we query how so many dots can be grasped in so brief an exposure, we are led back to

SPAN OF APPREHENSION FOR NUMBER OF DOTS

Data from Fernberger (1921), Oberly (1924), Glanville & Dallenbach (1929)

No. dots exposed	G_1	F_3	F_1	O_5	G_3	O_1	O_4	O_6	O_3	O_2	F_4	F_2	F_5	G_2	Group Average
2				100		100	100	100	100	100					
3	100			100	100	100	100	100	100	100				100	
4	100			100	100	98	100	98	100	100	100	98	90	98	
5	100			100	100	95	97	98	98	99	96	94	80	78	
6	100	99	99	97	98	86	82	90	94	94	91	87	62	49	
7	97	97	95	84	98	69	65	88	68	77	70	58	42	38	
8	84	92	80	79	63	57	63	49	59	58	22	9	34	3	
9	83	76	58	51	55	32	23	8	16	10	5	0	21	2	
10	74	63	43	34	16	20	13	3	2	0	0	0	17	4	
11	68	48	24	27	3		2	0						0	
12	58	24	16	17	2		0	0						0	
13	5				0									0	
14	8				0									0	
15	3				0									0	
Mean															
Normal curve	11.30	10.60	9.69	9.54	8.83	8.22	7.93	7.89	7.88	7.82	7.33	7.00	6.82	6.20	8.36
Summation	11.30	10.49	9.65	9.39	8.85	8.07	7.95	7.84	7.87	7.88	7.34	6.96	6.96	6.22	8.34
Graphic, Median	12.1	10.7	9.5	9.2	8.8	8.2	8.2	8.0	8.1	8.1	7.4	7.1	6.6	6.1	8.44
SD															
Normal curve	2.36	1.93	1.95	2.04	1.33	1.89	1.83	1.41	1.34	1.12	1.10	1.05	2.51	1.61	1.68
Summation	2.15	1.73	1.81	2.03	1.32	1.82	1.72	1.19	1.28	1.10	1.05	1.02	2.25	1.43	1.56
Graphic	1.9	2.0	2.1	2.4	1.2	1.9	1.8	.9	1.3	.9	.9	.8	2.5	1.3	1.56

Hamilton's suggestion that it may be done by *grouping*. Introspection shows that grouping often occurs. Some collections of dots fall readily into groups. One of Fernberger's subjects (F_3 in our table, whose span is very large) reported after a certain trial:

I had a clear auditory perception of the "ready" signal, which was followed immediately by the clear perception of the dots arranged in the form of an uneven square. The attention then shifted to the upper right-hand part of the figure. Rapid perception of four dots which stood out very clearly. Then I had a clear perception of three dots in the lower left-hand part of the figure. Then immediately I had a very clear perception of another group of three dots in the central part of the figure. Then followed the verbalization "ten" which was followed by intensive pleasantness.

When the dots are *objectively* well grouped, O's task is easier and his span greater (Freeman, 1916).

Actual *counting* of the dots—"One, two, three . . ."—is sometimes reported in these experiments. It cannot possibly get very far during an exposure of 100 ms, but the visual afterimage prolongs the time for counting, and what is called the primary memory image, or memory afterimage, makes still more time available. The primary memory image has less of definite sensory quality than the visual afterimage, and is distinguished by the fact that it does not move with the eye, but remains localized in the place where the objects were exposed. Of course neither of these afterimages affords any opportunity for the eyes to shift their fixation and so amplify the retinal data, but they do allow a few seconds extra for the cerebral response to the data supplied by the retina.

Grouping and counting may be combined in the process of discovering the number of dots exposed. Part of the collection may fall at once into a group or groups, and the remaining dots may then be added by counting.

An experiment of Oberly (1924) was so arranged as to yield three spans: for the apprehension of number without regard to the process; for apprehension that was free from counting and any noticeable use of the afterimages; and for apprehension that was immediate in the full sense, being achieved without either grouping or counting. O reported after each trial by what process he had gained his knowledge of the number of dots. As would be expected, the span is smallest for direct apprehension, intermediate for grouping, and largest when all cases were included without regard to the process. On the average of Oberly's six O's, the spans were as follows:

For direct apprehension	3.93 dots
For direct plus grouping	6.91 dots
For all forms inclusively	8.21 dots

When only two, three or four dots were shown, the apprehension was usually reported as immediate and without grouping. When the number was five or six, the commonest report was "grouping," but with "counting" also beginning to be frequent; above six, counting and grouping were about equally frequent, and both fell off rapidly with the larger numbers, giving way to failure. The average results from ten subjects are given in the following table.

RELATIVE FREQUENCY OF DIFFERENT FORMS OF APPREHENSION

(*Adapted from Oberly, 1924 and Cooper, 1928. Black dots on white.*)

	Number of dots exposed										
	2	*3*	*4*	*5*	*6*	*7*	*8*	*9*	*10*	*11*	*12*
Percents:											
apprehended without grouping or counting	88	80	54	18	2	0	0	0	0	0	0
apprehended by grouping	12	19	40	59	54	34	30	15	9	4	2
apprehended by counting	0	1	5	15	32	39	30	15	8	5	1
not apprehended	0	0	1	8	11	27	40	70	83	91	97
TOTAL	100	100	100	100	99	100	100	100	100	100	100

The table reads, for example, that when five dots were shown, they were reported as apprehended immediately, without grouping or counting, 18 percent of the time; as apprehended by grouping 59 percent of the time; as apprehended by counting 15 percent of the time; with failure in the other 8 percent of trials.

Practice increases the average span. Some Os become expert in grouping, others in counting. If the same arrangement of dots recurs frequently in an experiment, O comes to recognize it and thus to know the number directly without subdivision into groups.

Different spans. The variability of the span has been sufficiently emphasized, in opposition to the old idea of a fixed span. It varies from one individual to another, and with the same individual from moment to moment. It varies with internal conditions such as the duration of the afterimages, the momentary alertness of the individual, and his set and attitude. It varies with external conditions such as the arrangement of the dots on the card. It also varies according to the *amount of information* that must be obtained from the exposure. If more than the mere number of exposed objects is demanded, the span necessarily becomes smaller, as shown by Glanville & Dallenbach (1929). They exposed dots with instructions to report the number; letters to be read; geometrical figures to be named; and geometrical figures of different colors, with instructions to report both form and color of every figure. As in all span experiments, all the objects must be correctly reported in order that the trial may count as a success. If 7 letters are shown and 6 of them are correctly reported, the trial simply is a failure. The results obtained from three Os are combined into the following average spans:

Span for number of dots	8.8
Span for letters read	6.9
Span for geometrical forms	3.8
Span for report on both form and color	3.0

Can the span of apprehension be regarded as the "span of attention"? The question has often been raised, "How many objects can be attended to at once?" and the results on span of apprehension have been hastily accepted as the answer to this question. Meanwhile, introspective psychologists have been seeking a scientific definition of what is meant by attention. They wished to define it in terms of conscious content rather than as an act or function, and they have agreed to identify the content indicated by the word attention with what they have called clearness, vividness, prominence or insistence. "Clearness" has been the word most often used. To distinguish the clearness which is identified with attention from visual clearness due to objective distinctness or due to presence in the field of clear vision, the technical word "attensity" was suggested by Titchener. From this viewpoint, psychologists have defined the problem of the range of attention as follows: "How many objects can be simultaneously clear?" The question is of course not how many objects can be crowded into the field of clear vision, but how many can simultaneously have the attribute of attensity.

Glanville & Dallenbach (1929) sought to answer this question by a span experiment in which O reported not the number of dots nor any other objective fact, but simply whether the collection appeared equally clear throughout, or whether some part stood out more clearly than the rest. In the case of one O, the results could be used for computing an average span of about 18 dots; with fewer dots he reported "all equally clear," and with a more numerous collection he was likely to report "some clearer than others." But with some Os it was impossible to compute a span, because clearness did not change in any regular way with increase in the number of dots exposed. A small collection might fall apart into clearer and less clear portions, and a large collection might be uniformly clear. The number of dots seemed to have no decisive effect on clearness. There was no such thing as a clearness span, and we should therefore use the term "span of apprehension" rather than span of attention.

In reality, what we have been measuring is not even the span of apprehension. It is the span of apprehension-and-report. O may apprehend more letters, colors, or geometrical figures than he manages to report. Before the report is completed some of the observed facts may be forgotten. We find statements such as the following:

(8 letters exposed, 4 correctly named): "All were equally clear, could have reported all if report could have been instantaneous. Lost memory images of the last letters before I came to them."

(7 letters exposed, 4 correctly named): "Rapid pronunciation of S and Z

(the third and fourth letters) caused me to stutter—an inhibition sufficiently disturbing to obliterate partially the memory afterimage of the remaining letters."

The true span of apprehension must be larger than the measures which we have obtained—how much larger we cannot judge. The distinction is very important, since items momentarily grasped, even though not reportable, can serve as cues in perception. In reading, as we shall see (p. 742) this is almost certainly the case; a larger number of letters than can be reported are seen clearly during a momentary exposure and serve as the cue for recognizing a word.

All these spans are concerned with visually presented objects, and there are no equivalent experiments on the other senses. Touch and hearing might furnish comparable data. In the case of touch, however, there are complicating factors in the irregular surface and the varying spatial discrimination of the skin. In hearing, the masking of one sound by another simultaneous sound complicates the situation. Series of *successive* stimuli can be applied in hearing and touch, as well as in sight, and the three senses thus brought into direct comparison, but we have then to reckon with a more or less elaborate rhythmical series of successive groups. A regular series of sounds is almost certain to be heard in rhythmical form, with subjective accents and pauses, and the regular groups so formed can be used as an index of the number of sounds in a series. By compounding these rhythmical groups a long series of sounds can be organized without any use of number-words, and the number later deduced from the rhythmical structure. A series of sounds, or a series of one's own finger taps, represented by dashes as follows:

／　　　　／

－ － － － － － － －

can easily be apprehended, and afterwards calculated to be 8 in number, without any counting during the reception of the stimuli; and the same process, by aid of graduated accents, can be extended as far as this,

and afterwards calculated to be 46. Indeed, the rhythmical series can be carried much further than this. The effort to measure a span of number apprehension for series of sounds thus breaks down if the sounds occur at regular intervals. If the intervals were irregular, or very short (less than a tenth of a second) rhythmization would be difficult or impossible, and a span could be determined that would be somewhat comparable with one for visual objects. But there seem to be no data on this matter.

SHIFTS AND FLUCTUATIONS

Under this title may be included various remarkable changes of response, which are of two kinds when taken simply as phenomena: shifts from one response to another, and fluctuations in the efficiency of response. Shifts occur in binocular rivalry and in viewing ambiguous figures, and in the ordinary movement of attention from one object to another. Fluctuations appear as lapses from a high level of efficiency during continued work or observation. It is common to all these phenomena that the response changes though the stimulus remains the same. The change of response is forced by internal and not by external conditions. What these internal conditions may be is a difficult problem.

Ordinary shifting of attention. Confronted by a complex field of view you typically look about, noticing first one object and then another. If you set yourself to notice cutaneous sensations, first one then another emerges into prominence. If you close your eyes and notice what you think about, you find constant shifting from one thought to another. Even if you are thinking intently on some problem, the particular ideas come and go.

Billings (1914) undertook to discover how rapid this sequence of responses might be. He placed a picture before O, with instructions to attend to one particular point in the picture, and to press a telegraph key whenever his attention wandered from that point. By electrical connections a record was obtained on a smoked drum, along with a time line. On the average of several Os and many experiments, about 2 sec. were spent on one object or idea before shifting. The time varied from moment to moment. In the same O and the same brief experiment it might vary from 1/10 of a sec. to 5 sec. or more. Pillsbury (1913) in discussing these results (obtained in his laboratory) shows that the obtained average is too high because O always missed recording some of the shifts. He also urges that every recorded shift means two actual shifts: (1) from the point looked at to some other object or thought, and (2) from this to the recording movement. Consequently he believes that 1 sec. would be a better average than 2 sec. for the duration of a single pulse of attention. He further emphasizes the importance of the minimum times recorded, as indications of the maximum rate of shifting, and concludes that something like .1 or .2 sec. per item represents the greatest mobility of attention.

This maximum speed of attention can be compared with the maximum tapping rate which is about 9–11 taps per sec. However, it is certain that O does not by any means attend separately to each successive tap.

One of the most rapid processes that occur in human beings is silent reading. Photographs of the eyes (p. 724) show about 4 fixations per sec. in a moderately rapid reader, and 6 per sec. in some individuals. If we could regard each fixation as a separate attentive response, we should thus have .16–.26 sec. as the time of each response. But it appears that the perceptual and meaning-getting processes in reading are not cut up into separate units corresponding to the eye fixations. If we measure the speed of reading in terms of words, we find as many as 10–13 words per sec. covered by very rapid readers, but the separate words are not read in as many separate attentive responses. Though we can derive no exact measure of the speed of attention from these reading experiments, we are impressed with the probability that the movement can be very rapid—about as rapid as Pillsbury computed from the other type of experiment.

If we ask, not how quickly attention can move, but how long it can remain fixed, we get from Billings some such figure as 5 sec. You can attend to a complex object for a much longer time, but attention is shifting from one part of the object to another. You can pursue a goal for a much longer time, but while pursuing it you are making one particular response after another. Reading is another case where you do not lose the thread in spite of the rapid sequence of responses. Something—call it a "set"—remains steady through the shifting and holds it in leash, so that in a real sense we do have sustained attention.

Oscillations in the perception of ambiguous figures. An ambiguous figure or drawing can be seen as representing two or more different objects. The best known are drawn in reversible perspective (p. 628). Under steady scrutiny such a figure seems to change back and forth repeatedly. The oscillation can be controlled to some extent by directing the eyes to a part of the figure that you wish to have protrude. If no control is attempted, the rate of oscillation is very variable. At first one appearance may remain steady for many seconds or even for minutes, but after the changes have once begun they recur more and more rapidly during steady exposure of the eyes to the figure. After a rest they may commence slowly again. Usually one of the alternative appearances (phases) predominates over the others in total time of appearance. Bills (1931), after teaching O how to control the appearance of such a figure, directed him to shift back and forth as fast as possible, and secured an average of 72 phases per min. when O was fresh, decreasing to 60 phases per min. after 5 min. of steady effort.

Similar oscillations occur in viewing a *dot figure*, though the number of phases (different groupings) is not limited by any means to two. The rate of oscillation varies, and in some counts averages 20–30 phases per min. (p. 627).

Retinal rivalry (p. 573) is the most striking of all these varieties of oscillation. It is a very special kind of oscillation, depending on the particular physiology of the binocular apparatus.

None of the peculiar forms of shifting that have just been mentioned is to be identified with the ordinary shifting of attention. The following fact can easily be observed: while one of the phases is holding steady, attention may wander entirely away from the stimulus figure. Such wandering of attention does not force any change in the appearance of the figure.   The shifts in binocular rivalry or in viewing ambiguous figures are therefore not mere shifts of attention.

Fluctuation of attention.   The aurist Urbantschitsch (1875), in using the watch test for hearing, noticed that, when held at such a distance as to be barely heard, the watch did not remain steadily audible but "went out" and "came back" periodically.   Similar oscillations in attending to faint visual and tactile stimuli were soon observed, and the phenomenon received the name of fluctuation of attention.   If we think of attention as waxing and waning, rising and falling in an "attention

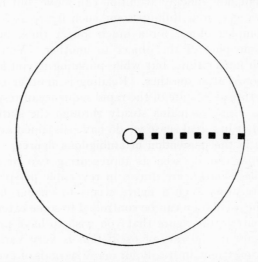

Fig. 226.   A Masson disk which when rotated gives a series of gray rings, fainter and fainter ones from the center out to the rim.   O selects a barely perceptible ring and fixates it steadily.   It disappears and reappears repeatedly.

wave," a barely perceptible stimulus will be sensed at the crest but not in the trough of the wave.

Instead of the watch an audiometer can be used for better control of the faint sounds.   In vision a stimulus is barely perceptible either when it is very small in area (as a black point on a white surface seen from a distance) or when it differs very little in brightness from its background.   The latter condition is obtained by laying a pale gray wash on part of a white surface, or by throwing a little extra light on a portion of an otherwise uniformly illuminated surface, or, conveniently, by using the color wheel.   As cutaneous stimuli, weak electric currents or light corks resting on the skin have been most used.   For critical notes on the history see Freiberg (1937 a, b).

Rate of fluctuation.   This varies widely from one individual to another.   One individual's average time for the complete "wave," including both the positive phase (when the stimulus is perceived) and the negative phase, was only 3 sec. (Slaughter, 1901), while another individual in the same laboratory gave an average as long as 26 sec. (Taylor, 1901). The typical time is about 8–10 sec. The rate is far from constant even for the same individual, as can be seen in the following continuous series of wave lengths obtained by Marbe (1893) from an O watching a small black spot on a white ground. Time in sec.:

17,4,14,3,9,8,6,11,13,9,8,13,6,7,8,7,9,19,12,4,11,3,10,10

The positive and negative phases vary irregularly, as seen in the following continuous series from Eckener (1893):

Positive phases	2.4	4.0	4.0	2.9	3.7	8.1
Negative phases	6.8	0.6	4.1	5.2	4.3	11.5

An experiment of Wiersma (1901) revealed one definite factor in determining the relative duration of the positive and negative phases. He held a watch sometimes so far from O's ear that it could scarcely ever be heard; sometimes so near that it was heard most of the time; and at several intermediate distances. Each test lasted 300 sec., and the table below shows the total time during which the watch was heard.

Time audible

Relative intensity of the stimulus	*Subject H.*	*Subject W.*
1	102 sec	126 sec
1.2	164	213
1.5	190	221
1.8	226	245
2.3	257	283
3	284	299

The duration of the positive phases increased with the strength of the stimulus. Exactly similar results were obtained with visual and auditory stimuli.

In very general terms, these fluctuations are explained by supposing that the whole receptive apparatus from sense organ to brain must be functioning perfectly in order to perceive a very weak stimulus. Any momentary lapse in efficiency interrupts the sensation. Of the different parts of the receptive apparatus, the sensory nerve is least likely to fluctuate in efficiency. The locus of the fluctuations may be the sense organ or the brain or both. One possible factor has been exploited by one investigator, and another by another.

Muscular unsteadiness. For the ear to have maximum receptivity for the ticking of a watch, the tympanic membrane needs perhaps (see p. 538) to be held at exactly the right tension by the little muscles of the middle ear; and if these muscles should relax periodically the sound would fail to register. But the importance of this factor was soon discounted when Urbantschitsch (1875) found that persons whose tympanic membrane had been removed still had typical fluctuations in listening to the ticking of a watch. Similarly, while unsteadiness of the ciliary muscle that controls the lens of the eye might conceivably be the cause of visual fluctuations, the importance of this factor was disproved by the finding (Pace, 1902; Slaughter, 1901; Ferree, 1906) that the fluctuations still occur when the ciliary muscle is paralyzed by atropin, and even in patients whose lenses have been removed.

In the case of touch, however, experiments with adequately controlled application of the stimulus show no fluctuation (Freiberg, 1937 a), so that the fluctuations reported in less precise work are probably due to the rapid adaptation characteristic of this sense, bringing on the negative phase, along with movements changing the stimulus to fresh receptors and so restoring the sensation.

Retinal adaptation. A rather probable factor in visual fluctuations is the "fatigue" of any part of the retina that is exposed to continued stimulation (p. 547). A steadily fixated pattern of light and dark fades out. The best indicator of this retinal adaptation is the negative afterimage which appears when the stimulus pattern is replaced by a plain gray field. Pace (1902) used this indicator. O gazed at a faint stripe of light which disappeared and reappeared periodically, and E removed the objective stripe at different phases of the fluctuation. A negative afterimage appeared if the objective stripe was removed at the beginning of the negative phase, but not if it was removed at the beginning of the positive phase. Retinal adaptation was therefore present at the beginning of the negative phase. The positive phase is a time of progressive adaptation and the negative phase a time of recovery. This conception of the matter was greatly strengthened by the more elaborate experiments of Ferree (1906, 1913) which revealed a thoroughgoing parallelism between the conditions favoring fluctuation and adaptation.

There are two good reasons against accepting adaptation of the sense organs as a complete explanation. (1) The auditory fluctuations cannot be so explained, since peripheral adaptation or fatigue is almost absent from the ear. (2) In the case of the eye, adaptation explains only the fading of the sensation, not its reappearance. How can the retina recover from its adaptation? The answer is that stimulation must change in order to wipe out adaptation.

Eye movements. There is one sure way of changing the retinal stimulation even while the external situation remains unchanged: simply move the eyes. As soon as they change their fixation point, the stimulus pattern falls on another part of the retina, and probably on a part not adapted to that particular pattern of light and shade. With a few successive eye movements the retina is usually left in a fairly uniform state all over and so is ready to take up any pattern of stimulation.

Some evidence that eye movements do contribute to the reappearance of a weak visual stimulus is furnished by Guilford's experiment (1927) which recorded eye movements and fluctuations simultaneously. While O was watching a faint square patch of light on a black ground, his eye movements were photographed, and his finger movements, signaling the disappearance and reappearance of the patch, were recorded on the same film. Examination of the records showed that eye movements were not confined to any single phase of the fluctuation, but they were most frequent just before the reappearance of the patch, and least frequent just before its disappearance. Relatively steady fixation during the positive phase favors adaptation and disappearance, and eye movements during the negative phase favor recovery and reappearance.

Central factors. A companion experiment by the same author indicates that adaptation may occur in the visual area of the cortex, as well as in the retina, and that cortical adaptation plays a part in the fluctuation. When O signaled the disappearance of the patch of light, the apparatus did one of three things with the stimulus:

1. The stimulus remained unchanged. The same part as before, in both retina and visual area, continued to be stimulated (until eye movement occurred). O signaled reappearance after 10–12 sec., the usual duration of his negative phase.

2. The stimulus was instantaneously shifted to another part of the retina. A fresh part of both retina and visual area was thus stimulated. O signaled reappearance in about 1 sec.

3. The stimulus was instantaneously shifted to the corresponding part of the other retina. A fresh bit of retina was thus stimulated, but the same part of the visual area as before was presumably affected, because of the projection of corresponding points of both retinas upon the same cortical point. O signaled reappearance in about 3 sec.

The comparatively slow reappearance in the last condition can probably be laid to some kind of cerebral adaptation.

Auditory fluctuations are the least explained. Their genuineness is reaffirmed by careful experiments with modern sound-producing apparatus. No appeal can be made to auditory adaptation which apparently does not exist, and muscular movements are apparently not a factor. Subjective sensation (tinnitus) makes the observations difficult and may be an important factor in producing the fluctuations (Freiberg, 1937 b).

Possible circulatory factor. The blood pressure and with it the blood supply to the brain are subject to a slight, periodic fluctuation sometimes called the Traube-Hering wave. It can be seen in a plethysmographic tracing from the arm (p. 268). Its period, while somewhat variable, agrees on the average with that of the still more variable "attention wave," and this agreement raised the suspicion that fluctuations of attention depended on these slight changes in blood pressure which might affect the efficiency of the brain. Early experimenters (Bonser, 1903) on recording the two waves simultaneously found what appeared like fair correspondence, phase by phase. Later critical examination showed so many exceptions as rather to spoil the rule. A large number of such simultaneous records were examined by Griffitts & Gordon (1924), who kept tally of the appearances and disappearances of a faint visual stimulus occurring at different phases of the Traube-Hering wave. They occurred almost impartially, though there was a slight (and statistically reliable) preponderance of reappearances during the rise of the Traube-Hering wave and a slight preponderance of disappearances during its crest. During its fall and trough there was no such preponderance. It is difficult to see any physiological reason for such a distribution, but the data are consistent with the conclusion that changes in brain circulation have a little, though not much, to do with the fluctuations which we have been considering.

Fluctuations of efficiency in continuous work. Approaching the question of oscillations from quite a different angle, students of work and fatigue have noticed momentary lapses scattered through the performance of uniform tasks. O pauses an instant now and then, and seems to be blocked or inhibited. An experiment on this matter of "blocking" (Bills, 1931) called for a rapid series of easy responses, such as naming 6 colors (repeated in irregular order in an unlimited series of little squares), substitution of designated letters for 6 digits (which were presented in a long series), and alternately adding and subtracting 3 from a long series of numbers. O responded orally, and E pressed a key as each response was heard, thus recording the time on a kymograph, but with some chance of error, since it is impossible to keep exact pace with a rapid and irregular series of sounds. A "block" was defined as an interval between two successive responses that was at least twice as great as O's average interval during the same minute of work.

There is no doubt of the reality of such blocks. The work proceeds at top speed for a time and then there is a gap. This state of affairs can be seen in a tapping record as well as anywhere. The gaps do not occur with rhythmical regularity, though one is prone to get that impression from inspection of the records. Bills gives 17 sec. as the average time between blocks, but he finds that individuals give averages all the way from 10–30 sec., and that practice decreases and fatigue increases the frequency of the blocks. Even the same individual in the same short section of his work may vary widely both in the length of the blocks and in the time between them.

The phenomenon of blocking may be akin to what we have called "ordinary shifting of attention." When the performance of a task demands a precise adjustment of some complex cerebral mechanism, any distraction or shift of interest to something outside the task will disturb this delicate adjustment and interrupt the performance.

In a similar experiment (Sterzinger, 1924) the tasks were more difficult and there were numerous lapses from perfect performance. O had before him a sheet containing a long series of letters and letter groups, such as:

abc fg h lnm nob ra b edif glo r ua wa amn o lo gm no e l
bb ban ac ha ho u es ab c d n erah fgh abc pm n ofm n o opp el i
u k xp pfab cam nob s fgh sgli b emno fan nix bw a bc abc
sal t ra o eo n u s e fgh ra bg fl abc cid ah a abc csa ab c

Three tasks, first learned separately, were then to be carried along together:

1. Cancel every letter that stands alone and between two vowels.
2. Cancel every letter that is identical with the one just before it.
3. Cancel every group of two letters that immediately follows another group of two.

O chose his own speed but was not allowed to retrace his steps. There were many errors of omission and they seemed to Sterzinger to show some periodicity. The successful responses seemed to occur in consecutive "runs" more than would be expected by chance. Some Os tended to miss 1 in every 3, others 1 in every 4, as if they had a habit of relaxing after just so many attentive acts.

Are these fluctuations properly called fluctuations of attention? When one ceases to attend to an object it does not ordinarily lapse altogether from the field of awareness, as the faint stimulus does in the negative phase of fluctuation, or as, in the rivalry experiment, the stimulus applied to one retina disappears when the stimulus applied to the corresponding part of the other retina emerges into view. The shifts in rivalry and fluctuation are more than shifts from the focus to the margin of attention—or from clearness to unclearness. They are shifts from awareness to unawareness.

It is also true that attention can shift in the ordinary way to and from a faint stimulus while it remains in the positive phase of fluctuation. One of Guilford's subjects reported after an experiment in watching a faint light:

I noticed during the first part of the experiment when the stimulus was present in the field, that I could direct my attention variously without in any way affecting the stimulus. I directed my attention to the biting-board, to the head-rest, to the light that seems to come in from the left side of the room, which I never noticed before. In spite of the fact that they seized my attention the stimulus persisted. . . . After it has disappeared I can, on the contrary, attend away from all those things and direct my whole efforts to the expecting and waiting for the stimulus, but to no avail.

In retinal rivalry there is a competition of the right and left eye stimuli for the subject's response; and in watching ambiguous figures there is a similar competition, in this way: the ambiguous figure is an adequate stimulus for either of two responses, for seeing the figure in either of two different ways. These responses are mutually exclusive; both cannot be executed at the same time. The same sort of competition is found between certain reflexes (Sherrington, 1906). Simultaneous scratching by both hind legs is impossible if the animal is standing, for one hind leg supports the trunk while the other is scratching. If irritating stimuli are applied simultaneously to both flanks, what happens is that one leg scratches for a time, then the other, and so on alternately. This is the result in the "spinal dog"; an intact dog with brain control of his spinal cord has a greater variety of responses at command and behaves less predictably. The competition between spinal reflexes is closely akin to that in retinal rivalry; that occurring in watching ambiguous figures is somewhat more complex, because there are more than two alternative ways of seeing such a figure.

In ordinary shifting of attention about a scene, as also in ordinary shifting of motor response from one movement to another, there is competition between alternative responses, but the behavior is more complex and more fluid than in rivalry, because the alternatives are more numerous and are not mutually exclusive in the full sense.

Two main facts—at least two—that come to light in the studies of attention are of great importance in understanding the dynamics of behavior: (1) the movement of attention, typified by shifts; and (2) the breadth of the field of simultaneous activity—a breadth which is genuine even though, as brought out by studying span and distraction, it is not unlimited in extent.

DISTRACTION

The principle of an experiment on distraction is simple: while an assigned task is being performed, irrelevant stimuli, "distractors," are introduced, so as to see whether the performance is impaired in any respect. O may be warned beforehand to pay no attention to the distractors, or they may take him by surprise. In either case he soon catches the point: he has nothing to do with the distractors except to neglect them. E is playing a game with him, trying to distract him, and he determines not to be distracted.

A distractor must not be such as would necessarily interfere with the performance. If the task calls for comparing two tones, extraneous sounds would be more than distractors since they would mask the tones. Visual distractors would be used in such a case. When the task demands use of the eyes, auditory distractors are usually employed.

With young adults, easily put on their mettle, the result of such an experiment is usually that the distractors do not distract, except perhaps for a short time while O is becoming adjusted to the situation. A convincing experiment of this sort is that of Hovey (1928). A class of college sophomores was divided into two matched groups on the basis of their scores in one Form of the Army Alpha test. Six weeks later the control group took another Form of Army Alpha under normal conditions, while the experimental group took it under conditions of auditory and visual distraction. The distraction was planned to be severe. Seven electric bells of different tones sounded intermittently from different parts of the room; besides, there were four efficient buzzers, two organ pipes and three whistles, a circular metal saw that was struck from time to time, and a phonograph playing lively music. A spotlight in the rear of the hall flashed continually here and there though not into the subjects' eyes, and E's accomplices entered noisily and strangely garbed, carrying strange pieces of apparatus. The conditions were disagreeable and fatiguing for the experimental group, but their test scores were scarcely affected. They did almost, not quite, as well as their mates in the control group. On the average the two groups, which had been equal in the first test, made the following scores in the second test:

Control group, working under normal conditions	137.6
Experimental group, working under distraction	133.9
Apparent loss through distraction	3.7

Whether an individual shall be stimulated or inhibited by such a distractor as a phonograph record of dance music may depend on his own attitude. If he is led to believe that the music will facilitate his work, he is likely to show a gain—a loss if the contrary belief is instilled into him (Baker, 1937).

How distraction is overcome. A reasonable supposition is that more energy must be thrown into the work in order to overcome the distraction. Morgan (1916) tested this hypothesis by recording the force of O's finger movements in performing a task somewhat like typewriting. O worked on a row of 10 numbered keys. The apparatus exposed a single letter which O translated into a number in accordance with a code. O struck the key labeled with this number and the apparatus immediately exposed another letter to be decoded and struck; and so on indefinitely. Without O's knowledge, the force with which he struck the key was recorded. A pneumograph about his chest furnished a breathing record. O was alone in the room, but E watched his behavior through a peekhole. When O had worked for a time in isolated quiet, bells, buzzers and phonograph records began to sound from all parts of the room. The distraction continued for 10 min. and was followed by 10 min. of quiet. Over 20 Os went through this experiment with results which differed in detail but agreed in important respects:

1. Having received only a little preliminary practice in the performance, O showed progressive improvement throughout the experiment.

2. At the onset of noise, there was some slowing of the work.

3. Within a very few minutes O regained his former speed and went on to further improvement.

4. When the noise ceased there was no sudden improvement, but often a momentary slump. The cessation of a noise to which O had become adjusted acted like a distraction. This fact is more clearly brought out by Ford (1929) who repeated the experiment with analysis of the results moment by moment.

5. As the quiet continued, there was further improvement in performance.

6. The force with which O struck the keys decreased during the first quiet period, increased sharply at the onset of noise, remained strong during the noise, and fell to a low level at the cessation of the noise.

7. The breathing record, along with E's peekhole observations, showed speech activity on O's part, especially during noise. The numbers and letters with which he was working were often spoken aloud.

We see here a genuine overcoming of distraction, along with increased muscular energy put into the work. Apparently it is almost instinctive to throw additional muscular force into an activity—the finger movement in this case—that is performed under distraction. The speaking of the numbers and letters was less instinctive, more like a device of O to reinforce the disturbed activity. In the same way one may add a column of numbers silently when all is quiet but feel compelled to speak or whisper the numbers if the place is noisy. Whether the extra muscular energy actually overcomes the distraction, and if so how, are questions on which opinions differ. The present author thinks of the matter in terms of a competition of different action systems for control of the organism; the bigger, more muscular activity presumably has an advantage.

Work in Noise and Quiet

(*Morgan, 1916*)

	Quiet.........				Noise.....			Quiet....	
Hundreds of reactions	1st	2nd	3rd	4th	5th	6th	7th	8th	9th
Time per reaction in seconds	4.9	4.5	4.1	4.0	4.8	3.6	3.5	3.6	3.4
Finger pressure in grams	293	197	150	115	300	302	235	180	165
Inspiration fraction (before work, .44)	.34	.30	.28	.28	.31	.25	.23	.30	.30

The "inspiration fraction" is the time occupied in inspiration expressed as a fraction of the complete breathing cycle (p. 262). In quiet breathing inspiration takes 40–45 percent of the time, as illustrated by the inspiration fraction of .44 before work in this table. In speaking aloud it goes down to .16, inspiration being quick and expiration slow because the breath is paid out gradually in producing voice. The table gives the record of one O which illustrates all the points made in the text. The average of 20 other Os shows the same changes.

To say that distraction is overcome by putting more energy into the work is not the whole story. If work under the same distraction is continued day after day, a second adjustment takes place and output is maintained under distraction *without* the consumption of extra energy. Harmon (1933) measured the energy consumed in terms of metabolic rate as determined by a respiration apparatus. The work was adding and the distractor was a phonograph record taken in a noisy office. For the first few days the metabolic rate was higher during noise, but after about 7 days of work under the constant distraction, 20 min. per day, the metabolic rate was the same during noise and quiet.

Distractions that are not overcome. In experiments such as have just been described, O is determined not to be distracted and is willing to put all the energy necessary into the work. In everyday life the determination to work is often not so strong. A novel stimulus will awaken curiosity and "time out" will be taken to investigate, just as Pavlov's dog (p. 96) responded to a distracting stimulus by the "investigatory reflex" and temporarily lost his conditioned response. In an experiment everything that E does is part of the game, while in ordinary life a similar distraction might make us angry; and anger is a worse distraction than noise. The intrinsic interest of bells and buzzers, and even of many phonograph records, is quite moderate; possibly something really interesting would really distract.

Following this last lead, Weber (1929) used for distractors good music and humorous anecdotes; and to avoid adaptation he set tasks calling for only a minute or two of intense mental activity: adding, cancelling, memorizing, defining, solving a riddle. All of the 16 Os showed a decrement of output (10–50 percent) and all reported a subjective sense of being at times distracted. Sometimes the distractor was a more or less disturbing background, and sometimes it broke in and became the center of interest, O forgetting his work and giving himself up to the music or story. At other times a background of music was felt to facilitate the work.

The subjective experience of overcoming a distraction, as reported by Weber's Os, consisted either in warding off the distractor or in positively concentrating on the work. The distractor could sometimes be warded off by treating it as valueless and ridiculous—even when it was attractive in itself—and by taking care not to notice the meaning of the story or the swing of the music. Some Os spoke of a sort of shutting of one's ears internally and so shutting out the distractor. Positive concentration consisted sometimes in hastening the tempo or intensity of work, sometimes in thinking aloud. The visible behavior during distraction, as recorded by E, included:

1. A general increase in muscular tension.

2. Increased energy of the work movements: loud speaking, vigorous hand movements, eyes glued to the work or fixed on vacancy, postures of concentration such as bending forward and holding the head in the hands.

3. Movements of defense or avoidance: shaking the head, shutting the eyes, covering the eyes with the hand, agitation of the shoulders, turning the face to the wall. These defense movements were so violent, sometimes, as to be "worse than the disease." O used up his energy

in warding off the distractor and had none left for the work. Some Os got into a momentary condition of nervous restlessness in which they could not work, or into a state of vacancy and complete inhibition.

Sensory acuity in relation to attention and distraction. One would expect better perception of weak stimuli, and a lowered stimulus threshold, when attention is closely directed to the stimulus than otherwise. The results of various experiments on this general problem have been divergent, probably because O is sometimes really distracted and sometimes keyed up by the distractor. The conditions in Newhall's experiment (1923) are free from this ambiguity because he used no distractor but depended on a fore-signal such as is used in reaction time work (p. 298) to vary O's readiness for the weak tactile stimulus. Sometimes there was no ready signal; O would then be least ready. Sometimes the ready signal allowed 1.7 sec. for getting ready; and sometimes O could tell *exactly* when the weak tactile stimulus was coming by watching a moving pointer which reached a certain mark just as the tactile stimulus was applied. This tactile stimulus was weak pressure on one finger. In a random half of the trials no pressure was applied. O's job was to report whether the stimulus had or had not been given. Combining the data from 2 Os, we have a table showing clearly that the greater the readiness (attention), the better the work. The closer the attention, the better the discrimination between faint stimulus and no stimulus. Similar results were obtained with weak visual stimuli.

PERCEPTION OF WEAK PRESSURE ON THE FINGER
(*Newhall, 1923*)

	Percent of pressure stimuli reported as felt	Percent of cases of no stimulus reported as felt	Net score
Condition I: no preliminary signal	52	8	44
Condition II: signal 1.7 sec. before the stimulus	76	7	69
Condition III: moving pointer indicating exact moment of stimulation	86	6	80

DOING TWO THINGS AT ONCE

The above is a noncommittal title for a line of investigation that often goes under the name, *division of attention*. Whether there is actually a division of attention in doing two things at once is a question which we will not try to answer at the outset. Division of attention would mean a simultaneous focusing upon two separate activities. If one of them is automatic and goes forward smoothly without conscious control, no division of attention is required. If both are combined into a single integrated performance, no division of attention is required. If two activities, while carried on simultaneously in a loose sense, are kept going by rapid shifting of attention from one to the other and back again, there is in the strict sense no division of attention. Whether or not the concept of attention can be given a fully scientific definition, certainly a problem of great importance in psychological dynamics is raised by the fact that the individual sometimes does two or more things at once.

We might better say that he always does more than one thing at once. Apart from internal activities of the glands and smooth muscles, he practically always has activity going on in his skeletal muscles and sense organs. He may be walking, holding something under his left arm, gesturing with his right hand, while all the time seeing and hearing. It is a fair question whether these simultaneous streams of activity run along independently or whether they are all interdependent parts of a single total activity.

Interaction between simultaneous performances. Experiments on this matter began as early as 1887, when Paulhan found himself able to recite one familiar poem orally, while writing another. Sometimes a word that was being recited would be written also, but on the whole the interference was rather slight. Without interrupting the flow of the oral recitation he could quickly rehearse the next line to be written and write that line with no further attention. He could recite a poem while performing very simple multiplication, and neither operation was retarded by the simultaneous execution of the other. An operation offering any difficulty was retarded even by so automatic a simultaneous performance as the recitation of a familiar poem.

In an experiment of Binet (1890) one of the simultaneous performances was the rhythmical squeezing of a rubber bulb held in the hand. The bulb was connected by tubing with a tambour which recorded the movements on a smoked drum. The simplest task was to give one squeeze a second in time with a metronome; another was to squeeze twice at each beat of the metronome; another, to squeeze 3 times at each beat. When O had obtained some facility in one of these motor performances, he was asked to continue it while reading aloud or doing mental arithmetic. Unless both tasks were very easy there was some interference and both were disturbed.

In another experiment, O did no reading or mental arithmetic, but squeezed two bulbs, the one in the right hand 5 times, the one in the left hand twice, at each beat of the metronome. Aside from the general difficulty of such a combination, what impressed Binet as specially significant was the way one hand would drag the other into its own rhythm. The hand that was supposed to squeeze in groups of 2 began to make groups of 3 or 4. In this connection Binet alludes to parlor games such as rubbing the stomach with a circular movement of one hand while patting the top of the head with the other hand. When, on the contrary, both hands make the same movement or cooperate toward the same result, there is mutual facilitation rather than interference.

These results were confirmed by Jastrow & Cairnes (1891–92) who added the suggestive fact, found with one subject only, that tapping at a rapid rate actually hastened the simultaneous adding or reading.

Does steady muscular contraction facilitate mental work? In solving a difficult problem, performing a novel task, or getting ready for any important act, one almost inevitably tenses the muscles (p. 329; Freeman, 1934). Is this tension of any positive value or is it merely an overflow of energy into primitive channels? We cannot answer this question by getting O into a thoroughly relaxed condition and then putting him to work, for either he stays relaxed and does not work or he starts to work and loses his relaxation (Jacobson, 1929). Nor can we hope for a clear answer from experiments in which O's normal condition is compared with one of increased tension induced by squeezing a dynamometer or pushing against a pedal; for there is a good chance that O normally uses his own optimal degree of tension. However, when Bills tried the experiment (1927) on college students, he obtained positive results. During the tense condition, O had a dynamometer in each hand and exerted a steady moderate pressure on both. During the relaxed condition his hands rested easily in his lap. In both conditions he memorized, added, or read disconnected letters, as rapidly as possible. The output in adding, for example, was 10 percent greater in the tense than in the relaxed condition. The difference was statistically reliable for the experiment as a whole and appeared in most of the individuals tested. Other investigators (Zartman & Cason, 1934; Block, 1936) have obtained much less uniform results. Block tested the same Os many times and found little consistency; an O who did better on one day with a fairly strong squeeze on the dynamometers would do better another day with a weak squeeze or none at all. It did not seem possible to determine an optimum tension for each individual, and it certainly was not true that the greater the tension the better the mental work. We noticed on p. 705 that O's attitude was a factor in a distraction experiment; probably the same is true here too.

Efficiency of double performances. Usually one or both of two simultaneous performances show some impairment. In a tachistoscope experiment the span of apprehension for number of dots was diminished by including in the exposure field other objects to be observed (Lorenz, 1912). When a free association test (p. 354) was combined with a simultaneous counting task, the associative responses tended toward the relatively low level of rhyming and word completion (as "Black— Board"), responses to the sound rather than the meaning of the stimulus words (Speich, 1927). An exception was found by Mitchell (1914):

one task was the comparison of two weights lifted successively by the hand; the other was the counting of a series of 1–6 clicks. The weights were even better judged when the clicks were given, and the counting was only a little disturbed. In order to count the clicks, O was inclined to judge the weights very promptly and this promptness was apparently an advantage. In all these cases, though the stimuli were simultaneous, the essential (cognitive) responses may have been successive.

In some occupations, as that of the telephone operator, it is necessary to do two or more things at once, or to switch rapidly back and forth between two or more performances. Vocational tests for ability to do this sort of thing have been tried, as by Sterzinger (1928). A story is read to O while he is adding columns of one-place numbers. The story contains 36 items and is read in 90 sec. O then stops adding and writes down all he remembers of the story. Control tests are made with adding alone, and with the story alone, so that O's score in the double and single performances can be compared. One O scored as follows:

(A) Numbers correctly added, single task   52
(B)   "   "   " , double task   43 = 83% of A
(C) Items of story recalled, single task   31
(D) "   "   "   " , double task   10 = 32% of C

The 83% and 32% must somehow be combined into a single index of efficiency in doing two things at once. The arithmetical mean of the two percents will not serve. For suppose O to be utterly unable to keep the two performances going. Let him become wholly absorbed in the story and forget to add; in this way he might score 100% in the story and zero in adding. The arithmetical mean would give him 50%, whereas he should be marked zero in combining the two activities, which is what we are trying to measure. This difficulty is overcome by taking the geometrical mean of the two percents, instead of the arithmetical. So computed, the index for the O whose data are given above is $\sqrt{.83 \times .32} = .52$. The index for Sterzinger's 26 Os ranged from .30 to .90, with a group average of about .60. Using similar tests on ten-year-old boys, Dambach (1929) obtained some indices of over 1.00, at least one of the tasks being better done in combination than alone.

Can two attentive acts be done at the same instant? This question has not been squarely met in the experiments so far described, since the possibility of rapid shifting between the tasks has not been excluded. Even when the exposure is very brief the sensory and memory after-images may make such a shift possible. If the stimuli are weak as well as brief, use of the afterimages will be minimized. In one experiment (Mager, 1920; Pauli, 1924) weak pressure was applied to one finger of each hand, and O had to say which pressure was stronger; at the same instant there was a brief visual exposure of 3–6 short lines to be counted. Either task was so easy that, when presented alone, it gave nearly 100 percent of correct responses; but, when the two tasks were presented simultaneously,

both were correct in	12% of cases
one was correct in	60% of cases
neither was correct in	28% of cases

The conclusion is that simultaneous performance of two attentive acts of cognition did not often if ever occur.

Besides the frequently reported alternation between two tasks which are being done "at once," there is sometimes the possibility of combining them into a single coordinated performance, and when this can be done it is the most successful and agreeable way of handling the problem (Westphal, 1911; Schorn, 1928).

CHAPTER XXVIII

READING

O NE reason for the prominence of reading as a field for experimental psychology is to be found in the social and educational importance of reading. A relatively late acquisition of the race, only now becoming general throughout the world's population, it has great potential value for individual welfare and group solidarity. To discover the conditions of easy and efficient reading is a task properly assigned to psychology. However simple and matter-of-course it may appear to one who has mastered it, reading is a highly elaborate and skillful performance not at all easy to analyze.

In its historical development reading had first to deal with picture writing such as is found very commonly among tribes that have no written language in the modern sense. From the examples, p. 714, it is clear that one had to learn to read picture writing. It is somewhat conventionalized and symbolic, though it symbolizes not words, but things and facts. Written by an Indian speaking one language it could be read by one speaking quite a different language, if only he knew how to read this sort of writing.

Picture writing was developed to an extraordinary extent by the ancient Egyptians and Chinese. The hieroglyphic writing finally died out in competition with the later alphabetic writing of the Mediterranean region, but the Chinese system still persists in a highly conventionalized form. Most of the Chinese characters now bear no obvious resemblance to the objects or ideas which they symbolize; but that they still represent objects rather than speech sounds is clear from the fact that the same character means the same object in the various dialects. Readers from different parts of China read the same page with very different spoken words and yet all get the same meaning.

In relatively a few countries—Egypt, Babylonia, China, Yucatan, Peru—picture writing developed into syllabic writing. A picture representing an object that had a monosyllabic name came to represent that syllable; two pictures combined stood for a two-syllable word; and with a sufficient assortment of syllables the whole written language could become syllabic, though this seems not to have occurred, object symbols persisting along with the syllabic symbols.

The shift from object symbols to syllable symbols was a decided jump; but a still bigger jump was from syllabic writing to the use of an alphabet. To look at all the alphabets now used in different parts of the world, one would think that several independent alphabets must have been invented, but the authorities tell us that only one original alphabet has ever appeared and that all the varieties are derived from that one, which originated among the Semitic peoples about 1,000 B.C.

Fig. 227. (Mallery, 1893.) Indian picture writing. In time of war between two tribes of Indians in Maine, in the early days, the scouts of one tribe leave a notice for their main body of warriors in the form of a piece of birch bark fastened to a tree, inscribed as follows: Ten canoeists of the "Fish" tribe (the enemy) have gone down a certain lake towards its outlet, the lake being identified by a map.

(See Encyclopedia Britannica under "Alphabet" for some of the variations.)

If we query why alphabetic writing was a more difficult achievement than syllabic writing, the answer is that the analysis of a word into syllables is no great task, while the elementary speech sounds that make up a syllable are very closely combined. Some of them cannot be pronounced separately. Besides, the spelling of a word is only a rough analysis of the pronunciation. A spoken word is not actually broken up into the speech sounds symbolized by the letters. The spelling catches the high points, that is all.

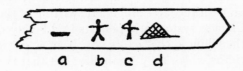

Fig. 228. (Mallery, 1893.) Indian Picture writing from Alaska. Fishermen have left their boat, *a*, and taken refuge in the shelter, *d*, where they have nothing (*b*, gesture sign for nothing) to eat (*c*, gesture sign for eating). This message, inscribed on a stick pointing the way to the shelter, is left on the shore in the hope of obtaining relief.

The facility with which a bright child learns to read is surprising in view of the obvious difficulties involved in alphabetic writing:

1. The written or printed symbols are two stages removed from their meaning. They represent speech sounds which in turn stand for objects.

2. The alphabet is phonetically very imperfect, even with "reformed spelling."

3. Instead of looking freely about the page as in the ordinary use of the eyes, one must regiment the eye movements so that they shall move along the lines of print.

Pioneer studies.   Experiments on reading started about 1880 and within a few years several fundamental facts were brought to light. Javal (1878) by watching the reader's eyes, found that they moved along the lines not with a smooth, steady movement, but in a series of jumps or "saccades" separated by fixation pauses.   Cattell (1885, 1886) showed by two lines of evidence that a familiar word is read "as a whole" and not by spelling out its letters: (1) in reaction time experiments, the response of naming a short word is fully as quick as that of naming a

心   "Heart," mind

理   "Ways"

學   "Study"

FIG. 229.   The Chinese equivalent of "Psychology."   It consists of three characters and is to be read downward, literally, "heart-ways study."

single letter; (2) in tachistoscope experiments, the span of apprehension for letters combined in words is very much greater than for unconnected letters.   The results of Javal and of Cattell were confirmed in the comprehensive study of Erdmann & Dodge (1898) who further showed that the fixation pauses are the time of effective exposure and stimulation of the eyes, the eye movements in reading being simply quick jumps from one fixation to the next.   These surprising results, tending to revolutionize the whole theory of reading, led to many further experiments which we shall not attempt to present in historical perspective.

SPEED OF READING

Something can be learned even from so simple an experiment as that of taking the time required to cover a known quantity of reading matter. The mere fact that easy material is read more rapidly than difficult proves at once that the limiting factors in speed of reading are to be sought, largely at least, in the process of comprehension rather than in the peripheral processes of retinal stimulation and eye movement.

Reading speed differs also with the individual. Huey (1908) measured the speed of 20 university students in reading an interesting novel, with results shown below.

Words Read per Second

(Huey, 1908)

	Group average	Range of individual averages
Oral reading, ordinary rate	3.6	2.2 to 4.7
Oral reading, maximum rate	4.6	2.9 to 6.4
Silent reading, ordinary rate	5.6	2.5 to 9.8

Approximately the same figures have been obtained by other experimenters. Dearborn (1906) found a professor whose average silent reading rate in *Robinson Crusoe* was 11 words per sec. The wide range of educated adults in speed of reading easy material is a challenge. Do the slow ones really know how to read? When college Freshmen are given a battery of reading tests and the slow ones examined individually, it is found that some of them have by no means mastered the technique and that they respond well to special training (Robinson, 1933; Anderson, 1937). Some children, though bright enough, have difficulty with reading and are helped by different forms of training (Gates, 1927; Monroe, 1932). Some do not readily grasp the phonetic values of the letters; some do not readily pick up the left-to-right eye movement; some have developed an emotional antipathy to reading from their early failures. All such cases, presumably, have something to teach regarding the process of reading.

The high speed of reading has important scientific implications. It enables us to rule out certain all-too-easy hypotheses. The most atomistic hypothesis would perhaps regard each letter as the stimulus for an elementary speech movement, so that reading would consist in a chain of such stimulus-response units. So, *p* would be a cue to close the lips, and *a* a cue to open the mouth and vocalize with the larynx. Confronted with the word *pa*, the reader would execute these two movements in succession. In reading aloud he certainly goes through the indicated sequence of movements, but he cannot be executing a series of distinct reactions, for even the speed of oral reading does not allow sufficient time. With visual stimulation we should have to allow a reaction time of at least 150 ms, probably nearer 300 ms (pp. 324, 355) for each letter sounded, so that not over 2 words per sec. could be read orally, instead of an average of 3.6 at the ordinary rate.

Also ruled out is the pure motor theory of silent reading. Oral reading, even when speeded to the maximum, does not reach the rate of silent reading—not by a wide margin in case of rapid readers. Something like telescoping or short-circuiting of the motor processes must take place;

some of the movements of oral speech must be omitted to enable the silent reading to attain such speed.

It might even be—to swing over to the opposite extreme—that silent reading escaped from motor speech altogether, in the skillful reader, and became what it probably was in case of picture writing, where the meaning was obtained directly from the visual characters without any intervening auditory-motor speech. Just as a picture, a gesture, a spoken word, suggests a meaning, why may not the printed word come to suggest its meaning directly instead of by the roundabout route of auditory-motor speech? The hypothesis of "purely visual reading" cannot be fully tested by introspection, because of the very speed of absorbed reading. Some rapid readers say they always hear the words or feel them in the throat, while others can detect only slight traces of such inner speech.

Speech movement a drag upon rapid reading. Being first taught oral reading children carry over some of the speech movements into silent reading, as audible whispering and later as silent lip and tongue movement. There is a chance that these movements, persisting sometimes into adult life, are one cause of slow reading.

SPEED AND EFFICIENCY OF READING WHILE AUTOMATICALLY REPEATING NUMBERS

(*Pintner, 1913*)

	First individual		Second individual	
	Reading time per passage	Ideas reproduced per second of reading time	Reading time per passage	Ideas reproduced per second of reading time
First 20 passages without "counting"	32 sec.	.10	13 sec.	.30
Passages read while "counting"				
first 9	32 "	.07	23 "	.11
second 9	27 "	.10	20 "	.20
third 9	27 "	.09	19 "	.26
fourth 9	31 "	.11	18 "	.26
fifth 9	24 "	.19	15 "	.32
sixth 9	28 "	.16	15 "	.32
seventh 9	28 "	.11	12 "	.39
Final 20 passages without "counting"	26 "	.18	12 "	.40

An experiment of Pintner (1913) throws some light on this question and on the possibility of "visual reading." He required O to read while repeating aloud the numbers, "13, 14, 15, 16, 13, 14, 15, 16" indefinitely. By preliminary practice this "counting" was made automatic so as not to distract the reader but it still prevented any enunciation of the words read. To insure genuine reading O was required after reading a passage to state its substance. Each passage consisted of about 70 words and contained 10 definite ideas to be reproduced. The number reproduced, divided by the time of reading the passage, furnished a measure of reading efficiency. The two Os practiced this performance for a series of days, with results shown in the table on page 717.

"Counting" hampered the reading at first but with practice both Os read more efficiently with the "counting" than they had read under normal conditions, and the final test showed greatly improved efficiency over the initial test, and also showed a decrease in visible lip movements. The evidence seems decisive that reading can go on without articulation of the words read. Secor (1900) had reached the same conclusion from a similar experiment in which whistling and repeating the alphabet were used to prevent articulation of the reading matter. In some cases of "motor" aphasia silent reading is possible. Head (1926) says of one such case, "All power of reading aloud was abolished. . . . There was not the slightest doubt, however, that he understood much of what he read to himself." He could carry out simple printed directions.

Practice directed toward increasing the speed of silent reading has given positive results with school children (Peters, 1917; Gray, 1917; O'Brien, 1921) and even with many college students (Harrelson, 1923). O'Brien's experiment was carried out in 40 schoolrooms in different Illinois towns. Each class was first given standardized reading tests and divided into an experimental and a control group matched in reading proficiency according to the test results. The control group continued their usual reading lessons, while the experimental group devoted all the reading periods to exercises in silent reading. The aim of these exercises, as explained to the children, was to increase the speed of silent reading. Easy and interesting passages were handed out by the teacher who allowed 2–3 min. for the reading and afterward gave a brief oral quiz on the substance of the passage. The ground covered by each child was recorded and a graph constructed showing his progress and motivating him to further efforts. At the end of two months the experiment was brought to a close by applying standardized reading tests. Both groups had gained, but the experimental group, in the grand average of all the 40 classes, had made a net gain of 31 percent in speed, with no loss in comprehension.

Exactly how these children gained cannot be discerned from the results. In some of the classes, the teacher urged the importance of eliminating lip movements, but it made no difference in the results whether this matter was brought to the children's attention or not. Other experimenters (Robinson, 1933) have sought to improve the eye movements of poor readers and have obtained increased speed in silent reading. In all such experiments, O is likely to be well motivated and to be devoting considerable time to an art which he ordinarily neglects. There is probably a good deal of slack to be taken up in his reading skill, and under the conditions of an experiment he takes up some of it, but exactly wherein his improvement lies is an unsettled question (Tinker, 1934).

DIRECT AND INDIRECT VISION IN READING

From the familiar fact that we look directly at anything we wish to see clearly, and from the introspective impression of a smooth sweep of the eyes along the line of print, the old conception of reading supposed that each letter in turn came into the center of clear vision. Then it was discovered (p. 591) that the eye moves in an entirely different way, fixating only a few points in the line and jumping from one fixation point to the next too rapidly to allow of any clear vision during the jump; and it was also found that several letters, or even a long familiar word, could be read from a tachistoscopic exposure too short to allow of more than one fixation. The inference is clear: not all the letters get into foveal vision; some use must be made of indirect vision.

How far out from the fovea can a letter be recognized? One way of attacking this problem is to expose a letter tachistoscopically at a certain distance from the fixation point, O being instructed to read the letter if possible. Ruediger (1907) used an exposure time of only 50 ms. On the pre-exposure field there was a fixation point and on the exposed card was a single letter, either n or u, located either to the right or the left of the fixation point. O could not beat the game by directing his eyes to the right or left of the assigned fixation point, for his guess would be wrong as often as right. The letters were printed from eleven-point type—a detail which it is necessary to specify, since the larger the letter the farther out into indirect vision it can be recognized. (Other specifications: white cards, distant 30 cm from O's eyes, well printed black letters, daylight illumination, pre- and post-exposure fields a dull "black," reflecting about 6% of the light.) After each exposure O was required at least to guess which of the two letters had been shown. A score of 50% right would be mere chance and show zero discrimination of the two letter forms.

READING OF LETTERS IN SLIGHTLY INDIRECT VISION
(*Ruediger, 1907*)

Distance of letter from fixation point, in mm	15	20	25	30	35	40
Same in angular degrees	2.9°	3.8°	4.8°	5.7°	6.7°	7.7°
Percent of right responses (average of 9 subjects)	98	95	90	84	74	66

There was no abrupt transition from distinct to indistinct vision. At a distance of an inch (25 mm) from the fixation point—a distance of 12–15 letters as they ordinarily run—vision is still quite good. In the vertical direction the extent of fairly clear vision is smaller—half or two-thirds of the horizontal extent—but still large enough to include at least two lines above and two below the line of print on which the eyes are fixated. In these measurements, however, the exposed field was bare except for the fixation point and a single letter. The presence of a whole page of letters might make a difference.

Masking of a letter by adjacent letters in indirect vision. Korte (1923) found that a group of letters, in comparison with a single letter, must be brought closer to the fixation point in order to be read. He was using the perimeter method, which consists in moving an object gradually from the periphery toward the center of clear vision, until O is just able to identify the object, maintaining steady fixation throughout. The capitals were read farther out than the lower case letters and some of these farther out than others; w could be read twice as far out as c. Isolated letters were read farther out than words, and the longer a word the closer it must be brought to the fixation point.

It seems strange that a word should need to be brought closer than a single letter. If the single letters can be read, why not the word composed of these letters? The answer is a mutual interference or masking of the letters, in indirect vision. Fixate the central o in each of the following lines, and try to read letters at the sides:

t   o   s

nte   o   hsx

The first and last letters in a group suffer less from masking than the interior letters. At either end, one side of the letter is free from the interference of adjacent letters. This statement can be tested in the following letter groups, the central o being always the fixation point.

o

bom

sbomk

asbomku

easbomkut

geasbomkutc

wgeasbomkutcz

dwgeasbomkutczh

idwgeasbomkutczhv

xidwgeasbomkutczhvp

fxidwgeasbomkutczhvpn

rfxidwgeasbomkutczhvpnj

yrfxidwgeasbomkutczhvpnjl

It is well to have some one watching your eyes in this experiment, to correct you when your eyes inadvertently shift their fixation to the point of momentary attention.

How much can be read in a single fixation? Hold the eyes fixed on the first letter in a line of print and discover how far into the line you can see the words distinctly, and what impression you get of words still farther to the right. You can perhaps see one long word or three short ones distinctly and beyond that you get some impression of the length of the next word or two, with perhaps a letter or two standing out. The experiment is rather difficult because of the inclination just mentioned to shift the eyes. Hamilton (1907) avoided this source of error by use of the tachistoscope. He exposed a whole line of print for too short a

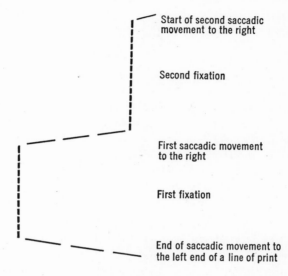

Start of second saccadic movement to the right

Second fixation

First saccadic movement to the right

First fixation

End of saccadic movement to the left end of a line of print

FIG. 230. Key diagram for photographic records of eye movement in reading. The records are to be read upward because the film or plate on which the movement was photographed moved downward. In the diagram, the eye arrives at the left end of a line of print, fixates there, makes a quick movement to the right and fixates there, and just starts another saccadic movement to the right. The recording light is supposed to be interrupted 100 times a second so as to leave dots by which the time occupied in each fixation and movement can be measured. For the method of recording, see p. 578.

time to allow of more than one fixation. O's task was to read from the left as far as possible and to report what he could regarding the rest of the line. Typically, he read the first word or two correctly and beyond that made a guess which had some resemblance to the next word; thus:

for "soon," seen in indirect vision, he guessed "some"
" "heard" " " " " , " " "board"
" "flowers" " " " " , " " "follows"

In continuous reading such incompletely perceived words would be immediately examined in direct vision and probably the partial perception would be a helpful step toward the complete perception. Instead of a very narrow field of clear vision moving along the line and picking up one letter at a time, we have a broad field of fairly clear vision supplemented by a margin of less clear but still useful vision, this whole field advancing by jumps along the line.

EYE MOVEMENTS IN READING

The movement of the eyes in reading is essentially the same saccadic movement as in examining an object or scene (p. 584), but is more regular in direction because it follows the lines of print. This regularity makes recording easier. When the lines of print are horizontal,

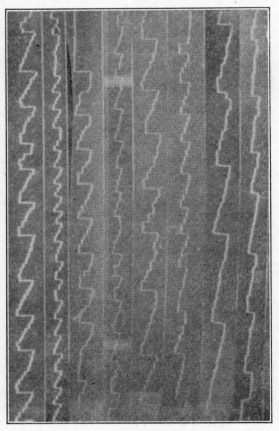

Fig. 231. (Dearborn, 1906.) Photographic records of eye movements in reading. These records are to be read upwards. The short, heavy vertical lines are the fixation pauses, and the lighter oblique lines (almost horizontal) are saccadic movements, the long ones to the left carrying the eye from the end of one line to the beginning of the next, and the little ones to the right carrying it from point to point in the reading of a line. Regressive movements can be seen in most of the records.

The records are from four educated adults, who differed greatly in speed of reading. Each is represented by two records, the first from his reading of material printed in long lines, and the second from his reading of short newspaper lines. In reading newspaper lines, the complete records of the four subjects, when measured, gave the following averages:

Subject	Fixations per line	Average duration of fixation
1	3.8	161 ms
2	3.9	216
3	5.5	255
4	5.4	402

the photographic film is made to move vertically at a known speed. Vertical distances in the record thus denote time, horizontal distances space. With additional attachments the apparatus will record also the vertical component of the eye's motion (Schmidt, 1917), or the movement of both eyes, as well as any head movement which may occur (for bibliography, see Tinker, 1936 a).

Examination of the records shows that the eyes of an experienced reader are well regimented, though such irregularities as the following occur:

1. Slight head movements are frequent, with compensatory eye movements (p. 587).

2. Imperfect convergence is responsible for corrective movements appearing in the records as a gentle sliding during the fixations. In the long jumps from the end of one line to the beginning of the next, convergence is often inaccurate and requires correction during the first fixation on the new line (p. 583).

3. The eye movement along a line is not always accurately horizontal; the vertical component is slight in experienced readers except, of course, when there is a definite movement from one line to another.

Regressive movements. Another frequent irregularity is a backward movement within a line. The child beginning to read explores the line backward and forward, much as he would a scene or object, but with experience his eyes become closely geared to the flow of speech, as represented by the orderly sequence of the printed words, and the regressive movements disappear for the most part. Even the expert reader makes a few such movements, especially at the beginning of a line, after the long jump to the left. Regressive movements in the interior of a line usually indicate difficulties or interesting details encountered in the reading. Some are demonstrably due to misreadings which do not make sense and are corrected by a second fixation (revealed by errors in oral reading, Fairbanks, 1937).

EYE MOVEMENTS IN READING, ACCORDING TO SCHOOL GRADE

(*Buswell, 1922*)

A sample of 8–19 children from each grade, of about medium reading ability, had their eyes photographed while reading, and the Mean for each grade is given.

School grade	Fixations per line of print	Mean duration of fixation	Regressive movements per line
I B	18.6	660 ms	5.1
I A	15.5	432	4.0
II	10.7	364	2.3
III	8.9	316	1.8
IV	7.3	268	1.4
V	6.9	252	1.3
VI	7.3	236	1.6
VII	6.8	240	1.5
High School I	7.2	244	1.0
H. S. II	5.8	248	0.7
H. S. III	5.5	224	0.7
H. S. IV	6.4	248	0.7
College	5.9	252	0.5

Fixations: their number and duration. Photographic records enable us to count the fixation points in a line of print, the distances between them and the duration of each fixation "pause." (The word "pause" conveys the false impression that the eye is simply resting from its job of moving along the line, the truth being that fixation is the time of exposure of the retina to the stimulus pattern which is wiped out during the saccadic movement, p. 591.) The number of fixations depends, of course, on the length of the line of print, and it depends on the ease or difficulty of the reading matter and on the expertness of the reader. The number of fixations, as shown by the table on p. 723, decreases greatly from the first school grade to the high school. A really rapid reader makes 3–5 fixations in a newspaper line, when the reading is going smoothly.

The average duration of the fixation also decreases from the first to the fifth school grades, and from that point on remains at about ¼ sec. The distribution is skew, with a few single fixations lasting as long as a second, even in good readers. Among college freshmen, the mode was about 210 ms for good readers, and about 260 ms for poor readers (Walker, 1933; Anderson, 1937). The mode is about the same for easy and moderately difficult reading matter, though there are more long fixations with the difficult matter. Training for rapid silent reading decreases the number of fixations much more than their average duration (Buswell, 1922; Robinson, 1933). All in all, the fixations are rather constant in duration, while varying much more in number.

We might suppose that the duration of fixation was determined by the need for adequate exposure of the retina; but from tachistoscopic experiments we know that exposures of very much less than ⅕ sec. are ample, provided the illumination is reasonably good. Some single fixations, in fact, last only 50–100 ms; and all of them could be as short as that so far as the demands of the retina are concerned.

Another false supposition is that the number of fixations is determined by the width of clear vision; results already considered under the head of indirect vision show that 2–4 fixations would be enough for most lines of print, while the actual number often runs far above the average of about 6 per line. The more difficult the reading matter, the more fixations and the more time per line—a fact which points to central rather than peripheral determiners.

Most of the reading time is devoted to fixation. Small saccadic movements occupy very little time (p. 584). Measurements made from records of reading (Dearborn, 1906; Schmidt, 1917) give an average of about 40 ms for the comparatively long return movement to the beginning of the next line, and an average of 22 ms for the interfixation movements within a line. The saccadic movement can neither be hastened nor slowed, except by such organic states as fatigue and drugs. To speed up reading you must decrease the number of fixations or their average duration. In rapid reading, with fixations of about 200 ms, the total fixation time will be about 90% of the whole reading time. In slower reading, with longer and more numerous fixations, the total fixation time may run as high as 95% or even higher (Tinker, 1936 b).

Placing beside this fact the other fact on which we have insisted so strongly (p. 591), that the retina during a saccadic movement receives only blurs and streaks as stimuli, we find that eye movements provide the reader with good visual data for 90% or more of the time and demand 10% or less for the operation of the ocular machine. The efficiency of the machine is thus very high. The limiting factors in speed of reading lie elsewhere.

Sometimes the duration of each single fixation has been called "recognition time" and the sum of all the fixations "perception time." Neither of these terms is correct. There is no reason to doubt that

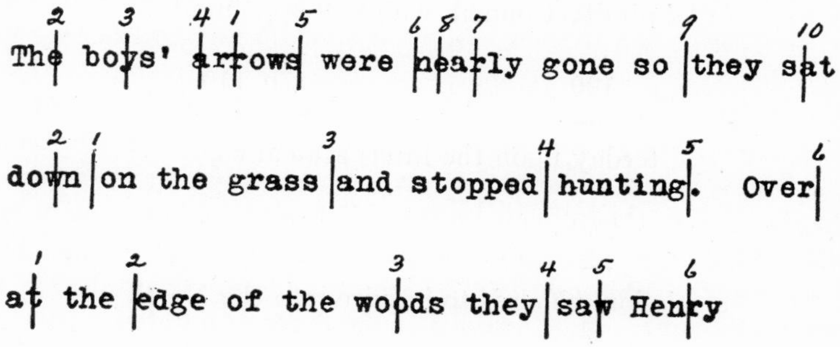

FIG. 232. (Buswell, 1920.) Location of the successive fixation points in three lines of reading. The vertical lines indicate the fixations, and the numbers above show the order in which the points were fixated. Thus, in the third line, the eye proceeded straight along, but in each of the other lines regressive movements occurred.

recognition and perception go on continuously, without interruption by the brief intervals of eye movement. Total fixation time might properly be called "exposure time"; it is usually longer than required for the mere perception and recognition of familiar words. If O has difficulty in understanding the meaning, or if his interest leads him to dwell on what he has just read, his eyes must be slowed down so as not to get ahead of his brain. His eyes must mark time by taking shorter steps or by delaying on each step. Exposure time may thus be greatly in excess of true perception and recognition time. Detailed study of the fixations sometimes reveals the reader's difficulties and interests.

The location of the fixations within the line of print. Presumably we can learn something regarding the process of reading by noticing exactly where the eye rests during each fixation. To discover where the eye does rest, it is necessary to superpose the photograph of the eye's movements and fixations upon the line which was being read. This apparently difficult experimental feat is quite simply accomplished by providing fixation points exactly even with the right and left edges of the printed matter, and having O fixate these points carefully before the reading matter is uncovered for him to read. These two preliminary fixations appear on the plate or film as two vertical lines at the right and left, and when the film is projected by a lantern upon the reading matter these two lines can be superposed upon the original fixation points. Having thus trued the photograph upon the printed lines, the investigator advances the film till the record of a fixation is projected

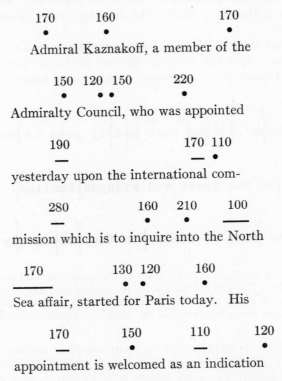

FIG. 233. (Modified from Dearborn, 1906.) Location of the fixations of a rapid reader in several successive lines of a newspaper. The dots indicate the positions of the center of fixation upon the line of print. When a horizontal line appears in place of a dot, the fixation slides over the distance indicated. The numbers indicate the duration of the fixations in milliseconds.

upon the line read and notes the place in the line where the fixation fell.

The records show much flexibility in the eye's behavior in reading. While the movements are regularized to the extent that they keep to the line of print and jump from the end of each line to near the beginning of the next, the fixations are by no means evenly spaced along the line, nor are they of uniform duration. More time is needed for grasping the material at some places than at others, and where more time is required, the eye must make longer stops or more of them. If the visual appearance of a word is obscure, the eye must explore it more minutely and probably by more numerous fixations. If the sense of a passage is obscure, the brain mechanism requires extra time to master it, and the eye must mark time.

Fully as impressive in the records as the irregularity of the fixations is the fact that most parts of any line are not directly fixated. The eye by no means fixates every letter or even every word. Slightly indirect vision is sufficient for most of the letters. With rapid readers, the first fixation is apt to fall some little distance from the beginning of the line.

We also notice that the first fixation is likely to last a longer time than most of the other fixations in the line. During this long fixation near the beginning of the line, what lies further to the right is already receiving some preliminary examination and consequently is passed over more rapidly in direct fixation.

How the total fixation time is distributed to successive quarters of the line. The same reasoning would lead us to expect fewer or briefer fixations near the end of the line than in the middle or near the beginning. The real question is not the mere number of fixations, nor the mere duration of the very last fixation, but the amount of time spent in fixating different parts of the line. If we divide a line into quarters, we can tell from the records how much time was spent in fixations falling within each quarter. Computing the fixation time for each quarter of 151 lines, from the records of about fifteen readers published by Dearborn (1906), Buswell (1922), and Judd & Buswell (1922), we have the following average result:

TIME SPENT IN FIXATIONS UPON EACH QUARTER OF A LINE, EXPRESSED IN PERCENT OF THE TOTAL FIXATION TIME PER LINE

First quarter	Second quarter	Third quarter	Last quarter
30	23	23	24

That is, 30 percent of the total time is spent in fixating the first quarter, while the other quarters receive on the average just about equal time. The different samples agree closely with regard to the proportion of time devoted to the first quarter, but differ considerably in the proportion for the last quarter, which comes out at 19% for one sample of 28 lines, and at 29% for another sample of 24 lines; from which we can conclude that the fraction of the total time devoted to the last quarter of the line is by no means well established by these samples. The definite finding is that the first quarter receives more than its proportional share of the fixation time.

Do the fixation points favor any particular parts of words, or any particular sorts of words? Cursory examination of the records may suggest that fixations tend to fall upon the short words, or on the ends of words, or on capital letters; and we might suspect that the eye was easily caught by such landmarks in indirect vision and jumped to them for its next fixations.

With regard to short and long words, we might argue either way: that the short word stands out and catches the eye or that the short words are too familiar to call for direct fixation. Similarly we might argue either that the ends of a word, by virtue of their sharp contrast with the adjoining white spaces, will catch the eye; or that the middle of a word, obscured by masking, will need the most precise fixation. The records provide the facts of the matter, if we start with a perfectly neutral hypothesis, and see whether the facts compel us to abandon it. The neutral hypothesis is that a fixation point is equally likely to fall at any point along the line—on a short or on a long word, at the beginning, middle or end of a word, or in the space between two words, simply in proportion to the space occupied by each. If we use as a rough unit the space occupied by a single letter, counting all letters as equal in width, and counting each punctuation mark and each space between words as a unit, then, according to the neutral hypothesis, fixations will in the long run fall equally on each unit in a line of print. If a newspaper line contains 40 unit spaces, and is read on the average with 5 fixations, that gives one fixation per 8 unit spaces. The probability of a fixation point falling upon any unit in any one reading is 1/8 or .125, under the special assumptions made.

In actual records, the general frequency of fixations is greater or less than the figure assumed above for purposes of illustration. Buswell (1922), and Judd & Buswell (1922), supply records from seven Os, who read a passage of six lines, containing 253 of our units, with 45 fixations on the average. Per unit, then, there were $45/253 = .178$ fixations. That was the general frequency of fixations per unit per reading, and we can compare with this general frequency or expectation the actual frequency of fixations on different letters, etc. What we find is as follows:

FREQUENCY OF FIXATIONS PER LETTER-SPACE PER READING

General frequency or expectation	.18
Frequency per empty space	.16
Frequency per capital letter	.08
Frequency per small letter projecting either above or below the line (b, d, f, g, h, i, j, k, l, p, q, t, y)	.18
Frequency per small letter not projecting (a, c, e, m, n, o, r, s, u, v, w, x, z)	.20

The evidence is rather slight, but so far as it goes fixation is nearly as likely to fall on a space between words as on any letter. Rather strangely, in view of the outstanding appearance of the capital letters, they have proportionally fewer fixations than the small letters. Even the projecting letters, which are sometimes believed to dominate the appearance of a word, seem to receive no more fixations than the non-projecting letters. The reason may be that indirect vision suffices for the more prominent letters.

A similar computation shows that the frequency of fixations is just about the same for the first and last letters of a word and any interior letter. The eye does not fixate a special part of the word more often than would be expected from the space occupied by that part.

When words of different lengths are compared in this way, it is necessary to assign to each word half of the empty space just before and after it. A word of two letters thus covers three spaces and is credited with any fixation that falls on or close beside it. Computing the incidence of fixation on words of different length from some of Dearborn's records, for about 85 lines of print, we have the following results:

FREQUENCY OF FIXATIONS PER LETTER-SPACE, IN WORDS
OF DIFFERING LENGTH

No. letters in word	Frequency of fixations per letter
1–2	.110
3	.110
4	.115
5	.086
6	.096
over 6	.096
General frequency	.102

As Dearborn's readers were specially expert, the general frequency of fixations is much less than in the preceding computations; but the question is, whether the short words get more fixations than they should according to the space occupied. The indication is that they do, but only slightly. Presumably a familiar long word, being a coherent whole, requires less scrutiny than an equal space filled with short words.

The general conclusion from the evidence at hand, which is indeed rather scanty, would run thus: the exact location of the fixation points in a line of print depends only slightly upon the particular filling of the various parts of the space covered. The eye seems to have no predilection for landing on any special part of a word or type of letter or length of word, though, if anything, it avoids capital letters and falls a little disproportionately upon the short words.

The location of fixations as dependent upon difficulties encountered in reading. Detailed examination of the fixations often shows spots where the reader found the passage difficult. The record of fixations yields a picture of his perplexities. The difficulty can often be traced to such factors as:

an unfamiliar word;

a word used in some other than its common conversational meaning;

an ambiguous word not sufficiently prepared for by the context;

a superfluous word from the reader's point of view; for example, the records indicate that in the sentence, "The moon shone in at the window," the word "at" gave trouble to children.

In the first line of the adjoining record beginning "A common violation," the eye progresses regularly till "the" is reached, when it turns back and lingers in the neighborhood of "illustrated." The reason may be that the most familiar use of "illustrated," as in "illustrated books," is to signify pictures, and that "illustrated by" most readily suggests that the illustrator is next to be named.

In the second line, progress is steady till the end of the word "expression"; the eye goes back and lingers on that word, as if time were needed to get its unusual meaning. At the beginning of the third line, "singular" seems to require time to make sure that it refers back to "expression" and not to "every one." Later in the third line, there is delay on the words "an idea," especially on "an," not because of the difficulty of those words, in all probability, but because of the accumulated difficulty of the whole passage.

The cause of delay may be at a different place from that suggested by the eye's record. The point *from* which the eyes regress is not the point that gives difficulty. The understanding of words and phrases necessarily lags a little behind the visual impression. The eye turns back at the time when understanding is blocked *to* the neighborhood where the difficulty seems to be located. When the eyes resume their forward march, they do not ordinarily skip the

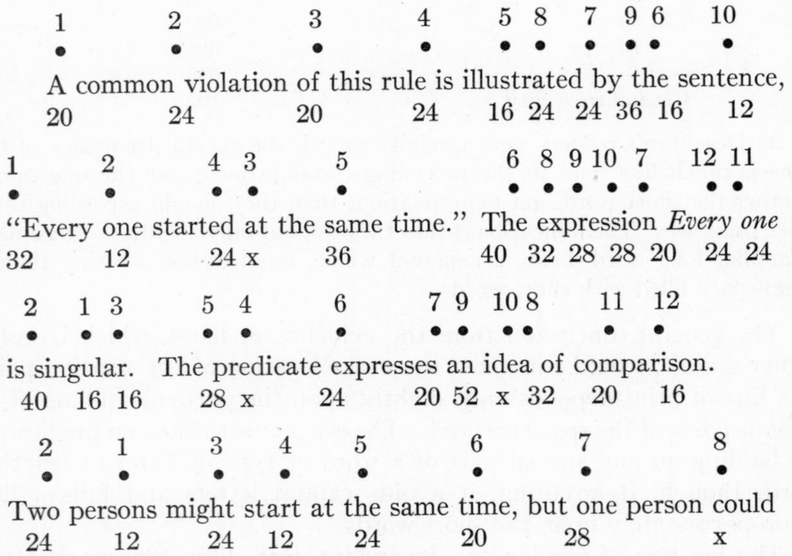

1	2	3	4	5	8	7	9	6	10
•	•	•	•	•	•	•	• •		•

A common violation of this rule is illustrated by the sentence,

| 20 | 24 | 20 | 24 | 16 | 24 | 24 | 36 | 16 | 12 |

1	2	4	3	5		6	8	9	10	7	12	11
•	•	•	•	•		•	•	•	•	•	•	•

"Every one started at the same time." The expression *Every one*

| 32 | 12 | 24 x | 36 | | 40 | 32 | 28 | 28 | 20 | 24 | 24 |

2	1	3	5	4	6	7	9	10	8	11	12
•	• •		•	•	•	• •		• •		•	•

is singular. The predicate expresses an idea of comparison.

| 40 | 16 | 16 | 28 x | 24 | 20 | 52 | x | 32 | 20 | 16 |

2	1	3	4	5	6	7	8
•	•	•	•	•	•	•	•

Two persons might start at the same time, but one person could

| 24 | 12 | 24 | 12 | 24 | 20 | 28 | x |

FIG. 234. (From Judd & Buswell, 1922.) Fixations in four lines of reading. The dots indicate the location of the fixations. The numbers above the dots give the order of fixations in each line, while the numbers below show the duration of each fixation in hundredths of a sec. Where an *x* occurs the duration could not be made out from the record. The reader was a university student.

words already fixated, but proceed through them in the regular way; and so it comes about that they may fixate once more an entirely inoffensive little word. The resulting double fixation of this little word should not be taken to indicate any difficulty connected with that word.

The eye-voice span in oral reading. In reading aloud the eyes keep ahead of the voice so that there is a "span" between the two. Reading word by word, as beginners do, does not make for natural conversational expression, and is also an inefficient procedure. While the processes of understanding and pronouncing one word are going on, the eyes can perfectly well move ahead and secure the visual stimulus for the next following response. Overlap of this sort occurs in all experienced readers.

The span can be measured in terms of space or of time. At a given instant when the eyes are fixating a certain word, the voice is speaking a word further back in the line of print, and the distance between the fixation point and the speaking point can be stated in millimeters, in letter spaces or in words. In terms of time, we have a certain word fixated at one instant and pronounced a little later, and the difference gives a sort of (prolonged) reaction time. The space and time measures need not correspond at every point though they must on the average of a passage: if the rate of the oral reading is 3 words per sec. and the voice

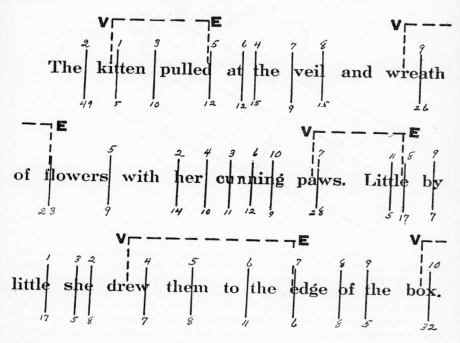

Fig. 235. (Buswell, 1920.) The eye-voice span in oral reading. Each connected pair of heavy letters, V and E, shows the simultaneous positions of voice and eye in the lines of print, at certain instants when the two records were directly synchronized. The first span determined extends from the first syllable of "kitten" to the end of "pulled," a distance of 11 letter-spaces. The vertical lines indicate the fixations; the numbers above show their sequence and the numbers below their duration in fiftieths of a second. Buswell published many fully worked-out records.

keeps on the average 1 sec. behind, it must be on the average 3 words behind.

Measurements of this general sort were made by Quantz (1897) and by Gray (1917). While O was reading aloud, the page was suddenly covered or the light extinguished, and O continued to say the words as far as he had seen them. Educated adults continued for 5.4 words or 4.4 words, on the average, according to the two investigators. So obtained the measure would exceed the eye-voice span proper, since some words to the right of the last fixation point could be got from indirect vision (p. 721).

A more exact study of the eye-voice span was made by Buswell (1920). He obtained simultaneous records of the eye movements by photography, and of the voice by a dictaphone. He synchronized the two records as they were being made by closing from time to time an electric circuit which operated two devices simultaneously: a shutter

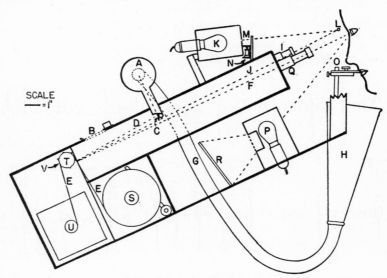

Fig. 236. (Tiffin & Fairbanks, 1937.) Setup for recording eye and voice on the same film. While the subject's eyes are directed toward the reading matter, R, a beam of light from the source, P, reflected from his cornea through the lens at Q and along the line FC, strikes the photographic film near T. A motor drive applied at V, draws the film, E, from the spool, S, around T to U. The voice is picked up by the horn, H, and carried through the tube, G, to the oscillograph, A, and the light from this instrument is reflected by a mirror at C to the film beside the eye record. A record of any head movements that occur is provided by a beam of light from the source, K, which is reflected by L, a bead on a spectacle frame worn by the subject, and passes through the lens at I and along the line marked J to the film at T. A time line is provided by a 60-cycle vibrator, N, which interrupts the head-beam at M. B is the focusing window.

The oscillograph, which is the Dorsey phoneloscope, is used here not for obtaining detailed pictures of the voice vibrations but simply for indicating the time when each syllable is spoken Fig. 237. For identification of the syllables, a phonograph record of the subject's oral reading is made simultaneously with the other records.

which cut off for an instant the light to the camera and so left a record of that instant on the moving film, and a tap bell caught by the dictaphone. A space-span was thus determined for certain instants and by interpolation for other parts of the record. Fig. 236 gives another method.

Variations in the eye-voice span. The eye-voice span is far from being a constant quantity. It varies from individual to individual. It is longer in good than in poor readers, and increases with experience in reading. Buswell (1920) measured it in six subjects from each school grade, three of whom were selected as good readers and three as poor readers for their grade. Samples of his results follow.

School grade	Average eye-voice span in letter-spaces	
	of three good readers	of three poor readers
II	11.0	5.4
VI	11.9	11.2
IX	15.8	11.5
XII	15.9	12.4

The eye-voice span is very elastic. It goes down almost to zero when unfamiliar or ambiguous words are encountered; the eyes mark time until the meaning is discovered. Where the material reads along smoothly,

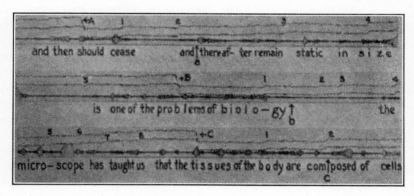

Fig. 237. (Tiffin, 1934.) Simultaneous eye-voice record combined with the reading matter. Both eyes are recorded. At A, B, C they swing back to the beginning of a new line; at 1, 2, 3 . . . they move forward along the line. The voice record is just above the printed matter, and the arrows marked a, b, c, show the position of the eyes when the voice has just reached A, B, C. The distances A–a, B–b, C–c show the spatial extent of the eye-voice span at the beginning of the three lines of print. The span is apt to be specially long at the beginning of a line.

the span lengthens and may become for an instant as long as a whole line of print. The span in terms of words varies from zero to eight. Measured in time, the eye-voice span for mature readers runs at about one or two seconds; the voice reaches a word one or two seconds after the eye has fixated it.

The reader is like a rotary printing press, or an automobile assembly line, that takes in raw material, performs a series of operations on it, and delivers a finished product. The operations in oral reading include perceiving, understanding and speaking. All these operations are going on simultaneously: while one word is being spoken, the one before it is being understood, and the one before that just being seen. The reading process is, to be sure, both more complex and more fluid and variable than that performed by a man-made machine. The time for passing a word through the machine is the eye-voice span which at its minimum is about 3/10 sec., as shown by reaction time experiments (p. 355), but in expressive oral reading runs up to 1–2 sec. or more.

Overlapping processes can be demonstrated in other similar performances such as typing from copy and taking down a telegraphic message from the sounder (pp. 159–160). The ear-hand span in receiving a telegraphic message is specially long because of the amount of organization needed to reduce a series of clicks to a meaningful message. In typing from printed copy, the eye-hand span averages only about 5–6 letter spaces, or about a second. In space it is much shorter than in oral reading, but in time it is about the same—typing being the slower motor process. The number of fixations is much greater in typing than in oral reading, and is least of all in silent reading. When the motor process is necessarily slow, the eyes have to put in the time somehow. (For determining the eye-hand span, the carriage of the typewriter made an electric contact at every tenth space, and these contacts were recorded on the film along with the eye movements; Butsch, 1932.)

Eye movements in special kinds of reading. Silent reading is the norm. Other sorts are slower because of some additional demand made on the reader, and this enforced slowness compels the eyes to tarry longer on a line of print, by increasing either the number or the duration of the fixations, or both. The average duration, as already mentioned, is less increased than the number of fixations.

Proofreading calls for detecting typographical errors as well as any obvious slips made by the writer in sentence construction or diction. The proofreader is not assimilating the reading matter for his own benefit and need not understand what he is reading except to a limited extent. He must not allow himself to become absorbed in the meaning if he is to succeed in detecting all the errors.

Crosland (1924) provided reading matter heavily loaded with typographical errors. Certain selections were to be read for errors, other selections for meaning, though in both cases any errors detected were to be marked. Reading for errors was much the slower process, and yielded a much greater count of errors detected.

PERCENT OF TYPOGRAPHICAL ERRORS DETECTED

(*Crosland, 1924*)

	by experts	by novices
in reading for errors	90	70
in reading for meaning	83	54

Another investigator (Vernon, 1931) photographed the eye movements during proofreading and found the number of fixations and the number of regressive movements much increased, while the average duration of a fixation was only a little longer than in ordinary reading.

Learning the spelling of a word (Abernethy, 1929; Gilbert, 1932). The number of fixations on a difficult 12-letter word may run as high as 25 with adult Os, or may be as small as 6. The average duration of a fixation is increased to 300–350 ms. The poor speller seems to wander aimlessly back and forth across the word, while the good speller is more methodical, going through the word repeatedly in the forward direction but with extra fixations on the difficult parts.

Reading and answering true-false and other "objective" examination questions (Frandsen, 1934). Both number and average duration of the fixations are greater than in reading scientific prose. The eye movements are adapted to the type of question; in true-false and completion questions they are rather like those in ordinary reading, while in analogies and multiple choice questions they diverge widely from this norm.

Reading numbers. A numeral, even though a single character, has the meaning of a complete word and often the precise meaning is important. Consequently the eyes spend more time on a series of numerals than upon the same space printed in words. Even though several digits can be clearly seen in one fixation, the eye usually fixates each in turn when they are presented in an unbroken series. If the digits are in groups of two, one fixation per group is usual; if in groups of three, 1–2 fixations per group; if in groups of four, 2–3 fixations per group. Terry (1922) found the time per digit to be greater than the time per word in ordinary reading. But a *familiar* combination such as 1492 or 3.1416 is often read in a single fixation (Rebert, 1932 a).

Reading formulas (Tinker, 1928; Rebert, 1932 b). A mathematical or chemical formula, like a numeral, is a very compact form of reading matter, and takes more time per inch, so that the number of fixations is increased. A familiar formula, like H_2SO_4, especially if it occurs repeatedly in a passage, is treated like a word and may receive but a single brief fixation.

Adding a column of figures. Buswell (1922) found in fifth grade children that the fixations in adding lasted 2 sec. on the average, as compared with ¼ sec. in the ordinary reading of these children. He says,

> It is not difficult to see the reason for such long fixations in arithmetic addition. The perceptual problem of recognizing the digits makes a very minor demand. . . . The difficult part of arithmetic addition consists of making the mental associations required for arriving at the correct answer. The child . . . simply lets his eye rest upon the same point while he is engaged in the mental labor of making the proper associations.

Reading a foreign language. Unless the language is quite familiar, the reading is slow and the fixations are consequently more frequent than in one's native language. Still the general pattern of eye movements will be the same, provided one is really reading, not digging out the meaning by a laborious back-and-forth exploration of the lines of print. Eye movement photographs can help in discovering what sort of reading is being done. Judd & Buswell (1922) found that some American students really read French, but there was no evidence in the eye movements that they did anything but decipher Latin. Futch (1935) found that the difficulty with Latin lay less in the peculiar order of words than in the endings which must be so carefully examined. Beginners make many regressive movements but graduate students of Latin were found to read straight through, though rather slowly.

Reading Chinese. Each Chinese character is a word, though often it takes two or three Chinese words to translate a long English word. On comparing the reading rates of Chinese and American students at Stanford University, Shen (1927) found that the Chinese read about 6 words per sec., as compared with 5 per sec. for the Americans. Taking account of the difference just stated between English and Chinese words, we see that approximately the same amount of thought is covered in the same time, in reading Chinese or English, in spite of the very different styles of language and printing. Once more we find that the speed of reading is determined by the rate at which the meaning is grasped, rather than by peripheral factors.

By photography Shen found the fixations closer together in reading Chinese than English. The reason is that the Chinese words are shorter and broader. The significant details of a Chinese character are often placed side by side, at right angles to the direction of the line of print. It is somewhat like English printed in a double-decked arrangement, each long word in two parts one above the other:

In	Chin	print	ev	char	repre	a	word
	ese	ing	ery	acter	sents		

While this style of printing does not suit the English words, it has some advantages. It conforms better to the shape of the field of clear vision which is by no means a narrow horizontal streak like an English line of print. As far as the eyes are concerned, we could easily read two lines at a time. The broad Chinese characters utilize the two dimensions of the distinct field to better advantage than in English.

Reading music. A pianist playing from printed music reads one staff for the right hand and one for the left, and as his eyes move along the score they cover a space an inch high instead of an eighth of an inch as in ordinary reading. Weaver (1930) found the pianist's eyes to fixate sometimes the upper and sometimes the lower staff, but not in regular alternation. The pattern of the eye movements differed with the kind of music. There is an eye-hand span here like the eye-voice span in oral reading, an elastic span which sometimes narrows to one or two notes, and sometimes expands to as many as eight, which seemed to be about the limit for sight reading.

Low correlation of reading ability with ability in other visual tasks. By all indications the speed and accuracy of reading are determined more by the central meaning-getting process than by peripheral factors. The normal eye, and even the eye with slight optical defects or with corrected optical defects, are more than adequate for reading purposes. This statement may need some qualification in case of prolonged reading, when defects may induce ocular fatigue. But as regards speed the reader can scarcely crowd his eyes to the limit either of their motor efficiency or of their field of fairly clear vision. Though individuals differ greatly in speed of reading and also in the width of their areas of distinct vision, there is almost a zero correlation between the two variables (Ruediger, 1907; Gray, 1917). Though poor readers show an excessive number of fixations and of regressive movements, this inefficient motor behavior is apparently the effect and not the cause of the slowness in understanding the material.

Visual acuity has a low positive correlation with reading ability in children, and to a slight extent the same seems to be true of other measures of elementary visual function (Fendrick, 1935; Wagner, 1937). Visual perception tests show a positive correlation with reading ability, a correlation which is quite low except when the exposed material approximates to ordinary reading matter. Gates (1922) tested school children for accurate observation of verbal and non-verbal material, and correlated their success in detecting small differences in such material with their reading ability, with results as follows:

Material	Correlation with reading ability
Drawings	+.05
Digits	+.14
Nonsense words	+.27
Words	+.39

These results were confirmed by Sister Mary (1929) who found appreciable correlation between reading ability and the "discrimination of minute details in words and groups of words," but not between reading and the perception of drawings or digits. Litterer (1933) correlated the reading ability of college sophomores with visual apprehension of more or less disconnected verbal material, and found average coefficients as follows:

Material	Correlation with reading ability
Digits	+.15
Letters	+.28
Words	+.36
Sentences	+.43

Reading correlates more closely with intelligence than with the sensory, perceptual and motor abilities that have been tested. Yet reading ability is not identical with intelligence; it seems to bring in a specific linguistic factor, or even a reading factor—as is to be expected from the peculiarly artificial and imperfect character of alphabetic writing when compared with either picture or syllabic writing.

CUES IN WORD PERCEPTION

Up to this point our attention has been directed to the peripheral rather than the cerebral process in reading. The roles of eye movements and of direct and indirect vision have been the chief topics. The cerebral process includes, we may assume, both knowing the words and getting the meaning of the passage. In some types of reading, as proofreading, the words are clearly perceived though the meaning is only dimly understood. More experimentation has been devoted to the perceptual process than to the process of getting the meaning. The main question has concerned the visual data which enable the reader to recognize a word.

The obvious answer was that the letters in their order—the spelling of the word—furnished the necessary and sufficient data for knowing the word. That this is not the true answer seemed to be demonstrated

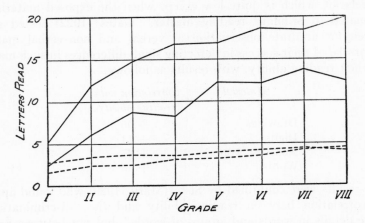

FIG. 238. (Hoffmann, 1927.) Increase of tachistoscope span for unconnected consonants and for familiar words with advance in school grade. Each grade is divided into an upper quarter, a medium half and a lower quarter, on the basis of intelligence as judged by the teachers. The curves give the average span for the upper and the lower quarters; the middle half and the general average may be imagined as lying between these paired curves. Full line, span for familiar words; dotted line, span for jumbled consonants; both spans being measured in terms of one letter as unit. The span for familiar words increases much faster and further than the span for letters.

by the early experiments of Cattell and of Erdmann & Dodge, already mentioned (p. 715). Cattell in 1885 used the tachistoscope for experiments on reading and found that, with an exposure of 10 ms,

    3–4 unconnected letters could be read,
    2 unconnected short words could be read,
    4 connected short words could be read.

Since even the 2 unconnected words exceeded the span for letters, it was clear that the words were not read by spelling them. What is perceived, Cattell reasoned, must be the "total word picture."

Erdmann & Dodge (1898), besides their important discovery that the cues in reading were obtained in the fixation pauses and not during actual eye movement, confirmed Cattell's findings. From a single brief exposure, only 4–5 unconnected letters can be reported with certainty. If O holds his fixation steady during a longer exposure he can often report 6–7 letters, but that is about the limit. If one letter is directly fixated, 2–3 letters on each side of that one can be seen distinctly enough to be read. But familiar words, even as long as 12–20 letters, were correctly read from a single exposure of 100 ms. Erdmann & Dodge therefore held that the "general shape of the word" must be the primary cue, with 6–7 letters close to the fixation point as supplementary cues.

Analysis of possible cues. "General word shape" need not mean precisely the same as Cattell's "total word picture." When Erdmann & Dodge emphasize the "crudity" of the general shape, they seem to have in mind simply the external configuration of the word. Messmer (1903) showed that internal characteristics should also be considered, such as the gridiron effect due to an accumulation of vertical strokes, and the lively effect of a sequence of curved letters like a, c, e, g, o and s. As far as external outline is concerned, these three word shapes are nearly identical:

consonants

consummate

consxxxxtx

The internal patterns and the total pictures are quite different.

Another possible cue is the "dominant letter" (Zeitler, 1900). Capitals and certain of the lower case letters, as b, p, f, g, extend above or below the general level, and might dominate the total shape and also might be visible farther into indirect vision than other letters and so increase the number of distinctly seen letters.

Even non-dominant letters can sometimes be seen farther from the fixation point than supposed by Erdmann & Dodge. The last letter in a word, being partly free from "masking" by adjacent letters, often stands out clearly; and the same is of course true of the first letter when the fixation point is in the middle of the word. Other letters occasionally stand out.

Experiment has then to test the claims of several cues that have been suggested:

1. External shape of the word.
2. Internal pattern.
3. The few letters adjacent to the momentary fixation point.
4. Dominant letters in other parts of the word.
5. The first and last letters of the word.
6. Still other letters at times.

The tachistoscope has provided the main type of experiment in this line of study. It affords, under control, the same sort of exposure as the eye gets in reading. The eyeball, with its saccadic movements and brief fixations, is in effect a variety of tachistoscope. The experimenter's tachistoscope can limit O to a single fixation. How much can O read in a single exposure? What errors will he make? Will he overlook misprints and confuse words of the same general shape or having the same dominant letters?

Misprints and misreadings. Some of the best evidence on reading cues has come from errors in reading long or mutilated words. Pillsbury (1897), whose work belongs among the pioneer studies, exposed type-written words with a letter omitted, a false letter substituted, or a letter blurred by typing "x" over it. These mutilations were usually not seen as such. The omission of a letter was detected in only 40% of the cases, the substituted false letter in 22%, and the blurred letter in 14%. The misprints were most often detected at the beginning of a word, probably because the eyes, or at least the attention, favored the left side of the exposure field.

Pillsbury distinguished three sorts of cues for word recognition:

1. The form of the whole word, determined by its length, by the projections produced by the high and low letters, and by the location of the clearly seen letters.

2. The clearly seen letters themselves, which are not confined to the immediate neighborhood of the fixation point.

3. The context. E sometimes supplied context by saying, just before the exposure, a word related in meaning to the mutilated word about to be shown. Once E said "sky" and exposed "eanth," expecting the response "earth." O however responded "zenith," which still shows the influence of context. Context often acted to conceal a mutilation.

O was asked to report, not only the word as read, but also the letters seen and how distinctly they were seen. Some of the reports are quoted here.

Letters exposed	Word read	Subject's comments
kommonly	commonly	"But I can't make out the first letter."
fashxon	fashion	"Didn't see the i."
duplably	culpably	"The c was not clear."
foyever	forever	"There is a hair across the r."
disal	deal	"There may be something between e and a, but I am not sure."
uvermore	evermore	"Seems to be an m before it."
danxe	danger	"The r seemed faint."
verbati	verbatim	"The last two letters seemed a little dim."

An important fact stands out in the comments: O sees details which he cannot use in reading the word. He gets the best word he can but he sees presented facts even when they do not fit into this word. He reads "foyever" as "forever," but thinks there must be a hair across the r; or he reads "danxe" as "danger" but admits that the r seemed faint. If O sees details that are inconsistent with his misreading, it follows that he sees similar details in an unmutilated word which is correctly read. His visual impression therefore is not limited to the general word shape. That the word form does not wholly control the response is clear also from a comparison of several of these responses with the presented material. There is a radical difference in general shape between "kommonly" and "commonly," and between "duplably" and "culpably." Dominant letters do not dominate completely. Nor are the correctly reported letters always adjacent to any possible fixation point: in three instances the first and last letters are correct though a middle letter is misread.

Dominant letters. Zeitler (1900), a strong supporter of the importance of the high, low and capital letters, gives many instances of misreadings in which these dominant letters are correctly reported. The fact that they are sometimes assigned a wrong position in the word shows, he believes, that they are seen as letters and not as mere projections in the general word shape. The evidence is not entirely convincing, since the word shape is usually well preserved in the misreadings, a few of which are given below.

Exposed	*Read*
Epaminondas	Epimenides
Kandelaber	Kanadabalsam
Praeglacial	Portugal
Agoraphobie	Agraphie
Hallneiuotiou	Hallucination
Meludie	Medulla
Trnuhxnckt	Trunksucht

General word shape. In a modified tachistoscope experiment, a series of exposures is given, the first being at too great a distance for any separate letters to be seen, and the succeeding exposures nearer and nearer to the eyes, till O finally reads the word correctly. Wiegand (1908) found that at a great distance a word was seen as a mere stripe of gray. As the tachistoscope was brought nearer, upward and downward projections from the stripe could be seen; and at about the same distance single letters began to make their appearance, usually at the beginning and end of the word; more letters and familiar letter combinations emerged till the word was entirely clear. At any stage in this process, a word was likely to suggest itself; it might be correct or incorrect. Kutzner (1916) found that misreadings at a distance preserved the approximate length of the exposed word (as would be expected), and also the approximate number of projecting letters. One projecting letter is substituted for another in many cases, as in the following instances from Grossart (1921) who regards them as proving the importance of general word shape:

Exposed:	ehelos	ausrufen	Lebenslust	fundieren
Read:	stehen	zuvordem	Lauterkeit	Interesse

The shape of a word can be seen, at a distance, when no letters are distinguishable, and the general shape may suggest some word. But the experiment proves little regarding ordinary reading because the stimulus is so different. When a word is near enough to show individual letters, the general word shape may cease to have any great importance as a cue.

The wide field of fairly distinct vision. One curious fact noted by several investigators (Cattell, Erdmann & Dodge, Pillsbury; see also p. 695) is that even when O can report but a few, he believes he has seen all the letters distinctly during the actual exposure. Unless they formed a familiar word, he forgot them before reaching them in his report. Nothing is more likely; unless some word suggested itself at once, brute memory would not hold all the disconnected letters. But if O is not

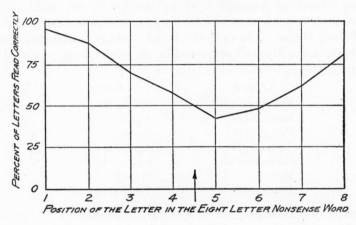

FIG. 239. (Wagner, 1918.) Letters near the ends of a series are better read than in the middle. Exposure, 100 ms. Fixation point indicated by arrow.

mistaken in this impression, he gets for an instant perfectly adequate cues of a correctly presented word. If for an instant he sees the whole word clearly, as he thinks he does, he has all the cues he could desire.

This possible explanation of word perception was taken seriously by Schumann (1921–22). It also seemed probable to him that O's attention is differently focused when he is expecting a row of unconnected letters and when he is expecting a word. Expecting mere letters, O would concentrate his efforts on a small region so as to make sure of a few of them; but expecting a word he would attempt to broaden his span so as to compass the entire word. To counteract the tendency to narrow the attentive field when unconnected letters are shown, Schumann instructed O to cover the whole field. His pupils, Heller (1911), Künzler (1913) and Wagner (1918), by use of these instructions, obtained results supporting the hypothesis. The results of Wagner are the most convincing.

Series of 8 unconnected letters were exposed for 100 ms, O's attention being adjusted to cover the whole series, though the fixation point was always in the middle of the series. The correctly reported letters were not closely grouped about the fixation point, but were more often near the ends of the series (where, according to what we have seen before, the masking effect is minimized). The adjoining diagram of Wagner's results could be practically duplicated from the work in other laboratories by Kutzner (1916) and Ipsen (1926 b).

Wagner exposed very long series of unconnected letters with the same instructions—to let attention cover the whole field. O was to report (1) how much of the series appeared distinct during the exposure, (2) how many of the letters he seemed to identify at the moment of exposure, and (3) what letters he remembered long enough to report. O often reported (1) that the whole of even a very long series appeared distinct, (2) that a large proportion of the letters seemed to be identified at the moment, although (3) comparatively few could be recalled immediately after the exposure. The letters reported came from all parts of a series, as shown in the following examples:

Letter-series exposed for 100 ms	*Letters reported*
L n z d w r r t s c h n f t s	L z d t s c h f t s
F r g h n w l y r h p k j s m	F h n w y j m
V a r w c z h u k z e w p o t	V a w h u z k p o t

It is certain that O read the first, the last, and part of the middle of each of the series of 15 letters. The letters reported were not concentrated about a single point. This objective result seems to dispose of the hypothesis that the only letters distinctly seen lie close to the fixation point, and to justify the assertion of many competent Os, who say that letters over a wide field are seen distinctly during the exposure. If they are seen distinctly, though only for an instant, they can act as cues for the recognition of a word; and thus we reach the conclusion that the most effective cue for reading a long word consists of a large share of the letters in the word, seen with fair distinctness for an instant.

This conclusion does not mean in the least that the word is read by spelling it out; evidence previously cited is enough to exclude that supposition. What the conclusion means is that an adequate *simultaneous* view of the word is afforded, and that this clear and detailed view of the entire word is the cue for recalling the word.

Further evidence for this conclusion is afforded by experiments with words printed all in capital letters. The word has then no characteristic shape aside from its mere length, and it is not so easy to read as when printed in lower case type. Yet Wagner (1918) found that words of 12–15 capital letters, exposed for 100 ms, were correctly read. In continuous reading, Tinker & Paterson (1928) found an advantage of 13 percent for lower case type as against all capitals. This difference in speed of reading is important from the practical point of view, but not large enough to indicate radically different perceptual processes in the two cases; and in reading words printed in capitals one simply must see the letters because the general shape fails as a cue.

Letter groups as cues. Intermediate between the single letter and the total word picture there are familiar combinations of letters, such as double letters and the prefixes and suffixes. Easily recognized groups are present in almost every long word. An experiment of Wilkins (1917) demonstrates their importance in reading. She exposed for 50–100 ms a phrase the syllables of which, if rearranged, gave a more familiar phrase. The presented words were typed in two lines, as shown below with some of the responses.

Words exposed	*Words read*
Washout at Irvington	Washington Irving
Woodson Wilrow	Woodrow Wilson
Psychment Departology	Psychology Department
Renaistecture Archisance	Renaissance Architecture
talder powcum	talcum powder
Shakesbeth Macpeare	Shakespeare Macbeth
Davfield Copperid	David Copperfield

Such misreadings are entirely spontaneous and occur often in hasty glimpses of outdoor signs. The reader is not bound to the general word shape; familiar syllables may instantly suggest a word or phrase in which the syllables are rearranged.

Easily recognized prefixes and suffixes, partially protected from masking by their positions at the ends of the word, doubtless furnish some of the clearest cues for word recognition.

Our general conclusion—to restate it—allows some cue value to the general shape of the word, especially in indirect vision before the eye reaches the word in continuous reading, but lays most emphasis on the clear view of letters and familiar letter groups, obtained for an instant during the direct fixation of the word.

Legibility. Optimal typographical conditions for ease of reading can presumably be worked out by experiment, though many interrelated variables need to be controlled: size and style of type, length of lines and space between them, gloss and color of paper. One difficulty is to secure precisely equivalent reading matter in different printing. Measures of relative legibility are found in:

1. Speed of continuous reading: the more quickly a given passage is read, the more legible.

2. Eye movements: number of fixations.

3. Brief exposure: percent of cases in which a letter or word is read correctly.

4. Distant presentation: at what distance the word or letter can be read.

5. Indirect vision.

6. Poor focus.

7. Low illumination.

Large type, heavy leads, short lines are less important for legibility than would be expected. Good brightness contrast between paper and letters is important. Some type faces are more legible than others. The experiments are well worthy of study from the standpoint of experimental technique (Paterson & Tinker, 1929; Tinker & Paterson, 1936; Hovde, 1929, 1930; Greene, 1934; Stanton & Burtt, 1935).

CHAPTER XXIX

PROBLEM SOLVING BEHAVIOR

Two chapters will not be too many for the large topic of thinking, and we may make the division according to the historical sources of two streams of experimentation, which do indeed merge in the more recent work. One stream arose in the study of animal behavior and went on to human problem solving; the other started with human thinking of the more verbal sort.

A problem is presented by some novel situation from which one has to escape or within which one wishes to achieve some result. There is a goal but the path to the goal is not clear and open. With so broad a definition a large share of the tasks assigned in psychological experiments could be included under the head of "problems." A list of nonsense syllables to be memorized offers a problem which is attacked by various devices, some of them quite intellectual (p. 33). The problems considered in the present chapter are mostly of the concrete, practical sort.

PROBLEM SOLUTION BY ANIMALS

The reasons for dipping here into animal psychology are partly historical, because human studies have grown out of experiments on animal intelligence, but partly psychological, since we need to examine a variety of problem-solving processes, including by all means some of the simplest. We do not obligate ourselves in the least to reach any conclusions on such questions of animal psychology as concern the relative intelligence of different species. Our interest in animals is much the same here as in the early chapter on maze learning (p. 124).

Animal trial and error. Controversy has centered around the expression "trial and error." This process of solution has been contrasted with "reasoning" and with "insight," but all these terms crept into psychology without any adequate definition. The question at issue in many discussions is not really whether animals, children and adults solve problems by trial and error or by insight, but what is meant by trial and error and by insight. Are they mutually exclusive and antithetical, or complementary and necessarily combined in any concrete process of problem solution? Rather than attempt to reach a formal definition at the outset we will follow the experimental work more or less historically and seek clarity of definition as we go along.

If we wished to treat the concept of trial and error historically we should need to go back at least to Alexander Bain (1855, 1864, 1870). He used the phrase in his theory of the "constructive intellect." An inventor or a creative artist needs, according to Bain, first a command of the elements to be used, and second a "feeling of the end to be served" and good judgment of when the end is satisfactorily attained. The actual process is one of "groping and experiment." "In all difficult operations for purposes or ends, the rule of trial and error is the grand and final resort."

In animal psychology we find the concept employed by Lloyd Morgan (1894). His predecessors had credited animals with reasoning power on the strength of anecdotes of cleverness in opening gates, etc., resulting, so it was assumed, from intelligent imitation of human acts. Lloyd Morgan adopted the rule (or "canon") of assuming only the simplest mental operations which could explain animal behavior, and he accordingly preferred to say that animals learned by trial and error. His meaning is made clear in discussing the question *whether animals perceive relations*. He made many informal experiments on animals, including a fox terrier that was quite fond of retrieving a stick. He tried this dog with a stick that had a heavy knob at one end.

At first he seized this by the middle; but to carry it thus was an awkward, lop-sided, unbalanced operation, and by the close of the afternoon he had profited by an hour or two of experience, and seized the stick near the knob end. Now such a proceeding can be completely explained in terms of sense-experience. The process was throughout one of trial and error; gradually he found the most comfortable way of carrying that stick, and adopted it. Incidentally he was solving in a practical way a problem in mechanics; he was finding the center of gravity of the stick. . . . But is there any reason to suppose that Tony perceived this relationship in even a rudimentary and indefinite way? I could see none. . . . The relations at most may be regarded as implicit in practical performance . . . not as explicit in focal perception.

Trial and error behavior, then, is directed toward a goal but is not controlled by any explicit perception of the relationships involved. Mastery of the problem is attained only gradually. In a later book (1900) the same author gave the following description of trial and error:

If such an animal [i.e., one capable of learning by experience] be placed in the midst of new circumstances he has to find out by a process of trial and error how they are to be met. After a longer or shorter period of trial, guided only by particular experiences, he chances to hit upon a mode of procedure which is successful. . . . The association is eventually established by repetition.

As examples of trial and error behavior, Lloyd Morgan gave the following instances: (1) A newly hatched chick pecks at small objects inaccurately but improves his aim in a few day's practice. (2) The young chick pecks indiscriminately at all small objects but after one or two trials of bees, caterpillars, etc., leaves them aside.   (3) A human being in acquiring skill in billiards, marksmanship, singing or any motor performance may receive some guidance from rules and principles but has to try, fail and try again.   (4) Lloyd Morgan's fox terrier Tony learned a number of tricks under his master's watchful eye, and always by the gradual process already described and illustrated.

Puzzle box problems.   Lloyd Morgan's lead was quickly followed by Thorndike (1898), who introduced the problem-solving experiment into the laboratory with cats, dogs, chicks and monkeys as subjects.   Thorn-dike strongly supported the reality of learning by trial and error or as he called it learning by trial and accidental success, which he contrasted with learning by ideas.   He devised a number of puzzle boxes, the doors of which were opened by pulling a string or loop inside or just outside the cage, by turning a door button, or by pressing down on a lever. He used as subjects 13 cats, mostly 3–11 months old, and also a few dogs.   His generalized description of the behavior of the cats is as follows:

The behavior of all but Nos. 11 and 13 was practically the same.   When put into the box the cat would show evident signs of discomfort and of an impulse to escape from confinement.   It tries to squeeze through any opening; it claws or bites at the bars or wire; it thrusts its paws out through any opening and claws at everything it reaches; it continues its efforts when it strikes anything loose and shaky; it may claw at things within the box. . . .   For eight or ten minutes it will claw and bite and squeeze incessantly.   With 13, an old cat (18 months), and 11, an uncommonly sluggish cat, the behavior was different.   They did not struggle vigorously or continually.   On some occasions they did not even struggle at all.   It was therefore necessary to let them out of some box a few times, feeding them each time.   After they thus associate climbing out of the box with getting food, they will try to get out whenever put in.   They do not, even then, struggle so vigorously or get so excited as the rest.   In either case . . . the impulse to struggle . . . is likely to succeed in letting the cat out of the box.   The cat that is clawing all over the box in her impulsive struggle will probably claw the string or loop or button so as to open the door.   And gradually all the other non-successful impulses will be stamped out and the particular impulse leading to the successful act will be stamped in. . . .

Vigor, abundance of movements, was observed to make differences between individuals. . . .   It works by shortening the first times, the times when the cat still does the act largely by accident. . . .   Attention, often correlated with lack of vigor, makes a cat form an association quicker after he gets started.   No. 13 shows this somewhat.   The absence of a fury of activity let him be more conscious of what he did do.

Thorndike bases his argument against reasoning in these animals, and against "seeing through the situation," mainly on the gradualness with which mastery was attained.   The learning curves show in the main a gradual, though irregular decrease in the time consumed per trial.   It is true that some animals mastered some puzzle-boxes in two or three trials, so that there was a rapid drop in their curves at the very outset. These were cases "where the act resulting from the impulse is very simple, very obvious, and very clearly defined." But there was a notable absence of learning curves which, after showing long times for many successive trials, dropped abruptly to short times, as if at a certain time the animal saw through the situation.

In his later work on monkeys, with somewhat similar puzzle boxes, Thorndike (1901) found all but the hardest problems to be solved "by a rapid, often apparently instantaneous, abandonment of the unsuccessful movements and a selection of the appropriate one. . . . It is natural to infer that the monkeys who suddenly replace a lot of general pulling and clawing by a single definite pull at a hook or bar have an idea of the hook or bar and of the movement they make." He admits, however, that this apparent "learning by ideas may also be possibly explained by general activity and curiosity, the free use of the hand, and superior quickness in forming associations of the animal sort."

Thorndike's work repeated. Thorndike's description of the behavior of cats in a puzzle box became classic, though usually the dramatic and impulsive activity of the younger animals was cited rather than the placid behavior of some older cats that mastered the problems. It is important to know whether later attempts to check this description make any important revision necessary. The work of Adams (1929) is sometimes said to compel a radical revision and to show that trial and error and the gradual elimination of false moves are really not characteristic of the animal's process of attacking and solving a problem. Adams gives detailed narratives of the cats' behavior in a near-duplicate of one of Thorndike's boxes. The door was bolted outside; a cord attached to the bolt passed up over a pulley and down into the front part of the cage where it terminated in a loop. Pulling the loop drew the bolt and allowed the door to swing open under the pull of a rubber band. A few abridged protocols are quoted.

Cat number 1, Ace, female, six months old, good condition; had been in laboratory from the age of three and one-half months.

Trial 1. Ace spent about 28 minutes sitting in the center looking around, and about 2 minutes in activity. . . . At the end of half an hour I . . . opened the door by depressing the loop with a pencil. She was allowed to eat about 10 grams of the food and was then replaced in the box.

Trial 2. After one or two exploratory gestures she sat quietly in the center for about 5 minutes . . . startled by a loud commotion . . . mewed and reached through the front to the pan, which I had inadvertently left just within reach, upset it, drew it in, and ate some of the food. . . . (Pan replaced in position by E.) She immediately tried to reach it again, but quickly desisted and sat quietly in the center for 5 more minutes. She then pawed the pulley casually, and in so doing caught the string with a claw . . . and in withdrawing the claw, opened the door. After looking around for a minute, she came out and was allowed to eat 10 grams. Time 13 minutes. After eating—about 2 minutes—she was replaced.

Trial 3. She first pulled on the elastic which was . . . used to open the door. . . . Her next movement was pulling the string just below the pulley, which opened the door. This time she came out at once and ate the reward. Time, 2 minutes.

Trial 4. Just after being put into the box, she pawed the latch . . . and in so doing knocked the loop with her head, but paid no attention to it. Twice she pulled in and bit the elastic, but for the remainder of the half hour period sat quietly . . . released and removed but not fed. . . .

Trial 5. Eight hours later . . . 50 minutes . . . only about 5 minutes of activity. . . . At no time did she scramble and claw indiscriminately. . . . I released the latch where she could see it, allowed her to leave through the door and to eat about 5 grams of the food, and replaced her in the box.

Trial 6. Immediately upon being put into the box, she pawed once at the elastic and then sat in the center of the box. After sitting there almost motionless for one hour and 7 minutes, she pawed the pulley, the door opened and she came out and was allowed to eat all she wanted—about 80 grams—of the food. . . .

Trial 7. Three days later. . . . Twice . . . she pawed at the latch . . . except for the two movements mentioned, all her activity was narrowly directed upon the elastic, which she broke five times. . . . After 40 minutes of this, she stopped working and sat in the center for the remaining 20 minutes. At the end of an hour she was taken out, but not fed.

Trial 8. 90 minutes later. . . . In the meantime I had taken off the elastic and substituted a piece of steel clock spring (under the door where she could not see it) as the means for opening the door. She sat in the center for 4 minutes, then pawed several times where the elastic used to be, stopped abruptly, and bit the string just above the loop. An instant later she pulled the string in this way, came out and ate about 20 grams of the food. Total time, 5 minutes; working time, 1 minute.

Trial 9. Four minutes later she was replaced in the box and immediately sat down. After a minute she pawed where the elastic had been, then toward the food pan, and sat down in the center. Five minutes later pawed . . . at the latch and after a few efforts raised the latch by pulling up the knob. She came out at once, but instead of going directly to the food she paused and looked over the latch . . . for 30 seconds. Time, 7 minutes; working time, 1 minute.

Trial 10. Two minutes later. . . . After one minute she pawed tentatively toward the pulley . . . sat down . . . pawed where the elastic had been and at the latch. After 3 minutes in all, she escaped by pulling the string with her teeth.

Trials 11–31 showed no extra or 'useless' movements and the total time varied from 6 to 70 seconds. The method used varied from time to time. . . . Pulls string with teeth . . . with teeth and paws. . . . Pulls loop with paw. . . . Pulls loop with teeth. . . . Pulls string with paw.

Evidently this animal was well adjusted—almost too well adjusted—to the laboratory monotony and feeding routine. All her activity was restricted to the neighborhood of the door and the food, but within this narrow range of varied reaction there did occur a gradual elimination of some movements and gradual concentration of activity upon the string and loop.

Very exceptional in the records of cat behavior is the following account.

Cat number 4, Pete, 7 months old, good condition, had been in the laboratory from the age of 5½ months.

Trial 1. Pete vigorously resisted being put into the box, but once in displayed no excitement. He sat in the center and looked around, then walked slowly and quietly around the box. He did not touch any part of the walls. . . . After nearly 10 minutes . . . he took hold of the loop with his right paw, drew it to his mouth, pulled, and came out as the door opened. . . .

Trial 2. Three minutes later, after eating his reward, Pete was replaced in the box with much less resistance than he had displayed the first time. He sat back center and washed for three minutes, then ceased washing and sat there looking around for two minutes more. Then he went to the loop, took the string in his teeth and pulled, opening the door. He continued to paw the loop for about half a minute, then came out and ate the reward.

Trials 3–18. Always pulled either loop or string, with no other activity, and got out in from 2 seconds to 2 minutes.

A litter mate of the preceding animal showed the opposite extreme of behavior:

Cat number 5, Fea, good condition.

Trial 1. When first put into the box, Fea walked all around it and looked apparently at the whole interior. She walked about and mewed occasionally for 15 minutes, pawing once through six different openings in the front and top, and once trying to jam her head through an opening. At the end of 15 minutes she abruptly went into a tantrum. . . . She 'scrabbled' all over the front of the box, pawing and clawing at everything she touched. In the course of this behavior (after 20 seconds of it) she clawed at the pulley . . . and in so doing caught the string with a claw . . . and opened the door. . . .

Trial 2. Two minutes later . . . first pawed vigorously through five different openings . . . then walked around, mewing occasionally, for 4 minutes, once pausing to paw through an opening. . . . Then she bit the string, but dropped it quickly. She then pawed excitedly at the pulley and after 20 seconds of this escaped. Time, 4 minutes, 30 seconds.

Trial 3. Immediately when put into the box the animal bit the loop repeatedly . . . without pulling. After 2 minutes of this, she did pull it hard, but at the same time held down the . . . bolt on the outside with a paw. . . . Naturally nothing happened. She gave up after a few tugs, and pawed at the pulley, escaping thereby as before. Time, 2 minutes, 30 seconds.

Trial 4. . . . Fea started immediately to paw the pulley and to bite the loop, again holding the latch on the outside. After 2 minutes of miscellaneous scrabbling, the door opened when the outside string caught on her paw and she pulled it in. Time, 2 minutes.

Trial 5. In this trial she pawed the latch and the pulley and bit the string, escaping after 1 minute, 20 seconds by pawing the pulley.

Trial 6. As soon as she was put into the box, she pulled hard on the outside string. . . . She suddenly released the tension and the string was jerked off the pulley. I . . . replaced it. She then sat quietly . . . for about 2 minutes, after which she bit the string once, decisively and pulled hard, opening the door. Time, 2 minutes, 45 seconds.

Trial 7. The next morning. . . . She sat . . . a moment, bit the string once but dropped it immediately and sat quietly . . . for 2 minutes. Then she thrust a paw through several openings . . . began to mew, sitting . . . for about 3 minutes. She then opened the door by pulling in the outside string with a paw, taking the same with her teeth and pulling.

Trial 8. Immediately . . . took the string in her teeth, but dropped it without pulling. After sitting quietly in the center for nearly 5 minutes, she seized it again in her teeth and escaped with one vigorous pull. Time, 5 minutes.

Trial 9. Pulls string at once with teeth, and persists until door opens. Time, 50 seconds.

Trials 10–23 were much like Trial 9, with times varying from 15 seconds to 19 minutes, but with reaction consisting usually in biting and pulling string, sometimes in pawing it.

Adams's cats thus showed about the same range of individual differences as Thorndike's, though they were on the whole less active and less successful. The main addition to our knowledge from these more detailed reports is that we see the animal not simply going through a variety of *movements*, but dealing with definite *objects*. Moreover, these objects lie in the general neighborhood of the door and the food, or are related to escape. The animal's activity, though varied, is restricted to one general sector, aside from exploration, mere sitting, and washing.

Behavior in relation to objects. Thorndike had spoken of "acts" or movements, which became associated with the situation as a whole, rather than of objects with which the animal dealt. Thus there grew up a picture of trial and error as consisting of varied motor responses to a total situation, those movements which resulted well gradually getting advantage over the rest. Whether or not this motor conception of trial and error is precisely what Thorndike meant, it is at least a definite hypothesis, capable of being checked by experiment; and we may note at once that the detailed behavior cited from Adams—as also observations by Muenzinger (1931), Lashley (1934) and other animal psychologists—rather rules out this purely motor conception of trial and error. The animal's solution of the problem does not consist in the adoption of a particular muscular movement (for the successful movement may vary from trial to trial) but in concentration of activity in a certain region or upon a certain object—string, button, etc.—and in the production of some change in this object. Some stereotypy of movement is indeed found under certain conditions (Guthrie & Horton, 1937).

Response to relations. An important contributor to the history of problem solution is Hobhouse (1901) whose work followed very promptly after that of Thorndike. Hobhouse complained that Thorndike had left a hiatus in mental evolution, since man depends so much on his perception of the relations among objects, whereas in Thorndike's picture of animal learning there seemed to be no perception of relations but only an association formed between a total situation and a certain motor response. Hobhouse believed that three stages could be distinguished in the evolution of response to relations. In the lowest stage behavior is influenced by the relation, but the relation is in no way perceived. In the second stage the relation while not apprehended as such is grasped in connection with the terms as a total pattern. In the third stage the relationship itself is abstracted, named and compared with other relations. The third stage is exclusively human. But Hobhouse believed that the second stage was present in animals as low as the cat. Such an animal, he believed, was aware of things in relation though not aware of relations in the abstract. This type of awareness he called "concrete experience" and behavior based upon such experience he called "practical judgment." Concrete experience amounts to acquaintance with *objects in relation*. When the animal utilizes such acquaintance in solving a problem he shows practical judgment. Hobhouse therefore set himself the task of determining whether animals perceived objects and objective changes and results. He experimented on cats, dogs, elephants, otters, a monkey and a chimpanzee. Thorndike had found that cats and dogs did not learn a trick by being put through it passively nor by seeing another animal perform the trick, that is by imitation. Hobhouse believed it possible however that the animal could learn by being shown, that is by having his attention called to the object and to the manner of manipulation. The difficulty, he found, was to secure the animal's attention to the necessary object. For example, in one of his early experiments, meat was placed upon a card to which was attached a string, the card was put on a shelf and the string allowed to hang down within reach of a cat. The cat appeared not to notice the string at first, but when it finally caught her eye she reacted promptly and appropriately. In general, Hobhouse found that an animal's activity at any time was concentrated upon a certain object, as a string or a bolt, though the motor character of the activity varied from moment to moment.

Non-puzzle problems. Hobhouse introduced a type of task which has been much used in later work on insight and trial and error—a type illustrated by several varieties which he devised:

1. String pulling. The lure is attached to a string; by pulling, the animal secures the reward.

2. String discrimination. The lure is attached to one of 2–3 strings; the animal sees the lure attached. The question is whether he will pull the right string.

3. Reaching-stick or poker, used to pull in an object which lies beyond the reach of the unaided paw.

4. Two sticks. The animal is provided with a short stick to use in reaching a longer stick with which in turn he can reach the lure.

5. Obstacle. A box or other obstacle is placed in the animal's way, the question being whether he will remove the box.

6. Tube and rod. The lure is placed inside the tube, and can be pushed or pulled out with the rod.

7. Footstool. A stool or box must be moved underneath the lure in order to reach the latter.

These problems differ from the puzzle boxes in that the mechanical device involved is very simple and open to view. There are no hidden parts. The objects-in-relation are clearly presented, provided the animal is able to discern the kinetic possibilities of the setup from its mere visual appearance. More of this later.

From Thorndike and Hobhouse to Yerkes and Köhler several investigators during a period of fifteen years made contributions to the subject of problem solution in animals. We will deal with them only briefly.

Transfer as a factor in problem solution. Thorndike had noticed that experience with one puzzle sometimes facilitated the solution of another puzzle. An animal that had mastered a loop hanging in one part of the cage readily mastered a similar or even a dissimilar loop hanging in another part. Experience in the laboratory by degrees made an animal more adaptable to the problems presented. This matter of transfer was considered systematically by Kinnaman (1902) in his work on the rhesus monkey. Various locks had to be unfastened in order to enter the boxes and obtain food. Experience greatly increased the directness of attack upon these fastenings. Where at first the animal would putter around a box and attack the edges and corners, later he concentrated his efforts upon each new lock. A fastening moved from the right to the left side of the door puzzled the animal somewhat but was learned much more quickly than in the original position. When two locks which had been learned singly were combined upon a single door the mastery of this double lock was comparatively easy. The fact that an animal carries over his mastery from one form to a somewhat different form of a device shows that he must have *isolated* the device to some degree. Transfer need not carry over any particular *movement* from one situation to another, but may consist in carrying over response to a particular *object*. Even to recognize an object in an unfamiliar setting involves some transfer.

Limitations of animal problem solving. In the earlier animal studies which we are still considering it became clear that certain problems could be mastered much more readily than others. It was futile to ask in general whether an animal solved problems by trial and error or by response to objects-in-relation; it depended on the problem, and on the animal. Some characteristics of a situation can be discerned directly by a given animal, some by exploration and manipulation, others not at all, though practical mastery may be achieved by a long process of trial and error.

With rhesus monkeys as subjects, Shepherd (1910) found it necessary to use quite simple mechanical arrangements if the animal were to show any direct attack, anything beside trial and error procedure. When tested under "conditions which are within his mental range," the monkey showed practical judgment in Hobhouse's sense. The animals reacted directly to the string problem, when a bucket containing food was attached to one end of the string and the other end placed within reach; they responded equally well when the food was attached to the far end of a stick.

The door button, which to the human adult seems perfectly self-evident, required trial and error from the monkeys. "The animals

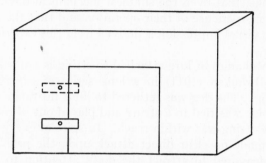

Fig. 240. A door-button puzzle box. The dotted button was added after the chimpanzee had mastered the other one.

scrambled about in a general way at first; they pulled and bit at the door and the adjacent parts of the partition, shook the door violently; but it is to be noted that after the first few experiments the attention of the animal was always directed to the door. Even after an accidental success in turning the button, the association was not at once set, but only after a number of trials."

The door button experiment had been tried on a young chimpanzee in 1902–03 in the laboratory of Sherrington at Liverpool, by the present author (reported in Ladd and Woodworth, 1911, p. 552). The chimpanzee had the run of the animal room. She saw a banana placed in the box, approached it and from the outset devoted most of her efforts to the door which could be moved slightly. She pulled, pushed and shook it. Soon she attacked the button and alternated for some time between it and the door, finally getting the button in the right position and pulling the door open. On a second trial she worked almost entirely at the door and the button and from the third trial her reaction was uniformly prompt and correct; she turned the button with one hand while pulling the door with the other. Several more trials were given for good measure and then E added a *second button* like the first, a few inches from it on the door jamb. The chimpanzee neglected the second button and concentrated all of her efforts on the first, turning it back and forth and pulling at the door. She kept this up for a long time before attacking the second button. Only by chance did she get both buttons right at the

same time. In the course of several trials no further progress was made.
"It seemed to be wholly a matter of chance whether both buttons should
be put right at once or not. The experiment showed a prompt narrowing
down of the field of effort to the right feature of the situation; but this
important factor in the process of learning seemed to be accompanied by a
complete absence of insight into the mechanical principle involved."

This chimpanzee behaved as if the door button were a means of
opening the door rather than a means of holding it closed. The experiment suggests, as is also suggested by the way young children tug their
coats from hooks, that even the simplest mechanical devices are understood only after experience of their operation and that the apparent self-
evidence of the visual impression is derived from this experience of operation.

That the mechanics of lure-attached-to-string is not self-evident was
discovered by Franken (1911) in a long series of experiments on his
Pomeranian dog. The dog was tethered to limit his range of movement,
a piece of sausage was tied to a string and placed out of reach, while the
near end of the string was within reach. In spite of every sign of eager-
ness, the dog made no clear direct attack upon the problem. The experimenter endeavored to attract the dog's attention to the string by
pointing to it and shaking it in front of the dog, but only at the end of a
long first trial did the dog impulsively take the string in his mouth and
jerk backward, so obtaining the lure. On a second trial he failed to
repeat this movement, but in scratching the floor his paw caught the
string and brought the meat within reach. Third and fourth trials were
similar. In further trials the dog usually secured the food either by
snapping at the string and pulling it or by scratching at it. The only
obvious effect of pointing out the string or shaking it before the dog was
to arouse his desire. The author sums up his results as follows: "When
his desire is aroused the dog behaves in an impulsive, variable, goal-
seeking manner . . . the dog seems also while in an emotional state to
be more easily stimulated and to be more eager for reaction. In the last
analysis it is this disposition which is the principal cause of his success
and not insight into the connection of the thing."

Insight in the anthropoid apes. From their anatomical similarity
to man, especially inside the skull, the chimpanzee, gorilla and orang-
utan have long been presumed to stand at the top of the animal scale
of intelligence. Intensive experimental study of their behavior was
started almost simultaneously by Yerkes in California (1916) and by
Köhler in Teneriffe (1917 a, 1924). Both employed the Hobhouse rather
than the Thorndike type of experiment and Köhler, especially, insisted
that all the essential conditions of the problem must lie open to the animal's inspection, if his intellectual level was to be revealed. The word
insight, used sporadically by previous students of animal behavior,
was adopted by Köhler as a fitting antithesis to *trial and error*.

An insightful solution, according to Köhler, is one which takes account of the situation confronting the animal and one which, not built up piecemeal, takes shape at a certain moment and then leads smoothly to the goal. The insightful performance is an integrated whole conforming to the configuration or structure of the situation. Such a solution may occur at the first contact with the problem or after other attempts, lacking insight, have been made. The suddenness with which the solution often emerges indicates insight, and another index is found in the transfer of the solution to a somewhat modified problem.

Yerkes, as well as Köhler, is fully convinced of the insightful character of much anthropoid behavior. As a result of manifold observations on all the anthropoids he lists (1927) the following characteristics of insightful problem solution: "(1) Survey, inspection or persistent examination of problematic situation. (2) Hesitation, pause, attitude of concentrated attention. (3) Trial of more or less adequate mode of response. (4) In case initial mode of response proves inadequate, trial of some other modes of response, the transition from one method to the other being sharp and often sudden. (5) Persistent or frequently recurrent attention to the objective or goal and motivation thereby. (6) Appearance of critical point at which the organism suddenly, directly and definitely performs the required adaptive act. (7) Ready repetition of adaptive response after once performed. (8) Notable ability to discover and attend to the essential aspect or relation in the problematic situation and to neglect, relatively, variations in non-essentials." This last criterion is equivalent to transfer.

Bierens de Haan (1931) regards sudden success as a poor criterion of insight. Mastery that makes its appearance suddenly may be the culmination of a gradual process of becoming acquainted with the situation; and mastery that seems very gradual may be insightful at the end. The latter case is illustrated by a turntable experiment on monkeys. Food was placed on the far side of the table in front of the cage. The first reaction was likely to be a reaching for the food or an attempt to pull the table nearer. When the rotation of the table was noticed most of the animals immediately started to turn it; some came to this procedure more gradually but after a few trials were acting as definitely as the rest. They seemed to understand the turntable as well, though not as quickly as the others.

A problem calls for a "detour." When there is a straight, open path to the goal there is no problem and consequently no solution. To quote Köhler: "We are not ordinarily inclined to speak of insightful behavior, when a man or animal reaches the goal by a direct route which offers him no problem. But we get the impression of insight when circumstances bar any such self-evident course but leave an indirect approach open, and when now the man or animal adopts this appropriate detour."

A typical though very simple problem is presented by a literal detour. Place a dog on one side of a fence and a lure near him on the other side. After first striking a posture as if to spring directly at the food, he may dash off around the end of the fence in a smooth, single curve. A hen in the same circumstances runs back and forth before the food but may gradually extend her run and finally reach the end of the fence from which a direct approach lies open. The dog, according to Köhler, has shown insight, the hen none. This author, it can be seen, approaches the study of problem solution from the side of perception rather than from the side of motor activity. Motor behavior is to him an index of how much the animal sees or discerns, and he distinguishes between detours which the animal does and does not see. (It would seem that he should allow insight also to the animal taking a direct, open route, for then if ever it is sure that the animal discerns the way to the goal. If he cannot discern a direct route, how can we assume him to discern the detour?)

The box stacking problem. This will serve as a sample of numerous experiments on insight performed by Yerkes, Köhler and their successors in the study of primates. Yerkes (1916), using a young orang as subject, found it necessary to demonstrate the process of box stacking repeatedly, but was convinced of the presence of insight by the ease with which the ape handled the situation after once fully succeeding. Yerkes concludes that trial and error played no essential part in the solution—"The ape had the idea."

Köhler first familiarized his subjects with the single box problem before passing to the box stacking. He used several young chimpanzees. At the first trial with a single box, he assembled six of the animals in a room which had smooth, unscalable walls, suspended a banana from the ceiling, and put the box in the middle of the room two or three yards away from the lure. All six chimpanzees leaped repeatedly for the banana, but Sultan, who in other tests showed himself the most apt, soon ceased jumping, paced up and down, suddenly stood still in front of the box, moved it quickly toward the objective, climbed, jumped and secured the banana, taking only twenty seconds in this final continuous act with the box. He repeated the performance the next day. The other apes acquired the box performance after being shown and with some difficulty.

When the lure was too high to be reached from the box in its flat position, several approaches were possible: stand the box on end, find a larger box, or put one box upon another. This last, less obvious, solution had to be enforced by removing all other possibilities.

The box stacking problem proved much more difficult than the use of a single box. It was solved *with assistance* by 4 apes of the 7 that mastered the single box. The (condensed) story of Sultan runs as follows:

Trial 1. The stick, which the animal tries first, is too short, and he throws it away in a rage. He sits down, begins to look around, scratching his head, his eyes rest on the boxes, he drags one of them underneath the lure, takes the stick, mounts the box and knocks down the fruit.

Trial 2. No sticks are present now. After futile attempts of various sorts he places one box in position, measures the distance with his eyes, does not mount but knocks the box around in a rage. Then he fetches the other box, but instead of placing it on the first, he does various things with it, placing it beside the first, and holding it up in the air toward the lure. He becomes enraged again, runs about the room dragging the box, discards it, and tries other objects. A complete failure in this trial.

Trial 3. Nothing is present now except two boxes and the suspended banana. He places one box, mounts, sits down again. Grabs the second box and runs around the room in a rage, comes to a halt, drags the second box to the first, places it on top, mounts, but does not jump. The lure is still too high.

Trial 4. (Immediately after the preceding.) The fruit is hung somewhat lower, but he pays no attention to the boxes, as if discouraged by his previous failure. The experimenter now places the boxes in position, and the ape mounts and obtains the fruit.

Trial 5. (Immediately after the preceding.) The ape stacks the two boxes but not under the lure; instead he places them in the exact spot where his first two-box structure had been erected (the lure had been moved). The experimenter again arranges the boxes.

Trial 6. On the next day, he puts only one box in position; the experimenter adds the second.

Trial 7. (Immediately after the preceding.) Sultan tries to use the experimenter as a ladder. The experimenter again stacks the boxes and Sultan gets the reward.

Trial 8. (Immediately after the preceding.) Sultan places one box in position, brings the second box, seems uncertain what to do with it, suddenly lifts it and places it on the first box and obtains the reward.

Trial 9. Two days later. Sultan places the first box in position, brings the second, lifts it, lowers it again and then tries other methods such as climbing the wall or using the experimenter as a ladder. Finally the animal returns to the boxes, gets one very unstably on the other, climbs but overturns the structure and falls. He lies down in a corner for a long time looking at the lure and the boxes, comes back, tries to reach from a single box, gets down, places a second box on the first but so unstably that it wobbles when he starts to mount: "Only after much experimenting in which the animal plainly is proceeding blindly and letting everything depend on the success or failure of planless movements, does the upper box finally get into position in which it does not wobble when he tests it with his foot, and so the goal is in his reach."

From that trial on Sultan always employed both boxes and never appeared altogether confused as to the proper method.

Why was box stacking so difficult for the chimpanzees? From a detailed study of their behavior, Köhler believes they had two problems to solve, one in geometry and then one in statics. The geometrical problem can be subdivided into: (a) a problem in quantity, (b) a problem in form.

1. (a) The problem of quantity is solved when the ape brings a second box to supplement the first. Instead of placing it on top he lays it beside the first, or holds it in the air toward the lure, as if the solution were formulated in the words: "If one box doesn't reach, get two." (b) The problem of form is solved when the animal places the second box

on top of the first; he is closing the gap between the ground and the lure. This problem like that of quantity is solved rather suddenly.

2. The problem of statics. The chimpanzees were poor builders. Such stability as a man would require was not necessary because of their agility. Their placing of the upper box was very crude, and yet one or

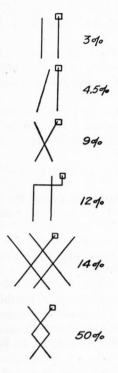

two of them succeeded in building structures of three and even four boxes, which would stand long enough for a rapid climb and a snatch at the food. Köhler concludes that the geometrical problem of box stacking was solved by insight but the static problem by trial and error.

Some difficulties encountered by animals in solving problems. While it is not easy to discern the process by which the animal reaches his solution, some light is thrown on the question by noticing the conditions which create difficulty.

1. **Intricate or unclear visual field.** The visual picture in the string-pulling problem can be complicated by introducing two or more strings, only one of which is attached to the lure though another or others lie near it, or cross each other, or run an indirect course (Fig. 241).

2. **Hidden characteristics of the field.** Hobhouse and Köhler were quite critical of puzzle boxes and insisted that the animal should be able to survey the whole problem. But they found it very difficult to live up to this principle. In the box stacking problem the animals did not see into the statics involved. When a ring hung from a hook they did not see the kinetics of the combination; they did not see that the ring could easily be lifted off the hook. In these matters of statics and kinetics, the visual field, apart from manipulation or past acquaintance, does not reveal the essential relations.

FIG. 241. (Harlow & Settlage, 1934.) String patterns tried on rhesus monkeys, with percent of errors. Each of 10 animals made 100 trials with each of these patterns.

3. **Resistance to detouring.** This source of difficulty can be observed in human beings as well as animals. To start out at 90° or 180° from the goal direction "goes against the grain." In apes and monkeys this difficulty is brought out by the "stick detour" problem. After the simple reaching-stick problem is mastered, the lure is placed in a box or drawer which is open at the top and at the far end, but closed at the near end and sides, so that the lure must first be pushed away from the animal— a detour of 180°. Köhler found this a difficult problem for chimpanzees,

as did Guillaume & Meyerson (1930). Their most intelligent animal tried every other possibility first: moving the drawer, poking the banana over one side of the drawer, which meant a 90° instead of a 180° detour, spearing the fruit with the stick, or smashing it and getting a taste from the stick. The "correct" solution occurred at first partly by accident, when some other line of attack brought the banana close to the open end of the drawer; then it was pushed out and around. The process of gaining

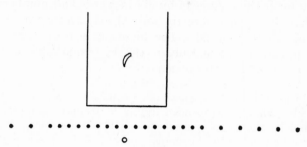

FIG. 242. Drawer detour problem. A fine-meshed wire netting prevents the animal from reaching directly into the drawer from inside his cage. He has a stick with which the banana can be pushed out of the far end of the drawer and then pulled within reach at the side.

mastery was gradual. It was a process not of fixing certain definite movements—for the movements continually varied according to the position of the lure—but rather a perceptual process in which the animal carefully watched the progress of the lure around the detour curve. The extent of the field which was apprehended as a unit increased by degrees, as did also the temporal span of planning or foresight. Transfer to similar stick-detour problems was good. The authors conclude that the solution was insightful, though it did not meet Köhler's criteria of suddenness and smoothness.

4. **Difficulties of temporal order.** The necessary sequence of moves is sometimes the main difficulty for the animal. Kinnaman (1902) devised a type of combination lock in which already familiar devices had to be operated in a definite order—a plug pulled out before a button could be turned, etc. The interlocking mechanism was concealed, and there was nothing in sight to reveal the order in which the devices had to be operated; this order could only be discovered by trial. Yet adult men mastered the order in one or two trials. Monkeys took many trials with very gradual dropping out of superfluous moves and without any evidence of insight into the necessary order.

Another combination lock, devised much later by McDougall & McDougall (1931) was all laid out in plain sight and proved much less difficult. The animal first learned to lift the lid of a box, finding food inside. The lid was then fastened by a simple bar, which was quickly mastered; another bar was now added which must be pushed aside before the first one could be moved; and as fast as one such problem was mastered another bar was added which must be moved first of all. With a raccoon as subject success continued up to as many as 24 bars. But in this problem the animal had much to guide him and was not learning a mere temporal sequence.

The best known problem demanding mastery of a mere time sequence is Hunter's temporal maze (p. 134) which is very difficult for animals though easy for human subjects by aid of words and numbers. Even a situation that lies open before the animal may cause trouble if the sequence of moves is essential. The following performance of a Cebus monkey in an experiment of Klüver (1933) is remarkable and yet shows some confusion in the matter of sequence.

The food was suspended above a table but beyond reach except by the use of a long stick. This was suspended from a horizontal bar and could not be reached except by the use of a short stick lying on the floor. But the short stick could not be reached by the animal, tethered as he was, except by the use of a small wire hook which lay within his reach. A smooth straightforward performance would require the animal to haul in the short stick with the hook, to knock down the long stick with the short one, and then, carrying the long stick, to mount the table and knock down the suspended fruit. The animal's actual behavior was as follows: Looks at food, reaches for the short stick, gazes at food again uttering sounds; picks up wire hook and drops it; climbs on table, does not reach for food, looks at long stick; climbs down to the floor, runs around the room; climbs on table and reaches for long stick; climbs down and reaches for long stick while standing beneath it; suddenly grasps wire hook and draws in short stick; climbs on table with short stick; tries to reach food with short stick but fails; knocks down long stick with the short one; leaves short stick on table, climbs down and gets long stick; climbs back on table but does not succeed in carrying long stick onto the table; tries to knock down the food with the short stick; failing in this, climbs down and finally succeeds in getting back on table with the long stick; knocks down food with long stick. Time, 5 minutes and 49 seconds.

Tentative conclusion on insight and trial and error. If these terms are both defined in the most extreme manner,—insight as equal to solution by mere inspection with no tentative movement, and trial and error as equal to mere movement with no inspection of the situation—then our survey of animal experiments has failed to reveal any case where either insight or trial and error was present. No behavior in problem situations has come to light in which the animal thrashes around in absolute blindness with no reference to the objective situation. Always he is reactive to objects and nearly all of his reactions have some degree of plausibility. Trial and error, as we find it, consists not in blind and purely random movement but in trying this and that lead toward the goal. As far as we can judge from the animal's behavior there is always some perception of the objective situation, as there is in the maze (p. 135).

The other side of the picture is that this perception is never complete at the outset, in any situation that can be called problematical. The situation needs to be explored and seldom can be satisfactorily explored without locomotion or manipulation. But even the first view of a situation reveals the outline of the problem sufficiently to limit in some degree the range of exploration and manipulation.

Our conclusion so far should be regarded as a hypothesis to be tested as we go on to consider human problem solution. We can put it in the form of a diagram: let a circle represent the whole range of the organism's possible activities. Faced with a problem, the organism does not deploy all these activities but only a certain sector of them related to the goal. Perception of the goal and of the situation has the effect of limiting the range of the organism's activity to a relatively narrow sector. Within that sector varied and tentative action is necessary. As exploration proceeds the situation is more fully perceived and the sector of trial and error is correspondingly narrowed, but even when the problem is solved "in principle" there remains a certain leeway for varied reaction in the finer details of manipulation. Only when the goal lies straight and open before the subject without detour of any sort—or only when through previous experience the problem has already been solved—is there a complete absence of trial and error.

PROBLEM SOLVING BY YOUNG CHILDREN

The experiments on primates have been a stimulus to the child psychologists, largely because the methods could easily be adapted. Sixteen infants were tested by Richardson (1932) with the single string and multiple string problems, once every four weeks from the age of 28 weeks to 52 weeks. The child was seated before a table which was separated from him by a grill with interstices 3 × 4 in. in size. Small toys were tied to the strings. At each sitting E presented first the single string problem and followed with the multiple strings just as long as the child's interest held. At the age of 28 weeks success in the single string problem seemed to occur only by chance, at 36 weeks there was often a prompt response, and at 44 weeks the response was definite. The time of those reactions which were successful went down from 72 sec. at 28 weeks to 20 sec. at 44 and to 12 sec. at 52 weeks.

What is meant by saying that the 28-weeks-old baby succeeded in the string pulling test only by accident is illustrated by the following abridged report of the behavior of a certain little boy confronted by a string attached to a toy cat:

He brings his right hand down on the string, scratches and picks up the string, releases it again, glances at the cat, scratches on the table top, again scratches at the string without picking it up, pounds the table top, finally secures the string between thumb and finger of his right hand and pulls on it, meanwhile however looking elsewhere. The cat comes half way across the table, but the child pays no attention to it and continues to pull in the string, watching the string move but not noticing the cat. Pounds the table top. Suddenly he jerks the string, bringing the cat within reach, then seizes it and carries it to his mouth, vocalizing satisfaction. Total time: 1 min., 55 sec.

Before the child reaches the stage of utilizing the string as a means of drawing the lure within reach, he seems to show 4 types of interest or perception: (1) interest in the string and in manipulating it, the lure being only incidental; (2) interest in the lure with a reaching motion toward it which accidentally affects the string; (3) interest in both the string and the lure but without seeing them as forming an integrated pattern; (4) experimentation, manipulating the string while watching the movement of the lure. The function of the string may be discovered in the act of pulling it.

Mastery of the multiple string problem, as one would expect, lagged behind that of the single string. In the simplest multiple string problem

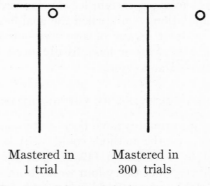

Mastered in   Mastered in
1 trial   300 trials

FIG. 243. Scheme of the hoe experiment.

(three strings reaching perpendicularly toward the subject, with one of the three tied to the lure), 42% of the babies were successful at 36 weeks and 73% at 48 weeks. The more complex multiple string problems, with converging or crooked strings, showed no definite progress up to the age of one year.

The gain in ability to master string problems during the last half of a child's first year may very well be a result of maturation, but maturation consists largely in development of the ability to learn. The behavior of the child certainly indicates that he has to learn the possibilities of strings by his own experimentation. There is no evidence that he sees the kinetic possibilities in advance of actual experience.

In their comparative study of the early development of a human child and a young chimpanzee, brought up together in the home and treated as nearly alike as possible, the Kelloggs (1933) made many observations on problem solving behavior. The hoe problem, a modification of the reaching-stick problem, was first presented when the child was 15 months old and the chimpanzee 2½ months younger but at about the same stage of development.   A piece of apple lay on the floor behind a wire screen which did not quite reach the floor but left a space through which O could reach with the hoe.   The small wooden hoe was a new tool, yet both subjects succeeded at once in the simplest problem, pulling the hoe and obtaining the apple which lay directly in the path of the hoe.   But when the apple was placed somewhat to the side, the response was not adjusted to this change of position and still consisted in a straight pull, missing the lure.   Both subjects behaved in this way.   A long practice series was begun, 10 trials a day, and the first success, apparently accidental in both cases, occurred in the chimpanzee's 99th trial and in the child's 120th.   Progress was so slow that E gave daily demonstrations in which O's movement was guided.   Thus assisted the chimpanzee achieved practical mastery in a total of 265 trials and the child in 337.   Each required still further experience to master the use of the hoe with the lure in a variable position.   Though the young chimpanzee appeared to have a slight advantage over the child in this and some other problems, on the whole their behavior and their development were quite similar. We are specially interested in the demonstrated need for experience in learning what seems to an adult a perfectly obvious relationship, namely, that the hoe must be behind the object which is to be pulled.

When somewhat older children, two or three years of age, are examined (as by Alpert, 1928), clues to the process of solution are afforded by their spontaneous comments as well as by their facial expressions.   For example here is the protocol of the first trial of a girl of 32 months with the single box or stool experiment:

The subject is ushered into a room in which a toy airplane is suspended from the ceiling to within about four feet of the floor, while five feet away on the floor is a hollow block or small box already familar to the subject in another setting.   The subject tries to reach the airplane with the right hand and with the left and then with both, shouting all the while "It's too high, I can't do it, how do you get it?"   She comes to the experimenter with this outcry and is told to try again.   She reaches up as before, complaining excitedly.   At the end of two minutes she perceives the block, pounces on it and says with a sob "I think this will help."   Places block in poor alignment but succeeds in swinging the objective.   Radiant with joy.

This author gave an ordered series of box tests, and a series of simple and complicated reaching-stick problems.   With 44 children as subjects, she found that their first attack upon a problem involving a *new principle* (as stacking two boxes or joining two sticks) almost always showed trial and error ("exploration and elimination").   When however the problem involved only slight change from the preceding one, so that transfer was easy, the solution was often immediate.   The author believed that some insight was always present whenever solution occurred.   The insight might be prompt or delayed, it might be partial or complete, it might be sudden or gradual.   In gradual insight O was apparently interested in the box or stick for some time before trying to use it. One trait often appearing in children as well as in chimpanzees and monkeys is a certain playfulness and liking for stunts. They become so interested in manipulating the tool as to lose sight of the goal.

Gottschaldt (1933) tried a variety of stick and string experiments, simple and complicated, on normal children up to 8 years of age and on feebleminded and psychopathic children. A problem which he regards as about on the six-year level is as follows: a short stick is placed within the child's play pen; outside are two sticks, a long and a short, which can be reached by using the short stick in the cage. But only the longer of these two outside sticks will reach to the lure beyond. Young children often pulled in both sticks and played with them, forgetting the original purpose, but a normal six-year-old showed an integrated and economical performance, disregarding the superfluous short stick, pulling in the long one, and with it pulling in the lure. This problem, curiously enough, is made more difficult by placing the toy almost within reach of the short stick which lies ready at hand. When the problem can *almost* be solved by an easy method the adoption of a more difficult method encounters unusual obstacles; the resistance to detour is high, the "vector" is too strong (Lewin, 1935, p. 83).

Gottschaldt also tried a block building problem which is analogous to the box stacking problem, but more complicated. The subject is supplied with 60 long, slender blocks and is told to build a tower which shall reach to the ceiling. A normal eight-year-old boy solved this problem as follows:

Starting with great confidence, he first lays the blocks flat but finds that there are not nearly enough of them to reach when laid thus. He clears away the first structure and tries a single pillar of the blocks, end to end, but this construction is too unstable to be carried high. He now pauses as if in thought and begins again with "arches" consisting of two uprights and a cross piece, repeating the arch vertically. Finding this structure unstable, he places blocks at the side to brace it, and also sets up a second arch on the floor parallel to the first. Then, apparently without seeing ahead, he lays two connecting blocks across from one arch to the other and at this moment seems to see how the problem can be solved. He proceeds in each successive story to set up two parallel arches tying them together by two cross pieces. This first attempt however collapses, but he does not change his method except to use more accuracy in placing the blocks.

An imbecile boy of eight years started in much the same way, but continued with blocks laid flat till all were used and then complained that there were not enough blocks. Being shown the blocks in a vertical position, he starts building pillar-wise and keeps this up for an hour, with thirty downfalls, till the experimenter gives him another lead. He develops no comprehensive plan for the whole problem and does not even set himself immediate goals, simply builds.

A psychopathic child approached the task in a halfhearted manner and tried various methods without ever setting to work on the tower.

The role of play in developing equipment for problem solution. If we were attempting to trace the child's development we should do well to observe him in his play, in the hope of discovering how he acquires the knowledge of things which he puts to use in problem solving. Interludes of playful activity have often occurred in the experiments already cited on problem solution by children and animals, and have seemed to result in new lines of attack. When the subject is baffled by the problem, he often compensates by engaging in playful activity, and in the midst of this play may hit upon something serviceable in the problem.

Guanella (1934) has traced the development of block building from two to six years in a preschool environment affording abundance of material with a minimum of adult restraint and teaching. Up to about two years (even in the superior group of children under observation) the child cannot be said to construct anything with his blocks. He is occupied with various manipulations such as pounding the blocks together, dropping them, throwing them, carrying them in the hands or on the head, handing them to someone else, taking blocks out of the box and putting them back. From about the age of two, children begin to construct something with blocks, not naming the structure and apparently not intending to represent anything. They are occupied with structural problems, problems of geometry and statics. They build horizontal rows of blocks, vertical rows, horizontal areas like a floor, vertical areas like a wall, three-dimensional solid constructions; and advance to the span or arch, the enclosed horizontal space, the roof. The "arch" or lintel unit, composed of two uprights and one horizontal block, is a great favorite which makes its appearance at about the age of three and is soon utilized in various elaborations, such as rows, walls and towers composed of arches or embodying arches along with other elements. Thus the young builder becomes familiar with conditions of stability and instability and with the possibilities of his materials. Along with this engineering interest there is apt to go a rudimentary esthetic interest. Often the question is, how to make something pretty. It is answered by the use of decoration, symmetry, repetition and rhythm, all of this being spontaneous with the child or at least not suggested by the adult. The stage of representative building comes on rather gradually during the third year. At first the child names his structures only after they are made, later he announces beforehand what he is building and starts with a definite idea to construct a particular sort of thing, as an ocean liner or a railroad station.

In brief, the child starts his block building career by making the acquaintance of single blocks and their properties, and advances to an exploration of the properties of combinations of blocks, after which he is prepared to utilize his knowledge in dramatic play and in representation. Undoubtedly there are many moments of discovery when the child first sees into a certain property of his material, but just as certainly his later achievements utilize what he has previously learned. His insights grow out of his knowledge and experience.

PROBLEM SOLUTION BY HUMAN ADULTS

The first use of puzzles as furnishing problems for human solution was made by Lindley (1897). He gave a useful survey of the great variety of puzzles, linguistic, mathematical, logical and mechanical, with which people amused themselves, and found by a questionnaire that the language puzzles were the most popular and the mechanical next. For experimental use he chose a unicursal puzzle, such as is shown in the adjoining figure. Each child or adult O was supplied with several copies of this puzzle to be traced without repeating any line or taking the

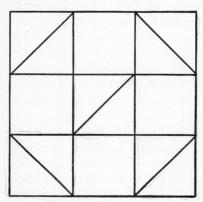

pencil off the paper. There was a tendency, derived probably from reading habits, to begin in the upper left hand corner of the puzzle, which beginning made success impossible. The younger children, when they succeeded, did so by a long series of slight variations with gradual exclusion of erroneous movements. Older persons made quicker shifts and wider variations. Asked for an introspective account, they reported methods which differed greatly from one O to another. Some started to draw with no preliminary examination of the puzzle, others analyzed the visible puzzle but used no abstract or mathematical concepts, still others were

FIG. 244. A unicursal puzzle used by Lindley (1897) and Bulbrook (1932).

guided by a sort of rudimentary mathematics. There is in existence an adequate mathematical analysis of unicursal puzzles by Euler, but these Os were not acquainted with it. The adults as compared with the children profited more promptly by their errors.

Ruger (1910) made an intensive study of puzzle solution by adults. He used the mechanical puzzle as an analogue of the puzzle box previously used on animals. In respect to method, this study is among the most complete. It includes behavior data obtained by watching O's manipulation, the running comments of O during the process of solution and O's retrospective account of each trial, which indeed did not attempt to go into any description of images and so on, but reported the difficulties encountered and the lines of attack. Finally, Ruger has the time of each trial and the learning curve obtained from the series of trials (p. 170).

An example will show the character of the data. The "heart and bow" puzzle consists of two rings interlinked, one ring having the shape of a bow. In place of the string of the bow there is a bar of wire passing loosely through two eyes at the ends of the bow and bent at each end into a square which prevents the bar from being slipped through the eye. The problem is to separate the heart from the bow. O's record is as follows:

Trial No.	Time of solution	O's report
1	351.0 sec.	"I have no idea in the world how I did it. I remember moving the loop of the heart about the end of the bar, and the two pieces suddenly came apart. I think I can do it sooner next time, not because I know just how to do it, but I remember the parts of the puzzle which I brought together in the first success."
2	256.4	"Do not yet know what movements to make."
3	155.0	"Success was still largely chance; did not anticipate except that I knew there was a certain part of the puzzle to work at. Hold the heart in the right hand and the bow in the left. Move the loop of the heart through the end of the bow. Can't describe the other movements; the rest is chance. Think I will get it next time."
4	27.0	
5	33.0	
6	50.0	
7	49.6	
8	28.0	
9	13.6	
10	13.7	
11	6.0	"It is easier to run the loop of the heart *under* the end of the bar. Had done this before but just realized its importance."
12	9.5	
13	8.0	"Noticed that when the bow is in a vertical position the bar on the upper side should be in a horizontal position. Pass the loop underneath, and with a sort of twist pass the end of the bar through the loop of the heart."
14	5.0	"Went through as anticipated. Feel that I understand solving the puzzle."
15	3.6	
16	4.8	
17	3.6	

Without attempting to follow this report in detail the reader can easily see certain of the main points which Ruger derives from the whole study.

1. *Locus analysis.* O noticed first the mere place or part of the puzzle where success was reached, and so was enabled to eliminate much superfluous experimentation in the following trials. Place analysis is obviously one of the easiest kinds. It is well illustrated in animal learning (p. 750).

2. *Analysis after the act.* Insight is often hindsight rather than foresight. In many cases O did not see ahead to the terminus of the solution, but being on the alert noticed how success occurred as or after it occurred. Some Os attempted to solve puzzles by inspection without manipulation, but no one was entirely successful, since, as Ruger puts it, the transformations in three dimensions required for the manipulation of these puzzles could not be envisaged without actual manipulation.

3. *Stages of analysis.* After O had mastered the puzzle in principle there still remained abundant opportunity for dissecting out the details, and such analysis led to greater skill.

Writing some years before Köhler had brought the word *insight* into prominence, Ruger used this word only incidentally. His equivalent terms are *analysis, conscious variation,* and the *setting up and testing of a hypothesis.* "The process of analysis or 'seeing through a thing' is a very distinct experience. In many cases it is an extremely sudden transformation, 'a flash.' " Again, "the term 'analysis' is used very broadly for the whole process of mental emphasis whether of the analytic or synthetic type in the narrow sense of the terms. The getting of a single organized view of a mass of details would thus be classed as 'analysis.' " *Analysis varies in explicitness* from a vague feeling of familiarity to a generalized formula available for use under varying conditions. *Analysis varies in completeness* from the mere locus analysis already mentioned, up through the mapping out of the successful procedure as a series of steps, and on up to the understanding of the principle in its application to the procedure as a whole and in detail. Again, *analysis varies from the purely perceptual to the purely ideational.* Perceptual analysis occurs when O in looking at the puzzle sees a relationship. The puzzle takes on a new appearance as a picture puzzle does when the hidden face is seen. Purely ideational analysis occurred in a few instances when O after working with the puzzle found the solution later with the puzzle no longer before him. Vivid imagery seemed to play no essential role in the process of analysis. The ideational type of analysis may be symbolic and verbalized or it may be schematic and spatial in character.

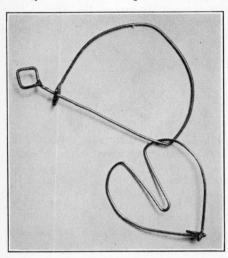

FIG. 245.   The "Heart and Bow" puzzle, used by Ruger (1910).

As conditions favorable for successful analysis, Ruger noticed two especially. One was an *objective attitude* of absorption in the problem, as distinguished from self-consciousness. In starting their first puzzles many Os had the feeling of being on trial. They felt that they were making fools of themselves. After one or two successful solutions they lost this hampering self-consciousness and were able to devote themselves fully to the task. The second general condition favoring the emergence of successful variations was a *freedom from fixed assumptions.* Very often the first glance at a puzzle gave the impression that a certain line of attack was necessary. This might be a radically false assumption, but difficult to shake off. In some cases, after prolonged failure, success was reached by the intervention of the experimenter with a simple question: What are your assumptions? Do you see any other possible assumptions? Sometimes a rest period freed O from false assumptions and enabled him to see fresh possibilities.

Both success and failure in different ways promoted analysis. Failure after some success stimulated O to examine the situation more closely. Success after monotonous failure freed him from a hopeless, inattentive routine of performance.

As indications of conscious analysis or insight, Ruger used the following: (1) O so reports; (2) O brightens up at a certain time; (3) O moves directly and precisely toward the goal; (4) O maintains this variation in later trials; (5) O transfers the variation to other situations, that is, to puzzles of similar principle.

With regard to this transfer criterion, however, Ruger found many cases where the transfer from one puzzle to another was a hindrance instead of a help because although the principle was the same the details differed and made new adaptations necessary. In some cases O was thrown altogether off the track by carrying over the exact procedure which had proved successful in a similar puzzle. Transfer may indicate lack of discrimination, lack of adequate insight.

The practice curve, constructed by plotting the time of each trial, afforded an objective check on the value of conscious analysis. When the practice curve showed a sudden drop to quicker and more uniform performance, the protocol was examined for indications of conscious analysis, and such indications were found just preceding 70–80 per cent of the instances of sudden improvement. *Nearly all the objective improvement could be traced to conscious analysis.*

Is all improvement in performance due to insight? Ruger's finding that conscious analysis occurs not only in discovering the main principle of a puzzle but also in details of manipulation raises an important question which was not indeed specifically raised by him. The question may be phrased in several different ways. May not all improvement in the practice curve, gradual as well as sudden, be due to insight on a large or small scale? Or, are not all variations in performance more or less conscious at the moment when they are initiated? Or again, is not the performance a perceptual as well as a motor process throughout? An affirmative answer to these questions would extend the range of problem solving and thinking down into the details of motor skill. At first thought an affirmative answer seems very improbable. Allowance would certainly have to be made for variations due to warming up and fatigue, physical and emotional condition, motivation and effort.

Swift (1903, 1908) from his experiments in learning ball tossing and the punching bag, and Book (1908) from his experiments on learning to typewrite, had concluded that improvements in method were hit upon *unconsciously* and not noticed until they had been in use for some time. After learning to manage a punching bag skillfully Swift reported that "it was quite clear that all of the delicate movements by which the bag is made continually to rebound with a rapidity that the eye cannot follow were happened upon quite unconsciously." The question remains whether these movements were initiated unconsciously in the full sense of the word. Methods adopted in the midst of active performance may be seen at the moment as possible leads but not formulated till later. Insight consists in the original seeing of a possible line of attack rather than in the later formulation of it. Swift, however, calls attention to the fact that in keeping two balls in the air the most important and delicate movements, made with the fingers, are less conscious than the grosser arm movements and scarcely susceptible of conscious analysis and modification.

Further studies on the role of insight in acquiring skill are discussed on pp. 158, 205.

Experimental methods in the study of human problem solution. Instead of considering one by one the more recent experiments, we may better take them up topically, beginning with improvements in method.

Thinking aloud or *reflexion parlée* as a means of obtaining data on O's process of solution was used to some extent by earlier experimenters and was strongly advocated by Claparède (1917, 1934). He distinguished it sharply from introspection, because the instructions call not for a description of the mental process but for free expression. O reports not sensations, images and feelings but usually the objects with which he is dealing, the situation as he sees it, and the results he is trying to accomplish. Individuals who do not like to talk while working are not suitable Os in this particular form of experiment. Several more recent experimenters have used this general method. Duncker (1926) instructed O to give expression to all his attempts at a solution, no matter how foolish. The reports, he found, were never complete, since some attempts at solution were too fleeting and too obviously foolish to be expressed. Therefore the protocols cannot be used to prove a negative conclusion. O's comments are taken down in longhand, shorthand or by use of a microphone-dictaphone assembly (Henry, 1934). Besides thinking aloud, O may be asked to refrain from manipulation till he has made and expressed a plan of attack (Durkin, 1937).

In order to bring the whole solution within the confines of the experiment, the device is used of supplying O with all the necessary data or material. So Duncker, setting physical or mathematical problems, prefaced the statement of the problem by the relevant information and instructed the subject not to go outside of this statement of facts.

The device of supplying aid by the intervention of E during the solution has been tried by several investigators. When O has come to a halt E supplies further data or suggests new lines of attack (Claparède, 1934). One object is to see how much use O makes of a given type of aid and thus to judge whether the corresponding process is important in his unaided solutions. For example, Duncker supplied a general abstract principle which could be used in the problem; as this aid was of little value the indication was that O's solutions were not proceeding in abstract terms. Henry in his geometrical originals supplied first the diagram without helping lines, then when the subject had come to a halt supplied helping lines and later other suggestions.

Types of problems used. Besides the mechanical and unicursal puzzles, already spoken of, a variety of practical problems have been employed. Many require the use of materials in new ways or depend on abandoning some preconceived notion or assumption. For example one problem used by Bulbrook (1932) required O to regularize the color pat-

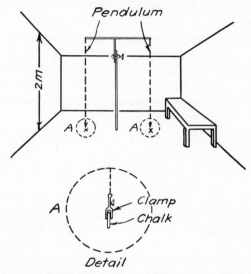

FIG. 246. (Maier, 1930.) The pendulum problem, solved.

tern of a string of beads without unstringing or restringing them or breaking the thread. The string as given can be represented in letters, X denoting one color and O another, as follows:

OXXOXXOXXXXXOXXOXXOXX

The problem consisted in getting rid of the superfluous beads in the center, and the only possible method was to break them with one of the tools provided. Before doing this O had to overcome his implicit assumption that the beads were to be left intact, though no such requirement was included in the instructions.

False assumptions were apparently the cause of difficulty in the following problem used by Maier (1930): To set up two pendulums at a specified distance apart, each of which shall mark the floor. Material supplied: wooden strips of different lengths, clamps, wire, and a heavy table which however must not be moved. In addition there were the walls and low ceiling of the room. E provided data in the form of "parts." (a) He showed how to make a plumb line by use of a wire attached to a clamp. (b) He showed how to lengthen a pole by clamping together two strips. (c) He showed how to wedge a strip against a door post by the use of another strip braced across the opening of the door. If these three devices were properly combined the solution was reached, but the Os all proceeded on the assumption that the table somehow would be used, or the walls, and none of them thought of using the ceiling until their attention was turned to that possibility by E's suggesting a "direction." Practically no one reached the solution without this direction which may also be called a line of attack upon the problem, an orientation, an organizing principle, or a frame of reference. The direction alone without aid in the form of "parts" was also not sufficient.

An old standard puzzle, used by several experimenters, supplies six matches and requires four equilateral triangles to be made without breaking the matches. O naturally assumes that the construction will lie in a plane, and on being shown the solution (a tetrahedron) he calls it a trick puzzle. The trick lies however in his own unnecessary assumption. Other trick puzzles depend on similar natural assumptions, as for example:

A Captain with 50 men comes to the edge of a river and finds the only boat to be one in which two children are playing but which is so small that it will hold only one man and not even a child in addition. How does the Captain manage to get all his men ferried across?

Another trick puzzle:

How can you bring up from the river exactly six quarts of water when you have only a four quart and a nine quart pail to measure with?

Yet another:

A man stopping at a hotel ran out of money and would have no more for 23 days. The landlord would not trust him, but as he had a heavy gold chain of 23 links, the landlord agreed to accept one link in payment on each successive day and to restore the chain on the receipt of the money. Problem, how many links does the owner have to cut in order to fulfill his engagement? The answer is 2 links.

The various puzzles of this type call for a twisting and turning, a back and forth action, a sort of detour, which is contrary to one's natural assumption of straightforward progress.

Regular arithmetical or geometrical problems would seem to be excellent material for the study of problem solution, provided of course that O has the proper background and knowledge. Henry (1934) first gave the students in a geometry class a review of certain basic propositions and then presented some original propositions to be demonstrated. He allowed only a short time for the solution of each original. His grist of correct solutions was small, as perhaps one would expect who remembers his own experience in geometry, and evidences of insight were scarce—only 17 "flash experiences" indicated in 193 correct solutions. Duncker (1935) besides geometrical propositions gave arithmetical problems such as: to prove that any six-place number having the form a b c, a b c (as 2 7 6, 2 7 6 or 5 3 8, 5 3 8) is divisible by 13.

The unnecessary assumption with which O loaded this problem consists in the habit of dividing right through from left to right disregarding the comma. Calling attention to the comma might be a steer in the right direction. Duncker found that introducing the abstract concept of com-

Fig. 247. (Claparède, 1934.) "Primitive cookery." Two protocols from this picture are appended.

1. Man in process of being roasted, another man turning the spit; two whites and two blacks, therefore the one who is turning the spit is destined also to be eaten. The two blacks are in a quarrel. The cook has an expression of woe, the other is reproaching him. For what reason? Perhaps because one should have begun by eating the other man, or perhaps the cook has forgotten something in the process of cooking, or has left some garments on the person being roasted, or perhaps the chief is scolding him because the one turning the spit is sweating and losing his fat (which will diminish his nutritive value) . . . There must be a feast given by the king of these savages, these two individuals have been kept to furnish food for the occasion and something on the menu corresponds to the dish composed of the old skinny man and the cook has roasted the fat one.

2. Some cannibals had the idea of eating a gentleman who has arrived on their island. No that is not it, I see that the thin gentleman is not doing that for his own pleasure, he has an air of a slave. Sweating, troubled, thin, he does not have the appearance of awaiting with pleasure making a meal of the fat man. I can't make out what the cook has done. This other man, the master, is in a rage because the cook has done something, but what? Perhaps the cook has made a mistake and cooked the guest.

mon divisor was of small assistance whereas calling attention to the number 1,001 helped considerably.

Simple problems calling for the application of physical principles were presented verbally by Duncker. For example, when a steel ball falls upon a steel plate and rebounds the impact against the plate flattens the ball which regains its shape in rebounding. How demonstrate that the ball is actually flattened? The solutions proposed were either to photograph the ball from the side just as it struck, or to coat the ball with chalk and examine the mark it left upon the horizontal plate.

Bulbrook called for an actual experiment in physics. Supplying a deflated toy balloon, a bottle, some pencils, a pen holder and a file, she instructed O to blow up the balloon inside of the bottle. All the Os attempted to do so without making provision for the escape of the air in the bottle! They were in the same position as regards the physical principle involved as Köhler's apes were in regard to the statics of box stacking.

Claparède obtained good protocols with quite a different type of problem. A story, usually humorous, is told in a series of pictures which are shown out of their right order; O at each stage makes what he can of the situation. A variant of this procedure was to show a single picture and ask O to supply a title for it or to diagnose the situation. An example is shown in Fig. 247.

The process of solution analyzed. These protocols certainly reveal something of the process of problem solution. We see the problem taking shape, a hypothesis emerging, and then a test of the hypothesis. There is observation of the situation, inference as to what must be the state of affairs, search or what Claparède calls *tâtonnement*, which might also be called trial and error.

This tentative exploratory process is twofold: the situation is explored to see what is given; the problem, to see what is required. Otherwise stated, O explores to see what has to be done and what there is to work with. His solution consists in discovering how to use what he has so as to accomplish what he desires. Duncker states the same general process in a slightly different form. In every problem there is something given and something required. The process consists in analyzing what is given and what is required till the two analyses come together into a solution. The nature of the process is suggested by several figurative expressions—restructuring, reorganizing, refiguring, recentering, revamping the situation. But, as Claparède urges, none of these figures of speech explains the process. In particular they do not explain *how the hypothesis originates*, which is a crucial question.

"Resonance." Claparède is inclined to believe that the process of generating a hypothesis can never be directly observed because, as he thinks, it is largely an unconscious process. He proposes a "resonance theory." "Our past experience is of an extraordinary richness . . . as soon as our need or present interest unearths from past experience anything that can serve its purpose, it is put to use. As if by a sort of internal resonance the need throws into vibration the elements which harmonize with itself."

Duncker uses "resonance" in almost exactly the same sense. When one is hunting for a lost knife anything having the general appearance of a knife jumps out of the background. If one is looking for a red object, red objects jump out. One may be looking for any object having a certain characteristic, as sufficient length for a certain purpose. In such cases one employs a "search model," to use Duncker's term, or a blank schema, to use a term of Selz (p. 798). O is searching for something which fits into this schema or model, and Duncker suggests that the model causes a vibration of the corresponding object in our visual cortical field. When we are searching in memory, he suggests a vibration of those residuals of past experience which fit into the present model.

Trial and error in human thinking. Whether problem solving is truly described as a trial-and-error process depends upon the definition of trial and error. If it means the trying of various leads because of inability to see in advance which lead will be successful, then every solution shows some trial and error. Confronted by a problem of any intricacy O cannot see through from the start to the finish, from what is given to what is required. He has to proceed step by step (Duncker), and his steps are often in the backward direction, from an analysis of the requirements back to the study of the facilities offered. As Claparède says, the process is decidedly a zigzag one.

But if trial-and-error is taken to mean absolutely random, blind groping, Claparède's protocols give little sign of any such blindness. In struggling with a difficult construction puzzle (Morgan, 1934) O tries only combinations of pieces that make sense. His behavior is "very well within the range of the plausible . . . the subject responds only to those elements of the situation which he has perceived to have some significance with respect to reaching the solution . . . the term 'plausible' places an important restriction upon the concept of variation and multiple response." Kubo (1933) in an extensive study of problem solution also finds a distinct absence of irrelevant behavior, though there were many false leads. In short the results with human adults confirm what was said on the basis of animal experiment, that the range of variation is limited by the set for the goal and by O's assumptions regarding the situation. The range of variation is often too much limited at the outset and needs to be widened by loosening up the assumptions.

Insight. When Köhler inquired as to insight in the chimpanzee, assuming its presence in human beings, he took over the word from common speech. With continued use it has acquired the flavor of a technical term. The question remains whether there is any useful technical definition for the word.

This question was considered by Bulbrook (1932) in a somewhat different form. She asked whether any process designated by the word insight was insufficiently covered by existing psychological terms. Summarizing her observations on a unicursal puzzle (compare Fig. 244) in which indeed sudden flashes of total insight are unlikely, she concluded that "apprehension of the object, search, and inspection and comment leading to action . . . were the essential characteristics of the procedure." The overt action was controlled by hypotheses invented and tested one after another. The process of solution could be fully described without the use of the word insight. Insight was a result rather than a process, or referred to a variety of processes, and therefore could not be regarded as a necessary addition to the list of psychological concepts. Claparède

(1934) makes similar remarks. The word seems to him a good one for signalizing the fact of perception of relations as distinguished from blind action, but it contains only a verbal explanation, and the question remains by what process insight is achieved.

Special interest attaches to Duncker's (1935) discussion since he follows the tradition of Wertheimer and Köhler who have specially insisted upon the importance of insight. Insight, Duncker finds, is not an all-or-none affair. It is both gradual and graduated. It is *gradual* in the sense that the solution of a complex problem proceeds by steps which are themselves insightful. O analyzes the situation he has to deal with and the goal he has to reach. There may come a dramatic snapping together of what he has observed at these two ends of the problem. Insight is *graduated* in the sense that one may see more or less deeply into a situation. Insight of the lower degree occurs when the individual knows a rule which works and sees that the present situation is one where the rule applies. Insight of the higher degree occurs when the individual sees the reason for the rule.

If degrees of insight are admitted, the ground is cleared of the old antithesis between insight and trial and error, considered as concrete phenomena. Reverting for a moment to the animal experiments, we recall that the string-pulling problem was supposed to lay all the cards on the table and so to be soluble by insight, whereas a puzzle box to be opened by turning a button was blind and only soluble by trial and error. But the results obtained with cats, dogs and young children show no essential difference between the two problems. Both have to be explored in the first instance and both can be "seen into," just as human adults showed insight in their quick solution of a perfectly blind combination lock (p. 761). Without attempting to comprehend the hidden interlocking mechanism they quickly discerned that a certain order of parts was necessary. Among Thorndike's learning curves (1898) there are a few which meet the sudden-improvement criterion of insight; curiously enough they come from an experiment in which he rewarded the cats whenever, being in a certain cage, they licked themselves. In this completely arbitrary situation they showed evidence of insight, and they continued to show it as the experiment progressed, by reducing the reward-bringing response to the dimensions of a merely symbolic or ritualistic lick (Fig. 248).

The relativity of insight must be acknowledged. The insight that suffices for a given problem may be inadequate when the problem is modified. The chimpanzee that quickly mastered the single door button (p. 755) had adequate insight so far but failed ingloriously when a second button was added, having apparently no insight into the obstructive character of a door button. In the same way the child who discovers that the electric switch turns on the light has adequate insight for that situation but not for wiring a room. The electrician may have adequate insight for ordinary wiring problems but not for devising a new radio circuit. The electrical engineer may have adequate insight for all engineering problems but not for the whole theory of electricity, and the physicists themselves with all their insight into the properties of the electrical field have not yet reached adequate insight for treating the electrical and gravitational fields under a single set of concepts, and they are now attempting by trial and error at the high level of mathematical physics to reach a solution of this great problem. No insight can safely be accepted as ultimate.

Insight and the utilization of past experience. Some psychologists have seemed, at least, to make a sharp distinction between insight and the

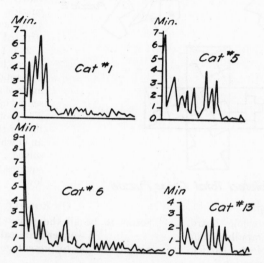

FIG. 248. (Thorndike, 1898.) Learning curves of cats rewarded for licking themselves.

use of past experience, as if insight must start every time from scratch with no help from anything previously learned, and as if all use of past experience must consist in the automatic performance of habitual acts. Experimental results give no warrant for such an antithesis. In the puzzle experiments it was often perfectly clear that fresh insight consisted in the application of a previously learned principle to a novel situation. A special study of this question was made by Durkin (1937). Her material consisted of flat construction puzzles, which proved to have several advantages in the study of problem solving. Everything was in sight; there were no hidden properties requiring to be learned by manipulation. The pieces were easy to identify so that "thinking aloud" and "retracing the solution" were comparatively easy. And an objective record could be made by sketches or photographs of the state of affairs at critical stages in the process. The five small squares were given separately and after each had been solved once, the pieces from all were presented in a mixed assemblage with instructions to construct a Maltese cross from

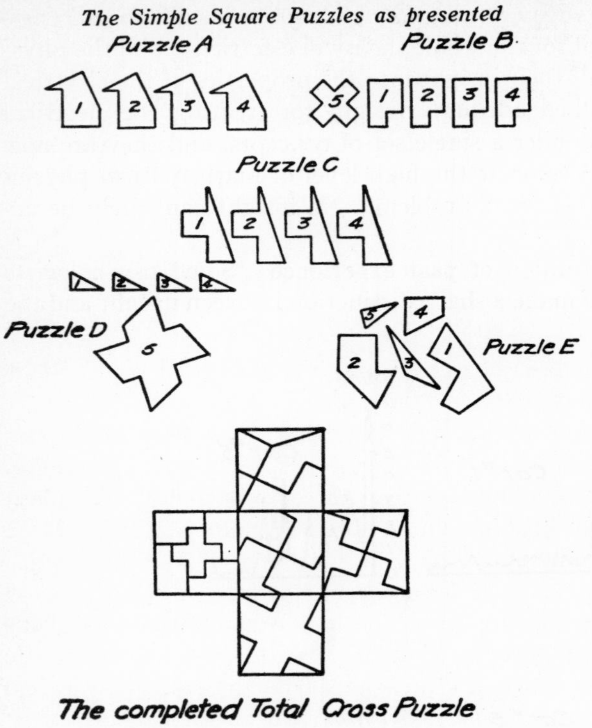

The Simple Square Puzzles as presented

Puzzle A   **Puzzle B**

Puzzle C

Puzzle D   **Puzzle E**

FIG. 249. (Durkin, 1937.) Flat construction puzzles. Puzzle A required a square to be constructed from the pieces 1, 2, 3, 4; and so with the other lettered puzzles. The total cross was to be made of all the pieces presented in disarrangement. The protocol of one solution of the large cross, by an O who had previously solved the five small squares, is presented below.

The completed Total Cross Puzzle

Moves	O's Remarks
1. Looks over whole board. Eyes move rapidly. Fingers many pieces, particularly D_5 (observation).	1. Seems to be all the pieces I've used before — — — — I wonder if all really here. (Recall, not in relation to present goal.)
2. Picks up D_5.	2. Logical to start with big cross (D_5) (implied Analysis)
3. Fingers B_5.	3. Maybe the little cross will complicate the thing. (Analysis)
4. Places D_5 at bottom center so it looks like a cross and would not make a square.	4. No ready solution but will start with this (D_5).
5. Piles them up in assorted order.	5. Get all similar pieces together so if one works all will.
6. Looks around at all pieces and fingers the little cross.	6. Maybe with little cross as center — — — This has to be much broader than these arms at center. (Analysis)
7. Fingers B_5.	7. Maybe this little cross ought to be started out as a square, because so many pieces need a big center. (Analysis)
8. Picks up B_5—stops, hesitates, and is very quiet a moment — — — —.	8. (Raised his voice and said excitedly) This is a good one, the real solution finally hits me. Make five squares and this can be the center.
9. Makes the five squares with only one error and puts them together to form the Greek cross.	

Retrace:

I was thrilled when it finally dawned on me, but should have thought of that first because I had been making squares. While working I had noticed there were 5 squares but didn't tie it up to the present problem. I recognized parts to go with the various squares. The clue came from the sq. to be used in center—because to use up all the pieces would have to get a large center. At that the idea came that I had the material for the square and the fact previously noted that with the little cross I had thought of using in the center none would fit in except the 4 used before as a square. Then it suddenly dawned on me that it would be one arm and I had the material for other arms. I remembered pieces very well to sort them. I had already sorted them at the beginning though with different plan in mind—merely that if one could be used probably the others of its kind could.

all the pieces. Some Os were given this last problem without the previous experience in constructing the small squares.

The protocol of one O who solved the large cross after experience with the small squares affords a vivid instance of the "flash" experience. This moment of insight or sudden reorganization was clearly dependent on the use of knowledge acquired in solving the small squares. More than that, the "flash" amounted to a realization that this knowledge could be now put to use. Such sudden reorganization did not appear in the protocols of Os who were given the large cross without previous experience with the small squares, though some of these Os solved the large cross by a process which the author called "gradual analysis" in which relevant relationships were discovered one after another.

Certainly the game of chess could not be played without insight and perception of relations. Cleveland (1907) made a study of learning to play chess and distinguished five stages in the process: (1) learning the names and moves of the pieces, (2) learning individual moves of offense and defense, (3) discovering the value of combinations of pieces, (4) becoming able to plan a game systematically in advance, (5) acquiring "position sense," a sense of the strategic implications of a given position of the whole board of chess men. The learning process shows a progressive combination of the elements into larger and larger complexes. The complexes become larger both spatially (in extent over the board) and temporally (in number of moves included in a single span of attention). The unit of perception becomes larger and more meaningful, the remote consequences of a move are more fully foreseen. The later stages in this process could certainly not be reached without passing through the earlier stages. In other words, insight in chess depends upon the utilization of past experience.

Do we have insight into necessary connections? This question has been regarded as settled ever since Hume (1739) announced his famous law that man never perceives any inherent connection of antecedent and consequent and that the feeling of a necessary causal connection results simply from habit based upon frequent observation of a uniform succession of events. Wertheimer (1922) holds that Hume's law is true only of the class of cases which Hume cited, such as the fall of an unsup-

ported body, where the cause is a hidden force. If however we start
with the whole path of a projectile the parts of that path belong together
from the concrete nature of the whole. Thus proceeding from the whole
to the parts one can see the necessary interrelation of the parts. Duncker
follows this line of thought and cites cases of ordinary observation in
which the cause and the effect have something in common. When you
strike a ball the motion of the ball *corresponds* to the force and direction
of your blow. The problem is perhaps one of logic rather than of psychology. However Claparède has made some psychological observations
bearing upon the question. He asks whether the feeling of necessity is
born altogether of habit and frequent repetition. On the contrary
he says the feeling of necessity inheres in the first experience and has
to be dispelled by varied experiences. The child has to learn not generali-
zations but distinctions. If baby's cat is black he assumes that another
cat must be black also. When he bites into sour fruit he does not simply
associate the sourness with the visual appearance but regards the taste
as a necessary attribute of the fruit. Thus association is formed between
items which are experienced as related. Perception of relation precedes
association. The past experience upon which the present insight depends is not an experience of unrelated items but of items originally
seen or felt to be in relation.

CHAPTER XXX

THINKING

THE present chapter as well as the preceding one is concerned with problem solution. Thinking, though not a sharply delimited concept in psychology, differs from routine mental work, such as adding a column of figures, in showing some degree of originality or at least dealing with a situation presenting some novelty. To think is typically to search for an answer—"Let me think"—though common usage includes other varieties of meaning. When a person hastily expressed himself as follows, "I thought, without thinking, that . . .," his meaning was perfectly clear.

Experiments on problem solution started, as we have seen, with the students of animal behavior. Those on thinking were concerned from the outset with human mental processes and were largely, though not exclusively, introspective in method. They have dealt with imagery and controlled association—topics considered elsewhere in this book— with the understanding of language, with finding the answers to simple and more difficult questions, with reasoning and generalization. Some of the main findings, along with the methods employed, will be considered in this chapter.

THE "THOUGHT EXPERIMENT" AND ITS RESULTS

Previous to 1900 psychological theories of the thinking process were based on the "laws of thought" as understood in formal logic, on language regarded as a faithful mirror of thought, and on the assumptions of the associationists and their rivals. About that year several psychologists attempted an experimental attack by a method which was certainly direct and obvious enough. O was asked to solve some simple problem and to recount his experience from the time when the problem was given till the solution was reached. He was to *describe* his experience, not to explain or interpret. His function was to serve as observer and provide the raw data which E would subsequently analyze and interpret. E sometimes questioned O as to imagery, silent speech and other content occurring during the period under retrospective observation; in general, however, since questions were likely to be suggestive, the instructions called simply for a free report. Strange to say, a ten-second period of thinking sometimes required as many minutes to recount and make clear to E. Experimental technique consisted mostly in putting O at his ease, in understanding his reports, and in selecting problems which would arouse genuine thought and still be solved quickly so as not to overtax O's immediate memory span for his experience. The time consumed in solving the problem was usually measured with a chronoscope or stop watch.

For so simple an experiment, the results obtained were rather startling. Conscious content was reported which, while characterized only negatively, as "imageless thought" especially, seemed to fall outside the accepted categories of sensation, image and feeling. This experiment was introduced by Binet (1903) and also by a group of investigators at the University of Würzburg, centering about Marbe (1901) and Külpe (1904) and including Ach (1905), Watt (1905), Messer (1906) and Bühler (1907 a, b). The present writer (1906 a) hit upon the same method independently.

Is the method valid? The thought experiment was in active use for several years before encountering serious criticism. The first of a rapid series of sharp attacks on the new method came from no less eminent a critic than Wundt (1907) who laid down several canons of genuine experimentation.

1. The observer should know exactly when and where to look for the phenomenon to be observed.

2. He should be in a state of close attention to the expected phenomenon.

3. Each observation should be repeated several times under identical conditions.

4. The conditions must be varied systematically so as to determine under what conditions the phenomenon occurs.

Wundt grants that strict obedience to all these rules is not always possible, and that experiments must be admitted that are only partially experimental, but if all the rules are flouted we have only a "Schein-experiment"—a pretended experiment. Now the so-called thought experiment, according to Wundt, breaks all the rules, and is forced to break them by the fluid and unpredictable nature of the thinking process. The observer cannot foresee the nature of the phenomenon and cannot focus his attention in advance nor make any truly scientific observation; his observation, like the unprepared observations of ordinary life, falls far short of scientific accuracy. You cannot secure the same phenomenon a second time, and you cannot conduct a planned series of experiments for testing a definite hypothesis.

Wundt admits, indeed, that the incidental observations of a trained psychologist, gleaned at moments of spontaneous thinking and immediately recorded in his notebook, have some value. "In such self-observations it became entirely clear to me that one does not form the thought at the moment when one starts to express it in a sentence. The thought is present as a whole in one's consciousness before the first word is uttered. At the outset the focus of consciousness does not contain a single one of the verbal and other images which make their appearance in running through the thought and giving it linguistic expression, and it is only in this process of unfolding the thought that its parts rise successively to distinct awareness."

What Wundt has done here amounts to this: he first demolishes the method of the thought experiment by his critique, and then proceeds to employ the same method himself and to reach the same results (as to "imageless thought") which had been reached by the Külpe school and which had seemed so objectionable.

Wundt further urges that the presence of an experimenter must hamper the thinker and prevent genuine thought from occurring, but this *a priori* judgment is not borne out in the laboratory, for the Os testify that they think quite normally. Genuine willing, choosing and conflict of impulses, occur in similar experiments (Martin, 1922).

Wundt's critique points rightly enough to the difficulties of experimenting on the thought processes, but does not succeed in proving that the experiments are valueless. Another line of criticism was undertaken by Dürr (1908), von Aster (1908) and Titchener (1909). The observer in these experiments is supposed to be giving a *description* of his experience while thinking, but he is prone to fall back into the everyday habit of merely giving *expression* to his thoughts. He reports that he "thought that" so-and-so, or "thought of" so-and-so. If pressed to describe his experience in "thinking of" a certain object, he sometimes answers that the experience is scarcely describable except in negative terms: in thinking of a certain object he did not have a visual image of it nor think of its name. The criticism is that such a report is not descriptive. In Titchener's terms, O has fallen into something akin to the "stimulus error" or object error (see p. 450), and instead of describing the thought-experience is merely designating the objects with which his thought was concerned. He should be forbidden to make any reference to external objects, and trained to analyze the content of the thought process without regard to its meaning.

In rejoinder to this criticism two points may be made. (1) The subject must *not* be forbidden to refer to objects, for certainly the thought of an object cannot be adequately described without designating that object. Titchener himself modified this prohibition (1912) and allowed his trained Os to include a "statement of meaning," provided the meaning was carefully distinguished from the sensations and other "existential content" of an experience. The meanings, being clearer and more rememberable, furnished a frame in which the rather elusive content could be placed. (2) Even though reference to the object is a very incomplete description of a particular instant of experience, a series of such statements does describe the *general course* of a thinking process— just as naming the towns through which you have driven maps the route you have taken. If O reports, "I thought of A, of B, of C, noticed that I was drifting away from the problem and went back to A," he gives a picture of the course of his thinking (Selz, 1913).

Consider, for example, a protocol obtained by Binet (1903, p. 14) from the older of his two daughters (who were 10 and 11½ years old at the beginning of the three-year series of experiments) after she had simply closed her eyes for a few minutes and allowed her thoughts to run as naturally as possible:

I thought of the pump in the garden which some one was operating and said to myself that it must be the cook, then I heard a rooster crow and thought of this rooster.

I asked myself whether Polly would be willing to lend me her bike so that Marge could take mine to ride with us to Fontainebleau.

I thought that I would like to be 16 years old and stop right there.

Here we have "thoughts of," "thoughts that" and "thoughts whether," not further described. In another example from the same source (p. 91), an attempt was made to report images as well as thoughts, and so to come closer to the requirements of "description."

During the course of an experiment, the subject, who was to have lessons in physics and in Molière's *Misanthrope* later in the morning and in another room of the house, suddenly exclaimed on looking at the clock, "Oh! Lessons at 11 o'clock!" E immediately inquired about her images, and got the answer: "I thought of the *Misanthrope:* I saw the word vaguely in a grayish color . . . and I saw the physics book, a little paragraph with its number, indistinctly. I saw the dining room just a bit, and my sister at her desk."

On being then asked to report her thoughts, O replied without hesitation: "I thought of asking you to let me go so that I could look over my lessons, for I was afraid of being unprepared. Then I thought of my sister's saying, 'Goodness, we have a lesson this morning!' As for the *Misanthrope*, I thought that I didn't know my lesson at all. As for the physics, I'm not sure what I did think. I also thought that I had very little time."

Binet makes the point that the experience is much better rendered by the report of "thoughts" than by that of "images." Certainly if we expunged from the record the thoughts, and left only the images, we should lose all that was characteristic of this particular experience. Also we may note that the account of images was itself contaminated with references to objects—"I saw the physics book . . . the dining room . . . my sister." It is almost impossible to induce a subject to eliminate all such objective reference from a report of images.

"Imageless thought." As regards the mere existence of moments of active thought in which no images could be detected, positive testimony has been given by many psychologists.[1] Bühler's contribution (1907 a, 1908) is especially noteworthy. For eliciting introspective reports of imageless thinking he found the following types of problem useful:

1. Paradoxical aphorisms, such as those of Nietzsche. These puz-

[1] Including Binet, 1903; Clark, 1922; Cordes, 1901; Fox, 1914; Grünbaum, 1908; Koffka, 1912; Moore, 1910, 1919; Revault d'Allonnes, 1934; Spearman, 1923; Taylor, 1906; Woodworth, 1906 a, 1907, 1908; Wundt, 1907.

zling assertions were read to O with instructions simply to try to understand them, to signal when he had done so, and then to recount his
experience during the process of reaching an understanding. The
meaning would sometimes "dawn," with an exclamation "Aha!" followed
by the unfolding of the thought into a sentence. For example:

E says, "Do you understand this: One must be both pitiful and cruel in
order really to be either"? O takes 13.5 sec. to reach the affirmative answer,
and his report of the process concludes with the statement, "Then after a little
pause there came like a flash, but entirely without words, the thought that
to be really cruel one must feel one's own harshness."

2. Matching proverbs as an exercise in recognition and recall of
thoughts. First a list of proverbs is read to O, then another proverb is
presented which has the same meaning as one in the list but in a different
picture; e.g.,

The donkey carries the grain to the mill and gets the straw for himself.
One man drives in the nail, another hangs his hat on it.

On hearing the second proverb O often recognizes the underlying
thought and after some delay recalls the form of the earlier proverb,
though usually in somewhat different words.
3. Proverbs recalled by aid of catchwords. The procedure is the
same as in the last experiment, except that after the list of proverbs
has been read, a single word from the proverb is presented as a cue.
Often the sense of the proverb is recalled before the words, and the
words are usually somewhat changed. Sometimes, but not always,
visual imagery plays a part.
Bühler concludes that there is abundant evidence of thought without either verbal or visual images, and believes that the "thoughts" are
the essential phenomena in thinking, the images being incidental.
According to Woodworth (1915 a) what is imageless is not thought
so much as recall. Even the most ordinary facts—the location and
style of a building, or the contents of one's pockets—are often recalled
without images. Any sort of observed fact is recalled in many cases
without the sensory background of the original experience and also,
for the first moment, without verbal images.
With Titchener the problem of imageless thought took a different
turn. He wished to make sure whether any new elements of conscious
content must be recognized in view of the results of Bühler and others.
Already recognized were the elements of sensation and feeling. Was
there also a thought element? Was there an independent feeling of
relation? His procedure in attacking this question was first to rule
out meaning and object reference as not genuine existential content,
and second to see whether his Os reported any genuine content which
did not fall under the accepted classes. He and his pupils and his pupils'
pupils came to a negative conclusion, since their Os reported (besides

meanings) only images, kinesthetic and organic sensations, and feelings (Clarke, 1911; Comstock, 1921; Crosland, 1921; Gleason, 1919; Jacobson, 1911; Okabe, 1910). They concluded that the reports of imageless thought emanating from other laboratories were due partly to the failure to separate meaning and content, and partly to the difficulty of observing vague images and sensations when one is actively thinking and intent upon meaning. The sensorial content may easily be overlooked, "so quick is the process of thought and so completely is the attention of the subject likely to be concentrated on meaning. We have a parallel case in the neglect of after-images . . . in everyday experience when other things are in the focus of attention" (Comstock, 1921).

The supporters of imageless thought were inclined to question the importance of such images as occurred in thinking. Images could occur as associative byplay without furthering the progress of thought. Comstock (1921) held that nearly all the images reported in her experiment had some use in "anchoring" the problem, carrying the meanings, providing leads for thought, or checking the conclusion. Hollingworth (1911, 1926) made the point that the logical irrelevance of many images need not interfere with their dynamic potency. When the objects that really stand in a certain relation are not easily imaged, substitute objects may take their place. This is the method of symbolic thinking. Words take the place of things, and a spatial diagram or a hand movement does service in thinking of many kinds of relation. Hollingworth reported that in his experience "present kinesthetic impressions or motor tendencies logically irrelevant are most frequently the vehicle or garment which plays the substantive role in relational consciousness."

Final comment on imageless thought. Tactual, kinesthetic and other sensations must always be present, and in the full sense there are therefore no moments of experience deprived of all sensory content. That visual or verbal images are usually present is also probable, except indeed when one is attentively looking or listening. The important question is whether at the dawning of a thought the meaning comes first, as Wundt said in the passage quoted, or the words or other symbolic and illustrative images. Even this question is not so important, the real question being whether meanings are present. If meanings are ruled out as non-existent and non-occurrent, then no imageless thoughts will be found, for the imageless thoughts are simply the meanings which the Os report with such ease and certainty.

It is curious what different semi-emotional reactions are made by different persons to the notion of imageless thought. To some it seems entirely natural and acceptable, while others shrink from it as a strange, mystical theory and insist that there simply must be some image or sensation to "carry the meaning." Since superfine introspection would be needed to establish the complete absence of all imagery at a moment of active thought, the whole question may well be shelved as permanently debatable and insoluble. The present writer would like, however, once more to record his own view that imageless thought is no more mysterious than the everyday perception of facts. Let us suppose that while you are reading in your room a sudden noise tells you that your neighbor has gone out of the adjoining room and slammed the door. The fact of which you thus become aware is very different from the mere occurrence of a sudden noise. If you have ready visual imagery, you may have an imaginal glimpse of your neighbor going out; if you are a ready verbalizer you may say to yourself, "So-and-so is going out"; and if his going suggests that you yourself must make haste, you may stiffen in your chair before continuing to read. A little later you recall the fact that your neighbor has gone out—perhaps with a revival of your previous visual or verbal image, perhaps without. Under cross-examination you might not be sure of the precise sensations, images and motor reactions occurring in the original experience, but you are sure of what the experience meant to you, that is, the fact of your neighbor's going out. Mysterious?

Conscious attitudes. Back in 1901, before the imageless thought controversy had got started, Marbe, his pupils Mayer and Orth at Würzburg and, quite independently, Cordes working in Wundt's laboratory, announced as the result of introspective experiments on association and judgment the existence of relatively indescribable states which could not be brought under the accepted categories of sensation, image and feeling. Examples were: expectancy, hesitation, doubt, sureness of being on the right track. These authors used the compound words, *Bewusstseinslage* and *Bewusstseinszustand*—literally, the "lay" or "condition of consciousness"—to designate these states. "Posture or attitude of consciousness" would be a fair English rendering, and "conscious attitudes" was soon adopted (Titchener, 1909). Washburn (1906) quickly offered the suggestion that these attitudes, or some of them, were *essentially motor*. James's famous "feeling of but," for example, might well be a kinesthetic sensation, arising from the suspended, baffled motor attitude of an organism called upon to make two incompatible reactions. This motor attitude becomes reduced to a mere vestige in the ordinary quick use of "but" in conversation. In Washburn's general motor theory of consciousness (1916) this conception of the conscious attitudes is impressively worked out and applied also to the imageless thoughts. Colvin (1910, 1911) early called attention to the importance of *mimetic gestures* in thinking. The orator brings out alternatives by gesturing right and left, and the silent thinker may make the same gesture on a small scale. Mimetic gestures are believed to be very primitive in the race and their use in thinking may be more fundamental than the use of words. In introspecting his own thought processes Colvin found "the actual 'mind-stuff' . . . in images which represent gestures, such as pointing, raising the index finger . . . or in more general symbols of bodily movements." Taking this question more definitely into the laboratory Clarke (1911) found that her Os could detect kinesthetic sensations or images in the conscious attitudes. *Seeking* seemed to consist of strain in the head and eyes and internal organs, *doubt* of the failure of an incipient movement to go on to its usual terminus. She concluded that "conscious attitudes can be analyzed into sensations and images and feelings . . . and do not warrant the proposal of an additional conscious element." Crosland (1921) later reached a similar conclusion by introspective analysis, though he emphasized not only the kinesthetic make-up of the attitudes but also their characteristic patterns of change.

In learning to typewrite by the touch system, one early builds up a clear image of the keyboard in which each letter can be located. Later, one loses this image and can no longer tell where the letters are, though one finds them readily with the fingers in writing, and has a sense of readiness and mastery which amounts to a conscious attitude. Book (1910) concludes that "conscious attitudes seem to represent a stage in a process of development which begins with vivid imaginal thought, and slowly and gradually passes downward to a stage of automatic or instinctive control."

Psychologists, so far as they have expressed themselves, are in pretty good agreement on the motor character of the typical conscious attitudes. The discovery of postural and gestural movements in silent thinking may be called one of the main achievements of this whole attempt to study thought introspectively. It should be said, indeed, that the motor theory of conscious attitudes remains a theory. It is not definitely an observed fact. The observed fact is that when O looks for kinesthetic experience he usually finds it present. The attitude may be primarily cerebral and the muscular contraction and kinesthesis may be an "overflow" or diffusion effect (May, 1917; Strohal, 1933).

Set as a factor in thinking. Another real achievement of the introspective study of thinking was the extension of the concept of "Einstellung" or set from reaction time and the comparison of weights (pp. 305, 440) to the process of thinking. Watt (1905) undertook a combined introspective-objective study of the process of controlled association (p. 309). He used word stimuli and alternated between six tasks:

genus—species—to name a concept subordinate to the one named in the stimulus word

species—genus—to name a supraordinate concept

species—species—to name a coordinate concept

whole—part—to name a part of the given whole

part—whole—to name a whole including the given part

part—part—to name another part of the same whole, when one part is given.

The procedure was: (1) task assigned, (2) short series of stimulus words presented visually by use of a card changer, (3) reaction times taken by use of a voice key and chronoscope, (4) retrospective review after each single response.

In the retrospections full account was taken of the distinction between foreperiod, main period, and after-period (p. 309). The Ready signal assigned the task; the foreperiod, during which O prepared to respond in the assigned manner, lasted from the Ready signal to the exposure of the stimulus word, and the main period (or reaction time) from the stimulus to the spoken response.

When O, in a simple reaction experiment, receives the Ready signal, he prepares to execute a certain prescribed movement. In the controlled association experiment, he cannot make so specific a preparation since he does not yet know the stimulus word. But he can make a generic preparation; he prepares a type of response that shall stand in the assigned relation to any stimulus word. How is such generic preparation possible? Watt's introspective reports showed the foreperiod occupied as follows when the task was relatively new and unfamiliar. O made the task clear to himself in a verbal, visual or kinesthetic form. He defined the relation, or found an example, or got a diagram or gesture symbolizing the relation. He also made appropriate motor adjustments, fixing his eyes on the card changer, bringing his mouth up to the voice key, and adopting an attitude of expectancy and muscular tension. When the stimulus word arrived, the reaction followed sometimes automatically, sometimes after an interval of waiting or searching, sometimes after false reactions had been suggested and rejected. Only in this last case did the definite consciousness of the task emerge again during the main period; usually it was confined to the foreperiod.

When the same task had continued for a series of stimulus words, the conscious awareness of the task faded out even from the foreperiod and was reduced to a mere feeling of readiness. The preparation lost its specificity as a conscious state, but not as an adjustment, for it still insured correctness of response according to the task. With practice the set became at once less conscious and more efficient.

Watt's main result was the efficiency of the task-set or preparation, along with the fact that this preparation was completed during the foreperiod. It worked by *selecting in advance*. It did not select during the main period from among several responses called up by the stimulus word, but it limited the field of response in advance of the stimulus word so that only responses conforming to the task were ordinarily called up.

Watt distinguished three factors determining the response in controlled association: (1) the stimulus word, (2) its associations, (3) the task-set or specific preparation. The demonstrated importance of the task makes it impossible, he urged, henceforth to accept any theory of the thought processes which is based wholly on the concept of association.

This experiment of Watt was repeated and amplified by May (1917) who used more Os and more stimulus words, varied the conditions in several ways and made more use of the objective results. He constructed apparatus for presenting both the task and the stimulus word visually and for controlling the length of the foreperiod mechanically or leaving its length to the option of O. He used tasks like those of Watt, but included opposites and the verb-object relation. The task was usually

I. When the task was assigned by giving the name of the required relation.

	Percent of cases	Foreperiod time
1. Immediate adjustment, no experience to report	22	0.9 sec.
2. "Conscious attitude" present, as readiness, confusion, easy or familiar task	35	1.0
3. Task schematized in motor adjustment, as by head movement to right or left, by downward shrinking feeling, upward expansive feeling, etc.	12	1.4
4. Task schematized in spatial diagram, as by small space inside larger space	5	1.3
5. Task carried verbally, as by repeating or dwelling on the key word	8	1.4
6. Miscellaneous	10	1.3
7. Failures and false reactions	8	
Whole no. of reactions = 400	100	

II. When the task was assigned by giving two words in the required relation.

	Percent of cases	Foreperiod time
1. Relation undifferentiated, with simple feeling of readiness	12	1.0
2. Awareness of definite relation, without naming it	22	1.2
3. Relation named	17	1.1
4. Relation schematized in spatial diagram	11	1.5
5. Relation schematized by motor adjustment	14	1.4
6. Visual image	8	1.5
7. Repetition of the two given words without clear awareness of their relation	6	1.1
8. Miscellaneous	6	1.2
9. Failures and false reactions	4	
Whole no. of reactions = 400	100	

changed for each successive stimulus word. Two ways of designating the task were employed: (1) exposing the name of the required relation, as "Give opposite of"—followed shortly by the stimulus word, "north"; (2) exposing a pair of words standing in a certain relation, "above-below"—followed shortly by the stimulus word, "north"—and requiring O to discern the relation from the first two words. (This last is the rule-of-three or analogy method.) The foreperiod introspections were somewhat different for the two modes of presenting the task, and the time required for the foreperiod was slightly longer with the rule-of-three method.

The varieties of *foreperiod* experience are tabulated on p. 792.

In this particular experiment the length of the foreperiod was controlled by O, who exposed the stimulus word when ready. Though the differences are not very reliable, on the whole the types of preparation entered as No. 1 in these lists show the shortest foreperiod. These are the most automatic and effective types of preparation.

The effect of practice to level down the conscious process of preparation was well illustrated by the reports of one O who started with a complete outfit of motor schemes or adjustments, one for each of the task relations. These adjustments felt definitely muscular at first, but "gradually lost their bodily or muscular aspect and became, as he termed it, 'more neural.' Later this neural process seemed to him to fade out" into mere spatial diagrams, which in turn faded into attitudes of readiness and finally gave way to an entirely automatic process. "We have here a descending series of processes with the length of the foreperiod getting shorter as the series descends."

Proceeding to the introspective reports of the *main period* of the associative reaction, May classified them as follows:

	Median reaction time when task was presented	
	I. by task-word	II. by rule-of-three
1. Reaction process automatic	1.0 sec.	0.9 sec.
2. Only conscious attitudes present in main period	1.1	1.1
3. Vacant interval present	1.5	1.2
4. Images present	1.3	1.2
5. Conflicting right responses suggested	1.2	1.5
6. Wrong responses suggested but inhibited	1.6	1.8

It will be seen that the reaction times here give some evidence for the reliability of the introspective reports, since the reactions reported as automatic are objectively the quickest, whereas those reported as reached only after the checking of false responses are the slowest.

Compound tasks and sets. In problem solution, in reading and in many sorts of "mental work" the set demanded is not so simple as in controlled association. For example, in multiplying a four-place by a one-place number, one has to alternate between simple multiplication and addition, all the time keeping one's general bearings. Jersild's experiment (1927) required a rapid *shifting* back and forth between two or more tasks, as between giving opposites and subtracting 3. College students, far from being disturbed, rather preferred the alternating to the more monotonous work, and actually worked faster in the combined tasks, provided the tasks and also the stimuli were *dissimilar*. (There was a loss of speed in shifting between adding 3 and subtracting 3, or between giving opposites of adjectives and opposites of verbs.) Jersild's main result is the demonstrated existence of sets of higher order in which one is prepared for two or more types of response.

SET AND SHIFT, ILLUSTRATIVE MATERIAL
(*After Jersild, 1927*)

Give opposites	Subtract 3	Alternately give opposite and Subtract 3
last	64	expensive
talkative	72	41
dangerous	47	timid
gay	30	59
broad	49	stale
past	35	26
secret	43	shaky
sharp	56	38
innocent	62	stormy
masculine	35	50
useful	44	thrifty
shallow	51	93
beautiful	67	wise
idle	73	25
silly	46	cloudy
public	25	67
coarse	53	rear
vague	29	82
gentle	72	noisy
fickle	98	74

Shifting set is a commonplace to the pianist. The keys to be struck are indicated by notes at different positions on the staff of five horizontal lines, but any given position on the staff means a different key according as the clef sign for treble or bass precedes, and one clef sign holds good until the other is encountered, whereupon the meaning of every note symbol is changed.

This and similar facts led von Kries (1895) to the first comprehensive discussion of set or *Einstellung,* and provided the suggestion for a laboratory experiment by Strohal (1933). Four symbols—square, circle, cross, triangle—were mounted in a long chance series on a paper belt and exposed one at a time through a window in a screen. Interspersed in the series of symbols were two "clefs," a red and a yellow rectangle, and, as in music, each clef controlled the following symbols until the other clef appeared. At sight of the square symbol O must say "rin" if the yellow sign was in force, but "tuk" if the red was in force; and similarly there were alternative responses for each symbol. The author's special interest lay in the question whether set is essentially unconscious, as often asserted. Whenever a buzzer sounded, O was to drop the work and report the experience of just that moment. When the buzzer came immediately after a clef sign, the typical report showed that O was aware of laying aside or pushing aside the previous task and getting a new adjustment. Interruption at other moments yielded reports of an awareness of the present task "running along with the work." The author reaches the conclusion that the task-set is typically conscious

FIG. 250. Shifting set in music reading.

and does not function automatically; he thinks it must be present as a conscious undercurrent if it is to be effective. It was not usually reported as a sensory, imaginal or motor experience but simply as a background awareness of what one is doing and of the conformity of one's responses to the task in hand.

Complex theory vs. constellation theory. Here we encounter one of the most insistent questions of recent psychology, a question which has become best known through the emphasis of the Gestalt psychologists on "organized wholes," but which is also present in Wundt's conception of "creative synthesis," in G. E. Müller's "collective apprehension," and in Spearman's "eduction of relations and of correlates." "Complex" as used in this connection has nothing special to do with the complexes of the psychoanalysts. Some of the best experimental evidence for the functional unity of complexes is found in the "higher units" of skilled performance in telegraphy, typewriting, etc. (p. 159).

As far as concerns the process of thinking, the leading exponent of the "complex theory" has been Otto Selz (1913, 1922, 1924). While working in Külpe's laboratory and following up the work of Watt and Bühler, he attacked a problem which we may formulate thus: Exactly what does a set place in readiness? In the controlled association experiment with word responses, does the set place in readiness certain response words, or certain *pairs* of words, e.g., pairs of opposites?

The factors in controlled association, according to Watt's analysis, already mentioned, are the task-set, the stimulus word and the associations of the stimulus word; and the set selects the right associate to fit the task. Two alternatives are shown diagrammatically in Figs. 251 and 252.

According to the constellation theory, the task-set in the species-genus test places in readiness the names of supraordinate classes such as "animal," "building," etc.; and the stimulus word "oak" (which has many other associates such as "wood" and "floor") brings the response "tree" because of the convergence of two forces upon this response.

According to the complex theory, the species-genus set places in readiness, not a class of single words, but a class of word pairs which

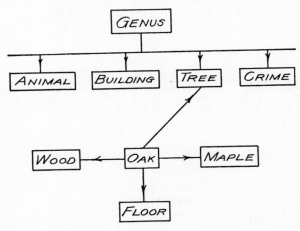

FIG. 251.   Diagram of the constellation theory

stand in the relation of species to genus—such pairs as "dog-animal," "church-building," etc.; and the stimulus word "oak" reinforces the pair "oak-tree."

At first thought the two theories may seem to differ very little. But Selz adduces both objective and introspective evidence tending to show that the constellation theory is impossible.

1. Regarded as a set for a class of *words* the task set is often ambiguous. Suppose the task is to name a whole of which a part is given, and the stimulus word is *page*. Why should not the response be *line* or even *word?* Each of these names a whole, the line being a whole made up of words and the word a whole made up of letters; and both are closely associated with the stimulus word *page*. The commonsense retort is, "Yes, but they are not wholes in relation to *page*." True enough, but the constellation theory does not assign any potency to this relation; it speaks only of associations between what we may roughly call elements, such as words, particular objects, etc. The complex theory, on the contrary, assumes that words-in-relation (or things-in-relation) are placed in readiness, such as *letter→word, word→line, page→book.* The stimulus-word reinforces one of these ready pairs.

For another example, let the task call for opposites, and the stimulus-word be *dark*. Why should not the response be, unhesitatingly, *night?* For *night* is a very familiar associate of *dark* and it is also a familiar opposite, the opposite of *day*.

Consider the task of finding a coordinate concept, with a list of stimulus words like this:

> apple
> oak
> dog
> green
> eat
> elbow
> Tuesday
> hammer
> copper
> lake
> memory

Almost any word can be used as a stimulus, since almost every object or action is paralleled by a coordinate object or action. According to the constellation theory, then, the set for coordinates would place in readiness the names of almost all objects and actions, and could have almost no selective influence.

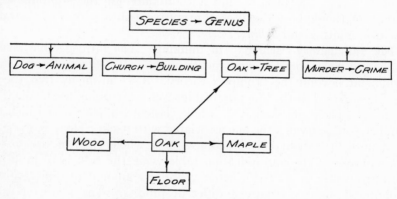

FIG. 252. Diagram of the complex theory

2. The constellation theory, assuming associations only between elements, breaks down if we push it so far as to suppose that the separate sounds in a spoken word, by the combination of their separate associations, arouse the meaning. The word *ten* immediately suggests a number; the word *net* suggests something entirely different; but the phonetic elements of the two words are the same, and the constellation theory has no way of taking account of the order of these elements. In the same way the words of a sentence or the notes of a tune arouse very different responses if arranged in a different order.

3. In experiments on the learning of lists of nonsense syllables

(p. 28) O tends to group the syllables, and one group can call up the next group as a whole, whereas the association between two adjacent syllables, one in one group and the other in the following group, is very weak.

4. Selz carried out experiments in controlled association, with a large variety of tasks, exposing the task-word and the stimulus word simultaneously, as for example:

Supraordinate?
Tiger
Coordinate?
Death
Wing
6 parts?
Voting
2 kinds?

The task was continually changed. The problems were intended to be fairly difficult and the instructions called for deliberation rather than speed, though time was taken (stopwatch).

Some of the introspective reports clearly indicated the recall of objects-in-relation or of complex wholes including two or more related objects. Given the task to find a coordinate for the stimulus word *hunting*, O thought of the life of primitive tribes with their parallel activities, hunting and *fishing*.

The anticipatory "schema" in thinking. The introspective results obtained by Selz from his experiments on difficult controlled association led him far beyond the "complex theory," if we mean by that theory what is expressed in the diagram of Fig. 252. According to the diagram the task-set places in readiness a whole class of complexes, of which the stimulus word activates the one associated with itself. There is a certain air of unreality about this "readiness of a whole class of responses," such as those of the multiplication table when the task is to multiply. The introspective reports, in cases where any amount of difficulty was encountered, point to quite a different process. The first step is to build up the "complete task," i.e., the problem, by combining the assigned task and the stimulus word. The problem is seen to be, for example, that of finding-a-supraordinate-to-*newspaper*. It has the character of a blank form or schema to be filled out. This word *schema* has been employed with a similar meaning in other studies of thinking by Betz (1932), Revault d'Allonnes (1934), and Flach (1925), and also in studies of memory for figures (p. 74). The word *frame* carries the same meaning, that of a performance in outline, needing to be filled in. The problem is schematically solved by being clearly formulated. The schema is "anticipatory," a mere start toward the complete performance. This concept lays claim to a position of fundamental importance in the psychology of thinking.

Sometimes the schema is symbolized by an imagined diagram, as in a case reported by Flach (1925), in which O was asked "What do we mean when we speak of exchange?" and reported: "At once a visual symbol appeared, not very precise in form but definite in meaning, a band connecting two bodies that might be persons, with movement understood to be taking place in both directions along the band and with no preference for one direction over the other."

FIG. 253. Type of a schema.

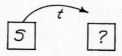

FIG. 254. (After Selz, 1922.) Schema of a simple operation. The relation t, prescribed by the task, and the stimulus word S are combined into a plan of operation.

An anticipatory schema is present in the reaction time experiment. O's readiness to react is a sort of blank check. It has a space for the stimulus (receptive readiness) and one for the response (motor readiness), and the cause-effect relation is also prepared in the readiness to react *to* the stimulus. Setting up this schema is an important step toward executing the complete reaction.

Another example given by Selz is seen in word completion. Suppose a school child is asked to name the capital of India and hesitates in his

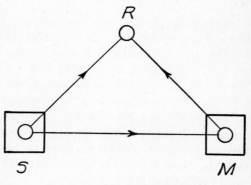

FIG. 255. (After Selz, 1922.) Schema of a compound operation. The problem is to find a response R, which shall stand to the stimulus word S in the relation of genus to species. M is an object coordinate with S, i.e., belonging under some common genus. The small circles denote the property common to S and M which is characteristic of the inclusive genus R.

reply. It may help him to be told the first letter or two, and if he knows the length of the word, so much the better. The more adequate the general schema, and the more filling is supplied, the better the chance of completion.

With the part-whole task and a rather difficult stimulus word, such as *painting*, *tomb*, or *clarinet*, the usual procedure was to visualize the object in its surroundings and search the surroundings for something that could be called a whole in relation to the object.

The schema is a plan of operation, a method of solution. Sometimes the operation is very direct and simple and amounts to Spearman's

(1923) "eduction of a correlate." The task prescribes a certain relation, the stimulus provides one "fundament," and the blank form needs only the other fundament to be complete (Fig. 254).

A difficult problem is one the schema of which cannot be completed in a direct manner. A detour is necessary, as Köhler puts it (p. 757). O is forced to complicate the operation by inserting auxiliary processes. The operation calls for a triangular diagram with three terms and (at least) three relations (Fig. 255). An abridged protocol gives an example.

Task, supraordinate; stimulus word, *nail;* reaction time, 13.6 sec. O's report: "First a visual image of an isolated nail, and response 'implement' rejected. Then search for some property of a nail from which I might arrive at a supraordinate. No such property occurred to me at first, but I had another image, that of a wooden wedge and of a wooden box with a wedge driven in at one corner. I noted in this picture the function of holding-firm and then thought that instead of this wedge a nail could have been used. Thus I grasped the similar function of the two, from which I formed a superior genus and designated it 'object for fastening'."

Errors are due mostly to inadequacy or false "direction" (p. 774) of the control schema. It may lack precision, as is often the case in finding a supraordinate; the schema may allow the intrusion of:

> a whole, as *nail—wall*
> a sphere of knowledge, as *star—astronomy*
> a higher rank, as *captain—general*

In other cases the schema is adequate at the start but is partly forgotten during a long process of solution. O loses his place; he may become so absorbed in an auxiliary problem as to forget the goal. Errors may also creep in because of strong irrelevant associations of the stimulus word (Wilcocks, 1928).

INDUCTION OR CONCEPT FORMATION

In logic a distinction is made between induction and deduction. Mathematics is said to be a deductive science, chemistry an inductive science. The properties of the circle are discovered, not by the inductive process of measuring many specimens and computing, for example, the average ratio of the circumference to the diameter, but by deduction from the definition of the circle combined with other geometrical definitions. The properties of oxygen were ascertained by discovering oxygen, obtaining as pure specimens as possible, and testing these specimens. If the chemist could be sure of the absolute purity of a single specimen and of the complete accuracy of his tests, he could determine the properties of oxygen once for all; but such an ideal has been approached only by a long series of approximations. In practice the chemist, like the biologist or the psychologist, has to advance from the particular to the general, from the specimen to the class.

Induction and deduction are not necessarily different intellectual processes. They are distinguished as problems rather than processes. A deductive problem calls for discovering the implications of certain given statements. What is given in an inductive problem consists of specimens, and the result to be attained is a definition, or at least a working knowledge, of the *class* represented by the given specimens. The process might be about the same in solving both sorts of problem; more probably, it will show much variation in both cases.

Problems of induction are obviously not confined to the sciences. The child gets acquainted not only with certain individual dogs but also with dogs as a class. He gains a practical acquaintance with the properties common to this class of objects as distinguished from the class of cats, for example. He develops responses suited to the common characteristics of each class of familiar objects. How he does this is an important psychological problem. From observation of children, and from the conditioning experiments on animals (p. 94), the great difficulty seems to lie rather in differentiation between classes than in generalization from the specimen to the class. See also p. 782.

In the laboratory a problem of induction or of "concept formation" calls for the mastery of more than a single concrete thing or situation. O must develop an effective response to a class of objects and a different response to objects not belonging to this class.

There are two theories to be tested. According to the "composite photograph" theory, the features common to a class of objects summate their impressions on the observer, who thus gradually acquires a picture in which the common features stand out strongly while the variable characteristics are washed out. The observer plays a passive or receptive role, simply letting himself be impressed by the objects. The other theory assigns to O the more active role characteristic of trial and error behavior. The concept is supposed to originate as a hypothesis, which O proceeds to test by trying it on fresh specimens of the class.

Objective experiments. Hull's experiment (1920) was patterned after the Paired Associates method in memory. Chinese characters were paired with nonsense names, and O learned to respond by the assigned name at sight of each character. These characters are compounds of smaller figures known as radicals. The same radical, varying somewhat in size and position, is embodied in many compound characters. Each of the characters used by Hull embodied one of 12 selected radicals, and all the characters containing the same radical were given the same name. The characters were written on separate cards and the cards made up into "packs" of 12 so that each pack contained all the radicals. The procedure was as follows. By aid of a memory apparatus Pack No. 1 was shown serially and in the middle of the 5 sec. exposure of any character its name was spoken by E and repeated by O. The second time around, O tried to anticipate E in saying the names, and the series was repeated till O had learned all the names for these 12 characters. Pack No. 2 was now substituted, and O was told that the same names

would be used and that he might "guess" the names the first time around.
The order of radicals was different in each new pack. Six packs were
learned and the percent of correct first-trial guesses increased from pack
to pack; thus, on the average of 18 Os:

Pack No.	2	3	4	5	6
Percent correct on first trial	27	38	47	55	56

This increasing ability to recognize new members of a class was due in
part to spontaneous efforts of O to analyze the figures and discover the
characteristic mark of each class. The 27 percent correct on first trial
of Pack No. 2 cannot be so explained because of O's ignorance of the
procedure. It was also true at the end that more characters were correctly

FIG. 256. (Hull, 1920.) Half of the radicals used in the experiment, with their
assigned nonsense names and some compounds containing each radical.

named than could be defined by sketching the common characteristic.
Something less analytical, more like ordinary recognition, was playing
a part. We recognize a person, we see a family resemblance, without
identifying the personal or family characteristics.

Another pioneer experiment using Chinese characters was that of
Kuo (1923). O learned the English meanings of several compound
characters containing the same radical and was then questioned to
ascertain whether he had noticed the radical and divined its meaning
from the meanings of its compounds. For example, a radical meaning
"mouth" was present in compounds meaning bite, kiss, whistle, cry,
sing, bark, etc. Though the instructions made no reference to radicals
and called simply for memorizing the meaning of the compounds, the
majority of the students tested spontaneously discovered the meaning

of this radical and of other radicals similarly presented. Fully as interesting is the failure of the minority to reach any generalization. The "common element" of form or meaning does not *necessarily* emerge from a collection of specimens, when O's attention is directed to the individual specimens.

In other experiments O has been given some steer toward finding the common characteristic in the varied specimens. Using polygons of 4–6 sides, with a right angle present as a common characteristic in half of them, Drever (1934) informed O that some of the polygons were alike in a certain respect. O was instructed to react with the right hand on sight of any polygon which possessed the (unknown) common characteristic, and with the left hand to any polygon not presenting this characteristic. At the outset the Os were quite in the dark and their reactions only 50 percent correct (chance) but some of them improved gradually while others remained at the chance level. The author drew two conclusions: mere repetition did not make the common feature stand out; some perception or insight was needed. Yet this insight worked gradually and gave no "sudden reorganization." Neither "composite photography" nor the clean testing of hypotheses truly described the inductive process. O's drawings and introspective reports indicated a gradual shaping of the concept, as in the case of an O who soon noticed a sort of right-angled character in several polygons and later observed the definite presence of the right angle.

Smoke (1932) presented in series several specimens of the same class with instructions to discover the common characteristic and define the class. He avoided common "elements," in the sense of parts such as the Chinese radicals, and made the common characteristic consist in certain relations of the parts. A "dax," for example, was a circle with one dot inside and one dot outside, differing from specimen to specimen in size and color of circle and exact position of dots. When O, after examining a number of specimens, one at a time, believed himself able to define the class, he was asked to give his definition, to draw some specimens, and to distinguish in a test series those figures which did and those which did not belong to the class. In agreement with Hull, Smoke found his Os sometimes able to pass the other tests but not able as yet to give an adequate definition. The faulty definitions were usually too inclusive. In one form of the experiment, "negative instances" were introduced—figures marked with a minus sign to indicate that they did not conform to the definition. On the whole the negative instances were of no assistance; some Os used them, others found them distracting. A frequent process of reaching the adequate concept involved the formulation, testing and rejection of hypotheses, till one was found that stood up for a series of specimens. Definite recall of previous members of the series played a role, as was shown by the "thinking out loud" required in this experiment. By aid of memory, similar specimens were grouped as a step toward definition of the whole class.

A classification problem introduced by Ach (1921) has been used by several experimenters including Hüper (1928) and Hanfmann & Kasanin (1937). A collection of blocks is to be sorted into 4 classes and the basis of classification must be discovered by O. In one form the blocks are of 5 different colors and of 6 different shapes, color and shape being irrelevant. They are tall or short, and large or small in horizontal size, and so, by cross-classification, fall into 4 classes. Grouping or "convergence" appears to be an important part of the process of reaching the concepts.

Introspective studies of concept formation. Full introspective reports were called for by Fisher (1916). Her trained psychological observers were shown a series of 10 drawings belonging to a class called, for example, "zalof," and were to discover the characteristics of this class and formulate a definition. In the first figure shown certain features stood out

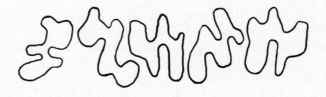

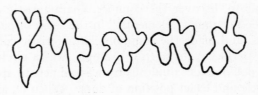

FIG. 257. (Stevanović, 1927.) Two classes of nonsense figures used in an experiment on induction. Each class consisted of the shadow outlines of a certain piece of cardboard held in different positions before the light. There were 7 classes and each was given a nonsense name. In the first round one specimen of each class was associated with the class name; in the second round, a second specimen of each class; and so on. Later, all the figures of the same class were presented together for study.

prominently in "focal awareness," and these same features were focal in each succeeding figure as long as they were present at all. If they were objectively inconspicuous, O searched for them. Any feature found present in the first few figures became, in effect, a hypothesis which was tested in the following figures. A feature found to be absent from some figure thereupon lost its subjective prominence. These changes in focality were very characteristic of the whole process. Naming and tracing, and muscular tensions in eyes and throat, were also reported.

A fresh specimen of an already well-known class was identified, not by comparison with an image representing the class concept, but, once more, by the focality of the class characteristics. In recalling the concepts after a lapse of time O was apt to get visual images of specimens of the class, except when the class had become quite familiar; in that

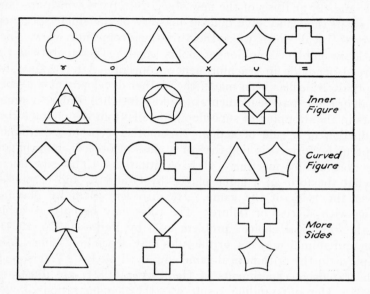

Fig. 258. (After Heidbreder, 1924.) Material for learning the rules of a game. O first learns the check mark assigned to each of the 6 figures. One of the compound figures in the second line is then presented with no further explanation. If O marks the inner figure with its particular check mark he is told "Right," otherwise "Wrong." Other double figures of this class are treated similarly, till O discovers the rule as proved by correct statement and responses. At the end of each trial, before being informed of its rightness or wrongness, O reports "everything that went on in his mind" during the trial. When the first game is mastered, the second follows. Here is an abridged protocol from the second game.

Trial 1, time 9.2 sec.—"It might as well be one as the other, but I marked the right hand one." (Wrong)

2, time 3.0 sec.—"I thought I'd try the left one then." (Right)

3, time 4.2 sec.—"Tried the same thing again, the left one." (Right)

4, time 3.2 sec.—"I marked the left one again." (Wrong)

5, time 15.8 sec.—"I thought then I'd try marking the one with curves. It seems to me that the ones I've had right have been curved." (Right)

6, time 2.2 sec.—"I tried the curve theory again." (Right)

7, time 6.2 sec.—"I am trying the curved lines again. They are not so much curved as the others (before) but I tried it." (Right)

8, time 3.2 sec.—"I stick to curves." (Right)

case the image was schematic or only verbal. A concept, the author concludes, is a readiness to respond appropriately to any member of a class of objects, and the response may be an overt movement or a verbal or visual image, so long as it conforms to the essential characteristics of the class.

Other introspective studies by English (1922), Stevanović (1927), and Chant (1933), while using quite different classes of material, agree in finding two main lines of attack in forming concepts of novel objects: (1) assimilation of the new object to some familiar object—a global attack; and (2) analysis of the new object into parts which are familiar. The first method may give quicker mastery of the single specimen but is likely to break down when the variations come into view, since the extrinsic resemblance no longer holds good. The analytical process is more dependable in reaching a new concept. After a start toward conceptualization has been made, the further development may be very gradual, or there may be moments of sudden insight. Progress sometimes consists in the dropping of superfluous details from the characterization.

Induction of a rule of action. In another type of experiment the concept to be formed is not that of a class of objects, but that of the correct formula for meeting a class of situations. The experiment has somewhat the form of a game played by O and E, and O's task is to discover the rules of the game. He discovers them by playing and meeting with success or failure. The rules may be entirely arbitrary, as in the "multiple choice" problem used by Yerkes (1921, 1934) with human and animal subjects, or the rules may depend on some discernible principle as in the arithmetical game employed by J. C. Peterson (1920).

The extensive experiments of Heidbreder (1924) are illustrated by Fig. 258. Her outstanding result was the demonstration of *spectator behavior*. The more usual *participant behavior* consists in trying out hypotheses. In spectator behavior O has no hypothesis; all his guesses have been proved erroneous, and he can only make some random response and remain on the watch for some new hypothesis to emerge. An example of spectator behavior is given by the protocol of an O occupied with a problem calling for marking *both* figures, whereas all the preceding problems had called for marking only one. After 8 trials, all failures, we find the following series:

9, time 61.5 sec.—"I don't know how to do this, really. It's no use fooling around with position, number of sides, straight and curved lines and all those things when you have no lead. I just marked this to get it out of the way. I have no ideas on the subject." (Wrong)

10, time 5.6 sec.—"I just marked it. I can't think of a thing." (Wrong)

11, time 4.2 sec.—"I think if I just keep marking and watching, I may catch on to something. I think you want something entirely new." (Wrong)

12, time 3.8 sec.—"Just the same. No principle at all. Just hoping it will bring out something." (Wrong)

13, time 3.3 sec.—"Same." (Wrong)

14, time 4.1 sec.—"Same." (Wrong)

15, time 5.4 sec.—"Same thing. But it isn't doing a bit of good." (Wrong)

16, time 59.7 sec.—"I thought I'd try marking both of them. I kept thinking it must be something entirely different because if it had anything to do with curves and number of sides and position and all those things I'd get some right by chance. I tried to dismiss all of them from my mind and the only thing left seemed to be to mark both." (Right)

Spectator behavior affords a clue toward answering the question (p. 776), how hypotheses arise. The receptive attitude may at times be just what is necessary to get us out of a rut and allow some hitherto neglected aspect of the situation a chance to exert its effect. The receptive phase of the inductive process is less observable, either objectively or introspectively, than the more active phase of trying out the hypothesis, but it may be no less essential.

DEDUCTION

If we could accept as good psychology the old idea that logic teaches the laws of thought, we should be far ahead in our knowledge of the process of thinking. Recent students of logic and of psychology agree that logic, or at least the formal logic which has come down from Aristotle, is not psychology to any great extent. It is more akin to mathematics. Its principles and rules afford essential checks on the validity of an act of reasoning but they do not picture the actual process of reasoning.

If the laws of logic were dynamic laws of the thinking process, they could not be broken. Every one obeys the law of gravitation, but we all are likely to disobey the laws of logic. Such disobedience results in a "fallacy," an error in reasoning, analogous to the errors of perception or judgment that are measured in psychophysics. Just as we use an accurate balance or other physical instrument to discover the objective fact which the psychophysical observer is trying to perceive, so we can use the laws of logic to determine the objective validity or invalidity of the inferences drawn by a reasoner from given premises.

The very fact that a syllogism, such as

> All S is M;
> All P is M;
> Therefore, all S is P,

will often be accepted though logically invalid, shows that we have here a type of material which can be of use in the study of thought processes. Especially when expressed in letter symbols, such problems have advantages akin to those of nonsense syllables in the study of memory. The solution of a syllogistic problem demands the use of the data presented and of nothing besides. The conclusion is to be drawn from the premises alone. Extraneous associations are reduced to a minimum.

A little logic. Before taking up the experiments that have employed syllogisms as problems to be solved, we may remind ourselves of a few of the terms and symbols of formal logic.

The syllogism consists of two premises and a conclusion. Each of these three propositions contains two terms, subject and predicate, connected by the copula, "is" or "are." The whole syllogism, however, contains only three different terms, since the "middle term" is present in both premises and not in the conclusion. The middle term is a bridge or link. The first premise links one of the other terms with the middle term, the second premise links the remaining term with the middle term, and then the middle term is eliminated, leaving only the two other terms linked in the conclusion.

Any words or letters can be used as the terms of a syllogism. A convenient standard form denotes the middle term by M, and the subject and predicate of the conclusion by S and P, respectively.

Besides the terms, M, S and P, and the copula, the word "not" may occur in any of the three propositions. Also, the quantifying words, "all" and "some," may occur. "Some" is understood to mean "at least some" and does not imply "not all." If "All A is B," it follows that "Some A is B."

A proposition, then, may be affirmative or negative, and it may be an all-statement or a some-statement. There are thus four types of propositions, commonly designated by letter symbols:

> A—All X is Y—universal affirmative—*all-yes* proposition
> E—No X is Y—universal negative—*all-no* proposition
> I—Some X is Y—particular affirmative—*some-yes* proposition
> O—Some X is not Y—particular negative—*some-no* proposition

To "convert" a proposition is to interchange the subject and predicate. The converted proposition is not valid, i.e., not implied in the original proposition, except in certain cases. The converse of an E proposition is necessarily valid: if no X is Y, obviously no Y can be X. The converse of an I proposition is necessarily valid. But an A proposition cannot be converted without changing *all* to *some;* and an O proposition cannot be converted at all. From "Some X is not Y" we cannot tell whether all, some or none of Y is X. If the truth of these assertions is not seen at once, the difficulty shows that such very elementary logical puzzles may be useful problems in examining the reasoning process.

Euler's diagrams. Back in the eighteenth century, the great Swiss mathematician, Euler, was conducting a correspondence course in logic, his pupil being a German princess. In the hope of removing some of the obscurities of the subject, he invented a set of diagrams which have proved a great help to successive generations of students. The diagrams are based on the relations of inclusion and exclusion. All the X's are supposed to be included in one circle, all the Y's in another circle. If the X circle is included in the Y circle, we see that all X is Y and, conversely, *some* Y is X. If the X and Y circles are entirely separate, no X is Y and, conversely, no Y is X.

So long as we stick to the diagrams, we have no difficulty with conversion. But when we attempt to translate the ordinary propositions into diagrams, we find our data often insufficient. There is no ambiguity in the E proposition, which means the same as the last diagram. But A can mean either of the first two diagrams, I can mean any one of diagrams 2–4, and O can mean any one of diagrams 3–5. To express the meaning of the overlapping diagram in ordinary propositions, we should need three: Some X is Y, Some X is not Y, Some Y is not X.

The errors committed in drawing inferences are largely due to the ambiguity of the standard propositions of logic. These propositions are however such as are used in ordinary speech. This ambiguity of common speech, as compared with the clarity of the diagrams, seems in itself a cogent argument against the theory that thinking is essentially silent speech. Often we have to get away from speech in order to think clearly.

In order to diagram a syllogism we need three circles. If we add

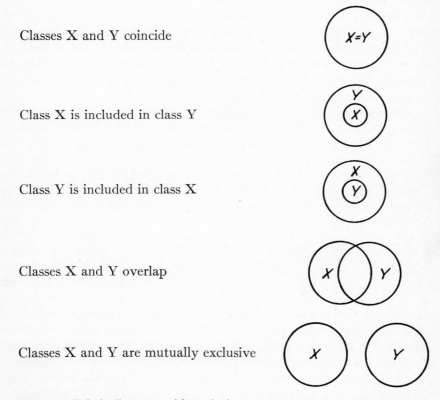

Classes X and Y coincide

Class X is included in class Y

Class Y is included in class X

Classes X and Y overlap

Classes X and Y are mutually exclusive

Fig. 259. Euler's diagrams, with equivalent verbal statements. These propositions can be simply converted. If X = Y, then Y = X. If X excludes Y, then Y excludes X. If X overlaps Y, then Y overlaps X. If X is included in Y, then Y includes X; and if X includes Y, then Y is included in X.

the proposition, Class Z is included in class Y, so making Y our middle term, we see that the relation of X and Z is clear in case of diagrams 1, 3 and 5, but ambiguous in the other two cases. If we know only that X and Z are both included in Y, we can make no further statement about the relations of X and Z. In many other cases the diagrams clarify relations that are obscure in ordinary propositions.

Besides the relations of inclusion and exclusion, there is a linear or unidirectional type of relation which is often used in syllogism problems. Such propositions as,

A is north of B;
P is older than Q;
X is the cause of Y,

are easily converted by use of words expressing the reverse relation. Two such propositions, using the same or opposite relation, sometimes do and sometimes do not yield a valid conclusion. A straight line makes a useful diagram for such syllogisms.

The rules of formal logic are worked out analytically, not geometrically, and apply directly to the ordinary propositions. One important rule demands that the middle term shall be "distributed" in at least one of the premises; something must be known regarding the whole class M. The syllogism given above as an example (p. 807) violates this rule, and represents a common type of fallacy.

Introspective studies of syllogistic reasoning. Syllogisms were introduced into the laboratory by Störring (1908) and were used repeatedly by him and his pupils in introspective experiments. The stimulus material is illustrated in the examples below. O was instructed to be perfectly sure of his conclusion, taking as much time as necessary. The time was measured with a stop watch. The simplest stimuli, used by Eidens (1929), contained only one premise and called for a converse. They were expressed as follows:

What can you say of P, given that all S are P?   (A)
What can you say of P, given that no S are P?   (E)
What can you say of P, given that some S are P?   (I)
What can you say of P, given that some S are not P? (O)

The letters varied from one stimulus to another. The important result was that most of the 11 subjects, who were highly educated adults though not trained in logic, converted all the propositions into their likes, though such conversion is legitimate only for the E and I propositions. Why is it so easy to fall into this error? We shall return to the question.

Störring (1908, 1925, 1926) presented two premises from which a conclusion was to be drawn. The time occupied in reaching the conclusion ranged usually from 5 to 30 seconds, and the process revealed by the introspective reports varied greatly. Most of the processes reported fell into three main classes.

1. The subject built up a pattern in which each of the three terms of the syllogism had its place. Then the middle term was left aside and the relation of the S and P terms was "read off" from the pattern. The pattern was sometimes a spatial diagram, more or less distinctly visual in character, and sometimes gestural and kinesthetic. Sometimes it consisted in an imagined temporal sequence. Some examples:

(a) Stimulus: Q is to the right of M,
                G is to the right of Q,
                Therefore...........

Subject's report: "Q was localized to the right of M on the exposed card; G was then localized to the right of this Q, so that there was an imaginary row, M...Q...G, from which total the fact was read off that G is to the right of M."

(b) Stimulus: *p* is larger than *o*,
                i is smaller than *o*,
                Therefore...........

Subject's report: "On reading the first premise, a sensation of expansion of the chest, as in inspiration, with a feeling of pleasure. On reading the second premise a sensation of contraction. First premise read again with renewed sensation of pleasurable expansion, and *p* was attached to the sensation of greatest expansion. On looking again at the second premise there were unpleasant sensations of contraction with both *o* and *i*, but *i* was attached to the strongest contraction. The conclusion was read off from the progressive sensation of contraction."

2. Verbal patterns. Here, without any distinct spatial diagram, the premises were combined into a total statement, from which the conclusion could be "lifted out." Examples:

(a) Stimulus: Many *i* belong to the class *f*,
                All *f* belong to the class *d*,
                Therefore...............

Subject's report: The two *f*'s were identified during the reading of the second premise, which was modified to take in the first premise, thus: "All *f*, including the many *i*, belong to the class *d*." Therefore, many *i* belong to the class *d*.

(b) Stimulus: If P does not exist, R does not exist;
                Only if V exists does P exist;
                Therefore...........

Subject's report: On first reading I recognize dimly the identity of the two P's and am clear that in the first premise there is negation, in the second affirmation, but see that I cannot fit the premises together without some modification of the second (here a false conversion of the second premise, leading to nothing). I experiment in this wise: If R exists, P exists; this puts P into the same place in both premises and should lead to some relation between R and V—but I find no sure conclusion. Now I start systematically from the second premise: "Only if V exists does P exist," which after some false leads I modify to read: "If V does not exist, neither does P"—that is the force of the "only." Aha! Now I can put them together nicely: If V does not exist, P does not exist; and if P does not exist, R does not exist. Therefore, if V does not exist, R does not exist.

This last process was carried on mostly in argumentative speech, but there was an "Aha-experience," a moment of insight, in which the two premises shot together into a unitary pattern.

3. Calculus of relations. Instead of building up a complete pattern in which each of the three terms had a place, the subject might operate

with relations, noting their likeness or opposition, and thus reaching a
conclusion.   Examples:

    (a) Stimulus: A is above B,
                    C is beneath B,
                    Therefore............

Subject's report: I noticed that the relation of C to B is the same as that
of B to A.   B is beneath A and so much the more is C beneath A.

    (b) Stimulus: A is part of B,
                    C is part of A,
                    Therefore.................

Subject's report: C is part of A which itself is part of something.   Therefore
C is the smallest of the lot, and it is smaller than the other term whatever
that is.   A look back at the first premise revealed the term wanted and gave
the conclusion, C is smaller than B, is a part of B.

There are two questions of theory which we may try to answer from
these results.   One is the question between talking and seeing, already
mentioned; and the other is a question between patterns and relations.

As between talking and seeing, the reports show many instances of
each kind.   Sometimes the subject uses diagrams or some concrete aid in
seeing the relationships of the terms and reaching a conclusion.   Sometimes he seems to talk the problem out.   The talking, to be sure, is anything but an automatism; it is a searchful talking, and shows moments
of insight.   There is really no clear evidence that verbal skill of itself is
the key to the solution of these problems.

As between patterns and relations, the question will have more point
if connected with two prominent groups of contemporary psychologists:
the Gestalt group, and the Spearman group.   While the two have not
come to grips on precisely this question, it is certain that Spearman
speaks of the seeing, or "eduction," of relations and correlates as the
essence of intellectual activity, whereas the Gestalt group emphasizes
organized wholes, total patterns.   A pattern includes relations as "dependent parts," but is not composed of relations, being psychologically
prior to relations, in the Gestalt view.

Taken at their face value, the reports of Störring's subjects support
now the pattern theory, now the relation theory, but more commonly
the pattern theory.   The calculus of relations seems almost too abstract
for ready use, though it is undoubtedly highly efficient where the material
is familiar and easy.

Objective studies of syllogistic reasoning.   Most experiments on
reasoning and most tests of reasoning ability have rather avoided the
syllogistic form, because probably of its artificiality.   In the hands of
certain experimenters, however, the syllogism has done good service in
revealing sources of difficulty.   Burt (1919, 1921) used this sort of material
in a test and regarded it the best single indicator of intellectual ability
in older children.   Without limiting himself to the exact form of the syl-

logism, he presented all the necessary data for drawing a conclusion, as in the examples:

7-year level   All wall-flowers have four petals: this flower has three petals. Is this a wall-flower?

10-year level   There are four roads here: I have come from the south and want to go to Melton:
The road at the right leads somewhere else:
Straight ahead it leads only to a farm.
In which direction is Melton—North, South, East, or West?

Each item was typed on a separate card and laid before O, who was asked for his reasons after he had replied. Comparison of easy with difficult items revealed some of the factors of difficulty. The formal logical structure made little difference. The fallacy of "undistributed middle term" seemed relatively easy to detect, and the "argumentum ad hominem" relatively difficult. On the whole the author concludes that "if put in a sufficiently glaring form, nearly every fallacy can be detected and avoided by children of seven; if sufficiently disguised, each will entrap even children of fourteen. The formal character of the fallacy has thus only a small influence upon the age at which it can be perceived." Much more important were the kind and quantity of the data presented. As to kind, the data must be within the range of the child's knowledge, or he will not reason about them correctly. As to quantity, some maturity was needed for handling a large mass of data.

Not quite so obvious is another non-logical factor which proved to be important—the linguistic form in which the problem was presented. This difficulty comes out clearly in the linear type of syllogism, and is essentially a difficulty in lining up the three terms. An example:

Three boys are sitting in a row: Harry is to the left of Willie: George is to the left of Harry. Which boy is in the middle?

This item was passed by 50% of the 9-year-olds. If the two premises are simply transposed, the item is passed by 61% of the same age-group. The same linguistic difficulty appears in the following item:

Edith is fairer than Olive: but she is darker than Lily. Who is darker, Olive or Lily?

In this form it was passed by 46% of the 8-year group, but the percent went up to 72 when a slight verbal change was made:

Lily is fairer than Edith: Edith is fairer than Olive. Who is the fairest, Lily or Olive?

The children who succeeded with the first form reported that they had to turn the first premise around (convert it) before seeing the answer. Much older subjects, in Störring's experiments, experienced the same difficulty when the premises had to be transposed or converted in order to bring out the linear relationship.

Another difficulty observed by Burt consists in the presence of irrelevant data which tend to confuse the pattern and suggest false conclusions. They have to be pushed aside.

Wilkins (1928) in an experiment on 81 college men presented logically identical syllogisms with letter terms and with word terms, in order to see whether the more abstract or the more concrete material was handled more correctly. She prepared her material in the form of a paper and pencil test. On opening his test booklet, O was confronted with a series of problems like the following:

All good ballet dancers have many years of training; some of the dancers in this musical comedy have many years of training;
therefore
    a. some of the dancers in this musical comedy are good ballet dancers.
    b. all good ballet dancers are in this musical comedy.
    c. some of the dancers in this musical comedy are not good ballet dancers.
Or, the same thing in symbols:
All a's are b's; some c's are b's;
therefore
    a. some c's are a's.
    b. all a's are c's.
    c. some c's are not a's.

The instructions were "to put a plus sign before every conclusion which you are sure follows necessarily from the given statements . . . a minus sign before every conclusion that does not necessarily follow from the given statements. If no conclusion can be drawn from the given statements, put a minus sign before each of the conclusions following."

Some of the conclusions submitted were valid, while some were examples of the different logical fallacies. The easiest fallacies to detect, according to the average results, were
    affirmative conclusion from negative premises;
    universal conclusion from particular premises.
The most difficult were:
    any conclusion from 2 particular premises;
    any conclusion when the middle term is undistributed
      in both premises.
The main result, however, was the greater difficulty of the syllogisms presented in letter terms. The average score was 76 percent correct for the letter terms, 84 percent for the syllogisms expressed in familiar words. The difference is statistically reliable, though not very great. A score of 50 percent correct in this test was no better than chance.

Why should college students accept so many invalid conclusions? A large share of the errors can be laid to the ambiguity of the word *some*. In logic, it means *at least some*, while in ordinary usage it often carries the implication, *not all*. It would ordinarily be rather misleading to say that

"Some soldiers were killed" if the truth were that all were killed. Following ordinary usage, many students believed it valid to infer from "Some X is Y" that, therefore, "Some X is not Y." This source of error is of no particular interest.

"Atmosphere effect." A valid conclusion is based on the exact pattern of relations inherent in the data—the relations of S, P and M as set forth in the premises. If one "sees" this pattern clearly, one sees the conclusion; or, if the pattern does not yield any usable relation between S and P, one sees that no valid conclusion can be drawn. But this well-articulated pattern has to be worked out, sometimes with much effort as shown by the introspections already quoted. Before the pattern is worked out, the premises produce a global impression of affirmation or negation, of universality or particularity. If the subject follows this global impression he is liable to error. Woodworth & Sells (1935) set up the hypothesis that this global impression or "atmosphere" of the premises was an important factor in erroneous reasoning. "An affirmative atmosphere in the premises makes it easy to accept an affirmative conclusion, etc." The atmosphere of a single premise makes it easy to accept the converse, as Eidens had found (p. 810). When the premises are alike, being both A propositions, or both E, or both I, or both O, the atmosphere corresponds. When the premises differ, the atmosphere is mixed, and supplementary hypotheses are required to predict the effect on the reasoner. The following hypotheses seemed reasonable:

1. A negative premise creates a negative atmosphere, even when the other premise is affirmative.

2. A particular ("some") premise creates a *some* atmosphere, even when the other premise is universal.

The atmosphere hypothesis, with these supplementary hypotheses, was subjected to a rigid test by Sells (1936). His test material appeared as follows:

1. AT	PT	I	AF	If all x's are y's;
				And if all z's are x's;
				Then all z's are y's.
2. AT	PT	I	AF	If no x's are y's;
				And if all z's are y's;
				Then some z's are x's.

Each conclusion was to be checked in the margin as "absolutely true," "probably true," "indeterminate," or "absolutely false." Abundant time was allowed. To avoid cluttering up the results with errors due to misinterpretation of "some," the meaning attached to this term in logic was carefully explained in advance. The subjects were 65 educated adults, not trained in formal logic. (Familiarity with the rules of logic would enable O to reject many conclusions instantly. Many of those presented violate the rule that no valid conclusion can be drawn from two negative premises.)

There were 180 items like the above, of which only 52 were valid syllogisms. The 128 invalid items included two examples of every possible combination of the propositions, A, E, I, and O. The results are shown in the adjoining table.

PERCENT OF INVALID CONCLUSIONS ACCEPTED BY 65 ADULTS

(*Sells, 1936*)

Premises presented	Conclusion favored by atmosphere	Invalid conclusion presented			
		A	E	I	O
AA	A	58	14	63	17
EE	E	21	38	25	34
II	I	27	9	72	38
OO	O	14	16	38	52
AE	E	11	51	13	63
EA	E	8	64	12	69
AI	I	33	4	70	32
IA	I	36	15	75	36
AO	O	15	26	42	76
OA	O	13	33	28	75
EI	O	8	40	22	62
IE	O	11	42	22	63
EO	O	13	29	29	44
OE	O	15	31	24	48
IO	O	12	19	31	64
OI	O	11	23	33	71

Since these conclusions were all invalid, their acceptance depended on non-logical factors. The data are fully in accord with the hypothesis that the atmosphere effect, or global impression, is a potent factor. Invalid conclusions favored by atmosphere are more often accepted than others. Some other factor must be invoked to account for the occasional acceptance of *any* conclusion from any premises. Sells suggested a factor of *gullibility*, a willingness to accept anything, and tested this suggestion by comparing the data from the brightest and dullest quarter of his group (as selected by an intelligence test). Miscellaneous acceptance was much more in evidence with the dull group. The bright group practically never accepted, for example, an A conclusion from negative premises. The bright group did, however, show the atmosphere effect, and showed it the more clearly because of freedom from "gullibility."

A demonstration of the atmosphere effect is provided by a brief syllogism test of Sells & Koob (1937). Instead of accepting or rejecting a ready-made conclusion, the subject in this test draws his own conclusion by filling in a blank. The instructions to "work quickly" are intended to favor the atmosphere effect. The material and results are shown in tabular form.

Percentage Distribution of Conclusions Drawn by 134 College Students

(*Sells & Koob, 1937*)

Item presented	Premises	Conclusion drawn				
		A	E	I	O	None
All x's are y's; And all y's are z's; Therefore —— x's —— z's.	AA	99	0	1	0	0
All x's are y's; And all x's are z's; Therefore —— y's —— z's.	AA	78	1	19	0	2
No x's are y's; And no z's are x's; Therefore —— z's —— y's.	EE	2	67	18	3	10
Some x's are y's; And some y's are z's; Therefore —— x's —— z's.	II	0	0	90	1	9
Some x's are not y's; And some z's are not x's; Therefore —— z's —— y's.	OO	0	2	14	70	14

In the first item, conclusions A and I are valid; in the second, only I is valid; the remaining three items admit of no valid conclusion, though the form of the test suggested that some conclusion could be drawn. The conclusion drawn is usually in accordance with the global impression of the premises.

The "atmosphere effect" is not confined to syllogisms. In speaking or hasty writing one is likely to make the verb agree with the singular or plural atmosphere of the subject phrase, instead of with the noun which is the grammatical subject; as in the following examples picked up from recent psychological literature (the present writer pleading guilty to the last two):

The laboratory equipment in these situations were in many instances essentially the same as those used before.

A common background of emotional conflict, repression, and abnormal reactions of a motor, visceral or perceptual nature have justified an inherent relationship.

Here a series of experiments were conducted with a knowledge of results as the only supposed variables.

Research on intelligence and motivation, on heredity and environment, are gradually clarifying what have always been matters of conflicting opinion.

Is trial and error blind or not?

How does atmosphere operate? Presumably one becomes quickly set or adjusted to the total impression of the presented situation, and responds accordingly. Accurate reasoning demands analysis of the situation, noting of relations, and building up of an articulated pattern.

"STAGES OF CREATIVE THOUGHT"

Helmholtz, a brilliant inventor and discoverer in several scientific fields, including, fortunately, psychology as well as physiology and physics, took occasion at a dinner in honor of his seventieth birthday to report something of his methods of work on original problems (1896).

I must say that those fields of work have become ever more agreeable to me in which one need not depend on lucky accidents and "happy thoughts." But as I have found myself pretty often in the uncomfortable position of having to wait for happy thoughts, the experience I have gained on the question, when and where they came to me, may perhaps be useful to others. Often enough they crept quietly into my thinking without my suspecting their importance at first; and then it was often impossible later on to recall under what circumstances they had come; they were simply there and that was all I could say. But in other cases they arrived suddenly, without any effort on my part, like an inspiration. So far as my experience goes, they never came to a fatigued brain and never at the writing desk. It was always necessary, first of all, that I should have turned my problem over on all sides to such an extent that I had all its angles and complexities "in my head" and could run through them freely without writing. To bring the matter to that point is usually impossible without long preliminary labor. Then, after the fatigue resulting from this labor had passed away, there must come an hour of complete physical freshness and quiet well-being, before the good ideas arrived. Often they were there in the morning when I awoke, just according to Goethe's oft-cited verses, and as Gauss also once noted. But they liked specially to make their appearance while I was taking an easy walk over wooded hills in sunny weather. The smallest amount of alcohol seemed to frighten them away.

Such testimony from Helmholtz is fully as good as a laboratory protocol, and the only question is whether it would hold good of other creative thinkers. Fortunately, again, the brilliant mathematician Poincaré (1908) was interested in the psychology of this matter and carefully noted the circumstances under which some of his discoveries were reached. His observations tally with those of Helmholtz, except that he added a certain amount of theory.

The part played by unconscious work in mathematical discovery seems to me indisputable. . . . Often when a man is working at a difficult question, he accomplishes nothing the first time he sets to work. Then he takes more or less of a rest, and sits down again at his table. During the first half-hour he still finds nothing, and then all at once the decisive idea presents itself to his mind. We might say that the conscious work proved more fruitful because it was interrupted and the rest restored force and freshness to the mind. But it is more probable that the rest was occupied with unconscious work. . . . There is another remark to be made regarding the conditions of this unconscious work, which is, that it is not possible, or in any case not fruitful, unless it is first preceded and then followed by a period of conscious work. These sudden inspirations are never produced . . . except after some days of voluntary efforts which appeared absolutely fruitless. . . . The necessity for the second period of conscious work can be even more readily understood. It is necessary to work out the results of the inspiration . . . but, above all, it is necessary to verify them.

Apart from the theory of unconscious work—unconscious cerebration, it has also been called—the facts observed by Poincaré in his thinking are essentially the same as those reported by Helmholtz. After the necessary preliminary period of intensive work in becoming familiar with the problem, there must be a period of rest, or perhaps of unconscious work, before a new idea can be expected. This new idea needs to be verified and elaborated before the discovery can be called complete. But what is really new about the discovery emerges suddenly after preparation and a period of inattention to the problem.

Graham Wallas (1926) definitely named the "four stages of creative thought" as Preparation, Incubation, Illumination and Verification. He believed however that "in the daily stream of thought these four different stages constantly overlap each other as we explore different problems. . . . Even in exploring the same problem, the mind may be unconsciously incubating on one aspect of it, while it is consciously employed in preparing for or verifying another aspect."

The word "incubation" rather implies the theory of unconscious work on a problem during a period of attention to other matters, but we can strip off this implication and use it simply to denote the fact—so far as it is a fact—that a period of inattention to a problem intervenes after preparation and before illumination. There is some resemblance between the meanings of "incubation" and of the "plateau" in the learning curve. Both are defined as periods of no apparent progress intervening between stages of rapid progress.

Inventors and scientists. Inquiries conducted by Rossman (1931) among inventors, and by Platt & Baker (1931) among chemists, show that the stages noted by Helmholtz and Poincaré are familiar to many solvers of original problems. First they "load up" with all available information and make determined efforts to reach a prompt solution; and sometimes they are successful in this first heat. But often they have to give up for the time, and days or weeks may elapse before the saving idea comes in a flash, while attention is on something remote from the problem, though sometimes during conversation on the problem, round-table discussion or attempts to explain the problem to some one else. About the earliest scientific discovery of which we have any psychological account was that of Archimedes, made during a bath—the original "eureka" experience— and exactly similar occasions are reported by some of these modern inventors. Others report illumination while riding on a train or automobile, while walking a city street, while dressing, shaving, gardening, fishing, golfing, playing solitaire, listening to a concert or sermon, reading, loafing at one's desk or on the beach, daydreaming, lying in bed after retiring, on awaking in the morning or in the middle of the night.

Most of the inventors seemed to adopt the easy hypothesis of unconscious work as the explanation of the illumination. One chemist who had considered the psychology of the matter more deeply, presents a different hypothesis along with some fresh facts (Platt & Baker, 1931):

The two factors that seem to be involved are, first, so thorough a study of the problem and of the data that your mind is quite completely saturated with the subject. Then, second, a period of intermission or rest, and an apparent solution or proper method of attack comes to your mind when you are not formally working on the problem and have no papers in front of you. . . . It is this period of intermission and the lack of any papers, diagrams, maps or whatever may be involved that causes one to refer to . . . a revelation or a hunch. Here I think is where we fall into error. This thing only occurs when your mind is completely saturated with the problem. . . . It can take up the matter at any time intelligently, without reference to data sheets, diagrams, maps, or such external aids. . . . I remember one morning I took my bath, shaved, took another bath, and in reaching out for a dry towel suddenly became aware that this was my second bath and that my mind had been deeply concentrated on a problem for half an hour. . . . I give this as an example . . . because it gives a clear picture of what is going on. The mind is fresh; it is so full of the problem that there is no need to refer to anything and it is in deep concentration. It is working at the problem. . . . If it works until the solution comes, we are liable to forget that it has worked at all. . . . With a rested mind soaked full of data on a problem, and in deep concentration, I would expect a man to solve a problem if he ever can solve it. (Statement by J. E. Teeple.)

These numerous observations appear well deserving of acceptance so far as concerns the necessity for intensive work on a problem followed by laying the problem aside. The last quotation raises an important question regarding the usually reported "flash" of illumination. If the flash is the climax of a short period of very intense thought, there is no need for the notion of unconscious work during the incubation period.

Closer to an experimental study of this general subject are the observations of Meinecke (1934) who assigned problems to a young inventor, kept watch on him during the process and obtained a retrospective report after the solution of each problem. In one case the problem called for an improved machine for portioning dough in bakeries. The task seemed easy at first and the inventor quickly worked out a solution which however did not satisfy him. He wished to get a radically new design that should be much simpler. "Because of similar experiences in other cases I laid the problem aside and turned to other occupation." Several days later the solution occurred to him on the street as he returned from a midday stroll by the river where he had been watching the paddle steamboats and also a new type of dredge. His solution had some similarity to these nautical machines, though at the actual moment of insight he did not think of this resemblance, being too excited and happy in the discovery itself.

Poets and artists. In an inquiry among living lyric poets, 55 of them, Patrick (1935) found the four-stage creative process to be typical; and she found the same in a similar inquiry among 50 pictorial artists (1937). Although a minority are accustomed to write a poem on the spur of the moment—or to sketch a picture of what they happen to see before them— 72% of the poets and 76% of the artists report a stage of incubation. For example:

I may get an idea for a poem from something that I see, which may be with me for a long time. For instance, I saw a nun leaning over a pool of flamingoes, and I got the idea of both being in captivity. I was a whole year trying to write that. I knew that it would be a sonnet or lyric, but that was all.

I saw the moon coming out of a cloud, which reminded me of a white owl. I carried that idea around several days before I finally wrote a poem on it.

I have an idea in the back of my mind for a long time, sometimes a week or two. I don't think constantly about it, but it keeps coming back.

I often carry an idea around for several weeks before I make a picture, though sometimes longer. I got ideas in Santa Fe last summer to do now. The ideas recur from time to time while I am occupied with other things.

Though Patrick accepts the four stages as a valid outline of the creative process, she adds the important point that the "idea" is not entirely absent from conscious thought during the stage of incubation. *"The incubated idea or mood recurs from time to time* during the incubation period. When the idea recurs, there is a chance of some work being done upon it." Some of the inventors made similar reports. The work done on the problem during incubation is however not seriously directed toward the main goal. "As soon as the mood or idea becomes definitely related to a specific goal, we have the third stage of illumination or inspiration."

This author went on to see whether the four stages could be found in miniature in an experimental situation. She had surprising success in obtaining from the poets and artists, as well as from control groups of non-poets and non-artists, the production of a lyric or picture under the experimenter's eye, with oral expression of their thoughts during the process, these remarks being taken down in shorthand. As a stimulus for the lyric, the picture of a mountain landscape was used; a poem was laid before the artists. The subject was requested to obtain any suggestion he pleased from the stimulus material, and to take as much time as he pleased in his composition. On the average, and with much variation, about 20 minutes was used by all classes of subjects.

That the poets and artists were not hampered by the experimental conditions appeared from their testimony and from the excellence of their products, some of which were later published.

The three overt stages, preparation, illumination, and revision, were easily identified in the protocols. At first manifold impressions and memories occurred, but usually nothing was committed to paper. After a time a decision emerged, and figures were rapidly blocked out or a series of lines roughly formulated. Revision of various kinds followed. A brief extract from the protocol of one of the poets will illustrate the first and third stages, and incubation can be read between the lines.

The first thing that I think of is the rush of water at the base of the picture and the cool blue heights feeling distance. The importance of the picture at the top and bottom. When I examine it in detail the mist of the waterfalls seems most interesting and the little evergreen trees suggest Christmas trees. The little clouds that float over the summit seem like desires that elude. Water has the suggestion of the timeless or eternal flowing on seeking something bigger than itself. I would say that the artist was outside of himself—that he had lost his personality in the vastness of nature.

5 min.: The figure of the man seems in keeping with the overpowering grandeur of nature. He is made so small that one discovers him only upon seeking him. The picture combines earth and unrest. It seems to bring the eternal quality of the hills and the changing of the water which reflects the mood of the sky. I call it a poem in colors. Well, let's see. (Pause)

1. The water swings to the timeless sea
2. And the peaks lift into eternity (Would be glad if they cut off that radio!)
3. While man is lost on the shores of time
4. Watching the changeless cool clouds climb (Pause)
5. Above the trees that top the rocks (And so on.)

Though the three overt stages overlapped in time, they came on the whole in that order. When each O's total time was divided into quarters and a count made of thoughts suggested, lines drafted (or shapes outlined), and revisions, the percent of the totals coming in each quarter was as follows for the poets (and much the same for the artists):

	Quarters of total time			
	1	*2*	*3*	*4*
Thoughts suggested	54	33	10	3
Lines drafted	9	36	33	22
Revisions	1	12	26	61

The thoughts or suggestions tended to come early, the first draft in the middle and the revisions late. There is time for a brief incubation between the suggestion of the thoughts and the first shaping of the poem or picture. On the average, 6–7 minutes was spent in obtaining suggestions before the lines began to take shape. The presence of incubation was regarded as shown "if an idea occurred early in the report, recurred one or more times, the subject meanwhile talking of other things, and at last appeared as the chief topic of the poem" or picture. By this criterion, incubation was surely present in 64% of the poets and 84% of the artists.

The process of creative thought seemed to run the same general course in the control groups, though their product was usually inferior.

Theories of incubation. The obvious theory—unconscious work, whether conceived as mental or as cerebral—should be left as a residual hypothesis for adoption only if other, more testable hypotheses break down. Several other hypotheses have been suggested in what precedes.

Since the problem does *consciously recur* from time to time during the period of incubation, though without effortful work done upon it, partial solutions may be obtained.

If it is true that the illumination comes in a period, short or long, of *intense concentration* on the problem, the assumption of previous unconscious work is gratuitous.

The *freshness* or lack of brain fatigue which seems to be necessary for illumination may furnish a sufficient explanation.

The parallel but simpler case of the recall of a name, after futile attempts followed by dropping the matter, suggests that an essential factor in illumination is the *absence of interferences* which block progress during the preliminary stage. When, as must often happen, the thinker makes a false start, he slides insensibly into a groove and may not be able to escape at the moment. He falls into certain assumptions which restrict his sector of exploratory activity, just as in other cases of problem solving (p. 771), and as long as he continues actively at work in this sector he does not escape from these assumptions, as he often does on coming back to the problem after giving it a rest. Several of the inventors noted a fact which favors this interpretation: the happy idea, when it came, amazed them by its simplicity. They had assumed a more complicated solution to be necessary. According to this line of evidence, incubation consists in getting rid of false leads and hampering assumptions so as to approach the problem with an "open mind."

BIBLIOGRAPHY

ABBREVIATIONS

Periodicals

Abh	Abhandlungen	*Mon*	Monograph
Akad	Akademie	*Ps*	Psychology
Am	American	*Q*	Quarterly
An	Annals	*R*	Review
Ar	Archives	*St*	Studies
Br	British	*U*	University
J	Journal	*Z*	Zeitschrift
Mo	Monthly		

Omitted are: *and, der, die, für, of, the, und.*

A

Abbott, E. *Ps Mon* 1914, 16, #68.

Abel, T. M. *J Exp Ps* 1930, 13, 47–60.

Abernethy, E. M. *J Educ Ps* 1929, 20, 695–701.

Abney, W. de W. *Researches in colour vision and the trichromatic theory.* 1913.

Ach, N. *Über die Willenstätigkeit und das Denken.* 1905.

Ach, N. *Über den Willensakt und das Temperament.* 1910.

Ach, N. *Über die Begriffsbildung.* 1921.

Achilles, E. M. *Ar Ps* 1920, #44.

Adams, D. K. *Comp Ps Mon* 1929, 6, #27.

Adrian, E. D. *Mechanism of nervous action.* 1932.

Adrian, E. D., Cattell, McK., Hoagland, H. *J Physiol* 1931, 72, 377–391.

Alechsieff, N. *Philos St* 1900, 16, 1–60.

Alechsieff, N. *Ps St* 1907, 3, 156–271.

Allesch, G. J. von *Ps Forsch* 1925, 6, 1–91; 215–281.

Allport, F. H. *Social psychology.* 1924.

Allport, G. W. *Br J Ps* 1924, 15, 99–120.

Allport, G. W. *Am J Ps* 1928, 40, 418–425.

Allport, G. W. *Br J Ps* 1930, 21, 133–148.

Allport, G. W. *Personality, a psychological interpretation,* 1937.

Alpert, A. *Solving of problem-situations by preschool children.* 1928.

Alrutz, S. *Z Ps* 1908, 47, 161–202; 241–286.

Anastasi, A. *Ps Mon* 1934, 45, #204.

Anderson, I. H. *Ps Mon* 1937, 48, #215, 1–35.

Anderson, M. *J Educ Ps* 1917, 8, 97–102.

Angell, F. *Am J Ps* 1911, 22, 86–93.

Angell, J. R. *Ps Mon* 1910, 13, #53, 61–107.

Angell, J. R., Fite, W. *Ps R* 1901, 8, 225–246.

Angell, J. R., Moore, A. W. *Ps R* 1896, 3, 245–258.

Angier, R. P. *Ps Mon* 1903, 4, #17, 541–561.

Ansbacher, H. *Ar Ps* 1937, #215.

Arnheim, R. *Ps Forsch* 1928, 11, 1–132.

Arrer, M. *Philos St* 1898, 13, 116–161; 222–304.

d'Arsonval, A. *Soc Biol Compt Rend* 1888, 40, 142–144.

Aschaffenburg, G. *Ps Arbeit* 1895, 1, 209–299.

Aschaffenburg, G. *Ps Arbeit* 1896, 1, 608–626.

Aschaffenburg, G. *Ps Arbeit* 1897, 2, 1–83.

Aster, E. A. v. *Z Ps* 1908, 49, 56–107.

Aveling, F. *Internatl Cong Ps* 1926, 8, 227–234.

B

Bacon, M. M., Rood, E. A., Washburn, M. F. *Am J Ps* 1914, 25, 290–293.

Bagley, W. C. *The educative process.* 1905.

Baier, D. E. *J Exp Ps* 1936, 19, 280–308.

Bain, A. *Senses and the intellect.* 1855. 1864.

Bain, A. *Mental science.* 1870.

Bair, J. H. *Ps Mon* 1902, 5, #19.

Baird, J. W. *Am J Ps* 1903, 14, 150–200.

Baird, J. W. *Color sensitivity of the peripheral retina.* 1905.

Baker, K. H. *J Genl Ps* 1937, 16, 471–488.

Baldwin, J. M. *Mind* 1896, 5, 81–90.

Baldwin, J. M., Shaw, W. J. *Ps R* 1895 a, 2, 236–239.

Baldwin, J. M., Shaw, W. J. *Ps R* 1895 b, 2, 259–273.

Baley, S. *Z Ps* 1914–15 a, 70, 321–346.

Baley, S. *Z Ps* 1914–15 b, 70, 347–372.

Ballachey, E. L., Buel, J. *J Genet Ps* 1934, 45, 358–370.

Ballachey, E. L., Krechevsky, I. *Calif U Pub Ps* 1932, 6, 83–97.

Ballard, P. B. *Br J Ps Mon* 1913, 1, #2.

Banister, H. *Br J Ps* 1926 a, 16, 265–292.

Banister, H. *Br J Ps* 1926 b, 17, 142–153.

Bappert, J. *Ps St* (Schumann) 1923, 1 abt, 7 heft, 78–114.

Barcroft, J., Florey, H. *J Physiol* 1929, 68, 181–189.

Bard, P. *Handbk genl exp ps* (Murchison) 1934, 264–311.

Barker, R. G. *J. Genl Ps* 1931, 5, 280–285.

Barrett, M. *Ps R* 1914, 21, 278–294.

Bartlett, F. C. *Remembering.* 1932.

Bartlett, R. J. *Br J Ps* 1927, 18, 30–50.

Barton, J. W. *J Exp Ps* 1921, 4, 418–429.

Bass, M. J., Hull, C. L. *J Comp Ps* 1934, 17, 49–65.

Batson, W. H. *Ps Mon* 1916, 21, #91.

Bayer, L. *Z Ps* 1933, 63 (2), 197–212.

Bayley, N. *Ps Mon* 1928, 38, #176, 1–38.

Bazett, H. C., McGlone, B., Brocklehurst, R. J. *J Physiol* 1930, 69, 88–112.

Bean, C. H. *Ar Ps* 1912, #21.

Beebe-Center, J. G. *Am J Ps* 1929, 41, 54–69.

Beebe-Center, J. G. *Psychology of pleasantness and unpleasantness.* 1932.

Beeby, C. E. *Br J Ps* 1930, 20, 336–353.

Beitel, R. J. *J Genl Ps* 1934, 10, 311–327.

Bekhterev, V. M. *General principles of human reflexology.* 1933.

Bell, Sir Charles *Anatomy and philosophy of expression.* 1806. 1844.

Bellis, C. J. *Soc Exp Biol Med Proc* 1932–33, 30, 801–803.

Benary, W. *Ps Forsch* 1924, 5, 131–142.

Bentley, M. *Am J Ps* 1899, 11, 1–48.

Benussi, V. *Unters Gegens Ps* (Meinong) 1904, 303–448.

Benussi, V. *Ar ges Ps* 1912, 24, 31–62.

Benussi, V. *Ar ges Ps* 1914 a, 31, 244–273.

Benussi, V. *Ar ges Ps* 1914 b, 32, 396–419.

Bergemann, R. *Ps St* 1906, 1, 179–218.

Berger, G. O. *Philos St* 1886, 3, 38–93.

Bergström, J. A. *Am J Ps* 1892, 5, 356–369.

Bergström, J. A. *Am J Ps* 1893, 6, 433–442.

Berkeley, G. *An essay towards a new theory of vision.* 1709.

Berkeley, G. *Principles of human knowledge.* 1710.

Bernstein, A. L. *J Genl Ps* 1934, 10, 173–197.

Berry, W. *Ps Bull* 1922, 19, 307–337.

Berry, W. *Am J Ps* 1927, 38, 584–596.

Berry, W., Imus, H. *Am J Ps* 1935, 47, 449–457.

Betts, G. H. *The distribution and functions of mental imagery.* 1909.

Betz, W. *Z ang Ps* 1932, 41, 166–178.

Beyrl, F. *Z Ps* 1926, 100, 344–371.

Bidwell, S. *Curiosities of light and sight.* 1899.

Bierens de Haan, J. A. *Z vergl Physiol* 1931, 13, 639–695.

Biervliet, J. J. van *Philos St* 1894, 10, 160–167. 1895, 11, 125–134.

Billings, M. L. *Ps R* 1914, 21, 121–135.

Billings, M. L., Shepard, J. E. *Ps R* 1910, 17, 217–228.

Bills, A. G. *Am J Ps* 1927, 38, 227–251.

Bills, A. G. *Am J Ps* 1931, 43, 230–245.

Bills, A. G., McTeer, W. *J Exp Ps* 1932, 15, 23–36.

Binet, A. *R philos* 1890, 29, 138–155.

Binet, A. *Psychologie des grands calculateurs.* 1894.

Binet, A. *L'étude expérimentale de l'intelligence.* 1903.

Binet, A., Henri, V. *Ann ps* 1894, 1, 1–23.

Binet, A., Simon, Th. *Ann ps* 1908, 14, 1–94.

Bishop, H. G. *J Genl Ps* 1928, 1, 177–178.

Blakeslee, A. F. *Science* 1935, 81, 504–507.

Blakeslee, A. F., Salmon, T. N. *Nat Acad Sci Proc* 1935, 21, 84–90.

Blank, G. *Indust Pstechnik* 1934, 11, 140–150.

Blatz, W. E. *J Exp Ps* 1925, 8, 109–132.

Bliss, C. B. *Yale St Ps* 1893, 1, 1–55.

Blix, M. *Upsala Läkareförenings förh* 1882–83, 18.

Blix, M. *Z Biol* 1884, 20, 141–156.

Block, H. *Ar Ps* 1936, #202.

Blodgett, H. C. *Calif U Pub Ps* 1929, 4, 113–134.

Boas, E. P. *Ar Internal Med* 1928, 41, 403–414.

Boas, E. P. *J Clinical Invest* 1931, 10, 145–152.

Boas, E. P., Goldschmidt, E. F. *The heart rate.* 1932.

Boas, E. P., Weiss, M. M. *J Am Med Assoc* 1929, 92, 2162–2168.

Bolton, T. L. *Am J Ps* 1892, 4, 362–380.

Bonnet, Ch. *Essai analytique sur les facultés de l'âme.* 1760. c xxxviii.

Bonser, F. G. *Ps R* 1903, 10, 120–138.

Book, W. F.   *The psychology of skill.*
1908.

Book, W. F.   *Ps R* 1910, 17, 381–
398.

Boreas, T.   *Praktika Acad Athènes*
1930, 5, 382–396.

Boring, E. G.   *Ps R* 1920, 27, 440–
452.

Boring, E. G.   *Am J Ps* 1921, 32,
449–471.

Boring, E. G.   *History of experimental
psychology.*   1929.

Boring, E. G.   *Am J Ps* 1930, 42,
446–449.

Boring, E. G.   *Philos Sci* 1935, 2,
236–245.

Boring, E. G., Stevens, S. S.   *Nat
Acad Sci Proc* 1936, 22, 514–521.

Boring, E. G., Titchener, E. B.   *Am
J Ps* 1923, 34, 471–485.

Botti, L.   *R Psicol* 1912, 8, 348–354.

Bourdon, B.   *R philos* 1893, 35,
225–260.

Bourdon, B.   *R philos* 1894, 38, 148–
167.   (See also *Ann ps* 1894, 1,
406–408.)

Bourdon, B.   *R philos* 1895, 40, 153–
185.

Bourdon, B.   *La perception visuelle de
l'espace.*   1902.

Bowditch, H. P., Warren, J. W.   *J
Physiol* 1890, 11, 25–64.

Bowers, H.   *Br J Ps* 1932, 23, 180–
195.

Bowie, W.   *Determination of time,
longitude, latitude, and azimuth.*
1913.

Bowlker, T. J.   *Philos Mag* 1908, (6)
15, 318–332.

Braly, K. W.   *J Exp Ps* 1933, 16,
613–643.

Bray, C. W.   *J Exp Ps* 1928, 11, 443–
467.

Breese, B. B.   *Ps Mon* 1899, 3, #11.

Breese, B. B.   *Ps R* 1909, 16, 410–
415.

Breitwieser, J. V.   *Ar Ps* 1911, #18.

Bressler, J.   *Ar Ps* 1933, #152.

Britt, S. H.   *Ps Bull* 1935, 32,
381–440.

Brown, C. H., Gelder, D. V.   *J Ps*
1938, 5, 1–9.

Brown, R. W.   *J Exp Ps* 1933, 16,
435–441.

Brown, T.   *Philosophy of human
mind.*   1820.

Brown, Warner   *Calif U Pub Ps* 1910,
1, 1–71.

Brown, Warner   *Calif U Pub Ps* 1914,
1, 199–268.

Brown, Warner   *J Exp Ps* 1923, 6,
377–382.

Brown, Warner   *J Educ Ps* 1924, 15,
229–233.

Brown, Warner   *Calif U Pub Ps* 1932,
5, 115–134.

Brown, Warner   *Am J Ps* 1935, 47,
90–102.

Brown, Wm., Thomson, G. H.   *The
essentials of mental measurement.*
1921. 1925.

Broyler, C. R., Thorndike, E. L.,
Woodyard, E.   *J Educ Ps* 1927, 18,
377–404.

Bruce, R. W.   *J Exp Ps* 1933, 16,
343–361.

Brunswik, E.   *Z Ps* 1929, 109, 40–
115.

Brunswik, E.   *Ar ges Ps* 1933, 88,
377–418.

Brunswik, E.   *Wahrnehmung und
Gegenstandswelt.*   1934.

Bryan, W. L., Harter, N.   *Ps R* 1897,
4, 27–53.

Bryan, W. L., Harter, N.   *Ps R* 1899,
6, 345–375.

Buel, J.   *J Comp Ps* 1934, 17, 185–
199.

Buel, J., Ballachey, E. L.   *J Genet Ps*
1934, 45, 145–168.

Buel, J., Ballachey, E. L.   *Ps R* 1935,
42, 28–42.

Bühler, K.   *Ar ges Ps* 1907 a, 9, 297–
365; 1908, 12, 1–122.

Bühler, K.   *Ar de Ps* 1907 b, 6, 376–
386.

Bühler, K.   *Die Gestaltwahrnehmung-
en.*   1913.

Bühler, K.   *Handbuch der psychologie.*   1922.

Bulbrook, M. E. *Am J Ps* 1932, 44, 409–453.

Burkamp, W. *Z Ps* 1923, 55 (2), 133–170.

Burnett, N. C., Dallenbach, K. M. *Am J Ps* 1927, 38, 418–431.

Burns, M., Dallenbach, K. M. *Am J Ps* 1933, 45, 111–117.

Burt, C. *J Exp Ped* 1919, 5, 68–77; 121–127.

Burt, C. *Mental and scholastic tests.* 1921.

Burtt, H. E. *J Exp Ps* 1921, 4, 1–23.

Burtt, H. E. *Employment psychology.* 1926.

Burtt, H. E., Clark, J. C. *J App Ps* 1923, 7, 114–126.

Burtt, H. E., Dobell, E. M. *J App Ps* 1925, 9, 5–21.

Burzlaff, W. *Z Ps* 1931, 119, 177–256.

Buswell, G. T. *Supp Educ Mon* 1920, #17.

Buswell, G. T. *Supp Educ Mon* 1922, #21.

Butsch, R. L. C. *J Educ Ps* 1932, 23, 104–121.

Buzby, D. E. *Am J Ps* 1924, 35, 602–604.

C

Calkins, M. W. *Ps R* 1894, 1, 476–483.

Calkins, M. W. *Ps Mon* 1896, 1, #2.

Cannon, W. B. *Bodily changes in pain, hunger, fear and rage.* 1915. 1929.

Cannon, W. B. *The wisdom of the body.* 1932.

Carmichael, L., Hogan, H. P., Walter, A. A. *J Exp Ps.* 1932, 15, 73–86.

Carpenter, W. B. *Principles of mental physiology.* 1877.

Carr, H. *J Animal Beh* 1917, 7, 259–306.

Carr, H. *Ps Bull* 1919, 16, 26–28.

Carr, H. *J Exp Ps* 1921, 4, 399–417.

Carr, H. *J Genet Ps* 1930, 37, 189–219.

Carr, H. *An introduction to space perception.* 1935.

Carr, H., Osbourn, E. B. *J Exp Ps* 1922, 5, 301–311.

Carr, H., Watson, J. B. *J Comp Neurol* 1908, 18, 27–44.

Cason, H. *J Exp Ps* 1922 a, 5, 108–146.

Cason, H. *J Exp Ps* 1922 b, 5, 153–196.

Cason, H. *J Exp Ps* 1926, 9, 195–227; 299–324.

Cason, H. *J Exp Ps* 1935, 18, 599–611.

Cason, H., Cason, E. *J Exp Ps* 1925, 8, 167–189.

Cattell, J. McK. *Philos St* 1885, 2, 633–650.

Cattell, J. McK. *Brain* 1885–86, 8, 295–312.

Cattell, J. McK. *Mind* 1886, 11, 63–65; 220–242; 377–392; 524–538.

Cattell, J. McK. *Philos St* 1886, 3, 305–336; 452–492.

Cattell, J. McK. *Mind* 1887, 12, 68–74.

Cattell, J. McK. *Philos St* 1888, 4, 241–250.

Cattell, J. McK. *Philos St* 1893, 8, 403–406.

Cattell, J. McK. *Philos St* 1902, 19, 63–68.

Cattell, J. McK. *Am J Ps* 1903, 14, 310–328.

Cattell, J. McK. *Science* 1906, 24, 658–665; 699–707; 732–742.

Cattell, J. McK., Bryant, S. *Mind* 1889, 14, 230–250.

Cattell, J. McK., Dolley, C. S. *Nat Acad Sci Mem* 1895, 7, 391–415.

Cattell, McK., Hoagland, H., *J Physiol* 1931, 72, 392–404.

Cattell, R. B. *Br J Ps* 1928, 19, 34–43.

Chandler, A. R. *Beauty and human nature.* 1934.

Chant, S. N. F. *Am J Ps* 1933, 45, 282–291.

Chapman, J. C. *Ps R* 1925, 32, 224–234.

Chappell, M. N. *Ar Ps* 1929, #105.

Chappell, M. N. *J Genet Ps* 1931, 39, 398–403.

Chen, L. K., Carr, H. A. *J Exp Ps* 1926, 9, 110–117.

Chiba, T. *Z Ps* 1923, 92, 177–226.

Churcher, B. G. *J Acoust Soc* 1935, 6, 216–226.

Claparède, E. *L'association des idées.* 1903.

Claparède, E. *Scientia* 1917, 22, 353–368.

Claparède, E. *Interméd Educat* 1924. (also, *L'éducation fonctionnelle*, 223–231.)

Claparède, E. *Ar de Ps* 1925, 19, 277–284.

Claparède, E. *Ar de Ps* 1934, 24, 1–155.

Clark, R. S. *Ar Ps* 1922, #48.

Clarke, H. M. *Am J Ps* 1911, 22, 214–249.

Cleveland, A. A. *Am J Ps* 1907, 18, 269–308.

Cobb, P. W. *J Exp Ps* 1916, 1, 410–425; 540–567.

Cobb, P. W. *Ps R* 1919, 26, 428–453.

Cobb, P. W. *J Opt Soc Am* 1934, 24, 107–113.

Cohn, J. *Philos St* 1894, 10, 562–603.

Cole, L. E. *Genet Ps Mon* 1929, 5, 335–450.

Colvin, S. S. *Ps R* 1910, 17, 260–268.

Colvin, S. S. *The learning process.* 1911.

Comstock, C. *Am J Ps* 1921, 32, 196–230.

Conklin, E. S. *Principles of abnormal psychology.* 1927. (191–207).

Conrad, H. S., Harris, D. *Calif U Pub Ps* 1931, 5, 1–45.

Converse, E. *Am J Ps* 1932, 44, 740–748.

Cook, S. A. *Ar Ps* 1928, #98.

Cook, T. W. *J Exp Ps* 1933 a, 16, 144–160.

Cook, T. W. *J Exp Ps* 1933 b, 16, 679–700.

Cook, T. W. *J Exp Ps* 1934 a, 17, 749–762.

Cook, T. W. *Ps R* 1934 b, 41, 330–355.

Cook, T. W. *Ps Mon* 1934 c, 45, #202.

Cook, T. W. *J Exp Ps* 1935, 18, 255–266.

Cook, T. W. *J Genet Ps* 1936, 49, 3–32.

Cook, T. W. *J Exp Ps* 1937 a, 20, 477–494.

Cook, T. W. *Br J Ps* 1937 b, 27, 303–312.

Cook, T. W., Morrison, S. H., Stacey, C. L. *J Genet Ps* 1935, 47, 218–232.

Cooper, S. F. *Am J Ps* 1928, 40, 254–274.

Coover, J. E. *Ps Mon* 1916, 20, #87.

Cordes, G. *Philos St* 1901, 17, 30–77.

Cox, J. W. *Br J Ps* 1933, 24, 67–87.

Crafts, L. W. *Am J Ps* 1929, 41, 543–563.

Crafts, L. W. *Am J Ps* 1930, 42, 591–601.

Cramer, T. *Z Ps* 1923, 54 (2), 215–242.

Crane, H. W. *Ps Mon* 1915, 18, #80.

Creed, R. S., Denny-Brown, D., Eccles, J. C., Liddell, E. G. T., Sherrington, C. S. *Reflex activity of the spinal cord.* 1932.

Creed, R. S., Granit, R. A. *J Physiol* 1928, 66, 281–298.

Creed, R. S., Ruch, T. C. *J Physiol* 1932, 74, 407–423.

Crosland, H. R. *Ps Mon* 1921, 29, #130.

Crosland, H. R. *Oregon U Pub* 1924, 2, #6.

Crosland, H. R. *Oregon U Pub St Ps* 1929, 1, 1–104.

Crowe, S. J., Guild, S. R., Polvogt, L. M. *Johns Hopkins Hosp Bull* 1934, 54, 315–379.

Crozier, W. J. *Handbk genl exp ps* (Murchison) 1934, 987–1036.

Cuff, N. B. *George Peabody Contr Educ* 1927, #43.

Culler, A. J. *Ar Ps* 1912, #24.

Culler, E. *Ar Ps* 1926, #81.

Culler, E. *Ps Mon* 1926, 35, #163, (Psychophysics.) 56–137.

Culler, E., Finch, G., Girden, E., Brogden, W. *J Genl Ps* 1935, 12, 223–227.

Culler, E., Mettler, F. A. *J Comp Ps* 1934, 18, 291–303.

D

Dahl, A. *Ps Forsch* 1928, 11, 290–301.

Dahlmann, R. *Ar ges Ps* 1934, 90, 504–560.

Dallenbach, K. M. *Am J Ps* 1927, 39, 402–427.

Dambach, K. *Z Ps* (Ergänzbd) 1929, 14, 159–236. (Dissertation, Tübingen).

Danzfuss, K. *Philos Ps Arbeiten* 1923, 5, 1–87.

Darrow, C. W. *J Exp Ps* 1927, 10, 197–226.

Darrow, C. W. *Am J Physiol* 1929 a, 88, 219–229.

Darrow, C. W. *J Genet Ps* 1929 b, 36, 172–173.

Darrow, C. W. *Internatl Cong Ps* 1929 c, 9, 136–137.

Darrow, C. W. *J Genl Ps* 1930, 4, 418–420.

Darrow, C. W. *J Genl Ps* 1932, 7, 261–273.

Darrow, C. W. *Ps R* 1935, 42, 566–578.

Darrow, C. W. *Ps Bull* 1936, 33, 73–94.

Darrow, C. W., Freemen, G. L. *J Exp Ps* 1934, 17, 739–748.

Darrow, C. W., Heath, L. L. *Studies in dynamics of behavior.* (Lashley). 1932, 57–261.

Darrow, C. W., Solomon, A. P. *Ar Neurol Psychiat* 1934, 32, 273–299.

Darwin, C. *Expression of the emotions in man and animals.* 1872.

Dashiell, J. F. *Psbiol* 1920, 2, 329–350.

Dashiell, J. F. *Ps Bull* 1927, 24, 174–175.

Dashiell, J. F. *Comp Ps Mon* 1930, 7, #32.

Dashiell, J. F., Bayroff, A. G. *J Comp Ps* 1931, 12, 77–94.

Daub, C. T. *J Comp Ps* 1933, 15, 49–58.

Davis, A., Meenes, M. *J Exp Ps* 1932, 15, 716–727.

Davis, F. C. *J Exp Ps* 1932, 15, 630–661.

Davis, F. C. *Am J Ps* 1933, 45, 298–302.

Davis, H. *Handbk genl exp ps* (Murchison) 1934, 962–986.

Davis, H., Derbyshire, A. J., Kemp, E. H., Lurie, M. H., Upton, M. *Science* 1935, 81, 101–102.

Davis, H., Forbes, A., Derbyshire, A. J. *Science* 1933, 78, 522.

Davis, R. C. *Ar Ps* 1930, #115.

Davis, R. C. *J Exp Ps* 1934, 17, 504–535.

Davis, R. C., Kantor, J. R. *J Genl Ps* 1935, 13, 62–81.

Davis, R. C., Porter, J. M. Jr. *J Genl Ps* 1931, 5, 115–120.

Davis, W. W. *Yale St Ps* 1898, 6, 6–50.

Dearborn, W. F. *Ar Philos Ps Sci Meth* 1906, #4.

Dearborn, W. F. *Ps Bull* 1909, 6, 44.

DeCamp, J. E. *Ps Mon* 1915, 19, #84.

DeCamp, J. E. *Psbiol* 1920, 2, 245–253.

Delabarre, E. B. *Am J Ps* 1898, 9, 572–574.

Delabarre, E. B., Logan, R. R., Reed, A. Z. *Ps R* 1897, 4, 615–631.

Dennis, W. *J Genet Ps* 1929, 36, 59–90.

Dennis, W. *Ps R* 1935, 42, 117–121.

De Silva, H. R. *Am J Ps* 1926, 37, 469–501.

Destutt de Tracy, A. L. C. *Éléments d'idéologie.* 1801–1815. (tome 1, 453).

Dick, L. *Ar Ps* 1938.

Diefendorf, A. R., Dodge, R. *Brain* 1908, 31, 451–489.

Dimmick, F. L. *Am J Ps* 1920, 31, 317–332.

Dimmick, F. L. *Ps R* 1927, 34, 321–335.

Dimmick, F. L. *Am J Ps* 1933, 45, 463–470.

Dixon, E. T. *Mind* 1895, 4, 195–212.

Dodge, R. *Am J Physiol* 1903, 8, 307–329.

Dodge, R. *Ps Bull* 1905, 2, 193–199.

Dodge, R. *Ps Mon* 1907, 8, #35.

Dodge, R. *J Exp Ps* 1921 a, 4, 165–174.

Dodge, R. *J Exp Ps* 1921 b, 4, 247–269.

Dodge, R. *J Exp Ps* 1923 a, 6, 107–137.

Dodge, R. *J Exp Ps* 1923 b, 6, 1–35.

Dodge, R. *J Exp Ps* 1923 c, 6, 169–181.

Dodge, R. *Elementary conditions of human variability.* 1927.

Dodge, R., Benedict, F. G. *Psychological effects of alcohol.* 1915.

Dodge, R., Cline, T. S. *Ps R* 1901, 8, 145–157.

Donaldson, H. H. *Mind* 1885, 10, 399–416 (408).

Donders, F. C. *Ar Anat Physiol* 1868, 657–681.

Dooley, L. A. *Am J Ps* 1916, 27, 119–151.

Dorcus, R. M. *J App Ps* 1932, 16, 277–287.

Dorcus, R. M., Gray, W. L. *J Comp Ps* 1932, 13, 447–451.

Dresslar, F. B. *Am J Ps* 1894, 6, 313–368.

Drever, J. I. *Br J Ps* 1934, 25, 197–203.

Drozyński, L. *Ps St* 1911, 7, 83–140.

Drury, A. N., Florey, H., Florey, M. E. *J Physiol* 1929, 68, 173–179.

Drury, M. B. *Am J Ps* 1933, 45, 628–646.

Dumas, G. et al. *Nouveau traité de psychologie,* 1930–

Dunbar, H. F. *Emotions and bodily changes.* 1935.

Duncker, K. *J Genet Ps* 1926, 33, 642–708.

Duncker, K., *Zur Psychologie des produktiven Denkens.* 1935.

Dunlap, K. *J Exp Ps* 1917, 2, 249–252.

Dunlap, K. *Psbiol* 1918, 1, 445–457.

Dunlap, K. *J Exp Ps* 1921, 4, 244–246.

Dunlap, K. *Genet Ps Mon* 1927, 2, 196–233.

Dunlap, K. *Paralogs.* 1933.

Dunlap, K., Wells, G. R. *Ps R* 1910, 17, 319–335.

Durkin, H. E. *Ar Ps* 1937, #210.

Dürr, E. *Z Ps* 1908, 49, 313–340.

Dusser de Barenne, J. C. *Handbk genl exp ps* (Murchison) 1934, 204–246.

Dwelshauvers, G. *Philos St* 1891, 6, 217–249.

Dysinger, D. W. *Ps Mon* 1931, 41, #187, 14–31.

E

Ebbecke, U. *Ar ges Physiol* 1929, 221, 160–212.

Ebbinghaus, H. *Über das Gedächtnis.* 1885. (translated by Ruger & Bussenius. *Memory.* 1913.)

Ebbinghaus, H. *Z Ps* 1897, 13, 401–457.

Ebbinghaus, H. *Grundzüge der Psychologie.* 1902.

Ebbinghaus, H. *Grundzüge der Psychologie.* 1911.

Ebert, E., Meumann, E. *Ar ges Ps* 1905, 4, 1–232.

Eckener, H. *Philos St* 1893, 8, 343–387.

von Ehrenfels, C. *Vierteljahrsch wiss Philos* 1890, 14, 249–292.

Ehrenstein, W. *Z Ps* 1930, 117, 339–412.

Eichler, W. *Z Ps* 1930, 60, 325–333.

Eidens, H. *Ar ges Ps* 1929, 71, 1–66.

Engel, P. *Z Ps* 1928, 107, 273–313.

Engel, R. *Ar ges Ps* 1928, 64, 1–36.

Engel, W. *Ps Forsch* 1930, 13, 1–5.

English, H. B. *Am J Ps* 1922, 33, 305–350.

English, H. B., Welborn, E. L., Killian, C. D. *J Genl Ps* 1934, 11, 233–260.

Erdmann, B., Dodge, R. *Psycho-logische Untersuchungen über das Lesen.* 1898.

Esper, E. A. *Ps R* 1918, 25, 468–487.

Eurich, A. C. *School Soc* 1930, 32, 404–406.

Ewert, P. H. *J Genet Ps* 1926, 33, 235–249.

Exner, S. *Ar ges Physiol* 1873, 7, 601–660.

Exner, S. *Ar ges Physiol* 1874, 8, 526–537.

Exner, S. *Ar ges Physiol* 1875, 11, 403–432.

Exner, S. *Entwurf zu einer physiologischen Erklärung der psychischen Erscheinungen.* 1894.

F

Fairbanks, G. *Ps Mon* 1937, 48, #215, 78–107.

Farmer, E., Chambers, E. G. *Br J Ps* 1925, 15, 237–254.

Fechner, G. T. *Poggendorf's Ann* 1840–50, 193–221; 427–465.

Fechner, G. T. *Sächs Akad Wiss Leip* 1858, 10, 70–78.

Fechner, G. T. *Elemente der Psychophysik.* 1860.

Fechner, G. T. *Abhand K Sächs Gessel Wiss Math-Phys* 1871, 9, 555–635.

Fechner, G. T. *Vorschule der Aesthetik.* 1876.

Fehrer, E. V. *Am J Ps* 1935, 47, 187–221.

Feinbloom, W. *Ar Ps* 1938.

Feingold, G. A. *Ps Mon* 1915, 18, #78.

Feleky, A. *Ps R* 1914, 21, 33–41.

Feleky, A. *J Exp Ps* 1916, 1, 218–241.

Feleky, A. *Feelings and emotions.* 1924.

Fendrick, P. *Columbia Univ T C Contr Ed T* 1935, #656.

Féré, C. *Soc Biol Compt Rend* 1888, 40, 28–33; 217–219.

Fernald, M. R. *Ps Mon* 1912, 14, #58.

Fernberger, S. W. *Am J Ps* 1921, 32, 121–133.

Fernberger, S. W. *Am J Ps* 1928, 40, 562–568.

Fernberger, S. W. *Ps R* 1930, 37, 107–112.

Fernberger, S. W. *Am J Ps* 1931 a, 43, 361–376.

Fernberger, S. W. *Am J Ps* 1931 b, 43, 560–578.

Fernberger, S. W. *Am J Ps* 1934, 46, 309–314.

Fernberger, S. W., Glass, E., Hoffman, I., Willig, M. *J Exp Ps* 1934, 17, 286–293.

Fernberger, S. W., Irwin, F. W. *Am J Ps* 1932, 44, 505–525.

Ferrall, S. C., Dallenbach, K. M. *Am J Ps* 1930, 42, 72–82.

Ferree, C. E. *Am J Ps* 1906, 17, 81–120.

Ferree, C. E. *Am J Ps* 1913, 24, 378–409.

Ferree, C. E., Rand, G. *Ps R* 1919, 26, 16–41, 150–163.

Fessard, A. *Ann ps* 1926, 27, 215–224.

Fessard, A. *L'Encéphale* 1927, 22, 214–215.

Fields, P. E. *Comp Ps Mon* 1932, 9, #42.

Finch, G., Culler, E.   *Science* 1934, 80, 41–42.

Finch, G., Culler, E.   *Am J Ps* 1935, 47, 656–662.

Findley, A. E.   *Am J Ps* 1924, 35, 436–445.

Finkenbinder, E. O.   *Am J Ps* 1913, 24, 8–32.

Finzi, J.   *Ps Arbeit* 1901, 3, 289–384.

Fischel, H.   *Z Ps* 1926, 98, 342–365.

Fischer, M. H., Löwenbach, H.   *Ar ges Physiol* 1935, 235, 609–657.

Fisher, R. A.   *Biometrika* 1915, 10, 507–521.

Fisher, R. A.   *Statistical Methods for research workers.* 1936.

Fisher, S. C.   *Ps Mon* 1916, 21, #90.

Fisher, S. C.   *Am J Ps* 1917, 28, 57–116.

Flach, A.   *Ar ges Ps* 1925, 52, 369–440.

Fletcher, H.   *Speech and hearing.* 1929.

Fletcher, H.   *J Acoust Soc* 1930, 1, 311–343.

Fletcher, H.   *J Acoust Soc* 1934, 6, 59–69.

Fletcher, H., Munson, W. A.   *J Acoust Soc* 1933, 5, 82–108.

Foley, J. P.   *Ar Ps* 1935, #184.

Folgmann, E. E. E.   *J Exp Ps* 1933, 16, 709–724.

Forbes, T. W.   *Am J Physiol* 1936, 117, 189–199.

Forbes, T. W., Bolles, M. M.   *J Ps* 1936, 2, 273–285.

Forbes, T. W., Landis, C.   *J Genl Ps* 1935, 13, 188–193.

Ford, A.   *Am J Ps* 1929, 41, 1–32.

Fossler, H. R.   *Ps Mon* 1930, 40, #181, 1–32.

Foster, W. S., Tinker, M. A.   *Experiments in psychology.* 1929.

Foucault, M.   *La psychophysique.* 1901.

Fox, C.   *Br J Ps* 1914, 6, 420–431.

Frandsen, A.   *Genet Ps Mon* 1934, 16, 79–138.

Frank, H.   *Ps Forsch* 1926, 7, 137–145.

Franken, A.   *Z ang Ps* 1911, 4, 1–64; 399–464.

Franz, S. I.   *Ps Mon* 1899, 3, #12.

Franz, S. I., et al   *Calif U Los Angeles Pub Ed Philos Ps* 1933, 1, 65–135.

Freeman, F. N.   *Ps Mon* 1907, 8, #34, 301–333.

Freeman, F. N.   *Ps Bull* 1911, 8, 43–44.

Freeman, F. N.   *Experimental education.* 1916.   (132–139, 209–212).

Freeman, F. N.   *J App Ps* 1920, 4, 126–141.

Freeman, G. L.   *Am J Ps* 1930, 42, 581–590.

Freeman, G. L.   *J Genl Ps* 1931, 5, 479–494.

Freeman, G. L.   *Am J Ps* 1933, 45, 17–52.

Freeman, G. L.   *Introduction to physiological psychology.* 1934.

Freeman, G. L., Darrow, C. W.   *Am J Physiol* 1935, 111, 55–63.

Freiberg, A. D.   *Am J Ps* 1937 a, 49, 23–36.

Freiberg, A. D.   *Am J Ps* 1937 b, 49, 173–197.

Frey, M. v.   *Ber Verhand K säch Wiss Leipzig, math-phys* 1894, 46, 185–196; 283–296.

Frey, M. v.   *Ber Verhand K säch Wiss Leipzig math-phys* 1895, 47, 166–184.

Frey, M. v.   *Z Biol* 1915, 65, 417–427.

Frey, M. v., Goldmann, A.   *Z Biol* 1915, 65, 183–202.

Freyd, M.   *Ps Mon* 1924, 33, #151.

Friedländer, H.   *Z Ps* 1920, 83, 129–210; 84, 258–291.

Friedrich, H.   *Ar ges Ps* 1928, 61, 355–416.

Friedrich, M.   *Philos St* 1883, 1, 39–77.

Fröbes, J.   *Lehrbuch der experimentellen Psychologie.* 1923. 2 vols.

Froeberg, S.   *Ar Ps* 1907, #8.

Fröhlich, F. W.   *Z Ps* 1921, 52(2), 60–88.

Fröhlich, F. W.   *Z Ps* 1922, 53(3) 79–121.

Fry, G. A., Bartley, S. H. *Am J Physiol* 1935, 112, 414–421.

Fuchs, W. *Z Ps* 1923, 91, 145–235.

Fullerton, G. S., Cattell, J. McK. *Penn U Philos Series* 1892, #2.

Futch, O. *J Genl Ps* 1935, 13, 434–463.

G

Galli, A. *Ar ital Ps* 1934, 12, 137–240.

Galli, A., Hochheimer, W. *Z Ps* 1934, 132, 304–334.

Galli, A., Zama, A. *Z Ps* 1931, 123, 308–348. (and) *U Cat Sacro Cuore Contr Lab Ps* 1931, 6, 29–76.

Galton, F. *Brain* 1879–1880, 2, 149–162.

Galton, F. *Inquiries into human faculty.* 1883.

Gamble, E. A. McC. *Am J Ps* 1898, 10, 82–142.

Gamble, E. A. McC. *Ps Mon* 1909, 10, #43.

Gamble, E. A. McC. *Ps Mon* 1916, 22, #96, 98–151.

Gamble, E. A. McC. *Am J Ps* 1927, 39, 223–234.

Gamble, E. A. McC., Calkins, M. W. *Z Ps* 1903, 32, 177–199.

Gamble, E. A. McC., Wilson, L. *Ps Mon* 1916, 22, #96, 41–97.

Garrett, H. E. *Statistics in psychology and education.* 1937.

Garrett, H. E., Schneck, M. R. *Psychological tests, methods, and results.* 1933. (pt. 2, 103–122).

Garth, T. R. *J Exp Ps* 1924, 7, 233–241.

Gates, A. I. *J Exp Ps* 1916, 1, 393–403.

Gates, A. I. *Ar Ps* 1917, #40.

Gates, A. I. *Columbia Univ T C Contr Educ* 1922, #129.

Gates, A. I. *The improvement of reading.* 1927, 1935.

Gates, A. I., Taylor, G. A. *J Educ Ps* 1925, 16, 583–592.

Gates, G. S. *J Educ Ps* 1923, 14, 449–461.

Gatewood, E. L. *Ps Mon* 1920, 28, #126.

Gault, R. H. *J Franklin Inst* 1927, 204, 329–358.

Gault, R. H. *J Franklin Inst* 1936, 221, 703–719.

Gelb, A. *Handbk normal path Physiol* 1929, 12 (1), 594–678.

Gelb, A. *Z Ps* 1932, 127, 42–59.

Geldard, F. A. *J Optical Soc Am* 1933, 23, 256–260.

Geldard, F. A., Gilmer, B. v. H. *J Genl Ps* 1934, 11, 301–310.

Gellermann, L. W. *J Genet Ps* 1931, 39, 197–226.

Gertz, E. *Z Ps* 1921, 52 (2), 1–51; 105–156.

Gesell, A., Thompson, H. *Genet Ps Mon* 1929, 6, 1–124.

Ghiselli, E. *J Exp Ps* 1936, 19, 91–98.

Gibson, J. J. *J Exp Ps* 1929, 12, 1–39.

Gibson, J. J. *J Genl Ps* 1934, 10, 234–236.

Gibson, J. J., Gibson, E. J. *Am J Ps* 1934, 46, 603–610.

Gibson, J. J., Jack, E. G., Raffel, G. *J Exp Ps* 1932, 15, 416–421.

Gilbert, J. A. *Yale St Ps* 1894, 2, 40–100.

Gilbert, L. C. *Ps Mon* 1932, 43, #196.

Gildemeister, M. *Handbk normal path Physiol* 1928, 8 (2), 657–702; 766–784.

Gilhousen, H. C. *J Comp Ps* 1933, 16, 1–23.

Girden, E., Culler, E. *J Comp Ps* 1937, 23, 261–274.

Glanville, A. D., Dallenbach, K. M. *Am J Ps* 1929, 41, 207–236.

Glaze, J. A. *J Genet Ps* 1928, 35, 255–267.

Gleason, J. M. *Am J Ps* 1919, 30, 1–26.

Goldscheider, A. *Ar Physiol* 1885, 340–345.

Golla, F. L., Antonovitch, S. *Brain* 1929, 52, 491–509.

Goodfellow, L. D. *J Franklin Inst* 1933, 216, 387–392.

Goodenough, F. L., Anderson, J. E. *Experimental child study.* 1931

Gottschaldt, K. *Ps Forsch* 1926, 8, 261–317.

Gottschaldt, K. *Ps Forsch* 1929, 12, 1–87.

Gottschaldt, K. *Z ang Ps* 1933, Beih #68.

Graham, C. H. *Handbk genl exp ps* (Murchison) 1934, 829–879.

Graham, C. H., Granit, R. *Am J Physiol* 1931, 98, 664–673.

Granit, R. *Br J Ps* 1921, 12, 223–247.

Granit, R. *Skand Ar Physiol* 1924, 45, 43–57.

Granit, R. *Am J Physiol* 1930, 94, 41–50.

Granit, R., Harper, P. *Am J Physiol* 1930, 95, 211–228.

Grannis, U. B., Walker, W. W. *J Exp Ps* 1936, 19, 417–428.

Gray, W. S. *Supp Educ Mon* 1917, #5.

Greene, E. B. *J App Ps* 1934, 18, 697–704.

Gregor, A. *Handbk biol Arbeitsmeth* 1927, 6(A), 1123–1148.

Grether, W. F. *J Comp Ps* 1938, 25, 91–96.

Griffitts, C. H., Gordon, E. I. *J Exp Ps* 1924, 7, 117–134.

Grindley, G. C. *Br J Ps* 1932, 23, 127–147.

Grossart, F. *Ar ges Ps* 1921, 41, 121–200.

Grünbaum, A. A. *Ar ges Ps* 1908, 12, 340–480.

Guanella, F. M. *Ar Ps* 1934, #174.

Guilford, J. P. *Am J Ps* 1927, 38, 534–583.

Guilford, J. P. *J Abn Soc Ps* 1929, 24, 191–202.

Guilford, J. P. *Psychometric methods.* 1936.

Guilford, J. P., Dallenbach, K. M. *Am J Ps* 1925, 36, 621–628.

Guilford, J. P., Helson, H. *Am J Ps* 1929, 41, 595–606.

Guilford, J. P., Park, D. G. *Am J Ps* 1931, 43, 589–599.

Guillaume, P., Meyerson, I. *J de Ps* 1930, 27, 177–236.

Gulliksen, H. *J Exp Ps* 1932, 15, 496–516.

Gulliksen, H. *J Genl Ps* 1934, 11, 395–434.

Gundlach, R., Bentley, M. *Am J Ps* 1930, 42, 519–543.

Günther, F. *Ps St* 1911, 7, 229–285.

Guthrie, E. R., Horton, G. P. *Ps Bull* 1937, 34, 774 (abstract).

H

Hahn, H. *Z Ps* 1930, 60 (2), 162–232.

Haines, T. H., Davies, A. E. *Ps R* 1904, 11, 249–281.

Hall, G. S., Kries, J. v. *Ar Anat Physiol* (Suppl) 1879, 1–10.

Hall, M. E. *J Exp Ps* 1928, 11, 65–76.

Halverson, H. M. *Ps Mon* 1922 a, 31, #140, 7–29.

Halverson, H. M. *Am J Ps* 1922 b, 33, 178–212.

Halverson, H. M. *Am J Ps* 1924, 35, 360–367.

Halverson, H. M. *Am J Ps* 1927, 38, 97–106.

Hambidge, J. *Dynamic symmetry.* 1920.

Hamel, I. A. *Ps Mon* 1919, 27, #118, 1–65.

Hamilton, F. M. *Ar Ps* 1907, #9.

Hamilton, Wm. *Lectures on metaphysics and logic.* 1859. 1. (lect. xiv)

Hammer, A. *Ps St* 1914, 9, 321–365.

Hanawalt, E. M. *Comp Ps Mon* 1931, 7, #35.

Hanawalt, E. M. *J Exp Ps* 1934, 17, 691–708.

Hanawalt, N. G. *Ar Ps* 1937, #216.

Hanes, O. H. *Ar ges Ps* 1929, 70, 371–417.

Haney, G. W. *Calif U Pub Ps* 1931, 4, 319–333.

Hanfmann, E. *Z Ps* 1928, 105, 147–194.

Hanfmann, E., Kasanin, J. *J Ps* 1937, 3, 521–540.

Harlow, H. F., Settlage, P. H. *J Comp Ps* 1934, 18, 423–435.

Harmon, F. L. *Ar Ps* 1933, #147.

Harrelson, P. V. *Peabody J Educ* 1923, 1, 77–84.

Harris, A. J. *Am J Ps* 1929, 41, 617–624.

Hartley, R. V. L. *Physiol R* 1919, 13, 373–385.

Hartley, R. V. L., Fry, T. C. *Physiol R* 1921, 18, 431–442.

Hathaway, S. R. *J Exp Ps* 1935, 18, 285–298.

Hauer, P. *Z Biol* 1926, 85, 265–274.

Haught, B. F. *Ps Mon* 1921, 30, #139.

Hausen, L. *Ar ges Ps* 1933, 88, 635–686.

Haycraft, J. B. *Brain* 1888, 11, 166–178.

Hazzard, F. W. *J Exp Ps* 1930, 13, 297–331.

Head, H. *Aphasia and kindred disorders of speech.* 1926.

Hecht, S. *J Genl Physiol* 1921, 4, 113–139.

Hecht, S. *J Genl Physiol* 1924 a, 6, 355–373.

Hecht, S. *J Genl Physiol* 1924 b, 7, 235–267.

Hecht, S. *Nat Acad Sci Proc* 1928, 14, 237–241.

Hecht, S. *Handbk genl exp ps* (Murchison) 1934, 704–828.

Heidbreder, E. *Ar Ps* 1924, #73.

Heider, F. *Ps Forsch* 1932, 17, 121–129.

Heider, G. M. *Ps Forsch* 1932, 17, 13–55.

Heigl, O. *Ar ges Ps* 1928, 64, 257–300.

Heimann, A., Thorner, H. *Ar ges Ps* 1929, 71, 165–184.

Heine, R. *Z Ps* 1914, 68, 161–236.

Heiser, F. *Ar Ps* 1932, #138.

Heller, R. *Untersuchungen über "Gesamtform" und ihre Bedeutung für das tachistoskopische Lesen im indirekten Sehen.* 1911. (Diss. Zürich).

Helmholtz, H. v. *Ar Anat Physiol* 1850, 276–364.

Helmholtz, H. v. *Über die Methoden, kleinste Zeittheile zu messen, und ihre Anwendung für physiologische Zwecke.* (Lecture). 1850 a.

Helmholtz, H. v. *Ar Anat Physiol* 1852, 199–216.

Helmholtz, H. v. *Philos Mag* 1853, s 4, 6, 313–325. (Translation of 1850 a).

Helmholtz, H. v. *Akad Wiss Berlin Ber* 1854, 328–332.

Helmholtz, H. v. *Handbuch der physiologischen Optik.* 1856–1866. (Trans. by J. P. C. Southall, 1924–25.)

Helmholtz, H. v. *Die Lehre von den Tonempfindungen als physiologische Grundlage für Theorie der Musik.* 1862.

Helmholtz, H. v., (N. Baxt) *Akad Wiss Berlin Monatsbr* (1867) 1868, 228–234.

Helmholtz, H. v. *Vorträge und Reden.* 1896. (1, 3–21).

Helson, H., Fehrer, E. V. *Am J Ps* 1932, 44, 79–102.

Hempstead, L. *Am J Ps* 1901, 12, 185–192.

Henderson, E. N. *Ps Mon* 1903, 5, #23.

Henmon, V. A. C. *Ar Philos Ps Sci Meth* 1906, #8.

Henmon, V. A. C. *J Exp Ps* 1917, 2, 476–484.

Henneman, R. H. *Ar Ps* 1935, #179.

Henning, H. *Z Ps* 1915, 73, 161–257. 1916, 74, 305–434; 75, 177–230; 76, 1–127.

Henning, H. *Der Geruch.* 1924.

Henning, H. *Handbk biol Arbeitsmeth* 1927, 6, A, 741–836.

Henry, L. K. *Iowa U St Educ* 1934, 9, #5, 65–102.

Hering, E. *Beiträge zur Physiologie.* 1861–1864.

Hering, E. *Akad Wiss Wien Sitzbr* 1874, 69 (3), 85–104 (101–103); 1876, 72 (3), 310–348 (335–338).

Hering, E. *Akad Wiss Wien Sitzbr* 1877, 75 (3), 108.

Hering, E. *Handbuch der Physiologie* 1879, 3 (1), 343–601.

Hering, E. *Grundzüge der Lehre vom Lichtsinn.* 1905–07. 1920.

Hermanides, J. *Over de constanten der in der olfaktometrie gebruikelijke negen Standaardgeuren.* 1909. (Thesis, Utrecht).

Hermann, L. *Ar ges Physiol* 1890, 47, 44–53.

Herrmann, J. *Neue ps St* 1926, 1, 473–506.

Heymans, G. *Z Ps* 1896, 9, 221–255.

Heymans, G. *Z Ps* 1897, 14, 101–139.

Heyninx, A. *Essai d'olfactique physiologique.* 1919. (Thesis, Bruxelles).

Hicks, V. C., Carr, H. *J Animal Beh* 1912, 2, 98–125.

Higginson, G. D. *J Exp Ps* 1926, 9, 228–252.

Hilden, A. H. *Ps Mon* 1937, 49, #217, 173–204.

Hilgard, E. R. *Ps Mon* 1931, 41, #184.

Hilgard, E. R. *Ps R* 1936 a, 43, 366–385.

Hilgard, E. R. *Ps R* 1936 b, 43, 547–564.

Hilgard, E. R. *Ps Bull* 1937, 34, 61–102.

Hilgard, E. R., Campbell, A. A. *J Exp Ps* 1936, 19, 227–247.

Hilgard, E. R., Campbell, A. A. *J Exp Ps* 1937, 21, 310–319.

Hilgard, E. R., Marquis, D. G. *J Comp Ps* 1935, 19, 29–58.

Hillebrand, F. *Z Ps* 1894, 7, 97–151.

Hirsch, A. *Soc Sci naturel Bull* (Neuchâtel) 1861–1864, 6, 100–114.

Hirsch, G. M. *Ar ital Ps* 1936, 13, 174–199. 1937, 14, 225–231.

Hobbes, T. *Leviathan.* 1651. (Pt. 1, chap. 3)

Hobhouse, L. T. *Mind in evolution.* 1901.

Höffding, H. *Vierteljahr wiss Philos* 1889, 13, 420–458.

Höffding, H. *Vierteljahr wiss Philos* 1890, 14, 27–54; 167–205; 293–316.

Höffding, H. *Philos St* 1893, 8, 86–96.

Hoffmann, J. *Ar ges Ps* 1927, 58, 325–388.

Hoffmann, P. *Handbk biol Arbeitsmeth* 1924, 5, B (3), 373–404; 405–426.

Hoisington, L. B. *Symposium on feelings and emotions.* (Wittenberg) 1928, 236–246.

Hollingworth, H. L. *Ar Ps* 1909, #13.

Hollingworth, H. L. *J Philos* 1910, 7, 461–469.

Hollingworth, H. L. *J Philos* 1911, 8, 688–692.

Hollingworth, H. L. *Ar Ps* 1912, #22.

Hollingworth, H. L. *The psychology of thought.* 1926. (152–167).

Hollingworth, H. L. *Psychology: its facts and principles.* 1928.

Hollingworth, H. L., Poffenberger, A. T. *Sense of taste.* 1917.

Holm, K. G. *Skand Ar Physiol* 1903, 14, 242–258.

Holmes, J. L. *Thesis (Ph.D.)* Columbia University. 1923.

Holt, E. B. *Ps Mon* 1903, 4, #17, 3–46.

Holway, A. H., Pratt, C. C. *Ps R* 1936, 43, 322–340.

Honzik, C. H. *Calif U Pub Ps* 1933, 6, 99–144.

Honzik, C. H. *Comp Ps Mon* 1936, 13, #64.

von Hornbostel, E. M. *Ps Forsch* 1923, 4, 64–114.

von Hornbostel, E. M., Wertheimer, M. *Akad Wiss Berlin Sitzbr* 1920, 388–396.

Hoskins, A. B. *George Peabody Contr Educ* 1936, #189.

House, E. R. *J Acoust Soc* 1935, 7, 127–134.

Hovde, H. T. *J App Ps* 1929, 13, 600–629.

Hovde, H. T. *J App Ps* 1930, 14, 63–74.

Hovey, H. B. *Am J Ps* 1928, 40, 585–591.

Hovey, H. B. *Am J Ps* 1936, 48, 434–445.

Howell, W. H. *Text-book of physiology*. 13th ed. 1936.

Hozawa, A. *Ar ges Physiol* 1928, 219, 111–158. (121).

Hubbard, L. M. *J Exp Ps* 1924, 7, 342–357.

Hudgins, C. V. *J Genl Ps* 1933, 8, 3–51.

Huey, E. B. *The psychology and pedagogy of reading*. 1908.

Hugony, A. *Z Biol* 1935, 96, 548–553.

Hulin, W. S. *J Exp Ps* 1935, 18, 97–105.

Hull, C. L. *Ps Mon* 1920, 28, #123.

Hull, C. L. *Ps R* 1932, 39, 25–43.

Hull, C. L. *Am J Ps* 1933 a, 45, 730–734.

Hull, C. L. *J Comp Ps* 1933 b, 16, 255–273.

Hull, C. L. *J Comp Ps* 1934 a, 17, 393–422.

Hull, C. L. *Handbk genl exp ps* (Murchison) 1934 b, 382–455.

Hull, C. L. *J Genl Ps* 1935, 13, 249–274.

Hull, C. L., Lugoff, L. S. *J Exp Ps* 1921, 4, 111–136.

Hume, D. *A treatise on human understanding*. 1739. (sec. vii).

Hume, D. *Inquiry concerning the human understanding*. 1748.

Hummel, E. *Ar ges Ps* 1926, 57, 305–394.

Hunt, W. A. *Am J Ps* 1931, 43, 87–92; 600–605.

Hunt, W. A., Hunt, E. B. *J Exp Ps* 1935, 18, 383–387.

Hunt, W. A., Landis, C. *Am J Ps* 1935, 47, 143–145.

Hunter, W. S. *Beh Mon* 1913, 2, #6.

Hunter, W. S. *Psbiol* 1920, 2, 1–17.

Hunter, W. S. *J Comp Ps* 1922, 2, 29–59.

Hunter, W. S. *J Genl Ps* 1928, 35, 374–388.

Hunter, W. S. *J Genet Ps* 1929, 36, 505–537.

Hunter, W. S. *Handbk genl exp ps* (Murchison) 1934, 497–570. (500)

Hunter, W. S. *Science* 1935 a, 82, 374–376.

Hunter, W. S. *Br J Ps* 1935 b, 26, 135–148.

Hunter, W. S., Nagge, J. W. *J Genet Ps* 1931, 39, 303–319.

Hüper, H. *Ar ges Ps* 1928, 62, 315–408.

Husband, R. W. *J Genl Ps* 1931 a, 5, 234–243.

Husband, R. W. *J Genet Ps* 1931 b, 39, 258–278.

Hylan, J. P. *Ps R* 1903, 10, 373–403.

I

Ingebritsen, O. C. *J Comp Ps* 1932, 14, 279–294.

Ipsen, G. *Neue ps St* 1926 a, 1, 171–278.

Ipsen, G. *Neue ps St* 1926 b, 1, 279–471.

Irwin, F. W., Seidenfeld, M. A. *J Exp Ps* 1937, 21, 363–381.

Isserlin, M. *Ps Arbeit* 1914, 6, 1–196.

Ivanov-Smolensky, A. G. *Brain* 1927, 50, 138–141.

J

Jablonski, W. *Ps Forsch* 1930, 13, 145–197.

Jackson, T. A. *Genet Ps Mon* 1932, 11, 1–59.

Jacobs, J. *Mind* 1887, 12, 75–79.

Jacobson, E. *Am J Ps* 1911, 22, 553–577.

Jacobson, E. *Progressive relaxation.* 1929. 1938.

Jaensch, E. R. *Kong exp Ps Ber* 1912, 5, 186–188.

Jaensch, E. R. *Z Ps* 1920, 85, 37–82.

Jaensch, E. R. *Kong exp Ps Ber* 1922, 7, 3–48.

Jaensch, E. R. *Über den Aufbau der Wahrnehmungswelt und die Grundlagen der menschlichen Erkenntnis.* 1927.

Jaensch, E. R. *Eidetic imagery and typological methods of investigation.* 1930.

James, H. E. O. *Br J Ps* 1930, 20, 322–332.

James, H. E. O., Massey, M. E. *Med Research Council special report* 1932, #166, 33–51.

James, H. E. O., Thouless, R. H. *Br J Ps* 1926, 17, 49–53.

James, Wm. *Principles of psychology.* 1890. 2 vols.

Jastrow, J. *Mind* 1886, 11, 539–554.

Jastrow, J. *Pop Sci Mo* 1897, 50, 361–368.

Jastrow, J., Cairnes, W. B. *Am J Ps* 1891–92, 4, 219–223.

Javal, E. *Annales d'oculistique* 1878, 1879.

Jeffress, L. A. *J Exp Ps* 1928, 11, 130–144.

Jenkins, J. G., Dallenbach, K. M. *Am J Ps* 1925, 35, 605–612.

Jenkins, T. N. *Ar Ps* 1926, #86.

Jenkins, T. N. *J Exp Ps* 1936, 19, 630–652.

Jersild, A. *Ar Ps* 1927, #89.

Jersild, A. *J Exp Ps* 1929, 12, 58–70.

Jevons, W. S. *Nature* 1871, 3, 281–282.

Johannsen, D. E. *J Genl Ps* 1930, 4, 282–308.

Johanson, A. M. *Ar Ps* 1922, #54.

Johnson, G. B. *J Genet Ps* 1927, 34, 118–128.

Johnson, H. M. *Ps Bull* 1923, 20, 562–589.

Johnson, H. M. *J Exp Ps* 1924, 7, 1–44.

Johnson, H. M. *Ps R* 1932, 39, 293–323.

Johnston, C. H. *Harvard Ps St* 1906, 2, 159–191.

Jones, H. E. *Ps Bull* 1928, 25, 183–184.

Jones, H. E. *Child Devel* 1930 a, 1, 106–110.

Jones, H. E. *J Genet Ps* 1930 b, 37, 485–498.

Jones, H. E., Wechsler, D. *Am J Ps* 1928, 40, 607–612.

Jost, A. *Z Ps* 1897, 14, 436–472.

Judd, C. H. *Ps R* 1897, 4, 374–389.

Judd, C. H. *Ps R* 1898, 5, 388–400.

Judd, C. H. *Ps R* 1899, 6, 241–261.

Judd, C. H. *Ps R* 1902, 9, 27–39.

Judd, C. H. *Ps Mon* 1905, 7, #29.

Judd, C. H. *Ps Mon* 1907, 8, #34.

Judd, C. H. *Educ R* 1908, 36, 28–42.

Judd, C. H., Buswell, G. T. *Supp Educ Mon* 1922, #23.

Judd, C. H., Cowling, D. J. *Ps Mon* 1907, 8, #34, 349–369.

Judd, C. H., others *Supp Educ Mon* 1918, #10.

Judd, D. B. *Am J Ps* 1927, 38, 507–533.

Jung, C. G. *Studies in word-association.* 1919.

Jung, C. G., Riklin, F. *J Ps Neurol* 1904, 3, 193–215.

K

Kanner, L. *Ps Mon* 1931, 41, #186.

Kao, Dji-Lih *Ps Mon* 1937, 49, #219.

Kappauf, W. F., Schlosberg, H. *J Genet Ps* 1937, 50, 27–45.

Kardos, L. *Z Ps* 1928, 108, 240–314.

Kardos, L. *Beitr Problemgeschichte Ps* (Bühler Festschrift) 1929, 1–77.

Kardos, L. *Z Ps Ergänzbd* 1934, #23.

Kasatkin, N. I., Levikova, A. M. *J Exp Ps* 1935 a, 18, 1–19.

Kasatkin, N. I., Levikova, A. M. *J Exp Ps* 1935 b, 18, 416–435.

Kästner, A., Wirth, W. *Ps St* 1907, 3, 361–392.

Kästner, A., Wirth, W. *Ps St* 1908, 4, 139–200.

Katona, G. *Z Ps* 1925, 97, 215–251.

Katona, G. *Ps Forsch* 1929, 12, 94–126.

Katz, D. *Z Ps Ergänzbd* 1911. 1930, #7.

Katz, D. *Z Ps* 1913, 65, 161–180.

Katz, D. *Der Aufbau der Tastwelt.* 1925.

Katz, D. *Zt Ps Ergänzbd* 1926, 11.

Katz, D., Révész, G. *Z ang Ps* 1921, 18, 307–320.

Katz, S. E., Breed, F. S. *J App Ps* 1922, 6, 255–266.

Katzaroff, D. *Ar de Ps* 1911, 11, 1–78.

Kelley, T. L. *Ps R* 1913, 20, 479–504.

Kelley, T. L. *Statistical method.* 1923.

Kellogg, C. E. *Ps Mon* 1915, 18, #79.

Kellogg, W. N. *Am J Ps* 1929 a, 41, 456–459.

Kellogg, W. N. *Ar Ps* 1929 b, #106.

Kellogg, W. N. *Ar Ps* 1930, #112.

Kellogg, W. N. *Am J Ps* 1931, 43, 65–86.

Kellogg, W. N. *J Exp Ps* 1938, 22, 186–192.

Kellogg, W. N., Kellogg, L. A. *The ape and the child.* 1933.

Kellogg, W. N., White, R. E. *J Comp Ps* 1935, 19, 119–148.

Kent, G. H., Rosanoff, A. J. *Am J Insan* 1910, 67, 37–96; 317–390.

Kiesow, F. *Philos St* 1894, 9, 510–527.

Kiesow, F. *Philos St* 1895, 11, 135–145.

Kiesow, F. *Z Ps* 1903, 33, 453–461.

King, J. L. *Br J Ps* 1934, 24, 389–402.

Kinnaman, A. J. *Am J Ps* 1902, 13, 98–148; 173–218.

Kirschmann, A. *Handbk biol Arbeitsmeth* 1927, 6, A, 952–971.

Kjerstad, C. L. *Ps Mon* 1919, 26, #116.

Klemm, O. *Ar ges Ps* 1919, 38, 71–114.

Klemm, O. *Ar ges Ps* 1920, 40, 117–146.

Kline, L. W. *J Educ Ps* 1914, 5, 259–266.

Kline, L. W. *Psbiol* 1920, 2, 255–328.

Klingler, G. *Ar ges Ps* 1931, 82, 105–152.

Klopsteg, P. E. *J Exp Ps* 1917, 2, 253–263.

Klüver, H. *Genet Ps Mon* 1926, 1, 71–230.

Klüver, H. *Ps Bull* 1928, 25, 69–104.

Klüver, H. *Ps R* 1930, 37, 441–458.

Klüver, H. *J Genet Ps* 1931, 39, 1–27.

Klüver, H. *Ps Bull* 1932, 29, 181–203.

Klüver, H. *Behavior mechanisms in monkeys.* 1933.

Knudsen, V. O. *Physiol R* 1923, 21, 84–102.

Knudsen, V. O. *J Genl Ps* 1928, 1, 320–352.

Koch, H. L. *J Exp Ps* 1923, 6, 366–376.

Koffka, K. *Zur Analyse der Vorstellungen und ihrer Gesetze.* 1912.

Koffka, K. *Ps Forsch* 1927, 9, 163–183.

Koffka, K. *Handbk normal pathol Physiol* 1931, 12 (2), 1166–1214; 1215–1271.

Koffka, K. *Ps Forsch* 1932, 16, 329–354.

Koffka, K. *Principles of Gestalt psychology.* 1935.

Koffka, K., Mintz, A. *Ps Forsch* 1931, 14, 183–198.

Köhler, W. *Z Ps* 1909, 54, 241–289.

Köhler, W. *Z Ps* 1910, 58, 59–140.

Köhler, W. *Z Ps* 1913, 64, 92–105.

Köhler, W.   *Abh preus Akad Wiss phys-math* 1915 a, #3, 1–70.

Köhler, W.   *Z Ps* 1915 b, 72, 1–192.

Köhler, W.   *Intelligenzprüfungen an Menschenaffen.* 1917 a.

Köhler, W.   *Z Ps* 1917 b, 77, 248–255.

Köhler, W.   *Ps Forsch* 1923, 4, 115–175.

Köhler, W.   *The mentality of apes.* 1924.

Köhler, W.   *Gestalt psychology.* 1929.

Köhler, W., Restorff, H. von   *Ps Forsch* 1935, 21, 56–112.

Kohlrausch, A.   *Handbk normal pathol Physiol* 1931, 12 (2), 1499–1594.

Komuro, K.   *Ar néerl Physiol* 1922, 6, 20–24.

König, A., Brodhun, E.   *Akad wiss Berlin Sitzbr* 1888, 37 (2), 917–932.

König, A., Dieterici, C.   *Z Ps* 1892, 4, 241–347.

Kopfermann, H.   *Ps Forsch* 1930, 13, 293–364.

Korniloff, K.   *Ar ges Ps* 1922, 42, 59–78.

Korte, W.   *Z Ps* 1923, 93, 17–82.

Kraepelin, E.   *Philos St* 1883, 1, 417–462; 573–605.

Kraepelin, E.   *Über die Beeinflussung einfacher psychischer Vorgänge durch einige Arzneimittel.* 1892.

Krauss, S.   *Z Ps* 1926, 100, 50–160.

Krauss, S.   *Ar ges Ps* 1928, 62, 179–240.

Krechevsky, I.   *Ps R* 1932 a, 39, 516–532.

Krechevsky, I.   *Calif U Pub Ps* 1932 b, 6, 27–64.

Krechevsky, I.   *J Comp Ps* 1933, 15, 429–433; 16, 99–116.

Krechevsky, I.   *J Comp Ps* 1935, 19, 425–468.

Kreezer, G.   *Am J Ps* 1931, 43, 659–664.

Kreezer, G.   *Am J Ps* 1932, 44, 638–676.

Kreezer, G.   *Am J Ps* 1934, 46, 1–18.

Kries, J. v.   *Z Ps* 1895, 8, 1–33.

Kries, J. v.   *Z Ps* 1896, 9, 81–123.

Kries, J. v.   *Z Ps* 1897, 13, 241–324; 15, 327–351.

Kries, J. v.   *Allgemeine Sinnesphysiologie.* 1923.

Kries, J. v.   *Handbk normal pathol Physiol* 1929, 12 (1), 679–713.

Kries, J. v., Auerbach, F.   *Ar Physiol* 1877, 297–378.

Kries, J. v., Nagel, W. A.   *Z Ps* 1896, 12, 1–38.

Kries, J. v., Nagel, W. A.   *Z Ps* 1900, 23, 161–186.

Kroh, O.   *Subjektive Anschauungsbilder bei Jugendlichen.* 1922.

Krueger, F.   *Philos St* 1900, 16, 307–379; 568–664.

Krueger, F., Spearman, C.   *Z Ps* 1907, 44, 50–114.

Krueger, W. C. F.   *J Exp Ps* 1929, 12, 71–78.

Krüger, H.   *Z Ps* 1925, 96, 58–67.

Kubo, Y.   *Jap J App Ps* 1933, 2, 82–183.

Kuhlmann, F.   *Ps R* 1906, 13, 316–348.

Kuhlmann, F.   *Am J Ps* 1907, 18, 389–420.

Kuhlmann, F.   *Am J Ps* 1909, 20, 194–218.

Külpe, O.   *Philos St* 1891, 6, 514–535; 1892, 7, 147–168.

Külpe, O.   *Philos St* 1902, 19, 508–556.

Külpe, O.   *Kong exp Ps Ber* 1904, 1, 56–68.

Künzler, W.   *Methodologische Beiträge zur experimentellen Untersuchung der Lesevorgänge bei kurzen Expositionszeiten.* 1913.

Kuo, Z. Y.   *J Exp Ps* 1923, 6, 247–293.

Kutzner, O.   *Ar ges Ps* 1916, 35, 157–251.

Kwalwasser, J.   *Ps Mon* 1926, 36, #167, 84–108.

L

Ladd-Franklin, C. *Colour and colour theories.* 1929.

Ladd, G. T., Woodworth, R. S. *Physiological psychology.* 1911.

Lakenan, M. E. *J Educ Ps* 1913, 4, 189–198.

Lalo, C. *L'esthétique expérimentale contemporaine.* 1908.

Lamansky, S. *Ar ges Physiol* 1869, 2, 418–422.

Landis, C. *J Comp Ps* 1924, 4, 447–509.

Landis, C. *Am J Physiol* 1925, 73, 551–555.

Landis, C. *J Comp Ps* 1926, 6, 221–242.

Landis, C. *Am J Physiol* 1927, 81, 6–19.

Landis, C. *Ps R* 1930, 37, 381–398.

Landis, C. *Ps Bull* 1932 a, 29, 693–752.

Landis, C. *Studies in dynamics of behavior.* (Lashley). 1932 b, 265–323.

Landis, C., DeWick, H. N. *Ps Bull* 1929, 26, 64–119.

Landis, C., Forbes, T. W. *Psychiat Q* 1933, 7, 107–114.

Landis, C., Gullette, R. *J Comp Ps* 1925, 5, 221–253.

Landis, C., Hunt, W. A. *J Exp Ps* 1935, 18, 505–529.

Landis, C., Wiley, L. E. *J Comp Ps* 1926, 6, 1–19.

Lange, K. *Deutsche med Wochenschrift* 1932, 58, 406–407.

Lange, L. *Philos St* 1888, 4, 479–510.

Langfeld, H. S. *J Abn Soc Ps* 1918, 13, 172–184.

Lanier, L. H. *J Exp Ps* 1934, 17, 371–399.

Larguier des Bancels, J. *Ann ps* 1902, 8, 185–213.

Larson, J. A. *J Exp Ps* 1923, 6, 420–454.

Larson, J. A. *Lying and its detection.* 1932.

Lashley, K. S. *Carnegie Instit Contr* 1915, #211, 105–128.

Lashley, K. S. *J Exp Ps* 1916, 1, 461–493.

Lashley, K. S. *J Animal Beh* 1917, 7, 139–142.

Lashley, K. S. *Psbiol* 1918, 1, 353–367.

Lashley, K. S. *Ar Neurol Psychiat* 1924, 12, 249–276.

Lashley, K. S. *Brain mechanisms and intelligence.* 1929.

Lashley, K. S. *Handbk genl exp ps* (Murchison) 1934, 456–496.

Lashley, K. S., Ball, J. *J Comp Ps* 1929, 9, 71–106.

Lashley, K. S., McCarthy, D. A. *J Comp Ps* 1926, 6, 423–432.

Lauenstein, O. *Ps Forsch* 1933, 17, 130–177.

Lebermann, F. *Z Biol* 1922, 75, 239–262.

Leeper, R. *J Genet Ps* 1935, 46, 3–40.

Leeper, R. *J Genet Ps* 1935 a, 46, 41–75.

Leeper, R., Leeper, D. O. *J Genl Ps* 1932, 6, 344–376.

Legowski, L. W. *Ar ges Ps* 1908, 12, 236–311.

Lehmann, A. *Philos St* 1888–89, 5, 96–156.

Lehmann, A. *Philos St* 1891–92, 7, 169–212.

Lehmann, A. *Die körperlichen Äusserungen psychischer Zustände.* 1899. 1901. 1905.

Lemmon, V. W. *Ar Ps* 1927, #94.

Lenk, E. *Neue ps St* 1926, 1, 573–612.

Leonardo da Vinci. *Trattato della pittura.* ab. 1500. (edition used 1735; German transl. 1882, vol. 2).

Lepley, W. M. *Ps Mon* 1934, 46, #205.

Leuba, J. H. *Am J Ps* 1892, 5, 370–384.

Lewin, K. *A dynamic theory of personality.* 1935.

Lewis, D., Larsen, M. J. *Nat Acad Sci Proc* 1937, 23, 415–421.

Lewis, F. H. *Ps R* 1933, 40, 90–96.

Liddell, H. S., James, W. T., Anderson, O. D. *Comp Ps Mon* 1934, 11, #51.

Linder, F. E. *Ps Mon* 1933, 44, #199, 1–20.

Lindley, E. H. *Am J Ps* 1897, 8, 431–493.

Lindley, S. B. *J Genet Ps* 1930, 37, 245–267.

Lindworsky, J. *Ar ges Ps* 1928, 61, 197–260.

Linnaeus, C. *Amoenitates academicae* 1756, 3, 183–201. (195).

Lipmann, O. *Z Ps* 1904, 35, 195–233.

Lipmann, O. *Z Ps* 1908, 49, 270–277.

Lipmann, O. *Handbk biol Arbeitsmeth* 1933, 6, C (2), 967–1056.

Litterer, O. F. *J App Ps* 1933, 17, 266–276.

Lobsien, M. *Beiträge Ps Aussage* 1903, 1 (2), 26–89.

Locke, N. M. *Ar Ps* 1935, #193.

Loeb, S. *Z Ps* 1912, 46, 83–128.

Long, L. *Ar Ps* 1937, #209.

Lorenz, J. *Ar ges Ps* 1912, 24, 313–342.

Lorge, I. *Columbia Univ T C Contr Educ* 1930, #438.

Loucks, R. B. *J Comp Ps* 1933, 15, 1–45.

Loucks, R. B. *Ps R* 1937, 44, 320–338.

Lowenstein, E., Dallenbach, K. M. *Am J Ps* 1930, 42, 423–429.

Lubrich, W. *Ar ges Ps* 1932, 84, 1–42.

Luckiesh, M., Moss, F. K. *Science of seeing.* 1937.

Luh, C. W. *Ps Mon* 1922, 31, #142.

Lumley, F. H. *Ps Mon* 1931, 42, #189.

Lumley, F. H. *J Exp Ps* 1932, 15, 195–205; 331–342.

Lund, F. H. *Am J Ps* 1926, 37, 372–381.

Lund, F. H. *J Exp Ps* 1927, 10, 424–433.

Lund, F. H., Anastasi, A. *Am J Ps* 1928, 40, 434–448.

Lundholm, H. *Ps R* 1921, 28, 43–60.

Luria, A. R. *The nature of human conflicts.* 1932.

Lyon, D. O. *Memory and the learning process.* 1917.

M

Macdonald, M. K. *Am J Ps* 1922, 33, 535–553.

Macdonald, P. A., Allen, J. F. *Philos Mag* 1930, 9, 817–827.

Macfarlane, D. A. *Calif U Pub Ps* 1930, 4, 277–305.

Mach, E. *Beiträge zur Analyse der Empfindungen.* 1886.

Mach, E. *The analysis of sensations.* 1914.

Macht, D. I., Isaacs, S. *Psbiol* 1917, 1, 19–32.

Macht, D. I., Isaacs, S., Greenberg, J. *Psbiol* 1918, 1, 327–338.

MacLeod, R. B. *Ar Ps* 1932, #135.

Mager, A. *St Ps Philos (Münchener)* 1920, 1, 497–657.

Maier, N. R. F. *J Comp Ps* 1930, 10, 115–143.

Maier, N. R. F. *J Comp Ps* 1931 a, 12, 181–194.

Maier, N. R. F. *Ps R* 1931 b, 38, 332–346.

Major, D. R. *Am J Ps* 1895, 7, 57–77.

Mall, G. D. *Z Ps* 1936 a, 138, 329–364.

Mall, G. D. *Z Ps Ergänzbd* 1936 b, #25.

Mallery, G. *Smithson Instit Bur Ethnol Rept* 1893, 10, 341; 352; 653.

Marbe, K. *Philos St* 1893, 8, 615–634.

Marbe, K. *Experimentell-psychologische Untersuchungen über das Urteil.* 1901.

Marquis, D. G. *J Comp Ps* 1935, 19, 29–58.

Marquis, D. P. *J Genet Ps* 1931, 39, 479–492.

Marsh, H. D. *Ar Philos Ps Sci Meth* 1906, #7.

Marston, W. M. *J Exp Ps* 1917, 2, 117–163.

Marston, W. M. *J Exp Ps* 1923, 6, 387–419.

Martin, A. H. *Ar Ps* 1922, #51.

Martin, L. J. *Ps Bull* 1911, 8, 36–37.

Martin, L. J. *Die Projektionsmethode und die Lokalisation visueller und anderer Vorstellungsbilder.* 1912.

Martin, L. J. *Z Ps* 1913, 65, 417–490.

Martin, L. J., Müller, G. E. *Zur Analyse der Unterschiedsempfindlichkeit.* 1899.

Martin, M. A. *Ar Ps* 1915, #32.

Martin, P. R., Fernberger, S. W. *Am J Ps* 1929, 41, 91–94.

Martius, G. *Philos St* 1889, 5, 601–617.

Martius, G. *Philos St* 1891, 6, 167–216; 394–416.

Marzynski, G. *Z Ps* 1921, 87, 45–72.

Matheson, E. *Child Devel* 1931, 2, 242–262.

Matsumoto, M. *Yale St Ps* 1897, 5, 1–75.

May, M. A. *Ar Ps* 1917, #39.

Mayer, A., Orth, J. *Z Ps* 1901, 26, 1–13.

Mayer, B. *Z Ps* 1927, 58 (2), 133–152.

Mayerhofer, G., Pauli, R. *Ar ges Ps* 1934, 91, 241–258.

McAllister, C. N. *Ps Mon* 1905, 6, #29, 17–54.

McClatchy, V. R. *J Exp Ps* 1922, 5, 312–322.

McClatchy, V. R., Cooper, M. *J Exp Ps* 1924, 7, 371–381.

McCulloch, T. L. *J Comp Ps* 1934, 18, 85–111.

McDougall, K. D., McDougall, W. *J Comp Ps* 1931, 11, 237–273.

McDougall, W. *Mind* 1901, 10, 52–97; 210–245; 347–382.

McDougall, W. *Br J Ps* 1904, 1, 78–113.

McFarland, R. A. *J Genl Ps* 1930, 3, 67–97.

McFarland, R. A. *Ar Ps* 1932, #145.

McFarland, R. A. *J Comp Ps* 1937, 23, 191–258; 24, 147–220.

McGeoch, G. O. *J Exp Ps* 1931, 14, 333–358.

McGeoch, G. O. *Am J Ps* 1935, 47, 65–89.

McGeoch, J. A. *Ps R* 1932, 39, 352–370.

McGeoch, J. A. *J Genl Ps* 1933, 9, 44–57.

McGeoch, J. A., McDonald, W. T. *Am J Ps* 1931, 43, 579–588.

McGeoch, J. A., Melton, A. W. *J Exp Ps* 1929, 12, 392–414.

McGeoch, J. A., Peters, H. N. *J Exp Ps* 1933, 16, 504–523.

McGinnis, E. *Genet Ps Mon* 1929, 6, 205–311 (294).

McGraw, M. B. *Growth: a study of Johnny and Jimmy.* 1935.

McKinney, F. *J Exp Ps* 1933, 16, 854–864.

McKinney, F. *J Exp Ps* 1935, 18, 585–598.

McTeer, W. *J Exp Ps* 1931 a, 14, 446–452.

McTeer, W. *J Exp Ps* 1931 b, 14, 453–476.

Meenes, M., Morton, M. A. *J Genl Ps* 1936, 14, 370–391.

Meinecke, G. *Ar ges Ps* 1934, 92, 249–254.

Menzerath, P. *Z Ps* 1908, 48, 1–95.

Menzies, R. *J Ps* 1937, 4, 75–120.

Merkel, J. *Philos St* 1885, 2, 73–127.

Merry, C. N. *Ps Mon* 1922, 31, #140.

Messenger, J. F. *Ps Mon* 1903, 4, #17, 123–144.

Messer, A. *Ar ges Ps* 1906, 8, 1–224.

Messmer, O. *Ar ges Ps* 1903, 2, 190–298.

Metfessel, M. *Ps Mon* 1928, 39, #178, 126–134.

Metzger, W. *Ps Forsch* 1930, 13, 6–29.

Meyer, H. W. *Z Ps* 1914, 70, 161–211.

Meyer, M. *Ps R* 1904, 11, 83–103.

Meyer, P. *Z Ps* 1913, 64, 34–91.

Meyer, W. *Z Ps* 1925, 98, 304–341.

Mibai, S. *Ps Mon* 1931, 42, #190.

Michaels, G. M. *Am J Ps* 1924, 35, 79–87.

Michotte, A., Fransen, F. *Études ps* 1914, 1, 367–414. (*Ann Instit Supérieur Philos* 1914, 3, 501–549).

Michotte, A., Portych, Th. *Études ps* 1914, 1, 237–364. (*Ann Instit Supérieur Philos* 1913, 2, 534–657).

Miles, W. R. *J Exp Ps* 1921, 4, 77–105.

Miles, W. R. *Carnegie Inst Contr* 1924, #333.

Miles, W. R. *J Genl Ps* 1928 a, 1, 3–14.

Miles, W. R. *J Genl Ps* 1928 b, 1, 373–374.

Miles, W. R. *Ps R* 1929, 36, 122–141.

Miles, W. R. *J Comp Ps* 1930, 10, 237–261.

Miles, W. R. *Am J Ps* 1931 a, 43, 377–391. (380–382).

Miles, W. R. *Nat Acad Sci Proc* 1931 b, 17, 627–633.

Miles, W. R. *J Exp Ps* 1931 c, 14, 311–332.

Miles, W. R. *Res Q Am Physical Educ Assoc* 1931 d, 2, #3, 5–13.

Miles, W. R. *Ps R* 1933, 40, 99–123.

Miles, W. R., Bell, H. M. *J Exp Ps* 1929, 12, 450–458.

Miles, W. R., Laslett, H. R. *Ps R* 1931, 38, 1–13.

Miles, W. R., Segel, D. *J Educ Ps* 1929, 20, 520–529.

Miles, W. R., Shen, E. *J Exp Ps* 1925, 8, 344–362.

Miller, D. C. *The science of musical sounds*. 1922.

Miller, J., Cole, L. E. *J Genet Ps* 1936, 48, 405–440.

Misbach, L. E. *J Exp Ps* 1932, 15, 167–183.

Mitchel, O. M. *J Franklin Instit* 1858, 66, 349–352.

Mitchell, D. *Ps Mon* 1914, 17, #74.

Mitchell, M. B. *Am J Ps* 1934, 46, 80–91.

Moldenhauer, W. *Philos St* 1883, 1, 606–614.

Monroe, M. *Children who cannot read.* 1932.

Moore, M. G. *Am J Ps* 1930, 42, 453–455.

Moore, T. V. *Ps Mon* 1904, 6, #24.

Moore, T. V. *Calif U Pub Ps* 1910, 1, 73–197.

Moore, T. V. *Ps Mon* 1919, 27, #119.

Morgan, C. *Iowa U St Educ* 1934, 9, #5, 105–143.

Morgan, C. Lloyd. *An introduction to comparative psychology.* 1894.

Morgan, C. Lloyd. *Animal behavior.* 1900.

Morgan, J. J. B. *Ar Ps* 1916, #35.

Mowrer, O. H. *Science* 1935, 81, 180–181.

Muenzinger, K. F. *Ps R* 1931, 38, 347–358.

Muenzinger, K. F. *J Exp Ps* 1934, 17, 439–448.

Müller, G. E. *Ar ges Physiol* 1879, 19, 191–235.

Müller, G. E. *Die Gesichtspunkte und die Tatsachen der psychophysischen Methodik.* 1904.

Müller, G. E. *Z Ps Ergänzbd* 1911, 5.

Müller, G. E. *Z Ps Ergänzbd* 1913, 8.

Müller, G. E. *Z Ps Ergänzbd* 1917, 9.

Müller, G. E. *Z Ps Ergänzbd* 1930, #17. #18.

Müller, G. E., Pilzecker, A. *Z Ps Ergänzbd* 1900, #1.

Müller, G. E., Schumann, F. *Ar ges Physiol* 1889, 45, 37–112.

Müller, G. E., Schumann, F. *Z Ps* 1894, 6, 81–190; 257–339.

Munn, N. L. *J Exp Ps* 1932, 15, 343–353.

Münnich, F. *Z Biol* 1915, 66, 1–22.

Münsterberg, H. *Z Ps* 1890, 1, 99–107.

Münsterberg, H. *Beiträge experimentellen Psychologie.* 1892, 4, (69–80).

Münsterberg, H., Bigham, J. *Ps R* 1894, 1, 34–44; 453–461.

Murphy, G. *Am J Ps* 1917, 28, 238–262.

Murphy, G. *Am J Insan* 1921, 77, 545–558.

Murphy, G. *Am J Psychiat* 1923, 2, 539–571.

Murphy, G., Murphy, L. B., Newcomb, T. M. *Experimental social psychology.* 1937.

Musatti, C. L. *Ar ital Ps* 1931, 9, 61–156.

Myers, C. S. *A text-book of experimental psychology with laboratory exercises.* 1911. 2 vols.

Myers, G. C. *Ar Ps* 1913, #26.

N

Nafe, J. P. *Am J Ps* 1924, 35, 507–544.

Nafe, J. P. *Am J Ps* 1927, 39, 307–389.

Nafe, J. P. *Handbk genl exp ps* (Murchison) 1934, 1037–1087.

Nagel, F. *Ar ges Ps* 1912, 23, 156–253.

Nagge, J. W. *J Exp Ps* 1935, 18, 663–682.

Needham, J. G. *Ps Bull* 1934 a, 31, 229–243.

Needham, J. G. *Am J Ps* 1934 b, 46, 558–567.

Needham, J. G. *Am J Ps* 1935 a, 47, 275–284.

Needham, J. G. *J Exp Ps* 1935 b, 18, 530–543.

Needham, J. G. *J Exp Ps* 1935 c, 18, 767–773.

Nellmann, H., Trendelenburg, W. *Z vergl Physiol* 1926, 4, 142–200.

Newhall, S. M. *Ar Ps* 1923, #61.

Newhall, S. M., Sears, R. R. *Comp Ps Mon* 1933, 9, #43.

Nicolai, F. *Ar ges Ps* 1922, 42, 132–149.

Nissen, A. E. *Thesis. M. A.* Columbia University. 1928. (Unpublished.)

Nutting, P. G. *Bull Bur Standards* 1907, 3, 59–64.

Nutting, P. G. *Bull Bur Standards* 1908, 5, 261–308. (286).

Nystrom, C. L. *Ps Mon* 1933, 44, #198, 61–82.

Nyswander, D. B. *J Genl Ps* 1929, 2, 273–289.

O

Oberholzer, E. E. *Elem School J* 1915, 15, 313–322.

Oberlin, K. W. *J Exp Ps* 1936, 19, 438–455.

Oberly, H. S. *Am J Ps* 1924, 35, 332–352.

Oberly, H. S. *Am J Ps* 1928, 40, 295–302.

O'Brien, F. J. *Am J Ps* 1921, 32, 249–283.

O'Brien, J. A. *Silent reading.* 1921.

O'Connor, J. *Born that way.* 1928.

O'Connor, J. *Psychometrics.* 1934.

Ogden, R. M. *Ar ges Ps* 1903, 2, 93–189.

Ohma, S. *Ar néerl Physiol* 1922, 6, 567–590.

Ohms, H. *Z Ps* 1910, 56, 1–84.

Okabe, T. *Am J Ps* 1910, 21, 563–596.

Orata, P. T. *The theory of identical elements.* 1928.

Ortner, A. *Ps Forsch* 1937, 22, 59–88.

Otis, M. *J Educ Ps* 1915, 6, 271–288.

P

Pace, E. A. *Philos St* 1902, 20, 232–245.

Panum, P. L. *Physiologische Untersuchungen über das Sehen mit zwei Augen.* 1858.

Parinaud, H. *C R Acad Sci* (Paris) 1881, 93, 286–287.

Passy, J. *Soc Biol Compt Rend* 1892, 44, 447–449.

Passy, J. *Soc Biol Compt Rend* 1893, 45, 479–481.

Paterson, D. G., Tinker, M. A. *J App Ps* 1929, 13, 120–130.

Patrick, C. *Ar Ps* 1935, #178.

Patrick, C. *J Ps* 1937, 4, 35–73.

Patterson, E. *Ps Mon* 1930, 40, #181, 85–108.

Paulhan, F. *R scient* 1887, 39, 684–689.

Pauli, R. *Z Biol* 1924, 81, 93–112.

Pavlov, I. P. *Conditioned reflexes.* 1927.

Peak, H. *Ps Mon* 1931, 42, #188.

Peak, H., Boring, E. G. *J Exp Ps* 1926, 9, 71–94.

Peak, H., Deese, L. *J Exp Ps* 1937, 20, 244–261.

Pearce, C. H. *J Exp Ps* 1937, 20, 101–113.

Pearson, K. *Tables for statisticians and biometricians.* 1, 1914. 2, 1931.

Pechstein, L. A. *Ps Mon* 1917, 23, #99.

Pechstein, L. A. *J Educ Ps* 1921, 12, 92–97.

Peckham, R. H. *Am J Ps* 1936, 48, 43–63.

Pendleton, C. R. *Am J Ps* 1928, 40, 353–371.

Pentschew, C. *Ar ges Ps* 1903, 1, 417–526.

Perkins, F. T. *Am J Ps* 1932, 44, 473–490.

Perkins, N. L. *Br J Ps* 1914, 7, 253–261.

Perkins, N. L. *Comp Ps Mon* 1927, 4, #21.

Perky, C. W. *Am J Ps* 1910, 21, 422–452.

Perrin, F. A. C. *Ps Mon* 1914, 16, #70.

Peter, R. *Ar ges Ps* 1915, 34, 515–564.

Peters, C. C. *J Educ Ps* 1917, 8, 350–366.

Peterson, F., Jung, C. G. *Brain* 1907, 30, 153–218.

Peterson, J. *J Exp Ps* 1917, 2, 178–224.

Peterson, J. *Ps R* 1918, 25, 443–467.

Peterson, J. *J Exp Ps* 1920, 3, 257–280.

Peterson, J. *J Exp Ps* 1922, 5, 270–300.

Peterson, J. C. *Ps Mon* 1920, 28, #129.

Petran, L. A. *J Genl Ps* 1932, 7, 381–404.

Pfaffmann, C. *Am J Ps* 1935, 47, 470–476.

Phelan, G. B. *Études Ps* 1925, 2 (1), 1–292.

Philip, B. R. *Am J Ps* 1934, 46, 379–396.

Philippe, J. *R philos* 1897, 43, 481–493.

Physical Society of London. *Report of a discussion on audition.* 1931.

Piderit, T. *Mimik und Physiognomik.* 1859. (1867, 1886, 1909, 1925).

Pierce, A. H. *Studies in auditory and visual space perception.* 1901.

Pierce, E. *Ps R* 1894, 1, 483–495.

Pierce, E. *Ps R* 1896, 3, 270–282.

Piéron, H. *Ann ps* 1913, 19, 91–193.

Piéron, H. *Soc Biol Compt Rend* 1919, 82, 1116–1118.

Piéron, H. *Ann ps* 1920, 21, 119–148.

Piéron, H. *Ann ps* 1929, 30, 87–105.

Piéron, H. *Ann ps* 1932 a, 33, 106–117.

Piéron, H. *Soc Biol Compt Rend* 1932 b, 111, 380–383.

Pikler, J. *Z Ps* 1928, 106, 316–326.

Pillsbury, W. B. *Am J Ps* 1897, 8, 315–393.

Pillsbury, W. B. *Am J Ps* 1903, 14, 277–288.

Pillsbury, W. B. *J Philos* 1913, 10, 181–185.

Pintner, R. *Ps R* 1913, 30, 129–153.

Piper, H. *Z Ps* 1903, 31, 161–214.

Platt, W., Baker, B. A. *J Chemical Educ* 1931, 8, 1969–2002.

Poffenberger, A. T. *Ar Ps* 1912, #23.

Poffenberger, A. T. *J Educ Ps* 1915, 6, 459–474.

Poffenberger, A. T., Barrows, B. E. *J App Ps* 1924, 8, 187–205.

Pohlmann, A. *Experimentelle Beiträge zur Lehre vom Gedächtnis.* 1906.

Poincaré, H. *Science et méthode.* 1908.

Ponzo, M. *Ar ital Biol* 1915, 64, 306–312.

Porteus, S. D. *Guide to Porteus maze test.* 1924.

Porteus, S. D. *The maze test and mental differences.* 1933.

Pratt, C. C. *Am J Ps* 1933 a, 45, 292–297.

Pratt, C. C. *J Exp Ps* 1933 b, 16, 798–814.

Pressey, L. C. *School Soc* 1926, 24, 589–592.

Prideaux, E. *Brain* 1920, 43, 50–73.

Prideaux, E. *Br J Ps Med Sec* 1921, 2, 23–46.

Priest, I. G. *J Optical Soc Am* 1920, 4, 402–404.

Puffer, E. D. *Ps Mon* 1903, 4, #17, 467–539.

Purdy, D. M. *Am J Ps* 1931, 43, 541–559.

Purdy, D. M. *J Genl Ps* 1936, 15, 437–454.

Purkinje, J. E. *Beobachtungen und Versuche zur Physiologie der Sinne.* 1823–1825.

Pyle, W. H. *J Educ Ps* 1914, 5, 247–251.

Pyle, W. H., Snyder, J. C. *J Educ Ps* 1911, 2, 133–142.

Q

Quantz, J. C. *Ps Mon* 1897, 2, #5.

R

Radosavljevich, P. R. *Das Behalten und Vergessen bei Kindern und Erwachsenen nach experimentellen Untersuchungen.* 1907.

Raffel, G. *J Exp Ps* 1934, 17, 828–838.

Ranschburg, P. *Monatschr Psychiat Neurol* 1901, 10, 321–333.

Ranschburg, P. *Die Lese-und Schreibstörungen des Kindesalters.* 1925.

Rawdon Smith, A. F. *Br J Ps* 1934, 25, 77–85.

Razran, G. H. S. *Ar Ps* 1933 a, #148.

Razran, G. H. S. *Ps Bull* 1933 b, 30, 261–324.

Razran, G. H. S. *Ps Bull* 1934, 31, 111–143.

Razran, G. H. S. *Ar Ps* 1935, #191.

Razran, G. H. S. *J Ps* 1936, 2, 327–337.

Rebert, G. N. *J Educ Ps* 1932 a, 23, 35–45.

Rebert, G. N. *J Educ Ps* 1932 b, 23, 192–203.

Reed, H. B. *J Exp Ps* 1917, 2, 315–346.

Reed, H. B. *Ps R* 1918, 25, 128–155; 257–285; 378–401.

Reed, H. B. *J Educ Ps* 1924, 15, 107–115, 592–595.

Reeves, P. *Ps R* 1918 a, 25, 330–340.

Reeves, P. *Astrophysical J* 1918 b, 47, 141–145.

Rehwoldt, F. *Ps St* 1911, 7, 141–195.

Reinhold, F. *Z Ps* 1909, 54, 183–214.

Renshaw, S., Hampton, I. L. *Am J Ps* 1931, 43, 637–638.

Restorff, H. von. *Ps Forsch* 1933, 18, 299–342.

Revault d'Allonnes, G. *J de Ps* 1934, 31, 27–87.

Reymert, M. L. *Scand Scient R* 1923, 2, 177–222.

Rich, G. J. *J Exp Ps* 1916, 1, 13–22.

Rich, G. J. *Am J Ps* 1918, 29, 120–121.

Rich, G. J. *Am J Ps* 1919, 30, 121–164.

Richardson, H. M. *Genet Ps Mon* 1932, 12, 195–359.

Richter, C. P. *Nat Acad Sci Proc* 1926, 12, 214–222.

Richter, C. P. *Brain* 1927, 50, 216–235.

Richter, C. P. *Am J Physiol* 1929 a, 88, 596–615.

Richter, C. P. *Johns Hopkins Hosp Bull* 1929 b, 45, 56–74.

Riedel, G. *Neue ps St* 1937, 10, 1–44.

Rieffert, J. *Kong exp Ps Ber* 1912, 5, 245–247.

Riesz, R. R. *Physical R* 1928, 31, 867–875.

Rikimaru, J. *Jap J Ps* 1934, 9, 87–107. (11–12).

Rikimaru, J. *Jap J Ps* 1937, 12, 33–54. (4).

Roberts, W. H. *J Franklin Inst* 1932, 213, 283–311.

Robinson, E. S. *Ps Mon* 1920, 28, #128.

Robinson, E. S., Brown, M. A. *Am J Ps* 1926, 37, 538–552.

Robinson, E. W., Wever, E. G. *Calif U Pub Ps* 1930, 4, 233–239.

Robinson, F. P. *Iowa Univ St (Series Aims Prog Research)* 1933, #39.

Robinson, F. P., Murphy, P. G. *Science* 1932, 76, 171–172.

Rodnick, E. H. *J Exp Ps* 1937, 20, 409–425.

Rolder, J. W. *Ar néerl Physiol* 1922, 6, 111–148.

Rosanoff, A. J., Martin, H. E., Rosanoff, I. R. *Ps Mon* 1918, 25, #109.

Rossman, J. *The psychology of the inventor.* 1931.

Rounds, G. H., Poffenberger, A. T. *Am J Ps* 1931, 43, 606–612.

Rubin, E. *Synsoplevede Figurer.* 1915.

Rubin, E. *Visuell wahrgenommene Figuren.* 1921.

Rubin-Rabson, G. *Ar Ps* 1937, #220.

Ruckmick, C. A. *Ps Mon* 1921, 30, #136, 30–35.

Ruckmick, C. A. *The mental life.* 1928. (124).

Ruckmick, C. A. *Psychology of feeling and emotion.* 1936. (345–372).

Rudeanu, A. *Trav humain* 1933, 1, 192–203.

Rudolph, H. *Der Ausdruck der Gemütsbewegungen des Menschen.* 1903. (2 v).

Ruediger, W. C. *Ar Ps* 1907, #7.

Ruediger, W. C. *Educ R* 1908, 36, 364–371.

Ruger, H. *Ar Ps* 1910, #15.

Ruger, H., Bussenius, C. E. (trans.) Memory. 1913.

Rupp, H. *Ps Forsch* 1923, 4, 262–300.

S

Saling, G. *Z Ps* 1908, 49, 238–253.

Salmon, T. N., Blakeslee, A. F. *Nat Acad Sci Proc* 1935, 21, 78–83.

Salow, P. *Ps St* 1913, 8, 506–540.

Sander, F. *Neue ps St* 1926, 1, 161–166.

Sander, F. *Kong exp Ps Ber* 1928, 10, 23–88.

Sanderson, S. *J Exp Ps* 1929, 12, 463–489.

Sanford, E. C. *Am J Ps* 1888–89, 2, 1–38; 271–298; 403–430.

Saul, L. J., Davis, H. *Ar Neurol Psychiat* 1932, 28, 1104–1116.

Schaefer, B. *Ps Mon* 1936, 48, #214, 57–73.

Schilder, P. *Ar Neurol Psychiat* 1929, 22, 425–443.

Schilling, W. *Ps R* 1921, 28, 72–79.

Schlieper, F. *Z ang Ps* 1929, 32, 454–499.

Schlosberg, H. *J Exp Ps* 1928, 11, 468–494.

Schlosberg, H. *J Genl Ps* 1932, 7, 328–342.

Schlosberg, H. *J Genet Ps* 1937 a, 50, 47–61.

Schlosberg, H. *Ps R* 1937, 44, 379–394.

Schmidt, F. *Z Ps* 1902, 28, 65–95.

Schmidt, W. A. *Supp Educ Mon* 1917, #2.

Schneider, C. *Neue ps St* 1928, 4, 85–159.

Schneirla, T. C. *Comp Ps Mon* 1929, 6, #30.

Schoen, M. *Ps Mon* 1922, 31, #140, 230–259.

Schoonhoven, G. O. *Thesis M. A.* Columbia University. 1925. (Unpublished.)

Schorn, M. *Z Ps* 1928, 108, 195–221.

Schriever, H. *Z Biol* 1926, 85, 67–84.

Schriever, H., Strughold, H. *Z Biol* 1926, 84, 193–206.

Schriever, W. *Z Ps* 1925, 96, 113–170.

Schultze, M. *Ar mikro Anat* 1866, 2, 175–286.

Schulze, R. *Die Mimik der Kinder bei künstlerischen Geniessen.* 1906.

Schulze, R. *Experimental psychology and pedagogy.* 1912. (154–162).

Schumann, F. *Z Ps* 1898, 17, 106–148.

Schumann, F. *Z Ps* 1900, 23, 1–32.

Schumann, F. *Z Ps* 1902, 30, 241–291; 321–339.

Schumann, F. *Ps St* (Schumann) 1904, 1, 1–32.

Schumann, F. *Z Ps* 1921–22, 88, 205–224.

Scott, J. C. *J Comp Ps* 1930, 10, 97–114.

Scott, T. C. *J Exp Ps* 1930, 13, 164–207.

Scripture, E. W. *Philos St* 1891, 7, 50–146.

Scripture, E. W. *Science* 1896, 3, 762–763.

Scripture, E. W., Burnham, J. L. *Yale St Ps* 1896, 4, 20–22.

Scripture, E. W., Smith, T. L., Brown, E. M. *Yale St Ps* 1894, 2, 114–119.

Sears, R. *Ar Ps* 1933, #155.

Seashore, C. E. *Iowa U St Ps* 1899, 2, 46–54.

Seashore, R. H. *J Genl Ps* 1930, 3, 38–66.

Secor, W. B. *Am J Ps* 1900, 11, 225–236.

Seibert, L. C. *Johns Hopkins U St Educ* 1932, #18.

Seifert, F. *Z Ps* 1917, 78, 55–144.

Sells, S. B. *Ar Ps* 1936, #200.

Sells, S. B., Koob, H. F. *J Educ Ps* 1937, 28, 514–518.

Selz, O. *Über die Gesetze des geordneten Denkverlaufs.* 1913.

Selz, O. *Zur Psychologie des produktiven Denkens und des Irrtums.* 1922.

Selz, O. *Die Gesetze der produktiven und reproduktiven Geistestätigkeit.* 1924.

Setzepfand, W. v. *Z Biol* 1935, 96, 236–240.

Seward, G. H. *Ar Ps* 1928, #99.

Seward, J. P., Seward, G. H. *Ar Ps* 1934, #168.

Seward, J. P., Seward, G. H. *J Exp Ps* 1935, 18, 64–79.

Shaxby, J. H., Gage, F. H. *Med Research Council special report* 1932, #166, 1–32.

Sheehan, M. R. *Ar Ps* 1938, #222.

Shen, E. *J Exp Ps* 1927, 10, 158–183.

Shepard, J. F. *Am J Ps* 1906, 17, 522–584.

Shepard, J. F. *Michigan U St Sci* 1914. (With Atlas.)

Shepherd, W. T. *Ps Mon* 1910, 12, #52.

Sherman, M. *J Comp Ps* 1927, 7, 265–284; 335–351.

Sherman, M. *J Comp Ps* 1928, 8, 385–394.

Sherrington, C. S. *J Physiol* 1897, 21, 33–54.

Sherrington, C. S. *Integrative action of the nervous system.* 1906.

Shipley, W. C. *J Genl Ps* 1934, 11, 46–64.

Shuey, A. *Am J Ps* 1924, 35, 559–582.

Shuey, A. *Am J Ps* 1926, 37, 528–537.

Siipola, E. M. *Ps Mon* 1935, 46, #210, 66–77.

Silleck, S. B., Lapha, C. W. *J Exp Ps* 1937, 20, 195–201.

Sinden, R. H. *J Opt Soc Am* 1923, 7, 1123–1153.

Sisk, T. K. *George Peabody Contr Educ* 1926, #23.

Sisson, E. D. *Am J Ps* 1935, 47, 309–311.

Sister Mary. *Catholic U Educ Res Bull* 1929, 4, #1.

Sivian, L. J., White, S. D. *J Acoust Soc* 1933, 4, 288–321.

Skaggs, E. B. *Ps Mon* 1925, 34, #161.

Skaggs, E. B. *J Comp Ps* 1930, 10, 375–419.

Skinner, B. F. *J Genl Ps* 1932, 7, 274–286.

Skinner, B. F. *J Genl Ps* 1933, 8, 114–129.

Skinner, B. F. *J Genl Ps* 1935, 12, 66–77.

Skramlik, E. v. *Z Ps* 1925, 56 (2), 69–140. (88–122).

Skramlik, E. v. *Ar ges Ps Ergänzbd* 1937, 4, (parts 1, 2).

Slattery, M. D. *Yale St Ps* 1893, 1, 71–79.

Slaughter, J. W. *Am J Ps* 1901, 12, 313–334.

Sleight, W. G. *Br J Ps* 1911, 4, 386–457.

Sloan, L. L. *Ps Mon* 1928, 38, #173.

Small, W. S. *Am J Ps* 1899–1900, 11, 80–100; 133–165. 1900–1901, 12, 206–239.

Smith, F. O. *J Genet Ps* 1927, 34, 394–405.

Smith, F. O. *Ps Mon* 1931, 41, #187, 142–152.

Smith, M. D. *Br J Ps* 1930, 21, 1–28.

Smith, M. D. *Br J Ps* 1934, 25, 63–76.

Smith, W. G. *Mind* 1895, 4, 47–73.

Smith, W. G. *Ps R* 1896, 3, 21–31.

Smith, W. G. *Mind* 1903, 12, 47–58.

Smith, W. G. *Br J Ps* 1905, 1, 240–260.

Smith, Whately. *The measurement of emotion.* 1922.

Smoke, K. L. *Ps Mon* 1932, 42, #191.

Snoddy, G. S. *Ps Mon* 1920, 28, #124.

Snoddy, G. S. *J App Ps* 1926, 10, 1–36.

Snoddy, G. S. *Evidence for two opposed processes in mental growth.* 1930.

Snygg, D. *J Genet Ps* 1935, 47, 321–336.

Snygg, D. *J Ps* 1936, 1, 153–166.

Southall, J. P. C. *Introduction to physiological optics.* 1937.

Spearman, C. *Ps St* 1906, 1, 388–493.

Spearman, C. *The nature of 'intelligence' and the principles of cognition.* 1923.

Spearman, C. *Br J Ps* 1925, 15, 211–225.

Speich, R. *Ar ges Ps* 1927, 59, 225–338. (254, 260).

Spence, K., Shipley, W. C. *J Comp Ps* 1934, 17, 423–436.

Spight, J. B. *J Exp Ps* 1928, 11, 397–398.

Spragg, S. D. S. *J Comp Ps* 1933, 15, 313–329.

Spragg, S. D. S. *J Comp Ps* 1934, 18, 51–73.

Stanton, F. N., Burtt, H. E. *J App Ps* 1935, 19, 683–693.

Starch, D. *Ps Mon* 1905, 6, #28, 1–45.

Starch, D. *Ps Mon* 1908, 9, #38, 1–55.

Starch, D. *Ps Bull* 1910 a, 7, 20–23.

Starch, D. *Ps R* 1910 b, 17, 19–36.

Starch, D. *J Educ Ps* 1915, 6, 1–24.

Starling, E. H. *Principles of human physiology.* 6th ed. 1933.

Steffens, Laura *Z Ps* 1900, 23, 241–308.

Steffens, Lottie *Z Ps* 1900, 22, 241–382, 465.

Stein, W. *Ar ges Ps* 1928, 64, 301–346.

Steinberg, J. C. *J Acoust Soc* 1934, 6, 16–24.

Steinhausen, W. *Ar ges Physiol* 1931, 228, 322–328; 1932, 229, 439–440; 1933, 232, 500–512.

Steinig, K. *Z Ps* 1929, 109, 291–336.

Sterzinger, O. *Z ang Ps* 1924, 23, 121–161.

Sterzinger, O. *Z ang Ps* 1928, 29, 177–196.

Stevanović, B. P. *Br J Ps Mon* 1927, 4, #12.

Stevens, S. S. *Am J Ps* 1934 a, 46, 397–408.

Stevens, S. S. *Nat Acad Sci Proc* 1934 b, 20, 457–459.

Stevens, S. S. *J Exp Ps* 1934 c, 17, 585–592.

Stevens, S. S. *Ps R* 1936, 43, 405–416.

Stevens, S. S., Davis, H. *Hearing: its psychology and physiology.* 1938.

Stevens, S. S., Davis, H., Lurie, M. H. *J Genl Ps* 1935, 13, 297–315.

Stevens, S. S., Newman, E. B. *Nat Acad Sci Proc* 1934, 20, 593–596.

Stevens, S. S., Newman, E. B. *Am J Ps* 1936 a, 48, 297–306.

Stevens, S. S., Newman, E. B. *Nat Acad Sci Proc* 1936 b, 22, 668–672.

Stewart, G. W. *Physical R* 1920, 15, 425–445.

Stewart, G. W. *Ps Mon* 1922, 31, #140, 30–44.

Stewart, G. W., Hovda, O. *Ps R* 1918, 25, 242–251.

Stoelting, C. H. *Psychological and physiological apparatus and supplies.* 1930, 86–88.

Stone, C. P., Nyswander, D. B. *J Genet Ps* 1927, 34, 497–524.

Stone, L. J., Dallenbach, K. M. *Am J Ps* 1936, 48, 117–125.

Störring, G. *Ar ges Ps* 1906, 6, 316–356.

Störring, G. *Ar ges Ps* 1908, 11, 1–127.

Störring, G. *Ar ges Ps* 1925, 52, 1–60.

Störring, G. *Ar ges Ps* 1926, 54, 23–84; 55, 47–110.

Stott, L. H. *J Exp Ps* 1935, 18, 741–766.

Stratton, G. M. *Ps R* 1902 a, 9, 444–447.

Stratton, G. M. *Philos St* 1902 b, 20, 336–359.

Stratton, G. M. *Ps R* 1906, 13, 81–96.

Street, R. F. *A Gestalt completion test.* 1931.

Stricker, S. *Studien über die Sprachvorstellungen.* 1880.

Stricker, S. *Studien über die Bewegungsvorstellungen.* 1882.

Strohal, R. *Z Ps* 1933, 130, 1–27.

Strohl, A. *Soc Biol Compt Rend* 1921, 84, 949–950. 85, 125–126; 948–949.

Strong, E. K. *Ar Ps* 1911, #17.

Strong, E. K. *Ps R* 1912, 19, 447–462.

Strong, E. K. *Ps R* 1913, 20, 339–372.

Strong, M. H., Strong, E. K. *Am J Ps* 1916, 27, 341–362.

Stroud, J. B. *Am J Ps* 1931 a, 43, 684–686.

Stroud, J. B. *J Exp Ps* 1931 b, 14, 184–185; 606–631.

Strughold, H. *Z Biol* 1926, 84, 311–320.

Strughold, H., Karbe, M. *Z Biol* 1925, 83, 297–308.

Stücker, N. *Akad Wiss Wien Sitzbr* 1907, 116 (2a), 367–388.

Stumpf, C. *Tonpsychologie.* 1, 1883. 2, 1890.

Suter, J. *Ar ges Ps* 1912, 25, 78–150.

Swenson, H. A. *J Genl Ps* 1932, 7, 360–380.

Swift, E. J. *Am J Ps* 1903, 14, 201–251.

Swift, E. J. *Studies in philosophy and psychology* (Garman) 1906, 297–313.

Swift, E. J. *Mind in the making.* 1908.

Switzer, S. C. A. *J Exp Ps* 1930, 13, 76–97.

Switzer, S. C. A. *J Genl Ps* 1933, 9, 77–100.

Switzer, S. C. A. *J Exp Ps* 1934, 17, 603–620.

Switzer, S. C. A. *J Genl Ps* 1935 a, 12, 78–94.

Switzer, S. C. A. *J Comp Ps* 1935 b, 19, 155–175.

Symonds, P. M. *Diagnosing personality and conduct.* 1931.

Syz, H. C. *Br J Ps* 1926 a, 17, 54–69.

Syz, H. C. *Br J Ps* 1926 b, 17, 119–126.

Syz, H. C., Kinder, E. F. *Ar Neurol Psychiat* 1928, 19, 1026–1035.

Syz, H. C., Kinder, E. F. *Ar Neurol Psychiat* 1931, 26, 146–155.

T

Tarchanoff, J. *Ar ges Physiol* 1890, 46, 46–55.

Taylor, C. O. *Z Ps* 1906, 40, 225–251.

Taylor, R. W. *Am J Ps* 1901, 12, 335–345.

Telford, C. W. *J Exp Ps* 1931, 14, 1–36.

Terry, P. W. *Supp Educ Mon* 1922, #18.

Thelin, E., Altman, E. R. *J Exp Ps* 1929, 12, 79–87.

Thiéry, A. *Philos St* 1895, 11, 307–370.

Thomson, G. H. *Br J Ps* 1912, 5, 203–241.

Thorndike, E. L. *Ps Mon* 1898, 2, #8.

Thorndike, E. L. *Ps Mon* 1901, 3, #15.

Thorndike, E. L. *Educational psychology.* 1903.

Thorndike, E. L. *Ps R* 1908, 15, 122–138.

Thorndike, E. L. *Educational psychology.* 1913. vol. 2.

Thorndike, E. L. *Teachers College Rec* 1914, 15, 1–66.

Thorndike, E. L. *J Educ Ps* 1917 a, 8, 323–332.

Thorndike, E. L. *Ps R* 1917 b, 24, 147–153.

Thorndike, E. L. *J Educ Ps* 1924, 15, 1–22; 83–98.

Thorndike, E. L. *The fundamentals of learning.* 1932.

Thorndike, E. L., Woodworth, R. S. *Ps R* 1901, 8, 247–261; 384–395; 553–564.

Thorne, F. C. *Ar Ps* 1934, #170.

Thorner, H. *Ar ges Ps* 1929, 71, 127–164.

Thouless, R. H. *Br J Ps* 1925, 16, 5–15.

Thouless, R. H. *Internatl Cong Ps* 1929, 9, 432–433.

Thouless, R. H. *Br J Ps* 1930, 20, 219–240; 309–321.

Thouless, R. H. *Br J Ps* 1931, 21, 339–359; 22, 1–30.

Thouless, R. H. *Br J Ps* 1932, 22, 216–241.

Thumb, A., Marbe, K. *Experimentelle Untersuchungen über die psychologischen Grundlagen der sprachlichen Analogiebildung.* 1901.

Thunberg, T. *Skand Ar Physiol* 1901, 11, 382–435.

Thurstone, L. L. *Ps Mon* 1919, 26, #114.

Thurstone, L. L. *J Genl Ps* 1930, 3, 469–493.

Tiffin, J. *Ps Mon* 1931, 41, #187, 153–200.

Tiffin, J. *Science* 1934, 80, 430–431.

Tiffin, J., Fairbanks, G. *Ps Mon* 1937, 48, #215, 70–77.

Tigerstedt, C. *Skand Ar Physiol* 1926, 48, 138–146.

Tinker, M. A. *Genet Ps Mon* 1928, 3, 68–182.

Tinker, M. A. *School Soc* 1934, 39, 147–148.

Tinker, M. A. *J Educ Res* 1936 a, 30, 241–277.

Tinker, M. A. *J Genet Ps* 1936 b, 48, 468–471.

Tinker, M. A., Paterson, D. G. *J App Ps* 1928, 12, 359–368.

Tinker, M. A., Paterson, D. G. *J App Ps* 1936, 20, 132–145.

Tischer, E. *Philos St* 1883, 1, 495–542.

Titchener, E. B. *Philos St* 1893, 8, 138–144.

Titchener, E. B. *Mind* 1895, 4, 74–81; 506–514. 1896, 5, 236–241.

Titchener, E. B. *Z Ps* 1899, 19, 321–326.

Titchener, E. B. *Experimental psychology.* 1901. (Qualitative).

Titchener, E. B. *Philos St* 1902, 20, 382–406.

Titchener, E. B. *Experimental psychology.* 1905. (Quantitative).

Titchener, E. B. *Lectures on the elementary psychology of feeling and attention.* 1908.

Titchener, E. B. *Lectures on the experimental psychology of the thought-processes.* 1909.

Titchener, E. B. *Am J Ps* 1912, 23, 165–182.

Titchener, E. B. *Am J Ps* 1916, 27, 435–436.

Titchener, E. B. *Am J Ps* 1920, 31, 212–214.

Todd, J. W. *Ar Ps* 1912, #25.

Tolman, E. C., Hall, C. S., Bretnall, E. P. *J Exp Ps* 1932, 15, 601–614.

Tolman, E. C., Honzik, C. H. *Calif U Pub Ps* 1930, 4, 257–275.

Toulouse, E. *R Paris* 1897, 6, 88–126.

Trautscholdt, M. *Philos St* 1883, 1, 213–250.

Trendelenburg, F. *J Acoust Soc* 1935, 7, 142–147.

Trimble, O. C. *Ps Mon* 1928, 38, #176, 172–225.

Troland, L. T. *J Genl Ps* 1929, 2, 28–58.

Troland, L. T. *Principles of psychophysiology.* 1930, v 2.

Troland, L. T. *Handbk genl exp ps* (Murchison) 1934, 653–703.

Trueblood, C. K., Smith, K. U. *J Genl Ps* 1934, 44, 414–427.

Tsai, C. *Comp Ps Mon* 1924, 2, #11.

Tsang, Y. C. *Comp Ps Mon* 1934, 10, #50.

Tsang, Y. C. *Comp Ps Mon* 1936, 12, #57.

Tschermak, A. *Handbk normal pathol Physiol* 1929, 12 (1), 478–497.

Tucker, Abraham *Light of nature.* 1768. c. xiv. sect. 5.

Tudor-Hart, B. *Ps Forsch* 1928, 10, 255–298.

Tufts, F. L. *Physical R* 1907, 25, 433–452.

Twitmyer, E. B. *Thesis. Ph. D.* U Penn 1902.

Twitmyer, E. M. *Am J Ps* 1931, 43, 165–187.

U

Uhlenbruck, P. *Z Biol* 1924, 81, 51–56.

Ulrich, J. L. *Beh Mon* 1913–15, 2, #10.

Urban, F. M. *The application of statistical methods to the problems of psychophysics.* 1908.

Urban, F. M. *Ar ges Ps* 1909, 15, 261–355. 16, 168–227.

Urban, F. M. *Ps R* 1910, 17, 229–259.

Urban, F. M. *Ar ges Ps* 1912, 24, 236–243.

Urbantschitsch, V. *Centralbt med Wissensch* 1875, 625–628.

Urbantschitsch, V. *Ar ges Physiol* 1882, 27, 446–453.

Urbantschitsch, V. *Über subjektive optische Anschauungsbilder.* 1907.

V

Valentine, W. L. *J Comp Ps* 1927, 7, 357–368.

Van Buskirk, W. L. *J Exp Ps* 1932, 15, 563–573.

Vance, T. F. *Ps Mon* 1914, 16, #69, 104–149.

Van der Veldt, J. *L'Apprentissage du mouvement et l'automatisme.* 1928.

van Ormer, E. B. *Ar Ps* 1932, #137.

Van Tilborg, P. W. *J Exp Ps* 1936, 19, 334–341.

Veraguth, O. *Kong exp Ps Ber* 1906, 2, 219–224.

Veraguth, O. *Das psychogalvanische Reflexphänomen.* 1909.

Vernon, M. D. *Br J Ps* 1931, 21, 368–381.

Vernon, P. E. *Br J Ps* 1934, 25, 123–139.

Vernon, P. E. *Br J Ps* 1935, 25, 265–283.

Vierordt, K. *Der Zeitsinn.* 1868.

Vigouroux, R. *Soc Biol Compt Rend* 1879, 31, 336–339.

Vincent, S. B. *Beh Mon* 1912, 1, #5.

Vincent, S. B. *J Animal Beh* 1915, 5, 1–24.

Vintschgau, M. v., Hönigschmied, J. *Ar ges Physiol* 1875, 10, 1–48. 1876, 12, 87–132. 1877, 14, 529–592.

Volkmann, A. W. *Sächs Akad Wiss Ber* Leipzig 1858, 10, 38–69.

Von Szeliski, V. *J Exp Ps* 1924, 7, 135–147.

Vörckel, H. *Z Biol* 1922, 75, 79–90.

W

Wada, Y. *Jap J Ps* 1932, 7, 505–537.

Wagner, A. H. *Ps Mon* 1930, 40, #181, 160–212.

Wagner, G. W. *Ps Mon* 1937, 48, #215, 108–146.

Wagner, J. *Z Ps* 1918, 80, 1–75.

Walker, R. Y. *Ps Mon* 1933, 44, #199, 95–117.

Wallas, G. *The art of thought.* 1926.

Waller, A. D. *R Soc London Proc* 1919, B, 91, 17–31.

Walton, A. *J Genet Ps* 1930, 38, 50–77.

Wang, G. H., Lu, T. W. *Chinese J Physiol* 1930, 4, 174–182; 303–326.

Wang, G. H., Pan, J. G., Lu, T. W. *Chinese J Physiol* 1929, 3, 109–122.

Wang, G. H., Richter, C. P. *Chinese J Physiol* 1928, 2, 279–284.

Warden, C. J. *Comp Ps Mon* 1923, 1, #3.

Warden, C. J. *J Exp Ps* 1924 a, 7, 98–116.

Warden, C. J. *J Exp Ps* 1924 b, 7, 243–275.

Warden, C. J. *J Comp Ps* 1925, 5, 365–372.

Warner, L. H. *J Genet Ps* 1932, 41, 57–115.

Warner, L. H., Warden, C. J. *Ar Ps* 1927, #93.

Warren, H. C. *Ps R* 1897, 4, 569–591.

Warren, H. C. *A history of the association psychology.* 1921.

Warren, H. C. *Dictionary of psychology.* 1934.

Washburn, M. F. *J Philos* 1906, 3, 62–63.

Washburn, M. F. *Am J Ps* 1911 a, 22, 114–115.

Washburn, M. F. *Am J Ps* 1911 b, 22, 578–579.

Washburn, M. F. *Movement and mental imagery.* 1916.

Washburn, M. F. *Am J Ps* 1921, 32, 145–146.

Waskom, H. L. *J Ps* 1936, 2, 393–408.

Waters, R. H. *J Ps* 1937, 4, 21–26.

Watson, J. B. *Ps Mon* 1907, 8, #33.

Watson, J. B. *Behavior.* 1914.

Watson, J. B. *Ps R* 1916, 23, 89–116.

Watson, J. B., Rayner, R. *J Exp Ps* 1920, 3, 1–14.

Watt, H. J. *Ar ges Ps* 1905, 4, 289–436.

Weaver, H. E. *Thesis. Ph. D.* Stanford University. 1930.

Weaver, H. E., Stone, C. P. *J Genet Ps* 1928, 35, 157–177.

Webb, L. W. *Ps Mon* 1917, 24, #104.

Weber, C. O. *J App Ps* 1931, 15, 310–318.

Weber, E. H. *De Tactu.* 1834. (Same paper in Annotationes anatomicae et physiologicae, 1851.)

Weber, E. H. *Handwörterbuch Physiol* (Wagner) 1846, 3 (2), 481–588. (Separate. *Tastsinn u Gemeingefühl* 1851.)

Weber, H. *Ar ges Ps* 1929, 71, 185–260.

Wechsler, D. *Ar Ps* 1925, #76.

Wechsler, D., Jones, H. E. *Am J Ps* 1928, 40, 600–606.

Wells, E. F., Hoisington, L. B. *J Genl Ps* 1931, 5, 352–367.

Wells, F. L. *Am J Ps* 1911 a, 22, 1–13.

Wells, F. L. *Ps R* 1911 b, 18, 1–23.

Wells, F. L. *Ps R* 1911 c, 18, 229–233.

Wells, F. L. *Ps R* 1912, 19, 253–270.

Wells, F. L. *J Exp Ps* 1924, 7, 59–66.

Wells, F. L. *Mental tests in clinical practice.* 1927.

Wells, F. L., Forbes, A. *Ar Ps* 1911, #16.

Wells, F. L., Kelley, C. M. *Am J Psychiat* 1922, 2, 53–59.

Wells, F. L., Kelley, C. M., Murphy, G. *J Exp Ps* 1921, 4, 57–62.

Wells, G. R. *Ps Mon* 1913, 15, #66.

Wendt, G. R. *Ar Ps* 1930, #123.

Wendt, G. R. *Ps R* 1936 a, 43, 258–281.

Wendt, G. R. *Ps Mon* 1936 b, 47, 311–328.

Wendt, G. R. *Ar Ps* 1938, #228.

Wendt, G. R., Dodge, R. *J Comp Ps* 1938, 25, 9–49.

Wenger, M. A. *Iowa U St Child Welfare* 1936, 12, 141–179.

Wenger, M. A. *Ps R* 1937, 44, 297–312.

Wenzl, A. *Ar ges Ps* 1932, 85, 181–218.

Wenzl, A. *Ar ges Ps* 1936, 97, 294–318.

Werner, H. *Z Ps* 1924, 94, 248–272.

Werner, H. *Am J Ps* 1935, 47, 40–64.

Werner, H. *Ps Mon* 1937, 49, #218.

Wertheimer, M. *Ar ges Ps* 1905, 6, 59–131.

Wertheimer, M. *Z Ps* 1912, 61, 161–265.

Wertheimer, M. *Ps Forsch* 1922, 1, 47–58.

Wertheimer, M. *Ps Forsch* 1923, 4, 301–350.

Wertheimer, M. *Drei Abhandlungen zur Gestalttheorie.* 1925.

Wertheimer, M., Klein, J. *Ar Krim-anthrop* 1904, 15, 72–113.

Westerlund, J. H., Tuttle, W. W. *Res Q Am Physical Educ Assoc* 1931, 2, #3, 95–100.

Westphal, E. *Ar ges Ps* 1911, 21, 219–434.

Wever, E. G. *Am J Ps* 1927, 38, 194–226.

Wever, E. G. *J Comp Ps* 1930, 10, 221–233.

Wever, E. G., Bray, C. W. *Nat Acad Sci Proc* 1930 a, 16, 344–350.

Wever, E. G., Bray, C. W. *Ps R* 1930 b, 37, 365–380.

Wever, E. G., Bray, C. W. *J Exp Ps* 1930 c, 13, 373–387.

Wever, E. G., Bray, C. W. *J Exp Ps* 1936 a, 19, 129–143.

Wever, E. G., Bray, C. W. *J Ps* 1936 b, 3, 101–114.

Wever, E. G., Bray, C. W. *J Exp Ps* 1938, 22, 1–16.

Wever, E. G., Bray, C. W., Horton, G. P. *Ann Otol Rhinol Laryng* 1935, 44, 772–776.

Wever, E. G., Bray, C. W., Willey, C. F. *J Exp Ps* 1937, 20, 336–349.

Wever, E. G., Zener, K. E. *Ps R* 1928, 35, 466–493.

Wheatstone, C. *R Soc London Philos Trans* 1838, 371–394.

Wheatstone, C. *R Soc London Philos Trans* 1852, Pt 1, 1–18.

Whipple, G. M. *Am J Ps* 1901, 12, 409–457.

Whipple, G. M. *Am J Ps* 1902, 13, 219–268.

Whipple, G. M. *Manual of mental and physical tests.* 1915, 2, 9–42.

Whipple, G. M. *Nat Soc St Ed 27th Yrbk* 1928, Pt 2, 179–209.

Whitely, P. L. *J Exp Ps* 1927, 10, 489–508.

Wickens, D. D. *J Exp Ps* 1938, 22, 101–123.

Wiegand, C. F. *Z Ps* 1908, 48, 161–237.

Wiersma, E. *Z Ps* 1901, 26, 168–200.

Wilcocks, R. W. *Am J Ps* 1928, 40, 26–50.

Wilkins, M. C. *Thesis M. A.* Columbia University 1917. (Unpublished).

Wilkins, M. C. *Ar Ps* 1928, #102.

Williams, O. *J Exp Ps* 1926, 9, 368–387.

Williams, R. D. *Ps Mon* 1914, 17, #75, 55–155.

Wilson, H. A., Myers, C. S. *Br J Ps* 1908, 2, 363–385.

Wiltbank, R. T. *Beh Mon* 1919, 4, #17.

Winch, W. H. *Br J Ps* 1908, 2, 284–293.

Winch, W. H. *Br J Ps* 1909, 3, 42–65.

Winch, W. H. *Br J Ps* 1924, 15, 64–79.

Wingfield, R. C., Dennis, W. *J Comp Ps* 1934, 18, 135–147.

Wirth, W. *Philos St* 1903, 18, 701–714.

Wirth, W. *Ps St* 1910, 6, 141–156; 252–315; 430–453.

Wirth, W. *Psychophysik.* 1912.

Wirth, W. *Handbk normal pathol Physiol* 1927, 10, 525–599.

Witasek, S. *Z Ps* 1907, 44, 161–185, 246–278.

Witmer, L. *Philos St* 1894, 9, 96–144; 209–263.

Witmer, L. *Analytic psychology.* 1902.

Wittmann, J. *Ar ges Ps* 1925, 51, 21–122.

Wohlfahrt, E. *Neue ps St* 1932, 4, 347–414.

Wohlgemuth, A. *Br J Ps Mon* 1919, #6.

Wolfe, H. K. *Philos St* 1886, 3, 534–571.

Wolff, W. *Ps Forsch* 1934, 20, 159–194.

Wolfle, D. L. *J Comp Ps* 1935, 19, 91–106.

Wolfle, H. M. *J Genl Ps* 1932, 7, 80–103.

Woodrow, H. *Ps R* 1915, 22, 423–452.

Woodrow, H. *J Exp Ps* 1916, 1, 23–39.

Woodrow, H. *J Educ Ps* 1927, 18, 159–172.

Woodrow, H. *J Exp Ps* 1932, 15, 357–379.

Woodrow, H. *Am J Ps* 1933, 45, 391–416.

Woodrow, H., Lowell, F. *Ps Mon* 1916, 22, #97.

Woodworth, R. S. *Studies philosophy psychology* (Garman). 1906 a, 351–392.

Woodworth, R. S. *Ps Bull* 1906 b, 3, 68–70.

Woodworth, R. S. *J Philos* 1907, 4, 169–176.

Woodworth, R. S. *Essays philosophy psychology in honor of William James.* 1908, 483–508.

Woodworth, R. S. *Ps R* 1912, 19, 97–123.

Woodworth, R. S. *Ps R* 1915 a, 22, 1–27.

Woodworth, R. S. *J Philos* 1915 b, 12, 246.

Woodworth, R. S. *Psychology.* 1929. 1934.

Woodworth, R. S., Poffenberger, A. T. *Text book of experimental psychology.* (Mimeographed.) 1920

Woodworth, R. S., Sells, S. B. *J Exp Ps* 1935, 18, 451–460.

Woodworth, R. S., Wells, F. L. *Ps Mon* 1911, 13, #57.

Wreschner, A. *Z Ps Ergänzbd* 1907–9, #3.

Wright, W. D. *R Soc London Proc* 1934, 115 B, 49–87.

Wulf, F. *Ps Forsch* 1922, 1, 333–373.

Wundt, W. *Beiträge zur Theorie der Sinneswahrnehmung.* 1862.

Wundt, W. *Vorlesungen über die Menschen und Thierseele.* 1863.

Wundt, W. *Grundzüge der physiologischen Psychologie.* 1874.

Wundt, W. *Grundzüge der physiologischen Psychologie.* 2nd ed. 1880.

Wundt, W. *Philos St* 1883, 1, 1–38.

Wundt, W. *Lectures on human and animal psychology.* 1894. (tr by J. E. Creighton & E. B. Titchener)

Wundt, W. *Grundriss der Psychologie.* 1896. (tr by C. H. Judd, 1896).

Wundt, W. *Ps St* 1907, 3, 301–360.

Wundt, W. *Grundzüge der physiologischen Psychologie.* 5th ed. 1911. Vol. 3, 507.

Wylie, H. H. *Beh Mon* 1919, 3, #16.

Y

Yamane, K. *Jap J Ps* 1935, 10, 327–390.

Yerkes, R. M. *The dancing mouse.* 1907.

Yerkes, R. M. *Beh Mon* 1916, 3, 1–145.

Yerkes, R. M. *J Comp Ps* 1921, 1, 369–394.

Yerkes, R. M. *Genet Ps Mon* 1927, 2, 1–193.

Yerkes, R. M. *Comp Ps Mon* 1934, 10, #47.

Yokoyama, M. *Am J Ps* 1921, 32, 81–107; 357–369.

Yoshioka, J. G. *J Comp Ps* 1928, 8, 429–433.

Young, P. T. *Am J Ps* 1918, 29, 237–271.

Young, P. T. *Br J Ps* 1925, 15, 356–362.

Young, P. T. *Am J Ps* 1927, 38, 157–193.

Young, P. T. *Am J Ps* 1928, 40, 372–400.

Young, P. T. *Motivation of behavior.* 1936.

Yule, G. U. *An introduction to the theory of statistics.* 9th ed. 1929.

Yum, K. S. *J Exp Ps* 1931, 14, 68–82.

Z

Zangwill, O. L. *Br J Ps* 1937 a, 27, 250–276.

Zangwill, O. L. *Br J Ps* 1937 b, 28, 12–17.

Zangwill, O. L. *Br J Ps* 1938, 28, 229–247.

Zartman, E. N., Cason, H. *J Exp Ps* 1934, 17, 671–679.

Zeigarnik, B. *Ps Forsch* 1927, 9, 1–85.

Zeitler, J. *Philos St* 1900, 16, 380–463.

Ziehen, Th. *Die Ideenassoziation des Kindes.* 1898, 1. 1900, 3.

Zigler, M. J. *Am J Ps* 1920, 31, 273–300.

Zigler, M. J., Cook, B., Miller, D., Wemple, L. *Am J Ps* 1930, 42, 246–259.

Zigler, M. J. *Am J Ps* 1932, 44, 709–720.

Zigler, M. J. *J Genl Ps* 1935, 13, 316–332.

Zimmer, A. *Z Ps* 1913, 47 (2), 106–158.

Zoll, P. M.　*Am J Ps* 1934, 46, 99–106.

Zurmühl, G.　*Z Ps* 1930, 61 (2), 40–86.

Zwaardemaker, H.　*Br Med J* 1888, 2, 1295.

Zwaardemaker, H.　*Die Physiologie des Geruchs.* 1895. (207–238).

Zwaardemaker, H.　*Ar néerl Physiol* 1922, 6, 336–354.

Zwaardemaker, H.　*L'odorat.* 1925.

INDEX

Only the first page of continuous passages is given.
Starred subheads appear also as main headings, with subdivision.
Abbreviations and symbols used in the text are defined in this Index.

B

B   Basal value of s, at and below which all the responses fall in category B 402

b   relative frequency of B responses

b′ cumulated relative frequency of B responses

Bacon, M. M. 449, 826
Bagley, W. C. 205, 826
Baier, D. E. 504, 826
Bain, A. 747, 826
Bair, J. H. 179, 224, 826
Baird, J. W. 543, 668, 669, 826
Baker, B. A. 819, 820, 849
Baker, K. H. 705, 826
Baldwin, J. M. 12, 307, 308, 826
Baley, S. 527, 826
Ball, J. 127, 843
Ballachey, E. L. 137, 138, 140, 826, 828
Ballard, P. B. 64, 826
Banister, H. 527, 528, 532, 826
Bappert, J. 672, 673, 674, 826
Barcroft, J. 273, 826
Bard, P. 257, 826
Barker, R. G. 147, 826
Barrett, M. 378, 826
Barrows, B. E. 391, 849
Bartlett, F. C. 69, 70, 73, 80, 826
Bartlett, R. J. 292, 293, 296, 826
Bartley, S. H. 637, 835
Barton, J. W. 218, 826
Bass, M. J. 100, 826
Batson, W. H. 165, 167, 168, 174, 826
Bayer, L. 562, 826
Bayley, N. 291, 826
Bayroff, A. G. 139, 831
Bazett, H. C. 463, 826
Bean, C. H. 826
Beats 514, 516
Beebe-Center, J. G. 240, 448, 449, 826
Beeby, C. E. 222, 826
Beitel, R. J. 564, 826
Bekhterev, V. M. 108, 109, 110, 826
Bell, Sir Charles 242, 243, 244, 827
Bell, A. G. 437
Bell, H. M. 846
Bellis, C. J. 338, 827
Benary, W. 571, 827
Benedict, F. G. 585, 832
Bentley, M. 11, 509, 827, 836
Benussi, V. 264, 265, 273, 274, 623, 649, 650, 827
Bergemann, R. 308, 827
Berger, G. O. 304, 305, 306, 310, 317, 318, 827
Bergström, J. A. 224, 827
Berkeley, G. 43, 653, 654, 665, 827
Bernstein, A. L. 111, 121, 827
Berry, W. 558, 561, 562, 827
Bessel 300
Betts, G. H. 40, 827

Betz, W. 798, 827
Bewusstseinslage 789
Beyrl, F. 827
Bidwell, S. 562, 827
Bierens de Haan, J. A. 757, 827
Biervliet, J. J. van 335, 827
Bigham, J. 12, 846
Billings, M. L. 696, 827
Bills, A. G. 176, 177, 697, 702, 710, 827
Binet, A. 8, 11, 19, 21, 22, 42, 400, 402, 709, 784, 786, 827
Binet tests 8, 400, 402
Binocular vision 572, 654, 659
  disparity 654, 660, 671
  double images 583, 662, 664, 667
  fusion 574, 659
  parallax 652, 654
  prevalence 574, 638, 659
  rivalry 573, 659, 697, 703
  superiority 321, 666f, 669
  superposition 660, 676
Bishop, H. G. 681, 827
Black and white 542, 598, 612f, 621
Blakeslee, A. F. 497, 827, 850
Blank, G. 334, 827
Blatz, W. E. 261, 264, 270, 827
Bliss, C. B. 321, 827
Blix, M. 455, 827
Block, H. 710, 827
Blocking 363, 702
Blodgett, H. C. 137, 827
Blood pressure, see Circulation
Boas, E. P. 268, 272, 827
Bolles, M. M. 279, 281, 834
Bolton, T. L. 8, 827
Bonnet, Ch. 685, 827
Bonser, F. G. 701, 827
Book, W. F. 159, 168, 212, 771, 790, 828
Boreas, T. 53, 55, 56, 60, 828
Boring, E. G. 182, 244, 245, 338, 392, 451, 510, 511, 828, 848
Botti, L. 828
Bourdon, B. 347, 658, 669, 670, 671, 673, 674, 828
Bowditch, H. P. 322, 828
Bowers, H. 43, 828
Bowie, W. 300, 828
Bowlker, T. J. 526, 530, 828
Brain, autonomic center 283
  circulation 267, 269, 701
  conditioning 100, 106, 115
  motor area 188
  potentials (waves) 107
  visual area 183
Braly, K. W. 639, 828
Bray, C. W. 186, 188, 517, 534, 536, 828, 857
Breed, F. S. 382, 841
Breese, B. B. 573, 574, 828
Breitwieser, J. V. 308, 314, 828
Bressler, J. 404, 405, 424, 426, 828

Equivalent stimuli 205
Erdmann, B. 577, 715, 738, 739, 742, 833
Error 643
  average 396
  constant 396, 421, 430, 438, 643
  cut tail 404, 420
  fallacy 807, 810, 813f
  * illusion 643
  maze 126, 137
  object 450, 785
  space 378, 438
  standard 396
  stimulus 450, 785
  time 378, 439
Esper, E. A. 343, 833
Esthetics 368, 448
  association 391
  balance 390
  color 381
  contrast 449
  division of line 389
  ellipse 389
  empathy 391
  form 383
  intensity 499
  measure of agreement or consistency 374, 379
  methods 369, 370
  practice effect 368, 388
  rectangle 383
  series effect 389, 448
  symmetry 390
  theories 384, 387f, 391
  time error 448
  triangle 389
Eurich, A. C. 833
Ewert, P. H. 186, 833
Examinations 271, 274
Excitation 94, 99
Exner, S. 305, 306, 681, 833
Expectancy 261, 270, 285, 288
Experience factor, in perception 84, 624f, 639f, 653
  in problem solving 756, 782
Experiment
  nature of 2
  planning 2
  reporting 690
  rules 784
Experimental factor 2
Experimental psychology 1
  beginnings 1, 6, 39, 92, 108, 114, 125, 181, 189, 235, 242, 276, 298, 340, 369, 384, 392, 445, 455, 469, 481, 589, 594, 596, 623, 651, 664, 680, 684, 698, 709, 715, 746, 783, 789
  scope 1
Exposure, apparatus 16, 632f, 682, 687
  repeated 72, 74
  reversed 689
Eye, see Sight, Vision

Eyeball 578
  muscles 576
  receptors and sensations 461–463, 584
Eye dominance 664
Eye movement 576
  accommodation 576f, 665
  compensatory 581, 586
  conjugate 576, 581, 583
  convergence 576, 581–583, 591, 655, 660, 665, 667
  coordination 576, 584, 587f, 591, 666
  fixation 579, 581f, 585f, 719
  in binocular rivalry 574
  in esthetic enjoyment 585
  in fluctuation 700
  in illusions 643, 648
  in perception of motion 682
  in reading 715, 718, 722
  in space perception 662, 672, 674
  latency 585, 588f
  muscles and nerves 576
  pursuit 581, 585, 591
  recording 577, 589, 648
  saccadic 577, 581, 584f, 588, 591, 719
  types 581
  vision 586, 591
  voluntary 585
  wink 111, 113, 581

F

f frequency within a step interval
Facial expression 242
  analysis 244, 247, 253
  antithesis 243
  conventional 252
  elementary 244
  individual differences 252, 254
  interpretation 245–253
  muscles 243, 253
  originally practical 242f
  originally sensory 244
  Piderit drawings 243
  posed 247
  scale 250
  spontaneous 252
  suggestion 245, 247f
Facilitation 305, 320, 357, 362, 707, 710f
Faculty 177
Fairbanks, G. 723, 732, 833, 854
Fallacy 807, 810, 813f
Farmer, E. 286, 293, 833
Fatigue 177, 354, 574, 702
Fechner, G. T. 39, 181, 369, 370, 371, 372, 384, 385, 386, 387, 388, 392, 393, 395, 400, 409, 412, 430, 433, 435, 436, 437, 438, 439, 558, 833
Feeling 234
  attitude 236, 238, 241
  bright vs. dull 237
  depression 236
  dimensions 235, 241